LIVES OF NORTH AMERICAN BIRDS

KENN KAUFMAN

LIVES OF

NORTH

AMERICAN

BIRDS

HOUGHTON MIFFLIN COMPANY ⚓ BOSTON • NEW YORK

Library of Congress Cataloging-in-Publication Data

Kaufman, Kenn.
Lives of North American birds / Kenn Kaufman.
p. cm. —
Includes bibliographical references (p.   ) and index.
ISBN 0-395-77017-3 (cloth)   ISBN 0-618-15988-6 (flexi)
1. Birds — North America.
II. Title.   III. Series.
QL681.K385   1996   598.297 — dc20   96-20285

Visit our Web site:
www.houghtonmifflinbooks.com.

Book design by Anne Chalmers
Typeface: Linotype-Hell Fairfield

Printed in the United States of America

RMT 10 9 8 7 6 5 4 3 2 1

CONTENTS

ACKNOWLEDGMENTS

This book's genesis was perhaps unique. I was on the team that developed the CD-ROM *Peterson Multimedia Guides: North American Birds.* To supplement the material from the Peterson Field Guides, we decided to add a brief life history for every bird. But when we looked for a source, we found that no book gave such information in up-to-date, usable form, so I took on the task of describing birds' lives for the Multimedia Guide. That text, with many revisions and about 50,000 words of additional information, developed into this book. So although there have been many multimedia products based on books, probably few books besides this one have started off in CD-ROM form.

In developing the original text for multimedia, I relied heavily on advice from Doug Eisenhart and Harry Foster and also received much good input from Eric Pozzo and Susan Kunhardt. The maps used in this book are adapted from the CD-ROM; originally based on maps by Virginia Marie Peterson (for the Peterson Eastern and Western Field Guides), they were adapted for multimedia by Jeff and Amy Price. (I made extensive changes in some of these maps, however, so any errors therein are my responsibility.) The photographs used in this book, also taken from the CD-ROM, were chosen by Doug Eisenhart and Lisa White, with some critical assistance from Shawneen Finnegan.

In the complicated process of turning all this into a book, I am grateful to Harry Foster for wise counsel at every step, to Anne Chalmers for designing the attractive layout, and to the talented Lisa White for her adroit handling of innumerable details.

But all of the preceding applies only to the process of putting the book together. A separate topic involves the information that went into it. The vast majority of this material came from published sources; I must thank the Science Library at the University of Arizona, Tucson, where I spent literally hundreds of hours in the course of researching this text. Although I have no official connection to the university, I was shown every courtesy by the library staff.

My single largest source of facts was the *Birds of North America* series, described elsewhere in this book, which gave me matchless information for almost 200 species. I have been privileged to take part in editing this series, and I'm grateful to everyone else involved. In particular, I had many worthwhile discussions of bird distribution and migration with Keith Russell, assistant editor of the series.

I will not attempt to list all the people from whom I have learned things relevant to this book's subject over the years. However, I must mention a few individuals in particular. Rick Bowers loaned me a number of references, provided unpublished information, and reviewed parts of the text. Jeff Cox gave a detailed critique to important sections of text and offered many improvements. Nora Mays researched and wrote partial drafts for many of the vireos and warblers and also reviewed other text sections. Sheri Williamson and Tom Wood provided much unpublished information and reviewed major sections of text. Others who provided unpublished data and/or reviewed portions of the text included Susan Roney Drennan, Jon Dunn, Pete Dunne, Victor Emanuel, Kimball Garrett, Jeff Gordon, John Madden, Jeremy and Leila Madeiros, Mark Robbins, Will Russell, Russ Schipper, Ella Sorensen, Sally Stebbins, Judy Toups, Janet Witzeman, and Dale and Marian Zimmerman.

As with anything I've accomplished in the last decade, I owe major thanks to my wife Lynn. In this project, her skills as a botanist sharpened my approach to discussing habitat, feeding, and nest building. She also researched and wrote initial drafts on a number of species, read portions of the text, and put up with my mental absence during the months that I was chained to my desk completing this book.

Finally, my biggest debt of gratitude is owed to the thousands of researchers, past and present, professional and amateur, who have been responsible for discovering the facts reported in these pages. The study of birds' lives is not a pursuit that brings wealth or renown, but it does add to our total knowledge of the world. My hat is off to those admirable people who have worked to give us this knowledge, and I can only hope that this book reflects at least a little of the wonders that they have discovered.

IMPORTANT NOTICE

Scientists often revise their ideas of how birds should be classified. Although the birds themselves have not changed in the short time since this book was written, some of them already have different classifications. For example, the tanagers (p. 558) are now considered to make up a family, not a subfamily; the Sage Grouse (p. 153) is now considered to be two species, not just one. For a complete list and discussion of all such recent changes in bird classification, see Kenn Kaufman's Web site at www.kknature.com.

INTRODUCTION: HOW BIRDS LIVE

For those lucky people who have discovered the world of birds around us, life is never dull. Everywhere outdoors — from just outside our windows to the farthest wilderness — hundreds of kinds of colorful, tuneful birds are leading fascinating lives.

When we see a new bird, our first question usually will be: What kind is it? . . . and a good field guide will give us the bird's name. But it may take longer to find the answer to our second question: What is the bird doing?

What the birds are doing turns out to be surprisingly varied. No two kinds of birds have exactly the same lifestyle. Even those that look very similar may be strikingly different in how they find their food, where they build their nests, when they migrate, whether they join flocks or travel alone. And the surprises do not end at that. There are birds that hibernate in winter, birds that can fly nonstop from Canada to South America, birds that may build nests out of human bones, birds that may dig tunnels 20 feet long. The plain little bird that hops across your windowsill may have its own remarkable secrets.

Most of the information published about the lives of birds, especially in recent years, has been quite technical in its approach. Scientists can find such information by searching through ornithological journals and reports, but these sources are not easily available to the general public. For most people, there has not been a ready source of facts, written in clear, nonscientific language, on how birds live. This book is intended to fill that gap.

In planning the format for this book, the editors and I focused on keeping everything as clear and accessible as possible. We wanted any reader to be able to open to any page and immediately understand it, without having to flip to some other part of the book for definitions or explanations of symbols, abbreviations, or scientific terms.

Thus, this introduction is not intended to tell you how to use the book, but to provide some further insight into how birds live and how we have gained an understanding of their lives.

HOW BIRDS ARE CLASSIFIED

How many kinds of birds are there? That depends on what you mean by "kinds," but the basic unit used by most scientists and birdwatchers is the *species*. At the moment, close to 10,000 species of birds are recognized worldwide. A little over 900 of those have been found in North America, and all of these are treated in this book.

Scientists still disagree on the exact definition of a species, and this leads to differences in how birds and other organisms are classified. For example, a few authorities suggest that various forms of Dark-eyed Junco, such as "Oregon" and "Gray-headed" juncos, should be considered different species. Baltimore Oriole and Bullock's Oriole were "lumped" into one species in 1973, and then "split" back into two species in 1995. This kind of taxonomic tinkering is not important to most of us, except that it sometimes changes birds' names.

Each species belongs to a larger group, called a genus, which in turn belongs to a family, and so on up the taxonomic ladder. For example, all the woodpeckers belong to one family, and all the sandpipers belong to another. Within these families, several of the noisy woodpeckers of open woods are placed in the genus *Melanerpes*, and several of the long-legged, slim sandpipers are classified in the genus *Tringa*. Family and genus are even less sharply defined scientifically than species, but they are very useful as a way of grouping related birds together.

In this book, each family of birds is described in a brief introduction that gives the characteristic aspects of behavior that apply to all or most members of the family. It also tells how many species there are in the family, where they live, and how the North American species compare with those found in the rest of the world. (For example, if you are accustomed to seeing just one type of kingfisher by the waterside here, it may be surprising to learn that there are dozens of kinds in the Old World, including some that are brilliantly colored, and that many of them do not eat fish.)

Within each family, the species are arranged by genus. Each major genus (plural: *genera*) is described in a short introduction that tells what is distinctive or notable about the birds of this genus, as observed in life.

For as much information as possible on a bird, read not only that species account but also the headings for its genus and family. Often these will contain information that is not repeated in the individual species description.

HABITAT

One of the most important things to know about a bird is its habitat. Most birds are quite choosy about their surroundings. Ordinarily we will not find a meadowlark or a pelican inside the forest, nor a Wood Thrush in an open field. Restriction to limited habitats is most notable in the tropics, where some species may occur only around huge fallen trees in dense upland forest, for example, and others only in dry scrub on islands in rivers. In the temperate zones, most birds cannot afford to be quite so particular. The variable climate forces them to be somewhat adaptable, but habitat preferences are still obvious usually.

Scientists have developed very precise terms and definitions for describing habitats, but in this book, habitats are described only in general terms, using words that are widely understood. I have used "marsh" to indicate an area of low nonwoody plants (such as grasses, sedges, cattails, etc.) growing in shallow water or very wet soil, and "swamp" for a wet area with some taller bushes or trees. "Forest," of course, indicates an area of tall trees growing fairly close together; "woodland" can mean almost the same thing, but in North America it is often applied to areas of shorter trees that may be more scattered or spread out. Most of the other habitat terms used should be clear in meaning.

During migration, the rules break down, and any birds often show up in unusual habitats. A snipe or a bittern may be found on a city sidewalk, or an ocean-going jaeger may appear on a small inland pond. Such odd variations in habitat cannot all be described here, of course.

TERRITORY

In many species accounts, you will read about how the bird defends its territory. Most species do have territories, at least in the nesting season. Ideally, the territory will supply everything needed to get the birds through the season: shelter, good nest sites, and enough food to sustain the pair of adult birds and their young. To protect these resources, the adults have an instinct to drive away other birds of their own kind that happen to stray into their territory.

Not all birds defend territories. In situations where nesting sites are concentrated and feeding areas may change from day to day, birds often nest in colonies. For example, seabird nests may be crowded together on islands, while the birds forage widely on the surrounding ocean. Many swallows may nest under the eaves of one building, spreading out over the surrounding countryside to seek flying insects. In these cases, the defended area may amount to only a few inches around the nest itself.

Although nesting territories are the best known, birds may defend territories at other seasons. This defense may last only a day or two (as in the case of a hummingbird that drives others away from a patch of flowers during migration), or it may last an entire winter. A bird that is solitary on the wintering grounds may be holding a winter territory, defending an area that may supply its needs during the season.

SOCIABLE VS. SOLITARY BIRDS

Birds that are quite defensive about their turf while they are nesting may become sociable at other seasons. For example, White-crowned Sparrows are aggressive in driving away others of their own kind in June; but by October, the White-crowns have gathered in large and peaceful flocks.

In North America, flocks form mainly in the nonbreeding season. The tendency to be either sociable or solitary at this time is often characteristic of a particular species. American Pipits, for instance, are usually in flocks in winter, while Sprague's Pipits are almost always found alone.

Flocks may be of two major kinds: those that are composed of just one species ("birds of a feather flock together"), and mixed flocks containing several species. There are two likely advantages to joining a flock. With more pairs of eyes and ears, the group may be quicker to spot an approaching predator; it may also be able to find new sources of food more readily. In mixed flocks, different kinds of birds have different feeding behaviors, so they may not be competing for exactly the same food even if they are foraging in the same trees.

SONGS AND CALLS

To us, the songs of birds may be simply sweet music for the outdoors. But to the birds, the songs mean serious business.

Usually it is the male that sings, and usually the main message of his song is to stake a claim to his territory. He is singing to warn rival males to stay away. A secondary purpose for the song may be to attract a female, or to communicate with his mate if he already has one. Some species are not very territorial and seem to use the song mainly for courtship or communication. There are also some birds (such as many of the warblers) that use one song in defense of the territory, and a second song in attracting a mate.

Many species, especially among the larger birds, do not have songs at all. For example, many hawks stake their claims by performing flight displays in the air above their territories. But most birds have *calls* of some sort. The difference between songs and calls is not always precise, but calls are usually shorter and have different functions than songs. Calls may express a variety of things, including alarm, aggression, or a simple "here-I-am" (a "contact note"). Birds that are sociable, living in family groups or flocks for much of the year, often have more different calls than do solitary birds.

PAIR-BONDS

In the breeding season a pair of birds, one male and one female, will typically stay together through at least one nesting cycle, more or less sharing the duties of nesting. But there are many exceptions to this standard. One common variation involves birds that have no lasting pair-bond. In these cases, the male and female go their separate ways after mating, and the female does all the work of caring for the eggs and young. A male of such a species might mate with several females. This is a common pattern among grouse, hummingbirds, and some other groups.

In another variation, a male may have two or more females sharing his nesting territory, and he may or may not help to care for the young in the multiple nests. This occurs with such familiar birds as Marsh Wrens and Red-winged Blackbirds. A far less common situation involves a female bird that mates with two or more males. In a few groups of shorebirds, a female may have several mates, laying a clutch of eggs for each one and leaving the males to incubate the eggs and care for the young.

Among the more typically monogamous birds, there are some species in which the same two birds will ordinarily remain paired as long as both survive. This is especially common among large birds such as geese, hawks, albatrosses, and loons. Such birds are said to "mate for life," but in general, if one member of the pair dies, the surviving bird will find a new mate.

COURTSHIP

Many birds perform rituals, or displays, as part of the process of pairing up, or to maintain the bond between two birds that are already a mated pair. For simplicity, both types are referred to here as "courtship displays." Many such displays are described in this book, especially if they are conspicuous and likely to be noticed by observers.

In some larger birds, and particularly waterbirds, displays are mutual, with both male and female taking part (the "dances" of some grebes are classic examples). Among many songbirds, the displays are unilateral: the male performs, and the female watches. But there are many variations.

A display seen in many groups of birds is courtship feeding, in which the male feeds the female. Often this is no more than a ritual, and sometimes in the stylized "feeding" no food is actually transferred. But in some groups of birds, courtship feeding is more than merely "romantic." Among hawks and owls, for example, when the female is getting ready to lay eggs, she may need to save her energy, and she may be too heavy to hunt effectively. In these species, the male often feeds the female not only before egg-laying but also while she is incubating the eggs.

Some of the most elaborate courtship displays involve birds that do not form any pair-bond at all. Male hummingbirds, for example, may perform spectacular courtship flights. Each male hummingbird will try to attract as many females as he can, so evolution has favored the development of bright colors and showy displays among these males.

Most impressive of all are the mass displays performed by groups of males on dancing grounds, or "leks." In North America, such displays are best known among certain grouse, such as prairie-chickens and Sage Grouse. Males of these species spend much of the spring on the lek, displaying with bizarre postures, motions, and sounds; females visit the site, mate with one of the males, and then go off to lay eggs and raise their young. Most females will choose the dominant males from the center of the lek — presumably the ones with the best genes.

NESTS

We sometimes think of birds' nests as if they were homes, but this is not accurate. Most birds do not live in their nests as we live in our houses. In the vast majority of cases, the nest is more like a cradle: a place for the eggs until they hatch, and for the young until they are strong enough to depart.

But these bird cradles can vary from extremely simple to remarkably complex. The simplest nests are nonexistent: some birds just lay their eggs on flat ground or cliff ledges. At the opposite extreme are the highly structured nests woven by the African birds known (appropriately) as weavers, or the nests of tailorbirds in Asia, with leaves actually sewn together.

Some larger birds, including many hawks and northern waterfowl, will use the same nest time after time, often continuing to add material to it annually. Most smaller birds tend to build a new nest for each brood of young; however, there are many exceptions to this.

In this book the nest of each species is described briefly, including its shape and the main materials used in its construction. For photographs and more detailed descriptions, see *A Field Guide to Birds' Nests* (1975) and *A Field Guide to Western Birds' Nests* (1979) by Hal H. Harrison, published by Houghton Mifflin Co. in the Peterson Field Guide series.

When describing materials used in nests, I often refer to "weeds." Of course, this term technically has no meaning, but most people understand it to mean low-growing, nonwoody plants that are not grasses. (Many a "weed" magically turns into a "wildflower" when it begins to bloom.) A scientist might refer to such plants as "forbs."

NEST SITES

Every kind of bird has a typical site for its nest. For example, meadowlarks typically nest on the ground among dense grass, grebes often build floating nests in shallow water, and Cerulean Warblers usually nest among the high branches of leafy trees. But many birds also can be somewhat flexible in their choice of sites. Around houses and farms, unusual sites are often recorded: finches nesting in hanging flowerpots, wrens nesting in a toolbox in a shed, and so on. Obviously, a book like this cannot list every possible nest site, so I have focused on the most typical sites.

For birds that nest in bushes or trees, the height of the nest above the ground is especially prone to variation; however, most species have distinct preferences. Here, again, I have emphasized the typical nest height, not the odd exceptions. Someone may have once seen an Eastern Towhee's nest 20 feet up in a tree, but the important thing to know is that the nests are *usually* lower than five feet. If we look long enough, it always will be possible to find a nest a little higher or lower than the range given in this or any other book.

For many kinds of birds, we do not know whether the nest site is chosen by the male or the female or both. In cases where the female does all the nest-building, we might guess that she also has chosen where to build it. Among birds that nest in holes in trees, choice of the site may play a role in courtship: the male leads a female around to show her potential nest sites in his territory; in choosing one of the sites, she also indicates her acceptance of the male.

NEST BUILDING

The species accounts tell who builds the nest, if that information is known. On the whole, female birds do most of the work of nest building. There are many species in which both sexes help to build the nest, and many in which the female does it alone, but relatively few in which the male is the main builder.

One interesting approach to sharing the task is seen in some birds, especially larger species: often the male does much of the gathering of material and brings it back to the site, but the female does the actual building. In another variation, the male starts the nest, building the foundation, but then the female completes the nest and adds a soft lining to it.

For some birds, "nest building" is largely a matter of excavating. For example, woodpeckers put a lot of effort into digging nest cavities in dead trunks or limbs of trees, but then they build no nest inside the hole: the eggs are laid on sawdust and wood chips on the floor of the cavity.

EGGS

For every species given full treatment in this book, I describe the color and markings of the eggs. For more thorough descriptions of eggs (and photographs of many), see Hal Harrison's *A Field Guide to Birds' Nests* and *A Field Guide to Western Birds' Nests*.

CLUTCH SIZE

The complete set of eggs laid by a female bird for one nesting attempt is known as the clutch. For most of our birds we have a good idea of the typical number of eggs per set, or clutch size. This varies widely among different groups of birds. Some of the seabirds invariably lay just one egg per clutch, many songbirds typically lay four or five, and many gamebirds and ducks may lay more than a dozen. In most cases, evolution probably favors a clutch size that will yield the maximum number of young that the bird is likely to raise successfully.

For this book, clutch size is often given as a range of numbers, such as "4–6, sometimes 3–7." In this example, most nests will have four, five, or six eggs, but some will have three or seven. Some birds have little variation in clutch size. For instance, many of the sandpipers lay four eggs almost every time. But most birds are more variable. Some species tend to lay more eggs in colder parts of their range. Some tend to lay more eggs early in the season; also, if a first clutch of eggs is destroyed, the replacement clutch may have fewer eggs. In some species, older females tend to lay more eggs than younger ones. Most fascinating is the pattern shown by a few birds such as some northern owls and a couple of warblers: these species tend to lay more eggs in years when food is abundant (as during population explosions of rodents or certain insects).

We may occasionally find a nest with a number of eggs outside the known extremes for clutch size. A very small clutch may occur if a predator takes some of the eggs. A very large clutch may result from two females laying in the same nest, as sometimes happens. In this book, I have focused on typical clutch sizes, not on the possible extremes.

INCUBATION

Many creatures besides birds lay eggs — for example, insects, fish, amphibians, and many reptiles. But actively incubating the eggs, sitting on them and keeping them warm until they hatch, is common only among birds. Not all birds actually sit on their eggs: the remarkable malleefowl of the Australasian region bury their eggs in huge mounds of earth, along with dead leaves; heat generated by the decaying plant material is enough to hatch the eggs. But no bird in our area is so inventive.

Most birds begin incubating about the time the last egg is laid, and all the eggs hatch at around the same time. But in some species, incubation begins as soon as the first egg is laid, and with each egg developing at its own speed, they hatch on different days. This happens with some owls, for example, and a brood of young owlets may look like a set of stair steps, with all different sizes from the oldest to the youngest.

In some species, both parents take part in incubation; in others, only the female incubates. There are only a few cases in which the male is the main incubator, and these are mostly among the shorebirds.

For transferring heat more effectively to the eggs, many birds develop a "brood patch" during incubation. This is an area on the belly that temporarily loses its feathers and develops extra, swollen blood vessels near the surface of the skin. Generally, if the female does all the incubating, only the female develops a brood patch, but both parents will develop one if they share the duties of incubation.

In this book I have given the typical length of the incubation period where it is known — defined as the number of days from the time the last egg is laid until that egg hatches. For most species this period is quite predictable, but for some it is quite variable. Among some seabirds, for example, incubation may take many days longer in years of bad weather: if the adults must spend more time away from the nest searching for food, the eggs are neglected for longer periods, and they develop more slowly.

There are still a number of species in North America for which the incubation period is unknown, especially among those whose nests are hard to find or hard to observe. This is a good opportunity for research by keen observers of birds.

NESTLINGS AND FLEDGLINGS

There is great variation in the appearance of newly hatched birds. A baby Mallard pops out of the egg covered with a downy coat and with its eyes wide open; within an hour or two it can walk and swim with ease. A baby sparrow struggles out of the egg scrawny and naked, with its eyes closed, barely able to hold its head up to beg feebly for food. These two types are referred to as "precocial" young (the active and wide-eyed ones) and "altricial" young (the blind and immobile ones). But there are various intermediate types between these two extremes.

In this book I have indicated whether one or both parents feed the young. In many cases, neither one does. Many precocial young find all their own food from the start, leaving the nest and following their parents as soon as their down has dried. On the other hand, many altricial young are fed throughout the time they spend in the nest, and even for up to several weeks after they leave it.

The term "nestling" is used for a baby bird that is still in the nest, while a "fledgling" is a young bird that has fledged (learned to fly) and has left the nest. Neither term applies well to young precocial birds that leave the nest soon after hatching and learn to fly sometime later.

Depending on the species (and on how much is known about it), I may give a figure for how old the young are when they leave the nest, or when they are first able to fly, or when they become independent. These milestones are quite variable from one group of birds to the next. Some baby grouse and quail can fly short distances when they are only a few days old and still tiny, but most birds do not fly until they are full-grown. In some species that nest in vulnerable spots (such as birds that nest on the ground in open fields), the young may leave the nest several days before they are able to fly, presumably because staying in the nest is so risky. Some larger birds abandon their young before they are old enough to fly, but in other cases, the young remain with their parents for many months and follow them in migration.

NUMBER OF BROODS PER YEAR

For many species, I indicate how many broods of young a pair of adults may raise per year. The maximum number of broods depends on the length of the available season (which is much shorter in cold climates, for example) and on the length of time needed to raise one brood to independence. The California Condor takes more than a year to raise its brood of one, so the condor can only nest every other year (the same is true of some albatrosses and penguins). On the other hand, some pigeons and doves living in warm climates may raise five or six broods in a year.

In every case, the number given is for the number of successful broods, not nesting attempts. Especially among smaller birds, if the early nests are destroyed, the birds may make repeated nesting attempts until they succeed in bringing up some young.

WHAT BIRDS EAT

Birds are remarkably varied in their food habits — both in what they eat and in how they get it. It is useful to consider these two aspects separately, so the species accounts divide information on feeding into "Diet" and "Behavior."

Considering birds' diets brings home one of the basic lessons of ecology: all living things are interrelated. Most of our birds eat insects at least part of the time, so wholesale poisoning of insects is bound to be bad for birdlife. Many birds eat weed seeds, and mass annihilation of weeds will be hard on them. And so on. We cannot claim to be protecting birds if we do not protect the whole ecosystem in which they live.

Birds' diets also lead us to think about some unfamiliar life forms. If I write that Barn Owls eat mice, or that Cedar Waxwings eat berries, everyone will understand; but a statement that Least Auklets eat copepods will draw a blank from most people. Birds have such varied diets that we cannot go into great detail about all the things they eat, but a few words about some items on the avian menu may be helpful.

PLANT MATERIAL EATEN BY BIRDS   Only a few of our birds are completely vegetarian, but many feed partly on plant material.

Seeds are very popular with many groups of birds, often those birds that have rather thick bills. Many species, such as various sparrows and grosbeaks, will feed mostly on insects in summer, switching over to feed mainly on seeds in winter. In describing diets, I often refer to "weed seeds." Again, by "weeds" I simply mean low-growing, nonwoody plants that are not grasses.

Many birds also feed on fruits. However, the way a botanist would define "fruit" is not the way most people understand it. Technically, "fruit" may include any plant structure that contains the seeds, and various kinds of fruits are referred to as capsules, achenes, nuts, berries, drupes, and so on. But most people seem to think of fruit mainly in terms of the large juicy things grown in orchards. To avoid confusion, in this book I have generally used the term "berry" for any small, fleshy fruits (including drupes and drupelets), although this is not always botanically correct.

Many birds also feed on buds and on fresh green shoots of plants. Only a few feed on twigs, dig up roots, or dine on leaves of land plants. However, many waterbirds will feed on various parts of aquatic plants, including their leaves, stems, and roots.

INSECTS EATEN BY BIRDS   If you read the "Diet" sections for enough species you will realize that, without insects, many birds would starve — and that, without birds, we soon would be knee-deep in insects! Insects are tremendously important in all habitats on land and in fresh water. They play a key role in turning plant material into protein, and they form the basis of the diet of many larger creatures, including a high percentage of birds.

Under many species accounts I have given a general idea of the kinds of insects that they eat. For more information on these, consult the excellent *Field Guide to the Insects* by Donald J. Borror and Richard E. White, in the Peterson series (Houghton Mifflin Co., Boston, 1970).

Here are a few general points to understand about the insects mentioned in this book. The term "larva" (plural: *larvae*) indicates the wormlike immature stages of many groups of insects, which look completely different from the adults. In this book I use the term "caterpillar" only for the larvae of butterflies and moths. Other kinds of larvae are also very important as bird food. For example, many of the sandpipers nesting on northern tundra feed heavily on the larvae of crane flies; these larvae live in water or damp soil, where they are easily found by sandpipers probing for food.

The word "bug" is sometimes used loosely for any insect, but it is correctly applied only to the insects of the order Hemiptera (including stink bugs, leaf bugs, and others); I have referred to these as "true bugs." The term "fly" as used here applies only to members of the order Diptera, such as house flies, horse flies, and so on. Other insects with "-fly" in the name, such as dragonflies, mayflies, and stoneflies, are unrelated creatures belonging to other orders.

Insects make up the major class of creatures within the larger phylum known as the arthropods. Birds in general do not care about such distinctions, and a bird that eats insects typically will also eat other arthropods, such as spiders.

AQUATIC CREATURES EATEN BY BIRDS   You may find that the most unfamiliar words in this book involve the diets of various waterbirds. Most of us are not well acquainted with the small creatures that live in the water (especially the ocean) or in the mud at the water's edge. Many of these are not insects and are not easily covered by any other familiar term. For these creatures I have simply used the most accurate general term in most cases.

I have used the catch-all term "marine worms" to describe various wormlike creatures that live in mud or water, including polychaete worms and nereid worms. Some of these creatures are not at all related to each other (nor to our familiar earthworms). The term "euphausiid shrimp" turns up often under the diets of various seabirds. Euphausiids are not exactly shrimp, but they are shrimplike crustaceans that are tremendously important as food for seabirds (and for many other sea creatures up to the size of whales). Other important crustaceans include the copepods and amphipods.

For the person who develops a special interest in the feeding habits of shorebirds or seabirds, the best advice is to find a good basic textbook on marine biology or invertebrate zoology, and look for illustrations of the creatures mentioned in the diets of those birds.

HOW BIRDS FIND THEIR FOOD

Just as varied as *what* birds eat is *how* they get it — in other words, how they forage. Many songbirds feed mainly on insects, for example, but some may fly out to capture those insects in midair, others seek them on foliage, and still others creep about looking for them on tree bark or on the ground. In this book I have described the most typical feeding behavior for each species. Some birds will use a wide variety of foraging methods, while others are much more stereotyped in their foraging.

MOLT

Although it is not mentioned in species accounts in this book, molt is an important part of every bird's annual cycle. Molt is simply the process in which old feathers drop out and new ones grow in their place. This takes place in an orderly way, so that the bird always has a covering of feathers.

Most birds molt at a specific time of year — usually when they are neither nesting nor migrating, since molt, like those activities, takes up energy. A typical pattern for many birds is to go through a complete molt in late summer or fall, replacing all the feathers, and then have a partial molt in early spring, replacing feathers of the body and head. We are not likely to notice the molt except when it brings about a change in color, as when the American Goldfinch molts from winter brown to summer yellow, and then back to brown in the fall.

In most cases, the flight feathers of the wings and tail are molted a few at a time, so that the bird remains capable of flying. But in some birds (including most ducks, for example), all the flight feathers are lost at once, and the birds are flightless until the new set grows in.

MIGRATION

Entire books have been written about bird migration, and with good reason — it is one of the most amazing and complicated phenomena of the natural world. In this book, we can only touch on a few aspects of migration.

Some birds are very sedentary, rarely moving more than a few miles from where they were hatched. But most, at least in the temperate zone, do at least some moving around.

The typical pattern of migration in North America is for birds to move north in spring and south in fall. But there is much variation in this. Some western hummingbirds, for example, move north through the deserts in late winter and move south through the mountains in late summer (and a few hummingbirds mainly move east and west). The southbound migration of shorebirds may be under way by the end of June, but some straggling migrants may still be on their way south in early January. Some migration is going on during every month of the year.

Some birds, such as geese and cranes, apparently learn the migration route by traveling with their elders. But for many, the route is instinctive. In many songbirds, shorebirds, and others, the young tend to migrate later in the fall than the adults; they are making the trip on their own, reaching their wintering grounds by sheer instinct.

The ways in which birds navigate are still being studied. Apparently they can use many different clues, such as the position of the sun at various times of day, and the positions of the constellations at night (many small birds migrate mostly at night). At least some birds can detect the Earth's magnetic field, and some can hear very low-pitched sounds (such as the crashing of the surf) from great distances. The glow on the horizon can help them find their way at dawn or dusk, and they can detect the angles of polarized light coming through heavy clouds. Birds probably have other clues that we have not yet discovered.

Sometimes a migratory bird will show up thousands of miles from where it is "supposed" to be. At one time it was believed that such birds had been blown off course by storms (and this is true in a few cases, such as those involving hurricanes); however, many of these strays now appear to have faulty navigational systems. Their instincts have gone awry, taking them to a place where the species does not normally occur at all.

In a different class from regular migrants are those birds that wander erratically, perhaps being present in large numbers in a certain region one year and being totally absent the next. Such "irruptive" migrants in North America include various northern finches and owls, waxwings, and a few others. The driving force behind such invasions seems to be food supply, not weather or anything else. If wild food crops are poor in the north, an invasion of northern birds may move south.

ROOSTING

For most kinds of birds, little is known about where they sleep, or roost, at night. In general, most seem to seek some sort of sheltered place. Some birds that place their nests in holes in trees, such as woodpeckers, also sleep in such cavities. Many songbirds probably roost among dense foliage in shrubs or trees.

Roosting habits are somewhat better known for those birds that roost en masse. Various kinds of birds are known to form communal roosts in the nonbreeding season. A familiar evening sight is a procession of herons, or crows, or flocks of blackbirds, all flying in the same direction, heading for a sheltered spot where large numbers will spend the night.

The reasons for communal roosting are still debated, but these gatherings may serve as information centers. Birds that have had good foraging are likely to head back to the same area the next day. Birds that have fared poorly in finding food may wait the next morning at the roost and then follow those that appear to be headed toward better feeding grounds. In other cases, communal roosts may help the birds to keep warm, or they may have other functions that we do not yet understand.

SURVIVAL AND LIFE SPAN

For some families of birds I have mentioned life expectancies in the wild. In most cases, such information comes from birds that have been banded and then recovered again later.

There is a major difference between the maximum life span and the average life span of a bird. Mortality is very heavy among young birds — many do not survive past their first few weeks out of the nest, and many more may die during their first migration or their first winter. Those that last through their first year may have a better survival rate for a few years thereafter, but in general, wild birds do not have long lives. A small bird that reaches 10 years, or a large bird that survives past 20 years, could be said to have lived to a ripe old age.

CONSERVATION STATUS

For most of the birds given full treatment in this book, I have included a brief statement on how well they are doing — whether their populations are increasing or decreasing, and what major threats they might face. When this section is missing, it means that populations of that species appear to be stable and not threatened. Some large birds such as waterfowl are censused regularly by government agencies involved in game management. But for most birds, our best data on population trends comes from two projects: the Breeding Bird Survey (BBS) and the Christmas Bird Count (CBC). The BBS, launched in 1969, involves randomly chosen routes that are censused in a very standardized way. The CBC has been run for almost a century; its approach is more free-form and variable, so the numbers are not always directly comparable, but it gives us a huge base of information about some trends. When I state here that a given bird is declining or increasing, this is usually based mainly on data from the BBS, often with backup from the CBC or from other census work.

RANGE MAPS IN THE TEXT

The primary subject of this book is *how* birds live, but that is usually affected by *where* they live. A bird that spends the summer in the far north and the winter in our southeastern states, for example, will have a very different lifestyle from another bird that lives all year in the deserts of the southwest. We have included small range maps for most species, to give you a general idea of where that bird is found.

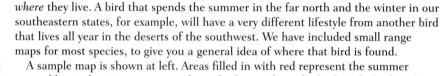

A sample map is shown at left. Areas filled in with red represent the summer range, blue is the winter range, and purple shows where the bird might be found at all seasons.

On some maps you will notice dotted lines of red or blue. These indicate areas where the bird may be found in very small numbers, or only in occasional years, during the summer (red) or winter (blue).

■ *Summer*

■ *Winter*

■ *All seasons*

Maps in this book are derived primarily from the maps used in the CD-ROM *Peterson Multimedia Guides: North American Birds*. Those, in turn, were adapted from range maps compiled by Virginia Marie Peterson for the Peterson Field Guides to *Eastern Birds* (1980) and *Western Birds* (1990), published by Houghton Mifflin Company. Anyone who wants detailed information on bird ranges should consult the original maps in the Multimedia Guide or the printed Field Guides. The process of reducing the maps to fit the format of this book inevitably resulted in some loss of detail, so they are meant only to give a general idea of bird distribution.

Because of the way the maps were produced, the ranges of many birds appear to end abruptly at the Mexican border. In real life, birds do not recognize international boundaries, of course. If the range of a species is shown extending to the border, in almost all cases the reader may assume that the bird is also found for some distance south into Mexico.

PHOTOGRAPHS IN THE TEXT

For most of the birds given full treatment in this book, we have included a photograph. These portraits were taken by many of North America's top bird photographers; a list of photo credits appears in the back of the book.

These photos are not intended to help you to recognize the birds you see. This is not a field guide. The best guides to bird identification, such as the Peterson Field Guides, are compact books designed to be carried easily into the field, and they are illustrated with paintings instead of photographs. In this book, the photos will serve to give a general idea of the birds' appearance. While you are reading the biography of a particular species, the photo will help to remind you of what it looks like. In most cases, the photo depicts an adult (usually a male) in summer plumage, but there are various exceptions.

The first pioneer ornithologists to explore North America were concerned mainly with cataloguing the variety of birdlife they found here, describing the physical appearance of the birds and giving them names. But serious attempts to describe the habits of the birds began not long afterwards — nearly two centuries ago.

COMPILATIONS OF BIRD LIFE HISTORIES

Alexander Wilson, often called "the father of American ornithology," explored eastern North America from 1794 to 1813, studying birds. He published a nine-volume work titled *American Ornithology, or the Natural History of the Birds of the United States*. This was largely a descriptive work, but he discussed the habits of the birds in as much detail as possible. Wilson's rival, John James Audubon, is best remembered as an artist, but Audubon also published a five-volume series called *Ornithological Biography, or an Account of the Habits of the Birds of the United States*. Both Wilson and Audubon were keen observers (even if Audubon sometimes strayed into exaggeration), and their works set the stage for later studies.

In the 1890s, Charles E. Bendire produced two volumes under the title *Life Histories of North American Birds*. These drew on Bendire's own observations and on material sent to him by various correspondents; they covered many species, but the series languished after Bendire passed away in 1897.

In 1910, the U.S. National Museum (which had published Bendire's work) invited Arthur Cleveland Bent to continue the series. Bent was a well-to-do businessman and amateur ornithologist with a reputation for getting things done, and he tackled the job immediately. It developed into a remarkable series of 26 volumes, published between 1919 and 1968 (the last four volumes posthumously). Each volume of Bent's *Life Histories of North American Birds* addressed one group of birds, with accounts drawn from numerous correspondents and from Bent's own studies. Many of these accounts were just anecdotes, but they pulled together a vast amount of information not available earlier, and they still make interesting reading today.

DETAILED STUDIES OF BIRD SPECIES

Since the time of Bent's compilations, studies of birds' lives have become more scientific. There is now less emphasis on simple description and more on measuring things precisely. For example, Bent might have written about how flocks of chickadees go trooping merrily through the winter woods. Professor Susan M. Smith also watches chickadees, but she has color-banded them for individual recognition, she knows each one's age, parentage, and social status, and she measures exactly how far they travel, where they forage, how they interact, and a host of other variables. Such an approach sounds daunting, but the resulting discoveries make the birds even more interesting.

Highly detailed studies have been carried out for several of our birds. For example, Val Nolan spent thousands of hours studying the behavior of Prairie Warblers. And for more than 25 years, the Florida Scrub-Jay has been the subject of intense study by Glen Woolfenden, John Fitzpatrick, and their students.

Other kinds of detailed studies have focused on certain aspects of birds' lives rather than on particular species. For example, Donald Kroodsma has studied the singing behavior of many birds. John Wiens has studied how whole communities of birds fit together. Stephen Rothstein has studied how various birds react to parasitism of their nests by cowbirds. All of these detailed projects, researching small pieces of the puzzle, help to bring greater understanding of birdlife in general.

THE NEW CLASSIC: *BIRDS OF NORTH AMERICA*

With the explosive growth in bird study during recent decades, Bent's *Life Histories* — especially the earlier volumes — had become hopelessly out of date. The American Ornithologists' Union (AOU) had discussed a plan to bring out individual life history accounts for each species in North America, but the idea was going nowhere until the late 1980s, when the AOU convinced Frank B. Gill to take on the project. Gill combined a worldwide reputation as a leading ornithologist with incredible energy and an unmatched talent for organization. As head of the bird department at the Academy of Natural Sciences of Philadelphia, Gill arranged for these new life histories to be published jointly by the Academy and the AOU. Funding was arranged, a standard format was worked out by Peter Stettenheim and others, Alan Poole was hired to edit the series, and the first numbers appeared in 1992.

Each species in *Birds of North America* (as the new series is called) is being published separately, in an account of up to 32 pages. The species accounts are released in the order in which they are ready, not in standard checklist order. Although it is only one-third completed (as of early 1996), *Birds of North America* is already being hailed as a landmark in science, an indispensable reference for anyone who studies birds. Each account gives a thorough summary of what is known about that bird, and — just as important — what is *not* known.

OPPORTUNITIES TO ADD TO OUR KNOWLEDGE

Amateur birders often assume that the lives of birds are already well known. This is far from true. A few species have been studied extensively, but for the vast majority of birds in North America, our information on life histories is fragmentary and sketchy. Practically all the accounts in *Birds of North America* contain numerous statements of "No information" or "Little information" under various headings.

While I was researching this book, fewer than 200 of the species accounts for *Birds of North America* had been published; for all the rest of the birds, I had to search widely for data. I often found that published statements were based on only a few observations.

For example, consider the height of the nest of the Golden-fronted Woodpecker. Charles Bendire, in his *Life Histories of North American Birds* published in 1895, stated that this woodpecker's nest is usually from 6 to 25 feet above the ground. This was quoted in A. C. Bent's *Life Histories of North American Woodpeckers*, published in 1939. Lester Short's *Woodpeckers of the World* (1982) says that Golden-fronted Woodpeckers in the northern part of their range usually nest 6 to 25 feet up, and *The Birder's Handbook* by Paul Ehrlich et al. (1988) gives the nest height as 6 to 25 feet. In this book I give a slightly different figure (usually lower than 20 feet) only on the basis of several nests I have seen in Texas, but this is certainly not definitive, and I would welcome better information. With all the bird observers on this continent today, we should be able to do better than simply quoting a source published over a century ago!

The fact is that anyone with time and interest can add to our knowledge of birdlife. For those who are ambitious enough to start their own study projects, a good start is to read the *Birds of North America* accounts and look for those designations of "No information" or "Little information." Those with less time, experience, or ambition can take part in cooperative studies of birds. Several such studies are under way, organized by professional scientists but dependent on the efforts of volunteers. Two organizations that sponsor such work are the National Audubon Society and the Cornell Laboratory of Ornithology. Everyone who is interested in the future of our birdlife should belong to both of these fine groups:

National Audubon Society
700 Broadway
New York, NY 10003

Cornell Laboratory of Ornithology
159 Sapsucker Woods Road
Ithaca, NY 14850

There are also educational opportunities available through the Roger Tory Peterson Institute:

Roger Tory Peterson Institute
311 Curtis Street
Jamestown, NY 14701

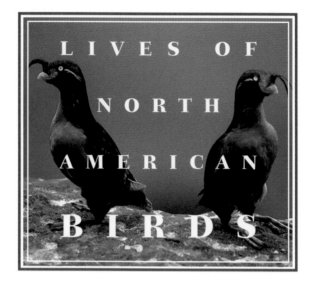

LIVES OF NORTH AMERICAN BIRDS

These are long-bodied, low-slung divers of northern waters. All five species of loons nest around lakes in the far north and spend the winter mostly on coastal waters in the north temperate zone. All of them show a seasonal change from rather plain gray and white winter plumage to a more strongly patterned breeding plumage.

Loons find most of their food underwater, diving with a forward lunge. They can also alter their buoyancy so that they float with only the eyes and bill above the surface. They fly strongly, but in taking flight they must patter along the water's surface to become airborne. As with many other diving birds, their legs are set far back on their bodies for better underwater propulsion. This structure makes them very awkward on land, and most loons (except the small Red-throated) cannot take off when "grounded."

Banding records indicate that loons may live 20–30 years.

Feeding
In general, loons forage by diving from the surface and swimming underwater. They often swim along the surface with their heads partly submerged, peering about underwater, watching for prey before they dive. They are propelled mainly by their feet but may sometimes also use their wings when turning or to get a burst of speed. Most of their dives last less than one minute and remain within about 30 feet of the surface, but they supposedly can dive to more than 200 feet below the surface. Loons find their food by sight, and their eyes are reported to have special adaptations for vision both in air and underwater.

Loons feed largely on fish at most times, but they also will take mollusks, crustaceans, insects, marine worms, frogs, and sometimes plant material. Their diets may tend to be more varied in summer than in winter.

Nesting
Loons apparently first breed at the age of 2 or 3 years, and the same two birds often remain paired year after year (in other words, they may mate for life). The nest site is on the ground at the water's edge, sometimes in shallow water, and the same site may be used for several years. Nest-building is usually accomplished by the sitting bird pulling surrounding plant material toward itself and forming it into a hollow mound around its body. Loons usually lay 2 eggs, olive to brown with darker spots. Both sexes incubate. Young leave the nest within a day or two after hatching and are fed by both parents; sometimes they ride on their parents' backs.

Displays
Nesting loons defend their territories mainly by voice, and their loud "yodeling" or wailing cries are often heard around northern lakes, especially at night. Some species also perform display flights, flying in wide circles over their territories. If intruders enter the nesting territory, loons can be very aggressive in defense. They may rush at intruders, rearing up out of the water with noisy splashing and wing-flapping.

Courtship displays often involve both members of a pair performing ritualized bill-dipping movements, dipping the tips of their bills in the water repeatedly. They also may dive with conspicuous splashing and swim rapidly past each other underwater.

RED-THROATED LOON   *Gavia stellata*

Red-throated Loon

The smallest of its family, the Red-throated also breeds farther north than any other loon, reaching the northernmost coast of Greenland. It may nest at very small ponds, doing much of its feeding at larger lakes or coastal waters a few miles away. This species takes flight from the water more readily than other loons, often taking off without a running start; unlike the others, it is also able to take off from land.

HABITAT   *Coastal waters, bays, estuaries; in summer, tundra lakes.* Breeding habitat includes small ponds as well as larger lakes, mostly on tundra but sometimes within edge of northern forest. Mainly on ocean in winter (a few on large lakes); often in shallower water than other loons, as in protected bays, large estuaries.

FEEDING   **Diet:** *Mostly fish.* Includes cod and herring on salt water, and trout, salmon, and char on fresh water. Also shrimps, crabs, snails, mussels, aquatic insects, leeches, and frogs. In early spring in high arctic, may also feed on plant material. Young are fed mainly insects and crustaceans for first few days. **Behavior:** See family introduction.

NESTING   May mate for life. Courtship displays include both birds rapidly dipping bills in water, diving and swimming past each other, making fast rushes underwater. Both members of pair defend nesting territory against intruding loons. **Nest:** Site, often reused from year to year, is on shore or in shallow water. Apparently both sexes help build nest. Nest is a heap of vegetation, or sometimes a simple scrape on top of a hummock; nest material may be added after incubation begins. **Eggs:** Usually 2, sometimes 1, rarely 3. Olive with blackish brown spots. Incubation by both sexes (though female may do more), 24–29 days. **Young:** Leave nest and take to water about 1 day after hatching. Both parents feed young, rarely carry young on their backs. Young can fly at about 7 weeks. One brood per year.

MIGRATION   Usually migrates singly, sometimes in small groups. Generally migrates along coast, a mile or two offshore. Rarely seen on inland waters south of Canada except on Great Lakes, where large numbers may stop on migration.

CONSERVATION STATUS   Populations probably stable, but vulnerable to loss of habitat due to development in high Arctic and to pollution in coastal wintering areas.

ARCTIC LOON   *Gavia arctica*

The Old World counterpart to our Pacific Loon, entering North America mainly as an uncommon summer resident in far western Alaska. The two are very similar, and until recently they were combined as one species under the name "Arctic Loon." The true Arctic Loon (of the form found in eastern Siberia and western Alaska) is larger than the Pacific Loon, but its habits are similar.

HABITAT   *Lakes, ocean.* In Alaskan breeding range, found mainly on large lakes surrounded by open tundra. In winter on ocean, probably usually within a few miles of land.

FEEDING **Diet:** *Mostly fish, but more varied in summer.* In winter and on ocean eats mainly small fish, including gobies, sticklebacks, herrings, cod, and others. In breeding season, diet also includes crustaceans, mollusks, aquatic insects. Rarely eats frogs, leeches, small amounts of plant material. **Behavior:** See family introduction.

NESTING May mate for life. Courtship displays include ritualized bill-dipping and splash-diving by both members of pair. **Nest:** Site is in shallow water, or on island or shore near water. Nest is a heap of vegetation, sometimes mixed with mud; may rarely build floating nest. Both sexes help build nest. **Eggs:** 2, sometimes 1–3. Olive to brown, with blackish spots. Both sexes incubate (although female does more), 28–30 days. **Young:** Leave nest shortly after hatching, return to nest to sleep for the first few nights, then sleep on water under parents' wings. Both parents feed young. Adults may fly several miles from nesting territory to other waters to eat and to bring back food for young. Age at first flight probably 60–65 days. One brood per year.

MIGRATION Movements of Alaska birds poorly known; may winter in waters around Aleutians. Numbers are seen flying past St. Lawrence Island, Bering Sea, in late spring.

PACIFIC LOON *Gavia pacifica*

Pacific Loon

This loon is hardly "Pacific" in summer—its breeding range extends across northern Canada as far east as Hudson Bay and Baffin Island. However, the great majority of these birds head west to the Pacific coast to spend the winter.

HABITAT *Ocean, open water; in summer, tundra lakes.* Breeds mainly on lakes surrounded by tundra, also lakes within forested country; often overlaps with Red-throated Loon, but requires larger and deeper bodies of water. In winter, mostly on ocean, often farther from shore than Red-throated or Common loons.

FEEDING **Diet:** *Includes fish, crustaceans, insects.* Diet varies with place and season. Apparently eats mostly small fish when these are available, especially in winter and on ocean. Also eats crustaceans, mollusks, aquatic insects, and some plant material, especially during breeding season. **Behavior:** Forages by diving from surface and swimming underwater, propelled mainly by feet. May dip head into water repeatedly, looking for prey, before diving.

NESTING May mate for life. Courtship displays include ritualized bill-dipping and splash-diving by both members of pair. Less aerial display than in Red-throated Loon. Very aggressive in defense of nesting territory, and has been seen to kill ducklings that strayed near nest. **Nest:** Site is almost always at edge of water, on shore or island, sometimes in shallow water. Nest (probably built by both sexes) is a heap of vegetation pulled up from around nest site, sometimes mixed with mud or with mud foundation; may rarely build floating nest. **Eggs:** 2, sometimes 1, rarely 3. Brown, with blackish brown spots. Both sexes incubate (although female does more), 23–25 days. **Young:** Leave nest shortly after hatching, return to nest for resting and sleeping during first few days. Both parents feed young. Adults may fly several miles from nesting territory to other waters to feed and to bring back food for young. Age at first flight probably 60–65 days. One brood per year.

Found inland rarely in fall and very rarely in spring. Therefore, birds may either make long overland flights or travel long distance around Alaska en route between wintering areas on Pacific coast and breeding grounds in central Canadian Arctic. Northbound migrants along Pacific coast may travel in flocks several miles offshore, usually less than 60 feet above water; they avoid flying on days with strong headwinds.

CONSERVATION STATUS Numbers apparently stable. Would be vulnerable to pollution in offshore wintering areas.

COMMON LOON *Gavia immer*

A long-bodied, low-slung diver. Many people consider the loon a symbol of wilderness; its rich yodeling and moaning calls, heard by day or night, are characteristic sounds of early summer in the north woods. In winter, silent and more subtly marked, Common Loons inhabit coastal waters and large southern lakes. In such places they are solitary while feeding but may gather in loose flocks at night.

HABITAT *Wooded lakes, tundra ponds, coastal waters.* In summer mainly on lakes in coniferous forest zone, also beyond treeline onto open tundra. Chooses large lakes with ample room for takeoff and with good supply of small fish. In winter mainly on ocean, usually fairly shallow waters close to shore; also on large lakes and reservoirs that remain ice-free.

FEEDING **Diet:** *Mostly small fish.* Includes fish up to about 10 inches long such as minnows, suckers, perch, gizzard shad, rock cod, killifish, many others. Also crustaceans, mollusks, aquatic insects, leeches, frogs. Sometimes aquatic plants such as pondweeds and algae. **Behavior:** Forages by diving and swimming underwater, propelled mainly by feet. Before diving, may swim on surface with head forward and partly submerged to peer underwater. Small fish are swallowed underwater, larger items are brought to surface and eaten there.

NESTING Apparently first breeds at age of 2 years. Nesting territory claimed by "yodeling" song, also by flying in circles over territory with loud calls. In courtship displays, pairs dip bills in water repeatedly; rear up to vertical posture with wings partly spread; race side by side across surface of water. **Nest:** Built by both sexes. Site always very near water, on island or shore, partly hidden by surrounding vegetation. Nest, often reused from year to year, is a mound

Common Loon

of grasses, twigs, reeds. **Eggs:** 2, rarely just 1. Olive, spotted with brown or black. Incubation by both sexes (female may do more), 24–31 days. **Young:** Leave nest within 1 or 2 days after hatching, can dive and swim underwater at 2–3 days. Young are tended and fed by both parents; when small, sometimes ride on parents' backs. Capable of flight at about 10–11 weeks after hatching. One brood per year.

MIGRATION In coastal areas, migrates singly or in small flocks just offshore, often low over water; usually flies higher when migrating over land. Large numbers may pause in migration on Great Lakes and other inland waters.

CONSERVATION STATUS Has disappeared from some former nesting areas owing to human disturbance on lakes in summer; acid rain may also reduce food supplies in breeding range. Has been protected on some breeding grounds in the northeast by volunteer "Loon Rangers" who patrol the lakes and help to educate the public about conservation.

YELLOW-BILLED LOON   *Gavia adamsii*

A big dagger-billed diving bird of wilderness waters. Closely related to Common Loon but even larger (the largest member of the family) and more northerly. Summers on high Arctic tundra, winters off wild northern shores, and occurs only in very small numbers south of Canada. Its great size, remote range, and general rarity give the Yellow-billed Loon an aura of mystery for many birders.

HABITAT   *Tundra lakes in summer; coastal waters in winter.* Breeds in high Arctic tundra region, often on large lakes but also on smaller lakes if good feeding areas are nearby; may fly up to 5 miles from nest site to feeding areas on rivers, coastal lagoons. In winter on ocean, generally on bays, inlets, among island groups; rarely on large lakes in interior.

FEEDING   **Diet:** *Probably mostly fish.* Diet not well known. Apparently feeds mainly on small to medium-sized fish, including sculpin, tomcod, rock cod; also crustaceans and mollusks, probably some insects in summer. Young may eat some plant material. **Behavior:** See family introduction.

NESTING   May mate for life. In courtship displays, pairs dip bills in water repeatedly; splash-dive and swim past each other underwater. **Nest:** Male may select site, both sexes probably help build nest. Site is always very near water, on island or shore, and may be partly hidden by surrounding vegetation. Nest, often reused from year to year, is a mound of tundra vegetation with depression at center; sometimes turf is overturned to form a mud foundation. **Eggs:** 2. Brown or olive, spotted with blackish brown. Incubation period 27–29 days; both parents incubate. **Young:** Leave nest 1–2 days after hatching. Adults very aggressive in defense of downy young. Young are fed by both parents, sometimes ride on parents' backs. Second chick of brood often disappears a few days after hatching. Age at first flight not known, probably about 12 weeks. One brood per year.

MIGRATION   Most winter in limited area of southern Alaska and coastal British Columbia, but route between wintering and breeding areas unknown; may follow coast around Alaska rather than flying overland. In recent years, single birds (usually immature) have been found wintering on reservoirs and lakes in interior as far east as Illinois and Arkansas, as far south as Arizona and Texas.

CONSERVATION STATUS   World population has been estimated at under 10,000, with half of these in Alaska. Vulnerable to oil spills and other pollution in the Arctic.

Yellow-billed Loon

GREBES (Family Podicipedidae)

Often compared to loons because members of both families are superb divers, grebes are much more widespread; their approximately 20 species inhabit every continent except Antarctica.

Grebes are adapted for spending almost all their time in the water. Their plumage is very thick and waterproof. Their feet are set far back on their bodies; this arrangement makes them almost helpless on land, but it is ideal for swimming underwater, when the birds hold their wings folded tightly against their bodies and push with their feet.

In diving from the water's surface, a grebe usually thrusts its head forward and down, and disappears with hardly a ripple. Sometimes it will lunge forward in diving, and it can also alter its buoyancy so that it sinks gradually out of sight or floats with only its head above the surface.

Grebes are not often seen flying except during migration. Awkward in takeoff, they must skitter across the water to become airborne. They generally cannot take off from land; sometimes a migrating grebe will land on wet pavement at night, mistaking the reflections for open water, and it may be stranded there unless rescued by a passing human. On some large lakes in the tropics, where the birds have no need to migrate, flightless species of grebes have evolved.

Feeding Most of the time, grebes do most of their foraging while swimming underwater, although they will also take some food from the water's surface or from plants hanging over the water. They feed on a wide variety of aquatic creatures. As a general rule, the smaller species eat more insects, while the larger ones take more fish. Other food items include crustaceans, tadpoles, leeches, and salamanders; small amounts of plant material in the diet may be swallowed incidentally along with other food.

Odd and unique is the grebes' habit of eating their own feathers. Adults of most species frequently pluck small feathers from their body plumage and swallow them, and they also feed feathers to their young. The purpose of this behavior is not well understood, but the soft mass of half-digested feathers in the stomach may provide some protection from sharp fish bones and other hard-to-digest items.

Nesting Because grebes are extremely awkward on land, their nests are usually surrounded by water. These may be mounds built up from the bottom in the shallows, or floating platforms of plant material. Typically both sexes help build the nest. The eggs are plain whitish to pale blue or buff at first, becoming stained darker in the nest; both parents help to incubate them. In many species, the incubating adult covers the eggs with nest material whenever it leaves the nest. The young can swim and dive shortly after hatching, and they soon leave the nest. They are fed by both parents and often ride on their parents' backs. At least in some species, the downy young have patches of bare skin on the head that turn red when the young are excited (such as when they are begging for food).

Displays Courtship displays of grebes are often complex and sometimes spectacular. In one common element of these displays, the members of a pair swim close to each other, turning their heads from side to side or nodding their heads up and down in a ritualized manner. Also common is the "weed dance": both birds dive underwater and come up with bits of weeds in their bills, and they then face each other with much posturing and bowing. Most elaborate is a "rushing" display, in which two birds rear up to a vertical position and then rush across the surface of the water side by side, with much pattering and splashing; this is most highly developed in Western and Clark's grebes.

Most courtship displays of grebes involve loud calls. Those species that live in dense marshy areas, such as Pied-billed and Least grebes, may have relatively simple physical displays; they may do more of their communication by voice, with members of a pair often calling in duet.

LEAST GREBE   *Tachybaptus dominicus*

A tiny diver of the American tropics, entering our area mainly in southern Texas. Seems to fly more readily than most grebes, and may quickly colonize temporary ponds or flooded areas. Often seen swimming and diving on small ponds or ditches in pursuit of aquatic insects, its main food. Sometimes the Least Grebe hides in dense marshes, where its presence may be revealed by metallic trilling calls, often given as a duet by members of a mated pair.

HABITAT   *Ponds, marshes.* In Texas, usually on shallow freshwater ponds and ditches, either fairly open or with heavy marsh vegetation. Often appears on small temporary ponds after rainy periods. In tropics, also on brackish marshes, lakes, slow-moving rivers, mangrove swamps.

FEEDING   **Diet:** *Mostly insects.* Feeds on wide variety of insects, including aquatic beetles, waterbugs, dragonfly larvae and adults, and others. Also small crustaceans, spiders, tadpoles, small fish. **Behavior:** Forages in several ways. Dives and swims underwater in pursuit of prey, captures insects on and above surface of water or takes them from waterside vegetation. May catch flying dragonflies by approaching them underwater and then erupting from beneath water's surface to snatch them from the air.

Least Grebe

NESTING   In Texas, breeds mainly spring and summer, sometimes at other seasons; nests year-round in the tropics. Courtship displays not well known, may include pair rising to upright position and gliding rapidly across surface of water. **Nest:** Site is in shallow water, usually 1–3 feet deep. Nest (built by both sexes) is a mass of decaying vegetation, either floating or resting on bottom, anchored to aquatic plants. Same nest often reused for subsequent broods. **Eggs:** 4–6, rarely 3–7. Whitish to very pale blue-green, becoming stained in nest. Incubation (by both sexes) about 21 days. **Young:** Can swim soon after hatching. Small young often ride on parents' backs; fed by both parents. Young may return to nest for sleeping and resting during first 2 weeks after hatching. Age at first flight not known. May raise 2–3 broods per year (possibly more in tropics).

MIGRATION   Not truly migratory, but moves around considerably, sometimes appearing quickly on newly formed ponds. Has strayed north to California, Arizona, and Louisiana. Has colonized many islands in Caribbean, and strays from Caribbean have reached Florida. Movements are probably mostly at night.

CONSERVATION STATUS   Numbers vary in limited range in United States. Many may be killed by exceptionally cold winters in Texas.

PIED-BILLED GREBE   *Podilymbus podiceps*

The most widespread grebe in the New World and the most familiar in most temperate parts of North America. Far less sociable than most grebes, almost never in flocks, sometimes found singly on small marshy ponds. When disturbed or suspicious, it may sink slowly until only head is above water. Rarely seen in flight. Often secretive in the breeding season, hiding in marsh, making bizarre whinnying, gobbling, cooing noises by day or night.

HABITAT   *Ponds, lakes, marshes; in winter, also salt bays.* In breeding season, chooses sites with heavy marsh vegetation but with some open water also. In migration and winter, still most likely on marshy freshwater ponds, but also on more open waters, including estuaries and coastal bays.

FEEDING   **Diet:** *Insects, fish, other aquatic life.* Diet highly variable with location and season; probably eats most small aquatic creatures in its habitat. Major food items include aquatic insects, crustaceans, small fish, leeches; also eats mollusks, frogs, tadpoles, salamanders, spiders, small amounts of aquatic plants. Like other grebes, swallows many feathers, and feeds feathers to its young. **Behavior:** Forages by diving from surface and swimming underwater, propelled mainly by feet.

Pied-billed Grebe

NESTING   Where climate allows, may have a long breeding season, from early spring to midautumn. Courtship displays less ritualized than in most grebes, involving much calling, sometimes in duet. **Nest:** Site is in shallow water in marsh, next to opening so that birds can approach nest underwater. Nest (built by both sexes) a dense mass of plant material, floating or built up from bottom, anchored to standing vegetation. **Eggs:** 4–7, rarely 2–10. Pale bluish white, becoming stained brownish. Incubation by both sexes (female does more), about 23 days. Eggs are covered with nest material when incubating bird departs. **Young:** Can swim soon after hatching. Young are fed by both parents, often ride on parents' backs when small; adults may swim underwater with young on back. Age at first flight not well known. One or 2 broods per year, possibly more in south.

MIGRATION   Southern populations may be permanently resident, northern ones strongly migratory. Apparently migrates mostly at night. Migration relatively late in fall, early in spring.

CONSERVATION STATUS   Still common and widespread, but surveys show declines in recent decades.

TYPICAL MEDIUM-SIZED GREBES — GENUS *Podiceps*

Unlike the Least and Pied-billed grebes, these birds inhabit marshes only in the nesting season; in winter they are typically on very open waters, with most Horned and Red-necked grebes wintering on coastal bays. All three of our species show a major seasonal change from bright breeding plumage to very dull winter plumage.

HORNED GREBE   *Podiceps auritus*

A small diver found mostly on northern marshes in summer, coastal bays in winter. Also widespread in Eurasia, where it is called Slavonian Grebe. Similar to Eared Grebe but much less gregarious; it seldom nests in colonies and seldom gathers in large flocks at other seasons. Like other grebes, it must patter across surface of water to become airborne; may become trapped when waters freeze quickly overnight.

HABITAT   *Lakes, ponds; coastal waters.* Summers on lakes having both open water and marsh vegetation, surrounded by northern forest, prairie, sometimes out onto southern

Horned Grebe

edges of tundra. Winters mainly on ocean, including protected bays and exposed shores. Also some in winter on large lakes and reservoirs, more commonly so in recent years.

FEEDING   **Diet:** *Mostly insects, crustaceans, fish.* Diet varies with habitat and season. In summer may eat mainly insects and crustaceans, also some fish, tadpoles, leeches, salamanders, small amounts of plant material. May eat mostly fish in winter, also crustaceans, mollusks, insects. Like other grebes, also swallows many feathers. **Behavior:** Forages by diving from surface and swimming underwater, propelled by feet. Also takes items from on or above water's surface. Usually solitary in feeding, but flocks may rarely forage cooperatively; has been seen foraging in association with Surf Scoters.

NESTING   Courtship displays involve posturing by both members of pair; both rise to vertical position on water with head feathers fully raised, turning heads rapidly; both dive and come up with bits of weed in bills, then rush across surface of water side by side carrying weeds. **Nest:** Site is in shallow water, usually among marsh growth. Nest (built by both sexes) a floating heap of wet plant material (with depression in middle for eggs), usually anchored to standing vegetation. **Eggs:** 4–6, sometimes 3–7. Whitish to very pale green or buff, becoming nest-stained. Both sexes incubate, 22–25 days. **Young:** Can swim shortly after hatching; fed by both parents, and often ride on parents' backs. Age at first flight 55–60 days. One brood per year, sometimes 2; young from first brood may help in feeding of second.

MIGRATION   Usually migrates singly. May migrate by day along coast, usually at night over land. A change in overall winter range detected in recent years, with more and more wintering on man-made reservoirs in the southeastern states.

CONSERVATION STATUS   Thought to have declined in recent decades, although solid data are mostly lacking.

RED-NECKED GREBE   *Podiceps grisegena*

A large grebe of northern marshes and coasts. Not especially wary when not molested by humans; nests on park lakes in some cities, such as Anchorage, Alaska.

Red-necked Grebe

Colorful, noisy, and conspicuous on its nesting territory, it seems a different bird in winter, when it is gray and silent, a solitary bird of offshore waters. Rather clumsy in takeoff and not often seen flying except in migration.

HABITAT   *Lakes, ponds; in winter, salt water.* **Summer:** On freshwater lakes or large ponds having some marsh vegetation, surrounded by prairie, northern forest, or sometimes tundra. **Winter:** Mostly on ocean, on protected bays but also miles offshore at times; also a few on some large lakes.

FEEDING   **Diet:** *Mostly insects and fish.* Diet varies with season. May feed mainly on small fish in winter on coastal waters; in summer on marshes and ponds, feeds mainly on insects. Also eats crustaceans,

mollusks, tadpoles, nereid worms, very small amounts of plant matter. Like other grebes, may eat feathers. **Behavior:** Forages while swimming underwater or while swimming on surface with head submerged. Also takes items (such as insects) from on or above water's surface or from waterside plants.

NESTING   Courtship displays are complex, with loud calls, raising of crest. Members of pair may face each other and rise partly out of water, chest to chest; sit close together while turning heads from side to side; bring up bits of weed from underwater and perform ritual dance while holding weeds. **Nest:** Site is in shallow water among marsh vegetation. Nest (built by both sexes) is a floating mass of plant material with a definite depression at the top, anchored to standing plants. **Eggs:** 4–5, sometimes 2–6. Bluish white or very pale buff, becoming nest-stained brown. Both sexes incubate, 20–23 days. **Young:** Are able to swim shortly after hatching; are fed by both parents, and may ride on parents' backs. Age at first flight not well known, may be 10 weeks in some cases. Usually 1 brood per year, rarely 2.

MIGRATION   Migration over land seems to be mostly at night, although migrates off coastlines during day. Apparently some normally winter on Great Lakes; during extremely harsh winters, these may be driven out when lakes freeze over.

CONSERVATION STATUS   Population status not well known, but may have declined in recent decades. Vulnerable to pollution in coastal wintering areas.

EARED GREBE   *Podiceps nigricollis*

A common grebe of freshwater lakes in the west. Gregarious at all seasons; nests in dense colonies, sometimes congregates in huge numbers on lakes during migration

and winter. Probably as an adaptation to life in the arid west, it is flexible in distribution, quickly taking advantage of temporary or man-made new bodies of water.

HABITAT   *Prairie lakes, ponds; in winter, open lakes, salt bays.* Favored nesting areas are lakes or large ponds with extensive marshy borders. Opportunistic, it may quickly occupy new or temporary habitats. During migration and winter, mainly on large freshwater or alkaline lakes. Also on coastal bays, but seen less often on ocean than Horned Grebe.

FEEDING   **Diet:** *Mostly insects and crustaceans.* Feeds on insects (such as aquatic beetles, dragonfly larvae, flies, mayflies), crustaceans, mollusks, tadpoles, a few small fish. During autumn stopover on large alkaline lakes, may feed mainly on brine shrimp. Young are fed mainly on insects. Like other grebes, sometimes

Eared Grebe

eats feathers. **Behavior:** Forages by diving and swimming underwater, propelled by feet. Also takes many insects and other items from surface of water.

NESTING   Courtship displays are complex. Male and female may swim side by side while turning heads and calling loudly; also face each other while rearing up out of water and turning heads from side to side; at climax of display, pair may rear up to vertical position and rush across surface of water side by side. **Nest:** Built by both sexes, a floating platform of weeds, anchored to standing vegetation in shallow water. **Eggs:** Usually 3–5, rarely 1–6. Whitish at first, becoming nest-stained brown. Incubation (by both sexes) about 21 days. **Young:** Leave nest after last egg hatches, are tended and fed by both parents. Adults may separate, each taking part of brood. Young may ride on parents' backs when small. May be independent by 21 days after hatching; age at first flight not well known. One brood per year, rarely 2.

MIGRATION Migration begins earlier in fall than in Horned Grebe. Generally migrates at night. Some birds migrate southeast from breeding range to winter near Gulf coast.

CONSERVATION STATUS Populations generally stable, but vulnerable because large numbers depend on just a few major lakes at some seasons (such as Great Salt Lake, Mono Lake, Salton Sea).

LARGE GREBES — GENUS *Aechmophorus*

These are graceful, swan-shaped diving birds of western waters. Western and Clark's grebes are famous for their spectacular courtship displays; in fact, their elaborate courtship rituals are among the most complex known for any birds. They eat fish more consistently than our other grebes. Their downy young are plain white and gray; the young of all other grebes are striped at first.

WESTERN GREBE   *Aechmophorus occidentalis*

Western Grebes are highly gregarious at all seasons, nesting in colonies and wintering in flocks. Their thin, reedy calls are characteristic sounds of western marshes in summer.

HABITAT *Rushy lakes, sloughs; in winter, bays, ocean.* Summers mainly on freshwater lakes with large areas of both open water and marsh vegetation; rarely on tidal marshes.

Western Grebe

Winters mainly on sheltered bays or estuaries on coast, also on large freshwater lakes, rarely on rivers.

FEEDING **Diet:** *Mostly fish.* Apparently feeds mainly on fish at all seasons and in all habitats. Also known to eat crustaceans, insects, polychaete worms, salamanders. Like other grebes, also eats feathers. **Behavior:** Forages by diving from surface and swimming underwater, propelled mainly by feet. Western and Clark's are only grebes having structure in neck allowing rapid spearlike thrusting of bill; may be useful in spearing fish, but use of this behavior is not well known.

NESTING Breeds in colonies. Courtship displays are elaborate and complex. Most conspicuous is a display in which two (or more) birds rear up to upright posture and rush across surface of water side by side, with loud pattering of feet, diving underwater at end of rush; other displays include "dancing" on water with bits of weed held in bill. **Nest:** Site is in shallow-water marsh. Nest (built by both sexes) a floating heap of plant material anchored to standing vegetation. **Eggs:** 2–4, rarely 1–6. Pale bluish white, becoming nest-stained brown. Incubation by both sexes, about 24 days. Hatching not synchronized; last egg may be abandoned in nest. **Young:** Climb onto back of parent within minutes after hatching, soon leave nest; are fed by both parents. Patch of bare yellow skin on head of young turns scarlet when young beg for food or are separated from parents. Age at first flight about 10 weeks. One brood per year.

MIGRATION Migrates at night, probably in flocks. Most birds from northern part of range migrate west to Pacific coast. Some southwestern and Mexican populations probably permanent residents.

Around beginning of 20th century, tens of thousands were killed for their feathers. Apparent recovery since, and has begun breeding in new areas not occupied historically. Mexican populations of both Western and Clark's grebes may be declining as cutting of tules on lakes removes nesting habitat.

CLARK'S GREBE *Aechmophorus clarkii*

Described to science in 1858, Clark's Grebe was soon dismissed as a mere variant of Western Grebe, and thereafter was ignored for over a century. Studies in the 1970s and 1980s, however, showed that although Western and Clark's are extremely similar, they are two distinct species.

Minor differences in face pattern, bill color, and voice seem to be enough to prevent the two from interbreeding most of the time, even where they nest in mixed colonies. Apparent hybrids have been found, but they are a minority of the population. Although Clark's may be found with Western Grebes at all seasons, it tends to associate more with its own kind.

In almost all aspects of behavior that have been studied, Clark's Grebe seems identical to Western Grebe. In one study on lakes in Oregon, Clark's tended to feed farther from shore and in deeper water.

ALBATROSSES (Family Diomedeidae)

Albatrosses are very large, long-winged seabirds, nesting on islands and spending most of their lives far out on the ocean, where they circle and soar gracefully on wind currents above the waves. Most of the 14 species are found in southern oceans; only three nest in the North Pacific and none in the North Atlantic.

These birds are built like sailplanes, not power fliers. They maneuver with ease in strong winds, but in calm weather they generally rest on the water. This is evidently why most kinds live in the windy southern oceans, avoiding the doldrums near the Equator. With only slight adjustments of its wings, an albatross can glide along in the trough between waves, then turn into the wind and circle high in the air before sailing down into the next wave trough. In this way, it can circle and glide for hours with hardly a flap of its long wings; it is thought that an albatross may even be able to sleep while flying.

Albatrosses may have very long life spans, more than 40 or 50 years for some species.

Feeding Unlike most birds, albatrosses and some other groups of seabirds apparently have a well-developed sense of smell, which helps them to find concentrations of food on the open ocean. After finding food, albatrosses usually feed by sitting on the water and grasping items on or near the surface with their bills. Sometimes they make shallow dives (typically within a few feet of the surface), with their wings extended for propulsion underwater.

Squid are among the main food items for most albatrosses, but some take more fish or crustaceans. Some also regularly feed on carrion, and they may follow ships to pick up scraps or refuse thrown overboard. Those that feed heavily on squid may forage at dusk or at night, when squid are often closer to the surface.

Nesting Albatrosses nest for the first time when they are several years old. They often mate for life, and the two birds may form a pair more than a year before their first actual nesting attempt.

Southern albatrosses build tall mounded nests of mud and vegetation, but those in the North Pacific make simpler scrapes on the ground with slightly raised edges. Only one egg is laid. Both parents take turns incubating the egg, for 9–11 weeks. For a few weeks after the egg hatches, the parents take turns brooding the chick and going to sea to bring back food. After that, the young bird is left alone between feeding visits. Age of the young when it flies out to sea averages 5 months, up to 9 months for the largest species. The breeding cycle of the largest albatrosses takes more than a year, so they nest only once every two years at most. Even the smaller species may not nest every year.

Displays Courtship displays of albatrosses are elaborate and conspicuous; they are usually performed only by birds in the process of forming a new pair, not by members of an established pair. While standing close together, the two birds may go through various motions such as bowing repeatedly, touching bills, preening under their wings, swinging their heads rapidly from side to side, or standing up on tiptoes and pointing the bill skyward while calling. In the largest species (such as Wandering Albatross), the birds may spread their wings wide during these displays.

GENUS *Diomedea*

WANDERING ALBATROSS *Diomedea exulans*

The 11-foot wingspan of this great seabird makes it one of the largest flying birds in the world. The Wandering Albatross is common in far southern oceans, riding easily on the endless winds, but it almost never wanders north of the Equator. One was once found on the coast of California.

SHORT-TAILED ALBATROSS *Diomedea albatrus*

This big seabird may have been the most numerous albatross off our Pacific coast at one time, but it was hunted almost to extinction on its nesting grounds, the Bonin Islands off Japan. It was thought to be possibly extinct in the 1940s, but in the 1950s a few pairs returned to Torishima Island and began to breed there. Numbers have gradually increased since, with the population over 250 birds by 1990. Now that their numbers are gradually increasing again, Short-tailed Albatrosses have been seen a few times recently off our coastline, especially in Alaskan waters.

BLACK-FOOTED ALBATROSS *Diomedea nigripes*

Restricted to the North Pacific, this is the only albatross seen commonly off the North American coastline. Its closest nesting colonies are in Hawaii. At sea it often follows ships, feeding on refuse in their wake.

HABITAT *Open ocean.* In foraging at sea, most common over upwellings or over continental shelf, but rarely close to shore. Nests on sandy beaches and other open flat areas on islands in Pacific.

FEEDING **Diet:** *Fish, squid, crustaceans.* Around Hawaii, feeds heavily on the eggs of flying fish. Also eats many squid, adult fish including flying fish, and crustaceans. Will scavenge carrion or refuse at sea. **Behavior:** Forages while swimming by seizing items at surface, upending to reach underwater or diving short distances underwater with wings partly spread. Feeds mostly early morning and evening.

NESTING First breeds at age 5 years or older. Courtship "dance" of pairs is

Black-footed Albatross

complex, includes many ritualized movements including bowing head, mutual preening, swinging head from side to side, pointing bill straight up while calling. **Nest:** Preferred nest sites are on higher parts of open sandy beaches. Nest is a simple, shallow depression with a slightly built-up rim. **Eggs:** 1. Creamy white, spotted with brown. Incubation (by both sexes) averages 65–66 days. **Young:** For about 18–20 days after hatching, one parent broods and guards the nestling while the other forages for food, taking turns every 1 or 2 days. Young is fed by regurgitation, by both parents, until it leaves the nest. Period from hatching to departure from island is about 140–150 days.

MIGRATION   Some can be found throughout North Pacific at all seasons, but adults concentrate near nesting islands (Hawaii and off Japan) from November to June; most restricted in February when feeding young nestlings. Most numerous off North American coast from June through August.

CONSERVATION STATUS   Far less abundant than Laysan Albatross. Total population estimated at about 100,000 pairs. Thousands may be killed annually by drift nets and longline fisheries.

LAYSAN ALBATROSS   *Diomedea immutabilis*

In total population, this species is more than 10 times as abundant as Black-footed Albatross. However, it is seen less often off the west coast of North America (and generally farther offshore), although sightings have increased in recent decades. Beginning in the 1980s, it has been found nesting on islands off the west coast of Mexico, a range extension of thousands of miles. Oddly, several Laysan Albatrosses have been found far inland in the southwestern United States.

HABITAT   *Open ocean.* Generally forages far from land, beyond continental shelf, and mainly over cold waters. Nests on open sandy or grassy areas on low, flat islands.

FEEDING   **Diet:** *Mostly squid.* Small squid are apparently staple fare, as they are for some larger albatrosses of southern hemisphere. Also eats fish and fish eggs, crustaceans, some carrion and refuse. **Behavior:** Forages by seizing prey near water's surface while swimming. Does much feeding at night (when squid are closer to surface), and eyes are adapted for night vision.

NESTING   First breeds at age of 7–9 years. Breeding season in Hawaii extends from November to

Laysan Albatross

July. Elaborate courtship "dance," performed only by first-time breeders and pre-breeders, includes many movements including bowing head, mutual preening, swinging head from side to side, pointing bill straight up while calling. **Nest:** Site is on open ground, preferably close to taller vegetation. Nest (begun by female, finished by both sexes) is shallow depression in ground, surrounded by built-up rim. **Eggs:** 1. Creamy white, spotted with brown. Incubation (by both sexes) averages 64–65 days. **Young:** For 12–24 days after egg hatches, one parent stays with young while the other forages

for food. Nestling fed by regurgitation, by both parents. Period from hatching to departure from island averages about 165 days.

MIGRATION   Birds leave Hawaiian breeding grounds in July; evidently most go northwest toward Japan, then northeast toward Aleutians, before turning south toward Hawaii again. Nonbreeders may wander anywhere in North Pacific at any season. Most numerous off Alaska in summer, off California in winter. Strays found in interior of American southwest are thought to be birds that moved north in Gulf of California and then attempted to continue north overland.

CONSERVATION STATUS   Several thousand may die in drift nets every year. Many colonies were decimated by feather hunters around beginning of 20th century, but population apparently now recovering and expanding range. Total population estimated at about 2.5 million.

BLACK-BROWED ALBATROSS   *Diomedea melanophris*

Very common in southern oceans, this seabird rarely strays into the North Atlantic. Has been seen a number of times off Britain and Europe, but on the American side of the ocean, most records involve Yellow-nosed Albatross instead.

SHY ALBATROSS   *Diomedea cauta*

In southern oceans, especially around Australia and New Zealand, this albatross is common. Hardly "shy," it often follows closely behind boats, looking for scraps. In North America it has been found only once, off the coast of Washington State.

YELLOW-NOSED ALBATROSS   *Diomedea chlororhynchos*

Mainly resident in the southern Atlantic and Indian oceans, this species sometimes strays north. It has been reported more than a score of times off our Atlantic and Gulf coasts, mostly during summer. Generally far off the coast, but has been seen from shore more than once.

GENUS *Phoebetria*

LIGHT-MANTLED SOOTY ALBATROSS   *Phoebetria palpebrata*

One of the most beautiful seabirds of the southern oceans, longer tailed and even more graceful in flight than the typical albatrosses. Lives mainly in the Antarctic Ocean and virtually never occurs as far north as the Equator; amazingly, one was found once on a birding boat trip off the California coast (July 1994).

SHEARWATERS AND PETRELS (Family Procellariidae)

This is the largest family of true seabirds, with about 70 species distributed throughout the oceans of the world. They are narrow-winged, fast-flying birds, able to maneuver with ease in high winds. Shearwaters and petrels spend most of their lives at sea, coming to land only to raise their young. Many species migrate long distances; some of the shearwaters seen most commonly off the North American coastline nest only south of the Equator.

Along with the related families of albatrosses and storm-petrels, these birds are known collectively as "tubenoses," because their nostrils are located in external tubes on their bills. Unlike most birds, many tubenoses have a well-developed sense of smell. This undoubtedly helps them find food at sea. For the many shearwaters and petrels that nest in burrows and visit them only at night, smell may also be a help in finding their own burrows in the darkness.

Shearwaters and petrels almost always nest in colonies on islands where there are few or no predators. Some colonies on large islands may run to literally millions of pairs. However, the nesting birds are quite vulnerable when their islands are invaded by humans or by introduced predators such as rats and cats. Some species are now seriously endangered because of such predators.

Feeding   Except for the two giant-petrels of the southern hemisphere, members of this family do all their feeding at sea. Foraging behavior varies. Some of the more agile species do much feeding on the wing, while others may feed more often while sitting on the water's surface. Many dive and swim underwater, using their wings to "fly" through the depths. Major items in the diet of shearwaters and petrels include squid, fish, and crustaceans. Some species also will scavenge on floating dead animals or scraps tossed from fishing boats.

Nesting   Breeding behavior of many species still poorly known. Most apparently do not breed until they are at least 3 years old, but then the birds may be paired for life and may use the same nest site every year. Activity around nesting colonies is mainly at night in most species, and most nest in burrows underground, digging the burrows themselves or taking over abandoned burrows made by other animals. Those that nest in the open (on the ground, on cliff ledges, or in simple crevices among rocks) are active around their colonies by day; the Northern Fulmar is a notable example. In some species, after a period of courtship, the adults may abandon the nesting colony for a couple of weeks before returning and beginning to nest. Only one white egg is laid. Both parents help incubate, and both parents help feed the chick. In many cases, the parents abandon the chick after it is full-grown; a few nights later, the young bird flies out to sea on its own.

Displays   Because so many species are nocturnal at colonies and nest underground, not much is known of their courtship displays. In some shearwaters, members of a pair may spend much time together in the nesting burrow before the egg is laid, calling and preening each other's feathers. Pairs of gadfly petrels may perform rapid display flights near the nesting colony. Fulmars, nesting in the open, use various head-waving displays between members of a pair and against potential intruders.

GENUS *Fulmarus*

NORTHERN FULMAR   *Fulmarus glacialis*

Patterned somewhat like a gull but very different in flight behavior, the fulmar flies fast, with quick wingbeats and stiff-winged glides, wheeling effortlessly in strong winds, often swinging up in high arcs over the waves. In North America, it breeds mainly in high Arctic Canada and on islands in the Bering Sea.

HABITAT   *Open ocean; breeds colonially on open sea cliffs.* Generally over cold waters, including around edges of pack ice in Arctic Ocean. Also south into temperate waters (especially around European nesting sites, and in winter off North America's west coast). Widespread at sea, often concentrated over outer continental shelf, upwellings.

FEEDING   **Diet:** *Varied, includes crustaceans, fish.* Feeds on a wide variety of marine creatures including crustaceans, small squid, marine worms, fish, and carrion. Follows fishing boats and other ships and feeds on offal, scraps, refuse. In North Pacific, also noted feeding on jellyfish. **Behavior:** Forages by seizing items at or just below surface of water while swimming. Also plunges into water and dives (to 12 feet or more below surface), propelled by feet and half-opened wings. May feed by day or night.

NESTING First breeds at age of 6–12 years. Breeds in colonies. Unlike many related birds, fulmars are active around nesting colonies in daylight. Birds at nest site display in variety of situations by opening bill wide, waving head back and forth while calling. Mated pairs nibble at each other's head and bill. **Nest:** Site is on ledge of cliff, or hollow in bank or slope. No nest formed on rock ledge, but on soil makes shallow scrape, sometimes adding pebbles as lining. **Eggs:** 1. White. Incubation is by both sexes, usually 49–53 days. **Young:** Both parents feed young, by regurgitation. One of the parents is usually present at nest for first 2 weeks after hatching; both adult and young can defend against intruders by spitting foul-smelling oil. Age at first flight 41–57 days, usually 46–51.

Northern Fulmar

MIGRATION Some may remain in winter as far north as there is open water. Others move south, commonly reaching latitude of New England on Atlantic coast, southern California on Pacific coast. Numbers on southerly winter range highly variable from year to year. Some may remain well southward into summer, especially after large winter invasions.

CONSERVATION STATUS Population in eastern part of North Atlantic (Iceland to Europe) has been increasing and spreading dramatically since the late 1700s. Expansion possibly linked to habit of following ships and feeding on offal. No such increase noted in western North Atlantic until 1960s and 1970s, when fulmars began to breed in Newfoundland, but apparently now increasing off eastern North America.

GADFLY PETRELS — GENUS *Pterodroma*

These are the true petrels, scimitar-winged fast fliers of midocean regions, not to be confused with the fluttery little storm-petrels. As a group, the *Pterodroma* petrels are among the most mysterious of birds. One widespread species was not described to science until 1949; the breeding grounds of two other species are still undiscovered. Their habits in general are not well known, but they seem to do much of their feeding in flight, dipping to the surface of the water to catch small squid and other creatures.

BLACK-CAPPED PETREL *Pterodroma hasitata*

At one time, this bird was known in North America only from scattered waifs blown inland by hurricanes. Now it is known to occur regularly in the Gulf Stream, far offshore from the southeastern states. It breeds only in the West Indies, and has disappeared from most former nesting areas; should be considered at risk of extinction.

HABITAT *Open ocean.* Forages over warm deep water far off southeastern coast of North America, especially over western edge of Gulf Stream. Also over seamounts or submarine ridges where turbulence may bring food nearer surface. Nests around steep forested cliffs in West Indies; may have nested in burrows on more level ground before exotic predators were introduced there.

FEEDING **Diet:** *Includes squid and fish.* Diet not well known. Besides small squid and fish, may scavenge floating carrion or refuse; attracted to slicks of natural oils. **Behavior:** Often in loose small flocks, associated with other seabirds. Forages by dipping to surface of water, with feet down and pattering on water, or by settling briefly on water with wings upstretched; sometimes feeds while swimming. May do most feeding early morning and late evening, when some prey items are closer to surface.

Black-capped Petrel

NESTING Breeding behavior still poorly known. Nesting season begins late fall, lasts to spring. Nests in colonies; known colonies today are on steep cliffs where forest holds enough soil in place for excavating nest burrows. Active around colonies only at night. Birds do much calling as they fly around cliffs in the darkness; courtship may involve flying in pairs. **Nest:** Site is evidently in burrow in soil. Adults undoubtedly dig their own nest burrow. **Eggs:** 1. White. Incubation period unknown; in the closely related Bermuda Petrel, incubation is by both parents, 51–54 days. **Young:** No details known. In Bermuda Petrel, both parents feed young, and young bird flies out to sea 90–100 days after hatching.

MIGRATION Waters of Gulf Stream far off southeastern United States seem to be the main nonbreeding distribution of this species. Some are present in these waters at all seasons; apparently most numerous (and farthest north) during the warmer months.

CONSERVATION STATUS Formerly an abundant nester on several islands, but numbers dropped sharply in middle of 19th century. Decline often blamed on introduction of mongoose, but that occurred in 1870s, after decline was already apparent. Introduced rats more likely responsible, along with humans catching petrels for food. Now known to nest in mountains in Haiti, Dominican Republic, and Cuba, and vulnerable in these few spots.

BERMUDA PETREL (CAHOW) *Pterodroma cahow*

One of the world's rarest seabirds. Once a common breeding bird in Bermuda, it was driven almost to extinction by human settlers (and by the associates of humans such as dogs and rats). The continued survival of the species is undoubtedly due to the heroic conservation efforts of Bermudian scientist Dr. David Wingate.

MOTTLED PETREL *Pterodroma inexpectata*

Nesting only on islands around New Zealand, this species wanders widely in the Pacific. A few reach Alaska's offshore waters in summer, and there are records far off the coast south to California, mostly in winter.

MURPHY'S PETREL *Pterodroma ultima*

This rather mysterious seabird, nesting on a few islands in the South Pacific, was not described to science until 1949. Not until the late 1980s was it learned that Murphy's Petrel may be a regular visitor far off the west coast of North America, mainly in late spring. Most sightings are more than 40 miles offshore.

HERALD PETREL   *Pterodroma arminjoniana*

This bird lives mainly in tropical regions, nesting on various islands in warmer parts of the Atlantic, Pacific, and Indian oceans. Years ago, a Herald Petrel was blown inland by a hurricane all the way to upstate New York. More recently, there have been several sightings far off the coast of North Carolina.

CAPE VERDE PETREL   *Pterodroma feae*

Related to the Soft-plumaged Petrel of the far southern oceans, this bird nests on the Cape Verde Islands and Desertas Islands off northwestern Africa. It is apparently scarce and is declining because of introduced predators on its nesting islands. The species has been reported several times on birding boat trips off the southeastern coast of the United States.

COOK'S PETREL   *Pterodroma cookii*

Breeding on islands around New Zealand, this petrel ranges over vast distances in the Pacific Ocean. Since the late 1970s, research cruises have revealed that Cook's Petrel occurs regularly off our west coast—but so far offshore that it is seldom seen on ordinary one-day birding boat trips, let alone from shore.

STEJNEGER'S PETREL   *Pterodroma longirostris*

A wanderer of deep midocean zones of the Pacific, nesting on islands off the coast of Chile, this fast-flying petrel has been found within 200 miles of the California coast only a few times. It may associate with the very similar Cook's Petrel.

LARGE SHEARWATERS — GENUS *Calonectris*

This genus includes only two species, which occur mostly at temperate and tropical latitudes, one in the Pacific and one in the Atlantic.

STREAKED SHEARWATER   *Calonectris leucomelas*

Often the most common seabird in waters around Japan, this large pale shearwater rarely comes to our side of the Pacific Ocean. Even as far east as Hawaii, it is only a rare visitor. Streaked Shearwater has been found a few times off California, mostly in Monterey Bay.

CORY'S SHEARWATER   *Calonectris diomedea*

This species has a stronger flight action than most shearwaters, with slower wing-beats and prolonged glides, sometimes soaring high above waves. Nesting on islands in the Mediterranean Sea and eastern Atlantic, it regularly visits waters off the east coast of North America. Although a few get as far north as Canada, the species is most common off the southeastern states.

HABITAT   *Open ocean.* Favors relatively warm waters, warmer than those sought by Greater Shearwater. May occur farther north off North American coast in warm-water years. At least off southern New England, may be seen from shore more often than other shearwaters. Occurs both over continental shelf and far out to sea. Nests on islands, often rocky or mountainous.

FEEDING **Diet:** *Mostly fish, squid, and crustaceans.* Diet not well known; fish eaten include herring and sand lance. At times may feed mainly on squid. Also eats crabs and other crustaceans, and scraps and offal around fishing boats. **Behavior:** Forages mainly by plunging into water from just above surface and by seizing items while swimming. Often may feed at night. Scavenges near fishing boats; may feed in association with whales or large predatory fish, which drive schools of small fish to the surface.

NESTING   Breeds in colonies on islands; on large islands, colonies may be several miles inland. Breeding season mostly from March to October. Activity in colonies mainly late afternoon to dawn; where persecuted by humans or other predators, may visit colonies only at night. In courtship, members of pair sit close together on ground, nibbling at each other's head and bill. **Nest:** Site is in burrow up to 3 feet long or in crevice in rocks; sometimes on ground under thick scrub. Nest is simple pile of pebbles, shells. **Eggs:** 1. White. Incubation is by both sexes, 52–56 days. **Young:** Both parents feed young, visiting at night. Eventually young is deserted and goes to sea on its own. Period from hatching to departure probably about 90 days.

Cory's Shearwater

MIGRATION   Winters mainly off southern Africa. Breeding adults are generally near colonies from March to October, so birds seen off east coast of North America (peak numbers June to November) apparently are immatures and nonbreeders.

CONSERVATION STATUS   Still numerous despite declines in some nesting areas. Colonies are vulnerable to disturbance and to pollution of nearby waters.

TYPICAL SHEARWATERS — GENUS *Puffinus*

Flying low over the sea with quick wingbeats and stiff-winged glides, these birds often tilt up so that one wingtip seems almost to cut the surface of the water, hence the name "shearwater." Some species (especially the smaller ones) commonly feed over waters fairly close to shore, but most are also regular farther out to sea. The shearwaters seen off the North American coastline mostly come from breeding grounds far away.

PINK-FOOTED SHEARWATER   *Puffinus creatopus*

The largest of the shearwaters to be commonly seen off our Pacific coast, with rather heavy and slow wingbeats, often gliding and wheeling above the waves, especially in windy conditions. May be solitary or randomly mixed with other seabirds, but not seen in pure flocks of its own species. Nesting only on islands off southern South America, it is a common summer visitor to our coastal waters as far north as southeastern Alaska.

HABITAT   *Open ocean.* Mainly found well offshore over relatively shallow waters of continental shelf. Rarely seen from shore, and rarely over deep midocean waters. Nests on islands with soil suitable for nest burrows.

FEEDING **Diet:** *Includes fish and squid.* Diet not well known; in addition to fish and squid, probably eats various crustaceans. **Behavior:** Forages mostly by plunging into water from flight or diving from surface, and swimming short distance underwater with wings spread; also seizes items while swimming on surface. May follow boats for scraps or offal.

NESTING Breeding behavior not well known. Nests in colonies on islands far off coast of Chile. Active at colonies mostly at dusk and at night. Adults gather near colonies in September; by October, some two months before eggs are laid, pairs may be resting together in burrows. Mated pairs may call softly in duet, preen each other's head and neck. **Nest:** Site is in underground burrow, often more than 4 feet long. Nest chamber may have sparse lining. Most eggs probably laid in early December. **Eggs:** 1. White. Both sexes probably incubate; incubation period not known. **Young:** Probably fed by both parents during nocturnal visits; age at first flight not known. Young depart nesting islands in April and May.

Pink-footed Shearwater

MIGRATION Migrates north after breeding, commonly seen off North America's west coast from May to November, with peak numbers in September. A few seen at other seasons at our latitudes are nonbreeders or immatures.

CONSERVATION STATUS Still numerous as a visitor to North American waters. Declining on some of its nesting islands because of the effects of introduced predators, including rats and coatis.

FLESH-FOOTED SHEARWATER   *Puffinus carneipes*

Among the hordes of Sooty Shearwaters off our Pacific coast, this larger bird is sometimes seen, especially in fall. It is closely related to the Pink-footed Shearwater and resembles it in shape and habits.

GREATER SHEARWATER   *Puffinus gravis*

A common seabird off our Atlantic coast, seldom coming close to shore except during storms. Often forages in flocks. Commonly feeds around fishing boats, fighting over scraps and offal, seemingly fearless of humans. Although Greater Shearwaters are often very numerous in North American waters, they nest only on a few islands in the South Atlantic.

HABITAT *Open ocean.* Favors cold waters at all seasons, moving rapidly across tropical zones during migration only. Tends to occur over colder waters than Cory's Shearwater. Perhaps most common over outer part of continental shelf, avoiding midocean and areas near shore. Nests on hilly islands with soil suitable for nesting burrows.

FEEDING **Diet:** *Mostly fish and squid.* Feeds mainly on small fish and squid that swim in schools near surface; also eats crustaceans and scavenges offal from fishing boats. **Behavior:** Forages by plunging into water from the air, by diving from surface and swimming underwater, or by seizing items while swimming on surface. Prey caught underwater is brought to surface and swallowed. May feed in association with whales and dolphins. Typically feeds by day but apparently also at dusk and at night.

Breeds mainly on Gough Island and islands in Tristan da Cunha group in South Atlantic. Arrives at colonies in September, most eggs laid in November, most young leave colony in May. Activity at colony is mainly at night. Courtship display includes pair sitting close together on ground, calling loudly and nibbling at each other's nape feathers. **Nest:** Site is in burrow, sharply angled and about 3 feet long; sometimes in crevice among rocks. Nest chamber at end of burrow lined with grass. **Eggs:** 1. White. Incubation is probably by both sexes, estimated at 55 days. **Young:** Both parents feed young, visiting at night. Age at first flight is reportedly about 84 days.

Greater Shearwater

MIGRATION   Adults leave breeding islands in April and move north rapidly, mostly along western side of Atlantic, becoming common off east coast of North America in June. Spread eastward across North Atlantic during summer, and southward migration is on broad front in August. Nonbreeders remain in North Atlantic at least through November. Two records off California presumably of birds that rounded tip of South America and went north in the "wrong" ocean.

CONSERVATION STATUS   Total population estimated at well over 5 million. Could be vulnerable because of its very limited breeding range; Tristan islanders harvest large numbers of adults and young every year from certain colonies.

WEDGE-TAILED SHEARWATER   *Puffinus pacificus*

Widespread in the tropical Pacific and Indian oceans, this seabird is a very rare visitor to our west coast. Underparts may be either light or dark; both color forms have reached California. The long, wedge-shaped tail makes this shearwater more graceful and maneuverable than many of its relatives.

BULLER'S SHEARWATER   *Puffinus bulleri*

A cleanly patterned seabird, nesting only near New Zealand but visiting waters off the west coast of North America in fall. Buller's seems more buoyant and graceful in flight than most shearwaters, with more gliding and less flapping. It often arcs up high first on one wingtip and then the other, and small flocks may turn and glide over the waves in unison.

HABITAT   *Open ocean.* Tends to concentrate at areas of strong upwelling, or where warm and cool water currents meet, bringing food to the surface. Rarely comes close to shore. Nests on islands with soil suitable for burrows or with crevices among rocky cliffs.

FEEDING   **Diet:** *Crustaceans, fish, squid.* Diet not well known. Near breeding grounds may feed mostly on euphausiid shrimp and other crustaceans. Off California, may eat mostly small fish and squid. **Behavior:** Food is taken at or just below surface of water. Forages by dipping to surface in flight, plunging into water from a few feet above surface, swimming with head submerged, sometimes upending with head down and tail up. Rarely dives underwater. May feed at night.

NESTING   Breeds on Poor Knights Islands off North Island, New Zealand. Adults arrive there in September, most eggs laid in late November, young depart in May. Breeds in dense

Buller's Shearwater

colonies. Adults noisy around colonies at night, may climb up into trees to take flight more easily. **Nest:** Site is in burrow under tree roots or rocks, or in cave or rock crevice. Both sexes help dig burrow. Nest chamber is lined with leaves, twigs, pebbles. Where birds nest in Maori burial caves, may use human bones as nest material. **Eggs:** 1. White. Incubation is by both sexes, roughly 51 days. **Young:** Both parents feed young, by regurgitation. Period from hatching to departure from nest probably about 100 days.

MIGRATION   Breeding adults move north in May, common in parts of North Pacific in summer, returning to New Zealand waters by September. Seen off Pacific coast of North America mainly June to November, most common September–October; evidently these are mostly nonbreeders and immatures.

CONSERVATION STATUS   On some islands, where colonies had been nearly wiped out by feral pigs, shearwaters recolonized after pigs were eradicated in 1936. Total population estimated at more than 2 million.

SOOTY SHEARWATER   *Puffinus griseus*

In calm weather, the Sooty Shearwater flies low over the ocean with quick, stiff beats of its narrow wings; in windy conditions, it glides and scales effortlessly over the waves. Sociable at sea, it is often seen in gatherings of hundreds or even thousands,

Sooty Shearwater

flying in long lines or resting in dense rafts on the water. Although it is often the most abundant seabird off the coast of California, the Sooty Shearwater nests only deep in the Southern Hemisphere, around Australia, New Zealand, and southern South America.

HABITAT   *Open ocean.* Widespread at sea, but concentrates around upwellings and over continental shelf in cooler waters, also where cold and warm water masses meet. May come close to shore if water is deep. Breeds on islands in southern oceans with soil for burrows or with suitable rock crevices for nest sites.

FEEDING   **Diet:** *Mostly fish, crustaceans.* Diet in North Pacific mainly small fish, also euphausiid shrimp and other crustaceans, squid, jellyfish. In North Atlantic may feed mostly on euphausiid shrimp and fish. **Behavior:** Forages by plunging into water from a few feet above the surface and swimming underwater, propelled by wings; also dives from surface, and seizes items at or just below surface while sitting on water. Sometimes feeds in association with whales, dolphins, or other seabirds.

NESTING   In Australia and New Zealand, nesting season is September to May. First breeding at age of 5–9 years. Breeds in colonies on islands, with most activity in evening and at night. In courtship, pairs may call in duet. **Nest:** Site is in burrow dug in soil, sometimes in natural crevice in rock. Burrow may be up to 10 feet long. Nest is loose foundation of leaves and grass. **Eggs:** 1. White. Incubation is by both sexes, averages 52–56 days. **Young:** Both parents feed young, visiting at night, feeding

frequently when chick is small and less often as it matures. Finally young bird is abandoned, and it eventually goes to sea. Period from hatching to departure from nest averages about 97 days. Young usually departs from island at night.

MIGRATION   Adults from southern colonies move north rapidly in April and May, passing Atlantic coast of North America mostly in late spring. Moves north on broad front in Pacific. Peak numbers off California in late summer, probably corresponding to southward movement. Some, possibly nonbreeders, are present at all seasons off our Pacific coast.

CONSERVATION STATUS   Abundant; total population probably in the tens of millions. Has disappeared from some former nesting islands because of habitat degradation. In southern New Zealand, some young are taken annually for food and oil by Maori people, but this controlled harvest has little or no impact on total population. In recent years, off parts of North American west coast, numbers of visiting Sooty Shearwaters have declined significantly; this may be related to a general rise in sea surface temperatures there.

SHORT-TAILED SHEARWATER   *Puffinus tenuirostris*

This dark, narrow-winged seabird occurs in large flocks over cold waters. It is very similar to the Sooty Shearwater and, like that species, is a visitor from far to the south. Short-tailed Shearwaters nest only around Australia, but in the northern summer they may penetrate north past the Bering Strait. Generally found off Alaska in summer, farther south off west coast in winter.

HABITAT   *Open ocean.* Concentrations at sea are over continental shelf and around upwellings in cool waters. Breeds on islands close to shore and locally on Australian mainland, where grass and shrubs cover soil soft enough for excavating nesting burrows.

FEEDING   **Diet:** *Mostly fish, crustaceans, squid.* Diet varies with region, but may include many small fish; crustaceans, including amphipods and euphausiid shrimp; small octopus and squid. Also some marine worms, jellyfish, insects, other items. **Behavior:** Forages mostly by diving from surface of water or by plunging from a few feet above surface, swimming underwater by rowing with wings; may dive as deep as 60 feet below surface. Sometimes forages in association with whales or dolphins.

NESTING   Breeds only around southern and eastern Australia. Nesting season extends from September to April. First breeds at age of 5–8 years. Nests in colonies on islands and locally on mainland, with most activity in colony at night. **Nest:** Sites are in burrows dug in soil under grass or scrub; both sexes help to excavate burrow, and same site may be used for several years. Nest chamber at end of burrow may be bare or lined with grasses. **Eggs:** 1. White. Incubation is by both sexes, 52–55 days. **Young:** Both parents feed young, visiting at night, feeding by regurgitation. Feeding visits become less frequent as chick matures. Adults then abandon young, and it goes to sea 82–108 days after hatching.

MIGRATION   Moves north through western Pacific in April and May, concentrating off southern Alaska in summer, with some moving north through Bering Strait to Arctic Ocean. Breeders move south again in August and September, crossing tropical waters rapidly. Nonbreeders may remain off Pacific coast of North America all year; occurs off California mainly in our winter months.

CONSERVATION STATUS   Total numbers estimated at more than 20 million. Young are harvested commercially for food in certain colonies around Tasmania; this controlled harvest has little or no impact on total population.

MANX SHEARWATER   *Puffinus puffinus*

Formerly a rare visitor to waters off northeastern North America, the Manx Shear-water has increased in recent decades and has been found nesting on this side of the Atlantic. Many small black and white shearwaters in other oceans are closely related and are sometimes classified as belonging to this same species.

HABITAT   *Open ocean.* Off North America, generally occurs over cooler waters (but it inhabits warm waters elsewhere, including waters off eastern South America). Often feeds closer to shore than other shearwaters. Nests on islands, mostly small islands near mainland.

FEEDING   **Diet:** *Mostly small fish.* Feeds on a variety of common small fish, especially herrings, sprats, sardines, sand lance; also squid, crustaceans. **Behavior:** Forages by plunging into water from low flight, by making shallow dives from surface, or by seizing items at or just below surface while swimming. Swims underwater better than some other shearwaters.

Manx Shearwater

NESTING   Breeding behavior known mostly from studies around Great Britain. Usually first breeds at age 5–6 years, and may mate for life. Nests in dense colonies on islands. Activity at colony entirely at night. Courtship not well known, but members of pair spend much time in nest several weeks before egg is laid. **Nest:** Site is in burrow, usually 3–6 feet long, excavated by both sexes; same burrow may be reused for several years. Nest chamber is usually lined with small amount of grass, leaves. **Eggs:** 1 per season. White. Incubation is by both sexes, 47–55 days, rarely up to 63 days. **Young:** Both parents feed young. Parents abandon young after about 60 days, and it leaves nest 8–9 days later, going to sea alone.

MIGRATION   Present in numbers off northeastern North America from May to October. Movements of these birds not well known. Large numbers move north past Bermuda in spring, peaking in March. A few have been recorded off the southeastern United States in winter. Birds from European colonies winter mainly off east coast of South America.

CONSERVATION STATUS   Apparently increasing off east coast of North America; first found nesting in Massachusetts in 1973, Newfoundland in 1976.

BLACK-VENTED SHEARWATER   *Puffinus opisthomelas*

Most shearwaters range widely over the ocean far from land, and most of those seen off our Pacific coast nest only in the Southern Hemisphere. The Black-vented Shear-water is an exception, nesting on islands off northwestern Mexico, traveling only short distances north along the California coast, and usually staying within a few miles of shore. Observers at coastal lookouts may see this bird in late fall, flying with rapid wingbeats and short glides low over the waves.

HABITAT   *Open ocean near coast.* Found closer to shore than most shearwaters, over continental shelf within a few miles of the coast. Favors warm waters at all seasons: fewer move north along California coast in years when sea surface temperature is lower. Nests on islands with enough soil for burrowing or with natural crevices in rock.

FEEDING **Diet:** *Probably mostly fish.* Diet not well known. Off southern California may eat mostly small fish, including herring and sardines. May also eat small squid, crustaceans. **Behavior:** Forages by seizing items at or just below surface while swimming, by plunging into water from low flight, or by making shallow dives from surface. Apparently does not dive as often nor swim as well underwater as the similar Manx Shearwater.

NESTING Breeding behavior not well known. Nests in colonies on islands. Active around colonies only at night. Both members of pair may rest in nest burrow during daytime before egg-laying. **Nest:** Site is in burrow in ground, sometimes in crevice in rock. Burrow may be more than 10 feet long, often with turns to the side rather than straight; probably both sexes help dig burrow, as in related species. Nest chamber at end of burrow may have a few bits of plant material or may be unlined. **Eggs:** 1. Dull white. Incubation probably by both sexes, as in other shearwaters; incubation period not well known. **Young:** Both parents probably feed young, by regurgitation. Development of young and age at first flight not well known, but young probably remains in nest at least 2 months.

MIGRATION Moves north from Baja into California's coastal waters in fall. Numbers and timing variable: when sea temperature is high, may arrive early and in large numbers. Some also may move well to south of breeding range, but southward migration poorly known.

CONSERVATION STATUS Numbers stable, but vulnerable to introduced cats and other predators on nesting islands.

Black-vented Shearwater

LITTLE SHEARWATER   *Puffinus assimilis*

From its range in the eastern North Atlantic, this small seabird has wandered very rarely to waters off our east coast. It flies with several shallow, fluttery wingbeats followed by a short glide.

AUDUBON'S SHEARWATER   *Puffinus lherminieri*

This small seabird is widespread in the Atlantic, Pacific, and Indian oceans, mostly in tropical waters; in North America, it is regular over warm waters off the southeastern coast. At sea it is usually solitary or in small groups.

HABITAT *Open ocean.* Almost exclusively over warm waters; follows warm current of Gulf Stream north. Very seldom comes near land in North America. Nests on islands, both along rocky coastal edges and in wooded areas farther inland.

FEEDING **Diet:** *Squid, fish.* Diet not well known, apparently mostly small squid and fish. Has been reported to eat many sardines at times. **Behavior:** Forages by diving and swimming underwater, rowing with wings; may be quite agile underwater. Also feeds by seizing items at surface. Probably feeds by night as well as by day. Does not ordinarily follow ships as some seabirds do.

NESTING Breeds in colonies on islands. Active at colonies only at night. Adults may arrive at colony 3 months before time of egg-laying. Members of mated pair spend much time

Audubon's Shearwater

together at nest site, rubbing bills together, often calling loudly. **Nest:** Site is in narrow natural crevice in rock, in underground burrow, or on ground under dense vegetation, usually with little or no nest lining added. **Eggs:** 1 per season. White. Incubation is by both sexes, about 51 days. **Young:** Chick is brooded or attended by one parent for several days after hatching. Both parents feed young, visiting at night. Last feeding of young is about 70 days after hatching; 3–5 days later, young departs from nest. Leaving at night, young climbs to highest point nearby, makes its first flight out to sea.

MIGRATION   Moves north in Gulf Stream in late summer and fall. Northernmost records (off New England) tend to coincide with periods of highest water temperature. Some also move into Gulf of Mexico. Dispersal distance is quite limited compared with long migrations of some shearwaters.

CONSERVATION STATUS   Populations in Caribbean vulnerable to disturbance as human population of that region continues to grow. Formerly a common breeder in Bermuda, last recorded in 1980s. Has probably declined on larger islands in the Bahamas and elsewhere.

STORM-PETRELS (Family Hydrobatidae)

They seem almost too small and frail for the open ocean, but the storm-petrels are true seabirds. About 20 species wander the oceans of the world, coming to land only to nest or when driven ashore by hurricanes.

When swimming, storm-petrels float buoyantly on the water's surface. In flight they are almost always very close to the water, but style of flight varies from quick fluttering to erratic bounding wingbeats or stiff glides. Some storm-petrels (such as Wilson's) often patter their feet on the surface of the water while flying. This is the source of the name "petrel": a diminutive of "Peter," it refers to the New Testament account of St. Peter walking on the water.

Some storm-petrels gather in flocks to rest on the water, but they are often seen singly as well. They are active around their nesting colonies at night, and many kinds may feed at night as well. Silent at sea, they make astonishing calls as they fly about their nesting islands in the darkness. Despite their small size, storm-petrels may live more than 20 years in the wild.

Feeding   In general, the diet of storm-petrels is poorly known. Apparently the birds can locate food by smell (like some other seabirds, but unlike most birds); birders on oceanic boat trips, baiting birds by putting out a slick of fish oil, often see storm-petrels arriving from downwind, following the scent. The birds seem to feed mostly on very small crustaceans and fish, but they are also much attracted to floating natural oils and fats from animal carcasses.

Much of their feeding is done in flight, as they flutter or hover just above the water, picking items from the surface. Only occasionally do they feed while sitting on the water, and they rarely dive even a short distance below the surface.

Nesting   Storm-petrels nest in colonies on islands, and they are active around their nesting colonies almost exclusively at night, probably to avoid predators. Nest sites are in protected spots, such as in crevices among boulders or in burrows underground. The same pair may use the same nest site year after year; after a period of renewing the pair-bond, the female may go off to sea for a couple of weeks before returning to lay the single egg. Both parents help to incubate the egg and feed the young. The length of time needed for incubation and fledging may be tremendously variable, because bad weather may prevent the parents from attending the egg or young for days at a time. The offspring are good survivors, however; the eggs have been known to hatch even after incubation was interrupted for 25 days, and the young can survive a fast of up to three weeks between feedings.

Displays   Not much is known of storm-petrel displays. When birds arrive at colony sites at the beginning of the breeding season, they fly about over the island at night, calling. In courtship, two birds may fly about rapidly together in the darkness. Later they will spend much time together inside the nest, preening each other's feathers and sometimes calling in duet.

GENUS *Oceanites*

WILSON'S STORM-PETREL   *Oceanites oceanicus*

Despite its small size and seemingly weak flight, this bird is at home on the roughest of seas, flying in the troughs of the waves during gales. It also travels huge distances—from the Antarctic to the edge of the Arctic. Although it nests only in far southern oceans, Wilson's Storm-Petrel is often the most common seabird off the Atlantic coast of the United States.

HABITAT   *Open ocean.* Widespread at sea, from tropical and subtropical waters to edges of pack ice. Off North America mainly over continental shelf, may concentrate over upwellings and where warm and cool water currents meet, as along edges of Gulf Stream. Seldom close to land in nonbreeding season.

FEEDING   **Diet:** *Small crustaceans, fish.* Feeds mainly on crustaceans (especially euphausiid shrimp and amphipods) and small fish, also small squid, marine worms, other small organisms. Scavenges at natural oil slicks and carrion, and will follow ships to pick at offal. **Behavior:** Takes food from surface of water. Forages mostly by hovering with feet touching water and picking at surface with bill, also by dropping into water and then resuming flight, sometimes by picking at items while swimming.

NESTING   Breeds on islands and cliffs of Antarctic region and around southern South America.

Wilson's Storm-Petrel

Nesting is generally November to May. Males may arrive at nesting sites first, and unmated males may sit near nest entrance and call to defend site and attract female. **Nest:** Site is in crevice or hole in cliff, among rock piles, or in burrow. Nest chamber usually lined with feathers and moss, sometimes bare. **Eggs:** 1. White, usually with reddish brown dots at larger end. Incubation is by both sexes, usually 40–50 days, sometimes 38–59. **Young:** Fed by both parents. Period from hatching to departure from nest (46–97 days) varies considerably, probably depends on rate of feeding. Young is independent of parents after leaving nest and going to sea.

MIGRATION   Moves north in March to May, most commonly in Atlantic and Indian oceans, many crossing Equator. Common off eastern North America

CONSERVATION STATUS   Total population certainly runs to many millions. Despite its abundance, this species (like many other seabirds) would be vulnerable to pollution, overfishing, or other degradation of the Antarctic Ocean.

GENUS *Pelagodroma*

WHITE-FACED STORM-PETREL   *Pelagodroma marina*

This pallid little seabird is sometimes found by birders who take boat trips far offshore from our southern Atlantic coast. It flies low with an odd rocking motion, wings held out to the sides, dropping its long legs repeatedly to push off against a wave with its feet.

GENUS *Hydrobates*

EUROPEAN STORM-PETREL   *Hydrobates pelagicus*

Nesting on islands around the coasts of Britain and Europe, this dark little seabird is purely accidental on our side of the Atlantic. One was found once on an island off Nova Scotia.

TYPICAL STORM-PETRELS — GENUS *Oceanodroma*

Along with the preceding species, these are often called the "northern" storm-petrels, although a few of them nest south of the Equator. Compared with the "southern" group (characterized by Wilson's), these birds tend to have longer wings and shorter legs, and they tend to do less foot-pattering on the water's surface while feeding.

FORK-TAILED STORM-PETREL   *Oceanodroma furcata*

A small, silvery seabird of cold waters off the Pacific coast, most common off southern Alaska. Flutters low over the waves offshore, sometimes in flocks. Its center of distribution is much farther north than those of other storm-petrels in Pacific; it is able to fly well even in serious winter storms, zig-zagging through wave troughs.

HABITAT   *Open ocean.* Favors cold waters, foraging over continental shelf and farther out to sea, sometimes fairly close to land. Extends north into Bering Sea, and may even occur around edges of floating ice. Nests on islands, mostly hilly islands with good cover of grass or shrubs.

FEEDING   **Diet:** *Includes fish, crustaceans.* Feeds mostly on small fish, crustaceans, and floating natural oils. Skims oily fat (from dead or wounded animals) from surface of water. Also may feed on carrion or floating refuse. **Behavior:** Takes food from surface of water. Forages mostly by hovering and picking at surface with bill, also by dropping into water and then resuming flight, sometimes by picking at items while swimming.

NESTING   Nests on islands, commonly in large colonies. Active around nesting sites only at night. **Nest:** Excavates burrow in soil or uses natural rock crevices, openings in rock piles, or old burrows of other species (such as puffins). Sometimes two or more pairs

have nests in side tunnels branching off from single entrance. Nest chamber usually with little or no lining added, sometimes small amount of grass. **Eggs:** 1. Dull white, with fine dark dots around larger end. Incubation is by both sexes. Incubation period averages about 50 days, ranges from 37–68 days. **Young:** Both parents feed young. At first young is fed an oily orange substance regurgitated by adults, later semidigested fish. Young fledges about 60 days after hatching, goes out to sea.

MIGRATION   Not strongly migratory, with most remaining in far northern waters all year. In some winters, fair numbers move south to central California, rarely farther.

Fork-tailed Storm-Petrel

CONSERVATION STATUS   Still abundant in the North Pacific, although some island colonies may have been affected by introduced rat populations.

LEACH'S STORM-PETREL   *Oceanodroma leucorhoa*

A small dark seabird that flies low over the water with erratic, bounding wingbeats. Unlike Wilson's Storm-Petrel, it seldom follows ships. Nests on islands off both coasts of North America, most commonly off eastern Canada. Silent and usually solitary at sea, it becomes very vocal when visiting its nesting islands at night, filling the darkness with spooky chattering, trilling, and sputtering cries.

HABITAT   *Open ocean; nesting colonies in turf on offshore islands.* Widespread at sea, concentrating around upwellings and areas where cold and warm currents meet. Forages over continental shelf but also far out to sea; off Pacific coast, generally seen farther offshore than other storm-petrels. Nests on islands with soil for nesting burrows.

FEEDING   Diet: *Mostly crustaceans.* Feeds mainly on small crustaceans, including euphausiid shrimp, amphipods, copepods, larval stages of spiny lobster; also small squid, possibly some small fish. Scavenges at slicks of oil and fat on sea surface.

Leach's Storm-Petrel

Behavior: Forages mostly by hovering or skimming low over water and taking items from surface. Seldom sits on water to feed. May feed by day or night. Sometimes associated with feeding whales or seals.

NESTING   First breeds at age of 4 or 5 years. Nests in colonies on islands, coming ashore only at night. **Nest:** Site is in burrow under grass, rocks, or tree roots; burrow is usually 1–3 feet long, sometimes more than 5 feet. Male digs burrow, mostly using feet. Several burrow entrances may be very close together, or several nests may be in side branches of one tunnel. May also use natural holes and crevices at times. Nest chamber usually lined with leaves, grass. **Eggs:** 1. White, some with band of purplish dots toward large end. Incubation is by both sexes, 38–46 days. **Young:** Both parents feed young, by regurgitation, visiting at night. Feeding rate declines as young matures. Period from hatching to young bird's departure from nest is about 9–10 weeks.

MIGRATION Movements not well known. Majority of birds in both Atlantic and Pacific apparently move south to spend winter months in tropical seas, although there are some winter reports at northerly latitudes.

CONSERVATION STATUS Total population probably in the millions, but thought to have declined in recent decades. On nesting islands, vulnerable to disturbance by predators, especially introduced mammals such as rats.

ASHY STORM-PETREL *Oceanodroma homochroa*

Ashy Storm-Petrel

A small seabird with a limited range, breeding only on offshore islands from central California to northern Baja and dispersing only short distances at sea. Flies low over the waves with relatively shallow wingbeats. Of the various all-dark storm-petrels on the west coast, this one is medium-sized and slightly paler than the others.

HABITAT *Open ocean.* During summer, favors relatively cool waters of the California Current, feeding mainly just off the edge of the continental shelf. In fall, concentrates where deep waters of the Monterey Submarine Canyon come relatively near shore in Monterey Bay. Nests on rocky islands with abundant crevices for nest sites.

FEEDING **Diet:** *Probably mostly crustaceans and small fish.* Diet is not well known. Includes small fish and crustaceans such as euphausiids. Once reported to feed heavily on the larval stage of spiny lobster off southern California. **Behavior:** Forages mostly by hovering or skimming low over water and taking items from surface; also will sit on water to feed. Probably forages mostly at dusk and at night.

NESTING Breeds in colonies on offshore islands. Active at colonies only at night, arriving there just after dark and departing before first light. Some adults may visit colony every month of year. At Farallon Islands off central California, nesting is not synchronized; egg-laying may occur any time late April to mid-July, rarely to September. Before eggs are laid, both members of pair may spend time in nest chamber, giving trilling and twittering songs. **Nest:** Site is in natural cavity or crevice under rock piles, under driftwood, or in old burrow of other species; usually no nest lining added. **Eggs:** 1. White or with faint reddish brown dots. Incubation is by both sexes, averages about 45 days. **Young:** Probably both parents feed young, by regurgitation. Young leaves nest and goes to sea on average about 84 days after hatching.

MIGRATION In fall, a high percentage of total population may concentrate on Monterey Bay, central California. Some are present in California waters at all seasons, but at northern end of range the species is least numerous in early winter; apparently some move a short distance south to waters off western Mexico. Unlike many storm-petrels, performs no long-distance migration.

CONSERVATION STATUS Reasonably common in limited range. Well protected at the largest and best-known colony (estimated 2,000 pairs) at the South Farallon Islands. Would be quite vulnerable to an oil spill or other disaster on Monterey Bay in fall, when most of world's population is present there.

BAND-RUMPED STORM-PETREL *Oceanodroma castro*

Until the late 1970s, this species was considered an accidental visitor to North America, with a few having been found inland after hurricanes. With increased surveys offshore, it has proven to be a regular visitor far off our southern Atlantic and Gulf coasts. It may have been overlooked in the past because of its great similarity to Leach's Storm-Petrel.

WEDGE-RUMPED STORM-PETREL *Oceanodroma tethys*

Nesting on islands off the west coast of South America, this bird wanders widely in offshore waters of the eastern Pacific. A few individuals have been known to stray as far north as California. The race of this species breeding in the Galápagos is the only storm-petrel that regularly visits its nesting colonies by day.

BLACK STORM-PETREL *Oceanodroma melania*

This is the largest of the dark storm-petrels found off the west coast and the one most likely to be seen from shore in southern California. It has a buoyant flight with deep wingbeats, low over the waves. The Black Storm-Petrel nests mainly on islands off western Mexico. The first breeding record for the United States was in 1976 on a rock near Santa Barbara Island, and a few may nest elsewhere in the Channel Islands.

Black Storm-Petrel

HABITAT   *Open sea.* Favors warm ocean waters; off central California, fewer appear during years of colder water temperatures. Generally far offshore, but in southern California and Mexico, may occur regularly within a few miles of the mainland coast. Nests on rocky islands.

FEEDING   **Diet:** *Includes crustaceans, small fish.* Diet poorly known. May eat many small fish at times, and has been reported feeding on larval form of the spiny lobster. May also eat small squid. Scavenges floating fat from dead animals at sea. **Behavior:** Forages mostly by hovering or fluttering low over water and taking items from surface.

NESTING   Breeding behavior poorly known. Nests on islands, often in small colonies. Both members of pair may spend part of time resting in nesting burrow for nearly 3 months before egg-laying. Active around colonies only at night. Adults give staccato calls while flying around colonies, changing to a musical trill when inside the nest. **Nest:** Site is in small opening among boulders, in crevice in cliff, or in burrow (especially abandoned burrow of Cassin's Auklet). Usually no nest built, sometimes a few bits of plant material. **Eggs:** 1. White, sometimes with small reddish brown spots around larger end. Incubation probably by both sexes. **Young:** Probably fed by both parents.

MIGRATION   After nesting, moves north regularly as far as central California. Common on Monterey Bay in late summer and fall during years of high water temperature. Most disappear after October, wintering south to waters off Panama and northwestern South America.

CONSERVATION STATUS   Numbers probably stable. Vulnerable to introduction of predators (such as rats and cats) on nesting islands.

LEAST STORM-PETREL   *Oceanodroma microsoma*

A tiny seabird, the smallest of the storm-petrels, no larger than a sparrow. It flies low over the waves with fast deep wingbeats, giving it a rather batlike look. Nests only on islands off western Mexico but moves north irregularly into California waters in late summer, sometimes in large numbers. On the rare occasions when hurricanes off western Mexico turn inland, this species may be carried along; Hurricane Kathleen in 1976 deposited hundreds on the Salton Sea in southern California.

HABITAT   *Open ocean.* Favors warm waters; more likely to move north along California coast in years when water temperature is higher. Generally over continental shelf, and may occur closer to shore than some other storm-petrels, often being seen from shore in Mexico. Nests on rocky islands.

FEEDING   **Diet:** *Probably tiny crustaceans and other very small marine life.* Diet very poorly known; presumably feeds mainly on zooplankton (general term for tiny creatures floating in water). Once reported to feed on larval stages of spiny lobster. **Behavior:** Forages mostly by fluttering low over water and taking items from surface. Seldom sits on water to feed.

Least Storm-Petrel

NESTING   Nesting behavior poorly known. Breeds in colonies on islands off northwestern Mexico. At San Benito Island, many nests reported to have eggs in July. Active around nesting colonies only at night. Makes whirring calls from inside nest. **Nest:** Site is reported to be usually among piles of rocks, or in crevices in cliffs. Apparently not in burrows as in many other storm-petrels. Several pairs may nest close together if good sites are clustered. No nest built, egg laid on bare rock. **Eggs:** 1. White. Incubation probably by both sexes. **Young:** Probably both parents feed young.

MIGRATION   Moves north irregularly into California waters, mostly August and September. Numbers quite variable; sometimes hundreds recorded, occasionally none. In midautumn moves south along coast of Central America, commonly as far as Panama, a few as far as Peru.

CONSERVATION STATUS   Numbers probably stable, but overfishing and pollution of Gulf of California could have negative impact. Vulnerable to introduced predators (such as rats and cats) on some nesting islands.

TROPICBIRDS Family (Phaethontidae)

The three species of tropicbirds are graceful, beautiful, long-tailed birds, flying high over tropical seas with strong, quick wingbeats. Often attracted to ships at sea, they may circle overhead before continuing on their way. When swimming, they float buoyantly on the water with tails cocked up, but they seem to spend more of their time on the wing.

Tropicbirds are not particularly sociable. They nest in colonies in some places, but only where good nesting sites are clustered close together. At sea they are usually solitary, never in flocks. Around their nesting sites they make a variety of rattling and shrieking cries, especially during courtship displays, but at sea they are generally silent.

WHITE-TAILED TROPICBIRD   *Phaethon lepturus*

In the United States, this beautiful bird is seen mostly in Hawaii and around the Dry Tortugas, Florida. This is the national bird of Bermuda, where the "Longtail" is familiar to all and is given complete protection.

White-tailed Tropicbird

HABITAT   *Tropical ocean, islands.* Found close to shore around nesting islands but otherwise spends most of its time far out at sea, over warm waters. Nests on islands, often those with rocky cliffs.

FEEDING   **Diet:** *Mostly fish.* Feeds on a wide variety of small fish but seems to favor flying-fish, which are common in tropical waters. Also eats small squid, snails, crabs. **Behavior:** Forages by plunging into water from flight, submerging briefly; sometimes by swooping down to surface without striking water, perhaps taking flying-fish in the air. May feed most actively in early morning and late afternoon.

NESTING   May nest as isolated pairs or in colonies, depending on spacing of available nest sites. Nesting season is spring and summer in Bermuda; may nest year-round at some tropical islands. Courtship displays include two birds flying gracefully in unison, one above the other, with higher bird bending tail down to touch tail of lower bird. **Nest:** Site is in crevice or hole in rock, on ledge, on ground under dense vegetation; in Old World tropics, may nest in hollow tree or log. Same site may be reused for several years. No nest built, egg laid on bare ground. **Eggs:** 1. Whitish to pale buff, with brownish and purplish spots. Incubation is by both sexes, 40–42 days, perhaps sometimes shorter. **Young:** Both parents feed young, by regurgitation. Age at first flight usually 70–85 days.

MIGRATION   Visits North American waters in spring and summer. Only a summer resident in Bermuda. Present year-round in some parts of Caribbean. Sometimes driven far inland in North America by hurricanes.

CONSERVATION STATUS   Nesting colonies in some parts of world have declined because of human disturbance, but still widespread and common in many areas.

RED-BILLED TROPICBIRD   *Phaethon aethereus*

The only tropicbird likely to be seen off the California coast, but rare even there; sometimes seen on boat trips to the southern Channel Islands. Common in parts of the Caribbean, the Red-billed Tropicbird very rarely strays to waters off Florida or elsewhere in the east.

RED-TAILED TROPICBIRD   *Phaethon rubricauda*

This graceful seabird ranges widely in the tropical Pacific and Indian oceans and may be seen by visitors to Hawaii. In North American waters it has been found far off the coast of California, where it may be a rare but regular visitor more than 100 miles from land. Even more than its relatives, it seems to wander great distances away from its nesting islands.

The three species of gannets and six species of boobies range widely over the oceans of the world. All are large birds, with long, pointed wings, fairly long tails, and pointed bills. They fly strongly, alternating powerful wingbeats with long glides. When feeding, they plunge from high in the air, diving into the water to catch fish. Although some (especially the gannets) can fly very well in strong winds, they are not dependent on wind like albatrosses and some other seabirds.

Most species are sociable, nesting in colonies (usually on islands) and often foraging together where there are concentrations of fish.

Feeding
The foraging of a flock of Northern Gannets is among the great spectacles to be seen off our Atlantic coast. These big birds (with six-foot wingspans) circle high above the waves, watching for fish near the surface, and then plunge headfirst into the water to catch their prey. This is typical feeding behavior for most members of the family. The smaller boobies may often make shallower plunges, hitting the water at an angle instead of diving straight down, and they sometimes catch flying-fish above the water's surface. At times they may also dive from the surface and swim underwater, using their wings for propulsion. Their eyes are set far forward on their heads, giving them better binocular vision straight ahead than most birds, a useful trait in high-speed pursuit dives.

Fish that gather in dense schools are the main food items for gannets, while boobies also eat many squid and some crustaceans as well as fish.

Nesting
These birds are sociable in nesting. Gannet colonies are often large and tightly packed, while booby colonies are often smaller and more spread out. Most species nest on the ground, while two booby species build stick nests in trees. One to three eggs are laid, white to pale blue, with very thick shells. Both parents take turns incubating, placing the egg(s) under the webs of their feet for more direct transfer of heat. Both parents also help feed the young.

Displays
Many different ritualized postures and movements are used as displays, both for courtship and for defending the area around the nest. The latter tend to be more highly developed in gannets, with their denser colonies. Displays include bowing, stretching the neck up with the bill pointed skyward, swinging the head from side to side, and many others. Some boobies, including the Blue-footed and Red-footed, have high-stepping displays that show off their colorful feet.

BOOBIES — GENUS *Sula*

The name "booby" was coined long ago by sailors, who considered these birds stupid because they showed no apparent fear of humans. Although boobies and gannets are quite similar, gannets tend to be larger and inhabit cooler waters, while the boobies are mainly tropical. Four species of boobies occur in our area, but none is common here.

MASKED BOOBY   *Sula dactylatra*

Widespread in tropical oceans, this large, long-winged seabird occurs regularly off our southern Atlantic and Gulf coasts; it is also common in Hawaii, mainly in the northwestern chain. Known as a visitor to the Dry Tortugas, Florida, for many years, the Masked Booby did not begin to nest there until the 1980s.

HABITAT   *Tropical seas.* Forages over warm waters, shallow or deep, sometimes hundreds of miles from land. Nests on islands, mainly low flat islands with little or no vegetation. In Florida, has nested on small sandy island barely above high-water level.

FEEDING   **Diet:** *Mostly fish.* Eats a variety of fish, with flying-fish often predominating; also some squid. **Behavior:** Forages by plunging into water from flight (from as high as 90 feet above the sea), striking water headfirst and catching prey within a few feet of the surface. May rest on water, watching for fish below and watching other seabirds in vicinity; when it spots prey, it takes flight and begins plunge-diving, and other birds hurry to join in feeding.

Masked Booby

NESTING   Usually first breeds at age of 4 years. Breeds in colonies. Courtship displays of male include stretching neck and pointing bill skyward. Paired birds present each other with pebbles or feathers, parade slowly forward with prominent display of feet. **Nest:** Site is on ground, often near edge of slope or cliff for ease of takeoff. Nest is a shallow depression surrounded by slight rim of pebbles, debris. **Eggs:** 1–2. Pale blue to chalky white, becoming nest-stained. Both sexes incubate, placing eggs under webs of feet; incubation period 38–49 days. When 2 eggs are laid, second young to hatch is attacked and ejected from nest by its older sibling and does not survive. **Young:** Both parents feed young, by regurgitation. Age at first flight 109–151 days. Young return to nest site and continue to be fed by parents for 30–60 days after able to fly.

MIGRATION   No regular migration, but wide dispersal at sea. Birds in Pacific have been known to visit sites more than 1,000 miles from breeding colony. Apparently present all year off southeastern United States, perhaps more common in warmer months.

CONSERVATION STATUS   Total population difficult to assess because colonies are numerous and widely scattered, but these factors probably also ensure its survival. No evidence of widespread decline.

BLUE-FOOTED BOOBY   *Sula nebouxii*

Often shown in documentaries about the Galápagos, where pairs bow and shuffle and show off their blue feet, the Blue-footed Booby also nests as far north as western Mexico. In some years, small numbers stray north into the southwestern United States, mainly to the Salton Sea, California.

BROWN BOOBY   *Sula leucogaster*

Tropical seas around the world are home to this large, long-winged, strong-flying seabird. In North America it is seen most often near the Dry Tortugas, Florida, where it perches in trees or on navigational markers. It may have nested on the Florida Keys in the past, but the only U.S. nesting sites today are in Hawaii.

HABITAT   *Tropical oceans.* Widespread at sea, including very far from land, over warm waters in tropics and subtropics. Also often found close to shore, especially around islands, sometimes foraging in very shallow or muddy waters. Nests on rocky or sandy islands.

FEEDING **Diet:** *Mostly fish.* In North American waters, diet includes flying-fish and mullet, also squid and shrimp. **Behavior:** Forages mostly by plunging headfirst into water from flight, usually diving at angle and from fairly low above surface. Sometimes hovers before diving, dives from perch, swoops low to take items from surface, or seizes items while swimming. May pursue flying-fish in the air. Also steals food from other birds.

NESTING Probably first breeds at age of 4 years, and may mate for life. Courtship displays by members of pair include bill-touching, bowing, throwing head back with bill pointing skyward. Nests in large or small colonies, sometimes isolated pairs, on tropical or subtropical islands. **Nest:** Site is on ground or cliff.

Brown Booby

Nest is shallow depression, sometimes sparsely lined, sometimes with large mound of twigs, grass, debris, built by both sexes. **Eggs:** 1–2, rarely 3. Whitish to pale blue-green, becoming nest-stained brown. Incubation is by both sexes, 40–47 days. **Young:** Both parents feed young, by regurgitation. When 2 eggs laid, second young to hatch rarely survives. Period from hatching to first flight varies, depending on food supply, 84–119 days. Juvenile returns to nest site and begs to be fed for many weeks after first flight, often 20 weeks or more.

MIGRATION Present year-round in most parts of range, with only local wandering at sea. Birds from western Mexico sometimes stray north into interior of American southwest (especially Salton Sea, Colorado River).

CONSERVATION STATUS Vulnerable to disturbance on islands where it breeds, but survival probably ensured by wide range and large number of nesting sites.

RED-FOOTED BOOBY *Sula sula*

Found in tropical seas around the world, this long-winged seabird is only a very rare visitor to North America. Most records are from Florida, especially around the islands of the Dry Tortugas, but the species has also been found off the California coast.

GENUS *Morus*

NORTHERN GANNET *Morus bassanus*

One of the largest seabirds of the North Atlantic, the gannet is spectacular as it plunges into the sea in pursuit of fish. With a spearlike bill and spiky tail, it looks "pointed at both ends." Nesting colonies are on northern sea cliffs; one at Bonaventure Island, Quebec, has become a famous tourist destination. In winter off southern coastlines, the gleaming white adults may be outnumbered by brown and patchy immatures; it takes four years for gannets to attain full adult plumage.

HABITAT *Oceanic; often well offshore. Breeds colonially on sea cliffs.* Forages at sea, from fairly close inshore to out of sight of land, but mostly over waters of continental shelf. In cold-water areas in summer, but winters to edge of tropics. Nests on cliffs and ledges of islands, sometimes on steep protected cliffs of mainland.

Northern Gannet

FEEDING   **Diet:** *Mainly fish.* Feeds mostly on small fish (1–12 inches long) of types that live in dense schools, including herring, sand lance, cod, pollock, menhaden. Also may eat some squid. Sometimes scavenges for scraps and offal around fishing boats. **Behavior:** Forages by plunging headfirst into water, sometimes from more than 100 feet above surface. Also forages while swimming, submerging head to peer below surface and then diving and swimming underwater. May take food at surface, or may steal food from other birds.

NESTING   Usually first breeds at age of 5–6 years, and may mate for life. Breeds in tightly packed colonies, with much competition for prime nest sites. Male claims nest territory and displays to attract mate, with exaggerated sideways shaking of head. Mated pairs greet each other by standing face to face, wings out, knocking bills together and bowing. **Nest:** Site is on ledge or flat ground, often within 2–3 feet of other nesting gannets. Nest (built mostly by male) is pile of grass, seaweed, dirt, feathers, compacted and held together by droppings, used by same pair for years and gradually building up to tall mound. **Eggs:** 1. Pale blue to white, becoming nest-stained. Incubation is by both sexes, 42–46 days. **Young:** Both parents feed young, by regurgitation. Age at first flight 84–97 days. Only one young raised per year.

MIGRATION   Migrates offshore southward along Atlantic coast, some going around southern end of Florida and along Gulf coast to Texas. Immatures tend to winter farther south than adults. Many (especially adults) are present in winter far offshore as far north as New England. Immatures and nonbreeders may remain south of breeding grounds in summer.

CONSERVATION STATUS   Population declined drastically during 19th century because of taking of eggs and slaughter of adults; this occurred over much of range but especially off eastern Canada. With protection, populations began to recover early in 20th century, with increase apparently continuing to present day.

PELICANS (Family Pelecanidae)

As a group, the pelicans are unmistakable. The eight species found around the world all have long bills with greatly expandable pouches in the lower mandible, which they use in the manner of fishing nets. Our Brown Pelican, with a wingspan of "only" seven feet, is the *smallest* member of the family; the largest pelicans are among the heaviest of flying birds, approaching 30 pounds.

In the wild, pelicans may often live more than 25 years.

Feeding   All members of the family feed mainly on fish. Brown Pelicans (and the closely related Peruvian Pelicans) differ from all other species in habitat and feeding. They are strictly coastal, and they fish from the air, making spectacular plunge-dives into the sea to catch fish. The other species all forage while swimming, using their long bills and big pouches to scoop up fish from below the surface. These larger pelicans often feed cooperatively, lining up to drive schools of fish ahead of them into the shallows.

The plunge-diving pelicans spot their prey from the air, while the other species may find fish by sight or by touch (allowing them to feed successfully at night).

After making a catch, a pelican drains the water from its pouch before swallowing the fish.

Nesting Most probably breed for the first time at three years or older. They nest in colonies, sometimes very large. Nests may be either stick platforms built in trees or scrapes on the ground. Usually two off-white eggs are laid. Both parents take turns incubating, holding the eggs on or under the webs of their feet. Both parents also feed the young. After the young are strong enough to stand, they feed by sticking their heads deep into the parent's throat to take partially digested fish; to anyone watching, it may seem that the young bird is about to be swallowed.

Displays In the breeding season, the colors of the bill and bare face skin become brighter, and some species grow short feathery crests. Courtship displays vary, but may include strutting, bowing, and pointing the bill straight up. In aggressive interactions, the pelican may point its bill at a rival and open its mouth very wide, making a gaping threat display. Some of the odd postures that pelicans adopt at times (with the bill pointed up or spread wide) appear to be displays but may be simply stretching exercises to keep the pouch flexible.

GENUS *Pelecanus*

AMERICAN WHITE PELICAN *Pelecanus erythrorhynchos*

One of the largest birds in North America, with a 9-foot wingspan. Similar to Brown Pelican in shape but much larger, and very different in habits: occurs far inland, feeds cooperatively in shallow lakes, does not dive from the air for fish. Despite its great size, it is a spectacular flier, with flocks often soaring very high in the air, ponderously wheeling and circling in unison.

HABITAT *Lakes, marshes, salt bays.* In breeding season mostly inland, nesting on isolated islands in lakes and feeding on shallow lakes, rivers, marshes. Feeding areas may be miles from nesting sites. Also breeds locally on coastal islands. Flocks in migration stop on lakes, rivers. Winters mainly along coast, on shallow, protected bays and estuaries, also on large lakes in warm climates.

FEEDING **Diet:** *Mostly fish.* Primarily eats "rough" fish of little value to humans, also crayfish, salamanders. **Behavior:** Forages by swimming on surface, dipping bill into water and scooping up fish in pouch. During breeding season does much foraging at night,

American White Pelican

locating fish by touch during frequent dipping of bill; by day, probably locates prey visually. May forage cooperatively, lining up and driving fish toward shallower water.

NESTING Courtship displays include two (or more) birds strutting with heads erect, bills pointed down; deep bowing with wings slightly raised; high, circling courtship flights by groups. Breeds in colonies. **Nest:** Site is on ground, usually open bare soil, sometimes among grasses or under trees. Nest (built by both sexes) is shallow depression surrounded by low rim of dirt, stones, plant material. **Eggs:** 2. Dull white, becoming nest-stained. Both sexes incubate, about 30 days. **Young:** Second young to hatch usually dies within 2 weeks, but sometimes both young fledge, especially in years with abundant food supply. Both parents feed young. Young leave nest

17–25 days after hatching, gather in groups. Age at first flight 9–10 weeks, leave colony at 10–11 weeks.

MIGRATION   Most populations are migratory; some populations on Texas coast and in Mexico are permanent residents. Migrates by day, in flocks. Breeders from northern plains migrate southeast and southwest to coastal lowlands. Some nonbreeding birds remain through summer on winter range, especially in Florida. Strays wander widely, including to northeast.

CONSERVATION STATUS   Colonies are vulnerable to disturbance and habitat loss. Total population probably declined through first half of 20th century, has substantially increased since 1970s.

BROWN PELICAN   *Pelecanus occidentalis*

An unmistakable bird of coastal waters. Groups of Brown Pelicans fly low over the waves in single file, flapping and gliding in unison. Their feeding behavior is spectacular, as they plunge headlong into the water in pursuit of fish. The current abundance of this species in the United States represents a success story for conservationists, who succeeded in halting the use of DDT and other persistent pesticides here; as recently as the early 1970s, the Brown Pelican was seriously endangered.

HABITAT   *Salt bays, beaches, ocean.* Mostly over shallow waters along immediate coast, especially on sheltered bays; sometimes seen well out to sea. Nests on islands, which may be either bare and rocky or covered with mangroves or other trees. Strays may appear on freshwater lakes inland.

FEEDING   **Diet:** *Almost entirely fish.* Types of fish known to be important in some areas include menhaden, smelt, anchovies. Also some crustaceans.

Brown Pelican

Behavior: Forages by diving from as high as 60 feet in the air, plunging into water headfirst and coming to surface with fish in bill. Tilts bill down to drain water out of pouch, then tosses head back to swallow. Will scavenge at times and will become tame, approaching fishermen for handouts.

NESTING   Nests in colonies. **Nest:** Site is on ground or cliff of island, or on low trees such as mangroves. Nest (built by female with material gathered by male) may be simple scrape in soil, heap of debris with depression at top, or large stick nest in tree. **Eggs:** 3, sometimes 2–4. White, becoming nest-stained. Incubation is by both sexes, roughly 28–30 days. **Young:** Both parents feed young. Young may leave ground nests after about 5 weeks and gather in groups, where returning parents apparently can recognize own offspring. Young may remain in tree nests longer (perhaps up to 9 weeks) before clambering about in branches. Age at first flight varies, reportedly 9–12 weeks or more. Adults continue to feed young for some time after they leave colony. One brood per year.

MIGRATION   After breeding season, flocks move north along both Atlantic and Pacific coasts. These birds return southward to warmer waters by winter. Small numbers of immatures regularly wander inland in summer, especially in southwest.

CONSERVATION STATUS   Declined drastically in mid-20th century, as effects of pesticides caused eggshell thinning and failure of breeding. By 1970, all North American populations were essentially gone except some in Florida. Following the banning of DDT, Brown

Pelicans made a strong recovery. They are now common and perhaps still increasing on the southeast and west coasts.

CORMORANTS (Family Phalacrocoracidae)

Slim and snaky-necked, with a rather prehistoric look, cormorants are diving birds that pursue fish and other prey underwater. About 30 to 40 species (depending on how some forms are classified) live along coastlines worldwide, including much of the Arctic and Antarctic. Several species are also very common around inland waters.

The feathers of cormorants become waterlogged after a short time in the water. This helps the birds in diving, as it makes them heavier, but it means that they must allow the plumage to dry out between feeding sessions. For this reason, cormorants spend little time in the water when they are not actively foraging; much of their time is spent resting on rocks, piers, dead trees, or other perches, often with their wings spread out to dry. Most species are sociable, and flocks are often seen flying in lines or V-formation.

Feeding   Cormorants catch most of their food underwater. While swimming along the surface they may dip their heads underwater repeatedly, looking for prey, before diving. During dives their wings are usually folded tightly against their bodies, and they propel themselves with their large webbed feet. Their eyes have special adaptations for vision both in water and in air; they seek their food visually and then swim rapidly in pursuit. Most food is brought to the surface and swallowed there.

Fish make up most of the diet at most times. However, cormorants also eat a variety of other things, especially on fresh waters, where they may take frogs, salamanders, crayfish, snakes, insects, and others. Fish and other large creatures are swallowed headfirst, and the very flexible neck and throat allow the cormorant to swallow items nearly as thick as its own head. Indigestible parts of the food, including scales and bones, are coughed up later as pellets.

Nesting   These birds almost always nest in colonies, often associated with other kinds of waterbirds. Nest sites are usually on rocky cliffs on the coast, or in trees near water in inland areas. Both sexes help build the nest; at least in some species, the male brings material but the female does most of the actual building. A pair may use the same nest for several years. Up to seven pale blue eggs are laid, and both parents take turns incubating, resting the eggs on the webs of their feet. Both parents help feed the young. In our species, each pair probably raises just one brood per year.

Displays   As expected in sociable birds, cormorants have many displays used in courtship and aggression. Males often display at the nest site to attract a mate and to drive off intruders. The bare skin areas of the face and throat pouch develop brighter colors in the breeding season, and these colors are shown off in many displays in which the bill is pointed up or opened wide. Some cormorants have white patches on their flanks in breeding plumage, and these species often display by rapidly raising and lowering the tips of the folded wings so that the white patches seem to flash on and off.

GENUS *Phalacrocorax*

GREAT CORMORANT   *Phalacrocorax carbo*

Widespread in the Old World, the Great Cormorant was once an uncommon and local breeder in a limited area of eastern Canada. In recent decades its North

American population has gone through a great increase and expansion, with the nesting range now extending south into New England.

HABITAT   *Sea cliffs (nesting); mainly coastal.* In North America mostly over shallow waters close to shore, especially in sheltered bays, rarely well out to sea. Nests on rocky cliffs of coasts and islands. Southerly wintering birds often around rock jetties. In recent years, as population has increased, has been found in winter on large rivers inland. In Old World regularly far inland on lakes, rivers, swamps.

FEEDING   **Diet:** *Fish.* Feeds almost entirely on fish, with small numbers of crustaceans, marine worms. In Old World, where found also on fresh water, diet may be more varied. **Behavior:** See family introduction. Most foraging is within 10 feet of surface, although can dive to 30 feet.

NESTING   Usually first breeds at age of 4–5 years. Breeds in colonies. Male chooses nest site and displays to attract female by waving wings up and down, flashing white rump patches. Pairs at nest display by writhing and intertwining necks. **Nest:** Site is usually on sheltered ledge of cliff, from just above water to 300 feet or higher. Rarely nests in trees in North America (but does so commonly in Old World). Nest is a pile of sticks, seaweed, debris, lined with finer materials. Female does most building, with material brought by male. **Eggs:** 3–5, rarely 1–6. Pale blue-green, becoming nest-stained. Incubation is by both sexes, 28–31 days. **Young:** Both parents feed young, by regurgitation. Age at first flight about 50 days; young may return to nest to be fed for another 40–50 days.

MIGRATION   Migrates in flocks. Migration parallels the coastline, usually a short distance offshore. Rarely strays inland in fall and winter.

CONSERVATION STATUS   In recent decades, North American population has increased dramatically, and breeding range has expanded southward along coast.

Great Cormorant

DOUBLE-CRESTED CORMORANT   *Phalacrocorax auritus*

This dark, long-bodied diving bird floats low in the water with its thin neck and bill raised; perches upright near water with wings half-spread to dry. The Double-crested (which rarely looks noticeably crested in the field) is the most generally distributed cormorant in North America and the only one likely to be seen inland in most areas.

Double-crested Cormorant

HABITAT   *Coasts, bays, lakes, rivers.* Very adaptable; may be found in almost any aquatic habitat, from rocky northern coasts to mangrove swamps to large reservoirs to small inland ponds. Nests in trees near or over water, on sea cliffs, or on ground on islands.

FEEDING   **Diet:** *Fish and other aquatic life.* Diet varies with season and place, includes very wide variety of fish, also crabs, shrimp, crayfish, frogs, salamanders, eels; sometimes snakes, mollusks, plant material. **Behavior:** Forages mostly by diving from surface and swimming underwater, propelled by feet (may sometimes use wings as well). May forage singly or in groups. May forage in clear or muddy water, at middle to upper levels of water more often than near bottom.

NESTING   Usually first breeds at age of 3 years. Nests in colonies, sometimes mixed with wading birds and others. Male displays to female on water by splashing with wings, swimming in zig-zags, diving and bringing up pieces of weeds. At nest site, male displays by crouching and vibrating wings while calling. **Nest:** Site is near water on cliff ledge, on ground on island, or at any height in tree. Nest (built mostly by female, with materials brought by male) platform of sticks and debris, lined with finer materials. **Eggs:** 3–4, sometimes 1–7. Bluish white, becoming nest-stained. Incubation is by both sexes, 25–33 days, typically 28–30. **Young:** Both parents feed the nestlings. After 3–4 weeks, young may leave ground nests and wander through colony, but return to nest to be fed. Usually first fly at about 5–6 weeks, probably independent at 9–10 weeks.

MIGRATION   Some in Florida and on Pacific coast may be permanent residents; most are migratory. Migrates in flocks, often following coastlines or rivers. Most probably travel by day.

CONSERVATION STATUS   Population has had ups and downs. Probably long-term decline (because of persecution at nesting colonies) until about 1920s, then gradual increase until 1950s. Numbers dropped again through 1960s, probably from effects of persistent pesticides. After DDT was banned in 1972, populations began increasing again; still increasing and expanding range through mid-1990s.

NEOTROPIC CORMORANT   *Phalacrocorax brasilianus*

Neotropic Cormorant

Found throughout the American tropics, this lanky diving bird is common in some areas near the Mexican border, and may be gradually extending its range north. Similar to the Double-crested Cormorant but a little smaller, and may be found with it, especially inland or in winter. Formerly called Olivaceous Cormorant.

HABITAT   *Tidal waters, lakes.* In United States on warm southern waters, mostly fresh or brackish. Even in coastal regions, mainly on protected estuaries, rivers, or ponds, although may nest on coastal islands. May nest far inland in dead trees around reservoirs. In Latin America found in wide variety of inland and coastal areas, on both warm and cold waters.

FEEDING   **Diet:** *Small fish.* Feeds mostly on abundant small fish of shallow protected waters; typical prey about 2 inches long, up to about 5 inches. Also eats tadpoles, frogs, aquatic insects. In wide range of tropical habitats, probably other prey as well. **Behavior:** Forages by diving from surface and swimming underwater, propelled mostly by feet. Rarely plunges into water from air after prey. May forage in groups, birds beating water with wings to drive fish forward into shallows.

NESTING   Breeds in colonies. Displays of male include sitting with tail raised, bill pointed up, while raising and lowering tips of folded wings. Both sexes display by stretching neck up, bill open, waving head back and forth. **Nest:** Site usually in live or dead bushes or trees, 3–25 feet above water; sometimes on ground on islands. Nest (probably built by both sexes) a solid platform of sticks, with depression at center lined with twigs, grass. **Eggs:** 3–4, sometimes 1–5. Bluish white, becoming nest-stained. Incubation apparently by both sexes, averages about 25–30 days. **Young:** Both parents feed young. Age at first flight not well known, but young raised on islands able to swim and dive at 8 weeks, fed until 11th week, independent at 12 weeks.

MIGRATION   Largely a permanent resident, but some birds nesting inland may move south in winter. Occasionally wanders north, mainly in warmer months.

CONSERVATION STATUS   Texas population dropped sharply in 1950s and 1960s, possibly from effects of persistent pesticides, but since then has increased again in Texas and Louisiana. May be increasing and spreading north inland; first found nesting in New Mexico in 1970s.

BRANDT'S CORMORANT   *Phalacrocorax penicillatus*

Along the Pacific coast, this cormorant is a common resident of wave-washed rocks and offshore waters. Sociable at all seasons, it is often seen flying in long lines low over the water. Groups roost together on rocks near water and feed in flocks offshore, often associating with other seabirds.

Brandt's Cormorant

HABITAT   *Ocean, coast.* Almost always on salt water, entering brackish water at mouths of estuaries. May forage fairly close to shore or well out to sea. Nests on islands and locally on mainland, mostly on slopes rather than ledges of vertical cliffs.

FEEDING   **Diet:** *Mostly fish.* Eats a wide variety of fish, including herring, rockfish; also some shrimp, crabs. **Behavior:** See family introduction. Reportedly able to dive deep, perhaps more than 150 feet below surface. Forages singly or in groups, sometimes in association with sea lions. May forage at all levels from near surface to near bottom, perhaps mostly the latter.

NESTING   Breeds in colonies. Male chooses nest site and displays there to ward off rivals and attract mate. Displays include drawing head back with blue throat pouch extended and bill pointed upward, spreading tail, and fluttering wings; also thrusting head forward and down in rapid repeated strokes. **Nest:** Site is on ground, either level or steeply sloped. Nest is mound of seaweed, eelgrass, algae, cemented by droppings. Most nest material is obtained underwater; male does most of gathering, female does most of building. Pair may use same nest every year, adding to it annually. **Eggs:** 4, sometimes 3–6. Whitish to pale blue, becoming nest-stained. Incubation is by both sexes, incubation period unknown. **Young:** Both parents feed young, by regurgitation. Age at first flight unknown.

MIGRATION   Mostly permanent resident. Some local movements; birds nesting on Farallon Islands off California mostly absent in winter, perhaps going to adjacent mainland. In southeastern Alaska, apparently only a summer resident in very small numbers. Sometimes wanders along Mexican coast south of breeding range. Almost never found inland.

CONSERVATION STATUS   Local populations fluctuate, but overall numbers are probably stable.

PELAGIC CORMORANT *Phalacrocorax pelagicus*

Pelagic Cormorant

The smallest cormorant of the Pacific coast. May be solitary in its feeding but gregarious at other times, with groups perching together on rocks near water, holding wings out to dry. During the nesting season, even non-breeding individuals come to roost at night around the edges of nesting colonies, but Pelagic colonies are often smaller than those of its relatives. Often more shy and harder to approach than other cormorants.

HABITAT   *Coast, bays, sounds.* On ocean usually rather close to shore, sometimes well out to sea. Favors rocky bays, areas of deep water near base of cliffs. Nests on islands or coasts on narrow ledges, steep slopes, other inaccessible locations.

FEEDING   **Diet:** *Fish, crustaceans.* Eats mainly small fish, including sculpins, herrings, greenlings, sand lance; also many crabs, shrimps. Also eats marine worms, amphipods, algae. **Behavior:** Forages by diving from surface and swimming underwater, propelled mainly by feet, though possibly sometimes may use wings as well. Forages singly, although may be attracted to concentrations of other feeding birds. Known to dive at least 120 feet below surface; takes much of food from near bottom in rocky areas.

NESTING   Nests in colonies. Male displays at nest site with bill pointed up, tail down, quickly raising and lowering tips of folded wings so that white flank patches appear to flash rapidly. **Nest:** Site is on cliffs with near-vertical slopes, narrow ledges. Parents not effective at defending eggs or young, rely on inaccessible location for protection. Nest is of seaweed, grass, moss, sometimes sticks. Both sexes help build nest; may use same nest each year, adding to it annually. **Eggs:** 3–5, sometimes 1–7. Bluish white, becoming nest-stained. Incubation is by both sexes, 26–37 days, typically about 30. **Young:** Probably both parents feed nestlings. Young may be capable of short flights at 35–40 days, leave nest at about 45–55 days (much variation). Parents may tend and feed young for a few weeks after they leave nest.

MIGRATION   Present year-round in most of range, but vacates northern-most breeding areas (western Alaska) in winter when waters freeze and becomes more common off southern California and Baja in winter.

CONSERVATION STATUS   Numbers probably stable. Reportedly increased in coastal British Columbia during this century. North American population in 1980s estimated at over 120,000, with close to ¾ of those in Alaska.

RED-FACED CORMORANT *Phalacrocorax urile*

This Alaskan specialty nests on islands in cold seas, associating with a wide variety of other seabirds. The bright red bare skin of its face becomes duller in winter. In recent years the Red-faced Cormorant has been increasing in numbers, expanding its range eastward along the coast of southern Alaska.

HABITAT   *Ocean, coast, islands.* Spends most of its time close to shore in cool ocean waters, favoring rocky bays, straits between islands. Nests on rocky islands or coasts, on ledges of cliffs or steep slopes.

FEEDING   **Diet:** *Mostly fish.* Feeds on a variety of fish, especially sculpins, also pollock, sand lance, others. Also eats crustaceans including crabs, shrimp, amphipods. **Behavior:** See family introduction. Solitary in foraging; may feed near bottom in rocky areas.

NESTING   Breeds in mixed colonies with other seabirds. In display, male perches with head over back, bill pointed up, moving head up and down, while quickly raising and lowering tips of folded wings so that white patches on flanks are rapidly covered and exposed, appearing to flash on and off. **Nest:** Site is on ledge (wide or narrow) of cliff or steep slope above water. Nest is mound of grass, seaweed, moss, debris, with deep hollow in center, sometimes lined with feathers. Nest may be reused in subsequent years. **Eggs:** 3–4. Bluish white, becoming nest-stained. Incubation is by both sexes, probably about 31–34 days. **Young:** Probably fed by both parents. Age at which young leave nest estimated at 50–60 days.

MIGRATION   Mostly permanent resident. Very rare straggler away from nesting areas (though may winter away from breeding sites in Kuril Islands, north of Japan).

CONSERVATION STATUS   Population in Aleutians thought to have been increasing for several decades. Since late 1950s has expanded range east along south coast of Alaska, becoming very common east to Prince William Sound. Despite increase, remains vulnerable to oil spills and other pollution.

Red-faced Cormorant

DARTERS (Family Anhingidae)

This small family is represented by one species in the Americas and by forms in the Old World that may constitute one to three species. Darters are related to cormorants but are less widespread, occurring mainly in tropical and subtropical regions. Like the cormorants (and unlike most waterbirds), darters have feathers that become waterlogged easily, so they must allow their plumage to dry out between sessions of fishing.

GENUS *Anhinga*

ANHINGA   *Anhinga anhinga*

A long-necked, long-tailed swimmer of southeastern swamps. Often seen perched on a snag above the water, with its wings half-spread to dry. Can vary its buoyancy in water, sometimes swimming with only head and neck above water (earning it the nickname of "Snakebird"). Often solitary when feeding, it roosts in groups and nests in colonies. Looks rather like a cormorant when perched, but not in flight, when the long tail may be spread wide as the Anhinga soars high on outstretched wings. Anhingas are silent at most times, but around nesting colonies they make various croaking and clicking sounds.

HABITAT   *Cypress swamps, rivers, wooded ponds.* Mostly on quiet and sheltered waters such as freshwater marshes, slow-moving rivers through cypress swamps, inlets and lagoons lined with mangroves, lakes with standing dead trees.

FEEDING   **Diet:** *Mostly fish.* Feeds primarily on "rough" fish of little value to humans, including catfish, mullet, pickerel, sucker, gizzard shad. Also aquatic insects, crayfish, shrimp, sometimes snakes, baby alligators, small turtles. **Behavior:** Hunts for fish while swimming underwater or at surface. Not usually a fast swimmer, mostly waits for fish to come near, then impales them with lightning-fast thrust of long, pointed bill. Structure of neck is specially adapted for this kind of rapid thrust. Fish often tossed in air, then swallowed headfirst.

NESTING Sometimes nests in isolated pairs, usually in groups, in mixed colonies with herons, ibises, cormorants. Male chooses site in colony and displays there to attract mate.

Displays include waving wings, raising tail up over back, pointing bill skyward and then bowing deeply. **Nest:** Built mostly by female, with material supplied by male. A platform of sticks, often lined with green leaves. Sometimes takes over an occupied nest of heron or egret. **Eggs:** 4, sometimes 2–5. Whitish to pale blue, becoming nest-stained. Incubation is by both sexes, 25–29 days. **Young:** Both parents feed young. After age of about 2 weeks, if young are disturbed, they will jump out of nest into water; at least sometimes, they are able to climb back up to nest. Young climb in nest tree using feet and bill. Age at first flight unknown.

MIGRATION Withdraws from northern breeding areas in winter. Many go to Mexico, migrating around Gulf of Mexico, with migrant flocks seen along Texas coast in spring and fall. Some remain all winter

Anhinga

in south, especially peninsular Florida. Lone strays occasionally wander far to north during warmer months.

FRIGATEBIRDS (Family Fregatidae)

Frigatebirds are the ultimate gliders among birds, able to hang in the air for hours with hardly a movement of their long, angular wings. Denizens of warm seas, they are seen soaring over tropical coastlines or perched like gaunt statues on dead trees or navigational towers. They never swim, because their long wings (adapted for soaring) and tiny feet render them unable to take off from water; all their food is snatched from the surface in flight or stolen from other birds.

As an adaptation for soaring flight, these birds have very lightweight, hollow bones. In fact, a frigatebird's feathers weigh more than its skeleton.

Five species inhabit the tropical and subtropical oceans of the world. All are similar in habits to our Magnificent Frigatebird. Silent and inscrutable at most seasons, they become noisy and showy around their nesting colonies. There they make various rattling and whinnying calls, and the males display by inflating their enormous red throat pouches.

GENUS *Fregata*

MAGNIFICENT FRIGATEBIRD   *Fregata magnificens*

In North America, Magnificent Frigatebirds are most commonly seen in Florida. However, they also appear regularly along the Gulf coast, and strays have turned up in many parts of the continent.

HABITAT *Oceanic coasts, islands.* Occurs over warm waters, usually along coast but also far offshore at times. Also soars inland in coastal areas (for example, crosses isthmus of

Panama from one ocean to the other). Strays are rarely seen far inland around fresh water. Nests on islands, usually small islands with dense growth of mangroves or other trees or shrubs.

FEEDING   **Diet:** *Mostly fish.* Feeds mainly on small fish, also squid, jellyfish, crustaceans. Takes hatchling turtles, young terns and other birds, sometimes eggs. Also scavenges for scraps around fishing boats, docks. **Behavior:** Forages in the air, swooping close to water to take items from on or near surface, making very little contact with water. Never swims. Forages in the same way over land, taking prey from beaches without landing. Also feeds by piracy, chasing other birds, forcing them to drop or disgorge their food.

NESTING   Breeds in colonies, with nests often very close together. Perched males display (often in groups) by inflating throat pouch to huge red balloon, raising bill high, vibrating partially spread wings, swiveling back and forth, and calling. Females flying overhead are attracted to group, choose one male as mate. **Nest:** Site usually in mangroves, trees, or bushes 2–20 feet above ground or water, sometimes on ground. Nest (built mostly by female, with materials brought by male) a flimsy platform of sticks. **Eggs:** 1. White. Incubation is by both sexes, probably 40–50 days. **Young:** Both parents feed young. Nest is never left unguarded until young are half-grown, as other members of colony will eat eggs or young at unattended nest. Male departs after about 12 weeks, female continues to feed young. Age at first flight 20–24 weeks; female will feed young for additional 16 weeks or more. Total breeding cycle for female thus lasts about a year; most females probably do not breed every year.

Magnificent Frigatebird

MIGRATION   Apparently not truly migratory. Present year-round in southern Florida; in northern Florida and along Gulf coast, more common in summer. Nesting colonies are widely dispersed among islands and coasts of tropical America (and very locally off west Africa), but nonbreeders and immatures are seen far from colonies at all seasons. Small numbers (mostly immatures) regularly wander inland in southwest in summer. Rarely wanders north along coasts or far inland.

CONSERVATION STATUS   Total population difficult to monitor; probably has declined at some tropical colonies. Although known as a common visitor to Florida since the 1800s, not confirmed breeding there until late 1960s (on Marquesas Keys). At the well-watched Dry Tortugas, did not begin nesting until 1988.

GREAT FRIGATEBIRD   *Fregata minor*

Although it nests in Hawaii and far off western Mexico, this species is strictly accidental in North America. The first record, oddly enough, was of a wandering individual found in Oklahoma.

LESSER FRIGATEBIRD   *Fregata ariel*

This species is widespread in tropical seas, but only far from our region. As if to prove that nothing is impossible, a Lesser Frigatebird once appeared in Maine, thousands of miles from its normal range, and was photographed there.

These are long-legged fishermen of the shallows, usually seen wading in still waters or stalking at the water's edge, waiting to spear fish. Members of the heron family, about 60 species, are found worldwide except in the Antarctic and the far north.

Although many kinds of herons and egrets nest in colonies, they tend to be more spread out in foraging. Even where food is abundant and many herons are present, an individual may defend a small "feeding territory," driving away other birds that venture too close. In the evening, however, even outside the breeding season, herons may fly long distances to spend the night in big communal roosts. Unlike cranes, storks, and some other wading birds, herons normally fly with their heads hunched back on their shoulders, not stretched out in front of them.

Feeding Almost all birds in this family feed mainly on fish and other aquatic life, and do most of their foraging around the water. Most of their foraging methods are passive: the birds stand motionless, waiting for fish to approach, or they wade slowly, watching for prey. Some are more active feeders, shuffling their feet about to stir up the creatures or even dashing about erratically in the shallows (a common habit of the Reddish Egret). Feeding at dusk and at night is typical of the night-herons and of the odd Boat-billed Heron of the American tropics.

Besides fish, herons feed on many other aquatic creatures, including frogs, snakes, crayfish, crabs, and many others. The larger species may catch rodents and small birds, sometimes hunting them out on land. The Cattle Egret represents a different approach: it eats mostly insects, and hunts them in dry fields, often following grazing animals to catch the insects flushed out of the grass by the herds. Other egrets and herons occasionally feed this way as well.

Nesting Most herons and egrets are sociable in nesting. Their colonies often include more than one species and may be mixed with other waterbirds such as cormorants, darters, or ibises. Some species, such as the Green Heron, may nest either in colonies or in isolated pairs, and the bitterns generally nest alone.

Nest sites vary: they may be on the ground on predator-free islands, low in marsh vegetation, or high in trees. In many of the typical herons (but not in the bitterns), the female does most of the actual nest-building while the male gathers much of the nest material. Most species lay 2–7 eggs, and both sexes usually help incubate the eggs and feed the young. Unless noted otherwise, our species mostly raise just one brood per year.

Displays In most species, brighter colors develop on the bill, bare face skin, and legs during the breeding season, and many also grow long plumes then. Males usually arrive at nesting areas first and begin displaying to defend a nest site and to attract a mate. Common displays include stretching the neck up with the bill pointed straight up, bowing deeply, and pulling the head far back and then rapidly thrusting it forward while snapping the bill shut. Plumes may be fully raised during these antics. Many males also make short circling display flights near the nest site.

Since bitterns live in dense marshes, they seem to have fewer visual displays, depending more on voice to advertise their presence. If a bittern is disturbed at its nest, it may perform an aggressive display, pointing its bill at the intruder, puffing out all its feathers, and spreading its wings to make itself appear larger.

BITTERNS — GENERA *Botaurus* and *Ixobrychus*

Each of these genera is represented by several species around the world, but only one breeding in our area. Unlike most herons, the bitterns are secretive marsh birds, more often heard than seen. They differ in other habits as well. When alarmed, a bittern will "freeze" with its neck stretched up and bill pointed skyward; its pattern of vertical stripes then provides camouflage against the background of marsh grasses. In the large bitterns (*Botaurus*), unlike other herons, females do most or all of the work of incubating the eggs and feeding the young.

AMERICAN BITTERN   *Botaurus lentiginosus*

Extensive freshwater marshes are the favored haunts of this large, stout, solitary heron. It is seldom seen as it slips through the reeds, but its odd pumping or booming song, often heard at dusk or at night, carries for long distances across the marsh.

HABITAT   *Marshes, reedy lakes.* Breeds in freshwater marshes, mainly large, shallow wetlands with much tall marsh vegetation (cattails, grasses, sedges) and areas of open shallow water. Winters in similar areas, also in brackish coastal marshes. Sometimes feeds in dry grassy fields.

FEEDING   **Diet:** *Mostly fish and other aquatic life.* Eats fish (including catfish, eels, killifish, perch), frogs, tadpoles, aquatic insects, crayfish, crabs, salamanders, garter snakes. Has been seen catching flying dragonflies. In drier habitats may eat rodents, especially voles. **Behavior:** Forages mostly by standing still at edge of water, sometimes by walking slowly, capturing prey with sudden thrust of bill. May forage at any time of day or night, perhaps most actively at dawn and dusk.

American Bittern

NESTING   Male defends nesting territory by advertising presence with "booming" calls. Courtship displays not well known; male may hold head low and fluff out white feathers on sides. One male may mate with two or three females. **Nest:** Site is usually in dense marsh growth above shallow water, sometimes on dry ground among dense grasses. Nest (apparently built by female alone) is a platform of grasses, reeds, cattails, lined with fine grasses. **Eggs:** 3–5, sometimes 2–7. Pale brown to olive-buff. Incubation is by female only, 24–28 days. **Young:** Evidently only female cares for young, feeding them by regurgitation of partly digested items. Young may leave nest after 1–2 weeks, but remain nearby and are fed up to age of 4 weeks. Age at first flight unknown, possibly 7–8 weeks.

MIGRATION   May be permanent resident in a few areas at southern edge of breeding range, but most are migrants. Some winter south to West Indies, Central America. May migrate mostly at night.

CONSERVATION STATUS   Has seriously declined in southern part of breeding range, mostly from loss of habitat. Still numerous as a breeder in parts of Canada. Vulnerable because of its reliance on large marshes. Acid rain may reduce food supplies in some areas.

LEAST BITTERN   *Ixobrychus exilis*

One of the smallest herons in the world, adapted for life in dense marshes. Rather than wading in the shallows like most herons, the Least Bittern climbs about in cattails and reeds, clinging to the stems with its long toes. Its narrow body allows it to slip through dense, tangled vegetation with ease. Because of its habitat choice, it often goes unseen except when it flies, but its cooing and clucking call notes

HERONS, EGRETS, AND BITTERNS

are heard frequently at dawn and dusk and sometimes at night.

HABITAT *Fresh marshes, reedy ponds.* Mostly freshwater marsh but also brackish marsh, in areas with tall, dense vegetation standing in water. May be over fairly deep water, because it mostly climbs in reeds rather than wading. Sometimes in salt marsh or in mangroves.

FEEDING **Diet:** *Mostly fish and insects.* Eats mostly small fish (such as minnows, sunfishes, and perch) and large insects (dragonflies and others); also crayfish, leeches, frogs, tadpoles, small snakes, and other items. **Behavior:** Searches for food by clambering about in vegetation above water and by jabbing downward with its long bill to capture prey at the water's surface. Sometimes flicks its wings open and shut, which may startle prey into motion. At especially good feeding sites, it may bend down reeds to build a hunting platform for itself.

NESTING Nests are usually widely scattered in marsh but are sometimes in loose colonies. In one South Carolina study, Least Bitterns often nested in close association with Boat-tailed Grackles. **Nest:** Site is well concealed in tall marsh growth. Nest (built mostly by male) is platform created by bending down marsh vegetation, adding sticks and grass on top. **Eggs:** 4–5, sometimes 2–7. Pale green or blue. Incubation is by both sexes, 17–20 days. **Young:** Both parents feed young, by regurgitation. In response to predators near nest, adult bird may make itself look larger by fluffing out its feathers and partially spreading wings. Legs and feet of young develop quickly, and young may leave nest as early as 6 days after hatching if disturbed; ordinarily remain in nest for about 2 weeks, and stay near nest for another week or more. 1 or 2 broods per year.

MIGRATION Not well known; probably migrates mostly at night. Although flight seems weak, some individuals travel long distances. Migrates north in mid to late spring and south in early fall.

CONSERVATION STATUS Thought to have declined in many areas because of destruction of marsh habitat. Runoff of agricultural chemicals into standing marsh is another potential problem. However, still abundant in some parts of North America.

Least Bittern

YELLOW BITTERN *Ixobrychus sinensis*

Several small herons related to our Least Bittern live in eastern Asia. Of these, the Yellow Bittern is the only one known to have strayed to our area, having occurred once on Attu Island in the outer Aleutian Islands, Alaska.

GENUS *Ardea*

GREAT BLUE HERON *Ardea herodias*

Widespread and familiar (though often called "crane"), the largest heron in North America. Often seen standing silently along inland rivers or lake shores, or flying high overhead with slow wingbeats, its head hunched back onto its shoulders. Highly adaptable, it thrives around all kinds of waters from subtropical mangrove swamps to desert rivers to the coastline of southern Alaska. With its variable diet it is able to spend the winter farther north than most herons, even in areas where most waters freeze. A form in southern Florida (called "Great White Heron") is slightly larger and entirely white.

HABITAT *Marshes, swamps, shores, tideflats.* Very adaptable. Forages in any kind of calm fresh waters or slow-moving rivers, also in shallow coastal bays. Nests in trees or shrubs near water, sometimes on ground in areas free of predators. "Great White" form is mostly in saltwater habitats.

FEEDING **Diet:** *Highly variable and adaptable.* Eats mostly fish, but also frogs, salamanders, turtles, snakes, insects, rodents, birds. Has been seen stalking voles and gophers in fields, capturing rails at edge of marsh, eating many species of small waterbirds. **Behavior:** Forages mostly by standing still or walking very slowly in shallow water, waiting for fish to swim near, then striking with rapid thrust of bill. Also forages on shore, from floating objects, and in grassland. May hunt by day or night.

NESTING Breeds in colonies, often of this species alone, sometimes mixed with other wading birds; rarely in isolated pairs. Male chooses nest site and displays there to attract mate. Displays include stretching neck up with bill pointing skyward, flying in circles above colony with neck extended, stretching neck forward with head and neck feathers erect and then snapping bill shut. **Nest:** Site highly variable, usually in trees 20–60 feet above ground or water; sometimes in low shrubs, sometimes on ground (on predator-free islands), sometimes well above 100 feet in tree. Nest (built mostly by female, with material gathered mostly by male) is a platform of sticks, sometimes quite large. **Eggs:** 3–5, sometimes 2–7. Pale blue. Incubation is by both sexes, 25–30 days. **Young:** Both parents feed young, by regurgitation. Young capable of flight at about 60 days, depart nest at about 65–90 days. 1 brood per year in north, sometimes 2 in south.

Great Blue Heron

MIGRATION Northern populations east of Rockies are migratory, some going to Caribbean, Central America, or northern South America. Migrates by day or night, alone or in flocks. Some wander well to the north in late summer. Populations along Pacific coast may be permanent residents, even as far north as southeastern Alaska.

CONSERVATION STATUS Formerly often shot simply because it made a conspicuous and easy target, but this rarely occurs today. Colonies may be disrupted by human disturbance, especially early in season. Still common and widespread, numbers probably stable.

GREAT EGRET *Ardea alba*

A tall, stately, white wader of quiet waters. Common, especially in the south, it may wander far to the north in late summer. Nearly wiped out in the United States in the late 1800s, when its plumes were fashionable on women's hats, the Great Egret made a comeback after early conservationists put a stop to the slaughter and protected its colonies; as a result, this bird became the symbol of the National Audubon Society.

HABITAT *Marshes, ponds, shores, mudflats.* Usually forages in rather open situations, as along edges of lakes, large marshes, shallow coastal lagoons and estuaries; also along rivers in wooded country. Usually nests in trees or shrubs near water, sometimes in thickets some distance from water, sometimes low in marsh.

HERONS, EGRETS, AND BITTERS

FEEDING **Diet:** *Mostly fish.* Aside from fish, also eats crustaceans, frogs, salamanders, snakes, aquatic insects. In open fields may catch grasshoppers, rodents. Has been seen catching small rails and other birds. **Behavior:** Forages mostly by standing or walking in shallow water, waiting for fish to come near, then catching them with rapid thrust of bill. May feed in flocks or in association with other herons, cormorants, ibises, sometimes stealing food from smaller birds. Also forages in open fields, sometimes around cattle.

NESTING Probably first breeds at age of 2–3 years. Sometimes nests in isolated pairs, usually in colonies, often mixed with other wading birds, cormorants, Anhingas. In mixed colonies, Great Egrets tend to nest high. Male selects nest area and displays there, at first driving away all other birds, later courting females. Courtship displays include calling, circular display flight, stretching neck up with bill pointed skyward. **Nest:** Site is in tree or shrub, usually 10–40 feet above ground or water, sometimes very low in thicket or marsh, sometimes up to 90 feet high in tall cypress.

Great Egret

Nest (built by both sexes) a platform of sticks, sometimes substantial. **Eggs:** 3–4, sometimes 1–6. Pale blue-green. Incubation is by both sexes, 23–26 days. **Young:** Both parents feed young, by regurgitation. Young may clamber out of nest at 3 weeks, able to fly at 6–7 weeks.

MIGRATION Withdraws in winter from northern breeding areas, wintering only where waters remain open. After breeding season, often wanders far to north in late summer. In 1930s and 1940s there were a few large northward invasions (over 1,500 reached Massachusetts in 1948), but not recorded in such numbers since.

CONSERVATION STATUS Populations were decimated by plume hunters in late 1800s, recovered rapidly with protection early in 20th century. In recent decades, breeding range has been expanding gradually northward, while there is some evidence that southern populations have declined.

EGRETS — GENUS *Egretta*

The terms "heron" and "egret" are somewhat interchangeable, as shown by the fact that the Little Blue Heron is an undoubted member of this genus. Birds that are called egrets are medium-sized herons, and most are white. In the breeding season, many develop long plumes, or "aigrettes," on the head, neck, back, or chest. This elaborate finery led to widespread extermination of egrets in the late 19th century. It became fashionable for women in Europe and North America to wear egret plumes on their hats; the plumes sold for as much as $32 an ounce, twice the value of gold at the time, and hundreds of thousands of birds were slaughtered to satisfy the demand. One of the first projects of the newly formed Audubon Society at the turn of the century was to bring about protection for these plume birds. Egret populations have since recovered, and some species are once again very common.

CHINESE EGRET *Egretta eulophotes*

This egret of eastern Asia is poorly known and considered an endangered species. It has strayed once to the western Aleutians (Agattu Island) but may be unlikely to occur in our area again.

LITTLE EGRET   *Egretta garzetta*

This Old World counterpart to our Snowy Egret was formerly only an accidental visitor to North America, with only one record before 1980. Since 1980 it has been recorded several times along our Atlantic coast during the warmer months. These strays probably make the crossing from West Africa to the Caribbean, and then migrate north on our side of the Atlantic.

WESTERN REEF-HERON   *Egretta gularis*

Native to tropical coasts in the Old World, a single Western Reef-Heron created a sensation in 1983 by spending more than four months on Nantucket Island, Massachusetts. Since then the species has been found several times in the Caribbean, suggesting it may occasionally stray across from West Africa, so it might turn up in our area again.

SNOWY EGRET   *Egretta thula*

A beautiful, graceful, small egret, very active in its feeding behavior in shallow waters. Known by its contrasting yellow feet; could be said to dance in the shallows on golden slippers. The species was slaughtered for its plumes in the 19th century, but protection brought a rapid recovery of numbers, and the Snowy Egret is now more widespread and common than ever. Its delicate appearance is belied by its harsh and raucous calls around its nesting colonies.

Snowy Egret

HABITAT   *Marshes, swamps, ponds, shores.* Widespread in many types of aquatic habitats, including fresh and salt water; in coastal areas, may seek sheltered bays. Inland, favors extensive marshes and other large wetlands. Sometimes forages in dry fields. Nests in colonies in trees, shrubs, mangroves, sometimes on or near the ground in marshes.

FEEDING   **Diet:** *Includes fish, insects, crustaceans.* Diet is varied, includes fish, crabs, crayfish, frogs, snakes, insects, snails, worms, lizards, rodents. **Behavior:** Often forages actively, walking or running in shallow water, also standing still and waiting for prey to approach. May stir bottom sediments with feet to startle prey into motion. Sometimes hovers and then drops to water. Also may feed in open fields, sometimes following cattle to catch insects flushed by the animals.

NESTING   Breeds in colonies, often or usually mixed with other species of wading birds. Male selects nest site and displays there to ward off rivals and attract a mate. Displays include pointing bill straight up, raising all plumes, and pumping head up and down while calling; variant of this sometimes given in short flight. Also flies in circles around nest site; flies high and then tumbles down. **Nest:** Site is in tree or shrub, usually 5–10 feet up, sometimes on ground or higher in tree. Nest (built by both sexes) is a platform of sticks. **Eggs:** 3–5, sometimes 2–6. Pale blue-green. Incubation is by both sexes, 20–24 days. **Young:** Both parents feed young. Last young to hatch may starve. Young may clamber out of nest after 20–25 days, probably unable to fly before 30 days.

After breeding season, may wander well north. Withdraws in winter from northern breeding areas; birds banded in United States have been recovered in Panama, Trinidad. Permanent resident in parts of Florida, southern coastlines, Pacific lowlands. On Pacific coast, some may winter slightly north of breeding range.

CONSERVATION STATUS Numbers were decimated in late 1800s by plume hunters. With protection, populations recovered. In recent decades, has expanded breeding range far north of historical limits. Probably still expanding range and increasing population.

LITTLE BLUE HERON   *Egretta caerulea*

Despite its different last name, the Little Blue Heron is probably a close relative of the Snowy Egret. It looks much like a Snowy when young, but molts to a dark slaty blue plumage as an adult. Generally wary and hard to approach. Nests in colonies, sometimes of this species alone; in large mixed heronries, Little Blues tend to nest along the edges. Some of its largest colonies are in the lower Mississippi Valley, where it often nests in association with Cattle Egrets.

HABITAT *Marshes, swamps, rice fields, ponds, shores.* In North America most numerous on fresh inland waters, around river swamps and marshy lakes. Also feeds in wet meadows and even dry fields. Less commonly feeds in salt water, although it may favor such habitat in the Caribbean. Nests in trees or in dense low thickets near water.

FEEDING   **Diet:** *Mainly fish and crustaceans.* Diet quite variable. Eats mostly small fish (including larger ones than those favored by similar-sized Snowy Egret) and crustaceans, including crabs and crayfish. Away from water eats many grasshoppers and other insects. Other food items include tadpoles, frogs, lizards, snakes, turtles, spiders. **Behavior:** Usually slow and methodical in its foraging, walking very slowly in shallows or standing still waiting for prey to approach. May feed in shallow water or on shore, also in grassy fields.

Little Blue Heron

NESTING   Breeds in colonies. Male establishes small territory within colony and displays there, driving away other males. Displays by male include neck-stretching and bill-snapping; pairs in courtship may nibble at each other's plumage and cross and intertwine necks. **Nest:** Site is in a tree or shrub, usually 3–15 feet above ground or water, sometimes up to 40 feet high. Nest (built by both sexes) is a platform of sticks, varying from flimsy to substantial, with depression in the center. **Eggs:** 3–5, sometimes 1–6. Pale blue-green. Incubation is by both sexes, 20–23 days. **Young:** Both parents feed young, by regurgitation. Young may climb out of nest onto nearby branches after 2–3 weeks, are capable of short flights at 4 weeks, become independent at 6–7 weeks.

MIGRATION   After nesting, adults and young disperse from colonies in all directions, including northward. Some may move well to the north in late summer before migrating south. Banding returns show that some migrate as far as South America, although others remain in southeastern United States in winter.

CONSERVATION STATUS Because of its dark plumage and lack of long plumes, this species was not a major target for the plume hunters that decimated the populations of most of the white egrets and herons in the late 1800s. During the 20th century, Little Blue Heron has extended its range northward and increased in population in many areas.

TRICOLORED HERON   *Egretta tricolor*

On the southeastern coastal plain, the Tricolored Heron is a characteristic bird of quiet shallow waters. Strikingly slender, with long bill, neck, and legs, it is often seen wading belly-deep in coastal lagoons. Although it is solitary in its feeding, it is sociable in nesting, often in very large colonies with various other herons and egrets. Formerly known as Louisiana Heron.

HABITAT   *Marshes, swamps, streams, shores.* Mainly in waters of coastal lowlands. In breeding season usually near salt water, on shallow, sheltered estuaries and bays, tidal marshes, mangrove swamps. Also locally inland around freshwater marshes, lakes, rivers. Nests in colonies in trees, mangroves, or scrub near water.

FEEDING   **Diet:** *Mostly fish.* Eats mainly small fish of no economic value, also crustaceans (crayfish, prawns), insects (aquatic insects and grasshoppers), tadpoles, frogs, salamanders, lizards, spiders. **Behavior:** Forages in shallow water by standing still and waiting for prey to approach or by walking very slowly; sometimes more active, stirring bottom sediments with one foot or dashing in pursuit of schools of fish. Solitary in foraging, driving away others from small "feeding territory."

NESTING   Breeds in colonies, often with other species of wading birds. Male selects site within colony and displays there to attract mate. Displays in-

Tricolored Heron

clude neck stretching, deep bowing, circular display flights. **Nest:** Site depends on colony location, which may be in trees, mangroves, willows, thickets of dry scrub, sometimes on ground; nest usually 2–10 feet above ground, sometimes up to 30 feet. Nest (built mostly by female, with materials gathered by male) is a platform of sticks with a shallow depression at center, lined with finer twigs and grasses. **Eggs:** 3–4, sometimes 2–7. Pale blue-green. Incubation is by both sexes, 21–25 days. **Young:** Both parents feed young. Young may begin climbing about near nest at age of 3 weeks, able to fly at about 5 weeks.

MIGRATION   Northward wandering after breeding not as pronounced as in some southern herons, but has strayed far to the north on occasion. Withdraws in winter from northernmost breeding areas, with some migrating far south; birds banded in South Carolina have been recovered in Cuba and Panama. Common all winter in south Florida and parts of Gulf coast, where some are probably permanent residents.

CONSERVATION STATUS   Despite some reported local declines, still very common in parts of southeast, and has expanded range northward in this century. In recent decades has nested at many new localities farther north and inland.

REDDISH EGRET   *Egretta rufescens*

A conspicuously long-legged, long-necked wader of coastal regions, more tied to salt water than any of our other herons or egrets. Often draws attention by its feeding behavior: running through shallows with long strides, staggering sideways, leaping in

Reddish Egret

air, raising one or both wings, and abruptly stabbing at fish. Also notable for its two color morphs. Reddish Egrets are either dark or white for life, beginning with the downy stage in the nest. Mated pairs may be of the same or different color morphs, and broods of young may include either or both morphs. Over most of range, dark birds are far more numerous.

HABITAT   *Coastal tidal flats, salt marshes, shores, lagoons.* Does most feeding in calm shallow waters along coast, in protected bays and estuaries. Nesting habitat is mostly in red mangrove swamps in Florida, on arid coastal islands covered with thorny brush in Texas.

FEEDING   **Diet:** *Mostly fish.* Primarily eats small fish, with minnows, mullet, and killifish reported as major percentages; also frogs, tadpoles, crustaceans, rarely aquatic insects. **Behavior:** Has a wide variety of feeding behaviors. Often very active, running through shallows with head tilted to one side, suddenly changing direction or leaping sideways. May stand still and partly spread wings; schools of small fish may instinctively seek shelter in the shaded area thus created. Also feeds more placidly at times.

NESTING   Generally breeds in spring in Texas; in Florida may breed mainly in winter or spring. In courtship, male perches in future nesting site, stretches head and neck up and back with shaggy feathers fully raised, then tosses head forward repeatedly. May perform a variant of this display in flight. Male also walks in circles around female standing in shallows, tossing his head and raising one or both wings. Breeds in colonies. **Nest:** Site is typically on ground in Texas, 3–15 feet above water in mangroves in Florida. Nest, built by both sexes, a platform of sticks or grass. **Eggs:** 3–4, sometimes 2–7. Pale blue-green. Incubation is by both sexes, probably about 25–26 days. **Young:** Both parents feed young. Young may leave ground nests at about 4 weeks and wander about island, but probably not capable of sustained flight until 6–7 weeks.

MIGRATION   Mostly permanent resident, but some Texas birds may move south in winter. Wanders north along Gulf and southern Atlantic coasts, very rarely inland. Birds from western Mexico wander north into California.

CONSERVATION STATUS   Numbers were decimated by plume hunters in late 1800s. Reportedly not seen in Florida between 1927 and 1937, but numbers have gradually increased under complete protection. Current United States population roughly 2,000 pairs. White morph apparently made up a higher percentage of population prior to persecution by plume hunters.

GENUS *Bubulcus*

CATTLE EGRET   *Bubulcus ibis*

The remarkable range expansion of the Cattle Egret represents one of the great avian success stories. Unknown in North America before 1952, it is now abundant over much of the continent. It spread from Africa to northeastern South America in the 1870s and 1880s; more recently it has colonized Australasian region. Unlike other herons and egrets, this species typically feeds in dry fields, often following cattle (or other animals) and waiting for them to flush insects into view.

HABITAT	*Farms, marshes, highway edges; often associates with cattle.* Widespread in any kind of open country, including pastures, plowed fields, lawns, roadsides. Also in aquatic habitats, including flooded fields, marshes. Nests in trees or shrubs, in colonies with other herons and egrets.
FEEDING	**Diet:** *Mostly insects.* When associating with grazing animals in fields, diet is mostly large insects, especially grasshoppers, crickets, flies; also frogs, spiders, moths. Elsewhere may feed on crayfish, earthworms, snakes, nestling birds, eggs, sometimes fish. May scavenge for edible refuse in dumps. **Behavior:** Usually forages in flocks in dry fields, very often in association with grazing animals—usually cattle or horses in North America, but on other continents also elephants, camels, zebras, deer, many others. Insects are flushed from grass by animals, caught by egrets. Cattle Egrets may follow tractors or even lawnmowers for the same result.

Cattle Egret

NESTING   Usually first breeds at age of 2–3 years. Breeds in colonies, usually joining colonies already established by other herons and egrets despite very different feeding habitat. Male establishes pairing territory (in or near colony) and displays there to attract mate. Displays include stretching neck and raising plumes while swaying from side to side, making short flights with exaggerated deep wingbeats. **Nest:** Site is in colony, in trees or shrubs, often in swamps or on island. Nest (built mostly by female, with materials mostly brought by male) is platform or shallow bowl of sticks, often with green leafy twigs added. **Eggs:** 3–4, sometimes 1–9. Pale blue. Incubation is by both sexes, 21–26 days. **Young:** Both parents feed young, by regurgitation. Young begin to climb about near nest after 15–20 days, begin to fly at 25–30 days, and become independent at about 45 days.

MIGRATION   Strongly migratory. Birds from northern breeding areas in North America may winter to West Indies, Central America, northern South America. Common at all seasons in Florida, Gulf coast, parts of southwest. Young birds may disperse over long distances, even thousands of miles, in random directions; this behavior probably helped the species colonize much of the world.

CONSERVATION STATUS	North American population may still be increasing, although not as rapidly as in earlier years. In northern heronries, may compete with native species for nest sites; thought to have crowded out native herons or egrets in some instances. In general, however, has had little negative impact on any native species.

GENUS *Butorides*

GREEN HERON   *Butorides virescens*

Along quiet streams or shaded riverbanks, a lone Green Heron may flush ahead of the observer, crying "kyow" as it flies up the creek. This small heron is solitary at most seasons and often somewhat secretive, living around small bodies of water or densely vegetated areas. Seen in the open, it often flicks its tail nervously, raises and lowers its crest. The "green" on this bird's back is an iridescent color and often looks dull bluish or simply dark.

HABITAT	*Lakes, ponds, marshes, swamps, streamsides.* May be found foraging in practically any aquatic habitat, but most common around small bodies of fresh water, especially

those lined with trees, shrubs, tall marsh vegetation. Nests in a wide variety of situations, including willow thickets, mangroves, dry woods, open marsh.

FEEDING **Diet:** *Mostly fish.* Eats small fish such as minnows, sunfishes, gizzard shad; also crayfish and other crustaceans, aquatic insects, frogs, tadpoles. Other items include grasshoppers, snakes, earthworms, snails, small rodents. **Behavior:** Forages mostly by standing still or stalking very slowly at edge of shallow water, waiting for prey to approach. Sometimes uses "bait," dropping feather or small twig on surface of water to lure fish within striking distance.

NESTING   May nest as isolated pairs or in small groups, rarely in large colonies. Male chooses nesting territory and calls repeatedly from prominent perch in tree or shrub. Displays of male include stretching neck forward and down and snapping bill shut, pointing bill straight upward while swaying back and forth. Male and female may perform display flights around territory. **Nest:** Site is usually in shrub or tree 5–30 feet above ground but sometimes on ground; often very close to water but can be quite distant. Nest is a platform of sticks; male begins construction, then female builds while male brings materials. **Eggs:** 3–5, sometimes 2–7. Pale green or blue-green. Incubation is by both sexes, 19–21 days. **Young:** Both parents feed young, by regurgitation. Young begin to climb about near nest by 16–17 days after hatching, usually make first flight at 21–23 days, but are fed by parents for a few more weeks. Young are reportedly capable of swimming well. 1 or 2 broods per year.

Green Heron

MIGRATION   Withdraws in winter from all except southern tier of United States. Northern birds known to migrate as far as Panama, northern South America. Permanent resident in Central America, West Indies. Closely related species common in tropical areas around the world.

CONSERVATION STATUS   Apparently stable. May be expanding its range northward in parts of the northwest.

NIGHT-HERONS — GENERA *Nycticorax* and *Nyctanassa*

Our two species are sometimes placed in the same genus. Both do much of their foraging at night and at dusk and dawn. However, they will also feed in the daytime, especially during the nesting season. Unlike most herons, immatures look strikingly different from adults.

BLACK-CROWNED NIGHT-HERON *Nycticorax nycticorax*

Seen by day, these chunky herons seem dull and lethargic, with groups sitting hunched and motionless in trees near water. They become more active at dusk, flying out to foraging sites, calling "wok" as they pass high overhead in the darkness. Some studies suggest that they feed at night because they are dominated by other herons and egrets by day. A cosmopolitan species, nesting on every continent except Australia and Antarctica.

HABITAT   *Marshes, shores; roosts in trees.* Found in a wide variety of aquatic habitats, around both fresh and salt water, including marshes, rivers, ponds, mangrove swamps, tidal

flats, canals, rice fields. Nests in groves of trees, in thickets, or on ground, usually on islands or above water, perhaps to avoid predators.

FEEDING **Diet:** *Mostly fish.* Diet quite variable; mostly fish, but also squid, crustaceans, aquatic insects, frogs, snakes, clams, mussels, rodents, carrion. Sometimes specializes on eggs and young birds, and can cause problems in tern colonies. **Behavior:** Usually forages by standing still or walking slowly at edge of shallow water. May perch above water on pilings, stumps, small boats. Forages mostly from late evening through the night, but also by day during breeding season or in unusual weather.

NESTING Usually first breeds at 2 years of age. Breeds in colonies, of this species alone or mixed

Black-crowned Night-Heron

with other herons, egrets, ibises, sometimes with Franklin's Gulls. Some colonies occupied for several decades. May begin nesting earlier in season than other herons. Male chooses nest site and displays there to attract mate. Displays include stretching neck up and forward with feathers ruffed up and slowly bowing while raising feet alternately, giving hissing buzz at lowest point in bow. **Nest:** Site varies with colony situation, from on ground to more than 150 feet high, in trees, shrubs, marsh vegetation; most commonly 10–40 feet up and on firm support. Nest (built mostly by female with materials supplied by male) a platform of sticks, flimsy or substantial. **Eggs:** 3–4, sometimes 1–7. Pale green. Incubation is by both sexes, 21–26 days. **Young:** Both parents feed young, by regurgitation. Young clamber about in nest tree at 4 weeks, able to fly at about 6 weeks. After 6–7 weeks, may follow parents to foraging areas and beg to be fed there.

MIGRATION Some wander northward after breeding season. Northern populations move south for winter; banded birds from eastern North America have been recovered in Mexico, Central America, West Indies. Some populations from Pacific coast and southern United States are probably permanent residents.

CONSERVATION STATUS Populations have probably declined in 20th century from habitat loss and, in midcentury, the effects of DDT and other persistent pesticides. Following the banning of DDT, many local populations have increased in recent years. Water pollution is still a problem in some areas, but overall population probably stable or increasing.

YELLOW-CROWNED NIGHT-HERON *Nyctanassa violacea*

More solitary and often more secretive than the Black-crowned Night-Heron, the Yellow-crowned is still quite common in parts of the southeast. Particularly in coastal regions, often feeds by day as well as by night. Its stout bill seems to be an adaptation for feeding on hard-shelled crustaceans — it is called "crab-eater" in some locales. The species was introduced into Bermuda in a successful attempt to bring land crabs under control there.

HABITAT *Cypress swamps, mangroves, bayous, streams.* Commonly occurs in shallow tidal waters, also along lowland rivers, where trees or other heavy cover nearby. Seldom in open marshes. Nests in mangrove or cypress swamps, riverside groves, thickets near water. Sometimes nests in trees within suburbs or cities.

FEEDING **Diet:** *Includes many crustaceans.* Specializes more than most herons. Feeds heavily on crustaceans, mainly crabs and crayfish, especially in coastal

HERONS, EGRETS, AND BITTERS

areas. Also some mollusks, frogs, insects, fish. On inland waters, diet may be more varied. **Behavior:** Forages by walking slowly on land or in shallow water, or standing still waiting for prey to approach. Feeds at dusk and at night, but also commonly by day. Feeding schedule near coast probably influenced by tides.

NESTING Breeding behavior not well known. Often nests in isolated pairs or in very small groups, especially in northern part of range. Where common, nests in colonies, sometimes mixed with Black-crowned Night-Herons or other waders. Displays include

stretching the neck upward with bill pointing skyward, crouching with all plumes erect, and giving a loud call. Pairs greet each other by raising crest, calling, touching bills, nibbling at each other's feathers. **Nest:** Site is usually in tree 30–40 feet above ground, but sometimes very close to ground or water in thickets, mangroves. Nest is a platform of sticks, lined with finer twigs and sometimes leaves. **Eggs:** 4–5, sometimes 2–8. Pale blue-green. Incubation is by both sexes, 21–25 days. **Young:** Both parents feed young. Age at first flight about 6 weeks.

MIGRATION May be permanent resident in southern Florida, but in most of United States range it is far less common in winter than in summer. Withdraws from most of northern and inland breeding range in winter, some migrants going as far south as Panama and Lesser Antilles. In late summer, a few wander far

*Yellow-crowned
Night-Heron*

to north. Strays from western Mexico reach southwestern United States.

CONSERVATION STATUS Apparently stable. In recent decades has expanded breeding range northward in some areas.

IBISES AND SPOONBILLS (Family Threskiornithidae)

Although they somewhat resemble herons, ibises and spoonbills are very different in their feeding styles. While herons watch for fish and then spear them with a rapid thrust, the ibises and spoonbills mostly probe in the muck or feel about in water for unseen prey. This foraging behavior is reflected in their highly distinctive bill shapes.

About 26 species of ibises and 6 of spoonbills are found around the world. Most inhabit marshy areas or lagoons, but some ibises are at home in dry fields, and some live along creeks within dense forest. Most are sociable, feeding in flocks and nesting in colonies, although some tropical ibises are exceptions. They fly with their necks fully extended, and flocks often fly in lines or V-formation. All the birds flying in a line may flap and glide in unison.

In the wild, ibises and spoonbills may live 15 to 20 years or more.

Feeding Most species forage in shallow water (although some ibises feed in dry places), and they find most of their food by touch. Ibises often use their bills to probe in the soft mud of marshes or lagoons; as soon as they contact prey, the bill tip is snapped shut to capture it. On drier ground they will probe in crayfish holes or in cracks in the soil, and they also catch insects and other creatures that they have spotted visually. Spoonbills usually sweep their heads back and forth with the wide bill tip just under water and slightly open, snapping the bill shut when they contact food items.

Nesting	Our species and most others around the world nest in colonies, often mixed with other waterbirds. Nest sites may be on the ground, in marsh growth, or in trees; the nest is generally a bulky platform of plant material. Both sexes help build the nest, although in some species the female does most of the actual building, with the male bringing much of the material. Usually two to four eggs are laid; both parents help with incubation, and both help to feed the young. The young birds feed by sticking their heads and bills into the open mouth of the adult and taking partly digested food. Our species raise only one brood per year.
Displays	Most displays seem to take place within the nesting colonies. Males often establish the nest site and perform aggressive displays directed at other males nearby. Courtship behavior may involve the male and female presenting sticks to each other, bowing, and clasping each other's bills.

GENUS *Eudocimus*

WHITE IBIS   *Eudocimus albus*

One of the most numerous wading birds in Florida and common elsewhere in the southeast. Highly sociable at all seasons, roosting and feeding in flocks, nesting in large colonies. When groups wade through shallows, probing with their long bills, other wading birds such as egrets may follow them to catch prey stirred up by the ibises.

HABITAT   *Salt, brackish, and fresh marshes, rice fields, mangroves.* May forage in any kind of shallow water, commonly flying to feed in fresh water even in coastal regions. Forag-

ing sites include marshes, mudflats, flooded pastures, lake edges, mangrove lagoons, grassy fields. Nests in mangroves, swamps, dense thickets, or marshes.

FEEDING   **Diet:** *Varied; includes many crustaceans.* Diet is quite variable, but crayfish and crabs are major items. Also eats insects, snails, frogs, marine worms, snakes, small fish. **Behavior:** Forages by walking slowly in shallow water, sweeping bill from side to side and probing at bottom. Also forages on land, especially on mud or in short grass. Finds food by touch while probing, by sight at other times, seizing items from surface. White Ibises may steal food from each other and in turn have food stolen from them by larger species.

NESTING   First breeds at age of 2 years.

White Ibis

Breeds in colonies, sometimes mixed with other wading birds. Displays of male include ritualized preening, leaning over and grasping twig in bill, pointing bill skyward and lowering head onto back. **Nest:** Sites in mangroves, trees, thickets, usually 2–15 feet above ground or water, sometimes higher or on ground. Nest built by both sexes, male bringing most material, female doing most of building. Material often stolen from nests of other pairs. Nest is usually platform of sticks, sometimes of cordgrass or reeds. **Eggs:** 2–3, up to 5. Pale blue-green to white, blotched with brown. Incubation is by both sexes, averages 21 days. **Young:** Both parents feed young, by regurgitation. Young may clamber about near nest after 3 weeks, can make short flights after 4–5 weeks, capable of sustained flight at 6 weeks, may leave colony to forage with adults after 7 weeks.

Present throughout year in most of breeding range, but numbers much lower in winter in northern areas; some banded birds from United States have been recovered in Mexico, Cuba, northern South America. Singles and small groups may wander far north and inland after breeding season. Strays from western Mexico sometimes appear in southwest.

CONSERVATION STATUS Florida population much lower than historical levels, and has continued to decline in recent decades. Total range in United States has increased somewhat, with northward spread on Atlantic coast. Vulnerable to loss of feeding and nesting habitat.

SCARLET IBIS *Eudocimus ruber*

This tropical species is very similar to the White Ibis in size, shape, and pattern, but has the white replaced by unbelievably bright glowing red. An experimental attempt to introduce Scarlet Ibises into Florida in the 1960s was unsuccessful, but birds are occasionally reported in the southeast, probably escapes from captivity.

DARK IBISES — GENUS *Plegadis*

These birds favor open country, especially marshes. Our two species, one eastern and one mainly western, are closely related and often difficult to tell apart. Flocks often fly in lines or V-formation, and they may soar on rising thermals.

GLOSSY IBIS *Plegadis falcinellus*

Flocks of Glossy Ibises wade in the shallows of eastern marshes, probing for food with their sickle-shaped bills. Widespread in the Old World, the species is found in the New World mainly in the West Indies and along our Atlantic coast, especially Florida, where it was quite scarce as recently as the 1930s. It may have invaded within the last few centuries, riding the trade winds across from West Africa to the Caribbean.

HABITAT *Marshes, rice fields, swamps.* Forages in shallow waters, favoring marshes (either fresh or salt), flooded fields, shallow ponds, estuaries. Nests in low stands of willows and other shrubs surrounded by marsh, on ground in spartina marsh, in dense thickets of trees and shrubs on higher ground, sometimes in mangroves.

FEEDING **Diet:** *Mostly insects and crayfish.* Feeds on beetle larvae in soft soil, also adults and larvae of many aquatic insects. Crayfish may be main food in some areas. In Florida, reported to eat many small snakes. Also may eat leeches, snails, crabs, frogs, small fish. **Behavior:** Forages mostly by wading in shallow water, probing in soft mud for food. Also picks up insects and other visible items from surface of water or soil.

NESTING Breeds in colonies, sometimes associated with other kinds of wading birds. **Nest:** Site is in shrub or low tree over water or land, or on ground on island. Nest (built by both sexes) is bulky platform of sticks and marsh plants with a shallow depression at center. Adults may continue adding to nest throughout the period of incubating the eggs and feeding the young. **Eggs:** 3–4, sometimes 1–5. Pale blue or green. Female

Glossy Ibis

does more of incubation than male: all night, part of day. Incubation period about 21 days. **Young:** Both parents feed young, by regurgitation. By age of 2–3 weeks, young may wander or climb about near nest. First attempt to fly at 4–5 weeks. At 6–7 weeks, young can fly well, may go to feeding areas with parents.

MIGRATION   Withdraws from northern part of breeding range in winter. Migrates in flocks, moving south relatively early. Singles and small flocks sometimes wander far north and inland, especially in spring and summer.

CONSERVATION STATUS   North American population greatly increased and expanded range northward during 20th century. In some areas, apparently has declined somewhat since 1970s.

WHITE-FACED IBIS   *Plegadis chihi*

Very similar to the Glossy Ibis and mostly replaces it west of the Mississippi River, although the two species occur together in parts of the southeast. White-faced Ibises wander through the west during the warmer months, and they may quickly find and take advantage of temporary new habitat after rains or flooding. Even their nesting sites often change from year to year with changes in local water levels.

White-faced Ibis

HABITAT   *Fresh marshes, irrigated land, tules.* For foraging, favors very shallow water, as in marshes, flooded pastures, irrigated fields. Sometimes in damp meadows with no standing water. Prefers freshwater marsh but sometimes forages in salt marsh.

FEEDING   **Diet:** *Mostly insects, crustaceans, earthworms.* Feeds on aquatic insects and their larvae, as well as those living in damp soil. Eats many crayfish and earthworms. Also eats frogs, snails, small fish, leeches, spiders. **Behavior:** Forages mostly by wading in shallow water, probing in soft mud for food. Also picks insects and other items from surface of water or soil or from plants above water.

NESTING   Breeds in colonies. Colony sites often shift from year to year with changes in water levels. **Nest:** Site is usually in dense marsh growth (such as bulrushes or cattails) or in low shrubs or trees above water, sometimes on ground on islands. Nest (built by both sexes) is bulky platform of bulrushes or other plant stems, with depression at center. Material gathered close to nest site, sometimes stolen from vacant nests of other birds. **Eggs:** 3–4, sometimes 2–5. Clutches of more than 5 probably result from other females laying eggs in nest. Eggs pale blue-green to dark turquoise. Incubation is by both sexes, 17–26 days, usually 21–22 days. **Young:** Both parents feed young, by regurgitation. At age of 3 weeks, young may move about outside nest; attempt to fly at 4 weeks, can usually fly fairly well at 5 weeks.

MIGRATION   Present all year in southern California and coastal Texas and Louisiana; migratory elsewhere. Birds from all populations are likely to wander. Strays have reached Atlantic coast often in recent decades.

CONSERVATION STATUS   Local numbers fluctuate, but total population in North America apparently increased from 1970s to 1990s. Has expanded breeding range somewhat eastward during same period.

ROSEATE SPOONBILL *Ajaia ajaja*

Roseate Spoonbills are gorgeous at a distance and bizarre up close. Locally common in coastal Florida, Texas, and southwest Louisiana, they are usually in small flocks, often associating with other waders. Spoonbills feed in shallow waters, walking forward slowly while they swing their heads from side to side, sifting the muck with their wide flat bills.

HABITAT   *Coastal marshes, lagoons, mudflats, mangrove keys.* Forages in shallow water with muddy bottom, in both salt and fresh water, including tidal ponds, coastal lagoons, extensive inland marshes. Nests in colonies, in Florida mainly in red mangroves, farther west in willows or on coastal islands in low scrub, including mesquite and salt-cedar.

FEEDING   **Diet:** *Small fish, aquatic invertebrates.* Diet is mostly small fish such as minnows and killifish, also shrimp, crayfish, crabs, aquatic insects (especially beetles), mollusks, slugs. Eats some plant material, including roots and stems of sedges. **Behavior:** Forages by wading in shallow muddy water, sweeping bill from side to side with mandibles slightly open, detecting prey by feel. Sometimes picks up items that it has found by sight.

Roseate Spoonbill

NESTING   Breeds mainly during winter in Florida, during spring in Texas. Nests in colonies. At beginning of breeding season, entire flock may suddenly fly up for no apparent reason and circle the area. In courtship, male and female first interact aggressively, later perch close together, present sticks to each other, cross and clasp bills. **Nest:** Site is in mangroves, tree, shrub, usually 5–15 feet above ground or water, sometimes on ground. Nest (built mostly by female, with material brought by male) a bulky platform of sticks, with deep hollow in center lined with twigs, leaves. **Eggs:** 2–3, sometimes 1–5. White, spotted with brown. Incubation is by both sexes, 22–24 days. **Young:** Both parents feed young. Young clamber about near nest, may leave nest after 5–6 weeks, capable of strong flight at roughly 7–8 weeks.

MIGRATION   Present all year in coastal Texas but more common in summer, with some migrating to Mexico in winter. There is thought to be some regular seasonal movement between Florida and Cuba. After breeding season, a few (mostly immatures) may stray far north and well inland. Rarely strays into southwest from western Mexico.

CONSERVATION STATUS   Very common in parts of the southeast until the 1860s, spoonbills were virtually eliminated from the United States as a side effect of the destruction of wader colonies by plume hunters. Began to recolonize Texas and Florida early in 20th century. Still uncommon and local, vulnerable to degradation of feeding and nesting habitats.

STORKS (Family Ciconiidae)

All members of this family are large birds with long legs, long necks, and long bills. Some of the biggest storks are among the largest of all flying birds. About 19 species are known, only three of them in the Americas. Storks fly with their necks outstretched, and they often soar on rising thermals; flocks may circle high above the ground. Although some species are quite sociable, nesting in large colonies, a few are solitary.

Many storks feed near water, but some forage in dry fields. Their methods of feeding are quite variable. Some (like our Wood Stork) find their food mostly by touch, feeling about with their bills in shallow water. Others hunt visually, in water or on dry land. Some catch many grasshoppers and other large insects, while some of the largest species do much feeding on carrion, and two are specialized for eating large snails.

The legend about storks bringing human babies is apparently centuries old. Origins of this myth are obscure, but it has worked to the birds' advantage in Europe, where storks are encouraged to nest on rooftops in many towns.

GENUS *Jabiru*

JABIRU   *Jabiru mycteria*

This huge tropical stork is found mainly in South America. It is an uncommon breeder in southern Mexico, but wanderers have strayed as far north as Texas a few times, and one has reached Oklahoma. Occurrences north of the border have been in late summer or fall.

GENUS *Mycteria*

WOOD STORK   *Mycteria americana*

Wood Stork

Our only native stork in North America, a very large, heavy-billed bird that wades in the shallows of southern swamps. Flies with slow wingbeats, and flocks often soar very high on warm days. Young Wood Storks have noisy begging calls, but adults are almost silent except for hissing and bill clappering. Florida populations have declined as water management there has become a more difficult problem.

HABITAT   *Cypress swamps (nesting colonies); marshes, ponds, lagoons.* Forages mainly in fresh water, including shallow marshes, flooded farm fields, ponds, ditches. Favors falling water levels (when fish and other prey are likely to be concentrated in remaining pools). Nests mainly in stands of tall cypress, also sometimes in mangroves, dead trees in flooded impoundments.

FEEDING   **Diet:** *Mostly fish.* Eats a wide variety of fish, especially minnows, killifish, mullet. Also crayfish, crabs, aquatic insects, snakes, baby alligators, small turtles, frogs, rodents, some seeds and other plant material. **Behavior:** Forages mainly by wading in shallow water with head down, bill in water and partly open; quickly snaps bill shut when it makes contact with prey. Can locate prey by touch or sight.

NESTING   Breeds in colonies. Nests in winter and spring in Florida, where water levels (because of their impact on food supply) may dictate timing. In some years, may not attempt to nest at all. **Nest:** Site depends on colony location; may be 10–15 feet above water in mangroves, 80 feet or higher in cypress, usually well out on horizontal limb. Nest is flimsy platform of sticks, lined with twigs and leaves; male brings most materials, female may do most of building. Some sticks added to nest even after

young hatch. **Eggs:** 3–4, sometimes 2–5. Whitish. Incubation is by both sexes, 28–32 days. **Young:** Fed by both parents. During first 5 weeks or so, one parent usually guards young; unguarded nests may be attacked by unmated storks wandering through colony. Young may make short flights at about 8 weeks but return to nest to be fed and to sleep until about 11 weeks old.

MIGRATION   Not strictly migratory but has a regular northward dispersal after nesting. Florida birds wander well north in eastern states; flocks of birds from eastern Mexico occur along Texas coast in summer; birds from western Mexico appear in summer at Salton Sea and elsewhere in southwest.

CONSERVATION STATUS   Population of southeastern United States reportedly over 150,000 at one time, but by early 1990s probably not much over 10,000. Destruction of habitat and disruption of water flow through southern Florida are major causes of decline. Breeding population of far southern Florida has dropped sharply since 1970s, some of these birds apparently shifting north; has expanded breeding range north to South Carolina recently.

FLAMINGOES (Family Phoenicopteridae)

Shockingly pink, with odd "broken-nose" bills, long necks, and long legs, flamingoes are among the most distinctive of birds. Five species are found in scattered areas around the world. The family seems to have no close relatives.

Flamingoes are gregarious at all seasons; in Africa, their concentrations may run to more than a million birds on certain large lakes. When feeding, they wade in the shallows, heads down and bills underwater, with their mandibles slightly opened. Small comblike structures inside their bills help them to strain tiny organisms out of water and mud. The pink color of their feathers comes from carotenoid pigments in their food; without the right diet, zoo birds may fade to white.

Nesting colonies of flamingoes are usually on wide-open mudflats of coastal lagoons or alkaline lakes. Their nests are mounds or flat-topped cones of mud. Typically only one egg is laid, and both parents take part in incubating the egg and caring for the young.

GENUS *Phoenicopterus*

GREATER FLAMINGO   *Phoenicopterus ruber*

Until about 1900, flocks of flamingoes from the Bahamas regularly migrated to Florida Bay in what is now Everglades National Park. Today, most flamingoes seen on the loose in North America are considered suspect, as possible escapees from aviaries or zoos. However, some of those appearing in Florida Bay may still be wanderers from Bahamian colonies, and some seen in coastal Texas may come from colonies on the Yucatan Peninsula of Mexico.

DUCKS, GEESE, AND SWANS (Family Anatidae)

Members of this family are among the most widely familiar of birds. About 150 species of ducks, geese, and swans are found worldwide. For convenience, they are often referred to collectively as "waterfowl" (as distinct from "waterbirds," which can include any birds found near water). They vary greatly in size, from huge swans to little teal, but all have webbed feet and dense waterproof plumage, and all spend much of their time swimming.

Waterfowl are typically social birds, often seen in large flocks. Most kinds fly strongly, but a few odd ducks of islands and far southern coasts are flightless. Almost all waterfowl, unlike most birds, molt all of the flight feathers of the wings at the same time, so that they are unable to fly for up to a month. Brightly colored male ducks generally molt into a dull plumage, called "eclipse plumage," before they enter this flightless stage, undoubtedly to make them less conspicuous during their vulnerable period.

Waterfowl are economically important to humans: several species have been domesticated, and many others are hunted for food or for sport. However, these birds may be most important for the life and color they add to waterside habitats around the world.

Feeding　As expected in such a large family, waterfowl have diverse feeding habits. Only a few ducks are fish-eaters; more consume mollusks, crustaceans, and aquatic insects, but plant material makes up the majority of the diet for the family as a whole. Swans and geese are almost entirely vegetarian, and so are the whistling-ducks and some species of true ducks.

Manner of feeding is as variable as diet in this family. Some species (especially among the geese) do most of their foraging on land, grazing on young grass or other plants or picking up seeds. Many waterfowl are dabblers, picking up items from on or near the water's surface as they swim. A common tactic is "upending," in which the bird tips up with its tail pointed skyward and its head and neck submerged and pointing straight down, maintaining this position for a few moments by paddling with its feet while it gleans items from underwater. By upending, a long-necked bird like a swan can take its food from a couple of feet below the surface. Quite a few ducks are adapted for deeper foraging, diving from the surface and swimming underwater.

Nesting　Typically waterfowl nest on the ground, not far from water, although several kinds place their nests in large tree cavities. Most kinds add some of their own down feathers to the lining of the nest, especially in cold climates. Eiderdown is famous for its insulating quality and is harvested commercially.

Generally, waterfowl lay large clutches of eggs. This is probably necessary to compensate for the large numbers of young that are lost to predators. In most species, incubation is by the female only. Among most ducks, the male deserts the female shortly after she begins to incubate. However, in the swans, geese, and some others, the male remains nearby during incubation and then helps care for the young after they hatch. Downy waterfowl chicks can take to the water shortly after hatching. From the start, they feed themselves, even though they are attended and guarded by their mother or by both parents. In many ducks, the female abandons the young before they are old enough to fly, but young swans and geese remain with their parents for many months.

Most of our waterfowl nest in the north, where summer is short, and almost invariably raise only one brood per season. However, some ducks nesting in the south may raise two broods.

Displays　The display activities of waterfowl have been studied extensively. Among geese and swans, most displays seem to focus on defending the nesting territory or strengthening the pair bond, and they are often performed by both members of a pair. Among the true ducks, males do most of the displaying, and almost all of the energy goes into attracting a mate. The displays of male ducks involve many bizarre postures and contortions, many of them seemingly designed to show off bright areas of the plumage.

Displays are described briefly under most of the species accounts below, but many of these actions are hard to describe in words. People who get to observe flocks of ducks in late winter and spring should watch for the fascinating courtship antics of the males.

SWANS, GEESE, AND WHISTLING-DUCKS (subfamily Anserinae)

The waterfowl of North America can be divided conveniently into two groups: the swans, geese, and whistling-ducks on one hand, and the true ducks on the other. In this first group, males and females look almost identical, and both sexes generally help to care for the young. Among the true ducks, males are usually much more brightly patterned, and females typically do all the work of incubating the eggs and tending the young. Swans and geese may mate for life, while in the true ducks the pair-bond may last only a few days.

WHISTLING-DUCKS — GENUS *Dendrocygna*

Despite the name, these odd birds are quite different from the true ducks. The eight species are found mostly in tropical and subtropical regions. They may feed either by day or by night; flocks are often seen flying to feeding sites at dusk or are heard overhead at night, making wild whistling cries. In contrast to most other waterfowl, males play an active role in incubating the eggs as well as helping care for the young.

FULVOUS WHISTLING-DUCK *Dendrocygna bicolor*

A lanky bird of shallow wetlands, widespread in the tropics of Africa, Asia, and the Americas. Known for its tendency to wander hundreds of miles in roving flocks. Unlike Black-bellied Whistling-Duck, this species seldom perches in trees.

HABITAT *Fresh marshes (mostly coastal), irrigated land.* At most seasons, favors shallow freshwater or brackish marshes in flat open country of coastal plain; also flooded rice fields, other agricultural fields, ponds, lakes. Migrants or strays may appear at any type of water, but most likely at marshy shallows.

FEEDING **Diet:** *Mostly seeds.* Diet apparently more than 95 percent plant material, mainly seeds of aquatic plants and grasses, including paspalum, wild millet, sedge, smartweed, and many others. Also eats a few aquatic insects. **Behavior:** When feeding in water, may dabble at surface or tip up with tail up and head and forepart of body submerged. Also sometimes dives to take food underwater. Does much of its foraging in damp fields (especially in rice fields in the U.S.).

NESTING May pair for life. In courtship, 2 (or more) may fly in large circles with much twisting and turning. Mated pairs may rear up on water with neck in tight S-curve and tread water side by side. **Nest:** Site is on ground next to water or in dense marsh just above water. Nest (built by female only?) woven of grass, sedges, cattails, sometimes with canopy of same materials above. Unlike most waterfowl, no down added to nest. **Eggs:** 12–14, sometimes 6–16. Whitish, becoming nest-stained. Females may lay eggs in each other's nests (or nests of other species); such "dump nests" can contain 60 eggs. Incubation by both sexes, 24–26 days. May leave eggs unattended for hours on warm days until close to hatching time.

Young: Can swim and dive well. Tended by both parents, but find their own food. Young fledge at about 2 months.

Fulvous Whistling-Duck

MIGRATION Some regular migration of Gulf coast birds to southern Mexico for winter; regular migration overshadowed by widespread wandering. Flocks have strayed far north, with records from at least six Canadian provinces. These wanderings can lead to extensions of breeding range. Beginning around 1950, species invaded eastward along Gulf coast from Texas; since 1960, has become a common nesting bird in Florida. A flock appeared in Hawaii in early 1980s and began nesting in 1984.

CONSERVATION STATUS In recent decades has declined in southwest, increased in southeast. In latter area, changes in rice farming may affect it. Impact of this species on rice growing is controversial: may damage crops, or may feed mainly on seeds of weeds growing in rice fields.

BLACK-BELLIED WHISTLING-DUCK *Dendrocygna autumnalis*

A spectacularly marked, sociable, noisy waterfowl. Often rests on low snags above water and may perch high in dead trees. In North America found mostly near Mexican border, but has increased in numbers recently, partly because it will use nest boxes put out for it. In some areas (such as coastal Texas), feeding of this species has become popular, with landowners tossing out corn near ponds to attract hundreds of whistling-ducks.

Black-bellied Whistling-Duck

HABITAT *Ponds, fresh marshes.* Favors shallow freshwater lakes; may come to those in open country but seems to favor ponds surrounded by trees. Will nest on ground or in tree cavities. When foraging, often in dry fields, also in irrigated land.

FEEDING **Diet:** *Mainly seeds and grains.* Feeds mostly on seeds of various grasses, also of smartweed and other plants. Insects, snails, and other invertebrates make up less than 10 percent of diet. **Behavior:** Does much foraging on land, and may feed by day or night. Flocks come to harvested fields to feed on waste grain, also to prairies and overgrown pastures. In shallow water may wade to reach emergent plants or may dabble at surface or tip up to reach under water.

NESTING May mate for life. Often nests in colonies. **Nest:** Site usually in tree cavity or broken-off stub, 4–20 feet above ground or water. Tree nests on land are usually close to water, but can be up to ¼ mile away. Also frequently nests on ground in dense low growth near water. Many now use nest boxes; have also nested in chimneys, barns. Cavity nests are bare or with a few wood chips, but ground nests are woven of grasses and weeds. **Eggs:** 12–16. Whitish. Females may lay eggs in each other's nests; such "dump nests" may have 50–60 or more eggs. Incubation is by both sexes, 25–30 days. **Young:** Ducklings in cavity nests can climb walls of cavity, jump to

ground 1 or 2 days after hatching. Young tended by both parents, find all their own food. Young fledge at about 2 months.

MIGRATION Not strongly migratory. Flocks disappear in winter from some but not all northern breeding areas. Small flocks may wander well to north of normal range.

CONSERVATION STATUS North American population has greatly increased since 1950s. In Texas and eastern Mexico, nest boxes have probably helped this expansion. In Arizona (where most nests apparently are on ground), species was very rare before 1949, has since become a common nesting bird.

SWANS — GENUS *Cygnus*

This group includes the largest of the waterfowl. Most swans are pure white, but the Black Swan of Australia and Black-necked Swan of South America are exceptions. Unlike most waterfowl, the male swan helps with incubating the eggs, sitting on the nest while the female goes off to feed; he also helps tend the young. Swans can be very aggressive in defending their nests, even attacking humans who venture too near.

TUNDRA SWAN *Cygnus columbianus*

Tundra Swan

Nesting on Arctic tundra and migrating long distances to favored wintering areas, this native swan was less affected by human settlement than was the Trumpeter Swan. Destruction of southern wetlands has reduced its former food sources in wintering areas, but it has adapted by shifting its habits to feed on waste products in agricultural fields. The North American race is often called Whistling Swan.

HABITAT *Tundra (summer), lakes, large rivers, bays, estuaries, flooded fields.* In summer on northern tundra with many lakes and ponds, generally near the coast. During migration and winter mainly on shallow lakes, wide slow-moving rivers, and coastal estuaries, especially those with agricultural fields nearby.

FEEDING **Diet:** *Seeds and other plant material.* Summer diet mainly stems, seeds, and roots of aquatic plants, including sedges, pondweeds, arrowleaf, algae, and others; also a few small invertebrates. At other seasons, eats much grain in harvested fields of corn, barley, and soybean. **Behavior:** In nesting season forages mainly in water by dabbling at surface, dipping head underwater, or upending with tail up and head straight down (can reach 3 feet below surface). On migration and in winter does much feeding on land in open fields. Sometimes feeds during moonlit nights.

NESTING In one display involving members of a pair, the birds face each other, wings partly spread and rapidly quivering, and call loudly. **Nest:** Site is near lake or other open water, on ridge or island with good visibility. Nest (built by both sexes) is low mound of plant material, 1 or 2 feet in diameter, with a depression in the center; may be used for more than 1 year. **Eggs:** 4–5, up to 7. Creamy white, becoming stained. Female does about ¾ of incubating, male does rest; eggs hatch in 31–32 days. **Young:** Both parents tend young, leading them to feeding sites in water. Adults may paddle with feet to bring submerged food to surface for young; may rarely feed young directly. Young fledge in 2–3 months, remain with parents at least through first winter.

MIGRATION Birds may leave nesting areas in late summer and concentrate in nearby estuaries. Southward migration begins midautumn. Migrating flocks (of up to 100 or more) are made up of family groups. May fly long distances between traditional staging areas in fall; spring migration may involve shorter flights and more stopovers.

CONSERVATION STATUS Population is stable, and large enough to sustain a limited hunting season in some areas.

WHOOPER SWAN   *Cygnus cygnus*

A huge Eurasian swan, near the size of our Trumpeter Swan. Birds from Siberia winter in small numbers in the Aleutian Islands, Alaska. Migrants occasionally stray to other points in western Alaska, and very rarely have been found in winter farther south along Pacific seaboard to California. Singles and small flocks seen rarely in the northeast may be either escapes from captivity or strays from Iceland.

TRUMPETER SWAN   *Cygnus buccinator*

Trumpeter Swan

Largest of the native waterfowl in North America, and one of our heaviest flying birds, the Trumpeter Swan was almost driven to extinction early in the 20th century. Its healthy comeback is considered a success story for conservationists. Ordinarily the Trumpeter is quite sensitive to human disturbance; in protected areas, such as some parks and refuges, it may become accustomed to humans and allow close approach.

HABITAT *Lakes, ponds, large rivers; in winter, also bays.* Favors large but shallow freshwater ponds, or wide, slow-flowing rivers, with lots of vegetation. Most of current range is in forested regions, but at one time was also common on northern prairies.

FEEDING **Diet:** *Mostly plant material.* Adults eat mainly stems, leaves, and roots of aquatic plants, including pondweed, sedges, rushes, arrowleaf, wild celery, bulrush, burreed, and many others. May eat terrestrial grasses and waste crops in winter. Young eat many insects and other small invertebrates, mainly during first 2 weeks after hatching. **Behavior:** Takes food from underwater or on or above water's surface; sometimes on land, especially in winter. To forage in deeper water, swans upend with tail up and neck extending straight down, finding food by touch with bill.

NESTING Usually forms pairs at age 2–4 years, but nests for first time at age 4–7 years. Often mates for life. **Nest:** Site is surrounded by water, as on small island, beaver or muskrat house, floating platform. Nest (built by both sexes, although female may do most of work) is a low mound of plant material several feet in diameter, with a depressed bowl in the center. Same nest may be used in subsequent years. **Eggs:** 4–6, up to 9. Whitish, becoming nest-stained. Female does most of incubating, but male often does some; eggs hatch in 32–37 days. **Young:** Can swim when less than 1 day old. Both adults tend young, leading them to feeding sites. Young not fully capable of flight until 3–4 months after hatching.

MIGRATION Most southern populations are nonmigratory. Northern Trumpeters move south in late fall as waters begin to freeze. Most migration is by day, flocks often in V-formation, flying low. Spring migration begins early, birds often reaching nesting territory before waters are free of ice.

CONSERVATION STATUS   Trumpeter Swans once nested over most of North America but disappeared rapidly as civilization advanced westward; by the 1930s, fewer than 100 remained south of Canada. With protection from hunting and disturbance, populations have rebounded in parts of the northwest. More recent efforts have focused on reintroducing the species to its former breeding range, including Minnesota, Wisconsin, Michigan, and Ontario.

MUTE SWAN   *Cygnus olor*

Brought from Europe as an ornamental addition to parks and estates, the Mute Swan has established itself in a feral state in some parts of North America, mainly in the northeast. In some places, it has become common enough to be unpopular and is considered a pest in a few areas. Not really "mute"; its voice is hoarse and much quieter than those of our native swans, but its wingbeats may be heard as much as a half mile away.

HABITAT   *Ponds, both fresh and salt; coastal lagoons, salt bays.* In North America found in wide variety of wetland areas including all types of marshes, lakes, park ponds; often in close association with humans, but also in some remote wild areas.

FEEDING   **Diet:** *Mostly plant material.* Feeds on seeds, stems, leaves, and roots of aquatic plants, including pondweeds, eelgrass, algae. Also grazes on grasses, feeds on waste grain. Sometimes eats insects, snails, worms, tadpoles, small fish. **Behavior:** Feeds by dabbling at water's surface, dipping head and neck below surface, and upending with tail up and head extending straight down; also grazes on land. Readily adapts to artificial feeding by humans.

NESTING   Pairs usually form at age of 2 years, first nesting usually at 3–4 years. Pairs in courtship face each other and turn heads from side to side in unison. In threat display to protect nesting area, wings arched over back, head laid far back with neck feathers fluffed out, while swan swims forward jerkily. **Nest:** Site on shoreline, small island, or mound built up in shallows. Nest (built by female, although male helps gather material) is mound of plant material, usually 5–6 feet in diameter, with shallow depression on top. **Eggs:** 5–7, up to 10, rarely 11. Very pale green, becoming nest-stained. Incubation period about 36 days. Female does

Mute Swan

almost all incubating; male will sit on nest while female forages. **Young:** Both adults tend young; small young often carried on parents' backs. Young fledge in 4–5 months, usually remain with parents through first winter.

MIGRATION   North American birds seem not to migrate farther than necessary. Those in northeast move southward or to coastal waters when breeding lakes freeze; more southerly birds may be sedentary. On native range in Eurasia, may migrate long distances.

CONSERVATION STATUS   North American populations are still increasing. These huge birds can be a nuisance, consuming great amounts of aquatic vegetation and competing with native waterfowl. By the early 1990s some biologists suggested control of the population in some areas, especially Chesapeake Bay region and southern New England, but general public opinion was still on the side of the swans.

GEESE — GENERA *Anser, Chen,* and *Branta*

The 15 species of true geese are all native to the Northern Hemisphere. In North America, most geese breed on northern tundra; only the Canada Goose is widespread farther south in summer. Male and female geese are almost identical. Unlike most ducks, geese may mate for life, and the young birds often remain with their parents for several months. Only the female incubates the eggs, but both parents tend the young.

Members of the first genus below, *Anser,* are often known as "gray geese." Several kinds nest across northern Eurasia, but only one is common in North America.

BEAN GOOSE   *Anser fabalis*

Widespread across northern Europe and Asia, this big gray-brown goose sometimes shows up in spring in far western Alaska: almost annually in the western Aleutians, very rarely on islands and coasts of the Bering Sea. Accidental elsewhere in North America, it has appeared a few times in eastern Canada and once with other migrant geese on the Iowa-Nebraska border.

PINK-FOOTED GOOSE   *Anser brachyrhynchus*

Although many Pink-footed Geese nest in Greenland and Iceland, these birds all migrate across the North Atlantic to spend the winter in Britain and northwestern Europe. Strays that have gone the wrong direction have been found in North America only a couple of times, in eastern Canada.

GREATER WHITE-FRONTED GOOSE   *Anser albifrons*

Greater White-fronted Goose

In North America, this gray goose is found mainly west of the Mississippi River. Nesting on Arctic tundra, it winters in open country in mild climates. Wintering flocks leave night roosts before sunrise to fly to feeding areas, and musical gabbling and honking can be heard from wavering lines of White-fronts passing overhead at dawn. Included in this species is a large, dark form known as the "Tule Goose," nesting in southern Alaska and wintering in central California marshes.

HABITAT   *Marshes, prairies, fields, lakes, bays; tundra in summer.* Generally in open country; most spend winter where agricultural fields (for foraging) are close to extensive shallow waters (for roosting). Breeds on tundra, both wet coastal areas and drier inland tundra. "Tule Goose" breeds in wet open sloughs and bogs in spruce forest region, winters mainly in marshes.

FEEDING   **Diet:** *Mostly plant material.* In winter, mostly eats seeds and waste grain in fields, also grazes on new growth. In summer, eats stems and roots of grasses, sedges, horsetail, and other plants, also berries and buds. Eats a few aquatic insects and sometimes snails, possibly swallowed accidentally along with plants. **Behavior:** Forages while walking on land by grazing and picking up items from ground. In water, submerges head and neck or upends with tail up and head straight down.

NESTING Usually first breeds at age of 3 years. "Triumph display" important in pair bond: male briefly attacks some other bird, then returns to female with neck outstretched and wings partly open, and both male and female call loudly. **Nest:** Site is on ground, usually near water, generally surrounded by grasses, sedges, low shrubs. Nest (built by female) is shallow depression lined with plant materials, with down added near end of egg-laying. **Eggs:** 3–6, sometimes 1–8. Dull white, becoming nest-stained. Incubation is by female only, 22–27 days. **Young:** Can walk and swim well shortly after hatching. Both parents tend young, leading them to feeding areas; young feed themselves. Age at first flight 38–45 days. Young remain with parents for first year of life and often are loosely associated with them for several years.

MIGRATION A long-distance migrant. Migrates by day or night. Follows established routes and relies on traditional stopover points on migration. Birds nesting in Greenland migrate east over North Atlantic, wintering mainly in Ireland; rarely stray to northeastern North America.

CONSERVATION STATUS Total population in North America fluctuates. Apparently declined in 1970s, increased again in late 1980s and later. Status of "Tule Goose" poorly understood, may be vulnerable because of small numbers and limited range.

LESSER WHITE-FRONTED GOOSE *Anser erythropus*

This small goose is uncommon (and apparently declining) in its native range in the Old World. Has strayed at least once to the western Aleutian Islands, Alaska. Birds seen elsewhere in North America probably have been aviary escapes.

SNOW GOOSE AND RELATIVES — GENUS *Chen*

These birds are very similar to the gray geese (*Anser*) in most ways except color, and they are often placed in the same genus.

SNOW GOOSE *Chen caerulescens*

Very localized, but abundant where they occur, Snow Geese typically are seen in large numbers or not at all. Included under this heading is the "Blue Goose," long considered a separate species, now known to be only a color morph of the smaller race of Snow (Lesser Snow Goose). The two color forms mate with each other and may produce young of either or both colors. A larger race, Greater Snow Goose, nests in far eastern regions of Canada and winters on the Atlantic coast.

HABITAT *Tundra (summer), marshes, grain fields, ponds, bays.* In summer on Arctic tundra usually within 5 miles of coast, near lakes or rivers. During migration and winter in coastal marshes, estuaries, freshwater marshes, agricultural country. Greater Snow Goose often nests in higher and drier tundra, and in migration and winter is more often in saltwater habitats than Lesser Snow.

FEEDING **Diet:** *Almost entirely plant material.* Feeds on seeds, leaves, and roots of many species of wild grasses, also of sedges, bulrushes, horsetail, others. Very young goslings may feed on insect larvae. In fall, may eat many berries. Winter

Snow Goose

flocks often feed on waste grain in agricultural fields. **Behavior:** Forages mostly by walking in shallow water or on land. Except when nesting, usually feeds in flocks, sometimes mixed with other kinds of geese.

NESTING   May mate for life. Usually first breeds at age of 3 years. In one courtship display, male and female face each other and stretch necks upward rapidly and repeatedly in unison. Often nests in colonies. **Nest:** Site (selected by female) usually on slight ridge or hummock, with good visibility. Same site may be used more than one season. Nest (built by female, mostly after first egg is laid) is shallow depression filled with bulky bowl of plant material, lined with down. **Eggs:** 3–5, sometimes 1–7, rarely 8. Whitish, becoming nest-stained. Incubation is by female only, 22–23 days, up to 25. **Young:** Usually leave nest within a few hours after hatching; they find their own food and are tended by both parents. Family group may travel miles on foot away from nest site. Young fledge at 42–50 days.

MIGRATION   Migrates long distances, in flocks, often flying very high. In many regions, Snows migrate along rather narrow corridors, with traditional stopover points en route.

CONSERVATION STATUS   Population of Greater Snows was reduced to only 2,000–3,000 around year 1900, has made satisfactory recovery. Total number of Lesser Snows apparently has increased greatly in recent decades. Population may vary because of Arctic summer weather: in series of exceptionally cold summers, Snow Geese may raise very few young.

ROSS'S GOOSE   *Chen rossii*

Ross's Goose

This pint-sized relative of the Snow Goose has been surrounded by mystery and surprise. Explorers recognized it as a different bird as early as 1770, but it was not described to science until 1861; its Arctic nesting grounds were not discovered until 1938. Once thought to be very rare, even on the brink of extinction, its population has greatly increased in recent decades. Not until the late 1970s was it discovered that Ross's, like Snow Goose, can occur in a "blue" morph. Blue Ross's Geese are still rarely detected.

HABITAT   *Tundra (summer), marshes, grain fields, ponds.* In summer on Arctic tundra, especially flat tundra with mix of grassy areas and low matted thickets of dwarf birch or willow. In migration and winter, shallow lakes, freshwater marshes, flooded stubble fields, other agricultural lands.

FEEDING   **Diet:** *Almost entirely plant material.* Diet for most of year is mainly green grasses and sedges. On arrival on breeding grounds, before new growth is available, does much grubbing for roots. In fall migration, feeds more on seeds and grains of wild grasses or cultivated crops. **Behavior:** Forages mainly by walking on land or wading or swimming in shallow water. During migration and winter, feeds in flocks, usually with Snow Geese.

NESTING   First breeds at age of 2 or 3 years. Courtship involves rapid head-dipping by both members of pair. Breeds in colonies, usually associated with colonies of Snow

Goose. **Nest:** Site is often on island or shore of tundra lake, usually on edge of low thicket. The same site is often used for more than 1 season. Nest is a bulky bowl of twigs, leaves, grass, moss, lined with down. Female builds nest, beginning about the time the first egg is laid, continuing after incubation begins. **Eggs:** 4, sometimes 2–6, rarely 1–8. Dull white, becoming nest-stained. Female does all incubating, usually 21–23 days. **Young:** Leave the nest shortly after hatching, following parents to water. Both parents tend the young; male is most active in defense against predators. Young fledge in 40–45 days.

MIGRATION   Main population migrates from Northwest Territories to central California, traveling along a rather narrow route with traditional stopovers, especially in Alberta and Montana. In recent years, numbers wintering in New Mexico and east of Rockies have increased markedly. Migrate in flocks, often mixed with Snow Geese, sometimes with other geese. Strays appearing far out of range may have arrived by traveling with other species.

CONSERVATION STATUS   Population apparently still increasing, as with some other Arctic-nesting geese (Snow and White-fronted). Ross's Goose often hybridizes with Snow Goose, but evidently not enough to be genetically "swamped" by the Snows.

EMPEROR GOOSE   *Chen canagica*

Emperor Goose

This tidewater goose of the Bering Sea region seems less wary than most other geese. Uncommon and localized, it ordinarily migrates only short distances, from the Alaskan and Siberian tundra to the Aleutian chain; only a few stragglers are seen south of Alaska. Generally does not mix with other geese, and usually travels in small groups, although large numbers may concentrate at a few key spots in migration and winter.

HABITAT   *In summer, tundra; in winter, rocky shores, mudflats.* Closely tied to salt water at all seasons. Most nesting areas on low marshy tundra within 10 miles of coast, near sloughs and rivers affected by tides. Flocks in migration stop over on large coastal estuaries. In winter, found along shorelines. Autumn strays south to Oregon and California may appear well inland.

FEEDING   **Diet:** *Varies with season.* On breeding grounds, mostly plant material: roots and bulbs early in season, fresh growth of sedges and other plants during summer. In late summer, may feed on crowberry or blueberry. During migration and winter feeds heavily on clams and mussels, also on marine algae and other plants. **Behavior:** On breeding grounds, forages mostly on land, grubbing for roots, grazing on fresh growth. During migration and winter, forages on mudflats exposed by falling tides, walking on wet mud or in shallow water.

NESTING   May mate for life, and pairs seem to be formed before arrival on breeding grounds. **Nest:** Site on small island in pond, raised hummock or shoreline, surrounded by low dead vegetation but with good visibility. Nest is a shallow scrape lined with dead plant material and with large amounts of down. **Eggs:** 4–6, sometimes 2–8. Creamy white, becoming nest-stained. Females frequently lay eggs in each other's nests. Incubation is by female only, typically 24 days, up to 27. **Young:** Goslings can walk and swim within hours after hatching, usually leave nest in less than a day, following parents to good feeding areas that may be several miles from nest site.

Both parents tend young. Adults with broods adopt a threat posture with neck outstretched and bill pointed toward source of disturbance. Young fledge in 50–60 days.

MIGRATION Short-distance migrant. Often migrates in large flocks. Timing of migration affected by weather. In spring and fall, flocks may stage for several weeks in large lagoons on north shore of Alaska Peninsula before moving on to breeding areas on west coast of Alaska or wintering areas in Aleutians.

CONSERVATION STATUS *Threatened.* Alaska population, estimated at 139,000 in 1964, declined to 42,000 by 1986. Causes for decline not well known; may be related to hunting, possibly also to oil pollution in wintering areas. Status of Siberian population not well known, but apparently has been declining for much of 20th century.

CANADA GOOSE AND RELATIVES — GENUS *Branta*

Very similar to other geese in habits, these species have darker bills and legs and more contrasting color patterns.

BRANT *Branta bernicla*

No other goose nests as far north as the Brant, and few migrate as far. These small geese are characteristic of coastal areas in summer and winter; most birdwatchers know them from seeing their wintering flocks along both of our coasts. Traveling between their summer and winter outposts, they may fly at altitudes of several thousand feet as they cross great expanses of land or open ocean.

HABITAT *Salt bays, estuaries; tundra (summer).* Usually on wet coastal tundra of high Arctic in summer, along coastlines in fairly mild climates in winter. Migrants may make regular stopovers on a few freshwater lakes in the interior of the continent.

FEEDING **Diet:** *Mostly plant material.* In migration and winter, eats aquatic plants; eelgrass heavily favored where available, also takes wigeon grass, rockgrass, green algae, others. On breeding grounds, grazes on sedges, grasses, pondweed, others. Also eats a few aquatic insects, mollusks, worms. **Behavior:** Forages by

Brant

wading or tipping up in shallow water, or by walking on tidal flats or on shore. Feeds in flocks at most times of year.

NESTING Pair bond usually formed on wintering grounds. Often breeds in loose colonies. **Nest:** Site is on small island in tundra pond, slight rise in low grassy flats, usually within 1–5 miles of coast and often subject to destruction by storm tides. Nest is a shallow bowl of grass and other materials, heavily lined with down. **Eggs:** 3–5, rarely up to 8. Creamy white to pale olive, becoming nest-stained. Incubation is by female only, 22–26 days, usually 24. When female leaves nest to feed, she covers eggs with down, keeping them warm. **Young:** Leave nest within 1–2 days after hatching, are tended by both parents and led to feeding areas, where young find their own food. In long daylight of high Arctic, young feed at all hours and develop rapidly, fledging at 40–50 days.

MIGRATION Long-distance migrant, traveling in flocks. Birds from central Canadian Arctic move down east side of Hudson Bay, then may make nonstop flight overland from southern James Bay to central Atlantic coast of U.S. In Alaska, large numbers gather at Izembek Lagoon and then depart almost simultaneously for long overwater flight to wintering areas on Pacific coast. Migrating flocks may fly very high. Wintering birds may linger later in spring than most geese, as coastal breeding areas in high Arctic remain unsuitable for nesting until summer.

CONSERVATION STATUS   In 1930s, a sudden die-off of eelgrass along Atlantic coast (the main winter food of Brant) may have had a serious impact on this species. No long-term damage to numbers, as Brant were able to switch to other food sources, and eelgrass has made partial recovery in these areas.

BARNACLE GOOSE   *Branta leucopsis*

An attractive small goose, nesting on Arctic coasts from northeastern Greenland east to Siberia and wintering in northwestern Europe. Greenland birds may occasionally go off course and reach northeastern North America. However, this is a popular aviary bird, and most Barnacle Geese seen on this continent have probably escaped from captivity.

CANADA GOOSE   *Branta canadensis*

This big "honker" is among our best-known waterfowl. In many regions, flights of Canada Geese passing over in V-formation—northbound in spring, southbound in fall—are universally recognized as signs of the changing seasons. Once considered a symbol of wilderness, this goose has adapted well to civilization, nesting around park ponds and golf courses; in a few places, it has even become something of a nuisance. Local forms vary greatly in size; the smallest, "Cackling Goose," may be a separate species.

HABITAT   *Lakes, ponds, bays, marshes, fields.* Very diverse, using different habitats in different regions; always nests near water, winters where feeding areas are within commuting distance of water. Nesting habitats include tundra, fresh marshes, salt marshes, lakes in wooded country. Often feeds in open fields, especially in winter. In recent years, also resident in city parks, suburban ponds.

FEEDING   **Diet:** *Mostly plant material.* Feeds on very wide variety of plants. Eats stems and shoots of grasses, sedges, aquatic plants, also seeds and berries; consumes many cultivated grains (especially on refuges, where crops are planted for geese). Also eats some insects, mollusks, crustaceans, sometimes small fish. **Behavior:** Forages mostly by grazing while walking on land; also feeds in water, submerging head and neck, sometimes upending. Feeds in flocks at most seasons.

Canada Goose

NESTING   May mate for life. Male defends territory with displays, including lowering head almost to ground with bill slightly raised and open, hissing; also pumps head up and down while standing. **Nest:** Site (probably chosen by female) is usually on slightly elevated dry ground near water, with good visibility. Much variation; may nest on cliff ledges, on muskrat houses, in trees, on artificial platforms. Nest (built by female) is slight depression with shallow bowl of sticks, grass, weeds, moss, lined with down. **Eggs:** 4–7, sometimes

2–11. White, becoming nest-stained. Incubation is by female, 25–28 days; male stands guard nearby. **Young:** Parents lead young from nest 1–2 days after hatching. Young are tended by both parents but feed themselves. Age at first flight varies—probably 6–7 weeks in smallest races, 8–9 weeks in largest forms.

MIGRATION   Historically, each local population followed a rigid migratory path, with traditional stopovers and wintering areas. Today many geese in urban areas and on refuges are permanent residents. Other populations have changed routes or wintering areas as habitats have changed.

CONSERVATION STATUS   Species as a whole probably still increasing: responds well to management on wildlife refuges and has become a common resident of city lakes and parks in many areas. Some distinctive populations are scarce or declining. The small Aleutian Canada Goose (almost exterminated by foxes introduced to those islands for the fur trade) is still endangered.

TRUE DUCKS (subfamily Anatinae)

This is the second major group of waterfowl in North America. Unlike the geese, swans, and whistling-ducks, males of the true ducks are usually more brightly colored than females, often in very ornate patterns. In all our species, the tasks of incubation and caring for the young are carried out entirely by the female; the male usually abandons her about the time she begins to incubate. Possibly because the pair-bond is so brief, these ducks seem to crossbreed with other species more readily than most birds do, and hybrid ducks are seen sometimes in the wild and often in captivity.

GENUS *Cairina*

MUSCOVY DUCK   *Cairina moschata*

Most birders know the Muscovy only from having seen the dumpy domesticated version. Wild Muscovies, native to the American tropics, are wary, fast-flying birds of wooded rivers and swamps. Most Muscovies seen in North America are of the barnyard variety, but small numbers of wild birds from northeastern Mexico may appear on the Rio Grande in southern Texas. These big ducks nest in cavities in trees, and cavities large enough have become harder to find as riverside trees have been cut. However, they will also use nest boxes, and many such boxes have been put in place in Mexico by the organization Ducks Unlimited.

GENUS *Aix*

WOOD DUCK   *Aix sponsa*

Beautiful and unique, this duck of woodland ponds and river swamps has no close relatives except for the Mandarin Duck of eastern Asia. Abundant in eastern North America in Audubon's time, the Wood Duck population declined seriously during the late 19th century because of hunting and loss of nesting sites. Its recovery to healthy numbers was an early triumph of wildlife management.

HABITAT   *Wooded swamps, rivers, ponds.* Favors shallow inland lakes, ponds, slow-moving rivers, swamps, mainly those surrounded by deciduous or mixed woodland. Often in

places where large trees overhang the water, creating shady conditions. Also in open marshes within generally forested country.

FEEDING　**Diet:** *Mostly seeds.* Feeds on aquatic plants and their seeds, fallen seeds of trees and shrubs, also insects and crustaceans. Acorns are a major part of diet in many areas. Also comes to fields to feed on waste grain. Young feed mainly on insects and other invertebrates. **Behavior:** Forages in water by taking food from surface, submerging head and neck, occasionally upending; also by walking on land.

NESTING　Courtship displays of male involve postures that show off colorful plumage. **Nest:** Sites are in large tree cavities near water, up to 65 feet above ground. Cavity lined with down. Rarely nests in hollow fallen logs, barn lofts, crevices in rocks. Uses artificial nest boxes, even when these are placed low and in open marsh. **Eggs:** 9–14, sometimes 6–15. Dull white to pale buff. Females frequently lay eggs in each other's nests, sometimes in "dump nests" where no incubation ever takes place. Incubation is by female only, 25–35 days. **Young:** Ducklings remain in nest until morning after hatching. Clinging with sharp claws and bracing with tails, young climb to cavity entrance, jump to ground. Female tends young. Two or more broods may combine. Young are tended by females for 5–6 weeks, capable of flight at about 8–9 weeks. 1 brood per year in north, often 2 in south.

MIGRATION　Northern birds are migratory; southern females may be permanent residents. Movements of males variable; pairs form on wintering grounds and male supposedly follows female to nesting range, so a male might migrate far north one spring and only a short distance the next, depending on the origin of his mate for that year.

Wood Duck

CONSERVATION STATUS　Early in 20th century, species was thought to be threatened with extinction. Main cause of decline probably loss of nest sites due to cutting of large trees, combined with hunting pressure. Legal protection and provision of nest boxes helped recovery; many thousands of nest boxes are now occupied by Wood Ducks in U.S. and southern Canada. In recent years, apparently has been expanding range in north and west.

DABBLING DUCKS — GENUS *Anas*

This important group includes many of the most familiar ducks of inland marshes and ponds. They take most of their food by dabbling at the water's surface or by upending with tail up and head submerged, but they will also feed on land in open areas. Several kinds have bills adapted for straining tiny items out of muddy water. Females are mostly brown with cryptic spots and stripes, good camouflage when they are nesting. Most males are much more brightly colored, but in a few close relatives of the Mallard, the male is patterned almost like the female.

GREEN-WINGED TEAL　*Anas crecca*

Our smallest dabbling duck. Very common and widespread, remaining through the winter farther north than other teal. Often rests out of water, even standing on low snags or branches. Flocks in flight appear very fast because of small size, with rapid twisting and turning in unison. Typically travels in small flocks, but in winter or at migration stopovers may gather in concentrations of thousands.

HABITAT *Marshes, rivers, bays.* In summer, open country near shallow freshwater lakes and marshes. In migration and winter, found on coastal estuaries and tidal marshes, also on shallow lakes and ponds inland, seeming to prefer those with much standing or floating vegetation.

FEEDING **Diet:** *Mostly plant material.* Diet quite variable with season and location. Feeds especially on seeds of grasses, sedges, pondweeds, many others. Also takes aquatic insects, crustaceans, mollusks, tadpoles; rarely earthworms, fish eggs. May feed more on animal matter in summer, seeds in winter. **Behavior:** Forages by wading or swimming in very shallow water while filtering mud with bill, upending, or picking items from water's surface. May feed by night or day.

NESTING Pairs usually arrive already mated on breeding grounds. In one courtship display, male rears up out of water, arching head forward and down to shake bill very rapidly in water while giving a sharp whistle. **Nest:** Site is usually among grasses and weeds of meadow, sometimes in open woodland or brush, within 200 feet of water. Well hidden by surrounding grasses or shrubs, which often form complete canopy. Nest (built by female) is a shallow depression filled with grasses, twigs, and leaves, lined with down. **Eggs:** 6–11, rarely up to 15 or 18. Cream to pale buff. Incubation is by female only, 20–24 days, usually 21. **Young:** Leave nest a few hours after hatching. Female cares for ducklings, which may return to the nest for the first few nights; young find all their own food. Young fledge at about 35 days.

Green-winged Teal

MIGRATION After breeding, adults may go through annual molt near nesting area or may move hundreds of miles in late summer before going through flightless stage of molt. Main fall migration much later, mostly October to early December. Females may move somewhat farther south than males, on average. Spring migration begins early, with mated pairs often traveling north together. The race of Green-wings on Aleutian Islands, Alaska, is mostly nonmigratory. American Green-wings regularly stray to Europe, and Eurasian Green-wings occur annually in North America.

BAIKAL TEAL *Anas formosa*

A beautiful small duck of eastern Asia, rarely wandering into Alaska. Has been reported at a few other sites in North America, but these birds could have been escapes from captivity. Baikal Teal apparently has been decreasing on its native range in recent decades, and it may be reaching Alaska less frequently now than in the past.

FALCATED TEAL *Anas falcata*

This Asian duck, seemingly too large to be called a teal, is a very rare stray into western Alaska. Sightings elsewhere in North America are likely to refer to escapes from captivity.

AMERICAN BLACK DUCK *Anas rubripes*

American Black Duck

A close relative of the Mallard, the Black Duck is better adapted to wooded country. With the clearing of forest, it has steadily lost ground to spreading populations of Mallards. In its stronghold along the Atlantic coast it is a hardy bird, wintering farther north than most dabbling ducks. It is among the few dabblers to prosper in tidewater areas; pairs and small parties of Black Ducks are often seen flying over the salt marsh, their white wing linings flashing in bright contrast to their dark bodies.

HABITAT *Marshes, bays, estuaries, ponds, rivers, lakes.* Wide variety of aquatic habitats; found on lakes in northern forest and in salt marsh more often than most dabblers. Majority in winter in coastal estuaries and tidal marshes, lesser numbers on inland lakes, tree-lined ponds, wooded swamps.

FEEDING **Diet:** *Omnivorous.* Diet varies with location and season. On fresh water, feeds mainly on plant material, including seeds, leaves, roots, berries. Seeds of various grasses, pondweeds, sedges, and others often a major part of diet. In tidal zones may feed mainly on mussels, clams, snails, small crustaceans, aquatic arthropods. Young ducklings eat many insects. **Behavior:** Feeds in water by dabbling, upending, rarely by diving; feeds on land by grazing, plucking seeds, grubbing for roots.

NESTING Older birds may form pairs by early fall and remain together until following summer. **Nest:** Site variable; usually near water, as on banks or small islands, but can be up to a mile distant. Generally on ground among clumps of dense vegetation, sometimes in raised situation as on top of stump, in large tree cavity, on duck blind in water. Typical ground nest (built by female) is a shallow depression with plant material added, lined with down. **Eggs:** 7–11, sometimes 6–12, rarely 4–17. Creamy white to greenish buff. Incubation by female only, 23–33 days, typically 26–29. **Young:** All eggs typically hatch in space of a few hours. Female leads young to water, often after dark. Ducklings find their own food. Young fledge at age of about 2 months and are abandoned by female about that time.

MIGRATION Those breeding in northern interior may migrate long distances, but coastal and southerly birds may move only short distances. Fall migration is often late in season, as waters freeze or food supply is depleted. Much of migration apparently occurs at night.

CONSERVATION STATUS Still abundant locally, but has declined drastically in interior parts of range. Clearing of forest has favored invasion by Mallards, which hybridize extensively with Black Ducks, leading to genetic "swamping" of population.

MOTTLED DUCK *Anas fulvigula*

A close relative of the Mallard, the Mottled Duck is the only dabbling duck specialized for nesting in southern marshes, far to the south of most of its relatives. Unlike most waterfowl, Mottled Ducks are almost never seen in large flocks, generally traveling in pairs or small groups. A major threat to their survival is the release of numerous pet Mallards in Florida and elsewhere in southeast; these feral birds interbreed with Mottled Ducks, diluting the wild population of the latter.

HABITAT *Marshes.* Open marshy country, wet prairies, rice fields. Favors treeless country, wide horizons. In coastal areas, usually found in fresh or brackish ponds adjacent to coast rather than in salt marsh.

FEEDING **Diet:** *Omnivorous.* Diet includes seeds of aquatic plants and grasses, insects, snails, occasionally small fish. Young ducklings feed almost entirely on insects and other invertebrates. **Behavior:** Forages in shallow water, mostly by dabbling with bill at mud just below water's surface, occasionally by up-ending. Young ducklings frequently dive underwater to feed; adults seldom do.

NESTING Pairs usually form in fall, with breeding activity beginning in January. Pairs may prospect for nest sites together, flying low over marsh. **Nest:** Site is in dense growth in marsh or prairie, sometimes on canal bank or in agricultural field, usually within 600 feet of water. Where supported in dense clumps of grass, nest may be several inches above ground. Nest is shallow bowl of grasses, reeds, lined with down and breast feathers. **Eggs:** 8–12, sometimes 5–13. Whitish to pale olive. Generally fewer eggs in later clutches. Incubation is by female only, 24–28 days. **Young:** Leave nest shortly after hatching; female leads them to feeding sites, and young feed themselves. Young can make short flights to escape danger at about 50 days; capable of sustained flight at 60–70 days.

MIGRATION Mostly nonmigratory, but makes local movements in response to changes in habitat conditions. Some birds from western Gulf coast may move southward along Mexican coast in winter.

CONSERVATION STATUS Draining and destruction of marshland has had serious impact on total population. Also, a major threat to survival of "pure" stock is interbreeding with Mallards. Although breeding range of wild Mallard does not overlap with that of Mottled Duck, released pet Mallards have formed large feral populations that have hybridized with Mottleds, especially in Florida.

Mottled Duck

MALLARD *Anas platyrhynchos*

Abundant over most of the northern hemisphere, the Mallard is the most familiar wild duck to many people and the ancestor of most strains of domesticated ducks. In many places this species has managed to domesticate itself, relying on handouts in city parks. Although barnyard and feral ducks may be dumpy and ungainly creatures, the ancestral wild Mallard is a trim, elegant, wary, fast-flying bird.

HABITAT *Marshes, wooded swamps, grain fields, ponds, rivers, lakes, bays, city parks.* May occur in any kind of aquatic habitat, but favors fresh water at all seasons; only sparingly on coastal waters, mainly in winter on sheltered bays and estuaries. Most abundant in summer on prairie potholes and in semi-open country north of the prairies. Most abundant in winter on swamps and lakes in lower Mississippi Valley.

FEEDING **Diet:** *Omnivorous.* Majority of diet is plant material, including seeds, stems, and roots of a vast variety of different plants, especially sedges, grasses, pondweeds, smartweeds, many others; also acorns and other tree seeds, various kinds of waste grain. Also eats insects, crustaceans, mollusks, tadpoles, frogs, earthworms, small fish.

Young ducklings may eat mostly aquatic insects. **Behavior:** Forages in water by dabbling, submerging head and neck, upending, rarely by diving; forages on land by grazing, plucking seeds, grubbing for roots.

NESTING   Pairs form in fall and winter. Displays of male include dipping bill in water and then rearing up, giving whistle and grunt calls as he settles back on water; raising head and tail while giving sharp call; plunging forepart of body deep in water and then flinging up water with bill. **Nest:** Female, accompanied by male, seeks and chooses site for nest. Site may be more than 1 mile from water; usually on ground among concealing vegetation, but may be on stump, in tree hollow, in basket above water, various other possibilities. Nest is shallow bowl of plant material gathered at the site, lined with down. **Eggs:** 7–10, sometimes 5–15. Whitish to olive buff. Incubation is by female, 26–30 days. **Young:** Leave nest within a day after hatching, are led to water by female. Young are tended by female but feed themselves. Age at first flight 52–60 days. 1 brood per year, perhaps rarely 2.

MIGRATION   Fall migration extends over long period; migrates relatively early in spring. Since pairs form in fall and winter, male probably follows female to breeding areas. Feral populations may be permanent residents, but all wild Mallards in North America are probably migratory.

CONSERVATION STATUS   Still one of the most abundant ducks in the world. Numbers fluctuate considerably, and population of northern Great Plains is probably permanently reduced from historical levels. Status of wild birds is clouded by large number of feral populations.

Mallard

SPOT-BILLED DUCK   *Anas poecilorhyncha*

Related to the Mallard, this Asian duck has the same general size, shape, and habits. Not a very long-distance migrant, it does not often wander outside its normal range, but strays have reached Alaska a few times. The name refers to red spots at the base of the bill, absent in the subspecies that has occurred in Alaska.

WHITE-CHEEKED PINTAIL   *Anas bahamensis*

Widespread in the Caribbean and South America, this marsh duck sometimes wanders to Florida, mainly in winter. Sightings elsewhere in eastern North America might pertain to escapes from captivity.

NORTHERN PINTAIL   *Anas acuta*

Widespread across North America, Europe, and Asia, the Northern Pintail is probably one of the most numerous duck species in the world (although outnumbered by the omnipresent Mallard). Slim and long-necked, it has an elegant appearance both on the water and in flight. Pintails are wary at all seasons and become very secretive during the flightless stage of their molt in late summer.

HABITAT   *Marshes, prairies, fresh ponds, lakes, salt bays.* Summers in wide variety of open habitats, including prairies, farmland, northern tundra, near bodies of water. In migration and winter around any shallow waters with exposed mudflats, including fresh and brackish marshes, lakes, flooded fields.

FEEDING **Diet:** *Mostly seeds, insects.* Diet mostly plant material in fall and winter, especially seeds of grasses, sedges, pondweeds, and others, and waste grain in fields. In spring and summer also feeds on roots and new growth. More animal matter in summer, mainly insects, mollusks, crustaceans; sometimes tadpoles, small fish. Young ducklings eat mostly insects. **Behavior:** Forages in shallow water by upending with tail up and head down, or by submerging head and neck while swimming, finding most food in underwater mud. Also forages by walking on land.

NESTING Pair formation begins on winter range and continues during spring migration, with some birds perhaps not paired until after arrival on breeding grounds. Several males often court one female, leading to pursuit flights. **Nest:** Site is on dry ground among short vegetation, usually near water but can be up to ½ mile away; often more exposed than nests of other ducks. Nest (built by female) a shallow depression lined with grasses, twigs, leaves, with addition of down. **Eggs:** 6–10, sometimes 3–12. Pale olive. Incubation is by female only, 21–25 days. **Young:** Female leads young from nest within a few hours after they hatch. Young feed themselves. Capable of flight at 38–52 days after hatching; in far north, where continuous daylight allows for feeding at all hours, young may develop faster.

Northern Pintail

MIGRATION Migrates in flocks. Northward migration begins early in spring, southward migration is underway for much of fall. Many pintails nesting in Siberia cross the Bering Strait to winter in North America.

CONSERVATION STATUS Widespread and abundant, but some surveys show a significant decline since the 1960s. Numbers vary considerably; series of drought years on the northern plains may drastically reduce nesting success there.

GARGANEY *Anas querquedula*

A long-distance migrant in the Old World, this small duck sometimes goes off course and might turn up almost anywhere in North America. Most likely to be seen in spring, on marshy ponds of the sort favored by Blue-winged Teal. In the western Aleutian Islands, Alaska, occurs as a rare migrant in spring and very rarely in fall.

BLUE-WINGED TEAL *Anas discors*

Teal are small ducks, fast in flight, flocks twisting and turning in unison. Seemingly a warm-weather duck, the Blue-winged Teal is largely absent from most of North America in the cold months, and winters more extensively in South America than any of our other dabblers. Small groups of Blue-wings often are seen standing on stumps or rocks at the water's edge.

HABITAT *Fresh ponds, marshes.* In summer on shallow freshwater marshes and ponds in open country, also brackish marshes near coast. In migration and winter on any kind of shallow waters, inland or coastal. Flocks in migration are sometimes seen over ocean, many miles offshore.

Blue-winged Teal

CONSERVATION STATUS

FEEDING **Diet:** *Mainly seeds.* Diet is mostly plant material, especially seeds of various grasses, sedges, pondweeds, smartweeds, and others. Snails, bivalves, insects, crustaceans, and other animal matter may be important in the diet at some seasons. **Behavior:** Forages in very shallow water, gleaning items from surface or swimming forward with head partly submerged; seldom upends, and seldom feeds away from water.

NESTING Pair formation begins in early winter and continues during spring migration. Male has varied courtship displays, including one in which whole forepart of body is submerged, tail raised, feet waved in air. **Nest:** Site is on ground in prairie, hayfield, coastal meadow, sometimes several hundred yards from nearest water. Nest is a shallow depression with some grass or weeds added, lined with down; usually well concealed by surrounding vegetation. **Eggs:** 9–13, sometimes 6–15. Dull white or tinged olive. Ring-necked Pheasants sometimes lay eggs in Blue-winged Teal nests. Incubation is by female only, 23–24 days. **Young:** Leave nest within 24 hours after hatching. Young find their own food, are tended by female for first few weeks, but broods of young are often left alone before old enough to fly. Young capable of flight 38–49 days after hatching.

MIGRATION Compared with most ducks, migrates relatively late in spring and early in fall. Migrates in flocks in fall, often in smaller flocks or isolated pairs in spring. Some southbound groups in fall are composed entirely of young birds, indicating that migratory route is instinctive, not learned. Blue-wings wintering in South America evidently migrate long distances over open ocean; flocks are sometimes seen many miles offshore.

Populations apparently stable. Most Blue-wings winter south of the U.S., so management requires cooperation with Latin American nations.

CINNAMON TEAL   *Anas cyanoptera*

While many of our marsh ducks are found from coast to coast, the Cinnamon Teal is strictly western. Unique among our northern dabbling ducks, this teal also has nesting populations in South America. A close relative of Blue-winged Teal (and sometimes hybridizing with it), the Cinnamon Teal has a slightly larger bill, better developed for straining food items out of water. In some ways this species seems intermediate between Blue-winged Teal and Northern Shoveler.

Cinnamon Teal

HABITAT *Marshes, fresh ponds.* Favors fresh or alkaline shallow lakes, extensive marshes. Generally not in coastal salt marshes. In migration, may pause on any kind of small pond or reservoir. South American races may use wider variety of habitats.

FEEDING **Diet:** *Mainly seeds.* Plant material in diet includes seeds of smartweeds, sedges, grasses, pondweeds, others. Also eats insects, snails, small crustaceans. In one study, migrants consumed mostly seeds and other plant material in fall, a higher proportion of

animal matter (mainly insects) in spring. **Behavior:** Usually forages in shallow water, swimming forward with head partly submerged, straining food from water. One feeding bird may follow another, taking advantage of food stirred up by paddling actions of first bird. Occasionally feeds on land near water.

NESTING   Several males may court one female, making ritualized mock feeding and preening movements. Short display flights may develop into pursuit flights, with males chasing female. **Nest:** Site usually close to water among good cover of sedges, weeds, salt grass, generally well concealed. Nest is a shallow depression with some dead grass and weeds added, lined with down. Female selects nest site and builds nest. **Eggs:** 9–12, sometimes 4–16. Whitish to very pale buff. Incubation is by female only, 21–25 days. **Young:** Female leads young to water after they hatch. Young find their own food; capable of flight 7 weeks after hatching. If danger threatens young, adult female may put on broken-wing act as a distraction display. Unlike most duck species, male may not abandon mate until near the time the eggs hatch, and sometimes is seen accompanying female and young brood.

MIGRATION   May migrate mostly by day. Less of a long-distance migrant than Blue-winged Teal. Some records of northern Cinnamons reaching South America, based on banding returns, may reflect misidentifications: some teal are very hard to identify in fall, even in the hand, so some Blue-wings may be banded under guise of Cinnamon Teal.

NORTHERN SHOVELER   *Anas clypeata*

Many of the dabbling ducks use their flat bills to strain food items from the water, but the big spatulate bill of the Northern Shoveler is adapted to take this habit to the extreme. Flocks of shovelers often swim along with their big bills barely submerged in front of them, straining food from the muddy soup of shallow waters. Despite their heavy-set build, shovelers are good fliers; at large gatherings, groups often are seen taking off, circling the area repeatedly, then alighting again.

HABITAT   *Marshes, ponds; in winter, also salt bays.* In summer in open country such as prairie, marsh, or tundra, in vicinity of shallow water. In migration and winter on alkaline lakes, fresh marshes, tidal estuaries, or any shallow waters with extensive muddy margins, including stagnant or polluted waters not much favored by other ducks.

Northern Shoveler

FEEDING   **Diet:** *Varies with season and habitat.* In winter, may feed mostly on seeds and other parts of aquatic plants, such as sedges, pondweeds, grasses, and others. Also (especially in summer) eats mollusks, insects, crustaceans, sometimes small fish. **Behavior:** Forages mainly by swimming slowly forward with the bill skimming the surface or with the head partly submerged, often swinging the bill from side to side as it sifts food from the muddy water. Seldom upends, rarely dives, seldom feeds on land.

NESTING   Pair formation begins in winter and continues during spring migration. Several males may court one female, gathering around her on water. Each male in turn attempts to lead female away, by swimming away or by short flight; female indicates acceptance by flying away with male. Male remains with female longer than in most ducks, often through part of incubation period. **Nest:** Site is usually close to water, generally in area of short grass. Nest (built by female) is a shallow depression partly filled with dried grasses and weeds, lined with down. **Eggs:** 9–12, sometimes 6–14. Shades of pale olive. If first clutch of eggs is destroyed, replacement clutch usually has fewer eggs. Incubation is by female only, 21–27 days. **Young:** Within a few hours after eggs hatch, female leads young to water, generally keeping them close to cover of marsh vegetation. Young are capable of flight 52–60 days after hatching.

MIGRATION   Migrates in flocks. Migratory period is quite prolonged in both spring and fall, with many birds moving late in spring and early in fall.

GADWALL   *Anas strepera*

In many of our dabbling ducks, the males have bright ornate patterns, while the females are plainly marked with brown and gray. In the Gadwall, even the male looks plain at a distance; only a close view reveals subtle but beautiful colors. Although it

is widespread in North America (and in Europe and Asia as well), the Gadwall is most common on inland waters west of the Mississippi River.

HABITAT   *Lakes, ponds, marshes.* In summer, mainly around fresh or alkaline lakes in prairie regions or western intermountain valleys where land is open, not forested; also locally in coastal marshes. In migration and winter on marshes, lakes, estuaries, but generally not on salt water.

FEEDING   **Diet:** *Mostly plant material.* Feeds mainly on aquatic plants. Compared with other dabbling ducks, eats more leaves and stems of these plants, fewer seeds. Also eats small numbers of mollusks, insects, crustaceans, rarely small fish. Very young ducklings eat many insects at first before shifting to more vegetarian diet. **Behavior:** Forages mainly while swimming by taking items from surface or by dabbling with head submerged, sometimes by upending, occasionally by diving. Rather seldom forages on land.

Gadwall

NESTING   In one courtship display, male pulls head far back on shoulders and raises rear part of body out of water, with wingtips lifted to show off white patch on wing. Compared with most ducks, nesting begins rather late. **Nest:** Female, accompanied by male, makes prospecting flights to seek site for nest. Site is usually near water, on dry land, surrounded by dense weeds or grass. Nest (built by female) is in a shallow depression, built of grasses, weeds, lined with down. **Eggs:** 8–11, sometimes 5–13. White. 2 or more females sometimes lay in same nest. Incubation is by female only, 24–27 days. **Young:** Leave nest shortly after hatching. Female leads young to water, where they find their own food; often seen on more open water than young of other dabbling ducks. Young are capable of flight 48–59 days after hatching.

MIGRATION   Migrates in flocks. Not a long-distance migrant, most wintering north of the tropics. Some southern breeders may be permanent residents.

CONSERVATION STATUS   Settlement of the northern Great Plains may have reduced Gadwall numbers more than those of most ducks. Current populations vary substantially from year to year, but not in serious decline.

EURASIAN WIGEON   *Anas penelope*

This Old World counterpart to our American Wigeon is a regular winter visitor to the Pacific lowlands from Canada to California. Small numbers are also seen in winter in the northeast and elsewhere. In parts of the Pacific Northwest, examination of any winter flock of wigeon is likely to reveal a male Eurasian among them, because the two wigeon species invariably flock together.

HABITAT **Marshes, lakes, bays, fields.** In winter in North America often on marshy ponds with open ground nearby or in flooded fields; also on shallow coastal estuaries and sheltered bays. Presence of American Wigeon is best key to good habitat for Eurasian Wigeon.

FEEDING **Diet:** *Almost entirely plant material.* Diet in North America not well known; in Europe, eats wide variety of leaves, stems, roots, seeds. Eats some insects in summer. **Behavior:** Forages by grazing on land, by dabbling at surface of water, sometimes by submerging head and neck. May steal food brought to surface by other species such as coots or geese. May feed by day or night.

Eurasian Wigeon

NESTING   Known to breed only in Old World, but likely to be found nesting in North America eventually. Several males may compete with each other in courting one female, jostling for position. Displays of male include lifting tips of folded wings to expose white wing patch, raising head while giving whistled call, lowering bill to display buffy crown patch to female. **Nest:** Site is on ground under dense vegetation, usually near water. Nest is shallow depression lined with grass and with large amount of down. **Eggs:** 8–9, sometimes 6–12. Whitish to pale buff. Incubation is by female only, 24–25 days. **Young:** Leave nest and go to water shortly after hatching. Young are tended by female but find all their own food. Age at first flight 40–45 days.

MIGRATION Reaches North America from both east and west. Birds banded in Iceland have been recovered in eastern Canada. Regular in migration in western and southern Alaska. Birds wintering in Pacific lowlands from British Columbia to California probably come from eastern Siberia.

CONSERVATION STATUS Numbers reported wintering in North America (mainly in west) have increased in recent decades, reflecting better observation or actual population increase. Possibly breeding at some undiscovered site on this continent.

AMERICAN WIGEON   *Anas americana*

While most dabbling ducks are denizens of the shallows, American Wigeon spend much of their time in flocks grazing on land. Paradoxically, they also spend more time than other marsh ducks on deep water, where they get much of their food by stealing it from other birds such as coots or diving ducks. This duck was once known as "Baldpate" because of its white crown.

HABITAT **Marshes, lakes, bays, fields.** In summer mainly on inland marshes, especially larger marshes, not often at small ponds. In migration and winter on coastal estuaries, fresh or salt marshes, inland lakes and ponds. May winter on large deep lakes.

FEEDING **Diet:** *Mostly plant material.* Eats aquatic plants such as pondweeds, sedges, wild celery, eelgrass, algae. Also eats some insects and snails. On land, grazes on young grass shoots and consumes seeds and waste grains. Very young ducklings eat many insects. **Behavior:** Versatile in foraging. Flocks feed on land or in shallow water, taking items from surface or submerging head and neck; also associates with diving birds on

deeper water, robbing them of their food when they come to the surface. May feed by day or night.

NESTING Pair formation begins on wintering grounds; most older birds are paired before spring migration. Several males often court one female. In one display, male extends neck forward with head low, bill open, while raising tips of folded wings, revealing white wing patches. Tends to begin nesting later in season than most dabblers. **Nest:** Site on dry land, sometimes on island, usually within 100 feet of water but sometimes up to ½ mile away; site concealed by tall vegetation. Nest (built by female) is shallow depression filled with grasses and weeds, lined with down. **Eggs:** 8–11, sometimes 5–12. Whitish. Incubation is by female only, 23–24 days. Male usually departs before eggs hatch.

American Wigeon

Young: Leave nest shortly after hatching, feed themselves. Female remains with brood for much of their preflight stage. Young capable of flight 45–63 days after hatching.

MIGRATION Migrates in flocks, and may travel mostly by day. In summer, when males leave their mates, they may fly great distances to large open marshes where they will stay while going through the flightless stage of their molt. In western U.S., southward migration seems to be gradual, with numbers in southern California peaking in December or January.

CONSERVATION STATUS Apparently stable. Since about the 1930s the breeding range has expanded eastward somewhat in eastern Canada and the northeastern states.

BAY DUCKS OR POCHARDS — GENUS *Aythya*

This genus begins the group known generally as "diving ducks." All of the waterfowl on the following pages do much of their feeding by diving from the surface and swimming underwater. They are propelled through the depths by powerful strokes of their feet, although some also hold their wings partly open when submerged.

Members of this genus are seen more often on fresh water than many of the other diving ducks, often wintering on large lakes. However, some of their biggest concentrations in winter are found on coastal bays and lagoons. Males have simple color patterns of dark and light; females tend to be evenly colored with shades of brown, without the spotting and barring typical of female dabbling ducks.

COMMON POCHARD *Aythya ferina*

A common diving duck of Europe and Asia, a counterpart to our Redhead or Canvasback and looking similar to those two species. A few Common Pochards reach the islands of western Alaska in migration. Accidental strays have been reported elsewhere, including southeastern Alaska, Saskatchewan, and California.

CANVASBACK *Aythya valisineria*

This big diving duck, the largest of its genus, is wary and swift in flight, earning the respect of sportsmen. It is a characteristic bird of prairie marshes in summer and saltwater bays in winter. The Canvasback dives for its food, mainly the bases and roots of plants growing underwater. Its specific name, *valisineria*, refers to the scientific name of wild celery, an aquatic plant that is among its favored foods.

HABITAT *Lakes, salt bays, estuaries; in summer, fresh marshes.* For nesting, shallow marshes in prairie regions. Also large marshy lake complexes to the north, in boreal forest regions, and a few to edge of tundra. In migration, mostly on large lakes. Winters mainly near coast, on protected bays and estuaries; also on lakes in interior.

FEEDING **Diet:** *Mostly plant material.* Mainly eats the leaves, roots, and seeds of aquatic plants: pondweeds, wild celery, sedges, grasses, and others. Also eats mollusks, insects, some small fish. In one study in summer, adult males continued to eat mostly plants, while females and young fed on aquatic insect larvae. **Behavior:** Dives for food, usually in water only a few feet deep. In very shallow water may stir up bottom sediments with feet, then upend to feed; also takes some food from surface of water.

NESTING Pair formation occurs mostly at stopover points during spring migration. Several males may court one female. Displays of male include snapping the head far back and then thrusting it forward while giving clicking and cooing call notes. **Nest:** Site is in marsh, in stands of dense vegetation above shallow water. Sometimes on dry ground. Nest (built by female) is basketlike and bulky, built of dead vegetation, lined with down. **Eggs:** 7–12. Olive-gray. Redheads often lay eggs in Canvasback nests; when this happens, female Canvasback is likely to lay fewer eggs. Incubation is by female only, 23–28 days. **Young:** Several hours after hatching, young are led to open water by female. Young feed themselves. Female remains with young for several weeks but departs before they fledge; young are capable of flight roughly 60–70 days after hatching.

MIGRATION Generally migrates late in fall and early in spring. Migrating flocks fly high, often in V-formation. During years of major drought on the northern Great Plains, many Canvasbacks continue moving north, with larger numbers appearing in Alaska.

CONSERVATION STATUS Numbers vary from year to year, but species has been generally declining for some time. Loss of nesting habitat may be main threat.

Canvasback

REDHEAD *Aythya americana*

Ducks in general often lay eggs in the nests of others, but the Redhead carries this to extremes. Female Redheads regularly parasitize each other's nests, as well as the nests of at least 10 other duck species. They also have been known to lay eggs in the nests of the American Bittern and even of the predatory Northern Harrier! Some females may be entirely parasitic, never incubating their own eggs. Such behavior is abetted by the social tendencies of the species, with many often nesting in close proximity. In winter, impressive flocks of Redheads concentrate on coastal lagoons; such gatherings may run to tens of thousands of individuals.

HABITAT *Lakes, saltwater bays, estuaries; in summer, fresh marshes.* For nesting season favors large marshes in prairies or intermountain valleys. Migrants gather on large lakes. In winter, mainly on coastal bays and lagoons, also on freshwater lakes inland.

Redhead

FEEDING **Diet:** *Aquatic plants, insects.* Diet is mainly leaves, stems, seeds, and roots of aquatic plants: shoalgrass, pondweeds, smartweeds, sedges, waterlilies, and others. Also eats many aquatic insects, especially in summer, plus mollusks, rarely small fish. **Behavior:** Forages by diving, usually in water a few feet deep, or by dabbling and upending in very shallow water. In winter on shallow coastal lagoons may do most feeding by simply dipping head underwater.

NESTING **Nest:** Site is in dense marsh (especially bulrushes) above shallow water, occasionally on dry ground. Bulky nest is built up of dead vegetation and anchored to standing growth, lined with down. Nesting is complicated by parasitic tendencies; females typically lay eggs in nests of other Redheads and other waterbirds. Most females apparently are semi-parasites, laying several eggs in nests of other birds, then raising a clutch of their own. Several may lay eggs in a nest that is never incubated; such "dump nests" have been reported with up to 87 eggs. **Eggs:** Usually 9–14, although true "normal" clutch size is difficult to determine. Dull white to pale olive-buff. Incubation is by female only, 23–29 days. **Young:** Female leads young away from nest about a day after they hatch. Young feed themselves; capable of flight at about 60–65 days.

MIGRATION Migrates in flocks. In summer, when males abandon their mates, they may fly hundreds of miles to the north to lakes where they go through the flightless stage of molt. Main migration is fairly late in fall and early in spring.

CONSERVATION STATUS Total population is evidently far below original levels, a sharper decline than for most ducks. Loss of nesting habitat is probably the main cause.

RING-NECKED DUCK *Aythya collaris*

Although it mixes freely with other diving ducks on large lakes in winter, the Ringneck is also found on small, tree-lined ponds, and associates with dabbling ducks on shallow waters. A strong and fast flier, it is able to take flight by springing up directly from the water, without the laborious take-off run of most diving ducks. Despite the name, the ring on its neck is almost never visible.

Ring-necked Duck

HABITAT *Wooded lakes, ponds; in winter, also rivers, bays.* In summer on freshwater marshes, ponds, and bogs, mainly in openings in forested country. In migration and winter on ponds, lakes, slow-moving rivers, sometimes on coastal estuaries, but generally not on saltwater bays.

FEEDING **Diet:** *Mostly aquatic plants, insects.* Diet varies with season and habitat. Feeds on seeds, stems, and roots of many aquatic plants, including pondweeds, sedges, smartweeds, grasses, algae, and others. Also eats aquatic insects and mollusks. Young ducklings feed mainly on insects. **Behavior:** Forages by diving, usually in water a few feet deep. Also forages at surface and sometimes upends in shallows. Opportunistic, it may move into flooded fields to feed.

NESTING   Pair formation activity begins in winter. Courtship displays by male include laying head far back and then thrusting it forward; also swimming with head feathers erect, nodding rapidly. **Nest:** Site is on dry hummock, clump of brush, or mat of floating vegetation, close to open water. Nest is shallow bowl of grasses, sedges, weeds, lined with down. **Eggs:** 8–10, sometimes 6–14. Color varies: olive-gray, pale brown, pale buff. Incubation is by female only, 25–29 days. **Young:** Female leads young to water 12–24 hours after they hatch; young may return to nest at night. Unlike many diving ducks, female and brood often hide in marsh rather than seeking safety on open water. Young find their own food, are capable of flight 49–55 days after hatching. Unlike most ducks, female may remain with young until they are old enough to fly.

MIGRATION   Migrates in flocks. Migration is relatively late in fall and early in spring.

CONSERVATION STATUS   Numbers apparently stable. Since about the 1930s, has become a much more widespread and numerous breeding bird in eastern Canada and northern New England.

TUFTED DUCK   *Aythya fuligula*

A common diving duck of the Old World, the Eurasian counterpart of our Ring-necked Duck. Tufted Ducks wander to North America from both directions, reaching the northeast from Europe and Iceland, reaching Alaska and the Pacific coast from Asia. Although they are turning up more often, they are still considered rare everywhere except western Alaska.

GREATER SCAUP   *Aythya marila*

Greater Scaup

The more northerly of our two scaup species, the Greater is also found across northern Europe and Asia. Winter flocks on coastal bays may number in the thousands. When a flock is feeding on waters where a tide is running, the birds generally face upcurrent; birds from the back of the flock may continuously take off and fly to the front, so that the flock stays in roughly the same position despite the downcurrent tidal drift of individuals.

HABITAT   *Lakes, rivers, salt bays, estuaries.* In summer on lakes and bogs in semi-open country near northern limits of boreal forest, and out onto tundra. In winter mainly on coastal bays, lagoons, estuaries; some on inland lakes. Overlaps with Lesser Scaup at all seasons, but in winter the Greater tends to be on more open bays, more exposed situations.

FEEDING   **Diet:** *Mostly mollusks and plant material.* Diet in winter is mainly mussels, clams, oysters, snails, and other mollusks. In summer (and perhaps in winter on fresh water) consumes plants including pondweeds, wild celery, sedges, grasses, and others; also insects and crustaceans. **Behavior:** Forages by diving and swimming underwater; large food items are brought to surface to be eaten. Occasionally forages by dabbling or upending in shallow water. May feed at any time of day or at night, with timing affected by tides in coastal regions.

NESTING   Pair formation occurs mostly in late winter and early spring. Several males may court one female. Display elements of the males include throwing the head back sharply

while giving a soft call; exaggerated bowing movements, with bill tip lowered to water and then raised high; flicking wings and tail while giving soft whistled notes. **Nest:** Site usually very close to water on island, shoreline, or mats of floating vegetation. Nest is a shallow depression, lined with dead plant material and down. Female chooses nest site and builds nest. Several nests may be close together in loose colony. **Eggs:** 7–9, sometimes 5–11. Olive-buff. Incubation is by female only, 24–28 days. **Young:** Female leads young to water shortly after hatching; two or more broods may join, tended by one or more females. Young feed themselves, are capable of flight 40–45 days after hatching.

MIGRATION   Migrates in flocks. Birds from Alaska may winter on either Pacific or Atlantic coast; banding records indicate that the same individual may go to opposite coasts in different winters, probably as a result of joining different flocks.

CONSERVATION STATUS   Abundant. Heavy concentrations in coastal bays in winter could be vulnerable to oil spills or other pollution.

LESSER SCAUP   *Aythya affinis*

Lesser Scaup

One of the most numerous and widespread diving ducks in North America, especially on inland waters. Can be very active when feeding, diving and surfacing repeatedly. In winter often seen on lakes and bays in dense flocks, numbering hundreds or even thousands, often with no other species of ducks associated with them. The two scaup species sometimes occur in the same places, but they tend to keep to themselves rather than mixing freely.

HABITAT   *Marsh ponds (summer), lakes, bays, estuaries.* Summers around large marshes in prairie or forested regions. Winters on lakes, reservoirs, rivers, sheltered areas of coastal bays. Overlaps extensively with Greater Scaup, especially in winter, but at that season the Lesser is far more likely to be found on freshwater lakes and ponds well inland.

FEEDING   **Diet:** *Includes mollusks, plant material.* Diet varies with season and habitat, but animal matter may predominate, especially mollusks such as clams and snails, also aquatic insects, crustaceans. Also eats plant material such as stems and leaves of sea lettuce, pondweeds, wild celery, plus seeds of pondweeds, sedges, grasses, and others. Birds on the Great Lakes may feed heavily on the introduced zebra mussel. **Behavior:** Forages by diving and swimming underwater, sometimes by dabbling or upending in shallow water. Sometimes feeds at night.

NESTING   Probably first breeds at age of 2 years in most cases. Elements of courtship display by male include a shake of the head, followed by throwing the head far back and bringing it forward very quickly; exaggerated bowing movements; ritualized preening. Some displays may be performed underwater. **Nest:** Site is usually on dry land close to water, often on islands in lakes, surrounded by good cover of vegetation. Stands of bulrush in marshes especially favored. Nest is a slight depression with addition of some dry grass, lined with down. **Eggs:** 9–11, sometimes 8–14. Olive-buff. Incubation is by female only, 21–27 days. **Young:** Leave nest shortly after hatching, go to water. Young are tended by female but feed themselves. Two or more broods of young may join under care of several adult females. Age at first flight 47–54 days after hatching.

MIGRATION Migrates in flocks. Main migration is rather late in fall and early in spring.
CONSERVATION STATUS Abundant. Fluctuation in numbers from year to year is less pronounced than in some ducks.

EIDERS — GENERA *Somateria* and *Polysticta*

These are stocky, hardy ducks of northern coastlines, able to survive year-round in very cold climates. Adult males have bold color patterns, while females and young are brown or gray. Flocks fly low over the sea or rest in tightly packed rafts offshore; they rarely go far inland. Eiders seek most of their food by diving and swimming underwater, with wings partly open but propelled mostly by their feet. The three larger species (genus *Somateria*) feed mainly on mollusks, while the diet of Steller's Eider is more generalized.

Most eiders probably nest for the first time at the age of 3 years. Their nests are very heavily lined with down; the incubating female often covers the eggs with down when leaving the nest.

COMMON EIDER *Somateria mollissima*

A big, lethargic, heavy-bodied duck of northern coastlines. Often seen floating offshore in flocks of up to several thousand birds. Sociable in breeding season also, and often nests in colonies. Eider down, famous for its insulating qualities, is used in

large amounts in the nest lining of these ducks, helping to keep the eggs warm in frigid northern climates. In some places, such as Iceland, the down is harvested at coastal "eider farms," where the wild birds are encouraged to nest in sheltered nooks built for them.

HABITAT *Rocky coasts, shoals; in summer, also islands, tundra.* Very close to coastlines at all seasons. For nesting, favors islands or coasts with rocky shoreline, either barren or forested, or coastal lagoons in tundra regions. At other seasons on shallow oceanic waters, usually not far from shore. Rarely on fresh water.

FEEDING **Diet:** *Mainly mollusks.* Feeds especially on mussels and other bivalves; also some crabs and other crustaceans, echinoderms, aquatic insects, small fish. On breeding grounds eats more insects and some plant material. **Behavior:** Forages mainly underwater; also forages in shallow water by upending or by swimming with only head submerged. May feed by day or night, most often on falling tide or at low tide.

NESTING Several males may court one female. Displays of male mostly involve exaggerated movements of head, accompanied by low cooing calls; also rearing up out of water, flapping wings. **Nest:** Site on ground, usually somewhat sheltered by rocks or plants, close to water. Occasionally on cliff ledge. Often breeds in colonies; may be associated with Arctic Terns or other birds. Nest is a shallow depression lined with plant material and large amounts of down. **Eggs:** 3–5, sometimes 1–8. Olive green to olive-gray. Incubation by female only, 24–25 days,

Common Eider

sometimes 23–30 days. **Young:** Leave nest shortly after hatching and go to water. Female tends young, but they find all their own food. Several broods often join in group called a "creche," accompanied by several adult females. Age at first flight 65–75 days.

MIGRATION   Northernmost breeders migrate rather long distances, southernmost breeders are more sedentary; total winter range does not extend far beyond southern edge of nesting range. Less likely than King Eider to appear far to the south. Hudson Bay birds remain there all year on openings in pack ice.

CONSERVATION STATUS   Abundant; total population probably several million. Local concentrations vulnerable to oil spills and other forms of pollution.

KING EIDER   *Somateria spectabilis*

King Eider

A big sea-duck of Arctic waters. Well adapted to frigid climates, diving and swimming underwater in seas near the freezing point, resting on ice floes. In its normal range, generally in large flocks, with the brown females and immatures outnumbering the strikingly ornate adult males. South of their main range, single King Eiders may associate with flocks of Common Eiders.

HABITAT   *Rocky coasts, ocean.* Nests on high Arctic tundra, both along coast and around freshwater lakes far inland. In winter on ocean, mostly in far north, including around edge of pack ice. Less tied to coast than Common Eider, may occur farther inland in summer and farther offshore in winter. Rarely on fresh water in winter, as on the Great Lakes.

FEEDING   **Diet:** *Mostly mollusks.* Diet varies with season. Mollusks are among main foods at most times. Also eaten are crustaceans, insects, echinoderms, and some plant material. Insect larvae may be main foods in summer. **Behavior:** Forages mainly underwater. Often forages in deep water and may dive more than 150 feet below surface.

NESTING   Most pairs are formed in spring, during migration or near breeding grounds. Several males may court one female, surrounding her on water. Displays of male include turning head rapidly from side to side, rearing up out of water while rotating head, flapping wings, also various head movements accompanied by cooing calls. Faster displays than in Common Eider. **Nest:** Site usually on raised dry ground not far from water. Nest is a shallow depression lined with bits of plant material and with large amounts of down. **Eggs:** 4–5, sometimes 3–7. Pale olive. Incubation is by female only, 22–24 days. **Young:** Leave nest shortly after hatching and go to water. Female tends young, but they find all their own food. Several broods of young often join (in group called a "creche"), accompanied by several adult females. Age at first flight not known, probably 50 days.

MIGRATION   Spring migration begins very early, flocks moving north over mostly frozen seas by early April. Those going to central Canadian Arctic apparently go around Alaska and northeast Canada, rather than flying overland. Although main wintering concentrations are very far north, winter strays have reached Florida, Louisiana, Kansas, southern California.

CONSERVATION STATUS   Abundant in its remote northern range, total population running to several million.

SPECTACLED EIDER *Somateria fischeri*

An uncommon and poorly known eider of the high Arctic, its distribution centered on the Bering Sea. Generally in small flocks. Tends to occur mainly in areas where travel is difficult for humans—boggy tundra in summer, at sea around pack ice at other times—but its winter range is still not well known. Its remote habitat and bizarre, ghostly appearance contribute to its aura of mystery.

HABITAT *Ocean, tundra.* In breeding season on wet low-lying tundra with many lakes and ponds, sometimes well inland. At other seasons on ocean. May be near coastline but often far offshore, along edges and openings of floating pack ice.

FEEDING **Diet:** *Mostly mollusks.* During most of year, when at sea, diet is mainly mollusks. In summer on tundra, diet includes many aquatic insects and some crustaceans, plus much plant material such as sedges, grasses, and berries. **Behavior:** During most of year forages mainly by diving and swimming underwater. Supposedly able to remain submerged longer than most diving ducks. On tundra in summer may forage by dabbling in shallow water or by walking on land.

Spectacled Eider

NESTING Most pairs evidently formed in winter, before spring migration to nesting grounds. Male's displays include rearing up out of water, wing-flaps, shaking head rapidly, stretching neck upward and then jerking head back in quick motion. **Nest:** Site is usually very close to edge of tundra pond, on a raised ridge or hummock; sites may be reused in subsequent years. Nest (built by female) is a shallow depression lined with plant material and large amounts of down. Eggs 3–6, sometimes 1–8. Olive-buff. Incubation is by the female only, about 24 days. **Young:** Leave nest shortly after hatching, are led to water by female. Young are tended by female but find all their own food. Age at first flight 53 days or less, a rapid development for such a large bird.

MIGRATION Flocks in migration usually fly low over sea. Winter range (recently discovered by radio-tracking and airplane surveys) is on Bering Sea, far from land. Body heat of eider flocks may keep holes open in pack ice.

CONSERVATION STATUS *Threatened or endangered.* In the Yukon-Kuskokwim delta of western Alaska, one of the main breeding areas, populations declined by 96 percent from 1970 to 1993. Status of Siberian populations not well known.

STELLER'S EIDER *Polysticta stelleri*

The smallest of the eiders. More agile than the others in flight and less clumsy on land; floats buoyantly on the water, often with its tail cocked up. Its distribution in the Arctic and Subarctic is centered on the Bering Sea. Sociable at most times of year. Flies in tightly packed flocks and often feeds in compact groups as well. When foraging on the sea, all birds in a flock may dive at the same time. Lone Steller's will sometimes associate with flocks of Harlequin Ducks or other divers.

HABITAT *Coasts, ocean.* In breeding season on low-lying tundra with many lakes and ponds, often some distance inland. At other seasons on ocean, in areas with clear water, as along rocky shores or around edges of pack ice.

FEEDING **Diet:** *Varies with season and habitat.* Diet at sea is mostly

mollusks and crustaceans, but also echinoderms, polychaete worms, small fish. On tundra in summer, eats many aquatic insects, also some plant material such as pondweeds and crowberries. **Behavior:** During most of year forages at sea by diving and swimming underwater. In summer, may forage in shallow water by wading or swimming, with head submerged or dabbling at surface.

NESTING   Pairs are formed in winter flocks. In courtship, several males may surround one female. Males' displays include rearing up out of water, turning head rapidly from side to side, tossing head back with rapid motion; may lead to courtship flight, with several males in pursuit of female. **Nest:** Site is on ground near water, on open tundra or surrounded by low scrub. Nest, built by female, is shallow depression lined with bits of plant material and large amounts of down. **Eggs:** 7–8, sometimes 5–10. Olive-buff. Incubation by female only, incubation period unknown. **Young:** Leave nest shortly after hatching and go to water. Female tends young, but young find all their own food. Two or more broods of young sometimes join under care of one or more females. Age at first flight not known.

MIGRATION   Most of world's population (from Alaska and Siberia) winters in southern Bering Sea, although a few go west to winter off northern Scandinavia. Migrates in flocks.

CONSERVATION STATUS   Alaskan population has declined significantly in recent decades.

Steller's Eider

GENUS *Camptorhynchus*

LABRADOR DUCK   *Camptorhynchus labradorius*

Formerly found along our northeastern coasts, this duck disappeared in the 1870s. Little is known of its habits in life, and even the reasons for its extinction are mysterious. It had fleshy flaps at the side of its bill, suggesting a specialized feeding habit; it might have used its bill to grub for mollusks along rocky shores. Perhaps it was always very uncommon, and was unable to survive any hunting pressure.

GENUS *Histrionicus*

HARLEQUIN DUCK   *Histrionicus histrionicus*

Turbulent northern waters are favored by this strikingly patterned little duck. It is often found in summer on rushing rivers, diving and swimming against the current, climbing easily on steep and slippery rocks above the water. When moving inland, pairs of Harlequins usually fly low, following every bend of the river rather than taking overland short cuts. In winter, seems to choose the roughest coastal water, with rocks pounded by the surf. Studies show that many adult Harlequins have had broken bones, probably a result of their rough surroundings.

HABITAT   *Mountain streams in summer; rocky coastal waters in winter.* Nests along shallow fast-moving rivers and streams, even around rapids and waterfalls, often in forested country. Generally not on streams fed by melting glaciers (where food may be scarce). At other seasons mostly on ocean, on exposed coastlines where waves pound on rocks, seldom on sheltered bays.

FEEDING **Diet:** *Mollusks, crustaceans, insects.* Diet at sea is mostly mollusks (including mussels and periwinkles) and crustaceans (including crabs and others); also a few small fish, marine worms. On rivers may eat mostly aquatic insects, and may eat small amounts of plant material. **Behavior:** Forages by swimming underwater or by diving and walking on the bottom; also by dabbling at surface or upending in shallow water. Uses bill to pry food items off of rocks underwater.

NESTING First breeds at age of 2 years. Pairs form during winter and spring. Several males may court one female, surrounding her on water. Displays of male involve raising tail and stretching neck, with ritualized head-bobbing movements. **Nest:** Site is on ground, usually close to water, well hidden under bushes or among rocks; in Pacific Northwest, rarely nests in tree cavity. Nest (built by female) is shallow depression with grasses, weeds, twigs, lined with down. **Eggs:** Usually 5–7, sometimes 3–10. Pale buff or cream. Incubation is by female only, 27–30 days. Female covers eggs with down when leaving nest. **Young:** Leave nest shortly after hatching. Young are tended by female but feed themselves; are able to dive when quite small, but take most food from water's surface at first. Broods often combine under care of multiple adult females. Age at first flight probably 5–6 weeks after hatching.

Harlequin Duck

MIGRATION Mostly a short-distance migrant, moving from inland nesting areas to nearby coasts. Migrates in small flocks, usually following rivers or coastlines.

CONSERVATION STATUS Apparently stable in Northwest. Population in eastern North America evidently has declined substantially over the last century.

GENUS *Clangula*

OLDSQUAW *Clangula hyemalis*

Oldsquaw

A long-tailed duck of cold northern waters. Often the most abundant bird in the high Arctic. Large flocks are often far out at sea; many spend the winter on such northern waters as Bering Sea, Hudson Bay, and Great Lakes. Flocks fly low over sea, with stiff shallow wing-beats, often tilting from side to side. Far more vocal than most ducks, and loud melodious calls of flocks can be heard from some distance. The name Oldsquaw, politically incorrect by any measure, refers to this "talkative" behavior—although it is the male of this duck that makes most of the noise.

HABITAT *Ocean, large lakes; in summer, tundra pools and lakes.* For breeding season favors both low-lying tundra and hilly areas, barren ground and edges of northern forest, as long as open water is nearby. At other seasons mostly on ocean, including far from shore among pack ice; also on Great Lakes and sometimes elsewhere on fresh water.

FEEDING	**Diet:** *Mollusks, crustaceans, insects.* Diet at sea mainly mollusks (including mussels, clams, periwinkles) and crustaceans (including amphipods and isopods); also a few small fish. In summer on breeding territory eats mostly aquatic insects, also crustaceans, mollusks, fish eggs, and some plant material including grasses and pondweeds. **Behavior:** Forages by diving and swimming underwater, with wings partly opened but propelled mainly by feet. Most feeding is within 30 feet of surface; supposedly able to dive more than 200 feet, deeper than any other duck.
NESTING	First breeds at age of 2 years. Courtship display begins by early winter, but most pairs form in early spring. Displays of male include shaking head back and forth, raising long tail high in air, tossing head back with bill pointed up while calling. **Nest:** Site is on dry ground close to water, often partly hidden under low growth or among rocks. Nest is a depression lined with available plant material and large amount of down, the down being added after some eggs are laid. **Eggs:** 6–8, sometimes 5–11. Olive-buff to olive-gray. Incubation is by female, 24–29 days. Female covers eggs with down when leaving nest. **Young:** Leave nest shortly after hatching, can swim and dive well when quite small. Young are tended by female but feed themselves; may feed on items dislodged to surface by diving of female. Age at first flight about 35–40 days.
MIGRATION	Migrates relatively late in fall and early in spring. May travel in flocks of hundreds. In travel over land, fly very high. Many migrate around coastlines rather than going overland; for example, huge numbers move north through the Bering Straits in spring.
CONSERVATION STATUS	Abundant, with population in the millions. Dense concentrations are vulnerable to oil spills and other pollution in northern seas. Large numbers are sometimes caught and killed in fishing nets.

SCOTERS — GENUS *Melanitta*

Scoters are dark sea-ducks that spend most of the year in large flocks on the ocean. They are swift in flight but must patter along the surface of the water to become airborne. Flocks fly low over sea in long irregular lines. On their breeding grounds around northern lakes and rivers they have a varied diet, but at sea they may feed mainly on mollusks brought up from the depths. They breed for the first time at the age of 2–3 years.

BLACK SCOTER *Melanitta nigra*

Once called "Common Scoter," but it is generally seen less often than the other two kinds of scoters in most parts of North America. Floats rather buoyantly on water, often with tail cocked up noticeably. On northern waters, more vocal than the other two scoters, giving clear whistled calls.

HABITAT   *Seacoasts; in summer, coastal tundra.* Breeding habitat includes low-lying wet tundra and higher slopes in treeless terrain, also openings around lakes in northern forest. In winter mostly on bays and along exposed coastlines, usually over shallow water within a mile of shore. Migrants stop on Great Lakes and other fresh waters, some remaining for winter.

FEEDING   **Diet:** *Mainly mollusks, insects.* At sea feeds mainly on mollusks, especially mussels and other bivalves; also crustaceans, marine worms, echinoderms. In summer on fresh water eats many aquatic insects, also fish eggs, mollusks, small fish, some plant material. **Behavior:** Forages by diving and swimming

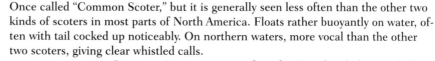

Black Scoter

underwater, propelled by feet; wings may be folded or partly opened.

NESTING   Several males may court one female, surrounding her on water. Displays of male include rushing along surface of water with back hunched and head low, bowing jerkily while calling, and quickly snapping tail up to vertical position over back. **Nest:** Site is on ground, usually near water, often on a hummock or ridge on tundra, generally hidden by grasses or low scrub. Nest (built by female) is a shallow depression lined with plant material and down. **Eggs:** 8–9, sometimes 5–11. Whitish to pale buff. Incubation is by female, roughly 27–31 days. **Young:** Leave nest shortly after hatching and go to water. Female tends young (and broods them at night while small), but young feed themselves. Age at first flight about 6–7 weeks.

MIGRATION   Tends to migrate early in spring and late in fall. In migration along coast, flocks fly low over sea well offshore. When traveling overland, may make long nonstop flights at high altitude.

CONSERVATION STATUS   Numbers apparently stable. Flocks at sea are vulnerable to oil spills and other pollution.

SURF SCOTER   *Melanitta perspicillata*

Surf Scoter

This duck is common in winter on both coasts; on Pacific coast, often seen around fishing piers and harbors. The male's strong head pattern earns the species the hunter's nickname of "skunk-head coot." When feeding, they usually spring forward and dive with wings partly opened. Silent at most times of year.

HABITAT   *Ocean surf, salt bays, marinas; in summer, fresh Arctic lakes, tundra.* Breeding habitat is near lakes and slow-moving rivers in far north, in sparsely forested or semi-open terrain, sometimes out on open tundra. In winter mostly on ocean in shallow bays or estuaries. Some may winter on Great Lakes, rarely on other bodies of fresh water.

FEEDING   **Diet:** *Mostly mollusks.* In addition to mollusks, also feeds on crustaceans, aquatic insects, small fishes, echinoderms, marine worms. Also eats some plant material, mainly pondweeds and sedges. Young eat mostly aquatic insects at first, also mollusks and some plant material, including sedges, pondweeds, and crowberries. **Behavior:** Forages by diving and swimming underwater, propelled mainly by the feet, with wings usually half-opened.

NESTING   Pairs are formed on winter range. Several males may surround one female in courtship. Displays of male include swimming rapidly back and forth with neck stretched upward, exaggerated bowing, short display flights; males may pursue female underwater. **Nest:** Site is often some distance from water, on ground, well hidden under low tree branches or in dense grass clump. Nest (built by female) is a shallow depression lined with down. **Eggs:** 5–9, usually about 7. Pale buff. Incubation is by female only, incubation period not known. **Young:** Leave nest and go to water shortly after hatching. Young are tended by female but feed themselves. Age of young at first flight not well known.

MIGRATION Migrates in flocks. When migrating overland to coastal wintering areas, usually flies high. Stopovers on inland lakes apparently are mostly for resting, not for feeding.

CONSERVATION STATUS May have gone through a serious decline early in the 20th century, but now stable and numerous. Wintering concentrations are vulnerable to oil spills and other pollution.

WHITE-WINGED SCOTER *Melanitta fusca*

The largest scoter. Flocks usually fly low over the sea in long, wavering lines, but in migration they may fly much higher, and a flock may suddenly drop hundreds of feet with a loud rushing noise. On the water, generally silent.

HABITAT *Salt bays, ocean; in summer, lakes.* In breeding season around lakes, ponds, and slow-moving rivers, generally in open country. In winter mainly on coastal waters, especially shallow water over shellfish beds; some remain on Great Lakes and other large bodies of fresh water.

FEEDING **Diet:** *Mostly mollusks.* In addition to mollusks, also feeds on crustaceans and aquatic insects, plus small numbers of fish. Also eats some plant material, including sea lettuce, pondweeds, and others. **Behavior:** Forages by diving and swimming underwater, propelled mainly by feet, with wings partly spread to aid in maneuvering and thrust. Small items are swallowed underwater, but large mollusks are brought to surface and swallowed whole there.

White-winged Scoter

NESTING In courtship, several males may surround one female. Male's displays include lowering head, arching back, and rushing forward short distance on water. Several males may pursue female on short underwater chases. Nesting activity begins late, with clutches often not complete until late June or early July. **Nest:** Site is on ground, usually close to water in patch of dense brush. On islands in lakes, several nests may be close together. Nest is shallow depression, sometimes with plant material added, lined with down. **Eggs:** Usually 9–10, sometimes 6–12. Pale buff or pinkish. Incubation is by female only, 25–30 days. Female covers eggs with down when leaving nest. **Young:** Leave nest shortly after hatching. Female tends young and broods them while they are small, but young feed themselves. Age at first flight not well known, may be 9–11 weeks or as young as 7–8 weeks.

MIGRATION Generally migrates in small flocks, although large numbers may congregate at stopover points. On overland passage to coastal wintering areas, may fly very high. On average, adult males tend to winter somewhat farther north than females or younger birds.

GOLDENEYES AND BUFFLEHEAD — GENUS *Bucephala*

These are diving ducks of cold waters, the males strikingly patterned in black and white. They nest in tree cavities in northern forests and winter on inland lakes and rivers as well as on protected coastal bays, rarely on exposed coastlines. In foraging they dive and swim underwater, propelled by their feet. Normally they first breed at the age of 2 years.

COMMON GOLDENEYE   *Bucephala clangula*

This is by far the more numerous of the two goldeneye species, often seen in small flocks, sometimes in large concentrations. When feeding, all birds in one section of a flock may dive at the same time. They tend not to mix freely with other waterfowl. Fast in flight, their wings make a whistling sound, earning them the hunter's name of "Whistler."

Common Goldeneye

HABITAT   *Forested lakes, rivers; in winter, also salt bays, seacoasts.* In breeding season requires large trees for nesting cavities close to clear, cold water, as around northern lakes, bogs, rivers. In winter mostly on shallow, protected bays and estuaries, also on rivers and lakes.

FEEDING   **Diet:** *Varies with season and habitat.* Eats crustaceans including crayfish, crabs, shrimps, amphipods, and others; also mollusks (including blue mussels), small fishes, marine worms, frogs, leeches. Aquatic insects are main food in summer (when lakes with no fish may be preferred). Also eats some plant material, such as pondweeds, especially in fall. **Behavior:** Forages mostly underwater; rarely by dabbling or up-ending in shallow water.

NESTING   First breeds at age of 2 years, but 1-year-old females go prospecting for future nest sites in early summer. Pair formation occurs mostly in late winter. Several males may court one female. In courtship, displays of male include throwing head far back with bill pointed skyward while uttering shrill call; also ritualized head-pumping and short flights with exaggerated takeoff and landing. **Nest:** Sites are in large tree cavities, 5–60 feet above ground, sometimes in abandoned buildings; will use nest boxes. Nest is depression in wood chips at bottom of cavity, lined with down. Where nest sites are scarce, females may lay eggs in each other's nests. **Eggs:** Usually 7–10, sometimes 5–17. Olive green to blue-green. Incubation is by female, usually 29–30 days. Female covers eggs with down when leaving nest. **Young:** Leave nest 1–2 days after hatching, are led to water by female. Young are tended by female but feed themselves. Age at first flight 56–66 days.

MIGRATION   Generally migrates late in fall and early in spring. Males tend to winter farther north than females.

CONSERVATION STATUS   Numbers apparently stable. Populations have increased in some areas where nest boxes are provided.

BARROW'S GOLDENEYE   *Bucephala islandica*

The less numerous of the two goldeneye species, found mainly in wild country of northwestern North America, with small populations in eastern Canada and Iceland. Occurs in small groups in winter on cold waters, sometimes associating with Common Goldeneye flocks. Since it does not always nest in tree cavities, Barrow's may nest farther north than Common Goldeneye, extending north of treeline.

HABITAT   *Lakes, ponds. In winter, coastal waters, rivers.* Breeds on cold inland waters, such as small lakes, rivers, beaver ponds, mostly in forested country but also in open terrain. In winter mainly on shallow, protected coastal waters, such as bays and estuaries. May winter far inland on lakes and rivers, even in very cold regions where hot springs keep water open.

Barrow's Goldeneye

FEEDING **Diet:** *Varies with season and habitat.* On fresh water, eats mainly aquatic insects, such as larvae of dragonflies and caddisflies. At sea eats mostly crustaceans and mollusks. Also eats much plant material, especially pondweeds, mainly in summer and fall. **Behavior:** Forages by diving and swimming underwater, rarely by dabbling in shallow water.

NESTING Pairs are formed mostly in winter. Several males may court one female in communal display on water. Displays of male include a circular pumping action of the head; also turning head from side to side, flapping wings. **Nest:** Female selects nest site and may reuse it for several years. Sites are mainly in large tree cavities, also in rock crevices, abandoned buildings, burrows, or on ground under bushes in treeless country. Will also use nest boxes. Nest is shallow depression lined with down and sometimes other materials. **Eggs:** 7–10, sometimes 5–14. Pale olive to blue-green. Incubation is by female, 28–34 days. Female covers eggs with down when leaving nest. **Young:** Leave nest 1–2 days after hatching, are led to water by female. Young are tended by female but feed themselves. Age at first flight about 8 weeks.

MIGRATION Migrates late in fall and early in spring. Able to adapt to changing conditions; in recent years some have wintered on cold waters just downstream from dams on lower Colorado River, south of any previous wintering area.

BUFFLEHEAD *Bucephala albeola*

Bufflehead

A diminutive diver, one of our smallest ducks, often very energetic in its feeding. Related to the goldeneyes and, like them, nests in cavities; but unlike other hole-nesting ducks, the Bufflehead is small enough to use unmodified old nest holes of Northern Flickers, giving it a ready source of good nest sites. Less sociable than most ducks, seen in pairs or small groups, almost never in large flocks. Takes wing easily from the water, flies with rapid wingbeats. The name Bufflehead is derived from "buffalo-head," for the male's odd puffy head shape.

HABITAT *Lakes, ponds, rivers; in winter, salt bays.* Preferred nesting habitat is around ponds and small lakes in rather open mixed coniferous and deciduous forest, also burned areas and aspen groves; less often in pure coniferous forest near rivers or larger lakes. In winter on sheltered bays and estuaries, also on lakes, ponds, and slow-moving rivers inland.

FEEDING **Diet:** *Varies with season and habitat.* In summer and on fresh water feeds mainly on aquatic insects; on ocean feeds mainly on crustaceans. Also eats many mollusks (especially snails) in winter and small amounts of plant material in fall. **Behavior:** Forages mostly underwater. All the birds in a small flock may dive at same time. Rarely feeds with only head submerged.

NESTING Males begin courtship displays by early winter, but most pairs form in spring. Displays of male include head-bobbing, wing-lifting, and short display flights, most with

crest feathers fully raised. **Nest:** Site, chosen by female, is in tree cavity (especially old flicker holes), usually 2–10 feet above ground, sometimes up to 50 feet. Sometimes uses nest boxes. Same site may be used for several years. Lining of down is only nest material. **Eggs:** 8–10, sometimes 6–12. Cream to pale buff. Incubation is by female, 29–31 days, sometimes 28–33. **Young:** Leave nest 1–2 days after hatching, are led to water by female. Young are tended by female but feed themselves. Two broods may join, or young separated from one brood may join another. Age at first flight 50–55 days.

MIGRATION   Migrates relatively late in fall; spring migration is protracted over long period. Overland migration, in small flocks, apparently occurs mostly at night.

CONSERVATION STATUS   Evidently much less numerous now than historically because of unrestricted shooting early in 20th century and loss of nesting habitat, but still fairly common and widespread. Current populations seem stable overall.

MERGANSERS — GENERA *Mergellus, Lophodytes,* and *Mergus*

Mergansers are our only ducks that specialize in eating fish. Sometimes called "sawbills," they have serrations (or "sawteeth") on the edges of their bills, which probably help them grasp slippery fish. In flight they look very slender and stretched-out, with very fast wingbeats. Most species nest in hollows in trees and will also use artificial nest boxes. Hooded Merganser and Smew are often placed in the genus *Mergus* along with the two larger species.

SMEW   *Mergellus albellus*

A small merganser of northern Europe and Asia. A few turn up during migration and winter in the western Aleutian Islands, Alaska. Very rare elsewhere in Alaska. There are scattered records of birds wintering along the Pacific coast south to California and in the northeast; some of these may have been escapes from captivity.

HOODED MERGANSER   *Lophodytes cucullatus*

The Hooded is the smallest of our three native merganser species and often seems to be the least numerous, as it tends to live around swamps and wooded ponds where it may be overlooked. A cavity nester along wooded waterways in the temperate parts of North America, it has probably benefited by taking advantage of nest boxes put out for Wood Ducks.

HABITAT   *Wooded lakes, ponds, rivers.* In summer in forested country, along creeks, narrow rivers, edges of ponds. May be in more open marsh habitats if artificial nest sites are provided. In winter on woodland ponds, wooded swamps, fresh and brackish coastal estuaries.

FEEDING   **Diet:** *Fish and other aquatic life.* Feeds mainly on small fish, crayfish and other crustaceans, and aquatic insects; also some tadpoles, a few mollusks, small amounts of plant material. Ducklings eat mostly insects at first. **Behavior:** Forages by diving and swimming underwater, propelled by feet. Apparently finds all its food by sight; eyes adapted for good underwater vision.

NESTING   Pairs may form in late fall or winter. In most courtship displays, male's crest is prominently raised and spread. **Nest:** Site is in tree cavity near water, usually 10–50 feet above ground, rarely up to 80 feet or more. Also uses artificial nest boxes. Nest of natural wood chips and debris in bottom of cavity, with down added. **Eggs:** 10–12, sometimes 7–13. White. Eggshell thicker than in most ducks. Females often lay eggs in each other's nests, also in nests of Wood Ducks and others. Incubation is by female only, 26–41 days, usually about 33 days. **Young:** Within 24 hours after hatching, young leave nest; female calls to them from below, young climb to cavity entrance and jump to ground. Young find their own food; female tends young for several weeks. Young fledge about 70 days after hatching.

MIGRATION   Mostly a short-distance migrant; southerly breeders may be permanent residents. Migration is relatively late in fall and early in spring.

Hooded Merganser

CONSERVATION STATUS   Undoubtedly declined in past with loss of nesting habitat (large mature trees near water). Now population seems to be increasing, helped by artificial nest boxes, including those intended for Wood Ducks.

COMMON MERGANSER   *Mergus merganser*

This fish-eating duck is the typical merganser of freshwater lakes. Its flocks are usually small, but these may combine into big concentrations sometimes at large reservoirs. Common Mergansers living along rivers may spend hours resting on rocks or on shore. The British call this bird the "Goosander." In some parts of Europe where artificial nesting sites are provided, the species has become a common nesting bird along city waterfronts; this has not yet happened in North America.

HABITAT   *Wooded lakes, rivers; in winter, rarely coastal bays.* Mainly around fresh water at all seasons. Summer: On shallow but clear rivers and lakes in forested country; avoids dense marshes and muddy waters. Winter: On lakes, large rivers; occasionally on bays along coast.

FEEDING   **Diet:** *Mostly fish.* Eats a wide variety of fish; also will eat mussels, shrimp, salamanders, rarely plant material. Adult males may swallow fish more than 1 foot long. Young ducklings eat mostly aquatic insects. **Behavior:** Forages by diving and swim-

Common Merganser

ming underwater, propelled by its feet, stroking with both feet in unison. Finds most food by sight; may swim along surface, dipping head underwater repeatedly until prey is spotted, then diving in pursuit.

NESTING   Courtship displays of male include swimming very rapidly in circles near female; suddenly stretching neck upward, pointing bill straight up, and giving soft call. **Nest:** Site is near water, usually in large tree cavity; also in crevices in rock, in holes under tree roots or undercut banks, or in nest boxes. Occasionally in buildings. Nest of wood chips or debris in cavity, plus lining of down. **Eggs:** 8–11, sometimes 6–13. Pale buff. Females often lay eggs in each other's nests. Incubation is by female only, 30–35 days. **Young:** May remain in nest a day or more after hatching;

then they climb to cavity entrance and jump to ground. Female tends young birds for several weeks, but they feed themselves; they may survive even if abandoned quite early. Young are capable of flight about 65–70 days after hatching.

MIGRATION   Migrates mostly in small groups. Adult males, on average, seem to winter farther north than females and young. Migration is late in fall and early in spring.

CONSERVATION STATUS   May be increasing in Europe; apparently stable in North America.

RED-BREASTED MERGANSER   *Mergus serrator*

Red-breasted Merganser

A slim, crested, fish-eating duck, commonly seen around jetties and piers along the coast. Superficially this species is quite similar to the Common Merganser. However, the Red-breasted Merganser nests farther north, winters mostly on salt water, and nests mainly on the ground, while the Common winters mostly on fresh water and nests in cavities.

HABITAT   *Lakes, open water; in winter, coastal bays.* During nesting season around lakes and rivers, within the northern forest and northward into tundra regions. In winter mostly on coastal waters, including bays, estuaries, and open ocean; a few winter on ice-free reservoirs and large rivers.

FEEDING   **Diet:** *Mostly fish.* Feeds mainly on small fish, also crustaceans, aquatic insects, and sometimes frogs, tadpoles, or worms. Young ducklings eat mostly insects. **Behavior:** Forages by diving and swimming underwater. Sometimes a group appears to hunt cooperatively, several birds lining up and driving schools of small fish into very shallow water, where the mergansers scoop them up without diving.

NESTING   In courtship display, male stretches neck forward and upward, then suddenly dips neck and forepart of body underwater, with head angled up out of water and bill open wide. **Nest:** Female selects site on ground, usually near water, in a spot sheltered by dense plant growth or debris. Sometimes nests inside hollow stump, under rock, or in shallow burrow. Nest is a simple depression lined with down. **Eggs:** Usually 7–10, sometimes 5–13. Olive-buff. Females sometimes lay eggs in each other's nests, occasionally in nests of other ducks. Incubation is by female only, 29–35 days. **Young:** Within a day after eggs hatch, female leads young to water, where they feed themselves. Two or more broods may join, tended by one or more females, but young are left on their own within a few weeks. Young are capable of flight about 2 months after hatching.

MIGRATION   May migrate later in spring and earlier in fall than the Common Merganser. Migrating flocks fly in V-formation or lines.

STIFF-TAILED DUCKS — GENUS *Oxyura*

These are odd little divers with a large flat bill, small wings, large feet set far back on the body, and spiky tail feathers that are often cocked up in the air. Often they seem reluctant to take wing; when they do fly, they whir along with very fast wingbeats. This genus includes only six or seven species, but they inhabit every continent except Antarctica.

RUDDY DUCK   *Oxyura jamaicensis*

Ruddy Duck

The main North American representative of the group of stiff-tailed ducks, with spiky tail feathers that are often cocked up in the air. Usually lethargic, and seems reluctant to fly. On takeoff it must patter across the surface of the water to become airborne, then whirs along on rapidly beating wings. On land it is almost helpless. Flocks of Ruddies wintering on lakes seldom mix freely with other ducks, although they may associate with American Coots.

HABITAT   *Fresh marshes, ponds, lakes; in winter, salt bays.* Breeds on fresh or alkaline lakes and ponds with extensive marshy borders and with areas of open water. In winter on protected shallow bays and estuaries along coast; also on ice-free lakes and ponds in the interior, including those with little or no marshy border.

FEEDING   **Diet:** *Mostly seeds, roots, insects.* Feeds on the seeds and roots of plants including pondweeds, sedges, smartweeds, coontail, and grasses. Also eats aquatic insects, mollusks, crustaceans, rarely small fish. Insects and their larvae may be main foods eaten in summer. **Behavior:** Forages by diving and swimming underwater, propelled by feet, using its bill to strain food items from mud at the bottom of ponds. Rarely forages by dabbling at the surface.

NESTING   Pairs form after arrival on breeding waters. Courtship displays of male include raising tail over back and bouncing head rapidly so that bill slaps against chest; short rushes across water with much splashing of wings and feet. **Nest:** Site is in dense marsh vegetation over shallow water. Nest (built by female) is a woven platform of grasses, cattails, lined with down, a few inches above water and anchored to standing marsh growth. Sometimes built on top of old muskrat house or coot nest. **Eggs:** 5–10, typically 8. Whitish, becoming nest-stained, with rough, granular surface; quite large for size of bird. Ruddies often lay eggs in each other's nests and in those of other ducks and marsh birds. Incubation is by female, 23–26 days. **Young:** Leave the nest within a day after hatching, are able to swim and dive well immediately. Young are tended by female but feed themselves. Age at first flight about 6 weeks. 1 brood per year in north, sometimes 2 in south.

MIGRATION   Apparently migrates mostly at night, in small flocks. Migration extends over considerable period in both spring and fall. Populations in Caribbean and South America may be permanent residents.

CONSERVATION STATUS   Current population apparently much lower than historical levels because of unrestricted shooting early in 20th century and loss of nesting habitat.

MASKED DUCK   *Oxyura dominica*

A tropical duck that periodically invades southern Texas and Florida. Smaller than the Ruddy Duck and able to take flight from the water much more easily, the Masked Duck may colonize small and temporary bodies of water. Generally easy to overlook, as it spends much time resting within dense marsh growth, and may clamber about through marsh like a rail. On open water, however, it can be rather tame.

HABITAT   *Marshes, ponds.* In United States mainly found on ponds and impoundments

Masked Duck

with extensive marsh growth and some open water. In tropics also found on mangrove lagoons, swamps, rice plantations.

FEEDING   **Diet:** *Probably mostly plant material.* Diet not well known. Apparently eats mostly plant material, including seeds and roots of smartweeds, sedges, grasses, and various other aquatic and waterside plants. Also eats some aquatic insects and crustaceans. **Behavior:** Forages mostly by diving and swimming underwater, propelled by feet.

NESTING   Breeding behavior not well known. The few known Texas nestings have been in fall. Displays of male apparently include raising tail and lowering bill onto chest while making soft calls, also making short rushes across surface of water. **Nest:** Site is among marsh vegetation in shallow water. Nest (built by female) is a woven bowl of reeds and grasses, perhaps with sparse lining of down. **Eggs:** 4–10. Smaller and smoother than those of Ruddy Duck, whitish to pale buff. Females sometimes lay eggs in each other's nests. Incubation is by female, about 4 weeks. **Young:** Not well known. Like other stifftails, probably leave nest shortly after hatching, are tended by female but feed themselves. Age at first flight not known.

MIGRATION   May travel mostly at night. Apparently not truly migratory, but wanders unpredictably. Seems to invade Texas from eastern Mexico after a series of unusually wet years creates much appropriate habitat. Strays have wandered far outside normal range, reaching Wisconsin, Massachusetts, Pennsylvania.

CONSERVATION STATUS   Despite wide range in American tropics, does not seem to be very common anywhere. Secretive behavior and nomadic movements make it difficult to estimate total population or to provide protection for species.

NEW WORLD VULTURES (Family Cathartidae)

These efficient scavengers play an important role as part of nature's cleanup crew, quickly disposing of dead animals. Very large birds with long, broad wings, they are able to soar for hours as they scan the ground for carrion. Their heads are bare, which is logical, since it would be impossible to keep head feathers clean during the messy work of dismembering carcasses.

The Old World has vultures too, but those birds belong to the hawk family. The seven species of New World vultures are in a family by themselves. Even though they look rather like large hawks, there is evidence to suggest that they are more closely related to the storks.

Often sociable, New World vultures may gather in large communal roosts at night, with anywhere from a dozen to hundreds of birds sleeping in a grove of large trees. After sunrise, before setting off on their daily rounds, the vultures often hold their wings spread out to the sun as if to warm themselves up before flying.

In the movies, when someone is lost in the desert, vultures often circle overhead giving harsh screams. In real life, our vultures generally search for creatures that are already thoroughly dead, and they have essentially no voice at all: hissing and puffing sounds are all they can manage.

Feeding   Vultures find carrion by scanning for it visually as they soar along, and by watching the actions of other scavengers. In some areas they seem to have learned to patrol the highways, looking for road kills. A curiosity in this family is that the Turkey Vulture can also find food by odor. The Black Vulture and California Condor apparently cannot; like most birds, they seem to have very little sense of smell.

Although dead animals make up the majority of the diet, vultures sometimes eat decaying plant material or garbage of various kinds; they may scavenge around garbage dumps in tropical areas. They will also capture helpless creatures such as large insects, fish stranded in drying pools, recently hatched turtles, and eggs and young birds. The Black Vulture seems to have a wider range of food items than the other species.

Nesting   Nesting sites of New World vultures are surprisingly hard to find, considering how large and common the birds can be. Sites chosen are usually on the ground in dense thickets, inside hollow logs, in caves or abandoned buildings, or sometimes in very large tree cavities. One or two eggs are laid, and both parents take turns incubating. Both parents also help feed the young, by regurgitation.

Displays   Courtship displays may involve high circling flight by two birds; there have been reports of displays on the ground as well, with two or more birds walking or hopping in circles with stiff, ritualized movements.

GENUS *Coragyps*

BLACK VULTURE   *Coragyps atratus*

Black Vulture

This broad-winged scavenger is abundant in the southeast, scarce in the southwest. In low flight, it proceeds with several quick flaps followed by a flat-winged glide; when rising thermals provide good lift, it soars very high above the ground. Usually seen in flocks. Shorter wings and tail make it appear smaller than Turkey Vulture, but looks are deceptive: body size is about the same, and aggressive Black Vultures often drive Turkey Vultures away from food.

HABITAT   *Open country; avoids higher mountains.* Mostly found in flat lowlands, such as coastal plain. Forages over open country, but typically roosts and nests in forest, so is scarce in open plains. In Latin America, often common around cities and towns. Less likely than Turkey Vulture to fly over open water, so absent on many islands (such as Florida Keys).

FEEDING   Diet: *Mostly carrion.* Feeds on carcasses of dead animals of all sizes. At times also eats eggs of other birds, turtles, lizards. May kill and eat young of some birds and sea turtles; sometimes eats newborn young of larger mammals. Also eats some plant material, such as coconuts and rotting vegetables. Will scavenge scraps from garbage dumps. Behavior: Often flies very high when foraging, watching for carrion or watching behavior of other vultures to locate food. May forage in family groups.

NESTING   In courtship display, birds may spiral high in air. On ground, male may walk in circles around female, neck extended, making hissing sounds. Nest: Site is on ground in thicket, inside hollow log, in large tree cavity up to several feet above ground, or in cave; sometimes in abandoned building. Formerly used hollow tree sites more often (when more were available in southeast). No nest built. **Eggs:** 2, rarely 1 or 3. Pale gray-green, blotched with brown. Usually one egg of clutch more heavily marked than the other. Incubation is by both sexes, typically 37–41 days. **Young:** Both parents feed young, by regurgitation. Young remain in nest about 60 days, then may move to higher areas nearby; capable of flight at about 75–80 days. May be partly dependent on parents for several more months.

MIGRATION   Some withdraw in winter from northern part of range (although increasing numbers now spend the winter in the north, usually with roosts of Turkey Vultures). Strays may wander north of breeding range at any season, especially late summer.

CONSERVATION STATUS   Has expanded range northward in the northeast, but has declined in parts of southeast. Loss of good nest sites (in large tree hollows) may be one cause.

GENUS *Cathartes*

TURKEY VULTURE   *Cathartes aura*

The dark, long-winged form of the Turkey Vulture, soaring high over the landscape, is a familiar sight in the sky over much of North America. Most birds are believed to have a very poor sense of smell, but the Turkey Vulture is an exception, apparently able to find carrion by odor.

HABITAT   *Widespread over open country, woods, deserts, foothills.* Most common over open or semi-open country, especially within a few miles of rocky or wooded areas providing secure nesting sites. Generally avoids densely forested regions. Unlike Black Vulture, regularly forages over small offshore islands.

FEEDING   **Diet:** *Mostly carrion.* Feeds mainly on dead animals, preferring those recently dead (that is, relatively fresh carrion). Occasionally feeds on decaying vegetable matter, live insects, or live fish in drying-up ponds. **Behavior:** Seeks carrion by soaring over open or partly wooded country, watching the ground and watching the actions of other scavengers. Can also locate some carrion by odor: unlike most birds, has a well-developed sense of smell.

NESTING   As a part of pair formation, several birds gather in circle on ground and perform ritualized hopping movements around perimeter of circle with wings partly spread. In the air, one bird may closely follow another, the two birds flapping and diving. **Nest:** Sites are in sheltered areas such as inside hollow trees

Turkey Vulture

or logs, in crevices in cliffs, under rocks, in caves, inside dense thickets, or in old buildings. Little or no nest built; eggs laid on debris or on flat bottom of nest site. **Eggs:** 2, sometimes 1, rarely 3. Whitish, blotched with brown and lavender. Incubation is by both parents, usually 34–41 days. **Young:** One parent remains with young much of time at first. Both parents feed young, by regurgitation. If young are approached in nest, they defend themselves by hissing and regurgitating. Age of young at first flight about 9–10 weeks.

MIGRATION   Present year-round in much of southern United States, but northern birds migrate long distances, some reaching South America. Migrates in flocks, and may travel long distances without feeding.

Thought to have declined during 20th century in parts of North America, but current populations apparently stable.

GENUS *Gymnogyps*

CALIFORNIA CONDOR *Gymnogyps californianus*

A holdover from prehistoric times, the great condor is one of our largest and most magnificent birds—and one of the rarest. Soaring over wilderness crags, feeding on carcasses of large dead animals, reproducing very slowly, it was ill suited to survival in modern-day southern California. Headed toward extinction in the 1980s, the last birds were brought in from the wild in 1987, to be bred in captivity for eventual release into the wild again.

HABITAT *Wild open country, rugged hills.* At one time, ranged over much of the west, from mountains and valleys to the coast. On its last stand in California, the condor foraged over open grassland and savanna and nested in rugged mountainous terrain with forest and steep cliffs.

California Condor

FEEDING **Diet:** *Carrion.* Prefers recently dead large animals, such as deer or cattle. Formerly occurred often on coast, feeding on dead whales and other marine creatures washed up on beach. **Behavior:** Generally forages only in warmer hours of day, spending morning and evening perched at night roost. Forages by soaring, often less than 2,000 feet above ground, looking for carrion. May find much of its food by watching actions of other scavengers such as vultures or ravens.

NESTING Apparently does not breed in the wild until about 7 years old. **Nest:** Site is usually in cave or large crevice in cliff; sometimes in crevice among large rocks on steep slope, or in burned-out cavity in huge tree, such as giant sequoia. On flat bottom of cave, adult condors may make "nest" of stones, debris, gravel. **Eggs:** 1. Whitish. Incubation is by both sexes, about 56 days. Members of pair trade places on the egg once every 1–5 days, rarely taking shifts up to 9–10 days. **Young:** Both parents bring food for young bird. Adult condors harass or chase away potential predators, such as ravens, Golden Eagles, and large mammals, from vicinity of nest. Young capable of flight about 5–6 months after hatching, may remain dependent on parents for at least another 6 months. This long period of dependence means that the nesting cycle takes more than a year, so after successfully raising one young the condors must skip a nesting season before trying again.

MIGRATION No definite migration proven, but individuals were known to have moved long distances within the breeding range.

CONSERVATION STATUS Decline in numbers was already evident to observers by 1890. Early causes included shooting; also, many condors died in traps or at poisoned carcasses put out to kill large predators. In more recent years, poisoning (including lead poisoning), shooting, and collisions with power lines were among causes of death. Numbers remaining were estimated at about 60 in 1965, fewer than 25 in 1982. In mid-1980s, all remaining wild condors were caught for captive breeding. This breeding program succeeded quite well in raising the numbers of captives, suggesting that it might be possible to reestablish a wild population again. By the mid-1990s, attempts were being made to introduce some of the captive-bred condors into the wild.

HAWKS, EAGLES, KITES, ETC. (Family Accipitridae)

Most birds of prey that are active by day belong to this large family, which includes about 240 species worldwide. These birds are quite variable, ranging in size from huge eagles to agile small hunters barely 10 inches long. In almost all the birds of this family, females are larger than males, the reverse of the usual situation with birds.

Birds of prey have very keen powers of vision, as suggested by the term "hawk-eyed." At a distance, a hawk's eyes may be able to see two or three times more detail than human eyes can. These birds also have good hearing, and they may come to investigate alarm calls of small birds or mammals. However, only one of our hawks, the Northern Harrier, regularly uses sound to pinpoint the location of its prey.

Unlike many other groups of birds, the members of this family (and a related family, the falcons) do virtually all their migrating by day. They often concentrate at favored points: where updrafts along a ridge provide easy flying, or where they must follow coasts or lake shores to avoid flying over water. Watching and counting hawks at such places has become a very popular activity, especially in fall.

Feeding
The great majority of these birds are hunters. Their particular prey varies widely, depending on the species. Large eagles may take animals as big as foxes, while some of the smaller hawks feed almost entirely on insects. Some kites feed mainly on snails. Hawks of the genus *Accipiter* catch many birds. The Old World vultures mostly eat carrion, but the Bearded Vulture eats bones and bone marrow, and the Palm-nut Vulture feeds on the fruits of various palms. The Osprey specializes in catching fish; various sea-eagles also eat fish, although they may be more likely to eat dead ones washed up on shore.

All of the hunters in this family find their prey mainly by sight and capture it with their feet, but methods of hunting are quite variable. Hawks with broad wings and short tails may soar high, scanning the ground, and then dive when prey is spotted. They also may wait and watch from a high perch. Hawks with short rounded wings and long tails may move quietly through dense cover, putting on a burst of speed at the last minute to ambush their prey.

Nesting
Many kinds of hawks apparently mate for life. Almost all defend nesting territories — very large for those that feed on large prey, much smaller for those feeding on small, abundant prey. Nests are usually placed in trees or on cliff ledges, although a few types will nest on the ground. A pair may use the same nest site year after year, or they may have two or three standard sites, alternating among them from year to year.

The largest eagles may lay only one or two eggs, while small hawks may lay five or six. Some hawks are known to lay more eggs in years when prey is abundant. The male and female may both help incubate, but in most species the female does most of the incubating and the male brings food to her. Often the female remains with the young for some time after they hatch, while the male continues to bring food for them.

Displays
To advertise their ownership of a breeding territory, many of these birds have flight displays. These may involve circling over the area with exaggerated slow wingbeats, or repeatedly flying high and then performing spectacular dives. In courtship, the male and female may fly high together, calling. Often the male feeds the female; this ritual serves a useful purpose, as the female may find it more difficult to hunt when she is getting ready to lay eggs.

OSPREY   *Pandion haliaetus*

A distinctive fish hawk, sometimes placed in a separate family of its own. Along coastlines, lakes, and rivers almost worldwide, the Osprey is often seen flying over the water, hovering, and then plunging feet first to catch fish in its talons. After a successful strike, the bird rises heavily from the water and flies away, carrying the fish head-forward in its feet. Bald Eagles sometimes chase Ospreys and force them to drop their catch. In many regions, landowners put up poles near water to attract nesting Ospreys.

Osprey

HABITAT   *Rivers, lakes, coast.* Found near water, either fresh or salt, where large numbers of fish are present. May be most common around major coastal estuaries and salt marshes, but also regular around large lakes, reservoirs, rivers. Migrating Ospreys are sometimes seen far from water, even over the desert.

FEEDING   **Diet:** *Almost entirely fish.* Typically feeds on fish 4–12 inches long. Type of fish varies with region; concentrates on species common in each locale, such as flounder, smelt, mullet, bullhead, sucker, gizzard shad. Aside from fish, rarely eats small mammals, birds, or reptiles, perhaps mainly when fish are scarce. **Behavior:** Flies slowly over water, pausing to hover when fish spotted below; if fish is close enough to surface, the Osprey plunges feet first, grasping prey in its talons.

NESTING   Courtship displays include pair circling high together; male may fly high and then dive repeatedly in vicinity of nest site, often carrying a fish or stick. **Nest:** Site is usually on top of large tree (often with dead or broken top) not far from water. Also nests on utility poles, duck blinds, other structures, including poles put up for them. May nest on ground on small islands, or on cliffs or giant cactus in western Mexico. Site typically very open to sky. Nest (built by both sexes) is bulky pile of sticks, lined with smaller materials. Birds may use same nest for years, adding material each year, so that nest becomes huge. **Eggs:** 3, sometimes 2–4. Creamy white, blotched with brown. Incubation is by both parents but mostly by female, about 38 days. **Young:** Female remains with young most of time at first, sheltering them from sun and rain; male brings fish, female feeds them to young. Age of young at first flight averages about 51–54 days. 1 brood per year.

MIGRATION   Some are permanent residents in southern Florida; migratory elsewhere. Migrants travel singly, not in flocks, often following coastlines, lake shores, rivers, or mountain ridges.

CONSERVATION STATUS   Was seriously endangered by effects of pesticides in mid-20th century. Since DDT and related pesticides were banned in 1972, Ospreys have made a good comeback in many parts of North America.

KITES — GENERA *Chondrohierax, Elanoides, Elanus, Rostrhamus,* and *Ictinia*

The name "kite" is rather loosely applied to several kinds of medium-sized to small hawks around the world. Most of these have a gliding or soaring flight (in fact, the paper kite flown on a string was named after the bird, not the other way around). However, they differ greatly in shape and especially in their choice of prey. Some in the Old World are mainly scavengers. Our five species of kites, no two in the same genus, are a varied lot: one feeds mainly on insects, one on rodents, two on snails, and one is more of a generalist.

HOOK-BILLED KITE   *Chondrohierax uncinatus*

Hook-billed Kite

A recent arrival north of the border, this sluggish tropical hawk was first found in southern Texas in 1964 and has been a regular resident there since 1975. May be seen sailing over the trees or sometimes soaring high, but spends much of its time down within the canopy of the woods, where it searches for its staple food of tree snails. Usually in pairs or family groups in Texas, but has been seen in flocks in South America.

HABITAT   In Texas, found in native deciduous woodland in subtropical zone along lower Rio Grande. Farther south found in various kinds of forest; in Mexico favors deciduous and semi-arid woodlands, but also found in humid tropical forest farther south. High numbers of tree snails may be most important aspect of habitat.

FEEDING   **Diet:** *Mostly tree snails.* Aside from snails, reported to eat frogs, salamanders, and insects. **Behavior:** Foraging behavior not well known. Apparently forages by climbing and walking about in upper branches of trees, looking for tree snails. On finding a snail, kite holds it against branch with left foot, uses hooked bill to break open shell. This species is remarkably variable in bill size, and smaller-billed birds tend to eat smaller snails.

NESTING   Details of breeding behavior not well known. Courtship display reportedly involves two birds flying in tight circles, diving at each other and calling. In Texas, nesting activity has been noted mostly in May and June. **Nest:** Site is in tree, 15–25 feet above ground. Nest (apparently built by both sexes) is a flimsy platform of sticks. **Eggs:** 2, sometimes 3. White, heavily marked with dark brown. Incubation is apparently by both sexes, with incubation period unknown. **Young:** Probably both parents feed the young. Age at first flight unknown; young may remain with parents for several months.

MIGRATION   Apparently permanent resident throughout its range; present year-round in southern Texas.

CONSERVATION STATUS   As a recent arrival in Texas, this kite seems to require nothing more than undisturbed nest sites and a good supply of tree snails. Probably has declined in many parts of tropical range with clearing of woods. Two races in West Indies (Cuba, Grenada) are endangered.

SWALLOW-TAILED KITE   *Elanoides forficatus*

Our most beautiful bird of prey, striking in its shape, pattern, and extraordinarily graceful flight. Hanging motionless in the air, swooping and gliding, rolling upside down and then zooming high in the air with scarcely a motion of its wings, the Swallow-tailed Kite is a joy to watch. At one time it was common in summer over much of the southeast, but today it is found mostly in Florida and a few other areas of the Deep South.

HAWKS, EAGLES, KITES, ETC.

HABITAT   *Wooded river swamps.* Requires tall trees for nesting and nearby open country with abundant prey. In North America found mostly in open pine woods near marsh or prairie, cypress swamps, other riverside swamp forest. In tropics, also found in lowland rain forest and mountain cloud forest.

FEEDING   **Diet:** *Insects, frogs, lizards, birds.* Adults apparently feed mostly on large insects at most times of year, including dragonflies, wasps, beetles, cicadas, grasshoppers, many others. Especially when feeding young, will capture many frogs, lizards, snakes, nestling birds. In tropics, also eats small fruits. **Behavior:** Extremely maneuverable in flight. Catches flying insects in the air. Takes much of its food by swooping low over trees or lower growth, picking small creatures from the twigs or leaves without pausing. Probably takes young birds of other species out of their nests.

Swallow-tailed Kite

NESTING   Courtship may involve aerial chases by both sexes; male may feed female. **Nest:** Site is in tall tree in open woodland, usually in pine, sometimes in cypress, cottonwood, or other tree. Typically places nest near top of one of the tallest trees available, more than 60 feet above ground. Nest (built by both sexes) is platform of small sticks lined with soft lichens and Spanish moss. **Eggs:** 2, sometimes 1–3. Creamy white, marked with dark brown. Incubation is by both parents, about 28–31 days. **Young:** During first week after hatching, young are brooded almost continuously by female. Male brings food to nest, and female feeds it to young. After about 2–3 weeks, female also may hunt and bring food to nest. Young may move about in nest tree after about 5 weeks, first fly at about 5–6 weeks.

MIGRATION   Migration is early in both spring and fall, with Florida birds arriving February–March, departing August–September. Some migrate around Gulf of Mexico, but most Florida birds apparently cross Caribbean; their migration is poorly known.

CONSERVATION STATUS   Formerly more widespread in southeast, north as far as Minnesota, but disappeared from many areas in early 20th century. Current population apparently stable.

WHITE-TAILED KITE   *Elanus leucurus*

As recently as the 1940s, this graceful hawk was considered rare and endangered in North America, restricted to a few sites in California and Texas. In recent decades, it has increased greatly in numbers and spread into many new areas. It is often seen hovering on rapidly beating wings over open fields, looking for small rodents, its main food source. The introduction of the house mouse from Europe may have played a part in its increase; formerly, the kite fed almost entirely on voles.

HABITAT   *Open groves, river valleys, marshes, grasslands.* Found in a wide variety of open habitats in North America, including open oak grassland, desert grassland, farm country, marshes. Main requirements seem to be trees for perching and nesting and open ground with high populations of rodents.

FEEDING   **Diet:** *Mostly small rodents.* Specializes on small rodents that are active by day in open country, particularly voles and house mice. Other items in diet, mostly of minor importance, include pocket gophers, harvest mice, rats, shrews, young rabbits, sometimes birds. Rarely may eat snakes, lizards, frogs, large insects. **Behavior:** Hunts mostly by flying over open country, pausing frequently to

GENERA *Chondrohierax, Elanoides, Elanus, Rostrhamus,* and *Ictinia* hover and study the ground; on sighting prey, it dives, catching prey in its talons.

NESTING   In courtship, male flies near female in odd hovering with wings in sharp "V," calling; male feeds female. **Nest:** Site is in top of tree, usually 20–50 feet above ground, sometimes higher or lower depending on available sites. Live oak often chosen as nest site. Nest (built by both sexes) is a good-sized platform of sticks and twigs, lined with grasses, weeds, Spanish moss. **Eggs:** Usually 4, sometimes 5, rarely 3–6. May tend to lay larger clutches in years when rodents are abundant. Eggs creamy white, blotched with shades of warm brown. Incubation is by female, 26–32 days. Male usually perches nearby, and brings food to female during incubation. **Young:** Female broods young while they are small; male brings food and female feeds it to nestlings. Later, prey is dropped into nest, and young feed themselves. Young are able to fly at about 30–35 days, but may return to nest to sleep or to be fed for some time after. Adults may nest a second time in same season, and if so, young from first nesting may be driven from territory.

MIGRATION   No regular migration, but wanders widely.

CONSERVATION STATUS   North American population has been increasing and spreading since about the 1930s, invading many new areas where it was never known historically. Has also spread and increased in American tropics with clearing of forest.

White-tailed Kite

SNAIL KITE   *Rostrhamus sociabilis*

In the wide-open marshes of central Florida, this broad-winged bird glides slowly and low over the sawgrass. It has no need for fast flight, because it seeks only snails—and only one particular sort, the apple snail. This snail is strongly affected by water levels, and drainage of wetlands has hurt populations of both the snail and the kite. The Florida race of this bird, formerly called Everglades Kite, is now endangered.

HABITAT   *Fresh marshes and canals.* In Florida, found at large freshwater lakes and marshes. Favors shallow waters, with stands of sawgrass and cattails mixed with areas of open water and with a few shrubs or low trees. In the American tropics, also in wet savannas, rice fields, sugarcane fields.

FEEDING   **Diet:** *Large snails.* Under normal conditions, Florida birds live almost entirely on large apple snails (genus *Pomacea*). When the snails become scarce, as during drought, the kites may eat many small turtles. Also rarely eat small snails, rodents, crabs. **Behavior:** Hunts by gliding slowly and low over marsh, dropping to pick up snail with one foot from surface of

Snail Kite

water or plants. Sometimes perches low, scanning surrounding area for snails, then flies to catch one. Kite flies to perch, holds snail with one foot while extracting snail from shell with long, curved upper mandible of bill.

NESTING   Usually nests in loose colonies. In courtship, male repeatedly flies up and dives short distance near female; flies with exaggerated deep wingbeats. Male may feed snails to female. **Nest:** Site is over water in shrub or low tree, sometimes in cattails

HAWKS, EAGLES, KITES, ETC.

or sawgrass, usually 3–15 feet above water, rarely up to 30 feet or higher. Nest (built mostly by male) is bulky platform of sticks and twigs, lined with vines and weeds. **Eggs:** Currently in Florida, usually 2–3. Formerly may have laid more eggs there, regularly 4, rarely 5–6; smaller clutches today may be response to lowered food supply. Eggs white, marked with brown. Incubation is by both parents, usually 26–28 days. **Young:** Both parents feed the young at first, bringing them snails. After 3–6 weeks, one parent (either one) usually departs, may find another mate and nest again. Remaining parent cares for young until they are 9–11 weeks old. Young may climb out of nest at 4–5 weeks, can fly well at 6–7 weeks.

MIGRATION Apparently not migratory, but nomadic, moving around in response to changing water levels.

CONSERVATION STATUS Florida population endangered; disruption of water flow (with impact on habitat and snail populations) main cause. Widespread in tropics but vulnerable to habitat loss.

MISSISSIPPI KITE *Ictinia mississippiensis*

Mississippi Kite

One of our most graceful fliers, this kite glides, circles, and swoops in pursuit of large flying insects. Despite the name, it is most common on the southern Great Plains. During recent decades, the planting of trees in shelterbelts and towns has made it possible for this bird to nest in many areas where it was formerly scarce; many towns on the southern plains now have their own nesting colonies of Mississippi Kites.

HABITAT *Wooded streams; groves, shelterbelts.* For nesting, requires trees (preferably tall) next to open country. In southeast, found mostly in groves of trees along rivers or swamps where surrounding country is more open. On plains and in southwest, nests in tall trees along rivers, in towns, or in groves or shelterbelts on prairie.

FEEDING **Diet:** *Mostly large insects.* Major items in diet include cicadas, grasshoppers, katydids, beetles, and dragonflies; also eats moths, bees, and other insects, mainly large ones. In addition, eats lesser numbers of frogs, toads, snakes, bats, rodents, small birds, turtles. **Behavior:** Catches many large flying insects high in the air in graceful maneuvers, often then holding these in one foot and eating them while soaring. Also skims low to catch prey on or near the ground. Sometimes flies out from a perch to catch passing insects. Pursues bats and flying birds (such as swallows and swifts) in the air. Sometimes catches insects that have been flushed from the grass by herds of grazing animals or by fire. Also scavenges road-killed animals at times (this may account for occasional large rodents or turtles in diet).

NESTING Usually nests in loose colonies. Courtship behavior not well known; may involve aerial acrobatics, posturing while perched. **Nest:** Site is in tree, usually near edge of woodlot, usually 20–35 feet above ground; can be up to 140 feet high. In oaks or mesquites on plains, may be as low as 6 feet. Nest (built by both sexes) is rather flimsy platform of dead twigs, lined with green leaves. Adults continue to add greenery to nest during season. **Eggs:** 1–2. White. Incubation is by both parents, 29–31 days. **Young:** Both parents care for young, brooding them in cool weather and shading them at midday. Both parents bring food for young. At first, may feed young mostly insects, regurgitated into nest; may bring larger prey later.

Young may climb out of nest onto nearby branches at age of about 4 weeks, may make first flights at about 5 weeks. Adults continue to feed them for at least 8 weeks after hatching.

MIGRATION   A long-distance migrant, wintering in southern South America. Migrates in flocks; sometimes seen in very large concentrations in Texas and Mexico.

CONSERVATION STATUS   Since about 1950, populations in some areas (such as southern Great Plains) have greatly increased, and range has extended into parts of the southwest where this kite was previously absent.

SEA-EAGLES — GENUS *Haliaeetus*

The eight members of this group, also known as fish eagles, are found in most parts of the world except the American tropics. Usually living near water, they often grab fish from the water's surface or feed on dead fish washed up on shore. Two species stray into our area, and a third is uniquely North American.

BALD EAGLE   *Haliaeetus leucocephalus*

Bald Eagle

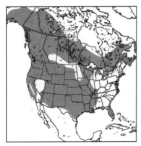

The emblem bird of the United States, majestic in its appearance. It is not always so majestic in habits: it often feeds on carrion, including dead fish washed up on shore, and it steals food from Ospreys and other smaller birds. At other times, however, it is a powerful predator. Seriously declining during much of the 20th century, the Bald Eagle has made a comeback in many areas since the 1970s. Big concentrations can be found wintering along rivers or reservoirs in some areas.

HABITAT   *Coasts, rivers, large lakes; in migration, also mountains, open country.* Typically close to water, also locally in open dry country. Occurs in a variety of waterside settings where prey is abundant, including swamps in Florida, edges of conifer forest in southeastern Alaska, treeless islands in Aleutians, desert rivers in Arizona. Also winters in some very dry western valleys.

FEEDING   **Diet:** *Mostly fish when available, also birds, mammals.* Feeds heavily on fish in many areas, including herring, salmon, carp, catfish, many others. When fish are scarce, may eat birds (ducks, coots, auklets, others) or mammals (jackrabbits, muskrats, others). Sometimes eats turtles, crabs, shellfish, other items. Often feeds on carrion; when fish or carrion readily available, may catch few birds or mammals. **Behavior:** Opportunistic; sometimes a predator, sometimes a scavenger. Does much hunting by watching from a high perch, then swooping down to catch prey in its talons. Also hunts by cruising very low over sea or land, taking prey by surprise. Where fish are abundant (as at spawning runs), may wade in shallow water to pursue them. Sometimes steals fish from Ospreys or other birds. Also lands on ground to feed on carrion.

NESTING   Usually first breeds at age 4–5 years, and may mate for life. **Nest:** Site is usually in tree, often on cliff in west, or on ground on northern islands. Tree nests are usually in very tall tree, standing above surrounding forest, up to 180 feet or more above ground. Nest (built by both sexes) usually a mound of sticks, lined with finer materials; nest may be reused and added to for years, becoming huge. Great Horned Owls sometimes take over nests. **Eggs:** 2, sometimes 1–3. White. Incubation is by both parents, 34–36 days. **Young:** At least one parent remains with young almost constantly for first two weeks. Both parents bring prey to nest, tearing food into small pieces and feeding it directly to young at first; after 3–6 weeks, young begin pecking at food dropped in nest. In seasons when prey is scarce, only largest young may survive. Age at first flight about 10–12 weeks.

MIGRATION Many southern and coastal adults are permanent residents (as far north as Aleutian Islands). Birds from far northern interior migrate south in winter. Immatures from Florida may migrate far north (even to Canada) during their first summer.

CONSERVATION STATUS Numbers declined seriously during the first two-thirds of the 20th century. Shooting was one major cause; even after the eagles were given full legal protection, they continued to decline, probably because of the effects of DDT and other pesticides. Following the banning of DDT, numbers have been increasing gradually since the 1970s.

WHITE-TAILED EAGLE *Haliaeetus albicilla*

This rarity actually has nested in the United States—but only on Attu, at the far western end of the Aleutian chain in Alaska. The Eurasian replacement for our Bald Eagle, its range extends from Siberia all the way around to Iceland and Greenland; in the past, when it was more common in the latter areas, strays reached Massachusetts a few times.

STELLER'S SEA-EAGLE *Haliaeetus pelagicus*

A huge, majestic eagle, native to the wild coastlines of northeastern Asia. Only a few individuals have been known to wander to Alaska, but a couple of those strays have taken up residence in one general area for several years.

GENUS *Circus*

NORTHERN HARRIER *Circus cyaneus*

Parts of Europe and Asia have several kinds of harriers, but North America has only one. Harriers are distinctive hawks, long-winged and long-tailed, usually seen quartering low over the ground in open country. At close range, the face of our Northern Harrier looks rather like that of an owl; like an owl (and unlike most other hawks) it may rely on its keen hearing to help it locate prey as it courses low over the fields.

HABITAT *Marshes, fields, prairies.* Found in many kinds of open terrain, both wet and dry habitats, where there is good ground cover. Often found in marshes, especially in nesting season, but sometimes will nest in dry open fields.

FEEDING **Diet:** *Mostly small mammals and birds.* Diet varies with location and season. Often specializes on voles, rats, or other rodents; also takes other mammals, up to size of small rabbits. May eat many birds, from songbirds up to size of flickers, doves, small ducks. Also eats large insects (especially grasshoppers), snakes, lizards, toads, frogs. May feed on carrion, especially in winter. **Behavior:** Usually hunts by flying low over fields, scanning the ground; males tend to fly lower and faster than females. May find some prey by sound. On locating prey in dense cover, may hover low over site or attempt to drive prey out into open.

NESTING Often nests in loose colonies; one male may have two or more mates. In courtship, male flies up and then dives, repeatedly, in a roller-coaster pattern. **Nest:** Site is on ground in dense field or marsh, sometimes low over shallow water. Nest built mostly by female, with male supplying some material. Nest may be

Northern Harrier

shallow depression lined with grass, or platform of sticks, grass, weeds. **Eggs:** 4–6, sometimes 2–7, rarely more. Pale bluish white, fading to white and becoming nest-stained; sometimes spotted with pale brown. Incubation is by female only, 30–32 days. **Young:** Female remains with young most of time at first; male brings food and delivers it to female, who feeds it to young. After young are about 2 weeks old, female does much of the hunting for them. Young may move short distances away from nest after about a week but return to nest to be fed; are able to fly at about 30–35 days.

MIGRATION   Some southern birds may be permanent residents, but northern ones migrate. At least in North America, always migrates singly. Time of migration is spread out over long season in both spring and fall.

CONSERVATION STATUS   Has disappeared from many former nesting areas, especially in southern parts of range, and surveys suggest that it is still declining in parts of North America.

ACCIPITERS OR BIRD HAWKS — GENUS *Accipiter*

This is a very successful genus, with about 50 species found worldwide, most in the tropics. Only three occur in our area, but they are very widespread, inhabiting woodlands all over the continent. Accipiters have short, rounded wings and rather long tails, a maneuverable shape for flying rapidly among branches inside the forest. Unlike most of our hawks, these three take many birds, surprising them with quick bursts of speed.

SHARP-SHINNED HAWK   *Accipiter striatus*

The smallest of our bird-hunting *Accipiter* hawks, this one is also the most migratory, breeding north to treeline in Alaska and Canada and wintering south to Panama. It is

Sharp-shinned Hawk

during migration that the Sharp-shin is most likely to be seen in numbers, with dozens or even hundreds passing at some favored points on coastlines, lake shores, and mountain ridges. At other seasons the hawks lurk in the woods, ambushing songbirds and generally staying out of sight.

HABITAT   *Mixed or coniferous forests, open deciduous woodlands, thickets, edges.* Usually nests in groves of coniferous trees in mixed woods, sometimes in dense deciduous trees or in pure coniferous forest with brush or clearings nearby. In winter found in any kind of forest or brushy area, but tends to avoid open country.

FEEDING   **Diet:** *Mostly small birds.* Feeds mostly on birds of about sparrow size up to robin size, sometimes up to the size of quail. Also eats small numbers of rodents, bats, squirrels, lizards, frogs, snakes, large insects. **Behavior:** Hunts mostly by perching inside foliage and waiting for small birds to approach, or by approaching stealthily through dense cover, then bursting forth with incredibly swift flight to capture prey in its talons. Sometimes hunts by flying rapidly among the trees or low over the ground, threading its way around obstacles, taking prey by surprise.

NESTING   In courtship, pairs may circle above the forest, calling; fluffy white undertail coverts may be spread out to side during some displays. Male may fly high and dive steeply into woods. **Nest:** Site is very well concealed, usually in a dense conifer (such as spruce or fir) within forest or thick grove; usually 20–60 feet above ground, but can be lower or higher in suitably dense cover. Sometimes builds on top of old nest of squirrel or crow. Nest is a platform of sticks lined with bark strips, twigs, grass. Both sexes bring nest material, female may do most of building. **Eggs:** Usually 4–5, sometimes 3, rarely 1–6. Bluish white fading to white, blotched and washed with brown. Incubation is mostly by female, 30–35 days. Male brings food to female on nest, and may sit on eggs while she is eating. **Young:** Female remains near young for first 1–2 weeks after they hatch; male brings food, female feeds it to nestlings. Young may move out of nest onto nearby branches after about 3–4 weeks, can fly at about 5–6 weeks.

MIGRATION   Some in northwest may be permanent residents, but most are migratory. Large numbers may concentrate at some points along coasts or ridges during migration, especially in certain weather conditions, but the birds are traveling as individuals, not in flocks.

CONSERVATION STATUS   Numbers dropped in mid-20th century, possibly as a result of DDT and other pesticides in the food chain, then recovered somewhat through early 1980s. Since that time, counts of migrants in the east have shown significant declines again.

COOPER'S HAWK   *Accipiter cooperii*

Cooper's Hawk

A medium-sized hawk of the woodlands. Feeding mostly on birds and small mammals, it hunts by stealth, approaching its prey through dense cover and then pouncing with a rapid, powerful flight. Of the three bird-eating *Accipiter* hawks, Cooper's is the mid-sized species and the most widespread as a nesting bird south of Canada.

HABITAT   *Mature forest, open woodlands, wood edges, river groves.* Nests in coniferous, deciduous, and mixed woods, typically those with tall trees and with openings or edge habitat nearby. Also found in trees along rivers through open country, and increasingly in suburbs and cities where some tall trees exist for nest sites. In winter may be in fairly open country, especially in west.

FEEDING   **Diet:** *Mostly birds and small mammals.* Feeds mainly on medium-sized birds, in the size range of robins, jays, flickers, also on larger and smaller birds. Also eats many small mammals, such as chipmunks, tree squirrels, ground squirrels, mice, bats. Sometimes eats reptiles, insects. **Behavior:** Usually hunts by stealth, moving from perch to perch in dense cover, listening and watching, then putting on a burst of speed to overtake prey. Sometimes cruises low over ground, approaching from behind shrubbery to take prey by surprise.

In courtship (and occasionally at other times), both sexes may fly over territory with slow, exaggerated wingbeats. Male feeds female for up to a month before she begins laying eggs. **Nest:** Site is in tree, either deciduous or coniferous, usually 25–50 feet above ground. Often placed on top of some preexisting foundation, such as old nest of large bird or squirrel, or clump of mistletoe. Nest (probably built by both sexes) is bulky structure of sticks, lined with softer material such as strips of bark. **Eggs:** 3–5, sometimes 1–7. Pale bluish white. Incubation is mostly by female, usually 34–36 days. Male brings food to female and then incubates for a few minutes while female is eating. **Young:** Female broods young during first 2 weeks after they hatch; male brings food, gives it to female at perch near nest, and she feeds it to young. Young may climb about in nest tree after about 4 weeks, can fly at about 4–5 weeks.

MIGRATION   Found all year in much of range, but northernmost breeders move south for winter. Migrates by day. Especially in fall, migrants often concentrate along ridges and coastlines in certain weather conditions.

CONSERVATION STATUS   Numbers declined in mid-20th century, possibly from effects of DDT and other pesticides. Some recovery since, and numbers probably stable in most areas.

NORTHERN GOSHAWK *Accipiter gentilis*

Northern Goshawk

A powerful predator of northern and mountain woods. Goshawks hunt inside the forest or along its edge; they take their prey by putting on short bursts of amazingly fast flight, often twisting among branches and crashing through thickets in the intensity of pursuit. In some years, perhaps when prey is scarce in the north, autumn invasions may bring Goshawks well to the south of their normal range in the east and into lowland valleys in the west.

HABITAT   *Coniferous and mixed forests.* Generally restricted to wooded areas, but may be in relatively open woods or along edges. Often more common as a breeding bird in mixed woods than in pure stands of coniferous trees. During winter incursions to the south, may be found in any forest type.

FEEDING   **Diet:** *Mostly birds and small mammals.* Feeds on many medium-sized birds, such as grouse and crows; also many squirrels, rabbits, snowshoe hares. Also eats some small birds, small rodents, snakes, insects. **Behavior:** Hunts by perching quietly at midlevels in trees, watching for prey, often moving from one perch to another. When prey is spotted, the hawk attacks with a short flight, putting on a great burst of speed and often plunging through tangled branches and thickets in pursuit of quarry. Sometimes searches for prey by flying low through woods.

NESTING   May mate for life. In display over nesting territory, adult glides and circles, often with fluffy white feathers under tail spread out to sides; also may do a series of shallow dives and upward flights. Male provides most or all food for female, beginning before eggs are laid. **Nest:** Site is in tree, often in deciduous tree in mixed forest, at a major crotch in the trunk. Height varies, commonly 25–50 feet above ground, sometimes 15–75 feet up. Nest (built mostly by female) is platform of sticks lined with finer material, including green foliage. Nest may be reused, with more material added each year, becoming quite large. **Eggs:** 2–4, rarely 5. Bluish white, fading to white. Incubation is mostly by female, 32–38 days; male brings food to her. **Young:** Female remains with young most of time at first; male brings food, and female feeds it to young. Adults (especially female) very bold in defense of nest, diving at intruders, including humans, and sometimes drawing blood. Age of young at first flight about 5–6 weeks.

MIGRATION   Some may remain through winter in north woods, others (especially young birds) move south. Sometimes big invasions move south of breeding range, possibly when prey is scarce in north. Migrates relatively late in fall, early in spring.

CONSERVATION STATUS   Expanding range and possibly increasing in northeast during recent decades. Populations in southwestern mountains may be threatened or endangered by loss of habitat.

GENUS *Geranospiza*

CRANE HAWK   *Geranospiza caerulescens*

A slim, gangly hawk of tropical woodlands. Sometimes it hunts over open fields, but more often it clambers about in trees, using its long legs to reach into cavities for prey, sometimes hanging upside down in the branches. A single Crane Hawk spent a winter in southern Texas in the 1980s.

GENUS *Buteogallus*

COMMON BLACK-HAWK   *Buteogallus anthracinus*

In the arid southwest, this hawk is limited to the edges of flowing streams. A bulky bird with very broad wings, short tail, and long legs, it usually hunts low along streams, even wading in the water at times, catching fish, frogs, and other small creatures. Although it seems sluggish, it is wary, calling loudly in alarm if people approach the nest. Common Black-Hawks have abandoned some former nesting areas because of too much human disturbance.

HABITAT   *Wooded streams.* Almost always found near water. In United States, breeds in tall trees (especially cottonwoods) along streams with more or less permanent water flow and relative lack of human disturbance. In tropics, found in wider range of habitats, including lowland rain forest, mountain rivers, coastal mangrove swamps.

Common Black-Hawk

FEEDING   **Diet:** *Includes fish, frogs, lizards.* Feeds on a wide variety of small creatures, especially those found in water. In United States, eats mostly fish, frogs, tadpoles, and lizards, plus some small birds, snakes, rodents, insects. In tropics, diet may include many crayfish, crabs, large insects. **Behavior:** Hunts mostly by watching from low perch, then gliding down to catch prey in talons. Sometimes hunts actively along streams by moving from rock to rock at water's edge, and sometimes wades in shallow water, stirring up prey.

NESTING   In courtship, pairs soar and dive, calling, with long legs dangling. Near nest site, male may feed female. **Nest:** In United States, site is in tree in grove along stream, usually in cottonwood or sycamore. Site usually 30–90 feet above ground. Nest is bulky platform of sticks, lined with green leaves; male brings much material, female adds it to nest. **Eggs:** 1–2, sometimes 3. White to greenish white, blotched with brown and lavender. Incubation is by both parents, with female incubating at night and much of day. **Young:** Female remains at nest almost constantly for first 2 weeks after eggs hatch and much of the time thereafter. Male hunts and brings food to nest, female feeds it to young. Young leave nest after about 6–7 weeks, move to nearby trees; can fly well at about 10 weeks; adults continue feeding them for a further 5–6 weeks.

MIGRATION   Nonmigratory in most of range, but only a summer visitor in United States, where it arrives mostly in March, departs mostly in September and October.

CONSERVATION STATUS   Possibly as many as 250 pairs in United States; vulnerable to disturbance and to loss of habitat.

GENUS *Parabuteo*

HARRIS'S HAWK   *Parabuteo unicinctus*

This strikingly patterned southwestern hawk is more sociable than most birds of prey. It is often seen in groups of three or more, the birds perching close together on poles or giant cactus. It may seem lethargic or tame when perched, allowing close approach; when hunting, however, it is dashing and powerful, pursuing prey in agile flight even through dense brush. Two or more Harris's Hawks may hunt cooperatively, working together to chase prey into the open.

HABITAT   *River woods, mesquite, brush, cactus deserts.* Found mostly in open dry country. Most common in saguaro cactus desert in Arizona and in mesquite brushland in Texas and New Mexico. Also found in trees along rivers, and recently has become resident in suburban areas of some southwestern cities.

FEEDING   **Diet:** *Small mammals, birds, lizards.* Feeds on a wide variety of small creatures. Common prey includes ground squirrels, rabbits, wood rats, kangaroo rats, and many medium-sized birds, such as quail and woodpeckers. Eats large lizards when they are common. Also sometimes large insects. **Behavior:** Hunts actively, in low flight, pursuing prey around bushes and thickets. Often two or three hunt together, and a fleeing animal that evades one hawk may be caught by the next; larger prey is often shared by the hawks.

Harris's Hawk

NESTING   Often nests in triads, with two males mated to one female, all three adults associating peacefully at the nest and cooperating in raising the young. Courtship (involving two, three, or more birds) includes soaring, circling, and diving. **Nest:** Site is usually in small tree (such as mesquite or paloverde) or in arms of giant saguaro cactus, usually 12–25 feet above ground; sometimes higher on powerline tower, tall tree. Nest (built by both sexes) is bulky structure of sticks lined with twigs and grass, with leafy twigs added throughout nesting cycle. Nest may be reused several times. **Eggs:** 3–4, sometimes 1–5. Pale bluish white, sometimes with a few brown spots. Incubation is mostly by female, 33–36 days. At nests with two males, both males bring food to incubating female and take shorter turns sitting on the eggs. **Young:** May be brooded and fed mostly by the female, but most food is brought by the

HAWKS, EAGLES, KITES, ETC.

male(s). Young move out of nest to nearby perches after about 40 days, gradually develop to strong flight. Adults may raise 2–3 broods per season, and young from earlier nesting may help feed the young in later broods.

MIGRATION No definite migration, although groups and individuals may wander widely, especially during times of prey shortage.

CONSERVATION STATUS Has disappeared from some former areas, such as lower Colorado River Valley; some attempts have been made to reintroduce the species. Threatened in some areas by illegal taking for falconry.

BUTEOS OR SOARING HAWKS — GENUS *Buteo*

With broad wings and short, wide tails, these hawks are built for soaring, and they are the ones most often seen in most areas. When they are not circling in the sky, they frequently perch on dead snags, telephone poles, or other prominent perches, watching for prey. Most kinds seldom feed on birds, but their diets may include rodents, reptiles, large insects, or various other creatures that are not too agile and quick for the hawks to capture. In Europe, hawks of this type are called "buzzards," but that name unfortunately has been used as a slang term for vultures in North America.

GRAY HAWK *Buteo nitidus*

Widespread and common in the tropics, this small hawk enters our area mainly in southeastern Arizona, where it is limited to cottonwood and mesquite forests along a few streams. It sometimes soars above the surrounding country, but often it perches within the branches of tall trees, where its presence may be given away by its loud whistling calls. Fast and agile in flight, the Gray Hawk may slip rapidly through the trees, plucking fast-running lizards from the branches.

HABITAT *Wooded lowland streams.* In United States, breeds only in tall trees along or near

Gray Hawk

permanent streams, especially in cottonwoods, with areas of dense brush (such as mesquite) nearby. In the tropics, much more widespread, found in any kind of brushy or semi-open habitat.

FEEDING **Diet:** *Mostly lizards and birds.* In Arizona, feeds heavily on spiny lizards (genus *Sceloporus*) that climb in trees; also other lizards, various small and medium-sized birds, snakes, mice, wood rats, small rabbits, ground squirrels, large insects. Diet in tropics not well known but apparently similar. **Behavior:** Surprisingly agile in flight, able to fly rapidly among tree limbs and dense brush, using its talons to pick off lizards or birds from the branches. May watch for prey from a perch, or may circle low over clearings or through the woods.

NESTING In courtship, pairs circle high in air, calling. In impressive aerial display, male may climb high, dive steeply, then repeat. At times both members of pair may fly high and then dive. Adults have loud whistling call, somewhat like cry of peacock, given near nest. **Nest:** In Arizona, nest site is in tall tree, usually in cottonwood but sometimes in sycamore, oak, or other species. Site is usually well hidden near top of tree, 40–60 feet up, to over 100 feet at times. Nest is a small platform of sticks, including green leafy twigs, lined with leaves. **Eggs:** Usually 2–3. Pale bluish white, fading to white, sometimes with a few brown spots. Incubation is mostly or entirely by female, about 32 days. **Young:** Apparently both parents bring food for young birds. Young may leave nest at about 6 weeks but may return to nest for resting or sleeping for some time thereafter.

MIGRATION   Mostly withdraws from Arizona in winter, but probably travels only a short distance south into Mexico; a few may linger near the border. In southern Texas, perhaps more frequent in winter than in summer.

CONSERVATION STATUS   Probably no more than about 50 pairs nest north of Mexico; vulnerable to loss of lowland stream forest habitat. Still fairly common and widespread in tropics.

ROADSIDE HAWK   *Buteo magnirostris*

This chunky small hawk of tropical roadsides and forest edges is a very rare stray into southern Texas. Seldom seen soaring like other *Buteo* hawks; it flies instead with several quick flaps followed by a glide, looking rather clumsy. On its native range in Mexico and southward, this hawk is noisy, often giving squealing calls.

RED-SHOULDERED HAWK   *Buteo lineatus*

A hawk of the woodlands, often heard before it is seen. The clear whistled calls of this hawk are conspicuous, especially in spring; in the east, Blue Jays often give a near-perfect imitation of this call. Over much of eastern North America the Red-shoulder has become uncommon, sticking closely to the remaining forests. Populations in Florida and California are often more visible, perhaps adapting better to open habitats.

HABITAT   *Bottomland woods, wooded streamsides, swamps.* In east, nests in deciduous and mixed forest, with tall trees and relatively open understory, often along rivers and swamps. May move into more open habitats in winter. In west, typically in riverside forest or oak woodland, sometimes in eucalyptus groves. Florida birds may be in pine woods, mangroves.

FEEDING   **Diet:** *Includes small mammals, amphibians, reptiles, birds.* Diet varies with region and season. Main items often mammals such as voles and chipmunks, at other times frogs and toads; may eat many crayfish in some areas. Also eats snakes, small birds, mice, large insects, occasionally fish, rarely carrion. **Behavior:** Usually hunts by watching from a perch,

Red-shouldered Hawk

either within forest or in open, swooping down when it locates prey. Sometimes flies very low in open areas, taking creatures by surprise. May use hearing as well as sight to locate prey.

NESTING   In courtship, male displays by flying upward, calling, then diving steeply. Pairs may soar together in circles, calling, high over nesting territory. **Nest:** Site is usually in deciduous tree, sometimes in conifer, located in fork of main trunk or at base of branches against trunk, usually 35–65 feet above ground. Nest (built by both sexes) is platform of sticks and other material, lined with bark, moss, and sprigs of green vegetation. Nest may be used for more than one season. **Eggs:** Usually 3–4, sometimes 2. Pale bluish white, blotched with brown and lavender.

Incubation is mostly by female, roughly 33 days. Male brings food to female at nest and may take a turn sitting on eggs while female eats. **Young:** Female remains with young most of time for first 1–3 weeks after they hatch; male brings food, female feeds it to nestlings. Young leave the nest at about 5–7 weeks after hatching and are fed by parents for another 8–10 weeks.

MIGRATION   Mostly a permanent resident in west and south; northern birds migrate but do not travel far. Some movement in winter as far south as central Mexico.

CONSERVATION STATUS   Far less numerous than historically in some areas, including upper Midwest and parts of Atlantic coast, but current populations thought to be stable in most regions.

BROAD-WINGED HAWK *Buteo platypterus*

A small hawk, common in eastern woodlands in summer. Staying around the edges of forest, Broad-wings are often not very noticeable during the breeding season, but they form spectacular concentrations when they migrate. In fall, almost all individuals leave North America in a mass exodus to Central and South America, and thousands can sometimes be seen along ridges, coastlines, or lake shores when wind conditions are right.

HABITAT   *Woods, groves.* Typically breeds in deciduous or mixed coniferous-deciduous forest, often near water and near clearings or edges. Migrants may be seen over any kind of open country but tend to stop for the night in forest or extensive groves of trees.

Broad-winged Hawk

FEEDING   **Diet:** *Includes small mammals, amphibians, reptiles, birds.* Varied diet includes mice, voles, squirrels, other small mammals; toads, frogs, snakes, lizards, young turtles; various small birds; large insects. Sometimes eats crayfish, fish, centipedes, earthworms. **Behavior:** Hunts by watching for prey from a perch, usually located along edge of woods or near water. When prey is spotted, the hawk swoops down rapidly to capture the creature in its talons. Occasionally hunts by flying through the woods or along watercourses, actively searching for prey.

NESTING   Early in breeding season, pairs circle high in the air, calling. In display, one bird may fly high, then dive steeply toward the ground. **Nest:** Site is usually in the lower part of a large tree (either deciduous or coniferous), typically 25–40 feet above ground. Nest (built by both sexes) is a rather small platform of sticks lined with softer materials such as bark and moss. Leafy green twigs often added during nesting cycle. Often uses existing nest of hawk, crow, or squirrel, adding material to it. **Eggs:** Usually 2–3, sometimes 1–4. Whitish, usually spotted with brown. Incubation is almost entirely by female, 28–31 days. Male brings food to female during incubation, then he may sit on eggs while she eats. **Young:** Female remains with young almost constantly for first 1–2 weeks after they hatch; male brings food, and female feeds it to nestlings. Young may climb out of nest onto nearby branches at about 4–5 weeks; can fly at about 5–6 weeks, and soon start learning to hunt.

MIGRATION   A long-distance migrant, most going to South America for the winter. Migrates in flocks. Birds from throughout the east travel southwest or south to go around, not across, the Gulf of Mexico.

CONSERVATION STATUS   Early in the 20th century, large numbers of these birds were sometimes shot during migration, but with legal protection their numbers now seem healthy.

SHORT-TAILED HAWK   *Buteo brachyurus*

This rather small tropical hawk enters our area only in Florida. Even there it is uncommon, with widely scattered pairs nesting along the edges of woods in the central part of the state. It seldom perches in the open; when hunting, it regularly soars very high, where it may go unnoticed by the observer on the ground. Unlike most of the *Buteo* hawks, the Short-tail feeds mostly on small birds, dropping from the sky to take them by surprise.

HABITAT   *Pines, wood edges, cypress swamps, mangroves.* Main feature of habitat in Florida is presence of open country next to woodland. Trees involved may be pines, cypress, mangroves, or mixed swamp forest, but must have large expanses of open prairie, farmland, or marsh nearby. In tropics, found in similarly semi-open country, in both lowlands and mountains.

Short-tailed Hawk

FEEDING   **Diet:** *Mostly small birds.* In Florida, eats birds ranging in size from small songbirds up to Mourning Dove and Sharp-shinned Hawk. Occasional items in diet (in Florida and elsewhere) include snakes, lizards, tree frogs, rodents, insects. **Behavior:** Searches for prey mainly in flight, rarely from a perch. Often appears to hang motionless in the air or glides very slowly into the wind. Dives steeply after prey is spotted. Usually attempts to catch birds perched in tops of trees or shrubs.

NESTING   Breeding behavior not well known; has been studied mostly in Florida, not much in wide tropical range. In spring, male displays over nesting territory with aerial acrobatics, alternately climbing and swooping, flying in high circles, diving head first. **Nest:** Site is in tree, especially pine or cypress, usually higher than 25 feet and often near top of tree but under canopy of foliage. Nest is bulky platform of sticks, twigs, Spanish moss, often with leafy green branches added for lining. Male brings most material, female builds nest. **Eggs:** 2, sometimes 1–3. White to pale bluish white, sometimes with brown spots. Incubation is apparently only by female, about 34 days. Male brings food to female during incubation period. **Young:** Female remains with young most of the time while they are small; male brings food, and female feeds it to young. Development of young and age at first flight not well known.

MIGRATION   Pairs nesting in southern Florida may be permanent residents, but those from northern Florida winter in southern part of peninsula. Migration is late in fall, early in spring. Birds from Mexico have very rarely strayed north to Texas.

CONSERVATION STATUS   Very uncommon in Florida (perhaps fewer than 500), but numbers probably stable. May be increasing in Mexico.

SWAINSON'S HAWK   *Buteo swainsoni*

This slim and graceful hawk is a common sight over grasslands of the Great Plains and the west, but only in summer: every autumn, most individuals migrate to southern South America. Although Swainson's Hawk is big enough to prey on rodents, snakes, and birds (and does so while it is raising young), at most seasons it feeds heavily on large insects instead. Flocks are often seen sitting on the ground in fields where there are many grasshoppers or caterpillars.

Plains, dry grassland, farmland, ranch country. Breeds most commonly on northern Great Plains, in prairie regions with scattered groves of trees for nest sites. Less common in dry grassland farther west and in heavily farmed country. In migration, often pauses in fields where insect larvae may have been turned up by the plow.

FEEDING **Diet:** *Mostly small mammals and reptiles in early summer, large insects at other seasons.* When feeding young, preys on ground squirrels, pocket gophers, mice, snakes, lizards, small birds; sometimes bats or carrion. At other seasons, diet shifts to mostly large insects. May feed heavily on grasshoppers and caterpillars in late summer. In winter in Argentina, follows and feeds on swarms of nomadic dragonflies.

Swainson's Hawk

Behavior: May hunt by soaring over grassland or by perching and scanning the ground. Skilled at catching flying insects in the air. When feeding on insects in fields, may catch them by running about on ground. May concentrate near grass fires, watching for prey driven into the open by the flames.

NESTING   In courtship, members of pair engage in display flights, with circling and steep dives. On prairies with scattered groves of trees, may have conflicts with Great Horned Owl where both species attempt to nest in same grove. **Nest:** Site is usually in a tree or large shrub in open country, usually 15–30 feet above ground, but may be lower or higher; generally well hidden within foliage. May be built on top of old magpie nest. Sometimes nests on ledge of cliff or steep slope. Nest is a platform of sticks lined with finer twigs, weeds. Often adds leafy green branches to nest. **Eggs:** 2–3, sometimes 1 or 4. Pale bluish white fading to dull white, usually lightly spotted with brown. Incubation is almost all by the female, about 34–35 days. Male brings food to female during incubation period. **Young:** Both parents bring food for young, but at first female may remain with young much of time while male hunts. Young can fly about 42–44 days after hatching; may remain with parents until fall migration.

MIGRATION   Long-distance migrant, with most going to southern South America for winter. Often migrates in large flocks. May travel for several days without feeding. Mostly western, but every fall a handful of individuals show up on Atlantic coast.

CONSERVATION STATUS   Has declined seriously in much of its nesting range, especially in California. Causes of decline not well understood.

WHITE-TAILED HAWK   *Buteo albicaudatus*

A hawk of tropical grasslands and savannas, the White-tail is fairly common in places on the coastal prairie of Texas. It is a rather bulky bird with noticeably broad wings and short tail, and it soars with the wings held in a shallow "V." Although it seems particular in its choice of habitat, it is a generalized feeder, preying on a wide variety of small animals.

HABITAT   *Dry grassland, coastal prairies.* In Texas, found mostly on open grassland with scattered shrubs or low trees such as mesquite, hackberry, and oak. Mostly on coastal prairie, also inland in ranch country. Generally not found where land is farmed or heavily grazed.

FEEDING   **Diet:** *Quite varied.* Known to eat rats, mice, pocket gophers,

White-tailed Hawk

rabbits, birds, snakes, lizards, frogs, crayfish, crabs, insects. Sometimes feeds on carrion. **Behavior:** Hunts by watching for prey either from a perch or while flying; dives steeply when prey is spotted. Sometimes catches flying insects in the air. Attracted to grass fires, where it catches creatures trying to escape the flames.

NESTING Breeding behavior not thoroughly studied. In one courtship display, both birds land on ground, male goes through act of pulling at grass blades and weeds. **Nest:** Site in Texas is usually on top of low tree or shrub, averaging about 10 feet above ground; sometimes as low as 3 feet, sometimes higher, rarely up to 40 feet. Nest (apparently built by both sexes) is a bulky platform of sticks, twigs, grasses, weeds. Nest may be used more than once. **Eggs:** 2, sometimes 3, rarely 1 or 4. White, sometimes lightly spotted with brown. Incubation is mostly by female, 29–32 days. **Young:** Apparently both parents bring food to young in nest, but roles of sexes in feeding young not well known. Young are able to fly at about 46–55 days after hatching; may remain with parents and be fed by them for up to 7 months or even longer.

MIGRATION Not truly migratory but may move to different areas for winter; for example, some winter on Padre Island, Texas, where they no longer nest.

CONSERVATION STATUS Declined in Texas from 1950s to 1970s, possibly as a result of pesticides. Numbers probably now stable in Texas. May be declining in Mexico, probably because of overgrazing of habitat.

ZONE-TAILED HAWK *Buteo albonotatus*

Seen soaring at a distance over rugged country in the southwest, the Zone-tail looks remarkably like a Turkey Vulture. It may be overlooked even by birders who are searching for it. This close resemblance may fool other creatures as well: small animals in the west learn to ignore the abundant and harmless Turkey Vultures, and they may fail to notice an approaching Zone-tailed Hawk until it is too late.

Zone-tailed Hawk

HABITAT *River woodlands, desert mountains, canyons.* Mostly forages over open country such as grassland, desert, chaparral, or areas with scattered trees. Seems to favor hilly or mountainous terrain and may soar on updrafts from cliffs. Nests in very large trees, often in isolated groves along rivers, in steep canyons, or near cliffs.

FEEDING **Diet:** *Mostly lizards, mammals, birds.* Diet varies with location. In some areas, may specialize on certain large lizards, such as spiny lizards or collared lizards. In other areas, birds are main items in diet. Also eats many small mammals, plus some frogs, snakes, insects, centipedes. **Behavior:** In hunting, it soars and circles like a vulture, and thus may be ignored by smaller animals below. When it spots prey, it continues to circle as before, but gradually moves off to side and lower; as soon as it is screened from the prey animal by cover, the hawk turns

HAWKS, EAGLES, KITES, ETC.

and makes a direct, powerful attack, taking the prey by surprise. Sometimes makes steeper direct dives without this kind of stealthy approach.

NESTING   In breeding season, pairs may circle high in air, calling. In another display, bird flaps to high elevation while calling and then dives steeply, almost to ground. **Nest:** Site is typically in tall tree such as cottonwood or pine, along river or near cliffs; tree is often somewhat isolated and is usually among the largest in the vicinity. Nest is usually more than 30 feet above ground, up to 100 feet or higher. Sometimes nests on cliff ledges. Nest is a bulky platform of sticks lined with green leafy twigs. Same nest site may be used for many years. **Eggs:** 2, sometimes 1–3. White (or pale bluish white when freshly laid), sometimes with a few spots of tan or gray. Incubation is probably by the female only, about 35 days. **Young:** Probably the female stays with the young during the first two weeks after they hatch, while the male brings food and female gives it to the young; later, both sexes hunt. Young are able to fly in about 6–7 weeks.

MIGRATION   Most withdraw from United States in winter, although a few are seen in southern Texas at that season.

CONSERVATION STATUS   Uncommon and local, and has disappeared from some former nesting areas. Loss of nesting sites, such as tall cottonwoods along streams, may be a factor in declines.

RED-TAILED HAWK *Buteo jamaicensis*

This is the most widespread and familiar large hawk in North America, bulky and broad-winged, designed for effortless soaring. An inhabitant of open country, it is commonly seen perched on roadside poles or sailing over fields and woods. Although adults usually can be recognized by the trademark reddish brown tail, the rest of their plumage can be quite variable, especially west of the Mississippi: Western Red-tails can range from blackish to rufous-brown to nearly white.

Red-tailed Hawk

HABITAT   *Open country, woodlands, prairie groves, mountains, plains, roadsides.* Found in any kind of terrain that provides both some open ground for hunting and some high perches. Habitats may include everything from woodland with scattered clearings to open grassland or desert with a few trees or utility poles.

FEEDING   **Diet:** *Varied, includes small mammals, birds, reptiles.* Diet varies with location and season. Mammals such as voles, rats, rabbits, and ground squirrels often major prey; also eats many birds (up to size of pheasant) and reptiles, especially snakes. Sometimes eats bats, frogs, toads, insects, various other creatures; may feed on carrion. **Behavior:** Does most hunting by watching from a high perch, then swooping down to capture prey in its talons. Also hunts by flying over fields, watching for prey below. Small prey carried to perch, large prey often partly eaten on ground.

NESTING   In courtship, male and female soar in high circles with shrill cries. Male may fly high and then dive repeatedly in spectacular maneuvers; may catch prey and pass it to female in flight. **Nest:** Site is variable. Usually in tree, up to 120 feet above ground; nest tree often taller than surrounding trees. Also nests on cliff ledges, among arms of giant cactus, or on artificial structures such as towers or buildings. Nest (built by both sexes) a bulky bowl of sticks lined with finer materials, often with leafy green branches added. **Eggs:** 2–3, sometimes 4, rarely 1–5. Whitish, blotched with brown. Incubation is by both parents, 28–35 days. **Young:** Female remains with young most of the time during first few weeks. Male brings most food, and female tears it into small pieces to feed to the young. After about 4–5 weeks, food is dropped into nest and the young feed themselves. Young leave the nest about 6–7 weeks after hatching, but not capable of strong flight for another 2 weeks or more. Fledglings may remain with parents for several more weeks.

MIGRATION   Northern Red-tails may migrate far to the south, while many at central or southern latitudes (especially adults) are permanent residents. Most migration is relatively late in fall and early in spring.

CONSERVATION STATUS   Widespread and common. Apparently has increased in some areas since the 1960s, and numbers now stable or still increasing.

FERRUGINOUS HAWK   *Buteo regalis*

This regal bird is the largest of our soaring *Buteo* hawks, a fitting raptor for the wide skies and windswept plains of the west. It soars with its broad wings held in a shallow "V," and swoops down to catch ground squirrels, snakes, young jackrabbits, and other good-sized prey. It is often seen sitting on the ground in open fields. Except when nesting, the Ferruginous Hawk seems curiously unafraid of humans, often allowing close approach.

Ferruginous Hawk

HABITAT   *Plains, prairies.* Found at all seasons in very open and dry country. Inhabits dry grassland, sagebrush plains, saltbush and greasewood flats, rangeland, desert. In winter, also in agricultural country, including over plowed fields.

FEEDING   **Diet:** *Mostly small to medium-sized mammals.* Feeds on most readily available small prey, such as young jackrabbits, ground squirrels, pocket gophers, kangaroo rats; also cottontails, mice, others. Also eats birds, snakes, large insects. **Behavior:** Hunts by watching for prey while soaring high, flying low, or from a raised perch. Sometimes waits on ground near active burrow of pocket gopher, then catches the rodent as it comes to surface.

NESTING   Pairs may circle high above nesting territory, calling. **Nest:** Site is usually in top of tree, 20–50 feet above ground, but can be as low as 6 feet (available trees may be very short). Sometimes nests on cliff or on ground. Nest is bulky structure of sticks and debris lined with finer materials, including cow dung. Historically, some nests were built of bison bones and lined with bison dung. Nest may be reused and added to annually until it becomes huge. **Eggs:** 2–4, sometimes up to 6 or more. Pale bluish white fading to white, usually marked with brown. Incubation is by both sexes, but female does more; male brings food to her. Incubation period 32–33 days. **Young:** Female remains with young at first; male brings food, female feeds it to young. After about 3 weeks, both parents hunt. Age of young at first flight about 40–50 days.

MIGRATION   Mostly a short-distance migrant; some southern breeders may be permanent residents. Very rarely strays east of normal range.

CONSERVATION STATUS   *Threatened.* Has declined seriously over most of its range; current population may be fewer than 4,000 pairs. Causes of decline include shooting, loss of habitat.

ROUGH-LEGGED HAWK   *Buteo lagopus*

Of our soaring *Buteo* hawks, this is the only one tied to cold climates. It nests in the Arctic, mostly in tundra regions north of the boreal forest; in winter, only a few move farther south than the central United States. Its breeding success on the tundra is often dictated by the population cycles of lemmings, which may provide most of the food for the young. The name "Rough-legged" refers to the feathering that extends down the legs to the base of the toes—a helpful adaptation for staying warm in frigid weather.

Rough-legged Hawk

HABITAT   *Tundra escarpments, Arctic coasts; in winter, open fields, plains, marshes.* Spends the winter in open country, including grasslands, coastal prairies and marshes, farmland, dunes. Breeds mostly on tundra, in areas having cliffs for nest sites; some breed along northern edge of coniferous forest zone.

FEEDING   **Diet:** *Mostly rodents.* On breeding grounds, feeds heavily on lemmings and voles. During high population cycles, lemmings may be more than 80 percent of summer diet. Also eats many birds. In winter and migration, eats voles, mice, ground squirrels, other small mammals, plus occasionally birds, frogs, insects. May readily feed on carrion in winter. **Behavior:** Often hunts by hovering over fields, watching for movement below. Also hunts by watching from a perch or patrolling low over ground.

NESTING   In breeding season, members of pair circle together high in air. One may perform sky dance, alternately flapping to high elevation and then diving steeply. **Nest:** Site is usually on a narrow ledge or niche in high cliff. Sometimes nests on slopes, atop large rocks, even on level ground. At edge of forest, may nest in top of tree. Nest is a bulky structure of sticks, bones, debris, lined with grasses and twigs. **Eggs:** Usually 3–5, sometimes 2–6. In some areas, supposedly may lay more eggs in years when rodents are abundant. Eggs pale bluish white, fading to white, blotched with brown and violet. Incubation is by female, roughly 31 days (male may sometimes sit on eggs briefly). During incubation, male brings food for female. **Young:** Female remains with young at first; male brings food, female feeds it to young. Later, both parents hunt. Age of young at first flight about 5–6 weeks, and they remain with parents for another 3–5 weeks.

MIGRATION   Migrates relatively late in fall and early in spring. Numbers appearing south of Canada are quite variable from one winter to the next.

CONSERVATION STATUS   Local populations in the Arctic go up and down, largely as a result of rodent populations there. Overall numbers of Rough-legged Hawks are apparently healthy.

GENUS *Aquila*

GOLDEN EAGLE   *Aquila chrysaetos*

This magnificent bird is widespread in the wilder country of North America, Europe, and Asia. About the same size as the Bald Eagle, the Golden is less of a scavenger and more of a predator, regularly taking prey up to the size of foxes and cranes. The Golden Eagle was important to many Native American tribes, who admired the eagle's courage and strength and ascribed mystical powers to the bird and even to its feathers.

HABITAT   *Open mountains, foothills, plains, open country.* Requires open terrain. In the north and west, found over tundra, prairie, rangeland, or desert; very wide-ranging in winter, more restricted to areas with good nest sites in summer. In forested eastern North America, often hunts over marshes or along rivers.

FEEDING   **Diet:** *Mostly small mammals.* Typically preys on mammals ranging in size from ground squirrels up to prairie-dogs, marmots, and jackrabbits. May take smaller rodents (voles and mice) or larger animals such as foxes, young pronghorns, or young deer on occasion. Also eats birds, mostly gamebirds such as grouse but rarely birds as large as cranes or as small as sparrows. Also some snakes, lizards, large insects. Will feed on carrion, including dead fish. **Behavior:** Searches for prey by soaring high or flying low over slopes; also watches for prey from high perches. When prey is spotted, the eagle plunges to capture it in talons. Members of a pair sometimes hunt together, with the second bird capturing prey that evades the first.

NESTING   May mate for life. In courtship, two birds circle high in air, making shallow dives at each other. Display to defend territory includes repeated high flight followed by steep dives, loops, rolls, and other acrobatics. **Nest:** Site is most often on cliff ledge, also frequently in large tree, rarely on ground. Sites may be used for many years. A pair may have two or more alternate nest sites, using them in different years. Nest (built by both sexes) a bulky platform of sticks lined with weeds, grass, leaves, moss. New material is added each year, and the nest may become huge. **Eggs:** 2, sometimes 1–3, rarely 4. Whitish to buff, marked with brown. Sometimes one egg in the clutch is unmarked. Incubation is by both parents (female does more), 41–45 days. **Young:** Female remains with young most of the time at first, while male does most hunting, bringing prey to nest. After young are half-grown, female also does much hunting. Age of young at first flight roughly 60–70 days.

MIGRATION   Northern birds are migratory, mostly moving late in fall and early in spring. In western United States and southwestern Canada, many adults may be permanent residents, but young birds may migrate south in fall.

CONSERVATION STATUS   Has undoubtedly declined from historical levels, but current populations thought to be stable. May not be able to tolerate human disturbance near the nest.

Golden Eagle

FALCONS AND CARACARAS (Family Falconidae)

Noble birds, magnificent hunters, some of the fastest of all fliers—falcons are universally admired. About 60 species are found worldwide. Indeed, one species, the famous Peregrine Falcon, nests on every continent except Antarctica.

Typical falcons are predatory birds with pointed wings and long tails, built for very fast flight. The larger kinds may dive from very high above the ground to catch birds in midair; it is in these power dives, or "stoops," that the falcons achieve their highest speeds, and it has been claimed that the Peregrine can reach 200 miles per hour. Falcons have relatively large eyes and very keen eyesight, necessary for their style of hunting.

The art of falconry—training falcons or hawks to hunt and bring back wild game—apparently goes back many centuries. Although there are still dedicated falconers today, the practice is strictly regulated by law, and only a few people are well qualified to care for these birds.

Aside from the typical falcons, the family also includes a few other groups. In the American tropics there are the slow-flying caracaras, most of which are scavengers; the Laughing Falcon, a snake-eater; and the forest-falcons, with short rounded wings like the *Accipiter* hawks, pursuing small birds in agile flight through dense forest. There are also several falconets and pygmy-falcons in the Old World tropics, feeding mainly on insects. The comments below apply only to the typical falcons unless noted otherwise.

Feeding All of the typical falcons are predators, but they are also opportunists, and a few are known to feed on carrion at times. The smaller species (such as kestrels) specialize on large insects but will take a wide variety of other small creatures. Larger falcons often specialize on birds but may take small mammals or other creatures given the opportunity.

Prey is located by sight and always caught with the feet, but hunting methods are quite variable. The birds may drop to capture prey on the ground, pursue their prey in level flight, or dive from above to strike birds in the air. Kestrels often hover while hunting, but the larger species do not.

Nesting The same pair of falcons may nest together, and use the same site, for several years. In fact, some good nesting sites have been used by falcons for generations. Larger falcons usually nest on cliff ledges or on old nests of other birds in trees, while kestrels usually nest in cavities. In any case, the falcons typically add no nest material themselves. Usually three to five eggs are laid. In many species, the female does most of the incubating, and the male brings food to her; after the eggs hatch, the female often remains with the young while the male hunts for the whole family. Male falcons usually are noticeably smaller than females and may be better suited to taking abundant small prey.

Displays Many of the typical falcons have courtship display flights, featuring spectacular dives and chases. Some of the same types of actions may be used as threat displays against other falcons that come too near the nest.

GENUS *Caracara*

CRESTED CARACARA   *Caracara plancus*

Related to the typical falcons but very different in shape and habits. The Crested Caracara is a strikingly patterned, broad-winged opportunist that often feeds on carrion. Aggressive; may chase vultures away from road kills. Found throughout the American tropics, it enters our area only near the Mexican border and in Florida. "Caracara" comes from a South American Indian name based on the bird's call.

HABITAT   *Prairies, rangeland.* Lives in a wide variety of semi-open habitats offering open ground for hunting and dense cover for nesting. In our area these include wet prairies of Florida, Texas coastal plain, desert in Arizona. Found in other kinds of open terrain in American tropics.

FEEDING   **Diet:** *Carrion, small animals.* Feeds on a wide variety of smaller creatures, either captured alive or found dead. Diet includes rabbits, ground squirrels, skunks, various birds (plus their eggs and young), frogs, snakes, lizards, turtles, young alligators, fish, large insects. **Behavior:** An opportunist, hunting and scavenging in a variety of ways. Often hunts by flying low, taking small animals by surprise. Flies along highways early in morning, searching for road kills. May steal food from other birds. May scratch on the ground for insects or dig up turtle eggs.

Crested Caracara

NESTING   In courtship, two birds may toss heads back repeatedly while giving guttural call. Members of a pair may preen each other's feathers. **Nest:** Sites vary, usually 8–50 feet above ground in top of shrub or tree, such as live oak, cabbage palm, acacia; in Arizona, sometimes in giant cactus. Nest is a bulky structure of sticks, weeds, debris, sometimes built on top of old nest of other species. Nest may be reused annually, with more material added each year. **Eggs:** 2–3, rarely 4. Pale brown, blotched with darker brown. Incubation is reportedly by both sexes (although female may do more), about 30 days. **Young:** Both parents bring food to young in nest. Age of young at first flight varies, probably usually 6–8 weeks. Young may remain with parents for several weeks after fledging.

MIGRATION   Adults are typically permanent residents on territory. Young birds may wander considerable distances.

CONSERVATION STATUS   Has declined in parts of U.S. range because of shooting and habitat loss. Some evidence of recent increases in Texas. The distinctive race on Guadalupe Island, Mexico, became extinct in 1900.

GENUS *Micrastur*

COLLARED FOREST-FALCON   *Micrastur semitorquatus*

Very different from typical falcons, the forest-falcons of the American tropics live in densely wooded areas, pursuing birds and other prey in agile flight among the trees. They are usually hard to see, but their voices are loud and distinctive. The Collared Forest-Falcon has strayed north from Mexico to spend the winter in southern Texas at least once.

TYPICAL FALCONS — GENUS *Falco*

All of the fast-flying falcons of open country belong to this genus, which includes some 35 species worldwide and almost all of the North American species. All have pointed wingtips and fairly long tails.

EURASIAN KESTREL   *Falco tinnunculus*

The Eurasian replacement for our American Kestrel is a larger bird (a little larger than a Merlin). Widespread across Europe and Asia, it has strayed to our area from both directions, with scattered records for the northeast and for Alaska and British Columbia.

AMERICAN KESTREL   *Falco sparverius*

Our smallest falcon, the kestrel is also the most familiar and widespread in North America. In open country it is commonly seen perched on roadside wires or hovering low over a field on rapidly beating wings, waiting to pounce on a grasshopper. Kestrels nest in cavities in trees; in places where there are few large dead snags to provide nest sites, they may rely on nest boxes put up for them by conservationists.

HABITAT   *Open country, farmland, cities, wood edges.* Inhabits any kind of open or semi-open situation, from forest clearings to farmland to desert, wherever it can find adequate prey and some raised perches. In breeding season, may be limited to habitats that also provide appropriate nesting sites. In winter, females may tend to be found in more open habitats than males.

FEEDING   **Diet:** *Mostly large insects; also some small mammals, birds, reptiles.* Grasshoppers are among the favored prey, but many other large insects are taken, including beetles, dragonflies, moths, caterpillars, others. Also feeds on mammals (including voles, mice, and sometimes bats), small birds (sometimes up to the size of quail), lizards, frogs, earthworms, spiders, crayfish, other items. **Behavior:** Hunts mostly by watching from a high perch, then swooping down to capture prey. Sometimes, especially when no good perch is available, hovers over fields to watch for prey. May pursue and catch insects, birds, or bats in flight. Individual kestrels often specialize on one particular kind of prey.

NESTING   During courtship displays, female flies slowly with stiff, fluttering wingbeats, wings held just below horizontal. Male repeatedly flies high, calling, and then dives. Male brings food for female, passes it to her in flight. **Nest:** Site is in cavity, usually in dead tree or snag, sometimes in dirt bank or cliff or in old magpie nest. In southwest, often in holes in giant cactus. Also uses artificial nest boxes. Sites usually 10–30 feet up, but may be at any height. **Eggs:** 4–6, rarely 2–7. White to pale brown, usually spotted with brown and gray. Incubation is by both parents, usually 28–31 days. **Young:** Female remains with young most of time at first, while male brings food; after 1–2 weeks, female hunts also. Age of young at first flight about 28–31 days. Parents continue to feed young up to 12 days after fledging; later, these juveniles may gather in groups with young from other nests.

MIGRATION   Many kestrels in southern or middle latitudes are permanent residents, while northern birds may migrate far to the south. Young birds may tend to migrate farther than adults.

CONSERVATION STATUS   Counts of migrants suggest declining numbers in the northeast in recent years, but numbers elsewhere still healthy. Provision of nest boxes has helped populations in some areas.

American Kestrel

MERLIN   *Falco columbarius*

A rather small falcon, compact and fast-flying, the Merlin is a common breeder across the northern forests of North America and Eurasia. It feeds mostly on small birds, capturing them in midair in rapid pursuit. The Merlin is generally found in wild places, but since about 1960 it has become a common urban bird in several towns on the northern prairies; there it nests and remains to winter, relying on a steady supply of House Sparrows as prey.

HABITAT   *Open conifer woodland, prairie groves; in migration, also foothills, marshes, open country.* Generally breeds in semi-open terrain having trees for nest sites and open areas for hunting. Habitat varies from coniferous forest in north and on northwest coast to isolated deciduous groves and suburban yards on prairies. May winter in more open areas such as grasslands, coastal marshes.

FEEDING **Diet:** *Mostly small birds.* Often specializes on locally abundant species of birds (such as Horned Larks on the plains, House Sparrows in urban settings, small sandpipers on coast). Also feeds on large insects (especially dragonflies), rodents, bats, reptiles. **Behavior:** Does most hunting by watching from a perch, then flying out to capture prey in the air. Also hunts by flying low among trees or over ground, taking prey by surprise; seldom dives steeply from above to capture prey. Birds, insects, and bats are usually caught in midair.

NESTING In courtship, male performs spectacular flight displays, with steep dives, strong twisting flight, glides, rolling from side to side, fluttering with shallow wingbeats. Male brings food and presents it to female. **Nest:** Site is usually in tree in old nest of hawk, crow, or magpie, 10–60 feet above ground. Sometimes in large tree cavity, on cliff ledge, or on ground. Usually little or no material added to existing nest. **Eggs:** 4–5, sometimes 2–6. Whitish, lightly or heavily marked with reddish brown. Incubation is mostly by female, 28–32 days; male brings food to female, then he incubates while she eats. **Young:** Female remains with young most of time, brooding them when they are small. Male brings food, female takes it from him near nest and feeds it to young. Age of young at first flight about 29 days.

Merlin

MIGRATION Most Merlins migrate, some northern birds reaching South America. Those of Pacific Northwest (race *suckleyi*) are mostly permanent residents. Some prairie birds (race *richardsonii*) have become permanent residents in cities on northern plains during recent decades, while others there still migrate.

CONSERVATION STATUS Apparently increasing in numbers on northern prairies, numbers probably stable in other areas.

APLOMADO FALCON *Falco femoralis*

This trim, elegant falcon once nested in desert grassland of the southwest, but it has been very rare north of the Mexican border since the 1920s or before. Recently a few have reappeared in New Mexico and western Texas, and there has been an attempt to reintroduce the species in southern Texas.

EURASIAN HOBBY *Falco subbuteo*

This Eurasian falcon spends much of its time in the air, pursuing aerial prey in swift, agile, acrobatic flight. It has reached Alaska a few times. Three of the records there were of birds ranging over the ocean and stopping to rest on ships off the Aleutian Islands.

PEREGRINE FALCON *Falco peregrinus*

One of the world's fastest birds; in power-diving from great heights to strike prey, the Peregrine may possibly reach 200 miles per hour. Regarded by falconers and biologists alike as one of the noblest and most spectacular of all birds of prey. Although it is found on six continents, the Peregrine is uncommon in most areas; it was seriously endangered in the mid-20th century because of the effects of DDT and other persistent pesticides.

HABITAT   *Open country, cliffs (mountains to coast); sometimes cities.* Over its wide range, found in wide variety of open habitats, from tundra to desert mountains. Often near water, especially along coast, and migrants may fly far out to sea. Limited by availability of nest sites and prey; thus, it often moves into cities, nesting on building ledges and feeding on pigeons.

Peregrine Falcon

CONSERVATION STATUS

FEEDING   **Diet:** *Mostly birds.* Feeds on a wide variety of birds. Pigeons are often favored prey around cities, and ducks and shorebirds are often taken along coast; known to take prey as large as loons, geese, large gulls, and as small as songbirds. Also eats a few small mammals, seldom insects, rarely carrion. **Behavior:** Often hunts by flying very high, then stooping in spectacular dive to strike prey out of the air. Large prey may be knocked out of the air, fed upon on the ground where it falls. Also pursues prey in level flight after spotting it from a perch or while flying. May fly very low over ground or sea, taking prey by surprise.

NESTING   May mate for life. Territorial and courtship displays include high circling flight by male, spectacular dives and chases by both sexes. Male feeds female. Breeding Peregrines defend the immediate area of the nest from intruders but hunt over a much larger area. **Nest:** Site is usually on cliff ledge, sometimes in hollow of broken-off tree snag or in old stick nest of other large bird in tree. In some areas, may nest on ground on hilltop. Also uses ledges of buildings, bridges, other structures. Some sites may be used for many years. No nest built, eggs laid in simple scrape. **Eggs:** 3–4, sometimes 2–5, rarely 6. Whitish to pale reddish brown, heavily marked with warm brown. Incubation is mostly by female, 32–35 days. Male brings food for female during incubation. **Young:** Female stays with young at first, while male brings food for her and for young; later, female hunts also. Age of young at first flight 39–49 days.

MIGRATION   Permanent resident on northwest coast and in some temperate regions; northern breeders are long-distance migrants, many going to South America. Migrants often travel along coastlines and regularly occur well out at sea. Concentrations of pesticides from prey caused widespread failure to reproduce during 1940s–1970s, and the species disappeared from much of its former breeding range. Has been reintroduced in many temperate areas in North America, and Arctic nesting populations have also recovered somewhat.

GYRFALCON   *Falco rusticolus*

This formidable predator, the largest falcon in the world, reigns over barren tundra and desolate coasts in the high Arctic. There it preys mostly on large birds such as ptarmigan and waterfowl, overtaking them in powerful flight. Most Gyrfalcons remain in the far north all year; only a few come as far south as the Canadian border in winter, providing thrills for birders. Variable in color, Gyrs may be blackish, gray, or stunningly white.

HABITAT   *Arctic barrens, seacoasts, open mountains.* Breeds in Arctic regions having open tundra for hunting and cliffs for nest sites. Often occurs along coasts and rivers, where prey may be more abundant. Mostly in treeless country, but occurs along the edges of northern forest in some places. Wintering birds south of Arctic tend to be either along coast or in very open country inland.

FEEDING   **Diet:** *Mainly birds, some mammals.* Feeds mostly on medium-sized to large birds. Ptarmigan are mainstays of diet on Arctic tundra, while coastal Gyrs may take more

gulls, ducks, and geese, but numerous other species eaten on occasion. Also some mammals, including lemmings, ground squirrels, hares. Wintering birds in west have been seen taking birds as large as Sage Grouse. **Behavior:** Hunts by scanning its surroundings from a perch on a high rock or while flying. Prey may be taken by surprise, the falcon approaching very low over the ground, or may be pursued relentlessly in flight over long distances.

NESTING   Pairs may occupy nest sites very early in season, even in late winter. Members of pair display at nest site with bowing and scraping motions; male brings food to female. **Nest:** Most nest sites are on cliffs, and most are on old nests built by other birds, such as ravens or Golden Eagles. Sometimes breeds on open ledges with no nest structure present, and some-

Gyrfalcon

times uses old nests in trees, such as spruce or poplar (tree nesting is frequent in some areas). Does not add material to existing nests. **Eggs:** Usually 3–4, sometimes 2–5. White or creamy white, spotted with reddish brown. Incubation is by both parents (but female does more), about 35 days. **Young:** For first 1–3 weeks, young are brooded most of time, mostly by female; male does all or most of hunting during this time, bringing food which female feeds to the nestlings. After 2–3 weeks, female hunts also. Age of young at first flight about 45–50 days.

MIGRATION   Many adults are permanent residents in far north, even above Arctic Circle, but many immatures move southward for winter. Northernmost adult breeders may also migrate.

CONSERVATION STATUS   Has declined in parts of Arctic Europe, but North American populations are probably stable. Illegal taking of young for falconry could be a problem in some areas, but most nest sites are remote from human disturbance.

PRAIRIE FALCON   *Falco mexicanus*

A large falcon of the arid west. The Prairie Falcon is nearly the size of the famous Peregrine but differs in its hunting behavior, often pursuing small prey in rapid flight maneuvers close to the ground. Although characteristic of desolate plains and desert wilderness, this falcon has also adapted to altered landscapes: in winter, it is often seen flying over southwestern cities or hunting Horned Larks in farm country.

HABITAT   *Open hills, plains, prairies, deserts.* Typically found in fairly dry open country, including grassland and desert. Also in open country above treeline in high mountains. In winter, often found in farmland and around lakes and reservoirs, and may regularly winter in some western cities. Avoids forested country, and usually scarce on the immediate coast.

FEEDING   **Diet:** *Mostly small birds and mammals.* Often will focus on one abundant and easily caught prey species at a time. May feed heavily on ground

Prairie Falcon

squirrels in early summer, shifting to young songbirds when many are fledging; in winter, may feed on common flocking birds like Horned Lark. Many other species eaten, up to size of grouse and jackrabbits; also lizards, insects. **Behavior:** Uses a wide variety of hunting techniques. Often hunts by flying fast and low over ground, taking prey by surprise. Also will dive steeply from the air or pursue birds in flight.

NESTING   Courtship involves much flying about and calling near potential nesting ledges. Male performs aerial acrobatics, struts back and forth at nest site. **Nest:** Site is typically on a ledge of a cliff, in a recessed site protected by an overhang of rock. Sometimes nests on dirt bank or uses an abandoned nest of raven or hawk on ledge; rarely uses nest in tree. No nest built; only a simple scrape in gravel or dirt on ledge. **Eggs:** Usually 3–5, sometimes 2–6. Whitish, spotted with brown. Incubation is mostly by female, about 31 days. Male brings food to incubating female, and he may sit on eggs temporarily while she is eating. **Young:** Female remains with young for about the first 4 weeks; male brings food, and female feeds it to young. After 4 weeks, female may do some hunting. Young leave the nest at about 5–6 weeks after hatching.

MIGRATION   Many adults may be permanent residents near their nesting sites. Others move short distances south for winter. Some also move eastward somewhat on Great Plains after nesting season.

CONSERVATION STATUS   Has undoubtedly declined in some developed areas, but current population probably stable.

GUANS, CURASSOWS, AND CHACHALACAS (Family Cracidae)

The wilder regions of the American tropics are home to the 50 species of guans, curassows, and chachalacas (often referred to as cracids, short for the family name of Cracidae). These birds look somewhat like slender, long-tailed turkeys, except that they spend much of their time up in trees, bounding from branch to branch with great agility. Cracids usually build stick nests up in bushes or trees, seldom on the ground; their diets are mostly vegetarian. Only a few species have been studied in detail in the wild, because they are common mainly in wilderness areas: unable to take much hunting pressure, guans and curassows tend to disappear after roads are put in unless they are strictly protected. The smaller chachalacas—wary, sociable, noisy birds—may adapt a little better to the advance of civilization. One chachalaca is the only member of the family to reach our area.

GENUS *Ortalis*

PLAIN CHACHALACA   *Ortalis vetula*

Our only representative of a distinctive tropical family. Plain Chachalacas are common in a limited area of southern Texas, where flocks live in thickets or riverside woods. Frequently, especially at dawn and dusk, a flock will perch in a tall tree and give voice to a disorganized clattering chorus of *cha-cha-lac* calls.

HABITAT	*Subtropical woods, river groves, dense brush.* In south Texas usually found near water, as around ponds, resacas, riverbanks. Generally in native woodlands of ebony, hackberry, huisache, and mesquite, but also found around edges of overgrown orchards and well-wooded suburbs of Rio Grande Valley towns.
FEEDING	**Diet:** *Mostly berries, leaves, buds, seeds.* Diet in south Texas is mostly vegetarian, eating various parts of a wide variety of plants; includes berries of coyotillo, pigeonberry, hackberry, and others, plus seeds, leaves, buds, and flowers. Also eats a few insects and snails. Where accustomed to humans in certain parks, will come to eat birdseed, popcorn, bread, and other junk food. **Behavior:** Forages on ground or in shrubs and trees, often climbing about precariously in thin branches.

Plain Chachalaca

NESTING In southern Texas, usually nests in woods very close to water. **Nest:** Site is on limb or in fork of branches, sometimes in vines or broken-off stub, in tree within dense cover. Usually 4–15 feet above ground, sometimes up to 35 feet. Nest is a flat platform of sticks, twigs, weeds, leaves, Spanish moss, with a depression in the center; an old nest of some other bird may be used as the foundation. **Eggs:** 2–3, sometimes 4. Creamy white. Incubation is by female only, about 25 days. **Young:** Downy young leave nest shortly after hatching. Both parents care for young, feeding them by regurgitation at first. Young can flutter short distances within a few days after hatching, can fly up into brush at 2–3 weeks, but not full-grown until sometime later.

MIGRATION	Permanent resident.
CONSERVATION STATUS	In Texas, numbers probably stable, with good populations at a few protected parks and refuges. In Mexico and Central America, probably declining but still locally common.

GROUSE, PARTRIDGES, PHEASANTS, TURKEYS, AND QUAIL (Family Phasianidae)

The diverse creatures under this heading could be loosely defined as "chickenlike birds." In the past, the 200 or so species included here have been divided among three to five different families. Several kinds are familiar to many people because they have been domesticated. The world's most important bird—from an economic standpoint—is undoubtedly a type of pheasant: the Red Junglefowl, wild ancestor of the domestic chicken.

All the birds in this group spend most of their time on the ground, although many will take refuge in trees if they are alarmed, and some kinds of grouse do much of their feeding up in trees. They have relatively short, rounded wings and fly with bursts of quick wingbeats. Usually, it seems, they would rather walk than fly. Most kinds do not migrate any major distance.

Feeding   For this family as a whole, plant material makes up the great majority of the diet, but the details differ widely. Many of the grouse are almost entirely vegetarian, and they are among the few birds to browse heavily on leaves and conifer needles. Partridges and quail may eat mostly plant parts (including seeds, berries, buds, roots), varying the diet with many insects in summer. Turkeys and pheasants may be omnivores, sometimes eating small reptiles or rodents. In many cases, the young birds eat more insects than the adults, taking in protein for fast growth.

Most species feed mainly on the ground, and some will scratch in the soil to turn up buried roots or other items. Many will also feed in trees. Some of the northern grouse, for example, spend the winter feeding on buds or needles in trees.

Nesting Most birds in this family form traditional pairs, with a male and female remaining together through one nesting season. But there are exceptions, more than in most groups of birds. A male Ring-necked Pheasant may have a harem of several females. Males of some grouse and turkeys will mate with as many females as they can attract with their courtship displays.

Nests are almost always placed on the ground, although there are a few types of pheasants and others that will nest among branches or in tree hollows. Most of these birds lay large clutches of eggs, often up to 12 or 15 or even more than 20. Incubation is entirely by the female in most species. Typically the eggs in a nest all hatch within the space of a few hours, and the chicks leave the nest soon afterwards. Although they are tended by one or both parents, the chicks feed themselves. In many species, the young can fly short distances when they are only a few days old and still very small.

Displays Courtship displays of some birds in this family are truly dazzling. The display of a peacock (a type of pheasant), raising his fan-shaped train with its bold eyespots, is one example. The strutting of a male turkey, body puffed up and tail spread wide, is another. Spectacular group displays are performed by some prairie grouse, with up to several dozen males strutting, posturing, and calling to entice females to approach.

Displays of quail and partridges are less theatrical. Males usually defend nesting territories with loud calls, and their courtship activities include walking or running about on the ground near the female with fluffed feathers and odd postures.

GENUS *Tetraogallus*

HIMALAYAN SNOWCOCK   *Tetraogallus himalayensis*

Native to the Himalayan region of southern Asia, this huge grouse was introduced as a game bird in the Ruby Mountains of northern Nevada beginning in 1963. There it lives on steep and barren slopes above treeline, in remote areas that birders may visit only with a major effort. Small flocks of snowcocks often move uphill during the day, feeding as they go on roots, tubers, and seeds, and then glide down the slopes again in the evening.

The nest is a simple scrape on the ground, often sheltered from wind by nearby rocks or grass clumps. Usually 4–6 eggs are laid, buffy to grayish, spotted with reddish brown. Incubation is by the female, about 4 weeks. Young leave the nest shortly after they hatch; they are tended by both parents but find all their own food.

GENUS *Perdix*

GRAY PARTRIDGE   *Perdix perdix*

Because of its popularity as a game bird in Europe, the Gray Partridge was brought to North America as early as the 1790s, although it was not really established here until later. It has been most successful on the northern prairies, where it often does very well in farm country. Gray Partridges live in flocks, or coveys, at most times of year. Even where they are common, they often go unseen as they forage in the tall grass.

HABITAT   *Cultivated land, hedgerows, bushy pastures, meadows.* Mostly lives in grasslands and agricultural fields. Farmland is excellent habitat as long as hedgerows and shelterbelts are left between fields. In winter often in stubble fields, moving into edges of woodlots in harsh weather.

Gray Partridge

FEEDING   **Diet:** *Mostly seeds, also leaves and insects.* Eats seeds from a wide variety of plants, including many grasses and weeds, also waste grain from crops such as wheat, oats, corn, sunflower. Seeds are most of diet in fall and winter; eats more green leaves in spring, insects in summer. Young chicks eat mostly insects. **Behavior:** Forages in coveys most of year, alone or in pairs in spring. Takes most food from ground. In winter, may burrow into snow to reach seeds on ground.

NESTING   In courtship, male stands upright, flicks tail up and down, puffs out chest feathers to display dark belly patch and barred flanks; female approaches with bobbing movements of head. **Nest:** Site is on ground among dense cover, sometimes in open field but more often under hedgerow or shelterbelt or on brushy roadside. Nest (built by female, with male keeping watch nearby) is a shallow scrape lined with grass, leaves. **Eggs:** Usually 12–18, sometimes up to 22 or more, sometimes fewer than 10. Fewer eggs in later clutches. Eggs buff, brown, or olive. Incubation begins after last egg is laid; until that time, eggs are covered with grass and weeds when female is away from nest. Incubation is by female only, 21–26 days, usually 25. **Young:** All eggs usually hatch on same day, and downy young leave nest together with parents. Both parents tend young and may lead them directly to food, but young feed themselves. Young can make short flights at less than 2 weeks, may be full-grown at 3–4 months, remain with parents through first winter.

MIGRATION   North American populations apparently do not migrate. Some in eastern Europe may move south in particularly harsh weather.

CONSERVATION STATUS   North American population may be lower now than in 1950s, but still widespread, common in many areas.

GENUS *Alectoris*

CHUKAR   *Alectoris chukar*

Native to the Middle East and southern Asia, the Chukar was brought as a game bird to North America, where it has thrived in some arid regions of the west. From late summer to early spring, Chukars travel in coveys, but they may be hard to see as they range through the brush of steep desert canyons. They become more conspicuous in spring, when the harsh cackling *chuk chuk chukar* of the territorial males echoes from the rocky cliffs.

HABITAT   *Rocky, grassy, or brushy slopes; arid mountains, canyons.* Successfully introduced mainly around rocky cliffs, steep canyon slopes where winter snow will melt quickly, grassland mixed with sagebrush or saltbush. Needs cover of grass, brush; introduced cheatgrass is key element. Often in very dry country, but may require access to water unless it can eat plenty of green leaves.

FEEDING   **Diet:** *Seeds, leaves, berries, insects.* Diet varies with season. Many of the Chukar's major food plants are also introduced from Eurasia. Grasses provide

Chukar

much of food (seeds, leaves). In winter may feed mostly on seeds, such as cheatgrass and Russian thistle. Eats berries of Russian-olive and other plants. Spring and summer diet includes many green leaves, insects. **Behavior:** Feeds mostly on ground but will climb into shrubs and trees for berries. Forages in flocks in winter.

NESTING   In courtship, male displays by tilting head, circling female. Both members of pair go through mock feeding movements; male may feed female. **Nest:** Site is on ground, usually hidden under shrub or overhanging rock. Nest is a depression with substantial lining of grass, twigs, feathers. **Eggs:** 8–14, sometimes 6–20 or even more. Pale yellow to buff, spotted with reddish brown. Incubation typically by female only, 22–24 days. Female may sometimes lay two separate clutches of eggs, and male may incubate one while female incubates the other. **Young:** Leave nest shortly after hatching. Tended by one parent (usually female) or by both; role of the male in raising young still not well understood. Young mostly find their own food. Able to fly at 7–10 days, reach full size in about 2 months.

MIGRATION   Apparently a permanent resident throughout North American range. On native range in Eurasia, may move downslope in some mountainous areas or invade some deserts in winter.

CONSERVATION STATUS   Firmly established in some regions of western North America.

GENUS *Phasianus*

RING-NECKED PHEASANT   *Phasianus colchicus*

Ring-necked Pheasant

Most kinds of pheasants are shy forest birds of Asia. The Ring-neck, better adapted to open country, has been introduced as a game bird to several parts of the world, including North America. Here it thrives in some areas, such as the northern prairies, where the iridescent colors and rich crowing calls of the males add much to the landscape. Winter flocks of these pheasants often are segregated—small groups of males, larger flocks of females.

HABITAT   *Farms, fields, marsh edges, brush.* May live in any semi-open habitat. Sometimes in open grassland but more often in brushy meadows, woodland edges, hedgerows, farmland with mixed crops. Access to water may be important; pheasants are often common around edges of marshes and are rarely found in very arid places.

FEEDING   **Diet:** *Omnivorous.* Diet varies with season and place. Feeds on wide variety of grains and smaller seeds, fresh green shoots, buds, roots, berries, insects, spiders, earthworms, snails; rarely eats lizards, snakes, frogs, rodents. Diet may include more seeds in winter, more insects in summer. **Behavior:** Typically feeds on ground, sometimes in trees. On ground, scratches with feet or digs with bill to uncover food.

NESTING   Male defends territory by taking raised perch, giving crowing call while briefly drumming with wings. One male may have several mates, the females associating with each other in a small flock on his territory. In courtship, male struts in half-circle around female with

back and tail feathers tilted toward her, near wing drooping, face wattles swollen. **Nest:** Site is on ground in dense cover. Nest (built by female) is shallow depression lined with grass, leaves, weeds. **Eggs:** Usually 10–12, sometimes 6–15 or more. Plain olive-buff, rarely pale blue. Females sometimes lay eggs in each other's nests or in those of other birds; clutches of more than about 18 probably result from two or more females. Incubation is by female only, 23–28 days. **Young:** Downy young leave nest with female shortly after hatching; mostly feed themselves. Male may rarely accompany female and brood. Young capable of short flights at about 12 days but stay with female for 10–12 weeks.

MIGRATION   Apparently a permanent resident everywhere, both on native range and where introduced.

CONSERVATION STATUS   Intensively managed as a game bird in most areas where it occurs in North America. Some populations here probably not self-sustaining but are maintained by releases of game-farm birds.

FOREST GROUSE — GENUS *Dendragapus*

These dark, chunky birds of coniferous and mixed forests are hard to spot but are often remarkably tame when they are found. They do most of their feeding on the ground in summer, up in trees in winter. In breeding season, males give deep thumping calls, so low-pitched as to be almost inaudible.

SPRUCE GROUSE   *Dendragapus canadensis*

Spruce Grouse

Common in the north woods but very easy to overlook, the Spruce Grouse eludes many birders who seek it. Absurdly tame, it may sit motionless while observers pass by just a few feet away, and it may thus go unnoticed. Spruce Grouse are usually solitary in summer, but in winter they may gather in loose flocks. They readily perch in trees and do most of their feeding there in winter.

HABITAT   *Conifer forest, pines, muskeg.* Almost always in conifer forest but not necessarily in spruce. Prime habitat includes burned areas grown up to dense stands of jack pine or lodgepole pine, also forests of spruce, subalpine fir, hemlock, with dense undergrowth. Also on blueberry barrens. During dispersal in fall, sometimes found in deciduous woods.

FEEDING   **Diet:** *Mostly conifer needles.* Adults are mostly vegetarian, feeding heavily on needles of pines, spruce, other conifers. Diet may be almost entirely conifer needles in winter. At other times also eats fresh green shoots and leaves of other plants, berries, flowers, insects, snails, and fungi. Very young birds may eat more insects. **Behavior:** Does much of its foraging on the ground in summer; forages almost entirely in trees in winter.

NESTING   Both females and males defend individual territories in breeding season. Male displays by drumming with wings, making deep thumping sound audible only at close range. Males of Franklin's race (northern Rockies and Cascades) also make a loud wing-clap in flight. In courtship, male raises and spreads tail, fluffs out feathers, postures in front of female. One male may mate with several females.

Nest: Site is on ground under dense cover. Nest (built by female) is shallow depression, lined with a few needles and leaves. **Eggs:** 4–10, usually 5–7. Olive to buff, usually blotched with brown. Females of Franklin's race tend to lay fewer eggs. Incubation is by female only, about 20–24 days. When leaving nest, female may partly cover eggs with dry needles and leaves. **Young:** Downy young leave nest shortly after hatching. Female tends young, brooding them at night and in cool weather; young find all their own food. Young can make short flights at 6–8 days old, are full-grown at about 10–11 weeks, become independent at about 10–15 weeks.

MIGRATION   Most individuals are permanent residents, but some move short distances (less than 10 miles) between summer and winter territories. This "migration" is accomplished on foot. Females more likely to move than males, and tend to go farther.

CONSERVATION STATUS   Local populations fluctuate in numbers. May have declined in parts of southern edge of range, but still common in far north.

BLUE GROUSE   *Dendragapus obscurus*

A large, dark grouse of western mountains and coastal forests. Slow-moving and inconspicuous but often surprisingly tame. Most likely to be noticed (at least by sound) in spring, when males "sing" incessantly to attract mates, a series of deep hoots. Those along the Pacific coast may do their singing from more than 100 feet up in a dense evergreen tree.

HABITAT   *Deciduous and mixed forests in mountains in summer; conifer forests at higher elevations in winter.* Prime summer habitat for inland birds is where forest meets open country, such as sagebrush flats. In winter, these birds favor dense forests of conifers. Coastal birds may be in semi-open coniferous forest (old-growth or recently logged) all year.

Blue Grouse

FEEDING   **Diet:** *Conifer needles, leaves, insects.* Diet in summer is mostly leaves, flowers, buds, berries, and conifer needles; also many insects. Very young birds may eat more insects than adults. In winter feeds mostly on needles of conifers, including pines, hemlocks, firs, Douglas-firs. **Behavior:** Forages mostly on ground in summer, mostly in trees in winter, especially in inland areas with heavy snow cover.

NESTING   In breeding season, male gives deep song punctuated with short flights, wings fluttering loudly. Coastal males usually sing in trees; those from the interior usually sing on ground. In peak display, male struts with tail raised and fanned, neck feathers spread to reveal patches of bright skin. Female mates with male, then departs. **Nest:** Site is on ground, under cover such as shrub, log, rock ledge. Nest a shallow scrape lined with dead twigs, needles, leaves, a few feathers. **Eggs:** 5–10, sometimes 2–12. Pale buff, usually speckled with brown. Incubation is by female only, 25–28 days. **Young:** Usually leave nest within a day after hatching and follow female; young find all their own food. Female often fearless in defense of eggs or young, standing her ground when approached closely. Young can make short flights at age of 8–9 days, are full-grown at about 13 weeks.

MIGRATION   Most birds move in autumn from fairly open breeding areas to dense coniferous forest. In most parts of range, this involves moving uphill to spend the winter, an unusual kind of altitudinal migration. Maximum known travel is about 30 miles, but most go shorter distances. Birds may migrate entirely by walking or may intersperse short flights.

CONSERVATION STATUS   Still fairly common. Affected by forest management. May increase after clearcuts, but then declines as these grow up; does very poorly in even-aged tree farms as compared with original old-growth forest.

PTARMIGAN — GENUS *Lagopus*

Ptarmigan are grouse of the tundra, adapted for life in the high Arctic and on the highest mountains. Molting their body feathers twice a year, they go from mottled brown or gray in summer to white in winter, so that they are camouflaged at all seasons. In winter their feet are heavily feathered to the tips of the toes; these feathers increase the surface area of the feet and act as snowshoes, allowing the birds to walk easily over fresh drifts. They have exceptionally thick, downy plumage in winter to hold in warmth. On winter nights, like some other kinds of grouse, they often burrow into drifts to sleep, letting the insulating properties of the snow keep them warm.

WILLOW PTARMIGAN   *Lagopus lagopus*

Willow Ptarmigan

Aptly named, this common northern grouse is closely associated with thickets of dwarf willow on the tundra at all seasons. It occurs in isolated pairs at the beginning of the nesting season, but gathers in flocks in winter.

HABITAT   *Tundra, willow scrub, muskeg.* Generally found north of timberline, in lower wet tundra with abundant thickets of dwarf willow. Also in brushy openings within northern forest. In mountainous regions, lives near timberline or in open valleys in shrubby willow growth.

FEEDING   **Diet:** *Mostly buds, twigs, leaves, and seeds.* Adult almost entirely vegetarian, feeding heavily on willow, alder, birch, and other plants, eating the buds, leaves, and twigs. Also eats many berries, such as crowberry and blueberry, and eats some insects. Regularly swallows grit to help digest rough plant material. Young chicks feed mostly on insects and spiders at first, soon beginning to eat more plant matter. **Behavior:** Forages while walking by picking at vegetation, nipping off food with bill.

NESTING   In spring, male defends territory by displaying: raises red combs over eyes, throws head back, fans tail, droops wings, and struts about. Makes short flights, circling back to starting point while uttering harsh call. **Nest:** Site on ground, sometimes completely in open but often under willow shrub, grass clump, or other shelter. Nest (built by female) a shallow depression lined with grass, leaves, moss, feathers. **Eggs:** 5–14, usually about 7. Red when first laid, but dry to blotchy blackish brown with some pale areas. Incubation is by female only, 21–22 days. **Young:** Downy chicks leave nest with female a few hours after hatching. Female tends young (and broods them while they are small), but young feed themselves. Young capable of short flights at age of 10–12 days, but not full-grown for several weeks; remain with adult female until late summer.

MIGRATION   Seems to be less migratory than Rock Ptarmigan on average, but sometimes appears well south of the breeding range in winter.

Goes through population cycles, abundant in some years and scarce in others; generally common over its vast northern range, mostly remote from the impacts of human disturbance.

ROCK PTARMIGAN *Lagopus mutus*

A hardy grouse of barren ground in the high Arctic, well adapted to harsh surroundings. Well camouflaged by white winter plumage and mottled brown summer plumage; male molts later in spring than female, so early in the breeding season he remains conspicuously white while she becomes almost invisible against the tundra.

HABITAT   *Above timberline in mountains; bleak tundra of northern coasts.* Summers on relatively dry, open tundra, with rock outcrops and arid ridges mixed with areas of dwarf willow and birch, sedge meadows. On islands (such as Aleutians), may occupy all open habitats. In winter, many remain in summer habitat, but some move into shrubby areas, openings in northern forest.

Rock Ptarmigan

FEEDING   **Diet:** *Mostly buds, leaves, and seeds.* Adults are almost entirely vegetarian, feeding on buds, catkins, leaves, flowers, berries, and seeds. Major food sources include willow, dwarf birch, alder, saxifrage, crowberry. Also eats some insects, spiders, snails; young chicks feed on these items heavily at first. Regularly swallows grit to help digest rough plant material. **Behavior:** Forages while walking by picking rapidly at vegetation, nipping off food with bill. In winter, may sometimes follow herds of caribou or musk-ox, feeding where animals have scraped away the snow.

NESTING   Male defends territory in spring with conspicuous display flight: flaps very rapidly, glides high, then flutters to ground while giving staccato call. In courtship display, male raises red combs above eyes, fans tail, and walks in circles around female, dragging one wing on ground. **Nest:** Site is on ground in relatively barren, rocky area, usually near large rock. Nest (built mostly by female) is shallow depression, lined with small amounts of moss, lichen, grass, feathers. **Eggs:** 4–13, usually 7–9. Pale buff with brown spots. Incubation is by female only, usually about 21 days; begins after laying next to last egg. **Young:** Downy chicks leave nest with adult female within a day after hatching. Female tends young, but young feed themselves. Capable of short flights at 7–10 days, can fly fairly well at 10–15 days. Young are independent at age of about 10–12 weeks.

MIGRATION   Leaves northernmost parts of breeding range and highest mountains in winter, moving to lower elevations and southward. A regular influx to some areas south of breeding range, but not extending much south of tundra regions. Migrates in flocks.

CONSERVATION STATUS   May become locally scarce near Arctic settlements, but still very common over vast areas of northern wilderness.

WHITE-TAILED PTARMIGAN *Lagopus leucurus*

This elusive little ptarmigan, the smallest member of the grouse family in North America, lives far above timberline in mountains of the west. While the other ptarmigan are strictly northern, this one follows the cordillera of the high Rockies as far south as New Mexico. Easily overlooked, it may crouch motionless as hikers pass close by.

HABITAT *Rocky alpine tundra; mountains above timberline.* Summers above timberline, on rocky slopes with low vegetation (a few inches tall) or damp alpine meadows near

streams or snowfields. Sometimes in stunted growth just below timberline. Elevations from under 4,000 feet in Alaska to almost 14,000 feet in Colorado. In winter often moves slightly lower, to areas where willows and other plants extend above snow.

FEEDING **Diet:** *Mostly buds, leaves, twigs, and seeds.* Adults are almost entirely vegetarian, feeding on all parts of low alpine plants, especially buds, twigs, and leaves of willows. Also favors birch, alder, sedges, crowberry, and others. Very young chicks eat mostly insects at first, soon switching to more plants. Regularly swallows grit to help digest rough plant material. **Behavior:** Forages while walking, nipping off pieces of plants with bill. Feeds in flocks at most times of year (from late summer through winter).

White-tailed Ptarmigan

NESTING During breeding season, males and females defend individual territories. In courtship display, male raises red combs above eyes, spreads tail, struts and bows. Male usually remains with female until sometime during incubation. **Nest:** Site is on ground, usually in rocky area, matted willow thicket, or sedge meadow. Nest (built by female) is shallow depression lined with plant material, with a few feathers added. **Eggs:** 2–8, usually about 5. Pale cinnamon, spotted with dark brown. Incubation is by female only, 22–26 days. **Young:** Downy chicks leave nest a few hours after hatching. Female tends young and leads them to food, but young feed themselves. If danger threatens brood, female puts on distraction display, running in zigzags with wings dragging. Young can fly at 10–12 days, reach full size at 12–14 weeks. Brood gradually breaks up in fall, young birds joining winter flocks.

MIGRATION Most birds move to slightly lower elevation in winter, with some traveling as much as 14 miles from summer to winter range. Females tend to move farther than males.

CONSERVATION STATUS Most of habitat is remote from human disturbance, so still present in most of original range. Has been introduced into new sites including some in Oregon, California, and Utah.

GENUS *Bonasa*

RUFFED GROUSE *Bonasa umbellus*

Our most widespread and familiar grouse, found in woodlands from Alaska to Georgia. The low-pitched, thumping "drumming" of the male is often heard in spring, but only a careful stalker is likely to see him perched on a horizontal log, neck ruffs puffed out, drumming the air with his wings. In the interior of brushy woods, Ruffed Grouse may be seen walking on the ground or perched in trees. Where they are not hunted, they may be surprisingly tame.

HABITAT *Ground and understory of deciduous or mixed woods.* Over its wide range, found in a variety of woodland types. May favor mixed coniferous-deciduous forest, using

coniferous trees for shelter, taking buds of deciduous trees as a staple winter food. Seldom found in pure coniferous forest.

FEEDING   Diet: *Omnivorous.* Feeds mostly on plant material. Diet includes buds, twigs, leaves, flowers, catkins, berries, seeds. Also eats insects, spiders, snails, occasionally small snakes or frogs. Diet varies with season, includes many fruits and berries in summer and fall. Buds of trees are important in diet in winter, especially in far north, where food on ground is buried by snow. Young eat mostly insects at first. **Behavior:** Forages on ground, in shrubs, or high in trees.

Ruffed Grouse

NESTING   In spring, male establishes territory for courtship display. On log or other raised perch, male fans tail, raises crest and neck ruffs, and struts back and forth. Uses rapid stiff beats of wings to make accelerating drumming sound. Female is attracted to sound, mates with male. One male may mate with several females. **Nest:** Site is on ground in dense cover, usually next to log, rock, or base of tree, or under dense shrubs. Nest (built by female) is a depression lined with leaves, grass, pine needles, often a few feathers. **Eggs:** Usually 9–12, sometimes 6–15. Buff, sometimes spotted with brown. Incubation is by female only, about 23–25 days. **Young:** Downy young leave nest soon after hatching. Female tends young and leads them to feeding sites, but young feed themselves. Young can make short flights at age of 1–2 weeks, but not full grown for several more weeks.

MIGRATION   Permanent resident, but may make short seasonal movements to areas with more dense cover for winter.

CONSERVATION STATUS   Local populations rise and fall in regular cycles, but generally widespread and common.

GENUS *Centrocercus*

SAGE GROUSE   *Centrocercus urophasianus*

Well-named, this very large grouse is found nowhere except in sagebrush country of the west. It nests on the ground among the sage, and sage leaves are its staple diet in winter. The Sage Grouse is best known for the spectacular courtship displays of the males: large numbers (up to 70 or more) will gather in spring on traditional dancing grounds and strut with their chests puffed out and spiky tails spread, hoping to attract females.

HABITAT   *Sagebrush plains; also foothills and mountain slopes where sagebrush grows.* Found on open plains, high valleys, rocky mesas, mountainsides, but only in vicinity of sagebrush. Prime nesting habitat includes some lower, wet areas where young can forage for insects. In very dry country, may fly several miles to water in morning and evening.

Sage Grouse

FEEDING   Diet: *Mostly sage leaves and buds, also insects.* Diet in fall and winter may be almost entirely the leaves and fresh shoots of sagebrush. At other seasons, also eats leaves, flowers, and buds of a wide variety of plants; also some insects in summer (young eat many insects at first). Unlike most grouse, digestive system is not adapted for digesting hard seeds. **Behavior:** Forages by walking on ground, browsing leaves and other plant parts, or picking up items from ground.

NESTING   Traditional display grounds may be used for years. In courtship display, male puffs out white chest, inflates two yellow air sacs, raises and spreads tail, droops wings; head is thrown back on shoulders as air sacs are deflated with loud popping sound. Females visit display ground to mate with one of the males. Oldest and most experienced males compete for positions at center of display ground, and these males are usually chosen by females. **Nest:** Site is on ground, under sagebrush or clump of grass. Nest (built by female) is shallow depression, sparsely lined with plant material. **Eggs:** Usually 7–9, sometimes 6–13. Olive-buff, evenly dotted with brown. Incubation is by female only, 25–27 days. **Young:** Downy young leave nest shortly after hatching. Young are tended by female but feed themselves. Able to make short flights at age of 1–2 weeks but do not reach adult size until much later.

MIGRATION   Mainly a permanent resident, but may perform some local movements, abandoning some high-elevation valleys in winter.

CONSERVATION STATUS   Has disappeared from much of former range. Loss of habitat (through clearing for farmland and overgrazing) is main cause. Probably still declining in some areas.

PRAIRIE GROUSE — GENUS *Tympanuchus*

Like the Sage Grouse, these three smaller species are best known for the courtship displays of the males. Large numbers gather in spring on traditional dancing grounds or booming grounds, where they display to attract females. All three of our species are far less common today than they were historically; they have declined mostly because of loss of habitat.

GREATER PRAIRIE-CHICKEN   *Tympanuchus cupido*

At one time, the eerie hollow moaning of male prairie-chickens displaying on their spring booming grounds was a common sound across much of central and eastern North America. Today the prairie-chickens are quite uncommon and localized; the race on the Atlantic seaboard, the Heath Hen, became extinct in 1932. Greater Prairie-Chickens still thrive on a few areas of native grassland in the Midwest.

Greater Prairie-Chicken

HABITAT   *Native tallgrass prairie.* Prime original habitat apparently was where prairie was intermixed with oak woodland. Currently found in areas of tallgrass prairie (especially native prairie, now a rare type), including places where such habitat is interspersed with agricultural fields.

FEEDING   **Diet:** *Mostly seeds, leaves, insects.* Winter diet is mostly leaves and seeds, also waste grain in agricultural fields. Historically, may have eaten many acorns in winter, and still may do so where they are available. In summer eats a variety of leaves, buds, seeds, berries, and insects. Young birds eat more insects. **Behavior:** Forages mostly on the ground, occasionally in trees. Most feeding in early morning and evening.

NESTING   In spring, males gather on booming grounds and display there to attract females. Booming ground often on low hill, with good visibility; typically 8–20 males present, exceptionally up to 70. In display, male lowers head and raises tail, inflates air sacs on neck, raises feather tufts, stamps feet rapidly while making hollow moaning sounds; may leap in the air with loud cackles. Female visits booming ground, mates with one of the males. **Nest:** Site is on ground, among thick tall grass. Nest (built by female) is shallow depression lined with grass, leaves, feathers. **Eggs:** Usually 10–12, sometimes 7–17. Olive to pale buff, speckled with dark brown. Incubation is by female only, 23–25 days. **Young:** Follow female away from nest shortly after hatching. Young find all their own food. Can make short flights at about 2 weeks, stronger flights at 3 weeks. Young usually remain with female for almost 3 months.

MIGRATION   Some individuals are permanent residents, others may move between breeding and wintering areas, traveling as much as 100 miles. No obvious or consistent differences in habitat between breeding and wintering sites.

CONSERVATION STATUS   Atlantic coast race (Heath Hen) became extinct in 1932; Texas coast race (Attwater's) is seriously endangered. Loss of habitat is single greatest threat to remaining populations in interior.

LESSER PRAIRIE-CHICKEN   *Tympanuchus pallidicinctus*

A little smaller and paler than the Greater Prairie-Chicken, this grouse is adapted to arid shortgrass regions of the southern Great Plains. At one time it was abundant in this region, but it has declined seriously and is now an uncommon bird found in a few local concentrations.

Lesser Prairie-Chicken

HABITAT   *Sandhill country, sage and bluestem grass, oak shinnery.* Found in sandy shortgrass prairie regions with scattered shrubs such as sand sage. Often found around stands of low, scrubby oaks (Havard and Mohr's oak, also called shin oak). Regularly comes to agricultural fields to feed on waste grain but disappears from areas where too much of native prairie is taken over by farmland.

FEEDING   **Diet:** *Includes seeds, acorns, insects, leaves.* Diet varies with season. Eats seeds and leaves of a wide variety of plants, including oak leaves and acorns. May eat much waste grain around agricultural fields in fall and winter. Eats many insects, including grasshoppers and beetles, especially in summer. Also eats some flowers, twigs, oak galls. **Behavior:** Forages mostly on ground, sometimes above ground in oaks. May move several miles every day from roosting areas to good feeding sites.

NESTING   In spring, at dawn and again in evening, males gather on booming grounds and display there to attract females. Booming ground on slight rise or level open ground with good visibility. In display, male raises feather tufts on neck, stamps feet rapidly while making hollow gobbling sounds; may leap in the air with loud cackles. Female visits booming ground, mates with one of the males. **Nest:** Site is on ground, usually under a shrub or clump of grass. Nest (built by female) is shallow depression lined with a few bits of grass, weeds. **Eggs:** Usually 11–13. Whitish to pale buff, finely speckled with brown and olive. Incubation is by female only, 22–24 days. **Young:** Downy young leave nest shortly after hatching. Female tends young, but young feed themselves. Young are able to make short flights at age of 1–2 weeks but are not full-grown for several more weeks.

MIGRATION   No regular migration, but some may move many miles between summer and winter ranges.

CONSERVATION STATUS   Has disappeared from most of former range and is probably still declining; considered to be threatened. Biggest problem is conversion of natural prairie to farmland.

SHARP-TAILED GROUSE   *Tympanuchus phasianellus*

The Sharp-tailed Grouse is typical of regions that have open grassland mixed with groves of trees or shrubs. Closely related to the prairie-chickens, it is found mostly farther north. On winter nights it may roost by burrowing into snowdrifts, where the snow helps insulate it from the cold.

HABITAT   *Prairie, brushy groves, forest edges, open burns in coniferous forest.* Prime habitat includes a mixture of open prairie with groves of deciduous trees or shrubs, such as aspen, birch, willow. Shifts habitat with season, occupying more open grasslands in summer, groves of trees and shrubs in winter.

FEEDING   **Diet:** *Mostly seeds, buds, leaves.* Largely vegetarian for most of year. In winter, when food on ground is often buried by snow, feeds heavily on buds of trees and shrubs. In spring, eats leaves, green shoots, large numbers of flowers. Varied diet in fall, with seeds, berries, leaves, waste grains. Insects eaten mainly in summer (especially by young

Sharp-tailed Grouse

birds), including many grasshoppers. **Behavior:** Forages mostly on ground in summer, mostly in trees and shrubs in winter.

NESTING   In early mornings in spring, males gather on display ground. Male points tail up, spreads wings, holds head low, stamps feet rapidly while moving forward or in circles. Male inflates neck sacs, then deflates them with hollow cooing sound; also rattles tail feathers. Female visits display grounds, mates with one of the males. **Nest:** Site is on ground, under shrub or thick clump of grass. Nest (built by female) is a shallow depression with a sparse lining of grass, leaves, ferns. **Eggs:** 5–17, typically about 12. Olive-buff to pale brown, usually speckled with various browns. Incubation is by female only, about 23–24 days. **Young:** Downy young leave nest shortly after hatching. Female tends young and leads them to feeding areas, but young feed themselves. Young can make short flights at age of 1–2 weeks but are not full-grown for several more weeks.

MIGRATION   No major migration, but birds may move several miles with the season to reach optimum habitat for summer or winter.

CONSERVATION STATUS   Has disappeared from some parts of former range (especially southern areas), and may still be declining. Loss of habitat is main cause.

GENUS *Meleagris*

WILD TURKEY   *Meleagris gallopavo*

Benjamin Franklin would have preferred to have the Wild Turkey, not the Bald Eagle, chosen as the national symbol of the United States. Although the barnyard

variety is a rather stupid creature (leading to the insulting tone of the word *turkey*), the original wild form is a wary and magnificent bird. Wild Turkeys usually get around by walking or running, but they can fly strongly, and they typically roost overnight in tall trees. Turkeys are sometimes considered to belong to a separate family from other chickenlike birds; there are only two species, ours in North America and the Ocellated Turkey in Central America.

HABITAT *Woods, mountain forests, wooded swamps.* Habitats vary in different parts of continent, include oak-hickory forest, pine-oak forest, cypress swamps, arid mesquite grassland, pinyon-juniper woodland, chaparral. Usually found near some kind of oak (acorns are a favorite food). Best habitat

Wild Turkey

includes a mixture of woodland and open clearings.

FEEDING **Diet:** *Omnivorous.* Diet varies with season but is mostly plant material, including many acorns, leaves, seeds, grains, berries, buds, grass blades, roots, bulbs. Also eats insects, spiders, snails. Sometimes eats frogs, lizards, snakes, salamanders, crabs. **Behavior:** Forages mostly by walking on ground. Often scratches in leaf litter to expose food items. Sometimes climbs in shrubs or trees to eat berries. May forage most actively in early morning and evening.

NESTING In spring, male gives gobbling call to attract females. In courtship, males puff out feathers, raise and spread tail, swell up face wattles, droop wings; in this exaggerated posture they strut, rattling the wing feathers and making humming sounds. One male will mate with several females. **Nest:** Site is on ground, often at base of tree, under shrub, or in tall grass. Nest is shallow depression, sparsely lined with grass, leaves. **Eggs:** Usually 10–15, sometimes 4–18, rarely more. White to pale buff, dotted with reddish brown. Sometimes more than one female will lay eggs in one nest. Incubation is by female only, 25–31 days. **Young:** Downy young leave nest soon after hatching. Female tends young and broods them at night for several weeks; young feed themselves. Young can make short flights at age of 1–2 weeks, but not full-grown for several months.

MIGRATION Not migratory, but may wander at some seasons, especially in fall.

CONSERVATION STATUS Numbers seriously depleted by beginning of 20th century, but has been reintroduced to most of former range and established in new areas. Apparently still increasing in many regions.

QUAIL — GENERA *Cyrtonyx, Colinus, Callipepla,* and *Oreortyx*

The quail of the New World are so different from other chickenlike birds that they are often placed in a separate family. Our species live in grassy or brushy areas and gather in small flocks called coveys at most times of year, when they are not nesting. Members of a covey often stay in contact with loud and distinctive call notes.

MONTEZUMA QUAIL *Cyrtonyx montezumae*

Despite its bold and bizarre pattern, this little quail of the Mexican border regions can be remarkably hard to see. When approached, pairs or coveys of Montezuma Quail may crouch motionless until they are practically stepped upon; then they explode into flight, to whir away across the hillsides. Fall and winter coveys usually

have fewer than 10 birds, and they often range over a very limited area.

HABITAT   *Grassy oak canyons, wooded mountain slopes with bunchgrass.* Presence of tall grass and usually oaks seem to be main requirements. Found in open oak or pine-oak woodland, open grassy hills with scattered trees, sometimes in openings in coniferous forest higher in mountains. Avoids low deserts.

FEEDING   **Diet:** *Bulbs, insects, seeds.* The bulbs of various plants (including wood sorrel and nut-grasses) may be a major part of the diet. Also eats many insect larvae and pupae, acorns and other nuts, various seeds, and berries and small fruits.
Behavior: Does much of its foraging by digging in soil with its feet to dig up bulbs, or scratching with its feet in leaf litter under the oaks to uncover insects or seeds. Forages in pairs or in family groups.

Montezuma Quail

NESTING   In Arizona, nesting is mostly in mid to late summer, timed to the summer rains. May nest earlier in spring farther east. Male defends nesting territory with a purring trill—soft, but audible for some distance. **Nest:** Site is on ground in tall grass. Nest (built by female, possibly with help from male) is well constructed; shallow depression lined with grass, with more grass domed over top and often hanging down over small entrance on side. **Eggs:** 10–12, sometimes 8–14. White, often becoming stained in nest. Has a longer incubation than most quail, 25–26 days. Incubation is probably by female only. **Young:** Downy young leave nest soon after hatching, are accompanied by both parents. Adults may lead young to food, but young feed themselves. Young are capable of making short flights at about 10 days, reach adult size in about 10–11 weeks.

MIGRATION   Generally a permanent resident, but in northern part of range may move to lower elevations in winter.

CONSERVATION STATUS   Has disappeared or become scarce in parts of the southwest because of overgrazing. The same is probably happening in Mexico, but its status there is not well known.

NORTHERN BOBWHITE   *Colinus virginianus*

The only native quail in the east. Its whistled *bob-white!* call is a familiar sound in spring in farmland and brushy pastures. The birds are heard more often than seen; although not especially shy, they often keep within dense low cover. During fall and winter, bobwhites live in coveys, averaging about a dozen birds. At night they roost on the ground in circles, tails pointed inward, heads pointed out.

HABITAT   *Farms, brushy open country, roadsides, wood edges.* Found in a wide variety of semi-open habitats, including brushy meadows, overgrown fields, or where pastures or agricultural fields are next to hedgerows or woodlots. "Masked Bobwhite" of southwest inhabits ungrazed native grasslands.

FEEDING   **Diet:** *Includes seeds, leaves, insects.* Diet varies with season and place. Eats many seeds (especially those of legumes), also leaves, buds, berries, acorns, roots, insects, spiders, and snails. May eat mostly seeds in winter, with more insects eaten in summer. Young birds may eat mostly insects at first. **Behavior:** Forages by walking on ground, head down, searching for food by sight; sometimes moves up into vines or shrubs. Feeds in flocks (coveys) at most seasons, alone or in family groups during breeding season.

NESTING In courtship, male turns head to side to show off pattern, droops wings, fluffs up feathers, makes short rushes at female; also walks slowly around female with tail fanned, feathers fluffed up. **Nest:** Site (apparently chosen by both members of pair) is on ground among dense growth. Nest (built by both sexes) is shallow depression lined with grass, leaves. Grass and weeds are often woven into an arch over nest, making it very well hidden, with entrance at one side. **Eggs:** Usually 12–16. White to pale buff. Incubation is by both sexes, 23–24 days. **Young:** Downy young leave nest shortly after hatching; are tended by both parents but feed themselves. If danger threatens young, parents may put on distraction display. Young can make short flights at 1–2 weeks, not full-grown for several more weeks.

Northern Bobwhite

MIGRATION Permanent resident throughout range, which extends south to Guatemala.

CONSERVATION STATUS At northern edge of range, many may be killed by unusually harsh winters. "Masked Bobwhite," extinct in Arizona and endangered in Mexico, is now being reintroduced into southern Arizona.

SCALED QUAIL *Callipepla squamata*

Scaled Quail

Dry southwestern grasslands provide a home for this blue-gray quail. Coveys of Scaled Quail travel about on foot; even when disturbed, they tend to run rather than fly. In the concealing cover of the short grass they can be inconspicuous except in spring, when males often call from atop fenceposts or exposed rocks. At night, coveys of Scaled Quail roost on the ground in dense low growth.

HABITAT *Grasslands, brush, arid country.* Prime habitat is flat open country or rolling hills, supporting a mix of grasses with annual weeds, with scattered shrubs for additional cover and shade. Also found where grassland grades into other open habitat types such as desert, juniper slopes, dry brush.

FEEDING **Diet:** *Seeds, insects.* Eats seeds of many annual and perennial weeds (such as snakeweed, Russian thistle, broomweed), seeds of woody plants (such as mesquite); seems to eat relatively few grass seeds, but perhaps more than some quail. Also feeds on green leaves, berries. Eats more insects than most quail, especially in spring and summer. **Behavior:** Forages in coveys at most seasons, in pairs or singly during early part of breeding season.

NESTING In breeding season, unmated males perch on tops of shrubs, rocks, or posts and give hoarse, single-noted call to defend territory and attract females. **Nest:** Site is on ground, usually well hidden under shrub, tumbleweed, cactus, or other cover. Nest (probably built by female) is shallow depression lined with grass and leaves, with tuft of standing grass arched over it. **Eggs:** Usually about 12, sometimes 5–16 or more. Whitish, speckled with light brown. Incubation is mostly by female, rarely by male, about 22–23 days. **Young:** Leave nest shortly after hatching. Both parents tend young, with male often standing guard on higher perch while female and young feed on the ground. Young feed themselves. Development of young and age at first flight not well known. One brood per year, rarely two.

MIGRATION Permanent resident throughout its range.

CONSERVATION STATUS Local populations rise and fall. Reproduction may be poor in dry years. Moderate grazing may improve habitat for this species, but overgrazing degrades habitat.

GAMBEL'S QUAIL *Callipepla gambelii*

The Sonoran desert is the home of this distinctive bird. Gambel's Quail is often abundant near desert streams and waterholes, with coveys walking to the water in the morning and evening, giving a variety of clucking and crowing notes. As cities have grown in the desert southwest, these birds have adapted to life in the surrounding suburbs, coming into backyards to eat grain scattered for them. At night, coveys of Gambel's Quail roost in bushes or low trees.

Gambel's Quail

HABITAT *Brushy desert, canyons.* May be in very dry country, but concentrates near sources of water. Favors typical Sonoran desert, with open ground and wide variety of shrubs, low trees, and cactus; often around mesquite thickets. Avoids unbroken grassland with no shrubs. May be common in open suburbs where some land is left undeveloped.

FEEDING **Diet:** *Mostly seeds, leaves, berries.* Adults apparently are largely vegetarian at most seasons. They eat many fresh plant shoots, leaves, and buds, especially in spring. Cactus fruits and the berries of mistletoe, hackberry, and other plants are eaten when available. Seeds are important in the diet at all times. Usually few insects are eaten, although young birds may eat more. **Behavior:** Forages in flocks from late summer to early spring. Does most feeding on ground but readily goes up into shrubs and low trees for berries, leaves, buds.

NESTING In breeding season, male gives clear descending note from high perch. Mated pairs spend much time exploring territory, apparently prospecting for good nest sites. **Nest:** Site is usually on ground, in shade of shrub or grass clump; sometimes above ground on stump or on old nest of thrasher or roadrunner. Typical ground nest (probably built by female) is shallow depression lined with grass, leaves, twigs. **Eggs:** 10–12, sometimes more. Dull white to pale buff, rather heavily marked with brown. Two females sometimes lay eggs in one nest. Incubation is by female only, 21–24 days. **Young:** Downy young leave nest within a day after hatching and follow parents. Both parents tend young and lead them to food sources, but young feed themselves. Young can fly short distances at age of 10 days but are not full grown until later. One brood per year, two in years with good food supply.

MIGRATION Permanent resident throughout its range.

CONSERVATION STATUS Local populations rise and fall, apparently reproducing poorly in very dry years. Overall population seems stable.

CALIFORNIA QUAIL *Callipepla californica*

This sharply marked bird with the curving topknot is common along the California coast and in a few other areas of the west. It has adapted rather well to the

GROUSE, PARTRIDGES, PHEASANTS, TURKEYS, AND QUAIL

increasing human population and is often found around well-wooded suburbs and even large city parks. California Quail live in coveys at most seasons and are often seen strutting across clearings, nodding their heads at each step. If disturbed, they may burst into fast low flight on whirring wings.

HABITAT   *Broken chaparral, woodland edges, coastal scrub, parks, farms.* May be most common in open oak woodland and in streamside growth bordered by chaparral, but also found in suburbs, semi-desert situations, pinyon-juniper woods, grassland, coastal sage scrub. Where introduced farther inland, may be in other brushy habitats. Avoids mountains.

FEEDING   **Diet:** *Mostly seeds and leaves.*

California Quail

Feeds on a wide variety of plants, especially annual weeds, eating the seeds, leaves, and fresh shoots. Also eats acorns, berries, flowers, bulbs, insects. **Behavior:** Forages mostly by picking up items from ground, often scratching on ground, and picking leaves from plants. Along roads, may feed on acorns that have been cracked open by passing cars. In neighborhoods with good plant cover, comes into yards to eat grain or birdseed.

NESTING   During breeding season, males call loudly to advertise territory. In courtship, male postures with wings drooped, tail spread; bobs head and may rush at female. **Nest:** Site is usually on ground, under a shrub or brushpile or next to a log or other cover. Sometimes nests above ground, on broken-off branch or in old nest of another bird. Typical nest on ground (probably built by female) is a shallow depression lined with grass and leaves. **Eggs:** 10–16, usually 13–14. Dull white to pale buff, variably marked with brown. Two females sometimes lay eggs in same nest. Incubation is by female only, about 18–23 days. **Young:** Downy young leave nest within a day after hatching. Both parents tend young, with female often brooding them when small, male perching high and acting as sentinel; young feed themselves. Young can fly short distances at age of 10 days but are not full grown until later. One brood per year, two in years with good food supply.

MIGRATION   Permanent resident throughout its range.

CONSERVATION STATUS   Adapts fairly well to the vicinity of civilization, but declining in some regions as coastal areas become more and more built up.

MOUNTAIN QUAIL   *Oreortyx pictus*

In foothills and mountains of the far west, coveys of these striking birds scurry through the manzanita thickets. Mountain Quail are often overlooked because they keep to dense cover; when approached, they often sit motionless in the brush, where they are very difficult to spot. They become more conspicuous in spring, when the rich call notes of the males, given at long intervals, echo across the slopes.

HABITAT   *Dense brush in wooded foothills and mountains.* Most common in pine-oak woodland, coniferous forest, and chaparral; sometimes in pinyon-juniper woods or in scrub at lower elevations. May be common in areas of second-growth brush after fires or clearcuts. Requires dense low thickets for cover. During hot weather, rarely found more than a mile from water.

FEEDING   **Diet:** *Includes seeds, bulbs, leaves, berries, insects.* Diet varies with season. Eats large amounts of seeds, bulbs, acorns; fair amounts of green leaves,

Mountain Quail

flowers, berries; also some insects, fungi. **Behavior:** Has a wide variety of foraging techniques. Picks up items from ground, often scratching among leaf litter; uses feet to dig for bulbs; climbs in shrubs and trees to pick berries, leaves; jumps up from ground to reach seeds and berries in low plants.

NESTING   Males call in breeding season to defend territory. In courtship, male faces female, fluffs feathers, droops wings. **Nest:** Site is on ground in dense cover, usually sheltered by a shrub, log, or grass clump. Nest is a shallow depression, lined with grass, pine needles, leaves, feathers. **Eggs:** 9–10, sometimes 6–15. Creamy white to pale buff. Incubation is apparently by both sexes (female may do more), about 24 days. **Young:** Downy young leave nest shortly after hatching; are tended by both parents and led to food, but young feed themselves. Parents are very active in defense of young, putting on distraction displays to lure away predators. Development of young and age at first flight not well known. Usually one brood per year, sometimes two at low elevations or in very good conditions.

MIGRATION   Unlike other North American quail, may regularly migrate in some areas, but only short distances. Migrates on foot, moving to lower elevations for winter.

CONSERVATION STATUS   Still reasonably common in highlands over most of its range. May have disappeared from northern limits in southwestern British Columbia (but possibly was introduced there, not native).

RAILS, GALLINULES, AND COOTS (Family Rallidae)

Rails and coots belong to the same family, but they represent opposite approaches to life near the water's edge. Coots (and their relatives the gallinules) behave like ducks, gathering in flocks, swimming conspicuously on open water, and walking about on shore. Rails, by contrast, are solitary and sneaky birds, hiding in dense marshes, frequently active at night, and more often heard than seen.

About 140 species in the family range over every continent except Antarctica and many islands, including some in midocean. Rails in general appear to be weak fliers, and some of the island forms are completely flightless; paradoxically, however, their ancestors must have flown great distances to colonize those islands in the first place. This points up one of the odd traits of the family: despite their seemingly weak flight, rails sometimes stray hundreds or even thousands of miles outside their normal ranges.

Feeding   Most members of the family are omnivores, although some concentrate on plant material (such as seeds, leaves, and roots) and some feed mainly on aquatic insects, crustaceans, and other invertebrates. Larger species may eat some frogs, fish, and the eggs or nestlings of other birds.

Rails forage mostly while walking about in damp areas of marshes, sometimes while swimming. Coots and gallinules forage while swimming or walking, and gallinules often climb about in shrubs above the water. Coots regularly dive and swim underwater to find food. Some rails and gallinules will carry food to edge of water and "wash" it before eating it.

Nesting   Nest sites are usually well hidden among dense growth in the marsh, either on the ground or up in reeds or shrubs above shallow water. Coots may build floating nests, anchored to standing marsh plants. Nests of many species have ramps of plant material leading down from the edge of the nest to the ground or the water. Usually 5–10 eggs are laid; incubation is by both parents or by the female only.

The downy chicks leave the nest soon after hatching, and young coots and gallinules can swim well almost immediately. Several birds in this family build additional nest platforms near the one used for incubating the eggs, and the young may be brooded at night on one of these extra nests. In most species, both parents help feed the young.

Displays   Many rails seem to defend their territories mainly by voice; intruders may be actively chased away. Chases also figure into the courtship activities of several species. Other courtship displays include both members of a pair preening each other's feathers; the male may posture and bow or strut back and forth, and he may feed the female. Many species repeatedly raise their short tails as they walk, flashing the white feathers under the tail; this action may be used as part of the display both in aggression and in courtship.

GENUS *Coturnicops*

YELLOW RAIL   *Coturnicops noveboracensis*

Yellow Rail

One of the most secretive birds in North America, almost never seen under normal conditions, although its metallic clicking calls may echo across northern prairie marshes on summer nights. Rarely flies in the daytime except under extreme pressure. Somewhat erratic in occurrence on the breeding grounds: may be common at a given locale in wet years, scarce or absent in dry years.

HABITAT   *Grassy marshes, meadows.* In summer, favors large wet meadows or shallow marshes dominated by sedges and grasses. Typically in fresh or brackish marsh with water no more than a foot deep. In winter mostly in coastal salt marsh, especially drier areas with dense stands of spartina; also rice fields, damp meadows near coast.

FEEDING   **Diet:** *Mostly insects, snails, seeds.* Diet not well known, but small freshwater snails reported to be important at some seasons. Eats a wide variety of insects (especially aquatic ones), also spiders, small crustaceans, probably earthworms. Also eats many seeds, at least in fall and winter. **Behavior:** Foraging of wild birds essentially unknown. Yellow Rails in captivity feed only by day, picking food from ground, plants, or water.

NESTING   Male defends territory by calling, mostly at night. In courtship, male and female may preen each other's feathers. **Nest:** Site is in shallow part of marsh, on damp soil or over water less than 6 inches deep. Nest is shallow cup of sedges and grasses with concealing canopy of dead plants above it. May build more than one nest, with extra(s) being used for brooding the chicks after they leave their hatching nest. Male takes part in starting nests, but female completes the work. **Eggs:** Usually 8–10. Buffy white, with reddish brown spots around larger end. Incubation is apparently by female only, about 17–18 days. Male may remain near nest during incubation. **Young:** Apparently fed by female only. Remain in nest only about 2 days, then follow female about in marsh. When not foraging, female and brood go to second nest (not the one in which the eggs hatched). Young find much of their own food after 2 weeks, all of it after 3 weeks; probably able to fly at about 5 weeks.

MIGRATION   Migrates at night. Very rarely detected in migration, but individuals are sometimes found when they stop over in city parks or other spots with little cover. Migrates south mostly in September and October, north mostly in April and early May.

CONSERVATION STATUS   Undoubtedly has declined in this century, especially at southern end of breeding range, because of loss of habitat. Localized race in central Mexico is probably endangered if not extinct.

GENUS *Laterallus*

BLACK RAIL   *Laterallus jamaicensis*

A tiny marsh bird, no bigger than a sparrow. Extremely secretive, it walks or runs through the marsh and is rarely seen in flight. In very dense cover, it may get around by using runways made by mice. The distinctive short song of the Black Rail is given mostly late at night, so the bird may go unnoticed in some areas. Fairly common at a few coastal points, its status inland in the east is rather mysterious.

HABITAT   *Tidal marshes and salicornia on coast; grassy marshes inland.* Favors very shallow water or damp soil with scattered puddles. In coastal marsh, upper limits of highest tides; inland, mostly wet meadows. Found in dense stands of spartina and other grasses, salicornia, rushes, sedges.

FEEDING   **Diet:** *Insects, snails, seeds.* Probably a generalized feeder on small items in its habitat. Feeds on wide variety of insects, including aquatic beetles. Also eats spiders, snails, small crustaceans. Eats many seeds of bulrush and other marsh plants, especially in

Black Rail

winter. **Behavior:** Foraging behavior poorly known. Although the birds often call late at night, they apparently feed mostly by day while walking through marsh.

NESTING   Nesting behavior not thoroughly studied. **Nest:** Site is usually a couple of inches above ground or shallow water in a clump of vegetation, often at a spot slightly higher than surrounding marsh. Nest is a well-constructed cup of marsh plant material, usually with a domed top woven over it. A ramp of dead vegetation leads from nest entrance down to ground. Adults may continue to add to nest, building it up to higher level, in areas where nest might be threatened by high tides. **Eggs:** 3–13, usually 6–8. White to pale buff, dotted with brown. Eastern race may tend to lay more eggs than western race. Incubation is by both sexes, 17–20 days. **Young:** Downy young leave nest within a day after hatching. Both parents probably care for young and feed them; details of development of young and age at first flight not well known.

MIGRATION   Eastern Black Rails are somewhat migratory, withdrawing from northern areas in winter, but those in the west apparently are permanent residents.

CONSERVATION STATUS   Has probably declined in most parts of North American range, drastically so in upper Midwest. Loss of habitat is main threat. Where habitat is protected, numbers probably stable.

CORN CRAKE   *Crex crex*

This chunky rail lives in rank weedy fields and damp meadows in Europe, sometimes in upland fields far from water. In former times it occurred as a very rare
stray to northeastern North America, but since the 1920s there have been only
two records.

TYPICAL RAILS — GENUS *Rallus*

These birds are medium-sized to large and have rather long, thin bills. (The smaller
rails, such as Sora, Yellow Rail, and Black Rail, are often referred to collectively as
crakes.) Typical rails tend to eat more animal life and less plant material than crakes.

CLAPPER RAIL   *Rallus longirostris*

A clattering cackle in the salt marsh is often our first clue to the presence of this
big rail. The Clapper Rail is usually hidden in dense cover, but sometimes we see it

stalking boldly along the muddy edge of the marsh,
twitching its short tail as it walks, or swimming across
a tidal creek. Historically it was abundant on the
Atlantic coast — Audubon reported that it was possible
to find a hundred nests in a day — but now much more
localized, as coastal marsh has been broken up
by development.

HABITAT   *Salt marshes, rarely brackish;
locally in mangroves in southeast, fresh marshes in
southwest.* Along most of Atlantic and Gulf coasts and
locally on Pacific coast, strictly a bird of salt marsh,
sometimes in adjacent brackish marsh. In Florida, also
found in shallow mangrove swamps. "Yuma" Clapper
Rail in southwest inhabits freshwater marsh along
Colorado River and nearby areas.

Clapper Rail

FEEDING   **Diet:** *Includes crustaceans, insects,
fish.* Diet varies with locality and includes a wide variety of small prey. Crustaceans
often favored, especially crabs, also crayfish and others. Also eats many aquatic insects, small fish, mollusks, worms, frogs. Eats seeds at times. **Behavior:** Forages by
walking in shallow water or on mud, especially on falling tide or at low tide, picking
up items from the ground or vegetation, sometimes probing in mud or water.

NESTING   In courtship displays, male approaches female, points bill down,
and swings head from side to side; also stands erect with neck stretched, bill open.
Male may feed female. **Nest:** Site is in clump of grass or other vegetation in marsh,
near the upper reaches of high tide or on bank near water. Nest (built by both sexes,
although male may do more) is well-built cup of grasses and sedges, lined with finer
material, often with vegetation woven into a canopy over nest. Often a ramp of plant
material leads from ground up to nest. **Eggs:** Usually 7–11, sometimes 5–12 or more.
Pale yellow to olive-buff, blotched with brown and gray. Incubation is by both sexes,
20–23 days. **Young:** Downy young may leave nest soon after hatching. Both parents
probably feed young. Parents may brood young in a separate nest from the one in
which the eggs hatched. Young can fly in about 9–10 weeks.

MIGRATION	Found all year in most parts of range. On Atlantic coast, some withdrawal in winter from northern end of range, and an influx of northern birds is noted in parts of the southeast in winter.
CONSERVATION STATUS	Western populations endangered; has seriously declined in parts of the east. Loss of habitat is main threat.

KING RAIL   *Rallus elegans*

King Rail

A chicken-sized marsh bird, the largest of our rails. Nesting in freshwater marshes of the east, the King Rail has become an uncommon species as many wetlands have been drained. It remains locally common near the Atlantic and Gulf coasts, where it is not especially shy, often stalking about at the marsh edge in full view of observers. Closely related to the Clapper Rail and may interbreed with it in zones where salt and fresh marshes meet.

HABITAT   *Fresh and brackish marshes, rice fields, swamps. Sometimes salt marshes in winter.* Will use a variety of habitats with shallow fresh or brackish water and dense cover. Important plants include cattails, bulrushes, spartina, and others. May be in brushy swamps with many willows or in flooded rice fields.

FEEDING   **Diet:** *Mostly insects and crustaceans.* Diet includes many aquatic insects, especially beetles. Eats many crayfish and crabs and sometimes many small fish. Also eats snails, clams, grasshoppers, frogs, spiders, and seeds of aquatic plants. **Behavior:** Mostly forages in shallow water, in or close to dense marsh cover. Large items such as big crayfish or crabs may be carried to solid ground and dismembered before being eaten.

NESTING   In courtship, male walks about with tail raised, showing off white undertail coverts. Male may feed female. **Nest:** Site is in a clump of grass or sedges, usually about a foot above water or land. Nest (apparently built mostly by male) is a solid platform of grass, sedges, other marsh plants, with a canopy woven over the top and a ramp leading down from the entrance. Additional simpler nest platforms may be built nearby. **Eggs:** Usually 10–12, sometimes 6–14. Pale buff, lightly spotted with brown. Incubation is by both sexes, 21–23 days. **Young:** Downy young leave nest a few hours after hatching. Both parents feed young; after about 3 weeks, young start to pick up much of their own food. While young are small, adults may brood them at simple nest platforms near where they hatched. Young are able to make short flights at about 9–10 weeks. May have two broods per year in south.

MIGRATION	Withdraws from most of northern and inland part of range in winter. Apparently migrates at night.
CONSERVATION STATUS	Has declined or disappeared in many areas because of loss of habitat. Also hurt by runoff of farm chemicals into wetlands. Numbers may be stable now at lowered population.

VIRGINIA RAIL   *Rallus limicola*

Seldom seen but often heard, this medium-sized rail lives in marshes across much of our continent. This bird and the Sora are often found together, but their diets differ: the short-billed Sora eats many more seeds, while the long-billed Virginia Rail eats

mostly insects. Virginia Rails communicate with a wide variety of calls, and some of these can be mystifying to listeners; one, dubbed the "kicker" call, was attributed to the elusive Yellow Rail for many years.

HABITAT *Fresh and brackish marshes; in winter, also salt marshes.* Nests in a variety of marshy situations, mostly fresh, but also brackish marsh near coast. Where this species and Sora breed in same marshes, Virginia Rail typically places its nest in drier spots. Often moves into salt marshes in winter. During migration, sometimes found in odd spots, even city streets.

FEEDING **Diet:** *Mostly insects, crayfish, snails; some seeds.* Feeds on a wide variety of aquatic insects and their larvae, especially beetles, flies, dragonflies, many others. Also eats crayfish, earthworms, snails,

Virginia Rail

slugs, a few small fish. Seeds may be important in diet at times. **Behavior:** Forages by probing in mud or shallow water, picking items from ground or from plants, or stalking small creatures and capturing them with a swift thrust of the bill.

NESTING In courtship, male runs back and forth near female with wings raised; male and female both make bowing motions; male feeds female. **Nest:** Site is in marsh, in dry area or over very shallow water, placed a few inches up in dense clump of vegetation. Nest (built by both sexes) is platform of cattails, reeds, grasses, usually with living plants forming a canopy over it. **Eggs:** 5–13. Pale buff, lightly spotted with brown and gray. Incubation is by both parents, about 18–20 days. **Young:** Downy young leave nest soon after hatching. Both parents feed young and brood them while they are small. Family remains on breeding territory until chicks are full-grown, then adults may depart, while young remain. Chicks are fed by parents until they are 2–3 weeks old, then become independent; are able to fly at about 25 days.

MIGRATION Some in west may be permanent residents. Most migrate as far as southern United States, northern Mexico; some as far as Guatemala. Another race is resident in South America.

CONSERVATION STATUS Has declined in many areas with loss of marsh habitat; still widespread and fairly common.

GENUS *Porzana*

SORA *Porzana carolina*

The Sora makes its presence known with plaintive whistles and whinnies rising from marshes all across North America. Despite its abundance, it is not often seen: as with other rails, it spends most of its time hidden in dense marshy growth or wet meadows. Occasionally it will walk about in full view at the edge of a pond, delighting any birders who happen to be nearby. Although Soras might seem like weak fliers when seen fluttering over the marsh, they regularly migrate long distances, many going to South America for the winter.

HABITAT *Fresh marshes, wet meadows; in winter, also salt marshes.* Occurs in a variety of marshy situations, from extensive river marshes to grassy edges of small ponds. Also in damp meadows, and sometimes in tall grass fields some distance from water. Breeds mostly in freshwater habitat with large stands of cattails, but moves into salt marshes at times, especially in winter.

Diet: *Mostly seeds, insects, snails.* At least at some seasons, feeds mainly on seeds, including those of smartweeds, sedges, grasses, other marsh plants. May feed heavily on wild rice in late summer and fall. Also eats a wide variety of insects, snails, other aquatic invertebrates. **Behavior:** Forages by picking items from surface of ground, water, or plants; sometimes probes with its bill in mud or among vegetation.

Sora

NESTING   Courtship displays by both members of a pair involve ceremonial preening, sometimes bowing, facing toward and then away from each other. **Nest:** Site is in dense marsh vegetation, especially cattails, sedges, bulrushes. Nest (built by both sexes) is well-built cup of dead cattails, grasses, other plants, lined with finer material, placed a few inches above water. Often has vegetation arched over top, and sometimes has ramp or runway of plant material leading to nest. **Eggs:** 10–12, sometimes 6–18. Rich buff, spotted with brown. Number of eggs is large for nest, so eggs are sometimes arranged in two layers. Incubation is by both sexes, 18–20 days. **Young:** Because incubation begins after first few eggs are laid, eggs do not hatch at same time; one parent may care for downy hatchlings while other continues to incubate remaining eggs. Young leave nest shortly after hatching, are fed by both parents. Age at first flight 21–25 days.

MIGRATION   Large numbers may gather in some marshes in late summer and early fall, feeding and building up fat reserves before migrating south. Apparently migrates mostly at night. Readily crosses bodies of water such as Gulf of Mexico, Caribbean Sea.

CONSERVATION STATUS   Apparently has declined in many parts of range with loss of freshwater marsh habitat. However, still widespread and common.

GENUS *Neocrex*

PAINT-BILLED CRAKE   *Neocrex erythrops*

This little rail is common but elusive in freshwater marshes in parts of South America. Although rails are known to be wanderers at times, scientists were surprised by the two North American occurrences of this species: once in Texas and once in Virginia, both in winter.

GENUS *Pardirallus*

SPOTTED RAIL   *Pardirallus maculatus*

A medium-sized rail, furtive in behavior but distinctive in pattern, inhabiting freshwater marshes in the American tropics. Apparently prone to wander; it has strayed once to Pennsylvania and once to Texas.

GENUS *Porphyrula*

PURPLE GALLINULE   *Porphyrula martinica*

This "swamp hen" is a striking bird, big, brightly colored, and noisy. With its strong legs and long toes, it runs about on open shorelines, walks on floating lily pads, and

clambers through marshes and waterside trees, flicking its short tail nervously. Nods its head as it swims; flies short distances with legs dangling conspicuously. Found mainly in the southeast and the tropics, but single birds sometimes stray far to the north at any season.

HABITAT *Fresh swamps, marshes, ponds.* In North America usually in extensive wetlands with still or slow-moving shallow water, lots of dense marsh cover and floating vegetation. In tropics may be found also on smaller ponds, ditches. During migration, individuals may stop over in odd habitats, even in cities.

FEEDING **Diet:** *Omnivorous.* Eats a wide variety of plant and animal matter, including seeds, fruits, and leaves of aquatic and terrestrial plants,

Purple Gallinule

also insects, frogs, snails, spiders, worms, fish. At times, eats the eggs and young of other birds. **Behavior:** Forages while walking on land, while climbing through marsh vegetation or waterside shrubs or trees, or while swimming.

NESTING Breeding behavior has been studied mostly in Costa Rica. May breed at any season in tropics, only in spring and summer in North America. **Nest:** Site is in dense marsh growth, over water that is often several feet deep. Nest (built by both sexes) is platform of cattails, grasses, sedges, firmly anchored to standing marsh vegetation, at water level or 1–3 feet above it. Often build extra nests. **Eggs:** 6–8, sometimes 5–10. Buff with brown spots. Incubation is by both sexes, 22–25 days. **Young:** May leave nest shortly after hatching, move to second nest.

In feeding young, parents are often assisted by other birds (as many as 8); these helpers evidently all are previous offspring of breeding pair, and juveniles less than 10 weeks old may help feed newly hatched chicks. Young are capable of flight at roughly 9 weeks.

MIGRATION Withdraws in winter from northern parts of breeding range. In United States in winter, found mostly in southern Florida. Strays may reach as far north as Canada at any season; these birds may originate from well to the south of us. Nomadic and migratory within South America as well. Despite seemingly clumsy flight, may travel long distances: strays sometimes cross the Atlantic, and this is one of the most frequent American wanderers to southern Africa.

CONSERVATION STATUS Still widespread in appropriate habitat, but undoubtedly has decreased with draining of swamps, and still vulnerable to loss of more wetlands.

AZURE GALLINULE *Porphyrula flavirostris*

A bird of South American swamps and marshes, strictly accidental in North America. The first record was of a bird found on Long Island, New York, in December. As surprising as this occurrence may seem, other members of its family have been known to wander very long distances at times.

GENUS *Gallinula*

COMMON MOORHEN *Gallinula chloropus*

Adaptable and successful, this bird is found in the marshes of five continents (it is replaced by similar moorhens in Australia). It swims buoyantly, bobbing its head; it also walks and runs on open ground near water and clambers about through reeds and cattails above the water. Related to the American Coot and often found with it, but not so bold, spending more time hiding in the marsh.

HABITAT *Fresh marshes, reedy ponds.* May be on still or slow-moving waters. Favors fresh marshes with some open water, ideally with some open ground and some dense cover along margins. Sometimes on more open ponds with only small amount of marsh cover. Found with American Coot in many places, but requires more marsh growth.

FEEDING **Diet:** *Omnivorous.* Major food items include leaves, stems, and seeds of various water plants, also fruits and berries of terrestrial plants. Also eats insects, spiders, earthworms, snails and other mollusks, tadpoles. Sometimes eats carrion, eggs of other birds. **Behavior:** Forages while swimming, walking on land, or climbing through marsh vegetation. While swimming, may dip head underwater or upend (tail up, head down); sometimes dives.

NESTING In courtship, male chases female on land; both stop, bow deeply, preen each other's feathers. Other displays involve lowering head and raising tail, exposing white patches under tail. **Nest:** Site is in marsh over shallow water, sometimes on ground or in shrub near water. Nest (built by both sexes) is solidly constructed platform (or wide, shallow cup) of cattails, bulrushes, reeds; often has a ramp of similar material leading down to water. Similar platforms built nearby may be used for resting or brooding. **Eggs:** 8–11, sometimes 5–13. Buff, irregularly spotted with brown. Incu-

Common Moorhen

bation is by both sexes, 19–22 days. **Young:** Can swim well shortly after hatching. Young fed by both parents, sometimes by older siblings from earlier broods; gradually learn to feed themselves, finding most of own food after about 3 weeks, though still fed sometimes by parents past 6 weeks. Young capable of flight at 40–50 days. One or two broods per year, rarely three.

MIGRATION Probably migrates at night. Some southern and coastal populations evidently permanent residents. Occasionally strays far from normal range.

CONSERVATION STATUS Undoubtedly has declined over much of range because of loss of wetlands. Still widespread and may be locally common where good marsh habitat exists within historical range.

COOTS — GENUS *Fulica*

About 10 species of coots are found worldwide, with the most variety in South America. These are the showoffs of the rail family, noisy and gregarious. They often quarrel among themselves as they swim about on open water or walk on the shore, nodding their heads as they go.

EURASIAN COOT *Fulica atra*

A common waterbird of Europe and Asia, where it replaces our American Coot. A massive winter storm that came across the Atlantic in December 1927 dropped a few Eurasian Coots in eastern Canada. There have been no records in North America since, aside from one bird in Alaska that undoubtedly strayed from Asia.

AMERICAN COOT *Fulica americana*

Coots are tough, adaptable waterbirds. Although they are related to the secretive rails, they swim in the open like ducks and walk about on shore, making themselves at home on golf courses and city park ponds. Usually in flocks, they are aggressive and noisy, making a wide variety of calls by day or night. They have strong legs and big feet with lobed toes, and coots fighting over territorial boundaries will rear up and attack each other with their feet. Often seen walking on open ground near ponds. When taking flight they must patter across the water, flapping their wings furiously, before becoming airborne.

HABITAT *Ponds, lakes, marshes; in winter, also fields, park ponds, salt bays.* For breeding season requires fairly shallow fresh water with much marsh vegetation. At other seasons may be in almost any aquatic habitat, including ponds or reservoirs with bare shorelines, open ground near lakes, on salt marshes or protected coastal bays.

Migrants sometimes are seen at sea some distance from land.

FEEDING **Diet:** *Omnivorous.* Eats mostly plant material, including stems, leaves, and seeds of pondweeds, sedges, grasses, and many others, also much algae. Also eats insects, tadpoles, fish, worms, snails, crayfish, prawns, eggs of other birds. **Behavior:** Wide variety of foraging methods—dabbles at surface of water, upends in shallows, dives underwater (propelled by feet), grazes on land. Also steals food from various ducks.

NESTING Very aggressive in defense of nesting territory. In courtship, male may pursue female across water. Displays include swimming with head and neck lowered, wings arched, tail raised to show off white patches. **Nest:** Site is among tall marsh vegetation

American Coot

in shallow water. Nest (built by both sexes) is floating platform of dead cattails, bulrushes, sedges, lined with finer materials, anchored to standing plants. Several similar platforms may be built, only one or two used for nesting. **Eggs:** 6–11, sometimes 2–12. Buff to grayish with brown spots. Nests with more than 12 eggs probably indicate laying by more than one female. Incubation by both sexes, 21–25 days. **Young:** Can swim well soon after hatching; follow parents and are fed by them. At night, young are brooded on a nestlike platform built by male. Young probably able to fly at about 7–8 weeks after hatching. One or two broods per year.

MIGRATION Some populations probably permanent residents, others migratory. May winter as far north as open water permits. Probably migrates mostly at night.

CONSERVATION STATUS Still abundant in many areas, but has decreased in recent decades in some areas, especially in east.

CARIBBEAN COOT *Fulica caribaea*

Coots nesting in parts of the Caribbean region are very much like our American Coot except for their swollen foreheads. Beginning in 1974, birds of this type were found repeatedly in Florida and were identified as Caribbean Coots. Since that time, however, similar birds have been found in several other areas, including Michigan and California, far from the Caribbean region. Many scientists now believe that these are all just variants of the American Coot.

LIMPKIN (Family Aramidae)

This odd wading bird is in a family by itself. The Limpkin is known for its wailing voice and its diet of giant snails.

GENUS *Aramus*

LIMPKIN   *Aramus guarauna*

Limpkin

Looking like something between a crane and a rail, this wader has no close relatives. It is widespread in the American tropics but enters our area only in Florida and southern Georgia, where it can satisfy its dietary requirement for a certain freshwater snail. Mostly solitary, Limpkins may be overlooked as they stalk about in marshes and swamps; they draw attention with their piercing banshee wails, often heard at dawn or at night.

HABITAT   *Fresh swamps, marshes.* In Florida, found in open freshwater marshes, along the shores of ponds and lakes, and in wooded swamps along rivers and near springs; locally in river swamps in Georgia. Throughout most of its tropical range, habitat and distribution are dictated by the presence of apple snails (*Pomacea*).

FEEDING   **Diet:** *Large snails.* Eats mostly large apple snails (genus *Pomacea*). In Florida, will also eat other kinds of snails and mussels; also sometimes insects, crustaceans, worms, frogs, lizards. **Behavior:** Forages by walking in shallow water, searching for snails visually, also by probing in mud and among floating vegetation. May feed at night, especially on moonlit nights. Moves to solid ground to remove snail from shell or to pound mussel open. The tip of the bill usually curves slightly to the right, which may help in removing snail from curved shell. The bill also usually has a slight gap just behind the tips of the mandibles, which may help in carrying and manipulating the snails.

NESTING   Breeding behavior not well known. May nest in loose colonies where food is abundant. **Nest:** Site varies; may be on ground near water, in marsh grass just above water, or in shrubs or trees above or near water, up to 20 feet high or sometimes much higher. Nest is a platform of reeds and grass, lined with finer plant material. **Eggs:** Usually 4–8. Olive to buff, blotched with brown and gray. Incubation is by both sexes, but incubation period not well known. **Young:** Downy young leave the nest within a day after hatching and follow one or both parents. Probably both parents feed young. Development of young and age at first flight not well known.

MIGRATION   In South America, may move around somewhat with wet and dry seasons. Permanent resident in limited range in United States. Strays have very rarely wandered farther north.

CONSERVATION STATUS   Limpkin had been hunted almost to extinction in Florida by beginning of 20th century; with legal protection, has made a fair comeback. Probably declining in parts of tropical range.

The name "crane" is often mistakenly applied to the Great Blue Heron, common all over North America. Real cranes are not so readily seen. Although they look superficially like herons or storks, the 15 species of cranes make up a distinct family with no close relatives.

Cranes are large and majestic birds. They walk on the ground with slow and stately tread, and fly with their long necks and legs fully extended, often giving a wild guttural bugling in flight. Widely admired by humans, they are considered to represent good luck in some Asian cultures. Despite being held in esteem, however, at least four species are now endangered; our own Whooping Crane came very close to extinction in the 1940s. Loss of appropriate wetlands habitat is the biggest problem facing the cranes of the world.

Most kinds of cranes gather in flocks outside the nesting season. For the most common species (such as our Sandhill Crane), these concentrations can run to spectacular thousands of birds. In migration they travel in flocks, pausing at traditional stopover points. Unlike many birds, which find their way by pure instinct in migration, young cranes apparently must learn their route from their elders.

In the wild, cranes may live 20–30 years or more.

Feeding Cranes are omnivores, feeding on a wide variety of small creatures as well as seeds, grain, roots, and berries. They forage while walking slowly in shallow water or on land. Much of their food is found by sight, but they also may use their bills to probe and dig in soil. They often forage in dry farm fields or prairies far from water.

Nesting Apparently often mate for life. Even cranes that feed in dry fields usually nest near water; the nest may even be built up in the shallows so that water surrounds it. The nest is a large mound or floating platform of plant material, sometimes mixed with mud, with a depression at the top for the eggs. Usually two eggs are laid, and both parents incubate, although the female may do more. Both parents tend and feed the young.

Displays The spectacular "dancing" displays of cranes involve two birds leaping in the air, flapping their wings, and calling. Although these are prominent as courtship displays in spring, they may be performed at other times of year by members of a mated pair. Cranes also have various postures used as threat displays against other members of their own species.

GENUS *Grus*

SANDHILL CRANE *Grus canadensis*

Found in several scattered areas of North America, Sandhill Cranes reach their peak abundance at migratory stopover points on the Great Plains. The early spring gathering of Sandhills on the Platte River in Nebraska is among the greatest wildlife spectacles on the continent, with over a quarter of a million birds present at one time. Although they are currently very common, their dependence on a few key stopover points makes them vulnerable to loss of habitat in the future.

HABITAT *Prairies, fields, marshes, tundra.* Habitat varies with region, but usually nests around marshes or bogs, either in open grassland or surrounded by forest. Northernmost birds nest on marshy tundra. In migration and winter, often around open prairie, agricultural fields, river valleys.

FEEDING **Diet:** *Omnivorous.* Diet varies widely with location and season. Major food items include insects, roots of aquatic plants; also eat rodents, snails, frogs, lizards, snakes,

Sandhill Crane

nestling birds, berries, seeds. May eat large quantities of cultivated grains when available. **Behavior:** See family introduction. Except in breeding season, forages in flocks.

NESTING   Courtship includes elaborate "dance," with birds spreading wings, leaping in air while calling. **Nest:** Site is among marsh vegetation in shallow water (sometimes up to 3 feet deep), sometimes on dry ground close to water. Nest (built by both sexes) is mound of plant material pulled up from around site; nest may be built up from bottom or may float, anchored to standing plants. **Eggs:** Usually 2, sometimes 1, rarely 3. Variably pale olive to buff, marked with brown or gray. Incubation is by both sexes, 29–32 days. Female does more of incubating (typically all night, part of day). **Young:** Leave the nest within a day after hatching, follow parents in marsh. Both parents feed young at first, but young gradually learn to feed themselves. Age at first flight about 65–75 days. Young remain with parents for 9–10 months, accompanying them in migration.

MIGRATION   Sandhill Cranes nesting in north migrate long distances (some cross the Bering Straits every spring and fall, en route to and from nesting grounds in Siberia). Populations nesting in Mississippi, Florida, and Cuba do not migrate.

CONSERVATION STATUS   Most populations now stable or increasing slightly, but still vulnerable to loss of habitat. Degradation of habitat at major stopover points for migrants could have serious impact on species. Localized races in Mississippi and Cuba are considered endangered.

COMMON CRANE   *Grus grus*

This crane is relatively common in parts of Eurasia, but strictly an accidental visitor to North America. Most records have been of birds in migrating flocks of Sandhill Cranes on the Great Plains; these are likely individuals that joined flocks of Sandhills in eastern Siberia and then traveled with them back across the Bering Strait and south to wintering areas on this continent.

WHOOPING CRANE   *Grus americana*

One of the rarest North American birds, and also one of the largest and most magnificent. Once fairly widespread on the northern prairies, it was brought to the brink of extinction in the 1940s, but strict protection has brought the wild population back to well over 100. The flock that winters on the central Texas coast flies 2,400 miles north to nest in Wood Buffalo National Park in central Canada; this remote breeding area was not discovered until 1954.

HABITAT   *Muskeg (summer); prairie pools, marshes.* Current breeding habitat is in remote northern forest, in areas of muskeg (swampy coniferous woods with numerous lakes and ponds). Formerly also nested in prairie marshes. Winters in coastal marsh, where adult pairs and families defend territories, returning to same territory each winter.

FEEDING   **Diet:** *Omnivorous.* In winter, eats insects, shrimp, crabs, clams, snails, frogs, snakes, small fish, seeds, acorns, roots, berries. Summer diet not well

CRANES

known, probably a similarly wide variety of animal and plant matter. **Behavior:** See family introduction.

NESTING In courtship, pairs "dance," leaping into air repeatedly with flapping wings, bills pointed upward, giving bugling calls; dance has a dignified look. Other displays include bowing, tossing tufts of grass in the air, and loud trumpeting or "whooping" calls. **Nest:** Site is on ground, typically on marshy island in lake or pond. Nest (built by both sexes) is a large mound of grass, weeds, mud, with depression at center. **Eggs:** 2, sometimes 1 or 3. Olive-buff, spotted with dark brown. Incubation is by both sexes, 29–31 days; female usually incubates at night. **Young:** Downy young leave nest within a few hours after hatching. Both parents feed young. Two eggs typically hatch, but very rarely or never does more than one young bird survive. Young able to fly at about 3 months after hatching.

Whooping Crane

MIGRATION Migrates by day, in family groups or small flocks. Travels along rather narrow corridors and makes traditional stopovers. Although they may travel in flocks, in winter they mostly separate into family groups, each pair of adults defending a feeding territory against intruding cranes.

CONSERVATION STATUS *Endangered.* Whoopers once nested on the northern prairies south to present-day Iowa and Illinois, but they disappeared as settlers moved in. As recently as 1912, about 90 birds wintered at various points in coastal Texas and Louisiana, and there was a nonmigratory population in southwestern Louisiana as well. By 1941, the Texas wintering flock was down to only 15 birds (another six were still resident in Louisiana, but that flock soon dwindled away). After 1941, numbers very gradually rose again, helped by protection on the wintering grounds and public education against shooting; by the mid-1990s, the Texas wintering flock approached 150. Attempts to start a new flock farther west (by putting Whooper eggs under Sandhill Cranes in Idaho) failed, but in the 1990s a new effort was undertaken to start a nonmigratory flock in Florida, using birds raised in captivity.

THICK-KNEES AND STONE-CURLEWS (Family Burhinidae)

The nine species in this family live at scattered points around the world, mostly at southern latitudes. They look rather like oversized plovers but with swollen leg joints (hence the name "thick-knee"), heavy bills, and staring yellow eyes. Most kinds live in dry fields, well away from the shore, and they are often active at night. They feed mostly on large insects, but also take some lizards, frogs, rodents, and other small creatures.

GENUS *Burhinus*

DOUBLE-STRIPED THICK-KNEE   *Burhinus bistriatus*

On open grasslands from eastern Mexico to northern South America, this odd bird is sometimes common. Easily overlooked by day, it becomes noisy and active at night, giving harsh high-pitched calls. A stray individual was once found in ranch country of southern Texas.

This is the first of several families that are collectively known as shorebirds (or "waders" in Europe). Although the sandpipers represent the largest family of shorebirds, plovers make up the second largest, with about 65 species found worldwide.

All plovers live on the ground in open habitats, but not all are found on the shore; some live out on dry plains, far from water. Our most familiar plover, the Killdeer, is often seen in plowed fields or on large lawns. However, most kinds live on shores, beaches, or mudflats for at least part of the year.

Plovers can usually be picked out among other shorebirds by their shape and behavior. All have round heads and short, straight bills. They typically run a few steps, stop abruptly, and then run again, in a jerky start-and-stop fashion. Strong and swift in flight, some plovers migrate long distances, from high Arctic tundra to lands far south of the Equator.

Feeding   Many kinds of shorebirds find their food by probing in mud or shallow water, but plovers apparently find almost all their food by sight. Typically they run a few steps and then pause, then run again, pecking at the ground whenever they spot something edible. Smaller plovers sometimes hold one foot forward and shuffle it rapidly over the surface of sand or mud, as if to startle small creatures into moving. Larger species, such as the Black-bellied, may sometimes probe with their bills in mud or short grass. Plovers have rather large eyes, and several kinds are known to forage at night as well as by day. Small invertebrates make up most of the diet for all species; depending on habitat, these may be mostly insects or may include crustaceans, marine worms, mollusks, or others. A few plovers also eat some berries or seeds.

Nesting   Plovers place their nests on the ground, usually in fairly dry spots such as upland tundra, sandy beaches well above high tide, or dry fields. In flat open terrain with few landmarks, they often choose to nest close to some conspicuous object: a large rock or grass clump, or even a dried cow chip for prairie species. The nest itself is very simple, usually a shallow scrape in the soil with a slight lining of pebbles, dry grass, or other debris. Usually three or four eggs are laid, and both parents normally help incubate. The downy young leave the nest soon after hatching, are usually tended by both parents, but find all their own food.

Displays   Males often advertise their ownership of a nesting territory by flying over it with deep, exaggerated wingbeats while calling. In courtship, a male may approach a female on the ground with various ritualized postures, such as crouching with his tail spread or raised, drooping his wings, or pattering his feet. Adult plovers may protect their eggs or young when a predator comes near the nest by putting on a broken-wing act, fluttering along the ground as if injured and luring the predator away.

GENUS *Vanellus*

NORTHERN LAPWING   *Vanellus vanellus*

Lapwings are large plovers, often with crests, and various kinds are found in most parts of the world except North America. They are often more at home in open fields than on shorelines. This species is common in Europe and Asia; it rarely wanders to eastern Canada or the northeastern United States. Such strays usually occur singly, but on a few occasions, major winter storms have brought small invasions.

The four species in this group are larger than most plovers, and they go through a striking change in pattern from bright summer plumage to dull winter plumage. All four nest in the north and migrate medium to long distances.

BLACK-BELLIED PLOVER   *Pluvialis squatarola*

This stocky plover breeds in high Arctic zones around the world and winters on the coasts of six continents. Some can be seen along our beaches throughout the year (including nonbreeding immatures through the summer). Although the Black-bellied Plover is quite plain in its nonbreeding plumage, it adds much to the character of our shorelines with its haunting whistles, heard by day or night.

HABITAT   *Mudflats, open marshes, beaches; in summer, tundra.* For nesting favors drier tundra, often more barren ridges above lowland lakes and rivers. Sometimes in lower wet tundra near coast. In winter mostly on open sand beaches, tidal flats. During migration will often stop in shortgrass prairie or plowed fields.

FEEDING   **Diet:** *Insects, mollusks, crustaceans, marine worms.* Diet on northern tundra is mostly insects, also some mollusks, and small amount of plant material. In coastal

situations (where it spends most of year), eats many polychaete worms, also mollusks, crustaceans, some insects. **Behavior:** See family introduction. Sometimes probes for hidden prey.

NESTING   Male displays on territory by flying with slow, deep wingbeats, giving clear whistled notes. Female may be attracted by this display. In courtship, male lands near female, runs stiffly toward her with head low. **Nest:** Site is on dry ground, often somewhat raised on ridge or hummock, with good visibility. Nest is a shallow scrape, lined with pebbles and bits of plant material; male begins scrape, female adds lining. **Eggs:** 4, rarely 3–5. Buff to gray-green, with darker blotches. Incubation is by both parents, 26–27 days. **Young:** Downy young leave nest shortly after hatching, find all their own food. Both parents tend young at first, then female

Black-bellied Plover

leaves before young are 2 weeks old. If predator threatens, adults may lure it away by putting on broken-wing act. Adults also mob predatory birds that come near nest area. Young are able to fly at 25–45 days; adult male may leave before young fledge.

MIGRATION   Most migrate along coast or over sea, but numbers stop over regularly at some inland sites. Winter range remarkably extensive, from New England and southwestern Canada to southern South America, Africa, Australia. Females may tend to winter farther south than males. Most immatures apparently do not go to breeding grounds in summer; may remain through season on more southerly coasts.

CONSERVATION STATUS   Population trends would be difficult to detect. No evidence of widespread change in numbers.

EUROPEAN GOLDEN-PLOVER   *Pluvialis apricaria*

A close relative of our American and Pacific golden-plovers, this species is common in Europe and strays to eastern Canada on occasion. Spring storms over the North

Atlantic have sometimes brought flocks of European Golden-Plovers to Newfoundland, with a few stragglers reaching other points in the Maritime Provinces.

AMERICAN GOLDEN-PLOVER *Pluvialis dominicus*

A trim, elegant plover. Swift and graceful in flight, probably one of the fastest fliers among shorebirds, and with good reason: it migrates every year from Arctic Alaska and Canada to southern South America. Flocks of northbound migrants, in their striking spring plumage, are seen mostly in the heartland of our continent, on the Great Plains and the Mississippi Valley; there they often forage in open fields and prairies, far from water.

HABITAT *Prairies, mudflats, shores; tundra (summer).* During migration, usually found on short-grass prairies, flooded pastures, plowed fields; less often on mudflats, beaches. Breeds on Arctic tundra. In western Alaska, where it overlaps with Pacific Golden-Plover, the American tends to nest at higher elevations, on more barren tundra slopes.

FEEDING **Diet:** *Mostly insects.* On breeding grounds, apparently feeds mostly on insects, including flies, beetles, and others, also some snails and seeds. In migration in open fields, eats wide variety of insects, including grasshoppers, caterpillars, larvae of beetles. On shores, also feeds on small crustaceans and mollusks. In late summer, may eat many berries. **Behavior:** See family introduction.

American Golden-Plover

NESTING Males perform flight display over breeding territory by flying high, with exaggerated slow, deep wingbeats, while repeatedly giving a short *kt-dlink* call. In courtship, male walks up to female in crouching posture with tail raised, neck stretched forward. **Nest:** Site is on ground on very open, dry tundra. Nest (probably built by male) is shallow depression in tundra lined with lichens, moss, grass, leaves. **Eggs:** 4, sometimes 3. Pale buff to cinnamon, boldly blotched with black and brown, well camouflaged when seen against varied tundra vegetation. Incubation is by both parents, about 26–27 days. Male reportedly incubates by day, female at night. **Young:** Downy young leave nest shortly after hatching. Both parents tend young, but young find all their own food. Age at first flight about 22–24 days.

MIGRATION Northward migration in spring is mostly through Great Plains. In fall, most birds apparently make nonstop flight from eastern Canada to northern South America; some pause along our Atlantic coast, especially after storms with northeast winds.

CONSERVATION STATUS Huge numbers were shot in late 19th century, and population apparently has never recovered to historic levels. May be limited now by loss of habitat on South American wintering range.

PACIFIC GOLDEN-PLOVER *Pluvialis fulva*

This bird is so similar to American Golden-Plover that the two were regarded as one species until 1993. However, the birds can tell the difference: where the two forms overlap in western Alaska, they seldom or never interbreed. Their migratory routes are strikingly different: American Golden-Plover migrates to South America, while

Pacific Golden-Plover flies from Alaska to islands in the Pacific and often on to Australia, regularly covering over 2,000 miles in a single nonstop flight.

Where these two golden-plovers overlap in western Alaska in summer, the Pacific typically nests at lower elevations than the American, on wetter tundra with taller vegetation. The flight display of the male includes a different call, a repeated, plaintive *teee-chewee* whistle. Other aspects of nesting behavior seem to be similar. In fall, most Pacific Golden-Plovers from Alaska probably make nonstop flight to Hawaii; some winter there, others continue to other islands, Australia, or New Zealand. Small numbers occur along west coast of Canada and United States, mostly in fall, a few spending the winter.

TYPICAL PLOVERS — GENUS *Charadrius*

About 30 species of plovers worldwide belong to this genus. Those that nest in the north are migratory, but many in the tropics or the Southern Hemisphere are permanent residents. Most of the plovers in this group have dark bands crossing the chest.

MONGOLIAN PLOVER   *Charadrius mongolus*

This Asian plover is found in very small numbers in western Alaska in spring, when its bright pattern makes it unmistakable; it has even nested there. The species has also occurred as a rare stray in scattered areas south of Alaska, including Oregon, California, Alberta, Ontario, New Jersey, and Louisiana.

COLLARED PLOVER   *Charadrius collaris*

Widespread in the American tropics, from northern Mexico to central Argentina, this small plover lives on gravel bars along rivers far inland, as well as on coastal beaches. The first one ever found north of Mexico was at a pond far inland in south-central Texas in May 1992.

SNOWY PLOVER   *Charadrius alexandrinus*

An inconspicuous, pale little bird, easily overlooked as it runs around on white sand beaches or on the salt flats around lakes in the arid west. Where it lives on beaches, its nesting attempts are often disrupted by human visitors who fail to notice that they are keeping the bird away from its nest; as a result, Snowy Plover populations have declined in many coastal regions. In Europe, it is known as the Kentish Plover.

HABITAT   *Beaches, sandy flats.* At all seasons, tends to be found in places where habitat matches the pale color of its back: dry sand beaches along coast, salt pans or alkaline flats in interior. Usually in places with very little vegetation, not around marshes. Also sometimes forages on open mudflats.

FEEDING   **Diet:** *Includes crustaceans, insects, marine worms.* Along coast, may feed mostly on tiny crustaceans, mollusks, and marine worms, also some insects. At inland sites, diet may be mostly insects, including various flies and beetles. **Behavior:** See family introduction.

NESTING   May nest in loose colonies or as isolated pairs; sometimes nests close to tern colonies. Unlike many shorebirds, male seems to have no aerial display over territory. **Nest:** Site is on open bare ground, sometimes close to a grass clump or piece of driftwood. Nest is shallow scrape in ground, lined with bits of shell, grass, pebbles, other debris, sometimes surrounded with similar items. **Eggs:** 3, sometimes 2, rarely 4. Pale buff, dotted with black. Incubation is by both parents, 26–32 days. Male usually incubates at night, female most of day. **Young:** Downy young leave nest a few hours after hatching, feed themselves, can fly at age of 28–32 days. In some areas,

Snowy Plover

both parents tend young. In other areas, female may depart in less than 6 days, leaving male to raise young; female may then find another mate and raise another set of young. In these cases, male from first nest may also find a new mate and renest after first young have fledged.

MIGRATION   Most birds nesting inland migrate to coast for winter; many on coast are permanent residents. Generally only a short-distance migrant.

CONSERVATION STATUS   Declining in some areas, especially along Gulf coast and parts of Pacific coast; considered threatened in parts of range. Human disturbance on beaches often causes failure of nesting attempts.

WILSON'S PLOVER   *Charadrius wilsonia*

Several of our plovers are small birds with single dark neck rings. Wilson's Plover is slightly larger than the others and has a more southerly distribution, living on

beaches along the southern Atlantic and Gulf coasts. Its oversized bill is not only its best field mark but also a clue to its feeding behavior: some studies have shown that it tends to capture and eat slightly larger creatures than the other plovers on the beach.

HABITAT   *Open beaches, tidal flats, sandy islands.* Found only in coastal regions, typically in very open areas such as white sand or shell beaches, estuaries, tidal mudflats. May favor islands, such as offshore barrier beaches, dredge spoil islands.

FEEDING   *Diet: Many crustaceans, also worms, insects.* Crustaceans in diet include many crabs, such as fiddler crabs and others, also crayfish, shrimp. Also eats small mollusks, marine worms, many insects and their larvae. **Behavior:** See family introduction.

Wilson's Plover

NESTING   Nests as isolated pairs or in loose colonies. In courtship, male goes through ritualized nest-scrape making; male postures near female with wings drooped, tail held low and spread, pattering with feet. **Nest:** Site is on dry part of beach, often near piece of driftwood, clump of grass, or other conspicuous object. Nest is simple scrape in sand or shell of beach, usually with sparse lining of pebbles, pieces of shell, grass, debris. Male makes several scrapes, female chooses one. **Eggs:** 3, sometimes 2, rarely 4. Buff, blotched with brown and black. Incubation is by both parents, 23–25 days. Male usually incubates at night, female most of day. **Young:** Downy young leave nest soon after hatching. Both parents tend young, but young feed themselves. Age at first flight roughly 21 days.

Only a short-distance migrant, with northernmost breeders (and those on parts of Gulf coast) withdrawing in winter. Rarely wanders north along coast (including from western Mexico into California), and very rarely wanders inland.

CONSERVATION STATUS Uncommon and local, probably has declined in parts of its range.

COMMON RINGED PLOVER   *Charadrius hiaticula*

This small shorebird is very much like our Semipalmated Plover and replaces it in Europe and Asia. The breeding range of the Ringed Plover extends to Greenland and to some islands in the high Canadian Arctic, and a very few also come into western Alaska, but these birds apparently all cross to the Old World in fall before migrating south.

SEMIPALMATED PLOVER   *Charadrius semipalmatus*

Semipalmated Plover

The most common of the small plovers on migration through most areas. On its breeding grounds in the north, it avoids the tundra habitat chosen by most shorebirds, nesting instead on gravel bars along rivers or ponds. In such surroundings, its seemingly bold pattern actually helps to make the plover inconspicuous, by breaking up its outline against the varied background. The name "semipalmated" refers to partial webbing between the bird's toes.

HABITAT   *Shores, tideflats.* Favors very open habitats on migration, including broad mudflats, sandy beaches, lake shores, pools in salt marsh; sometimes in flooded fields or even plowed fields with other shorebirds. Tends to avoid flats overgrown with too much marsh vegetation. Breeds in the north, mostly on open flats of sand or gravel near water.

FEEDING   Diet: *Insects, crustaceans, worms.* Diet varies with season and location. In breeding season and during migration inland, may feed mostly on insects, including flies and their larvae, also earthworms. On coast, eats many marine worms, crustaceans, small mollusks. **Behavior:** See family introduction.

NESTING   In breeding season, male displays over territory by flying in wide circles with slow, exaggerated wingbeats, calling repeatedly. On ground, male may display by crouching with tail spread, wings open, and feathers fluffed up, calling excitedly. **Nest:** Site is on ground, amid sparse plant growth or on bare open gravel or sand, sometimes placed close to large rock or other landmark. Nest is shallow scrape in ground, sometimes lined with small leaves, other debris. **Eggs:** 4, rarely 3. Olive-buff to olive-brown, blotched with black and brown. Incubation is by both sexes, 23–25 days. **Young:** Downy young leave nest soon after hatching. Both parents tend young, but young find all their own food. Age at first flight about 23–31 days.

MIGRATION Migrates mostly late in spring and early in fall, with peak southbound flights in August. Has a very extensive winter range, along coasts from United States to southern South America.

CONSERVATION STATUS Seriously depleted by unrestricted shooting in late 19th century, but has recovered well; currently widespread and common.

PIPING PLOVER *Charadrius melodus*

A small plover with a very short bill. Its pale back matches the white sand beaches and alkali flats it inhabits. While many shorebirds have wide distributions, this one is a North American specialty, barely extending into Mexico in winter. Many of its nesting areas are subject to human disturbance or other threats, and it is now considered an endangered or threatened species in all parts of its range.

HABITAT *Sandy beaches, tidal flats.* Nests in open sandy situations near water, in a variety of settings: beaches along Atlantic coast and Great Lakes; sandbars along major rivers on northern Great Plains; gravel or sand flats next to alkali lakes. Winters along coast, on tidal flats and beaches.

FEEDING **Diet:** *Includes insects, marine worms, crustaceans.* Diet not well known. On coast, feeds on marine worms, small crustaceans, insects, other marine invertebrates. Inland, feeds mostly on insects, including small beetles, water boatmen, shore flies, midges, and many others. **Behavior:** See family introduction.

NESTING Males perform display flights over breeding territory, with slow wingbeats and piping call note. On the ground, male approaches female, stands upright with neck stretched, and rapidly stamps feet with odd high-stepping gait. **Nest:** Site is on open ground some distance away from water, often with large rock or clump of grass nearby, but no direct shelter or shade. May nest very close to breeding colonies

Piping Plover

of terns. Nest is shallow scrape in sand, sometimes lined with tiny shells and pebbles. **Eggs:** 4, sometimes 2–3, rarely 5. Pale buff, blotched with black and dark brown. Incubation is by both sexes, averages 26–28 days. **Young:** Downy young may leave nest a few hours after hatching. Young feed themselves. Both parents brood young during cool weather at first, but female often deserts them within a few days, leaving male to care for young. Development of young not well known; able to fly at 21–35 days.

MIGRATION Most birds from northern plains and Great Lakes probably winter on Gulf coast. Not often seen in migration; may travel from breeding to wintering grounds in one nonstop flight.

CONSERVATION STATUS *Threatened or endangered.* Almost gone from Great Lakes as a breeder and has declined elsewhere. Increased human activity on beaches affects Great Lakes and Atlantic coast birds. Irregular water releases from dams often flood out nesting attempts on rivers in the interior.

LITTLE RINGED PLOVER *Charadrius dubius*

A small relative of the Semipalmated and Common Ringed plovers, widespread in the Old World, where it is often found on inland mudflats. Although its normal range does not extend into far eastern Siberia, a few strays have made it to Alaska, appearing in the western Aleutians.

KILLDEER *Charadrius vociferus*

Widespread, common, and conspicuous, the Killdeer calls its name as it flies over farmland and other open country. Like other members of the plover family, this

Killdeer

species is often found at the water's edge, but it also lives in pastures and fields far from water. At times, it nests on gravel roofs or on lawns. Many a person has been fooled by the bird's broken-wing act, in which it flutters along the ground in a show of injury, luring intruders away from its nest.

HABITAT *Fields, airports, lawns, river banks, mudflats, shores.* Often found on open ground, such as pastures, plowed fields, large lawns, even at a great distance from water. Most successful nesting areas, however, have some shallow water or other good feeding area for the chicks. Also commonly found around water, on mudflats, lake shores, coastal estuaries.

FEEDING **Diet:** *Mostly insects.* Feeds on a wide variety of insects, including beetles, caterpillars, grasshoppers, fly larvae, many others; also eats spiders, earthworms, centipedes, crayfish, snails. Eats small amounts of seeds as well. **Behavior:** See family introduction. May follow farmers plowing fields and feed on grubs turned up by the plow.

NESTING In breeding season, male flies high over nesting territory in floating, wavering flight with slow, deep wingbeats, giving *kill-dee* call repeatedly. On ground, courtship displays include ritualized nest-scrape making. **Nest:** Site is on ground in open area with good visibility, as on bare soil, field of short grass, gravel road; sometimes on gravel roof. Nest is shallow scrape in soil or gravel, either unlined or lined with pebbles, grass, twigs, bits of debris. **Eggs:** Usually 4, sometimes 3–5. Buff, blotched with black and brown. Incubation is by both parents, 24–28 days. In very hot climates, adults shade eggs in midday, may soak belly feathers to help cool eggs. **Young:** Downy young leave nest soon after hatching. Young are tended by both parents but feed themselves. Age of young at first flight roughly 25 days. In some warmer parts of range, Killdeers raise two broods per year.

MIGRATION Migratory in north, may be permanent resident in south. Spring migration is very early, returning to some northern areas in February or March.

CONSERVATION STATUS Despite local declines in some urbanized areas, still widespread and abundant.

MOUNTAIN PLOVER   *Charadrius montanus*

Poorly named, this pallid plover is a bird of flat open plains, not mountains. Of all of our "shorebirds," this is the one most disconnected from the shore, generally living miles from water in the dry country of the west. The shortgrass prairie where it once thrived has been largely converted to farmland, but the Mountain Plover has found new habitat in grassland overgrazed by cattle.

HABITAT *Semi-arid plains, grasslands, plateaus.* Favors areas of very short grass, even bare soil. Typically far from water. Nests mostly in shortgrass prairie, including overgrazed pasture and very arid plains. In some areas, nests mainly on the rather barren open ground found in large prairie dog towns. Winter habitats include desert flats, plowed fields.

FEEDING **Diet:** *Mostly insects.* Diet is not well known, but in the dry upland habitats where this plover lives, it probably feeds almost entirely on insects, including grasshoppers, beetles, flies, and crickets. **Behavior:** See family introduction.

NESTING In breeding season, male may display by flying high over territory with exaggerated slow wingbeats, calling. Female may lay one clutch of eggs and leave male to care for eggs and young, then lay another clutch and incubate it herself. **Nest:** Site is on flat open ground (flat sites chosen even in hilly country). On featureless plain, nest

Mountain Plover

is often placed close to some conspicuous object, such as a pile of cow manure. Nest is shallow scrape in soil. Nest lining (including pebbles, grass, rootlets, chips of cow manure) added mostly during incubation. Several nest scrapes are made, only one is used. **Eggs:** 3, sometimes 2, rarely 1–4. Olive-buff with many black marks. Incubation is by one or both sexes, 28–31 days. On very hot days, adult will stand over eggs, shading them from intense sun. **Young:** Downy young leave nest soon after hatching, are tended by one or both parents but feed themselves. Adults shade young on hot days, and family may seek out any available shade at midday. Young can fly well at about 33–34 days.

MIGRATION   Most apparently migrate southwest from breeding grounds; some go straight south to Texas, northern Mexico. Very rarely strays to eastern United States, mostly in fall and winter.

CONSERVATION STATUS   Has disappeared from much of former breeding range as former shortgrass prairie is converted to farmland. In some areas, decline may be linked to decline in prairie dogs (whose colonies formerly furnished good nesting habitat).

EURASIAN DOTTEREL   *Charadrius morinellus*

Across northern Europe and Asia, this beautiful small plover nests on high, dry tundra, and it has been found nesting a few times on similar terrain in western Alaska. Strays have been found very rarely south of Alaska on the Pacific coast in fall.

OYSTERCATCHERS (Family Haematopodidae)

These are stocky shorebirds with stout legs and colorful, knifelike bills, living mostly in coastal areas around the world. Depending on how they are classified, the various local forms make up anywhere from 5 to 11 species. Named for their feeding habits, oystercatchers use their bills to "catch" oysters and other shellfish by surprise.

Feeding   Although they will eat a variety of other small invertebrates, the diet is mainly shellfish, especially bivalves such as mussels, clams, and oysters. The birds have two methods of opening the shells of bivalves: Finding a mussel with its shell slightly open, the oystercatcher quickly jabs its bill into the opening, cutting the muscles and then cleaning out the contents. In the other method, the bird simply hammers on the shell to break it open. (At least in some species, an individual will specialize on one method or the other.) Other mollusks such as limpets or chitons may be pried off rocks and flipped over to be eaten. Oystercatchers find much of their food by sight, but they will also probe in mud for marine worms and other items. Our two species are strictly coastal, but in some parts of the world, oystercatchers occur on inland fields, where they probe for earthworms.

Nesting   Nest sites are on the ground, often on a raised rocky area or well above the high tide mark; Eurasian Oystercatcher sometimes nests on flat gravel roofs. Nest is a simple scrape with sparse lining of pebbles or debris. Two or three eggs are laid, and both parents help to incubate. In most other shorebirds, the chicks find all their own food from the start, but oystercatchers feed their young for several weeks.

Displays In the "piping" display, two birds stand, walk, or run side by side, giving loud piping calls, often holding their heads forward and bills pointed down. They may take off and fly together, continuing to call, and sometimes they are joined in the air by other pairs. Variations on the piping display may be used in courtship, in maintaining the pair bond, and in warning other pairs of oystercatchers away from the nesting territory.

GENUS *Haematopus*

EURASIAN OYSTERCATCHER   *Haematopus ostralegus*

Very common in Europe, this big shorebird occurs regularly as close to our area as Iceland, but it is strictly accidental in North America. A single bird found in New-foundland in 1994 furnished the first record. American Oystercatcher is only a rare visitor as far north as eastern Canada; stray oystercatchers seen in the maritime provinces could be either species.

AMERICAN OYSTERCATCHER   *Haematopus palliatus*

A very large, unmistakable shorebird of Atlantic and Gulf coast beaches. Solitary or in family groups in summer, American Oystercatchers may gather in large flocks in winter.

HABITAT   *Coastal beaches, tidal flats.* Strictly coastal, in areas with extensive sand beaches, tidal mudflats, salt marsh. Key element is presence of good food supply, such as oyster beds, clam flats. May nest among dunes, on islands in salt marsh, or on dredge spoil islands.

FEEDING   **Diet:** *Mostly shellfish and marine worms.* Feeds mostly on mussels, clams, oysters; also marine worms, sand crabs, limpets, sea urchins, jellyfish, and other small creatures of the intertidal zone. **Behavior:** See family introduction. Often forages by walking in shallow water, searching for food by sight.

NESTING   First breeds at age of 3–4 years. Sometimes may mate for life. In areas with high populations, may form trios, with one male and two females attending one nest or two nearby nests. **Nest:** Site is on ground, on marsh island or among dunes,

American Oystercatcher

usually well above high tide mark. Nest (apparently built by both sexes) is shallow scrape in sand, sometimes lined with pebbles, shells. **Eggs:** 1–4. Buffy gray, usually speckled with dark brown. Nests attended by two females and one male may have 5–6 eggs. Incubation is by both sexes, 24–28 days. **Young:** Downy young leave nest shortly after they hatch. Both parents feed young for at least 2 months after hatching, although young may attempt to forage on their own well before parents stop feeding them. Age at first flight about 5 weeks.

MIGRATION   Southern birds apparently permanent residents. Northern breeders move south, probably to southeastern United States, for winter.

CONSERVATION STATUS   Numbers declined seriously in 19th century, have recovered well in 20th century. Despite disturbance in beach habitats, the species is currently doing well, often nesting on dredge spoil islands.

BLACK OYSTERCATCHER   *Haematopus bachmani*

Where the Pacific Ocean breaks against rocky shorelines, pairs of these big black birds stalk about on the rocks and nearby flats. If disturbed, they take flight with loud, ringing whistles easily heard above the sound of the waves. Their range stretches from Alaska to Baja, but Black Oystercatchers are scarce along the coast of southern California, where the shoreline is mostly sandy, not rocky.

Black Oystercatcher

HABITAT   *Rocky coasts, sea islets.* Found at all seasons along rocky shorelines, especially on small off-shore islands where predators are fewer; chooses areas with abundant shellfish and other marine life. In winter, also commonly found on mudflats close to rocky coastlines, but uses mudflats less in summer.

FEEDING   **Diet:** *Mostly mussels, limpets, other shellfish.* Diet varies with place and season, but feeds mostly on mussels where they are abundant; also limpets, whelks, urchins, crabs, marine worms, beetle larvae. Young birds, newly independent, may eat fewer mussels at first, perhaps lacking the skill to open them. **Behavior:** Forages mostly near low tide, resting at high tide. When feeding on mussel beds, typically removes the mussel from its shell and leaves the shell in place.

NESTING   May mate for life. Almost always nests on islands. Pairs typically defend a breeding territory that includes both an elevated area for nesting, well above high tide, and an adjacent feeding area with mussel beds or other food source. **Nest:** Site is on ground well above high tide mark, on gravel, grassy area, or depression in rock. Nest (built by both sexes) is slight scrape, with sparse lining of pebbles, pieces of shell. **Eggs:** 2–3, sometimes 1. Pale buff to olive, spotted and scrawled with brown and black. Incubation is by both parents, 24–29 days. **Young:** Downy young remain near nest at first; parents take turns guarding the young and catching food for them, walking back and forth to nearby intertidal zone. Older chicks follow their parents to feeding areas and are fed by them there. Young can fly at age 5 weeks or older; begin to catch some of their own food then but are still fed by parents for some time thereafter.

MIGRATION   Mostly permanent resident. No regular migration, but wanderers away from breeding areas are most likely to be seen in spring and fall.

CONSERVATION STATUS   Still widespread along Pacific coast, numerous in some areas. Vulnerable to effects of oil spills and other pollution in intertidal zone. Also very vulnerable to disturbance at nesting sites.

STILTS AND AVOCETS (Family Recurvirostridae)

These are slender, graceful, long-legged shorebirds, wading in the shallows of six continents, usually in warmer climates. In general, stilts have thin, straight bills, while avocets have upcurved bills. The family contains anywhere from 6 to 12 species, depending on how one classifies the various forms of stilts. (Some scientists also include in this family the Ibisbill, an odd shorebird living along rocky streams in southern Asia.)

Feeding　Stilts seem to find most of their food visually, picking up items from the surface of water or land. Avocets find much of their food by touch; the upcurved tip of the bill is held just under the water's surface and slightly opened as the bird sweeps its head back and forth. Tiny insects and crustaceans make up most of the diet.

Nesting　Unlike many shorebirds, avocets and stilts often nest in loose colonies, on wide-open flats close to water. The nest may be either a simple scrape in the ground with sparse lining or a built-up mound with a depression on top, the latter apparently more likely where there is a strong chance of flooding. The usual clutch is four eggs, spotted and mottled for better camouflage. Both parents help incubate and care for the chicks, but the young feed themselves.

Displays　The most attention-getting antics of these birds are their distraction displays, given when an intruder wanders too close to a nesting colony. Several adults may fly a short distance away, then land and wander about at random, feigning injury of one wing and then the other. This behavior gives no clue to the exact whereabouts of the nests, and it may help to lure predators away. Stilts will also hover overhead, making demented yapping calls, and avocets may fly directly at an intruder's head in a most unnerving way. Courtship displays are generally much simpler and may include ritualized preening by both members of a pair.

GENUS *Himantopus*

BLACK-WINGED STILT　*Himantopus himantopus*

This is the Old World replacement for our Black-necked Stilt, very similar and closely related (some scientists consider them to belong to the same species). A single Black-winged Stilt that once showed up on the Aleutian Islands, Alaska, was far from its normal haunts in Asia.

BLACK-NECKED STILT　*Himantopus mexicanus*

Everything about the Black-necked Stilt seems delicate—from its incredibly thin stilt-legs to its slim wings and its needlelike bill—yet it manages to thrive on the

Black-necked Stilt

sun-baked flats around shallow lakes, some of them in searing climates.

HABITAT　*Grassy marshes, mudflats, pools, shallow lakes (fresh and alkaline).* Found at all seasons at the margins of shallow water in very open country, especially where there is much marsh growth. For nesting, requires bare open ground, with little vegetation, near water. Often found in the same places as American Avocet, but the stilt is more partial to fresh water.

FEEDING　**Diet:** *Mostly insects and crustaceans.* Feeds on very small creatures that live on or near surface of water, including many flies, beetles, and other insects, shrimp, crayfish, snails; sometimes eats tadpoles or tiny fish. Also eats some seeds of aquatic plants. On some western lakes, may feed heavily on brine shrimps and brine flies. **Behavior:** Finds most food visually, picking items from surface of water or mud with bill; may spot items underwater and plunge head into water to take them. A standing bird may grab insects as they fly past.

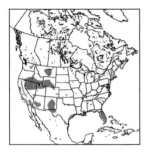

NESTING Typically nests in loose colonies, sometimes mixed with avocets. If predators approach a colony on foot, several adults may fly to a spot some distance away and perform a distraction display there. **Nest:** Site is on bare open ground near water or on slight rise surrounded by water. Nest (built by both sexes) variable; may be a simple scrape in soil or a mound built up above water level, lined with pebbles, shells, debris. **Eggs:** 4, sometimes 3–5. Buff, heavily blotched with brown and black. Incubation is by both parents, about 25 days; female may incubate by night, both sexes taking turns by day. On very hot days, adult may go to water and wet belly feathers to cool eggs. **Young:** Downy young leave nest shortly after hatching; are tended by both parents but feed themselves. Age at first flight about 4–5 weeks.

MIGRATION Vacates most inland areas in winter, moving to coasts, and some may migrate well to the south. Strays sometimes wander far beyond breeding range, especially in late spring.

CONSERVATION STATUS Numbers may be increasing as range expands. Quick to take advantage of artificial habitat (sewage ponds, dikes, etc.), so has recently extended breeding range into new areas.

GENUS *Recurvirostra*

AMERICAN AVOCET   *Recurvirostra americana*

American Avocet

Around lake shores and tidal flats, especially in the wide-open spaces of the west, flocks of elegant American Avocets wade in the shallows. They often feed while leaning forward, with the tips of their bills in the water and slightly open, filtering tiny food items from just below the surface. Sometimes a flock will feed this way in unison, walking forward, swinging their heads rhythmically from side to side.

HABITAT *Beaches, flats, shallow lakes, prairie ponds.* Widespread on shallow waters and extensive mudflats, both along coast and in the interior. Typically in very open situations with little vegetation. Inland, often favors salty or alkaline lakes more than fresh waters.

FEEDING **Diet:** *Mostly small crustaceans and insects, also some seeds.* Feeds on abundant tiny creatures that live in or near shallow water. Diet includes many midge larvae and other aquatic insects, small crustaceans. On lakes in west may feed heavily on brine shrimp and brine flies. **Behavior:** Forages in a variety of ways. Often sweeps head from side to side, with upturned tip of bill barely submerged in shallow water, finding food by touch. Also finds food visually, picking items from surface of water or mud or plunging head into water; sometimes snatches passing insects out of the air.

NESTING Typically nests in loose colonies, sometimes mixed with Black-necked Stilts. If predators approach a colony on foot, several adults may perform a distraction display nearby, running about in a crouch with both wings spread. If eggs or young are directly threatened, adult avocets may fly straight at an intruder, calling loudly. **Nest:** Site is on bare open ground, not far from water. Nest (built by both sexes) may be a simple scrape in soil, a scrape lined with pebbles and other debris, or a mound built up to more than a foot tall. **Eggs:** 4, sometimes 3–5. Olive-buff, blotched with brown and black. Incubation is by both parents, 23–25 days. Female incubates at night, both sexes take turns during day. **Young:** Downy young leave nest soon after hatching, find all their own food. Both parents tend young. Age at first flight about 4–5 weeks.

MIGRATION   Most migrate to the coast (or to valleys of California) in winter. Some migrate well to the east, wintering along much of Atlantic coast, with flocks of nonbreeders remaining through the summer there.

CONSERVATION STATUS   Population probably stable or possibly increasing. Numbers occurring in east (as migrants and wintering birds) have increased greatly during recent decades.

PRATINCOLES AND COURSERS (Family Glareolidae)

Pratincoles are long-winged, fork-tailed shorebirds that look somewhat like terns or giant swallows. They run on the ground, feeding like plovers, but they also do much of their feeding in the air, swooping about acrobatically to catch flying insects. Pratincoles nest only in the Old World, but one species has reached Alaska.

GENUS *Glareola*

ORIENTAL PRATINCOLE   *Glareola maldivarum*

When a single pratincole appeared on Attu Island, Alaska, in 1985, it added a new family to the North American list. At the time it seemed a unique record, unlikely to be duplicated; but just a year later, another individual was found farther north and east in Alaska, at Gambell on St. Lawrence Island.

JACANAS (Family Jacanidae)

The eight species of jacanas are bizarre shorebirds, found around marshes in tropical and subtropical regions. Their very long toes allow them to run about on floating vegetation, such as lily pads. This behavior earns them the nickname of "lily-trotters," which would be easier to pronounce than "jacana" (a Portuguese and South American Indian word, variously pronounced *ja-SAH-nah, ja-CAH-nah, ha-SAH-nah,* and *zha-sha-NAH*)! In most species the female jacana is larger than the male, and one female may have several mates. She lays eggs in a separate nest for each of her males, and the males tend to the eggs and young.

GENUS *Jacana*

NORTHERN JACANA   *Jacana spinosa*

At marshy ponds from Mexico to Panama, this odd shorebird is common. Its long toes allow it to run about on lily pads and other floating vegetation. When it flies, the feet trail behind it; on landing, it may hold the wings high for a moment, showing off the yellow flight feathers. This species has turned up several times in Texas and has even nested there.

Northern Jacana

HABITAT   *Marshes, overgrown ponds.* In the tropics, found on wide variety of shallow freshwater ponds and lake margins, especially those with much floating vegetation. In United States, has occurred mostly in Texas, on large fresh ponds surrounded by extensive marsh and with floating plants such as lily pads, water hyacinth.

FEEDING   **Diet:** *Mostly insects.* Diet in Texas not well known. In Costa Rica, reported to feed almost entirely on insects; occasionally eats small fish. **Behavior:** Forages by walking about on mats of floating vegetation, picking insects from surface of plants or water, sometimes from just below water's surface. Also forages on mud or open ground near water.

NESTING   One female may have up to 4 mates; she lays eggs in separate nests for each, and males do almost all the work of incubating the eggs and caring for the young. **Nest:** Site is on top of marsh vegetation, either standing or floating, in shallow water. Nest (built by male) is a flimsy and simple open cup made of available plant material; male continues to add to nest during incubation period. **Eggs:** Usually 4, sometimes 3–5. Almost round; brown, scrawled with black lines. Incubation is by male only, 22–24 days. During hot part of day, male will shade eggs from sun (female occasionally shades eggs also). **Young:** Downy young leave nest within 1–2 days after hatching. Male tends young and leads them to feeding sites, but young feed themselves; male broods young during rain or cool weather. Female sometimes accompanies or broods young, but always far less than male. Age at first flight about 4 weeks.

MIGRATION   No regular migration, but wanders irregularly. Seems to stray into Texas most often after a series of seasons with good rainfall have created much good habitat in northeastern Mexico and southern Texas. Has also strayed to Arizona, possibly Florida.

CONSERVATION STATUS   Very common in parts of its normal range, but could be vulnerable to loss of wetland habitat.

SANDPIPERS AND RELATED BIRDS (Family Scolopacidae)

The 88 species belonging to this diverse family range in size and shape from small, compact stints or "peeps" up to long-legged, long-necked waders like yellowlegs, curlews, and godwits. All are short-tailed, thin-billed birds, and almost all of them live at the water's edge.

Except for some kinds of snipes and woodcocks, almost all sandpipers nest in northern areas and move south for the winter. In fact, long-distance migration could be considered a typical trait of the family. In their lengthy travels, they sometimes go off course and appear far outside their normal ranges. Most of the sandpipers (63 species) have been found in North America, but nearly half of those (27 species) are only rare visitors from Europe or Asia. The chance of finding something rare is one reason why sandpipers and other shorebirds are often very popular with experienced birders.

Feeding   The varied bill shapes of sandpipers provide a clue to their feeding habits. Some have very short bills and feed on tiny creatures that they find by sight. Some have very long bills and do most of their feeding by probing in the mud; the tips of the bills of such birds are very sensitive and somewhat flexible, allowing the bird to grasp whatever items it detects below the surface. Many employ both approaches: even very long-billed sandpipers will pick up items that they see, and even short-billed species occasionally probe in mud. Many kinds of shorebirds in coastal areas feed at low tide and rest at high tide, so their daily schedule may be dictated more by tides than by time. Some (such as the Dunlin) are known to do more visual hunting by day, more probing at night.

    The small invertebrates eaten by sandpipers are classified in various groups, including insects, crustaceans, mollusks, marine worms, and many others. Some species also will eat seeds or other plant material.

Nesting   Sandpipers practice several different approaches to the roles of the parents in raising young. At one extreme are the phalaropes, in which females are larger and more colorful than males; after the female phalarope has courted a mate and laid her eggs, the male does all the incubating and cares for the young. At the opposite extreme is the Ruff, in which males gather on group display grounds to attract females, and then the females go off to do all the work of tending to the eggs and young.

    More than in most families of birds, however, male sandpipers often wind up with the child-rearing duties. In many species, the female departs soon after the eggs hatch, leaving the male with the young. In the familiar Spotted Sandpiper, one female may have several mates, laying a separate clutch of eggs to be cared for by each of her males.

    Almost all sandpipers nest on the ground (but there are exceptions—see Solitary Sandpiper). They are surprisingly consistent in their clutch size, with most species laying four eggs. In most species, the young find all their own food from the start, though they are tended by one or both parents. Exceptions include the snipes and woodcocks, which feed their young at first.

Displays   To advertise their nesting territories, males of most sandpipers perform aerial displays, flying over the territory and singing. These flight songs are among the typical sounds of northern tundra in summer but are seldom heard from migrant birds farther south. Some of the most spectacular flights (but hardest to watch, since they are performed at night) are those of the snipes and woodcocks, in which much of the "song" is made by the vibration of certain feathers in the tail or wings.

    Courtship displays are variable, but they are usually performed on the ground, often with the male holding odd postures (tail spread, wings drooped, and so on). Sandpipers often raise one wing high, showing off the color of the underwing; this may be used in either aggression or courtship.

    If predators approach a nesting area, adults of the larger sandpipers may harass the intruder, flying about nearby and calling. Smaller species are more likely to perform a distraction display, fluttering away as if injured to lure the predator away.

SHANKS — GENUS *Tringa*

These are mostly medium-sized sandpipers, often common around the edges of fresh water. Active in their feeding, they may dash about, picking up items from on or near the surface of shallow water; many have noisy call notes. The brightly colored legs of some species (such as the redshanks and greenshanks) explain the name "shanks" for the group as a whole.

COMMON GREENSHANK   *Tringa nebularia*

A big shorebird, common in Europe and Asia. There it seems to fill the same niche as our Greater Yellowlegs; it is not too different in appearance, and it even sounds similar. Common Greenshanks show up in small numbers on the Alaskan islands, mostly during spring migration.

GREATER YELLOWLEGS   *Tringa melanoleuca*

Greater Yellowlegs

At ponds and tidal creeks, this trim and elegant wader draws attention to itself by bobbing its head and calling loudly when an observer approaches. In migration, the Greater Yellowlegs is common from coast to coast. Sometimes it may annoy the birder by spooking the other shorebirds with its alarm calls; usually it is a pleasure to watch as it feeds actively in the shallows, running about on trademark yellow legs.

HABITAT   *Open marshes, mudflats, streams, ponds; in summer, wooded muskeg, spruce bogs.* During migration and winter, found in wide variety of settings, including tidal flats, estuaries, open beaches, salt and fresh marshes, shores of lakes and ponds, riverbanks. Breeds in boggy and marshy places within northern coniferous forest.

FEEDING   **Diet:** *Includes insects and small fish.* In breeding season, probably feeds mostly on insects and their larvae. In migration and winter, often feeds on small fishes such as killifish, minnows. Diet also includes crustaceans, snails, tadpoles, marine worms, sometimes berries. **Behavior:** Typically forages in shallow water. Often feeds very actively, sometimes running after minnows. May forage by walking forward while swinging its head back and forth with the tip of the bill in the water.

NESTING   On breeding grounds, male performs display flight, alternately rising and falling with flutters and glides as it gives a loud, ringing, whistled song. **Nest:** Site is on ground, usually close to water, often placed close to log or other object. Nest is well concealed in hummock of moss, a shallow depression lined sparsely with grass or leaves. **Eggs:** Usually 4. Buff, blotched with gray and dark brown. Incubation is probably by both parents, about 23 days. **Young:** Downy young are able to leave nest soon after hatching. Both parents tend young, and protest noisily with attacks or distraction displays if predators or humans come anywhere near. Young find all their own food. Age at first flight probably about 18–20 days.

MIGRATION   Usually migrates in small flocks. In fall, a few may linger in the north quite late in the season.

LESSER YELLOWLEGS   *Tringa flavipes*

At first glance, the two species of yellowlegs look identical except for size, as if they were put on earth only to confuse birdwatchers. With better acquaintance, they turn out to have different personalities. The Lesser is often at smaller ponds, often present in larger flocks, and often seems rather tame. Perhaps a more delicate bird (as it appears to be), it does not winter as far north as the Greater Yellowlegs.

HABITAT *Marshes, mudflats, shores, ponds; in summer, open boreal woods.* Occurs widely in migration, including coastal estuaries, salt and fresh marshes, edges of lakes and ponds; typically more common on freshwater habitats. Often in same places as Greater Yellowlegs, but may be less frequent on tidal flats. Breeds in large clearings, such as burned areas, near ponds in northern forest.

FEEDING **Diet:** *Insects, small fish, crustaceans.* Eats many aquatic insects, including beetles, water boatmen, dragonfly nymphs, crane fly larvae, and others; also terrestrial insects. Also feeds on crustaceans, snails, worms, small fish. Insects make up most of diet in summer. **Behavior:** Typically forages in very shallow water, picking at items on or just below water's surface.

Lesser Yellowlegs

Sometimes swings its head back and forth with the tip of the bill in the water.

NESTING Nesting behavior not well known. On the breeding territory, male performs a rising and falling display flight while giving a ringing song that can be heard from some distance. Adults may perch on top of dead trees and call, especially when humans intrude on territory. **Nest:** Site is on ground in open, typically in dry spot and sometimes far from water; may be placed close to log, burned stump, brushpile. Nest is a shallow depression sparsely lined with leaves, grass. **Eggs:** 4, sometimes 3. Buff to yellowish or gray, blotched with brown. Incubation is probably by both parents, roughly 22–23 days. **Young:** Downy young are able to leave nest soon after hatching; are tended by both parents but feed themselves. Age at first flight probably about 18–20 days.

MIGRATION Tends to migrate a little later in spring and earlier in fall than the Greater Yellowlegs.

MARSH SANDPIPER   *Tringa stagnatilis*

A trim, delicate sandpiper that wades in freshwater marshes in the Old World. Although it is a long-distance migrant, its breeding range does not extend very far east in Asia; one that appeared once on the western Aleutian Islands, Alaska, was far from its normal haunts.

SPOTTED REDSHANK   *Tringa erythropus*

The dark color of this big sandpiper makes it almost unmistakable in breeding plumage (although an oiled yellowlegs was once identified as a Spotted Redshank). The species is a rare migrant in western Alaska, and strays have shown up at scattered points elsewhere in North America—not only on both coasts but also at some far inland sites, such as Ohio and Kansas.

COMMON REDSHANK   *Tringa totanus*

Native to Eurasia, this big red-legged sandpiper is a regular nesting bird as close to our area as Iceland. It had long been expected to show up somewhere on our side of the Atlantic, and there had been possible sight records in the northeast, but the first confirmed records for North America involved storm-driven birds that reached Newfoundland in the spring of 1995.

WOOD SANDPIPER   *Tringa glareola*

A very common sandpiper of Europe and Asia, found most often around freshwater ponds, streams, and estuaries. It is a regular migrant in small numbers in western Alaska; sometimes it occurs in flocks on the outer Aleutian Islands, and it has even nested there. Strays have reached New York State twice.

GREEN SANDPIPER   *Tringa ochropus*

The Old World replacement for our Solitary Sandpiper. This trim, rather dark wader is found mostly around small freshwater streams and ponds across Europe and Asia. It has strayed a few times to islands in western Alaska.

SOLITARY SANDPIPER   *Tringa solitaria*

Almost all of our sandpipers migrate in flocks and nest on the ground, but the Solitary Sandpiper breaks both rules. In migration, as its name implies, it is usually encountered alone, along the bank of some shady creek. If approached, it bobs nervously, then flies away with sharp whistled cries. In summer in the northern spruce bogs, rather than nesting on the wet ground, the Solitary Sandpiper lays its eggs in old songbird nests placed high in trees.

HABITAT   *Streamsides, wooded swamps and ponds, fresh marshes.* In migration generally along shaded streams and ponds, riverbanks, narrow channels in marshes. Sometimes along the edges of open mudflats, but generally avoids tidal flats and salt marsh. Nests in muskeg region, with bogs and ponds surrounded by forest of spruce and other trees.

FEEDING   **Diet:** *Insects and other small aquatic creatures.* Feeds on many insects of water and shore, including beetles, dragonfly nymphs, grasshoppers; also crustaceans, spiders, worms, mollusks, occasionally small frogs. **Behavior:** Mostly forages in shallow water, moving about actively, picking items from surface; also

Solitary Sandpiper

probes in water and mud. While walking in water, may pause and quiver one foot, presumably to stir up small creatures from the bottom.

NESTING   Breeding behavior not well known. In breeding season, male gives repeated call while perching on tops of trees or while performing display flight over nesting territory. **Nest:** Uses nests built by songbirds such as American Robin, Rusty Blackbird, Bohemian Waxwing, Eastern Kingbird, Gray Jay. Nest chosen is usually in spruce or other conifer, sometimes in deciduous tree, 4–40 feet above ground. Sandpipers may sometimes take over a freshly built nest. Female may add lining material to original nest. **Eggs:** 4, rarely 5. Olive to buff, marked with brown. Incubation details poorly known, may be by both parents, roughly 23–24 days. **Young:** Development and behavior of young poorly known. Since parents are not known to feed young, apparently the chicks must jump to the ground; probably tended there by one or both parents. Age of young at first flight not known.

MIGRATION A long-distance migrant, wintering mostly in South America, especially around swamps and riverbanks in the Amazon Basin. Apparently migrates mostly alone and at night.

CONSERVATION STATUS Population very difficult to census because birds are so dispersed at all seasons, but no obvious decline in numbers.

GENUS *Catoptrophorus*

WILLET   *Catoptrophorus semipalmatus*

A Willet standing on the beach is simply a large plain shorebird; but its identity is obvious as soon as it spreads its patterned wings, and it even calls its name in flight.

Willet

Two distinct populations inhabit North America, one nesting in prairie marshes, the other in salt marshes along the Atlantic and Gulf coasts. In favorable areas in the middle Atlantic states, Willets are abundant, nesting in colonies, their ringing calls echoing across the tidelands on spring mornings.

HABITAT   *Marshes, wet meadows, mudflats, beaches.* Eastern race nests in areas of extensive salt marsh along coast; western race nests inland, around fresh marshes in open country, especially native grassland. In migration and winter, both forms occur on mudflats, tidal estuaries, sandy beaches.

FEEDING   **Diet:** *Includes insects, crustaceans, marine worms.* Diet varies with location. On inland waters, may feed largely on aquatic insects. On coast, eats many crabs, including fiddler crabs. Also feeds on other crustaceans, small mollusks, sometimes small fish; eats some plant material, including grass, fresh shoots, and seeds. **Behavior:** Forages by walking on shore, in marsh, or in shallow water, probing with its bill in mud or water or picking items from the surface.

NESTING   Often nests in colonies, especially along Atlantic coast. In breeding season, unpaired males perform flight displays, flying over nesting area with wings fluttering through shallow arc, while giving *pill-will-willet* calls. **Nest:** Site is on ground, usually among dense short grass, sometimes on open ground. Usually well hidden, sometimes conspicuous. Nest is shallow depression with grass bent down to form foundation, lined with finer grasses. **Eggs:** 4, rarely 5. Grayish to olive-buff, blotched with brown. Incubation is by both parents, with male incubating at night and sometimes during midday, female at other times. Incubation period 22–29 days. **Young:** Downy young leave nest within a day after hatching, are led by parents to marshy pond areas. Young find all their own food. Female parent departs after 2–3 weeks, leaving male to care for young. Age of young at first flight not well known, probably about 4 weeks.

MIGRATION Willets breeding on the northern Great Plains and the interior of the northwest migrate to coastal regions for the winter. Some of these western birds migrate far to the east, occurring all along the Atlantic coast in fall and winter.

CONSERVATION STATUS Eastern population was much reduced by hunting in late 19th century, has made good recovery. Loss of habitat has reduced numbers in some areas, but birds tolerate some disturbance of habitat.

WANDERING TATTLER   *Heteroscelus incanus*

Along rocky shorelines on the west coast, this gray sandpiper clambers actively over the boulders. If an observer approaches too closely, the bird gives a loud

"tattling" call and flies away, spooking the other shorebirds on the rocks. The name "Wandering" refers to the wide distribution of this species: in winter it is found along Pacific coastlines from North America to Australia, including innumerable islands in the southwest Pacific. In summer, for a change of pace, it goes to high mountains in Alaska and northwestern Canada.

HABITAT   *Rocky coasts, pebbly beaches. Nests near mountain streams above timberline.* In migration and winter usually on rocky coastline or similar areas, such as rock jetties or breakwaters. Occasionally feeds on nearby mudflats or sand beaches. In breeding season, found along rocky or gravelly streams in northern mountains.

Wandering Tattler

FEEDING   **Diet:** *Includes insects, crustaceans, mollusks.* On northern breeding grounds, feeds on insects, including flies, beetles, and caddisflies, also amphipods and small mollusks. During migration and winter, eats a variety of mollusks, marine worms, crabs and other crustaceans, and other invertebrates. **Behavior:** Forages more actively than other shorebirds of rocky coasts, moving about quickly over rocks, picking items from surface. Also probes among rocks or in mats of algae. On breeding grounds, forages by walking or wading along mountain streams.

NESTING   Early in breeding season, male displays over nesting habitat with high flight, giving whistled song; flight path is long and straight, may extend well beyond limits of nesting territory. **Nest:** Site is on ground among rocks or gravel near mountain stream. Nest is shallow depression; may be unlined or may have substantial lining of small twigs, rootlets, and dry leaves. **Eggs:** Usually 4. Olive to green, heavily blotched with brown. Incubation is by both parents, about 23–25 days. The incubating adult may sit motionless on the nest even when approached very closely. **Young:** Downy young leave nest soon after hatching. Both parents tend the young at first, but after 1–2 weeks usually only one adult is present. Young feed themselves, following parents along edge of stream; young can swim well even when small. Age at first flight not well known.

MIGRATION   Mostly a long-distance migrant. Some winter along our Pacific coast, but many go as far as Australia in a series of long flights across the Pacific. Small numbers also winter along South American west coast.

CONSERVATION STATUS   Widely dispersed range makes species difficult to census, but also probably helps to ensure survival.

GRAY-TAILED TATTLER   *Heteroscelus brevipes*

A close relative of our Wandering Tattler, replacing it as a breeding bird in Siberia; the two may sometimes winter together in coastal Australia. The Gray-tailed Tattler is not so tied to rocky shorelines as its American counterpart, being found more often on mudflats. It occurs as a rare but regular migrant in western Alaska.

GENUS *Actitis*

COMMON SANDPIPER   *Actitis hypoleucos*

The name Common Sandpiper is appropriate only in the Old World; in North America this is a rare bird, occurring in small numbers in western Alaska during migration. This is the Eurasian counterpart to our Spotted Sandpiper, and it walks with a similar teetering action along the edges of streams and ponds.

SPOTTED SANDPIPER   *Actitis macularia*

Most sandpipers nest only in the far north, but the little "Spotty" is common in summer over much of North America. As it walks on the shores of streams, ponds, and marshes, it bobs the rear half of its body up and down in an odd teetering motion. When startled, it skims away low over the water, with rapid bursts of shallow wingbeats and short, stiff-winged glides. Even where it is common, it is seldom seen in flocks.

Spotted Sandpiper

HABITAT   *Pebbly lake shores, ponds, streamsides; in winter, also seashores.* Breeds near the edge of fresh water in a wide variety of settings, including lakes, ponds, rivers, streams, in either open or wooded country. In migration and winter also found along coast on mudflats, beaches, breakwaters; also on such inland habitats as sewage ponds, irrigation ditches.

FEEDING   **Diet:** *Insects, crustaceans, other invertebrates.* Feeds on wide variety of insects, also earthworms, crabs, crayfish, small mollusks, small fish, sometimes bits of carrion. **Behavior:** Forages in a variety of ways. Picks up items from surface of ground or water; snatches flying insects out of the air; plucks small items from shallow water. On open flats, may crouch low, stalk slowly, then dash forward to catch insects or small crabs.

NESTING   Has a complicated mating system. Females are slightly larger and much more aggressive, actively defending breeding territory with displays in flight and on ground. At least in some parts of range, one female may mate with up to five males during a season; each time, female lays a clutch of eggs, leaving male to incubate the eggs and care for the young. **Nest:** Site is near water or some distance away, on ground under shrubs or weeds, next to fallen log, etc. Nest (built by both sexes) is shallow depression lined with grass, moss, sometimes feathers. **Eggs:** 4, sometimes 3, rarely 5. Buff, blotched with brown. Incubation is usually by male only, 20–24 days; female may help incubate final clutch of the season. **Young:** Downy young leave nest soon after hatching. Young feed themselves, are usually tended by male only. Age at first flight about 17–21 days.

MIGRATION   Some are only short-distance migrants, wintering in southern United States and along our Pacific coast; others go as far as southern South America.

CONSERVATION STATUS   Numbers are thought to have declined in many parts of range during recent decades, probably from loss of habitat. However, still widespread and common.

TEREK SANDPIPER *Xenus cinereus*

An odd shorebird from Eurasia with short legs and a long, upcurved bill. On a mud-flat with other sandpipers, the Terek often draws attention by its animated behavior, running about more actively than the other birds. It occurs in small numbers in western Alaska during migration, occasionally in flocks.

GENUS *Bartramia*

UPLAND SANDPIPER *Bartramia longicauda*

The ghostly, breathy whistle of the Upland Sandpiper is a characteristic sound of spring on the northern Great Plains. The bird sings sometimes from the tops of fenceposts or poles but more often on the wing, flying high with shallow, fluttering wingbeats. When it lands, it may be hard to see in the tall grass of its typical habitat. Because of its short bill and round-headed shape, it was once called "Upland Plover," but it is a true sandpiper and apparently a close relative of the curlews.

HABITAT *Grassy prairies, open meadows, fields.* Favored nesting habitat is native grassland, with mixture of tall grass and broad-leafed weeds. In the northeast, where natural grass-land is now scarce, may be found most often at airports. In migration, stops on open pastures, lawns. Almost never on mudflats or other typical shorebird habitats.

FEEDING **Diet:** *Mostly insects, some seeds.* Feeds on a wide variety of insects, including many grasshoppers, crickets, beetles and their larvae, moth caterpillars, and many others; also spiders, centipedes, earthworms, snails. Also eats some seeds of grasses and weeds, and waste grain in fields. **Behavior:** Forages by walking through the grass with rather abrupt or jerky movements, picking up items from ground or from vegetation.

NESTING Male displays over breeding terri-tory in song-flight, with shallow, fluttering wingbeats and drawn-out whistles, often very high above the ground. May nest in loose colonies, with all the pairs in a local area going through stages of nesting (egg-laying, hatching, etc.) at almost exactly the same time. **Nest:** Site is on ground among dense grass, typically well hidden, with grass arched over it. Nest (probably built by both sexes) is shallow scrape on ground lined with dry grass. **Eggs:** 4. Pale buff to pinkish buff, lightly spotted with reddish brown. Incubation is by both sexes, 22–27 days. **Young:** Downy young leave nest soon after hatching. Both parents tend young, but young feed themselves. If nest or young are threatened, adults perform distraction display to lead predators away. Age of young at first flight about 30–31 days.

Upland Sandpiper

MIGRATION A long-distance migrant, vacating North America entirely in winter. Migrates mostly through Great Plains in both spring and fall.

CONSERVATION STATUS Numbers probably increased in the early days of settlement, up through the early 1800s, as forest was turned into farmland in eastern North America. During the period of commercial hunting in the late 1800s, great numbers were shot, and the population dropped sharply. Since that time, Upland Sandpipers have recovered in a few areas. Their numbers are apparently holding steady on parts of Great Plains, but in much of the east and northeast they are now very local.

CURLEWS — GENUS *Numenius*

Eight species of medium-sized to large sandpipers, all with downcurved bills. The word *curlew* was originally an interpretation of the wild whistled calls of the big Eurasian Curlew. Although a few kinds are common, some of the rarest shorebirds in the world belong to this group.

LITTLE CURLEW *Numenius minutus*

An uncommon Asian shorebird, smallest of the curlews. Closely related to the nearly extinct Eskimo Curlew, and like that species it forages in grassy fields more often than on shores or mudflats. Stray migrants, far off course, have been found a few times in California and once in Alaska.

ESKIMO CURLEW *Numenius borealis*

At one time, great flocks of Eskimo Curlews migrated between the pampas of Argentina and their nesting grounds on the tundra of Arctic Canada. In spring they passed north through the Great Plains, pausing to feed on open prairies along with flocks of American Golden-Plovers. In fall they would fly east to the coast of Labrador in eastern Canada, and then often fly nonstop to northern South America. Major storms with northeast winds would bring flocks of Eskimo Curlews to the coast of New England, along with golden-plovers, Hudsonian Godwits, and other shorebirds traveling the same route.

Unfortunately, the late 1800s was an era when wild game was hunted for the market, with little or no legal protection. Tremendous numbers of shorebirds were shot, and these small curlews were especially sought after (they were often called "dough-birds" because they are so plump). Their numbers had dropped drastically by the beginning of the 20th century. Even after the hunting was halted and other shorebirds seemed to make a comeback, this species continued to decline. Birders still hope that a few may survive, but there have been no confirmed sightings of Eskimo Curlews since 1963.

WHIMBREL *Numenius phaeopus*

The most widespread of the curlews, nesting in the Arctic across North America and Eurasia, wintering on the coasts of six continents. Whimbrels tend to concentrate in flocks at a few favored spots in migration, so that the observer sees either many of them or else very small numbers. The name "Whimbrel," originating in England, apparently began as a loose interpretation of the bird's call.

HABITAT *Shores, mudflats, marshes, tundra.* Found on a wide variety of habitats on migration. Most common on mudflats, but also found on rocky shores, sandy beaches, salt marshes, flooded agricultural fields, grassy fields near coast. In summer, breeds on Arctic tundra.

FEEDING **Diet:** *Includes insects, crustaceans, berries.* On breeding grounds may feed mostly on insects at first, but berries (such as crowberry and cranberry) become major part of diet by late summer. On coast, often eats many crabs, also amphipods and other crustaceans, marine worms, small mollusks. **Behavior:** Forages by walking on open flats, picking up items from surface or probing just below surface; despite long bill, does not seem to probe deeply. When feeding on crabs, may break off legs and crush shell before swallowing body of crab.

NESTING Early in breeding season, male performs flight display over nesting territory: flies in large circles, alternately fluttering higher and gliding down, while giving whistling and bubbling song. On ground, members of pair may call together. **Nest:** Site is on ground, usually in dry raised area near low-lying wet tundra. Nest (probably built mostly by female) is shallow depression lined with bits of lichen, moss, grass. **Eggs:** 4, sometimes 3. Olive to buff, blotched with shades of brown. Incubation is by both sexes, roughly 24–28 days. **Young:** Downy young leave nest soon after hatching. Both parents tend young, but young feed themselves. Adults actively attack predators flying over nesting area and will fly straight at human intruders, swerving aside at last moment. Age of young at first flight about 5–6 weeks.

MIGRATION Has a wide wintering range, from our Pacific and southeastern coasts to southern South America. Whimbrels from European and Asian races, with white on lower back and rump, sometimes stray to North America.

Whimbrel

CONSERVATION STATUS Numbers were seriously depleted by market hunters in late 19th century, have recovered somewhat since.

BRISTLE-THIGHED CURLEW *Numenius tahitiensis*

A rare and enigmatic bird. It was discovered wintering on South Pacific islands in 1769, but its nesting grounds were not found until almost 180 years later—in the late 1940s. It is now known to nest in a few hilly areas of western Alaska. During the winter, molting its feathers, it is unable to fly for a time—the only shorebird known to have a flightless molt. This is no problem on remote islands with no predators, but becomes a serious handicap when humans settle on those islands.

HABITAT *Tundra (Alaska); reefs and beaches in winter.* Nests at a few sites in western Alaska, well inland in steep hilly country, on open tundra with scattered small shrubs. Winters on islands in tropical Pacific, on beaches, coral reefs, mudflats, grassy fields.

FEEDING **Diet:** *Includes crustaceans, insects, berries.* Summer diet not well known, probably includes many insects. In late summer, may feed heavily on berries. On Pacific islands where it winters, feeds on crustaceans, snails, small fish; also eggs of seabirds nesting there. **Behavior:** Forages mostly by walking on ground, picking up items from surface, probably also probing in soil or mud with long bill. In feeding on thick-shelled eggs of albatrosses on winter range, may pick up a piece of rock and use it to crack the shell, a rare case of tool-using by a bird.

NESTING Early in breeding season, male displays by flying over nesting territory, calling. **Nest:** Site is on the ground on hilly upland tundra with scattered small shrubs, with nest often placed directly under a dwarf willow. Nest is a shallow depression in tundra, lined with bits of lichen, moss, and leaves. **Eggs:** Usually 4. Olive-buff, blotched with brown. Incubation is by both sexes, roughly 25 days. **Young:** Downy young leave nest soon after hatching, are tended by both parents. Young feed themselves. Adults are very aggressive in defending the nest and young; may put on "distraction display" to lure predators away or may directly attack even large predators. After a few days, families with young move away from nest site, eventually gathering with other families on hilltops. Adult females usually depart before young fledge, leaving males to care for young.

Bristle-thighed Curlew

MIGRATION   After nesting, most individuals gather on the Yukon Delta in western Alaska to feed heavily on berries and insects, building up fat reserves, then depart on nonstop flight of over 2,500 miles to Hawaii and other islands in Pacific.

CONSERVATION STATUS   Rare; population probably well under 10,000. Most threats are on wintering range, where the curlews are very vulnerable during the flightless stage of their molt.

SLENDER-BILLED CURLEW *Numenius tenuirostris*

Breeding in central Asia and wintering in northwest Africa, this curlew is now among the world's rarest shorebirds, probably close to extinction. A lone Slender-billed Curlew strayed to Ontario once in the 1920s, but it is almost certain that the species will never be seen in North America again.

FAR EASTERN CURLEW *Numenius madagascariensis*

One of the largest shorebirds in the world, with an incredibly long bill, averaging even longer than that of our Long-billed Curlew. Migrating impressive distances in the Far East, it travels from southern Australia to eastern Siberia in spring; one or two sometimes go off course and appear on the Aleutian Islands of Alaska.

EURASIAN CURLEW *Numenius arquata*

Almost as large as our Long-billed Curlew, this big wader is common in Europe and across much of Asia. Very rarely strays to northeastern North America. In Europe it sometimes forages in marshes or wet fields inland, but records in our area have been on the outer coast.

LONG-BILLED CURLEW *Numenius americanus*

This incredibly long-billed sandpiper is the largest of our shorebirds; more often than not, however, it is seen away from the shore. It spends the summer on the grasslands of the arid west, appearing on coastal mudflats only in migration and winter, and even then likely to be on prairies instead. It often occurs alongside the Marbled Godwit, which is very similar in size and color pattern, but the godwit's bill curves up, not down.

Long-billed Curlew

HABITAT   *High plains, rangeland. In winter, also cultivated land, tideflats, salt marshes.* Breeding habitat is mostly native dry grassland and sagebrush prairie; may favor areas with some damp low spots nearby, to provide better feeding area for the young. May nest in pastures that are not too heavily grazed, rarely in agricultural fields. In migration and winter often in farm fields, marshes, coastal mudflats, in addition to grasslands.

FEEDING   **Diet:** *Mostly insects.* On grasslands, feeds mostly on insects, including beetles, grasshoppers, caterpillars, many others; also eats spiders, toads, and sometimes the eggs and young of other birds. May eat many berries at times. In coastal areas, also eats crabs, crayfish, mollusks, marine worms, other large invertebrates. **Behavior:** Forages by walking rather quickly over grassland or mudflats, using long bill to reach ahead and pick up insects or probe just below the surface of mud or soil. On coastal mudflats, often probes into small burrows for mud crabs, ghost shrimps, and other creatures.

NESTING   Male displays over nesting territory with spectacular undulating flight, fluttering higher and then gliding lower, while giving loud ringing calls. **Nest:** Site is on ground on open prairie, usually in rather dry surroundings. On mostly featureless terrain, often chooses site close to conspicuous rock, shrub, pile of cow manure, or other object. Nest is shallow scrape in ground, usually with sparse lining of grass, weeds; may have slight rim built up around edge. **Eggs:** 4, rarely 3–5. Pale buff to olive-buff, evenly spotted with brown and dark olive. Incubation is by both parents, 27–30 days. Incubating bird may sit motionless on nest even if approached closely. **Young:** Downy young leave nest soon after hatching. Both parents tend young, often leading them to marshy or damp area for better feeding; young feed themselves. Age of young at first flight varies, 32–45 days.

MIGRATION   Only a short-distance migrant, most wintering in southern United States and northern Mexico.

CONSERVATION STATUS   Was once much more common and widespread; in the mid-1800s, occurred as a common migrant along much of the Atlantic coast. Hunting of wild game for market caused a serious decline in this species and other shorebirds in the late 1800s. In more recent decades, has decreased in many parts of its nesting range as grassland has been converted to agriculture.

GODWITS — GENUS *Limosa*

The ringing cries of these big sandpipers may suggest the word *godwit!* Members of the genus can be recognized by their long, slightly upcurved bills. Of the four godwit species, three nest in our area and the other is a rare visitor.

BLACK-TAILED GODWIT   *Limosa limosa*

The rarest of the four godwits in our area, the Black-tail nests in Eurasia and is only a stray to North America. In Alaska it may be a rare but regular migrant in spring in the Aleutian Islands. On our Atlantic coast it is only casual or accidental, but strays have been found in several states and provinces from Newfoundland to Florida.

HUDSONIAN GODWIT   *Limosa haemastica*

Once thought to be very rare, even endangered, this big sandpiper was probably just overlooked on its long migration between the Arctic and southern South America. In spring it moves north across the Great Plains, pausing at marshes and flooded fields more often than at the mudflats thronged by other shorebirds. In fall, most fly non-stop from James Bay, Canada, to South America. Some stop in fall on our Atlantic coast, especially when driven there by northeasterly winds.

Hudsonian Godwit

HABITAT   *Marshes, prairie pools, mudflats; edge of tundra in summer.* Spring migrants are usually on shallow marshy lakes, flooded pastures, rice fields, mudflats around ponds. Fall migrants on Atlantic coast may be on marshy ponds or tidal flats. Nesting habitat in far north is near treeline, where patches of tundra, open woods, and ponds are mixed.

FEEDING   **Diet:** *Insects, mollusks, crustaceans, marine worms.* Diet not well known. On breeding grounds, may feed mostly on insects, including many flies and their larvae. During migration, may feed on marine worms, mollusks, and crustaceans on coast, mostly insects inland. **Behavior:** Forages mostly by walking in shallow water, probing with bill in mud of bottom. Often wades so deeply that head is underwater part of the time.

NESTING   In display over nesting territory, male flies high, calling; at peak of display, he glides with wings in shallow "V" while calling intensely for up to a minute or more, then dives toward ground. Male often perches on treetop; in courtship, pursues female in flight. **Nest:** Site is on ground in sedge marsh, usually on top of hummock under prostrate dwarf shrub, sometimes in tussock of grass. Very well concealed, extremely hard to find. Nest is shallow depression in vegetation, with sparse lining of leaves. **Eggs:** 4, rarely 3. Dark olive-brown, with rather obscure brown blotches. Incubation is by both sexes, about 22–25 days. **Young:** Downy young leave nest soon after hatching. Young find all their own food but are tended by both parents. Adults are very aggressive in defense of young. Young are able to fly at about 30 days.

MIGRATION   Migrates north mostly through Great Plains. Southward migration mostly off Atlantic coast, most apparently flying nonstop from James Bay, Ontario, to northern South America. Adults migrate south earlier than juveniles in fall.

CONSERVATION STATUS   Numbers were seriously depleted in late 19th century by unrestricted shooting. Current population probably stable.

BAR-TAILED GODWIT   *Limosa lapponica*

Widespread in summer across northern Europe and Asia, this godwit also crosses the Bering Strait to nest in western Alaska. Big, noisy, and cinnamon-colored, it is conspicuous on its tundra nesting grounds. Bar-tailed Godwits from Alaska spend the winter in the Old World. A few may show up on either coast of North America in migration; such strays, in dull winter plumage, often associate with flocks of other godwits, where they are easily overlooked.

HABITAT   *Mudflats, shores, tundra.* In Alaska, nests on rolling hills of tundra, on slopes with hummocky ground cover and low stunted shrubs, a habitat shared with Whimbrels;

Bar-tailed Godwit

adults may feed on coastal lagoons some distance from nesting sites. In migration and winter mainly on tidal mudflats along coast.

FEEDING   **Diet:** *Includes insects, crustaceans, mollusks.* In summer in Alaska, feeds mainly on aquatic insects, also occasionally seeds and berries. On mudflats and shores at other seasons, feeds on crustaceans, mollusks, insects, annelid worms. **Behavior:** Forages by probing in mud of exposed flats or in shallow water. Females have longer bills and may feed in deeper water than males.

NESTING   First breeds at age of two years. Territorial and courtship display of male involves loud calls and aerial acrobatics, deep wingbeats alternating with glides as he circles high above tundra. **Nest:** Site is usually on a raised hummock, surrounded by grass. Nest is a shallow depression lined with bits of grass, moss, lichens. **Eggs:** Usually 4. Olive or pale brown, usually with a few brown spots. Incubation begins with laying of last egg; both male and female incubate, and eggs hatch in about 3 weeks. **Young:** Shortly after hatching, young are led to nearby marshy areas, where they stay until able to fly. Both parents tend young, and young find all their own food. Age at first flight probably about 30 days. One brood per year.

MIGRATION   Alaskan and Siberian birds winter from southeast Asia south to Australia and New Zealand. Those from Alaska thought to migrate long distances over water rather than following Asian coastline. Strays in the lower 48 states may come from either Asia or Europe.

MARBLED GODWIT *Limosa fedoa*

Marbled Godwit

This big cinnamon-colored sandpiper inhabits the northern Great Plains in summer. When it leaves the prairies, the Marbled Godwit goes to coastal regions and becomes quite gregarious. Large flocks roost together in the salt meadows at high tide or stand together in shallow water above the flats, probing deeply in the mud with their long bills.

HABITAT   *Prairies, pools, shores, tideflats.* Breeds mostly on northern Great Plains, in areas of native prairie with marshes or ponds nearby. Localized populations also nest on tundra at James Bay, Ontario, and on Alaska Peninsula. In migration and winter around tidal mudflats, marshes, ponds, mainly in coastal regions.

FEEDING   **Diet:** *Includes insects, mollusks, crustaceans.* In summer on prairies, feeds mostly on insects, including many grasshoppers; also roots and seeds of various aquatic plants, such as sedges and pondweeds. On coast, feeds on mollusks, marine worms, crustaceans, other invertebrates. **Behavior:** On mudflats and in marshes, forages mostly by probing in water or mud with long bill. Often wades and probes so deeply that head is underwater. Finds most food by touch; may feed by day or night. On prairies, also picks up insects from surface of ground or plants.

NESTING   May nest in loose colonies. Male displays over breeding territory by flying over area, calling loudly. On ground, members of pair may go through ritualized nest-scrape-making display. **Nest:** Site is on ground, usually in short grass on dry spot fairly close to water (sometimes far from water). Nest is slight depression, lined with dry grass. Occasionally has slight canopy of grass arranged above nest. **Eggs:** 4, rarely 3–5. Greenish to olive-buff, lightly spotted with brown. Incubation is probably by both parents, 21–23 days. Incubating bird may sit motionless even when approached closely. **Young:** Downy young leave nest soon after hatching. Both parents tend young, but young find all their own food. Age of young at first flight roughly 3 weeks.

MIGRATION   Migrates in flocks. Most birds move to coastal regions in winter. Some reach South America, but most winter north of Panama. A few birds (possibly one-year-olds) remain on winter range throughout the summer.

CONSERVATION STATUS   Numbers were reduced by market hunting during 19th century; some recovery since, but now declining again as more of its nesting habitat is converted to farmland.

TURNSTONES — GENUS *Arenaria*

Turnstones are tough, aggressive little sandpipers, adept at using their short, chisel-like bills to probe under debris or turn over stones in search of food. Although the Ruddy Turnstone has a very wide range around the world, its close relative the Black Turnstone is limited to our Pacific coast.

RUDDY TURNSTONE   *Arenaria interpres*

A chunky, short-legged sandpiper wearing a bright harlequin pattern in summer, dark brown in winter. The Ruddy Turnstone nests on high Arctic tundra of North America and Eurasia and winters along the coastlines of six continents. In migration it is seen mainly along the coast, although numbers may stop over at favored points inland, especially along the Great Lakes.

HABITAT   *Beaches, mudflats, jetties, rocky shores; in summer, tundra.* Mostly coastal in migration and winter, favoring rocky shorelines, rock jetties, or beaches covered with seaweed or debris. May also feed on mudflats or on plowed fields near coast. Nests on open ground in Arctic, including wet tundra and dry rocky ridges.

FEEDING   **Diet:** *Variable; includes insects, crustaceans, mollusks.* In breeding season mostly insects, also spiders, seeds, berries, moss. At other seasons eats crustaceans (including barnacles, crabs, amphipods), mollusks, worms, sea urchins, small fish. Will eat carrion, also food scraps at garbage dumps. Sometimes eats eggs of other birds. **Behavior:** Best known for habit of inserting bill under stones, shells, etc., and flipping them over to find food underneath.

Ruddy Turnstone

Several birds may work together to overturn a larger object. Often probes under seaweed or debris. Can be a nuisance in tern colonies at times, including on wintering grounds on Pacific islands, where it may puncture and eat the contents of many eggs.

NESTING   In courtship, male pursues female in the air and on the ground. Male may approach female in hunched posture, raising and lowering tail. **Nest:** Site is on ground, either in the open or concealed among rocks or under plants. Nest (built by female) is shallow depression with slight lining of leaves. **Eggs:** 4, sometimes 2–3. Olive green to olive-buff, blotched with dark brown. Incubation is by both sexes (but female does more), 22–24 days. **Young:** Downy young leave nest shortly after hatching. Both parents care for young at first, but male takes greater role, and female usually departs before young are old enough to fly. Male leads young to food at first, but young feed themselves. Age at first flight 19–21 days, usually independent thereafter.

MIGRATION   Usually scarce inland in migration. Winters on coasts from United States to South America, southern Africa, Australia. Birds from western Alaska winter from west coast of North America to Australia and New Zealand, some making long overwater flights from Alaska to Hawaii and then on to southwest. Birds from northern Canada winter on coasts from United States to southern South America. Those from northeasternmost Canadian islands (and Greenland) winter in western Europe.

CONSERVATION STATUS   Common and widespread. Very wide winter range and remote breeding range help to ensure survival.

BLACK TURNSTONE *Arenaria melanocephala*

Black Turnstone

This is a characteristic bird of wave-washed rocky shorelines along the Pacific coast in winter. Against the background of dark rocks it is hard to see when it sits still, but it is usually moving, clambering about in search of barnacles and limpets.

HABITAT   *Strictly coastal. Rocky shores, break-waters, islets; nests on coastal tundra.* In migration and winter, typically found in rocky sites along coast, such as rocky shoreline, jetties, breakwaters; also on mudflats and sand beaches at times. Breeds in Alaska on wet tundra near estuaries or lagoons, very close to coast.

FEEDING   **Diet:** *Includes barnacles, mollusks, insects.* On breeding grounds, may feed heavily on insects, also some seeds and berries. On coast (where it spends most of year), barnacles and limpets are among main foods. Also eats other crustaceans and mollusks, marine worms. **Behavior:** On coast, forages mostly by walking slowly on rocks. Feeding on acorn barnacle, may insert bill in shell opening and pry it open or hammer on shell to break it. Limpets and other mollusks are pried from rocks with pointed bill. On beaches, may turn over rocks, shells, or seaweed to look underneath for food.

NESTING   Adults often come back to exact same sites and nest with same mate each year. Male displays with circular flight over territory. **Nest:** Site is on ground, usually close to water among grasses or sedges, either in open or hidden by tall vegetation. Nest (probably built by both parents) is shallow depression lined with grasses. **Eggs:** 4, sometimes 3. Yellowish green to olive, blotched with dark brown. Incubation is by both sexes, usually 22–24 days. **Young:** Downy young leave nest soon after hatching. Both parents tend young at first, but female usually leaves after about 2 weeks, leaving male to care for them; young find all their own food. Young can make short flights after about 23 days, can fly well at about 28–30 days.

MIGRATION   Apparently follows the coastline closely in spring migration. In fall, some birds may take a shortcut across the Gulf of Alaska, flying southeast across the water from western Alaska rather than taking the long way along the coast.

CONSERVATION STATUS   Some data from the Pacific Northwest suggest declining numbers over the last two decades.

GENUS *Aphriza*

SURFBIRD   *Aphriza virgata*

Surfbird

Named for its winter haunts, the Surfbird spends the winter (as well as migration seasons) on rocky coastlines pounded by the surf, often clambering about the rocks barely above the reach of the waves. But this stocky little sandpiper leads a double life, abandoning the coast in late spring. Its nesting grounds, high in the mountains in Alaska and the Yukon Territory, were not discovered until the 1920s.

HABITAT   *Rocky coasts; nests on mountain tundra.* During migration and winter, mostly on rocky outer coasts and islands, also on stone jetties and breakwaters. Sometimes on sandy beaches or mudflats, especially during brief stops on migration. In summer, breeds on rather barren, rocky tundra above treeline in northern mountains.

FEEDING   **Diet:** *Mostly insects, mollusks, barnacles.* In summer on tundra, feeds mostly on insects; also spiders, snails, a few seeds. On coast (where it spends most of year), feeds on mollusks, such as mussels, limpets, and snails, as well as barnacles and other crustaceans, and other small invertebrates. **Behavior:** Major feeding method on coast involves removing barnacles, limpets, and young mussels from rocks with a quick sideways jerk of the head; the Surfbird's thick bill is adapted for this behavior. Also picks up snails and insects from ground or rocks, sometimes probes in mud.

NESTING   Breeding behavior is not well known. In display over nesting territory, male makes long flight, fluttering wings through shallow arc, then gliding while giving repeated calls or harsh song. **Nest:** Site is on ground, in natural depression in rocky surface of high, dry ridge, in area surrounded by very low ground cover. Nest (probably built by both sexes) is simple lining of dead leaves, lichens, and moss added to nest depression. **Eggs:** 4. Buff, spotted with dark reddish brown. Incubation is by both sexes, incubation period not well known. **Young:** Downy young leave nest soon after hatching. Both parents tend young, but they find all their own food. Development of the chicks and age at first flight not well known.

MIGRATION   Considering the limited size of the breeding range, wintering range is remarkably stretched out, from southeastern Alaska to southern Chile. Some can be found on wintering range at least from late July to early May. On our southern Pacific coast, the only noticeable peak in migrant numbers occurs in spring, mainly in April.

CONSERVATION STATUS   Generally an uncommon bird, but numbers probably stable.

This group includes the tiniest of the sandpipers and also many of the most common kinds. They are often called "stints" in Europe or "peeps" in North America—especially the seven smallest members of the genus, which can be very difficult to tell apart. Some of the larger species are more distinctive. All members of this group nest in the far north, and some are very long-distance migrants.

GREAT KNOT   *Calidris tenuirostris*

The biggest of the "peeps," nearly the size of a Black-bellied Plover, this robust sandpiper nests in the mountains of eastern Siberia. It is a rare stray to western Alaska in spring, occurring most often on St. Lawrence Island and the Seward Peninsula.

RED KNOT   *Calidris canutus*

This chunky shorebird has a rather anonymous look in winter plumage but is unmistakable in spring, when it wears robin red on its chest. It nests in the far north, mostly well above the Arctic Circle (the first known nest was discovered during Admiral Peary's expedition to the North Pole in 1909); its winter range includes shorelines around the world, south to Australia and southern South America. Where it is common, the Red Knot may roost in densely packed flocks, standing shoulder to shoulder on the sand.

HABITAT   *Tidal flats, shores; tundra (summer).* In migration and winter on coastal mudflats and tidal zones, sometimes on open sandy beaches of the sort favored by Sanderlings. Nests on Arctic tundra, usually on rather high and barren areas inland from coast, but typically near a pond or stream.

FEEDING   Diet: *Includes mollusks, insects, green plants, seeds.* In migration and winter, feeds on small invertebrates that live in mud of intertidal zone, especially small mollusks, also marine worms, crustaceans. On breeding grounds, feeds mostly on insects, especially flies. Also eats much plant material, especially early in breeding season when insects may be scarce, including shoots, buds, leaves, and seeds.

Red Knot

Behavior: On tidal flats, forages mostly by probing in mud with bill, finding food by touch. On dry sand and on tundra breeding grounds, forages mostly by sight, picking items from surface.

NESTING   Early in breeding season, male flies in high circles above territory, hovering on rapidly quivering wings and then gliding, while giving mellow whistled calls. Female may fly around territory with male. On ground, male displays with wings held high. Nest: Site is on ground on open tundra, usually near water. Nest is a shallow scrape lined with leaves, lichen, moss. Eggs: 3–4. Pale olive green with small brown spots. Incubation is by both sexes (although male may do more), 21–22 days. Young: Downy young leave nest soon after hatching. Both parents tend young at first, but female leaves before young are old enough to fly. Young feed themselves. Young are able to fly at about 18–20 days after hatching, become independent about that time.

A few winter on southern coasts of the United States, but many go to southern South America for the winter. Some birds nesting in far northern Canada apparently fly across Greenland ice cap in fall to winter in Britain and Europe.

CONSERVATION STATUS Once far more numerous in North America, but huge numbers were shot on migration in late 1800s. Some populations have declined sharply since 1960s; reasons not well understood.

SANDERLING *Calidris alba*

This is the little sandpiper that runs up and down the beach "like a clockwork toy," chasing the receding waves. Plumper and more active than most small sandpipers

and quite pale at most times of year, a good match for dry sand. Sanderlings nest only in limited areas of the far north, but during migration and winter they are familiar sights on coastal beaches all over the world.

HABITAT *Outer beaches, tideflats, lake shores; when nesting, stony tundra.* At most seasons, found on sandy beaches washed by waves. Sometimes on rocky shorelines, less often on mudflats. Typically coastal, but a few stop over on lake shores inland. In breeding season, mostly far above Arctic Circle on rather dry, rocky tundra with growth of moss, lichens, low plants, generally close to lakes or ponds.

FEEDING **Diet:** *Mostly sand crabs and other invertebrates.* Feeds on a wide variety of small creatures on beach, including sand crabs, amphipods, isopods, insects, marine worms, small mollusks; also

Sanderling

may eat some carrion. Wintering birds on southern coasts may eat corn chips and other junk food left by people. In spring, may feed heavily on eggs of horseshoe crab. On tundra, feeds mostly on flies and other insects, also some seeds, algae, and leaves. **Behavior:** Chases the waves mostly to find sand crabs, which lie buried in intertidal zone and are easiest to spot just after a wave retreats. Sanderlings also probe in sand and mud for other creatures and move rapidly while picking items from surface.

NESTING In breeding season, unmated male performs low display flight, alternately fluttering and gliding while giving harsh chirring song. On ground, male runs up to female with feathers ruffled, head hunched down on shoulders. **Nest:** Site is on ground, usually in open and rather barren spot that may be higher than surroundings. Nest is shallow scrape, often lined with small leaves. **Eggs:** 4, sometimes 3. Olive green to pale brown, sparsely spotted with brown and black. Incubation is by both sexes, 24–31 days. Sometimes female lays two clutches in separate nests; male incubates one set, female the other. At other times, female may have two mates, leaving each male to care for a set of eggs and young, while female departs. **Young:** Downy young leave nest shortly after hatching, are tended by one or both parents. If both parents are present at first, female may leave within a few days. Young feed themselves. Age at first flight about 17 days.

MIGRATION Much of migration is accomplished in long nonstop flights between key stopover points. Studies show that many individuals return year after year to same wintering sites. One-year-old birds may remain through summer on the southern wintering grounds.

May be seriously declining; some surveys show more than 80 percent drop in numbers in the Americas since early 1970s. Relies heavily on a few staging areas in migration and is vulnerable to destruction of those sites.

SEMIPALMATED SANDPIPER   *Calidris pusilla*

Small and plain in appearance, this sandpiper is important in terms of sheer numbers. It often gathers by the thousands at stopover points during migration. Semipalmated Sandpipers winter mostly in South America, and studies have shown that they may make a nonstop flight of nearly 2,000 miles from New England or eastern Canada to the South American coast. The name "Semipalmated" refers to slight webbing between the toes, visible only at extremely close range.

Semipalmated Sandpiper

HABITAT   *Beaches, mudflats; tundra in summer.* During migration along coast found on mudflats in intertidal zone, shallow estuaries and inlets, beaches. Inland, occurs on edges of lakes and marshes next to very shallow water. Nests on low Arctic tundra near water.

FEEDING   **Diet:** *Mostly tiny aquatic insects and crustaceans.* Diet varies with season and place. In breeding season eats mostly insects, especially flies and their larvae, also some spiders, snails, seeds. During migration, feeds on a wide variety of small crustaceans that live in shallow water or wet mud, also many insects, small mollusks, worms. **Behavior:** Forages mostly by walking on wet mud, looking for prey; sometimes probes in mud with bill. In coastal areas, does most feeding while tide is falling or at low tide. May forage at night.

NESTING   Male defends territory with display flight, fluttering wings and singing a sputtering trill (sounds like a tiny outboard motor). Females are attracted by song; male and female may chase each other around territory. **Nest:** Site is on ground, often at top of low mound or on island, under small shrub. Nest is shallow depression lined with leaves, grass, moss. Male makes potential nest scrapes, female chooses one and adds nest material. **Eggs:** 4, sometimes 3. Variable in color, whitish to olive-buff blotched with brown and gray. Incubation is by both parents, usually 20 days. **Young:** Downy young leave nest within hours after hatching. Young are tended by both parents at first, but female usually deserts them within a few days. Male remains with young until they are about old enough to fly, but young feed themselves. Young can make short flights at about 2 weeks after hatching, can fly fairly well at 16–19 days, when not quite full-grown.

MIGRATION   Migrates in flocks. May make very long nonstop flights between major feeding areas on migration. In fall, adults move south about a month before juveniles on average. One-year-old birds mostly stay on wintering grounds through first summer.

CONSERVATION STATUS   Still abundant, but vulnerable because of heavy dependence on a few key stopover points in migration. Several special reserves have been established to protect this and other migratory shorebirds.

WESTERN SANDPIPER   *Calidris mauri*

A close relative of the Semipalmated Sandpiper. Western Sandpipers nest mostly in Alaska and migrate mostly along the Pacific coast, but many reach the Atlantic coast

in fall and remain through the winter. Of the various dull gray sandpipers to be found commonly on coastal beaches in winter, Western is the smallest.

HABITAT   *Shores, beaches, mudflats; in summer, dry tundra.* Migrants and wintering birds are typically on open shorelines, mudflats, sandy beaches, tidal estuaries. In winter mostly along coast, few remaining inland then. Breeds on tundra slopes, choosing dry sites with low shrub layer and with marshes nearby for feeding.

FEEDING   **Diet:** *Includes insects, crustaceans, mollusks, marine worms.* On breeding grounds, eats mostly flies and beetles, also other insects, spiders, small crustaceans. Diet in migration and winter varies. On coast eats many amphipods and other crustaceans, small mollusks, marine worms, insects. Inland migrants eat mostly insects, some seeds. **Behavior:** Forages by walking in shallow water or on mud and probing in mud with bill; also feeds by searching visually and picking up items from surface of shore.

Western Sandpiper

NESTING   Male sings while performing display flight over breeding territory. On ground, unmated male approaches female in hunched posture, tail raised over back; repeatedly gives trilled call. **Nest:** Site is on ground, usually under low shrub or grass clump. Nest is shallow depression with sparse lining of sedges, leaves, lichens. Male makes several nest scrapes, female chooses one. **Eggs:** 4, sometimes 3, perhaps rarely 5. Whitish to brown with darker brown spots. Incubation is by both parents, about 21 days. At first, female incubates from late afternoon to midmorning, male only during midday, but male's share increases later. Female sometimes departs before eggs hatch. **Young:** Downy young leave nest a few hours after hatching. Sometimes both parents care for chicks, but often female deserts them after a few days, leaving male to care for the young. Young feed themselves. Age at first flight about 17–21 days.

MIGRATION   From breeding grounds in Alaska and eastern Siberia, migrates southeast to wintering areas on both coasts of North and South America. Apparently migrates in series of short to moderate flights, without the long overwater flights of some shorebirds.

CONSERVATION STATUS   Still abundant, but vulnerable because high percentage of population may stop during migration at a few key points, such as Copper River Delta in Alaska. Declining numbers noted in some areas.

RED-NECKED STINT   *Calidris ruficollis*

This rusty-headed little sandpiper is mostly an Asian bird, but every summer, small numbers cross the Bering Strait to nest in western Alaska. Rarely, a few individuals will migrate south in the Americas rather than taking their usual route south to the Australasian region. Such strays have been seen on both coasts and at points in between. Most Red-necked Stints found south of Alaska have been adults migrating south in July, still in distinctive breeding plumage.

HABITAT   *Mudflats, shores; tundra in summer.* In Alaska found on coastal tundra or dry foothills tundra not far from coast, also at nearby river mouths and shores. In migration, occurs in the same kinds of situations as those favored by Semipalmated and Western sandpipers, including coastal estuaries and tidal flats, also muddy edges of ponds and lakes inland.

FEEDING   **Diet:** *Mostly insects and crustaceans.* Diet not well known, probably similar to that of Semipalmated Sandpiper. In breeding season may feed mostly on insects, especially

Red-necked Stint

flies and their larvae. During migration, probably eats a wide variety of small crustaceans that live in shallow water or wet mud, also insects, small mollusks, worms. **Behavior:** Forages by walking, usually on shore rather than in shallow water, picking rapidly at tiny items on surface. Sometimes probes in mud with bill.

NESTING Breeding behavior not well known. Male displays over breeding territory by fluttering and gliding, giving a repeated nasal call; at the end of the display, he holds his wings high over his back in a sharp "V" and drops to the ground. **Nest:** Site is on ground, often on moss hummock in rocky tundra with dwarf willows nearby. Nest is shallow depression in moss or other vegetation, typically lined with willow leaves. **Eggs:** Usually 4. Olive to buff, blotched with brown. Incubation is apparently by both parents; incubation period not well known, probably about 3 weeks. **Young:** Downy young leave nest soon after hatching, probably find all their own food. Young may be tended by both parents at first, but female often abandons them shortly after hatching, leaving male to care for the young. Age at first flight not well known.

MIGRATION Adults migrate south earlier than juveniles, often migrating during July. Most migrate through Asia, wintering abundantly to southern Australia. Strays in all parts of North America, even on east coast, undoubtedly come via Siberia and Alaska, not across the Atlantic.

LITTLE STINT *Calidris minuta*

Rare and difficult to identify, this Eurasian shorebird was not detected in our area until 1975, but it may have been overlooked before that. There now have been well over two dozen North American records, about half of them either in the northeast or along the Pacific coast, the rest in Alaska.

TEMMINCK'S STINT *Calidris temminckii*

Of the seven species of tiny "peeps" and "stints" around the world, Temminck's is the most distinctive, with its horizontal look, long tail, and white outer tail feathers. Unlike the others, it usually occurs singly or in very small groups, in marshy places instead of open mudflats. Widespread in Eurasia, it is a rare migrant in western Alaska.

LONG-TOED STINT *Calidris subminuta*

The Asian replacement for our Least Sandpiper, usually poking about in marshy places and the muddy edges of freshwater ponds. It shows up every year on the Aleutian Islands of Alaska during migration, usually in small numbers, sometimes in flocks. At least one lost bird has strayed to California.

LEAST SANDPIPER *Calidris minutilla*

The smallest member of the sandpiper family, no bigger than a sparrow. This is the sandpiper most likely to be seen on small inland bodies of water. On sandy riverbanks, lake shores, and edges of sewage treatment ponds, little flocks of Least Sandpipers fly up to circle the area and then settle again, giving thin, reedy cries as they go. On the outer coast, outnumbered by bigger shorebirds, they seek out sheltered places on the muddy edges of the marsh.

HABITAT *Mudflats, grassy marshes, rain pools, shores.* In migration, often more common inland than on coast, favoring muddy edges of marshes, ponds, rivers; sometimes in flooded fields or damp meadows. On coast, usually avoids sandy beaches and wide-open tidal flats, being found instead on narrow tidal creeks and edge of salt marsh. Breeds on tundra, sedge meadows, northern bogs.

FEEDING **Diet:** *Tiny crustaceans, insects, snails.* Diet varies with season and place. On breeding grounds, may feed mostly on larvae of various flies. During migration on coast, may

feed mostly on small crustaceans called amphipods and isopods; in inland areas, may eat mostly insects. Diet also includes small snails, marine worms, seeds. In spring on Atlantic coast, may join other shorebirds in feeding on eggs of horseshoe crab. **Behavior:** Forages mostly by walking slowly and picking up tiny items from surface of ground. Sometimes probes in mud with bill.

NESTING In display flight over breeding territory, male circles with alternating flutters and glides while singing. During courtship on ground, male approaches female, leaning forward with tail lifted, sometimes raising one or both wings over his back. **Nest:** Site is on ground near water, usually in clump of grass or on hummock of moss. Nest (begun by male, completed by female) is shallow depression lined with bits of grass,

Least Sandpiper

leaves, moss. **Eggs:** 4, rarely 3. Pale buff, blotched with shades of brown. Incubation is by both sexes, with female incubating at night and early morning, male most of day at first. In later stages, male may do most or all of incubating. **Young:** Downy young leave nest soon after hatching. Young are usually tended by both parents at first, but female usually deserts them before male does, sometimes departing even before eggs hatch; male typically stays with young at least until they can fly. Young feed themselves, can fly about 14–16 days after hatching.

MIGRATION Migrates in flocks. Birds from eastern Canada may make nonstop flight over ocean to northern South America; others move south through interior of North America, probably with short flights and frequent stops. Large numbers winter in southern United States.

CONSERVATION STATUS Widespread and common, and numbers probably stable. Less dependent than some other shorebirds on key stopover points in migration, so perhaps less vulnerable.

WHITE-RUMPED SANDPIPER *Calidris fuscicollis*

The trademark white rump patch is usually hidden by the long wings, which are a clue to this bird's long migrations. Many fly annually from Canada's Arctic islands to the southern tip of South America; some have gone even farther, to islands near the Antarctic Peninsula. In North America, White-rumped Sandpipers are seen in greatest numbers during northward migration through the Great Plains. At some stopover points, such as Cheyenne Bottoms, Kansas, many thousands may be present in late spring.

HABITAT *Prairies, shores, mudflats; in summer, tundra.* During migration, found in a variety of situations, including flooded fields, shallow ponds, edges of freshwater marshes, tidal flats, gravel beaches. Breeds mostly on low-lying wet tundra with grassy areas and dwarf willows; sometimes on higher and drier tundra.

FEEDING **Diet:** *Includes insects, mollusks, marine worms, seeds.* Diet not well known. On breeding grounds, probably eats mostly insects, including crane flies, beetles. During migration and winter, eats insects, marine worms, snails and other mollusks, crustaceans, leeches. Also eats many seeds and other plant material at various times of year. **Behavior:** On mudflats, forages by probing in mud or in shallow water, also picks up some items from surface. On tundra, often probes deeply in moss and other vegetation.

NESTING Male displays over breeding territory by gliding and fluttering, making rattling and oinking sounds. On ground, male stretches wings out to side, raises tail high to show off white rump patch, and walks and runs while giving repeated call. **Nest:** Site is on ground, usually well hidden in clump of grass or moss on tundra. Nest (built by female) is a cup-shaped depression; lining material, bits of lichen, moss, and leaves, may be present naturally, not added by female.

White-rumped Sandpiper

Eggs: 4, rarely 3. Olive to green, sometimes buff, blotched with brown, olive-brown, or gray. Incubation is by female only, about 22 days. **Young:** Downy young leave nest less than a day after hatching. Female tends young and broods them to keep them warm, but young apparently find all their own food. Age at first flight about 16–17 days; become independent soon thereafter.

MIGRATION A very long-distance migrant. In fall, many make nonstop flight from eastern Canada to northern South America. In spring, most move north through Great Plains and Mississippi Valley. A late migrant in spring, with peak numbers in central United States in late May, some lingering into June.

CONSERVATION STATUS Because migration often involves long flights, species is dependent on stopover points to feed and refuel for next flight; loss of these staging areas could cause serious problems.

BAIRD'S SANDPIPER *Calidris bairdii*

Nesting in the high Arctic, this sandpiper is seen by birders mostly in its migrations through the Great Plains. Many other shorebirds that migrate north through the prairies in spring go south off our Atlantic coast in fall; however, Baird's follows the plains route at both seasons, although a few spread out to either coast in fall. A long-winged, long-distance migrant, this is one of the few shorebirds that regularly stops at lakes in the high mountains.

HABITAT *Rain pools, mudflats, shores, fields.* In migration, often chooses slightly drier or more open habitats than related small sandpipers: dry and sandy shores, nearby grassy areas, even open fields. Also found on mudflats, flooded fields. Breeds on dry upland tundra in Arctic.

FEEDING **Diet:** *Mostly insects.* Diet not well known. On northern breeding grounds, eats many insects, especially flies and beetles; also spiders, other invertebrates. During migration, feeding in drier habitats, probably continues to feed mostly

Baird's Sandpiper

on insects, including caterpillars. Also takes some amphipods and other crustaceans. **Behavior:** Forages mostly by picking items from surface, not by probing; moves about actively on flats, looking for insects and other prey.

NESTING Male flies high over breeding habitat in slow hovering flight, fluttering wings continuously, giving trilled song. At beginning of breeding season, males may tend to be clustered fairly close together, perhaps to help in attracting females to area. **Nest:** Site is on ground on dry tundra, in area with rocks and only low ground cover. May be well hidden under grass clump. Nest (probably built mostly by male) is a shallow scrape lined with lichens, grass, dry leaves. **Eggs:** Usually 4, sometimes fewer. Pinkish buff to olive, blotched with dark brown. Incubation is by both parents, 19–22 days. **Young:** Downy young leave nest soon after hatching. Young are tended by both parents at first, but female may depart before male. Age of young at first flight about 16–20 days.

MIGRATION In late summer and early fall, large numbers congregate on the Great Plains and in the central valleys of Mexico; then most apparently fly nonstop to South America.

PECTORAL SANDPIPER *Calidris melanotos*

This is one of the "grasspipers," more likely to be seen in grassy marshes or wet fields than on open mudflats. Its spring migration is mostly through the Great Plains, with smaller numbers east to the Atlantic; the species is found coast to coast in fall but is still scarcer in the west. The name "Pectoral" refers to the inflatable air sac on the male's chest, puffed out during his bizarre hooting flight display over the Arctic tundra.

Pectoral Sandpiper

HABITAT *In migration, prairie pools, muddy shores, fresh and tidal marshes; in summer, tundra.* Migrants favor grassy places rather than open mudflats. Often seen along grassy edges of shores, at edges of tidal marsh, in flooded fields or wet meadows. Sometimes on dry prairie or even plowed fields. On breeding grounds, favors wet grassy areas of tundra.

FEEDING Diet: *Mostly insects.* Diet not well known. On breeding grounds, feeds mostly on insects, especially flies and their larvae, also beetles and others. Also eats amphipods, spiders, some seeds. Diet in migration may include small crabs and other crustaceans, plus other aquatic invertebrates, but insects may still be main food. **Behavior:** Forages by picking up items from surface of ground, also by probing in mud or shallow water.

NESTING In flight display, male puffs out chest sac so that chest looks like a feathered balloon. As the male flies low over a female on the ground, he gives a low-pitched, throbbing, hooting noise; after passing female he circles, alternating flutters and glides, back to his starting point. On ground, male approaches female with tail raised, wings drooping, chest puffed out. One male may mate with several females, and he takes no part in caring for the eggs or young. **Nest:** Site is on ground in

grassy tundra, often in dry upland site but sometimes near water, usually well hidden in grass. Nest (built by female) is shallow depression with cup-shaped lining of grass and leaves. **Eggs:** 4. Whitish to olive-buff, blotched with dark brown. Incubation is by female only, 21–23 days. **Young:** Downy young leave nest soon after hatching. Female tends young, but young feed themselves. Age at first flight about 21 days.

MIGRATION   The winter range is mostly in South America, but some (probably from nesting grounds in Siberia) migrate to Australia and New Zealand. Compared with other shorebirds, migration is relatively early in spring and late in fall. Adults migrate south at least a month before juveniles, on average, with adults peaking in late August, young birds in late September.

SHARP-TAILED SANDPIPER   *Calidris acuminata*

This Asian shorebird is related to our Pectoral Sandpiper, and like that species it is a long-distance migrant, traveling from Siberia to Australia and New Zealand. A few reach North America every year, mostly fall migrants in Alaska and the Pacific Northwest; a casual stray in other areas, very rare in spring.

PURPLE SANDPIPER   *Calidris maritima*

This stout, short-legged sandpiper is seemingly adapted to tough conditions. It winters farther north on the Atlantic coast than any other shorebird, and its chosen habitat is on coastal rocks pounded by the surf. When an especially large wave hits the rocks, the lowest birds in a flock may simply hop or flutter up far enough to evade the incoming water. Few birders ever see this species on its remote breeding grounds in the Canadian high Arctic.

HABITAT   *Wave-washed rocks, jetties.* In winter almost always on rocky shores or rock jetties and breakwaters, foraging in zone below high-tide mark. Sometimes in areas of seaweed washed up on beaches. In summer on barren northern tundra, especially in rocky areas or ridges.

Purple Sandpiper

FEEDING   **Diet:** *Mostly insects and mollusks.* On breeding grounds eats mostly insects, also some crustaceans, spiders, worms. Unlike most sandpipers, also eats some plant material, including berries, buds, seeds, leaves, and moss. On migration and in winter, diet is mostly small mollusks, including mussels and snails, also some crustaceans and insects. **Behavior:** Clambers over rocks, seaweed, beaches, or tundra, looking for prey. Occasionally probes in mud but usually finds food visually.

NESTING   In territorial display, male flies in wide circles with fluttering wings held above horizontal. Displays to intruders on ground by raising one wing high above back. Male may pursue female on ground or in the air. **Nest:** Site is on ground on open tundra, either in high rocky area or lower wet site, often among lichen or moss. Nest is shallow depression, with or without lining of grass, leaves. Male makes up to five nest scrapes, female chooses one. **Eggs:** 4, sometimes 3. Olive to buff, blotched with brown. Incubation is by both sexes (but male often does more), 21–22 days. **Young:** May leave nest within a few hours after hatching.

Young are cared for mostly or entirely by male; young find their own food from the beginning. Age at first flight not well known, probably about 3 weeks.

MIGRATION Apparently follows coast in migration, seldom appearing inland. Fall migration much later than that of most sandpipers, not appearing on wintering grounds in numbers until November.

CONSERVATION STATUS Numbers apparently stable or perhaps increasing. Breeding range is mostly remote from human impact. Building of rock jetties along Atlantic coast may have increased available wintering habitat.

ROCK SANDPIPER *Calidris ptilocnemis*

Very similar to the Purple Sandpiper, replacing it in the west. Spends the winter on coastal rocks, sharing this habitat with other "rockpipers" like Black Turnstone and Surfbird. Rock Sandpiper is more effectively camouflaged than these birds in winter plumage and is often hard to spot against the gray boulders. Although it nests

in places on the mainland of Alaska, it seems most numerous on islands such as the Pribilofs and the Aleutians.

HABITAT *Rocky shores; nests on mossy tundra.* In winter typically on rocky shores or rock jetties, foraging mostly in zone below high tide mark, especially on mats of algae or among mussels or barnacles. Breeds on tundra, generally on drier and more barren stretches with sparse cover of lichen, moss, grasses.

FEEDING Diet: *Mostly insects and other invertebrates.* Insects may be main part of diet on breeding grounds, but also eats crustaceans, mollusks, marine worms. Unlike most sandpipers, also eats some plant material, including berries, seeds, moss, and algae. On migration and in winter, diet is mostly small mollusks, crustaceans, and insects. **Behavior:** Forages by

Rock Sandpiper

moving about slowly on rocks or walking on mudflats or tundra. Finds food visually.

NESTING Male defends territory by flying in wide circle with fluttering wingbeats, giving trilled calls. In aggressive display on ground, male raises one wing. **Nest:** Site is on ground on open dry tundra, often on a raised area of lichen or moss. Nest is a deep scrape, usually lined with lichen, leaves, grass. Male begins scrape, female may add some lining. **Eggs:** Usually 4. Olive to buff, blotched with brown. Incubation is usually by both sexes, about 20 days. Occasionally only one parent (either one) incubates. If predators threaten nest, adult may perform distraction display, fluttering away as if wing were broken. **Young:** May leave the nest within a few hours after hatching. Usually tended by male, rarely by female or both parents. Young find all their own food. Age at first flight not well known, probably about 3 weeks.

MIGRATION Those nesting on Pribilofs and Aleutians are apparently short-distance migrants or permanent residents. Mainland breeders go farther south. Some of those wintering on our west coast south of Alaska probably come from Siberia.

CONSERVATION STATUS Numbers wintering in the Pacific Northwest have declined since the 1970s.

DUNLIN *Calidris alpina*

The name, first applied long ago, simply means "little dun-colored (gray-brown) bird," a good description of the Dunlin in winter plumage. Spending the winter farther north than most of its relatives, this species is a familiar sight along the outer beaches during the cold months, as far north as New England and even southern Alaska. It is often in large flocks; in flight, these flocks may perform impressive aerial maneuvers, twisting and banking in unison. In breeding plumage, the Dunlin is so much more brightly colored as to seem a different bird.

HABITAT *Tidal flats, beaches, muddy pools; wet tundra in summer.* During migration and winter, widespread in coastal habitats; mainly mudflats, but also sand beaches, rocky shores. Inland, occurs on lake shores, sewage ponds, flooded fields. Breeds on wet tundra, especially areas with hummocks, tussocks, and low ridges interspersed with ponds and marshy spots.

Dunlin

FEEDING **Diet:** *Mostly insects on tundra, other small invertebrates on coast.* Diet varies with season and location. On breeding grounds feeds heavily on insects, including larvae of midges, crane flies, beetles, and others. On coast eats wide variety of small creatures found in intertidal zone, including marine worms, snails and other mollusks, amphipods and other crustaceans, sometimes small fish. Sometimes eats seeds and leaves. **Behavior:** Forages by picking at items on surface or by probing in mud, sometimes with very rapid "stitching" motion, probing several times per second. May feed by day or night.

NESTING In display flight, male circles slowly over breeding territory, fluttering and gliding while singing. On ground, reacts to intruding males by advancing, pausing to raise one wing high over back. Courtship may involve ritualized nest-making movements. **Nest:** Site is on ground, usually well hidden in or under grass clump or in hummock. Nest is a shallow scrape lined with leaves and grass. Both sexes make scrapes, but female chooses one and completes nest. **Eggs:** 4, sometimes 2–3, perhaps very rarely more than 4. Olive or blue-green to buff, with brown blotches concentrated at larger end. Incubation is by both sexes (mostly female during night, male during day), 20–23 days. **Young:** Downy young leave nest soon after hatching. Both parents tend young at first, but female often departs after a few days. Young feed themselves, are able to fly at age of 18–26 days.

MIGRATION A short-distance migrant, wintering commonly on North American coast, almost never reaching the Equator. Generally a much later fall migrant than most shorebirds.

CONSERVATION STATUS Numbers wintering in some coastal areas have declined noticeably since the 1970s; reasons are unknown.

CURLEW SANDPIPER *Calidris ferruginea*

A few Curlew Sandpipers turn up on the Atlantic coast every year, rewarding birders who scan the shorebird flocks. Elsewhere in North America, this Eurasian wader is only a rare visitor. It has nested at Point Barrow, Alaska, but in most years it is completely absent there. Most of those seen as migrants are adults in bright rusty red breeding plumage; young birds and adults in winter plumage are more likely to be overlooked.

HABITAT *Tidal flats, beaches; wet tundra in summer.* In migration, found in places where other small sandpipers congregate, including mudflats and beaches along coast, muddy edges of ponds and lakes. Nesting habitat in Alaska is along low ridges and slight rises in wet, grassy tundra.

FEEDING **Diet:** *Insects, crustaceans, mollusks, worms.* Diet in New World not well known. In Old World, eats wide variety of insects (especially flies and beetles), mainly in breeding season; also crustaceans (including amphipods and shrimp), small mollusks, marine worms, a few seeds. **Behavior:** Forages mostly in shallow water, probing in mud with bill, sometimes picking items from surface. When feeding with Dunlins, Curlew Sandpiper often wades in slightly deeper water and tends to eat larger items.

NESTING Male proclaims territory by calling from raised mound, performing low flight display. Courtship displays are more complex than those of most small sandpipers. Male often pursues female in air; both birds perform ritualized nest-making movements; male runs around female in zigzag pattern with wings raised, tail spread, white rump patch displayed prominently. After elaborate courtship, male apparently departs, leaving female to care for eggs and young.

Curlew Sandpiper

Nest: Site is on ground on hummock or low mound on tundra. Nest is shallow depression lined with bits of moss, lichens, leaves. **Eggs:** Usually 4. Creamy to pale olive, blotched with brown and reddish brown. Incubation is apparently by female only, roughly 21 days. **Young:** Downy young leave nest soon after hatching. Young are tended by female but feed themselves. Development of young and age at first flight not well known.

MIGRATION A very long-distance migrant, nesting in high Arctic Siberia and wintering to southern coasts of Africa, Australia.

CONSERVATION STATUS Population trends not well known. May have better nesting success in years with high lemming populations, when predators concentrate on lemmings and leave the sandpipers alone.

STILT SANDPIPER *Calidris himantopus*

This wader is related to our very smallest sandpipers, but it is much more stretched out in shape, designed for feeding in deeper water. In its drab winter plumage the Stilt Sandpiper is often overlooked, passed off as either a yellowlegs or a dowitcher, depending on what it is doing. Standing or walking, it looks rather like a yellowlegs; feeding, it acts like a dowitcher, probing the mud with a sewing-machine motion.

HABITAT *Shallow pools, mudflats, marshes; tundra in summer.* Typically on fresh water, including ponds and marshes with extensive shallows. Even in coastal areas, tends to occur on lagoons or ponds, not on tidal flats. Breeds on tundra, especially in sedge meadows with raised ridges for nest sites.

FEEDING **Diet:** *Includes insects, mollusks, seeds.* Diet not well known but includes a wide variety of aquatic insects (including fly larvae and beetles), marine worms, snails; also the seeds, leaves, and roots of aquatic plants. **Behavior:** Forages mostly by wading in shallow water and probing vertically with its bill in the mud of the bottom, often thrusting its head underwater. Sometimes picks insects from surface of water. Feeding is similar to that of dowitchers, and it often associates closely with dowitcher flocks.

Stilt Sandpiper

NESTING   Male displays over breeding territory by flying slowly with shallow wingbeats, calling incessantly, then gliding with wings in shallow "V" while giving guttural song. In courtship, spectacular aerial displays; male pursues female in the air, gets in front of her and then raises wings high over his back, singing as he plummets. **Nest:** Site is in a dry spot on low ridge or on top of sedge hummock, often surrounded by water or wet ground. Nest is shallow depression in vegetation, with little or no lining; male makes nest scrapes, female chooses one. **Eggs:** 4. Pale cream to olive green, heavily dotted with brown. Incubation is by both parents, 19–21 days. Female incubates at night, male during the day. **Young:** Downy young leave nest soon after hatching, find all their own food. Both parents may tend young at first, but female usually departs in less than a week, male after about 2 weeks. Young can fly at about 17–18 days.

MIGRATION   Migrates mostly through Great Plains; uncommon on east coast, rare on west coast, mostly in fall. A few winter as far north as United States (Florida, Texas, Salton Sea), but most apparently go to South America. In fall, adults migrate south about a month before juveniles on average.

CONSERVATION STATUS   Counts of migrants in some areas suggest that the species may have increased in recent decades.

GENUS *Eurynorhynchus*

SPOONBILL SANDPIPER   *Eurynorhynchus pygmeus*

A rare little sandpiper, nesting in eastern Siberia and wintering in southern Asia. It has strayed to western and northern Alaska, where it is among the most sought-after rarities. The Spoonbill Sandpiper feeds mostly in shallow water, walking with its head down, sweeping its unique spoon-tipped bill from side to side.

GENUS *Limicola*

BROAD-BILLED SANDPIPER   *Limicola falcinellus*

An uncommon shorebird, nesting in bogs across northern Europe and Asia and wintering at marshes and coastal mudflats from Africa to Australia. It forages rather slowly, probing like a Dunlin with its oddly flattened bill. A few autumn strays have reached the Aleutians.

GENUS *Tryngites*

BUFF-BREASTED SANDPIPER   *Tryngites subruficollis*

A beautiful but strange little sandpiper, its short bill and round head giving it the look of a plover. On migration it typically stops on prairies, fields of short grass, and even dry plowed fields, seemingly odd settings for a shorebird. Formerly an abundant bird, the Buff-breasted Sandpiper suffered serious declines around the beginning of the 20th century, with many shot during their long migration from the Arctic tundra to the pampas of Argentina.

HABITAT *Shortgrass prairies; in summer, tundra ridges.* Migrants in North America mostly on dry open ground, such as prairies, pastures, airports, stubble fields, plowed fields. Sometimes on shores of lakes or ponds or on coastal flats, but even there it tends to be on higher and drier sections. Breeds on tundra slopes and ridges with ponds or streams nearby.

FEEDING **Diet:** *Mostly insects.* Diet not well known, but probably mostly insects at all seasons. On breeding grounds, eats many flies (including crane flies and midges), also beetles and other insects. During migration, besides insects, also eats spiders and small crustaceans; sometimes eats seeds. **Behavior:** Searches for food by sight, standing still and then making short run forward to capture prey, picking up insects and other items from surface of ground.

NESTING Males gather on display grounds, or "leks," to attract females. These leks are spread out, each male defending an area of up to several acres; rarely more than 10 males present. Male displays by raising one wing, showing off white underside. If females approach, male spreads both wings wide, points bill up, shakes body. One male may mate with

Buff-breasted Sandpiper

several females, and male takes no part in caring for the eggs or young. **Nest:** Site is on ground, usually near water, often on a hummock of moss. Nest (built by female) is shallow depression lined with leaves, sedges, lichens, moss. **Eggs:** 4, rarely 2 or 3. Whitish to buff or olive, with brown marks concentrated at larger end. Incubation by female only, 23–25 days. **Young:** Downy young leave nest less than a day after hatching. Female tends young, but young feed themselves. Age at first flight about 16–20 days.

MIGRATION Migration route through Great Plains is used by most birds in fall and almost all in spring. During fall, uncommon on Atlantic coast, rare on Pacific coast. Adults migrate south earlier in fall than juveniles, on average.

CONSERVATION STATUS Formerly abundant, now very uncommon. Many were killed by market hunters in late 1800s and early 1900s. Much of habitat for migrating and wintering birds has been destroyed or degraded.

GENUS *Philomachus*

RUFF *Philomachus pugnax*

Of the various Eurasian shorebirds that stray into North America, this one is the most regular and widespread in its occurrence. Ruffs are best known for their bizarre courtship plumage and rituals. In spring, male Ruffs are wildly variable in color and pattern of their neck ruffs and head tufts; they gather on display grounds, or "leks," and display to attract females. Rudimentary displays are occasionally seen from spring migrant Ruffs in North America.

HABITAT *Grassy marshes, mudflats, flooded fields.* Migrants in North America often are seen on marshes or ponds a short distance inland; on the coast, they favor estuaries, lagoons, mudflats at inlets, salt marshes. Generally not on open sandy beaches.

FEEDING **Diet:** *Mostly insects and other invertebrates, also seeds.* Diet in North America not well known. In Eurasia, eats many insects, especially flies, beetles, caddisflies. Also eats small mollusks, crustaceans, spiders, worms, small fish, frogs. During migration and winter may eat many seeds, sometimes forming major part of diet. **Behavior:** Forages while walking or wading, by picking up items from surface or probing in water or mud. Sometimes forages actively, running about on open mudflats. May feed by day or night.

Ruff

NESTING Has nested once in Alaska, but information here applies to Eurasian birds. Males gather in spring on "leks" and display to attract females. In display, male raises head tufts and neck ruff, flutters wings, may leap in air; many other elaborate postures including bowing, crouching with feathers fluffed up, standing tall. Usually silent during display. Males often fight. Female visits lek, mates with one of the males; male takes no part in caring for eggs or young. **Nest:** Site is on ground, well hidden in grass or marsh. Nest (built by female) is shallow depression lined with grasses. **Eggs:** 4, sometimes 2–3. Olive to green, blotched with brown. Incubation is by female only, 20–23 days. **Young:** Downy young leave nest soon after hatching. Female feeds young at first, but they learn to feed themselves after a few days. Age at first flight about 25–28 days.

MIGRATION In North America, a regular stray near both coasts, less frequent in the interior. Found somewhat more often in fall than in spring.

CONSERVATION STATUS Has decreased in some parts of European range because of loss of wetland habitat.

DOWITCHERS — GENUS *Limnodromus*

Dumpy sandpipers with rather short legs and long bills, dowitchers wade in shallow water, probing the mud with their bills in a vertical "sewing-machine" motion. Our two species are very similar but tend to use different habitats, one favoring fresh water and the other more common in salt water. Dowitchers are sociable, often feeding in densely packed flocks.

SHORT-BILLED DOWITCHER   *Limnodromus griseus*

The name of this species could be misleading: it is "short-billed" only in comparison with the Long-billed Dowitcher and is longer-billed than the average shorebird. Flocks of Short-billed Dowitchers wade in shallow water over coastal mudflats. They often seem rather tame, allowing a close approach when they are busy feeding.

HABITAT *Mudflats, tidal marshes, pond edges.* Migrants and wintering birds favor coastal habitats, especially tidal flats on protected estuaries and bays, also lagoons, salt marshes, sometimes sandy beaches. Migrants also stop inland on freshwater ponds with muddy margins. Breeds in far north, mostly in open bogs, marshes, and edges of lakes within coniferous forest zone.

FEEDING **Diet:** *Small aquatic invertebrates.* Diet probably varies with season. Eats many insects and their larvae, especially on breeding grounds. In migration and winter also eats mollusks, marine worms, crustaceans. At times, may feed heavily on seeds of grasses, bulrushes, pondweeds, other plants. In spring, also feeds

on eggs of horseshoe crab. **Behavior:** Typically forages by wading in shallow water (sometimes walking on wet mud), probing deeply in the mud with its bill. Usually deliberate in its feeding, standing in one spot or moving forward slowly.

NESTING Much of nesting area is far inland, generally south and east of the breeding range of Long-billed Dowitcher. **Nest:** Site is on ground in bog, forest clearing, or edge of tundra, often near water. Nest is a shallow depression in moss or in a clump of grass, lined with small twigs, leaves, fine grasses. **Eggs:** 4, sometimes 3. Olive-buff to brown, marked with brown. Incubation is by both sexes, about 21 days. **Young:** Downy young leave nest shortly after hatching. Roles of parents in caring for young not well known, but reportedly female departs, leaving male to tend the chicks. Young find all their own food. Their development and age at first flight are not well known.

MIGRATION Breeds in three distinct regions, with distinct migratory routes and wintering areas. Alaska birds winter on Pacific coast, central Canada birds migrate through Great Plains and along Atlantic coast, eastern Canada birds stay east, winter as far south as Brazil.

LONG-BILLED DOWITCHER *Limnodromus scolopaceus*

Although the two dowitcher species are strikingly similar in appearance, they tend to segregate by habitat. The Long-billed prefers fresh water at all seasons; it is a common migrant through much of North America (but scarce in the northeast).

HABITAT *Mudflats, shallow pools, margins; mostly on fresh water.* Even in coastal regions, migrants and wintering birds tend to occur on freshwater habitats, such as ponds, impoundments, upper reaches of estuaries. Sometimes on open tidal flats with Short-billed Dowitchers. Breeds in far north on wet, hummocky tundra.

FEEDING **Diet:** *Small aquatic invertebrates.* Diet probably varies with season. Particularly on breeding grounds, eats many insects and their larvae, including many flies, beetles, others. In migration and winter also eats mollusks, marine worms, crustaceans. At times, may feed heavily on seeds of grasses, bulrushes, pondweeds, other plants. **Behavior:** Typically forages by wading in shallow water (sometimes walking on wet mud), probing deeply in the mud with its bill. Usually deliberate in its feeding, standing in one spot or moving forward slowly.

Long-billed Dowitcher

NESTING Breeding range is mostly in Arctic coastal regions, generally farther north and west than that of Short-billed Dowitcher. **Nest:** Site is on ground, usually near water, often on raised hummock or tussock in wet meadow. Nest is a depression sparsely lined with sedges, grasses; bottom of nest is often wet. **Eggs:** 4, sometimes 3. Olive to brown, marked with brown. Incubation is by both sexes at first, then mostly or entirely by male in later stages. Incubation period 20–22 days. **Young:** Downy young leave nest shortly after hatching. Female reportedly departs near the time the eggs hatch, leaving male to care for young. Young find all their own food; development of young and age at first flight not well known.

MIGRATION From breeding range in far northwest, many migrate southeast to reach Atlantic seaboard. On both coasts, this species may linger later in fall and winter farther north than the Short-billed Dowitcher.

Still widespread and common. Numbers of migrants reportedly have increased in some areas during recent decades.

GENUS *Lymnocryptes*

JACK SNIPE *Lymnocryptes minimus*

This very small snipe is an elusive bird of marshes in the Old World. It has been found only a few times in North America, in such scattered sites as Alaska, Labrador, and northern California.

GENUS Gallinago

COMMON SNIPE *Gallinago gallinago*

Often overlooked in migration and winter, the snipe is a solitary creature of wet fields and bogs, seldom seen on open mudflats. Flushed from the marsh, it darts away in zigzag flight, uttering harsh notes. The Common Snipe becomes more flamboyant in the breeding season, when it often yammers from atop a fencepost or dead tree. At night on the nesting grounds, the ghostly winnowing flight sound of the males often echoes across the marshes.

HABITAT   *Marshes, bogs, wet meadows.* In migration and winter, found in a variety of damp habitats including fresh and salt marshes, muddy banks of rivers and ponds, wet pastures, flooded agricultural fields. In breeding season mostly around fresh marshes and bogs, shrubby streamsides, northern tundra.

FEEDING   **Diet:** *Mostly insects and earthworms.* Eats many insects that burrow in damp soil or live in shallow water, such as larvae of crane flies, horse flies, various beetles, many others. At some places, diet includes many earthworms. Also eats some leeches, crustaceans, mollusks, spiders, frogs, leaves, seeds. **Behavior:** Forages mostly by probing in soft mud; bill tip is sensitive and flexible, allowing the snipe to detect and capture prey underground. Also captures some food in shallow water or from surface of ground.

Common Snipe

NESTING   In breeding season, especially at night, male performs "winnowing" display: flies in high circles, periodically making shallow dives; during dive, vibration of outer tail feathers produces a hollow whinnying sound. In aggressive and distraction displays on ground, bird crouches, raising and spreading tail to show off pattern. **Nest:** Site is on ground, usually well hidden in clump of grass or buried in tundra vegetation. Nest (built by female) is shallow depression lined with fine grasses, leaves, moss, sometimes with overhanging plants woven into a kind of canopy. **Eggs:** 4, sometimes 3. Brown to olive-buff, marked with dark brown. Incubation is by female only, 18–21 days. **Young:** Downy young leave nest shortly after hatching. Parents may split brood, each caring for 1–2 of the chicks. Parents feed young at first, before they learn to find own food. Age at first flight about 19–20 days.

MIGRATION   Winters commonly in North America, but some travel longer distances; birds banded in Canada have reached Lesser Antilles and South America. Probably migrates alone, not in flocks.

CONSERVATION STATUS   Probably far more abundant at one time, reduced by market hunting in late 19th century and by loss of habitat; however, still widespread and common.

PINTAIL SNIPE   *Gallinago stenura*

North American birders may count themselves lucky to have only one Common Snipe to identify. Asia has several snipe species, all very hard to tell apart. The Pintail Snipe has been proven to occur once at Attu (outer Aleutian Islands), but even there other sight records have been controversial.

GENUS *Scolopax*

EURASIAN WOODCOCK   *Scolopax rusticola*

Larger than our American Woodcock, this chunky bird probes the mud in forests across Europe and Asia. In the 19th century it occurred a number of times as a rare visitor to northeastern North America, with records from several states and provinces, but it has not been found here since 1935.

AMERICAN WOODCOCK   *Scolopax minor*

American Woodcock

Related to the sandpipers but strikingly different in habits. This rotund, short-legged bird hides in forest thickets by day, where it uses its long bill to probe in damp soil for earthworms. Its eyes are set far back on its head, allowing it to watch for danger even with its bill buried in the dirt. Males perform a remarkable "sky dance" on spring and summer nights, in a high, twisting flight, with chippering, twittering, bubbling sounds.

HABITAT   *Wet thickets, moist woods, brushy swamps.* Favors a mix of forest and open fields, often spending day in the forest, night in the open. Mostly in deciduous or mixed woods with much young growth and moist soil, such as thickets along streams. At night may be in open pastures, abandoned farm fields, open swamp edges.

FEEDING   **Diet:** *Mostly earthworms and insects.* Earthworms are major prey at most times and places. Insects also important, especially insect larvae that burrow in soil, such as those of many beetles, crane flies, and others. Also eaten are millipedes, spiders, snails, and other invertebrates. Consumes some plant material, including seeds of grasses, sedges, smartweeds. **Behavior:** Feeds mostly by probing with bill in soft soil. Tip of bill is sensitive and flexible, allowing bird to detect and then grab creatures in the soil. Sometimes performs odd rocking motion while standing; possibly the vibration from this will disturb earthworms into moving; it has been suggested that the woodcock can hear sounds of creatures moving underground.

NESTING   Males display at night in spring and summer to attract females. Often several males are close together in meadow, brushy field. Male gives nasal beeping call on ground, then performs high, twisting flight display. In this "sky dance," musical twittering sounds made by certain modified wing feathers, chirping calls made vocally. Female visits area, mates with one of the males. Male takes no part in caring for eggs or young. **Nest:** Site is on ground, usually in open woods or overgrown field, in area with many dead leaves. Nest (made by female) is a scrape lined with dead leaves, other debris. **Eggs:** 4, sometimes 1–3; rarely 5 or more (possibly resulting from more than one female laying in same nest). Eggs pinkish buff, blotched with brown and gray. Incubation is by female only, 20–22 days. **Young:** Downy young leave nest a few hours after hatching. Female tends young and feeds them. After a few days, young may begin probing in soil, learning to search for food. Young can make short flights at age 2 weeks, fly fairly well at 3 weeks, independent at about 5 weeks.

MIGRATION Migrates at night. Fall migration influenced by weather, with many driven south by major cold fronts. Spring migration begins very early, some males moving north in January in warm years.

CONSERVATION STATUS Probably declining in eastern United States, may be increasing in parts of Canada as coniferous forests are cut and grow up to thickets. Still reasonably common overall.

PHALAROPES — GENUS *Phalaropus*

Phalaropes reverse the usual sex roles in birds: females are larger and more colorful than males; females take the lead in courtship, and males are left to incubate the eggs and care for the young. Unlike any other sandpipers, they forage mostly while swimming, by picking items from water's surface or just below it. Often they spin in circles on shallow water, probably to stir things up and bring food closer to surface. In general, they feed very rapidly on very small prey. For example, many shorebirds feed heavily on fly larvae, but phalaropes are notable for catching lots of adult flies. Two of the three species of phalaropes spend the winter far out at sea. With their very distinctive behavior, phalaropes sometimes have been placed in a separate family of their own.

WILSON'S PHALAROPE *Phalaropus tricolor*

An odd shorebird that swims and spins on prairie marshes. The other two species of phalaropes nest in the Arctic and winter at sea, but Wilson's is a bird of inland waters, nesting mostly on the northern Great Plains. Huge numbers may gather in fall on some salty lakes in the west, such as Mono Lake and Great Salt Lake, before migrating to South America.

Wilson's Phalarope

HABITAT *Shallow prairie lakes, fresh marshes, mudflats; in migration, also salt marshes.* Nests mostly at shallow freshwater marshes in open country. In migration, may stop at ponds, coastal marshes, sewage treatment plants, but biggest concentrations are at salty or alkaline lakes. Winters mostly on salty lakes in South America.

FEEDING **Diet:** *Mostly aquatic insects and crustaceans.* Eats a variety of flies and their larvae, beetles, true bugs, and other insects, mainly aquatic species. Also eats shrimp, copepods, seeds of marsh plants. During autumn and winter on salty lakes, may feed mostly on brine shrimp and brine flies. **Behavior:** Forages mostly while swimming (but does more walking on shore than other phalaropes). Picks up small items from surface of water, sometimes probes in soft mud. Sometimes stands still and catches flying insects; rarely pursues insects in the air.

NESTING Females compete for males; one female may mate with more than one male during the season, leaving each of her mates to care for a set of eggs. In courtship, female stretches neck, puffs out neck feathers, makes chugging call. **Nest:** Site is usually on ground near water, sometimes a couple of inches above ground in marsh plants. Typical nest is shallow depression with slight lining of grass. Female may take the lead in choosing nest site, but male finishes nest. **Eggs:** 4, sometimes 3. Buff, blotched with brown. Incubation is by male only, 18–27 days, usually about 23 days. **Young:** Downy young leave nest within a day after hatching. Male tends young and broods them while they are small, but young find all their own food. Male may try to lure predators away from nest or young by performing broken-wing act. Age of young at first flight and age at independence unknown.

MIGRATION Migrates in flocks. Winters mostly on salty lakes in highlands of South America, and may travel there in long nonstop flight from staging areas on lakes in western North America. Spring migration in North America is mostly through Great Plains.

CONSERVATION STATUS Has lost some nesting areas to drainage of prairie marshes, but still numerous. Protection of staging areas for migrants (such as Mono Lake, California) important for survival.

RED-NECKED PHALAROPE *Phalaropus lobatus*

Red-necked Phalarope

Red-necked Phalaropes nest around Arctic tundra pools and winter at sea. During migration they pause on shallow ponds in the west, where they spin in circles, picking at the water's surface. Most, however, apparently migrate offshore, especially in the east. Despite their small size and delicate shape, they seem perfectly at home on the open ocean.

HABITAT *Ocean, bays, lakes, ponds; tundra in summer.* At sea, often concentrates over upwellings or tide rips, sometimes around edges of kelp beds. Inland, stops on ponds or lakes with abundant small creatures to eat; often favors sewage ponds where insects are numerous. Breeds in tundra regions, mainly on marshy edges of ponds and lakes.

FEEDING **Diet:** *Insects, crustaceans, mollusks.* Diet varies with season and habitat. On breeding grounds and on fresh waters in migration, eats mostly insects, including adults and larvae of flies, beetles, caddisflies. During stopovers on alkaline lakes, may eat many brine shrimp. Winter diet on ocean poorly known, probably includes small crustaceans and mollusks. **Behavior:** See genus introduction.

NESTING Female seeking mate makes short flights, with whirring of wings and calling. In courtship, female swims around male, tries to make him follow her; male usually reluctant, shows interest only gradually. In some cases, after leaving male to care for eggs and young, female finds another mate and lays another clutch of eggs.

Nest: Site is on ground, usually in low vegetation near water. Nest is a shallow scrape lined with grass, leaves. Both sexes make scrapes, female chooses one, probably both sexes then help build nest. **Eggs:** 4, sometimes 3. Olive to buff, blotched with dark brown. Rarely 2 or 3 females will lay eggs in one nest. Incubation is by male only, 17–21 days. **Young:** Downy young leave nest within a day after hatching, go to shore of pond. Male tends young and broods them while they are small, but young feed themselves. Male departs after about 2 weeks, young are able to fly at about 3 weeks.

MIGRATION   Common in migration off both coasts. A common migrant through the interior of the west (locally abundant in fall), but quite rare inland in the east (where most records are in fall). Western birds winter at sea, mainly south of Equator off western South America; wintering areas of east coast migrants not well known.

CONSERVATION STATUS   Population difficult to monitor. Some evidence of recent declines in some areas, such as off the coast of New England.

RED PHALAROPE *Phalaropus fulicaria*

Red Phalarope

The Red Phalarope nests in the high Arctic and winters in flocks on southern oceans. It is rarely seen inland in most parts of North America.

HABITAT   *Ocean; tundra in summer.* For most of year found only out at sea, often very far from land. Favors areas with upwellings or tide rips, or where warm and cold currents converge; may regularly associate with whales. In summer on low-lying wet tundra near coast in high Arctic.

FEEDING   **Diet:** *Includes insects, mollusks, crustaceans.* On tundra, eats many insects, especially aquatic ones; also small mollusks, crustaceans, worms, bits of plant material, rarely small fish. Diet in winter poorly known. **Behavior:** See genus introduction. At sea, may land on mats of floating seaweed, and may pick parasites from backs of whales. On breeding grounds, also forages while walking or wading, and flutters up to catch insects in the air.

NESTING   In courtship, female flies in wide circle, calling. Female may chase male in the air or on water, head hunched down between her shoulders. After leaving male to care for eggs, female will sometimes find a second mate and lay a second clutch of eggs. **Nest:** Site is on ground among low vegetation, usually near water. Nest is a shallow scrape lined with grass, lichens, moss. Both sexes make scrapes, female selects one, male adds nest lining. **Eggs:** 4, sometimes 2–3. Olive to buff, blotched with black or dark brown. Sometimes 2 females lay eggs in one nest. Incubation is by male only, 18–20 days. **Young:** Downy young leave nest within a day after hatching; male leads them to edge of nearby pond. Young are tended by male (rarely joined by female) but mostly feed themselves. Male may remain with young until they can fly, or may abandon them after just a few days; abandoned young can care for themselves. Age at first flight about 16–18 days.

MIGRATION   Migrates mostly offshore; rarely seen inland south of breeding grounds. A few winter off North American coast, but most apparently are well south of Equator in winter. Migrates later in fall than Red-necked Phalarope.

SANDPIPERS AND RELATED BIRDS

JAEGERS, GULLS, TERNS, AND SKIMMERS (Family Laridae)

Some of the most conspicuous birds of the waterside belong to this large family, which includes about 105 species nesting on every continent, including Antarctica. The family comprises four rather different groups of birds, each of which has been placed in its own separate family at times in the past.

Most familiar are the gulls, noisy denizens of the shore. They are often seen along beaches or on lakes, swimming on open water, resting in flocks on parking lots, or fighting over scraps at garbage dumps. Most of them are sociable at all seasons, nesting in colonies and occurring in large mixed flocks at good feeding sites. Although they are often called "seagulls," only a few kinds actually venture far out on the ocean.

More seagoing in their habits are the jaegers and skuas, predatory relatives of gulls. These birds nest in colder climates of both the Northern and Southern hemispheres and spend much of the year far out at sea, often migrating long distances. They are not very sociable, usually seen singly or in small groups.

Terns are mostly smaller than gulls and more graceful in the air, often foraging in flight as they swoop to catch fish or insects. They spend far less time swimming than gulls do. However, many terns range widely at sea, and they are generally more common than gulls in tropical areas. In a tropical midocean island group like Hawaii, for example, several kinds of terns are common, while gulls of any sort are only rare visitors.

Skimmers are large and long-winged birds recognized by their odd bill shape, with the lower mandible much longer than the upper one. Inhabiting warm climates, they are strictly coastal in our area, but they go far inland in South America, Africa, and southern Asia. Although they look unique, they are probably close relatives of the terns.

In the wild, some gulls and terns may live to be more than 30 years old.

Feeding   Gulls (at least some of the larger kinds) will eat practically anything, and they use a wide variety of foraging methods. They will feed while swimming, while walking or wading, or while hovering in midair. Gulls often act as scavengers, feeding on garbage or carrion, and they sometimes steal food from other birds. Jaegers and skuas are less omnivorous; they hunt live prey, harass other seabirds to make them drop their catch, and sometimes scavenge on carrion. Most kinds of terns feed mainly on small fish, with insects and crustaceans also important for some. They do most of their foraging in flight, diving into the water headfirst to catch fish or swooping to pick items off the surface of the water or out of the air. Skimmers have the strangest feeding habits of all. A skimmer will fly very low, with the very long lower mandible of its bill plowing through the water; when it makes contact with a fish, it quickly snaps the bill shut and then swallows the fish. More details on feeding are presented under the heading for each group.

Nesting   These birds do not nest until they are more than one year old: two years in some of the smallest gulls and terns, more typically three or four years in larger species. Except for the jaegers and skuas, most members of this family nest in colonies; and except for a few of the smaller gulls, most kinds nest on the ground. They almost always lay eggs with patterns of spotting or mottling, which helps to provide camouflage. Incubation is typically by both parents. The downy young usually remain in the nest for at least a few days and are fed by both parents. A few kinds of terns sometimes raise two broods per year, but all the rest of our species raise only one brood.

Displays   As expected in such a varied group, courtship displays take a variety of forms. The terns and jaegers, which do much of their feeding on the wing, also may perform spectacular courtship flights, while gulls may carry out most of their courtship on the ground. Species that nest in colonies display to warn other birds not to stray too close to their nests. Courtship feeding is also practiced by many members of this family. A male tern will bow and posture elegantly as he presents a fish to his intended. Male jaegers and gulls, in a less elegant ritual, feed their mates by regurgitating partly digested food; it may look unromantic to us, but these birds are scavengers, and they feed their young in the same way.

JAEGERS — GENUS *Stercorarius*

Jaegers are fast-flying seabirds, predatory and piratical. The three species nest in the Arctic zone of North America and Eurasia and spend the rest of the year at sea. Only rarely are lost migrants seen inland. Even along the coast they are not seen very often, although a patient watcher with a telescope may see Parasitic Jaegers flying well offshore. On the tundra areas where they breed, jaegers (and their relatives the skuas) can be very aggressive in defense of their nests, even attacking humans who come too close.

POMARINE JAEGER   *Stercorarius pomarinus*

Powerful and fast-flying, a predator and pirate of the ocean and the far north. The largest of the three jaeger species. Seen from shore less often than Parasitic Jaeger, but usually the one seen in greatest numbers on boat trips offshore. In northern Alaska, this is a major predator on the brown lemming: during summers when these rodents are in low numbers, many Pomarine Jaegers do not attempt to nest.

Pomarine Jaeger

HABITAT   *Open sea, coasts (offshore); tundra (summer).* Spends most of year at sea, often over continental shelf, but usually stays farther from land than Parasitic Jaeger and may occur far out in midocean. Concentrates over upwellings and boundaries of currents. In summer on tundra, generally low-lying areas near coast.

FEEDING   **Diet:** *Includes fish, rodents, birds.* Diet varies with location. At sea, usually eats fish, also smaller birds and some carrion or refuse. Breeding birds feed heavily on lemmings and other rodents; nonbreeding birds in summer around tundra have more varied diet, including birds, eggs, fish, carrion, insects. **Behavior:** Forages at sea by dipping to surface in flight to catch fish, by catching small birds in flight, also by harassing other birds and forcing them to drop their food. Forages over land mostly by hovering and dropping on prey.

NESTING   At least in some regions, much more likely to nest in years when rodent populations are high. Birds younger than 4–5 years old attempt nesting only in such good seasons. Defends nesting territory against other species of jaegers. In courtship, members of pair face each other, vibrating wings and calling. Male may feed female. **Nest:** Site is on open ground, sometimes on slightly raised ridge or hummock. Nest (built by both sexes) a shallow depression, often lined with bits of plant material. **Eggs:** 2, rarely 1–3. Olive to brown, blotched with dark brown. Incubation is by both parents, 25–27 days. **Young:** May leave nest a few days after hatching, but remain in general area and are fed by both parents. Age at first flight about 21–27 days; dependent on parents at least 2 more weeks.

MIGRATION   Most migration is offshore. Migrates later in fall than other jaegers, especially young birds, with juveniles rarely seen south of the Arctic before October. Some apparently migrate to far southern oceans, but others remain off North American coasts in winter. Very rare inland, but such strays may appear in summer as well as during migration seasons.

CONSERVATION STATUS   Local breeding numbers fluctuate strongly along with population cycles of lemmings and other rodents. Worldwide jaeger population difficult to monitor, but no evidence of major declines. Most of breeding range is remote from impact of human activity.

PARASITIC JAEGER   *Stercorarius parasiticus*

Parasitic Jaeger

This is the mid-sized member of the jaeger trio and the most familiar, as it is the one most likely to be seen from shore. Variable in plumage, it occurs in dark, light, and intermediate morphs.

HABITAT   *Ocean, coastal bays, lakes (rarely); tundra (summer).* Spends most of year at sea, concentrating over continental shelf within a few miles of land, rarely far out in midocean. Breeds in open country of far north, mostly tundra, also rocky barrens and coastal marshes. Immatures and nonbreeders may remain at sea all year.

FEEDING   **Diet:** *Includes fish, birds, rodents.* Diet at sea and at coastal nesting areas is mostly fish stolen from other birds. On land, also eats many birds and their eggs, rodents, insects, berries. Less dependent on lemmings and other rodents than the other jaegers. **Behavior:** At sea, does much of foraging by chasing other birds and forcing them to drop their catch; also dips down in flight to catch fish at surface. On breeding grounds, also hovers and swoops down to catch prey and feeds while walking.

NESTING   Usually first breeds at age of 4–5 years; in one study in Europe, birds of pale morph tended to start nesting younger than dark birds. May nest in colonies or in isolated pairs. Early in breeding season, pairs or groups perform acrobatic display flights. Courtship involves upright posturing, calling; male feeds female. **Nest:** Site (selected by male) is on the ground in the open, sometimes on a slight rise. Nest (built mostly by female) is a shallow depression, usually with a sparse lining of plant material. **Eggs:** 2, sometimes 1–3. Olive to brown, rarely blue, spotted with brown. Incubation is by both sexes, 25–28 days. **Young:** Downy young may leave nest a few days after hatching, but remain in vicinity. Both parents feed young, by regurgitation. Young can fly at 25–30 days, but remain with parents for a few more weeks.

MIGRATION   Often seems to follow general trend of coastline, a few miles offshore; some may regularly migrate over land. A few remain in winter as far north as North American waters, but most go farther south, some reaching southern Australia, Africa, South America.

CONSERVATION STATUS   Most of breeding range is remote from human impact. No evidence of major changes in population.

LONG-TAILED JAEGER *Stercorarius longicaudus*

A swift-flying seabird, extremely graceful and agile in flight. When swimming, it floats buoyantly, and it takes flight from the water easily. Of the three jaeger species, the Long-tail is the smallest and the one that migrates farthest offshore; south of the Arctic, it seldom comes within sight of land.

HABITAT *Open sea; tundra (summer).* Spends much of year far out at sea, generally out of sight of land. In breeding season on tundra, both near coast and well inland, but tends to prefer higher and drier areas rather than marshy coastal tundra. Young birds and nonbreeders may remain at sea all year.

FEEDING **Diet:** *Includes fish, rodents, birds, berries.* Summer diet is mostly small rodents, especially lemmings and voles when they are in high part of population cycle; also insects, small birds, fish, squid, carrion, and berries (especially crowberries). Diet during rest of year poorly known; includes fish, carrion, refuse. **Behavior:** In summer on tundra, hunts by hovering and then swooping down on prey; sometimes picks up items while swimming or catches insects in flight. May steal food from other birds.

NESTING Probably does not breed until at least 3–4 years old. More likely to nest successfully in years when lemmings are abundant. Has spectacular courtship flight with rapid swoops and zigzags, often three birds together, or one male chasing one female. In courtship on ground, male feeds female. **Nest:** Site

Long-tailed Jaeger

is on ground on open tundra, often on slightly raised spot. Nest (built mostly by female?) is simple depression, usually with sparse lining of plant material. **Eggs:** 2, sometimes 1, rarely 3. Brown to olive, blotched darker brown and gray. Incubation is by both sexes, 23–25 days. **Young:** Both parents feed young, by regurgitation. Parents defend nest by diving at predators or humans, even landing on intruder's head and pecking. Young can fly at 22–27 days; remain with parents another 1–3 weeks.

MIGRATION Typically migrates farther offshore than other jaegers. In early fall, a very few (mostly first-autumn immatures) show up on lakes well inland. Fall migration earlier than in other jaegers, with many adults southbound by mid-August. Wintering areas not well known, but apparently mostly at sea south of the Equator.

CONSERVATION STATUS Local breeding populations fluctuate sharply with changes in food supply; overall numbers probably more or less stable. No evidence of widespread trends in population.

SKUAS — GENUS *Catharacta*

British birders use the word "skua" for the jaegers as well, but North Americans apply the term only to the big predators in this genus. Skuas lack the long central tail feathers of adult jaegers, and they are mostly brown at all ages. Although they are shaped like bulky, broad-winged gulls, they are very powerful and fast in flight, easily overtaking other birds. One species nests in the North Atlantic, and up to five closely related forms nest in the Antarctic region.

GREAT SKUA *Catharacta skua*

A big, broad-shouldered, predatory seabird of the North Atlantic. Usually solitary at sea, although may concentrate where food is abundant. Breeds mainly in Iceland and on islands north of Great Britain; in North America, very seldom seen from shore, although it may be common far offshore during the winter. Closely related forms are common in the Southern Hemisphere, mostly in subantarctic regions.

HABITAT   *Open ocean.* Except during breeding season, usually far offshore, out of sight of land. With wide range at sea, occurs over cold and warm waters, from subarctic to equatorial regions. Nests mainly on treeless northern islands with low vegetation, close to colonies of other seabirds.

FEEDING   **Diet:** *Mainly fish, birds, carrion.* At sea eats mostly fish, particularly species such as sand lance that gather in dense schools. Around breeding colonies often preys heavily on smaller seabirds, including kittiwakes and puffins, and eats eggs and chicks of many species. Also eats carrion, insects, and small mammals up to size of rabbits. **Behavior:** Forages in flight by dipping to surface of water or by picking up items while swimming; scavenges on land and catches smaller birds in the air. Often harasses other birds, forcing them to drop their food.

NESTING   Usually first breeds at age of 7–8 years. Nests in loose colonies. Pair formation occurs in neutral social areas within or near colony, with much posturing and calling. **Nest:** Site is on ground, in open area. Nest (built by both sexes) is shallow depression lined with bits of plant material. In aggressive display near nest, both wings are raised together over back, head extended forward while bird gives harsh calls. **Eggs:** 2, rarely 1. Brownish to olive or pale blue, usually with dark brown spots around larger end. Incubation is by both sexes, 26–32 days. **Young:** May leave nest shortly after hatching but remain in vicinity. Female stays with young most of time, while male brings back food to feed them by regurgitation. Young capable of flight about 40–50 days after hatching; may become independent soon thereafter or not for almost 3 weeks.

MIGRATION   Disperses widely at sea, south to West Africa and Brazil. In North American waters, most common off eastern Canada and New England from October through February. A few nonbreeders may be present off North America at any season.

CONSERVATION STATUS   Population increasing in northern British Isles, possibly declining in Faeroes, stable in Iceland. Few direct threats to survival other than disturbance at nesting sites.

SOUTH POLAR SKUA *Catharacta maccormicki*

It occurs regularly off both our coasts, but this predatory seabird nests only far to the south of us, around the edges of Antarctica. When it reaches North American waters it remains far offshore, pirating food from other seabirds or catching its own fish.

HABITAT   *Open ocean.* Ranges widely at sea, over both warm and very cold waters. Appears far off North American coast where there are concentrations of other birds from which to steal food. Almost never seen from shore on this continent. Nests in Antarctica, on islands and mainland, on barren ground.

FEEDING   **Diet:** *Mainly fish.* Diet in North American waters not well known, but feeds mostly on fish while at sea. On breeding grounds, some feed mainly on the eggs and young of penguins and on carrion around penguin colonies. **Behavior:** Forages at sea by plunging into water from flight or by seizing items while

South Polar Skua

sitting on surface. Often steals food from other seabirds: may grab a shearwater or gull with its bill and shake the other bird violently to make it disgorge its catch.

NESTING   In Antarctica, some nest close to penguin colonies, feeding on eggs and chicks. Where this species overlaps with the larger Brown Skua, the Browns effectively "control" the penguin colonies, and the South Polars must forage at sea. Courtship involves much posturing and calling; male feeds female. Usually first breeds at age of 5–6 years; birds usually have same mates and nest sites every year thereafter. In aggressive display near nest, both wings are raised together over back, head extended forward while bird gives harsh calls. **Nest:** Site is on ground. Nest is simple scrape in soil or moss; often begun by male and completed by female. **Eggs:** 2, sometimes 1. Olive to brown, blotched with darker brown. Incubation is by both sexes, but female does more. Incubation period 24–34 days, usually 28–29. **Young:** Both parents feed young, by regurgitation. Young may leave nest soon after hatching, wander in immediate vicinity. Although both eggs usually hatch, usually only one young survives to fledging. Age at first flight 49–59 days.

MIGRATION   From Antarctic nesting grounds, moves far to the north in both Atlantic and Pacific. Perhaps most common off southern California in late spring, off northern California in early fall, and off New England in early summer, but details still poorly known.

CONSERVATION STATUS   Numbers apparently stable. Except near a few Antarctic research stations, the haunts of the species are usually remote from the impact of human activities.

TYPICAL GULLS — GENUS *Larus*

Of the 50 or so species of gulls in the world, all but six are now classified in this genus. Many of the larger gulls are common and familiar and are becoming more so: several have been increasing in numbers and expanding their ranges during recent decades.

The behavior of these birds can be easy and interesting to watch. Often they are quite tame, especially where people have fed them. Some gulls, especially the larger ones, can be very aggressive, and seem to be constantly fighting over food even when they have an unlimited supply.

Gulls use a wide variety of displays around their nesting colonies. These are at least slightly different in every species, but some elements of display are so common that they may be seen in most species. Most conspicuous is the "long call" display, in which an adult gives a loud, long series of calls, with the head stretched forward and often bowing in the middle of the long call. Adults also often throw their heads back over their backs repeatedly. Another display, called "choking," involves the bird pointing its bill at the ground and moving its head up and down while making a guttural choking noise. Any of these displays may be used in either courtship or aggression. Finally, the male often feeds the female in courtship. This courtship feeding is practiced by various other kinds of birds as well. With gulls, however, it seems less romantic to the casual observer, because the male feeds the female by coughing up food he has already partly digested!

LAUGHING GULL *Larus atricilla*

The strident laughing calls of this well-named gull are among the most characteristic sounds around tidewater along the Atlantic and Gulf coasts, especially in summer. It seems to be mostly a warm-weather bird, with the majority departing from Atlantic coastal areas north of Florida in winter. Its nesting colonies are localized but often large, sometimes with thousands of nests.

HABITAT *Salt marshes, coastal bays, piers, beaches, ocean.* Generally found only in coastal regions, especially common around beaches and salt marshes but also ranging several miles inland to rivers, fields, dumps. Found well inland in Florida and at Salton Sea, California. Nests on beaches and dredge spoil islands among grass and bushes.

FEEDING **Diet:** *Includes crustaceans, insects, fish.* Diet varies with location and season. Eats many small fish, crustaceans, and insects, also earthworms, snails, refuse. In late spring, gathers to eat eggs of horseshoe crabs. Also eats eggs and sometimes young of other birds, especially Royal Terns. **Behavior:** Forages

Laughing Gull

while walking, wading, or swimming, or may forage in flight by plunging into water or dipping to surface. May steal food from Brown Pelican, landing on pelican's head and snatching fish from the larger bird's bill pouch.

NESTING Breeds in colonies, sometimes with thousands of nests; sometimes associated with other species of gulls or terns. **Nest:** Site is on ground among grass or bushes. In more southerly areas, may be among denser growth or under shrubs or vines, perhaps for protection from sun. Nest (built by both sexes) may be a scrape in ground with sparse lining or a shallow cup of grass, sticks, debris, lined with finer grass. Adults may continue adding to nest during incubation. **Eggs:** 3, sometimes 2–4. Olive to buff or brown, blotched with brown. Incubation is by both sexes, about 20 days. **Young:** Remain in nest for a few days after hatching, then wander nearby, hiding under vegetation. Both parents feed young, giving them half-digested food at first, solid food later. Age at first flight about 5 weeks.

MIGRATION Withdraws in winter from northern areas, with many migrating as far as northern South America. Rarely straggles far inland.

CONSERVATION STATUS Numbers were seriously depleted during 19th century by hunting for feather trade, recovered well in early 20th century, then some decline at northern colonies because of competition with larger gulls. Current populations probably stable.

FRANKLIN'S GULL *Larus pipixcan*

The typical nesting gull of the northern Great Plains, sometimes called "Prairie Dove." Rare on either coast but familiar in the interior, with flocks often seen following plows in farm fields. Locations of nesting colonies shift from year to year with changes in marsh conditions. Nesting colonies may be very large, some running to thousands of pairs. Highly migratory; most Franklin's Gulls spend the winter south of the Equator along the west coast of South America.

HABITAT *Prairies, inland marshes; in winter, coasts, ocean.* Nests on prairie marshes where habitat is extensive and water is fairly deep; forages during summer and migration over agricultural fields, prairie, flooded pasture, marshes, estuaries. In winter mostly along coast, in protected bays, estuaries; sometimes far offshore or on lakes well inland.

Franklin's Gull

FEEDING   **Diet:** *Mainly insects, fish.* Diet in summer is mostly insects (especially aquatic insects and grasshoppers) and earthworms, also seeds, leeches, snails, crayfish. In some regions, young are fed mostly earthworms. During winter may eat many small fish and crustaceans in addition to insects. **Behavior:** Forages by walking on ground, wading in shallow water, by swimming, or by catching insects in flight.

NESTING   Breeds in colonies. In courtship, pairs stand upright and alternately turn heads toward and away from each other; male may feed female. **Nest:** Site is in marsh, where water may be several feet deep. Nest (built by both sexes) is large floating mass of bulrushes, cattails, other plant material, often anchored to standing vegetation. Much of nest material is stolen from other nests in colony. **Eggs:** 3, sometimes 2, rarely 4. Buff to olive or brown, blotched with brown or black. Incubation is by both sexes, 23–26 days. **Young:** Both parents feed young and brood them while they are small; one parent remains with young at all times. Young remain in nest at least 20 days, then may swim short distances around nest. Capable of flight at about 35 days but fed by parents for at least another week.

MIGRATION   Migrates in flocks. Most go south through Great Plains and along eastern coastal plain of Mexico, crossing to Pacific at Isthmus of Tehuantepec. A few may linger into early winter on southern Great Plains. Strays have reached Europe, Africa, Australia, Japan.

CONSERVATION STATUS   Because of nesting in large freshwater marshes, local numbers fluctuate with cycles of rainfall and drought. Overall population trend uncertain; thought to have declined sharply in some areas but stable in others, and has expanded breeding range to new areas in recent decades.

LITTLE GULL   *Larus minutus*

Little Gull

This smallest of the gulls is a recent arrival in North America, having invaded from Europe during this century. Although records of stragglers go back many decades, the species was first found nesting on this continent in 1962. Since then it has nested at several points around the Great Lakes and Hudson Bay. Single birds often associate with flocks of Bonaparte's Gulls, sometimes with terns.

HABITAT   *Lakes, bays.* In summer, mostly inland around low marshy areas near lakes, also fresh or brackish marshes close to coast. Winters along coast, concentrating at protected shallow estuaries, mudflats, beaches, fresh ponds close to shore.

FEEDING   **Diet:** *Mostly insects.* During summer and migration feeds mostly on insects. Also eats brine shrimp and other crustaceans, small mollusks, spiders, marine worms, and some small fish. **Behavior:** Often forages by flying rather slowly and low, dipping to surface of water or land to pick up items. May land on water to feed; sometimes wades in shallow water.

NESTING Breeds in colonies, those in North America usually small, sometimes isolated pairs. In courtship, two birds may walk around each other, heads tilted away, then go through ritualized preening or pecking at ground. **Nest:** Site is on ground near water. Nest (built by both sexes) is a shallow depression lined with grass, leaves, weeds; may be more built up if on wet ground. **Eggs:** 2–3, sometimes 1–5. Olive to buff, marked with brown and gray. Incubation is by both sexes, 23–25 days. **Young:** Tended and fed by both parents; may leave nest when a few days old but remain in general area. Young capable of flight at 21–24 days, may leave nest area with parents but become independent soon thereafter.

MIGRATION Movements on this continent not known in detail. Primarily around Great Lakes in summer, on Atlantic coast in winter, probably with some regular movement between these two areas. Scattered records for other parts of North America, at various seasons, mostly in winter. Those seen in west may come from Asia via Alaska, but Alaska records are almost nil.

CONSERVATION STATUS Still has a shaky hold in North America, with nesting attempts scattered and irregular. Population here possibly not self-sustaining, probably supplemented by additional strays from Europe. The Little Gull invasion represents a natural experiment, one that may or may not succeed. Other birds must have crossed the Atlantic in this way in ages past.

BLACK-HEADED GULL *Larus ridibundus*

Black-headed Gull

One of the most abundant gulls in Europe and Asia and a recent invader to North America. It was first recorded on this continent in the 1920s and 1930s and first found nesting in Newfoundland in 1977. Still mostly a winter visitor to tidewater areas in the northeast and a summer visitor to western Alaska.

HABITAT *Mostly coastal waters.* In North America mostly along coast, on protected bays, shallow estuaries; generally rare on fresh waters well inland. In Eurasia found commonly on fresh marshes, lakes, ponds in interior, especially during summer.

FEEDING **Diet:** *Omnivorous.* Eats mostly animal material, including wide variety of insects, also earthworms, marine worms, mollusks, crustaceans, small fish, carrion. During summer may eat many seeds and small fruits. **Behavior:** Versatile in feeding. Searches for food while walking or swimming, or swoops down to take items from surface while flying; sometimes catches insects in high flight. Black-headed Gulls also steal food from each other and from other birds.

NESTING Usually nests in colonies, sometimes in isolated pairs. **Nest:** Site is usually on ground among vegetation, sometimes on bare soil or above ground. Nest (built by both sexes) usually a scrape lined with bits of plant material, sometimes a mound with depression at top. **Eggs:** 2–3, sometimes 1–4. Variable, gray-green to tan or yellowish, blotched with brown or olive. Incubation is by both sexes, 23–26 days.

Young: Both parents feed young. Young may leave nest after about 10 days but remain in general area; capable of flight at about 5 weeks and independent soon thereafter.

MIGRATION   Of the hundreds that winter in Newfoundland and Nova Scotia (and the dozens that winter elsewhere in the northeast), most probably come from Iceland: the appearance of the species in eastern North America followed a sudden growth of the Icelandic nesting population in the 1930s. Strays from Asia also show up regularly in Alaska.

CONSERVATION STATUS   Future of North American nesting population still uncertain, but species is abundant across Europe and Asia.

BONAPARTE'S GULL   *Larus philadelphia*

This is the smallest gull usually seen over most of North America. Delicate in flight, it suggests a tern more than it does the larger gulls. It differs from large gulls in other ways as well: it seldom scavenges in garbage dumps, and it nests in trees, not on the ground. The name honors French zoologist Charles Lucien Bonaparte, a distant cousin of Napoleon.

HABITAT   *Ocean bays, lakes, muskeg.* Breeds in edges of northern forest where coniferous trees are near lakes or bogs. In migration and winter on many kinds of waters, including rivers and lakes inland, coastal estuaries and lagoons, sometimes well offshore on ocean. Often concentrates at sewage treatment ponds, probably to feed on the abundant insects.

Bonaparte's Gull

FEEDING   **Diet:** *Insects, crustaceans, fish.* Around inland nesting areas, apparently feeds mostly on insects. In coastal regions, where it spends most of the year, diet includes small fish (such as sand lance, herring, and pollock), crustaceans (especially euphausiid shrimp), insects, marine worms, and other invertebrates. **Behavior:** Forages in flight by plunging into the water or dipping to the surface; also picks up items while swimming or wading. Often catches insects in the air. Unlike larger gulls, seldom scavenges at carrion or garbage dumps.

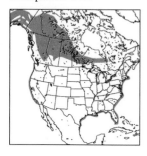

NESTING   Breeding behavior is not well known. Nests in isolated pairs or small colonies in sparse northern forest near water. **Nest:** Site is in coniferous tree, on horizontal branch usually 4–15 feet above ground, sometimes up to 20 feet or higher. Sometimes may build nest on ground. Nest is usually a rather small platform or open cup of sticks, lined with finer materials such as grass and moss. **Eggs:** 3, sometimes 2 or 4. Olive to buff, blotched with brown. Incubation is probably by both parents, about 24 days. **Young:** Both parents feed young in nest. Development of young and age at first flight not well known. If intruders approach the nest, the adults perch on nearby treetops or fly about calling in protest.

MIGRATION   Many birds from central Canada apparently move east or west toward nearest coast in fall. In winter, flocks may move around a lot in response to changing food supplies.

CONSERVATION STATUS   Numbers apparently stable. Has not benefited from human activities as much as some gulls (e.g., does not feed at dumps). However, most of its nesting areas are remote from human disturbance.

HEERMANN'S GULL *Larus heermanni*

Every summer, flocks of these distinctive gulls move north along the Pacific coast from their nesting grounds in western Mexico. This movement is timed with the northward flight of Brown Pelicans; when a pelican comes to the surface after plunging into the water for fish, a Heermann's Gull is often waiting to try to snatch the fish from the pelican's pouch. Although this gull is not large, it is aggressive, harrying other birds to make them drop their catch.

HABITAT *Coast and nearby open ocean.* Favors the immediate coast, including beaches, rocky shores, estuaries, coastal lagoons, offshore kelp beds. Unlike some other coastal gulls, seldom visits freshwater ponds or garbage dumps even a short distance inland. May occur far offshore, out of sight of land.

FEEDING **Diet:** *Fish and other small marine life.* Eats many small fish, also crustaceans, mollusks, insects. Sometimes eats eggs of other birds, refuse, or carrion. **Behavior:** Forages in flight over sea, dipping to surface or plunging into water for fish. Pirates much food from other birds: steals fish directly from bill pouch of pelican, harasses other birds to force them to drop or disgorge their catch. Also will take eggs of other birds and will scavenge refuse or carrion, but seems to do so less than some gulls.

Heermann's Gull

NESTING Breeding behavior not well known. Nests during spring in colonies on islands off west coast of Mexico. Some colonies very large; only a few scattered nesting records on U.S. coast. **Nest:** Site is on level ground, usually in colony on island. Nest (probably built by both sexes) may be shallow scrape in soil with very little lining, or more substantial cup of grass and weeds, lined with feathers. **Eggs:** 2–3. Variable in color, pale gray to blue-gray, blotched with brown, lavender, olive. Incubation is by both sexes, probably about 28 days. Adults incubate eggs in cool temperatures, shade them during day; eggs could easily overheat in intense sun of hot desert islands. **Young:** Fed by both parents. Age at first flight not well known.

MIGRATION Moves north along our Pacific coast after nesting, first appearing in numbers in late May, remaining common until early February when most return to Mexico. Some may also disperse south of nesting areas along Mexican coast.

CONSERVATION STATUS Vulnerable to disturbance on nesting islands, where fishermen sometimes land to harvest eggs.

BLACK-TAILED GULL *Larus crassirostris*

Common along the coastlines of eastern Asia, this gull has wandered to western Alaska a few times. Isolated birds have been found elsewhere in North America (such as Maryland, Rhode Island, southern California). Although these far-flung strays may have been assisted in their arrival, perhaps resting on ships for part of their journey, they also might have wandered there on their own.

BAND-TAILED GULL *Larus belcheri*

Native to the west coast of South America, this gull has been found a few times in Florida. Such strays may have been assisted in arrival, perhaps crossing the isthmus of Panama and then riding north on ships. However, it is possible that these wanderers arrived without human help.

MEW GULL *Larus canus*

Of several similar gulls having white heads and black wingtips with white spots, this one is the smallest. Its small bill and dark eyes give it a gentle expression. Mew Gulls are common all along the Pacific coast in winter, but they spend the summer in

Alaska and northwestern Canada, where they are often seen perched on top of spruce trees. Other races live in Europe and Asia, and European birds rarely stray to our Atlantic coast in winter.

HABITAT *Coastal waters in winter, lakes in summer.* Along Pacific coast, concentrates in winter around river mouths and lagoons and freshwater ponds near the shore. Not as common at garbage dumps as many larger gulls, and seldom occurs any distance offshore. In summer, mostly around lakes in northern forest.

FEEDING **Diet:** *Omnivorous.* Diet may be mostly small fish along coast, mostly insects around inland lakes, but also eats crustaceans, mollusks, sea urchins, earthworms, small rodents, young birds of other species, carrion, refuse. May eat many berries

Mew Gull

in late summer, and eats grain at times. **Behavior:** Forages while walking, wading, or swimming, or dips down to surface of water in flight. May catch flying insects in the air. Sometimes carries hard-shelled mollusks into the air and drops them on rocks to break them open.

NESTING   Breeds in small colonies or in isolated pairs. In courtship, female approaches territorial male in a hunched posture, wagging head from side to side. **Nest:** Site is on high ground near water, or on top of stump or dense low spruce up to 20 feet above ground. May build floating nest in marsh; in Europe, may nest on gravel roofs. Ground nest is shallow scrape lined with grass; tree nest is platform or shallow cup of twigs, grasses. Both sexes help build nest. **Eggs:** 3, sometimes 2. Olive to buff, blotched with brown. Incubation is by both sexes, 23–28 days. **Young:** May leave ground nests when a few days old but remain nearby. Both parents feed young. Age at first flight about 5 weeks.

MIGRATION   Inland breeders apparently move directly to coast and then south; rarely found inland south of breeding range. Fall migration is relatively late, not reaching many wintering areas until November.

CONSERVATION STATUS   Numbers apparently stable. Less affected by human activities than some of the larger gulls.

RING-BILLED GULL *Larus delawarensis*

Often the most common and widespread gull in North America, especially inland, and numbers are probably still increasing. Sociable at all seasons; concentrations at nesting colonies or at winter feeding sites may run into the tens of thousands. The Ring-bill has adapted thoroughly to civilization. Flocks are often seen resting in parking lots, scavenging scraps around fast-food restaurants, or swarming over landfills.

Lakes, bays, coasts, piers, dumps, plowed fields. Associated with water at all seasons, although it does much of its feeding on land. Favors fresh water as much as salt water, but often common along coast, especially at harbors and estuaries; rarely any distance offshore. Common around cities, docks, farm fields, landfills, other human-altered habitats.

FEEDING **Diet:** *Omnivorous.* Diet varies with location and season, but major items include insects, fish, earthworms, grain, rodents, and refuse. Forages in freshly plowed fields for grubs and earthworms. **Behavior:** Opportunistic. Wide variety of foraging behaviors while walking, wading, swimming, flying. May steal food from other birds. Often scavenges in garbage dumps and other places where food scraps may have been tossed out.

NESTING Breeds in colonies, sometimes associated with California or Herring gulls. In court-ship, both birds stretch upright and alternately face

Ring-billed Gull

toward and away from each other; male feeds female. **Nest:** Site is on ground near water in area with sparse plant growth. Nest (built by both sexes) is shallow cup of grasses, twigs, moss. **Eggs:** 2–4, sometimes 1–8. Gray to olive, blotched with brown. (Clutches of more than 4 eggs result from more than one female. Sometimes two females form "pair" and share nest.) Incubation by both sexes, 23–28 days. **Young:** Both parents bring food for young and brood them while they are small. Young may wander out of nest by second day, but remain in immediate area. Young capable of flight about 5 weeks after hatching, become independent 5–10 days later.

MIGRATION Migrates in flocks, often following coastlines or major river systems. Tends to fly higher when migrating over land. Less hardy than Herring Gull, tends to move farther south in winter.

CONSERVATION STATUS Seriously depleted by human persecution during late 19th century, but has made strong comeback. Population in 1990 estimated at 3–4 million and probably still increasing. Has benefited from food provided by garbage dumps and farming practices. High populations may have negative impact on nesting Common Terns and other birds.

CALIFORNIA GULL *Larus californicus*

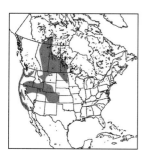

Part of a complex of similar gulls, this bird closely resembles the Herring Gull or Ring-billed Gull and is intermediate between those two in size. It nests around lakes in the interior of the west and winters commonly along the Pacific coast, including offshore waters. This was the species that came to the rescue of the Mormon settlers whose crops were threatened by a grasshopper plague in 1848, inspiring the seagull monument in Salt Lake City.

HABITAT *Seacoasts, lakes, farms, urban centers.* Breeds in the interior at lakes and marshes, often foraging for insects around farms, plowed fields. Some winter inland around major lakes and rivers, but most are coastal at that season, frequenting beaches, docks, garbage dumps, fields. Sometimes common well offshore in winter.

FEEDING **Diet:** *Varied; includes insects, fish, eggs, refuse.* Summer diet inland is mostly insects; also worms, spiders, rodents, eggs and young of other birds, and carrion. On coast, eats fish and other marine life, also scavenges for refuse around garbage dumps, fishing piers. **Behavior:** Forages while walking, wading, swimming, or flying. May hover and dip down to pick items from surface of land or water. Sometimes follows plows to pick up insects exposed in the furrows.

NESTING   Breeds in colonies, sometimes very large, and sometimes mixed with Ring-billed Gulls or other birds; the nests may be quite close together. **Nest:** Site is on ground near lake or marsh, often on island. Nest (built by both sexes) is shallow depression, usually lined with weeds, grass, debris, feathers. **Eggs:** 2–3, sometimes 1–5. Clutches of more than 3 result from two females laying in same nest. Eggs brown, olive, gray, or buff, blotched with dark brown or gray. Incubation is by both parents, 23–27 days. **Young:** May leave nest when a few days old, but remain in immediate area. Both parents feed young, by regurgitation. Young can fly at about 45 days after hatching.

California Gull

MIGRATION   From breeding grounds in interior, most migrate west or southwest to Pacific coast. Surprisingly few move south to Gulf coast; extremely rare east to Atlantic coast. Birds too young to breed may remain along Pacific coast through the summer.

CONSERVATION STATUS   Has increased in many areas during recent decades.

HERRING GULL   *Larus argentatus*

Large, abundant, and widespread, the Herring Gull is among the most familiar members of its family, especially in the northeast. It has been extending its range toward the south along the Atlantic coast in recent decades. In the west, where there are several similar large gulls, no such range expansion seems to be taking place.

HABITAT   *Ocean coasts, bays, beaches, lakes, piers, farmlands, dumps.* Wide variety of habitats, typically associated with water. Most numerous along coast and around large lakes, also along major river systems. Forages at sea, on beaches, mudflats, plowed fields, marshes, or where human activity provides food (garbage dumps, picnic grounds, docks, fishing operations). Nests on islands, sometimes on gravel roofs.

FEEDING   **Diet:** *Omnivorous.* Diet varies with place and season, includes fish, crustaceans, mollusks, sea urchins, marine worms, birds, eggs, insects. Scavenges refuse and carrion. At sea, may feed on schools of fish driven to surface by foraging whales. **Behavior:** Opportunistic. Forages while walking, swimming, or flying, dipping down to take items from surface of water or land, sometimes plunge-diving into water. May

Herring Gull

steal food from other birds. May carry hard-shelled items (such as crabs, mollusks) high in air and drop them on rocks to break them open.

NESTING   Usually first breeds at age of 4–5 years. Nests in colonies (often with other species of gulls), sometimes in isolated pairs. In courtship, female approaches male with hunched posture and begging calls; male displays with upright posture, "choking"

JAEGERS, GULLS, TERNS, AND SKIMMERS

motions; feeds female. **Nest:** Site on ground, next to object such as shrub or rock which protects from prevailing wind. Nest (built by both sexes) is shallow scrape, usually lined with grass, feathers, debris. **Eggs:** 3, sometimes 1–2, rarely 4. Buff to olive, blotched with black, brown, dark olive. Incubation is by both sexes, 27–30 days. **Young:** May leave nest a day or two after hatching, remain in immediate area. Both parents feed young, by regurgitation. Young capable of flight 45–50 days after hatching, may be fed by parents for another month.

MIGRATION   Present year-round as far north as New England, Great Lakes, southern Alaska. Some move south as far as Mexico, a few to West Indies and Panama. Young birds tend to migrate farther south in winter than adults.

CONSERVATION STATUS   Numbers declined sharply during 19th century when hunted for eggs and feathers. With protection, has increased greatly during 20th century, expanding breeding range far to the south along Atlantic coast. May have been aided in expansion by availability of food in garbage dumps, around fishing operations, etc., but such simple reasons may not be whole explanation.

YELLOW-LEGGED GULL   *Larus cachinnans*

Long considered just a yellow-legged race of the Herring Gull, this form was recently recognized as a full species. Native to southern Europe, it has strayed very rarely to eastern North America.

THAYER'S GULL   *Larus thayeri*

Thayer's Gull

Wintering commonly along parts of the Pacific coast, this bird was largely overlooked for years because of its resemblance to Herring Gull (it was once considered a race of that species). Thayer's is a gull of the Canadian high Arctic in summer. It is closely related to the Iceland Gull, and the two are sometimes very difficult to tell apart; they may be only forms of the same species.

HABITAT   *Coastal waters, bays.* Winters mostly in coastal regions, especially around estuaries and protected bays, also well offshore at times. May regularly visit freshwater ponds and garbage dumps in coastal plain. Rare in winter farther inland around lakes, rivers. Nests on rocky coasts of northern islands.

FEEDING   **Diet:** *Omnivorous.* Diet includes many small fish, also carrion, mollusks, crustaceans, berries. Around colonies of smaller seabirds, may take eggs or young. Also may feed on refuse around garbage dumps, docks, fishing boats. **Behavior:** Forages in flight by dipping to surface of water or by plunging to just below surface; also feeds while swimming or walking.

NESTING   Breeding behavior not well known. Probably does not breed until 4 years old. Nests in colonies, sometimes with other species of gulls. **Nest:** Site is on ledge of rocky cliff close to ocean, usually facing fjord or sound on Arctic island. Nest (probably built by both sexes) is a low mound of plant material with a depression at the center. **Eggs:** 2, sometimes 3. Buff to olive or gray, with darker brown blotches. Incubation is probably by both sexes; incubation period not known. **Young:** Both parents probably feed young. Age of young at fledging and at independence not known.

MIGRATION	Most birds from central Canadian Arctic move southwest to Pacific coast. Rare farther east in winter. Young birds tend to move farther south than adults; most found in southern California and northwestern Mexico are first-winter immatures.
CONSERVATION STATUS	Nesting range is mostly remote from impact of human activities. No obvious trends in population.

ICELAND GULL   *Larus glaucoides*

A pale northern gull, about the size of Herring Gull but more graceful and maneuverable in flight. Despite its name, it occurs in Iceland only during the winter. The typical white-winged form nests only in Greenland, while the "Kumlien's" form, with gray in the wingtips, nests in northeastern Canada. Very closely related to Thayer's Gull, and probably should be considered the same species. The "Kumlien's" form seems to intergrade with Thayer's where their nesting ranges come in contact in the Baffin Island region of Arctic Canada.

HABITAT   *Coastal, less frequent inland.* During most seasons found in coastal regions, both in protected bays and estuaries and well offshore. Some occur in winter on Great Lakes and other large bodies of water inland. Nests on rocky cliffs, mostly in protected bays and fjords rather than on exposed coastline.

FEEDING   **Diet:** *Mostly fish.* Aside from a variety of small fish, also feeds on mollusks, crustaceans, carrion, berries, seeds. Around colonies of smaller seabirds, may take eggs or young, and often scavenges dead young birds. Also may feed on refuse around garbage dumps, docks, fishing boats. **Behavior:** Forages in flight by dipping to surface of water to pick up items or by plunging to just below surface; also feeds while swimming or walking.

Iceland Gull

NESTING   Breeding behavior not well known. Probably does not breed until 4 years old. Nests in colonies, often in same colonies with Black-legged Kittiwakes, sometimes with Glaucous Gulls. In such mixed colonies, Iceland Gulls usually nest higher than kittiwakes, lower than Glaucous Gulls. **Nest:** Site is usually on ledge of a cliff facing the sea. Nest (probably built by both sexes) is a bulky mound of grasses, moss, and debris, with a shallow depression at the top. **Eggs:** 2–3. Buff to olive, blotched with darker brown. Incubation is probably by both sexes; incubation period unknown. **Young:** Both parents probably feed young. Age of young at fledging not known.

MIGRATION   Moves short distance south from Arctic breeding range, mostly wintering in coastal eastern Canada (from Labrador south to New England) and around Iceland. Smaller numbers winter to northwestern Europe.

CONSERVATION STATUS   Mostly remote from effects of human activities. Populations apparently stable or perhaps increasing. Numbers wintering in New England seem to have increased during last century or so.

LESSER BLACK-BACKED GULL   *Larus fuscus*

Once a very rare stray to North America, this European gull has become a regular visitor here, with several dozen found every winter scattered along the eastern seaboard. This increase may be related to the growing population of the species in Iceland, where it first nested in the 1920s and is now present by the thousands. Similar in appearance and habits to the Herring Gull, but slightly smaller, and may be more agile in flight.

HABITAT *Beaches, bays, coasts, garbage dumps.* Mostly along coast, including bays, estuaries, coastal islands; also around lakes inland, especially Great Lakes and elsewhere in northeast. Concentrates around sources of food, such as garbage dumps, fishing harbors.

FEEDING **Diet:** *Omnivorous.* Diet includes a wide variety of fish, insects, mollusks, crustaceans, marine worms, small birds, nestlings, eggs, rodents; also eats berries, seeds, seaweed. Also scavenges refuse around garbage dumps. **Behavior:** Forages by swooping down to sea surface in flight, or picks up items while swimming, walking, or wading. May steal food from other birds.

NESTING Not yet proven to nest in North America. Usually first breeds at age of 4 years. Nests in colonies. **Nest:** Site is on ground, sometimes on cliff ledge or on roof of building. Nest (built by both sexes) a mound of grasses, seaweed, debris, with shallow depression at top lined with finer materials. **Eggs:** 3, sometimes 1–4. Brown or olive to bluegreen, usually blotched with dark brown. Incubation is by both sexes, 24–27 days. **Young:** Both parents feed young. Downy young may leave nest after a few days, but remain in vicinity. Age at first flight about 30–40 days.

MIGRATION May be found in North America during every month of the year, but most are seen during winter. Some move quite far south; regular in Florida and coastal Texas. Many of those wintering in North America may come from Iceland.

CONSERVATION STATUS Has increased numbers and expanded range in Europe during last century. May eventually colonize northeastern North America as a breeding bird.

SLATY-BACKED GULL *Larus schistisagus*

Resident along the coastlines of northeastern Asia, this big gull is a regular summer visitor to western Alaska, usually in small numbers. In winter, it has appeared as a very rare stray at widely scattered points in North America, as far east as Niagara Falls and as far south as Texas.

YELLOW-FOOTED GULL *Larus livens*

Passed over for years as a local race of Western Gull, the Yellow-footed Gull is actually a distinct species. It nests only in the Gulf of California, that long narrow arm of sea between Baja and the Mexican mainland. Every summer after nesting, many Yellow-footed Gulls move north across the desert to the landlocked Salton Sea in southern California.

HABITAT *In U.S., barren shoreline of Salton Sea.* Visitors to Salton Sea concentrate on west side, mostly on open shoreline, sometimes foraging in flooded fields nearby. In Gulf of California, found around islands and shoreline, sometimes well out to sea but almost never inland.

FEEDING **Diet:** *Fish, other marine life.* Diet poorly known. On Gulf of California, probably includes fish, crabs, shrimp, clams, wide variety of other sea creatures. Also takes eggs and young of other birds. Will eat carrion, and scavenges around dumps and docks for scraps and refuse. **Behavior:** Feeding behavior not well known. Forages while walking, wading, or swimming, sometimes plunging into water in flight.

NESTING Breeding behavior not well known, probably similar to that of Western Gull. Nests in colonies, with different arrangement from those of Western Gull: nests are arranged in a line along beach just above the reach of the highest tides, and each pair may defend a narrow territory from the nest down to the water. **Nest:** Site is on ground, on beach or at base of cliffs, a short distance above the high tide line. Nest is a shallow depression lined with seaweed, grass, or other plant material. **Eggs:** Usually 3. Olive to buff, marked with dark brown. Incubation is probably by both parents. **Young:** Probably fed by both parents. Probably able to fly at about 6–7 weeks after hatching.

MIGRATION   Most are probably permanent residents within Gulf of California. Some (up to several hundred) move north to Salton Sea, California, after nesting season. Main arrival typically late June, with peak numbers in August; small numbers usually remain through winter.

CONSERVATION STATUS   Numbers probably stable at the moment. Overfishing and pollution of the Gulf of California could cause problems for this species and other seabirds nesting there.

Yellow-footed Gull

WESTERN GULL *Larus occidentalis*

The only gull nesting along most of the Pacific coast from Washington to Baja, this large species is common at all seasons. An opportunist, it often nests around colonies of other seabirds, where it can steal unguarded eggs or chicks. It will also nest near colonies of California sea lions, scavenging any sea lion pups that die of natural causes. At the northern end of its range it hybridizes with Glaucous-winged Gull, and many intermediate birds are seen.

HABITAT   *Coastal waters, estuaries, beaches, city waterfronts.* Mostly along immediate coast, but regularly found well out at sea, especially between coast and nesting islands. Visits garbage dumps, ponds, and flat open areas (such as parking lots) within a few miles of coast, but almost never found farther inland. Nests on islands and locally on mainland cliffs.

FEEDING   **Diet:** *Fish and other marine life, eggs, carrion, refuse.* Feeds on a wide variety of aquatic life, including fish, crabs, squid, clams, sea urchins.

Western Gull

Eats eggs and young (and sometimes adults) of other birds. Around sea lion colonies, scavenges dead pups and afterbirth. Also eats other carrion, and scavenges in dumps and around docks for refuse. **Behavior:** Forages while walking or swimming, or may plunge into water from flight. May drop hard-shelled clams and crabs onto rocks while in flight to break them open.

NESTING   First breeds at 4 years or older. Nests in colonies. **Nest:** Site is on ground or on cliff ledge, sometimes on boat or building, sometimes under overhanging rock. Nest (probably built by both sexes) is shallow depression, usually with lining of grass, other plants. **Eggs:** Usually 3, sometimes 1–5, rarely 6. Clutches of more than 3 eggs result from two females laying in same nest, which happens fairly often at some colonies. Eggs buff to olive or gray, blotched with darker brown. Incubation at normal nests is by both parents (female may do more), 29–32 days. In very hot weather, adults may fly to water and soak belly feathers to cool eggs. **Young:** Fed by both parents. May leave nest when a few days old and hide in nearby vegetation. Capable of flight at about 6–7 weeks after hatching. Young depart from some colonies at about 10 weeks, becoming independent then; at other colonies, young may be fed by parents longer.

MIGRATION   Present all year throughout its breeding range, but banding records show that individuals wander widely within this range. Some move north into British Columbia and south to southern Baja, especially in winter. Almost never found inland.

CONSERVATION STATUS   Common, and overall numbers apparently stable. Nesting at some colonies has been affected in the past by pesticides in the food chain.

GLAUCOUS-WINGED GULL   *Larus glaucescens*

The typical large gull of the northern Pacific coast, nesting mainly from southern Alaska to Washington. Common all along the Pacific coast in winter, it very rarely strays any distance inland. Part of a complex of closely related forms, it interbreeds freely with Western Gull at the southern end of its range and often with Herring Gull and Glaucous Gull in Alaska.

HABITAT   *Primarily coastal.* Most common around bays, estuaries, beaches, rocky shorelines. Visits fresh ponds and garbage dumps near coast. Sometimes far offshore over continental shelf, well out of sight of land. Very rare around inland lakes and rivers. Nests mainly on low, flat islands.

FEEDING   **Diet:** *Omnivorous.* Diet includes fish, limpets, chitons, clams, mussels, sea urchins, barnacles, crabs, squid. Also smaller birds, eggs, small mammals, some plant material. Scavenges refuse in garbage dumps and eats carrion. **Behavior:** Forages while walking or swimming, or may plunge into water from flight. May drop hard-shelled clams and crabs onto rocks while in flight to break them open. Associates with feeding bears and other predators to pick up scraps they leave behind.

Glaucous-winged Gull

NESTING   First breeds at age of 4 years or older. Breeds in colonies, often densely packed. **Nest:** Site is on ground, sometimes on cliff or roof. Nest (built by both sexes) is a shallow scrape lined with grass, moss, seaweed, debris. Pair may begin building several nests, but complete only one. **Eggs:** 2–3, sometimes 1–4. Olive to yellow-green, marked with scrawls and blotches of brown and gray. Incubation is by both sexes, 26–29 days. **Young:** Downy young may leave nest 2 days after hatching, remain in vicinity. Both parents feed young. Age at first flight 37–53 days after hatching; leave colony about 2 weeks later on average.

MIGRATION   Present all year in much of range, but some withdrawal in winter from northernmost areas in western Alaska. Many disperse well to the south in winter, reaching northwestern Mexico. Very rare migrant inland.

CONSERVATION STATUS   Has been steadily increasing in numbers in recent decades. Since it is a predator on eggs and young, its increase may cause problems for populations of other coastal bird species.

GLAUCOUS GULL *Larus hyperboreus*

A big, pale, ghostly gull of the far north. The only large gull common in the high Arctic, although a couple of small gulls are successful there as well. At various times it may fill the role of either predator or scavenger. Generally found around cold waters, but a few Glaucous Gulls (mostly young birds) may leave the Arctic and move far south in winter, sometimes reaching Florida, Texas, or northwestern Mexico.

HABITAT *Mainly coastal.* At most seasons favors coastal bays and estuaries, but also occurs well offshore at times; small numbers may be found around large lakes well inland in winter. Nests on cliff ledges, islands, beaches.

FEEDING **Diet:** *Omnivorous.* Diet highly variable, includes fish, mollusks, crustaceans, marine worms, sea urchins, insects, birds, eggs, berries, seaweed, carrion. Often scavenges refuse around towns, fishing boats. **Behavior:** Feeds as both a predator and a scavenger; also steals food from other birds. Forages while walking or swimming; in flight, may swoop down to pick items from surface of water, or may catch smaller birds in the air.

Glaucous Gull

NESTING Breeds in colonies or in isolated pairs. **Nest:** Site is on cliff top, flat rocky ground, rocky outcrop; sometimes on ice or snow. Nest (built by both sexes) is a mound of grasses, moss, seaweed, and debris, with a shallow depression at the top. **Eggs:** 3, sometimes 2–4. Olive to buff, blotched with dark brown. Incubation is by both sexes, 27–28 days. **Young:** Both parents feed young. Downy young may leave nest a few days after hatching, but remain in general area. Age at first flight probably about 45–50 days, with young becoming independent soon thereafter.

MIGRATION Many remain in winter as far north as there is open water. A few move well south along both coasts of United States and to Great Lakes; scattered singles may turn up anywhere inland or on Gulf coast.

CONSERVATION STATUS Widespread and common in far north; not much affected by human activities. No obvious trend in population.

GREAT BLACK-BACKED GULL *Larus marinus*

The largest gull in North America. Primarily a bird of the Atlantic coast, seldom seen inland except around the Great Lakes. Because of its large size and omnivorous feeding habits, the Great Black-back can be a significant predator on other species of birds during the nesting season. It has benefited from certain human activities (such as the establishment of garbage dumps) and has expanded its range southward along the Atlantic seaboard in recent decades.

HABITAT *Mainly coastal waters, estuaries; a few on large lakes.* Close to coast at most seasons, but will forage far offshore in winter over the continental shelf. Some regularly move inland along St. Lawrence River to Great Lakes, rarely other fresh waters. Nests mostly on islands, tops of sea cliffs, sometimes on mainland beaches and marsh edges.

FEEDING **Diet:** *Omnivorous.* Diet includes carrion, fish, mollusks, crustaceans, marine worms, insects, rodents, and berries, as well as other birds and their eggs and young. **Behavior:** Opportunistic. Forages on foot, while flying, or while

swimming. May steal food from other birds. May break open hard-shelled mollusks and eggs by flying high and dropping them on rocks. Often scavenges refuse around fishing boats, docks, garbage dumps.

NESTING   Usually first breeds at age of 4–5 years. Generally nests in colonies, often mixed with Herring Gulls or other birds; sometimes nests in isolated pairs. **Nest:** Site is on ground, often on top of or beside a rocky outcropping. Nest (built by both sexes) is mound of grass, seaweed, moss, debris, with shallow depression in center. **Eggs:** 2–3, sometimes 1–5. Olive to buff with brown blotches. Incubation is by both sexes, 27–28 days. **Young:** Both parents care for and feed young. Downy young may wander from nest after

Great Black-backed Gull

a few days, but remain in general area. Young are capable of flight at 7–8 weeks after hatching, become independent soon thereafter.

MIGRATION   Present all year in most parts of breeding range, but withdraws in winter from coast of Labrador, and a few move south as far as Florida. Numbers in southeast and on Great Lakes increase in winter. Very rare on Gulf coast and in most inland areas.

CONSERVATION STATUS   Has been increasing its population in North America at least since the 1930s, with the breeding range steadily expanding southward along the Atlantic coast and inland to some areas of the Great Lakes.

KITTIWAKES — GENUS *Rissa*

These small gulls, named for their nasal *ki-ti-waak* call notes, nest on the cliffs of northern islands. Unlike most gulls, they spend most of the year out at sea. One of the two kittiwake species is very widespread and common, while the other is scarce and local, found in a few areas around the Bering Sea.

BLACK-LEGGED KITTIWAKE   *Rissa tridactyla*

A very common small gull of northern and offshore waters. Seldom comes to land south of its nesting range, but may be seen from shore on either coast, especially during storms. Often abundant on the northern islands where it nests. There the kittiwakes are seen on narrow cliff ledges, perched facing the wall, their tails sticking out over the edge.

HABITAT   *Chiefly oceanic.* Spends most of year at sea, with wide range of conditions, from edge of pack ice to moderately warm waters off Baja. Favors areas of upwellings, and sometimes concentrates over edge of continental shelf, but may occur from coast to hundreds of miles out. Nests on ledges of steep cliffs on northern islands and mainland.

FEEDING   **Diet:** *Mostly fish.* Feeds mainly on small fish, often concentrating on one or two locally abundant species (such as sand lance or pollock). If fish numbers are low, eats many crustaceans, often including many euphausiid shrimp. Also eats marine worms, mollusks, small squid, insects, rarely plant material. Unlike most gulls, does not feed at garbage dumps. **Behavior:** Does much foraging in flight, dipping down to take items at surface or plunging into water to take prey below surface; also feeds by seizing items at surface while swimming.

NESTING   First breeds at age of 3–5 years. Male displays to attract female by making "choking" motions, jerking head up and down with bill gradually opening. Pairs display by

Black-legged Kittiwake

nodding heads, crossing necks; male feeds female. **Nest:** Site is on cliff ledge, often quite narrow; sometimes on boulders or on ground. (In Europe, also nests on building ledges and roofs.) Nest (built by both sexes, with male bringing most of material) is mound of mud, grasses, seaweed, with shallow depression at center. **Eggs:** 1–3. Variable, olive or pale blue to tan, speckled with darker brown and gray. Incubation is by both parents, 25–28 days. **Young:** Remain in nest until ready to fly, are fed by both parents. Age at first flight 34–58 days; young may return to nest at night for several weeks.

MIGRATION   Most migration is offshore. A few, mostly young birds, come south through interior in autumn. In winter, ranges from Labrador and southern Bering Sea south to Florida and northwestern Mexico. Very irregular in numbers off Pacific coast in winter, numerous some years, almost absent in others. Strays have reached Hawaii and Peru.

CONSERVATION STATUS   Local populations fluctuate considerably. In recent decades, major increases in some eastern Canadian colonies, major decreases at some in Bering Sea.

RED-LEGGED KITTIWAKE *Rissa brevirostris*

This small gull is an uncommon specialty of the Bering Sea, nesting in only four island groups. Its limited range is surprising because its close relative, Black-legged Kittiwake, is abundant in northern waters; even in the general region of the North Pacific and Bering Sea, Black-legged outnumbers Red-legged by more than 10 to 1.

Red-legged Kittiwake

Red-legged Kittiwake is known to birders mainly from colonies on the Pribilof Islands, Alaska.

HABITAT   *Ocean, islands.* At sea found mostly over deep water, at and beyond edge of continental shelf. May forage farther from nesting colonies than Black-legged Kittiwake. Especially in winter may be very far from land, in North Pacific or near edge of pack ice in Bering Sea. Nests on ledges of steep cliffs above sea on islands.

FEEDING   **Diet:** *Fish, squid, crustaceans.* Feeds mainly on lampfish, pollock, squid, and small crustaceans such as amphipods. Fish eaten are mostly under 4 inches long. **Behavior:** Forages by dipping to surface of water or plunging into water from flight low over surface. Often forages in flocks, mixed with Black-legged Kittiwakes, over schools of fish. Red-legged Kittiwake has larger eye, possibly adaptation to feeding in dim light; may feed by day or night. Some food items such as lampfish and squid may be closer to surface at night.

NESTING   Breeds in colonies, associated with other seabirds. Courtship displays similar to those of Black-legged Kittiwake. **Nest:** Site is on ledge of vertical cliff, often smaller ledges than used by Black-legged Kittiwake. Nest (built by both sexes) is shallow cup of mud, grass, kelp. Same site may be reused each year, although nest must be rebuilt after winter storms. **Eggs:** 1, sometimes 2. Variable, gray to buff or greenish with blotches or scrawls of brown. Incubation by both sexes, probably about 30 days; may incubate slightly longer than Black-legged Kittiwake on Pribilofs. **Young:** Both parents care for young, brooding them for first 2 weeks after hatching, feeding them by regurgitation. Young capable of flight at about 37 days; may return to nest to be fed for at least several more days.

MIGRATION Movements not well known; may winter in Gulf of Alaska and near edge of pack ice in Bering Sea. Almost never occurs south of Alaska, but one was found once in summer in southern Nevada.

CONSERVATION STATUS Total population in 1970s estimated at a little over 230,000, with 95 percent of these in Pribilofs. Since then, evidence of major declines in Pribilofs, small increases at some other colonies. Decline probably related to unreliable food supply, but causes for this not well known. Also vulnerable to accidental introduction of rats to nesting islands. May have been much more numerous historically, but no reliable data.

GENUS *Rhodostethia*

ROSS'S GULL *Rhodostethia rosea*

A beautiful small gull of the far north, named after the great Arctic explorer James Clark Ross. Breeds mainly in remote stretches of northern Siberia, spending other seasons among the ice pack of the Arctic Ocean. Was considered almost mythical by most North American birders until 1980, when it began nesting near a paved road at Churchill, Manitoba. Still regular only at Churchill and a few points in Alaska, but rare winter strays turn up farther south.

Ross's Gull

HABITAT *Pack ice, northern coasts, tundra.* Nests (in Siberia and Manitoba) mainly on wet, boggy tundra and marsh near southern limits of tundra regions; also some on high Arctic tundra farther north. Spends remainder of year at sea, mostly around areas of pack ice, also along Arctic coastlines. Very rare visitor farther south, both along coast and on inland waters.

FEEDING **Diet:** *Insects, crustaceans, fish.* Diet on breeding grounds mostly insects. At sea, feeds on crustaceans, small fish, mollusks, marine worms; may also eat carrion, refuse. **Behavior:** Forages mostly by flying low over water, dropping to surface and partly submerging, or picking items from surface while hovering. Also feeds while swimming or while wading or walking along shore. May paddle its feet in water while wading or hovering, perhaps to stir up prey.

NESTING May nest in loose colonies, often associated with colonies of Arctic Tern. Aggressive nest defense of terns may benefit Ross's Gulls nesting nearby. Courtship displays include two birds facing each other, raising their tails and giving soft calls; also standing side by side, circling each other on foot. **Nest:** Site is on an island or hummock in a marshy area, close to water. Nest is a shallow depression lined with bits of plant material. **Eggs:** 2–3. Olive with brown blotches. Incubation is by both parents, probably 21–22 days. **Young:** After the young are a few days old, parents visit only briefly and infrequently to feed them; nesting colony may look deserted. Age at first flight not well known, probably more than 3 weeks.

Movements poorly known. After breeding, moves north to Arctic Ocean, where apparently spends most of year associated with openings in pack ice. Every fall, many (hundreds or even thousands) move past Point Barrow, Alaska, apparently heading northeast, mostly during September and October. Present at Churchill, Manitoba, only in summer. Rare strays south of Arctic in North America may be either on coast or inland.

CONSERVATION STATUS   Most of breeding range is remote from human impact. Should be considered vulnerable, however, since world population has been estimated at under 10,000.

GENUS *Xema*

SABINE'S GULL   *Xema sabini*

A small gull with a spectacular wing pattern. Generally a prized sighting for birders, because it nests on tundra of the high Arctic and migrates south at sea, often well offshore. A young Sabine's that goes astray in fall may cause excitement by showing up on a pond far inland. Delicate in its feeding, this species often floats low in the air over water, dipping down to take food from the surface without landing. Its flight action may suggest a tern more than a gull.

HABITAT   *Ocean; nests on tundra.* In summer on low, marshy tundra close to coast, especially areas with many ponds and shallow tidal flats. In migration and winter mostly at sea, typically a few miles offshore over continental shelf; concentrates in winter where there are upwellings of cold water near coastlines south of the Equator.

FEEDING   **Diet:** *Insects, fish, crustaceans.* Diet in summer mostly insects and aquatic insect larvae, also some crustaceans, mollusks, marine worms, small fish. Winter diet not well known, includes small fish, crustaceans. **Behavior:** During migration and in winter (mostly at sea), forages by dipping to surface of water in flight or by picking up items near surface while swimming. In summer, also does much feeding while walking on tidal flats or in marshes. In shallow water may spin in circles, stirring up items from bottom.

NESTING   Male on territory lures female by giving long call, arching neck, bowing. In courtship, male may feed female. **Nest:** Site is on open ground, in small colony, typically close to water. Usually located in or near a colony of Arctic Terns. Nest is a shallow depression, either unlined or with a lining of seaweed, moss, feathers. **Eggs:** 2, sometimes 1–3. Olive with darker olive-brown spots. Incubation is by both sexes, 23–25 days. Parents may defend nest by dive-bombing intruders, or may try to lead predators away with distraction display. **Young:** Shortly after young hatch, parents lead them to area near water; young mostly feed themselves. Age at first flight unknown.

MIGRATION   Birds from Alaska and Siberia migrate south along our Pacific coast to spend winter off western South America. Those from eastern Canada and Greenland mostly migrate eastward across North Atlantic and then south, wintering mostly off South Africa. Thus migrants are often seen on boat trips off our west coast, rarely off our east coast. Every fall, a few (mostly young birds) show up on lakes in the interior of North America.

Sabine's Gull

Remote summer range and seagoing habits probably help ensure survival. Like other seabirds, could be vulnerable to pollution in coastal waters during migration or winter.

GENUS *Pagophila*

IVORY GULL   *Pagophila eburnea*

A gleaming white bird of the frozen north, spending most of its life along shifting edges of pack ice in the Arctic Ocean. Its pristine appearance is belied by its feeding habits: the Ivory Gull often is a scavenger, eating carrion and even the droppings of other animals and aggressively fighting over food. Seems to swim less often than most gulls. Only a very rare stray south of the Canadian border.

Ivory Gull

HABITAT   *Arctic Ocean, barren northern coasts.* Usually around edges of floating ice at sea, also along shores of northern islands in vicinity of pack ice. Rarely farther south along coast, and very rare inland in winter. Nests on cliff ledges, bare rocky ground.

FEEDING   **Diet:** *Carrion, small marine life.* Diet includes many small fish, crustaceans, insects. Sometimes is a scavenger, feeding on carrion (including kills left by polar bears) and on the droppings of walrus, seals, polar bears, and others. May feed on refuse around northern coastal towns. **Behavior:** Does much of its feeding while walking on ice or beach. Forages in flight by dipping to surface of water; sometimes forages by swimming or wading.

NESTING   Usually breeds in colonies. Courtship displays include long calls, tossing head back so that bill points up, lowering head and making "choking" movements. In courtship feeding, male regurgitates to feed female. **Nest:** Site is usually on cliff ledge, either coastal or inland; may be on flat rocky ground. Has been found nesting on patches of rock imbedded in floating icebergs. Nest (built by both sexes) is usually a bulky mound of seaweed, mud, debris, with shallow depression at top; sometimes little or no nest built. **Eggs:** 1–2, rarely 3. Buff to olive, blotched with dark olive, brown, or black. Incubation is by both sexes, roughly 24–26 days. **Young:** Both parents feed young, and brood them while they are small. Young usually remain in nest until ready to fly; age at first flight not well known, but at least 5 weeks.

MIGRATION   Moves south in winter to waters around Newfoundland and into Bering Sea, but mainly around edges of pack ice. Very rare stray south to New England and Great Lakes; in west, almost never found south of Alaska.

CONSERVATION STATUS   Has declined at nesting areas at Spitsbergen (north of Norway) and probably at a few other spots, but North American population and trends difficult to determine.

TYPICAL TERNS — GENUS *Sterna*

Sometimes called "sea swallows," these are graceful fliers that patrol above lakes, coastal marshes, and offshore waters. Most of the approximately 45 species of terns worldwide are now classified in the genus *Sterna*. Although almost all their feeding is done on the wing, they have at least two distinct foraging styles: hovering and then plunging headfirst into the water, or making shallow swoops to pick items from the surface. Most kinds of terns specialize in one or the other of these methods. Some (especially the Gull-billed Tern) also catch many flying insects in the air.

As befits such graceful fliers, many terns perform courtship displays in the air. Often two birds will fly very high and then glide down together. On the ground, a pair will perform elaborate bowing and posturing, and the male often brings small fish to feed the female.

GULL-BILLED TERN *Sterna nilotica*

Besides the thick bill that gives it its name, this tern has a relatively stocky build and broad wings. Typically seen in leisurely flight over marshes, hawking for insects in the air or swooping down to take prey from the water or the ground; unlike typical terns, rarely dives into water for fish. On the ground, walks better than most terns. Widespread in warmer parts of the world, but local in North America, mainly in southeast. Generally found only in small numbers.

HABITAT *Salt marshes, fields, coastal bays.* Restricted to seacoast in North America (except in Florida and at Salton Sea, California), but does most foraging over marshes, pastures, farmland, and other open country just inland from coast. Nests mostly on beaches, islands. Reportedly used to nest more often in salt marshes, abandoned those sites because of human persecution.

FEEDING **Diet:** *Mostly insects.* Feeds on a wide variety of insects caught on ground, in air, or at surface of water; also spiders, crabs, shrimp, mollusks, earthworms, marine worms, small fish, lizards, frogs, toads, rodents, small birds. **Behavior:** Forages by flying slowly into wind, dipping to surface of land or water to pick up items, or by catching flying insects in the air. Sometimes forages while walking on ground; rarely plunges into water.

NESTING Colonial breeder. Colonies usually small, not as densely packed as those of many terns. Has some aerial displays, but much of courtship display takes place on ground, involving elaborate posturing, bill-pointing, male feeding female. **Nest:** Site is on open ground, sometimes on gravel roof. Nest (built by both

Gull-billed Tern

sexes) is shallow depression, often with rim of soil, addition of some plant material and debris. **Eggs:** 2–3, sometimes 1–4. Pale buff, spotted with dark brown. Incubation is by both parents (although female may do more), 22–23 days. **Young:** Leave nest a few days after hatching, move to dense plant cover if nearby. Both parents bring food for young. Age at first flight 4–5 weeks. Young may remain with parents 3 months or more, beginning southward migration with them.

MIGRATION Mainly a summer resident in California and on Atlantic coast; some remain through winter on Gulf coast.

CONSERVATION STATUS Evidently far less numerous on the Atlantic coast today than it was historically. Human disturbance and loss of nesting sites among likely causes. Has begun nesting on rooftops in some Gulf coast areas. Colonized southern California, apparently from western Mexico, beginning to nest at Salton Sea in 1920s and at San Diego in 1980s.

CASPIAN TERN *Sterna caspia*

Caspian Tern

The largest of the terns, larger than many gulls. Cosmopolitan, nesting on five continents. In North America, it is common along both coasts and locally inland, mainly around large bodies of water. Noted for its long adolescence, with the young dependent on their parents for many months; even in late winter, many an adult Caspian is trailed by a begging youngster from the previous nesting season.

HABITAT   *Large lakes, coastal waters, beaches, bays.* Found on both fresh and salt water, favoring protected waters such as bays, lagoons, rivers, lakes, not usually foraging over open sea. Inland, more likely on large lakes than on small ponds. Nests on open ground on islands, coasts.

FEEDING   **Diet:** *Mostly fish.* Often concentrates on a few abundant fish species in a given locale (for example, shiner perch on California coast, alewife on Great Lakes). Also eats insects, sometimes eggs or young of other birds. **Behavior:** When foraging flies high over water, hovers, then plunges to catch fish below surface. Less often flies low, dips down to catch prey at water's surface. May steal food from other birds.

NESTING   First breeds at age of 3 years. Nests in colonies, sometimes in isolated pairs. Male may fly low over colony carrying fish; female follows. On ground, courtship feeding (male feeds female). **Nest:** Site is on bare ground, among driftwood or debris, perhaps sometimes on floating mats of dead vegetation. Nest (built by both sexes) is shallow depression, sometimes with rim or lining of debris. **Eggs:** 1–3, rarely 4 or 5. Pale buff, spotted with brown or black. Incubation is by both parents (female may do more), 20–22 days. **Young:** May leave nest a few days after hatching, move to nearby shore. If colony is undisturbed, young may remain at nest until ready to fly. Both parents bring food for young. Age at first flight about 30–35 days; young may remain with parents as long as 8 months.

MIGRATION   Inland breeders move to coast and southward for winter. Some winter south to West Indies, northern South America.

CONSERVATION STATUS   Overall population probably stable, perhaps increasing slightly; range has expanded recently to include southern Alaska.

ROYAL TERN *Sterna maxima*

Common along tropical and subtropical shores, the Royal Tern is a characteristic sight along the Gulf coast and southern Atlantic coast, less numerous in California. Aside from a few interior localities in Florida, it is almost never found inland except after hurricanes.

HABITAT   *Coasts, sandy beaches, salt bays.* Favors warm coastal waters, especially those that are shallow and somewhat protected, as in bays, lagoons, estuaries. Also found well offshore at times, and travels freely between islands in the Caribbean. Usually nests on low-lying sandy islands.

FEEDING   **Diet:** *Fish, crustaceans.* Feeds mostly on small fish (up to 4 inches long, sometimes up to 7 inches) and crustaceans, especially crabs. Eats wide variety of small fish, also shrimp, squid. Soft-shelled blue crabs are major items in diet on Atlantic coast.

Behavior: Forages mostly by hovering over water and plunging to catch prey just below surface. Sometimes flies low, skimming water with bill; occasionally catches flying-fish in the air or dips to water's surface to pick up floating refuse. May steal food from other birds. Sometimes feeds at night.

NESTING   Usually first breeds at age of 4 years. Nests in colonies. Courtship involves high spiraling flights by two or more birds. On ground, male presents food to female; both birds bow, strut in circles. **Nest:** Site is on ground (usually sandy) in the open. Nest (probably built by both sexes) is a shallow depression, with or without sparse lining of debris. **Eggs:** 1, rarely 2. Whitish to brown, blotched with reddish brown. Incubation is by both sexes, 28–35 days, usually

Royal Tern

30–31. **Young:** Within 2–3 days after hatching, young leaves nest and joins others in group called a "creche." Both parents bring food; parents and offspring are able to recognize each other by voice, so that adults feed only their own young. Age at first flight about 4–5 weeks. Young remain with parents for up to 8 months or more, migrating south with them.

MIGRATION   Present year-round in most of breeding range, scarcer northward in winter. On Atlantic coast, some wander north of breeding range in late summer. In California, more common in winter than in summer. Some southward migration occurs, as the species reaches Ecuador and Argentina in winter.

CONSERVATION STATUS   Populations declined seriously in late 1800s and early 1900s when eggs were harvested from many colonies for food; made substantial comeback during 20th century. Still vulnerable to loss of nesting sites. Has declined in California since 1950, coinciding with decline in population of Pacific sardine there.

ELEGANT TERN   *Sterna elegans*

Formerly just a late-summer visitor to our Pacific coast from its Mexican breeding colonies, the Elegant Tern has been reaching California in increasing numbers since about 1950, nesting there since 1959. A medium-sized tern, slim and long-billed, strictly coastal in its occurrence. In size, shape, and call notes, very similar to the Sandwich Tern of the Atlantic coast.

Elegant Tern

HABITAT   *Coast, bays, beaches.* Generally on ocean, close to shore over shallow waters, concentrating around bays and estuaries. Sometimes far out to sea. Extremely rare on fresh waters inland. Nests on sandy or rocky islands.

FEEDING   **Diet:** *Small fish.* Feeds mostly on small fish, probably also taking some small crustaceans. In California waters, preys heavily on northern anchovy; increasing population of anchovies there coincided with increase in Elegant Terns. **Behavior:** Forages by flying over water, hovering and plunge-diving to catch prey below the surface.

NESTING   Breeds in colonies. Sometimes associated with other terns (or, in Mexico, with Heermann's Gulls). In California, appears to prefer nesting close to the larger Caspian Terns, which may help in defense against predators. Courtship displays on ground involve both members of pair drooping wings, stretching neck upward, raising and lowering bills. **Nest:** Site is on open bare ground. Nest (probably built by both sexes) is a simple scrape in the soil. **Eggs:** 1, rarely 2. Buff to white, blotched or spotted with dark brown. Incubation is probably by both parents; incubation period not well known, but more than 20 days. **Young:** May leave nest after a few days, gather in group (called a "creche"). Both parents probably feed young. Age at first flight and at independence not well known.

MIGRATION   Moves north along coast to northern California or farther in late summer and early fall, after breeding. Most move south again in October. Winter range extends as far south as Peru and northern Chile. Very rarely strays inland, but perhaps somewhat more likely in the interior than Royal Tern.

CONSERVATION STATUS   Has increased and spread northward in California in recent years, first nesting at San Diego in 1959 and in Orange County in 1987. At the same time, has disappeared from some former nesting sites in western Mexico. Considered vulnerable because nesting is restricted to very few sites.

SANDWICH TERN   *Sterna sandvicensis*

A slim, long-billed tern, swift and graceful in flight. Strictly coastal in the southeastern states. Larger than the typical terns of the Forster's or Common sort, but distinctly smaller than Royal or Caspian terns. Might be thought of as the Royal Tern's sidekick; typically found with that species, usually even nesting in mixed colonies with it, but tends to be less numerous. Named after the town of Sandwich in County Kent, England, where this tern was first discovered.

HABITAT   *Coastal waters, jetties, beaches.* Favors warm waters near coastlines, often fairly shallow areas such as bays and estuaries near extensive beaches, mudflats. Sometimes forages farther out to sea. Nests on sandy islands, beaches, sandbars, in coastal lagoons or offshore.

Sandwich Tern

FEEDING   **Diet:** *Mostly fish.* Feeds mainly on smaller fish such as sand lance and mullet; also eats shrimp, squid, marine worms, and many insects. **Behavior:** Forages by plunging headfirst into water from flight (often hovering first) and emerging immediately with fish in bill. Sometimes catches insects in flight.

NESTING   Usually first breeds at age of 3–4 years. Nests in colonies, very often associated with Royal Terns. Early in courtship, high spiraling flight with long descending glides. On ground, male feeds fish to female; both birds may point bills up, droop wings, turn heads from side to side. **Nest:** Site is on ground in open spot. Nest (built by both sexes) is shallow scrape, sometimes lined with bits of debris. **Eggs:** 1–2, rarely 3. Pale cream, blotched with black, brown, gray. Incubation is by both parents, 21–29 days. **Young:** If colony subject to disturbance, young may leave nest after a few days and gather in group (called "creche") with others. Young bird recognizes its own parents by voice, comes out of creche to be fed when they approach. Age at first flight about 28–32 days; young may remain with parents another 4 months.

MIGRATION	Withdraws in winter from most of Atlantic coast north of Florida. Along much of Gulf coast, more common in summer than winter, indicating some southward migration from there. Very rare inland except in Florida, where occasional in migration and after storms.
CONSERVATION STATUS	Probably went through serious decline in late 1800s when eggs were harvested from many colonies. Has made a slow comeback in many areas, but still uncommon. Still vulnerable to disturbance or destruction of nesting sites.

ROSEATE TERN   *Sterna dougallii*

Widespread but very local on the coasts of six continents. In North America, only on Atlantic seaboard, mainly in northeast and Florida. More strictly coastal and oceanic than most similar terns. Has a very light and buoyant flight, with relatively fast and shallow wingbeats, and often gives a musical call note in flight. Its numbers on this continent are in a long-term decline, probably from a combination of reasons, and it is now considered an endangered species.

Roseate Tern

HABITAT   *Coastal; salt bays, estuaries, ocean.* Nests on sandy or rocky islands with some low plant cover, close to shallow waters for feeding, especially in protected bays and estuaries. Forages in coastal waters and sometimes well offshore; seems to prefer warmer waters.

FEEDING   **Diet:** *Mostly fish.* Feeds mainly on small fish, including many sand lance and herring off eastern North America; also a few crustaceans, mollusks, rarely insects. **Behavior:** Forages mostly by patrolling in flight above water and then plunging to catch fish below surface. Sometimes dips down in flight to take prey from surface of water. May hover less than most terns.

NESTING   Usually first breeds at age of 3 years. Nests in colonies, associated with Common Terns in northeast. Early in breeding season, groups fly high, glide down. On ground, birds display with tail raised, neck arched. Male may feed female. **Nest:** Site on ground under cover such as grass, shrubs, or rock ledge, sometimes in abandoned burrow or in open on bare sand. In Florida, some nest on gravel roofs. Nest (built by both sexes) is shallow scrape, usually lined with bits of debris. **Eggs:** 1–2, sometimes 3. Cream to pale olive, blotched with blackish brown. Incubation is by both sexes (female may do more), 21–26 days. **Young:** Are fed by both parents; may move away from nest to better shelter a few days after hatching. Age at first flight usually 27–30 days, but remain with parents at least 2 more months.

MIGRATION   Leaves North America entirely in winter for Caribbean and northern coast of South America. Migrates along coast or well out to sea. Birds younger than 3 years old may remain all year on wintering grounds.

CONSERVATION STATUS   Now considered an endangered species in the northeast. Apparently was once far more numerous along much of Atlantic coast, but today nests at only a few sites. Initial decline may have been caused by hunting for plume trade in late 1800s. After partial recovery, some colonies disappeared after 1930s when islands were overrun by expanding populations of Herring Gulls in northeast. Continuing decline may involve hunting of terns on wintering grounds in northeastern South America.

JAEGERS, GULLS, TERNS, AND SKIMMERS

COMMON TERN *Sterna hirundo*

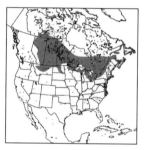
Common Tern

One of four very similar terns on this continent. The species lives up to its name as a "common" tern mainly in the northeast; over much of the continent it is outnumbered by the similar Forster's Tern. Also widespread in the Old World.

HABITAT   *Lakes, ocean, bays, beaches.* Wide range of aquatic habitats in summer, both coastal and inland waters in low-lying open country, where shallow waters for fishing are close to undisturbed flat islands or beaches for nesting. Winters mostly along coastlines in warm subtropical or tropical waters.

FEEDING   **Diet:** *Mostly fish.* Feeds on a wide variety of small fish, focusing on whatever types are most easily available, sometimes concentrating on shrimp instead. Also eats other crustaceans, insects, marine worms, small squid, leeches. **Behavior:** Forages mostly by flying over water, hovering, and plunging to catch prey below surface. Sometimes dips down to take items from surface of water or pursues flying insects in the air. Occasionally steals food from other terns.

NESTING   Usually first breeds at age 3–4 years. Nests in colonies, sometimes in isolated pairs. In aerial courtship, groups and pairs perform high flights. Male may fly over colony carrying fish; female follows. On ground, pair postures, bows, struts in circles; male presents fish to female. **Nest:** Site is on bare ground or surrounded by low vegetation; sometimes on floating mat of dead vegetation. Nest (built by both sexes) is shallow scrape in soil, usually lined with bits of plant material and debris. **Eggs:** 1–3. Variable, buff to pale blue or olive, marked with brown and black. Incubation is by both parents (female may do more), 21–25 days. **Young:** Leave nest after a few days but remain nearby, are fed by both parents. Age at first flight about 22–28 days; may remain with parents another 2 months or more. One brood per year, rarely two.

MIGRATION   After breeding, may move a short distance north before beginning southward migration. Almost never actually overwinters in North America, although fall migrants may linger to the beginning of January. Winter range is along tropical coasts as far south as Peru and Argentina. Stray Common Terns in Alaska are from a dark-billed race in eastern Asia.

CONSERVATION STATUS   Northeastern populations probably much lower than they were historically. Numbers reduced by plume hunters in late 1800s, increased with protection early in 20th century, then declined again as populations of predatory large gulls increased in that area. Coastal Common Terns are more and more concentrated in a few well-protected colonies. Some inland populations are declining as well.

ARCTIC TERN *Sterna paradisaea*

Famous as a long-distance champion: some Arctic Terns may migrate farther than any other birds, going from the high Arctic to the Antarctic. Breeds on coasts and tundra from New England, Washington, and Britain north to the northernmost limits of land, and spends the rest of the year at sea. Its migrations take it to every ocean and to the vicinity of every continent. In North America, seldom seen from land south of its breeding grounds.

HABITAT *Open ocean, rocky coasts, islands; in summer, also tundra lakes.* At sea for most of year, in wide variety of situations, but seems to spend most time over cold waters and well offshore. Nests on islands, gravel beaches, coastal tundra; also far inland around lakes, rivers, ponds in tundra regions.

FEEDING **Diet:** *Fish, crustaceans, insects.* Diet varies with season and location; mostly small fish and crustaceans, also many insects in summer on breeding grounds. Also known to eat mollusks, marine worms, earthworms, rarely berries. **Behavior:** Forages mostly by flying slowly upwind, hovering briefly, then plunging to catch prey below water's surface. Sometimes dips down in flight to take items from surface, or chases flying insects in the air. Despite its small size, may steal food from other birds, swooping at them to startle them into dropping their catch.

Arctic Tern

NESTING Usually first breeds at age of 3–4 years. Nests in colonies, sometimes with other terns. Much of courtship is aerial, with groups and pairs performing high flights. Male may fly over colony carrying fish, wings beating high above back. On ground, pair of birds posture, bow, strut in circles; male presents fish to female. **Nest:** Site is on ground in the open. Nest (built by both sexes) is a shallow scrape, usually lined with a few bits of plant material, debris. **Eggs:** 1–3. Buff to pale olive, blotched with black and brown. Incubation is by both parents, 20–24 days. Parents are vigorous in defense of nest, will dive at and strike intruders. **Young:** Leave nest 1–3 days after hatching, find place to hide nearby. Both parents bring food for young. Age at first flight 21–28 days; young remain with parents another 1–2 months.

MIGRATION Most migration is offshore. In spring migration, some may move up the St. Lawrence River and then fly overland to James Bay and Hudson Bay; others may come overland from farther south on Atlantic coast, but very few records inland in spring. Strays found in the interior in fall are mostly young birds.

CONSERVATION STATUS Steadily declining at southern end of breeding range on Atlantic coast. Elsewhere no obvious trend. Most of very extensive range is remote from effects of human activities.

FORSTER'S TERN *Sterna forsteri*

Several of the terns are very similar in appearance. Forster's Tern looks so much like a Common Tern that it was largely overlooked by Audubon and other pioneer birders. However, Forster's is more of a marsh bird at most seasons, especially in summer, when it often nests on top of muskrat houses. Unlike Common Tern, Forster's regularly winters along our southern coasts.

HABITAT *Marshes (fresh or salt), lakes, bays, beaches.* During summer is mostly around marshes, either coastal salt marsh or large marshy lakes in the interior. May visit any waters during migration. Winters mostly along coast, especially around estuaries, inlets, coastal lagoons, sheltered bays.

FEEDING **Diet:** *Fish, insects, other small aquatic life.* Diet is mostly fish at all seasons, but in summer on marshes may eat many insects. Also eats small crustaceans, frogs. **Behavior:** Forages by flying and hovering over water, plunging to take fish from just below surface. Also may dip down in flight to take items from surface and will forage in the air, catching insects in flight.

NESTING   May breed in loose colonies, with spacing dictated by arrangement of good nesting sites. Sometimes associated with colonies of Yellow-headed Blackbird. Aggressive toward other birds in vicinity of nest. **Nest:** Site is in marsh, on top of dense vegeta-

tion or mats of floating dead plants, often on top of muskrat house. Sometimes placed on ground near marsh or on abandoned nest of grebe. Where it nests in same marsh as Black Tern, Forster's tends to choose higher and drier nest sites. Nest (built by both sexes) is platform of reeds and grasses, with deep hollow at center lined with finer material and shells. **Eggs:** 3, sometimes 1–4. Olive to buff, variably marked with brown. Incubation is by both sexes, 23–25 days. **Young:** Both parents feed young in nest. Development of young and age at first flight not well known.

MIGRATION   Much less migratory than Common Tern, wintering regularly along southern coastlines of United States.

CONSERVATION STATUS   Has declined in some areas with loss or degradation of marsh habitat.

Forster's Tern

Recreational boating on nesting lakes may have impact as well, since wakes from speedboats often flood nests.

LEAST TERN   *Sterna antillarum*

Least Tern

Our smallest tern. Often seen flying low over the water, with quick deep wingbeats and shrill cries. Usually hovers before plunging into water for tiny prey; hovers more than most terns. Populations are endangered in many areas because of human impact on nesting areas, especially competition for use of beaches. However, Least Terns in some parts of the east are now nesting successfully on gravel roofs near the coast.

HABITAT   *Sea beaches, bays, large rivers, salt flats.* Along coast generally where sand beaches are close to extensive shallow waters for feeding. Inland, found along rivers with broad exposed sandbars, lakes with salt flats nearby. In winter found along tropical coasts, sometimes well out to sea.

FEEDING   **Diet:** *Fish, crustaceans, insects.* Diet varies with season and location; mostly small fish, crustaceans, and insects, also some small mollusks and marine worms. **Behavior:** Forages by flying over water, hovering, and plunging to catch prey just below water's surface. Sometimes dips down to take prey from surface of water or land, and may catch insects in flight.

NESTING   Nests in colonies, sometimes in isolated pairs. In courtship, male (carrying fish in bill) flies upward, followed by female, then both glide down. On ground, displays include courtship feeding. **Nest:** Site is on open ground (or on gravel roof). Nest is shallow scrape, sometimes lined with pebbles, grass, debris. **Eggs:** 1–3, perhaps rarely more. Buff to pale green, blotched with black, brown, gray. Incubation is by both sexes; female may do more in early stages, male more later.

In very hot weather, adult may dip into water and wet belly feathers to cool eggs. Incubation period 20–25 days. **Young:** Leave nest a few days after hatching, find places to hide nearby. Both parents feed young. Age at first flight about 19–20 days; young may remain with parents another 2–3 months. One brood per year, sometimes two in south.

MIGRATION
Leaves North America and northern Mexico entirely in winter, moving to tropical waters as far south as Brazil.

CONSERVATION STATUS
Several populations are endangered. On coasts, nesting areas often disturbed by beachgoers. On inland rivers, fluctuating water levels (from releases from major dams) often flood out nesting sites on sandbars.

ALEUTIAN TERN *Sterna aleutica*

An uncommon bird, nesting around the Bering Sea and nearby waters, including much of the southern Alaskan coast and Aleutian Islands. May associate with Arctic Tern but is far less numerous. Its habits have not been thoroughly studied. Its winter range was completely unknown until the late 1980s; now it is known that many Aleutian Terns spend the winter near the Equator in the western Pacific.

HABITAT *Northern coasts (summer); open ocean (winter).* During most of year apparently at sea, moving south to tropics in winter, although details poorly known. In breeding season found along northern coastlines, foraging mostly offshore and nesting on open islands, sandbars, or beaches with dense low ground cover.

FEEDING **Diet:** *Includes crustaceans, fish, insects.* Diet in summer includes many euphausiid shrimp and other crustaceans, small fish, and insects. Winter diet essentially unknown. **Behavior:** Forages

Aleutian Tern

mostly by flying or hovering low over water, dipping down to take items from surface; apparently seldom plunge-dives into water.

NESTING Usually nests in small colonies, often associated with Arctic Terns. Unlike most terns, parents do little or nothing to defend nest against predators or intruders, simply departing at approach of danger. May benefit by nesting with Arctic Terns, which are more aggressive in defense of colony. **Nest:** Site is close to water on low sandspit, island, or beach, among grasses or other vegetation. Nest is inconspicuous, a shallow depression in moss, matted grass, low vegetation. **Eggs:** 1–2, sometimes 3. Buff to olive, heavily marked with dark brown. Incubation is probably by both sexes, about 22–23 days. **Young:** Both parents probably bring food for young. Age at first flight about 25–31 days. Young may remain around colony a week or two after fledging; age at independence unknown.

MIGRATION
Winter range still poorly known, was completely unknown until late 1980s; most apparently winter at sea near the Philippines or Indonesia. Arrives on Alaska breeding grounds in May, departs mostly in August. One seriously lost individual once was found in Britain.

CONSERVATION STATUS
Uncommon and local, colonies vulnerable to disturbance. No obvious trends in population.

BRIDLED TERN *Sterna anaethetus*

A widespread seabird of the tropics and subtropics. Sometimes common over the warm waters of the Gulf Stream but seldom seen from land in North America except after hurricanes. A handful of pairs have nested in southern Florida since 1987. Very light and buoyant in flight. Almost never seen resting on ocean; birds at sea may perch on driftwood or floating debris.

HABITAT   *Warm oceans.* Spends most of year at sea, over warm waters, generally in offshore waters rather than far out in midocean. In Florida waters often forages along weed lines on landward side of Gulf Stream, so may be found closer to shore than Sooty Tern. Nests on islands with areas of rock rubble, limestone caves, bushes, or other shelter.

FEEDING   **Diet:** *Mostly fish.* Feeds mainly on small fish, also small squid, crustaceans, insects. **Behavior:** Forages mostly by flying low, hovering, and dipping down to take items from surface of water; seldom plunge-dives into water. May concentrate where schools of predatory fish are chasing smaller fish to surface. May sometimes feed at night.

NESTING   Breeds in isolated pairs or in colonies, often with other terns. Florida nesters were associated with Roseate Terns. Courtship involves high flight by groups or pairs. Male may fly slowly and low over colony, carrying stick or fish, to be pursued by other birds. On ground, two birds bow, strut, turn in circles. **Nest:** Site is usually in sheltered spot such as under ledge, among rock rubble, in small limestone cave, under shrub; sometimes on open ground. Nest is slight scrape in soil with little or no lining added. **Eggs:** 1. Pale buff, spotted with dark brown or reddish brown. Incubation is by both parents, 28–30 days. **Young:** May leave nest after a few days and hide in nearby cover. Both parents feed young, regurgitating small fish. Age at first flight about 55–63 days; may become independent about a month later.

MIGRATION   Movements of most populations at sea not well known. Present off southeastern states mainly in warmer months, with few records for midwinter.

SOOTY TERN *Sterna fuscata*

Sooty Tern

While most terns inhabit marshes and shores, the Sooty Tern leads the life of a true seabird. A long-winged flier, it wanders tropical oceans, nesting on remote islands. Many nest in Hawaii, but North American birders often seek the species by visiting the islands of the Dry Tortugas, west of the Florida Keys. Noisy around its nesting colonies by day and night; a sailors' name for the bird is "wide-awake."

HABITAT   *Warm tropical seas.* Generally far out at sea, wandering widely but often following warm-water currents. Avoids shallow waters and areas near mainland coast. Nests mostly on small islands, on open sandy beaches with sparse vegetation.

FEEDING   **Diet:** *Mostly fish, some squid.* Feeds mainly on small fish that live in dense schools far out at sea. Also some small squid. **Behavior:** Forages by dipping down in flight to take fish from surface of water (or may take flying-fish from above surface). Rarely or never plunges into water for prey below surface. Feeds mainly where small fish have been driven to surface by schools of large predatory fish, congregating quickly where such temporary concentrations of food exist.

NESTING May not breed until age of 6 years or older. At Dry Tortugas, arrives in numbers two months before first eggs laid. At first, flocks visit site at night, circling over islands and calling, departing at dawn. Courtship involves high flight and gliding descent; on ground, birds strut and bow. **Nest:** Site is on ground, usually in open, sometimes under edge of shrubs. Nest (probably built by both sexes) is shallow scrape in soil, sometimes lined with a few leaves. **Eggs:** 1. Whitish, variably marked with brown, lavender, gray, sometimes black. Incubation is by both sexes, 28–30 days. On hot days, parents stand and shade the eggs. **Young:** Both parents feed young, regurgitating small fish. Young wanders in vicinity of nest, may return to it to be fed. Capable of flight at about 8–9 weeks, may stay around colony another 2–3 weeks.

MIGRATION Young birds from Tortugas may move south through Caribbean and then east to equatorial waters off West Africa, not returning for several years. Adults probably do not go as far, mostly dispersing in Gulf of Mexico and elsewhere in general region.

CONSERVATION STATUS Abundant and widespread in tropical oceans around the world. Colonies on Tortugas and some in Hawaii are strictly protected.

GENUS *Phaetusa*

LARGE-BILLED TERN *Phaetusa simplex*

A large tern of South American rivers, known by its striking pattern. On its native range it is found mostly in the interior, not on the coast, and it is not considered to be migratory, but lost individuals have strayed north to New Jersey, Ohio, and Illinois.

MARSH TERNS — GENUS *Chlidonias*

The three species in this genus have shorter tails than most *Sterna* terns, and they show a more striking change from dark summer plumage to pale winter plumage. All three are widespread in the Old World; only the Black Tern also nests in the Americas. These terns may be coastal or even out at sea in winter, but in summer they inhabit inland marshes, often building their nests on mats of floating vegetation. Their downy young are more brightly marked than the young of most terns.

WHISKERED TERN *Chlidonias hybridus*

A tern of the marshes, looking like a cross between a Black Tern and a Common Tern. Widespread in the Old World from Europe to Australia. The first Whiskered Tern found in North America wandered the shoreline of New Jersey and Delaware in the summer of 1993.

WHITE-WINGED TERN *Chlidonias leucopterus*

This Eurasian species, rare in our area, is similar to Black Tern and usually associates with it. Most often seen with flocks of migrant Black Terns on the Atlantic coast in late summer; recently, one or two have been found there almost every year. It has also strayed from Asia to Alaska. There are a couple of instances of adults summering around marshes in the interior, and an adult once paired with a Black Tern in Quebec and nested there.

BLACK TERN *Chlidonias niger*

A small, graceful marsh tern, black and silver in breeding plumage. In its choice of surroundings, it leads a double life: in North America in summer it is a typical bird of freshwater marshes, but in winter it becomes a seabird along tropical coasts.

Black Tern

Vulnerable to loss of marsh habitat, its numbers have decreased in many areas during recent decades.

HABITAT *Fresh marshes, lakes; in migration, coastal waters.* For nesting favors fresh waters with extensive marsh vegetation and open water, also sometimes in smaller marshes and wet meadows. In migration found on larger lakes and along coast. Winters in tropical coastal regions, mostly just offshore or around salt lagoons and estuaries.

FEEDING **Diet:** *Mostly insects, fish.* Diet on breeding grounds is mostly insects, also small fish, tadpoles, frogs, spiders, earthworms, crustaceans, leeches. In migration and winter at sea, eats mostly small fish, also some crustaceans and insects. **Behavior:** Forages in flight, dipping to surface of water or shore to pick up items, sometimes pursuing flying insects in the air, seldom plunging into water after prey.

NESTING Breeds in scattered colonies, often associated with Forster's Terns. Early in season, pairs or small groups ascend in spiraling high flight above colony, then glide down. **Nest:** Site is low in marsh, on floating mat of plant material, old muskrat house, or debris, or on ground close to water. Nest (built by both parents) may be substantial platform of marsh plants, or simple depression with a few bits of vegetation added, very close to water level; eggs often damp. **Eggs:** 2–4. Pale buff to olive, blotched with brown and black. Incubation is by both sexes, 21–22 days. **Young:** Develop rapidly; after 2–3 days, may leave nest but remain in vegetation nearby. Capable of flight 19–25 days after hatching; may be fed by parents for up to two more weeks. One brood per year, sometimes two in south.

MIGRATION Most apparently migrate north through interior of North America. In late summer, many move east to Atlantic coast before turning south; those from farther west may move south to coasts of Mexico and continue southward offshore. Winters mostly along north and northwest coasts of South America.

CONSERVATION STATUS North American population has declined sharply since the 1960s. Loss of nesting habitat because of drainage of wetlands is one likely cause. Runoff of farm chemicals into nesting marshes may affect hatching success. Loss of food supply on the wintering grounds because of local overfishing may also be a factor.

NODDIES — GENUS *Anous*

BROWN NODDY *Anous stolidus*

Most terns are white with dark caps and have forked tails. The Brown Noddy, like an anti-tern, is dark with a white cap and has a wedge-shaped tail. At sea it flies low, with deep wingbeats; when perched, it has a solemn and lethargic look. Widespread in tropical oceans, including around Hawaii. Birders know this species mostly from its colony at the Dry Tortugas, Florida, where it nests alongside the much noisier and more numerous Sooty Tern.

HABITAT   *Tropical oceans.* Found over warm seas, often very far from land. Seldom comes near mainland coast anywhere, except when driven there by storms. Nests on tropical islands, in bushes on beach or on rocky ledges.

FEEDING   **Diet:** *Small fish.* As far as known, feeds on small fish, often catching them when schools of large predatory fish drive the smaller ones to the surface. **Behavior:** Forages in flight by dipping to take items from surface of water. Sometimes makes shallow plunges for prey just below surface, but does not plunge-dive forcefully as some terns do. Rarely settles on water to feed. At Tortugas, adults nesting close together in colony may fly out to sea to forage together.

NESTING   Courtship involves bowing and nodding movements (leading to name of "Noddy"); also swift high flight by pairs. **Nest:** On Tortugas, nest site is in bay cedar or cactus, a few inches to 12 feet above ground. Nest (built by both sexes) is a platform of sticks and seaweed, often with bits of rock or coral

Brown Noddy

added as lining. Nest may be reused and added to every year, growing to large size. In some other regions, nests on cliffs and among stone crevices, laying eggs on bare rock. **Eggs:** 1. Pale buff, lightly spotted with reddish brown and pale lavender. Incubation is by both sexes, 35–38 days. **Young:** Both parents feed young, by regurgitation. At Tortugas, adult noddies often forage closer to colony than Sooty Terns, feeding their young more often, and the young mature faster (able to fly at 6–7 weeks).

MIGRATION   Movements not well known. Present around the Tortugas January to October. May be seen well offshore elsewhere in Florida waters during warmer months. Sometimes driven to shore or inland in southeast by tropical storms.

CONSERVATION STATUS   Formerly more numerous on Tortugas, numbers probably hurt by commercial egg harvesting in 19th century. Current numbers there apparently stable. Widespread and common in tropical seas around the world.

BLACK NODDY   *Anous minutus*

Among the thousands of Brown Noddies at the Dry Tortugas, Florida, one or two Black Noddies have been found in most years since 1960. This tropical tern, slightly smaller and darker than the Brown Noddy, has not yet been proven to nest there.

SKIMMERS — GENUS *Rynchops*

BLACK SKIMMER   *Rynchops niger*

The strange, uneven bill of the skimmer has a purpose: the bird flies low, with the long lower mandible plowing the water, and snaps the bill shut when it contacts a fish. Strictly coastal in most areas of North America, Black Skimmers are often seen resting on sandbars and beaches. Unlike most birds, their eyes have vertical pupils,

narrowed to slits to cut the glare of water and white sand. Flocks in flight may turn in unison, with synchronized beats of their long wings. The world's three species of skimmers are sometimes placed in their own separate family, although they are clearly related to the terns.

HABITAT *Mostly ocean beaches, tidewater.* Favors coastal waters protected from open surf, such as lagoons, estuaries, inlets, sheltered bays. Locally on inland lakes in Florida and at Salton Sea, California. Nests on sandy islands, beaches, shell banks. In South America, occurs far inland along major rivers.

FEEDING **Diet:** *Mostly fish.* Feeds mostly on small fish that live just below surface of water. Also eats some small crustaceans. **Behavior:** Well-known for its

Black Skimmer

skimming habit, furrowing the water with lower mandible, the upper mandible snapping down immediately when contact is made with a fish. Finds food by touch, not by sight; often forages in late evening or at night, when waters may be calmer and more fish may be close to surface. Rarely may forage by wading in very shallow water, scooping up fish.

NESTING Breeds in colonies. Courtship not well studied, may involve zigzagging flight with two or more males pursuing one female. **Nest:** Site on ground on open sandy beach, shell bank, sandbar; sometimes on gravel roof. Nest is shallow scrape in sand. **Eggs:** 4–5, sometimes 3, rarely 6–7. Variable in color, whitish to buff to blue-green, marked with dark brown. Incubation is by both sexes (male may do more), 21–23 days. **Young:** Both parents feed young, by regurgitation. Upper and lower mandibles of young are same length at first, so they are able to pick up food dropped on the ground by parents. Young wander in vicinity of nest after a few days; if danger threatens, may attempt to look inconspicuous by lying flat on beach, even kicking up sand to make a hollow to lie in. Able to fly at about 23–25 days.

MIGRATION Withdraws from northern part of breeding range in winter. Sometimes pushed north along coast by tropical storms, rarely driven inland. Has colonized southern California (from western Mexico) since 1960s, now nests at Salton Sea and San Diego.

CONSERVATION STATUS In late 19th century, eggs were harvested commercially and adults were killed for their feathers, leading to a reduction of Atlantic coast populations; good recovery of numbers since. Still very sensitive to disturbance in nesting colonies. Range expanding in west.

AUKS, MURRES, PUFFINS, AND RELATED BIRDS (Family Alcidae)

Swimming and diving birds of the coast and the open sea, the members of the family Alcidae go by various names: murres, murrelets, auklets, guillemots, puffins, and so on. As a group, they are often simply called "auks" or "alcids" for short. Most are birds of cold northern waters. The Bering Sea is the family's center of distribution; of the 22 species, 16 can be found in Alaska.

Auks appear to fly only with great effort, whirring along over the water with very rapid wingbeats. However, their wings serve them better underwater, as they "fly" through the depths with great speed and agility. The larger and heavier species can probably dive deeper; the largest of all, the extinct Great Auk, was specialized for diving and could not fly at all. It was like a northern counterpart to the penguins, flightless divers of the Southern Hemisphere.

Some of the large auks may live more than 25 years in the wild.

Feeding   Most auks do all or most of their foraging underwater. They dive from the surface, using their wings to "fly" underwater; their feet may be used for steering but usually not to provide extra push. Before diving, some species will lower their faces below the surface and peer about underwater, as if looking for prey or predators.

Auks catch their prey in rapid pursuit. The largest species may dive to more than 200 feet; most apparently feed closer to the surface. The diets of auks vary by species, but most seem to specialize on either crustaceans or small fish.

Nesting   Auks are superbly adapted to life in the water, but on land, where they must come to lay their eggs, they are clumsy and vulnerable. Therefore, some aspects of their nesting behavior seem designed to help them evade predators. Most auks nest on islands, where they are safe from many mammals. Almost all except the largest auks lay their eggs in protected places, such as underground burrows or crevices among rocks. Several species, particularly at southern latitudes, evade predatory gulls by entering and leaving their nests mainly at night. Remarkable defenses are practiced by some of the little murrelets. The Marbled Murrelet often nests on the mainland, but it may lay its single egg on a mossy tree branch more than 100 feet off the ground. Xantus's, Craveri's, and Ancient murrelets get their young away from the dangers of the nest site as soon as possible, leading them out to sea when they are little balls of fluff only a couple of days old.

Some auks apparently mate for life and use the same nest sites year after year. Most kinds lay only one egg (guillemots and some murrelets lay two). Both male and female generally share in incubating the egg and feeding the young. Most auks raise only one brood per year.

Displays   Several of the auks have notable colors or patterns on their bills. These may be important in many courtship displays, as the members of a pair often nibble at each other's bills or even clash them together. Other common displays include both birds bowing or turning their heads from side to side and often calling, sometimes in duet.

GENUS *Alle*

DOVEKIE   *Alle alle*

The smallest member of the auk family in the North Atlantic. Feeds on abundant tiny crustaceans in icy waters, and nests by the millions far above Arctic Circle, such as northwest Greenland; its center of abundance is farther north than that of any other auk. Small numbers come as far south as New England waters in winter, rarely farther, but the vast majority remain farther north. On the water, Dovekies bob about buoyantly; flocks fly low over the waves. Winter storms sometimes drive them close to the coast or even inland.

HABITAT   *Oceanic; offshore to pelagic.* Usually in cold Arctic waters, often around edges of pack ice; may rest on ice. Even when moving farther south in winter, favors cold waters, avoiding warm currents. Often very far from land over deep water. Nests on northern coasts and islands on deeply fissured cliffs, talus slopes, boulder piles.

FEEDING   **Diet:** *Small crustaceans.* Feeds almost entirely on small crustaceans, mainly very small species that occur in swarms near surface in cold waters, including calanoid

copepods, mysids, amphipods, euphausiids, others. Also eats small numbers of fish, mollusks, marine worms, plus bits of algae. **Behavior:** Forages by diving and swimming underwater, evidently using both wings and feet. Does most foraging just below surface.

NESTING   Breeds in colonies; northernmost colonies may be very large. On arrival at colony in spring, flocks may circle over site for hours, giving trilled calls. Members of pair display by bowing rapidly and repeatedly, wagging head from side to side, touching bills. **Nest:** Site is well hidden among rocks or in crevice in cliff; same pair may use site in subsequent years. Nest is thin layer of pebbles, sometimes with bits of grass or lichen. **Eggs:** 1. Pale blue-green, sometimes with buff and brown spots. Incubation is by both sexes, 28–31 days. **Young:** Both parents feed nestling, bringing back food in throat pouch; young is brooded continuously for first 2–4 days after hatching. Young leaves nest 23–30 days after hatching, usually departing in evening or at night, flying out to sea alone or accompanied by adults.

Dovekie

MIGRATION   Many remain in winter as far north as open water permits, around pack ice north of Arctic Circle; southernmost big concentrations in winter are on Grand Banks of Newfoundland. Smaller numbers irregularly come south to waters off New England, small invasions rarely reaching Florida. Major winter storms sometimes drive numbers inland in northeast.

CONSERVATION STATUS   Total population undoubtedly in millions, but hard to census and trends would be difficult to detect. Natives in Greenland and elsewhere harvest many for food, but this is unlikely to affect total population. Would be vulnerable to oil spills or other pollution in northern waters.

MURRES — GENUS *Uria*

The two murres are the largest living auks and the only ones that regularly nest out on open ledges of cliffs. They feed mainly on fish. Despite their names, the Common Murre may actually be less numerous than the Thick-billed, but the Thick-billed generally lives farther north, so it may be seen less often by most birders.

COMMON MURRE   *Uria aalge*

Widespread on the Pacific coast from Alaska to California but more local in the east, being found mainly off eastern Canada. This large auk sits upright on sea cliffs, looking like a northern version of a penguin. It swims and dives expertly, but its flight appears labored. For its size, the Common Murre has the most densely packed nesting colonies of any bird species; nests may be so close together that incubating adults actually touch other adults on both sides.

HABITAT   *Ocean, large bays; colonies on sea cliffs.* Favors cool ocean waters, both offshore and rather near coast, generally over continental shelf. Unlike Thick-billed Murre, tends to avoid pack ice. Nests on coasts and islands, on ledges of cliffs and on flat bare rock atop sea stacks.

FEEDING   **Diet:** *Mostly fish.* Feeds on wide variety of fish, including herring, cod, capelin, sand lance, haddock, many others. Also eats various crustaceans,

marine worms, squid. **Behavior:** Forages while swimming underwater (see family introduction). May dive to more than 150 feet below surface when foraging.

NESTING First breeds at age of 4–5 years. Nests in colonies. Displays by members of pair include pointing bill skyward, bowing deeply, clashing open bills together, preening each other's feathers. One (usually female) may return to nest site from sea with fish, present it ceremonially to mate. **Nest:** Site is on cliff ledge or on flat stony surface near water. Nests may be very close together, incubating birds well within touching distance. No nest built, egg laid on bare rock. **Eggs:** 1. Very variable, usually whitish, tan, blue, or green, with markings of brown, reddish, black. Incubation is by both sexes, 28–37 days. **Young:** Fed by both parents. Young leaves nest at 15–25 days, before able to fly; flutters down to water, is cared for and fed by parents at sea for several more weeks. Young is probably capable of flight at about 50–70 days.

Common Murre

MIGRATION Permanent resident in many areas. Must leave vicinity of northern colonies in western Alaska in winter, when waters freeze solid. Some southward movement off both coasts, birds reaching New England waters and southern California in winter.

CONSERVATION STATUS Still abundant, but populations are known to have declined in many areas. Vulnerable to effects of pollution; a frequent victim of oil spills.

THICK-BILLED MURRE *Uria lomvia*

Thick-billed Murre

A large, robust auk, swimming and diving deep in cold ocean waters. Very similar to Common Murre. The two are found together in many areas, even nesting on the same ledges of rocky northern islands, but the Thick-billed has its center of abundance farther north. Despite major recent declines, its population in the eastern Canadian Arctic undoubtedly runs into the millions.

HABITAT *Ocean, nesting colonially on ledges of sea cliffs.* Favors very cold ocean waters of Arctic; when not nesting, often very far from land over deep water. May associate with edges of or openings in pack ice. Nests on rocky coasts or islands with steep cliffs.

FEEDING **Diet:** *Mostly fish.* Diet is primarily fish in summer (and young are fed almost entirely on fish); may include more crustaceans in winter. Fish in diet include cod, herring, capelin, sand lance, sculpin, many others. Crustaceans eaten include shrimp, amphipods, mysids, copepods. Also eats some marine worms, squid. **Behavior:** Forages while swimming underwater (see family introduction). May dive to more than 200 feet below surface.

NESTING Probably older than 3 years at first breeding. Nests in colonies, some very large. Some pair formation may occur before arrival at colony. At nest site, members of pair bow, nibble at each other's bills; may pick up pebbles and present them to each

other. **Nest:** Site is on cliff ledge; may use narrower and smaller ledges than Common Murre. No nest; egg laid on bare rock. **Eggs:** 1. Very variable, usually whitish, tan, blue, or green, with markings of brown and black. Incubation is by both sexes, 30–35 days. One parent is almost always at nest throughout nesting cycle. **Young:** Fed by both parents. Adults often forage many miles away from colony. Young leaves nest at 15–30 days, before able to fly; glides down to sea, accompanied by adult male. Young evidently is accompanied and cared for by male for several weeks after leaving nest.

MIGRATION   Some remain through winter as far north as open water allows, including around openings in pack ice. Others move south. Regular in winter on waters off New England, has strayed farther south. In west, very rare south of Alaska in winter.

CONSERVATION STATUS   Population still in the millions, but declines reported in recent decades of 20–50 percent in some large colonies are cause for concern. Eggs and adults harvested for food by natives in some Arctic areas. Bigger threats to survival are large numbers killed in fishing nets and vulnerability to pollution and oil spills.

GENUS *Alca*

RAZORBILL   *Alca torda*

Razorbill

This stocky, thick-billed auk is found only in the North Atlantic. It nests on northern islands and coasts, often in the same colonies as murres. It is similar to the murres but has a longer tail, often cocked up above the water when swimming. In winter it lives in flocks well offshore. Hardy observers who go out to the coast during winter storms may see flocks of Razorbills sweeping past, low over the water. This species is probably the closest living relative of the extinct Great Auk.

HABITAT   *Open ocean; nests on sea cliffs.* Tends to forage in cool waters less than 200 feet deep, so often concentrates over offshore shoals or ledges; sometimes closer to shore than other large auks. Nests on islands or mainland on cliffs or rocky shorelines.

FEEDING   **Diet:** *Mostly fish.* Feeds mainly on small fish, especially sand lance, also herring, sprat, capelin, stickleback, cod. Also eats crustaceans and marine worms. **Behavior:** Forages while swimming underwater (see family introduction). Catches most food 5–20 feet below surface, rarely may dive to 30 feet. May catch several fish during one dive. Sometimes steals fish from puffins or other auks.

NESTING   Usually first breeds at age of 4–5 years. Nests in colonies. May mate for life. Pair formation may take place within flocks on water or on common ground near colony. In display, male raises head, pointing bill up while giving growling call, then bows deeply; female sometimes does same. Members of pair also touch bills, preen each other's feathers. **Nest:** Site is in crevice in cliff, under boulders, on ledge, or in abandoned burrow of other species. Sometimes no nest built, usually small collection of pebbles, grass. **Eggs:** 1, perhaps rarely 2. Tan or greenish to white, variably marked with brown. Incubation is by both sexes, 32–39 days. **Young:** Both parents bring fish in bills to feed nestling. Young leaves nest 14–25 days after hatching, before able to fly. Late in evening, young follows adult to cliff edge and then flutters down to water, and adult and young swim away.

MIGRATION   Winters well offshore, mainly from Grand Banks of Newfoundland to southern New England, in small numbers south to Virginia. Very rare south to Florida. Winter distribution varies, depending on food supply and weather. European birds may winter farther south, reaching northwest Africa.

CONSERVATION STATUS   Far less numerous than the murres; world population in 1970s estimated at a little over 200,000. Distribution is mostly near shore, so is vulnerable to oil spills and other pollution. Thought to have declined in some areas recently, perhaps reflecting increasing pollution of North Atlantic.

GENUS *Pinguinus*

GREAT AUK   *Pinguinus impennis*

Formerly found in the North Atlantic, this largest member of its family was heavy-bodied and flightless. In evolutionary terms, the Great Auk apparently had sacrificed flying ability for the capacity to dive and swim more effectively underwater, rather like penguins in the Southern Hemisphere. It ranged widely at sea, wintering as far south as the Carolinas. Since it could not fly up to cliff ledges like other auks, it nested only on low islands where it could walk ashore, such as Funk Island off the coast of Newfoundland and a few small islands around Iceland and Scotland. In such places it was vulnerable to sailors with clubs. The last Great Auk was killed in 1844.

GUILLEMOTS — GENUS *Cepphus*

These medium-sized auks are less sociable than most members of their family and are generally seen singly or in pairs, not in flocks. They are also more likely to be seen in the immediate vicinity of the coast, rather than far offshore.

BLACK GUILLEMOT   *Cepphus grylle*

In the northeast, this bird may be seen swimming and diving around rocky shorelines. A "Black" Guillemot only in summer, it looks mostly frosty white in winter. Very similar to Pigeon Guillemot of Pacific coast and overlaps with it locally in Alaska.

Black Guillemot

HABITAT   *Inshore waters of ocean; breeds on rocky shores, islands.* Usually close to shore in shallow waters, but may be far offshore, especially around edges of pack ice. Sometimes feeds on freshwater lakes near coast. Nests along rocky shores, low cliffs, among debris on beaches.

FEEDING   **Diet:** *Varies with place and season.* May include more fish in southern part of range, more crustaceans farther north. Fish in diet (mainly those living near bottom in shallow waters) include butterfish, blennies, sculpins, gobies, sand lance, cod, many others. Crustaceans include crabs, shrimps, mysids, amphipods, copepods, isopods. Also eats some mollusks, insects, marine worms, bits of plant material.

Behavior: Forages while swimming underwater (see family introduction). Most foraging within 30 feet of surface, may rarely dive more than 100 feet.

NESTING Usually first breeds at age of 4 years. Nests as isolated pairs or in colonies. May perform communal display: one or several birds strut with high-stepping walk, neck upstretched; may assume similar posture in water, leading to chases and diving. Members of pair face each other and bob heads, calling, sometimes touching bills. **Nest:** Site is in boulder pile, crevice near base of cliff, under driftwood or debris; usually close to water, rarely more than a mile inland. Pair may reuse same site each year. Nest is thin layer of pebbles or debris, sometimes mere scrape in soil. **Eggs:** 1–2. Whitish to pale blue-green, spotted with black, brown, gray. Incubation is by both sexes, 23–39 days. **Young:** Both parents feed young, carrying fish in bill to nest. Young depart from nest 31–50 days after hatching, before able to fly; scramble down to water alone, are apparently independent after leaving.

MIGRATION Largely permanent resident, overwintering as far north as open water allows, including openings and edges in pack ice. Small southward movement in winter brings some annually to Massachusetts, rarely farther.

CONSERVATION STATUS Wide range and scattered nesting sites probably help ensure survival. Has declined in some areas after introduction of mink or rats to nesting areas. Since 1960s, numbers wintering in Massachusetts have increased noticeably.

PIGEON GUILLEMOT   *Cepphus columba*

Along the Pacific coast from Alaska to California, this auk is generally found very close to rocky shores. Pairs may nest in colonies or in isolation. It is strikingly patterned in breeding season, when the red-orange legs and mouth lining may be important signals in courtship.

Pigeon Guillemot

HABITAT   *Rocky coasts, inshore waters.* Breeds on rocky islands and on mainland cliffs inaccessible to predators. At sea usually close to rocky shorelines, less often far out over continental shelf. In Bering Sea, may be far from land around openings and edges of pack ice.

FEEDING   **Diet:** *Fish and other marine life.* Diet varies with season and location. Eats mostly small fish, also shrimps, crabs, polychaete worms, mollusks, small octopus. **Behavior:** Forages by diving and swimming underwater, propelled mainly by wings. Uses feet mostly for steering but also, unlike most auks, for some propulsion underwater. Mostly forages by searching sea bottom; can dive as much as 150 feet below surface, but most feeding is probably within 60 feet of surface.

NESTING   First breeds at age 3–5 years. Courtship displays by members of pair include mutual circling and bill-touching. Rapid zigzag chases on water near colony may also be involved in courtship. **Nest:** Site, probably chosen by male, is in crevice or cave, among boulders, in abandoned burrow, under driftwood or debris. May also excavate own nest burrow. Same site usually reused for several years. Nest is shallow scrape in pile of dirt, pebbles, shells. **Eggs:** 1–2. Creamy to pale blue-green, with gray and brown blotches concentrated near large end. Incubation is by both sexes, 26–32 days. **Young:** Both parents feed young, bringing them small fish at all hours of day, especially in early morning. Young leave nest 29–54 days after hatching, usually at night, scrambling or fluttering down to water. Able to swim and dive immediately, but not capable of strong flight for another 2–3 weeks.

MIGRATION   Northernmost breeders in Alaska move south in winter to edge of pack ice. Birds from center of range (British Columbia to Oregon) may be permanent residents of that region. Many California birds apparently move north after breeding, as far as British Columbia.

CONSERVATION STATUS   Total population not well known, but probably has declined in recent decades. Vulnerable to oil spills and other pollution. Breeding attempts may fail in years of unusually warm water temperatures.

MURRELETS — GENUS *Brachyramphus*

In breeding season, these two species differ from all other auks by wearing a cryptic plumage of mottled brown. This is clearly for camouflage, because these remarkable birds nest in places that could be very vulnerable. Often they are well inland, and they usually nest in the open—on the ground or (in the case of the Marbled Murrelet) high in trees. Unlike most auks, they do most of their feeding in protected bays close to shore, not out at sea.

MARBLED MURRELET   *Brachyramphus marmoratus*

Marbled Murrelet

A strange, mysterious little seabird. Although it is fairly common off the northern Pacific coast, its nesting behavior was essentially unknown until the 1970s. In the Pacific Northwest, now known to nest high in trees in old-growth forest several miles inland from coast. Even where numerous, it is usually seen on the water in pairs or aggregations of pairs, not in large flocks; pairs flush from the water in front of approaching boats, fly away low with very rapid wingbeats.

HABITAT   *Coastal waters, bays. Breeds inland on mountains near coast.* Generally on ocean on calm protected waters near coast, as in bays, inlets, among islands; does most foraging in fairly shallow water. Sometimes found on lakes near coast. Nests on mountainsides on islands or well inland in mature forest.

FEEDING   **Diet:** *Fish, crustaceans.* Diet varies with place and season, mostly small fish and crustaceans. Fish in diet include many sand lance, capelin, and herring, mostly small but up to 5 inches in length. Crustaceans include euphausiid shrimp, mysids, amphipods. **Behavior:** Forages while swimming underwater (see family introduction). Does most feeding in waters less than 100 feet deep, fairly close to shore.

NESTING   Very few nests have been found, so breeding behavior poorly known; details given here probably incomplete. Solitary nester, not in colonies. **Nest:** Site varies. In north, may be on ground on mountainside among sparse or dense growth. In south, may be on tree branch in dense forest, up to 150 feet above ground. Site may be close to coast or up to 15 miles inland. Nest is no more than shallow depression in lichens or moss on ground or tree branch; droppings of young bird build up into low rim. **Eggs:** 1. Variable, yellowish to olive to blue-green, marked with brown, black, lavender. Incubation is by both sexes, probably about 4 weeks. **Young:**

Both parents apparently feed young, making feeding visits at night. Young leaves nest at about 27–28 days, probably flies directly to sea or at least to lake near coast.

MIGRATION   Generally resident near breeding areas, but some move south in winter, rarely with small numbers "invading" coast of southern California. Strays found far inland in North America have turned out to be of the Siberian race, not birds from our own Pacific coast.

CONSERVATION STATUS   Still fairly numerous, but vulnerable. Continues to lose nesting habitat with cutting of old-growth forest in northwest. Habit of feeding near shore makes it especially vulnerable to coastal oil spills.

KITTLITZ'S MURRELET *Brachyramphus brevirostris*

Kittlitz's Murrelet

A compact little seabird of Alaskan waters. Closely related to Marbled Murrelet and, like that species, rather mysterious and poorly known. Much more limited in range, being common mainly from Kodiak Island east to Glacier Bay. Solitary in nesting; only a few nests have been found, so its breeding behavior is not well known.

HABITAT   *Ocean, glacial waters; nests on barren slopes in coastal mountains.* Found on cold sea waters, mostly in calm, protected bays and among islands. Usually fairly close to shore. Nests on islands and mainland, on steep barren mountainsides, talus slopes, rock slides, sometimes near glaciers.

FEEDING   **Diet:** *Not well known.* Has a shorter bill than that of Marbled Murrelet, suggesting a different diet; known to eat small crustaceans, and possibly eats fewer fish than Marbled Murrelet. **Behavior:** Forages while swimming underwater (see family introduction). Does most feeding in cold waters fairly close to shore, probably where relatively shallow.

NESTING   Solitary in breeding, on islands and mainland; few details known. **Nest:** Site is on ground on steep rocky slope with little vegetation, often 1,000–3,000 feet above sea level and several miles inland from ocean (can be more than 45 miles inland). Often at base of large rock, and may be fairly near stream flowing toward ocean. No nest built, egg laid on bare rock or ground. **Eggs:** 1. Pale olive with brown and gray spots. Incubation probably by both sexes, but details (including length of incubation period) unknown. **Young:** Probably fed at nest site by parent(s) for at least 2–3 weeks. Some young then may travel along streams and rivers to reach sea, probably before old enough to fly strongly; others may fly directly from nest to ocean.

MIGRATION   Mostly permanent resident, although must leave northernmost breeding areas in western Alaska in winter (when seas freeze solid). Extremely rare straggler south of southeastern Alaska.

CONSERVATION STATUS   Total population not large, but its rugged and remote range probably helps ensure survival. Would be vulnerable to spills and other pollution in coastal waters.

MURRELETS — GENUS *Synthliboramphus*

The four species in this genus (including one in Japan) live mainly in temperate parts of the Pacific, not ranging as far north as most auks. Unlike most members of the family, they typically lay two eggs, not one. Some other auks lead their young out to sea when they are not yet full-grown, but these murrelets take that habit to the extreme.

XANTUS'S MURRELET   *Synthliboramphus hypoleucus*

Most members of the auk family favor cold northern waters, but this one is found mostly off Baja and southern California. It nests on offshore islands and is almost never seen from the mainland. Generally uncommon, it occurs at sea in pairs or family groups, not in flocks. Young Xantus's Murrelets start their seagoing life early; they leave the nest only one or two days after hatching and often must jump more than 200 feet down from cliffs into the surf before swimming away with their parents.

Xantus's Murrelet

HABITAT   *Ocean, islands.* Generally in relatively warm waters and well offshore. May be close to nesting islands but almost never close to mainland; may go far out beyond continental shelf. Nests on islands with steep cliffs, rocky slopes, dense cover of bushes.

FEEDING   **Diet:** *Poorly known.* In some areas in nesting season, eats mostly very small fish (larval anchovies and others); also eats some small crustaceans. **Behavior:** Forages by diving and swimming underwater, propelled by wings. Pairs often forage together.

NESTING   Breeds on islands in small colonies. Birds typically have same mate and same nest site each year. **Nest:** Site is in rock crevice, under dense bush, under debris, or in abandoned burrow of other species; no nest built. **Eggs:** 2, rarely 1. Large for size of bird, pale blue to dull green with few or many brown spots, sometimes solid brown. Incubation is by both sexes, 27–44 days. **Young:** Parents do not feed young in nest. 1–2 nights after hatching, downy young are led from nest by parents, who then fly away; young make their own way to water, often jumping from cliffs more than 200 feet down to surf. Parents and young reunite in water and swim away from island. Young remain with parents and are fed by them for lengthy period. One brood per year, but may lay a second clutch if first clutch is lost.

MIGRATION   A few are present off southern California all year, but common mainly March through June. Numbers drop sharply in midsummer, with many of these birds evidently going north (at least to central California). Whereabouts in winter poorly known. Probably migrates mostly by swimming, not flying.

CONSERVATION STATUS   Total population probably low. Vulnerable to predators, even small ones, on nesting islands; in one study, almost half of all eggs were destroyed by deer mice. Accidental introduction of rats could devastate colonies.

CRAVERI'S MURRELET   *Synthliboramphus craveri*

Nesting on islands off the west coast of Mexico, this small seabird wanders north irregularly into California's offshore waters in late summer. Its numbers vary, with more seeming to show up in seasons with warmer water temperatures, and in some years not one is found north of the border. In appearance and habits, Craveri's is very similar to Xantus's Murrelet.

AUKS, MURRES, PUFFINS, AND RELATED BIRDS

ANCIENT MURRELET *Synthliboramphus antiquus*

Ancient Murrelet

Elegantly marked, a diving bird of the northern Pacific coast. More agile in flight than most auks; able to take off directly from water, flocks often banking and turning in unison. Breeding behavior unusual for a seabird: males "sing" at night from tree branches and other high perches at nesting colonies; the species regularly raises two young (most auks raise only one); and it raises its young at sea, leading them away from the nest within a few days after they hatch. The name "Ancient" comes from the gray back, which has a fancied resemblance to a shawl draped across an old person's shoulders.

HABITAT   *Open ocean, sounds, rarely salt bays.* Mostly on cool waters out of sight of land, sometimes concentrating over edge of continental shelf; may feed close to shore, especially in straits or near islands where tidal currents concentrate food near surface. Nests in burrows on islands with good cover of grass, shrubs, trees.

FEEDING   **Diet:** *Crustaceans, fish.* Diet not well known, but euphausiid shrimp appears to be primary food for much of year, mainly those about 1 inch long. At some seasons eats mostly very small fish, including sand lance, capelin, herring, smelt, saury, rockfish, and shiner perch. **Behavior:** Forages while swimming underwater (see family introduction). Probably catches all food within about 60 feet of surface.

NESTING   Breeds in colonies on islands; active at colonies mostly at night. Males come ashore after dark and sing a simple song of repeated chirps from high perches, such as tree branches or stumps. **Nest:** Site is burrow in ground under trees or grass, usually on slope and close to sea. Burrow (excavated by both sexes) usually 2–5 feet long; nest chamber at end lined with twigs, grass, leaves. **Eggs:** 2, rarely 1. Pale buff or olive, spotted with brown. Incubation is by both parents, 29–37 days. **Young:** Not fed in nest. 1–3 days after eggs hatch, parents come to nest at night and call near entrance; young leave nest and scramble down to sea, often over 1,000 feet through dense vegetation. Parents and young recognize each other by voice, reunite at sea and swim away from colony. Young are fed by parents until fully grown, at least 4 weeks.

MIGRATION   Some remain all year off southern Alaska, others move south to waters off California in winter. Disperses widely at sea after breeding. Of North American auks, this one is most likely to appear far inland. Records exist for many states and provinces east to Quebec and New York, south to Nevada and New Mexico. A few such records virtually every year, most in October or November.

CONSERVATION STATUS   World population probably still over 1 million, but has been declining for many years. Foxes and raccoons (introduced for fur production) and rats (introduced accidentally) have wiped out or reduced nesting populations on many islands, in both North America and northeast Asia.

GENUS *Ptychoramphus*

CASSIN'S AUKLET *Ptychoramphus aleuticus*

A small, dark seabird, nesting on islands along the Pacific coast from Alaska to Mexico. Sociable at all seasons, feeding in flocks at sea and nesting in large colonies.

Its small size makes it vulnerable to predators, so it visits its nesting colonies mainly under the protection of darkness. A Cassin's Auklet colony at night may resound with the squealing and peeping of the birds in their burrows.

HABITAT   *Ocean; colonizes sea islands.* May use any kind of island for nesting (barren or forested, steep or level) as long as no predatory mammals are present. Otherwise at sea, often near nesting islands or in upwellings over continental shelf, but also far out over deep water.

FEEDING   **Diet:** *Mostly small crustaceans.* Diet in breeding season includes euphausiid shrimp, amphipods, copepods, some small fish and squid; diet at other seasons not well known. **Behavior:** Forages while swimming underwater (see family introduction). May feed by day or night. Can dive to more than 120 feet below surface.

NESTING   Usually first breeds at age of 3 years, sometimes earlier. Pairs usually form in late winter. Courtship displays include mutual bowing and head-bobbing, moving head from side to side, touching bills. **Nest:** Site is in burrow excavated in soil or in natural crevice, sometimes under debris or driftwood. Both members of pair take part in excavating burrow. Little or no nest material added. Nest reused in following years by same pair. **Eggs:** 1. Creamy white, sometimes becoming nest-stained. Incubation is by both sexes, usually 38–39 days, sometimes as long as 57 days. **Young:** Both parents visit at night to feed young by regurgitation. Young bird nibbles at white spot on parent's bill to elicit feeding. At 41–50 days after hatching, young make first flight and go to water, are able to swim and dive immediately. Usually one brood per year, sometimes two.

MIGRATION   Northern birds apparently move south in winter, but details not well known. Southern breeders may remain close to colony site all year.
Still abundant in parts of range (especially islands off British Columbia), but has disappeared from many former breeding islands in Alaska and elsewhere because of introduction of foxes or other predators. Vulnerable to disturbance on nesting islands and to oil spills and other pollution at sea.

Cassin's Auklet

CONSERVATION STATUS

GENUS *Cyclorrhynchus*

PARAKEET AUKLET   *Cyclorrhynchus psittacula*

A small swimming and diving seabird, summering in the Bering Sea and south coastal Alaska. Usually in pairs or small groups, not large flocks. Often nests on same islands with Crested and Least auklets but is usually less abundant. Little known in winter, when it may disperse far out in the middle of the North Pacific.

HABITAT   *Ocean; nests on sea cliffs.* Found in cold ocean waters in summer, but may move into more temperate seas in winter. Apparently mostly very far from land in midocean when not breeding. Nests on rocky islands around cliffs, pinnacles, talus slopes.

FEEDING   **Diet:** *Mainly jellyfish, also crustaceans.* At least in summer, apparently specializes on jellyfish and other gelatinous creatures; odd bill shape may be adapted to handling such slippery prey. Also eats crustaceans, including euphausiid shrimp and amphipods, and some small fish. **Behavior:** Forages by diving from surface and swimming underwater, or may forage while swimming at surface.

NESTING   Breeds in isolated pairs or loose colonies, less densely packed than those of Crested or Least auklets but often near those species. Adults arrive in vicinity of colonies 4–6 weeks before egg-laying begins. **Nest:** Site is in deeply cracked or decomposed cliff,

ridge, rocky outcrop, or in talus slope partly covered with vegetation. Thus often in places where rock is mixed with soil, not pure rock as in Crested Auklet. Nest is in deep crevice; no nest material added, egg laid on bare soil or rock. **Eggs:** 1. Whitish to pale blue. Incubation is by both sexes, about 36 days. **Young:** Both parents feed young, bringing food to nest in throat pouch. Young leaves nest and goes to sea about 5 weeks after hatching.

Parakeet Auklet

MIGRATION   Apparently disperses widely in North Pacific in winter. Reaches waters as far south as California, but irregularly, perhaps more often in the past. Perhaps more regular in occurrence very far offshore. A number of strays have reached the northwestern Hawaiian Islands. One once turned up on a lake in Sweden, half a world away from its normal range.

CONSERVATION STATUS   Very difficult to census, so trends in population hard to detect. Undoubtedly has declined on some islands following introduction of foxes or rats. Accidental introduction of rats to more islands is potential threat.

NORTHERN AUKLETS — GENUS *Aethia*

These three small auks live mainly in the Bering Sea region. They nest in colonies on islands, sometimes in very large numbers. All have tufts or plumes of feathers on their heads in breeding season, although those of the Least Auklet are inconspicuous.

LEAST AUKLET   *Aethia pusilla*

The tiniest member of the auk family, no bigger than a sparrow. Abundant around islands in Bering Sea, where scores at a time can be seen perched on rock piles above the beach, chirping and chirring. Sometimes in huge flocks, winging low over the waves on very rapid beats of their small wings or circling in the air near nesting colonies. Least Auklets are oddly variable in the pattern of their underparts, which can be anything from white to spotted to solid dark gray.

HABITAT   *Ocean, northern islands.* May forage close to shore or far out at sea. Favors areas with turbulent water, upwellings, strong gradients of water temperature or salinity, edges of currents, or tide rips. Nests on islands in boulder fields, talus slopes, lava flows, rock crevices.

FEEDING   **Diet:** *Crustaceans and other marine invertebrates.* Diet in summer is small creatures that occur in swarms in cold waters, mostly very small crustaceans known as calanoid copepods, also some euphausiid shrimp, amphipods, others. Diet at other seasons not well known. **Behavior:** Forages while swimming underwater (see family introduction). Fast and agile underwater but probably not able to dive very deep.

NESTING First breeds at age of 3 years. In courtship, male perches upright and makes chattering calls; female approaches in exaggerated stretching and crouching postures, then both birds engage in bill-touching and chattering in duet. Pair-bond often lasts more than one season. **Nest:** In colonies located in talus slopes, rock piles, other areas with abundant small rock crevices for nest sites. No nest built, egg laid on bare rock, soil, or pebbles. Pair may reuse nest site for several years. **Eggs:** 1. White, becoming nest-stained. Incubation is by both sexes, 25–39 days, usually about 30 days. **Young:** Both parents feed young, bringing food to nest in throat pouch. Young develops faster than young of most auks, leaves nest 25–33 days after hatching.

Least Auklet

MIGRATION Birds from northernmost colonies move south to evade the solid ice that surrounds their colony sites in winter. Those from Pribilof and Aleutian islands may be permanent residents in general region of colonies. Very rare stray as far south as British Columbia and Washington.

CONSERVATION STATUS Abundant, with North American population estimated at 9 million in late 1980s. Accurate counts very difficult, however, so trends in numbers hard to detect. Many populations have disappeared or declined after introduction of foxes or rats to their islands. Accidental introduction of rats to additional islands may be single greatest threat.

WHISKERED AUKLET *Aethia pygmaea*

Poorly known to most birders, the Whiskered Auklet is a small seabird confined to remote areas of the Aleutian Islands, Alaska (as well as the Commander and Kurile islands off eastern Asia). Relatively scarce and secretive, it is active around its nesting colonies mostly at night. Unlike most auks, it seldom ventures more than a few miles away from shore. Shares an odd distinction with its relative, Crested Auklet: the plumage has a noticeable citruslike odor.

Whiskered Auklet

HABITAT *Ocean, tide rips, rocky coasts.* Usually at sea within a few miles of islands, in relatively shallow water. Favors rough water where currents converge or where tidal currents race across shallows or through narrow passes between islands. Nests on islands among rocks or cliffs.

FEEDING **Diet:** *Small crustaceans.* Diet not well known, primarily small crustaceans including copepods, euphausiid shrimp, amphipods; also marine worms, mollusks. May concentrate on copepods in summer, euphausiids in winter. **Behavior:** Forages while swimming underwater (see family introduction). Depth of dives unknown, but usually feeds in fairly shallow water.

NESTING Breeds in colonies, less densely packed than in related small auks. Active at colonies mostly at night, especially when not nesting in association with other species. Courtship behavior not well known, includes pairs calling in duet. **Nest:** Sites in small openings in talus slopes, boulder piles, or crevices in cliffs, sometimes in areas of soil

AUKS, MURRES, PUFFINS, AND RELATED BIRDS

mixed with rock. No nest built, egg laid on bare rock or soil. **Eggs:** 1. Dull white. Incubation is by both sexes, roughly 35–36 days. **Young:** Both parents feed young, visiting nest at night, bringing food back in throat pouch. Age of young bird at departure from nest not well known, may be about 40 days. Fledgling departs by flying away from nest site at night.

MIGRATION   Apparently permanent resident of waters near its nesting islands.

CONSERVATION STATUS   Total population probably very low compared with most auks. Attracted to lights at night, may be killed by crashing into lighted fishing boats. Accidental introduction of rats to nesting islands may be biggest threat.

CRESTED AUKLET   *Aethia cristatella*

A chunky seabird of Alaskan waters with a loose crest that hangs down in front of its face. Gregarious at all seasons, often feeds in dense concentrations, large numbers swimming and diving together in deep waters. Its nesting colonies are noisy places, with birds honking, barking, and whistling from their secure crevices among the rock

piles. Crested Auklets usually fly in tightly packed flocks and sometimes engage in mass circling maneuvers in the air near their colonies.

HABITAT   *Open sea; nests in colonies on sea cliffs.* Often over deep water far from land, but may forage near shore where there is turbulence caused by upwellings, tide rips, or tidal flow in passes between islands. Nests on rocky islands among boulders, talus slopes, lava flows, cliffs with many openings and crevices.

FEEDING   **Diet:** *Mostly small crustaceans.* Diet not well known, but includes many small crustaceans that occur in swarms (especially euphausiid shrimp and copepods), also probably small numbers of fish and squid. **Behavior:** Forages while swimming underwater (see family introduction). Underwater behavior poorly known, but maximum dive depth thought to be about 100 feet below surface. Often forages in flocks.

Crested Auklet

NESTING   First breeds at age of 3 years or older. In courtship, male puffs out chest, points bill up, and makes honking sounds; female approaches, and pair engages in bill-touching, preening each other's neck feathers, intertwining necks. **Nest:** Site is in deep crevice in cliff or among boulders, may be several feet below surface of rock pile. Nest is shallow depression in soil or pebbles at bottom of crevice. **Eggs:** 1. White, becoming nest-stained. Incubation is by both sexes, 29–40 days, usually about 34. **Young:** Both parents feed young (although female may do more), bringing back food in throat pouch. Young is noisy, making peeping sounds when parents present and whistling when they are absent. Age at first flight 27–36 days; young comes out of nest for a few days before fledging to exercise wings.

MIGRATION   Undoubtedly migrates from northern colonies, which become surrounded in winter by solid ice. Winters regularly around Kodiak Island, Alaska, outside known breeding range, and Siberian birds winter to northern Japan. Has strayed to British Columbia and once to north Atlantic near Iceland.

CONSERVATION STATUS   North American population estimated at 3 million in late 1980s, but accurate censusing very difficult. Probably has declined in Aleutians because of introduced foxes and rats. Vulnerable to oil spills and other pollution.

RHINOCEROS AUKLET *Cerorhinca monocerata*

A chunky dark seabird related to the puffins, common at times off the northern Pacific coast. Often unsuspicious, and boats may approach it rather closely on the water. If pressed, it dives and swims powerfully underwater. Although its takeoff appears clumsy and laborious, it is a fast flier, and may fly long distances to feeding areas daily. The "horn" on the bill, responsible for the bird's name, grows annually in early spring and is shed in late summer.

HABITAT *Ocean, tide rips; nests in burrows on islands.* Often far from land but may feed close to shore, especially where tidal currents near islands cause upwellings or concentrations of food. In winter, flocks may spend night on coastal bays, flying farther out to sea to forage by day. Nests on islands, in burrows in soil under grass, shrubs, trees.

FEEDING **Diet:** *Fish, crustaceans.* Food brought to nestlings is mostly small fish, particularly sand lance, herring, and anchovy, also rockfish, smelt, saury, and others. Favors fish that gather in dense schools. Diet of adults probably similar. Also eats crustaceans. **Behavior:** Forages while swimming underwater (see family introduction). Can remain submerged for up to 2 minutes. May tend to forage closer to shore than puffins.

NESTING Breeds in colonies, mostly on islands. Generally active around colonies only in evening and at night, although at some colonies the adults visit by day as well. Courtship displays include members of pair nibbling at each other's bills. Advertise ownership

Rhinoceros Auklet

of nest site by standing upright with wings partly opened, pointing bill up and hissing. **Nest:** Site is in burrow in ground, typically on slight slope covered with grass, shrubs, trees, sometimes in steep slope or cliff. Burrow up to 20 feet long, usually 5–10 feet, with one or more side branches. Nest is in chamber in burrow, a shallow cup of moss, twigs. **Eggs:** 1. White, usually spotted with brown and gray. Incubation is by both sexes, 39–52 days, average 45 days. **Young:** Both parents feed young, carrying fish in bill to nest. Young leaves nest about 7–8 weeks after hatching.

MIGRATION More strongly migratory than most western auks. Although summer and winter ranges overlap widely, mostly vacates northern part of breeding range in winter, and large numbers move into California waters then.

CONSERVATION STATUS Less abundant than some Arctic auks but still fairly numerous. On Farallon Islands, California, where the species ceased to breed for almost a century, it reestablished itself in the 1970s after introduced rabbits were eliminated (rabbits may have competed for burrows).

PUFFINS — GENUS *Fratercula*

Puffins are famous even among people who have never seen one. Perching upright on sea cliffs, these football-shaped auks with big, colorful, triangular bills look almost comical. Their big bills are used very deftly for catching fish in swift underwater pursuit.

TUFTED PUFFIN   *Fratercula cirrhata*

This dark-bodied puffin is common along the northern Pacific coast, nesting on islands offshore, where it may be seen sitting on rocks in an upright posture. Although it flies strongly, it must work hard to take off from the water, thrashing along the surface before becoming airborne. The colorful tufts of feathers on the head are present mostly in summer.

HABITAT   *Ocean, nesting colonially in burrows on sea cliffs.* Ranges widely at sea, from fairly near shore to far out of sight of land. Even during breeding season, may be at sea far from nesting colonies. Nests on islands, primarily on grassy steep slopes or cliff tops (steep dropoff may help birds take flight). Prefers treeless islands throughout its range.

Tufted Puffin

FEEDING   **Diet:** *Mostly fish.* Feeds mainly on small fish, especially sand lance and capelin; also small squid and miscellaneous fish such as saury, rockfish, smelt. Reported to eat some crustaceans, mollusks, sea urchins, small amounts of algae. **Behavior:** Forages by diving and swimming underwater, using wings to "fly" through the depths, with tail spread and feet back to aid steering. Swims rapidly through schools of small fish, catching them in bill.

NESTING   Breeds in colonies on islands; active at colonies by day. **Nest:** Site is in burrow, mostly in grassy areas on slopes or cliffs. Sometimes in deep natural crevice among rocks, or on ground under shrubs. Burrows (excavated by both sexes) usually 2–7 feet long, occasionally longer. Nest chamber at end of burrow may have lining of grass, feathers, or may be unlined. **Eggs:** 1. Dull white to bluish white, often spotted with gray and brown. Incubation is by both sexes, about 40–42 days. **Young:** Both parents feed nestling, carrying fishes in bill and dropping them on ground in nest or near entrance. Tufted Puffin may forage farther from colony than Horned Puffin, and sometimes 1–2 days pass between feeding visits to nest. Young leave nest about 6–7 weeks after hatching. One brood per year, possibly two in south.

MIGRATION   Not well known. Must leave northernmost breeding colonies, where surrounding seas freeze solid in winter. Most may spend winter very far offshore, where seldom observed.

CONSERVATION STATUS   Disappeared from former nesting sites off southern California decades ago; numbers nesting off northern California much lower than historical levels. Farther north, some island populations probably reduced by introduced foxes or rats. Still, Alaska population estimated at over 1 million pairs in late 1970s.

ATLANTIC PUFFIN   *Fratercula arctica*

Nesting around the edges of the North Atlantic, this puffin is sought by birdwatchers who visit Maine or eastern Canada in summer. At its colonies, the bird may fly back to its nest carrying a dozen small fish lined up in its bill, making us wonder how the puffin holds onto 10 slippery fish while grabbing two more. Gregarious at its nesting sites, the Atlantic Puffin is often solitary in winter, far from land on the open ocean.

HABITAT   *Coastal and offshore waters, open sea.* Colonial; breeds in burrows and among rocks of sea islands. Favors cool or cold waters off North America. Outside of breeding season usually well offshore, even far out in midocean. Nests on islands where nesting sites are provided by soil for burrows or crevices among rocks.

FEEDING   **Diet:** *Fish, crustaceans.* Food brought to young in nest is mostly small fish, especially sand lance, herring, capelin, cod, many others. Diet of adults (especially in winter) poorly known; in addition to fish, may include many crustaceans (such

as euphausiid shrimp, mysids, copepods) as well as mollusks and marine worms. **Behavior:** Forages while swimming underwater (see family introduction). Does most foraging within 50 feet of surface but can dive to about 200 feet.

NESTING   Usually first breeds at about 5 years. Breeds in colonies. Birds often have same mates each year. In courtship, male repeatedly flicks head up and back so that bill points up; may continue for minutes. Members of pair swing bills sideways and clash them together repeatedly. **Nest:** Site is in burrow 3–7 feet long, or in natural crevice or under rocks. Sometimes one entrance leads to side branches and multiple nests. Both sexes help excavate. Nest in chamber in burrow usually has sparse lining of grass, feathers.

Atlantic Puffin

Eggs: 1 (rarely 2, probably laid by two females). White, sometimes faintly marked with brown, purple. Incubation is by both sexes (female may do more), 36–45 days, usually 39–42. **Young:** Both parents feed nestlings, carrying fish in bill; may feed fish directly to young at first, later drop them on floor of nest. Young leave nest about 38–44 days after hatching; usually leave at night, flying directly out to sea.

MIGRATION   In North American waters, winters from edge of pack ice south to Maryland, far offshore, mostly just seaward from edge of continental shelf. Has strayed south to Florida. European birds may move into warmer waters, reaching western Mediterranean and northwest Africa. Capable of moving long distances; young birds banded in Iceland and Europe have been recovered in eastern Canada.

CONSERVATION STATUS   Major declines during 19th century were due to overharvesting of eggs and adults. During 20th century, has continued to decrease at southern end of breeding range in both North America and Europe. Vulnerable to introduction of predators (such as rats) to nesting islands. Since the 1980s, an ambitious project to reintroduce puffins on former nesting islands off Maine has had some success.

HORNED PUFFIN   *Fratercula corniculata*

Very similar to the famous Atlantic Puffin but with different bill colors and a longer fleshy "horn" above each eye. Found mainly on islands around the coastline of Alaska, where pairs perch upright on rocks and stare quizzically at human visitors. In winter, likely to be on ocean waters far out of sight of land. Often found with the Tufted Puffin, but in general has a more northerly distribution, rarely wandering as far south as California.

HABITAT   *Ocean, nesting colonially in burrows or crevices on sea cliffs.* During summer usually on ocean waters fairly close to shore of nesting islands; at other seasons may be very far offshore. Nests mainly on rocky islands.

FEEDING **Diet:** *Mostly fish.* Favors small fish, especially sand lance and capelin, also sticklebacks, smelt, and others. Food brought to young almost entirely fish. Adults also eat many squid, marine worms, and crustaceans. **Behavior:** Forages while swimming underwater (see family introduction). Swims rapidly through schools of small fish, catching them in bill.

NESTING Breeds in colonies on islands, usually with other species of auks. **Nest:** Site is in burrow in ground, 1–3 feet or longer, perhaps sometimes with two entrances; also in natural crevice in cliff or among boulders. Burrow (apparently excavated by both sexes) may be reused in subsequent years. Nest chamber may be bare or lined with grasses. **Eggs:** 1. Dull white, usually with faint spots of gray, lavender, brown. Incubation is by both sexes, 38–43 days. **Young:** Both parents feed nestling, carrying fish in bill and dropping them in nest or near entrance. Adults generally forage in waters close to colony, may make more frequent feeding visits than Tufted Puffins. Young depart from nest at about 38–44 days; unable to fly well at departure, they flutter or tumble down to water and swim out to sea, apparently independent from then on.

MIGRATION Poorly known. Departs from vicinity of northern colonies in winter (when surrounding waters are frozen solid). Some reportedly winter near Aleutians, others may be far out at sea. In some years, numbers found off California in spring, suggesting that they may have wintered very far offshore (perhaps hundreds of miles) and come closer to coast on northward migration. An "invasion" once reached the northwestern Hawaiian Islands.

Horned Puffin

CONSERVATION STATUS Still abundant in Alaska, but undoubtedly has declined on some islands where foxes or rats have been introduced. Puffins are considered especially vulnerable to effects of oil spills.

PIGEONS AND DOVES (Family Columbidae)

This is a large and important family, with more than 300 species found worldwide except for the coldest regions. The name "pigeon" is often used for the larger species and "dove" for the smaller ones, but the terms are loosely applied and there are no precise definitions. Members of the family are recognized by their stout bodies, small heads, short bills, and rather short legs. Most pigeons and doves in our area are fairly drab, but some colorful gems in this family inhabit the tropics, especially in the Old World.

Members of the pigeon family are among the few birds that can drink by suction, sticking their bills in the water and drinking continuously; most other birds must take one billful of water at a time and then tilt the head back to swallow.

A more remarkable trait of pigeons and doves is that they produce "milk" to feed their young; unlike mammals, however, they make this substance within the digestive system of adults of both sexes. See below under "Nesting."

Some pigeons and doves in the wild may live 20 years or longer.

Feeding As a rule, pigeons and doves are mainly vegetarians. Depending on the species, they may feed mostly on seeds or mostly on fruits and berries, or they may take a variety of plant material including buds and green leaves. Many species also eat a few insects, snails, or other invertebrates, but such animal fare rarely amounts to more than a small fraction of the diet.

Even large, hard seeds are swallowed whole, not broken up first. Doves that feed mainly on such seeds may also swallow large quantities of small, rough gravel or grit, which probably helps in the process of internally grinding up these seeds for digestion.

Nesting One reason why many pigeons and doves are so common is that they may nest repeatedly, raising several broods in a season. In mild climates, some species may raise as many as six broods in a year. So even though they usually lay only one or two eggs per clutch, they may succeed in producing a lot of offspring.

Most kinds of pigeons and doves build rather flimsy stick nests in trees or bushes, although some will nest on building ledges or cliffs or on the ground. Normally both parents help incubate the eggs and feed the young.

Birds that are mostly vegetarians as adults often feed their young mostly on insects. But pigeons and doves have another way to give their young protein: by producing "pigeon milk." This substance is produced in the crop, an enlarged pocket of the upper esophagus. During the nesting season, the walls of the crop secrete a milky fluid that is rich in fat and protein. For the first few days after hatching, the young are fed a pure diet of pigeon milk. Then they begin to receive a mixture that includes some partially digested seeds or fruit, but their diet continues to include some pigeon milk for at least a couple of weeks. To be fed, the young bird will insert its bill into the corner of the parent's mouth, and the adult will regurgitate the pigeon milk or the mixture for the young to eat.

Displays Most male pigeons and doves defend their nesting territories by calling in low-pitched, cooing voices. Many species also have a flight display in which they fly up with noisy wingbeats and make a long circular glide back to their starting point. In courtship, the male often puffs out his chest and performs deep bowing motions, while calling.

PIGEONS — GENUS *Columba*

The common park pigeon is a typical member of this group in shape and size, although most wild species are far more wary. These pigeons are fast fliers, frequently seen in flocks, and they often feed on berries in trees. This genus is an important and widespread group, with about 50 species found worldwide.

ROCK DOVE *Columba livia*

Few birds have been associated with humans as closely as the Rock Dove, better known as the common city pigeon. It has been domesticated and taken around the world, raised for food, trained for homing, racing, and carrying messages, and used in research. Originally native from Europe to North Africa and India, it now lives in a wild or semi-wild condition in cities all over the world, including most of North America. In places it has reverted to wild habits, nesting on cliffs far from cities.

HABITAT *Sustains itself in the wild around cities, farms, cliffs, bridges.* In North America most common around cities, also in suburban areas and on farms, occasionally in wild places far from human dwellings. In native range, nested on cliffs along coast and in inland mountains and gorges.

286

FEEDING **Diet:** *Mostly seeds.* Away from cities, feeds on waste grain, seeds of many grasses and other plants, sometimes berries or acorns; may eat a few earthworms or insects. In cities, may live largely on bread, popcorn, or other junk food provided by humans. **Behavior:** Forages mostly by walking on the ground. Sometimes forages for berries in trees or shrubs, climbing about awkwardly. Often feeds in flocks.

Rock Dove

NESTING May mate for life. In courtship, male spreads tail, puffs up chest, and struts about, often strutting in circles around female, repeatedly bowing and cooing. **Nest:** Natural sites are on sheltered cliff ledges. In cities and around human dwellings, uses artificial replacements such as window ledges of tall buildings, barn lofts, rain gutters, many others. Nest (built by female, with material supplied by male) is platform of twigs, grass. Pair may use same site repeatedly, adding to nest each time. **Eggs:** 2, sometimes 1. Incubation is by both parents, 16–19 days. **Young:** Both parents feed young "pigeon milk" (see family introduction). Young leave nest at about 25–32 days, or later in cold weather. A pair may raise up to 5 or more broods per year.

MIGRATION Not migratory. If displaced from nesting area, has good homing ability; trained homing pigeons can return to home loft from long distances away.

CONSERVATION STATUS Sometimes a nuisance in cities, but not proven to have much negative impact on native bird species. A favorite prey of Peregrine Falcon, supporting Peregrines that stay around cities.

SCALY-NAPED PIGEON *Columba squamosa*

On many islands in the Caribbean, this large, dark pigeon lives in humid tropical woods. It has strayed to Florida twice in the past. With clearing of forest in the West Indies, this pigeon probably is becoming scarcer, and it may be unlikely to reach Florida again.

WHITE-CROWNED PIGEON *Columba leucocephala*

A strong and fast flier, the White-crowned Pigeon regularly undertakes long flights over water, and it has been able to colonize islands almost throughout the Caribbean. It occurs commonly in parts of southern Florida, but most of its Florida nesting colonies are on small offshore islands. Flocks are usually seen flying swiftly overhead or perched in treetops, feeding on berries.

HABITAT *Mangrove keys, wooded islands.* Moves about freely among wooded habitats in south Florida. Usually nests in mangroves on small offshore islands, sometimes in outer fringe of mangroves along mainland, but generally avoids areas having raccoons (apparently a major nest predator). Feeds in tropical hardwood groves on islands and mainland.

FEEDING **Diet:** *Mostly fruits and berries.* Feeds on the fruits and berries of a great variety of native trees and shrubs of the Caribbean region, also sometimes those of introduced plants. May eat seeds at times, and perhaps rarely insects or snails. **Behavior:** Forages almost entirely in trees, clambering about with an agility surprising for size of bird,

leaning and stretching and sometimes hanging upside down momentarily to reach berries. Seldom comes to the ground to feed.

NESTING   In Florida, breeds most commonly during July and August. Often nests in colonies. Male calls to attract female while perching erect, chest puffed out. In courtship, male struts and nods. **Nest:** Site is usually on fork in horizontal branch, low (below 15 feet) in mangroves or other shrubs, sometimes on cactus; may be up to 30 feet above ground or water or on ground on small islands. Nest (probably built by both sexes) is loosely constructed platform of twigs, lined with grasses or other fine material. **Eggs:** 2, sometimes 1. White. Incubation is by both parents, mostly by female at night and male by day; incubation period not well known. **Young:** Both parents feed young "pigeon milk" (see family introduction). Young leave nest at about 3 weeks. In parts of range, may raise 3 broods per year.

MIGRATION   Somewhat nomadic, moving about in Florida (and in Caribbean) with changing food supplies. Banding returns show that some Florida birds winter in West Indies, but many also winter on Florida Keys and some on southern Florida mainland.

CONSERVATION STATUS   Florida population estimated at about 10,000 pairs and probably stable or increasing. Numbers apparently declining on many islands in Caribbean because of overhunting and habitat loss.

White-crowned Pigeon

RED-BILLED PIGEON *Columba flavirostris*

A common bird of dry woods in Mexico and Central America, this big pigeon enters our area only in southern Texas. There it inhabits native woods along the Rio Grande, where it is uncommon in summer and rare in winter. The rich cooing song of the male may help the observer to discover the Red-bill as it perches half hidden in the top of a dense low tree.

HABITAT   *River woodlands, tall brush.* In Texas, found mostly in relatively undisturbed native woods of hackberry, mesquite, huisache, ebony, and other trees. Farther south, inhabits dry woodlands of various types, generally avoiding more humid regions of rain forest.

FEEDING   **Diet:** *Includes berries, seeds, nuts.* Diet not known in detail. Feeds on many wild fruits and berries, including those of hackberry, mistletoe, wild fig, and many other plants. Also eats many acorns when available, and seeds of a variety of plants. **Behavior:** Forages mostly in trees and shrubs, climbing about among the branches to reach berries. Will also come to the ground to feed, including on waste grain in fields. Usually forages in pairs or small flocks.

NESTING   Nesting behavior is not well known. **Nest:** Site is in tree, large shrub, or tangled vines, usually 8–30 feet above the ground on horizontal fork in branch. Nest (probably built by both sexes) is flimsy platform of sticks lined with grasses and stems. **Eggs:** 1, rarely 2. White. Incubation apparently by both parents, incubation period not well known. If adults are disturbed on nest, they put on a distraction display, dropping from the nest and fluttering low over the ground. **Young:** Both parents probably feed young "pigeon milk" (see family introduction). Development of young and age at first flight not well known. May raise several broods per year in the tropics.

MIGRATION   Probably permanent resident in much of its range; some withdrawal from northernmost part of range (in Texas) during winter.

CONSERVATION STATUS   Has declined with loss of native habitat in Texas. In Mexico and Central America, vulnerable to overhunting.

BAND-TAILED PIGEON *Columba fasciata*

This big pigeon, larger than the familiar park pigeon, is common in parts of the west. It lives along much of the Pacific coast and in the mountains, moving about nomadically to feed on acorns, berries, or other wild food crops. Band-tails are sociable, foraging in flocks at most seasons and often nesting in small colonies. Unlike many doves, they do much of their feeding up in trees, clambering about with surprising agility to pluck berries.

HABITAT   *Oak canyons, foothills, chaparral, mountain forests.* Mainly in wooded or semi-open habitats; moves around to take advantage of changing food supplies. Breeds in oak woodland along the coast and in mountains, also in pine-oak woods and fir forest. May forage along streams in lowland desert. Increasingly regular in suburban areas on Pacific coast.

FEEDING   **Diet:** *Mostly nuts, seeds, berries.* Diet shifts with season. Acorns are major part of diet when available. Eats many berries, including those of elderberry, manzanita, juniper, wild grape, many others. Also eats seeds, tender young spruce cones, buds,

Band-tailed Pigeon

young leaves, flowers, occasionally insects. **Behavior:** Will forage on ground or in trees. Can climb about with great agility in small branches, even hanging upside down to reach berries. Usually forages in flocks, even during breeding season.

NESTING   Several pairs may nest close together in loose colony. In courtship, male flies up and then glides in a wide circle, giving a wheezing call and fluttering wings toward end of glide. On perch, male coos with chest and neck puffed up, tail lowered and spread. **Nest:** Site is in coniferous or deciduous tree, usually 15–40 feet above ground, can be lower or much higher. Placed on fork of horizontal branch or at base of branch against trunk. Nest is a bulky but loosely built platform of sticks; male brings material, female builds. **Eggs:** 1, sometimes 2. White. Incubation is by both parents, 18–20 days. **Young:** Both parents feed young "pigeon milk" (see family introduction). Young leave nest about 25–30 days after hatching, are tended by parents for some time thereafter. Two broods per year, sometimes three.

MIGRATION   Present all year in some areas, especially on Pacific coast; mainly summer resident elsewhere, including northwestern coast and southwestern interior. Often nomadic, flocks concentrating where food supplies are good. Strays have reached Atlantic coast.

CONSERVATION STATUS   Numbers were once seriously depleted by overhunting. With protection, made a fair comeback; in recent decades declining again, undoubtedly for different reasons.

TURTLE-DOVES — GENUS *Streptopelia*

The 15 species in this genus are all native to the Old World, where they are often very common in open country. One or two species have strayed to our area, and two more have established feral populations here after escaping from captivity.

ORIENTAL TURTLE-DOVE *Streptopelia orientalis*

Very common in eastern Asia and migratory in the northern part of its range, this dove has strayed to Alaska several times. Records elsewhere in North America might have involved birds that had escaped from captivity.

EUROPEAN TURTLE-DOVE   *Streptopelia turtur*

A single European Turtle-Dove was found in April 1990 on the Florida Keys, far from its normal range in Europe, western Asia, and North Africa. It might have strayed there naturally (since the species is a strong flier), or it might have escaped from captivity not far away.

EURASIAN COLLARED-DOVE   *Streptopelia decaocto*

During the 20th century, this pale dove expanded its range spectacularly from the Middle East all the way across Europe. Introduced accidentally into the Bahamas in 1974, it soon spread to the Florida mainland. Currently it is increasing and spreading through the southeastern United States, and it is already abundant in parts of Florida. If it spreads in North America as it did in Europe, the Eurasian Collared-Dove may soon be among our most familiar backyard birds.

HABITAT   *Suburbs, farmland, wood edges, open country.* Apparently very adaptable. In original Asian range, found in semi-open dry country with scattered trees and groves. In Europe, favors suburbs and farmland. North American population found mostly around residential areas or farmland having combination of trees and open ground.

FEEDING   **Diet:** *Mostly seeds, some berries and insects.* Diet in North America not yet well known. In Europe, feeds on waste grain of many cultivated crops, also seeds of many plants; eats some berries and small insects, rarely snails. Also eats bread crumbs and other foods provided by humans. **Behavior:** Forages mostly while walking on the ground. When not breeding, usually forages in flocks. Sometimes flutters among branches of trees or shrubs to take berries.

Eurasian Collared-Dove

NESTING   Male displays by flying up at steep angle with noisy wingbeats, then gliding down in spiral with wings and tail fully spread, giving harsh call during glide. Also attracts female by calling and by ritualized bowing display. **Nest:** Male leads female to potential nest sites, female chooses. Site is in tree or shrub, sometimes on man-made structure, 6–70 feet (usually 10–40 feet) above ground. Nest is flimsy platform of sticks and twigs; male gathers material, female builds. **Eggs:** 2, sometimes 1. White. Incubation is by both parents, 14–18 days. **Young:** Both parents feed young "pigeon milk" (see family introduction). Young leave nest at about 15–20 days, are tended by parents about another week. In Europe, reported to raise up to 6 broods per year; may also do so in Florida, where it may breed almost throughout the year.

MIGRATION   No regular migration, but young birds may disperse long distances (thus aiding in spread of populations).

CONSERVATION STATUS   Newcomer in North America, spreading rapidly. Possible interactions with native species not yet well understood, but no obvious negative impacts have been noted so far.

RINGED TURTLE-DOVE   *Streptopelia "risoria"*

Not even a full species, this bird is a domestic-bred variant of the African Turtle-Dove (S. *roseogrisea*). It can be found living in a semi-wild condition in some North

American cities, where it relies on handouts from humans to survive. Nowhere is it as hardy or vigorous as its relative the Eurasian Collared-Dove, which is now spreading rapidly in the southeast.

SPOTTED DOVE   *Streptopelia chinensis*

Native to southern Asia, this dove was introduced into the Los Angeles area around 1917. Since then it has gradually spread, occupying areas north to Santa Barbara and Bakersfield and south to San Diego. Living mostly in residential areas, it is usually rather tame, feeding on the ground on lawns and gardens. When disturbed, it flies almost straight up from the ground with noisy flapping of its wings.

HABITAT   *Residential areas, parks, river woods.* Found mostly in altered habitats of suburbs, especially well-watered areas with trees and lawns. Also found around farms and in groves of trees (including eucalyptus) along streams.

Spotted Dove

FEEDING   **Diet:** *Mostly seeds.* Diet in North America not studied in detail, but includes seeds of many plants. **Behavior:** Forages mostly on the ground, walking about and picking up seeds. Usually forages in pairs or small groups. Will come to bird feeders but often picks up seeds from ground under feeders.

NESTING   In territorial and courtship display, male flies up steeply with noisy clapping of wings, then glides down in wide circle with wings and tail fully spread. When perched, male displays by bowing and cooing, lowering head to show off spotted collar. **Nest:** Site is usually in large shrub or tree, on horizontal branch or fork of branch, 8–40 feet above ground. Nest (probably built by both sexes) is loose platform of twigs. **Eggs:** 2. White. Incubation probably by both parents; incubation period 2 weeks or more. **Young:** Both parents probably feed young "pigeon milk" (see family introduction). Development of young and age at first flight not well known.

MIGRATION   Permanent resident in its limited range in California, rarely straying east or north within the state.

CONSERVATION STATUS   Numbers in California currently stable or possibly now declining in some areas. Apparently still very common in native range in Asia.

LARGE AMERICAN DOVES — GENUS *Zenaida*

These are mainly birds of open or brushy country. Quick to take advantage of man-made changes in the landscape, they are now among the most common birds in many regions.

WHITE-WINGED DOVE   *Zenaida asiatica*

Related to the Mourning Dove but larger and bulkier, the White-wing is mainly a summer resident in the southwestern states. It is abundant in some regions, and streamside groves or desert washes may echo with the crowing calls of males on spring mornings. In some desert areas, this dove often feeds on the fruits of cactus and visits their flowers for nectar; it is an important pollinator of the giant saguaro cactus.

River woods, mesquites, saguaros, groves, towns. Found in a variety of semi-open habitats in southwest, including native brushlands in Texas and deserts farther west, plus chaparral and open oak woods; also adapts quickly to altered habitats such as farmland, suburbs, citrus groves, plantings of trees in grassland. In winter, those remaining north of Mexico are mostly in towns.

White-winged Dove

FEEDING **Diet:** *Mostly seeds, some fruits and berries.* Feeds on seeds of many wild plants, also some cultivated grains; may eat acorns where available. Feeds on fruits, especially those of cactus, also smaller berries. Will come to large flowers, apparently for nectar. **Behavior:** Forages mostly on ground, also up in trees, shrubs, cactus. Often seen at top of giant saguaro cactus, feeding on fruit or flowers (may get much of its water that way in desert areas).

NESTING May nest in colonies, especially where nest sites in isolated grove are surrounded by good feeding areas. In courtship display, male flaps up and then glides down in wide circle. While perched, male raises tail and quickly fans it open and shut to flash black and white tail pattern. Both members of pair go through ritualized nodding and preening motions. **Nest:** Site is in shrub, tree, or cactus, usually 4–30 feet above ground. Placed on horizontal limb or fork in branch, sometimes on top of old nest or on tangle of thorns. Nest is a flimsy platform of sticks. Male brings most material, female builds. **Eggs:** 2, sometimes 1–4. White to very pale buff. Incubation is by both parents, 13–14 days. **Young:** Both parents feed young "pigeon milk" (see family introduction). Young leave nest at about 13–16 days, are fed by parents for some time thereafter. Two to three broods per year.

MIGRATION Most of those nesting in southwest move south in fall. Migration is early in both seasons, most birds arriving by March and leaving in September. A few remain through winter north of the border, especially in suburban areas. Strays sometimes wander far north of breeding range. Regular along Gulf coast in winter. Florida birds are mostly permanent residents.

CONSERVATION STATUS Probably declined originally with clearing of native habitat, but has adapted well to altered environment, now abundant and probably expanding range to the north.

ZENAIDA DOVE   *Zenaida aurita*

When Audubon explored Florida in the 1830s, he apparently found Zenaida Doves nesting on the Florida Keys. Today the species is only a rare visitor to Florida from the islands of the Caribbean. Like its relatives, the Mourning and White-winged doves, it usually feeds on the ground in brushy or semi-open areas.

MOURNING DOVE   *Zenaida macroura*

The mournful cooing of the Mourning Dove is one of our most familiar bird sounds. From southern Canada to central Mexico, this is one of our most common birds, often abundant in open country and along roadsides. European settlement of the continent, with its opening of the forest, probably helped this species to increase. It also helps itself by breeding prolifically: in warm climates, Mourning Doves may raise up to six broods per year, more than any other native bird.

HABITAT *Farms, towns, open woods, roadsides, grasslands.* Found in almost any kind of open or semi-open habitat in temperate parts of North America, including forest clearings, farmland, suburbs, prairies, deserts. May be most common in edge habitats having both trees and open ground, but also found in some treeless areas. Avoids unbroken forest.

FEEDING **Diet:** *Seeds.* Feeds almost entirely on seeds (99 percent of diet). Favors seeds of cultivated grains, also those of grasses, ragweeds, many other plants. Occasionally eats snails, very rarely any insects. **Behavior:** Forages mostly on ground; sometimes will perch on plants to take seeds. Will come to bird feeders, often eating on the ground below them. Fills crop quickly with seeds, then digests them while resting.

Mourning Dove

Regularly swallows grit (small gravel) to aid in digestion of hard seeds.

NESTING In courtship, male flies up with noisy wingbeats and then goes into long circular glide, wings fully spread and slightly bowed down. On ground, male approaches female stiffly, his chest puffed out, bowing and giving emphatic cooing song. Members of mated pairs may preen each other's feathers. **Nest:** Male leads female to potential nest sites; female chooses one. Site is usually in tree or shrub, sometimes on ground, sometimes on building ledge or other structure; usually lower than 40 feet, rarely up to 100 feet or more above ground. Nest is very flimsy platform of twigs; male brings material, female builds. **Eggs:** 2. White. Incubation is by both parents, about 14 days. **Young:** Both parents feed young "pigeon milk" (see family introduction). Young leave nest at about 15 days, usually wait nearby to be fed for next 1–2 weeks. One pair may raise as many as 5–6 broods per year in southern areas.

MIGRATION Some remain through winter over most of breeding range, but many move south from northern areas in fall. Migration is mostly by day, in flocks.

CONSERVATION STATUS Does very well in human-altered habitats. Numbers probably have increased greatly with increasing settlement of North America.

GENUS *Ectopistes*

PASSENGER PIGEON *Ectopistes migratorius*

When the Pilgrims landed, the mighty Passenger Pigeon was one of the most abundant birds in North America. Ranging over the eastern two-thirds of the continent, it nested in immense colonies in the forest, and enormous flocks would sometimes darken the sky. Pioneer ornithologist Alexander Wilson, who was not given to exaggeration (unlike the flamboyant Audubon), estimated one flock in 1808 at more than *two billion* pigeons. The species was a "passenger" in the old sense of the word, as a bird of passage; the great flocks moved around the continent, feeding on acorns, beechnuts, and other bountiful food of the forest.

During the 1700s and 1800s, huge numbers were slaughtered for food; no one thought of trying to protect such an abundant bird until its population suddenly crashed in the late 1800s. The last lone Passenger Pigeon died in a zoo in 1914.

The extinction of this species is somewhat mysterious, because humans obviously did not hunt down every last one. Perhaps the Passenger could nest successfully only when it had safety in numbers. Small colonies or isolated pairs might have been easy marks for natural predators, while in a huge colony the predators could have taken only a small percentage of the hordes of pigeons. Whatever the reasons for its demise, it reminds us that the best time to protect a species is while it is still numerous.

GROUND-DOVES — GENUS *Columbina*

The eight or nine species in this group live mostly in warmer regions of the Americas. All are small doves that do most of their feeding on the ground. They are sociable, living in pairs or small flocks. Two or more birds will often perch close together on a branch, even huddled together so that their bodies are touching.

INCA DOVE *Columbina inca*

The soft, whistled *no-hope* of the Inca Dove is a familiar sound in southwestern cities. These little doves are often seen walking about on lawns with dainty steps, or fluttering up with a rattle of wings. In much of their range, they are found around human dwellings and rather seldom seen in natural habitats away from towns or farms. Probably absent originally from areas north of Mexico, they have spread northward as settlements have grown up in the southwest.

HABITAT *Towns, parks, farms.* In the United States found mostly around human dwellings, especially where there are green lawns and plantings of trees. Will inhabit desert yards or very urbanized areas as long as water is available. Sometimes nests away from human habitations along lowland streams or rivers.

Inca Dove

FEEDING **Diet:** *Mostly seeds.* Feeds on a wide variety of seeds, including waste grain, grass seeds, birdseed. May sometimes eat fruits, such as those of cactus. **Behavior:** Forages almost entirely on the ground, walking about on bare soil or among short grass or weeds. Will also come to bird feeders (which may be important in maintaining city flocks). Regularly swallows grit (small gravel) to aid in digestion of hard seeds.

NESTING Male defends breeding territory against other males, displaying with one wing raised over back; males will sometimes fight vigorously. In courtship, male bobs head, raises tail high over back and spreads it wide to show off black and white markings. **Nest:** Site varies, usually in tree or shrub 5–20 feet above ground, sometimes as high as 50 feet or on ground. May be on building ledge, wire, other artificial site. Nest (built by female, with material gathered by male) a small platform of twigs, stems, leaves, sometimes lined with grass. **Eggs:** 2. White. Incubation is by both parents, 15–16 days. Male incubates mostly during middle of day, female at other times. **Young:** Both parents presumably feed young "pigeon milk" (see family introduction). Young leave nest at about 12–16 days, are tended by parents for another week or so. A pair may raise up to 4–5 broods per year.

MIGRATION Mostly a permanent resident. Sometimes wanders northward in fall and winter; birds that stray north and then remain to breed help to expand the species' range.

CONSERVATION STATUS Abundant, and still expanding its range to the north.

COMMON GROUND-DOVE *Columbina passerina*

Common Ground-Dove

Quiet and unobtrusive, the little Ground-Dove walks on the ground in open bushy places in the southern states. If startled, it flies up into the brush with a fluttering rattle, showing a short black tail and a flash of rusty red in the wings. The male may repeat his short cooing song incessantly, even in the heat of the day.

HABITAT *Farms, orchards, wood edges, roadsides.* Mostly in semi-open habitats with low brush and grass. In the southeast, found mostly in brushy fields, understory of open pine woods, forest edges. In southwest, occurs in similar habitats including orchards, ranch yards, mesquite thickets along streams.

FEEDING **Diet:** *Mostly seeds.* Feeds on a wide variety of seeds, especially those of grasses and weeds, also waste grain in farm fields. Also eats small fruits and berries, and reportedly eats some insects. **Behavior:** Forages mostly on the ground, walking about and picking up seeds. Often forages in pairs, sometimes in small flocks; may associate with Inca Doves where their habitats overlap. Will come to bird feeders for seeds, especially in the southeast.

NESTING In courtship, male struts with stiff steps, chest puffed out and head bowed, while cooing. Several males may compete for attentions of one female. Members of mated pairs often perch very close together and may preen each other's feathers. **Nest:** Site varies; may be on ground or in shrubs or low trees up to 25 feet above ground; usually 3–12 feet up on horizontal fork of branch. Nest (probably built by both sexes) is flat, flimsy platform of sticks. **Eggs:** 2, sometimes 3. White. Incubation is by both parents, 12–14 days. **Young:** Both parents presumably feed young "pigeon milk" (see family introduction). Young leave nest after 11–12 days or more. 2–3 broods per year, sometimes 4.

MIGRATION Permanent resident in most areas, but in parts of the southwest it is much more common in summer, suggesting a regular migration to the south.

CONSERVATION STATUS In recent decades has declined seriously in many areas, especially in the southeast. Reasons are not well understood.

RUDDY GROUND-DOVE *Columbina talpacoti*

Very common in the tropics, this little dove ranges north to northern Mexico, and recently it has been showing up increasingly often in our Southwest. These visitors appear mainly in fall and often stay through the winter. They have been found at various points from southern California to southern Texas, often associating with Inca Doves.

TROPICAL FOREST DOVES — GENUS *Leptotila*

WHITE-TIPPED DOVE *Leptotila verreauxi*

The birder visiting woods of southern Texas may be startled to realize that some of the doves walking about on the ground are of an unfamiliar type. Round-bodied and short-tailed, they keep close to cover; if disturbed, they walk away rapidly through the undergrowth or fly away low with a whistle of wings. These White-tipped Doves are the northernmost representatives of a distinctive group, the genus *Leptotila*, that is widespread in wooded areas in the American tropics.

HABITAT *Shady woodlands, river thickets.* In southern Texas, found in any kind of dense low growth; most common in native woodland but also found in second growth. Within its wide range (from Texas to Argentina) found in many habitats, but mostly drier or more open woods, avoiding unbroken rain forest.

FEEDING **Diet:** *Probably seeds and berries.* Diet not well known. Evidently eats many seeds, including those of grasses, mesquites, and elms; also berries and fruits, including those of hackberry and prickly-pear cactus. May eat some insects. **Behavior:** Forages mostly on ground, walking about in woodland undergrowth; may sometimes forage in low trees or shrubs. In some parks in southern Texas, will come for birdseed or other food put out for them. Several may concentrate at sources of food, but usually solitary, not sociable like many doves.

NESTING In courtship on ground, male may hunch shoulders, lower head, run a few steps toward female, then stop and coo. Also may have bowing display. **Nest:** Site is in dense low tree, thorny shrub, or tangle of vines, usually less than 15 feet above the ground, perhaps sometimes on the ground. Usually placed on horizontal fork of branch. Nest (probably built by both sexes) is a platform of sticks and weed stems, usually quite flimsy. **Eggs:** 2. Pale buff, fading to white. Incubation is probably by both parents, about 14 days. **Young:** Both parents presumed to feed young "pigeon milk" (see family introduction). Development of young and age at first flight not well known.

White-tipped Dove

MIGRATION Permanent resident throughout its range.

CONSERVATION STATUS Numbers holding up very well in undisturbed habitats in southern Texas. As long as habitat remains, probably not too vulnerable to hunting pressure in tropics.

QUAIL-DOVES — GENUS *Geotrygon*

KEY WEST QUAIL-DOVE *Geotrygon chrysia*

Although it was named for Key West, Florida, where it probably nested in the 1800s, today this bird is only a rare visitor to Florida from islands in the Caribbean. A chunky, rotund bird, it walks quietly on the ground under very dense cover and is often difficult to find even where it is common.

RUDDY QUAIL-DOVE *Geotrygon montana*

Quail-Doves are shy inhabitants of the forest floor in tropical regions, related to other doves and pigeons but as round-bodied as quail. This species is found almost throughout the American tropics; it has strayed to southern Florida several times.

PARROTS (Family Psittacidae)

When Columbus sailed, North America had one common native parakeet in the southeast, a parrot that ranged the mountains of the southwest, and perhaps a couple of parrots in the area that is now southern Texas. All of those birds are gone now. But parrots and parakeets are still seen flying wild in parts of North America, because many kinds have escaped from captivity and some have established flocks in the wild.

With more than 300 species around the world, the parrot family (which also includes parakeets, parrotlets, macaws, cockatoos, and others) is most diverse in South America and in the Australian region. Parrots have zygodactyl feet (two toes forward, two pointing back); most have thick bills for cracking hard seeds, and most have colorful feathers. They often use one foot as a "hand," to pick up and hold items they are eating.

Nest sites for parrots are usually in holes in trees, sometimes in crevices in cliffs or even in underground burrows, although the Monk Parakeet builds a bulky stick nest among tree branches. Most kinds of parrots live in flocks, communicating with shrill or harsh cries.

Some parrots are famous for their ability to mimic human words. (They cannot "talk" in a human sense, but research has shown that they can be specially trained to associate meanings to words.) With their skills as mimics and their bright colors, many kinds are popular as pets. Unfortunately, the capture of birds for the cagebird trade, along with the cutting of tropical forests, has had a serious impact on numbers of parrots. Some kinds are now rapidly disappearing and may even be threatened with extinction in the wild.

GENUS *Melopsittacus*

BUDGERIGAR   *Melopsittacus undulatus*

The little "budgie," native to Australia, is a very popular cagebird, so it was probably inevitable that some would escape and establish a wild colony in our area. The west coast of Florida has a sizeable population, and there are some elsewhere in Florida as well. Lone escapees may be seen almost anywhere in North America.

GENUS *Conuropsis*

CAROLINA PARAKEET   *Conuropsis carolinensis*

Although it is hard to imagine it today, native wild parakeets were once common in the southeastern states. The Carolina Parakeet, a long-tailed, bright green bird with an orange-yellow head, sometimes ranged as far north as New York and Wisconsin. Gaudy and noisy, it gathered in shrill flocks in the trees along rivers and forest edges. Unfortunately, these birds also gathered in orchards and grainfields, and many were shot by irate farmers; others were shot for their colorful plumage or captured to be sold as cagebirds. The species could not survive this relentless persecution, and the last Carolina Parakeets died out early in the 20th century. The last definite records in the wild were in 1904, but there were possible sightings in the late 1920s and even later.

GENUS *Rhynchopsitta*

THICK-BILLED PARROT   *Rhynchopsitta pachyrhyncha*

This large parrot feeds on pine cones in the mountains of Mexico, moving nomadically with changes in the cone crop. It was formerly a sporadic visitor to the mountains of Arizona and New Mexico, but the last big invasions were in the 1920s. Recently, small numbers from Mexico have been released into the Chiricahua Mountains, Arizona, with the hope that a resident population will become established.

GENUS *Brotogeris*

CANARY-WINGED PARAKEET   *Brotogeris versicolurus*

Native to South America, this parakeet became common around Miami and else-where in southern Florida during the 1960s and 1970s after large numbers escaped from captivity. It has become less numerous there since the early 1980s. A few feral birds also live in California. Populations in Florida include two distinct forms, the typical Canary-winged and the "Yellow-chevroned" Parakeet.

GENUS *Myiopsitta*

MONK PARAKEET   *Myiopsitta monachus*

Most parrots and parakeets nest in holes in trees, but this South American native builds bulky stick nests among the branches, both for raising young and for sleeping in at night. Many North American cities now have local colonies of Monk Parakeets, established by birds escaped from captivity. Despite some dire past predictions, these noisy but colorful birds have not yet spread to take over the countryside.

GENUS *Amazona*

RED-CROWNED PARROT   *Amazona viridigenalis*

When these stocky parrots fly overhead, they may be recognized by their loud cries of *heeeyo, cra-cra-cra*. Birds escaped from captivity are free-flying (and sometimes nesting) locally in Florida and California; those seen in southern Texas include es-capees and possibly also wild strays from Mexico. Ironically, on its limited native range in northeastern Mexico, the species has declined seriously and might even be considered threatened.

CUCKOOS (Family Cuculidae)

Included in this family are about 140 species found throughout the warmer parts of the world. The majority of species live in the Old World. Most kinds of cuckoos are rather slim and long-tailed. Most live among dense foliage of bushes and trees, but some spend their time walking and running on the ground; the roadrunner of our southwest is an example.

   Cuckoos are typically solitary birds, often shy and hard to observe (the anis are ex-ceptions to these rules). The habit of sneaking about through the trees may come naturally to cuckoos that lay their eggs in the nests of other birds. The Common Cuckoo of Europe is famous for this trait; it never tends to its own eggs or young, leaving them instead to be hatched and raised by unwitting "hosts" that may be smaller than the cuckoo. This kind of parasitism is practiced by many other mem-bers of the family, including a few in the American tropics.

Most cuckoos in the Americas are fairly plain and drab, but some in tropical Africa and Asia are brilliantly colored.

Feeding Insects are the mainstay of the diet of most cuckoos. Particularly sought out by many species are caterpillars, including large hairy caterpillars that most birds avoid. They may also take a variety of other small creatures, including lizards, snails, spiders, and sometimes the eggs of other birds. Some large species such as our roadrunner are more predatory, catching snakes, rodents, and small birds, as well as smaller fare. This kind of feeding requires the roadrunner to be active and speedy, but most cuckoos are rather slow-moving and lethargic while foraging.

Nesting The most notable "nesting" habits in the family are those of the species that build no nests and do not care for their own young. Over a third of the species in the family are brood parasites, mostly in the Old World. A slight tendency in this direction is shown by our Black-billed and Yellow-billed cuckoos, which sometimes lay eggs in each other's nests or in those of other birds.

Among species that do raise their own young, the nest is usually a bulky platform of sticks in a shrub or tree. Both parents usually take part in incubating the eggs and feeding the young. The anis take cooperation even farther, with several adults sharing a communal nest and all adults helping to care for the eggs and young in the nest.

Displays Males of many cuckoo species advertise their claim to nesting territory by singing. Other kinds of displays are quite variable. In some species, the male may feed the female in courtship, or he may present her with a stick or other object. Cuckoos that live in trees may display by bobbing head, lowering wings, spreading tail, or swaying from side to side; roadrunners, living on the ground, have more active displays involving much running and chasing.

OLD WORLD CUCKOOS — GENUS *Cuculus*

COMMON CUCKOO   *Cuculus canorus*

This is the famous bird of Europe whose voice is imitated by cuckoo clocks (and whose call, *coo-coo*, gave the name to the entire cuckoo family). It is well known as a brood parasite: females lay their eggs in the nests of smaller birds, and their hapless "hosts" raise only young cuckoos. A common migratory bird across most of Europe and Asia, it regularly strays to the western Alaskan islands in late spring and early summer.

ORIENTAL CUCKOO   *Cuculus saturatus*

This Asian bird is very similar to the Common Cuckoo; like that species, it sometimes strays to Alaska during migration, but the Oriental Cuckoo seems to show up less often. On the treeless Alaskan islands where such vagrants occur, these wary birds are very hard to approach, and some cuckoos there are never identified to species.

AMERICAN CUCKOOS — GENUS *Coccyzus*

Generally shy birds that hide in leafy woods, dining on caterpillars. They move about rather sluggishly in the trees but are swift in flight, zipping rapidly across clearings in the woods. Yellow-billed and Black-billed cuckoos are known for their habit of eating hairy caterpillars of the sort avoided by most birds. An outbreak of tent caterpillars or gypsy moths may bring an invasion of cuckoos as well.

BLACK-BILLED CUCKOO *Coccyzus erythropthalmus*

Slipping furtively through leafy thickets, this slim, long-tailed bird is heard more often than seen. It seems even more elusive than the Yellow-billed Cuckoo and is generally seen less often during migration, although the Black-billed is the more common nesting bird toward the north.

HABITAT   *Wood edges, groves, thickets.* Breeds mostly in deciduous thickets and shrubby places, often on the edges of woodland or around marshes. Also in second growth of mixed deciduous-coniferous woods or along their brushy edges. In migration, seeks any kind of dense cover, usually among young trees or tall shrubs.

FEEDING   **Diet:** *Caterpillars and other insects.* Feeds heavily on caterpillars when available, including hairy types such as tent caterpillars; also other insects such as beetles, grasshoppers. Also may eat some snails, small fish, eggs of other birds, and berries and small fruits. **Behavior:** Forages by moving about through shrubs and trees, clambering and hopping among the branches, gleaning insects from foliage.

Black-billed Cuckoo

NESTING   In courtship, male feeds female. **Nest:** Site is in shrub or low tree, 1–20 feet above the ground, usually lower than 10 feet, placed among dense branches. May sometimes nest on the ground. Nest (probably built by both sexes) a loose platform of sticks, usually well lined with leaves, grass, pine needles, catkins, other soft material. **Eggs:** 2–3, sometimes 4–5. May lay more eggs in seasons when caterpillars are abundant. Eggs blue-green, occasionally mottled darker. Incubation is by both parents, 10–14 days. Occasionally lays eggs in nest of Yellow-billed Cuckoo or other bird. **Young:** Fed by both parents. May leave nest within a week after hatching, climb about in branches; if disturbed, young bird may "freeze" in upright position, with neck stretched and bill pointed straight up. Age of young at first flight about 3 weeks.

MIGRATION   A long-distance migrant, wintering in South America. Migrates at night; sometimes heard calling in flight overhead at night during spring.

CONSERVATION STATUS   Local numbers rise and fall as birds move around in response to caterpillar outbreaks. Surveys suggest no major change in overall population in North America.

YELLOW-BILLED CUCKOO *Coccyzus americanus*

Sometimes common but usually hard to observe, the Yellow-billed Cuckoo inhabits dense leafy groves and thickets during the summer. Its stuttering, croaking calls, audible at a great distance, are often heard on hot, humid afternoons; people sometimes call this bird the "rain crow," imagining that it is calling for rain.

HABITAT   *Woodlands, thickets, orchards, streamside groves.* Breeds mostly in dense deciduous stands, including forest edges, tall thickets, dense second growth, overgrown orchards, scrubby oak woods. Often in willow groves around marshes. In the west,

mostly in streamside trees, including cottonwood-willow groves in arid country.

FEEDING **Diet:** *Caterpillars and other insects.* Feeds heavily on caterpillars when available, including hairy types such as tent caterpillars; also other insects such as cicadas, beetles, grasshoppers, katydids. Also may eat some lizards, frogs, eggs of other birds, and berries and small fruits. **Behavior:** Forages by clambering about through shrubs and trees, gleaning insects from foliage and branches. May fly up and hover momentarily to pluck a caterpillar or other creature from foliage; sometimes flies out from a perch to catch a flying insect.

Yellow-billed Cuckoo

NESTING In courtship, male feeds female. **Nest:** Site is in tree, shrub, or vines, usually 4–10 feet above the ground, sometimes up to 20 feet or higher. Nest (built by both sexes) is a small, loosely made platform of twigs and stems with thin lining of grass, pine needles, leaves, and other materials. **Eggs:** 3–4, sometimes 1–5 or even more; may lay more eggs in seasons when caterpillars or other insects are abundant. Occasionally lays eggs in nest of Black-billed Cuckoo or other bird. Eggs pale bluish green. Incubation is by both parents (but female may do more), 9–11 days, perhaps sometimes longer. **Young:** Fed by both parents. Young may leave nest and climb about in branches after about a week; can fly in about 3 weeks. In some cases, first young to leave the nest are tended by male, last ones by female.

MIGRATION Mostly arrives late in spring and departs early in fall. A long-distance migrant, some going as far as Argentina in winter. Sometimes heard calling overhead at night during migration.

CONSERVATION STATUS Local numbers rise and fall with insect outbreaks; however, surveys show a general decline in recent decades, especially in parts of the west, where loss of habitat is a likely cause.

MANGROVE CUCKOO *Coccyzus minor*

Birders who seek the Mangrove Cuckoo in Florida may have to contend with heat, humidity, mosquitoes, and long hours of searching. This bird is a shy denizen of dense mangrove swamps, living in impenetrable tangles, where its presence is often betrayed only by its throaty calls.

HABITAT *In our area, mostly in mangroves.* In Florida, lives in mangrove swamps and in groves of tropical hardwoods on the Keys and the southern mainland. Elsewhere in range, found in mangroves and various kinds of scrubby woods, including dry forest far from water.

FEEDING **Diet:** *Mostly insects.* Diet not known in detail. As with other cuckoos, seems to eat many caterpillars. Also feeds on grasshoppers,

Mangrove Cuckoo

praying mantises, moths, flies, and other insects; also some spiders and small frogs, and probably some berries and small fruits. **Behavior:** Forages rather slowly and deliberately among mangroves or other dense growth, peering about, sometimes making short leaps or flutters to take insects from the foliage.

NESTING   Breeding behavior not well known. Male gives low, throaty song in spring, presumably to defend territory and attract a mate. **Nest:** So far as known, site is in mangrove or other low tree, usually fairly low over the water or ground (probably lower than 10 feet in most cases), among dense foliage. Nest is a flimsy platform of sticks. **Eggs:** 2, sometimes 3. Pale blue-green, fading to greenish yellow. Incubation is probably by both parents; incubation period not well known. **Young:** Development of young and age at first flight not well known. Probably fed by both parents, as in other cuckoos.

MIGRATION   Migratory status in Florida uncertain. Recorded at all seasons and thought to be permanent resident, but more conspicuous in summer. Rare stray from Mexico north into Texas and Gulf coast.

CONSERVATION STATUS   Probably declining in Florida Keys as habitat is lost to development, but may be expanding north slightly along coast. Still widespread in Caribbean and elsewhere in tropics.

ROADRUNNERS — GENUS *Geococcyx*

GREATER ROADRUNNER   *Geococcyx californianus*

The most famous bird in the southwest, featured in folklore and cartoons, known by its long tail and expressive crest. The Roadrunner walks and runs on the ground, flying only when necessary. It can run 15 miles per hour, probably with much faster spurts when chasing a fast-running lizard or other prey. Its prowess as a rattlesnake fighter has been much exaggerated, but it does eat a remarkable variety of smaller creatures.

HABITAT   *Deserts, open country with scattered brush.* Most common in Sonoran desert and in other kinds of brushy country, including chaparral and Texas brushlands, in areas with a mix of open ground and dense low cover. At limits of range, found in dry grassland, forest edges, and limestone hills with scattered junipers.

FEEDING   **Diet:** *Includes insects, reptiles, rodents, birds.* Feeds on many large insects, plus other arthropods including scorpions, tarantulas, and centipedes. Also catches many lizards, snakes, mice, young ground squirrels, small birds (including baby quail and adult sparrows), sometimes snails. Eats some fruits (especially cactus fruit) and seeds. **Behavior:** Usually hunts by walking rapidly, looking for prey, then making very rapid dash forward to catch prey in its bill. May leap straight up from ground to catch insects or birds flying over (has been seen catching hummingbirds this way).

Greater Roadrunner

NESTING   May mate for life, pairs defending territory all year. Courtship includes chases on foot, with frequent pauses to rest. One bird (either sex) approaches the other with stick or blade of grass and drops it on the ground or gives it to other bird. In other displays, male runs away from female with tail and wings raised over back, gradually lowers wings; male wags tail from side to side while slowly bowing. **Nest:** Site is in dense bush, low tree, or cactus, usually 2–12 feet above ground, rarely on ground. Nest is platform of sticks, lined with grass, leaves, feathers, sometimes with snakeskin or pieces of cow manure. **Eggs:** 3–5, sometimes 2–6. White to pale yellowish. Incubation is by both parents (male does more), about 20 days. **Young:** Fed by both parents; leave the nest after about 18–21 days. May begin catching own food soon after leaving nest, but still fed by parents up to another 30–40 days.

MIGRATION   Permanent resident, but some (young birds?) may wander considerable distances.

CONSERVATION STATUS   Periodically expands range to north and east, is killed back by severe winters. May be in long-term decline in California.

ANIS — GENUS *Crotophaga*

These tropical members of the cuckoo family are odd in both appearance and habits. They look like disjointed blackbirds with huge, puffinlike bills, and they breed in communal groups, several pairs placing their eggs in one group nest. Seen in flight, anis look loose-hinged, flapping floppily and then gliding, the long tail trailing behind.

SMOOTH-BILLED ANI   *Crotophaga ani*

Smooth-billed Ani

Audubon and other early naturalists failed to find the Smooth-billed Ani in Florida, but it has been a regular nesting bird there at least since 1938.

HABITAT   *Brushy edges, thickets.* In Florida, usually found where dense brush stands next to open fields, pastures, or marshes. In its tropical range, found in a variety of brushy or semi-open habitats in the lowlands, mainly in humid areas. Generally avoids unbroken forest.

FEEDING   **Diet:** *Mostly large insects.* Feeds on insects including grasshoppers, beetles, moths, caterpillars, and others. May take external parasites from cattle. Also eats spiders, snails, and often small lizards. Will consume many small fruits and berries at some seasons, also seeds. May sometimes eat eggs of other birds. **Behavior:** Forages mostly on the ground, hopping and running rather clumsily; will also forage well up in bushes. In pastures, often associates closely with cattle or other grazers, catching insects flushed by the larger animals.

NESTING   Often nests communally: one or more pairs (perhaps as many as five pairs) will work together to build one large nest; then each female lays eggs there, and all the adults help to incubate the eggs and care for the young. **Nest:** Site is in dense shrub or tree, 5–30 feet above ground, usually fairly low. Nest (built by both sexes, apparently by all adult members of group) is a bulky bowl of twigs and weeds, lined with leaves. **Eggs:** About 4 blue eggs laid by each female in group; nest may have up to 20 or more eggs. Incubation is by both sexes and apparently involves all adults in group, about 14 days. **Young:** Apparently fed by all adults in group; may climb out of nest before old enough to fly. Age at first flight not well known.

MIGRATION   Present in southern Florida at all seasons, but some may move back and forth between Florida and Cuba.

CONSERVATION STATUS   In Florida, apparently increased through middle part of 20th century; has declined again since 1970s. In tropics, has increased as clearing of forest has created more open habitat.

GROOVE-BILLED ANI   *Crotophaga sulcirostris*

These ungainly cuckoos are sociable at all seasons, feeding in flocks on the ground in south Texas pastures. When resting, several may sit hunched side by side on the same branch. Sometimes members of a flock will perch in the sun with their wings spread out as if to dry.

HABITAT   *Thick brush, overgrown pastures.* In the United States, found mostly where dense thickets are next to open grassland, pastures, or marshes, or at edges of low riverside woods. In the tropics, inhabits any kind of semi-open country in the lowlands, avoiding unbroken forest.

Groove-billed Ani

FEEDING   Diet: *Mostly large insects.* Feeds on insects including grasshoppers, beetles, and others. May take external parasites from cattle. Also eats spiders, lizards, other small creatures. Will feed on small fruits and berries. **Behavior:** Forages mostly by hopping and running on the ground; will also forage in bushes, especially to eat berries. Often associates closely with cattle in open pastures, catching insects flushed by the larger animals. In a similar way, at the edges of tropical forest, will follow swarms of army ants to eat insects or other creatures flushed by the ants.

NESTING   In courtship, male feeds female. Often uses communal nest: 1–4 pairs will work together to build nest, then the female of each pair will lay eggs in the nest, and all adults will help incubate the eggs. In addition to breeding pairs, group may include extra adult "helpers." **Nest:** Site is in low tree, usually 5–15 feet above ground, sometimes lower or higher. Nest (built by both sexes) is bulky and bowl-shaped, made of twigs, lined with green leaves. **Eggs:** 3–4 (perhaps sometimes more) laid by each female in group. Pale blue. Females may attempt to throw out each other's eggs. Incubation is apparently by all adults in group (dominant male usually incubates at night), 13–14 days. **Young:** Fed by all adults in group. Young climb out of nest after about 6–7 days, can fly poorly at about 10 days, can fly well at about 17 days. Sometimes two broods per year.

MIGRATION   Found year-round in southern Texas but more common there in summer. In winter, small numbers move north and east along Gulf coast. Sometimes strays well north of breeding range, especially in fall.

CONSERVATION STATUS   Numbers in United States probably stable. Has probably increased in tropics as clearing of forests has created more habitat for them there.

BARN OWLS (Family Tytonidae) AND TYPICAL OWLS (Family Strigidae)

Scientists classify these birds into two distinct families, with about 15 species of barn owls and about 165 of typical owls found worldwide. These two families differ in some details of structure, but they are similar in habits, so they are treated together here.

The myth of the "wise owl" is probably based on human conceit: we tend to think of owls as intelligent because, with their upright stance and forward-facing eyes, they look more human than most birds. On the other hand, the owls' reputation as superb nighttime hunters is well deserved.

Owls cannot see in complete darkness (no creature can), but they do have excellent vision in low light. The retina of an owl's eye is packed with receptors for making out details in dim light; the tradeoff is that they probably have a poor sense of color. But although they may be colorblind, they can see perfectly well in daylight, contrary to one popular myth.

A further advantage for a nocturnal hunter is the owl's ability to find prey by sound. Humans (like most animals) can tell whether a noise is coming from the left or right: if it comes from the left, it will strike our left ear more strongly and a fraction of a second sooner. But many owls can judge the direction of a sound in terms of its height as well. Because their ear openings are asymmetrical, higher on one side of the head than the other, they can pinpoint the source of a sound both horizontally and vertically, something we cannot do. Experiments have shown that a Barn Owl can strike its prey in total darkness, locating it by sound alone. The conspicuous round "facial disk" of feathers framing each side of an owl's face is thought to help funnel sounds into the ear openings.

Of course, many of the creatures that owls hunt are also listening in the dark; to be effective hunters, an owl must be silent. The leading feather in each wing is modified, with a serrated edge, and the rest of the flight feathers have softened edges, deadening the sound of the wingbeats. The very soft and fluffy feathers of the owl's body also help to muffle the sounds of movement.

In the wild, some of the larger owls may live 20 years or more, and smaller species may live more than 10 years.

Feeding All owls are predators, but they vary widely in their choice of prey. Some of the smaller species live entirely on insects and other arthropods. At the opposite extreme, large hunters like Great Horned Owl and Snowy Owl may take animals as large as rabbits, skunks, and even geese. Some fast-flying species like the pygmy-owls may capture many small, agile songbirds. In Africa and Asia, several owls live along streams and prey on fish.

Although most owls hunt at night, there are many exceptions. These include some that live in the far north, where daylight is continuous in summer. Pygmy-owls, Burrowing Owls, and others may also hunt by day.

In most kinds of owls, the indigestible parts of their prey—bones, fur, feathers, insect wings, and the like—are coughed up later in the form of pellets. Naturalists can learn much about what owls are eating by collecting these pellets from underneath an owl roost and examining their contents.

Nesting Choice of nest site varies widely. Many owls, especially the smaller kinds, nest in holes in trees, either natural cavities or old woodpecker holes (and they will also use birdhouses at times). Others take over old stick nests built by other birds, such as hawks or crows; the Great Horned Owl will even take over nests built by Bald Eagles. Still other owls nest on the ground, and the Burrowing Owl nests in underground burrows.

Typically, owls do no nest-building at all, simply laying their white eggs on whatever debris lies in the bottom of the hole or old stick nest. The female usually does all or most of the incubating, while the male brings food for her. After the eggs hatch, the female often remains with the young at first while the male hunts to provide food for all of them.

In many owls, the female begins incubating soon after she lays the first egg, so that the first egg may hatch many days before the last. A brood of young owls may look like a set of stair steps from largest to smallest, with the oldest owlet perhaps fully feathered while the youngest is still covered with down.

Displays   As expected for birds that are active mostly at night, owls do most of their communicating by voice. Most kinds have a wide variety of calls used in different circumstances; for example, some may be used mainly for defending the territory, others for communication between mates. Members of a pair may call in duet. Males of many species also perform courtship display flights. Some owls perform wing-claps in flight, bringing the wings together sharply below the body with a whipcrack sound that may be heard a hundred yards away; this may be used either in courtship or in defense of the nesting territory. Finally, courtship feeding may be typical of most owls, with the male bringing food to the female, beginning well before the first egg is laid.

BARN OWLS — GENUS *Tyto*

BARN OWL   *Tyto alba*

With its ghostly appearance, rasping shrieks, and habit of roosting in such places as church belfries, this bird has attracted much superstition. However, it is really a good omen for farmers who find it in their barns, for it preys chiefly on mice and rats. Discovered in its daytime retreat, the Barn Owl bobs its head and weaves back and forth, peering at the intruder. At night it is often heard calling as it flies high over farmland or marshes. One of the most widespread of all landbirds, found on six continents and many islands.

HABITAT   *Woodlands, groves, farms, barns, towns, cliffs.* Typically in open or semi-open country in lowlands. May nest in forest or city if nearby area has good open foraging territory, such as farmland, marsh, prairie, desert.

FEEDING   **Diet:** *Mostly rodents.* Feeds heavily on voles; also takes various kinds of mice, small rats, shrews, young rabbits, other mammals. Eats very small numbers of birds, lizards, insects, rarely frogs or even fish. **Behavior:** Hunts at night, seldom by day. Seeks prey

Barn Owl

mostly by flying low over open ground, watching and listening; sometimes hunts by flying down from a perch. Has excellent vision in low light levels, and hearing is so precise that it can strike prey in total darkness.

NESTING   In courtship, male performs display flight, including loud wing-claps; male feeds female. **Nest:** Uses sites in caves and hollow trees, also many artificial sites such as barn lofts, church steeples, abandoned houses, dry wells, crevices under bridges, nest boxes. Where no existing cavities available, will dig holes in dirt banks. No real nest built, but will arrange debris into crude depression. **Eggs:** Usually 3–8, sometimes 2–12 or even more. Whitish, sometimes becoming nest-stained. Incubation is by female only, 29–34 days; male brings food to female during incubation. **Young:** Female remains with young at first and broods them while they are small; male brings food, female feeds it to young. After about 2 weeks, female hunts also. Age of young at first flight roughly 55–65 days. Young return to sleep at nest or nearby for several more weeks. One or two broods per year, sometimes three.

MIGRATION   Some remain all winter near northern edges of range, but some (perhaps especially young birds) move long distances southward in fall. A regular October migrant at Cape May, New Jersey.

CONSERVATION STATUS   In recent decades, has declined slightly in some regions, drastically in others. Numbers are apparently stable or increasing in a few sites. May be helped in some areas by provision of nest boxes.

SCREECH-OWLS AND SCOPS-OWLS — GENUS *Otus*

This genus includes about 40 or 50 species of owls, found in most areas of the world except Australia and Antarctica. All are small, and many are very common, although some tropical forms are scarce or poorly known. The number of species in the genus is uncertain because scientists are still debating how to classify various forms; our Eastern and Western screech-owls were "split" only recently.

ORIENTAL SCOPS-OWL   *Otus sunia*

The scops-owls are Old World relatives of our screech-owls. This species is migratory in eastern Asia, and strays have reached the western Aleutian Islands of Alaska on a couple of occasions.

FLAMMULATED OWL   *Otus flammeolus*

The soft, low-pitched hoots of this little owl can be heard (if one listens carefully) in mountain pine forests over much of the west. Seeing the bird is another matter; its variegated pattern of brown and rust makes perfect camouflage when it perches close to a pine trunk. Because it is so inconspicuous, the Flammulated Owl was long overlooked in many areas and was considered rare until recently.

HABITAT   *Open pine forests in mountains.* Nests in relatively open forest, typically of ponderosa pine, in cool and fairly dry zones such as mountains of the interior. In some areas, favors groves of aspen. Upper level of forest usually quite open, but may be brushy understory of oaks and other plants. In migration, sometimes found in dense thickets at lower elevations.

FEEDING   **Diet:** *Large insects.* Feeds almost entirely on insects, especially moths, beetles, and crickets. Also eats a few spiders, centipedes, scorpions, and other arthropods. Almost never eats vertebrates, but once proven to have eaten a shrew. **Behavior:** Hunts most actively just after dark and near dawn, less in

Flammulated Owl

middle of night. Forages by perching and looking for insects, then flying out to catch them. May catch prey in the air or on the ground, but apparently most often takes insects from foliage, hovering momentarily and grabbing them with feet.

NESTING   Male hoots at night early in season to defend territory and attract a mate. In courtship, female begs, male feeds her. **Nest:** Site is in cavity in tree, usually old woodpecker hole, usually 15–40 feet above ground. Will also use artificial nest boxes. **Eggs:** 2–3, sometimes 4. White or creamy white. Incubation is by female only, 21–24 days. Male brings food to incubating female at nest. **Young:** Female remains with nestlings for about 12 days after they hatch; male brings food for female and young. After about 12 days, female also hunts. Young leave nest by about 25 days after hatching, perch in trees nearby. At least sometimes, brood splits up after fledging, each parent tending 1–2 of the young for about another 4 weeks.

MIGRATION   Strongly migratory, with North American birds going to Mexico and Central America for winter. May tend to migrate north through the lowlands in spring (when insects may be scarce at upper elevations), and south through the mountains in fall.

CONSERVATION STATUS   Still widespread, and common in many areas, but probably has declined in some regions. Cutting of dead trees in forest removes potential nesting sites.

EASTERN SCREECH-OWL   *Otus asio*

This robin-sized nightbird is common over much of the east, including in city parks and shady suburbs, where many human residents are unaware they have an owl for a neighbor. The owl spends the day roosting in holes or in dense cover, becoming active at dusk. Despite the name, screech-owls do not screech; the voice of this species features whinnies and soft trills.

HABITAT   *Woodlands, farm groves, shade trees.* Generally favors deciduous or mixed woods, but may be found in any habitat having some open ground and some large trees, from forest to isolated groves to suburban yards. May be absent from some areas because of lack of dead snags with suitable nesting holes.

FEEDING   **Diet:** *Mostly large insects and small rodents.* Wide variation in diet. Eats many beetles, moths, crickets, other large insects. Catches mice and other rodents, shrews, sometimes bats; also some small birds, lizards, frogs, spiders, earthworms, crayfish,

Eastern Screech-Owl

many other small creatures. Some catch many small fish. **Behavior:** Forages at dusk and at night. Hunts mostly by watching from a perch and then swooping down to take prey from the ground or from foliage. Also catches flying insects in the air. Can locate prey by sound as well as by sight.

NESTING   Courtship displays of male include bowing, raising wings, clicking bill. Male brings food to female. Mated pairs preen each other's feathers, call in duet. **Nest:** Site is in cavity in tree, including natural hollows and abandoned woodpecker holes; will also use artificial nest boxes. Usually 10–30 feet above ground, can be 5–80 feet up. **Eggs:** 4–5, sometimes 2–8. White. Incubation is mostly by female, averages about 26 days. Male brings food to female during incubation. **Young:** Both parents bring food for young. Adults may bring back small, wormlike Blind Snakes and release them in nest, where the snakes burrow in debris in bottom of cavity, feeding on insects there, perhaps helping protect the young from parasites. Young leave the nest about 4 weeks after hatching, are fed by parents for some time thereafter.

MIGRATION   Apparently a permanent resident throughout its range. Especially in north, may wander somewhat in fall and winter.

CONSERVATION STATUS   Still widespread and fairly common but thought to have been gradually declining in various parts of range. Helped in some areas by provision of nest boxes.

WESTERN SCREECH-OWL   *Otus kennicottii*

This little owl is inconspicuous but locally very common. In the varied terrain of the west, its haunts range from coastal forests in southeastern Alaska to cactus groves in the Arizona desert, and it is often found in suburban areas. Until the 1980s, Western and Eastern screech-owls were considered to belong to the same species because they look so similar; however, their voices differ, and they apparently recognize their own kind by sound.

HABITAT   *Wooded canyons, desert mesquites, farm groves, shade trees.* Found in a wide variety of wooded or semi-open habitats, including forest edges, wooded suburbs, canyons, mesquite groves and saguaros in the desert, streamside groves in arid country. Mostly in deciduous or mixed woods. Avoids extreme desert situations and higher elevations in mountains.

FEEDING   **Diet:** *Mostly small mammals and large insects.* Diet varies with habitat and region. Includes many beetles, moths, other insects, as well as spiders, scorpions, centipedes; also many small mammals, such as mice, voles, pocket gophers. Also eats small birds, lizards, snakes, frogs, fish. **Behavior:** Forages at dusk and at night. Hunts mostly by watching from a perch and then swooping down to take prey from the ground or from foliage. Also catches flying insects in the air. Can locate prey by sound as well as by sight.

NESTING   Courtship displays of male while perched include bowing, clicking bill. Male brings food to female. Mated pairs preen each other's feathers, call in duet. **Nest:** Site is in cavity in tree, pole, or giant cactus, typically in old woodpecker hole but also in natural hollows in trees. May also use old magpie nests. Sites usually 5–35 feet above ground. **Eggs:** 2–5, sometimes 6. White. Incubation is mostly or entirely by female, averages about 26 days. Male brings food to female during incubation. **Young:** Both parents bring food for young. If intruders (including humans) come too close to nest, adults may attack or may put on distraction display. Young leave nest about 4 weeks after hatching, are cared for by parents for some time thereafter.

MIGRATION   Permanent resident throughout its range.

WHISKERED SCREECH-OWL   *Otus trichopsis*

In mountains near the Mexican border, this little owl is common in the oak woodlands. Although its voice is distinctive, it looks very much like the Western Screech-Owl, which is common in the same general region. The Whiskered is a little smaller and lives mostly at higher elevations. Western and Whiskered screech-owls are often found side by side in the lower parts of canyons in Arizona, where the desert gives way to oaks and sycamores.

HABITAT   *Canyons, pine-oak woods, oaks, sycamores.* Favors habitat with relatively dense, broadleaved oaks, both in pure stands and in mixed woodland with pines, generally above 5,000 feet. In Arizona canyons, often common in groves of sycamores next to oak woodland.

FEEDING   **Diet:** *Mostly large insects.* Eats many caterpillars, beetles, moths, crickets, katydids, and other insects; also other arthropods, including centipedes and scorpions. Sometimes eats small rodents. **Behavior:**

Whiskered Screech-Owl

Hunts at dusk and through the night. Hunts by watching from a perch and then making short flights out to take prey from foliage or from the ground; may fly back and forth or hover among vegetation to take insects. Captures most prey with feet.

NESTING   Breeding behavior is not well known. Males defend breeding territory by singing at night, and may vigorously attack intruding males. Members of mated pairs call in duet, also nibble at each other's bills and preen each other's feathers. **Nest:** Site is in cavity in tree such as oak or sycamore, either an abandoned woodpecker hole or a natural hollow; nest sites often 10–30 feet above ground. **Eggs:** 3, sometimes 4. White. Incubation is probably mostly by female, incubation period not well known. **Young:** Both parents probably bring food for young. Development of young and age at first flight not well known. Parents feed young for some time after they leave nest.

MIGRATION   Permanent resident.

CONSERVATION STATUS   Locally common, and numbers apparently stable in limited range in United States.

EAGLE-OWLS — GENUS *Bubo*

GREAT HORNED OWL   *Bubo virginianus*

This big owl is found almost throughout the Americas. Aggressive and powerful in hunting (sometimes known by nicknames such as "tiger owl"), it takes prey as varied as rabbits, hawks, snakes, and skunks, and will even attack porcupines, often with fatal results for both prey and predator. Great Horned Owls begin nesting very early in the north, and their deep hoots may be heard rolling across the forest on midwinter nights.

Great Horned Owl

HABITAT   *Forests, woodlots, streamsides, open country.* Found in practically all habitats in North America, from swamps to deserts to northern coniferous forest near treeline. In breeding season avoids tundra and unbroken grassland, since it requires some trees or heavy brush for cover.

FEEDING   **Diet:** *Varied, mostly mammals and birds.* Mammals make up majority of diet in most regions. Takes many rats, mice, and rabbits, also ground squirrels, opossums, skunks, many others. Eats some birds (especially in north), up to size of geese, ducks, hawks, and smaller owls. Also eats snakes, lizards, frogs, insects, scorpions, rarely fish. **Behavior:** Hunts mostly at night, sometimes at dusk. Watches from high perch, then swoops down to capture prey in its talons. Has extremely good hearing and good vision in low light conditions. In north in winter, may store uneaten prey, coming back later to thaw out frozen carcass by "incubating" it.

NESTING   May begin nesting very early in north (late winter), possibly so that young will have time to learn hunting skills before next winter begins. In courtship, male performs display flight, also feeds female. **Nest:** Typically uses old nest of other large bird, such as hawk, eagle, crow, heron, usually 20–60 feet above ground; also may nest on cliff ledge, in cave, in broken-off tree stump, sometimes on ground. May take over newly built hawk nest. Adds little or no nest material, aside from feathers at times. **Eggs:** 2–3, sometimes 1–5, rarely 6. Dull whitish. Incubation mostly by female, 28–35 days. **Young:** Both parents take part in providing food for young owls. Young may leave nest and climb on nearby branches at 5 weeks, can fly at about 9–10 weeks; are tended and fed by parents for up to several months.

No regular migration, but individuals may wander long distances in fall and winter, some of them moving southward.

Widespread and common, numbers apparently holding up well in most areas.

GENUS *Nyctea*

SNOWY OWL   *Nyctea scandiaca*

Snowy Owl

A large, powerful owl of the high Arctic tundra, colored for camouflage in northern winters. In summer it may be nomadic, concentrating and nesting where there are high populations of the small rodents called lemmings. At other times it takes a wide variety of prey, including birds as big as geese. In some winters, large numbers of Snowy Owls appear south of the Canadian border; those that stop in towns and cities invariably cause a stir and attract media attention.

HABITAT *Prairies, fields, marshes, beaches, dunes; in summer, Arctic tundra.* Breeds on tundra, from just north of treeline to the northernmost land. Prefers very open tundra, either in hilly country or wetter areas near coast. Winters in open country, including prairies, farmland, coastal marshes, beaches, large airports.

FEEDING **Diet:** *Varied, includes lemmings, plus other mammals and birds.* In Arctic, may feed almost exclusively on lemmings when these are available. Otherwise, feeds on wide variety of prey. Takes mammals including rabbits, hares, voles, ground squirrels. In coastal areas may feed heavily on birds, including ducks, geese, grebes, murrelets, and sometimes songbirds. Also may eat fish, carrion. **Behavior:** Often hunts by day. Usually hunts by watching for prey from a perch, then pursuing it in swift flight and catching prey in talons. Sometimes seeks prey by flying low, or by hovering and watching ground. May locate prey by sight or sound.

NESTING In many regions of Arctic, may breed mainly in years when lemmings are abundant, failing to nest at all when lemmings are scarce. Male defends territory with deep hooting in early spring. In courtship, male flies with deep, slow wingbeats, often carrying a lemming in his bill; landing near female, he leans forward, partly raising wings. **Nest:** Chooses a raised site on top of mound or ridge in hilly country or on hummock in low-lying areas, always with good visibility in very open tundra. Site may be used for several years. Nest (built by female) is simple depression in tundra with no lining added. **Eggs:** 3–11. Clutch size quite variable, with more eggs laid in years when prey is abundant. Eggs whitish, becoming nest-stained. Incubation is by female only, 31–33 days; male brings food to incubating female. Eggs hatch at intervals, so that female cares for first young while still incubating last eggs. **Young:** Female remains with young; male brings food, female takes it and feeds them. Young may leave nest after 2–3 weeks, but not able to fly well until about 7 weeks; fed by parents up to at least 9–10 weeks.

Migration not well understood. Nomadic in breeding season, concentrating where prey is abundant. Numbers moving south in winter quite variable from year to year, probably relating to populations of prey in the north.

Formerly, many were shot during southward invasions in winter. Most North American breeding areas are remote from effects of human disturbance. Has declined in parts of breeding range in northern Europe.

NORTHERN HAWK OWL *Surnia ulula*

Northern Hawk Owl

In the northern forest, a lucky observer may spot this long-tailed owl perched upright at the top of a spruce. Rather hawklike in both appearance and behavior, it often hunts by day. Going from tree to tree, it flies fast and low, swinging up at the last moment to alight on the topmost twigs. The occasional Hawk Owl that wanders into the northeastern United States in winter may remain for weeks, attracting birders from far and wide.

HABITAT   *Open conifer forests, birch scrub, tamarack bogs, muskeg.* Found in northern forest of spruce and other conifers mixed with aspen or birch, north to treeline. Generally in semi-open sites, as around edges of clearings, bogs, burned areas.

FEEDING   **Diet:** *Mostly rodents.* Especially in summer, eats mostly voles, mice; also some small squirrels, weasels, shrews. Also eats small birds, especially in winter. May take insects, frogs, even small fish at times. **Behavior:** Hunts mostly by day, or at dawn and dusk. Watches for prey from a prominent raised perch, often moving from one hunting perch to another; when prey is spotted, attacks in very fast flight. May hover while hunting. Sometimes catches birds in the air. May sometimes locate prey by sound alone, plunging into snow to catch unseen rodents.

NESTING   Members of mated pair call in duet, sometimes bow stiffly. Male feeds female and may store uneaten prey near nest. **Nest:** Site varies, includes large cavities in trees, broken-off tops of snags, or old nests of other birds, such as crows or hawks. In northern Europe, may use artificial nest boxes. Usually 10–40 feet above ground. **Eggs:** 5–7, sometimes 4–9, rarely 3–13. May lay more eggs in years when rodents are abundant. Eggs white. Incubation is by female only, 25–30 days. **Young:** Female stays with young most of time for about first 2 weeks; male brings food for them. Later, both parents bring food. Young climb around in nest tree before capable of flight, may be able to fly at about 5–6 weeks. Young may remain with parents for several months after fledging.

MIGRATION   No regular migration, but somewhat nomadic, moving around to track available prey. A few may move well southward in winter.

CONSERVATION STATUS   Most of North American breeding range is remote from effects of human disturbance.

PYGMY-OWLS — GENUS *Glaucidium*

Tiny but formidable, pygmy-owls are fast-flying hunters that are often active by day. They have longer tails than most small owls, perhaps helping them to maneuver in flight as they pursue their prey, which may include many small birds as well as rodents and insects. When perched, a pygmy-owl often bobs its head and flicks its tail up and down. Most kinds have tooting calls. At least 20 species occur around the world, most in the tropics, but they are often uncommon and hard to find.

NORTHERN PYGMY-OWL *Glaucidium gnoma*

In western forests, this little owl is often active by day. It may fly fast and low from one tree to the next and then swoop up to take a high perch, rather like a shrike. An aggressive hunter despite its small size, it catches more birds than most small owls. Little gangs of chickadees and other songbirds often gather to "mob" a pygmy-owl discovered in daylight, and they will react the same way to a birder who imitates the owl's whistled call.

HABITAT   *Open coniferous or mixed woods, wooded canyons.* Found in a wide variety of forest types, including open oak groves, sycamores in canyons, pine-oak woodland, coniferous forest of far north and high mountains. Generally in partly open habitats rather than solid unbroken forest.

FEEDING   **Diet:** *Includes rodents, birds, insects, lizards.* Diet varies with location and season. Rodents such as voles and mice are often major prey, also catches mammals as large as gophers and squirrels. During warm weather, eats many large insects such as grasshoppers, crickets, cicadas, beetles. Small songbirds are sometimes up to one-third of diet. In southern parts of range, may catch many lizards. **Behavior:** Hunts most actively near dawn and dusk, but also at other times. Watches for prey from a perch, then makes very rapid pursuit flight.

NESTING   Some birds defend territories all year; in breeding season, pairs defend very large nesting territories. Courtship displays at dusk may involve rapid aerial chases near potential nest sites. In courtship on perch, male feeds female. **Nest:** Site is in cavity in tree, either in natural hollow or (perhaps more often) in abandoned woodpecker hole, usually 8–25 feet above ground. Nests often hard to find because adults enter and exit rapidly. **Eggs:** 3–4, sometimes 2–7. White. Incubation apparently is by female only, about 28 days. **Young:** Both parents take part in providing food for young, with male bringing much of prey, female feeding it to young. Female may roost in nest hole with young at first. Age of young at first flight about 27–28 days.

MIGRATION   No regular migration, but may wander away from breeding areas in fall and winter, including some downslope movement by mountain birds.

CONSERVATION STATUS   Generally uncommon, but widespread; no evidence of general declines.

Northern Pygmy-Owl

FERRUGINOUS PYGMY-OWL   *Glaucidium brasilianum*

Common and widespread in the American tropics, this little owl enters our area only in southern Texas and Arizona, where it is now uncommon to rare. It is often active by day and may feed on small birds at times; songbirds in its range all recognize its whistled call and will gather to mob and harass the owl when they discover it.

HABITAT   *Mesquite thickets, desert riverine woods, saguaros.* In United States, currently most numerous in low stands of live oak and mesquite in southern Texas. Was formerly common in mesquite forest along rivers and in desert dominated by saguaro cactus. In tropics, found in wide range of lowland habitats, mostly in semi-open country.

FEEDING   **Diet:** *Includes insects, birds, rodents, lizards.* Diet not well known, probably varies by region. Among known foods

Ferruginous Pygmy-Owl

are large insects (including crickets, caterpillars, and beetles), scorpions, small birds, rodents and other small mammals, and lizards. **Behavior:** Apparently hunts most actively near dawn and dusk. Hunts by watching from raised perch, then darting out in very rapid flight to capture prey in talons. Notably bold and aggressive for its small size.

NESTING   Breeding behavior is not well known. Male defends nesting territory with song of monotonous repeated whistles, mostly at dusk and dawn, also at night, sometimes by day. **Nest:** Site is in cavity in tree or in giant cactus, usually old woodpecker hole but sometimes natural hollow in tree. Typically low, 10–30 feet above ground. **Eggs:** 3–4, sometimes 5. White. Apparently incubation is mostly or entirely by female, about 28 days; male brings food to female during incubation. **Young:** Both parents take part in providing food for young; male may do most of hunting at first. Age of young at first flight about 27–30 days.

MIGRATION   Apparently permanent resident throughout its range.

CONSERVATION STATUS   Now considered endangered or threatened in limited range in United States. Still widespread in tropics, although undoubtedly has declined in some areas.

GENUS *Microthene*

ELF OWL   *Microthene whitneyi*

Elf Owl

Regions near the Mexican border are home to this gnome, the tiniest owl in the world, no bigger than a sparrow. On moonlit nights in late spring, its yapping and chuckling calls (surprisingly loud for the size of the bird) echo among the groves of giant cactus and through the lower canyons. The Elf Owl feeds almost entirely on insects and other invertebrates, which become harder to find in cold weather, so it migrates south into Mexico for the winter.

HABITAT   *Saguaro deserts, wooded canyons.* Within its United States range, found in any lowland habitat providing cover and good nesting cavities. Most common in deserts with many tall saguaro cactus or large mesquites, and in canyons in the foothills, especially around sycamores or large oaks. Locally along streamsides in higher mountains.

FEEDING   **Diet:** *Insects and other arthropods.* In summer, feeds heavily on moths, beetles, and crickets, as well as katydids and other insects active at night. Also feeds on scorpions and spiders. Rarely eats lizards and other small vertebrates. **Behavior:** Hunts only at dusk and at night. Watches from a perch and then swoops down to take prey off the ground, or flies low, pausing to hover before pouncing. Also flies out from a perch to catch flying insects. May hover among foliage and then catch insects that are flushed from the leaves. Apparently catches all prey with its feet. May remove the stinger before eating scorpions.

NESTING   Early in breeding season, male sings loudly and persistently at night to defend territory and attract female. In courtship, male feeds female. Male sings from inside potential nest hole to lure female to it. **Nest:** Site is almost always in old woodpecker hole in tree or giant cactus (or in utility pole). Height varies: usually 15–50 feet above ground in streamside sycamores, 10–30 feet up in saguaros. May use same nest for many years. **Eggs:** 3, sometimes 2–4, rarely 1–5. White. Incubation is by female only, about 24 days; male brings food to female during incubation. **Young:** Female remains with young most of the time at first, while male brings food for female and young. After about 2 weeks, female hunts for food also. Young leave nest at about 27–28 days, are cared for by parents for at least several days thereafter.

MIGRATION   North of the Mexican border, strictly a summer resident, arriving early in spring and departing fairly early in fall.

CONSERVATION STATUS   Has become scarce along the lower Colorado River and in southern Texas, probably because of loss of habitat. Still abundant in many parts of southern Arizona.

GENUS *Speotyto*

BURROWING OWL   *Speotyto cunicularia*

Cowboys sometimes called these owls "howdy birds" because they seemed to nod in greeting from the entrances to their burrows in prairie dog towns. Colorful fiction once held that owls, prairie dogs, and rattlesnakes would all live in the same burrow at once. A long-legged owl of open country, often active by day, the Burrowing Owl is popular with humans wherever it occurs, but it has become rare in many areas because of loss of habitat.

HABITAT   *Open grassland, prairies, farmland, airfields.* Favors areas of flat open ground with very short grass or bare soil. Prairie dog towns once furnished much ideal habitat in west, but these are now scarce, and the owls are found on airports, golf courses, vacant lots, industrial parks, other open areas.

FEEDING   **Diet:** *Mostly insects and small mammals.* Diet varies with season and location. In summer in many areas, eats mostly large insects, including grasshoppers, beetles, crickets, moths, caterpillars; also scorpions, centipedes, other arthropods. For much of year, may feed mostly on small mammals (such as voles, mice, ground squirrels), some small birds. May eat many frogs, toads, lizards, and snakes, perhaps especially in Florida. **Behavior:** Hunts mostly at dusk and at night, but does much hunting by day during breeding season. Hunts by a variety of methods, including swooping down from a perch, hovering over fields, or running along ground, then clutching prey in its talons. May catch flying insects in the air.

Burrowing Owl

NESTING   Birds in courtship may repeatedly fly up, hover, and descend. On ground near nest burrow, male feeds female; members of pair nibble at each other's bills and preen each other's feathers. **Nest:** Site is in burrow in ground, in area surrounded by bare soil or short grass. Florida birds usually dig their own burrows, but those in west usually use old burrow left by prairie dogs, ground squirrels, kangaroo rats, armadillos, or other animals. Burrows excavated by the owls may be up to 6–10 feet long, with nest in chamber at end. May line burrow entrance and nest chamber with cow manure, but no real nest built. **Eggs:** Typically 7–10 in west, 4–6 in Florida; can range from 3 to 12. Eggs white, becoming nest-stained. Incubation by female only, 28–30 days; male brings food for female during incubation. **Young:** Female remains with young most of time at first; male brings food and female feeds it to young. After 1–2 weeks, female begins hunting also. Young may leave nest at about 6 weeks or sometimes

earlier, but not capable of strong flight at first. One brood per year, sometimes two in Florida.

MIGRATION   Birds in Florida and parts of southwest may be permanent residents, but northern birds migrate south, some reaching southern Mexico and Central America. Strays sometimes have wandered north from Florida or east from the Great Plains.

CONSERVATION STATUS   Has been declining for many years because of prairie dog and ground squirrel control programs, also habitat loss and accidental mortality (many are killed by cars). Now considered endangered or threatened in some areas.

GENUS *Ciccaba*

MOTTLED OWL   *Ciccaba virgata*

Common in wooded areas throughout the American tropics, this medium-sized owl approaches our area closely in northeastern Mexico. A single stray was once found as a road kill in southern Texas. A live Mottled Owl could turn up sometime in woods along the Rio Grande.

WOOD OWLS — GENUS *Strix*

These are medium-sized to large owls with a round-headed look, lacking the "ear" tufts of many owls. All have hooting calls with a rich tone. Unlike many owls that thrive in open country, they are mostly found deep in the forest.

SPOTTED OWL   *Strix occidentalis*

Because it requires old-growth forest, this owl has become a center of fierce controversy between conservationists and the logging industry in the west. The owl itself seems anything but fierce: it has a gentle look, and it preys mostly on small mammals inside the forest. Its deep hooting calls carry far on still nights, especially in southwestern canyons where they may echo for more than a mile. Found on their daytime roosts, Spotted Owls may allow close approach.

Spotted Owl

HABITAT   *Mature old-growth forests, conifers, wooded canyons.* Along Pacific seaboard, mainly in undisturbed old-growth timber, including Douglas-fir and redwoods. In southwest, generally in forested mountains and canyons, especially where tall trees grow close to rocky cliffs.

FEEDING   **Diet:** *Mostly small mammals.* Specializes on small forest mammals, including woodrats, deer mice, voles, red tree mice (*Phenacomys*), small rabbits, bats. Also takes some small birds, reptiles, large insects. **Behavior:** Hunts mostly at night, but also by day while nesting. Hunts mostly by watching from a perch, then swooping out to capture prey in talons. Prey is taken from the ground and out of trees, and bats may be captured in the air.

NESTING   Male defends nesting territory by calling at dusk and at night. Pairs typically use same nest site for life, but often do not nest every year. **Nest:** Chooses a sheltered site inside

large hollow tree in deep forest, in cave or crevice in cliff, sometimes in old stick nest of hawk or other large bird. No nest built, makes simple scrape in debris in bottom of site. **Eggs:** 2, sometimes 1–3, rarely 4. Whitish. Incubation is by female only, 28–32 days. Male feeds female during incubation. **Young:** Female remains with young at first; male brings food for female and young. After about 2 weeks, female hunts also. If humans approach nest, adults perch nearby but make no active defense. Young leave nest at about 5 weeks, are tended and fed by parents for some time thereafter.

MIGRATION   A permanent resident in many areas, but some mountain populations move to lower elevations for the winter.

CONSERVATION STATUS   Endangered in Pacific Northwest, possibly threatened in southwest. Requires undisturbed habitat and old-growth forest, does poorly in second-growth.

BARRED OWL   *Strix varia*

The rich baritone hooting of the Barred Owl is a characteristic sound in southern swamps, where members of a pair often will call back and forth to each other. Although the bird is mostly active at night, it will also call and even hunt in the daytime. Only a little smaller than the Great Horned Owl, the Barred Owl is markedly less aggressive, and competition with its tough cousin may keep the Barred out of more open woods.

Barred Owl

HABITAT   *Woodlands, wooded river bottoms, wooded swamps.* Favors mostly dense and thick woods with only scattered clearings, especially in low-lying and swampy areas. Most common in deciduous or mixed woods in southeast, but in north and northwest may be found in mature coniferous trees.

FEEDING   **Diet:** *Mostly small mammals.* Eats many mice and other small rodents, also squirrels (including flying squirrels), rabbits, opossums, shrews, other small mammals. Also eats various birds, frogs, salamanders, snakes, lizards, some insects. May take aquatic creatures such as crayfish, crabs, fish. **Behavior:** Hunts by night or day, perhaps most at dawn and dusk. Seeks prey by watching from perch, also by flying low through forest; may hover before dropping to clutch prey in talons.

NESTING   Courtship involves both male and female bobbing and bowing heads, raising wings, and calling while perched close together. Male may feed female in courtship. Members of pair often call in duet. **Nest:** Site is in large natural hollow in tree, broken-off snag, or on old nest of hawk, crow, or squirrel. Rarely nests on ground. In east, often uses old Red-shouldered Hawk nest; hawk and owl may use same nest in alternate years. **Eggs:** 2–3, rarely 4. White. Incubation is mostly or entirely by female, about 28–33 days; male brings food to incubating female. **Young:** Female may remain with young much of time at first, while male hunts and brings back food for her and for young. Age of young at first flight about 6 weeks.

MIGRATION   Permanent resident throughout its range, although individuals may wander away from nesting habitat in winter.

CONSERVATION STATUS   Still widespread and common, but may have declined in parts of south with loss of swamp habitat. In recent decades, has expanded range in northwest, possibly competing there with Spotted Owl.

GREAT GRAY OWL   *Strix nebulosa*

A big nightbird, haunting woods of the far north and certain high mountains of the west. Its great size is partly illusion: it has very thick fluffy plumage, and its body size is smaller than it would appear, so it preys mostly on tiny rodents. When there is a population crash of voles and other rodents in the boreal forest, numbers of Great Gray Owls may drift into the northeast, causing excitement among birders.

HABITAT   *Dense conifer forests, adjacent meadows, bogs.* Generally favors country with mix of dense forest for nesting and roosting and open areas for hunting. In the north, mostly around bogs, clearings, and burns in extensive coniferous woods; in the west, mostly around meadows in mountain forest.

FEEDING   **Diet:** *Mostly small mammals.* Feeds mainly on voles in many northern areas; in western United States, pocket gophers may be main prey. Also eats mice, shrews, squirrels, weasels, small birds, rarely frogs. **Behavior:** May hunt by day or night. In summer, daytime feeding is usually near dawn or dusk. Usually hunts by listening and watching from a perch, swooping down when it locates prey; sometimes hunts by flying low over open areas. Can locate prey by sound, and will plunge into snow to catch rodents more than a foot below the surface.

NESTING   In courtship, male may feed female; members of pair preen each other's feathers. **Nest:** Usually uses old abandoned nest of other large bird, such as goshawk, raven, Osprey; sometimes nests

Great Gray Owl

on top of broken-off snag or stump, rarely on the ground. Site usually 10–50 feet above ground. A pair may reuse the same nest for several years. **Eggs:** 2–5. White. At times, may lay more eggs in years when food is abundant. Incubation is by female only, 28–36 days. Male brings food to incubating female on nest. **Young:** Female broods young for first 2–3 weeks. Male brings food to nest, female feeds it to young. Young may climb out of nest and perch in nest tree or nearby trees after 3–4 weeks, are able to fly 1–2 weeks later. In some areas, adult female departs after young fledge, while male remains with them and feeds them for up to 3 months.

MIGRATION   No regular migration, but nomadic. Large numbers may move south or southeast in some winters in eastern Canada and extreme northeastern United States; this is apparently in response to a sudden drop in rodent populations.

CONSERVATION STATUS   Much of range is remote from impact of human activities. In southern parts of range, has probably declined because of habitat loss and disturbance.

"EARED" OWLS — GENUS *Asio*

The "ear" tufts of the six owls in this genus may be long or short. Our two species live in different habitats and have different patterns, but they can look surprisingly similar in flight, when they flap along with buoyant wingbeats. Less vocal than many owls, they are not often heard outside the nesting season.

LONG-EARED OWL   *Asio otus*

This medium-sized owl is widespread but not particularly well known in North America. It seems to call less often or less conspicuously than many of our other owls, so it may be overlooked in some areas where it nests. In winter, groups of a dozen or more may sometimes be found roosting together in groves of conifers, willows, mesquites, or other trees.

HABITAT   *Woodlands, conifer groves.* Favored habitat includes dense trees for nesting and roosting, open country for hunting. Inhabits a wide variety of such settings, including forest with extensive meadows, groves of conifers or deciduous trees in prairie country, streamside groves in desert. Generally avoids unbroken forest.

FEEDING   **Diet:** *Mostly small mammals.* Usually feeds heavily on common local rodents. Depending on region, may be mostly voles, deer mice, kangaroo rats, pocket gophers, etc. Also known to eat small birds, shrews, bats, lizards, snakes, other small creatures. **Behavior:** Hunts mostly at night, sometimes before dusk, especially when feeding young. Forages over fields or in open woods, flying back and forth a few feet above the ground. Locates prey by sound or by sight, then swoops down to capture it with talons.

NESTING   Early in breeding season, male performs aerial display, flying in zigzags around nesting area with deep wingbeats and glides, occasionally clapping wings together loudly below body. **Nest:** Site is usually in tree, 4–30 feet above ground, usually at about midlevel in tree; sometimes in giant cactus or on cliff ledge. No nest built; uses abandoned nest built by other birds, such as crows, ravens, magpies, various hawks. **Eggs:** 2–10, usually 4–6. White. Incubation is by female only, usually 26–28 days. Male brings food for female during incubation period. **Young:** Female remains with young almost continuously for first 2 weeks, while male brings food for female and young. Later, female also hunts. Young climb out of nest onto nearby branches after about 3 weeks, can make short flights at about 5 weeks. Adult male feeds young until they are 10–11 weeks old, when they disperse from area.

Long-eared Owl

MIGRATION   Some withdrawal in winter from northern part of breeding range, and some movement south into southeastern United States and Mexico, but species is found year-round in many regions. May be nomadic at times, moving about in response to changing food supplies.

CONSERVATION STATUS   Status not well known; local numbers rise and fall, but some surveys and migration counts suggest that overall population in North America is declining. Loss of habitat may be part of cause.

SHORT-EARED OWL   *Asio flammeus*

Easier to see than most owls, the Short-ear lives in open terrain, such as prairies and marshes. It is often active during daylight, especially in the evening. When hunting it flies low over the fields, with buoyant, floppy wingbeats, looking rather like a giant moth. Aside from its North American range, it also nests in South America and Eurasia and on many oceanic islands, including Hawaii.

HABITAT   *Prairies, marshes, dunes, tundra.* Found in open country that supports high numbers of small rodents. Nests most commonly on tundra, inland and coastal prairies, extensive marshes, farmland. In winter also found in stubble fields, small meadows, coastal dunes, shrubby areas.

FEEDING   **Diet:** *Mostly rodents.* Feeds mainly on voles, also other rodents such as lemmings, deer mice, pocket mice. Also eats shrews, rabbits, gophers; rarely bats, muskrats. Eats birds, especially in coastal regions. **Behavior:** Hunts by flying low over the ground, often hovering before dropping on prey. Reportedly finds prey mostly by sound but also by sight. May hunt by day, especially in far north, but mostly active at dawn and dusk.

In courtship, male spirals up into the air, hovers while giving series of short rapid hoots, then dives, clapping wings together loudly under his body. **Nest:** Site is on dry ground, often on a raised hummock or ridge, especially in marshy country. Usually among tall grass or under a shrub. Very rarely above ground. Nest (built by female) is a depression in soil, lined with grass and feathers. **Eggs:** 3–11, usually 6–8. White, becoming stained in nest. Incubation is apparently by female only, 24–37 days. Male brings food to female during incubation period. **Young:** Male brings food for young, gives it to female, who feeds the young (and broods them in cold weather). If nest is threatened, adults may fly at intruder and make loud wing-clap or sit on ground with feathers ruffed up, wings spread and tilted forward to look as large as possible. Young may leave nest on foot after 12–18 days, can fly at 27–36 days.

MIGRATION   Northern birds are strongly migratory. Also somewhat nomadic, concentrating where there are temporary high populations of rodents.

CONSERVATION STATUS   Has disappeared from many southern areas where it formerly nested. Loss of habitat is probably the main cause.

SMALL ROUND-HEADED OWLS — GENUS *Aegolius*

These two northern species (like the other two members of the genus in the American tropics) are forest birds that are often hard to find. Strictly nocturnal in their activities, they feed mostly on rodents.

BOREAL OWL   *Aegolius funereus*

A rather mysterious owl of dense northern woodlands. Except when calling at night in very early spring, it is easily overlooked. Until the 1970s it was not known to breed anywhere south of Canada; recent explorations have shown that it is a resident in

many mountain ranges in the western United States, nesting in forest at the highest elevations. In the northeast, winter invasions sometimes bring a few Boreal Owls south to areas frequented by birders.

HABITAT   *Mixed and conifer forests, muskeg.* Nests mostly in forests where coniferous trees such as spruce or fir are mixed with deciduous trees including aspen or birch. Such habitats are found at low elevations in the north, only in high mountains toward the south. During winter invasions, usually found in groves of conifers.

FEEDING   **Diet:** *Mostly small mammals.* Feeds mostly on voles and mice, also small squirrels, shrews, pocket gophers. Also eats small birds of various kinds, and insects, especially crickets. **Behavior:** Hunts mostly

Boreal Owl

at night (although summer nights are not entirely dark in far north). Hunts by moving through forest from one perch to another, watching for prey, then swooping down to take prey in its talons. Can capture prey hidden under snow or under dense vegetation because ears are adapted for precise location of sounds.

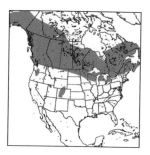

NESTING   Beginning in late winter or early spring, male sings at night to defend territory and attract female. In courtship, male feeds female. Male sings at potential nest holes, and female apparently makes final choice of site. **Nest:** Site is in cavity in tree, usually old woodpecker hole (Northern Flicker or Pileated Woodpecker) or natural hollow, 20–80 feet above ground. Also will use artificial nest boxes (some populations in northern Europe nest mostly in boxes). Usually chooses new nest site each year. **Eggs:** 3–4, sometimes 2–5 (European birds may lay more eggs). White. Incubation is by female only, 26–32 days. **Young:** Female remains with young most of time at first; male brings food, female feeds it to young. After about 3 weeks, female also hunts and brings back food. Young leave nest about 28–36 days after hatching, are fed by parents for at least 2 more weeks.

MIGRATION   Apparently no regular migration, but stages irregular invasions south of nesting range during some winters, probably when food is scarce on breeding grounds.

CONSERVATION STATUS   Northern populations in North America probably face no immediate threats. Status of western mountain populations still not well known.

NORTHERN SAW-WHET OWL   *Aegolius acadicus*

Birders who prowl through conifer groves in winter sometimes find this round-headed little gnome perched there, sitting still as if to avoid notice. Avoiding notice is a task at which this owl often succeeds; it is overlooked in many places where it occurs. Late at night in the breeding season, males give a rhythmic tooting song that

may go on for hours with scarcely a break. The bird was named for this song, which reminded settlers of the sound of a whetstone sharpening a saw.

HABITAT   *Forests, conifers, groves.* Breeds most commonly in coniferous forest of various kinds, including open pine forest, spruce-fir associations, white cedar swamps; also mixed woods such as pine-oak, spruce-poplar, and others. In some places, breeds in oak woodland or in streamside groves in arid country. Winters in habitats with dense cover, especially groves of conifers.

FEEDING   **Diet:** *Mostly small rodents.* Feeds mostly on mice that live in forest, especially deer mice; also many voles. Also eats other mice, shrews, young squirrels, sometimes small birds and large insects.

Northern Saw-whet Owl

Resident race on Queen Charlotte Islands, British Columbia, may eat crustaceans and insects in intertidal zone. **Behavior:** Hunts almost entirely at night, mostly by waiting on low perches and then swooping down on prey. Finds its prey both by sound and by sight.

NESTING   Early in breeding season, male sings incessantly at night to defend territory and attract a mate. **Nest:** Site is in cavity in tree, usually 15–60 feet above ground. Mostly uses abandoned woodpecker holes, especially those of flickers and Pileated Woodpeckers. Will also use artificial nest boxes. Apparently will not use same site two years in a row. **Eggs:** 5–6, sometimes 4–7, rarely 3–9. White. Incubation is by female only, 27–29 days. Female remains in nest almost constantly from time first egg is laid; male brings food to her throughout this time. **Young:** At first, adult male brings all food to nest, female feeds it to young. Female remains with chicks until youngest is about 18 days old; then she may begin to hunt for them also, or may depart. Young leave nest at about 4–5 weeks, remain together near nest and are fed (mostly by male) for at least another 4 weeks. Female may sometimes find another mate and nest a second time in one year.

MIGRATION　　Some remain all year on breeding range, others move south in autumn. Some western mountain birds may move downhill for winter. Migration is relatively early in spring, late in fall. Migrates at night.

CONSERVATION STATUS　　Probably some slight declines in numbers with loss of habitat, but still widespread and fairly common.

NIGHTJARS (Family Caprimulgidae)

The 80 or so species in this family are mostly creatures of night, seldom seen but often heard; some, like the Whip-poor-will, are named for their voices. The nighthawks (which are not at all related to real hawks) are often seen flying high in broad daylight, but most other members of the family are shadowy figures that stay out of sight.

Every nightjar has a very short bill opening into a very wide mouth. When the bill is open, it gapes nearly as wide as the bird's head; the bird uses this big mouth to scoop flying insects out of the air as it flies about. A nightjar typically has large wings and a large tail, making it buoyant and maneuverable in flight, but its legs are very short and its feet small. When perched in a tree, it sits lengthwise on a limb, not across the branch like most birds. Whether it rests on a branch or on the ground, it is camouflaged by its mottled brown plumage.

Nightjars are sometimes seen sitting on roads at night, when their eyes reflect the glare of headlights with glowing orange or pink eyeshine. The road-sitting habit is indicated in the Spanish name for the family, *tapacaminos*.

In English, these birds are sometimes called "goatsuckers," a bizarre term also reflected in the scientific name of the family (Caprimulgidae). An ancient myth, going back at least to the third century B.C. in Greece, claimed that these birds milked goats; the idea probably got started because people saw nightjars flying low in pastures at dusk.

Feeding　　All nightjars feed mainly on insects, especially large and common types likely to be flying at night, such as moths and beetles. Some larger species occasionally catch small birds, perhaps mostly songbirds that are migrating at night.

Birds that feed on flying insects have two general strategies for foraging: either they fly about continuously, watching for insects and then intercepting them, or they wait on a perch and then sally out when an insect flies past. Nightjars may use one method or the other, or both, depending on the species. Many members of the family are reported to swallow small rocks on occasion, perhaps to help with the grinding up of beetles and other hard-shelled insects in the gizzard.

Nesting　　Nest sites for nightjars are usually on the ground, although nighthawks in some areas often nest on gravel roofs. Typically no nest at all is built, the female simply laying her eggs on the flat ground; sometimes she may make a slight scrape in the leaf litter or soil. The normal clutch for most species is two eggs, usually white with some darker mottling. Incubation is by the female alone or by both parents. In most species, apparently, both parents help to feed the young.

Displays　　Most nightjars advertise their claims to nesting territory mainly by calling loudly and repeatedly at night. A few species also have flight displays, perhaps used both in territorial defense and in courtship. Our Common Nighthawk, with its "booming" power dives, provides one example. Other flight displays are performed by tropical species that have special adornments shown off in flight, such as Lyre-tailed

Nightjar in South America or Pennant-winged Nightjar in Africa. Males of some species also perform courtship displays on the ground, strutting about on their short legs, posturing and head-bobbing.

If disturbed at the nest, adults of some species will put on a distraction display, feigning injury and fluttering away as if to lure predators away from the nest.

NIGHTHAWKS — GENUS *Chordeiles*

Far less secretive and less nocturnal than most family members, nighthawks are often seen flying high in the open sky in daylight, especially near dawn and dusk but also sometimes at noon. They do not call as loudly or persistently as most nightjars, but voice is the best way to tell the various kinds apart, because they look very similar.

LESSER NIGHTHAWK   *Chordeiles acutipennis*

A denizen of the arid southwest, the Lesser Nighthawk flies low over deserts and grasslands at dusk, capturing insects in flight. Very similar to the more widespread Common Nighthawk, it is a much quieter bird, without the sharp calls and "booming" display flights of its larger cousin. Only occasionally does one hear the odd whinnying and trilling calls of the Lesser.

Lesser Nighthawk

HABITAT   *Arid scrub, dry grassland, desert washes.* Found in open arid habitats including desert, grassland, brushy country. Where it overlaps locally with Common Nighthawk in southwest, Lesser is more common at lower elevations and in drier country.

FEEDING   **Diet:** *Insects.* Feeds mainly on flying insects, including beetles, moths, grasshoppers, flies, and many others. Will feed heavily on swarms of winged ants. **Behavior:** Forages most actively near dusk; also at night and sometimes by day. Forages mostly in flight, usually flying fairly low, scooping up flying insects in its wide mouth. Also may feed by sitting on the ground at night and fluttering up short distances to catch flying insects as they pass. Will feed around bright lights at night, taking the insects attracted there.

NESTING   In courtship, male flies about with stiff wingbeats, following female, his white throat puffed out conspicuously as he gives trilling and whinnying calls. **Nest:** Site is on ground, sometimes in shade of small shrub but often on fully exposed open spot. Sometimes on roof of building. No nest built, eggs laid on bare dirt or gravel. **Eggs:** 2. White to pale gray, finely dotted with gray, brown, and lavender. Incubation is mostly or entirely by female, about 18–19 days. **Young:** Both parents feed young, by regurgitating insects. If approached, adults put on "broken-wing" act to lure intruders away; in case of disturbance, young often move to new spot, able to crawl over ground with surprising speed. Age of young at first flight probably about 3 weeks.

MIGRATION   Some northern breeders migrate as far as Colombia, others remain north to central Mexico. In southwestern United States, lingers late in fall and returns early in spring; a few may spend the winter. May become torpid in cool weather.

CONSERVATION STATUS   Numbers seem to be doing well overall in southwestern United States.

COMMON NIGHTHAWK *Chordeiles minor*

This widespread and familiar bird may hunt by day or night, catching flying insects high in the air. Its bounding, erratic flight and angular wings make it unmistakable except in the southwest and in Florida, where two other types of nighthawks occur. Originally nesting on open ground, Common Nighthawks have learned to nest on flat gravel roofs; their nasal calls and "booming" display dives may be heard over many cities.

Common Nighthawk

HABITAT *Open country to mountains; open pine woods; often seen in the air over cities, towns.* Inhabits any kind of open or semi-open terrain, including clearings in deciduous or coniferous forest, prairie country, farmland, suburban areas, city centers.

FEEDING **Diet:** *Insects.* Feeds mostly on flying insects, including beetles, moths, grasshoppers, flies, mosquitoes, and many others. Will feed heavily on swarms of winged ants. **Behavior:** May forage most actively near dawn and dusk; also during day and at night, perhaps especially on moonlit nights. Will feed around bright lights at night, taking the insects attracted there. Forages mostly in flight, scooping up flying insects in its wide gaping mouth. May rarely take insects from the ground.

NESTING In male's courtship display flight, his wingbeats become even more stiff and choppy as he circles and hovers high in air, calling repeatedly; then he goes into a steep dive, with a rushing or "booming" sound made by air passing through wing feathers at bottom of dive. Landing near female, he spreads tail, rocks back and forth, and calls. **Nest:** Site is on ground on bare open soil, often in sandy place; also on gravel roof, sometimes on top of stump or other raised object. No nest built, eggs laid on flat surface. **Eggs:** 2, rarely 1–3. Whitish to pale buff or gray, heavily dotted with gray and brown. Incubation is mostly by female, about 19 days. Incubating bird may shift position during day so that sun is always at her back. **Young:** Both parents care for young, feeding them regurgitated insects. Age of young at first flight about 21 days.

MIGRATION A long-distance migrant, wintering mostly in South America. Often migrates in flocks, sometimes numbering in the hundreds.

CONSERVATION STATUS Apparently declining in numbers in several parts of North America. Reasons for this decline not well known. May be affected by pesticides, also by changes in land use.

ANTILLEAN NIGHTHAWK *Chordeiles gundlachii*

A common nesting bird on islands in the Caribbean, this nighthawk enters our area only in southern Florida. When it was first discovered there in 1941, it was considered only a race of the Common Nighthawk, as it looks very similar; however, its voice is different. Where Antillean and Common nighthawks meet on the upper Florida Keys, they appear to compete and to defend territories against each other.

In Florida this species is concentrated around undeveloped open ground, such as airports, vacant lots, fields. In West Indies, inhabits semi-open terrain including open woods, fields, farmland. Its feeding behavior is much like that of the Common Nighthawk. Nesting behavior is also similar, but the "booming" noise in flight display is thinner and quieter. Its eggs are often more heavily and darkly marked than those of Common Nighthawk.

Antillean Nighthawk is strictly a summer resident in Florida, present late April to September. Its winter range is not well known, probably northern South America. A rare spring and summer stray north of southernmost Florida. The species probably increased in Florida through the 1970s as land was cleared on the Keys, now declining again as land is developed. May be losing ground to Common Nighthawks spreading south.

GENUS *Nyctidromus*

PAURAQUE   *Nyctidromus albicollis*

Pauraque

After sunset, in the brushy woods of southern Texas, a hoarse wheezing whistle is heard from here and there in the undergrowth. As dusk settles in, a silhouetted bird flutters and glides silently through the clearings. This is the Pauraque, a common tropical nightjar. If disturbed by day at its resting place in dense thickets, it flutters away on a zigzag course, showing white flashes in the wings and tail.

HABITAT   *Woodlands, brush, river thickets.* In Texas, most common in native woodland, dense thickets, and areas of tall brush, foraging along edges and over adjacent open fields. In American tropics, widespread in semi-open habitats, mainly in lowlands.

FEEDING   **Diet:** *Insects.* Diet not known in detail, but feeds mostly on night-flying insects, especially beetles, also moths and probably many others. **Behavior:** Seems to forage most actively at dusk and dawn, also on moonlit nights. Forages by perching on branch or on ground and flying out to catch passing insects; also sometimes forages in continuous flight along edges of woods. May sometimes pick up insects on ground; has longer legs than most nightjars (still quite short) and can run with surprising speed for short distances.

NESTING   Breeding behavior is not well known. Males call at night, probably to defend territory and attract a mate. Courtship displays may involve birds facing each other on ground, bobbing heads and fluttering. **Nest:** Site is on ground, usually in fairly open woods, often placed at the base of a shrub. No nest built, eggs laid on dead leaves lying on ground. **Eggs:** 2. Buff to pale pink, finely marked with reddish brown. Incubation is by both parents, incubation period not well known. **Young:** Cared for and fed by both parents. Adults feed young by regurgitation, placing bill into widely opened mouth of young. If site is disturbed, adult may call to young with low throaty calls, young respond by hopping rapidly along ground toward parent. Age of young at first flight not well known.

MIGRATION   Permanent resident, but less conspicuous in winter.

CONSERVATION STATUS   Some evidence of declines where habitat is cleared, but still locally common in southern Texas. Widespread and abundant in American tropics.

GENUS *Phalaenoptilus*

COMMON POORWILL   *Phalaenoptilus nuttallii*

In dry hills of the west, a soft whistled *poor-will* carries across the slopes on moonlit nights. Drivers may spot the Poorwill itself sitting on a dirt road, its eyes reflecting orange in the headlights, before it flits off into the darkness. This species is famous as the first known "hibernating" bird: in cool weather it may enter a torpid state, with lowered body temperature, heartbeat, and rate of breathing, for days or even weeks at a time. Science discovered this in the 1940s, but apparently the Hopi people knew it long before that; their name for the Poorwill means "the sleeping one."

HABITAT — *Dry hills, open brush.* Inhabits various kinds of open dry terrain at low elevations in the west, including rocky mesas with scattered shrubs, washes and hills in Sonoran desert, scrubby areas in dry open pine forest. May be found in open grassland, but usually only around rocky outcrops.

FEEDING — **Diet:** *Insects.* Feeds mainly on night-flying insects, especially moths and beetles, also some grasshoppers, flies, and others. Insects up to one and a half inches long can be swallowed whole. **Behavior:** Forages mostly by sitting on the ground or on a low perch and making short upward flights to catch passing insects. Occasionally forages in longer, extended flights. Does most foraging at dawn and dusk and on moonlit nights, when sky is light enough for the bird to spot flying insects by silhouette. Sometimes picks up insects (and possibly spiders) from ground.

NESTING — Male calls at night in spring to defend territory and attract a mate, sitting on ground or low perch and calling *poor-will* repeatedly. (Females may also give this call at times.) **Nest:** Site is on ground, on bare open soil, rock, or gravel, sometimes on leaves or pine needles. Often shaded by a shrub or overhanging rock and sometimes in secluded rock shelter. No nest built, though bird may make slight scrape in soil. Same site may be used more than one year. **Eggs:** 2.

Common Poorwill

White, sometimes with a few spots. Incubation is by both parents, 20–21 days. **Young:** Both parents feed young, by regurgitating insects. If nest site is disturbed, adults can move either the eggs or the young to new site. Downy young can move on their own by hopping or somersaulting across the ground. Age of young at first flight 20–23 days. May raise two broods per year; female may be incubating eggs of second clutch while male is still feeding first brood.

MIGRATION — Departs from northern part of breeding range in fall; migratory route and winter range of these birds not well known. In southwest, may be present all year, remaining torpid in cooler weather.

CONSERVATION STATUS — Still widespread, and numbers probably stable. In some areas, overgrazing or logging may improve habitat for this species.

TYPICAL NIGHTJARS — GENUS *Caprimulgus*

The most important genus of nightjars, occurring on six continents and containing well over half the species in the family. Unlike the nighthawks, these birds are probably all strictly nocturnal, with loud and distinctive voices.

CHUCK-WILL'S-WIDOW   *Caprimulgus carolinensis*

The rich, throaty chant of the Chuck-will's-widow, singing its name, echoes through southern woodlands on summer nights. By day, the bird is seldom detected as it rests on horizontal tree limbs or on the ground, where its cryptic dead-leaf pattern offers good camouflage. If disturbed, it flaps away on silent wings, sometimes giving low clucking calls in protest.

HABITAT *Pine forests, river woodlands, groves.* Breeds in shady southern woodlands of various types, including open pine forest, oak woodland, edges of swamps. Winter habitats not well known but include subtropical woods and lowland rain forest in tropics.

FEEDING **Diet:** *Mostly large insects.* Feeds on large night-flying insects, especially beetles and moths, also members of various other insect orders. Also occasionally takes small birds, including warblers, sparrows, hummingbirds. **Behavior:** Forages at night, perhaps most actively near dusk and dawn and on moonlit nights. Forages by flying out from a perch high in a tree or from the ground to catch flying insects; also forages in continuous flight along the edges of woods. Captures food in its wide, gaping mouth; insects and small birds are swallowed whole.

NESTING In courtship during daytime, male struts or sidles up to female with his body plumage puffed up, wings drooping, and tail spread; moves with jerky actions, and calls. **Nest:** Site is on ground, in rather open area within shady understory of forest. Same site may be used more than one year. No nest built, eggs laid on flat ground on leaves or pine needles. **Eggs:** 2. Creamy white, usually blotched with brown and gray. Incubation is probably by female only, about 3 weeks. If the nest is disturbed, the adult may move the eggs some distance away (several feet or more). **Young:** Apparently cared for by female alone. Female broods young and shelters them during the day; feeds them by regurgitating insects. Age of young at first flight 17 days or more.

MIGRATION Some winter in southern Florida, but most migrate well south, wintering in the West Indies, Mexico, Central America, and northern South America.

CONSERVATION STATUS Thought to be declining in parts of range, possibly because of loss of habitat.

Chuck-will's-widow

BUFF-COLLARED NIGHTJAR *Caprimulgus ridgwayi*

Buff-collared Nightjar

Birders hearing it for the first time may have trouble believing that the Buff-collared Nightjar is a relative of the Whip-poor-will. Staccato, unbirdlike, the call sounds like the voice of an insect—a very large insect, perhaps, audible up to half a mile away over the dry hills at night. First found north of the Mexican border in 1958, this bird now spends the summer in several arid canyons in southern Arizona and southwestern New Mexico.

HABITAT *Desert canyons, rocky slopes.* In United States, found mostly around 4,000 feet elevation, in rocky canyons that have trees or dense brush along drainage and sparse growth on hillsides. In Mexico, found in various kinds of dry tropical forest and brush.

FEEDING **Diet:** *Insects.* Diet not known in detail, but undoubtedly includes large night-flying insects such as beetles and moths. **Behavior:** Apparently forages at dusk and dawn, also on moonlit nights. Does much of its foraging by sitting on exposed perch at top of shrub or small tree and flying out to catch passing insects in midair. Also makes long flights of a minute or two, patrolling for insects. May also forage by flying up from the ground.

NESTING   Nesting behavior is poorly known; only a few nests have been found, mostly in Mexico. Male calls at night, most actively at dusk and dawn and when moon is up. **Nest:** Site is on ground, usually in the shade of a shrub and often surrounded by dense thickets. No nest built, eggs laid on dead leaves or open soil. **Eggs:** 2, perhaps sometimes 1. Pale buff, heavily marked with spots of lilac and brown. Incubation behavior not well known; in related nightjars, incubation is mostly or entirely by female and lasts about 3 weeks. **Young:** Development of young and age at first flight are not well known. If danger threatens, adult may put on a distraction display, feigning a broken wing to lure intruders away from nest.

MIGRATION   Probably permanent resident over most of its range. In Arizona and New Mexico, apparently arrives mostly in May, remaining through August.

CONSERVATION STATUS   Numbers and range north of Mexican border may be gradually expanding. Still widespread and reasonably common in parts of Mexico.

WHIP-POOR-WILL   *Caprimulgus vociferus*

Often heard but seldom observed, the Whip-poor-will chants its name on summer nights in eastern woods. The song may seem to go on endlessly; a patient listener

once counted 1,088 *whip-poor-wills* given rapidly without a break. By day, the bird sleeps on the forest floor. Whip-poor-wills in the southwestern mountains have a slower and rougher song and may represent a different species.

HABITAT   *Leafy woodlands; in west, pine-oak woods in mountains.* In the east, breeds in rich moist woodlands, either deciduous or mixed; seems to avoid purely coniferous forest. In the southwest, breeds in mountain forest, mostly in pine-oak zone. Winter habitats are also in wooded areas.

FEEDING   **Diet:** *Insects.* Feeds on night-flying insects, especially moths, also beetles, grasshoppers, mosquitoes, many others. **Behavior:** Forages at night, especially near dusk and dawn and on moonlit nights.

Whip-poor-will

Forages by flying out from a perch in a tree or in low continuous flight along the edges of woods and clearings; sometimes by fluttering up from the ground. Captures insects in its wide, gaping mouth and swallows them whole.

NESTING   Nesting activity may be timed so adults are feeding young primarily on nights when moon is more than half full, when moonlight makes foraging easier for them. Male sings at night to defend territory and attract mate. Courtship behavior not well known; male approaches female on ground with much head-bobbing, bowing, and sidling about. **Nest:** Site is on ground, in shady woods but often near the edge of a clearing, on open soil covered with dead leaves. No nest built, eggs laid on flat ground. **Eggs:** 2. Whitish, marked with brown and gray. Incubation is apparently mostly by female, 19–20 days. **Young:** Apparently cared for by both parents. Adults feed young by regurgitating insects. Age of young at first flight about 20 days.

One or two broods per year; female may lay second clutch while male is still caring for young from first brood.

MIGRATION Many spend the winter in southeastern states, in areas where Chuck-will's-widows are resident in summer. Others migrate south to Central America; few occur in the West Indies. Southwestern birds are probably only short-distance migrants.

CONSERVATION STATUS Numbers apparently have decreased over much of the east in recent decades. Reasons for decline not well understood.

JUNGLE NIGHTJAR *Caprimulgus indicus*

This Old World relative of the Whip-poor-will is common in eastern Asia. Despite its name, it is found in many habitats besides jungle—especially in summer, when it reaches northern Japan and eastern Russia. As an overshooting migrant, it has strayed to the western Aleutians.

SWIFTS (Family Apodidae)

The name "swift" is no misnomer. All members of this family are fast fliers, and speeds well above 100 miles per hour have been claimed for several kinds. The roughly 90 species of swifts range over six continents, and many islands as well.

All swifts have streamlined bodies, long narrow wings, and short wide bills. With their mouths open wide, they pursue flying insects as they zoom about in high-speed flight. Their feet are very small (the Latin name of the family, Apodidae, is based on Greek words meaning "without feet"), making them unable to perch on twigs, so they cling to vertical surfaces when not flying.

They are flying most of the time, however. These may be the most aerial of all birds. Swifts feed while flying; drink while flying, by dipping to the surface of ponds; gather nest material while flying, by breaking dead twigs from trees; and some are even thought to be able to sleep while flying. Some types that nest in caves in Asia are thought to be able to use sonar, sending out sharp clicking sounds and using the echoes to navigate in the darkness.

As might be expected of such strong fliers, swifts sometimes appear far outside their normal ranges. Some of the larger swifts may live more than 20 years in the wild.

Feeding Essentially all their food is captured in flight, so swifts feed mainly on a wide variety of flying insects. Usually they seem to spot and pursue specific insects, but where they encounter dense concentrations they may simply zoom through the swarms with their mouths open wide.

Swifts often forage in flocks, and often quite high (typically higher than most swallows, for example). During wet weather they will fly much lower, presumably because the insects are also lower then.

The diets of many swifts are known to include spiders, which may seem odd for birds that forage only in the air. However, young spiders of some types put out long silken threads (or "parachutes") and allow themselves to be wafted aloft by the wind, a practice that helps to disperse the spiders but also raises their odds of becoming bird food. In other cases, spiders and flightless insects may simply be carried aloft by strong updrafts.

Nesting Swifts are notable for choosing nest sites that are hidden or inaccessible or both. As a result, nesting habits of many species around the world remain unknown. Some typical known sites include inside hollow trees, in caves, behind waterfalls, or among hanging palm fronds. Some kinds have adapted to artificial sites such as the insides of chimneys or buildings.

The most common type of swift nest known is a shallow half cup (or half saucer) adhered to a vertical surface. Common nest materials include small twigs, moss, and feathers. These may be cemented together with mud by some swifts, but most species use their own remarkably sticky saliva to hold the nest together and to its vertical support. The fluid of their large salivary glands dries into a hard, translucent substance so strong that some swifts make their nests of nothing but saliva. Bird's-nest soup, a delicacy in parts of Asia, is produced by boiling down the nest of a species officially known as the Edible-nest Swiftlet.

Many swifts may lay only one or two eggs, but clutches of up to seven are recorded for some smaller species. As far as is known, both parents typically help to incubate the eggs and feed the young.

Displays   Courtship displays, like most other activities, may take place in the air. In some species they involve two birds flying close together, one after the other, with wings held high. Actual mating may take place in the air, although at least some species apparently mate only at the nest site. If threatened at the nest, a swift may react by raising both its wings and perhaps by calling harshly.

GENUS *Cypseloides*

BLACK SWIFT   *Cypseloides niger*

Black Swift

The largest swift normally found in North America, uncommon and local in the west. Where it occurs, it may be seen flying very high, gliding and wheeling gracefully in pursuit of flying insects. The Black Swift seems to be limited in range by its very particular choice of nesting sites: it requires shady, sheltered spots on vertical cliffs totally inaccessible to predators; often nests on the damp rock behind waterfalls.

HABITAT   *Open sky over mountain country, coastal cliffs.* Forages widely over any kind of terrain but is still very local in its occurrence, probably limited to regions with suitable nesting sites. Nests on ledges or in crevices in steep cliffs, either along coast or near streams or waterfalls in mountains.

FEEDING   **Diet:** *Flying insects.* Feeds on a wide variety of flying insects, including wasps, flies, mayflies, caddisflies, beetles, leafhoppers, moths, and others, also spiders. At times may feed heavily on emerging swarms of winged adult ants or termites. **Behavior:** Forages only while flying. Flight is rapid and often very high; bird scoops insects out of the air with its wide bill. May forage singly or in small flocks.

NESTING   Courtship apparently involves long aerial chases, and the birds also mate while flying. May nest in small colonies. **Nest:** Site is on ledge sheltered by overhang or in protected crevice on cliff, along rocky coast or in mountainous country. Mountain nest sites are often behind or near waterfalls, in spots where nest is continuously damp from spray. Sites are usually inaccessible. Nest is small saucer of mud, moss, ferns, sometimes lined with fine plant material. Same site may be reused for years, with material added each time. **Eggs:** 1. White, becoming nest-stained. Incubation is by both parents, 24–27 days. **Young:** Both parents feed and care for young bird, which remains in nest until ready to fly (not climbing about like the young of some other swifts). Age at first flight about 45–49 days. Probably just one brood per year.

MIGRATION Summer resident in North America, arriving in late spring, departing in early fall. Winter range of North American birds not well known. Permanent resident populations occur in Mexico, Central America, West Indies.

CONSERVATION STATUS Uncommon and local, but numbers probably stable.

GENUS *Streptoprocne*

WHITE-COLLARED SWIFT *Streptoprocne zonaris*

This big swift is common and widespread in the American tropics, where it is often seen in large, noisy flocks over any kind of terrain. Stray individuals have wandered north to the United States on several occasions, appearing at various points along the Gulf coast and once in California.

SMALL DARK SWIFTS — GENUS *Chaetura*

The nine species in this genus, all found in the Americas, are among the smallest and plainest members of the family. Several kinds that originally built their nests inside hollow trees have adapted to nesting in chimneys or other man-made structures—a habit reflected in the name of the well-known Chimney Swift.

CHIMNEY SWIFT *Chaetura pelagica*

Chimney Swift

The only swift occurring regularly in the east. It once nested in hollow trees, but today it nearly always nests in chimneys or other structures. Because large numbers can be captured and banded in such situations, it has been studied much more thoroughly than other North American swifts. In late summer, hundreds or even thousands of individuals may roost in one large chimney, gathering in spectacular flocks overhead near dusk.

HABITAT *Open sky, especially over cities and towns.* Forages in the sky over any kind of terrain, wherever there are flying insects. Now most common over towns and cities; within its range, few forests remain with hollow trees large enough to serve as nest sites.

FEEDING **Diet:** *Flying insects.* Feeds on a wide variety of insects, including beetles, flies, true bugs, and moths; also spiders. Will concentrate at times on swarming insects, such as emergences of winged adult ants. **Behavior:** Forages only while flying, pursuing insects and scooping them out of the air. Often flies high but will forage very low during wet weather. Typically seen foraging in small flocks.

NESTING Courtship involves aerial displays; in one display, two birds fly close together, one following the other, both gliding with wings held up in V. Often nests in colonies. Breeding pair is often assisted by an extra adult "helper." **Nest:** Site is inside chimney or similar hollow tower; usually well down from opening, in well-shaded area. Originally

nested (and sometimes still does) inside large hollow trees. Nest (built by both sexes) is shaped like half a saucer, made of twigs glued together with the birds' saliva. Adults break off short dead twigs from trees while zooming past in flight. **Eggs:** 4–5, sometimes 3–6. White. Incubation is by both parents, 19–21 days. **Young:** Both parents feed young, by regurgitating insects. Young may climb out of nest after about 20 days, creeping up vertical walls. Age of young at first flight about 28–30 days.

MIGRATION   Migrates in flocks, apparently by day. A long-distance migrant, wintering in eastern Peru and perhaps elsewhere in the Amazon Basin of South America.

CONSERVATION STATUS   Probably increased greatly after adapting to nesting in chimneys, much more readily available than hollow trees. In recent decades has declined in some areas, but still widespread and common.

VAUX'S SWIFT   *Chaetura vauxi*

A small, dark aerialist of the west, often overlooked as it flies high over northwestern forests or low over lakes and rivers with stiff, rapid wingbeats. Similar to the well-known Chimney Swift of the east, but only occasionally nests in chimneys. Because of its reliance on large hollow trees for nest sites, it has become scarce as old-growth forest in the northwest has been destroyed.

HABITAT   *Open sky over woodlands, lakes, and rivers.* Often feeds low over water, especially in morning or evening or during unsettled weather. Nests in coniferous and mixed forest, mainly old-growth forest, including redwood, Douglas-fir, grand fir. Resident forms in American tropics in other habitats; in Yucatan, may nest in wells around Mayan ruins.

FEEDING   **Diet:** *Mostly flying insects.* Feeds on a wide variety of flying insects, including flies, winged ants, bees, moths, aphids, beetles, mayflies, true bugs. Also some spiders and flightless insects. **Behavior:** Forages in rapid flight, pursuing flying insects and capturing them in wide bill. May forage singly or in flocks. Spiders and sedentary insects in diet may have been captured after being carried high by air currents or taken from trees by swifts while hovering briefly in flight.

NESTING   May nest in solitary pairs or in colonies. Courtship involves much aerial chasing, sometimes gliding with wings up in sharp V. **Nest:** Site is usually inside hollow tree, reached via broken-off top or woodpecker hole. Sometimes nests in chimneys. Both sexes gather nest material by breaking off small twigs from trees while flying. Twigs are carried in mouth to nest site, cemented into place with sticky saliva. Nest is a shallow half cup glued to inside wall of tree. **Eggs:** 6, sometimes 3–7. White. Incubation is by both sexes, 18–19 days. **Young:** Both parents care for and feed young. At some nests, one or two additional adults may help parents incubate eggs and feed nestlings. Young may be brooded during first week after hatching. Feeding visits to nest frequent; average once every 12–18 minutes, perhaps less often as young get older. Young capable of flight at 28–32 days, may return to roost at nest site for several days after fledging. One brood per year.

MIGRATION   Migrates by day. North American breeders move south in fall, probably most to Mexico. Small numbers winter in coastal California, and some may migrate southeast to winter along northern coast of Gulf of Mexico. Populations in southern Mexico, Central America, and Venezuela may be permanent residents.

CONSERVATION STATUS   Populations known to be declining in Oregon and Washington, probably elsewhere. Major threat is loss of nesting sites from cutting of large and mature trees.

WHITE-THROATED NEEDLETAIL   *Hirundapus caudacutus*

Needletails are big Asian swifts named for fine spines that extend past the tips of the tail feathers (not visible in the field). A strong and incredibly fast flier, this species occasionally overshoots its normal summer range in northeastern Asia, reaching the Aleutian Islands.

EURASIAN SWIFTS — GENUS *Apus*

COMMON SWIFT   *Apus apus*

The most common swift in Europe, where it nests around cities, in holes in buildings and under roof tiles. It also breeds across much of Asia, but not in eastern Siberia; one that appeared once in the Pribilof Islands, Alaska, was quite far outside its normal range.

FORK-TAILED SWIFT   *Apus pacificus*

This big swift is widespread in Asia, and its summer range extends far east in Siberia, where it often occurs around coastal cliffs as well as in mountainous areas. It has strayed to Alaska a number of times, mostly to the Aleutian and Pribilof islands, once as far east as Middleton Island in the Gulf of Alaska.

GENUS *Aeronautes*

WHITE-THROATED SWIFT   *Aeronautes saxatalis*

White-throated Swift

Around rocky cliffs and canyon edges in the west, little groups of these elegant swifts go hurtling past the crags, calling in shrill voices. This species has been claimed to be one of our fastest flying birds, and any observer who has seen them pass at close range will believe it. White-throated Swifts are very wide-ranging, probably foraging in the air many miles from their nesting sites at times.

    HABITAT   *Open sky, cruising widely.* May be seen in the air over virtually any western habitat, wherever there might be flying insects. Breeds in crevices in cliffs, mostly in dry mountains and canyons, locally on sea cliffs.

    FEEDING   **Diet:** *Flying insects.* Feeds on a wide variety of flying insects, including flies, beetles, true bugs, wasps, bees, leafhoppers. May feed heavily on winged adult ants during an emergence of these insects. **Behavior:** Forages only in flight. May forage high or low, depending on weather conditions. Typically seen foraging in flocks.

    NESTING   Many details of nesting remain unknown, partly because nests are so inaccessible. Courtship involves aerial displays; birds also mate while in flight, sometimes joining and then tumbling down together for hundreds of feet. **Nest:** Site is usually in narrow

vertical crevice in high cliff, in very inaccessible place. Sometimes nests in crevices in buildings. Same site may be used for years. Nest is shaped like shallow half saucer; made of feathers, weeds, grasses, glued together and to wall of crevice with the birds' saliva. **Eggs:** 4–5, sometimes 3–6. White, often becoming stained or spotted in the nest. Incubation timing not well known. **Young:** Probably fed by both parents. Young are probably able to climb about inside nesting crevice before old enough to fly. Age at first flight not well known.

MIGRATION   Northern breeders move south in fall; found all year in much of southwest (only swift likely to be seen in North America in winter). During cool winter weather, may become torpid to conserve energy.

CONSERVATION STATUS   Like other swifts, could be affected by insecticides. Currently common and widespread, numbers apparently stable.

GENUS *Tachornis*

ANTILLEAN PALM-SWIFT   *Tachornis phoenicobia*

On several islands in the Caribbean, this small swift is common in the lowlands. It flies low in rapid, twisting flight, and it nests and roosts among the hanging dead fronds in palm trees. In 1972, a pair of Antillean Palm-Swifts stayed for several weeks in Key West, Florida.

HUMMINGBIRDS (Family Trochilidae)

Tiny glittering gems with feathers, hovering at blossoms to sip nectar, hummingbirds seem like creatures of magic. They live only in the Americas, and most of the 300-plus species live in the tropics, where the dazzling beauty of their colors is suggested by their names: Hillstar, Sunbeam, Sapphirewing, Goldenthroat, Blossomcrown, Comet, Sylph, Sunangel.

This family includes the smallest birds in the world (although some of the largest hummingbirds are bigger than sparrows). It also includes some of the most colorful, and some of the most amazing fliers.

Many of the bright iridescent colors of hummingbirds are created more by the structure of the feather than by pigments. The pigment may be brown or gray, but it is overlaid by transparent cells that are structured to reflect only certain colors of light. When there is just the right angle between the observer, the feather, and the light source, a brilliant color becomes visible. This is why some of the bright reds, blues, purples, or greens of hummingbird throats seem to flash on and off as the birds move, turning to dull black in the shade. The green feathers on the backs of many hummingbirds are also iridescent, but they are structured to reflect the color in more directions, so that the green is usually visible.

Hummingbirds can control their position in midair like no other birds — flying backwards, sideways, up or down, as well as hovering in one spot. High-speed films and studies of anatomy reveal their secrets. When hovering, a hummingbird beats its wings very fast (up to 80 times per second), but it moves the wings backward and forward, not up and down, in a motion like a sideways figure eight. The shoulder joint is very flexible; the wing is partly rotated for each sweep, so that the forward edge of the wing always leads. The resulting change in angle means that the wing is pushing down against the air on both the forward and backward strokes — on the backstroke, the upper surface of the wing is actually turned underneath.

With microscopic changes in wing angle, the bird can control its position and motion precisely.

Because it burns energy so fast, a hummingbird could run dangerously low on "fuel" in the course of a single night. At times, especially in cold weather, these birds conserve energy by entering a torpid condition at night, lowering their body temperature and slowing their heartbeat and breathing.

The oldest known hummingbird in the wild lived more than 11 years, but most probably have much shorter life spans.

Feeding   Hummingbirds are uniquely adapted for hovering at flowers to feed on nectar. In North America, all species have long narrow bills and tend to be most attracted to long tubular flowers, especially those that are red, orange, or violet. Many such flowers may have evolved to be pollinated by these birds. Some tropical hummingbirds have strongly curved bills and specialize on feeding at curved tubular flowers, but those in the temperate zone cannot afford to be so specialized.

Hummingbirds will come to feeders filled with sugar-water mixtures, and they also come to other sweet food sources: several kinds have been seen taking the oozing sap at drillings made by sapsuckers. In addition to such sugary items, hummingbirds also eat many tiny insects. They will fly out from a perch to take insects in the air or from foliage, and will take small spiders (or trapped insects) from spider webs.

In between bouts of feeding, hummingbirds usually perch quietly, processing the food they have taken in. Given an unlimited supply of food, some kinds will feed an average of about 15 times per hour, resting in between.

Such rests may be broken to chase away other hummingbirds; these birds are remarkably aggressive. There is a good reason why such behavior would have evolved. A flower will produce only so much nectar per day; if a hummingbird can defend a large patch of flowers, keeping other nectar-eaters away, that patch may provide all the food it needs.

Nesting   The female hummingbird has a simple role in nesting: she does everything. After mating, the male and female go their separate ways. Considering the amount of feeding that a hummingbird must do just to keep itself alive, it seems remarkable that one adult is able to raise young all by herself.

The nest is usually a compact, open cup. Materials include plant down, spider webs, fine grasses, plant fibers, moss, and other soft items, so that the nest has a velvety texture; in many species, the walls of the nest will stretch as the young grow larger. Often the outside of the nest is decorated with pieces of lichen, adding to its camouflage. Typically two white eggs are laid. The female does all incubating and all feeding of the young. Both incubation and raising the young may take longer in cold or wet seasons, when the female must spend more time away from the nest to find food for herself.

In feeding the young, the female inserts her bill deep into the wide open mouth of the nestling and regurgitates food from her crop (an enlarged area of the upper esophagus). In most cases, this food probably consists mostly of tiny insects, perhaps mixed with nectar.

Nesting habits of many tropical hummingbirds are unknown or poorly known. Some build domed nests of moss, some attach their nests to the undersides of hanging fronds, and various other kinds of nests have been found.

Displays   Because male hummingbirds take no part in the actual raising of young, all of their energies in the breeding season are poured into trying to attract females, and many of them have evolved spectacular displays for that purpose. Several of our species perform displays in the air, often flying high and diving at tremendous speed, with distinctive sounds made either by voice or by the vibration of certain feathers.

VIOLET-EARS — GENUS *Colibri*

GREEN VIOLET-EAR *Colibri thalassinus*

In the highlands of the American tropics, from Mexico to Bolivia, this dark hummer is often common in forest clearings and edges. It is apparently somewhat nomadic, moving around among mountain ranges, and some wanderers reach our area. Recorded more than a dozen times in Texas, it has also strayed as far east as North Carolina and has reached Canada twice.

MANGOS — GENUS *Anthracothorax*

GREEN-BREASTED MANGO *Anthracothorax prevostii*

Mangos are rather large hummingbirds with slightly curved bills, living around forest and clearings in tropical lowlands. This species is widespread in the American tropics and ranges as far north as northeastern Mexico. It has wandered north into southern Texas at least twice.

GENUS *Cynanthus*

BROAD-BILLED HUMMINGBIRD *Cynanthus latirostris*

In a very limited area of southern Arizona, this colorful Mexican species is common, even abundant, during the summer. It is mostly a bird of the foothills and streamsides, seldom venturing into the higher mountains. The name "Broad-billed" refers to the fact that the base of the bill is somewhat widened and flattened, a feature not apparent in the field.

Broad-billed Hummingbird

HABITAT   *Desert canyons, streamsides, foothill oak woodlands.* Breeds mostly in semi-open habitats at around 3,000–5,000 feet in Arizona. Favors areas with streamside groves of sycamore or cottonwood and with dense mesquite thickets, or open oak woodlands in lower canyons. In winter may be found along streams in desert country.

FEEDING   See family introduction. Favors red or orange tubular flowers such as bouvardia or desert honeysuckle.

NESTING   Breeding biology is not well known. Male has soft jumbled song, not often heard; seems to defend territory mostly by perching high, watching for intruders and chasing them away. **Nest:** Site is in deciduous shrub or low tree, saddled on horizontal or drooping branch or placed in fork, usually 3–9 feet above the ground. Nest (built by female) is rather loosely made cup of grasses and spider webs, lined with plant down, the outside camouflaged with bits of bark and leaves. Unlike most hummingbird nests, outside usually not decorated with lichens. **Eggs:** 2. White. Incubation is by female only; incubation period not well known, probably about 2 weeks or more. **Young:** Female feeds young. Development of young and age at first flight not well known. Often raises two broods per year.

MIGRATION   Present in southern Arizona mostly March to September. In areas north and west of breeding range (including central Arizona and southern California), very small numbers may be present mainly in fall and winter.

CONSERVATION STATUS   Very common in limited range in United States and in parts of Mexico; no evidence of decline in numbers.

GENUS *Hylocharis*

WHITE-EARED HUMMINGBIRD   *Hylocharis leucotis*

Abundant at times in the high mountain forests of Mexico, this little jewel is an uncommon visitor to the southwestern United States. In southern Arizona canyons where hummingbird feeders are maintained, lone White-ears sometimes show up and remain for weeks at a time. Although the species has been known as a summer visitor to Arizona at least since the 1890s, there are still very few proven records of its actually having nested there.

White-eared Hummingbird

HABITAT   *Pine-oak woods near streams, montane forest.* In Mexico and Central America found mostly in clearings and edges of coniferous forest in higher mountains, as well as pine-oak woods at middle elevations. In the United States, has been seen most often coming to feeders in mountain canyons, in areas dominated by oak, pine, or Douglas-fir.

FEEDING   See family introduction.

NESTING   Has been known to nest only a few times in United States. Where species is common, males gather in loose groups (scattered about 60–100 feet apart) and perch in trees singing short songs to attract females. When female visits, male follows her back to her nesting territory and performs flight display. **Nest:** Site is 5–20 feet above ground in shrub or tree, saddled on twig or placed in fork. Nest (built by female) is cup of plant fibers, moss, pine needles, spider webs, lined with fine plant down. Outside of nest camouflaged with lichens and moss. Female may continue adding to nest after incubation begins. **Eggs:** 2. White. Incubation is by female only, 14–16 days. **Young:** Fed by female. Age of young at first flight about 23–26 days.

MIGRATION   Probably a permanent resident over most of its range. Occurs north of Mexico mostly in summer; has wintered at feeders in Arizona at least once.

CONSERVATION STATUS   Widespread and locally very common south of the United States. Could be vulnerable to major clearing of forest in mountains.

XANTUS'S HUMMINGBIRD   *Hylocharis xantusii*

Related to the White-eared Hummingbird but found only in Baja California, this hummer is the most distinctive of the few Baja specialty birds. A female of this species has occurred once in southern California (Ventura), where it actually nested and laid eggs that did not hatch.

MID-SIZED GENERALISTS — GENUS *Amazilia*

In most North American hummingbirds, males are more brightly colored than females; but in the tropical genus *Amazilia*, the sexes look very similar. Members of this group are widespread and very common in forest and edge habitats in most areas of the American tropics. A few species enter our area only locally near the Mexican border.

BERYLLINE HUMMINGBIRD   *Amazilia beryllina*

Common in the uplands of Mexico, this colorful hummer first appeared in the United States in 1964. Since then it has become almost a regular visitor, with one or two found almost every summer in the mountains of southeastern Arizona, and it has nested there a few times. In canyons near the border it may visit feeders or flowers. While perched in trees, it sometimes gives a soft three-noted call, sounding like a tiny trumpet.

HABITAT   *Mountain forest, canyons.* Arizona occurrences have been mostly at 5,000–7,000 feet in mountains, in open pine-oak forest or among sycamores in shady canyons. In Mexico, occurs widely in foothills and lower slopes of mountains, especially in oak woodland.

FEEDING   See family introduction.

NESTING   Breeding behavior is not well known. In Arizona, has nested during summer rainy season. **Nest:** Site is in deciduous tree or shrub, sometimes coniferous tree. Two Arizona nests were both in sycamores, 17–25 feet above the ground, on horizontal branch or in near-vertical fork of branch. Nest (probably built by female alone) is cup of plant fibers, spider webs, the outside covered with green lichens, sometimes with bits of grass trailing below. **Eggs:** 2. White. Incubation is apparently by female only. Incubation period not well known, probably more than 2 weeks. **Young:** Apparently cared for and fed by the female only. Age of young at first flight about 18–20 days.

MIGRATION   Probably not migratory over most of its range; strays north into United States during summer. In parts of Mexico, may move to lower elevations for the winter.

CONSERVATION STATUS   Common and widespread in Mexico, but may be vulnerable to loss of habitat as lower mountain slopes are cleared.

BUFF-BELLIED HUMMINGBIRD   *Amazilia yucatanensis*

Buff-bellied Hummingbird

Our most common *Amazilia* representative, the Buff-bellied Hummingbird, is the only hummingbird to nest regularly in southern Texas.

HABITAT   *Woods, thickets, citrus groves.* In Texas found mostly in semi-open habitats, such as woodland edges or clearings, areas of brush and scattered trees. Sometimes around citrus groves. A regular resident of suburban neighborhoods, especially those with trees and extensive gardens.

FEEDING   See family introduction. Often visits red tubular flowers such as turk's-cap and red salvia.

NESTING   Breeding behavior not well known. The nesting season in Texas extends at least from April to August. **Nest:** Site is usually in large shrub or small deciduous tree, such as hackberry or Texas ebony, usually low (3–10 feet above ground). Saddled on horizontal or drooping branch or placed in horizontal fork of twig. Nest (probably built by female alone) is cup of plant fibers, fine stems, shreds of bark, and spider webs, lined with plant down.

Outside is decorated with lichens, small flower petals. May refurbish or build on top of old nest. **Eggs:** 2. White. Incubation is probably by female only; incubation period not well known, probably 2 weeks or more. **Young:** Probably cared for and fed by female only. Development of young and age at first flight not well known. May raise 2 broods per year, possibly more.

MIGRATION   In southern Texas, more common in summer, but some remain through winter. A few move north along coast in fall, to winter on upper Texas coast and in Louisiana.

CONSERVATION STATUS   Numbers probably declined in the past with loss of habitat, but current population in United States seems to be stable.

CINNAMON HUMMINGBIRD   *Amazilia rutila*

In parts of western and southern Mexico, this colorful hummer is very common in semi-open country and around woodland edges. It was not recorded definitely in our area until 1992, when one appeared at a hummingbird feeder in southern Arizona; since then there has also been one record in western Texas.

VIOLET-CROWNED HUMMINGBIRD   *Amazilia violiceps*

This good-sized Mexican hummingbird was not found nesting in the United States until 1959. It is now uncommon but regular in summer in a few sites in southeastern Arizona and extreme southwestern New Mexico. In places where flowers are not abundant, the Violet-crown may be discovered flying about or hovering in the shady middle levels of tall trees, catching small insects in flight.

HABITAT   *Sycamore groves in canyons, streamside woods.* In its limited range in the United States, found mostly near groves of tall trees (especially sycamores and cottonwoods) with brushy understory, along flowing streams through the lowlands or lower parts of canyons.

FEEDING   See family introduction.

NESTING   Breeding behavior not well known. Has a squeaky song, heard especially at dawn in breeding season. In Arizona, most nesting is in mid- to late summer. **Nest:** Site is in deciduous tree, especially sycamore, or large shrub; placed on horizontal branch or in forked twig, in open but shaded spot, 4–40 feet above the ground, typically about 20 feet up. Nest (probably built by female alone) is a cup of cottony plant down and other fibers, bound with spider webs, lined with fine plant down. Outside of nest is camouflaged with lichen, small twigs. **Eggs:** 2. White. Incubation probably by female alone; incubation period not well known, probably 2 weeks or more. **Young:** Probably fed by female only. Development of young and age at first flight not well known.

Violet-crowned Hummingbird

MIGRATION   Probably permanent resident over most of its range, but present in United States mostly in summer (a few have been known to winter).

CONSERVATION STATUS   A relative newcomer to United States, where range and numbers seem to be very gradually increasing.

BLUE-THROATED HUMMINGBIRD *Lampornis clemenciae*

The largest hummingbird breeding in the United States. Its normal range north of Mexico is limited to canyons in a few mountains near the border. Where it occurs, it is usually conspicuous: bold and aggressive, it dominates other hummingbirds, chasing them away from its favored flowers or sugar-water feeders. The blue on the male's throat is not easily seen, but the flashy white tail corners are hard to miss as the bird flies swiftly past or hovers in the shadows.

Blue-throated Hummingbird

HABITAT *Wooded streams in lower canyons of mountains.* In its limited range in United States, almost always found near flowing water in shady mountain canyons. Inhabits streamside sycamores, pine-oak woods, coniferous forest.

FEEDING See family introduction. Often feeds heavily on small insects and spiders and can survive dry seasons when few flowers are blooming.

NESTING Especially during breeding season, males perch at midlevels in trees and call with monotonous repeated squeak. **Nest:** Site varies, may be 1–30 feet above ground, but typically well sheltered from above. May be on branch sheltered by overhanging limb, sometimes on exposed root on undercut stream bank. Also often places nest on wire or ledge under eaves of building or bridge. Nest may be added to and reused several times. Nest (built by female) is cup of plant fibers, moss, spider webs. Outer covering of green moss is unique among North American hummer nests. **Eggs:** 2, sometimes 1. White. Incubation by female only, 17–18 days. **Young:** Cared for and fed by female only. Age of young at first flight about 24–29 days. Up to three broods per year.

MIGRATION Probably a permanent resident over most of its Mexican range, but most United States birds depart in fall. Sometimes winters (or attempts to) at feeders in canyons in Arizona.

CONSERVATION STATUS Range in United States may have expanded slightly during 20th century. Vulnerable to loss of habitat in Mexico.

MAGNIFICENT HUMMINGBIRD *Eugenes fulgens*

A big, long-billed hummingbird of forests in the southwestern mountains. Almost as large as the Blue-throated Hummingbird found in the same ranges, the Magnificent is not usually so aggressive or conspicuous, but some individuals are very pugnacious in defending flower patches or feeders, even fighting with the Blue-throat at times. In hovering flight, the wingbeats are almost slow enough for the human eye to see.

HABITAT *Mountain glades, pine-oak woods, canyons.* In range in southwestern United States, usually in mountains at elevations of 5,000–9,000 feet. Inhabits shady canyons with sycamore and maple, open hillsides with pine-oak woodland, coniferous forest of higher mountains. Less restricted to streamsides than Blue-throated Hummingbird.

FEEDING   See family introduction. Does much foraging in woodland away from flowers, watching from a perch and then flying out to catch passing insects. Will also pick insects from foliage or from bark, and will take spiders (and trapped insects) out of spider webs.

NESTING   Breeding behavior and courtship displays not well known. Male sings a squeaky, scratchy song from a favorite perch between bouts of chasing rivals. **Nest:** Site is in tree such as pine or maple, 10–60 feet above the ground, saddled on horizontal branch in rather open part of tree. Nest (built by female only) is a compact cup of plant fibers, moss, spider webs, lined with fine plant down and sometimes feathers, outside camouflaged with bits of lichen. **Eggs:** 2. White. Incuba-

Magnificent Hummingbird

tion is by female only, probably about 16 days. **Young:** Female feeds young. Development of young and age at first flight not well known.

MIGRATION   Summer resident in southwest, probably migrates only a short distance south into Mexico for winter; occasionally winters (or attempts to) at feeders in Arizona canyons. Strays have wandered north of breeding range, even as far north as Minnesota.

CONSERVATION STATUS   Common within its breeding range in United States. May be vulnerable to loss of mountain forest habitat in Mexico and Central America.

STARTHROATS — GENUS *Heliomaster*

PLAIN-CAPPED STARTHROAT   *Heliomaster constantii*

A native of dry forest in Mexico and Central America, this big hummingbird strays northward into Arizona on occasion. Here it usually occurs in lowland areas near streams or in the open lower parts of canyons; most records have been in summer. Despite the evocative name "Starthroat," the throat color is very hard to see without perfect lighting, and the bird usually looks quite dull overall.

GENUS *Calliphlox*

BAHAMA WOODSTAR   *Calliphlox evelynae*

The normal range of this small hummingbird includes only various islands in the Bahamas, but it has wandered several times to southern Florida. It seems to have no regular seasonal pattern, with records scattered through the year, but some of the Florida strays have remained for several weeks at hummingbird feeders.

GENUS *Calothorax*

LUCIFER HUMMINGBIRD   *Calothorax lucifer*

A hummingbird from Mexico's central plateau that enters our area in the Big Bend area of Texas and locally farther west. Adapted to desert regions, it is most often seen feeding at flowering agave stalks on arid hillsides. Although small in body size, it has a relatively long, curved bill and long tail. The tail of the male Lucifer is deeply forked, but this is rarely visible except when he spreads the tail wide during his display flight.

HABITAT *Arid slopes, desert canyons, agaves.* In southwestern United States, mostly on very dry hillsides with scattered ocotillos, agaves, cacti, and thorny shrubs. Also moves into some less arid areas, including dry grassland with scattered oaks.

Lucifer Hummingbird

FEEDING See family introduction. Often visits tubular flowers such as agave, penstemon, and paintbrush.

NESTING Male has unique habit of performing courtship display to female while she is at her nest, during nest-building or egg-laying stage. In display, male shuttles back and forth several times in short flight, with loud rustling noise of wings, then flies high and dives steeply past nest. **Nest:** Site is in open cholla cactus, on stem of ocotillo, or on agave stalk, 2–10 feet above ground. Nest (built by female) a compact cup made of plant fibers, pieces of flowers, leaves, fine stems, spider webs, with outside decorated with leaves or lichens. **Eggs:** 2. White. Incubation is by female only, about 15 days. **Young:** Fed by female. Age of young at first flight about 19–24 days. Female may continue to feed young for 2–3 weeks after they leave nest. Sometimes raises two broods per year, and may build nest and even begin incubating second clutch while still feeding fledglings from first nest.

MIGRATION Birds from southwestern United States and northern Mexico apparently move to south-central Mexico for the winter.

CONSERVATION STATUS Uncommon but possibly increasing in limited range in United States. Status of Mexican populations not well known.

GENUS *Archilochus*

These two close relatives are extremely similar in call notes and in the appearance of the females. They divide up the continent in summer, one in the east, one in the west.

RUBY-THROATED HUMMINGBIRD *Archilochus colubris*

Hundreds of kinds of hummingbirds nest in the American tropics, and more than a dozen in the American west, but east of the Great Plains there is only the Ruby-throat. There it is fairly common in summer in open woods and gardens. Hovering in front of a flower to sip nectar, it beats its wings almost 80 times per second. Impressive migrants despite their small size, some Ruby-throats may travel from southern Canada to Costa Rica.

HABITAT *Gardens, wood edges.* Summers in a variety of semi-open habitats, including open woods, clearings and edges in forest, gardens, city parks. Winters mostly in rather open or dry tropical scrub, not usually in rain forest. Migrants may pause in any habitat with flowers.

FEEDING   See family introduction. Favors red tubular blossoms such as those of trumpet vine, also many other flowers.

NESTING   In courtship display, male flies back and forth in wide U-shaped "pendulum" arc, making whirring sound on each dive; also buzzes back and forth in short passes in front of perched female. Male and female may fly up and down, facing each other. **Nest:** Site is in tree or large shrub (usually deciduous), 5–50 feet above ground, usually 10–20 feet. Placed on horizontal branch or one that slopes down from tree, usually well surrounded by leafy cover. Nest (built by female) is deep cup of plant down and plant fibers, held together with spider webs, the outside camouflaged with lichens and dead leaves. May refurbish and reuse old nest. **Eggs:** 2. White. Incubation is by female only, 11–16 days. **Young:** Female feeds young. Nest stretches as young grow. Age of young at first flight about 20–22 days. Usually 1–2 broods per year, sometimes 3.

Ruby-throated Hummingbird

MIGRATION   Almost all leave North America in fall, wintering from Mexico to Costa Rica or Panama. Some may cross Gulf of Mexico but apparently most go around Gulf, concentrating along Texas coast. In spring, males move north earlier than females.

CONSERVATION STATUS   Thought to have declined in some areas in recent decades, but surveys show no distinct downward trend in numbers.

BLACK-CHINNED HUMMINGBIRD   *Archilochus alexandri*

Over much of the west, this species is widespread in many habitats at low elevations, often coming into suburban gardens and nesting in backyards within its range. Several other western hummers may stay through the winter, at least in small numbers, but the Black-chin is almost entirely absent from the west in winter.

HABITAT   *Semi-arid country, river groves, chaparral, suburbs.* Breeds in many kinds of semi-open country in the lowlands, including streamsides, towns, brushy areas, open woods, oak groves in canyons. In the southwest, avoids most open desert but may be found along dense washes or desert rivers. After breeding, may move to higher elevations in mountains.

FEEDING   See family introduction.

NESTING   In courtship, male performs "pendulum" display, flying back and forth in wide U-shaped arc, making whirring sound on each dive. Also buzzes back and forth in short passes in front of perched female. **Nest:** Site is in tree or shrub (usually deciduous),

Black-chinned Hummingbird

typically 4–8 feet above ground, sometimes lower or higher (up to 30 feet). Placed on horizontal or diagonal branch. Nest (built by female) is deep cup of plant down and plant fibers, held together with spider webs, the outside camouflaged with lichens, dead leaves, and other debris. May build on top of old nest. **Eggs:** 2, sometimes 1–3. White. Incubation is by female only, 13–16 days. **Young:** Female feeds young. Nest

stretches as young grow. Age of young at first flight about 20–21 days. Usually 1–2 broods per year, sometimes 3. Female may begin building second nest while still feeding fledglings from the first.

MIGRATION   Strictly migratory, arriving in spring and leaving in fall, virtually never remaining to winter in western United States. Almost all winter in Mexico. Very small numbers stray east in fall, and a few may winter near Gulf coast.

CONSERVATION STATUS   Widespread and common, and numbers probably stable.

SINGING HUMMINGBIRDS — GENUS *Calypte*

These two species are common in parts of the west and southwest. Unlike most of our hummingbirds, males of both have songs that are often heard during the breeding season, and they have iridescent feathers on top of their heads as well as on their throats.

ANNA'S HUMMINGBIRD   *Calypte anna*

Anna's Hummingbird

This hardy little bird is a permanent resident along our Pacific coast, staying through the winter in many areas where no other hummingbirds are present. More vocal than most hummers, males have a buzzy song, often given while perched. In recent decades it has expanded its range, probably helped along by the flowers and feeders in suburban gardens; it now nests north to British Columbia and east to Arizona.

HABITAT   *Gardens, chaparral, open woods.* Found in a wide variety of habitats within its range, including streamside groves, chaparral, open oak woodland, coastal sage scrub, arid brush, gardens, city parks. Most common in lowlands and lower slopes, but may be found in high mountain meadows in late summer.

FEEDING   See family introduction.

NESTING   May begin nesting in December. In courtship display, male hovers in midair, giving buzzy song, then flies much higher; he then dives steeply and rapidly toward the female, making a loud explosive popping sound at bottom of dive. Also buzzes back and forth in front of perched female in short shuttling flights. **Nest:** Site is variable, usually on branch of tree or shrub, sometimes in vines, on wires, under eaves. Usually 4–25 feet above ground, can be lower or higher. Nest (built by female alone) is cup of plant fibers and spider webs, lined with fine plant down and sometimes feathers, the outside camouflaged with lichens. Rather large for a hummingbird nest. Female may continue building after eggs are laid. **Eggs:** 2, rarely 1–3. White. Incubation is by female only, 14–19 days. **Young:** Fed by female. Age of young at first flight about 18–23 days.

MIGRATION   Southwestern birds perform some east-west migration, many Arizona birds moving west to California in midspring after nesting, returning in late summer. Others are permanent residents. Sometimes wanders far north or east of usual range.

CONSERVATION STATUS   Since the 1950s, has expanded its breeding range both north and east. Very common in much of its range, adapting well to suburban areas.

COSTA'S HUMMINGBIRD *Calypte costae*

The desert might seem like a bad place for a creature that feeds at flowers, but it is the favored habitat of Costa's Hummingbird. In Arizona and California deserts, this species nests during late winter and spring, and most then avoid the hot summer by migrating to coastal California and Baja. The thin, high-pitched whistle of the male is often heard over desert washes in early spring.

HABITAT   *Deserts, washes, mesas, sage scrub, arid hillsides.* Mostly in dry and open habitats having good variety of low plant life, such as washes and streamsides in Sonoran desert, lower parts of dry canyons, coastal sage scrub areas. Rarely moves up into mountain meadows when not breeding.

FEEDING   See family introduction. Feeds on nectar from flowers, including those of desert natives such as agave, chuparosa, desert honeysuckle, fairy-duster.

NESTING   In courtship display, male flies high, then zooms down past perched female and climbs again, making shrill high-pitched whistle during dive; also gives same whistled song while perched. One male may mate with several females. **Nest:** Site is in rather open or sparsely leafed shrub or small tree, sometimes in yucca or cactus, usually 2–8 feet above ground. Placed on horizontal or diagonal branch, usually in open spot with good visibility. Nest (built by female) is open cup of

Costa's Hummingbird

plant fibers, bits of leaves and flowers, feathers, spider webs; usually has a gray look. Female continues to add to nest during incubation period. **Eggs:** 2. White. Incubation is by female only, 15–18 days. **Young:** Female feeds young. Age of young at first flight about 20–23 days.

MIGRATION   Many that nest in deserts in spring migrate west to coast for other seasons. However, where flowers are present all year (as in suburban gardens), increasing numbers of Costa's now remain all year.

CONSERVATION STATUS   Common within its range. Undoubtedly has declined where desert is cleared for development, but in some places has adapted to nesting in suburbs.

GENUS *Stellula*

CALLIOPE HUMMINGBIRD *Stellula calliope*

This is the smallest bird in North America, measuring about 3 inches long and weighing about one-tenth of an ounce. Despite its tiny size, it is able to survive cold summer nights at high elevations in the northern Rockies, and some migrate every year from Canada to southern Mexico. In migration it may be overlooked, often feeding at low flowers and avoiding the aggression of larger hummingbirds.

HABITAT   *Forest glades, canyons, usually in mountains.* Breeds mostly from 4,000 feet up to near treeline. Favors open shrubby areas, especially near streams, and may be most common in second growth several years after fire or logging. Winters mostly in pine-oak woods of mountains in Mexico, and migrants occur both in mountains and in lowlands.

FEEDING See family introduction.

NESTING Male establishes breeding territory, drives away other males. Male has U-shaped courtship flight, rising 30–100 feet and diving steeply with popping and zinging sound at bottom of dive, then rising again. Male hovers before female with throat feathers fully spread. **Nest:** Site is usually in pine or other conifer, sometimes in deciduous shrub. At any height, usually 6–40 feet up, can be 2–70 feet above ground. Usually saddled on twig or branch directly under large overhanging branch or foliage for shelter; site may be used more than one year. May be built on base of old pine cone, making nest look like cone. Nest (built by female alone) is compact cup of plant down, moss, bark fibers, with lichens on outside and held together with spider webs. **Eggs:** 2. White. Incubation is by female only, 15–16 days. **Young:** Fed by female only. Female broods young to warm them between feeding bouts and at night. Age of young at first flight about 18–21 days.

Calliope Hummingbird

MIGRATION Moves northwest in early spring mostly through Pacific lowlands, and moves southeast in very early fall (beginning in July) mostly through Rocky Mountains region. Adult males migrate slightly earlier than females or young in both seasons.

CONSERVATION STATUS Common in its range, numbers probably stable. Could be affected by loss of habitat on breeding or wintering range.

GENUS *Atthis*

BUMBLEBEE HUMMINGBIRD   *Atthis heloisa*

An incredibly tiny bird (even smaller than our Calliope Hummingbird), native to the mountains of Mexico. Well named, it suggests a large insect in flight. A century ago (in 1896), two Bumblebee Hummingbirds reportedly were found in southern Arizona. Some experts doubt this record.

SELASPHORUS HUMMINGBIRDS — GENUS *Selasphorus*

Serious birders in the west become accustomed to using the tongue-twisting name of this group, because many individuals cannot be identified to species in the field — especially females of Rufous and Allen's hummingbirds. The various members of this genus are found from southeastern Alaska to Panama; most are small hummingbirds with some reddish brown in the tail, and many of them seem unnervingly aggressive for their size.

BROAD-TAILED HUMMINGBIRD   *Selasphorus platycercus*

The metallic wing-trill of the male Broad-tailed Hummingbird is a characteristic sound of summer in the mountain west. This sound is often heard as a flying bird zings past unseen. The birds are seen easily enough, however, at masses of flowers

in the high meadows, where they hover and dart around the blossoms, often fighting and chasing each other away from choice patches.

HABITAT   *Mountain meadows and forests.* Breeds mostly in mountains, up to over 10,000 feet elevation. Mostly in rather open forest, especially near streams, including pine-oak and pinyon-juniper woods, and associations of spruce, Douglas-fir, and aspen. Migrants occur in all semi-open habitats of mountains and also make stopovers in lowlands.

FEEDING   See family introduction. Favors red tubular flowers; in winter in Mexico, larger resident hummingbirds may monopolize these favored blooms, and Broad-tails may then feed at less desirable flowers.

Broad-tailed Hummingbird

NESTING   Male defends territory by perching high, scanning for and then chasing intruders. In courtship display, male repeatedly climbs high in air (up to 60 feet) and then dives, with loud wing-trill. **Nest:** Site is in tree, on near-horizontal twig or branch, typically sheltered from above by overhanging branch. Usually 4–20 feet above ground, sometimes higher. Nest (built by female alone) is neatly constructed cup of spider webs and plant down, outer edge covered with lichen, moss, bits of bark. **Eggs:** 2, sometimes 1, very rarely 3. White. Incubation is by female only, 16–19 days. **Young:** Female feeds young. Female sleeps on nest at night until young are 10–12 days old. Nest stretches as young grow. Age of young at first flight about 21–26 days; female feeds them for at least a day after they leave nest.

MIGRATION   Migration is early in both spring and fall, with many moving north in early March, south in early August. Adult males migrate before females and young in both spring and fall. Tends to move north through lowlands, south through mountains.

CONSERVATION STATUS   Common in its range; no indications of overall change in numbers.

RUFOUS HUMMINGBIRD   *Selasphorus rufus*

Although it is one of the smaller members in a family of midgets, this species is notably pugnacious. The male Rufous, glowing like a new copper penny, often defends a patch of flowers in the mountain meadows, vigorously chasing away all intruders (including larger birds). The Rufous also nests farther north than any other hummingbird: up to south-central Alaska. Of the various typically western hummingbirds, this is the one that wanders most often to eastern North America.

HABITAT   *Forest edges, streamsides, mountain meadows.* Breeding habitat includes forest edges and clearings, and brushy second growth within region of northern coast and mountains. Winters mostly in pine-oak woods in Mexico. Migrants occur at all elevations but more commonly in lowlands during spring, in mountain meadows during late summer.

FEEDING   See family introduction. Often visits red tubular flowers such as penstemons, red columbines, paintbrush, scarlet sage, gilia, many others.

NESTING   Male's courtship display flight traces a steep U or vertical oval, climbing high and then diving steeply, with whining and popping sounds at bottom of dive; also buzzes back and forth in front of perched female. Male may mate with several females. **Nest:** Site is usually well concealed in lower part of coniferous

trees, deciduous shrubs, vines. Located 3–30 feet above ground, usually less than 15 feet, although nests may be higher later in season. Old nests may be refurbished and reused. Nest (built by female alone) is compact cup of soft materials, lined with plant down, outside camouflaged with lichens and moss, held together with spider webs. **Eggs:** 2, sometimes 1, perhaps rarely 3–4. White. Incubation by female only, 15–17 days. **Young:** Female feeds young. Age of young at first flight about 21 days.

MIGRATION   Moves northwest in early spring mostly through Pacific lowlands, and moves southeast beginning in late June, mostly through Rocky Mountains region. Adult males migrate slightly earlier than females or young. Some winter regularly in Gulf coast states. Strays occur widely in east.

Rufous Hummingbird

CONSERVATION STATUS   Widespread and abundant, although surveys suggest possibility of slight recent declines.

ALLEN'S HUMMINGBIRD   *Selasphorus sasin*

A close relative of the Rufous Hummingbird, Allen's has a more limited range, nesting mostly in California. This is one of the two common nesting hummingbirds in northern California gardens (Anna's is the other). Females and immatures of Allen's Hummingbird are almost impossible to separate from Rufous females without close examination, so the status of the species in migration is still being worked out by dedicated hummingbird banders.

HABITAT   *Wooded or brushy canyons, parks, gardens, also mountain meadows.* Breeds in a variety of semi-open habitats, including open oak woods, streamside groves, well-wooded suburbs, city parks. Winters mostly in foothill and mountain forest in Mexico. Migrants may occur in high mountain meadows in late summer.

Allen's Hummingbird

FEEDING   See family introduction. Favors red tubular flowers such as penstemon, red monkey-flower, red columbine, paintbrush, scarlet sage; also flowers of other colors, such as tree-tobacco.

NESTING   Male's courtship display flight is in J-shaped pattern: flying high, diving steeply with metallic whine at bottom of dive, then curving up to hover at moderate height; often preceded by back-and-forth pendulum flight in front of female. **Nest:** Site is in tree or shrub, rarely in weed stalks, usually low (but up to 90 feet above ground), on horizontal or diagonal branch. Nest (built by female alone) is neatly constructed cup of green mosses and plant fibers, lined with fine plant down, the outside camouflaged with pieces of lichen, held together with spider webs. May recondition and reuse old nest. **Eggs:** 2. White. Incubation is by female only, 17–22 days. **Young:** Female feeds young. Nest stretches as young birds grow. Age of young at first flight about 22–25 days.

Moves north up Pacific coast in late winter; at least some go south through mountains in late summer. Tends to migrate a little earlier than Rufous Hummingbird. Population on California's Channel Islands and nearby mainland is nonmigratory. May have declined with increasing urbanization of its range, but in many places seems to adapt fairly well to residential areas.

TROGONS (Family Trogonidae)

Trogons are gorgeous birds of the forest, living in a tropical realm that barely touches the United States. Only in Arizona can a diligent searcher expect to find a trogon north of the border.

About 40 species of trogons live in the tropics of Asia, Africa, and the Americas. The apex of trogon beauty is the big Resplendent Quetzal, brilliant emerald and scarlet with a flowing train of feathers two feet long; the Quetzal was sacred to the Mayas and is now the national bird of Guatemala. But even the "ordinary" trogons are striking creatures.

These birds have a distinctive shape, with big heads, short necks, and rather long tails. Seemingly lethargic, trogons will perch for minutes at a time in one spot with a vertical posture, tails pointed straight down. When going from place to place they have an undulating flight, fluttering their wings in quick bursts.

Feeding Insects and small fruits are the main items on the trogons' menu (some species in the Old World tropics may be strictly insect-eaters). Many other birds feed on the same things, but few forage for their food in the same way. A trogon will perch quietly, turning and tilting its head very slowly as it peers about. After spotting a choice berry or an insect sitting on a leaf, the bird will fly out and hover for a few seconds as it plucks the item, and then swoop away to another perch. Trogons have small feet, so hopping about among the branches would be less practical for them than this style of aerial foraging.

Nesting Trogon nests are in enclosed places, often in cavities in trees (natural hollows or old woodpecker holes); some tropical species may hollow out their own cavities inside termite or wasp nests or rotten snags. Little or no nest material is added to the inside of the cavity. Usually two or three eggs are laid, whitish in typical trogons, pale blue in quetzals. Both parents typically share in incubating the eggs and feeding the young.

Displays To defend their nesting territories, trogons seem to rely mainly on voice. In a few kinds of tropical trogons, several males may perch fairly close together and call, perhaps a sort of group display. Quetzals may perform display flights. Among typical trogons, courtship may involve visits to potential nest sites.

GENUS *Trogon*

ELEGANT TROGON *Trogon elegans*

Since the 1890s, the possibility of seeing a trogon has lured birdwatchers to southern Arizona. With its brilliant metallic colors and odd croaking call, the Elegant Trogon brings an exotic touch to the wooded canyons and streamside sycamores where it lives. The observer who finds one may get to watch it at leisure: rather sluggish, the trogon may sit upright on one perch for several minutes.

HABITAT *Mountain forests, pine-oak or sycamore canyons.* In Arizona, breeds in canyons through the pine-oak zone of mountains, almost always where sycamores grow along flowing streams. In Mexico and Central America, lives in canyons and scrubby lowland woods in relatively dry areas, avoiding tall rain forest.

FEEDING **Diet:** *Mostly insects and fruits.* Feeds on a wide variety of insects, especially big ones such as katydids, cicadas, walkingsticks, and large caterpillars. Will also eat small lizards. Also eats many small fruits and berries, such as chokecherry and wild grape, especially in late summer and fall. **Behavior:** See family introduction.

NESTING Male defends nesting territory with repeated calls in spring. In courtship, male leads female to potential nest sites, calling from inside cavity; female enters to indicate acceptance. **Nest:** Site is in cavity in tree. In Arizona, usually in old flicker hole in dead tree or limb, especially in sycamores; 8–50 feet above the ground, typically about 25–26 feet up. Sometimes competes actively for nest sites with other birds, such as Sulphur-bellied Flycatchers. Little or no nest

Elegant Trogon

material added, eggs laid on bottom of cavity or on accumulated debris. **Eggs:** 2, sometimes 3, occasionally 4. Incubation is by both parents, 22–23 days; female incubates at night and at midday, male in early morning and late afternoon. **Young:** Cared for and fed by both parents. Young leave the nest about 20–23 days after hatching but are dependent on their parents for a few more weeks.

MIGRATION In Arizona, most arrive in April and May, depart during September and October. One or two sometimes remain through winter along streams at low elevations. Throughout most of range, a permanent resident. Sometimes strays into Texas from northeastern Mexico.

CONSERVATION STATUS Probably has gradually increased in Arizona during the 20th century; up to 50 pairs now nest there. Vulnerable to disturbance by observers while nesting.

GENUS *Euptilotis*

EARED TROGON *Euptilotis neoxenus*

Long regarded as a rare and elusive specialty of the Mexican mountains, this big trogon stunned birders by appearing north of the border in 1977, with a family group in Arizona's Chiricahua Mountains. Since then it has occurred several more times in Arizona, in at least four ranges, and has been found nesting. Only a distant relative of the Elegant Trogon, this species is more closely related to the quetzals.

HABITAT *Pine forests in mountains.* In Arizona, has been found in several canyons, all with pine-oak forest and other conifers such as Douglas-fir. In Mexico, occurs mostly at elevations of 6,000–10,000 feet in the mountains, in coniferous and pine-oak forest, often near sheer rocky cliffs.

FEEDING **Diet:** *Mostly insects and fruits.* Diet not known in detail. Feeds on a wide variety of insects, especially big ones such as katydids and large caterpillars. Also eats many small fruits and berries, such as those of madrone, especially late summer through

Eared Trogon

winter. **Behavior:** See family introduction. At times may fly up to catch insects in midair.

NESTING Breeding behavior is poorly known. Only a few nests have been observed, including one in Arizona. Breeding activity seems to be concentrated in late summer and early fall. **Nest:** Site is in cavity in tree. Those found so far have been in apparent old flicker holes in large dead or partly dead trees, often growing well up on slopes of canyons. Nest cavities have been 25–70 feet above the ground. **Eggs:** Apparently 2 eggs make up the usual clutch; eggs are pale blue. Incubation is probably by both parents, but details and incubation period not well known. **Young:** Fed by both parents. Adults are very wary around the nest and are easily disturbed by human intruders. Development of young and age at first flight are not well known.

MIGRATION Probably no regular migration anywhere in its range. Has proven itself capable of wandering long distances, however, covering the open stretches of dry lowlands between mountain ranges in Arizona.

CONSERVATION STATUS A recent arrival in United States, still present in extremely low numbers. Rare on native range in Mexico, probably threatened by loss of habitat.

HOOPOES (Family Upupidae)

Nothing else looks like a Hoopoe. Widespread in Europe, Asia, and Africa, this bird (sometimes separated into two species) has no close relatives.

HOOPOE *Upupa epops*

A bizarre and unique Old World bird with a long bill, long fanlike crest (usually lowered), and bold black and white pattern in the wings and tail. It can be surprisingly inconspicuous as it walks about on the ground, probing for insects in the soil or in crevices. For a nest site, it uses a cavity in a tree or a hole in a dirt bank. A single Hoopoe once strayed to western Alaska.

KINGFISHERS (Family Alcedinidae)

Members of this distinctive family have large heads (often crested), large bills, small feet, and usually short tails. Only six species live in the Americas, but in the Old World there are about 80, many of them incredibly colorful. The greatest variety of kingfishers is found in the Australasian region, with 22 species in New Guinea alone. Many kingfishers have loud and raucous voices; the famous Laughing Kookaburra of Australia is a member of this family.

Feeding Kingfishers are named for the habit, shared by many species, of plunging into the water to catch fish. Species in the New World and in Europe feed mostly on fish and other aquatic life, including insects, frogs, tadpoles, crayfish, and others. All of our species forage by perching or hovering above the water and then diving head first to capture their prey in their bills.

In the Old World, the name "fisher" does not always fit. Many species there live far from water, feeding on lizards, insects, rodents, and other dry-land creatures. Like the fishing members of the family, however, they forage mostly by watching from a high perch and then flying down rapidly to capture prey with their bills. There are a few odd exceptions, like the Shovel-billed Kingfisher, which digs in the soil for grubs and earthworms in New Guinea rain forests.

Nesting Apparently all kingfishers nest in holes of some sort. Many of those that feed on fish or other aquatic life make their own nest sites by excavating burrows in dirt banks. In the Old World, many species (especially among those that forage away from water) nest in holes in trees or in holes excavated in termite nests. Most kinds apparently add little or no nest material to the inside of the hole. The white eggs are usually incubated by both parents, and both parents also help to feed the young.

Displays In excitement and in aggressive displays, kingfishers often raise their crest feathers; some also spread their wings and adopt postures that show off their large bills. The early stages of courtship may be marked by aerial chases in some species. Later, in courtship feeding, the male feeds the female.

GENUS *Ceryle*

RINGED KINGFISHER *Ceryle torquata*

Common in the American tropics, the Ringed Kingfisher was considered rare north of Mexico until the 1960s. It is now found commonly along the lower Rio Grande and locally elsewhere in southern Texas. Larger than our familiar Belted Kingfisher, the Ringed usually hunts from higher perches and takes bigger fish. When going from place to place, it flies high, often following the river, giving a measured *tchack.... tchack* call in flight.

HABITAT *Rivers, large streams, ponds; nests in banks.* In Texas, most common along Rio Grande in areas where tall trees and brush border the river; also increasingly on ponds, streams elsewhere in southern part of state. In the tropics, found around almost any body of fresh water in lowlands, also in mangrove swamps on coast.

Ringed Kingfisher

FEEDING **Diet:** *Mostly fish.* Feeds mainly on fish, especially those 2–6 inches long. Also eats some frogs, small snakes, probably other aquatic creatures. **Behavior:** Seeks its food mostly by perching high (usually 15–35 feet up, higher than other kingfishers) and watching the water. When it spots a fish (or other prey) close to the surface, it plunges head first, catching the fish in its bill. Seldom hovers over the water before diving.

NESTING In the tropics, sometimes nests in loose colonies where a large dirt bank is especially favorable for nesting. Such sites are not always near water; sometimes in road cuts or other artificial banks more than a mile from water. Apparently nests only as isolated pairs in United States. **Nest:** Site is in burrow excavated in steep or vertical dirt bank. Both sexes help to dig burrow, which may be 5–8 feet long, with an enlarged nest chamber at the end. Little or no nest material added, but debris may accumulate in chamber. **Eggs:** 4–5, sometimes 3–6. White. Incubation is by both parents; incubation period not well known. **Young:** Evidently fed by both parents. Young leave the nest about 5 weeks after hatching, are probably cared for by the adults for some time thereafter.

MIGRATION   Apparently a permanent resident throughout its range, but individuals may wander widely.

CONSERVATION STATUS   Has gradually increased and spread in Texas since the 1960s. Widespread and common in the American tropics.

BELTED KINGFISHER   *Ceryle alcyon*

The Belted Kingfisher is often first noticed by its wild rattling call as it flies over rivers or lakes. It may be seen perched on a high snag or hovering on rapidly beating wings, then plunging head first into the water to grab a fish. Found almost throughout North America at one season or another, it is the only member of its family to be seen in most areas north of Mexico.

HABITAT   *Streams, lakes, bays, coasts; nests in banks.* During winter and migration, may be found in almost any waterside habitat, including the edges of small streams and ponds, large rivers and lakes, marshes, estuaries, and rocky coastlines; seems to require only clear water for fishing. During breeding season, more restricted to areas with suitable dirt banks for nesting holes.

FEEDING   **Diet:** *Mostly small fish.* Typically feeds on small fish, usually those less than 4–5 inches long. Also eats crayfish, frogs, tadpoles, aquatic insects. Occasionally takes prey away from water, including small mammals, young birds, lizards. Reported to eat berries at times. **Behavior:** Forages by plunging head first into water, capturing fish near surface with bill. Watches for fish from branch, wire, rock, or other perch above water, or may hover above water before diving. Bones, scales, and other indigestible parts of prey are coughed up later as pellets.

Belted Kingfisher

NESTING   In courtship display, male brings fish, feeds it to female. **Nest:** Site is in steep or vertical dirt bank, usually with higher content of sand than clay. Both sexes take part in digging a long horizontal tunnel with nest chamber at end. Tunnel is generally 3–6 feet long and usually slopes upward from entrance. Rarely nests in tree cavity. Usually no lining added to nest chamber, but debris and undigested fish bones and scales may accumulate. **Eggs:** 6–7, sometimes 5–8. White. Incubation is by both sexes, 22–24 days. Female incubates at night, with male taking over early in morning; male may or may not incubate less than female. **Young:** Both parents feed young, at first giving them partially digested fish, later whole fish. Male may make more feeding visits than female. Young depart from nest 27–29 days after hatching, are fed by parents for about another 3 weeks. One brood per year, perhaps sometimes two in south.

MIGRATION   A few may overwinter as far north as water remains open, including southern coast of Alaska. Some from North America migrate as far south as Central America, West Indies, northern South America. Migrants may tend to follow rivers, lake shores, coastlines.

CONSERVATION STATUS   Recent surveys indicate slight declines in population. May be vulnerable to loss of nesting sites and to disturbance during breeding season.

GENUS *Chloroceryle*

GREEN KINGFISHER   *Chloroceryle americana*

This little kingfisher seems oddly proportioned, rather like a sparrow with the bill of a heron. Living along streams and rivers near the Mexican border, it is often overlooked because it tends to perch low among vegetation near the water; its sharp ticking call notes may give it away. When moving up or downstream, the Green Kingfisher flies fast, with quick wingbeats, very low over the water.

HABITAT   *Rivers, streams.* Always found near water, but sometimes near very small streams with only intermittent pools. Also around edges of ponds and larger rivers. Favors areas where there is dense low growth on the banks, providing low perches close to the water.

FEEDING   **Diet:** *Small fish.* Feeds on minnows and other small fish, mostly those about 1–2 inches long. May also take some aquatic insects. **Behavior:** Forages mostly by perching low, typically on an overhanging branch or root 3–6 feet above the water, sometimes on a rock in midstream, watching for small fish swimming close to the surface. When prey is spotted, bird flies down and plunges into water head first to take fish in its bill. Seldom hovers before diving.

Green Kingfisher

NESTING   Nesting pair defends territory along stream, maintaining good distance from other pairs. **Nest:** Site is in burrow in vertical dirt bank near water. Burrow (probably excavated by both sexes) is usually 2–3 feet long, 5–8 feet above the water level, and no more than about 2 inches in diameter. The entrance to the burrow is usually hidden by overhanging vegetation or roots (in other kingfishers, entrance is usually exposed). At the end of the burrow is a slightly enlarged nest chamber, usually with no nest material added. **Eggs:** 3–6, usually 5. White. Incubation is by both parents, 19–21 days; female incubates at night, male part of day. **Young:** Fed by both parents. Young leave nest about 22–26 days after hatching, may be fed by parents for several days thereafter.

MIGRATION   Permanent resident. Sometimes wanders slightly north of range.

CONSERVATION STATUS   May have declined in parts of Texas with loss of streamside habitat. Recently has begun nesting locally in southern Arizona, spreading north from adjacent Mexico.

WOODPECKERS (Family Picidae)

Woodpeckers are found practically everyplace in the world where there are trees (except in the Australian region), with a total of about 215 species. Uniquely adapted for a life of climbing and pounding on trees, typical woodpeckers are tough birds with strong muscles and thick skin. Strong zygodactyl feet (two toes forward, two back) in most species provide a solid grip on vertical surfaces. Stiff tail feathers are pressed against the tree as a brace while the bird is pecking, or as an additional prop as it hitches its way upward. The skull and the chisel-shaped bill are designed to spread and absorb the shock of repeated pounding on hard wood.

Aside from the typical woodpeckers, the family also includes the odd wrynecks of the Old World and the piculets, smaller birds that clamber about on branches in the manner of nuthatches in many tropical forest areas.

The effects of woodpeckers on trees are almost entirely beneficial or neutral. Most of their diet consists of insects, and they keep many potential forest pests in check. Their deeper excavations (for nesting holes or in pursuit of wood-boring insects) are typically in trees or branches that are already dead, dying, or diseased.

Some woodpeckers may live more than 15 years in the wild.

Feeding Woodpeckers typically seek insects on the trunks and limbs of trees. Foraging methods include visual searching, probing in crevices, scaling off bits of bark, or excavating into dead wood. Some species also may feed on the ground or catch insects in flight. Nuts, fruits, and seeds figure heavily in the diet of some; tree sap is a big item for the four species of sapsuckers.

Woodpeckers are among the birds that most regularly eat ants—in fact, ants may form the major part of the diet at some seasons for flickers, Pileated Woodpeckers, sapsuckers, and others.

Nesting All of our woodpeckers nest in holes in trees, usually excavating these themselves. (In the desert southwest, giant cactus may be used in place of trees.) Sometimes they will occupy existing cavities or nest boxes, but in general they are far less likely to use artificial sites than most hole-nesting birds. They bring no nest material, so the eggs rest only on wood chips and sawdust in the bottom of the cavity. All of our woodpeckers lay white eggs. As far as is known, both sexes take turns incubating. In many species, males incubate at night and the sexes take turns during the day. Both parents bring food to the young in the nest.

Displays Courtship behavior of many species has not been studied yet; but as a general rule, woodpeckers seem to have many aggressive displays (used in defense of territory or feeding sites), and minor variations of these may be used in courtship. Indeed, the initial encounters between prospective mates may appear very hostile, with the male and female gradually becoming more tolerant of each other.

Few displays will be mentioned in the following accounts, but some common elements are used by a number of species. Most woodpeckers employ some kind of motion of the head: bowing, bobbing, turning the head from side to side, or pointing the bill up and swinging the head back and forth. The feathers of the head are frequently raised. Partial spreading of the wings and tail are often seen. Many species have a sort of display flight, with an odd fluttering, floating motion.

Males of some woodpecker species advertise their territories mainly by drumming, pounding out a loud rapid burst on a dead branch. Others with louder voices may advertise mainly by calling, or by both calling and drumming. Males and females may drum back and forth to each other in duet during pair formation. Ritualized tapping at potential nest sites may be a part of courtship for some species.

GENUS *Jynx*

EURASIAN WRYNECK *Jynx torquilla*

This is a strange little woodpecker that hops about in the branches like a songbird and often forages on the ground. It is named for its habit of twisting its neck into odd positions as it peers about in a rather reptilian way. Wrynecks are widespread and strongly migratory in the Old World, and a lone bird once strayed to western Alaska.

MEDIUM-SIZED GENERALISTS — GENUS *Melanerpes*

Members of this group are omnivores, generally eating more plant material (nuts, fruits, seeds) than most woodpeckers and searching for their insect food in a wider variety of ways (for example, most are adept at catching flying insects in the air). As a rule they avoid dense unbroken forest, favoring edges, clearings, even isolated groves in open country. Most of these species have loud voices, and they may do more advertising of their territories by calling, not as much drumming as in some woodpeckers.

Several tropical members of this genus are cooperative breeders, with multiple adults helping to care for the young in each nest. In our area, the Acorn Woodpecker practices the same kind of sociable nesting.

LEWIS'S WOODPECKER   *Melanerpes lewis*

One of our oddest woodpeckers—and not only because of its colors, which include pink, silver, and oily green. Although it climbs trees in woodpecker style, it feeds mostly by catching insects in acrobatic flight: swooping out from a perch like a flycatcher, circling high in the air like a swallow. Wide rounded wings give it a more buoyant flight than most woodpeckers. In fall, Lewis's Woodpecker chops up acorns and other nuts, stores them in crevices, then guards the storage area for its winter food supply. Discovered on the Lewis and Clark expedition of 1804–1806 and named for the expedition's co-leader.

Lewis's Woodpecker

HABITAT   *Scattered or logged forest, river groves, burns, foothills.* Because of aerial foraging, needs open country in summer, with large trees for nest sites and foraging perches. Often in cottonwood groves, open pine-oak woods, burned or cut-over woods. Winter habitat chosen in autumn for food supply, usually groves of oaks, sometimes date palms, orchards of pecans, walnuts, almonds, fruit.

FEEDING   **Diet:** *Mostly insects, nuts, fruits.* Feeds on a wide variety of insects; also eats fruits and berries, plus acorns and other nuts. **Behavior:** During spring and summer, forages mainly by catching insects in flight: sallying forth from a perch or circling high in air to catch flying insects, or swooping down to catch those on the ground. Also gleans some insects from tree surfaces, and takes small fruits in trees. In fall, harvests acorns or other nuts, breaks them into pieces by pounding with bill, then stores them in bark crevices or holes in trees for winter.

NESTING   Pairs may mate for life, and may use the same nest site repeatedly. Displays (used in both aggression and courtship) include perching with wings spread, head lowered, neck feathers ruffed out; floating circular flight around nest tree. **Nest:** Site is cavity excavated in tree (tree or limb usually dead), sometimes in utility pole, at site apparently chosen by male. Height of nest varies, from 5 feet to well over 100 feet above ground, probably usually lower than 60 feet. **Eggs:** 6–7, sometimes 4–9. White. Incubation is by both sexes (with males incubating at night and part of day), 12–16 days. **Young:** Both parents bring back insects in bill to feed nestlings. Young leave nest 4–5 weeks after hatching, remain with parents for some time thereafter.

MIGRATION   Some may be permanent residents, others move south and to lower elevations in winter. Quite variable from year to year; in some winters, large numbers invade lowlands of southwest. May migrate singly or in flocks.

CONSERVATION STATUS   Localized and erratic in occurrence, so populations are hard to monitor. Has disappeared from many former nesting areas. There are some indications of a continuing decline in population in recent years.

RED-HEADED WOODPECKER   *Melanerpes erythrocephalus*

Red-headed Woodpecker

This striking and unmistakable bird was a favorite of early ornithologists such as Alexander Wilson and Audubon. Often conspicuous because of its strong pattern, harsh calls, and active behavior in semi-open country, it tends to occur in small colonies. Although it migrates only short distances, little groups of migrants may be noticeable in early fall and late spring. Once a very common bird in eastern North America, the Red-headed Woodpecker is now uncommon and local in many regions.

HABITAT   *Groves, farm country, orchards, shade trees in towns, large scattered trees.* Avoids unbroken forest, favoring open country or at least clearings in the woods. Forest edges, orchards, open pine woods, groves of tall trees in open country are likely habitats. Winter habitats influenced by source of food in fall, such as acorns or beechnuts.

FEEDING   **Diet:** *Omnivorous.* Perhaps the most omnivorous of woodpeckers. Diet includes wide variety of insects, also spiders, earthworms, nuts, seeds, berries, wild and cultivated fruit, rarely small rodents. Sometimes eats eggs and nestlings of other birds. Also sometimes eats bark. **Behavior:** Opportunistic, with several foraging techniques. Flies out from a perch to catch insects in the air or on ground; climbs tree trunks and major limbs; clambers about in outer branches; hops on ground. Gathers acorns, beechnuts, and other nuts in fall, storing them in holes and crev-ices, then feeding on them during winter.

NESTING   Male establishes territory and advertises there with calling, drumming. In resident birds, male's winter territory may become breeding territory. **Nest:** Male's winter roosting cavity may be used for nest, or new cavity may be excavated (mostly by male); female indicates acceptance of site by tapping on tree. Nest cavity is in bare dead tree or dead limb, from a few feet above ground to 65 feet or higher. **Eggs:** 4–5, sometimes 3–7, rarely more. White. Incubation is by both sexes (with male incubating at night), 12–13 days. **Young:** Are fed by both parents, leave the nest at about 27–31 days. Pairs may be starting a second nesting attempt while still feeding the fledglings from the first; second brood may be raised in same nest but more often in new cavity, freshly excavated. One or two broods per year.

MIGRATION Some are probably permanent residents, but others, especially from northern and western areas, travel to wintering areas in southeastern states. Migrates by day. A short-distance migrant, not known to occur south of United States.

CONSERVATION STATUS Once very common throughout the east, but has been decreasing in numbers for years, and recent surveys show that this trend is continuing. Reasons for decline not well known, probably include loss of potential nest sites (from cutting of dead trees), competition with starlings for nest cavities. When swooping out to catch insects in flight along roadsides, often struck by cars.

ACORN WOODPECKER *Melanerpes formicivorus*

A clown-faced western woodpecker with a complicated social structure, living in small colonies. Best known for its habit of hoarding acorns: the birds drill small holes in a dead snag, then harvest acorns in fall and store them in these holes, to be

eaten during winter. Such a "granary tree" may be used for generations and may be riddled with up to 50,000 holes. Nesting is a group activity, with several adults (up to 12 or more) taking part in incubating the eggs and feeding the young in a single nest.

HABITAT *Oak woods, groves, mixed forest, oak-pine canyons, foothills.* Seldom away from oaks. Most common where several species of oaks occur together (this insures against total failure of local acorn crop, as different oaks respond to different conditions). May be in open oak groves near coast, pine-oak woods in mountains, streamside sycamores next to oak-covered hillsides.

FEEDING **Diet:** *Omnivorous, eats many acorns and insects.* Acorns make up about half of annual diet and are of major importance in winter. Also feeds on in-

Acorn Woodpecker

sects, particularly ants. Diet also includes various nuts, fruits, seeds, sometimes eggs of other birds. **Behavior:** Members of group harvest acorns in fall, store them in hole-studded trees, feed on them in following seasons. Insects are gleaned from surface of tree or caught in swooping, acrobatic flight. Unlike most woodpeckers, rarely or never excavates in wood for insects. May feed on sap, digging pits in bark or visiting those made by sapsuckers.

NESTING Nesting group consists of 1–7 breeding males and 1–3 breeding females, often assisted by additional nonbreeding adults (generally earlier offspring from same group). Members of group defend communal food stores and nesting territory year-round. **Nest:** Site is a cavity in tree (almost always dead tree or dead branch of live tree), 5–60 feet above ground, usually 12–30 feet. Excavated by both breeders and helpers. **Eggs:** 3–7. White. Nests with more eggs (up to 17 recorded) result from more than one female laying. Incubation mainly by breeders at first, with helpers soon joining in; incubating birds take turns, with rapid turnover, sometimes changing places many times per hour. Incubation period 11–14 days. **Young:** Are fed by both parents and helpers, and leave nest at about 30–32 days. 1–2 broods per year, possibly sometimes 3.

MIGRATION Mostly permanent resident throughout range (which extends south to Colombia). Stragglers may appear far from nesting areas at any season. If acorn crops fail, may stage small invasions to lowland valleys in fall and winter.

GILA WOODPECKER   *Melanerpes uropygialis*

Gila Woodpecker

A brash, noisy woodpecker of desert regions. Common and conspicuous in stands of saguaro, or giant cactus, it also lives in the trees along desert rivers and is quick to move into towns and suburbs. This species and the Gilded Flicker are the two main architects of desert "apartment houses": the holes they excavate in giant cactus are later used as nesting sites by many other birds, from flycatchers and martins to owls and kestrels.

HABITAT   *Desert washes, saguaros, river groves, cottonwoods, towns.* Generally in dry country, but requires suitable sites for nesting cavities: cottonwood groves along rivers, large mesquites or willows, palms, giant cacti such as saguaro or cardon. Readily adapts to suburbs of southwestern cities. Also dry tropical forest in Mexico.

FEEDING   **Diet:** *Omnivorous.* Diet includes wide variety of insects, also cactus fruit, other wild and cultivated fruit, berries of shrubs and mistletoe, nectar from flowers, seeds, small lizards, earthworms, eggs and sometimes young of smaller birds. **Behavior:** Forages on tree trunks and cacti, in outer branches of trees or shrubs, or on ground. When seeking insects on tree trunks, generally probes or gleans at surface, rarely excavating for food. Often drinks sugar-water from hummingbird feeders.

NESTING   Displays, used largely in aggression, include exaggerated bowing and head-swinging, accompanied by loud calls. **Nest:** Site is a cavity excavated in giant cactus or in tree (cottonwood, willow, or large mesquite), sometimes in palm trunk. Cavity usually 8–30 feet above ground. Both sexes take part in excavating. Cavity in giant cactus cannot be used for several months, as inner pulp of cactus must dry to solid casing around cavity; holes may be excavated one year, used the next. **Eggs:** 3–4, up to 6. White. Incubation is by both sexes, about 14 days. **Young:** Both parents feed young. Age at which young leave nest not well known, probably about 4 weeks; accompany parents for some time thereafter. 2–3 broods per year.

MIGRATION   Mostly permanent resident, but some move short distances north or uphill in winter. Also makes local movements, concentrating at sources of food when not nesting.

CONSERVATION STATUS   Declined seriously in California during 20th century. Still abundant in southern Arizona.

GOLDEN-FRONTED WOODPECKER   *Melanerpes aurifrons*

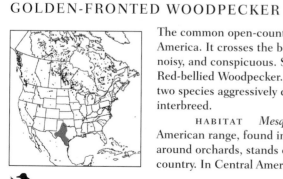

The common open-country woodpecker of eastern Mexico and northern Central America. It crosses the border mainly in southern Texas, where it is very common, noisy, and conspicuous. Similar in appearance and behavior to its relative, the Red-bellied Woodpecker. Where their ranges meet in Texas and Oklahoma, the two species aggressively defend territories against each other, and they sometimes interbreed.

HABITAT   *Mesquites, stream woodlands, groves.* In its limited North American range, found in most open woodlands, especially along rivers; also around orchards, stands of mesquite along dry washes, groves of trees in open country. In Central America, also around edges of tropical forest.

FEEDING   **Diet:** *Omnivorous.* Feeds on a wide variety of insects. Also eats nuts, berries, fruits, and seeds of many plants; will eat many acorns where they are available. **Behavior:** Searches for insects on tree trunks and limbs, gleaning them from bark or probing below surface. Clambers about in branches of trees or shrubs to pick nuts, berries, or fruits. May forage on ground, and sometimes catches insects in flight. Cracks open mesquite pods to eat the seeds.

NESTING   Advertises nesting territory with loud calls, sometimes with drumming. **Nest:** Site is a cavity in trunk of tree (live or dead) such as mesquite or oak, or in telephone poles or fenceposts. Cavities are usually fairly low, typically less than 20 feet above ground. Both sexes help excavate the cavity, which may be used for more than one season. **Eggs:** Usually 4–5, up to 7. White. Incubation is by both sexes (with male incubating at night and part of day), 12–14 days. **Young:** Both parents feed nestlings. Young leave nest about 30 days after hatching, may associate with parents for some time thereafter. 1–2 broods per year, rarely 3.

MIGRATION   Permanent resident, with some local movements, concentrating at good feeding areas in winter. A lone male once strayed to western Florida and remained several months, mating with a local Red-bellied and raising two young.

CONSERVATION STATUS   Was once persecuted as a pest because of its excavations in telegraph poles; many were shot in Texas in early part of 20th century. Current population apparently stable.

Golden-fronted Woodpecker

RED-BELLIED WOODPECKER   *Melanerpes carolinus*

Primarily a bird of the southeast, where its rolling calls are familiar sounds in swamps and riverside woods. Omnivorous and adaptable, this woodpecker has also adjusted to life in suburbs and city parks, and in recent years it has been expanding its range to the north. Despite the name, the red on the belly is not often visible in the field.

HABITAT   *Woodlands, groves, orchards, towns.* Most common in deciduous forest, especially along rivers and in swamps. Also in mixed coniferous and deciduous forest, less often in pure stands of pine. May be found in rather open areas, such as forest edges and clearings, groves of trees in farm country, shade trees in suburbs.

FEEDING   **Diet:** *Omnivorous.* Like most woodpeckers, eats many insects. Diet may be more than 50 percent plant material at some seasons, including acorns and other nuts, wild and cultivated fruits, seeds. Occasional items in diet include tree frogs, eggs of small birds, oozing sap, and even small fish. **Behavior:** Forages by searching for insects on tree trunks and major limbs. Climbs and perches among branches to pick berries and nuts, and sometimes catches flying insects in the air. Nuts and seeds taken in fall may be stored in bark crevices, eaten during winter.

NESTING   Uses many antagonistic displays in defending territory, including spreading wings, slow floating flight, and raising head feathers. **Nest:** Site is in cavity excavated in dead wood (tree, pole, fencepost, or stump), usually less than 50 feet above ground but can be as high as 120 feet. Male may begin excavating several holes, with female selecting which one

Red-bellied Woodpecker

is completed and used. Also may use natural cavity, abandoned hole of other wood-pecker, or nest box. **Eggs:** 4–5, sometimes 3–8. White. Incubation is by both sexes (with male incubating at night and part of day), 12–14 days. **Young:** Are fed by both parents, leave the nest about 22–27 days after hatching. Parents may continue to feed young for 6 weeks or more after they leave nest. 1 brood per year in north, 2–3 in south.

MIGRATION   Not truly migratory, wintering throughout its range. Some wander north in fall and remain through winter. Performs local movements, concentrating in areas of good food supply outside the breeding season.

CONSERVATION STATUS   Apparently the species was declining in some northern areas during the first half of the 20th century, but in recent decades the trend has reversed and it has extended its range to the north. Overall population seems stable or may be increasing slightly.

SAPSUCKERS — GENUS *Sphyrapicus*

These are woodpeckers with the odd habit of drilling tiny holes in tree bark, usually in neatly spaced rows, and then returning to them periodically to feed on the sap that oozes out. They also eat bits of cambium and other tree tissues, as well as insects that are attracted to the sap, but the sap itself may account for up to 20 percent of the total diet. A study published in 1911 listed over 280 kinds of trees and vines attacked by sapsuckers. The sap wells may be visited by other birds including other woodpeckers, warblers, and even hummingbirds, as well as by chipmunks and squirrels.

YELLOW-BELLIED SAPSUCKER   *Sphyrapicus varius*

Yellow-bellied Sapsucker

Although its name sounds like a cartoonist's invention, the Yellow-bellied Sapsucker does exist. This species is common in the north and east, and is replaced by close relatives in the west. Quiet in winter, it becomes noisy in spring, with catlike calls and staccato drumming.

HABITAT   *Woodlands, aspen groves; in winter, also orchards, other trees.* In summer mostly in mixed coniferous and deciduous woods, especially around aspens. May be found in any kind of woods or even dry brush in migration. Winters mostly in deciduous trees.

FEEDING   **Diet:** *Includes insects, tree sap, fruit.* Feeds on a wide variety of insects, including many ants (taken from tree trunks). Also regularly feeds on tree sap, and on berries and fruits. **Behavior:** See genus introduction. Besides drilling sap wells, also gleans insects from tree trunks in more typical woodpecker fashion, and sallies out to catch insects in the air. Berries and fruits are eaten at all seasons, and birds may concentrate in fruiting wild trees in winter.

NESTING   Males tend to arrive on breeding grounds before females. Courtship displays include pointing bill up to show off colored throat patch, ritualized tapping at nest site. **Nest:** Site is cavity in tree, usually deciduous tree such as aspen, poplar, birch, 6–60 feet above ground. Often uses same tree in consecutive years, rarely same nest hole. Favors trees affected by tinder fungus, which softens heartwood while leaving outer part of trunk firm. Both sexes help excavate. **Eggs:** 5–6, sometimes 3–7. White. Incubation is by both sexes (with male incubating

at night and part of day), 12–13 days. Both parents feed young, bringing them insects, sap, and fruit. Young leave nest 25–29 days after hatching. Parents teach young the sapsucking technique, feed them for about 10 days after they leave nest. One brood per year.

MIGRATION   One of the most migratory of woodpeckers. Essentially no overlap between summer and winter ranges. Northwestern breeders migrate east as well as south. Winters commonly in southeastern United States but also south to Central America, West Indies.

CONSERVATION STATUS   Has disappeared from several southerly areas where it formerly nested, but still widespread and numerous.

RED-NAPED SAPSUCKER   *Sphyrapicus nuchalis*

A western bird, common in the Rocky Mountain and Great Basin regions. Very similar to Yellow-bellied Sapsucker; for most of the 20th century it was considered only a race of that species. Its differences in behavior have not been much studied.

In summer the Red-naped Sapsucker is found in mountains in mixed coniferous and deciduous forest, especially around aspens. During migration and winter it occurs in both mountains and lowlands, in deciduous trees, riverside willow groves, pine-oak woods, orchards. Feeding habits are apparently much as in Yellow-bellied Sapsucker. Nesting is not well studied but also apparently much as in Yellow-bellied. May nest in dead or dying conifers a bit more often.

This species migrates southward and to lower elevations in winter. It generally travels shorter distances than Yellow-bellied Sapsucker, reaching central Mexico only.

RED-BREASTED SAPSUCKER   *Sphyrapicus ruber*

A very close relative of the Yellow-bellied and Red-naped sapsuckers, replacing them on the Pacific slope. It was considered to belong to the same species for some time, so differences in behavior have not been well studied.

Red-breasted Sapsucker

In summer on the northwest coast, the Red-breasted Sapsucker is often in forest of hemlock or spruce. Farther south in the mountains it is found in pine forest, always with a mixture of deciduous trees such as aspen, alder, willow. In winter some move south or into lowlands, occurring in deciduous or coniferous trees. Feeding habits are apparently much as in Yellow-bellied Sapsucker.

Nesting behavior is not well known; apparently much as in Yellow-bellied. Probably has different courtship displays: since male and female Red-breasted look alike, they may need to recognize each other by behavior. Nest site is usually in deciduous tree such as aspen, alder, cottonwood, or willow, but also in firs and other conifers. Nest cavity is often high, may be 50–60 feet or more above ground.

Living in a relatively temperate climate, this is the least migratory of the sapsuckers. In Pacific Northwest, birds from interior may move to coast or southward;

coastal birds may be permanent residents. Southern populations may move to lower elevations or short distance south in winter.

This species may interbreed with either the Red-naped or Yellow-bellied sapsuckers in the limited areas where their summer ranges come in contact. Hybrids produced in these areas may appear east of the range of Red-breasted Sapsucker in winter.

Overall numbers of Red-breasted Sapsuckers have probably declined somewhat because of cutting of forest in northwest, but the bird is still fairly numerous.

WILLIAMSON'S SAPSUCKER *Sphyrapicus thyroideus*

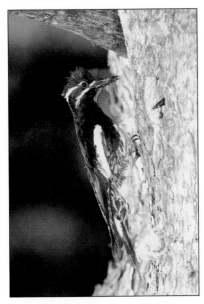

Williamson's Sapsucker

A strikingly marked woodpecker of western mountains. May be found nesting in the same aspen groves as Red-naped or Red-breasted sapsuckers, but also occurs in pure coniferous forest. Quiet and inconspicuous at most times, although its staccato drumming and nasal mewing calls may be noticeable in spring. Males and females of this woodpecker look so different that they were first described as two separate species.

HABITAT *Higher conifer forests, burns.* In summer found in mountains in conifer forests including spruce, fir, and lodgepole pine; also in aspen groves near conifers. Winters mostly in pine and pine-oak woodland in mountains. Even those few that wander to lowlands in winter are likely to be found in conifers.

FEEDING **Diet:** *Includes insects, tree sap, fruit.* Eats many kinds of insects; ants may form a very high percentage of diet during breeding season. Also feeds heavily on tree sap and eats some small fruits and berries. **Behavior:** See genus introduction. Besides drilling sap wells, also takes insects gleaned elsewhere in trees, sometimes catches insects in the air or on ground, and perches among twigs to eat berries.

NESTING Courtship displays include exaggerated floating and fluttering flight near nest site; members of pair also face each other while bobbing and swinging heads. **Nest:** Site is cavity in tree, often in aspen, pine, or fir, usually 5–60 feet above ground. Favors trees with dead heartwood and live outer layer, and may return to dig new nest holes in same tree year after year. Excavation of cavity is by male. **Eggs:** 4–5, sometimes 3–7. White. Incubation is by both sexes (with male incubating at night and part of day), 12–14 days. **Young:** Both parents feed young, carrying food in bill and throat; young are fed mostly ants. Young leave nest 3–4 weeks after hatching, may disperse from territory very soon afterward. Apparently one brood per year.

MIGRATION Seems to migrate south along mountain ranges in fall, tending to winter at upper elevations, as far south as west-central Mexico. A few move to lowlands; has wandered as far east as Louisiana. Females may winter a little farther south than males, on average.

GENUS *Dendrocopos*

GREAT SPOTTED WOODPECKER *Dendrocopos major*

A medium-sized woodpecker, like an Old World counterpart to our Hairy Woodpecker. Since it is essentially nonmigratory, it is not likely to wander far out of normal limits. However, its range includes the Kamchatka Peninsula of eastern Russia, probably the source for the single Great Spotted Woodpecker that once appeared on Attu Island, Alaska.

PIED OR SPOTTED WOODPECKERS — GENUS *Picoides*

Small to medium-sized species, most with strong black and white patterns. Mostly found in forest, not in semi-open country like some woodpeckers (the Ladder-backed Woodpecker of the arid southwest is an exception). Hairy and Downy woodpeckers are widespread and adaptable, but others are more specialized: Nuttall's and Strickland's woodpeckers being closely associated with oaks, Red-cockaded and White-headed occurring strictly in pines. The exacting habitat requirements of Red-cockaded Woodpecker have been its downfall, and it is now an endangered species.

LADDER-BACKED WOODPECKER *Picoides scalaris*

A small woodpecker of arid country. Because of its size, it is able to make a living even in scrubby growth along dry washes (other desert woodpeckers, like Gila Woodpecker and Gilded Flicker, require giant cactus or larger trees for nest sites). Closely related to Nuttall's Woodpecker of the Pacific coast; their ranges meet in California foothills, and they sometimes interbreed there.

HABITAT   *Deserts, river woods, groves, dry woods, arid brush.* In the United States in dry areas of southwest, including brushland, desert washes, mesquites, riverside trees in prairie country, towns. Moves into adjacent habitats such as oaks and pinyon-juniper stands in foothills, woods on Texas coast. In Central America also in thorn forest, pine-oak woods, even coastal mangroves.

FEEDING   **Diet:** *Mostly insects.* Feeds on a variety of insects, including beetles and their larvae, caterpillars, true bugs, ants. Also eats some berries and fruit, including cactus fruit. **Behavior:** Forages on trees, shrubs, cacti, tree yuccas, agave stalks, tall weeds, and sometimes on ground. Male and female often forage together, concentrating on different spots: male more on trunks and big limbs, female more on outer twigs, bushes, cacti. (Male is larger than female, with noticeably longer bill.)

Ladder-backed Woodpecker

NESTING   Pairs may remain more or less together throughout year. Displays (used mostly for territorial defense) include raising head feathers, bobbing and turning head, spreading of wings and tail, fluttering display flight. **Nest:** Site is cavity in tree (such as mesquite, hackberry, willow, oak) or in Joshua tree (a yucca) or agave stalk, sometimes in giant cactus, utility pole, fencepost. Both sexes probably excavate but male may do most of work. Cavity usually 4–20 feet above ground, sometimes higher. **Eggs:** 3–4, sometimes 2–7. White. Incubation is by both sexes, about 13 days. **Young:** Both parents feed young, bringing insects in their bills to nest. Age when young leave nest not well known.

MIGRATION   Permanent resident throughout its range, which extends as far south as Nicaragua.

CONSERVATION STATUS   Surveys suggest a slight decline in recent years, but still fairly common and widespread.

NUTTALL'S WOODPECKER *Picoides nuttallii*

A California specialty, Nuttall's Woodpecker extends only a short distance into Baja and rarely strays to Oregon. Within its limited range, it is often common wherever oak trees grow. It may go unseen at times because of its habit of foraging among densely foliaged oaks, but it frequently announces itself with sharp calls. Despite its close association with oaks, it tends to dig its nesting holes in other kinds of trees, and it eats only small numbers of acorns.

Nuttall's Woodpecker

HABITAT *Wooded canyons and foothills, river woods.* In much of range almost always around oaks, especially where oaks meet other trees along rivers, also in pine-oak woods in foothills. In southern California also in riverside cottonwoods, sycamores, willows, even if no oaks present. At eastern edge of range may venture out into mesquite or other dry woods.

FEEDING **Diet:** *Mostly insects.* Feeds on a wide variety of insects, especially beetles, also caterpillars, ants, true bugs. Also eats some nuts, seeds, fruits, berries. Despite close association with oaks, eats only small numbers of acorns. **Behavior:** Forages mainly in dense trees such as oaks and ceanothus, also in cottonwood, willow, sycamore, and others; sometimes in yuccas, mesquites (at eastern margin of range). The sexes sometimes forage differently in trees, with males focusing on trunk and large limbs, females working on smaller branches and twigs. Occasionally catches insects in flight.

NESTING Members of pair may remain more or less together all year. Displays include raising head feathers, swinging head from side to side, and a fluttering display flight. **Nest:** Site is cavity in live or dead tree, usually cottonwood, willow, or sycamore near oak woods, sometimes in utility pole, fencepost, or oak or other tree. Cavity usually 3–35 feet above ground, sometimes up to 60 feet or higher. Male does most of excavating; new nest cavity every year. **Eggs:** 3–4, up to 6. White. Incubation is by both sexes (with male incubating at night and part of day), about 14 days. **Young:** Both parents feed young. Young leave nest about 4 weeks after hatching, may remain with parents for several weeks thereafter.

MIGRATION Permanent resident throughout its range, rarely wandering any distance from nesting areas.

DOWNY WOODPECKER *Picoides pubescens*

The smallest woodpecker in North America, common and widespread, although it avoids the arid southwest. In the east this is the most familiar member of the family, readily entering towns and city parks, coming to backyard bird feeders. Its small size makes it versatile, and it may forage on weed stalks as well as in large trees. In winter it often joins roving mixed flocks of chickadees, nuthatches, and other birds in the woods.

HABITAT *Forests, woodlots, willows, river groves, orchards, shade trees.* Found in wide variety of habitats, from wilderness areas to second-growth woods to suburban yards, but generally favors deciduous trees. In far north and in mountains (areas dominated by conifers), restricted to groves of deciduous trees such as aspens or willows.

FEEDING **Diet:** *Mostly insects.* Feeds on a variety of insects, especially beetles and ants, also gall wasps, caterpillars, others. Also eats seeds and berries. Will eat suet at bird feeders. **Behavior:** Can forage not only on trunks and major limbs of trees but also on minor branches and twigs (often climbing about acrobatically and hanging upside down), as well as on shrubs and weed stalks. Male and female forage differently at times, but this varies with place and season. Feeding on trees, does more tapping and excavating in winter, more gleaning from surface in summer.

NESTING Male and female have separate feeding areas in fall and early winter, with pairs forming by late winter. Male and female take turns drumming loudly on dead limbs on their separate territories; male gradually approaches. **Nest:** Site is cavity (excavated by both sexes) in dead limb or dead tree, usually 12–30 feet above ground, sometimes 5–60 feet. Cavity entrance is often surrounded by fungus or lichen, helping to camouflage site. **Eggs:** 4–5, sometimes 3–6. White. Incubation is by both sexes, about 12 days. **Young:** Both parents bring billfuls of insects to feed the nestlings. Young leave the nest about 20–25 days after hatching, may follow parents around for a few weeks thereafter. One brood per year, possibly two in south.

MIGRATION Permanent resident in many areas, but northern-most populations may move some distance south in winter. Some birds from the Rockies and other western mountains may move down to valleys in winter, and may move short distance south as well.

Downy Woodpecker

HAIRY WOODPECKER *Picoides villosus*

This species and the Downy Woodpecker are remarkably similar in pattern, differing mainly in size and bill shape. They often occur together, but the Hairy, a larger bird, requires larger trees; it is usually less common, especially in the east, and less likely to show up in suburbs and city parks. In its feeding it does more pounding and excavating in trees than most smaller woodpeckers, consuming large numbers of wood-boring insects.

HABITAT *Forests, woodlands, river groves, shade trees.* Accepts wide variety of habitats so long as large trees present; found in deciduous, coniferous, and mixed forest, groves along rivers in prairie country, open juniper woodland, swamps. In southwest and from Mexico to Panama found in mountain forests, mostly of pine but also in cloud forest in Central America.

FEEDING **Diet:** *Mostly insects.* Feeds especially on larvae of wood-boring beetles, also other beetles, ants, caterpillars, and others. Also eats some berries, seeds, nuts. Will feed on sap at damaged trees or at sapsucker workings, and will come to bird feeders for suet. **Behavior:** Forages mainly on the trunks and limbs of trees, sometimes on vines, shrubs. Energetic in its search, often probing, scaling off bark, and excavating into dead wood in pursuit of insects. Males may forage more deliberately than females, working longer in one spot.

Hairy Woodpecker

NESTING   Male and female may maintain separate territories in early winter, pairing up in mid-winter, often with mate from previous year. Female's winter territory becomes focus of nesting territory. Courtship includes both birds drumming in duet; ritualized tapping at symbolic nest sites by female. **Nest:** Site is cavity (excavated by both sexes), mainly in deciduous trees in east, in aspens or dead conifers in west. Cavity usually 4–60 feet above ground. **Eggs:** 4, sometimes 3–6. White. Incubation is by both sexes (with male incubating at night, female most of day), about 14 days. **Young:** Both parents feed the nestlings. Male may forage farther from nest, making fewer feeding trips with more food each time. Young leave nest 28–30 days after hatching, are fed by parents for some time afterward. 1 brood per year.

MIGRATION   Mostly a permanent resident. Some birds from northern edge of range may move well south in winter, and a few from western mountains move to lower elevations.

CONSERVATION STATUS   Although still very widespread and fairly common, thought to have declined from historical levels in many areas. Loss of nesting sites (with cutting of dead snags in forest) is one potential problem. Starlings and House Sparrows may sometimes take over freshly excavated nest cavities.

STRICKLAND'S WOODPECKER   *Picoides stricklandi*

Strickland's Woodpecker

A brown-backed woodpecker of oak woodland, living in mountains near the Mexican border, mainly in southeastern Arizona. Foraging quietly at midlevels in the oaks, it is often easy to overlook. Much of its behavior is like that of the Hairy Woodpecker, but it is quieter, often forages lower in the trees, and does not dig as deeply into dead wood for insects.

HABITAT   *Oaks in mountains, pine-oak canyons.* In its United States range (Arizona and New Mexico only) found exclusively in oaks of foothills and midlevels of mountains, up into mixed pine-oak woods. At southern end of range (central Mexico), found higher in mountains, mainly in pines.

FEEDING   **Diet:** *Mostly insects.* Feeds on a variety of insects, especially larvae of wood-boring beetles; also some berries and small fruits, a few acorns. **Behavior:** Forages by climbing oaks, pines, other trees, tapping and probing, flaking off bits of bark, searching for insects. Also climbs acrobatically among branches, sometimes hanging upside down, and probes at flowers of agaves and other plants. Male (slightly larger and longer-billed than female) spends more time foraging on trunk, female does more on branches and twigs.

NESTING   Birds may pair up and begin working on nest cavity by midwinter. Members of pair may drum and tap near potential nest site, and make short gliding display flights nearby. **Nest:** Site is cavity in dead stub of large tree, usually 9–50 feet above ground, sometimes lower in agave stalk. In Arizona, nest cavity is often in walnut (easier to excavate than oak). Excavation is by male or by both sexes. **Eggs:** 3–4. White. Incubation is by both sexes, about 14 days. **Young:** Both parents feed nestlings. Age at which young leave nest is not well known; young may follow parents for several weeks after fledging.

MIGRATION   Generally permanent resident, but very rarely may wander to lowlands in winter.

RED-COCKADED WOODPECKER   *Picoides borealis*

Once fairly common in the southeastern United States, this bird is now rare, local, and considered an endangered species. It requires precise conditions within mature pine forest, a habitat that is now scarce. Lives in isolated clans, each clan an extended family group with one pair of adults assisted in their nesting by up to four additional birds. The red "cockade," a small patch of feathers behind the eye of the male, is usually hard to see in the field.

Red-cockaded Woodpecker

HABITAT   *Open pine woodlands.* Ideal habitat is mature pine woods (trees 80–100 or more years old), with very open understory maintained by frequent fires (the pines are fire-resistant). Most common in longleaf pine, but inhabits other pines as well, rarely cypress adjacent to pine woods.

FEEDING   Diet: *Mostly insects.* Feeds mainly on insects and other arthropods, especially ants and beetles, also termites, roaches, centipedes, and others. Also eats some wild fruits and pine seeds. **Behavior:** Forages mainly on pine trunks and branches, flaking off bits of bark in search of insects underneath. Family groups may forage together, males tending to forage on branches and upper trunk, females on lower trunk.

NESTING   Taking part in nesting with the breeding pair are 1–4 "helpers." These are mostly males (70–95 percent of those studied) and mostly the breeding pair's offspring from previous seasons. **Nest:** Preferred sites are cavities excavated in large live pines infected with red heart fungus (which gives tree a soft center inside a solid outer shell). Cavity usually 30–40 feet above ground, can be much lower or higher (to well above 100 feet). Entrance surrounded by tiny holes from which sticky resin oozes out, protecting nest from climbing predators. **Eggs:** 3–4, sometimes 2–5. White. Incubation is by both parents and to some extent by additional helpers; breeding male is on nest at night. Incubation period notably short, about 10–11 days. **Young:** Are fed by both parents and by helpers. Young leave nest at about 26–29 days. One brood per year, rarely two.

MIGRATION   Generally permanent resident; may wander some distance, perhaps after habitat destruction. Young females often disperse farther away from birthplace than young males.

CONSERVATION STATUS   *Endangered.* Has disappeared from many areas of former occurrence, with ongoing decline documented in several regions. Total population perhaps under 10,000, many of these in isolated groups facing local extinction. Causes for decline include suppression of natural fires, over-cutting of pine forest in southeast.

WHITE-HEADED WOODPECKER   *Picoides albolarvatus*

Boldly marked but quiet in its behavior, the White-headed Woodpecker is a specialty of mountain pine forests in the far west. At some times of year it feeds heavily on pine seeds, more so than any other North American woodpecker. Perhaps because of the high proportion of dry seeds in its diet, it is often seen coming down to the edge of water to drink.

HABITAT   *Mountain pine forests.* Seldom found away from pines, and favors those with large cones or prolific seed production, such as Coulter, ponderosa, Jeffrey, and sugar

pines. Also forages in incense-cedars, sequoias, and other conifers, and ranges very uncommonly up to elevations dominated by firs.

FEEDING **Diet:** *Mostly insects and pine seeds.* At some seasons, eats mostly pine seeds. Diet also includes wood-boring beetles, ants, and other insects, as well as spiders. **Behavior:** Obtains pine seeds by prying open cones in trees. Also forages for insects on trunk and limbs, and among needle clusters in conifers. Typically pries off flakes of bark rather than knocking them off, so foraging tends to be quiet. Sometimes catches insects in flight. Males and females often have different foraging behaviors, but this varies with place and season.

White-headed Woodpecker

NESTING Both sexes tap at potential nest site, and other displays around nest are apparently important in pair formation. **Nest:** Site is in cavity in heavy dead stub of tree (especially pines, also aspens, oaks, and others), usually 6–15 feet above ground, sometimes 2–25 feet, rarely up to 50 feet. New cavity each year, but often in same tree as used in previous years. Nest hole is excavated by both sexes. **Eggs:** 4–5, sometimes 3–7. White, often becoming stained by pine pitch on parents' plumage. Incubation is by both sexes, about 14 days. **Young:** Both parents feed young, and young leave the nest about 26 days after hatching.

MIGRATION Generally permanent resident, although a few may move to lower elevations for winter.

THREE-TOED AND BLACK-BACKED WOODPECKERS

Close relatives with several characteristics in common. Both are woodpeckers of the far north and high mountains, with only three toes on each foot (typical woodpeckers have four). They often forage on dead conifers, flaking off bits of bark to get at insects, and they may gradually remove all the bark from a standing dead tree. Often they will move into an area after many trees have been killed by fires or by flooding, or during population explosions of certain insects. They are thus somewhat nomadic; usually uncommon, they may become locally numerous when such prime conditions for them are created.

These two species may have hostile interactions where they meet. Although their ranges seem to overlap widely, in most places one or the other is by far the more common.

THREE-TOED WOODPECKER *Picoides tridactylus*

Often quiet and inconspicuous, and may perch motionless against a tree trunk for minutes at a time, making it easy to overlook. In some places the Three-toed Woodpecker provides the most effective control of the spruce bark beetle, a major forest pest.

HABITAT *Conifer forests.* Often closely associated with spruce, also found in pine, fir, tamarack, sometimes mixed with deciduous trees such as aspen or willow. Favors areas with many standing dead trees, as after fire or floods. May concentrate in areas with big infestations of wood-boring insects.

FEEDING **Diet:** *Mostly insects.* Diet is mainly wood-boring beetle larvae, also moth caterpillars and various other insects. Eats some fruit, and may visit sapsucker diggings to feed

on sap. **Behavior:** Forages on live or dead conifers, especially spruces. Often scales off flakes of bark to get at insects, and may gradually remove all bark from a dead tree. Members of a pair forage together at times, but usually separately while nesting.

NESTING   Same pairs may remain together for more than one season. **Nest:** Site is cavity in tree, typically dead conifer, sometimes in aspen, in live tree, or in utility pole. Cavity (new one each year, excavated by both sexes) usually 5–15 feet above ground, sometimes 2–50 feet up. Adult birds often quite unwary around nest, ignoring nearby observers. **Eggs:** 4, sometimes 3–6. White. Incubation is by both sexes (with male incubating at night and part of day), 12–14 days. **Young:** Both parents feed nestlings. Young leave nest about 22–26 days after hatching, may remain with parents for another 4–8 weeks. One brood per year.

Three-toed Woodpecker

MIGRATION   Populations in far north and high mountains may move short distance south or downslope in winter. Irregularly may stage southward irruptions in winter, with a few moving well south of breeding range.

CONSERVATION STATUS   Local populations vary considerably; usually uncommon but may become locally abundant during insect infestations. Extensive range in remote northern forest probably provides for secure future.

BLACK-BACKED WOODPECKER   *Picoides arcticus*

Generally uncommon, but not so quiet or inconspicuous as the Three-toed Woodpecker. Where the two species are found together, the Black-backed usually dominates, perhaps driving the Three-toed away from choice feeding or nesting areas.

HABITAT   *Boreal forests of firs and spruces.* Favors areas of dead or dying conifers, and may concentrate at burned or flooded areas with many standing dead trees. Also in undamaged forests of pine, Douglas-fir, hemlock, tamarack, and spruce, especially spruce bogs. Frequents lowlands in north, mountains in west.

FEEDING   **Diet:** *Mostly insects.* Feeds mainly on the larvae of wood-boring beetles; also eats other insects, spiders, some fruits and nuts. **Behavior:** Typical foraging behavior involves methodically flaking the bark off dead trees, searching for insects. May gradually remove the bark from an entire snag; may forage this way on fallen logs as well. Also gleans insects from bark of live trees, rarely catches insects in flight.

NESTING   Many aggressive displays, with complex harsh calls; some of these displays may also be used in courtship. **Nest:** Site is in cavity in dead tree or stub, usually conifer such as spruce or pine, sometimes birch or other deciduous tree; occasionally in live tree or utility pole. Usually 2–15 feet above ground, rarely 50 feet or higher. Cavity excavated by both sexes, with male often doing most of work. Bark

Black-backed Woodpecker

usually cleared away from area around entrance hole. **Eggs:** 3–4, sometimes 2–6. White. Incubation is by both sexes (male incubating at night and part of day), probably 12–14 days. **Young:** Both parents feed nestlings. Male forages farther from nest, may make fewer feeding trips with more food each time. Young thought to leave nest about 25 days after hatching. One brood per year.

MIGRATION   Not strictly migratory but may move around in response to changing conditions, often moving into a region after fires kill many standing trees. Eastern birds occasionally stage southward irruptions in winter, with scattered individuals showing up well south of breeding range.

CONSERVATION STATUS   Local populations rise and fall with changes in feeding conditions, but total population may be more or less stable.

FLICKERS — GENUS *Colaptes*

Flickers are large brown woodpeckers that spend much of their time on the ground, where they hop about searching for ants. There are several kinds in North and South America, most of them found in semi-open country, not in deep forest.

NORTHERN FLICKER   *Colaptes auratus*

This brown woodpecker flashes bright colors under its wings and tail when it flies. Its ringing calls and short bursts of drumming can be heard in spring almost throughout North America. Two very different-looking forms—Yellow-shafted

Northern Flicker

Flicker in the east and north, and Red-shafted Flicker in the west—were once considered separate species. They interbreed wherever their ranges come in contact. On the western Great Plains, there is a broad zone where *all* the flickers are intergrades between Red-shafted and Yellow-shafted.

HABITAT   *Open forests, woodlots, groves, towns, semi-open country.* With its wide range, from Alaska to Nicaragua, the flicker can be found in almost any habitat with trees. Tends to avoid dense unbroken forest, requiring some open ground for foraging. May be in very open country with few trees.

FEEDING   *Diet: Mostly ants and other insects.* Probably eats ants more frequently than any other North American bird. Also feeds on beetles, termites, caterpillars, and other insects. Eats many fruits and berries, especially in fall and winter, and eats seeds and nuts at times. **Behavior:** Forages by hopping on ground, climbing tree trunks and limbs, occasionally flying out to catch insects in the air. Also will perch in outer branches to eat fruits and berries. Has been reported catching young bats leaving their roost in Wyoming.

NESTING   Males defend nesting territory with calling, drumming, and many aggressive displays, including swinging head back and forth, flicking wings open and spreading tail to show off bright underside. Courtship displays mostly similar. **Nest:** Site is cavity in tree or post, rarely in a burrow in the ground. Tree cavities usually in dead wood; pine, cottonwood, and willow are among favored trees. Cavity excavated by both sexes, typically 6–20 feet above ground, sometimes much higher (to 100 feet or more). **Eggs:** 5–8, sometimes 3–12. White. Incubation is by both sexes (with male incubating at night and part of day), 11–16 days. **Young:** Both parents feed young, by regurgitation. Young leave nest about 4 weeks after hatching, are fed by parents at first, later following them to good foraging sites. One brood per year, or two in south.

MIGRATION   Northern Yellow-shafted Flickers from Alaska and Canada strongly migratory, most traveling east and then south. Big flights move down Atlantic coast in fall, migrating by day. Red-shafted Flickers often migrate shorter distances, moving southward and from mountains into lowlands; some spread eastward on Great Plains in winter.

CONSERVATION STATUS   Although still abundant and widespread, recent surveys indicate declines in population over much of the range since the 1960s. Introduced starlings compete with flickers for freshly excavated nesting sites, may drive the flickers away.

GILDED FLICKER   *Colaptes chrysoides*

In its color pattern, this bird combines some elements from both the Yellow-shafted and Red-shafted forms of Northern Flicker. However, it is slightly smaller than either, and it lives in the lowlands of the southwest—mainly in the desert, where it nests in holes in giant saguaro cactus. Its habits are mostly similar to those of the Northern Flicker.

Gilded Flickers are essentially permanent residents, with only local movements. In a few places, they overlap in breeding range with Red-shafted Flickers at middle elevations (Sonoita Creek near Patagonia, Arizona, is one good example). In such places, the Red-shafted and Gilded flickers interbreed freely, producing a summer population that is nearly all hybrids.

GENUS *Dryocopus*

PILEATED WOODPECKER   *Dryocopus pileatus*

A big, dashing bird with a flaming crest, the largest woodpecker in North America (except the Ivory-bill, which is almost certainly extinct). Excavating deep into rotten wood to get at the nests of carpenter ants, the Pileated leaves characteristic rectangular holes in dead trees. This species became rare in eastern North America with clearing of forests in centuries past, but has gradually increased in numbers again since about the beginning of the 20th century. Where unmolested, it even lives in parks and woodlots around the edges of large cities.

HABITAT   *Conifer, mixed, and hardwood forests; woodlots.* Favors mature deciduous or mixed deciduous-coniferous forest, also coniferous forest.

Pileated Woodpecker

Wide variety of specific forest types from southern swamps to old-growth Douglas-fir forest of northwest. Also in second growth and fragmented woodlots, as long as some large trees are present.

FEEDING   **Diet:** *Mostly ants and other insects, also fruits, nuts.* Carpenter ants may be up to 60 percent of diet; also eats other ants (rarely digging into anthills on ground), termites, larvae of wood-boring beetles, other insects. About one-quarter of the diet may be

wild fruits, berries, and nuts. **Behavior:** Forages mainly by probing, prying, and excavating in dead wood in search of insects. May gouge deep holes in rotten wood to get at ant nests, sometimes tearing apart stumps and big sections of fallen logs. May clamber about acrobatically in small branches to get at berries.

NESTING   Territory is defended with loud drumming and ringing calls. Courtship displays include spreading wings (showing off white wing patch), raising crest, swinging head back and forth, gliding display flight. At prospective nest site, both sexes may tap or drum on wood. **Nest:** Site is a cavity in a dead tree or in dead branch of a live tree, sometimes in utility pole, usually 15–80 feet above ground. Generally makes a new cavity each year, with both sexes helping to excavate. **Eggs:** 3–5. White. Incubation is by both sexes (male incubating at night and part of day), about 18 days. **Young:** Both parents feed nestlings, by regurgitation. Young leave nest 26–28 days after hatching, may remain with parents 2–3 months.

MIGRATION   Permanent resident, but individuals sometimes wander far from breeding areas.

CONSERVATION STATUS   Numbers in eastern United States declined sharply in 18th and 19th centuries with clearing of eastern forest. Since about 1900, has made a gradual comeback, with the species becoming common again in some areas. May be adapting to second-growth woods and proximity of humans.

GENUS *Campephilus*

IVORY-BILLED WOODPECKER   *Campephilus principalis*

A huge woodpecker that once ranged over much of the southeast. Now almost certainly extinct; last undoubted records in the United States were in 1950s, although reports in Cuba persisted into 1980s.

May have been somewhat nomadic at one time, moving into areas of virgin forest where numbers of trees were dying or recently dead. It foraged by scaling off the bark of such trees and by excavating in dead wood, feeding mainly on beetle larvae.

Pairs may have mated for life. Nest cavities were excavated 15–70 feet above ground, and the 1–5 white eggs were incubated by both sexes, for roughly 20 days. Both parents fed the young, which left the nest at about 5 weeks but remained with the parents for several months thereafter.

Unlike the Carolina Parakeet and Passenger Pigeon, which were essentially gone by the beginning of the 20th century, the Ivory-bill survived almost into the modern era. There are even good photographs and tape recordings of Ivory-bills in the wild — haunting reminders that the environmental movement arrived just too late to save this magnificent bird from extinction.

TYRANT FLYCATCHERS (Family Tyrannidae)

Tyrant flycatchers make up a purely New World family, unrelated to the Old World flycatchers, a few of which have strayed into Alaska. Birders in North America know the tyrant flycatchers as birds that are often difficult to identify — but the challenge becomes much greater as one ventures into the tropics, where most of the 400-plus species are found.

Voices are very important for most flycatchers. Evidently, many of them recognize their own species largely by sound. Many other types of songbirds have to learn to sing their songs by hearing them from adults of their own kind; but research has shown that at least some flycatchers are born knowing their songs and can sing them perfectly even if raised in isolation. A characteristic of many flycatchers is a "dawn song," given often before sunrise and seldom later in the day. These early morning performances can sound very different from the daytime songs and can be puzzling to birders.

Feeding   The best-known foraging method of this family involves sitting still and watching for flying insects to go past, then sallying out in fast, agile flight to capture them. The strategy is so typical of this family that it is called "flycatching" even when other kinds of birds do it.

Special adaptations for the flycatching habit can be seen in the shape of the bill, usually wide and flat, making a bigger surface area for grabbing elusive insects. Most typical flycatchers have long bristles at the corners of the mouth that may act as "feelers" in the critical last split second before the bill snaps shut on its fleeing prey. These birds usually perch bolt upright, peering about as they wait for insects to appear, and they evidently have very keen eyesight.

Almost all of our species feed by flying out from perches, but not all of their insect prey is caught in midair; some kinds regularly take insects and spiders from foliage while hovering momentarily, and some will drop to take insects from the ground. Some large flycatchers have been seen catching hummingbirds—reflecting the fact that some small hummingbirds are about the size of large insects. Some of our species also will eat berries on occasion.

In the tropics, where the family is much more diverse, flycatchers have several very different modes of feeding. Some run about on the ground in open country, some search for insects by hopping about among foliage in trees, and some feed primarily on berries and small fruits.

Nesting   This family is so varied that it is hard to generalize about nesting habits. In North America, most flycatchers build open cup nests among the branches of trees or shrubs or use cavities in tree trunks, but some build enclosed globular nests with an entrance on one side. In the tropics, some flycatchers nest on the ground or build long hanging nests; at least one species takes over active nests of other birds, driving away the rightful owners (and kicking out their eggs) before laying their own eggs in the nest.

In most North American flycatchers, the female does most or all of the incubating, but the male defends the nesting territory and generally takes part in feeding the young.

Displays   Male flycatchers mostly advertise their claims to nesting territory by voice, especially with their distinctive dawn songs. Some have flight-song displays; these are not often seen in most species, but some, like the Vermilion Flycatcher, perform these flights very frequently in the breeding season. Early courtship activities in some flycatchers may involve the male and female chasing each other in high-speed flight among the trees.

GENUS *Camptostoma*

NORTHERN BEARDLESS-TYRANNULET   *Camptostoma imberbe*

A standing joke among birders is that this bird's name is longer than the bird itself. This tiny flycatcher occurs in thickets and streamside woods near the Mexican border, where it is easily overlooked until one learns its piping calls. It perches upright and often flips its tail like an *Empidonax* flycatcher, but it may feed differently, moving along twigs to glean insects from the foliage. The name "Beardless" reflects the lack of bristles around the base of the bill (present in most of our flycatchers).

HABITAT *Low woods, mesquites, stream thickets, lower canyons.* In United States, often in woods near streams through dry country. Favors stands of mesquite or cottonwood-willow groves in Arizona, native woodland of huisache, ebony, hackberry, and mesquite in southern Texas. In tropics found in a variety of semi-open habitats and dry woods.

FEEDING **Diet:** *Mostly insects.* Diet not known in detail. Apparently feeds mostly on very small and slow-moving insects; known items include scale insects, treehoppers, beetle larvae, moth caterpillars, fly pupae. Also reported to eat some seeds and berries. **Behavior:** Especially in summer, often forages in typical flycatcher style, flying out from a perch to catch insects in its bill, taking them either in the air or from foliage. Often, however, forages more like a vireo, moving slowly and taking insects from surface of twigs or leaves.

Northern Beardless-Tyrannulet

NESTING Nesting behavior is not well known. Male sings whistled song in spring and summer to defend nesting territory. **Nest:** Site is in outer branches of tree or large shrub, 4–50 feet above the ground, usually 10–30 feet up. Often placed where it will be well camouflaged: inside a clump of mistletoe or in an old tent caterpillar web, in a tree that has many such clumps. Nest is the size and shape of a baseball, with an entrance high on one side; made of grasses and weeds, lined with soft plant down and feathers. **Eggs:** 3, sometimes 1–2. White, finely marked with dots of brown and gray, especially around the larger end. Details of incubation poorly known. **Young:** Probably fed by both parents. Development of young and age at first flight not well known.

MIGRATION Only a short-distance migrant. In Arizona more common in summer, but small numbers winter regularly at lower elevations. A few present at all seasons in southern Texas, perhaps more numerous in summer.

CONSERVATION STATUS May have declined with loss of streamside habitat in the southwest, but still locally common.

GENUS *Myiopagis*

GREENISH ELAENIA *Myiopagis viridicata*

Widespread in the American tropics, this small flycatcher is mostly a forest bird, easily overlooked. It has strayed into our area once, reaching the upper Texas coast.

GENUS *Elaenia*

CARIBBEAN ELAENIA *Elaenia martinica*

The various tropical flycatchers of the genus *Elaenia* are mostly very similar, challenging to tell apart. When a single Caribbean Elaenia reached northwestern Florida, it was identified mostly by voice. Its normal range comes no closer to our area than islands off the coast of the Yucatan Peninsula.

TUFTED FLYCATCHER   *Mitrephanes phaeocercus*

In mountain pine forests in Mexico, this distinctive little flycatcher is common at all seasons. In winter, a few also move down to lower elevations. Presumably such migrants account for the couple of records in our area, in western Texas.

PEWEES — GENUS *Contopus*

These are rather nondescript, medium-sized flycatchers that live in woodlands, better known by their voices than their looks. The name "pewee" comes from the song of the most common species in the east.

OLIVE-SIDED FLYCATCHER   *Contopus borealis*

This compact, big-headed flycatcher sits bolt upright on top of the highest dead branch of a tree, calling *pip-pip* at intervals, as if to ensure that birders notice it. A long-distance migrant, the Olive-sided Flycatcher breeds mostly in northern coniferous forest and winters in the tropics. It has become noticeably less common in recent years, perhaps because of a loss of habitat on the wintering grounds.

Olive-sided Flycatcher

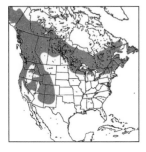

HABITAT   *Conifer forests, burns, clearings.* Breeds mostly in coniferous forest of the north and the higher mountains, especially around the edges of open areas including bogs, ponds, clearings. Also nests near the coast in California, in tall trees (including eucalyptus) in foothill canyons.

FEEDING   **Diet:** *Insects.* Apparently feeds almost entirely on flying insects. In summer, a high percentage of these are various kinds of wasps, winged ants, and bees, including many honeybees. Also eats beetles, grasshoppers, true bugs, moths, and others. Winter diet not well known. **Behavior:** Forages by watching from a high, exposed perch, often on a dead branch at very top of tree, flying out to catch passing insects in the air, then returning to its perch to eat them. Always or almost always takes insects in midair, not from foliage or ground.

NESTING   Male defends nesting territory by singing incessantly in spring. Courtship behavior not well known, probably involves active chasing through the treetops. **Nest:** Site is in tree, usually on horizontal branch well out from the trunk. Conifers preferred in most areas, but in other areas will often nest in deciduous trees; height also quite variable, 5–70 feet above ground. Nest usually well hidden among dense twigs or needles. Nest (probably built by female) a flat open cup of twigs, grass, weeds, lined with finer materials. **Eggs:** 3, rarely 2–4. White to pinkish buff, with brown and gray spots concentrated at larger end. Incubation is by female only, 16–17 days, sometimes reported as 14 days. **Young:** Fed by both parents. Age of young at first flight about 21–23 days.

MIGRATION   Tends to migrate late in spring and early in fall, but migration is spread over a long period. Winters mostly in South America, a few in Central America.

Evidently has been declining in some regions for many years, particularly so in recent decades. Loss of wintering habitat has been suggested as one possible cause.

GREATER PEWEE *Contopus pertinax*

In mountain forests of Arizona (and locally in western New Mexico), this chunky flycatcher is fairly common in summer. It is often seen perched on a dead twig high in a pine, watching for flying insects. In color and markings, the Greater Pewee is as plain as a bird can be; but it has a beautifully clear, whistled song, *ho-say, ma-re-ah*, giving rise to its Mexican nickname of "José Maria."

HABITAT   *Pine and pine-oak forests of mountains, canyons.* Breeds in relatively open forest with tall pines and scattered understory (often of oaks). Also in sycamores and other trees along canyons through pine-oak woods. The few that winter in the United States are in groves or woodlots in the lowlands.

Greater Pewee

FEEDING   **Diet:** *Insects.* Diet is not known in detail, undoubtedly includes a wide variety of flying insects. **Behavior:** Forages mostly by watching from a perch within a tree, especially an open tree such as a pine, choosing perches at most levels but usually fairly high. Flies out to capture flying insects in midair. Apparently has very good eyesight, sometimes flying out after insects up to 50 feet away from its perch.

NESTING   Breeding behavior is not well known. Both members of pair are quick to attack jays or other potential nest predators that come near nest tree. Some observers have reported that smaller birds (such as warblers and vireos) prefer to nest near the Greater Pewee to gain protection from predators. **Nest:** Site is at fork in horizontal branch of pine, sycamore, oak, or other tall tree, usually 10–40 feet above the ground. Nest (probably built by female) is a well-built cup of grass, weeds, leaves, and other plant fibers, often held to the branch with spider webs. Inside of nest is lined with fine grasses, and outside is camouflaged with lichens. From the ground, nest may look like a lichen-covered bump on the branch. **Eggs:** 3–4. Dull white to creamy white, lightly marked with brown and gray, mostly near larger end. Details of incubation not well known. **Young:** Probably fed by both parents. Age of young at first flight not well known.

MIGRATION   Probably only a short-distance migrant; present all year in most of Mexican range. One or two individuals often remain through winter in Arizona and sometimes in southern California.

CONSERVATION STATUS   Numbers in the United States apparently stable.

WESTERN WOOD-PEWEE   *Contopus sordidulus*

Small and plain, but often very common, this flycatcher of western woodlands is best known by its voice. Its burry, descending whistle has a hazy sound, well suited to hot summer afternoons. The bird also sings at dawn and dusk, including late in the evening when most other songbirds are quiet. This species and the Eastern Wood-Pewee look almost exactly alike; however, like some other small flycatchers, they evidently recognize their own kind primarily by voice.

HABITAT   *Woodlands, pine-oak forests, open conifers, river groves.* Breeds in a wide variety of open wooded habitats, mostly from the lowlands up to middle elevations in mountains. Favored habitats include aspen groves, pine-oak woods, and cottonwood-willow groves along streams. Winters at forest edges and in scrubby woods in the tropics.

FEEDING   **Diet:** *Insects.* Feeds almost entirely on insects, mostly flying ones, only occasionally eating a few berries. Diet features various kinds of flies, also wasps, bees, winged ants, moths, beetles, and others, including a few caterpillars. **Behavior:** Does most foraging by watching from an exposed perch within the shady middle or lower levels of a tree, then flying out to catch an insect in the air. Also flies out and hovers while taking insects from foliage or twigs, sometimes from tall grass.

Western Wood-Pewee

NESTING   Male sings in spring, especially at dawn and dusk, to defend nesting territory. Courtship behavior is not well known, may involve active chasing through treetops. **Nest:** Site is in tree (perhaps more often deciduous than coniferous), usually on a horizontal branch well out from the trunk. Usually 15–40 feet above ground, can be lower or much higher. Nest (probably built by female) is flat open cup of grass, plant fibers, plant down, the outside decorated with gray mosses, leaves, and sometimes lichens. From the side or below, nest may look like a bump or knot on the branch. Some observers report that nest of Western is typically larger than that of Eastern Wood-Pewee. **Eggs:** 3, sometimes 2, rarely 4. Whitish, with brown and lavender blotches often concentrated toward larger end. Incubation is by female, 12–13 days. **Young:** Both parents feed young. Age of young at first flight probably about 14–18 days.

MIGRATION   Strictly a summer resident in North America, arriving mostly late April and May, departing before mid-October. Probably migrates at night.

CONSERVATION STATUS   Still common to abundant in some areas, but apparently declining in parts of California and elsewhere.

EASTERN WOOD-PEWEE   *Contopus virens*

In eastern woods in summer, the plaintive whistled *pee-a-wee* of this small flycatcher is often heard before the bird is seen. The bird itself is usually somewhere in the leafy middle story of the trees, perched on a bare twig, darting out to catch passing insects. The Wood-Pewee sings most often at dawn and dusk, and it may continue singing quite late in the evening, after most songbirds have fallen silent.

HABITAT   *Woodlands, groves.* Breeds in forest (mainly deciduous, sometimes mixed, seldom coniferous forest). Favors margins of clearings, such as around meadows, roadsides, ponds, or small openings in forest. Winters at forest edges and in scrubby woods in tropics.

FEEDING   **Diet:** *Mostly insects.* Feeds almost entirely on insects and other arthropods, taking only small numbers of berries. Diet in summer includes various kinds of flies, also wasps, bees, winged ants, beetles, moths, true bugs, and grasshoppers; also some spiders and millipedes. **Behavior:** Does most foraging by watching from an exposed perch within a tree, then flying out to catch an insect in the air. Also takes insects from foliage or twigs while hovering, and may descend to pick insects from grass or other plants close to the ground.

NESTING	Male sings in spring, especially at dawn and dusk, to defend nesting territory. Courtship behavior is not well known, may involve male actively chasing female through treetops. **Nest:** Site is in tree (usually deciduous), saddled on a horizontal branch well out from the trunk. Usually 15–45 feet above ground, can be lower or much higher. Nest (probably built by female alone) is compact open cup of grass, plant fibers, and spider webs, the outside usually decorated with lichens. Nest seems small for size of bird. From the side or below, nest may look like a bump or knot on the branch. **Eggs:** 3, sometimes 2, rarely 4. Whitish, with brown and lavender blotches often concentrated toward larger end. Incubation is by female, 12–13 days. **Young:** Both parents feed young. Age of young at first flight about 14–18 days.
MIGRATION	Strictly a summer resident in North America, arriving on breeding grounds mostly in May, very few remaining after beginning of October. Probably migrates at night.
CONSERVATION STATUS	Still widespread and fairly common, but surveys show a slight decline in recent decades. Reasons for decline are not well known.

CUBAN PEWEE   *Contopus caribaeus*

Common in the Bahamas and Cuba, this rather drab flycatcher was first found in our area in 1995, when a single bird appeared in Florida. Looking somewhat like an Empidonax flycatcher with only a partial eye-ring, it might have been overlooked as a stray to Florida in the past.

EMPIDONAX FLYCATCHERS — GENUS *Empidonax*

The name of the genus means "king of the gnats," but birders often use less complimentary names for these little flycatchers as they struggle to identify them. Our 11 species of Empidonax are notoriously similar: little olive-gray birds with eye-rings and wing bars, safely recognized mainly by their voices. They mostly divide up by habitat in summer, when one or more species can be found in most wooded or brushy areas in North America.

YELLOW-BELLIED FLYCATCHER   *Empidonax flaviventris*

Yellow-bellied Flycatcher

While some of its relatives are often found in sunny open places, the Yellow-bellied Flycatcher is a bird of deep shade. It spends the summer in spruce bogs and other damp northern forests, where it places its nest on the ground in sphagnum moss or among tree roots. Although the Yellow-bellied is not as hard to identify in spring as some small flycatchers, birders may miss it because it moves north late, after most of the spring migrants have passed.

HABITAT   *Woods; in summer, boreal forests, muskegs, bogs.* Breeds in wet northern forest, especially in spruce bogs with ground cover of sphagnum moss, also in tamarack-white cedar swamps and in willow-alder thickets along streams in dense coniferous forest. In winter, lives in undergrowth of tropical forest.

FEEDING   **Diet:** *Mostly insects.* Feeds on a variety of small insects, both flying types and those taken from foliage, including many ants and small wasps, also flies, beetles, true bugs, caterpillars, moths, and others. Also eats many spiders, and

eats small numbers of berries and sometimes seeds. **Behavior:** Forages by watching from a perch, usually at low to middle levels in the forest, and then flying out to catch insects in the air. Also takes some food (such as caterpillars and spiders) from foliage or twigs while hovering. May sometimes take some insects while perched.

NESTING   Male defends nesting territory by singing, often from an exposed perch. Adults tend to be quiet and inconspicuous around the nest. **Nest:** Site is usually in dense sphagnum moss on or just above the ground in boggy places; sometimes placed among the upturned roots of a fallen tree or in other sheltered low spot. Generally well hidden within mosses with only a small entrance showing, and very difficult to find. Nest is bulky cup of mosses, mixed with weeds and rootlets, lined with grass, sedges, and many fine rootlets. **Eggs:** 3–4, sometimes 5. White, lightly spotted with brown. Incubation is by female only, 12–14 days. **Young:** Both parents bring food for nestlings. Age of young at first flight about 13–14 days. Probably only one brood per year.

MIGRATION   Spring migration is notably late, with most northbound migrants passing through in mid- to late May. Almost all migration is through the east, even for birds nesting in far western Canada.

CONSERVATION STATUS   Could be vulnerable to loss of habitat, especially on wintering grounds. Currently numbers appear to be stable.

ACADIAN FLYCATCHER *Empidonax virescens*

In southern woods in summer, the short explosive song of the Acadian Flycatcher comes from shady spots along streams or near swamps. This is the only member of the confusing Empidonax group to nest in most parts of the Deep South. Its range extends north to the Great Lakes and southern New England, and it has been gradually expanding this range toward the north.

HABITAT   *Deciduous forests, ravines, swampy woods, beech groves.* Breeds mostly in wet deciduous forest, such as in swamps or dense riverside woods; also in the understory of drier woods. Often nests in beech trees where they occur. Winters in the tropics in woodland or along its edges.

FEEDING   **Diet:** *Mostly insects.* Feeds on a wide variety of insects, especially wasps, bees, ants, caterpillars, and beetles, also flies, moths, true bugs, and others. Also eats some spiders, millipedes, and some small fruits and berries. **Behavior:** Forages by watching from a perch, usually at middle levels within the forest, and then flying out to catch insects in the air. Also takes some food (such as caterpillars and spiders) from foliage or twigs while hovering.

Acadian Flycatcher

NESTING   Courtship displays involve rapid aerial chases through the trees; male may hover above female when she stops to perch. **Nest:** Site is in tree or large shrub, usually deciduous, averaging 13 feet above ground, sometimes 4–50 feet up. Usually suspended within horizontal fork of branch well out from trunk. Nest (built by female) is a rather loosely made cup of weed stems, twigs, grass, and other plant fibers, sometimes lined with finer materials such as rootlets and plant down. Webs of spiders and caterpillars probably help to hold nest together. Usually has trailing strands of weeds or other materials hanging below, giving nest a sloppy or abandoned

appearance. **Eggs:** 3, sometimes 2–4. Creamy white, lightly spotted with brown. Incubation is by female, 13–15 days. **Young:** Fed by both parents. Age of young at first flight about 13–15 days. Male may continue to feed fledglings from first nest while female begins incubating the second clutch of the season.

MIGRATION Unlike other Empidonax flycatchers, the Acadian regularly migrates north across the Gulf of Mexico in spring. Most migration is at night.

CONSERVATION STATUS Would be vulnerable to loss of habitat, but no significant decline noted so far. In some regions, Brown-headed Cowbirds often lay eggs in nests of this species.

ALDER FLYCATCHER *Empidonax alnorum*

A small bird that spends the summer catching flying insects in northern thickets. This bird and the Willow Flycatcher are so similar that they were considered one species until the 1970s. The only differences apparent in the field are in their voices. However, voice is important to these birds: many other kinds of songbirds have to learn their songs, but Willow and Alder flycatchers are born instinctively knowing the voice of their own species.

HABITAT *Willows, alders, brushy swamps, swales.* Breeds in thickets of deciduous trees and shrubs, usually near water, as around streams, ponds, or bogs. Especially common in thickets of willows or alders. Winters in woodland edges or second growth in the tropics, especially near water.

FEEDING **Diet:** *Mostly insects.* Differences in diet, if any, between this species and Willow Flycatcher are not well known. Apparently eats mostly insects, including wasps, bees, winged ants, beetles, flies, caterpillars, moths, true bugs, and others. Also eats some spiders, a few berries, and possibly some seeds. **Behavior:** Forages by watching from a perch and then flying out to catch insects. Usually forages from perches within tall shrubs or low trees; catches insects in midair, or takes them from foliage while hovering.

NESTING Male defends nesting territory by singing. Courtship behavior is not well known, probably involves male actively chasing female through the trees. **Nest:** Site is usually low in a deciduous shrub, averaging about 2 feet up, usually lower than 6 feet above the ground. Placed in a vertical or diagonal fork in a branch. Nest (probably built by female alone) is an open cup, usually built rather loosely of grass, weeds, strips of bark, small twigs, rootlets, lined with plant down or other soft materials. Nest may have strips of grass or bark dangling from the bottom. **Eggs:** 3–4, rarely 2. White, with brown spots concentrated toward larger end. Incubation is by female, 12–14 days. **Young:** Both parents bring food for nestlings. Age of young at first flight about 13–14 days.

MIGRATION More of a long-distance migrant than Willow Flycatcher, tending to nest farther north and winter farther south. Migrates late in spring and early in fall.

CONSERVATION STATUS Much of breeding habitat in the north is remote from effects of human disturbance. Numbers probably stable.

WILLOW FLYCATCHER *Empidonax traillii*

Until the 1970s, this bird and the Alder Flycatcher masqueraded as just one species under the name "Traill's Flycatcher." They are essentially identical in looks, but their voices are different. Either kind may be found in thickets of either willow or alder shrubs, but their ranges are largely separate: Alder Flycatchers spend the summer mostly in Canada and Alaska, while Willow Flycatchers nest mostly south of the Canadian border.

Willow Flycatcher

HABITAT *Bushes, willow thickets, brushy fields, upland copses.* Breeds in thickets of deciduous trees and shrubs, especially willows, or along woodland edges. Often near streams or marshes (especially in southern part of range), but may be found in drier habitats than Alder Flycatcher. Winters around clearings and second growth in the tropics, especially near water.

FEEDING **Diet:** *Mostly insects.* Differences in diet, if any, between this species and Alder Flycatcher are not well known. Apparently eats mostly insects, including wasps, bees, winged ants, beetles, flies, caterpillars, moths, true bugs, and others. Also eats some spiders, a few berries, and possibly some seeds. **Behavior:** Forages by watching from a perch and then flying out to catch insects. Usually forages from perches within tall shrubs or low trees; catches insects in midair or takes them from foliage while hovering.

NESTING Male defends nesting territory by singing (female may sing also). Courtship behavior is not well known, probably involves male actively chasing female through the trees. In some regions, Brown-headed Cowbirds often lay their eggs in nests of this species. **Nest:** Site is in a deciduous shrub or tree, especially in willow, 4–15 feet above the ground. Placed in a vertical or diagonal fork of a branch or on top of a horizontal branch. Nest (built by female alone) is an open cup of grass, strips of bark, plant fibers, lined with plant down and other soft materials. Nest often has strips of plant material dangling from the bottom. **Eggs:** 3–4. Pale buff to whitish, with brown spots concentrated toward larger end. Incubation is by female, 12–15 days. **Young:** Both parents bring food for nestlings. Age of young at first flight about 12–14 days.

MIGRATION Migrates relatively late in spring and early in fall. In North America, migrants are seen moving north mostly during mid- to late May, moving south in August and September.

CONSERVATION STATUS Has declined in some areas with loss of streamside habitat. The race that nests along streams in the southwest is now considered threatened or endangered.

LEAST FLYCATCHER   *Empidonax minimus*

Least Flycatcher

The 11 Empidonax flycatchers in North America are notorious for causing trouble for birders. All are small birds with wing bars and eye-rings, and most are very hard to tell apart. The Least Flycatcher is the smallest and grayest of this group in the east, and it is often common near woodland edges, where it perches in the open and raps out its snappy song, *chebeck!*

HABITAT *Open woods, aspen groves, orchards, shade trees.* Breeds in deciduous or mixed woodlands, seldom in purely coniferous groves. Usually around clearings or edges, but sometimes in the interior of dry woods. Winters in the tropics around woodland edges and second growth.

FEEDING **Diet:** *Mostly insects.* Summer diet is mostly insects, including many small wasps, winged ants, beetles, caterpillars, midges, and flies, with smaller numbers of true bugs, grasshoppers, and others. Also eats spiders and occasionally a few berries.

Behavior: Forages by watching from a perch and flying out to catch insects. Often perches on dead twigs within the middle to lower levels of trees, in fairly open spots. Catches most insects in midair, but also takes food (including caterpillars and spiders) from foliage while hovering.

NESTING   May nest in loose colonies. Courtship behavior not well known, but may involve male chasing female through the trees. Least Flycatchers often actively chase American Redstarts out of nesting territory. **Nest:** Site is usually in deciduous sapling or small tree such as maple, birch, or ash, placed in a vertical fork in a branch. May be 2–65 feet above ground, but heights usually average 12–25 feet, varying with habitat. Nest (evidently built by female only) is a tidy cup of grass, strips of bark, twigs, lichens, plant fibers, often bound together with webs of spiders or caterpillars; lined with fine grass, plant down, animal hair, feathers. **Eggs:** 4, sometimes 3, occasionally 5. Creamy white. Incubation is by female only, 13–15 days. **Young:** Both parents bring food for nestlings. Age of young at first flight about 12–17 days; may be fed by parents for another 2–3 weeks after fledging.

MIGRATION   Migrants are rare in the west, so many of those breeding in western Canada apparently migrate east and then south. In fall, adults tend to migrate south earlier than young birds. A few may winter in southern Florida.

CONSERVATION STATUS   Surveys show some declining populations in southern part of breeding range; however, still widespread and common.

HAMMOND'S FLYCATCHER   *Empidonax hammondii*

Hammond's Flycatcher

The first claim to fame of Hammond's Flycatcher is that it is hard to tell apart from its relatives, especially the Dusky Flycatcher. However, although its range overlaps with that of the Dusky, Hammond's seems to prefer cooler surroundings at all seasons. It nests higher in the mountains and farther north; even on its main wintering grounds south of the border, it is usually in the mountains, not the hot lowlands.

HABITAT   *High conifer forests; in migration, other trees.* Breeds in cool coniferous forests, often where conifers such as Douglas-fir or spruce are mixed with aspens or other deciduous trees. In some areas, may breed in pure stands of aspens. Winters mostly in pine-oak woods of mountains in Mexico and Central America.

FEEDING   **Diet:** *Insects.* Apparently feeds only on insects. Summer diet includes beetles, caterpillars, moths, flies, leafhoppers, and small wasps. Winter diet not well known. **Behavior:** Forages by watching from a perch and then flying out to catch insects, usually returning to perch to eat them. Uses feeding perches at various heights in forest, often low; may take insects in midair, from surface of foliage or branches, or from the ground.

NESTING   In courtship, male approaches female, giving trilled call and fluttering wings. **Nest:** Site is on horizontal branch of tree (often Douglas-fir, pine, fir, or aspen), 10–100 feet above ground, averaging about 25–35 feet up. Nest (built by female, rarely with help from male) is cup of weed stems, grass, strips of bark, lichens, and other items, lined with finer materials such as feathers, fur, and plant down. Spider webs often worked into nest. Nest looks more like those of wood-pewees than those of other Empidonax flycatchers. **Eggs:** 4, sometimes 3. Creamy white, sometimes lightly spotted with reddish brown. Incubation is by female only, 15–16 days. **Young:** Female broods young when they are small, and both parents bring food to nestlings. Age of young at first flight about 16–18 days. Young may remain in a group, tended by parents, for a week or more after fledging.

MIGRATION Migration is spread over long period in both spring and fall, with some lingering late in fall. In spring, adult males migrate north earlier than females.

CONSERVATION STATUS Has lost some habitat with cutting of forests in the northwest, but still widespread and common.

DUSKY FLYCATCHER *Empidonax oberholseri*

Among the confusing Empidonax flycatchers in the west, birders know the Dusky as a bird in the middle. It is intermediate in size and shape between the Hammond's and Gray flycatchers; its breeding habitat is also intermediate, at middle elevations in the mountains, where tall conifers stand among shrubby low thickets. Pioneer ornithologists in the west often confused the Dusky and Gray flycatchers, and they debated for years whether there really were two species.

HABITAT *Breeds in mountain chaparral (Canadian-zone brush) with scattering of trees.* Favored habitat includes both trees and low bushes: varies from open conifer forest with understory of deciduous shrubs to brushy slopes with a few taller trees. In migration, often in foothills. Winters in streamside woods in southwest or in a variety of semi-open habitats in Mexico.

FEEDING **Diet:** *Insects.* Diet not known in detail, but so far as known feeds entirely on insects, including moths, bees, wasps, grasshoppers, damselflies, caterpillars, butterflies, and undoubtedly others, probably all of rather small size. **Behavior:** Forages by watching

Dusky Flycatcher

from an exposed perch (often on a dead branch), then flying out to capture insects, usually in the air. Sometimes drops to ground or hovers next to foliage or bark to capture insects.

NESTING Male defends nesting territory by singing from prominent perch; occasionally performs short flight-song display. In courtship, both sexes hop about in branches, fluttering wings. **Nest:** Site is usually in deciduous shrub, less often in conifer; usually 3–6 feet above ground, rarely up to 16 feet. Placed in vertical fork among dense foliage. Nest (probably built by female only) is cup of grasses, weeds, shreds of bark, lined with plant down, feathers, animal hair, and other soft materials. **Eggs:** 4, sometimes 2–3, rarely 5. Smaller clutch may be laid on second attempt if first nesting fails. Eggs dull white, rarely dotted with brown. Incubation is by female only, usually 15–16 days. **Young:** Brooded by female, fed by both parents. Young leave the nest about 15–20 days after hatching, may be fed by parents for another 3 weeks. One brood per year.

MIGRATION Arrives on breeding grounds mostly in May, departs mostly in August. Evidently migrates at night.

GRAY FLYCATCHER *Empidonax wrightii*

The high desert of the Great Basin is the summer stronghold of this pale little bird. The Gray Flycatcher nests in sagebrush country and in open woods of juniper and pinyon pine, in drier territory than most of its relatives. It also regularly winters farther north than any other Empidonax flycatcher: it is common in winter in the mesquite thickets and streamside groves of southern Arizona.

HABITAT *Sagebrush; also pinyon and juniper. In winter, willows, brush.* Breeds in open and rather arid habitats, especially sagebrush plains with a few taller trees or shrubs, also scrubby woods of juniper and pinyon pine. Winters in mesquite groves and in streamside willows and other trees, in lowlands.

FEEDING **Diet:** *Insects.* Diet not known in detail, but reported to feed only on insects, including beetles, wasps, moths, grasshoppers, and others. **Behavior:** Forages by watching for insects from exposed perch, then flying out to catch them in bill. Typically perches low and often flies down to ground for insects; also catches many insects in midair and takes some from foliage and twigs while hovering.

NESTING May sometimes nest in loose colonies in good habitat. In places, this species and Dusky Flycatcher overlap in nesting habitat, and they will defend territories against each other. **Nest:** Site is typically in vertical crotch of sagebrush or on horizontal branch of juniper or pinyon pine, 3–20 feet above the ground. Nest (built mostly by female, perhaps sometimes with help from male) is a deep cup, rather bulky and loosely constructed. Made of weeds, strips of bark, grasses, twigs; lined with plant down, fine bark fibers, animal fur, feathers. Nest is usually in dense part of plant and is not conspicuous. **Eggs:** 3–4. Creamy white. Incubation is probably by female only, about 14 days. **Young:** Both parents bring food for nestlings. Young leave nest and make first flights about 16 days after hatching.

MIGRATION Migrates shorter distance than most Empidonax flycatchers. Moves rather early in both spring and fall, with some arrivals on breeding range in April and on wintering range in August. Probably migrates at night.

Gray Flycatcher

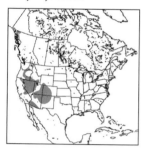

PACIFIC-SLOPE FLYCATCHER *Empidonax difficilis*

In humid woods along the Pacific coast, this little flycatcher is very common in summer. It favors deep shade, often in the groves along streams; it often places its beautiful mossy nest under a bridge or under the eaves of a cabin in the woods. This species and the Cordilleran Flycatcher are almost identical except for call notes and range, and were regarded as one species (called "Western Flycatcher") until the late 1980s.

HABITAT *Moist woods, mixed forests, shady canyons.* Breeds in wet forested regions. Often common in zones of coniferous forest, but there it seems to concentrate in deciduous growth, such as maples and alders, along streams. Also found in canyon groves of oak, sycamore, or willow. May tend to be in wetter forest than Cordilleran Flycatcher.

FEEDING **Diet:** *Mostly insects.* Differences in diet between this bird and Cordilleran Flycatcher poorly known. For the two species combined, diet is mostly insects, including small wasps, bees, flies, true bugs, caterpillars, moths, beetles, and others. Also spiders and a few berries and seeds. **Behavior:** Forages by watching from a perch at any level within shady parts of the forest, then flying out to catch insects in the air. Also takes some food (such as caterpillars and spiders) from foliage or twigs while hovering.

NESTING   In the Pacific Northwest, this species and Hammond's Flycatcher may defend territories against each other. **Nest:** Site is sometimes in the fork of a small tree but usually in other situations: in a cleft of a vertical streambank, on a stump, among the upturned roots of a fallen tree, under a small bridge, or on shed rafters. Natural sites are usually near (or on) the ground, but on artificial structures the nest may be more than 10 feet up. Nest (built by female) is cup of moss, grass, rootlets, strips of bark, lichens, and leaves, lined with finer material such as plant fibers, hair, feathers. **Eggs:** 3–4, rarely 5. Whitish, with brown blotches concentrated near larger end. Incubation is by female only, about 14–15 days. **Young:** Both parents bring food for nestlings. Age of young at first flight about 14–18 days.

MIGRATION   During migration, occurs commonly in the lowlands of southern Arizona, on its way to and from mainland Mexico. Winters mostly in the lowlands of western and southern Mexico.

CONSERVATION STATUS   May be affected by cutting of forests in northwest; however, still widespread and common.

CORDILLERAN FLYCATCHER   *Empidonax occidentalis*

Cordilleran Flycatcher

Among the look-alike Empidonax flycatchers, the two most difficult to tell apart are this species and the Pacific-slope Flycatcher. Males usually can be recognized by their call notes, but females can hardly be identified at all except by their ranges in summer. They were regarded as one species (under the name "Western Flycatcher") until the late 1980s, and differences between them are still poorly understood.

HABITAT   *Moist woods, forests, shady canyons.* Breeds in forested regions, mostly in the mountains, and mostly in deciduous growth along streams through mixed or coniferous forest. Often forages in conifers such as pines or Douglas-firs, but not common in purely coniferous forest. May tend to be in slightly drier or more open forest than Pacific-slope Flycatcher.

FEEDING   **Diet:** *Mostly insects.* Differences in diet between this bird and Pacific-slope Flycatcher poorly known. For the two species combined, diet is mostly insects, including small wasps, bees, flies, caterpillars, moths, beetles, and others. Also spiders and a few berries and seeds. **Behavior:** Forages by watching from a perch and then flying out to catch insects in the air. Also takes some food from foliage or twigs while hovering. Often forages quite high among the branches of tall conifers but will also feed low, especially among streamside trees.

NESTING   Differences in nesting (if any) between this species and Pacific-slope Flycatcher are poorly known. **Nest:** Site is sometimes in the fork of a small tree but usually in other situations: in a cleft of a vertical streambank, on a stump, among the upturned roots of a fallen tree, under a small bridge, or on shed rafters. Natural sites are usually near (or on) the ground, but on artificial structures the nest may be more than 10 feet up. Nest (built by female) is cup of moss, grass, rootlets, strips of bark, lichens, and leaves, lined with finer material such as plant fibers, hair, feathers. **Eggs:** 3–4, rarely 5. Whitish, with brown blotches concentrated near larger end. Incubation is by female only, about 14–15 days. **Young:** Both parents bring food for nestlings. Age of young at first flight probably about 14–18 days.

MIGRATION   Arrives on breeding grounds mostly in May, departs in September. Winters mostly in foothills and mountains of Mexico.

CONSERVATION STATUS   Could be affected by cutting of forests in the west; however, still widespread and common.

BUFF-BREASTED FLYCATCHER   *Empidonax fulvifrons*

Of our 11 little Empidonax flycatchers, this is the smallest and the easiest to identify by color. It is also the one with the most limited range in our area, nesting in only a few canyons in Arizona. At one time, this species ranged more widely in

Buff-breasted Flycatcher

the southwest. It favors open, grassy pine forest, a habitat maintained by occasional forest fires; fire prevention may have reduced the number of Buff-breasted Flycatchers north of the border.

HABITAT   *Open pine woods.* In Arizona, breeds in open areas in the mountains at elevations of 6,000–9,000 feet. Mostly in pines and oaks with very open, grassy understory. Tends to be concentrated along canyons, near trees growing along streams. In Mexico, summers in open pine woods, may winter in streamside trees at lower elevations.

FEEDING   **Diet:** *Insects.* Diet not known in detail. Apparently feeds only on small insects and other arthropods, including ants, wasps, true bugs, beetles, moths, spiders, and others. **Behavior:** Forages by watching from a perch, then flying out to capture insects, returning to the same perch or a new one. May forage high or low. Captures insects in midair or takes them from foliage while hovering; may also drop to the ground to capture food there.

NESTING   Often nests in loose colonies. Male sings to defend nesting territory. Courtship behavior involves male and female exploring potential nest sites together. **Nest:** Site is in tree (often pine), either at base of branch against trunk or well out on horizontal branch, averaging about 25 feet above ground. Usually placed directly under an overhanging branch or group of leaves. Nest (built by female only) is open cup of spider webs, rootlets, and leaves, the outside decorated with lichens, leaves, flakes of bark, and feathers. Lined with fine grasses, feathers, pine needles. **Eggs:** 3–4, sometimes 2, rarely 5. Creamy white. Incubation is by female only, 14–16 days. **Young:** Both parents bring food for nestlings. Young leave nest about 15–17 days after hatching. For several days after fledging, young stay close together, are fed by parents.

MIGRATION   Summer resident in Arizona, arriving in early April and departing in September. In Mexico, may regularly move to lower elevations in winter.

CONSERVATION STATUS   Arizona population probably under 30 pairs, but thought to be gradually increasing after a low point in the late 1960s. Fire may help create more nesting habitat.

PHOEBES — GENUS *Sayornis*

The three species of phoebes are medium-sized flycatchers, often found near water or near human habitations, sometimes nesting under the eaves of houses or barns. While perched, they often dip their tails down and then up in a gentle motion.

BLACK PHOEBE *Sayornis nigricans*

The sharp whistled call of the Black Phoebe is a typical sound along creeks and ponds in the southwest. The birder who explores such areas is likely to see the bird perched low over the water, slowly wagging its tail, then darting out in rapid flight to snap up an insect just above the water's surface. Related to the familiar Eastern Phoebe of eastern North America, this species has a much wider range, living along streams from California to Argentina.

HABITAT   *Shady streams, walled canyons, farmyards, towns; near water.* Occurs in a variety of semi-open habitats. Rarely found far from water, which ensures the availability of mud for nests; may be natural streams or ponds, irrigation ditches, or even water troughs.

FEEDING   **Diet:** *Almost entirely insects.* Feeds on a wide variety of insects including beetles, grasshoppers, crickets, wild bees, wasps, flies, moths, caterpillars. Occasionally eats small fish. **Behavior:** Forages by watching from a perch and darting out to catch insects, often just above water. Catches insects in midair, or may hover

Black Phoebe

while picking them from foliage or sometimes from water's surface. May also take insects from the ground, especially in cool weather. Indigestible parts of insects are coughed up as pellets. Male and female maintain separate feeding territories in winter.

NESTING   In courtship, male performs song-flight display, fluttering in the air with rapidly repeated calls, then descending slowly. **Nest:** Mud nests are usually plastered to sheltered spot such as cliff face, bridge support, culvert, or under eaves of building. Occasionally in well a few feet below ground level. Often returns to same nest site year after year. Nest (probably built by female) is an open cup, semi-circular if attached to vertical wall, circular if placed on flat beam. Nest is made of mud mixed with grass and weeds, lined with soft materials such as plant fibers, rootlets, hair. **Eggs:** 4, sometimes 3–6. White; some (thought to be the last laid) may have reddish brown dots. Incubation is by female only, 15–17 days. **Young:** Fed by both parents. May leave nest 2–3 weeks after hatching. Usually 2 broods per year, rarely 3.

MIGRATION   Mostly a permanent resident, but departs in fall from highest elevations and from northern edge of range in southwest.

CONSERVATION STATUS   Numbers apparently stable, possibly increasing in some areas where artificial ponds have added to nesting habitat.

EASTERN PHOEBE *Sayornis phoebe*

Despite its plain appearance, this flycatcher is often a favorite among eastern birdwatchers. It is among the earliest of migrants, bringing hope that spring is at hand. Seemingly quite tame, it often nests around buildings and bridges, where it is easily observed. Best of all, its gentle tail-wagging habit and soft *fee-bee* song make the Phoebe easy to identify, unlike many flycatchers.

HABITAT   *Streamsides, farms, woodland edges.* In breeding season, typically found near water in woodland or semi-open country. May be limited mostly by availability of good nest sites, which are often along streams. In migration and winter, found around edges of woods, brushy areas, often near water.

FEEDING   **Diet:** *Mostly insects, some berries.* Insects make up great majority of summer diet; included are many small wasps, bees, beetles, flies, true bugs,

388

Eastern Phoebe

grasshoppers, and others. Also eats some spiders, ticks, and millipedes. Small fruits and berries are eaten often in the cooler months and are probably an important part of the winter diet. **Behavior:** Forages by watching from a perch and flying out to catch insects. Most are caught in midair, some are taken from foliage while hovering briefly. Also drops to the ground to pick up insects. Perches in shrubs or trees to eat berries.

NESTING   Male defends nesting territory by singing, especially at dawn. Occasionally one male may have two mates and may help feed the young in two nests at once. **Nest:** Original sites were probably always on vertical streambanks or small rock outcrops in the woods, with a niche providing support below and some shelter above. Now often builds nest under bridges, in barns or culverts, or in other artificial sites. Same site may be used repeatedly, and may build on top of old nest. Nest (built by female) is an open cup with a solid base of mud, built up with moss, leaves, and grass, lined with fine grass and animal hair. **Eggs:** 4–5, sometimes 2–6. White, sometimes with a few dots of reddish brown. Incubation is by female only, about 16 days. **Young:** Both parents bring food for nestlings. Young usually leave nest about 16 days after hatching. Adults typically raise two broods per year.

MIGRATION   Migrates quite early in spring and late in fall, especially compared with other flycatchers.

CONSERVATION STATUS   Population probably increased as buildings and bridges provided many more potential nesting sites. Current numbers are apparently stable.

SAY'S PHOEBE   *Sayornis saya*

This soft-voiced flycatcher of the west is like the other two phoebes in its tail-wagging habit; but unlike them, it often lives in very dry country, far from water. It is

Say's Phoebe

typical of prairies, badlands, and ranch country, often placing its nest under the eaves of a porch or barn. In open terrain where there are few high perches, Say's Phoebe may watch for insects in the grass by hovering low over the fields.

HABITAT   *Scrub, canyons, ranches.* Found in open or semi-open terrain, often in dry country, avoiding forested areas. Often in farmland, savanna, or prairie in south, dry upland tundra in northern part of range. Unlike the other two phoebes, has no special attachment to water.

FEEDING   **Diet:** *Almost entirely insects.* Often feeds heavily on wild bees, wasps, winged ants. Other insects in diet include beetles, moths, grasshoppers, crickets, and dragonflies. Also eats spiders and millipedes, and occasionally berries. **Behavior:** Forages by perching on low shrub or rock and darting out to capture insects. May catch its food in midair or take it from low foliage or from ground. Also often hovers low over fields until prey is spotted, then drops to ground to capture it. Indigestible parts of insects are coughed up as pellets.

NESTING   Males are thought to arrive on breeding grounds before females. Male sings to defend nesting territory, usually from exposed perch, sometimes in flight-song display. **Nest:** Site varies; may be on rocky ledge or crevices in cliffs or caves, in wells or mine shafts, under bridges or eaves; occasionally in natural tree cavity or hole in bank. May take over old swallow nest. Nest (probably built by female, but details not well known) is a flat open cup made of grass, weeds, moss, spider webs, wool, and other materials. Unlike other phoebes, usually uses no mud in nest. **Eggs:** 4, sometimes 3–7. White; some (thought to be the last laid) may have small brown or reddish spots. Incubation is by female only, 12–14 days. **Young:** Both parents bring food to nestlings. Young leave nest about 14–16 days after hatching. 1–2 broods per year, sometimes 3 in the south.

MIGRATION   Migrates north relatively early in spring. Occasionally strays to Atlantic coast (once even to Bermuda), mostly in fall.

CONSERVATION STATUS   Adapts well to changes in landscape, often nesting in residential areas. Numbers apparently stable.

GENUS *Pyrocephalus*

VERMILION FLYCATCHER   *Pyrocephalus rubinus*

Most flycatchers are drab, but the male Vermilion Flycatcher is a brilliant exception. It is usually seen perched fairly low in open areas near water, dipping its tail gently

like a phoebe. As if the male's bright colors were not advertisement enough, he also displays by puffing up his feathers and fluttering high in the air while singing repeatedly. Fairly common in parts of the southwest, the Vermilion Flycatcher is also widespread in Central and South America.

HABITAT   *Streamsides in arid country, savanna, ranches.* In some areas may be found in dry grassland or desert with scattered trees, but much more frequent near water: short trees along streams, edges of ponds. Winter strays in the southeast are in open clearings or brushy areas near water.

FEEDING   **Diet:** *Insects.* Diet not known in detail, but apparently feeds entirely on insects, including beetles, flies, wasps, grasshoppers, and many others. **Behavior:** Forages by watching for prey from exposed

Vermilion Flycatcher

perch, then sallying out to capture flying insects in the air, also by hovering and dropping to the ground for small insects. If beehives are placed close to favored foraging sites, sometimes consumes many bees. Indigestible parts of insects are coughed up later as pellets.

NESTING   Male performs flight-song display above territory: fluffing out body and head feathers and rising high in air (up to 50 feet or more) in peculiar fluttering flight while singing rapidly and repeatedly, then swooping back down to perch. **Nest:** Female builds nest in horizontal fork of tree, usually 6–20 feet above ground, rarely up to 50 feet or more. Nest is a compact cup of twigs, grass, weeds, often held together with spider webs and decorated with lichens. Nest lining is of finer plant materials, hair, and feathers. **Eggs:** Usually 3, sometimes 2–4. Whitish with bold spots of brown, olive, lavender. Incubation is by the female (male may rarely take a turn on the nest), 14–15 days. **Young:** Both parents feed the young. Young fledge in 14–16 days, and male may tend the full-grown young while female begins second nest. Two broods per year.

MIGRATION   Found all year in most parts of range, but some withdraw in winter from northern and higher-elevation areas. Every year, a few spend the winter well to the east along the Gulf coast and west to the California coast.

CONSERVATION STATUS   Surveys have shown recent declines in the Texas breeding population.

CRESTED FLYCATCHERS — GENUS *Myiarchus*

This genus includes more than 20 species, widespread in the American tropics, including islands of the Caribbean. Most species have slight shaggy crests, and most have some reddish brown in the wings or tail and some yellow on the underparts. Several species are most easily told apart by voice. Members of this group usually nest in holes in trees.

DUSKY-CAPPED FLYCATCHER   *Myiarchus tuberculifer*

Dusky-capped Flycatcher

The mournful whistle of the Dusky-capped Flycatcher is a common sound in woodlands almost throughout the American tropics. This bird reaches its northern limits in Arizona and New Mexico, where it is common in summer in canyons and pine-oak forest. There are places in the lower canyons of Arizona where it can be found side by side with two close relatives in the crested flycatcher group, the Ash-throated and Brown-crested flycatchers.

HABITAT   *Oak slopes, pine-oak canyons, junipers.* In United States, usually found around tall oaks or pine-oak woods in the mountains. Also found along streams at middle elevations among tall cottonwoods and sycamores. In the tropics, inhabits many types of forest.

FEEDING   **Diet:** *Mostly insects.* Diet not known in detail but includes many small insects such as various flies, moths, caterpillars, beetles, treehoppers, wasps, and bees. Also some small fruits and berries. **Behavior:** Forages mostly within the foliage of tall trees. Flies out from a perch, hovers a moment while taking an insect from the leaves or twigs, then lands on another perch to eat it. Sometimes catches insects in midair.

NESTING   Nesting behavior not well known. Male defends nesting territory in spring with conspicuous calls and song. **Nest:** Site is in hole in tree (often oak or sycamore), either a natural cavity or an old woodpecker hole. Height varies, 10–60 feet above the ground, usually fairly high. Nest built inside cavity is a bulky mass of weeds, grass, twigs, strips of bark, plant fibers, leaves, and feathers, with a lining of softer material such as animal hair or plant down. **Eggs:** 4–5. Creamy white, finely but distinctly marked with brown, lavender, and olive-gray. Details of incubation not well known, lasts about 2 weeks. **Young:** Probably both parents bring food for nestlings. Age of young at first flight not well known, probably about 2 weeks.

<table>
<tr><td>MIGRATION</td><td>Probably a permanent resident over most of its range. Summer resident only in southwestern United States. Departs early; most are gone before the end of August.</td></tr>
<tr><td>CONSERVATION STATUS</td><td>Numbers in Arizona vary from year to year, but no obvious long-term trend.</td></tr>
</table>

ASH-THROATED FLYCATCHER   *Myiarchus cinerascens*

This pale flycatcher is common and widespread in arid country of the west. Like its close relatives, it nests in holes in trees. Because it lives in dry terrain where trees are often small or scarce, however, it will resort to other sites; nests have been found in such odd places as exhaust pipes, hollow fenceposts, mailboxes, and even in trousers hanging on a clothesline.

HABITAT *Semi-arid country, deserts, brush, mesquites, pinyon-juniper, dry open woods.* Found in a wide variety of lowland habitats, usually open and rather arid, avoiding mountains and forests. Often most common in mesquite groves, pinyon-juniper hillsides, and other open woods, it may live in wide-open grassland if nest sites are available. In winter, found along dense desert washes.

FEEDING   **Diet:** *Mostly insects.* Feeds on insects, including caterpillars, beetles, grasshoppers, wasps, true bugs, and flies, also some as large as cicadas. Eats spiders and rarely small lizards. Also feeds

Ash-throated Flycatcher

on fruits and berries, including those of desert mistletoe and saguaro cactus. Fruits of elephant-tree may be important in winter diet. **Behavior:** Forages mostly by flying out from a perch to hover and pick insects from foliage. Sometimes takes insects from trunks or branches or from the ground; seldom catches them in midair. Usually feeds low. Will perch in shrubs or cactus to feed on fruits.

NESTING   Male's song, given in spring to defend nesting territory, is a simple repetition of the usual call notes. **Nest:** Site is usually in hole in tree or post, either natural cavity or old woodpecker hole, 2–25 feet above ground. In its range, often uses old holes made by Ladder-backed Woodpecker. Also will use holes in giant cactus or in agave stalks, and such sites as birdhouses, metal drain pipes, old Cactus Wren nests, and others. Nest (built by both sexes) is a mass of weeds, grass, twigs, rootlets, lined with softer material such as hair and feathers. **Eggs:** 4–5, sometimes 3–7. Creamy white, blotched with brown and lavender. Incubation is by female only, about 15 days. **Young:** Both parents bring food for nestlings. Age of young at first flight about 14–16 days; parents feed young for at least several days after they fledge. Often raises two broods per year.

<table>
<tr><td>MIGRATION</td><td>Withdraws from most of United States range in fall, but some spend the winter in southwestern Arizona and southern California. A few wander east as far as Atlantic coast almost every year, mostly in late fall.</td></tr>
<tr><td>CONSERVATION STATUS</td><td>Numbers in the United States are apparently stable or possibly increasing. Will use nest boxes put out for bluebirds, and may be benefiting from "bluebird trails" in the west.</td></tr>
</table>

NUTTING'S FLYCATCHER   *Myiarchus nuttingi*

In the Southwest, where three very similar species of crested flycatchers are common, a fourth has been found as an accidental stray. Nutting's Flycatcher is

TYRANT FLYCATCHERS

extremely difficult to recognize unless its distinctive calls are heard, so it might be overlooked. So far it has been confirmed in our area only a couple of times, in Arizona.

GREAT CRESTED FLYCATCHER   *Myiarchus crinitus*

In dense leafy forests of the east, the Great Crested Flycatcher lives within the canopy of tall trees in summer. It is more easily heard than seen, its rolling calls echoing through the woods. The birder who pursues and sees the bird is likely to be impressed; this species is much more colorful than most flycatchers in the east. It nests in holes in trees, and it has the odd habit of adding pieces of shed snakeskin to its nest.

HABITAT   *Woodlands, groves.* Breeds mainly in deciduous forest or mixed forest, but avoids pure stands of conifers. May be found in either continuous deep forest or in more open wooded areas, around edges of clearings or abandoned orchards. Winters in the tropics mostly around edges of forest or second growth.

FEEDING   **Diet:** *Mostly insects.* Feeds on a wide variety of insects, including caterpillars, moths, butterflies, katydids, tree crickets, beetles, true bugs, and others. Also eats spiders and sometimes small lizards, and regularly eats fruits and berries. Small fruits may be a major part of diet in winter in the tropics. **Behavior:** Forages by flying out from a perch to catch insects. May hover momentarily while taking insects from foliage or twigs, or may catch them in midair. Sometimes drops down to take food from on or near the ground, but usually feeds rather high.

Great Crested Flycatcher

NESTING   Male defends nesting territory with loud calls, sometimes by fighting with other males. Courtship may involve male chasing female among the trees. **Nest:** Site is usually in hole in tree, either natural cavity or old woodpecker hole, usually 20–50 feet above the ground. Sometimes nests in artificial sites such as birdhouses, drainpipes, or hollow fenceposts. Both sexes help build nest; in deep cavities, they may carry in large amounts of material, bringing the nest level up close to the entrance. Nest foundation is made of grass, weeds, strips of bark, rootlets, feathers, or other debris, lined with finer materials. Usually includes a piece of snakeskin in lining (sometimes a piece of clear plastic instead). **Eggs:** 5, sometimes 4–6, rarely more. Creamy white to pale buff, marked with brown, olive, lavender. Incubation is by female only, about 13–15 days. **Young:** Both parents bring food for nestlings. Age of young at first flight about 12–18 days.

MIGRATION   Winters mainly from Mexico to Colombia; also winters regularly in southern Florida. Migrates mostly at night.

CONSERVATION STATUS   Could be vulnerable to loss of forest habitat, but current populations apparently stable.

BROWN-CRESTED FLYCATCHER   *Myiarchus tyrannulus*

Of the three similar crested flycatchers in the west, this is the largest. It is a common summer resident in the southwest, mainly in southern Texas and Arizona. Brown-crested Flycatchers are conspicuous and aggressive in the nesting season;

they arrive late in spring, after most other hole-nesting birds, and may have to compete for nest sites. Typically they feed on large insects such as beetles or cicadas, but they also have been seen catching hummingbirds on occasion.

HABITAT *Sycamore canyons, saguaros, river groves.* In Texas, mostly in dry woodlands and groves of taller trees along streams and rivers. Farther west, found in tall sycamores or cottonwoods along streams, in lowlands or in canyons; also common in open desert where giant saguaro cactus grows. Limited to areas with large cavities (in trees or saguaros) for nesting.

FEEDING **Diet:** *Mostly insects.* Feeds mainly on insects, especially cicadas, grasshoppers, and beetles, also other large insects such as dragonflies, praying mantises, and others. Will take small lizards, and has been seen catching and eating hummingbirds. Also feeds on fruit and berries, including the fruit of saguaro cactus. **Behavior:** Forages mostly by flying out from a perch and hovering while taking insects from foliage. Usually forages fairly high. Also catches some insects in midair or from branches or trunks of trees, and occasionally descends to take them on or near the ground. Will perch in shrubs or cactus to eat fruit.

NESTING Very aggressive during the nesting season, competing with other pairs of their own species and with other hole-nesting birds. Unlike many native birds, is able to compete successfully against starlings for nest sites. **Nest:** Site is in cavity in tree or in giant cactus, usually in holes made by good-sized woodpeckers (such as Gila or Golden-fronted) or flickers. Cavities used are 5–50 feet above the ground, usually 10–30 feet up. Both sexes help build nest in cavity, a bulky mass of plant fibers, animal hair, feathers, other debris, lined with softer materials. Pieces of snakeskin often added to lining. **Eggs:** 4–5, sometimes 3–6. White to pale buff, blotched with brown and lavender. Incubation is by female only, about 13–15 days. **Young:** Both parents bring food for nestlings. Age of young at first flight probably about 12–18 days. One brood per year.

MIGRATION In its United States range, arrives mostly in May and leaves mostly in August. Apparently only a short-distance migrant; present all year in most parts of Mexico. In fall and winter, a few wander east along Gulf coast; rare but almost regular in southern Florida in winter.

LA SAGRA'S FLYCATCHER *Myiarchus sagrae*

This native of the western Caribbean was first found in our area in central Alabama, where it has never occurred again. Since the early 1980s, however, La Sagra's Flycatcher has appeared several times in southeastern Florida, probably having strayed across the narrow gap from the Bahamas.

GENUS *Pitangus*

GREAT KISKADEE *Pitangus sulphuratus*

Named for its ringing *kis-ka-dee* calls, this bird seems to break the rules for the flycatcher family. Besides flying out to catch insects in the air, it also grabs lizards from tree trunks, eats many berries, and even plunges into ponds to catch small fish. Its bright pattern is unique in North America, but in the tropics there are several other flycatchers that look almost identical. The Great Kiskadee is found from Texas to Argentina and is also very common in Bermuda, where it was introduced in the 1950s.

HABITAT *Streamside thickets, groves, orchards, towns.* In its limited Texas range, found most commonly in open woodlands near water, but may occur in any habitat with good-sized trees. In the tropics, occurs widely in many semi-open habitats, usually avoiding dense unbroken forest.

FEEDING **Diet:** *Omnivorous.* Feeds mostly on large insects such as beetles, wasps, grasshoppers, bees, and moths; also eats lizards, mice, baby birds, frogs, tadpoles, and small fish. Also many berries and small fruits and some seeds. **Behavior:** Forages in various ways. Often flies out from a perch to catch flying insects in the air. Will perch on branch low over water and then plunge into water for fish, tadpoles, or insects. Often hops about in trees and shrubs to eat berries.

Great Kiskadee

NESTING Breeding behavior not well known. Both members of pair actively defend nesting territory against intruders of their own species and are quick to mob any predators that come close. **Nest:** Site is usually among dense branches of a tree or large shrub, 6–50 feet above the ground, usually 10–20 feet up. Nest is a large bulky structure, more or less round, with the entrance on the side. Nest is built of grass, weeds, strips of bark, Spanish moss, and other plant fibers, lined with fine grasses. **Eggs:** 4, sometimes 2–5. Creamy white, dotted with dark brown and lavender. Details of incubation are not well known. **Young:** Apparently both adults help to feed the young in the nest. Development of young and age at first flight not well known.

MIGRATION Permanent resident throughout its range. Very rarely strays north to Arizona (from western Mexico) and Louisiana.

CONSERVATION STATUS Numbers stable or increasing in Texas. May be increasing and spreading in tropics as rain forest is cut, as it does well around clearings, edges, and second growth.

GENUS *Myiodynastes*

SULPHUR-BELLIED FLYCATCHER   *Myiodynastes luteiventris*

One of the last spring migrants to arrive in southern Arizona, the Sulphur-bellied Flycatcher brings an unmistakable touch of the tropics. Colorful, strongly patterned, and noisy, it seems far more exotic than most of the drab North American flycatchers. Its shrill calls, sounding like rusty hinges or squeaky rubber toys, are typical sounds of summer among the sycamores in lower canyons near the Mexican border.

HABITAT *Sycamore-walnut canyons.* In our area, found mainly in lower parts of canyons in the mountains, where tall sycamores and other trees grow along streams through pine-oak forest. Also locally in sycamores and cottonwoods along streams at lower elevations. In the tropics, found in open woods, groves, and forest edges.

Sulphur-bellied Flycatcher

FEEDING **Diet:** *Mostly insects.* Diet not known in detail, but feeds mainly on insects, probably including large caterpillars, beetles, katydids, and others. Also some small fruits and berries. **Behavior:** Forages by watching from a perch, then flying out to capture insects. Usually forages fairly high, perching on a twig within the shady upper levels of a tree. Flies out and hovers while taking an insect from foliage or branches, or may catch insects in midair.

NESTING   In courtship, male and female perch close together, shaking their heads back and forth and calling in duet. Very aggressive during the nesting season; pairs of Sulphur-bellies may compete for choice cavities with other hole-nesting birds, even Elegant Trogons. Nests mainly in midsummer in Arizona, most eggs probably hatching in July. **Nest:** Site in Arizona is usually in large natural cavity of sycamore, 20–50 feet above ground. Female builds nest. If cavity is deep, she fills it most of the way with twigs and bark strips, then builds nest atop this foundation, mostly of fine leaf stems and pine needles. **Eggs:** 3–4. White to pale buff, heavily spotted with reddish brown. Incubation is by female only, 15–16 days. **Young:** Both parents bring food to nestlings. Age of young at first flight about 16–18 days.

MIGRATION   A long-distance migrant, going to South America for the winter. Arrives in Arizona in late May or early June, and departs for the south in September.

CONSERVATION STATUS   In its limited range in the United States, numbers seem stable or possibly increasing.

GENUS *Empidonomus*

VARIEGATED FLYCATCHER   *Empidonomus varius*

A long-distance migrant within South America, this flycatcher sometimes makes serious errors in navigation and shows up in our area. The first such stray, found in Maine in 1977, seemed outlandish and unique at the time; but since then, other individuals have turned up in Tennessee, Florida, and Ontario.

KINGBIRDS — GENUS *Tyrannus*

Kingbirds are medium-sized flycatchers of open or semi-open country. Their group name probably comes from their aggressive nature: seemingly fearless in nesting season, they attack any larger bird that comes near the nest, even hawks or herons. In addition, most species have a hidden patch of colorful feathers on top of the head; this "crown" may be raised during aggressive encounters, adding to the kingly aura. The family as a whole is referred to as the tyrant flycatchers because of these birds.

TROPICAL KINGBIRD   *Tyrannus melancholicus*

One of the most widespread birds of the American tropics, this species reaches the United States regularly only in southern Arizona. There it is the quietest and most inconspicuous of the four kingbird species present. Beginning in the early 1990s, a few Tropicals were also found in southern Texas, where they overlap with their close relative, Couch's Kingbird. Unlike most kingbirds, Tropicals are seldom found in flocks.

HABITAT   *River groves, scattered trees.* Breeding habitat in Arizona is in groves of cottonwoods near water at low elevations. Farther south in the tropics, found in any kind of open or semi-open habitat, from savannas and farms to towns and cities.

FEEDING   **Diet:** *Mostly insects.* Diet not known in detail, but feeds mostly on insects, including beetles, flies, grasshoppers, and many others. In the tropics, also eats many berries and small fruits. One Costa Rica study found that it rarely also eats small frogs. **Behavior:** From a perch on a tree, wire, fence, etc., the bird sallies out to capture insects in flight; also hovers and drops to ground for insects.

NESTING Both parents may chase away larger birds from vicinity of nest, but often seem to tolerate other kingbirds (Western and Cassin's) near nest tree in Arizona; three species of kingbirds may nest in same grove of trees. **Nest:** Placed on horizontal branch or in fork of tree, 6–40 feet above the ground, usually lower than 25 feet. Nest (built by female) is a shallow cup of twigs, grasses, stems, bark, plant fibers, lined with plant down, moss, other fine materials. **Eggs:** 3–4, sometimes 5. Creamy buff or pinkish, with blotches of brown and purple often concentrated at large end. Incubation is by female only, about 15–16 days. **Young:** Both parents bring food for nestlings. Young leave the nest about 18–19 days after hatching. Apparently just one brood per year in United States part of range.

Tropical Kingbird

MIGRATION Over most of its tropical range, probably a permanent resident. Those found recently in southern Texas have remained through the winter. Arizona birds strictly migratory, arriving in late spring and departing in early fall. Every fall, small numbers of young birds wander north (probably from western Mexico) along Pacific coast to California (rarely farther north), sometimes remaining through winter.

CONSERVATION STATUS Numbers in United States increasing slightly. Farther south, has become much more abundant and widespread as tropical forest has been cleared and turned into open country.

COUCH'S KINGBIRD *Tyrannus couchii*

This Texas specialty is almost identical to the Tropical Kingbird and was considered a race of that species until the 1980s. However, their voices are quite different, and they live side by side in eastern Mexico without interbreeding. Couch's Kingbirds are common around woodland edges and near ponds and rivers in southern Texas during the summer, and a few remain all winter there.

HABITAT *River groves, scattered trees.* In southern Texas, found mainly in native woodland near rivers, also in dense brushland or chaparral, especially near water. May also occur around larger trees in towns. In Mexico, found in semi-open country, roadsides, forest edges.

FEEDING **Diet:** *Mostly insects.* Diet not known in detail, but apparently feeds mostly on insects, including large ones such as beetles, grasshoppers, wasps, and large flies. Also eats some berries and small fruits. **Behavior:** Forages mostly by watching from a perch, then flying out to capture insects, returning to perch to eat them. Many insects are caught in midair; also hovers briefly while taking them from foliage and may swoop down to take insects from just above (or on) the ground.

NESTING Nesting behavior is not well known, probably similar to that of Tropical Kingbird. Adults are aggressive in chasing larger birds away from the vicinity of the nest. **Nest:** Site is usually on horizontal limb of tree, 8–25 feet above the ground. Nest (probably built by female) is a bulky flat cup of twigs, leaves, Spanish moss, weeds, and strips of bark, lined with fine materials such as plant down, rootlets, and softer parts of Spanish moss. **Eggs:** 3–4, sometimes 5. Pinkish to warm buff, blotched with brown and lavender. Details of incubation not well known, but probably by female, a little over 2 weeks. **Young:** Probably both parents feed young. Age of young at first flight not well known, probably between 2 and 3 weeks.

MIGRATION Present all year in southern Texas but more common in summer; winter numbers are variable. Rarely strays north along Gulf coast; accidental east to Florida.

CONSERVATION STATUS Numbers in Texas probably stable. In Mexico, may have increased in some areas with partial clearing of forest, decreased in other areas where clearing has been total.

CASSIN'S KINGBIRD *Tyrannus vociferans*

As suggested by its scientific name *vociferans*, Cassin's is our noisiest kingbird (except for the very localized Thick-billed). Possibly it has more need for vocal communication because it lives in denser habitat than most. Males have a strident "dawn song," a rising *berg-berg-berg-BERG*, often heard at first light but rarely later in the day, sometimes confused with song of Buff-collared Nightjar. Where present in numbers (as on wintering grounds in Mexico), flocks may gather to roost in large concentrations.

HABITAT *Semi-open high country, pine-oak mountains, groves.* In breeding season favors more wooded habitat than most kingbirds, and ranges to higher elevations, although in places it overlaps with Western Kingbird. Nests in open pine forest, pinyon-juniper woodland, oak woodland, and streamside trees; at lower elevation may nest in groves of eucalyptus. During migration and winter can be found in more open habitats.

Cassin's Kingbird

FEEDING **Diet:** *Mostly insects, some berries.* Feeds on a wide variety of insects, including wasps, beetles, caterpillars, moths, grasshoppers, true bugs, flies, and many others, as well as some spiders. Also eats some berries and fruits, more than most flycatchers. **Behavior:** From a perch in a tree or on an exposed wire, flies out to capture flying insects in midair. May also fly out and hover while picking insects or other arthropods from leaves or from the ground.

NESTING Male has a fast zigzag courtship flight. Members of pair may perch together in nest tree, calling, wings quivering. Adults actively harass larger birds such as ravens and hawks in vicinity of nest, but may tolerate other species of kingbirds nearby. **Nest:** Site is in a large tree such as sycamore, cottonwood, oak, or pine, placed on a horizontal or near-horizontal branch, often well out from the trunk. Usually 20–50 feet above the ground but occasionally lower and sometimes much higher. Nest is a bulky cup of twigs, weed stems, rootlets, leaves, feathers, hair, and debris, lined with finer plant fibers and other material. **Eggs:** 3–4, up to 5. Creamy white with brownish mottling, markings often concentrated near large end. Incubation is by female, about 18 days. **Young:** Both parents feed nestlings. Young leave the nest after 14–17 days. Usually one brood per year, may raise two in southern part of range.

MIGRATION Often lingers later in fall than other kingbirds. South of United States, may migrate in large flocks.

THICK-BILLED KINGBIRD *Tyrannus crassirostris*

Brash and noisy, the Thick-billed Kingbird perches high in streamside sycamores, fluttering its wings as it gives voice to incredibly loud metallic calls that echo through the canyons. This big tropical flycatcher is a recent immigrant to our area, first found in 1958 in Guadalupe Canyon, on the Arizona–New Mexico border. It has since become more widespread as a summering bird north of Mexico, but it is still found mainly at a few Arizona sites.

Thick-billed Kingbird

HABITAT *Sycamores and cottonwoods along streams.* In the United States, breeds along permanent streams in the lowlands and lower canyons; mostly where big sycamores and cottonwoods grow, occasionally in pure stands of cottonwoods. In Mexico, widespread in dry woods and semi-open country in lowlands.

FEEDING **Diet:** *Insects.* Diet not well known, but probably mostly or entirely insects. Large bill size suggests the ability to feed on very large insects; has been seen eating large beetles, cicadas, and others. **Behavior:** Forages by watching from a perch and flying out to capture insects, returning to perch to eat them. Captures most prey in midair, often in long, swooping flights. Usually hunts from high perches near tops of trees, but will forage low, especially in cool weather.

NESTING Breeding behavior not well known. Aggressive in defense of nesting territory, attacking larger birds that come near nest. Both members of mated pairs often perch close together, wings quivering, calling loudly. **Nest:** Site is usually high in tall tree (in Arizona, typically in sycamore, sometimes in cottonwood), 50–80 feet above ground. Nest is a large but loosely built open cup of twigs, grasses, weeds, leaves, plant down. Nest has a ragged look, with twigs sticking out in all directions; from below, eggs may be visible through bottom of nest. **Eggs:** 3–4. Whitish, blotched with brown. Details of incubation not well known. **Young:** Both parents bring food for young in nest. Development of young and age at first flight not well known.

MIGRATION Summer resident in southeastern Arizona and southwestern New Mexico, arriving in May and departing in September. Strays sometimes wander to lower Colorado River or southern coastal California in fall and winter.

CONSERVATION STATUS Has gradually increased in limited range in United States since first arrival in 1950s. Status of Mexican populations not well known.

WESTERN KINGBIRD *Tyrannus verticalis*

In open country of the west, the Western Kingbird is often seen perched on roadside fences and wires, flying out to snap up insects—or to harass ravens, hawks, or other large birds that stray too close to the kingbird's nest. Spunky and adaptable, this flycatcher has adjusted well to advancing civilization within its range. It frequently builds its nest where wires attach to utility poles, and may be seen tending its young there even along busy city streets.

HABITAT *Semi-open country, farms, roadsides, towns.* Breeds in open terrain with trees to provide nest sites; may be in farmland, groves or streamside trees in prairie country, semi-desert scrub; avoids true desert. Also in towns; where trees are lacking, will nest on artificial structures. Where ranges overlap, typically in more open country than Eastern or Cassin's kingbirds.

FEEDING **Diet:** *Mostly insects.* Feeds on a wide variety of insects, especially wasps, bees, beetles, and grasshoppers, also flies, true bugs, caterpillars, moths, and many others. Also eats some spiders and millipedes, and regularly eats small numbers of berries and fruits. **Behavior:** Forages mostly by watching from a perch and then flying out to snap up insects in its bill. May perch low or high; may catch insects in midair or may hover and then drop to the ground to catch them.

NESTING Male defends territory by singing, giving "dawn song" incessantly at first hint of daylight. In courtship, male performs flight display, rapidly flying up and down in vertical zigzags, giving rapid sputtering calls. **Nest:** Site varies, usually in tree in vertical fork or on horizontal limb, 15–30 feet above ground. Also often nests on utility poles, sometimes on building ledges or towers, in empty sheds, on cliff ledges, or in abandoned nests of other birds. Nest (probably built by both sexes) is a cup of grass, weeds, twigs, plant fibers, lined with finer materials such as feathers, plant down, animal hair, bits of paper. **Eggs:** 3–5, rarely up to 7. Whitish, heavily blotched with brown, lavender, and black. Incubation is mostly or entirely by female, about 18–19 days. **Young:** Both parents feed nestlings. Young leave nest about 16–17 days after hatching.

MIGRATION Often migrates in small flocks. A few stray eastward every fall, appearing along Atlantic coast, some of these birds moving south to winter in Florida.

CONSERVATION STATUS Has expanded breeding range eastward and increased in numbers during 20th century. Population now stable or possibly still increasing.

Western Kingbird

EASTERN KINGBIRD *Tyrannus tyrannus*

Eastern Kingbird

This species is the only widespread kingbird in the east. Common and conspicuous in summer, it is often seen perched jauntily on a treetop or fence wire, or sallying out with shallow fluttering wingbeats to catch an insect in midair. In winter in South America it takes on a different personality, living in flocks in tropical forest and dining on berries.

HABITAT *Wood edges, river groves, farms, shelterbelts, orchards, roadsides.* In summer, requires open space for hunting and trees for nesting; habitat ranges from clearings within forest to open grassland with few scattered trees. Often common around edges of marshes, farmland, native tallgrass prairie. Winters in tropical forest, especially around edges and along rivers.

FEEDING **Diet:** *Mostly insects, some fruit.* Insects make up majority of summer diet; included are many beetles, wasps, bees, winged ants, grasshoppers, flies, leafhoppers, and others. Sometimes claimed to be a serious predator on honeybees,

but there is little evidence for this. Also eats many berries and wild fruits. Winter diet not well known, but feeds heavily on berries in tropical forest. **Behavior:** Forages by watching from a perch and then flying out to catch insects. May capture food in midair, or may hover while taking items (insects, berries) from foliage. In cold weather, when few insects are flying, may feed on ground.

NESTING   In courtship, male displays with rapid up-and-down flight, zigzags, backward somersaults, and other aerial acrobatics. The red patch of crown feathers, usually concealed, may be visible during displays. **Nest:** Site is usually in deciduous tree or large shrub, 7–30 feet above ground, sometimes lower or much higher. Sometimes on power-line towers, on dead snags standing in water, on top of fencepost, or other odd site. Nest (built by female, perhaps with help from male) is a bulky cup of weed stalks, twigs, grass, lined with fine grass and sometimes animal hair. **Eggs:** 3–4, sometimes 2–5. White to pinkish white, heavily blotched with brown, lavender, and gray. Incubation is mostly or entirely by female, 16–18 days (perhaps sometimes shorter). **Young:** Both parents bring food for nestlings. Age of young at first flight about 16–18 days; young may be tended by parents for more than a month after fledging.

MIGRATION   A long-distance migrant, wintering entirely in South America. Migrates in flocks. Unlike many of the migratory songbirds, kingbirds may travel mostly by day.

GRAY KINGBIRD *Tyrannus dominicensis*

Widespread in the Caribbean, this big flycatcher enters our area mainly in Florida. There it is numerous in summer, mainly along the coasts, less common toward the

north. The Gray Kingbird is often conspicuous, perching in the open and giving loud, arresting calls. Its original nesting habitat along the coast has been partly taken over by development, but the bird has adapted, and it now nests in residential areas, farmland, and even cities.

HABITAT   *Roadsides, mangroves, edges.* In Florida, breeds in a variety of habitats, from undisturbed mangrove swamps to centers of cities near coast, also in farmland and vacant lots. In the Caribbean, found in a similarly wide range of wooded and open habitats.

FEEDING   **Diet:** *Mostly insects, some berries.* Feeds on a variety of insects, including beetles, wasps, bees, and many others, some as large as dragonflies. Also eats small lizards, and has been seen catching hummingbirds in the Caribbean. At some seasons,

Gray Kingbird

berries and small fruits may be more than one-fifth of the diet. **Behavior:** Forages by watching from an exposed perch and then flying out to catch insects in the air. May also hover and take insects or other items from foliage, and sometimes catches prey just above (or at) surface of water.

NESTING   Nesting behavior poorly known. Adults are very active and bold in defense of their nest, even attacking humans who come too close. **Nest:** Site is often among branches of coastal mangroves, 4–12 feet above water or ground. Also nests in taller trees inland, such as pines or oaks, up to 40 feet above ground. In cities, may build nest where wires cross utility poles. Nest is a cup of twigs, grasses, rootlets, lined with finer grass; usually loosely built, so that eggs may even be visible from below.

Eggs: 3–4, rarely 5. Pale pink to buff, blotched with brown, lavender, and gray. Details of incubation not well known. **Young:** Evidently both parents bring food for nestlings. Development of young and age at first flight not well known.

MIGRATION   Only a summer resident in southeastern United States (with a few winter records for Florida). Rarely wanders far to the north of breeding range, mainly in fall.

CONSERVATION STATUS   Surveys show declines in parts of Florida range, but still locally very common there and in Caribbean.

LOGGERHEAD KINGBIRD *Tyrannus caudifasciatus*

This chunky, big-headed flycatcher is widespread in the Caribbean. It has strayed into Florida several times, mainly to the southeastern coast and the Keys; some individuals have remained for up to several weeks.

SCISSOR-TAILED FLYCATCHER *Tyrannus forficatus*

Scissor-tailed Flycatcher

On the southern Great Plains, this beautiful bird is common in summer, often resting on roadside fences and wires. Seen perched at a distance it might suggest a slim, long-tailed Mockingbird—until it flies, showing off the salmon pink under the wings, its long tail streamers flaring wide as it maneuvers in midair to catch an insect. Although it looks unique, the Scissor-tail is closely related to the kingbirds, and like them it will fearlessly attack larger birds that come near its nest.

HABITAT   *Semi-open country, ranches, farms, roadsides.* Favors grassland or farmland with scattered trees or isolated groves. May breed in open grassland with no trees in some areas, where utility poles provide artificial nest sites. Winters in open or semi-open country in the tropics.

FEEDING   **Diet:** *Insects.* Feeds mostly on insects, including many grasshoppers, also beetles, wasps, bees, true bugs, flies, caterpillars, moths, and others. Also eats some spiders. Small numbers of berries and wild fruits are eaten occasionally. **Behavior:** Forages mostly by watching from a perch, flying out to catch insects, then returning to perch to eat them. May take insects in midair or pick them from foliage or from ground while hovering; very agile and maneuverable in flight.

NESTING   Male has spectacular courtship display, sharply rising and descending in flight, his long tail streamers opening and closing, while he gives sharp calls. May perform backward somersaults in the air. **Nest:** Site is usually in a tree or tall shrub, placed on a horizontal limb or less often in a vertical fork, usually 7–30 feet above the ground. Often also places nest where wires attach to utility poles or on other artificial sites such as towers or bridge supports. Nest (built by female) is a ragged open cup of twigs, weeds, rootlets, and grass, lined with finer materials such as hair and plant down. **Eggs:** 3–5, rarely 6. Whitish, blotched with brown and gray. Incubation is by female, about 14–17 days. **Young:** Both parents bring food to nestlings. Young leave the nest about 14–16 days after hatching.

MIGRATION   On the breeding grounds, often arrives early (by early April) and stays late (to October, even a few through November). Strays wander to either coast, and small numbers winter regularly in southern Florida.

Probably increased in some areas as planting of shelterbelt trees provided more nesting sites. Has declined in some areas in recent decades.

FORK-TAILED FLYCATCHER   *Tyrannus savana*

This spectacular wanderer from the tropics occurs virtually every year in North America. Although it is impossible to predict just where it will appear, the majority of records are along the Atlantic coast. Most Fork-tailed Flycatchers reaching our area probably come from southern South America, long-distance migrants that have made major errors in navigation.

BECARDS — GENUS *Pachyramphus*

ROSE-THROATED BECARD   *Pachyramphus aglaiae*

This is a tropical bird, distantly related to our typical flycatchers, that barely extends north of the Mexican border in summer. In our area it occurs regularly only along a few streams in southern Arizona. Quiet and inconspicuous, it is easily overlooked as it perches high within the canopy of the trees, occasionally fluttering out to pick an insect from the foliage. Its massive, football-shaped nest, swinging at the end of a dangling branch, is often the first clue that becards are present.

HABITAT   *Wooded canyons, river groves, sycamores.* In Arizona, usually along streams at middle elevations, especially in groves of sycamores and cottonwoods; sometimes in pure cottonwood groves with understory of mesquites. In Texas, generally in native woodland near Rio Grande. In Mexico and Central America, widespread in dry woods, canyons, locally up into mountain forest.

Rose-throated Becard

FEEDING   **Diet:** *Includes insects and berries.* Diet not well known. In summer in United States, probably feeds mostly on insects. Also known to eat many small fruits and berries, perhaps especially in southern parts of range. **Behavior:** Forages mostly by watching from a perch, then making short flights out to capture insects, returning to perch to eat them. Takes most insects from foliage while hovering briefly; also catches some in midair. Does much of its foraging within the shady canopy of tall trees.

NESTING   Male defends nesting territory by singing. Has a thin, rhythmic "dawn song," usually heard only before sunrise. **Nest:** Usually suspended at the end of a long hanging branch, under the shady canopy of a large tree (sycamore or cottonwood in Arizona), up to 50 feet above ground. Nest (built mostly by female, with some help from male) is a very large globular mass of vegetation, with the entrance low on one side; made of bark strips, grass, weeds, vines, spider webs, and other materials. More material may be added even after incubation begins. **Eggs:** 4–6. Whitish to buff, heavily blotched with brown. Incubation is by female; incubation period not well known. **Young:** Both parents bring food for nestlings. Young leave nest about 3 weeks after hatching.

MIGRATION   In Arizona, generally arrives in May and leaves in September. Probably permanent resident over most of its range. May wander into southern Texas at any season.

In Arizona, may have increased slightly since 1950s, but still very scarce and local. Widespread and common in Mexico and Central America.

GENUS *Tityra*

MASKED TITYRA *Tityra semifasciata*

Common in the tropics, the Masked Tityra is easily recognized by its strong pattern, woodpecker-like flight, and soft oinking call notes. Usually traveling in pairs, it may feed mainly on berries; it was formerly classified in the Cotinga family. This species has strayed into our area once, reaching southern Texas.

LARKS (Family Alaudidae)

In the Old World there are about 80 species of larks, but only one of these, the Horned Lark, spills over into the Americas to any great extent (our "meadowlarks" are actually related to the blackbirds and orioles). Larks are songbirds that live on the ground in open country, although a few species will perch readily in trees. Most are either brown and streaky (for camouflage among dry grass) or plain and pale (for camouflage against bare soil). Many are impressive songsters, often singing in flight high above the ground.

Feeding Larks generally feed on insects and seeds in varying proportions. Many species in temperate climates tend to feed mostly on seeds in winter, varying the diet with many insects in summer. Larks forage while walking or running on the ground, occasionally fluttering up to take items from low plants.

Nesting As expected for such terrestrial birds, larks place their nests on the ground, usually in a very open area but close to a small grass clump or other minor shelter. Nests are typically shallow open cups made of grass. In many species, only the female incubates the eggs, but both parents help feed the young.

Displays Living in open country where there are often no high perches from which to sing, many larks have developed flight song displays, flying or hovering high above the ground while singing to advertise their claims to nesting territory on the ground below. The most famous performer is the Sky Lark of Europe and Asia (in fact, singing in flight is often referred to as "skylarking"). In courtship, males of some species strut about on the ground near the female, often with wings drooped or with tail raised high.

GENUS *Alauda*

SKY LARK *Alauda arvensis*

This is one of the most famous songbirds in the world, celebrated by British poets and naturalists. English settlers in North America tried repeatedly to introduce the Sky Lark to this continent, but they succeeded only on southern Vancouver Island, British Columbia. Present since the early 1900s, there are still a few Sky Larks around the edges of Victoria, but they are gradually disappearing as development takes over their habitat.

HABITAT *Open country, fields.* Introduced population on Vancouver Island lives in open areas with fairly tall grass. On native range in Eurasia, found in any kind of open country, farmland, extensive lawns, edges of marshes.

FEEDING   **Diet:** *Seeds, insects.* Diet in North America not known in detail. In Europe, feeds mostly on seeds of grasses and weeds, grain in agricultural fields, and leaves of various ground plants. Also eats many insects (including beetles, caterpillars, and others) and some spiders, millipedes, and snails, mostly in summer. Young birds are fed mainly insects at first. **Behavior:** Forages by walking on ground in open areas, picking up items from ground and pecking at plant stalks and seed heads.

Sky Lark

NESTING   Male may sing at any season, most intensively in early spring to defend nesting territory and attract a mate. In typical song-flight display, male takes off from ground and flies up in steep spiral to as high as 150–300 feet, singing most of the way up; then hovers and circles for several minutes, singing continuously, before gradually spiraling down to ground while continuing to sing. **Nest:** Site is on ground in an open area among short grass. Nest (probably built by female only) is a slight depression in the ground lined with grass and rootlets, with an inner lining of finer grass and sometimes animal hair. **Eggs:** Usually 3–5. Pale gray, sometimes with greenish tinge, heavily spotted with olive or brown. Incubation is by female only, about 11 days. **Young:** Fed by both parents. Young often leave nest after 8–10 days, but not able to fly well until 10 days later.

MIGRATION   Introduced birds are permanent residents. Migratory birds from northeastern Asia have reached Alaska, and one has wintered in California.

CONSERVATION STATUS   Introduced population in North America is gradually declining. On native range in Eurasia (and where introduced in New Zealand and Australia), still widespread and abundant. Also introduced and common in Hawaii.

GENUS *Eremophila*

HORNED LARK   *Eremophila alpestris*

On open fields in winter, flocks of Horned Larks walk and run on the ground, examining the soil and stubble in search of seeds. If disturbed, the flock departs in swift, twisting flight, making soft lisping call notes. This species, the only native lark in North America, begins nesting very early in spring in those same barren fields, and the tinkling songs of the males come from high overhead as they perform their flight-song display. The "horns" of the Horned Lark are little tufts of feathers visible only at close range.

HABITAT   *Prairies, fields, airports, shores, tundra.* Inhabits open ground, generally avoiding areas with trees or even bushes. May occur in a wide variety of situations that are sufficiently open: shortgrass prairies, extensive lawns (as at airports or golf courses), plowed fields, stubble fields, beaches, lake flats, dry tundra of far north or high mountains.

FEEDING   **Diet:** *Seeds and insects.* Feeds on small seeds from a great variety of grasses and weeds, also waste grain. Many insects are also eaten, especially in summer, when they may make up half of the total diet. Also eats some spiders and snails, and eats berries of low-growing plants in some regions. **Behavior:** Forages entirely by walking and running on the ground, picking up items from ground or from plants low enough to reach. Except when nesting, usually forages in flocks.

Often nests quite early in spring. Male defends nesting territory by singing, either on ground or in flight. In flight song display, male flies up steeply in silence, often to several hundred feet above ground, then hovers and circles for several minutes while singing; finally dives steeply toward ground. **Nest:** Site is on open ground, often next to grass clump, piece of dried cow manure, or other object. Nest (built by female) is slight depression in ground, lined with grass, weeds, rootlets, with inner lining of fine grass or plant down. One side of nest often has flat "doorstep" of pebbles. **Eggs:** 3–4, sometimes 2–5. Pale gray to greenish white, blotched and spotted with brown. Incubation is by female, about 10–12 days. **Young:** Fed by both parents. Young may leave nest after 9–12 days, not able to fly for another week. One brood per year in far north, 2–3 farther south.

Horned Lark

MIGRATION   Present all year in most areas from southern Canada south; some are probably permanent residents (in many areas, different individuals are present at different seasons). Strictly migratory in far north. One of the earliest of spring migrants.

CONSERVATION STATUS   Does well on overgrazed or abused land, so has probably increased in North America with advance of civilization. Also widespread in Europe, Asia, and North Africa.

SWALLOWS (Family Hirundinidae)

With their graceful flight, soft musical voices, and habit of living around human houses and farms, swallows are perennially popular. Their return every year to northern climates is welcomed as a sure sign of spring.

The approximately 90 species of swallows are found worldwide except in the Antarctic, with the greatest variety of species occurring in Africa. All have long, pointed wings, short bills, and fairly small feet. Although they do not fly as fast nor as continuously as swifts, they are probably more aerial than any other songbirds. They avoid perching among foliage in trees, so when at rest they are usually on bare branches or on wires where they are easy to observe.

Many kinds of swallows are gregarious, foraging in flocks and nesting in colonies. As a group, swallows have benefited from the advance of civilization in North America. Several species build their nests on man-made structures — on the sides of buildings, under bridges, in culverts — while others, birds that dig burrows in dirt banks, take advantage of road cuts. In parts of the east, many Tree Swallows and practically all Purple Martins now nest in birdhouses.

Feeding   Swallows do almost all of their foraging in the air, pursuing insects in long, continuous flights. A swallow's very short, wide bill opens into a wide gaping mouth, good for scooping insects out of the air. The birds often fly low over water, since insect life is often concentrated there, and most species will forage in flocks. In very bad weather, they may resort to seeking insects on the ground. Among our species, only the Tree Swallow regularly eats berries.

Nesting   Several kinds of swallows typically breed in colonies, with many nests close together. In these cases the birds defend no territory except the nest itself, and all the birds from the colony forage together over the surrounding countryside.

Swallows build several kinds of nests, some of them quite impressive. In fact, the type of nest built has sometimes been used as a way of classifying the species into groups. Three general types are common: open cup-shaped nests placed inside cavities (usually holes in trees or birdhouses); burrows excavated in vertical dirt banks; and sturdy structures built of mud, plastered against a vertical surface. To make the latter sort, the adults land on the ground to scoop up mouthfuls of mud, form these into pellets, and then fly to the colony to plaster the mud pellets in place. The eggs are either white or lightly spotted. Incubation is by both parents or by the female only, but both parents generally help feed the young.

Displays Because many swallows do not defend territories, the songs of the males may be used mainly for attracting or communicating with a mate. Many species perform what appear to be courtship flights, but much of the courtship behavior may center on the actual site of the nest.

AMERICAN MARTINS — GENUS *Progne*

These are the largest swallows in the New World. They nest in cavities, usually in dead trees but also holes in buildings, cliffs, or giant cactus; the Purple Martin is famous for using birdhouses. Unlike most swallows, males and females are often strikingly different in pattern.

PURPLE MARTIN *Progne subis*

Purple Martin

Graceful in flight, musical in its predawn singing, this big swallow is one of our most popular birds. Almost all Purple Martins in the east now nest in birdhouses put up especially for them. Martin housing has a long history: some Native American tribes reportedly hung hollow gourds around their villages to attract these birds. Purple Martins migrate to South America for the winter, but before leaving, they may gather to roost in groups of thousands in late summer.

HABITAT *Towns, farms, semi-open country near water; in west, also mountain forest, saguaro desert.* In the east, breeds in any kind of semi-open area where nest sites are provided, especially near a pond or river. More local in the west, with isolated colonies breeding around woodland edges, clearings in mountain forest, and lowland desert with giant saguaro cactus.

FEEDING **Diet:** *Insects.* Feeds on a wide variety of flying insects, including many wasps and winged ants, and some bees; also many true bugs, flies (including house flies and crane flies), beetles, moths, and butterflies. Dragonflies may be an important part of diet. Also eats some spiders. The old claim of martins eating "2,000 mosquitoes a day" apparently has no basis in fact. **Behavior:** Forages almost entirely in the air. May forage very low over water or quite high at times. Occasionally walks about on ground to pick up insects, perhaps mostly in harsh weather.

NESTING Males return to nesting areas first in spring, establish nesting territories. Usually nests in colonies, especially in east, where almost all are in multiple-roomed nest boxes put up for them. Western martins may nest in looser colonies or as isolated pairs. Male will sometimes have more than one mate. **Nest:** Natural sites are cavities, mostly old woodpecker holes in trees (or in giant cactus in southwest). In the east, most martins now use nest boxes. Sometimes nests in holes in buildings or cliffs. Nest (built by both sexes) is cup of leaves, grass, twigs, debris, and usually mud. Nest may have raised dirt rim in front to help keep eggs from rolling out. **Eggs:** 4–5, sometimes 3–8. White. Incubation is by female, 15–18 days. **Young:** Both parents feed nestlings. Young leave nest about 26–31 days after hatching.

MIGRATION
A long-distance migrant, most wintering in Amazon Basin. Returns very early in spring in the east (often in February in southern states), usually later in spring in the west (mainly April and May).

CONSERVATION STATUS
Has declined seriously in parts of the west, and currently declining in the east. Reasons are not well known, but competition with starlings for nest sites may be involved.

CUBAN MARTIN *Progne cryptoleuca*

A close relative of the Purple Martin (possibly just a localized race) and very similar to it, probably not safely identifiable in the field. Nesting mostly in Cuba, this form was collected in southern Florida three times in the 19th century, but there have been no records since the 1890s.

GRAY-BREASTED MARTIN *Progne chalybea*

Very widespread in the American tropics, this smaller relative of the Purple Martin comes close to our area in northeastern Mexico. Although it might be expected to wander across the border occasionally, it is known here definitely only from two old records in the 1880s in extreme southern Texas.

SOUTHERN MARTIN *Progne elegans*

A counterpart to our Purple Martin, nesting in southern South America and migrating north after the breeding season. A single migrant, overshooting its normal range, was found many years ago at Key West, Florida.

BROWN-CHESTED MARTIN *Progne tapera*

This tropical species has the shape of a Purple Martin and the colors of a Bank Swallow. Migratory within South America, it has strayed north to our area once, with a single bird having appeared on the outer coast of Massachusetts.

WHITE-BELLIED SWALLOWS — GENUS *Tachycineta*

The six members of this group are all glossy above and white below. They are found only in the Americas; all nest in cavities, and all do most of their foraging in open country, especially near water.

TREE SWALLOW *Tachycineta bicolor*

The popularity of the bluebird has been a boon to the Tree Swallow, which nests in holes of exactly the same size and has taken advantage of bluebird houses over much of North America. In regions with no such ready supply of artificial nest sites, the swallows must compete with other cavity-nesting birds, arriving early in spring to stake out territories. Unlike other swallows, Tree Swallows eat many berries (especially bayberries), allowing them to survive wintry spells when other insect-eaters might starve.

HABITAT *Open country near water, marshes, meadows, lakes.* May breed in any kind of open or semi-open area that provides both nesting sites and a good supply of flying insects.

Typically breeds close to water, as around ponds or marshes, but also nests away from water around meadows or brushy areas. In winter, mainly around marshes and near bayberry thickets along coast.

FEEDING **Diet:** *Mostly insects, some berries.* Diet is mostly insects, especially in summer. Feeds on many flies, beetles, winged ants, and others. Also eats some spiders, and will eat sand fleas (which are crustaceans). Unlike our other swallows, eats much vegetable material (up to 20 percent of annual diet, mostly eaten in winter). Bayberries are main plant food, also eats other berries and seeds. **Behavior:** Forages mostly in flight, often low over water or fields. May pick items from surface of water while flying. Perches in bushes to eat berries, and sometimes feeds on ground, especially in cold weather.

Tree Swallow

NESTING Male arrives on nesting territory before female; courtship involves male showing female potential nesting sites. Birds often choose new mates each year. **Nest:** Natural nest sites are in holes in dead trees or in old sapsucker holes in live trees; also very frequently uses nest boxes. Sometimes in odd sites such as holes in buildings, old Cliff Swallow nests, or holes in ground. Nest (built mostly by female) is cup of grass, weeds, rootlets, moss, pine needles, other plant materials. Usually lined with many feathers (from other kinds of birds), mostly added after first eggs are laid. **Eggs:** 4–7, sometimes 2–8. Very pale pink at first, fading to white. Incubation is by female only, usually 14–15 days. **Young:** Both parents feed nestlings, and female broods them while they are small. Young usually leave the nest about 18–22 days after hatching.

MIGRATION Migrates north relatively early in spring. Southward migration begins as early as July, peaks in early fall. Migrates by day, in flocks.

CONSERVATION STATUS Widespread and common, and population apparently increasing in many areas.

VIOLET-GREEN SWALLOW   *Tachycineta thalassina*

A small swallow of the west, nesting from Alaska to central Mexico. Similar to the Tree Swallow in appearance and also in behavior, nesting in tree cavities and birdhouses; it also will nest in rock crevices of cliffs in rugged terrain. Flocks are often seen flying high over mountain pine forests or steep canyons.

HABITAT *Widespread when foraging; nests in open forests, mountains, towns.* During migration, often near water, as along rivers, lakes, coastline. Wide range of nesting habitats, mainly in semi-open situations, including aspen groves, pine forest, canyon walls, sometimes open prairie if nest sites exist. In Mexico, also in low desert, nesting in holes in giant cactus.

FEEDING **Diet:** *Insects.* Feeds on a wide variety of flying insects, such as flies, true bugs, wasps, winged ants, wild bees, beetles, moths, and many others. **Behavior:** Forages in flight, catching insects in the air. Often flies higher than other

Violet-green Swallow

swallows, although it will feed low over ponds, especially in bad weather. Usually forages in flocks; may associate with other swallows or White-throated Swifts.

NESTING   May nest in isolated pairs or in small colonies. **Nest:** Site is in a cavity, usually an old woodpecker hole or natural cavity in tree, sometimes in hole or crevice in rock. Will use birdhouses. In northwestern Mexico, will nest in holes in giant cactus. Nest (built by both sexes, with female doing most of work) is a cup of grass, twigs, rootlets, lined with many feathers. **Eggs:** 4–6, rarely 7. White. Incubation is evidently mostly or entirely by the female, about 13–18 days. **Young:** Both parents feed nestlings, but female often does more. Young leave the nest about 23–24 days after hatching. Parents continue to feed the young for some time after they leave the nest. One brood per year, perhaps sometimes two.

MIGRATION   Migrates in flocks. Very rarely overwinters north of Mexico, except for some on California coast. Spring migration very early, returning to southwest in large numbers by February.

CONSERVATION STATUS   Numbers probably stable. Benefits in some areas from supply of artificial nest sites, including nest boxes. In other areas, may suffer from competition for nest sites with introduced starlings and House Sparrows.

BAHAMA SWALLOW   *Tachycineta cyaneoviridis*

Normally nesting only on a few pine-clad islands in the Bahamas, this fork-tailed swallow has strayed to southern Florida a number of times, mostly in spring and summer. It may have nested on the Florida Keys, possibly elsewhere, but this has not been proven.

GENUS *Stelgidopteryx*

NORTHERN ROUGH-WINGED SWALLOW   *Stelgidopteryx serripennis*

Two kinds of brown-backed swallows nest in holes in dirt banks. The Rough-wing is the solitary one, not nesting in colonies like the Bank Swallow. It is usually seen singly or in small groups, even during migration, in rapid low flight over rivers or fields. The name "Rough-winged" comes from small serrations on the outermost wing feathers. The function of these is unknown, but they may produce sounds during courtship flights.

HABITAT   *Near streams, lakes, river banks, also arroyos in dry country.* Widespread in any kind of open country, but most commonly near water, nesting in vertical dirt banks (as along streambanks, river bluffs, gravel pits). May also nest along dry washes in arid country, but usually feeds over water, fields, or dense brush.

FEEDING   **Diet:** *Insects.* Feeds on a wide variety of flying insects, including many flies, wasps, winged ants, bees, true bugs, and beetles. Also eats some moths, caterpillars, mayflies, damselflies, spiders. **Behavior:** Forages mostly in the air, patrolling over rivers, ponds, and fields in swift flight. Usually forages low. Often solitary in foraging, but may join concentrations of other swallows at good feeding areas.

NESTING   Solitary in nesting; unlike Bank Swallow, does not form colonies, although several pairs may nest in favorable site. In courtship, male flies after female, spreading the white feathers under the base of his tail so that they are prominently displayed. **Nest:** Site is usually in burrow in vertical dirt bank; may be bank along running stream, or road cut or similar bank miles from water. Birds may dig tunnel themselves, 1–6 feet long, or may use old burrow of Bank Swallow, kingfisher, or ground squirrel. Sometimes in other kinds of cavities, such as drainpipe, culvert, crevice in bridge support, hole in side of building. Bulky nest at end of burrow made of twigs, weeds, bark fibers, lined with finer grasses, occasionally with fresh horse manure added. **Eggs:** 5–7, sometimes 4–8. White. Incubation probably by female, 12–16 days. **Young:** Both parents feed nestlings. Young leave nest about 19–21 days after hatching. One brood per year.

MIGRATION   Generally an early migrant in spring. In parts of the southwest it is absent mainly in late fall, reappearing in January or even late December.

CONSERVATION STATUS   Because it will nest in artificial sites, including road cuts and holes in bridges, may have increased with the spread of civilization.

Northern Rough-winged Swallow

GENUS *Riparia*

BANK SWALLOW   *Riparia riparia*

Bank Swallow

The smallest of our swallows, the Bank Swallow is usually seen in flocks, flying low over ponds and rivers with quick, fluttery wingbeats. It nests in dense colonies in holes in dirt or sand banks. Some of these colonies are quite large, and a tall cut bank may be pockmarked with several hundred holes. Despite their small size, tiny bills, and small feet, these swallows generally dig their own nesting burrows, sometimes up to 5 feet long.

HABITAT   *Near water; fields, marshes, streams, lakes.* Typically seen feeding in flight over (or near) water at all seasons, even in migration. Nests in colonies in vertical banks of dirt or sand, usually along rivers or ponds, seldom away from water.

FEEDING   **Diet:** *Insects.* Feeds on a wide variety of flying insects. Eats many flies (including house flies and crane flies), beetles, wasps, winged ants, small bees, and true bugs, plus some dragonflies, stoneflies, moths, caterpillars, and others. **Behavior:** Feeds almost entirely in flight. Often forages in flocks, and typically flies rather low, doing much feeding over water. Rarely feeds on ground, mainly in severe weather.

NESTING   Almost always nests in colonies in vertical banks of sand or dirt; may be along riverbanks, lake shores, road cuts, gravel pits, or similar sites. Colonies are often dense, with entrances to holes no more than a foot apart. All the pairs in a colony may be synchronized in timing of their nesting activities. **Nest:** Site is in burrow excavated in steep bank. Both sexes help dig burrow, beginning by clinging to bank and digging with bill, later crawling inside burrow and kicking out dirt with feet. Burrows usually

2–3 feet long, sometimes 1–5 feet long. Nest at end of horizontal burrow is made of grass, weeds, rootlets, with a lining of feathers added after eggs are laid. **Eggs:** 4–5, sometimes 3–7. White. Incubation is by both parents, 14–16 days. **Young:** Both parents feed nestlings. Young leave nest about 18–24 days after hatching.

MIGRATION   Migrates north relatively late in spring compared with other swallows. A long-distance migrant, wintering in lowlands of South America. In late summer, may gather in huge flocks before southward migration.

CONSERVATION STATUS   Local populations vary with availability of good colony sites, but overall numbers high, population probably stable.

MUD-NEST SWALLOWS — GENUS *Hirundo*

Members of this group are varied in appearance, but most are glossy blue-black on the back, and several in the Old World have long, forked tails ("swallow-tailed"). Most kinds build nests out of dried mud, plastered against a vertical surface or under an overhang.

CLIFF SWALLOW   *Hirundo pyrrhonota*

This swallow is probably far more common today than when the Pilgrims landed. Originally it built its jug-shaped mud nests on the sides of cliffs. However, the sides of barns and the supports of bridges provided sheltered sites that were far more

Cliff Swallow

widespread than the natural ones. Taking advantage of these artificial locations, the species has invaded many areas where it never nested before. It continues to spread in the east and is still more common in the west, where practically every culvert and highway bridge seems to have its own Cliff Swallow colony.

HABITAT   *Open to semi-open land, farms, cliffs, river bluffs, lakes.* Widespread in all kinds of semi-open country, especially near water, from prairies to desert rivers to clearings in northern forest. Breeds where it can find sheltered vertical cliffs or other surfaces for nesting and a supply of mud for building the nest; still unaccountably scarce or missing in some seemingly suitable areas.

FEEDING   **Diet:** *Insects.* Feeds mostly on a wide variety of flying insects, particularly beetles (including June beetles and adult weevils), true bugs, flies, winged ants, bees, and wasps. Also eats grasshoppers, mayflies, lacewings, and various other insects, plus some spiders. Occasionally eats berries. **Behavior:** Feeds mostly on the wing. Often forages in flocks, and may feed low over the water or very high over other terrain. In bad weather, may feed on ground.

NESTING   Typically nests in colonies, sometimes with hundreds of nests crowded close together. **Nest:** Site is usually on vertical surface with some overhead shelter. Natural sites were on cliffs; most sites today on sides of buildings, under bridges, in culverts, or similar places. Nest is made of dried mud and shaped like a gourd, with large chamber for nest, narrowing to small entrance on side. Both sexes help build nest; inside of nest sparsely lined with grass and feathers. May repair and reuse old nest, sometimes that of another species. **Eggs:** 4–5, sometimes 3–6. White to pale pinkish, spotted with brown. Incubation is by both parents, 14–16 days.

Young: Both parents bring food for nestlings. Young leave nest about 21–23 days after hatching.

MIGRATION A long-distance migrant, wintering in southern South America. Migrates in flocks, traveling by day. This is the famous swallow that returns to the mission in San Juan Capistrano, California, every spring; traditionally the return is celebrated on March 19th, although the birds actually return to the general area in late February.

CONSERVATION STATUS Declines have been noted in a few areas, but general continent-wide trend is toward wider range and higher numbers.

CAVE SWALLOW *Hirundo fulva*

As recently as the 1960s, this was a rare bird in the United States. It nested only in a few southwestern caves, plastering its cuplike mud nest against the walls in the dimly lit interior. Since then it has "learned" to nest in artificial sites, in culverts and under bridges, and it has become a common summer bird across much of Texas and southern New Mexico (with an outlying colony in Florida). In some places, Cave Swallows may actively compete with Cliff Swallows for these artificial nest sites.

Cave Swallow

HABITAT *Semi-open country.* Forages over any kind of open or semi-open terrain, especially near water. Breeding was formerly limited by scarcity of nest sites in natural caves or sinkholes. Now nests under bridges and in culverts, buildings, silos, many other artificial sites, allowing species to spread into new habitats.

FEEDING **Diet:** *Insects.* Diet not known in detail, but feeds on a wide variety of flying insects, including beetles, flies, true bugs, wasps, bees, winged ants, grasshoppers, lacewings, moths. **Behavior:** Forages almost entirely in flight. May forage low over water or much higher, mainly in clear warm weather. Often forages in flocks.

NESTING Typically nests in colonies, sometimes with hundreds of pairs. **Nest:** Natural site is on steep wall of cave or sinkhole, in area away from entrance but with at least some light. Artificial sites are on vertical surfaces in culverts, under bridges, or in buildings; in Yucatan Peninsula, may nest in ancient Mayan temples. In well-sheltered sites, nests may last for years and are used repeatedly. Nest (built by both sexes) is an open cup of mud plastered against wall. Birds in natural sites gather mud on cave bottom, where it often contains much bat guano. Nest is lined with grass, bark fibers, plant down, and feathers. **Eggs:** 3–4, sometimes 2–5. White, finely spotted with brown and purple. Incubation is probably by both parents, thought to be about 15 days. **Young:** Both parents bring food for nestlings. Young leave nest at about 20–26 days.

MIGRATION Small Florida population supposedly winters in West Indies. Winter range of southwestern birds poorly known. In recent years, has begun wintering regularly in southern Texas.

CONSERVATION STATUS Range has expanded and population apparently has greatly increased in recent decades.

BARN SWALLOW *Hirundo rustica*

One of our most familiar birds in rural areas and semi-open country, this swallow is often seen skimming low over fields in flowing, graceful flight. It seems to have

adopted humans as neighbors, typically placing its nest in barns and garages or under bridges or wharves; indeed, it is now rare to find a Barn Swallow nest in a site that is *not* man-made. The species is also common across Europe and Asia, wintering to southern Africa and South America.

HABITAT   *Open or semi-open land, farms, fields, marshes, lakes.* May occur in any kind of open or partly open terrain, especially near water, generally avoiding very dry country and unbroken forest. Often breeds around farms, buildings, towns, and forages over fields or ponds.

FEEDING   **Diet:** *Insects.* Feeds on a wide variety of flying insects, especially flies (including house flies and horse flies), beetles, wasps, wild bees, winged ants, and true bugs. Also eats some moths, damselflies, grasshoppers, and other insects, and a few spiders and snails. Only occasionally eats a few berries or seeds. **Behavior:** Food is mostly captured and eaten in the air. Often forages quite low over water or fields. In bad weather, may sometimes feed on the ground.

NESTING   Courtship involves aerial chases. On perch, mated pair sit close together, touch bills, preen each other's feathers. Several pairs may nest in same immediate area, but does not form dense colonies as some swallows do. **Nest:** Original natural sites were in sheltered crevices in cliffs or shallow caves. Sites used today are mostly in open buildings, under eaves, under bridges or docks, or similar places. Nest (built by both sexes) is a cup of mud and dried grass, lined with feathers. **Eggs:** 4–5, sometimes 6, rarely 7. White, spotted with brown. Incubation is by both sexes (female does more), 13–17 days. **Young:** Both parents feed young. One or two additional birds, the pair's offspring from previous broods, may attend the nest and sometimes feed the nestlings. Young leave the nest about 18–23 days after hatching. One or two broods per year.

MIGRATION   Migrates in flocks, mostly by day. Southward migration is well under way by mid-August.

CONSERVATION STATUS   Local declines noted in a few areas, but still widespread and abundant.

Barn Swallow

GENUS *Delichon*

COMMON HOUSE-MARTIN   *Delichon urbica*

Very common across Europe and Asia, where it builds its mud nest under the eaves of buildings, this swallow has strayed several times to Alaska. Records there are for the Bering Sea area, mostly on islands but also on the mainland at Nome. The House-Martin has also wandered once to the islands of St. Pierre et Miquelon, near Newfoundland, so it could probably turn up elsewhere in the northeast.

CROWS, JAYS, AND MAGPIES (Family Corvidae)

Anyone who watches these birds for long may get the impression that they are crafty and cunning creatures. Science bears this out: experiments have shown that some members of the family, especially crows and ravens, may be among the most intelligent of birds.

Besides the ravens, crows, jays, magpies, and nutcrackers, the family also includes species like jackdaws, choughs, and treepies in other parts of the world. For convenience, they are all often referred to as "corvids" (short for the family name, Corvidae). Corvids are mostly medium-sized to large birds, varying in color from all black to brilliant blue or green. They generally have strong bills, strong legs, and loud voices. Many kinds are sociable creatures, living in flocks when they are not nesting; some nest in colonies or even have group nests. The 100-plus species are found worldwide except in the Antarctic.

Some corvids may live more than 15 years in the wild.

Feeding Most members of this family are omnivores, with remarkably varied diets. Many species, however, especially among the jays and nutcrackers, tend to rely heavily on just a few types of food when available. Several of our jays that live around oaks eat large quantities of acorns; the Pinyon Jay specializes on seeds of pinyon pine, and Clark's Nutcracker feeds mainly on pine seeds in winter. The crows and ravens, by contrast, will eat practically anything, with an emphasis on animal matter.

Many of the jays in the New World have special modifications of the bones near the base of the jaw, which help to brace the lower mandible when the bird pounds on something hard. When pounding on an acorn, for example, some of these jays will hold the bill slightly open so that they hit the acorn with the lower mandible only.

Quite a few corvids also have the habit of storing food and then finding it later. Clark's Nutcracker is a champion at this behavior, but several of the jays do it too.

Nesting Most corvids nest in isolated pairs, but some kinds form loose colonies. Most notable is the cooperative breeding practiced by various kinds of jays, with several adults often tending to the young in a single nest.

Nests built by corvids are usually shaped like bulky open cups or globular masses with an entrance at the side. Eggs are often pale green to buff, with darker spots. In most species, the female does most or all of the incubation, but both parents help to feed the young. Often the male will feed the female during incubation.

Displays Especially among the more sociable corvids, many different call notes and displays may be used for communication with other flock members. Courtship displays are varied. Ravens and crows may perform impressive display flights, with soaring, diving, and tumbling. In many species, two birds perch close together and perform ritualized bowing and other motions in courtship, and the male often feeds the female.

GENUS *Perisoreus*

GRAY JAY *Perisoreus canadensis*

A hiker in the north woods sometimes will be followed by a pair of Gray Jays, gliding silently from tree to tree, watching inquisitively. These fluffy jays seem fearless, and they can be a minor nuisance around campsites and cabins, stealing food, earning the nickname "camp robber." Tough enough to survive year-round in very cold climates, they store excess food in bark crevices all summer, retrieving it in harsh weather. Surprisingly, they nest and raise their young in late winter and early spring, not during the brief northern summer.

HABITAT *Spruce and fir forests.* Found in various kinds of coniferous and mixed forest, but rarely occurs where there are no spruce trees. Habitats include black spruce bogs in eastern Canada, forests of aspen and Engelmann spruce in Rockies, Sitka spruce and Douglas-fir on northwest coast.

FEEDING **Diet:** *Omnivorous.* Diet is remarkably varied, includes insects, spiders, berries, seeds, fungi, small rodents, birds' eggs, and carrion. **Behavior:** An opportunist in its foraging, flying from tree to tree searching for food. Boldly enters campsites and even cabins to steal food. Will attack rodents and small birds. Sometimes flies out to catch insects in midair. Regularly eats carrion, especially in winter, coming to kills left by wolves or other predators. Stores food items throughout the year, especially in summer, and may live on these caches in severe winter weather; the bird's sticky saliva helps it stick pieces of food in bark crevices and other spots. Can carry food items, even fairly large ones, in flight, sometimes carrying them with its feet.

NESTING   Mated pairs stay together all year and defend permanent territories. Early in breeding season, male may perform courtship feeding of female. Nesting begins remarkably early, in late winter, while breeding grounds still snow-covered. **Nest:** Site is in dense conifer, close to trunk at base of branch; usually fairly low, averaging about 15 feet above the ground. Nest (built by both sexes) is a bulky flat cup of twigs, lichens, strips of bark, and caterpillar webs, lined with softer materials including animal hair and feathers.

Gray Jay

Eggs: 3–4, sometimes 2–5. Pale gray to greenish, dotted with brown, olive, or reddish. Incubation is by female only, about 18–22 days. Male sometimes brings food to female on nest. **Young:** Female broods young most of time at first while male brings food; later, both parents bring food to nest. Young leave nest at about 22–24 days, remain with parents for at least another month.

MIGRATION   No regular migration. Birds in high mountains of west rarely move to lower elevations in winter. On rare occasions, small invasions of Gray Jays will move a short distance out of boreal forest in winter.

CONSERVATION STATUS   Most of breeding range is not subject to human disturbance. Has declined in a few areas after clearcutting of forest.

CRESTED JAYS — GENUS *Cyanocitta*

These two jays are both regionally common, one in the east and one in the west, often living in suburbs and city parks. They sometimes interbreed where their ranges meet along the eastern base of the Rockies.

STELLER'S JAY   *Cyanocitta stelleri*

A common bird of western forests. Steller's Jay is most numerous in dense coniferous woods of the mountains and the northwest coast, where its dark colors blend in well in the shadows. Except when nesting it lives in flocks, and the birds will often fly across a clearing one at a time, in single file, giving their low *shook-shook* calls as they swoop up to perch in a tall pine.

HABITAT   *Conifer and pine-oak forests.* Most numerous as a breeder in the mountains and along the northern coast in forests of pine, spruce, and fir; also lives in pine-oak forest, and locally in riverside groves of oaks and other deciduous trees. Especially when not nesting, will range into other woodland types, orchards, and well-wooded suburbs.

FEEDING   **Diet:** *Omnivorous.* Diet is about two-thirds vegetable and one-third animal matter. Feeds heavily on pine seeds, acorns, and other nuts and seeds, especially during fall and winter; also eats many berries and wild fruits, sometimes

cultivated fruit. Especially in summer, eats many insects, including beetles, wasps, and wild bees. Also eats spiders, birds' eggs, table scraps, sometimes small rodents or lizards. **Behavior:** Forages mostly high in trees but also low or on ground. Opens hard seeds and acorns by pounding on them with bill.

NESTING   In courtship, male feeds female. Adults are quiet and secretive while nesting but become noisy and aggressive if nest is threatened. **Nest:** Site is in tree, usually coniferous; sometimes in deciduous tree or shrub. Height varies, usually 10–30 feet above the ground, sometimes lower or much higher. Nest (built by both sexes) is a bulky ragged cup of twigs, weeds, moss, dry leaves, cemented together with mud and lined with fine grass, rootlets, and pine needles.

Steller's Jay

Bits of paper often added to nest. **Eggs:** 4, sometimes 3–5, rarely 2–6. Pale bluegreen, finely spotted with brown or olive. Incubation is mostly or entirely by female, about 16–18 days. **Young:** Both parents bring food for nestlings. Age of young at first flight not well known, about 3 weeks.

MIGRATION   Often a permanent resident, but may move to lower elevations in winter. Occasionally stages large invasions into lowlands, perhaps when food crops fail in the mountains.

BLUE JAY   *Cyanocitta cristata*

One of the loudest and most colorful birds of eastern backyards and woodlots, the Blue Jay is unmistakable. Intelligent and adaptable, it may feed on almost anything, and it is quick to take advantage of bird feeders. Besides their raucous *jay! jay!* calls,

Blue Jays make a variety of musical sounds, and they can do a remarkable imitation of the scream of a Redshouldered Hawk. Not always conspicuous, they slip furtively through the trees when tending their own nest or going to rob the nest of another bird.

HABITAT   *Oak and pine woods, suburban gardens, groves, towns.* Breeds in deciduous or mixed woods, avoiding purely coniferous forest. May be in fairly low or scrubby forest in southern part of range. Favors habitat with many oak or beech trees. Often common in well-wooded suburbs or city parks.

FEEDING   **Diet:** *Omnivorous.* Most of diet is vegetable matter (up to 75 percent of diet for year, higher percentage in winter), including acorns, beechnuts, and other nuts, many kinds of seeds, grain, berries, small fruits, sometimes cultivated fruits. Eats

Blue Jay

many insects, especially caterpillars, beetles, grasshoppers, and others; also eats spiders, snails, birds' eggs, sometimes small rodents, frogs, baby birds, carrion, other items. **Behavior:** Forages in trees and shrubs and on ground. Comes to feeders for seeds or suet. Pounds on hard nuts or seeds with bill to break them open. Will harvest acorns and store them in holes in ground.

NESTING   Courtship may involve aerial chases; male may feed female. Blue Jays become quiet and inconspicuous around the nest, but will attack with loud calls if the nest is

threatened by a predator. **Nest:** Site is in tree (either coniferous or deciduous), placed in vertical crotch of trunk or at horizontal fork in limb well out from trunk; usually 8–30 feet above ground, sometimes 5–50 feet. Nest (built by both sexes) is a bulky open cup made of twigs, grass, weeds, bark strips, moss, sometimes held together with mud. Nest is lined with rootlets and other fine materials, often decorated with paper, rags, string, or other debris. **Eggs:** 4–5, sometimes 3–7. Greenish or buff, sometimes pale blue, spotted with brown and gray. Incubation is by both parents (but female does more), about 16–18 days. **Young:** Both parents bring food for nestlings. Young leave nest 17–21 days after hatching.

MIGRATION   Present all year in most of range, but variable numbers migrate south in fall; big southward flights in some years, with thousands on the move, although they do not go south of the United States. Migrates by day.

CONSERVATION STATUS   May have declined initially with clearing of eastern forest, before it adapted to nesting in cities. Now common, expanding range toward northwest.

TROPICAL JAYS — GENUS *Cyanocorax*

Widespread in the American tropics, these birds often look strikingly different from the bluish jays of North America: in Texas, for example, this group produces a Green Jay and a Brown Jay, and some found farther south are black and white. Many members of this genus are cooperative breeders, with nesting attempts involving multiple adults, not just one pair.

GREEN JAY   *Cyanocorax yncas*

Green Jay

Unmistakably tropical, the Green Jay enters our area only in southern Texas. There it is common in native woods and mesquite brush. Around some parks and refuges it is very tame, coming to picnic tables for scraps; but at other places it can be elusive and surprisingly hard to see despite its bright colors. Green Jays live in pairs or social groups at all seasons, communicating with each other with a bizarre variety of calls.

HABITAT   *Brush, woodlands.* In Texas, most common in dense native woodlands in the lowlands dominated by acacia, ebony, and hackberry; also lives in more open mesquite brush and stands of short oaks, and in some suburbs with native vegetation nearby. In the tropics, often in humid forest in foothills and lower mountain slopes.

FEEDING   **Diet:** *Omnivorous.* Feeds on a wide variety of insects, including beetles, grasshoppers, crickets, true bugs, wasps. Also spiders, centipedes, small rodents, lizards, eggs and young of small birds. Feeds on plant material including various seeds, nuts, berries, and small fruits. **Behavior:** Forages by moving actively through trees and shrubs, examining the foliage for food; drops to the ground for some items and sometimes flies out to catch insects in midair. Cracks open hard seeds and nuts by pounding them with bill. Will come to bird feeders for a variety of items.

NESTING   Pair or family group may defend territory throughout the year. **Nest:** In Texas, site is in dense tree or shrub, usually 5–15 feet above the ground. Nest (built by both sexes) is a bulky but loose cup of sticks, thorny twigs, lined with rootlets, grass, moss, and sometimes leaves. **Eggs:** 2–6, usually 3–5. Pale gray to greenish white, heavily spotted with brown and lavender. Incubation is by female only, about 17–18 days. Male may feed female during incubation. **Young:** Both parents bring food for nestlings. Young leave nest about 19–22 days after hatching.

CROWS, JAYS, AND MAGPIES

Young remain in parents' territory through nesting season of following year, then are evicted. In some tropical areas, these one-year-olds help with feeding young in nest, but apparently those in Texas do not.

MIGRATION Permanent resident. Rarely wanders any distance from nesting areas.

CONSERVATION STATUS Probably declined in southern Texas with initial loss of habitat, but current population seems stable.

BROWN JAY *Cyanocorax morio*

At dawn in the woods of south Texas, a shrill, explosive *pyow! pyow!* announces a flock of Brown Jays. These big birds, much larger than our other jays, are almost always in flocks, and their calls can be heard for more than a quarter of a mile; but they can be surprisingly inconspicuous when they stop calling and slip away

Brown Jay

through the trees. Common in Mexico, Brown Jays crossed into Texas in the 1970s; they are still uncommon and local there, found only on a stretch of the Rio Grande below Falcon Dam.

HABITAT *Dense riverside woods.* In Texas, found locally in relatively tall, dense, native woods along Rio Grande. In Mexico and Central America, lives in a variety of woodland habitats, especially around clearings, open woods, forest edges.

FEEDING **Diet:** *Omnivorous.* Feeds on a wide variety of insects, also spiders, small lizards, rodents, eggs and nestlings of smaller birds. Also feeds on berries, fruits, seeds, nectar. **Behavior:** Usually forages in flocks. Forages on the ground in dense cover or in shrubs or trees, hopping about actively through the branches. Visits large flowers to feed on nectar and possibly insects there. Will break open hard nuts or seeds by pounding on them with bill.

NESTING Nesting habits in Texas not well known. Farther south, has complicated social system. Each flock has only one nest; eggs in nest may be laid by only one female or by more than one; all adults in flock help to feed young in nest. **Nest:** Site is in tree or shrub, usually fairly low in Texas, probably in the range of 15–30 feet above the ground. Nest may be built by pair or by several adults. Often placed out at fork in horizontal limb. Nest is a bulky cup of sticks and twigs, lined with bark fibers, weeds, other soft material. **Eggs:** 3–4, sometimes 2–8. Blue-gray, spotted with brown. Incubation is by female (or by multiple females), about 18–20 days; other adults in flock may feed incubating female. **Young:** Fed by all adults in flock. Young leave nest about 3–4 weeks after hatching.

MIGRATION Permanent resident.

CONSERVATION STATUS Widespread and fairly common in Mexico and Central America. Recent arrival in southern Texas, still uncommon and local there.

SCRUB JAYS — GENUS *Aphelocoma*

These are rather large jays without crests and with no strong pattern in the wings or tail. Most of them live around oaks and eat many acorns. Two species in our area have developed cooperative breeding, with the young birds in the nest often being fed by adults other than their parents.

WESTERN SCRUB-JAY *Aphelocoma californica*

Western Scrub-Jay

In brushy western foothills, pairs of Western Scrub-Jays are often seen swooping across clearings, giving harsh calls, their long tails flopping in flight. Along the Pacific coast, they are often common around suburban yards or well-wooded city parks. The scrub-jays living in Florida and on Santa Cruz Island, California, are now considered to be two separate species from the widespread form in the west.

HABITAT *Foothills, oak-chaparral, river woods, pinyons, junipers, some suburbs.* Found in many kinds of brushy country, but typically where scrub oaks are common; in parts of the west, lives in pinyon-juniper woods with few oaks, the pinyon pine seeds perhaps taking the place of acorns in the bird's diet.

FEEDING **Diet:** *Omnivorous.* Diet varies with season and region. Eats a wide variety of insects, especially in summer, as well as a few spiders and snails. Winter diet may be mostly acorns, pine seeds, and other seeds, nuts, and berries. Also eats some rodents, eggs and young of other birds, and small reptiles and amphibians. **Behavior:** Forages on the ground and in trees, usually in flocks. Often harvests acorns and buries them, perhaps to retrieve them later.

NESTING Unlike Florida Scrub-Jay and Mexican Jay, this species breeds in isolated pairs, not in cooperative flocks. **Nest:** Site is in tree or shrub, usually fairly low, 5–30 feet above the ground. Nest (built by both sexes) is a well-built, thick-walled cup of twigs, grass, and moss, lined with fine rootlets and sometimes with animal hair. **Eggs:** 3–6, sometimes 2–7. Usually light green, spotted with olive or brown; sometimes paler gray or green with large reddish brown spots. Incubation is by female, about 15–17 days. Male feeds female during incubation. **Young:** Fed by both par-ents. Young leave nest about 18–19 days after hatching. One brood per year, sometimes two.

MIGRATION Mostly permanent resident. Those in the southwest sometimes stage invasions of the lowlands in fall and winter, probably when wild food crops fail in their usual foothill haunts.

FLORIDA SCRUB-JAY *Aphelocoma coerulescens*

This bird is noteworthy on several counts: it lives nowhere in the world except Florida, it has a complicated social system, it has been the subject of very detailed field studies, and it is threatened by loss of habitat. Formerly considered just a race of the scrub-jays found in the west, it is now classified as a full species.

Its name is appropriate, for it lives only in Florida scrub, areas of short scrubby oaks growing on sandy soil. This habitat occurs mostly as isolated pockets, and the jays rarely wander away from their own little patch of scrub, making them extremely sedentary. In their feeding habits they are similar to Western Scrub-Jays.

Florida Scrub-Jay is a cooperative breeder: each nesting territory is occupied by an adult pair and often by one to six "helpers," usually the pair's offspring from previous years. These additional birds assist in defending the territory and feeding the young.

CROWS, JAYS, AND MAGPIES

Studies have shown that a pair with "helpers" is likely to raise more young than a pair without.

As of the early 1990s, the total population was estimated at about 4,000 pairs, probably a reduction of more than 90 percent from original numbers. Loss of habitat has been the main problem. Prime Florida oak scrub is maintained by occasional fires, so fire prevention has added to the effect of ongoing development in squeezing out the jay's habitat.

ISLAND SCRUB-JAY   *Aphelocoma insularis*

This very localized species is larger, darker, and more richly colored than the Western Scrub-Jay. It lives only on Santa Cruz Island, a little over 20 miles long and up to 5 miles wide in places, one of the Channel Islands off the coast of southern California. Its feeding and nesting habits are apparently similar to those of the Western Scrub-Jay.

MEXICAN JAY   *Aphelocoma ultramarina*

Also known as the Gray-breasted Jay, this bird enters the United States in two areas: in much of southeastern Arizona and adjacent New Mexico, and in the Big Bend area of Texas. These two populations are not closely connected in Mexico, and they differ in a number of ways, including egg color, bill color of the young, voice, and aspects of nesting behavior. The nesting habits in Arizona are surprisingly complicated, with various members of the flock more or less involved with several nesting attempts at once.

HABITAT   *Open oak forests (Arizona); oak-pine woods (Texas)*. In Arizona, found in various oak woodlands, including those mixed with pines, in canyons and lower slopes of mountains (up to about 7,000 feet). Elsewhere in range, in Texas and Mexico, found in a variety of forests dominated by pines and oaks.

FEEDING   **Diet:** *Omnivorous; mostly acorns, seeds, insects.* Diet is largely acorns and seeds of pinyon

Mexican Jay

pine from fall through winter, mostly insects in summer. Eats grasshoppers, beetles, caterpillars, and many other insects; also lizards, small snakes, birds' eggs, rarely mice or birds. **Behavior:** Forages on the ground or in trees, usually in flocks. May visit large flowers in summer for nectar and insects. Rarely catches insects in flight. Breaks open acorns by holding them against branch with feet and pounding with bill. Harvests acorns in fall and buries them in ground, often remembering location and retrieving them later.

NESTING   Flocks defend permanent territories that may remain the same for generations. Within each flock, 2–4 females may nest at one time; each is attended by one male, but may mate with other males in flock as well. In Texas, where flocks are smaller, may nest as isolated pairs. **Nest:** Site is in tree, often oak, juniper, or pine, usually well hidden among foliage. Height averages about 20 feet above ground, can be 6–60 feet up. Nest (built by both sexes) is bulky cup of sticks and twigs lined with fine rootlets and plant fibers. **Eggs:** 4–5, sometimes 1–6. Eggs pale unmarked green in Arizona; in Texas, pale blue-green, usually with pale brownish spots. Incubation is by female only, about 18 days. Other adults in flock feed incubating female on nest. **Young:** Fed by both parents and by other members of flock. Young leave nest at about 25–28 days, may be fed for several weeks thereafter.

MIGRATION   Almost never moves away from immediate breeding territory; one of the most sedentary bird species in North America.

GENUS *Gymnorhinus*

PINYON JAY   *Gymnorhinus cyanocephalus*

This odd jay, looking more like a small blue-gray crow, lives mainly in the Great Basin region of the west. Appropriately named, it feeds heavily on the seeds of pinyon pines, and its distribution is tied closely to the range of these trees. Pinyon Jays are sociable at all seasons, traveling in flocks, nesting in colonies. When on the move they fly close together, giving harsh nasal calls.

Pinyon Jay

HABITAT   *Pinyon pines, junipers; ranges into sagebrush.* Under normal conditions, seldom found far from pinyon pines in pinyon-juniper woods. At times, perhaps when the pinyon cone crop fails, flocks are seen elsewhere in streamside groves, oak woods, or other habitats.

FEEDING   **Diet:** *Omnivorous, but especially pinyon pine seeds.* Feeds heavily on seeds of pinyon pine; also eats seeds of other pines and many other plants, berries, small fruits, nuts, waste grain. Especially in summer, eats many insects, including beetles, caterpillars, and grasshoppers, also sometimes eggs and young of smaller birds. Young are fed mostly insects. **Behavior:** Does much foraging on ground, also feeds in trees, and occasionally flies out to catch insects in the air. Almost always forages in flocks. Stores many pine seeds in late summer and fall, burying caches in ground, and is able to find them and feed on them later.

NESTING   Nests in colonies, close together but usually no more than 1–3 nests in any one tree. Breeds mostly in late winter, the adults feeding largely on stored seeds; may nest again in late summer if pinyon pines produce an exceptional seed crop. In courtship, several males may pursue one female in flight. **Nest:** Site is usually 3–20 feet above the ground in juniper, oak, or pinyon, sometimes much higher in other kind of pine. Nest (built by both sexes) has foundation of twigs, inner cup of shredded bark, grass, rootlets, pine needles, animal hair. Often steals material from unattended nests of neighbors. **Eggs:** 4–5, sometimes 3–6. Very pale blue-green to grayish, finely dotted with brown. Incubation is by female, about 16–17 days. Male feeds female during incubation. **Young:** Both parents bring food for nestlings. Young leave nest about 3 weeks after hatching.

MIGRATION   Not truly migratory, but nomadic. May remain in one area if cone crops are consistently good, or may wander widely, especially in fall and winter.

CONSERVATION STATUS　Local numbers may change drastically from year to year, but overall population probably stable.

NUTCRACKERS — GENUS *Nucifraga*

CLARK'S NUTCRACKER　*Nucifraga columbiana*

This bird often lives in places remote from human contact, near treeline on windy western peaks. Where it does encounter people, however, it seems fearless, striding about in picnic grounds and scenic-view parking lots, looking for handouts. Nutcrackers are champions at burying pine seeds (sometimes tens of thousands) in hidden caches in fall, then finding them during winter; these seed stores allow them to nest in late winter, when the forest is still covered with snow.

Clark's Nutcracker

HABITAT　*High mountains, conifers near treeline.* Generally breeds at high elevations in the mountains, in open or broken forest of pine, spruce, or Douglas-fir. May also breed in lower-elevation pine or pinyon-juniper woods when there is a good cone crop. Wanders to above treeline in summer, and may move to lower elevation woods in fall.

FEEDING　Diet: *Omnivorous.* Much of diet is pine seeds; remainder of diet quite varied, including other seeds, nuts, berries, insects, snails, eggs and young of other birds, carrion. **Behavior:** Forages on ground and in trees. Occasionally catches flying insects in the air or digs insect larvae out of wood by pounding with bill. Will pry open pine cones to extract seeds. Harvests pine seeds in late summer and fall, carrying up to 90 at once in throat pouch and burying them in soil on exposed slopes; may store 30,000 or more seeds in one season. Has a remarkable ability to find these caches later, feeding on them through winter.

NESTING　Breeding activity often begins in late winter, when territory is still snow-covered. Courtship may involve long flights, male following female. **Nest:** Site is in coniferous tree, usually away from trunk on horizontal limb, 8–40 feet above the ground. Nest (built by both sexes) is large and deep; has a platform of twigs and bark fibers supporting a cup of grass, bark strips, pine needles. **Eggs:** 2–4, sometimes up to 6. Pale green, lightly spotted with brown and gray. Incubation is by both parents, about 16–18 days. Incubating adult sits tightly on nest even when closely approached. **Young:** Both parents care for and feed young. Food for nestlings often consists of pine seeds stored the preceding autumn. Young leave the nest about 18–21 days after hatching.

MIGRATION　Movements are complex and variable. Often a permanent resident but may move to lower elevations in mountains in fall, even out into lowlands, perhaps in years when food crops are poor in the mountains.

MAGPIES — GENUS *Pica*

These are noisy, sociable birds of partly open country. Magpies are often seen walking, hopping, or running on the ground in search of insects, or swooping from tree to tree, their white wing patches flashing like beacons. One of the two species occurs on four continents, the other only in California.

BLACK-BILLED MAGPIE *Pica pica*

Black-billed Magpies add much to western landscapes, both with their flashy appearance and with their big bushel-basket nests in trees. In an earlier era, farmers and ranchers tried to exterminate this species, but to no avail, and it is common today in open country and even in towns in the mountain west.

HABITAT *Rangeland, conifers, streamsides, forest edges, farms.* Found in many kinds of semi-open country in the west. Avoids unbroken forest, and not found in treeless grasslands or extreme desert situations. Most common in streamside groves of trees in open terrain, farm country, and some suburban areas.

Black-billed Magpie

FEEDING **Diet:** *Omnivorous.* Diet is quite varied, but feeds on insects more consistently than most members of the crow family; eats many grasshoppers, caterpillars, flies, beetles, and others. Also eats carrion, rodents, eggs and young of other birds, sometimes small snakes. Vegetable matter such as berries, seeds, and nuts may be eaten more in winter. **Behavior:** Forages mostly by walking on ground; may use bill to flip over items in search of food. Sometimes steals food from other birds, and supposedly may follow predators at times to pick up scraps they leave. May take ticks from the backs of elk and other animals.

NESTING Often nests in small loose colonies. In courtship, males pursue females, often flashing their white wing patches. **Nest:** Site is among the branches of tree or large shrub (generally deciduous), 5–60 feet above the ground, usually 15–30 feet up. Nest is a huge structure, a globular canopy of sticks about 3 feet in diameter, with entrance holes on either side. Inside is a cup-shaped nest with base of mud or manure and lining of weeds, rootlets, grass, and hair. Both sexes help build nest. **Eggs:** 6–7, sometimes 5–9, rarely more. Greenish gray, heavily spotted with brown. Incubation is by female, 16–21 days, usually about 18. Male feeds female during egg-laying and incubation period. **Young:** Both parents bring food to nestlings. Young leave nest about 25–29 days after hatching. One brood per year.

MIGRATION Mostly permanent resident. Some upslope movement in fall, and a few birds move southward or downslope in winter. Individuals rarely wander well to east of breeding range.

CONSERVATION STATUS In early part of 20th century, many were killed as pests or poisoned by baits set out for predators. In spite of this, remains common and widespread.

YELLOW-BILLED MAGPIE *Pica nuttalli*

A bird of open country in California's central valleys. While its Black-billed relative lives across Europe, Asia, and North Africa, as well as western North America, the Yellow-billed Magpie lives only in California—in an area about 500 miles from north to south and less than 150 miles wide. Within this limited region, Yellow-billeds nest in colonies in groves of tall trees.

HABITAT *Stream groves, scattered oaks, ranches, farms.* Most numerous in open oak savanna and where riverside groves of oaks, cottonwoods, and sycamores border open country such as pastures or farmland.

CROWS, JAYS, AND MAGPIES

FEEDING **Diet:** *Omnivorous.* Diet varies with season, but year-round may average about 30 percent plant material, 70 percent animal material (mainly insects). May feed heavily on acorns in fall and winter, cracking them open by pounding with bill; also eats carrion in winter. Eats many grasshoppers in late summer. **Behavior:** When foraging on ground, may use bill to flip over cow dung, wood chips, etc., to look for food. Magpies also steal food from each other and from other animals. Sometimes cache food items (such as acorns) in shallow holes in ground, tree crevices, etc.

NESTING Nests in small colonies. Pair formation may begin in fall, although birds remain in flocks during winter. Main courtship ritual involves

Yellow-billed Magpie

male feeding female. **Nest:** Both sexes build nest, placing it far out on high limb (usually 40–60 feet above ground). Nest often built on top of mistletoe clump; even if not, may resemble such a clump from a distance. Nest is bulky domed structure (2–3 feet in diameter) with entrance on side, made of sticks and twigs. Interior of nest has base usually made of mud, lined with fine plant materials. **Eggs:** 4–8, usually 6–7. Olive-buff, marked with brown or olive. Incubation is by female, about 16–18 days. Male brings food to incubating female. **Young:** Both parents feed young. Time to fledging not well known, but parents may continue to feed young for several weeks after they leave nest. One brood per year.

MIGRATION Mostly a permanent resident. Rarely wanders away from breeding areas, perhaps most often in winter.

CONSERVATION STATUS Surveys suggest slight decline within its very limited range. Has disappeared from some former areas of occurrence.

CROWS AND RAVENS — GENUS *Corvus*

Adaptable and intelligent, these birds have managed to thrive even in many areas where the habitat has been severely altered by humans. Most crows and ravens are mostly or entirely black, and most are fairly large—the Common Raven, for example, is as big as a hawk. The roughly 40 members of this genus are widespread around the world, including some midocean island groups like Hawaii, but they are curiously absent from South America.

EURASIAN JACKDAW *Corvus monedula*

This small Eurasian crow staged a minor invasion of northeastern North America in the early to mid 1980s, with singles and small groups found in several states and provinces, and up to 50 at one spot in Quebec. These birds may have ridden on ships for part or all of their crossing of the Atlantic. There have been only a few records since 1986.

AMERICAN CROW *Corvus brachyrhynchos*

Crows are thought to be among our most intelligent birds, and the success of the American Crow in adapting to civilization would seem to confirm this. Despite past attempts to exterminate them, crows are more common than ever in farmlands, towns, and even cities, and their distinctive *caw!* is a familiar sound over much of the continent. Sociable, especially when not nesting, crows may gather in communal roosts on winter nights, sometimes with thousands or even tens of thousands roosting in one grove.

HABITAT *Woodlands, farms, fields, river groves, shores, towns.* Lives in a wide variety of semi-open habitats, from farming country and open fields to clearings in the woods. Often found on shores, especially where Fish Crow and Northwestern Crow do not occur. Avoids hot desert zones. Is adapting to towns and even cities, now often nesting in city parks.

FEEDING **Diet:** *Omnivorous.* Seems to feed on practically anything it can find, including insects, spiders, snails, earthworms, frogs, small snakes, shellfish, carrion, garbage, eggs and young of other birds, seeds, grain, berries, fruit. **Behavior:** Opportunistic, quickly taking advantage of new food sources. Feeds mostly on the ground, sometimes in trees. Scavenges

American Crow

along roads and at dumps. Will carry hard-shelled mollusks high in air and drop them on rocks to break them open. Indigestible parts of food are coughed up later as pellets.

NESTING In courtship on ground or in tree, male faces female, fluffs up body feathers, partly spreads wings and tail, and bows repeatedly while giving a short rattling song. Mated pairs perch close together, touching bills and preening each other's feathers. Breeding pair may be assisted by "helpers," their offspring from previous seasons. **Nest:** Site is in tree or large shrub, 10–70 feet above the ground, usually in vertical fork or at base of branch against trunk. Rarely nests on ground or on building ledge. Nest (built by both sexes) is a large bulky basket of sticks, twigs, bark strips, weeds, and mud, lined with softer material such as grass, moss, plant fibers, feathers. **Eggs:** 4–6, sometimes 3–9. Dull blue-green to gray-green, blotched with brown and gray. Incubation is probably mostly or entirely by female, about 18 days. **Young:** Fed by both parents and sometimes by "helpers." Young leave nest about 4–5 weeks after hatching.

MIGRATION Permanent resident in many areas; withdraws in fall from northern regions, and flocks spend the winter in some areas a short distance south of the breeding range.

CONSERVATION STATUS Attempts at extermination in past have included dynamiting of winter roosts. However, the crow remains abundant and is increasingly adapting to life in towns and even cities.

NORTHWESTERN CROW   *Corvus caurinus*

Along the immediate coast in the Pacific Northwest lives this smaller, hoarse-voiced version of the American Crow. Typically associated with tidewater, it raids seabird colonies for unattended eggs, explores tidepools for stranded marine creatures, and scavenges on the beach along with gulls. It is often hard to tell Northwestern and American crows apart where their ranges meet; they may interbreed, and some observers believe they are merely forms of the same species.

HABITAT *Near tidewater, shores.* Generally found close to the immediate coastline. Often along open beaches, rocky shores, tidal estuaries, coastal ponds, inshore islands. Also forages in woods and fields close to shore. Only occasionally moves to fields several miles inland.

CROWS, JAYS, AND MAGPIES

FEEDING **Diet:** *Omnivorous.* Seems to feed on anything it can find in its habitat, including fish, crabs, shellfish, carrion, garbage, various insects, berries, nuts, seeds, and birds' eggs (especially in seabird colonies). **Behavior:** Forages mostly while walking on ground or in very shallow water; also sometimes forages in trees. May concentrate at salmon runs along with other birds. Carries mussels aloft and drops them on rocks to break them open. May store food on territory and retrieve it later.

NESTING Usually solitary in nesting, not in colonies. Offspring from previous year may remain on nesting territory of adult pair; these "helpers" assist in mobbing predators, may or may not assist with feeding the nestlings. **Nest:** Site is usually in fork of tree or shrub; sometimes placed on the ground (sheltered by rocks) on islands. Nest (built by both sexes) is a bulky platform of sticks, bark, plant fibers, and mud, lined with softer material such as grass, animal fur, and rootlets. **Eggs:** 4–5. Dull blue-green to gray-green, blotched with brown and gray. Incubation is by female only, about 18 days. **Young:** Fed by both parents and sometimes by one-year-old "helpers." Age when young leave nest not well known, probably close to 4 weeks.

MIGRATION Permanent resident. Smaller crows sometimes seen along Oregon coast in winter may or may not be this form.

CONSERVATION STATUS Common within its range, numbers probably stable.

MEXICAN CROW *Corvus imparatus*

This small crow has a very limited range in the dry country of northeastern Mexico. In the United States it occurs mostly as a winter visitor to southernmost Texas, mainly around the garbage dump at Brownsville, where it scavenges for food along with Chihuahuan Ravens, gulls, and many other birds. The Mexican Crow has a surprisingly low-pitched voice for its small size. A close relative in western Mexico, the Sinaloa Crow, is now considered a separate species because its high, shrill calls are very different.

Mexican Crow

HABITAT *Semi-open country.* In Texas, seen mostly in and near the Brownsville garbage dump. In Mexico, found in dry brushland, arid scrub, farms, ranches, towns. Avoids unbroken forest, mountains, and extreme desert situations, and not often found on seashore.

FEEDING **Diet:** *Probably omnivorous.* Diet not known in detail, but probably like other crows in eating a wide variety of items. Scavenges for refuse, and known to eat carrion, insects, seeds; probably also birds' eggs, berries, nuts, various other things. **Behavior:** Forages mostly by walking on ground; also probably does some foraging in trees. Except when nesting, usually forages in flocks.

NESTING Has been known to nest only a few times in Texas. Breeding behavior is not well known. May nest in loose colonies. Courtship may involve two birds perching close together, touching bills and preening each other's feathers; one bird (male?) may feed the other. **Nest:** Site is usually in tree; the first nests found in Texas were built in the open on a framework of steel beams. Both sexes help build nest, a substantial platform or shallow basket of sticks and plant fibers, lined with softer materials. **Eggs:** 4. Pale blue, streaked with pale olive-buff. Incubation is apparently by female only, 17–18 days. **Young:** Both parents bring food for nestlings. Development of young in the wild not well known; may leave the nest roughly 30–35 days after hatching.

MIGRATION   Mostly a permanent resident; disperses somewhat in winter, with small flocks moving north into Texas.

CONSERVATION STATUS   Despite its adaptability, might be vulnerable because of ongoing destruction of habitat in its very limited native range.

FISH CROW   *Corvus ossifragus*

Like a smaller edition of the American Crow, but with a more nasal voice and typically found near water, the Fish Crow is very common in parts of the southeast. On the coast, it hunts in salt marshes and tidal flats, and scavenges on the beach. Inland, it ranges through swamps and along rivers. In recent decades it has extended its range farther and farther inland in some areas, especially on the Atlantic coastal plain and far up the Mississippi Valley.

HABITAT   *Tidewater, river valleys, swamps, woodland, farmland.* Overlaps in habitat with American Crow, but more likely to be near water, especially along coast, where it forages on beaches, marshes, and estuaries. Inland from coast, usually follows the drainages of large rivers, although it may feed in woods or fields a few miles from the water.

FEEDING   **Diet:** *Omnivorous.* May feed on practically anything it can find, including carrion, crabs, shrimp, crayfish, a wide variety of insects, berries, seeds, nuts, bird eggs, turtle eggs, and garbage.

Fish Crow

Behavior: Usually forages in flocks. Does most foraging by walking, especially on shores or in very shallow water, also in fields; sometimes forages in trees. May carry mollusks aloft, then drop them on rocks to break the shells. In colonies of herons and other waterbirds, if adults are frightened from their nests, Fish Crows may destroy many eggs.

NESTING   Often a few pairs nest in a loose colony. Courtship may involve male and female flying close together in gliding display flight. **Nest:** Site is in upright fork of tree or shrub. May be very low in coastal growth of pines, cedars, or quite high in deciduous trees in inland swamps; nest may be 5–70 feet above ground or even higher. Nest (probably built by both sexes) is a bulky platform of sticks and strips of bark, lined with softer materials such as grass, rootlets, hair, feathers, paper, pine needles, even manure. **Eggs:** 4–5. Dull blue-green to gray-green, blotched with brown and gray. Incubation is by female, possibly assisted by male, about 16–18 days. **Young:** Both parents probably bring food to nestlings. Age when young leave the nest not well known, probably 3–4 weeks.

MIGRATION   Mostly permanent resident. Withdraws from some inland parts of range in winter.

CONSERVATION STATUS   Probably increasing as it expands its range farther north and inland.

CHIHUAHUAN RAVEN   *Corvus cryptoleucus*

In the dry grasslands of the southwest, the Common Raven is replaced by this smaller species, about the size of an American Crow. Chihuahuan Ravens are often more sociable than Common Ravens, and flocks of up to several hundred may be

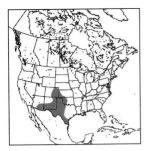

seen soaring over the plains on warm winter days or scavenging at garbage dumps. In treeless terrain, they often build their nests on the crossbars of utility poles.

HABITAT *Arid and semi-arid grassland, scrub, yucca flats.* Mostly a bird of dry grasslands. Generally avoids both wooded areas and true deserts, but occurs in brushy country in the lowlands. In the southwest, Common Raven lives in both drier areas (extreme deserts of lowlands) and wetter areas (mountain forests) than the Chihuahuan Raven, but is seldom in the grasslands.

FEEDING **Diet:** *Omnivorous.* Diet is highly varied but mostly animal matter, including large insects, spiders, earthworms, snails, rodents, lizards, and eggs and young of other birds. Often eats carrion and garbage. Also feeds on grain, seeds, berries, and fruits, including cactus fruit. **Behavior:** Mostly forages on ground, sometimes above ground in shrubs or cactus. Except during nesting season, usually forages in flocks. Often gathers at garbage dumps, and may patrol highways looking for road kills.

NESTING Sometimes nests in loose colonies where good nesting sites are concentrated. In some areas, breeds mostly in summer, perhaps to take advantage of better food supply after summer rains begin. **Nest:** Site is in tree, shrub, or large yucca, or on utility pole; sometimes on buildings, towers, other artificial supports. Height varies, 5–40 feet above ground. Nest (thought to be built by female) is a bulky mass of sticks and thorny twigs lined with grass, bark fibers, animal hair. Sometimes works in debris such as rags, paper, barbed wire. **Eggs:** 5–6, sometimes 3–8. Pale olive to gray-green, blotched with brown and lavender. Incubation is thought to be by both parents, about 18–21 days. **Young:** Both parents bring food for nestlings. Young leave nest about a month after hatching.

MIGRATION Mostly permanent resident. Some may withdraw in fall from northern part of range, but status in this area is poorly known. Flocks move around in winter, gathering in good feeding areas.

CONSERVATION STATUS At northern end of range (eastern Colorado, western Kansas), far less common today than in 1800s. Still very common farther south.

COMMON RAVEN *Corvus corax*

Of the birds classified as perching birds or "songbirds," the Common Raven is the largest, the size of a hawk. Often its deep croaking call will alert the observer to a pair of ravens soaring high overhead. An intelligent and remarkably adaptable bird, living as a scavenger and predator, it can survive at all seasons in surroundings as different as hot desert and high Arctic tundra. Once driven from much of its eastern range, the raven is now making a comeback.

Common Raven

HABITAT *Boreal and mountain forests, coastal cliffs, tundra, desert.* Can live in a very wide array of habitats, from tundra above the Arctic Circle to hot desert areas of the southwest. Often in heavily forested country; may also live on prairies if good nest sites (on cliffs) exist nearby.

FEEDING **Diet:** *Omnivorous.* May feed on practically anything, but majority of diet apparently is animal matter. Feeds on a wide variety of insects, including beetles, caterpillars, and others; also rodents, lizards, frogs, and eggs and young of other birds. Regularly eats carrion and garbage. **Behavior:** Typically

forages in pairs, the two birds sometimes cooperating to flush out prey. Searches for nests to eat the eggs or young birds. An opportunist, taking advantage of temporary food sources. Does most feeding on the ground. Often feeds as a scavenger, searching for carrion or visiting garbage dumps. In northern Alaska (Pt. Barrow) during endless nights of winter, seen feeding at dump under artificial lights.

NESTING   In courtship display, male soars, swoops, and tumbles in midair. Pair may soar high together; when perched, they touch bills, preen each other's feathers. **Nest:** Site is usually on ledge of rock cliff or high in tall tree (especially conifer). May use same site year after year, adding material on top of old nest. Both sexes help build. Nest is a bulky basket of large sticks and twigs, with deep depression in center lined with grass, bark strips, moss, animal hair. **Eggs:** 4–6, sometimes 3–7. Greenish, blotched with olive or brown. Incubation is mostly or entirely by female, about 18–21 days. Male feeds female during incubation. **Young:** Both parents bring food for nestlings, and female broods them while they are small. Young leave nest about 5–6 weeks after hatching.

MIGRATION   Mostly permanent resident, but some wander in fall and winter, appearing south of breeding range.

CONSERVATION STATUS   Ravens disappeared from much of the east and midwest before 1900. In recent decades they have been expanding their range again, especially in the northeast, spreading south into formerly occupied areas.

CHICKADEES AND TITMICE (Family Paridae)

They have cute-sounding names, and not by accident: these fluffy, sociable, cheery-voiced, rather tame little birds are popular with bird-lovers, welcome visitors at backyard bird feeders. About 50 species of titmice and chickadees live in woodlands around the world. Most are in the Northern Hemisphere, although a few reach southern Africa.

Members of this family generally do not migrate, and some of them live in the far north, displaying an impressive ability to endure very cold winters. One survival strategy common to many species is their habit of storing food—hiding items such as seeds or dead insects in holes or bark crevices—and then going back to retrieve it later. This food-stashing trait is similar to that practiced by some jays, and both groups have shown a remarkable ability to remember and find their stores.

Among our 10 species, there are only slight differences in behavior between those with crests (called titmice) and those without (called chickadees). As expected for such small birds, they seldom live more than 10 years, although a few have reached 12 or 13.

Feeding   These birds are little omnivores, feeding on a wide variety of insects and seeds and sometimes berries. In many species, insects and other small arthropods make up the majority of the summer diet, with many seeds also being eaten in winter. They are readily attracted to bird feeders for either suet or seeds.

Chickadees and titmice are quite agile and acrobatic in feeding, clambering about on heavy branches and fine twigs. They have specialized leg muscles that help them hang upside down to feed, so they can reach the undersides of twigs easily, finding insect eggs and other morsels possibly missed by other birds. As mentioned above, when food is plentiful, many of them will store excess food in hidden crannies, going back to find it later.

Nesting   Although many of these birds gather in small flocks in winter, all break up into pairs and defend territories in the nesting season. All nest in holes, such as natural hollows in trees, old woodpecker holes, or birdhouses; often they will find a small opening in a dead branch and enlarge it, or dig out a hollow in a rotten stub. The nest inside the hole is usually built by the female. The usual clutch numbers at least half a dozen eggs; typically the female does all the incubating, but the male may feed her during this period. Both parents usually help to feed the young.

Displays In winter flocks, chickadees and titmice communicate with various postures as well as calls. Aggression (as when competing for food items) may be expressed by raising the head feathers or ruffling up the body feathers. If approached too closely, one bird may stretch forward with its open bill pointed at another. Other postures are used by a bird that is backing down after having been threatened. Courtship displays may be simple but sometimes involve ceremonial visits to possible nest sites. The male often feeds the female, beginning early in the nesting season; at first this may be only a ritual, but it becomes important in sustaining her after she begins incubating the eggs.

GENUS *Parus*

BLACK-CAPPED CHICKADEE *Parus atricapillus*

Little flocks of Black-capped Chickadees enliven the winter woods with their active behavior and their cheery-sounding *chick-a-dee* call notes as they fly from tree to tree, often accompanied by an assortment of nuthatches, creepers, kinglets, and other birds. This is a very popular bird across the northern United States and southern Canada, always welcomed at bird feeders, where it may take sunflower seeds one at time and fly away to stuff them into bark crevices.

HABITAT *Mixed and deciduous woods; willow thickets, groves, shade trees.* Most common in open woods and forest edges, especially where birches or alders grow; avoids purely coniferous forest. Where it overlaps with other chickadee species in the north and west, Black-capped is mostly restricted to deciduous groves. Will live in suburbs as long as nest sites are available.

FEEDING **Diet:** *Mostly insects, seeds, and berries.* Diet varies with season; vegetable matter (seeds and fruits) may be no more than 10 percent of diet in summer, up to 50 percent in winter. Summer diet is mostly caterpillars and other insects, also some spiders, snails, and other invertebrates; also eats berries. In winter, feeds on insects (especially their eggs and pupae), seeds, berries, small fruits. Will eat fat of dead animals. **Behavior:** Forages mostly by hopping among twigs and branches and gleaning food from surface, often hanging upside down to reach underside of branches. Sometimes takes food while hovering, and may fly out to catch insects in midair. Readily comes to bird feeders for seeds or suet. Often stores food, recovering it later.

Black-capped Chickadee

NESTING Pairs typically form in fall and remain together as part of winter flock. Flocks break up in late winter, and both members of pair help defend nesting territory. Male often feeds female, beginning very early in spring. **Nest:** Site is in hole in tree, typically enlargement of small natural cavity in rotten wood, sometimes old woodpecker hole or nesting box; usually 5–20 feet above the ground. In natural cavity, both sexes help excavate or enlarge the interior. Nest (built by female) has foundation of moss or other matter, lining of softer material such as animal hair. **Eggs:** Usually 6–8, sometimes more or fewer. White, with fine dots of reddish brown often concentrated around larger end. Incubation is by female only, 12–13 days. Female covers eggs with nest material when leaving nest. Male often brings food to female during incubation. **Young:** Female remains with young most of time at first, while male brings food; later, both parents bring food. Young leave nest at about 16 days. Normally one brood per year.

MIGRATION   Mostly a permanent resident, but occasionally stages "invasions" in fall, with large numbers seen flying southward (mostly in northeastern states and southeastern Canada). These invasions usually do not penetrate much beyond southern limit of breeding range.

CONSERVATION STATUS   Widespread and common, and numbers apparently stable, possibly increasing in some areas.

CAROLINA CHICKADEE   *Parus carolinensis*

Very similar to the Black-capped Chickadee, this bird replaces it in the southeastern states. Living in milder climates, it has been reported to visit bird feeders less often, but it does come into suburban yards for sunflower seeds. Where the ranges of Black-capped and Carolina chickadees come together, they sometimes interbreed.

However, perhaps more often, they learn to imitate each other's songs—causing great confusion for birdwatchers.

HABITAT   *Mixed and deciduous woods, river groves, shade trees.* Mostly in deciduous forest, also in pine woods with good mixture of oak or other leafy trees, and will nest in well-wooded suburbs. Habitat like that of Black-capped Chickadee; where the two species overlap in the Appalachians, Carolina Chickadee lives at lower elevations.

FEEDING   **Diet:** *Mostly insects, seeds, and berries.* Probably eats more vegetable matter (seeds and berries) in winter than in summer. Caterpillars make up major part of diet in warmer months; also feeds on moths, true bugs, beetles, aphids, various other insects and spiders. Also eats weed and tree seeds, berries,

Carolina Chickadee

small fruits. **Behavior:** Forages mostly by hopping among twigs and branches and gleaning food from surface, often hanging upside down to reach underside of branches. Sometimes takes food while hovering, and may fly out to catch insects in midair. Stores food items, retrieving them later. Comes to bird feeders for seeds or suet.

NESTING   May mate for life. Pairs probably form in fall and remain together as part of winter flock. When flocks break up in late winter, pair establishes nesting territory. **Nest:** Site is in hole in tree, typically enlargement of small natural cavity in dead wood, sometimes old woodpecker hole or nesting box, usually 5–15 feet above the ground. In natural cavity, both sexes help excavate or enlarge the interior. Nest (probably built by female) has foundation of bark strips or other matter, lining of softer material such as plant down and animal hair. **Eggs:** 5–8. White, with fine dots of reddish brown often concentrated around larger end. Incubation is probably by female only, 11–13 days. Adult bird disturbed on nest makes loud hiss like that of a snake. **Young:** Both parents feed nestlings. Young leave nest about 13–17 days after hatching.

MIGRATION Permanent resident.

MEXICAN CHICKADEE   *Parus sclateri*

The southernmost of the chickadees, this bird is common in mountain forests over much of Mexico. It barely enters our area, crossing the border only to the Chiricahua Mountains of Arizona and the Animas Mountains of New Mexico. Most birders encounter it in the Chiricahuas, where it ranges through the Douglas-firs at high elevations. In late summer, after nesting, Mexican Chickadees join mixed flocks with various warblers and other birds.

HABITAT   *Conifers in mountains.* In limited range in United States, breeds in mountains in open ponderosa pine forest and in higher, denser forests of spruce and Douglas-fir. May range down into pine-oak forest and sycamore groves in winter. Farther south, in Mexico, lives in various habitats from high mountain fir forest down into oak woodlands.

FEEDING   **Diet:** *Mostly insects, probably some seeds.* Diet is not well known, but probably consists mostly of insects, including caterpillars, beetles, and others. Probably also eats seeds. **Behavior:** Forages mostly by hopping among twigs and branches and gleaning food from surface, often hanging upside down to reach underside of branches. Sometimes takes food while hovering, and occasionally catches flying insects in midair. May hammer on galls with bill to break them open and pull out insect larvae. Unlike many chickadees, not known to store food.

NESTING   Breeding behavior is not well known. **Nest:** Site is in hole in tree, usually 10–40 feet above ground, sometimes higher; can be just a few inches up in stumps. Adults may enlarge natural cavity, but details poorly known. Also will use nest boxes. Nest (apparently built by female) has foundation of bark fibers and moss, lining of soft moss, animal hair. **Eggs:** 5–9. White, with reddish brown dots concentrated at larger end. Incubation is by female only, incubation period not well known. Female may cover eggs with nest material when leaving nest. Male feeds female during incubation period. **Young:** Female broods young at first, while male brings most food; later, both parents feed young. Adult may sweep outside of nest entrance with crushed beetles; chemicals from these insects may help repel predators. Age of young when leaving nest not well known.

Mexican Chickadee

MIGRATION Mostly a permanent resident. In Chiricahua Mountains, Arizona, some birds move down into lower canyons in winter.

CONSERVATION STATUS Numbers probably stable in limited range in United States. May be vulnerable to loss of habitat in Mexico.

MOUNTAIN CHICKADEE   *Parus gambeli*

Almost throughout the higher mountains of the west, this chickadee is common in the conifer forests. It is not always easy to see, because it often feeds very high in the trees. However, except during the nesting season, any mixed flock of small birds moving through the highland pines is likely to include a nucleus of Mountain Chickadees.

HABITAT *Mountain forests, conifers; lower levels in winter.* Breeds in a variety of coniferous stands, including forests of pine, spruce, fir, or Douglas-fir, also groves of aspen in coniferous zones. Sometimes in lower habitats such as pine-oak or pinyon-juniper, and rarely breeds in cottonwood groves in lowlands. May wander to lowlands in winter, occupying planted conifers if available.

FEEDING **Diet:** *Mostly insects, seeds, and berries.* Feeds on a wide variety of insects, including many caterpillars and beetles; often feeds on insect eggs and pupae as well as spiders and their eggs. Also eats many seeds, some berries and small fruits. **Behavior:** Forages actively in trees, often feeding very high in conifers. Forages by gleaning food from twigs, often hanging upside down. Works along trunk or major branches, probing in bark crevices; has been seen using a wood splinter to probe deep cracks. Sometimes takes food while hovering. Will come to bird feeders for seeds or suet.

NESTING In some areas, numbers may be limited by a scarcity of good nesting sites. **Nest:** Site is usually in hole in tree, either natural cavity or old woodpecker hole, or a cavity enlarged or excavated by the chickadees. Usually 5–25 feet above ground, sometimes in stumps only a few inches up. Same site may be used more than one year. Sometimes uses nest box, occasionally even nests in holes in ground. In natural site in tree, both sexes help excavate. Nest (built by female, probably with help from male) is soft foundation of bark fibers, moss, hair, feathers. **Eggs:** 7–9, sometimes 5–12. White, dotted with reddish brown, sometimes unmarked. Incubation is probably by female only, about 14 days. Adult disturbed on nest will give a loud hiss, sounding like a snake. **Young:** Female spends much time with young at first, while male brings most food; later, both parents feed young. Age of young at first flight about 3 weeks.

MIGRATION Mostly a permanent resident. Some (mainly young birds) move to lower elevations in winter, sometimes out into lowland valleys and plains.

Mountain Chickadee

GRAY-HEADED CHICKADEE *Parus cinctus*

This is the rarest and most poorly known of North America's chickadees, living only in remote areas of northern Alaska and northwestern Canada. Determined birders who seek it, traveling by bush plane or wilderness road, may find it at a few sites where spruces and willows grow along Arctic streams. In northern Europe, where the species is known as "Siberian Tit," its habits are better known.

HABITAT *Streamside thickets, spruce forest.* In North America, found very locally in stunted spruce forest of far north, close to treeline. Perhaps mainly where narrow strips of spruce and groves of willows grow along streams through generally barren country. Similar habitats in northern Eurasia, but more widespread.

FEEDING **Diet:** *Mostly insects and seeds.* Diet in North America poorly known. Feeds on insects, including caterpillars, flies, beetles, and the eggs and pupae of many insects, as well as spiders. Also probably eats seeds of many conifers. Has been seen feeding on carcass of dead caribou in winter. **Behavior:** Forages in small flocks or family groups, moving actively from tree to tree. May prefer feeding in conifers at most seasons. Forages by clambering about in branches and twigs and on trunk, hanging upside down to examine undersides of twigs. Sometimes feeds on ground. At least in northern Europe, often stores food, retrieving it later.

NESTING   Nesting behavior in North America very poorly known; most details given here are from Europe. Members of pair remain together throughout year on permanent territory. This territory may be quite large and may be shared by 2 pairs. Male feeds female from before egg-laying until nestlings are about half-grown. **Nest:** Site is in hole in tree, either natural cavity or old woodpecker hole, usually low (1–15 feet above ground). May clean out cavity before starting nest building. Nest (built by female) has foundation of decaying wood, then layer of grass or moss, then cup of animal hair. **Eggs:** 6–10, sometimes 4–15. White, finely spotted with reddish brown, with some pale spots of olive-brown or gray. Incubation is by female, 14–18 days. **Young:** Female broods young most of time at first, while male brings food; later, both parents bring food. Young leave nest at about 19–20 days.

MIGRATION   As far as known, mostly a permanent resident in North America. Rarely seen away from breeding areas in winter.

CONSERVATION STATUS   Scarce and local in North America, but probably faces no serious threats in its remote haunts. In Scandinavia, apparently declining, possibly because of loss of habitat. No information from most of Russian range.

BOREAL CHICKADEE   *Parus hudsonicus*

This dusty-looking chickadee lives in spruce forest of the north, mostly north of the Canadian border. A hardy permanent resident, it survives the winter even as far north as the Arctic Circle. Like other chickadees, this species becomes much more quiet and inconspicuous during the nesting season. Because that is the time of year when birders most often search for it, the Boreal Chickadee has gained a reputation as an excessively elusive bird.

HABITAT   *Conifer forests.* Mainly in forests of conifers, especially spruces, but also in some mixed forest. Occurs in low stunted spruces as far north as treeline. At southern edge of range, found in spruce bogs in east, high mountain forest in west, barely south of Canadian border in either region.

FEEDING   **Diet:** *Mostly insects and seeds.* Feeds on a variety of insects, including many caterpillars in summer, plus moths, beetles, and others, also spiders. Eats many insect eggs and pupae, especially in winter. Also eats seeds of various trees. **Behavior:** Forages

Boreal Chickadee

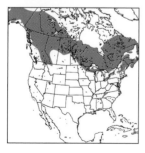

mostly by moving about in dense conifers, gleaning insects from surface of twigs, needles, or trunk. May probe in bark crevices, and may take food while hovering briefly. Also will extract seeds from cones and take seeds from deciduous trees such as birches. May store food and retrieve it later.

NESTING   May mate for life, the birds remaining together all year. **Nest:** Site is in hole in tree, either natural cavity or old woodpecker hole; chickadees may also excavate their own site or enlarge an existing hole. Site is usually low, 1–12 feet above the ground. Both sexes help with excavation, but only female builds nest inside. Nest has foundation of moss, bark strips, lichens, feathers, lining of animal hair and plant down. **Eggs:** 5–8, sometimes 4–9. White, with fine reddish brown dots often concentrated at larger end. Incubation is by female, 11–16 days. Male feeds female during incubation. **Young:** Female stays with young and broods them much of time at first, while male brings food. Later, both feed nestlings. Young leave nest at about 18 days. One brood per year.

MIGRATION   Generally a permanent resident. Occasional small southward invasions in fall, with a few appearing south of breeding range; may occur in same seasons when Black-capped Chickadees stage similar invasions.

CONSERVATION STATUS   Wide range in remote forests of far north probably helps secure this species' future.

CHESTNUT-BACKED CHICKADEE   *Parus rufescens*

The most colorful of the chickadees, the Chestnut-backed is common in the northwest. Inland, it may overlap in range with up to three other close relatives; but in the very humid coastal belt, in wet forests of hemlock and tamarack, this is the only chickadee present. In those shadowy surroundings its rich chestnut colors may be hard to see, but it can still be recognized by its husky, fast *chick-a-dee* calls.

Chestnut-backed Chickadee

HABITAT   *Moist conifer forests; adjacent oaks, shade trees.* In much of its range, a bird of dense, moist coniferous forest with trees such as spruce, fir, tamarack, hemlock, and others. In southern part of range, lives in pine-oak woods and in redwood forest with understory of alders and willows, also in oak woods and streamside willow groves.

FEEDING   **Diet:** *Mostly insects, seeds, berries.* Feeds on a wide variety of insects, including caterpillars, moths, beetles, leafhoppers, scale insects, small wasps. Also eats spiders, seeds (especially of conifers), and berries. **Behavior:** Forages mostly by hopping among twigs and branches and gleaning food from surface, often hanging upside down to reach underside of branches. Often probes in crevices in bark, and sometimes takes food while hovering. Readily comes to bird feeders for seeds or suet. May store food, recovering it later.

NESTING   Nesting behavior not well known. Members of pair may remain together all year. **Nest:** Site is in hole in tree, usually low, 2–20 feet above ground; can be much higher (reportedly up to 80 feet). Will nest in the same site more than one year. Uses natural cavity in dead or rotten wood, the chickadees often excavating or enlarging it themselves; also will nest in old woodpecker holes or nest boxes. Nest has foundation of moss, lichens, feathers, bark fibers, plant down, lined with soft materials such as animal hair. **Eggs:** 6–7, sometimes 5–9. White, with fine reddish brown dots concentrated at larger end; sometimes unmarked white. Incubation is probably by female, but details not well known. If disturbed, adult on nest flutters wings and makes loud hissing noise. **Young:** Probably cared for by both parents. Development of young and age at first flight not well known.

MIGRATION   Mostly permanent resident. Individuals may wander short distances in fall and winter.

BRIDLED TITMOUSE   *Parus wollweberi*

An active little crested bird of southwestern woodlands. In lower canyons of the Arizona mountains, the Bridled Titmouse is often one of the most common birds at all seasons, with small flocks moving about and chattering in the oaks as they search the branches for insects. The call notes and behavior of this species (and even its head markings) may suggest a chickadee more than the other titmice.

HABITAT *Oak and sycamore canyons, pine-oak woods.* Breeds mostly in areas with many live oaks, often in pine-oak woodland. In some areas, will breed in streamside groves of cottonwoods and willows at middle elevations. In winter, small numbers are regularly found in such cottonwood-willow groves.

FEEDING **Diet:** *Mostly insects, some seeds.* Diet is poorly known. Apparently feeds mostly on insects, including caterpillars, beetles, probably many others, including insect eggs and pupae. Also eats various seeds. **Behavior:** Forages in various trees and bushes but especially in oaks, hopping actively among branches and twigs, pecking at bases of leaves, often hanging upside down. Will feed on the ground briefly

Bridled Titmouse

as well. Will come to bird feeders for seeds or peanut butter mixtures; opens seeds by holding them with feet and pounding with bill.

NESTING Nesting behavior is poorly known. Pairs may remain together at all seasons, establishing nesting territory after flocks break up in late winter. In Arizona and adjacent New Mexico, nesting activity is mostly from April to June. **Nest:** Site is in hole in tree, often in dead limb or stump; may be either natural cavity or old woodpecker hole. Nest height varies, 4–30 feet above ground. Will also use artificial nest boxes. Nest has extensive soft lining of grass, leaves, spider webs, lichens, plant down, catkins, animal hair, and other items. **Eggs:** 5–7. Unmarked white. Details of incubation not well known, but probably mostly or entirely by female. **Young:** Probably both parents bring food for young. Development of young and age at first flight not well known.

MIGRATION Mostly a permanent resident. Small flocks regularly move to lower elevations in winter and occasionally appear in streamside groves far from mountains.

CONSERVATION STATUS Within its limited range in United States, very common, numbers apparently stable.

PLAIN TITMOUSE *Parus inornatus*

As plain as a bird can be, marked only by a short crest, the Plain Titmouse nonetheless has personality. Pairs or family parties travel about the woods together, exploring the twigs for insects and calling to each other frequently. Recent research suggests there may be two species under this name, one living in oaks along the Pacific coast, the other mostly in pinyon-juniper woods in the arid interior; the two forms look almost identical.

HABITAT *Oak woods, pinyon-juniper; locally river woods, shade trees.* Along Pacific seaboard, occurs most commonly in oak woodland, including areas where oaks meet streamside trees or pines; also in well-wooded suburbs, rarely in coniferous forest in mountains. In the interior, found mainly in open woods of pinyon pine and juniper as well as in oak or pine-oak woods.

FEEDING **Diet:** *Insects, nuts, seeds.* Feeds mainly on insects, including many caterpillars, beetles, true bugs, leafhoppers, aphids, and scale insects, as well as some spiders. Also eats pinyon nuts, acorns, weed seeds, and sometimes berries

Plain Titmouse

or small fruits. **Behavior:** Forages by hopping about in branches and larger twigs, sometimes hanging upside down, searching for insects among foliage and on bark. Opens nuts and acorns by holding them with feet and pounding with bill. Comes to bird feeders for seeds or suet.

NESTING   At least in some areas, pairs or family groups may defend territories all year. **Nest:** Site (selected by female) is usually in hole in tree, sometimes hole in stump, fencepost, or pole. May be natural cavity or old woodpecker hole. In rotten wood, both members of pair may work to enlarge small cavities. Also will use nest boxes and sometimes crevices in buildings or other cavities. Nest has foundation of grass, weeds, moss, bark fibers, and lining of soft material such as feathers or animal hair. **Eggs:** Usually 6–8. White, sometimes lightly dotted with reddish brown. Incubation is probably by female only, 14–16 days. **Young:** Both parents bring food to nestlings. Young leave nest about 16–21 days after hatching.

MIGRATION   Permanent resident, rarely wandering even short distances away from nesting areas.

CONSERVATION STATUS   Very common in parts of its range, numbers probably stable.

TUFTED TITMOUSE   *Parus bicolor*

This rather tame, active, crested little bird is common all year in eastern forests, where its whistled *peter-peter-peter* song may be heard even during midwinter thaws. It is related to the chickadees, and like them it readily comes to bird feeders, often carrying away sunflower seeds one at a time. Feeders may be helping it to expand its range: in recent decades, Tufted Titmice have been steadily pushing north. A very distinctive form, the "Black-crested" Titmouse, lives in southern and western Texas.

HABITAT   *Woodlands, shade trees, groves.* Mostly in deciduous forest with tall trees, sometimes in mixed forest. Can live in orchards, suburbs, or even city parks if trees are large enough. In southern Texas, "Black-crested" Titmouse inhabits brushlands and low woods as well as taller trees along rivers.

FEEDING   **Diet:** *Mostly insects and seeds.* Insects make up close to two-thirds of annual diet, with caterpillars the most important prey in summer; also eats wasps, bees, sawfly larvae, beetles, true bugs, scale insects, and many others, including many insect eggs and pupae. Also some spiders, snails. Seeds, nuts, berries, and small fruits are important in diet especially in winter. **Behavior:** Forages by hopping actively among branches and twigs of trees, often hanging upside down, sometimes hovering momentarily. Often drops to the ground for food as well. Comes to bird feeders for seeds or suet. Opens acorns and seeds by holding them with feet and pounding with bill. Will store food items, retrieving them later.

Tufted Titmouse

NESTING   Pairs may remain together all year, joining small flocks with other titmice in winter. Flocks break up in late winter, and pairs establish nesting territories. Male feeds

female often from courtship stage until after eggs hatch. Breeding pair may have a "helper," one of their offspring from the previous year. **Nest:** Site is in hole in tree, either natural cavity or old woodpecker hole; averages about 35 feet above ground, ranging from 3 to 90 feet up. Unlike the chickadees, apparently does not excavate its own nest hole. Will also use nest boxes. Nest (probably built by female) has foundation of grass, moss, leaves, bark strips, lined with soft materials, especially animal hair. Bird may pluck hair from live woodchuck, dog, or other animal, even from humans. **Eggs:** 5–6, sometimes 3–9. White, finely dotted with brown, reddish, or purple. Incubation is by female only, 12–14 days. **Young:** Female stays with young much of time at first, while male brings food; later, young are fed by both parents, sometimes by additional helper. Young leave nest about 15–16 days after hatching.

MIGRATION   Permanent resident. Young birds may disperse some distance away from where they were raised (in any direction, including north).

CONSERVATION STATUS   Continuing to expand its range to the north, and surveys suggest that populations are increasing in much of range.

VERDIN AND RELATED BIRDS (Family Remizidae)

An odd little bird of the southwestern desert, the Verdin was once classified with the chickadee family, but at the moment it is placed with a handful of Old World birds called penduline tits. Some scientists think it may be more closely related to the gnatcatchers. At any rate, it is unique among North American birds.

GENUS *Auriparus*

VERDIN   *Auriparus flaviceps*

Tiny but tough, Verdins are adaptable little birds of hot desert regions. They are usually seen singly or in pairs, flitting about actively in the brush, sometimes giving sharp call notes. The birds may build several nests per year, including new ones to sleep in on winter nights. These conspicuous, bulky stick nests may last for several seasons in the dry desert air and often seem more numerous than the Verdins themselves.

HABITAT   *Brushy desert valleys, mesquites.* Most common in Sonoran desert and mesquite woods at lower elevations. Also lives in other kinds of low open brush, including desert stands of acacia and paloverde, thickets of saltcedar, low riverside woods. Common in suburbs of some southwestern towns.

FEEDING   **Diet:** *Mostly insects.* Feeds on many kinds of tiny insects, including aphids, caterpillars, scale insects, leafhoppers, beetle and wasp larvae. Small spiders are also important in diet. Eats berries, small fruits, and sometimes seeds; regularly takes nectar. **Behavior:** Forages actively in shrubs and low trees, mostly among smaller branches. Takes most of its food from leaf surfaces, sometimes hanging upside down to reach undersides of leaves. Often visits flowers for nectar, and will come

Verdin

to hummingbird feeders for sugar-water. Sometimes catches insects in the air, on the ground, or on bark of branches.

NESTING   Male may build several nests, with female choosing one to use for raising the young. **Nest:** Placed well out on branches of thorny shrub or low tree or in cholla cactus, usually 4–12 feet above the ground. Nest is a conspicuous hollow oval or sphere, surprisingly large for size of bird, made of thorny twigs. Entrance is low on one side; interior is well insulated with lining of feathers, grass, leaves, spider webs. Nests built late in spring tend to have entrance facing prevailing wind, may help cool the interior. **Eggs:** 4–5, sometimes 3–6. Pale green to blue-green, with reddish brown dots often concentrated around larger end. Incubation is by female, reportedly about 10 days. **Young:** Both parents feed the nestlings. Young leave the nest about 21 days after hatching but continue to return to nest to sleep at night.

MIGRATION   Permanent resident.

LONG-TAILED TITS (Family Aegithalidae)

The seven members of this family are very small birds with moderately long tails, foraging actively for insects in bushes and trees. Six of the species are found only in the Old World. The seventh, the Bushtit, was once (like the Verdin) considered to belong to the chickadee family; but it differs from the chickadees in behavior and especially in the type of nest it builds.

GENUS *Psaltriparus*

BUSHTIT   *Psaltriparus minimus*

Tiny, drab birds with light ticking and lisping call notes, Bushtits are common in woods and mountains of the west, but they are often inconspicuous. A flock feeding in a tree may go almost unnoticed until the birds fly out, perhaps 20 or 30 of them, in straggling single file to the next tree. They are very sociable at most seasons, and groups will roost huddled close together in a tight mass on cold nights.

HABITAT   *Oak scrub, chaparral, mixed woods, pinyons, junipers.* Lives in many kinds of wooded or brushy habitats, from the lowlands to middle elevations in the mountains, including chaparral, oak forest, pinyon-juniper and pine-oak woods, streamside groves, and well-wooded suburbs and city parks. Avoids high mountains and hot desert regions, but may appear in cottonwood-willow groves along desert streams in winter.

FEEDING   *Diet: Mostly insects.* Feeds on a wide variety of tiny insects, especially leafhoppers, treehoppers, aphids, scale insects, caterpillars, and beetles; also wasps, ants, and many others, including eggs and pupae of many insects. Also eats some spiders, berries,

Bushtit

and sometimes seeds. **Behavior:** Forages very actively in trees and shrubs, moving rapidly among foliage and small twigs, often hanging upside down at the ends of twigs while probing among pine needles or the bases of leaves. Except when nesting, usually forages in flocks.

NESTING   After winter flocks break up, pairs establish territories but do not defend them strongly, tolerating other Bushtits even near nest. If pairs are disturbed during early stages of nesting, they reportedly may abandon the effort and build a new nest, perhaps with a different mate. **Nest:** Site is in a tree or shrub, 8–35 feet above ground, sometimes lower or higher. Nest (built by both sexes) is firmly attached to twigs and branches, a tightly woven hanging pocket, up to a foot long; small entrance hole near top leads to narrow passage that opens into nest chamber. Nest is made of spider webs, moss, grass, lichens, leaves, rootlets, twigs; inside lined with plant down, animal hair, feathers. **Eggs:** 5–7. White. Incubation is by both parents, about 12 days. Both parents may sleep in nest at night. **Young:** Fed and brooded by both parents. Young leave nest about 14–15 days after hatching. Two broods per year.

MIGRATION   Mostly a permanent resident. In the southwestern interior, where it breeds in foothills and mountains, small flocks may move into the lowlands in winter, even to many miles away from breeding habitat.

NUTHATCHES (Family Sittidae)

Nuthatches are widely known as "upside-down birds" because they can walk down trees head first. Compact and short-tailed, they rely on their strong toes and claws to grip the bark as they walk up, down, and around the trunk and branches. Unlike woodpeckers or creepers, they do not use their tails to prop themselves up against trees.

About 20 species of nuthatches live around the world, mostly in the Northern Hemisphere. Most live on the trunks of trees, but a couple in the Old World live among rocks.

Feeding   Nuthatches feed on both insects and seeds, typically eating more seeds in winter, mainly insects and other arthropods in summer. Their best-known foraging habit involves climbing actively about on trees—walking up, down, and around the trunk and branches and hanging upside down on the underside of limbs. The smaller species also clamber about in the outer twigs of pines and other trees. By going down trees head first, nuthatches may spot insects in hidden bark crevices that have been overlooked by woodpeckers or other birds moving up the trees.

To crack open a hard seed, a nuthatch will wedge it into a crevice and then pound on the seed with its bill, rearing back and putting its whole body into the downstroke (this behavior, "hacking" on nuts, is probably responsible for the name applied to this family).

Like some chickadees, jays, and other birds, nuthatches often store seeds or other food items in hidden crevices in tree bark, going back to eat them later.

Nesting   Nest sites are mostly in cavities in trees, although some species will nest in birdhouses (and two in the Old World nest among rocks). Nuthatches sometimes alter the entrances to their nest holes by adding mud to make the entrance smaller or by smearing the area around it with pine pitch or crushed insects. Such alterations may help to keep predators out of the nest. Usually the female incubates and the male brings food for her; both parents feed the young.

Displays   Nuthatches have a variety of postures used as aggressive displays in encounters with other birds. Courtship displays vary, but in some species the male droops his wings and spreads his tail while bowing or swaying back and forth. The male often feeds the female in courtship, and this continues through the egg-laying and incubation periods.

RED-BREASTED NUTHATCH   *Sitta canadensis*

With its quiet calls and dense coniferous forest habitat, this nuthatch may be overlooked until it wanders down a tree toward the ground. It often shows little fear of humans and may come very close to a person standing quietly in a conifer grove. Red-breasted Nuthatches nest farther north and higher in the mountains than their relatives; when winter food crops fail in these boreal forests, they may migrate hundreds of miles to the south.

HABITAT   *Conifer forests; in winter, also other trees.* Nesting habitat almost always has many conifers, such as spruce, fir, hemlock, either in pure stands or mixed with deciduous trees. Mature forest preferred, perhaps because old decaying wood is needed for nest sites. In migration and winter may appear in any wooded habitat, but always chooses conifers if available.

FEEDING   **Diet:** *Includes both insects and seeds.* Feeds mainly on insects and spiders in summer; in winter, eats many seeds, especially those of conifers. Young are fed mostly or entirely on insects and spiders. **Behavior:** Forages by climbing up and down trunk and branches of trees. Sometimes catches flying insects in midair. May cache food items in bark crevices.

NESTING   Unlike other nuthatches, has a soft musical song, used especially in courtship by male. In courtship display, male turns his back toward female, raises head, droops wings, and sways from side to side. Male also feeds female in courtship. **Nest:** Both

Red-breasted Nuthatch

sexes excavate nest cavity in rotten stub or snag, usually 5–40 feet above ground, rarely much higher. Rarely use old woodpecker holes or birdhouses. Sticky pitch is smeared around entrance to nest hole; this may prevent other creatures from entering. Adults avoid getting stuck in pitch by flying straight into hole. Apparently female does most of work of nest building. Nest in cavity made of soft grass, moss, bark fibers, feathers. **Eggs:** 5–6, sometimes 4–7. White, spotted with reddish brown. Female incubates, male brings food to female on and off nest. Incubation period about 12 days. **Young:** Both parents feed nestlings; young leave nest about 2–3 weeks after hatching. Probably one brood per year.

MIGRATION   Winter range varies tremendously from year to year, especially in east. Big southward invasions occur in fall of some years, perhaps mainly when cone crops are very poor in the northern forest. In years with good food supply, may remain all winter on nesting territory.

CONSERVATION STATUS   Numbers probably stable. Has expanded breeding range southward in some eastern states by nesting in plantings of ornamental conifers.

WHITE-BREASTED NUTHATCH   *Sitta carolinensis*

Readily attracted to bird feeders for sunflower seeds or suet, the White-breasted Nuthatch may spend much of its time industriously carrying seeds away to hide them in crevices. Its nasal calls are typical and familiar sounds of winter mornings in deciduous woods over much of North America.

HABITAT   *Forests, woodlots, groves, shade trees.* Typically in mature deciduous forest, also in mixed forest with some conifers; rarely found in pure coniferous forest. Often favors woodland edge along rivers, roads, clearings; may be in suburbs or parks if large trees are present.

FEEDING   **Diet:** *Mostly insects, also seeds.* Eats mostly insects (and spiders) during summer, supplementing these with seeds in winter. Proportion of seeds in diet may vary from zero in summer to more than 60 percent in winter. Will also feed on suet and peanut butter mixtures at feeders. Young are fed entirely on insects and spiders. **Behavior:** Forages mainly on trunk and larger limbs of trees, climbing about and exploring all surfaces. Sometimes feeds on ground. During fall and winter, regularly caches food items in bark crevices on territory.

NESTING   Pairs remain together on nesting territory all year, may mate for life. Courtship behavior begins by late winter. In courtship display, male raises head, spreads tail, droops wings, sways back and forth, and bows deeply. Male also performs much courtship feeding of female. **Nest:** Site is large natural cavity or old woodpecker hole, usually 15–60 feet above ground; may rarely use birdhouses; may sometimes excavate own nest cavity. Female builds nest in cavity, a simple cup of bark fibers, grasses, twigs, hair. Adults may spend minutes at a time

White-breasted Nuthatch

sweeping the outside and inside of nest with a crushed insect held in bill; chemical secretions of insects may help repel predators. Also sometimes adds mud to rim of nest entrance. **Eggs:** 5–9, rarely 10. White, spotted with reddish brown. Female incubates, is fed on nest by male. Incubation period 12–14 days. **Young:** Both parents feed young. Age when young leave nest uncertain, or perhaps quite variable; reported as 14–26 days. One brood per year.

MIGRATION   Usually a permanent resident. In occasional years, numbers may move south in the western and northern parts of the range, in an unexplained irruptive movement; this is far less frequent and less pronounced than in the Red-breasted Nuthatch.

PYGMY NUTHATCH   *Sitta pygmaea*

An acrobatic little bird of western pine forests, most likely to be seen in small, talkative flocks, clambering over the highest twigs, cones, and needle clusters. Sociable at all seasons, Pygmy Nuthatches spend the winter foraging in flocks of 5 to 15 birds, all roosting together at night in one cavity. Even when nesting, a pair may have as many as three additional "helpers" bringing food to the young.

HABITAT   *Yellow pines, other pines, Douglas-fir.* Yellow pine (the commercial name for ponderosa and Jeffrey pines) is main habitat element throughout mountains of west; also occurs in Monterey pine on California coast. In some places extends into pinyon-juniper woodland and redwood canyons. On rare visits to lowlands of interior, likely to be in planted conifers.

FEEDING   **Diet:** *Mostly insects and seeds.* Diet in summer is primarily insects, especially beetles, wasps, caterpillars, and true bugs, also many others. In winter, also eats many seeds, especially pine seeds. Nestlings are fed mostly insects. **Behavior:** Forages mainly on outermost and highest branches of pines, including cones and needle clusters; also on main branches and trunks. Sometimes sallies out to

catch flying insects in midair. Often stores seeds in holes or crevices in bark.

NESTING   Nesting pairs often joined by 1–3 additional birds, usually their previous offspring, which help defend the territory and raise the young; these helpers may roost in nest hole with the pair before the eggs hatch. Pairs with helpers tend to fledge more young than pairs without. **Nest:** Both sexes help excavate nest cavity in dead limb or snag, 8–60 feet above ground, usually higher than 20 feet. May tolerate some hole-nesting birds quite nearby (bluebirds, swallows) but not chickadees or other nuthatches. Nest in cavity is made of bark fibers, plant down, feathers. Pair usually roosts at night in nest cavity before egg-laying. **Eggs:** Usually 6–8, rarely 4–9. White, lightly dotted with reddish brown. Female incubates (15–16 days), is fed on nest by male and sometimes by additional helpers. **Young:** Fed by both parents and often by helpers. Young leave the nest at about 20–22 days. One brood per year, occasionally two.

MIGRATION   Mostly a permanent resident. In years with poor cone crops, mountain birds sometimes wander to lowlands and very rarely move far out onto plains.

Pygmy Nuthatch

BROWN-HEADED NUTHATCH   *Sitta pusilla*

A small nuthatch of the southeastern pine forests. It is often heard before it is seen; found in pairs or family groups all year, the birds call to each other constantly as they busily clamber about on the branches. In winter, small groups of Brown-headed Nuthatches often join mixed foraging flocks including chickadees, woodpeckers, and Pine Warblers.

HABITAT   *Open pine woods.* Pine species (such as loblolly, longleaf, slash, and pond pines) virtually always present in habitat; also other conifers including baldcypress and Atlantic white-cedar. Often in pine woods mixed with deciduous trees such as sweetgum, oak, hickory, or sycamore.

FEEDING   **Diet:** *Mostly insects and seeds.* Eats more insects and spiders in summer, more seeds (mainly pine seeds) in winter. **Behavior:** Forages mainly on trunk and large limbs of pines, also on higher branches and twigs. Males may forage lower than females, descending on trunks almost to ground. May use a chip of bark as a tool to pry off other pieces of bark while searching for insects. Sometimes catches flying insects in the air. May store seeds in bark crevices.

NESTING   Some nests aided by "helper," an additional male that brings food to female on nest, also to young after eggs hatch. **Nest:** Both sexes help exca-

Brown-headed Nuthatch

vate nest cavity in dead tree, usually in pine, sometimes in deciduous tree or fence-post near pine forest. Pair may begin several excavations before completing one for nest. Will also use birdhouses, old woodpecker holes; sometimes competes for nest

sites with Eastern Bluebird. Nest sites average about 5 feet above ground, rarely more than 15 feet high. Nest in cavity made of grass, bark fibers, hair, feathers, also "wings" of pine seeds. **Eggs:** Usually 4–6, sometimes 3–7. White, marked with reddish brown. Typically lays 4 or 5 eggs in Florida, 5 or 6 elsewhere. Female incubates, about 14 days. Male brings food to female during incubation; male roosts in nest with female and eggs at night. **Young:** Both parents feed young (so does additional "helper" at some nests). Young leave nest in 18–19 days. Usually one brood per year, rarely two.

MIGRATION   Mostly a permanent resident, very rarely wanders north.

CONSERVATION STATUS   Probably the least numerous nuthatch in North America. Has lost ground in some areas because of habitat loss, but still common where southern pine forest exists.

CREEPERS (Family Certhiidae)

This odd but well-named family includes only six species, five of them limited to Asia and Europe. All of the species are very similar to our Brown Creeper in appearance, and evidently in behavior as well. No other birds spend their lives in such intimate contact with tree bark.

GENUS *Certhia*

BROWN CREEPER   *Certhia americana*

Looking like a piece of bark come to life, the Brown Creeper crawls up trunks of trees, ferreting out insect eggs and other morsels missed by more active birds. It is easily overlooked until its thin, reedy call gives it away. Reaching the top of one tree, it flutters down to the base of another to begin spiraling up again. Creepers even place their nests against tree trunks, tucked under loose slabs of bark, where they are very difficult to find.

Brown Creeper

HABITAT   *Woodlands, groves, shade trees.* Breeds in mature forest, either coniferous or deciduous, with many large trees, ranging from mountain pine woods to lowland swamp forest. In migration, may be found in any habitat with at least a few good-sized trees, even suburbs or city parks.

FEEDING   **Diet:** *Mostly insects.* Feeds on a wide variety of insects, especially insect eggs and pupae hidden in bark; also weevils and other beetles, true bugs, leafhoppers, scale insects, aphids, caterpillars, ants, and many others. Also feeds on spiders and pseudoscorpions. Eats some seeds, and will feed on suet or peanut butter mixtures. **Behavior:** Does almost all foraging on trunk and limbs of trees, climbing slowly with tail braced against surface, examining bark visually and probing in crevices. Occasionally forages on ground or snow.

NESTING   Male defends nesting territory by singing. In courtship, male may perform rapid twisting flight among trees; may pursue female in the air and around tree trunks. **Nest:** Usual nest site is behind a large strip of bark still attached to a tree;

occasionally in cavity in tree. May be at any height from very low to 50 feet or more above ground. In typical sites, nest is a shallow half cup closely fitting the available space behind the bark slab. Nest (built by female, with male bringing some material) is made of twigs, bark strips, moss, leaves, lined with finer materials. **Eggs:** 5–6, sometimes 4–8. Whitish, dotted with reddish brown. Incubation is by female, about 14–17 days. Male may feed female during incubation. **Young:** Both parents bring food for nestlings. Young leave nest about 13–16 days after hatching.

MIGRATION   May migrate in small flocks. In many areas, migration peaks in April and in late September to early October.

CONSERVATION STATUS   Declined as a breeding bird in much of eastern United States with cutting of forests; nests mainly in mature forest, not young second growth. Still common locally in north and west.

BULBULS (Family Pycnonotidae)

This is strictly an Old World family of about 130 species, found mainly in Africa and southern Asia. Bulbuls feed mostly on berries and small fruits. Many of the species fall into one of two general types: drab olive birds that often hide in forest (including the greenbuls of Africa) and less elusive, more colorful birds that live around clearings and semi-open country. One of the latter sort has escaped from captivity and established a wild population in Florida.

GENUS *Pycnonotus*

RED-WHISKERED BULBUL   *Pycnonotus jocosus*

When a few Red-whiskered Bulbuls escaped from an aviary in the Miami area in 1960, they found an environment perfectly suited to their needs. The climate was not too different from that of eastern India, where they originated, and the suburb of Kendall, Florida, was heavily planted with exotic trees and shrubs, providing the bulbuls with abundant berries throughout the year. The birds quickly became established, but they have not spread much beyond Kendall. Another introduced population is common around Honolulu, Hawaii.

Red-whiskered Bulbul

HABITAT   *Suburbs with plantings of exotic fruiting trees.* Introduced in North America, found only in residential areas with wide variety of exotic trees and shrubs that provide berries and small fruits at all times of year. In native range in southern Asia, found in forest edges, semi-open areas, towns.

FEEDING   **Diet:** *Berries, small fruits, insects.* With its small bill, usually does not feed on large fruits until they are overripe or punctured by other birds. Important items in Florida include berries and fruits of Brazilian pepper, figs, lantana, jasmine, and others. Takes nectar, eats pieces of flowers and green shoots of vegetation. Also eats many insects. **Behavior:** Except when nesting, travels in flocks to feed at fruiting plants. Takes insects by flying out to capture them in midair, hovering to pick them from bark, or searching among foliage.

NESTING   In Florida, breeding season is mainly February to June. Florida birds seem not to defend territories strongly, often tolerating other bulbuls near the nest. In courtship display, one bird may approach the other, fluttering its wings and bowing; both birds raise and lower crests repeatedly. **Nest:** Site is usually fairly low in shrub, vine, or small tree, typically about 2–8 feet above the ground, often well concealed. Nest, placed in fork of branch, is a cup made of grass, weeds, rootlets, and casuarina needles. Outside of nest usually decorated with pieces of paper or plastic, large flakes of bark, or other debris. **Eggs:** Usually 3. Pinkish, profusely mottled with purple or reddish spots. Incubation is by both parents, 12–14 days. **Young:** Both parents feed nestlings. Age of young at first flight not well known.

MIGRATION   Apparently permanent resident throughout its native range, and introduced populations seem to do very little wandering.

CONSERVATION STATUS   Does not seem to compete seriously with native birds in Florida.

WRENS (Family Troglodytidae)

Busy little brown birds, creeping about in thickets or peering out furtively from brush piles, wrens always appear to be up to something. Various kinds of wrens are common and familiar almost throughout the Americas. There are about 70 species, most of them in the tropics (Mexico, for example, has more than 30), but only one is found in the Old World. That one is our Winter Wren, which undoubtedly crossed from Alaska to Asia in eons past and has since spread westward all the way to Britain, where it lives in gardens and is simply called "the Wren."

Although they generally lack bright colors, many of the wrens are superb singers, with rich or complicated melodies. Their songs are especially well developed in the tropics (where some have names like Flutist Wren, Nightingale Wren, and Musician Wren). In our Carolina Wren, the male and female sometimes sing a simple and disorganized "duet." Some tropical relatives of this species have remarkable duets, with male and female each singing only parts of the song with such precision that the whole performance sounds like it comes from just one bird.

Most of our wrens are solitary or live in pairs, but some in the tropics are found in small groups.

Feeding   All wrens feed mainly on insects and other invertebrates; some that live on the ground or around rocks may eat many spiders. They forage very actively, hopping or running about at various levels from the ground to the treetops, although most species tend to stay low. Most wrens have long, slender bills, well suited to probing into crevices in dead wood or under rocks. Plant material usually makes up only a minor part of the diet, but some kinds regularly eat a few berries or seeds. The larger wrens may catch small lizards or tree frogs.

Nesting   Most wrens lay their eggs in enclosed spaces. Some choose existing cavities in trees, holes among rocks, or sometimes holes in buildings. Others build their own covered spaces, making football-shaped or globular masses of twigs or grass with side entrances. In most species, the whitish eggs are dotted with brown or reddish brown. Incubation is typically by the female only, but both parents help to feed the young. Some of the tropical wrens practice cooperative breeding, with additional helpers taking part in feeding the young in the nest.

An odd habit of many male wrens is the building of "dummy" nests in their territories, occasionally as many as 20 nests that are never used. Another trait, even harder for us to understand, is that wrens of several species often sneak into the nests of other birds and puncture their eggs — not eating them, just destroying them. These two activities might seem pointless, but scientists have suggested one way in which they might benefit the wrens. Adding fake nests and destroying the contents of other nests will both increase the number of empty nests in the territory; if a predator checks several nests and finds them empty, it may stop looking for food in such places before it discovers the actual nest of the wren.

Displays   Wrens seem to communicate mostly by voice, but they also have some visual displays used in close encounters. In courtship displays, the male may spread his wings and raise or spread his tail while singing, and he may hop about stiffly near the female. In aggressive displays while defending his territory, a male may adopt threatening postures (such as crouching with his bill pointed at an intruder) before a chase or a fight develops.

LARGE WRENS — GENUS *Campylorhynchus*

CACTUS WREN   *Campylorhynchus brunneicapillus*

Big and bold, with strong markings and a harsh rasping voice, this bird is very different from our other temperate-zone wrens. It represents a tropical group of large, sociable wrens, with eight species in Mexico and a few more farther south. Cactus Wrens are common in our desert southwest. They are usually seen in pairs or family parties, strutting on the ground or hopping in the brush, often posturing with spread wings and tails as they call to each other. Their bulky nests are conspicuous in cholla cactus and desert trees; after the breeding season, the wrens may sleep in these at night.

Cactus Wren

HABITAT   *Cactus, yucca, mesquite; arid brush, deserts.* Lives in a variety of low dry habitats. Most numerous in desert, in areas with thorny shrubs and cactus, especially where cholla cactus is common; also found in mesquite brush, in towns, and locally in coastal chaparral where cactus grows.

FEEDING   **Diet:** *Mostly insects, some fruits and seeds.* Feeds on a wide variety of insects, including beetles, ants, wasps, true bugs, grasshoppers. Also eats a few spiders, and occasionally small lizards. Eats more plant material than other wrens (up to 20 percent), including berries, cactus fruits, seeds, some nectar. **Behavior:** Forages on the ground and in low trees, probing in bark crevices and among leaf litter on ground. Often forages in pairs or family groups. On the ground, often inserts bill under a leaf or small rock and lifts up to look for food underneath. Adaptable and curious, will explore possible new sources of food, learning to probe in cones of planted pines and to pick smashed insects from the front ends of parked cars.

NESTING   May mate for life, pairs remaining together all year on permanent territory. Members of pair have greeting display, perching upright with wings and tail partly spread, giving harsh calls. Male may build extra "dummy" nests while female is incubating. Adults sometimes puncture eggs of other birds nesting nearby. **Nest:** Site is in cactus (especially cholla), tree yucca, or thorny low tree such as mesquite, acacia, or paloverde; usually less than 10 feet above the ground, rarely up to 30 feet. Sometimes nests in hole in building or in large cavity in giant cactus.

Nest (built by both sexes) is a bulky mass of weeds, grass, twigs, lined with feathers, animal hair, plant down. Nest is shaped like football lying on its side; entrance at one end, with narrow tubular passage leading to nest chamber. **Eggs:** 3–4, sometimes 2–5. Whitish to pale pink, heavily spotted with brown. Incubation is by female only, about 16 days. **Young:** Both parents feed nestlings. Young leave nest about 19–23 days after hatching, may remain on parents' territory for some time thereafter.

MIGRATION Permanent resident.

CONSERVATION STATUS Surveys suggest numbers are declining in parts of Texas. Scarce population on coastal slope of southern California may be threatened. In main southwestern range, still widespread and abundant.

GENUS *Salpinctes*

ROCK WREN   *Salpinctes obsoletus*

Rock Wren

Arid rocky canyons and seemingly barren piles of boulders are home to this active little bird, the palest of our wrens. Birders who explore such places may spot the Rock Wren bouncing up and down on its short legs as if on springs, while it gives a metallic call note that echoes among the rocks. The nest of this wren can sometimes be located by its curious "front porch," a paving of small pebbles on the ground in front of the nest entrance.

HABITAT *Rocky slopes, canyons.* Breeds in a variety of rocky places. Found at elevations from low canyons to high in mountains, wherever surroundings are very open and arid, but scarce in hot desert regions in summer. Winters in rocky places at low elevations; sometimes on rock levees or on stone riprap below dams, especially when the bird wanders east. In the absence of rocks it may establish winter territory around stacks of hay bales, pieces of farm equipment, or other landmarks.

FEEDING **Diet:** *Mostly insects and spiders.* Diet is not well known. Probably feeds mostly on insects, including beetles, ants, grasshoppers, and many others, also spiders and probably other arthropods. **Behavior:** Forages on the ground in dry places and on steep dirt banks and rocky cliffs with many cracks and openings. Uses long bill to probe crevices among rocks. Sometimes forages among tangles of low vegetation or low on trunks of trees.

NESTING Nesting behavior not well known. Male sings to defend nesting territory. **Nest:** Site is usually in crevice among boulders, in hole in dirt bank, under a rock ledge, in crevice in stone building, or similarly sheltered site; rarely in low tree cavity. Nest (probably built by both sexes) is cup of grass, weeds, bark strips, twigs, rootlets, lined with finer materials such as animal hair, spider webs, feathers. Often marked by "paving" of small stones, sometimes with bones and other debris, laid out on ground in front of the entrance to the cranny where the nest is located. **Eggs:** 5–6, sometimes 4–8. White, lightly dotted with reddish brown. Incubation is probably by female, incubation period not well known. **Young:** Both parents feed nestlings. Age at which young leave the nest is not well known.

MIGRATION Strongly migratory, departing from northern part of range for the winter. Strays sometimes wander east in fall and have even reached the Atlantic coast.

Widespread and common, numbers probably stable. Most of nesting habitat is little affected by human activities.

GENUS *Catherpes*

CANYON WREN   *Catherpes mexicanus*

One of the best songsters in the west, the Canyon Wren is usually heard before it is seen. Surprisingly elusive and skulking even in open terrain, this dark rusty wren appears and disappears as it creeps about the jumbled rocks of an eroded cliff or steep canyon wall. If the observer waits, the bird will eventually jump to the top of an exposed boulder to pour out another song, a rippling and musical cascade of notes well suited to beautiful wild canyons.

HABITAT   *Cliffs, canyons, rockslides; stone buildings.* Generally around areas with steep rock faces and some dense low growth, as in steep-walled canyons or around the bases of cliffs; also in boulder fields and sometimes around stone buildings. May move into denser streamside vegetation away from cliffs in winter.

FEEDING   **Diet:** *Mostly insects and spiders.* Feeds on a variety of insects, including termites, ants, beetles, leafhoppers, and others, also spiders. **Behavior:** Forages by hopping actively about in rock piles, up and down faces of steep rocky cliffs, or through very dense undergrowth in canyons. Does much of its foraging in sheltered spots, such as under rocks or in crevices. Uses its very long bill to probe deep into crevices among the rocks. Usually forages alone, sometimes in pairs. Has been seen stealing spiders from the nest of a predatory wasp.

NESTING   Male defends nesting territory by singing. **Nest:** Site is usually in hole or crevice in rocky cliff, among rock piles, on ledge in cave; sometimes in crevices in stone buildings, abandoned sheds, hollow

Canyon Wren

stumps, or similarly protected sites. Nest (built by both sexes) has foundation of twigs, grass, bark chips, and other coarse items, topped with cup of softer materials such as fine grass, moss, leaves, spider webs, plant down, animal hair, feathers. May add odd debris to nest. **Eggs:** 5, sometimes 4–6, rarely 3–7. White, lightly dotted with reddish brown. Incubation is by female, 12–18 days. Male may feed female during incubation. **Young:** Both parents feed nestlings. Young leave nest at about 15 days, may remain with parents for several weeks or more.

MIGRATION   Unlike the Rock Wren, a permanent resident throughout its range, but may move into denser habitats in winter.

CONSERVATION STATUS   Common within its range, but some indications of declining numbers recently. Was formerly more numerous around towns; may have declined after invasion of other cavity-nesting birds such as House Sparrows.

GENUS *Thryothorus*

CAROLINA WREN   *Thryothorus ludovicianus*

More brightly colored than most wrens and with a rich musical song, Carolina Wrens are common in open woods and backyards in the southeast. There they busily explore brushpiles and low tangles. The adults live in pairs all year, and they may sing "duets" at any season, with the female giving a chattering note while the male sings. The northern edge of this species' range varies over time: it gradually expands northward during series of mild years, then gets knocked southward again by very severe winters.

HABITAT   *Tangles, undergrowth, suburbs, gardens, towns.* Common in the undergrowth of deciduous or mixed woods and in thickets along forest edges. Also lives in suburban areas, especially where some dense low growth and tangles have been left undisturbed.

FEEDING   **Diet:** *Mostly insects.* Feeds primarily on insects of many kinds, especially caterpillars, beetles, true bugs, grasshoppers, crickets. Also feeds on many spiders, some millipedes and snails. Sometimes catches and eats small lizards or tree frogs. Also eats berries and small fruits, especially in winter, and some seeds. **Behavior:** Usually forages in pairs, actively exploring low tangles, foliage, bark of trunks and branches, and the ground. Sometimes comes to bird feeders for suet, peanuts, other items.

Carolina Wren

NESTING   May mate for life. Pairs remain together all year, defending permanent territories; male and female often sing in duet. **Nest:** Site is in any kind of cavity, including natural hollows in trees or stumps, old woodpecker holes, crevices among upturned roots of fallen trees, sometimes in middle of brushpile; also in nest boxes, crevices in buildings, on shelf in garage, many other artificial sites. Usually less than 10 feet above ground. Nest is bulky mass of twigs, leaves, weeds, with lining of softer material such as moss, grass, animal hair, feathers. A piece of snakeskin is frequently added. Often a domed nest, with entrance on side. Both sexes help build, female adds most of lining. **Eggs:** 4–5, sometimes 3–8. White, with brown blotches usually concentrated at larger end. Incubation is by female only, 12–16 days; male may feed female during incubation. **Young:** Both parents bring food for nestlings. Young leave nest about 12–14 days after hatching. Two broods per year, or three in south.

MIGRATION   Permanent resident. May wander north of breeding range, especially in fall.

CONSERVATION STATUS   Populations rise and fall in northern part of range, decreasing after harsh winters. Overall population probably stable, perhaps even expanding.

GENUS *Thryomanes*

BEWICK'S WREN   *Thryomanes bewickii*

In dry thickets and open woods of the west, this is often a very common bird. Pairs of Bewick's Wrens (pronounced like "Buick") clamber about actively in the brush, exploring tangles and bark crevices, waving their long tails about, giving harsh scolding notes at any provocation. In the east, this species is far less common, apparently declining everywhere east of the Mississippi River and considered endangered in some areas.

HABITAT   *Thickets, underbrush, gardens.* In the west, found in many brushy or wooded habitats at lower elevations, including undergrowth in woods of oak and pine, streamside groves, chaparral, desert washes, suburban areas. In the east (where now scarce), mostly in brushy areas around the edges of woods.

FEEDING **Diet:** *Mostly insects.* Feeds on a wide variety of insects, including beetles, ants, wasps, true bugs, caterpillars, grasshoppers. Also eats many spiders and occasionally some berries or seeds. **Behavior:** Forages very actively by climbing and hopping about on trunks, branches, and twigs of trees, probing into bark crevices or gleaning insects from the surface. Also feeds on the ground, flipping over leaves and probing among leaf litter.

NESTING   Male defends nesting territory by singing; songs of eastern birds quite different from those of the west. Adults sometimes puncture eggs of other birds nesting nearby. **Nest:** Site is in any kind of cavity, including natural hollows in trees, old woodpecker holes; also in artificial sites, including nest boxes, holes in buildings, mailboxes, tin cans, and many others. Site is usually less than 20 feet above the ground. Male may build incomplete "dummy" nests; female probably chooses site and completes one nest for raising young. Nest has a foundation of twigs, leaves, bark strips, and trash, topped with a softer cup

Bewick's Wren

of moss, leaves, animal hair, feathers. Sometimes adds bits of snakeskin to nest. **Eggs:** 5–7, sometimes 4–11. White, with brown and gray blotches often concentrated at larger end. Incubation is probably by female only, about 14 days. **Young:** Both parents feed nestlings. Young leave the nest about 2 weeks after hatching.

MIGRATION   Some are present all year in most parts of breeding range, but many depart from northern areas and higher elevations in winter; may be more migratory in east than in west.

CONSERVATION STATUS   In the west, widespread and common, expanding range northward in some areas. In the east, scarce and declining, considered locally endangered east of the Mississippi River.

Small Dark Wrens — GENUS *Troglodytes*

The most widespread genus of wrens, found from Alaska to Argentina and also across Eurasia (where the Winter Wren is the only wren). Members of this group live in wooded areas; they are all rather plain, but most have complicated, musical songs.

HOUSE WREN   *Troglodytes aedon*

A familiar backyard bird, the House Wren was named long ago for its tendency to nest around human homes or in birdhouses. Very active and inquisitive, bouncing about with its short tail held up in the air, pausing to sing a rich bubbling song, it adds a lively spark to gardens and city parks despite its lack of bright colors. Various forms of this wren are found from central Canada to southern South America.

HABITAT   *Open woods, thickets, towns, gardens.* Breeds in a wide variety of semi-open habitats, including suburbs, orchards, woodlots, open forest, streamside groves, mountain pine-oak woods, and many others. Winters mostly in areas of dense low growth, including thickets and streamside brush.

FEEDING   **Diet:** *Mostly insects.* Feeds on a wide variety of insects, including beetles, true bugs, grasshoppers, crickets, caterpillars, moths, flies. Also eats many spiders, plus some

millipedes and snails. **Behavior:** Forages very actively in dense vegetation. Forages at various levels, sometimes high in trees but usually low, searching for insects among foliage, on twigs and branches, in the bark of tree trunks, and on the ground.

NESTING   Male defends territory by singing. Courtship involves male singing, showing the female potential nest sites. Adults often puncture the eggs of other birds nesting nearby (including other House Wrens). Male may have more than one mate; female may leave male to care for young from first brood while she moves to another male's territory and nests again. **Nest:** Site is in any kind of cavity, including natural hollows in trees and stumps, old woodpecker holes, crevices in buildings, often in nest boxes. May nest in almost any kind of enclosed space (flowerpots, parked cars, shoes, drainpipes, etc.). Site is usually low, may be high in trees, especially in western mountains. Male builds incomplete "dummy" nests in several cavities; female chooses one and finishes nest by adding lining. Nest has a foundation of twigs topped with softer cup of plant fibers, grass, weeds, animal hair, feathers. **Eggs:** 6–7, sometimes 5–8, occasionally more. White, heavily dotted with reddish brown. Incubation is probably mostly or entirely by female, about 12–15 days. **Young:** Probably both parents feed nestlings. Young leave the nest about 12–18 days after hatching. Two broods per year, rarely three.

House Wren

MIGRATION   Probably migrates at night. Males apparently migrate north slightly earlier in spring than females.

CONSERVATION STATUS   Declined in some areas in 19th century after introduction of House Sparrow, which competed for nest sites. Currently widespread and common, numbers probably stable.

WINTER WREN   *Troglodytes troglodytes*

A secretive little bird of dense woods. It often creeps about among fallen logs and dense tangles, behaving more like a mouse than a bird, remaining out of sight but giving an occasional *kimp-kimp* call note. Winter Wrens usually live close to the ground; but in spring in the northern woods, males ascend to high perches in the conifers to give voice to a beautiful song of long-running musical trills.

HABITAT   *Woodland underbrush; conifer forests (summer).* Breeds mostly in moist coniferous forest with an understory of dense thickets, often close to water. Winters in very dense low growth in woods, especially along streambanks or among tangles, brushpiles, and fallen logs.

FEEDING   **Diet:** *Mostly insects.* Feeds on a wide variety of insects, including many beetles, caterpillars, true bugs, ants, small wasps. Also eats many spiders, plus some millipedes and snails. Occasionally may eat tiny fish. Also sometimes eats berries, perhaps mainly in fall and winter. **Behavior:** Usually forages very low among dense vegetation, searching for insects among foliage, on twigs and trunks, and on ground. When feeding low along streambanks, may take items from water's surface.

NESTING   Male sings in spring to defend territory and attract a mate. In courtship, male perches near female, wings half-opened and fluttering, tail spread and moving from side to side, while he sings or calls. Male may have more than one mate. **Nest:** Site is in any kind of natural cavity close to the ground (lower than about 6 feet),

Winter Wren

including holes among upturned roots of downed trees, cavities in rotten stumps, old woodpecker holes, crevices among rocks, holes in streambanks, sometimes under cabin porches. Within cavity, both sexes help build nest of grass, weeds, moss, rootlets, lined with animal hair and feathers. Male may also build several unlined "dummy" nests. **Eggs:** 5–6, sometimes 4–7. White, with reddish brown dots often concentrated toward larger end. Incubation is by female, about 14–16 days. **Young:** Probably both parents feed nestlings. Young leave the nest about 19 days after hatching.

MIGRATION   Despite the name, leaves most northern areas in winter, except on Pacific coast where it is a permanent resident as far north as Alaska. Migration is relatively early in spring and late in fall.

GRASS AND MARSH WRENS — GENUS *Cistothorus*

These birds are specialists of low vegetation, particularly marshes and grass growing in damp places, where they often stay out of sight. They are less musical than many wrens, with dry or sputtering songs. Various close relatives of our Sedge Wren are found widely in South America.

SEDGE WREN   *Cistothorus platensis*

Related to the Marsh Wren but different in some key habits, the Sedge Wren is a rather mysterious creature for many birders. It is often hard to see as it creeps about in damp sedge meadows of the east and midwest, occasionally coming up to give its

Sedge Wren

dry rattling song. As a summer resident it is oddly erratic in many areas, showing up and breeding one summer and then vanishing again. Overall, its numbers seem to be gradually declining.

HABITAT   *Grassy marshes, sedgy meadows.* Breeds mostly in damp meadows of grass or sedges, also in lush hayfields and other fields with dense low growth and scattered bushes. Generally not in deep-water marsh, but may be along their grassy edges. Winters in rank weedy meadows, coastal prairies.

FEEDING   **Diet:** *Mostly insects.* Diet is not known in detail, but feeds on a wide variety of insects including true bugs, beetles, moths, caterpillars, grasshoppers, ants, flies. Also eats many spiders. **Behavior:** Forages very low in dense growth of sedges and grass, creeping about and searching for insects among the vegetation and on the ground. May sometimes make short flights to catch insects in the air.

NESTING   Very erratic in its choice of nesting territory, little colonies springing up one year and vacated the next. Male may have more than one mate. Adults often puncture the eggs of other birds nesting nearby (including those of other Sedge Wrens). **Nest:** Male may build several incomplete "dummy" nests that are never used. Real nest is built very low among standing grass or sedges in wet meadow, up to 3 feet above the

ground, usually hard to find. Nest is a round globular ball woven of sedges and grasses, with a small entrance on the side. The inside is lined with fine grass, plant down, animal hair, feathers. **Eggs:** 4–8. White, unmarked. Incubation is by female only, about 14 days. **Young:** Both parents feed young, but female may do more. Young leave nest about 12–14 days after hatching.

MIGRATION   Somewhat nomadic in summer, appearing and breeding where habitat conditions are favorable in a given year.

CONSERVATION STATUS   Local numbers vary from year to year; overall population in North America apparently has been declining in recent decades, but reasons are poorly understood.

MARSH WREN   *Cistothorus palustris*

A sputtering, bubbling song among the cattails is a giveaway that the Marsh Wren is at home. A patient watcher eventually will see the bird as it slips furtively through the reeds or bounces to the top of a stem for a look around. Industrious male Marsh Wrens build "dummy nests" in their nesting territories, occasionally up to 20 or more; most of these are never used for raising young, but the adults may sleep in them during other seasons.

HABITAT   *Marshes (cattail, bulrush, or brackish).* Breeds in many fresh and brackish marsh situations, usually with a large area of cattails, bulrushes, or cordgrass; also in other kinds of low rank growth along shallow water. Winters in a wider variety of large and small marshes, including salt marshes and brushy edges of ponds or irrigation ditches.

Marsh Wren

FEEDING   *Diet: Mostly insects.* Feeds on a wide variety of insects, including beetles, flies, moths, caterpillars, ants, grasshoppers. May include various aquatic insects and their larvae, including those of mosquitoes and damselflies. Also eats spiders and snails. **Behavior:** Forages very actively in dense low growth, taking insects from the stems of marsh plants or from the ground. Often picks items from surface of water. Sometimes makes short flights to catch flying insects in midair.

NESTING   Male defends nesting territory by singing; western males have far more song types than those in the east. One male may have two or more mates. Adults often puncture the eggs of other birds nesting in marsh (including those of other Marsh Wrens). **Nest:** Male builds several incomplete or "dummy" nests in territory; female chooses one and adds lining, or may build a new one. Nest is anchored to standing cattails, bulrushes, or bushes in marsh, usually 1–3 feet above water, sometimes higher. Nest is oval or football-shaped mass with entrance on side, woven of wet grass, cattails, rushes, lined with fine grass, plant down, feathers. **Eggs:** 4–5, sometimes 3–6, rarely more. Pale brown, heavily dotted with dark brown; sometimes may be all white. Incubation is by female only, about 13–16 days. **Young:** Both parents feed young, but female probably does more. Young leave nest about 12–16 days after hatching. Two broods per year.

MIGRATION   Probably migrates at night. Migrants sometimes stop over in odd habitats, away from water.

Undoubtedly has declined with loss of freshwater wetlands, but still fairly widespread and common.

DIPPERS (Family Cinclidae)

These are songbirds that live like waterbirds, getting most of their food underwater in rushing mountain streams. They can dive and swim against the current, flapping their wings underwater and walking on the bottom, probing for insect larvae under stones. The five species of dippers are distributed locally across the Americas and Eurasia, with one barely reaching northwest Africa. Apparently all are fairly similar in habits.

GENUS *Cinclus*

AMERICAN DIPPER   *Cinclus mexicanus*

This distinctive bird is locally common along rushing streams in the west, especially in high mountains. It is usually seen bobbing up and down on a rock in midstream or flying low over the water, following the winding course of a creek rather than taking overland shortcuts. The song and call notes of the Dipper are loud, audible above the roar of the water.

HABITAT *Fast-flowing streams in mountains.* Breeds along swift, rocky streams, seeming to favor clear, cold water, often in narrow canyons. Mostly lives in mountainous areas, but sometimes (especially in Alaska) may be along streams through level country, even near sea level. In winter, may move to streams at lower elevations, sometimes accepting narrow creeks or slower-moving rivers.

FEEDING   **Diet:** *Mostly aquatic insects.* Feeds on many kinds of aquatic insects, including larvae of caddisflies, mayflies, beetles, bugs, and mosquitoes, as well as adults of these insects and many others; also some worms and snails. Also eats fish eggs and very small fish (less than 3 inches long). **Behavior:** Most food is caught underwater. The Dipper may walk with only

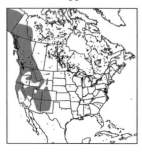

American Dipper

its head submerged, or may dive, "flying" underwater and walking on the bottom, probing under stones in streambed. Also will swim on surface to pick up floating insects. Occasionally takes insects from streamside rocks, rarely makes short flights to catch insects in midair.

NESTING   In courtship, either male or female may strut and sing in front of other bird, wings drooping and bill pointed up. **Nest:** Natural sites include slight ledge on mossy rock wall just above stream, among roots on dirt bank, or behind waterfall; often placed where nest remains continuously wet from flying spray. Many nests today are built under bridges that cross mountain streams. Nest (probably built by female) is a domed structure about a foot in diameter, with a large entrance low on one side; made of mosses, some of them still green and growing, often with some twigs, rootlets, or grass woven in. **Eggs:** 4–5, sometimes 3–6. White. Incubation is by female, 13–17 days. **Young:** Both parents feed nestlings (but female may do more). Young leave the nest at about 18–25 days and are able to swim and dive almost immediately.

Permanent resident in many areas, some staying through winter even in far north, wherever fast-flowing streams remain unfrozen. Some move to lower elevations and slightly southward in winter.

Has declined or disappeared in some former haunts where streams have become polluted. The species is a good indicator of water quality.

THRUSHES AND THEIR RELATIVES (Family Muscicapidae)

This is a large and varied family—so varied, in fact, that the birds in it were formerly divided up among several different families. Some scientists still doubt that all these birds really belong together, and it is possible that they will be classified differently in the future. As currently defined, the family contains such a wide variety of species that generalizations about them are almost useless; for our purposes, they are divided and discussed by subfamilies.

OLD WORLD WARBLERS (subfamily Sylviinae)

Despite the shared last name, these birds are not at all related to the American warblers. Members of the two groups are similar only in being small, active birds that feed mainly on insects.

The "true" Old World warblers (such as the first five species below) are mostly very plain in color and pattern and are often difficult to identify, although most have distinctive songs. The Arctic Warbler is the only one of the several hundred species that occurs regularly in the Americas. Also currently included in this subfamily are two small groups, the kinglets (widespread in the Northern Hemisphere) and the gnatcatchers (found only in the New World, mainly in the tropics).

GENUS *Locustella*

MIDDENDORFF'S GRASSHOPPER-WARBLER   *Locustella ochotensis*

In coastal regions of northeastern Asia in summer, this plain warbler skulks in dense grass and low scrub. It is a rare stray to the islands of western Alaska, perhaps occurring more regularly in fall (when there are far fewer birders there to notice it).

LANCEOLATED WARBLER   *Locustella lanceolata*

In rank brushy fields in Asia, this little brown warbler creeps about in the undergrowth, typically staying out of sight. Lanceolated Warblers briefly "invaded" Attu Island, Alaska, in summer 1984, with up to 25 found there, but the species has not been found there since. Remarkably, a single individual once appeared on Southeast Farallon Island, off the coast of California.

LEAF-WARBLERS — GENUS *Phylloscopus*

Among birders in the Old World, these birds are famous for causing headaches in identification. The genus includes about 40 species, many of them very plain and very similar. Only one crosses the Bering Strait to nest in Alaska, but two others have strayed in and others probably will appear in the future.

WOOD WARBLER *Phylloscopus sibilatrix*

This rather bright yellow-green little warbler nests in woodlands of Europe and adjacent western Asia, and winters in Africa. One that appeared once in the western Aleutian Islands (Shemya) was very far outside its normal range, and the species is not expected to reach our area again soon.

DUSKY WARBLER *Phylloscopus fuscatus*

Common in Asia, this plain warbler skulks in thickets, its presence revealed by its sharp low call note. The Dusky Warbler is known as a very rare visitor to western Alaska, but it might be found more often if more birders visited that region in fall, when the species is most likely to stray; there are at least five fall records for California.

ARCTIC WARBLER *Phylloscopus borealis*

Arctic Warbler

Along willow-lined streams in Alaska in summer, the song of the Arctic Warbler is unmistakable: a slow trill with an insistent or hammering sound. When the bird hops into view among the branches, it is less distinctive — plain olive and whitish with a pale eyebrow. In fall, the Arctic Warbler crosses the Bering Strait and migrates south in Asia.

HABITAT   *Willow scrub.* In Alaska, breeds in dense low thickets (4–10 feet tall) of willow, dwarf birch, or alder, mainly along streams. In Eurasia, breeds in similar habitat but also in open forest of conifers mixed with deciduous shrubs.

FEEDING   **Diet:** *Mostly insects.* Diet in North America not well known. In Eurasia, feeds on a wide variety of insects, especially beetles, mosquitoes, flies, leafhoppers, caterpillars, true bugs, mayflies, sawflies. Also eats some spiders and snails. **Behavior:** Forages very actively among the foliage of bushes and trees, examining twigs and leaves for insects. Sometimes hovers to glean insects from foliage. Flies out to catch insects in midair, and may do so repeatedly when midges or mayflies are swarming.

NESTING   Nesting behavior in Alaska not well known; information here includes data from Eurasia. Male sings to defend nesting territory; in aggressive encounters, males may flap wings slowly while singing. **Nest:** Site is on ground, usually in mossy ground cover under dense shrubs or in crevice among roots, sometimes tucked into side of grass tussock. Typically well hidden. Nest (thought to be built by female) is a domed structure with the entrance on the side; made of grass, weeds, moss, leaves, lined with fine grass. **Eggs:** 6–7, sometimes 5. White, finely dotted with brown. Incubation is by female only, 11–13 days. **Young:** Both parents feed nestlings. Young leave nest about 12–14 days after hatching. One brood per year.

Alaskan birds winter especially in the Philippines, also in nearby areas of Southeast Asia and Indonesia. Unlike some other Alaskan breeders, this species almost never strays southward in the New World.

CONSERVATION STATUS Small population in Alaska probably stable; could be affected by loss of habitat on wintering grounds.

KINGLETS — GENUS *Regulus*

These are among the smallest of all songbirds, weighing less than one-third of an ounce. Seemingly hyperactive, they flit about constantly in the trees, often flicking their wings slightly open and then closed again in a very quick motion.

GOLDEN-CROWNED KINGLET *Regulus satrapa*

Golden-crowned Kinglet

One of our tiniest birds, the Golden-crowned Kinglet is remarkable in its ability to survive in cold climates. Nesting in northern forest, wintering throughout much of the continent, it is usually in dense conifers which undoubtedly help provide shelter from the cold. This choice of habitat also makes the Golden-crown hard to see, but it may be detected by its high, thin call notes and then glimpsed as it flits about high in the spruce trees.

HABITAT *Mostly conifers; in winter, sometimes other trees.* Breeds in dense coniferous forest, especially spruce, fir, and hemlock, less often in Douglas-fir or pines. In migration and winter may be found in deciduous trees, but tends to seek out conifers even then, including pine groves and exotic conifers planted in cemeteries and parks.

FEEDING **Diet:** *Mostly insects.* Feeds on a wide variety of tiny insects, including small beetles, gnats, caterpillars, scale insects, aphids. Also eats spiders. Diet includes many eggs of insects and spiders. Will feed on oozing sap; rarely feeds on fruit. **Behavior:** Forages very actively in trees and shrubs, mainly in conifers. Hops among branches, often hanging upside down from tips of twigs. Occasionally hovers to glean an insect from foliage or bark; rarely flies out to catch an insect in midair. Compared with Ruby-crowned Kinglet, does less hovering and flycatching, more hanging upside down.

NESTING Male defends nesting territory by singing. In aggressive encounters with other males, he may lean far forward and down with crown feathers raised, wings and tail flicking while he sings. **Nest:** Placed in spruce or other conifer, 6–60 feet up but usually high, averaging about 50 feet above the ground. Nest is attached to hanging twigs below a horizontal branch, close to trunk, well protected by foliage above. Female builds deep hanging cup of moss, lichens, bark strips, spider webs, twigs, leaves, lined with feathers, plant down, rootlets, other soft materials. **Eggs:** 8–9, sometimes 5–11. A surprising number of eggs for small size of bird, often arranged in two layers in nest. Eggs whitish to pale buff, with brown and gray spots often concentrated toward larger end. Incubation by female only, about 14–15 days. Male may feed female during incubation. **Young:** Both parents feed nestlings. Young leave nest about 14–19 days after hatching.

Generally migrates late in fall and early in spring. Some on northern Pacific coast are probably permanent residents.

Populations may drop after very harsh cold seasons on wintering grounds. Long-term numbers seem healthy. Has expanded breeding range into some new areas in northeast, nesting in planted conifers.

RUBY-CROWNED KINGLET *Regulus calendula*

This tiny bird is often hard to see in summer, when it lives high in tall conifers. During migration and in winter, however, it often flits about low in woods and thickets, flicking its wings nervously as it approaches the observer. When it is truly excited (by a potential mate, rival, or predator), the male may erect his ruby red crown feathers, hidden at other times. The song of the Ruby-crown is jumbled and loud, all out of proportion to the size of the bird.

Ruby-crowned Kinglet

HABITAT *Conifers in summer; other trees and brush in winter.* Breeds in coniferous forest, including those of spruce, fir, Douglas-fir, and some pine woods. Winters in a wide variety of habitats, mainly in open deciduous woods, also in coniferous and mixed woods, mesquite brush, streamside thickets.

FEEDING **Diet:** *Mostly insects.* At all seasons, diet is primarily small insects, the birds concentrating on whatever is most readily available; includes many small beetles, flies, leafhoppers, true bugs, caterpillars. Also eats spiders and pseudoscorpions, eggs of insects and spiders. In winter, also eats some berries and seeds. Sometimes takes oozing sap or visits flowers, possibly for nectar. **Behavior:** Forages actively at all levels, from treetops to low brush, examining foliage, twigs, and major limbs for foods. Often hovers while taking items from foliage, and sometimes flies out to catch insects in midair. Compared with Golden-crowned Kinglet, does more hovering and flycatching, less hanging on twigs.

NESTING In courtship, male may crouch horizontally, fluttering wings and raising red crown feathers while singing. **Nest:** Usually in spruce, sometimes in other conifer; nest averages about 40 feet above ground, can be up to 90 feet, or very low in far northern forest where trees are short. Nest is attached to hanging twigs below a horizontal branch, well protected by foliage above. Female builds deep hanging cup of moss, lichens, bark strips, spider webs, twigs, rootlets, and conifer needles, lined with feathers, plant down, animal hair. **Eggs:** 7–8, sometimes 4–9. In Pacific Northwest, 9–10 eggs, sometimes 7–12, a remarkably large clutch for small size of bird. Eggs whitish to pale buff, with brown spots often concentrated at larger end. Incubation is by female only, about 13–14 days. Male may feed female during incubation. **Young:** Both parents feed nestlings. Young leave nest about 16 days after hatching. One brood per year.

Migrates a little earlier in fall and later in spring than Golden-crowned Kinglet. In many areas, peak migration periods are October and April.

Populations rise and fall, with many apparently being killed during exceptionally harsh winters. Overall, however, species is widespread and common.

These are very small birds, with long tails that are often held cocked up or flipped about as the gnatcatchers move actively among the foliage, seeking tiny insects. Most members of this group are permanent residents in warm climates. The Blue-gray Gnatcatcher, by migrating, has been able to spread over much of the United States and even southeastern Canada in summer.

BLUE-GRAY GNATCATCHER *Polioptila caerulea*

A very small woodland bird with a long tail, usually seen flitting about in the tree-tops, giving a short whining call note. Often it darts out in a short, quick flight to snap up a tiny insect in midair. Widespread in summer, its breeding range is still expanding toward the north.

HABITAT   *Open woods, oaks, pines, thickets.* Breeding habitat varies with region. In east, mostly in deciduous forest dominated by oak, ash, or maple, or in southern pine woods with understory of oak. In west, often in more scrubby habitat, including pinyon-juniper woods, chaparral, streamside trees, oak forest. Winters in wooded or brushy areas, often near water.

FEEDING   **Diet:** *Mostly insects.* Feeds on a wide variety of small insects, including leafhoppers, treehoppers, plant bugs, leaf beetles, caterpillars, flies, small wasps. Also eats many spiders. **Behavior:** Forages actively in trees and shrubs. Searches for insects among leafy outer twigs of deciduous trees and on branches and trunk of pines. Takes most food while perched, also hovers to pick items from surface, and often flies out to catch insects that it flushes from foliage. Large insects are beaten against a branch before being eaten.

Blue-gray Gnatcatcher

NESTING   Male arrives first in breeding areas and sings to defend territory and attract a mate. Courtship involves male leading female around to potential nest sites. **Nest:** Site is in tree, often deciduous. Nest saddled on top of horizontal limb of tree, less often in fork of horizontal limb; height above ground is quite variable, 2–80 feet up, but 20–40 feet may be typical. Nest (built by both sexes) is a compact open cup of grass, weeds, plant fibers, strips of bark, lined with plant down, animal hair, feathers. Outside of nest coated with spider webs and decorated with pieces of lichen, making nest well camouflaged. **Eggs:** 4–5, sometimes 3–6. Bluish white, dotted with reddish brown. Incubation is by both parents, 11–15 days, usually 13. **Young:** Female broods young much of time at first, while male brings food; later, both feed nestlings. Young leave nest about 10–15 days after hatching. 1–2 broods per year.

MIGRATION   Probably all in North America are migratory, with different individuals present in summer and winter. Some in Mexico and Bahamas may be permanent residents. Peak migration periods in many areas are April and September. May migrate by day.

CONSERVATION STATUS   Has expanded its breeding range through much of the northeast during the 20th century, and expansion may be continuing. Current population probably stable or increasing.

BLACK-TAILED GNATCATCHER *Polioptila melanura*

This long-tailed little insect-eater is at home in the desert southwest, even in arid scrub and creosote bush flats where there are few other birds. Black-tailed Gnatcatchers live in pairs all year, foraging together actively in the low brush. They stay in contact with each other using a wide variety of calls; some of these calls sound suspiciously like imitations of other desert birds, such as Verdin or Black-throated Sparrow.

HABITAT *Desert brush, ravines, dry washes, mesquites.* Found in many dry, scrubby habitats. Most common in Sonoran desert with varied growth of mesquites, acacias, and paloverdes, but also found in low acacia scrub and on open flats of creosote bush.

FEEDING **Diet:** *Mostly insects.* Feeds on a wide variety of small insects, including beetles, true bugs, caterpillars, wasps, ants, flies, moths, small grasshoppers; also some spiders. Eats small berries at times. **Behavior:** Forages by moving about actively in shrubs and low trees, searching for insects. Often feeds more among leaves during summer and fall, more on bare twigs and branches during winter and early spring. Sometimes hovers to pick items from foliage. Unlike Blue-gray Gnatcatcher, rarely flies out to catch insects in midair.

NESTING Pairs may remain together all year, defending permanent territories. Cowbirds often lay eggs in nests of this species, and some gnatcatcher pairs wind up raising only young cowbirds. **Nest:** Site is in a low shrub, usually in a vertical fork less than 5 feet above the ground. Nest (built by both sexes) is a compact open cup of plant fibers, grass, weeds, strips of bark, spider webs, plant down, and other items, lined with softer materials such as fine plant down, feathers, and animal hair. **Eggs:** 4, sometimes 3–5. Bluish white, very lightly dotted with reddish brown. Incubation is by both parents, about 14 days. **Young:** Both parents feed the nestlings. Young are reported to leave the nest about 10–15 days after hatching.

MIGRATION Permanent resident.

CONSERVATION STATUS Although many nesting attempts fail because of cowbirds, numbers of this species seem to be holding up well.

Black-tailed Gnatcatcher

CALIFORNIA GNATCATCHER *Polioptila californica*

Until the late 1980s, this bird was regarded as just a local form of the Black-tailed Gnatcatcher. With its recognition as a full species, it also became an endangered species: its limited habitat along the southern California coast is being taken over by housing tracts and other developments. California Gnatcatchers live in coastal sage scrub, a low shrubby habitat that is also home to other specialized animals and plants.

HABITAT *Coastal sage scrub.* In limited range on California coast, found only in coastal sage scrub. This is a habitat of low shrubs (mostly 3–6 feet tall), generally dominated by California sagebrush, buckwheat, salvia, and prickly-pear cactus. In Baja California, also found in other kinds of scrub.

FEEDING **Diet:** *Mostly insects.* Feeds on a wide variety of small insects, including true bugs, beetles, caterpillars, scale insects, wasps, ants, flies, moths, small grasshoppers;

California Gnatcatcher

also some spiders. May eat small berries at times.
Behavior: Forages by moving about actively in shrubs and low trees, searching for insects. Sometimes hovers to pick items from foliage. Unlike Blue-gray Gnatcatcher, rarely flies out to catch insects in midair.

NESTING   Adults often remain together in pairs throughout the year on permanent territories. In California, nesting season is from late February to mid-July. Brown-headed Cowbirds often lay eggs in nests of this bird, and the gnatcatchers may wind up raising only young cowbirds. **Nest:** Site is in dense low shrub, usually less than 4 feet above the ground. Nest (built by both sexes) is a compact cup of grass, bark strips, leaves, spider webs, plant down, and other items, lined with fine plant fibers, feathers, and animal hair. **Eggs:** 4, sometimes 3–5. Bluish white, finely dotted with reddish brown. Incubation is by both parents, about 14 days. On hot days, adults may stand on nest and shade the eggs. **Young:** Fed by both parents. Young leave the nest about 15–16 days after hatching.

MIGRATION   Permanent resident.

CONSERVATION STATUS   *Endangered.* The small amount of remaining habitat in California is being rapidly turned into housing developments. Nesting attempts often fail, partly because of cowbird parasitism.

BLACK-CAPPED GNATCATCHER   *Polioptila nigriceps*

This small songbird from western Mexico has been flirting with the Arizona border since the early 1970s. It has appeared in a number of canyons in southeastern Arizona, and it has nested several times, but it has not become firmly established anywhere; in most years, it is not found in our area at all.

OLD WORLD FLYCATCHERS (subfamily Muscicapinae)

The 100-plus species in this group are widespread in the Old World. They are not at all related to the tyrant flycatchers of the Americas, but most of them feed in a similar way, watching and waiting on a perch and then flying out to catch passing insects. Six species have wandered from Asia into Alaska.

COLORFUL OLD WORLD FLYCATCHERS — GENUS *Ficedula*

NARCISSUS FLYCATCHER   *Ficedula narcissina*

This brightly colored little flycatcher is migratory in eastern Asia. It nests mostly in Japan, and winters in the Philippines and Southeast Asia. The Narcissus Flycatcher has occurred as an accidental stray on Attu in the western Aleutians.

MUGIMAKI FLYCATCHER   *Ficedula mugimaki*

Small and colorful, this flycatcher is migratory within eastern Asia. A single individual once strayed well off-course to arrive on Shemya Island in the western Aleutians.

RED-BREASTED FLYCATCHER *Ficedula parva*

In wooded areas across Europe and Asia, this small flycatcher is common in summer. Both the orange-throated males and the plainer females can be recognized by their habit of flicking the tail sharply upward, showing off the white patches in the outer tail feathers. Red-breasted Flycatchers sometimes stray into western Alaska during migration.

DRAB OLD WORLD FLYCATCHERS — GENUS *Muscicapa*

SIBERIAN FLYCATCHER *Muscicapa sibirica*

This plain and dark little flycatcher is fairly common in woodlands of eastern Asia, and it has strayed a few times to the western Aleutians. Remarkably, it has also occurred once in Bermuda, halfway around the world from its normal range, proving that migratory birds can go seriously off course.

GRAY-SPOTTED FLYCATCHER *Muscicapa griseisticta*

Three kinds of grayish flycatchers from eastern Asia have strayed into Alaska. This one is the most frequent of these rare visitors. It often appears in May or June in the western Aleutians, and sometimes several have been present at once on Attu Island.

ASIAN BROWN FLYCATCHER *Muscicapa dauurica*

Small and very plain is this Old World flycatcher. Migratory within eastern Asia, it is strictly an accidental visitor to islands of western Alaska, with single birds having strayed to Attu and Gambell.

THRUSHES (subfamily Turdinae)

Ranging over six continents and innumerable islands, this subfamily includes many common and well-known birds worldwide. The 300-plus species currently classified here may be separated into two categories: the small thrushes or "chats," an Old World group represented in North America by the Wheatear, Bluethroat, and their relatives; and the true thrushes, including the bluebirds and the American Robin.

All of the thrushes have rather thin bills, and most have strong legs. Some are brightly patterned while others are very plain, but the youngest birds typically have spots or other cryptic markings, giving them better camouflage. Several of the thrushes are considered to be among the finest singers in the bird world. Large thrushes like the American Robin sometimes live more than 13 years in the wild, but most probably have shorter life spans.

Feeding Both insects and berries play major parts in the diets of many of the true thrushes. A typical seasonal pattern is for the birds to eat mostly insects in early summer, and then begin to eat more wild fruits and berries in late summer and fall (continuing through winter, at least for those that do not migrate to the tropics). Some species also feed heavily on other invertebrates besides insects, such as earthworms or snails.

Most thrushes have rather long legs, and they may do much of their foraging on the ground, especially when seeking insects or other animal life. When feeding on berries, they forage at all heights in bushes and trees. As a general rule, the small thrushes or chats of the Old World may tend to eat fewer fruits and berries than the true thrushes.

Nesting Sites chosen for nests are quite variable. Old World chats or small thrushes often nest on the ground, or in holes among rocks or in stumps; true thrushes often build open cup-shaped nests among the branches of low trees or shrubs. However, there are many exceptions: for example, bluebirds usually nest in holes in trees, while solitaires usually nest on the ground on steep dirt banks. Most of the nest building is usually done by the female. The eggs (averaging four or five to the clutch) are usually pale blue or blue-green, with or without darker spots. Incubation is generally by the female, but both parents take part in feeding the young.

Displays In aggressive interactions, many of the thrushes adopt a posture with the feathers sleeked down and the bill pointed forward or up. In excitement, thrushes may also raise their head feathers and flick their wings rapidly open and shut. Courtship displays are quite variable, but song evidently plays an important part in courtship as well as in defending the nesting territory against rivals. Early courtship activities in several species may involve the male chasing the female in flight around the territory.

SMALL THRUSHES — GENUS *Luscinia*

SIBERIAN RUBYTHROAT *Luscinia calliope*

This small Asian thrush is a rare migrant in western Alaska. Rather furtive and hard to approach, it looks plain and brown as it flies away from the observer; reaching the edge of a thicket, it may pause to look back, revealing (if it is a male) the startling ruby-red spot on the throat.

BLUETHROAT *Luscinia svecica*

A prize find for birders who visit northwestern Alaska is this elusive little thrush. Bluethroats usually skulk in low dense shrubbery, but sometimes a male will perch up conspicuously to sing, or even sing in brief flights above the thickets. The song is quite variable, often including imitations of other birds. The colorful throat patch of males is prominently shown off in aggressive encounters between rivals, as well as in courtship.

Bluethroat

HABITAT *Dwarf willows, thick brush.* In Alaska, breeds in areas where open tundra is broken by dense low thickets of willow and dwarf birch, especially along drainages or near water. In Eurasia found in various kinds of low brushy habitats, including thickets near water or along forest edge, or scrub in drier hills.

FEEDING Diet: *Mostly insects.* Diet in North America not well known. In Eurasia, feeds on many insects, especially beetles, caterpillars, ants, sawfly larvae, crane flies and other flies, and others. Also eats spiders, plus some snails and earthworms. Eats berries and a few seeds, perhaps mainly in fall. **Behavior:** Forages mostly on the ground under dense cover, picking up insects from the soil or from low plants. Sometimes flies up short distances to catch insects in the air.

NESTING	Nesting habits in Alaska not well known, probably similar to those in Eurasia, described here. Male sings to defend territory, from hidden perch or from top of shrub; sometimes performs short flight-song display. In courtship, male faces female, points bill up to show off throat pattern, raises tail, hops around female while singing. **Nest:** Site is on ground under dense low shrubs or tucked into side of grass tussock. Nest (built mostly or entirely by female) is an open cup of grass, weeds, twigs, moss, rootlets, lined with plant down and animal hair. **Eggs:** 5–6, sometimes 4–8. Pale blue-green, finely dotted with reddish brown. Incubation is mostly or entirely by female, about 13–14 days. **Young:** Both parents feed nestlings. Young can fly at about 14 days, may leave nest 1–2 days earlier.
MIGRATION	Alaska nesting birds winter in southeast Asia. Migrants apparently come across Bering Strait; seldom seen in Aleutians, although regular farther north on St. Lawrence Island.
CONSERVATION STATUS	Small population in Alaska probably stable or possibly increasing. Widespread and common in Eurasia.

SIBERIAN BLUE ROBIN *Luscinia cyane*

Much smaller than our American Robin, and not a close relative, this bird is a shy skulker of thickets in eastern Asia. When perched, it often quivers its tail up and down continuously. In our area, the Siberian Blue Robin is known only as an accidental visitor to the outer Aleutians.

GENUS *Tarsiger*

RED-FLANKED BLUETAIL *Tarsiger cyanurus*

This small thrush is a very rare visitor from Asia to islands of Alaska; a single bird once appeared on California's Farallon Islands. The Red-flanked Bluetail generally stays low in bushes or on the ground, and it often bobs its tail up and down while perched.

WHEATEARS — GENUS *Oenanthe*

NORTHERN WHEATEAR *Oenanthe oenanthe*

On fall weekends in the northeast, birders sometimes hope (but never expect) to find a Wheatear. This small thrush enters the North American Arctic from both directions, via both Greenland and Alaska, but almost all go back to the Old World in winter; only the occasional straggler appears south of Canada. Northern Wheatears can be found in summer on rocky tundra, where they are inconspicuous until they fly, flashing their tail pattern. In the Old World there are almost 20 species of wheatears, most of them in desert regions.

    HABITAT *In summer, rocky tundra, barren slopes.* Breeds on dry northern tundra with many exposed rocks and boulders, especially where these are near mats of dwarf shrubs a few inches high. Migrants may be seen on any kind of open ground, including vacant lots, barren fields, coastal meadows. In Eurasia, very widespread in open country.

    FEEDING **Diet:** *Mostly insects, some berries.* Diet in North America not known in detail. In Eurasia feeds mostly on insects, especially beetles, also ants, caterpillars, grasshoppers, true bugs, flies. Also eats spiders, centipedes, snails. Often feeds on berries, perhaps mainly in summer and fall. **Behavior:** Forages mostly on the ground, running short distances and then stopping to pick up items. May run and flutter in pursuit of active insects. Also often watches from a perch a couple of feet up, then flies down to take item on ground. Sometimes flies out to catch insects in midair.

Northern Wheatear

NESTING   Male defends territory by singing, often in song-flight display. Song often includes imitations of other birds. In one courtship display, female crouches on ground while male leaps back and forth above her, very rapidly, with wings and tail spread. Also other postures and displays, many showing off tail pattern. **Nest:** Site is on ground on dry tundra, usually in hole under rock, in crevice among large stones, or in old rodent burrow. Nest, probably built by female, is placed within this shelter; variable cup of grass, twigs, weeds, lined with finer material such as moss, lichens, rootlets, fine grass. **Eggs:** 5–6, sometimes 3–8. Pale blue, either unmarked or with fine reddish brown dots at larger end. Incubation is mostly or entirely by female, about 13–14 days. **Young:** Both parents feed nestlings, but female may do more. Young leave nest about 15 days after hatching. Probably one brood per year.

MIGRATION   Birds from eastern Canada migrate east via Greenland and Europe, to winter in Africa. Birds from Alaska and northwestern Canada cross Bering Strait and make long westward flight across Asia, also going to wintering grounds mostly in Africa.

CONSERVATION STATUS   North American population probably stable; may be increasing as a breeder in northeastern Canada.

GENUS *Saxicola*

STONECHAT   *Saxicola torquata*

This rather tame little thrush is very common in open fields across Europe and Asia, but it is strictly an accidental visitor in our area. The first one in North America was found in eastern Canada, on New Brunswick's Grand Manan Island; it has since been found in Alaska, on St. Lawrence Island and on the mainland.

BLUEBIRDS — GENUS *Sialia*

Found only in North America, bluebirds are among our most popular birds, with their bright colors and soft musical songs. Their habit of nesting in cavities put them in jeopardy when introduced starlings and House Sparrows competed with them for nest sites, but fortunately they will accept artificial cavities; many thousands of bluebird houses have been put up across the continent.

EASTERN BLUEBIRD   *Sialia sialis*

This is the most widespread of the three bluebirds. Although it is mostly "eastern" in our area, its total range extends south to Nicaragua. A high percentage of Eastern Bluebirds in North America today nest in birdhouses put up especially for them along "bluebird trails." When they are not nesting, these birds roam the countryside in small flocks.

HABITAT   *Open country with scattered trees; farms, roadsides.* Breeds in many kinds of semi-open habitats, including cut-over or burned areas, forest clearings, farm country, open pine woods; locally in suburbs where there are extensive lawns and good nest sites. Wanders to other habitats in winter.

FEEDING   **Diet:** *Mostly insects and berries.* Feeds on a wide variety of insects, including crickets, grasshoppers, beetles; also spiders, earth-worms, snails, rarely small lizards or treefrogs. Also eats many berries, especially in winter. **Behavior:** Does much foraging by perching low and fluttering down to ground to catch insects, often hovering to pick up items rather than landing. Also catches some insects in midair and may take some while hovering among foliage. Feeds on berries by perching or making short hovering flights in trees.

NESTING   As a courtship display, male may sing and flutter in front of the female with his wings and tail partly spread. While perched close together, pairs may preen each other's feathers; male may feed female. **Nest:** Placed in cavity, typically in natural hollow in tree, in old woodpecker hole, or in birdhouse. Usually nests fairly low (2–20 feet above the ground), occasionally up to 50 feet. Nest in cavity (built mostly by female) is a loosely constructed cup of weeds, twigs, and dry grass, lined with finer grass, sometimes with animal hair or feathers. **Eggs:** 4–5, sometimes 3–7. Pale blue, unmarked; sometimes white. Incubation is mostly by female, about 13–16 days. **Young:** Both parents bring food to the nestlings, and young from a previous brood also help to feed them in some cases. Young leave the nest at about 18–19 days on aver-age. Two broods per year, sometimes three.

MIGRATION   Permanent resident in many southern areas. In the north, arrives quite early in spring and lingers late in fall.

CONSERVATION STATUS   In the past, declined seriously in many areas with loss of habitat and loss of nesting sites. During recent decades has been in-creasing again, undoubtedly helped by birdhouses in many areas.

Eastern Bluebird

WESTERN BLUEBIRD   *Sialia mexicana*

In partly open terrain of the west, from valley farms and orchards to clearings in mountain pine forest, this bluebird is often common. In summer it is often seen perching alone on fence wires by open meadows, fluttering down to pluck insects from the grass. In winter, small flocks of Western Bluebirds are often heard flying overhead or seen feeding on berries in trees. Sometimes, as when juniper woods have heavy berry crops, the bluebirds may gather by the hundreds.

HABITAT   *Scattered trees, open conifer forests, farms; in winter, semi-open terrain, brush, deserts.* Breeds in semi-open areas including pine woods, oak woods, streamside groves, ranch country, sometimes in pinyon-juniper woods, but avoids hot dry re-gions. Winters in many kinds of open or semi-open habitats, especially in pinyon-juniper, also in desert, farmland, others.

FEEDING   **Diet:** *Mostly insects and berries.* Insects make up majority of diet, especially in sum-mer; feeds heavily on grasshoppers, caterpillars, beetles, ants, also many other in-sects. Berries and small fruits are important in diet especially in winter; among those eaten are fruits of mistletoe, juniper, and elderberry. **Behavior:** Often forages

by perching fairly low and flying down to ground to capture insects, sometimes hovering briefly before pouncing. May catch insects in midair or may seek them among foliage. Perches or flutters among branches to take berries.

NESTING Male typically arrives on breeding grounds before female, and defends nesting territory by singing. In courtship, male may flutter in front of female with wings and tail partly spread, while singing. Male may also feed female. **Nest:** Site is in cavity, such as natural hollow in oak or pine, old woodpecker hole, birdhouse, sometimes hole in building. Usually nests fairly low, rarely up to 50 feet above ground. Nest in cavity is probably built mostly by female, but male may take part. Nest is a rather loose cup of twigs and weeds,

Western Bluebird

lined with finer grass. **Eggs:** 4–6, sometimes 3–8. Pale blue, unmarked; occasionally white. Incubation is by female, incubation period not well known. **Young:** Both parents bring food to nestlings. Age of young at first flight is not well known, probably between 2 and 3 weeks. Probably two broods per year.

MIGRATION Permanent resident in some southern areas; migratory in the north, arriving rather early in spring and lingering late in fall. Winter range varies from year to year depending on food supplies.

CONSERVATION STATUS In recent decades, numbers have declined over much of range. Provision of birdhouses probably has not kept pace with loss of natural nest sites.

MOUNTAIN BLUEBIRD   *Sialia currucoides*

The powder blue male Mountain Bluebird is among the most beautiful birds of the west. Living in more open terrain than the other two bluebirds, this species may nest in holes in cliffs or dirt banks when tree hollows are not available. It often seeks its food by hovering low over the grass in open fields. During the winter, Mountain Bluebirds often gather in large flocks, even by the hundreds, sometimes associating with Western Bluebirds.

HABITAT *Open country with some trees; in winter, also treeless terrain.* Often in more open areas than other bluebirds. Breeding habitats not always in mountains; found in lowland prairies and sagebrush flats as well as alpine zones above treeline. In winter, most common in pinyon-juniper woods but also in open grassland, desert, farmland, even barren plowed fields.

FEEDING **Diet:** *Mostly insects and berries.* Feeds heavily on insects, including beetles, grasshoppers, caterpillars, crickets, ants, bees, and others. Also eats some berries, including those of mistletoe, juniper,

Mountain Bluebird

hackberry, and other plants. Berries are particularly important in the diet in winter. **Behavior:** Often forages by hovering over open field, then dropping to the ground when prey is spotted. Hovers more than other bluebirds. Also perches on rock or low branch and darts out to catch flying insects.

NESTING Sometimes interbreeds with Eastern Bluebird where their ranges overlap. **Nest:** Apparently the female selects the nest site. Site is in cavity, usually a natural hollow or old woodpecker hole in tree, or in birdhouse. Sometimes nests in holes in dirt banks, crevices in cliffs or among rocks, holes in sides of buildings, old nests of other birds (such as Cliff Swallow or Dipper). Nest in cavity (probably built by both sexes) is loose cup of weed stems, grass, twigs, rootlets, pine needles, sometimes lined with animal hair or feathers. **Eggs:** 5–6, sometimes 4–8. Pale blue, unmarked (occasionally white). Incubation is by female, about 13–17 days. **Young:** Both parents feed nestlings. Young leave the nest about 17–23 days after hatching, are tended by parents for another 3–4 weeks. Two broods per year.

MIGRATION Migrates relatively late in fall and early in spring. Winter range varies from year to year, depending on food supplies. Flocks sometimes wander east on Great Plains, and lone strays occasionally go as far as the Atlantic coast.

CONSERVATION STATUS Nests in many remote areas, where it is less affected than the other bluebirds by competition for nest sites with starlings and other invaders. Numbers are apparently stable.

SOLITAIRES — GENUS *Myadestes*

TOWNSEND'S SOLITAIRE *Myadestes townsendi*

Townsend's Solitaire

Solitaires are slim, long-tailed thrushes that perch upright in trees. As the name suggests, they are usually seen alone. Feeding mostly on berries in winter, each bird maintains its solitary status by defending a winter territory, staking out a supply of berries in a juniper grove or similar spot. These wintering birds often give a soft bell-like call note; in summer (and sometimes in winter as well) they give voice to a complex song of clear musical warblings.

HABITAT *Conifer forests in mountains, rocky cliffs; in winter, chaparral, pinyon-juniper, open woods, wooded streams.* Breeds mostly in open conifer forest in mountains, where exposed rocky slopes or dirt banks provide nesting sites; in far north, may be in burned areas or open scrub habitat near such banks. In winter, inhabits semi-open woods and brush, especially around junipers.

FEEDING **Diet:** *Mostly insects and berries.* Feeds on many insects, especially in summer, including caterpillars, beetles, ants, true bugs, and others, also spiders and other invertebrates. In winter, majority of diet may be berries and small fruits, including those of juniper, mistletoe, hackberry, and others. **Behavior:** Does much foraging by watching from a perch, then flying out to catch insects in midair or fluttering down to catch them on the ground. Also may hover momentarily while plucking insects or berries from foliage.

NESTING Male defends territory by singing, often from a high perch; sometimes sings in flight. **Nest:** Usually on ground in shallow depression in dirt bank or road cut, in crevice in cliff, under a log or stump, or among upturned roots, placed in a protected spot with some overhanging shelter. Sometimes in hollow in dead snag a few feet above ground. Nest is a bulky and loosely made open cup of twigs, grass, pine needles, bark strips, lined with finer grass. **Eggs:** 4, sometimes

47°

THRUSHES

3–5, rarely 6. Whitish to pale blue, blotched with pale gray, overlaid with darker brown spots. Details of incubation not well known; incubation period about 11 days. **Young:** Both parents feed nestlings. Young probably leave the nest about 2 weeks after hatching.

MIGRATION   Migrates relatively late in fall and early in spring, although odd individuals may be seen out of season. Winter range varies from year to year depending on berry supply. Small numbers winter well east of breeding range on Great Plains.

CONSERVATION STATUS   Seldom parasitized by cowbirds, and faces no other obvious threats. Current numbers seem stable.

BROWN THRUSHES — GENUS *Catharus*

Shy forest birds with beautiful voices, these thrushes are heard more often than they are seen. They usually stay low, foraging quietly on the forest floor, but they will also feed on berries in the treetops. All five of our species are strongly migratory, with four of them wintering entirely south of the United States. Several more kinds are permanent residents in the American tropics, where they are called "nightingale-thrushes."

VEERY   *Catharus fuscescens*

In moist leafy woods across the northern states and southern Canada, the breezy spiraling song of this thrush is a common sound in summer. An observer who waits patiently inside the woods may see the Veery itself, bounding across the forest floor with long springy hops or perching quietly in the undergrowth. Staying with us for less than half the year, the bird spends the balance of its time in the shadowy undergrowth of tropical rain forest.

HABITAT   *Damp deciduous woods.* For breeding, favors dense understory and leafy low growth near water. Surrounding habitat usually deciduous woods, sometimes mixed or coniferous woods, or open country on northern Great Plains. In mature forest, avoids areas with little understory, concentrating along streams or other openings. During migration, found mainly in deciduous woods. Winters in undergrowth of lowland tropical forest.

FEEDING   *Diet: Mostly insects and berries.* Diet is mainly insects during breeding season, including beetles, ants, small wasps, caterpillars, and crickets, also spiders, centipedes, snails; rarely eats small frogs or salamanders. Berries and small fruit may be majority of diet in late summer and fall. Winter diet poorly known. **Behavior:** Forages mostly by hopping about on the ground or in low vegetation. Sometimes flips dead leaves over with bill; often hovers briefly to take insects from foliage and may make short flights to catch insects in midair. Also watches from low perch and drops to ground for items. Feeds on berries up in shrubs and trees.

Veery

NESTING   Male arrives first on breeding grounds and defends nesting territory by singing. Courtship involves male chasing female, both birds calling back and forth. **Nest:** Typically placed on or near the ground in dense forest. Nests above ground are usually in base of shrub or sapling, less than 5 feet up; nests on ground are often placed against

stump or log or in clump of grass or weeds. Nest (built by female) has foundation of dead leaves, cup made of weeds, twigs, fine strips of bark, lined with rootlets and bark fibers. **Eggs:** 4, sometimes 3–5. Pale greenish blue, usually unmarked, sometimes spotted with brown. Incubation is apparently by female only, about 10–14 days. **Young:** Both parents feed nestlings; female may spend much time brooding them at first. Young leave nest about 10–12 days after hatching. Some pairs may raise two broods per year.

MIGRATION Migrates mostly at night. Winters east of the Andes in South America. Those nesting in west apparently migrate east in fall before turning south, as they are virtually unrecorded in the southwest south of breeding areas.

CONSERVATION STATUS Nests are frequently parasitized by Brown-headed Cowbirds, probably reducing nesting success. Surveys suggest that numbers of Veeries may be declining.

GRAY-CHEEKED THRUSH *Catharus minimus*

All the brown-backed thrushes can be shy and hard to see, but the Gray-cheek is perhaps the most elusive. During migration it hides in dense woods, slipping away when a birder approaches. On its far northern nesting grounds it may be more easily seen, especially in late evening, when it sings from treetops.

HABITAT *Boreal forest, tundra scrub; in migration, other woodlands.* Breeds in northern spruce forest, often rather open and stunted, and north of treeline in thickets of willow and alder on tundra. Winters in tropical forest.

FEEDING **Diet:** *Mostly insects and berries.* Diet through the year is not known in detail. In North America, feeds on a variety of insects, including beetles, caterpillars, ants,

Gray-cheeked Thrush

wasps, fly larvae; also spiders and some other invertebrates. Also eats many berries and wild fruits. Winter diet in tropics poorly known. **Behavior:** Forages mostly on the ground, hopping about under cover of dense thickets. Sometimes seen feeding on berries up in shrubs or trees.

NESTING Male arrives first on breeding grounds and establishes territory, defending it by singing. In courtship, male pursues female in swift flight among the trees. **Nest:** Often placed very low or even on the ground; usually less than 10 feet up, sometimes up to 24 feet. Ground nests are often among bases of willow or alder shoots, while higher nests may be against trunk of conifer at base of branches. Nest (built by female) is a well-made open cup of grass, moss, twigs, weeds, strips of bark, sometimes with some mud added; lined with fine grass and rootlets. **Eggs:** 4, sometimes 3–5, perhaps rarely 6. Pale blue, with vague brown spots, sometimes almost unmarked. Incubation is by female, 12–14 days. **Young:** Both parents feed nestlings. Young leave nest about 11–13 days after hatching.

MIGRATION Migrates mostly at night. Birds from Alaska (and eastern Siberia) apparently migrate far east in fall before turning south. Many probably make a nonstop flight from northeastern North America to northern South America.

CONSERVATION STATUS Southern breeding populations of Gray-cheeks may be declining.

BICKNELL'S THRUSH *Catharus bicknelli*

Extremely similar to the Gray-cheeked Thrush, this bird was only recently recognized as a distinct species. It has a limited summer range in the northeast, from upstate New York to Nova Scotia and Quebec, where it nests in short, stunted conifers near the tops of mountains and in dense second-growth woods with many young conifers. Gray-cheeked and Bicknell's thrushes have slightly different songs and different call notes in flight, but differences in their behavior have not been thoroughly studied. They have separate wintering areas: Bicknell's migrates south to the West Indies, especially the island of Hispaniola, while the Gray-cheeked goes on to South America. With its very limited range, Bicknell's Thrush merits close study and attention from conservationists.

SWAINSON'S THRUSH *Catharus ustulatus*

During the peak of migration, Swainson's Thrushes are often very common in wood-lots and parks, lurking in the thickets, slipping into fruiting trees to pluck berries.

Although they tend to stay out of sight, the patient birder eventually can see them well enough to discern the bold buffy eye-rings that give these birds their alert or startled look. Like the other brown thrushes, Swainson's migrate mostly at night, and their distinctive call notes can be heard from overhead on clear nights during spring and fall.

HABITAT *Spruce forests and dense streamside woods; in migration, other woods.* Breeds in far north and in mountains in coniferous forest with extensive leafy undergrowth; on Pacific coast, also breeds in deciduous trees and thickets growing along streams. Occurs in many kinds of woodlands in migration. Winters in tropical forest.

FEEDING **Diet:** *Mostly insects and berries.* In North America, feeds on a variety of insects including

Swainson's Thrush

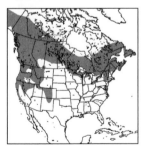

beetles, ants, caterpillars, crickets, wasps, flies, and moths, also spiders and other invertebrates. Berries and fruits amount to over one-third of summer diet. Winter diet in tropics not well known, but often found in fruiting trees there. **Behavior:** Does much feeding on ground, but not as much as the other brown thrushes. Also forages in trees, and may hover momentarily to take insects from foliage or may catch them in midair.

NESTING Male arrives on breeding grounds and establishes territory, defending it by singing. In aggressive display during encounters with intruders on territory, he sleeks down his feathers and points bill up. **Nest:** Usually placed on a horizontal branch, 2–10 feet above the ground, sometimes lower or much higher (rarely up to 30 feet). Often nests in conifers in the east and north, deciduous trees or shrubs in the west. Nest (built by female alone) is a bulky open cup of twigs, bark strips, moss, grass, leaves, sometimes with some mud added. Lined with bark fibers, lichens, animal hair, other soft materials. **Eggs:** 3–4, rarely 5. Pale blue, with brown spots sometimes concentrated at larger end; sometimes almost unmarked. Incubation is by female, about 12–14 days. **Young:** Both parents feed the nestlings. Young leave the nest about 10–13 days after hatching.

Spring migration is relatively late and spread over a long period; some northbound birds are still passing through southern states at beginning of June.

CONSERVATION STATUS Has declined as a breeding bird along parts of the Pacific coast and elsewhere. Over-all populations probably stable. Could be vulnerable to loss of habitat on breeding or wintering grounds.

HERMIT THRUSH *Catharus guttatus*

A more hardy bird than the other brown-backed thrushes, the Hermit migrates north earlier in spring and lingers later in fall than the others; it is the only one likely to be seen in winter in North America. If startled from the ground in the forest interior it often perches low and stares at the observer, flicking its wings nervously and slowly raising and lowering its tail. In summer, its clear, pensive song is heard in forests of the mountains and the north.

HABITAT *Conifer or mixed woods, forest floor; in winter, woods, thickets, parks.* Breeding habitats vary in different regions; included are spruce woods, sphagnum bogs, dry pine woods, second growth in burns with standing dead trees, thickly wooded canyons, mountain forests of spruce and fir. In migration and winter, found in any kind of woodland.

FEEDING **Diet:** *Mostly insects and berries.* Feeds on a variety of insects, including beetles, ants, caterpillars, true bugs, grasshoppers, crickets; also spiders, earthworms, rarely small salamanders. Also eats many berries, especially in winter; diet includes elder-

Hermit Thrush

berries, pokeberries, serviceberries, grapes, mistletoe berries, many others. **Behavior:** Does much foraging on ground, picking up insects from leaf litter or soil; also feeds up in shrubs and trees, often hovering momentarily while grabbing an insect or berry.

NESTING Male defends nesting territory by singing, especially in morning and evening. **Nest:** Site for nest varies with region. To the east and north, often on the ground, in a natural hollow on the side of a hummock and well hidden by overhanging branches or surrounding low vegetation. To the west, usually in a tree, especially a conifer, 3–12 feet above the ground. Nest (built by female alone) is a bulky, well-made open cup of moss, weeds, twigs, bark strips, ferns, lined with softer materials such as pine needles, rootlets, and plant fibers. **Eggs:** 4, sometimes 3–5, rarely 6. Pale blue or greenish blue, occasionally flecked with brown or black. Incubation is by female, about 12 days. **Young:** Both parents feed nestlings. Young are ready to fly at about 12 days. Usually 1–2 broods per year, perhaps sometimes 3 in south.

MIGRATION Migrates early in spring and late in fall; very little overlap in timing of migration with the other brown thrushes. Probably migrates mostly at night.

CONSERVATION STATUS Numbers seem to be holding up well. Winters farther north than other brown thrushes, less dependent on tropical forest for wintering.

GENUS *Hylocichla*

WOOD THRUSH *Hylocichla mustelina*

Seemingly not as shy as the other brown thrushes, not as bold as the Robin, the Wood Thrush seems intermediate between those two related groups. It sometimes

nests in suburbs and city parks, and it is still common in many eastern woodlands, where its flutelike songs add music to summer mornings. However, numbers of Wood Thrushes have declined seriously in recent decades, focusing the attention of conservationists on the problems facing our migratory birds.

HABITAT *Mainly deciduous woodlands.* Breeds in the understory of woodlands, mostly deciduous but sometimes mixed, in areas with tall trees. More numerous in damp forest and near streams than in drier woods; will nest in suburban areas where there are enough large trees. In migration, found in various kinds of woodland. Winters in understory of lowland tropical forest.

Wood Thrush

FEEDING **Diet:** *Mostly insects and berries.* Feeds on many insects, especially in breeding season, including beetles, caterpillars, ants, crickets, moths; also spiders, earthworms, and snails. Berries and small fruits are eaten at all seasons. Young are fed mostly insects but also some berries. **Behavior:** Forages mostly on ground, usually in forest undergrowth but occasionally on open lawns. Will use its bill to flip leaf litter aside as it seeks insects. Feeds on berries up in shrubs and trees.

NESTING Male arrives first on breeding grounds, establishes territory, and defends it by singing. Often reacts aggressively to other thrushes in territory, such as Robin or Veery. In courtship, male may chase female in fast circular flights among the trees. **Nest:** Placed in vertical fork of tree (usually deciduous) or saddled on horizontal branch, usually about 10–15 feet above the ground, sometimes lower, rarely as high as 50 feet. Nest (built by female) is rather like Robin's nest, an open cup of grass, leaves, moss, weeds, bark strips, mixed with mud; has lining of soft material such as rootlets. Often adds pieces of white paper or other trash to nest. **Eggs:** Usually 3–4. Pale greenish blue, unmarked. Incubation is by female only, 13–14 days. **Young:** Both parents feed nestlings. Young leave the nest about 12 days after hatching. 1–2 broods per year.

MIGRATION Migrates mostly at night. Many migrate across Gulf of Mexico in spring and fall.

CONSERVATION STATUS Numbers have declined seriously in recent decades. Cowbirds lay many eggs in their nests, so the thrushes often raise mainly cowbirds, with few young of their own. As forests are cut into smaller fragments, it apparently becomes easier for cowbirds to penetrate these small woodlots and find more of the thrush nests. The Wood Thrush is probably also losing wintering habitat in the tropics.

ROBINS AND LARGE THRUSHES — GENUS *Turdus*

A globe-trotting naturalist will find birds that act just like American Robins running on lawns in many parts of the world: Song Thrush in London, Rufous-bellied Thrush in Buenos Aires, Olive Thrush in Nairobi. All are members of this genus, which includes more than 60 species found almost worldwide. Our familiar American Robin originally was named after the European Robin, a much smaller thrush that is not closely related, simply because both had orange chest feathers.

EYEBROWED THRUSH *Turdus obscurus*

This Asian thrush is similar to our American Robin in shape and colors, but it is somewhat smaller with a pronounced pale eyebrow. It occurs as a rare migrant in the western Aleutian Islands, mostly in spring, and has also turned up on the Pribilofs, St. Lawrence Island, and the Alaskan mainland.

DUSKY THRUSH *Turdus naumanni*

A relative of the American Robin, the Dusky Thrush is a long-distance migrant in Asia, and it has strayed to Alaska several times. Although most records there are for the outer islands, it has also occurred twice in far southeastern Alaska, and one once spent the winter eating berries in a suburb of Vancouver, British Columbia.

FIELDFARE *Turdus pilaris*

This big robinlike thrush is common in Europe and parts of northern Asia, nesting in open woods and foraging on the ground in meadows and fields. Capable of long flights, the Fieldfare colonized southern Greenland in 1937, following a strong gale across the North Atlantic. Strays sometimes turn up in eastern Canada and the northeastern United States, and there are some Alaska records as well.

REDWING *Turdus iliacus*

Inhabiting open woods and fields across Europe and northern Asia, this medium-sized thrush occurs regularly as close to our area as Iceland. Contrary to what its name might suggest, the red in its wing is only on the underside; on the perched bird, it shows up only as a rust color along the flanks. The Redwing has strayed to northeastern North America several times, mostly in winter.

CLAY-COLORED ROBIN *Turdus grayi*

From eastern Mexico to northern Colombia, this plain gray-brown thrush is very common in lowland habitats, including parks and gardens. In recent years it has become a fairly frequent visitor to southernmost Texas, especially in winter, and it has even nested there.

WHITE-THROATED ROBIN *Turdus assimilis*

This shy forest robin lives in tropical mountains as far north as northern Mexico. Exceptionally harsh winter weather may sometimes drive it into the lowlands; twice during such conditions, single White-throated Robins have been found in extreme southern Texas.

RUFOUS-BACKED ROBIN *Turdus rufopalliatus*

This Mexican specialty is similar to our American Robin in appearance, but it is much more elusive, hiding in woods or dense thickets. First found in our area in 1960, it recently has become almost an annual visitor. Practically every winter, one or two are found somewhere in southern Arizona; strays also have reached Texas, New Mexico, and California.

AMERICAN ROBIN *Turdus migratorius*

A very familiar bird over most of North America, running and hopping on lawns with upright stance, often nesting on porches and windowsills. The Robin's rich caroling is among the earliest bird songs heard at dawn in spring and summer, often beginning just before first light. In fall and winter, robins may gather by the hundreds in roaming flocks, concentrating at sources of food.

HABITAT *Cities, towns, lawns, farmland, forests; in winter, berry-bearing trees.* Over most of continent, summers wherever there are trees for nest sites and mud for nest material. In arid southwest, summers mainly in coniferous forest in mountains, rarely in well-watered lowland suburbs. In winter, flocks gather in wooded areas where trees or shrubs have good crops of berries.

FEEDING **Diet:** *Mostly insects, berries, earthworms.* In early summer, insects make up majority of diet; also feeds on many earthworms, snails, spiders, other invertebrates. Feeds heavily on fruit, especially in winter (fruit accounts for perhaps 60 percent of diet year-round); mainly wild berries, also some cultivated fruits. Young are fed mostly on insects and earthworms. **Behavior:** Does much foraging on the ground, running and pausing on open lawns; apparently locates earthworms by sight (not, as had been suggested, by hearing them move underground). When not nesting, usually forages in flocks.

NESTING Males arrive before females on nesting grounds and defend territories by singing, sometimes by fighting. In early stages of courtship, female may be actively pursued by one or several males. **Nest:** Female does most of nest building with some help from male. Site is on horizontal branch of tree or shrub, usually 5–25 feet above ground, rarely on ground or up to 70 feet high; also nests on ledges of houses, barns, bridges. Nest is a cup of grasses, twigs, debris, worked into solid foundation of mud, lined with fine grasses and plant fibers. **Eggs:** Usually 4, sometimes 3–7. Pale blue or "robin's-egg blue." Incubation by female, 12–14 days. **Young:** Both parents feed young, though female does more. Parents very aggressive in defense of nest. Young leave the nest about 14–16 days after hatching. Male may tend the fledged young while female begins second nesting attempt. Two broods per season, sometimes three.

MIGRATION Migrates in flocks, often by day. Although some robins winter as far north as Canada, they are in localized concentrations then. Flocks break up before the nesting season; a northerner's "first robin of spring" may be a bird that has wintered only a few miles away, not one that has just arrived from southern climates. To the south, winter range is highly variable from year to year, depending on local food supplies.

American Robin

GENUS *Ixoreus*

VARIED THRUSH *Ixoreus naevius*

The haunting songs of the Varied Thrush echo through the dense humid forests of the Pacific Northwest. Long minor-key whistles repeated after deliberate pauses, they seem like sounds without a source; only a careful searcher will find the bird itself. Although it looks superficially like a robin, the Varied Thrush is far more elusive, usually feeding on the ground among dense thickets. Typical of the far west, it sometimes surprises birders by straying all the way to the Atlantic coast in winter.

HABITAT *Thick, wet forest, conifers; in winter, woods, ravines, thickets.* Breeds in coniferous forest of various types, but most common in dense, wet forest near the coast, in areas of fir, hemlock, and spruce with dense understory. In migration and winter favors coniferous woods but also occurs in undergrowth of other woods, especially near streams.

FEEDING **Diet:** *Mostly insects and berries.* Feeds on many insects, especially in summer, including beetles, ants, caterpillars, crickets; also eats many millipedes, sowbugs, snails, earthworms, spiders, other invertebrates. Berries and wild fruits make up majority of winter diet, also some seeds and acorns. **Behavior:** Does much foraging on the ground, usually under dense cover but sometimes on open lawns; may use its bill to toss leaf litter aside as it searches for insects. Feeds on berries either in trees and shrubs or after they fall to ground.

NESTING Male sings in spring to defend territory, singing most frequently at dawn and dusk and

Varied Thrush

after a rain. **Nest:** Usually placed in conifer, at base of branches against trunk, 5–15 feet above the ground. Sites vary: Occasionally much higher; especially in far north, may nest very low in deciduous thickets or on the ground. Nest (probably built by female) is a bulky open cup of twigs, moss, leaves, and bark fibers, lined with softer materials such as grass and rootlets. **Eggs:** 3–4, sometimes 2–5. Pale blue, lightly dotted with brown. Incubation is by female, probably about 2 weeks. **Young:** Both parents feed nestlings. Development of young and age at which they leave the nest are not well known. Probably two broods per year.

MIGRATION Migrates relatively late in fall and early in spring. Numbers present in southern wintering areas quite variable from year to year. A few stray far to the east every year in fall and winter, some reaching New England.

CONSERVATION STATUS Could be vulnerable to loss of habitat through cutting of northwestern forests. Currently still common.

GENUS *Ridgwayia*

AZTEC THRUSH *Ridgwayia pinicola*

An uncommon resident of mountain pine forests of Mexico. Quiet and shy, it is easily overlooked despite its striking pattern. Aztec Thrush was never found in our area until the late 1970s, but in recent years one or two have shown up almost annually in mountains near the Mexican border, especially in late summer in southeastern Arizona.

BABBLERS (subfamily Timaliinae)

Well over 200 species belong to this group, all but one of them restricted to the Old World, mainly in tropical areas. They tend to be rather short-winged birds that seldom fly long distances, but beyond that, they are quite varied. Some live in noisy flocks in open country or in forest undergrowth; some colorful types travel with mixed flocks of small birds in mountain forests; some live in pairs and hide in dense cover, where their presence is revealed by their distinctive voices. Our one species seems to fit in with the latter type.

WRENTIT   *Chamaea fasciata*

In the chaparral, the dense low brush that grows along the Pacific seaboard, Wrentits are often heard and seldom seen. Pairs of these long-tailed little birds move about actively in the depths of the thickets, rarely perching in the open or flying across small clearings. They are remarkably sedentary; a bird may spend its entire adult life in an area of just a couple of acres.

HABITAT   *Chaparral, brush, parks, garden shrubs.* Within its range, the Wrentit inhabits most kinds of dense low growth. Most common in chaparral, thickets of poison-oak, and coastal sage scrub; also lives in streamside thickets and in shrubby areas in suburbs and city parks. Extends very locally to edge of desert.

FEEDING   **Diet:** *Mostly insects and berries.* Feeds heavily on insects, especially in spring and summer, including ants, small wasps, caterpillars, beetles, scale insects, leafhoppers, and others, plus spiders. Eats many berries, especially in fall and winter, including those of poison-oak. Will come to bird feeders for bread crumbs or other soft items, and takes sugar-water from hummingbird feeders. **Behavior:** Forages actively in dense low growth, gleaning insects from twigs, sometimes hanging upside down to examine foliage. Sometimes hovers briefly while taking an item. Will hold a large insect with one foot while breaking off the wings.

Wrentit

NESTING   May mate for life. Pairs remain together on nesting territory at all seasons. **Nest:** Well hidden by foliage in a dense low shrub, usually 1–4 feet above the ground, rarely above 10 feet in small tree. Firmly lashed into place, attached to clusters of twigs or built in fork of branch. Nest (built by both sexes) is a neatly constructed, compact cup, typically made of strips of bark and spider webs, lined with fine plant fibers and sometimes animal hair. Outside of nest may be decorated with bits of lichen. **Eggs:** 4, sometimes 3–5. Pale greenish blue, unmarked. Incubation is by both parents, about 16 days. Female reportedly incubates at night, both sexes taking turns during the day. **Young:** Both parents feed nestlings. Young leave the nest about 15–16 days after hatching, are tended by parents for another 2–3 weeks.

MIGRATION   Permanent resident and very sedentary, seldom wandering away from breeding areas; rarely, a few may wander to higher elevations in late summer.

CONSERVATION STATUS   Has declined in some areas with increasing development of coastal regions. Still fairly widespread and common.

MOCKINGBIRDS AND THRASHERS (Family Mimidae)

The song of the Mockingbird is famous, but all members of this family have noteworthy voices. Some of their songs include artful imitations, some are richly melodious, and others are discordant or simply bizarre.

Mockingbirds, catbirds, and thrashers (often called "mimic thrushes" or "mimids" for short) make up a family of about 34 species, found only in the New World. All are fairly large songbirds with slim bodies, rather long tails, and short wings. All have strong legs, and most of them spend much time on the ground. Most have fairly heavy bills.

In general, the mimids are solitary birds; they may be seen in pairs or family groups, but seldom in flocks. Some of the larger species may live more than 12 years in the wild.

Feeding   Insects and berries are both important in the diet of most mimids. The summer diet usually leans heavily toward insects, while more berries are eaten in fall and winter. In addition to insects, some species will eat spiders, snails, earthworms, small lizards, even small fish. Some will also eat seeds and nuts, and they will probably take a variety of other foods (Gray Catbirds, for example, will try almost anything at a bird feeder).

Although berries are generally taken in shrubs and trees, the birds often do much of their foraging while walking or running on the ground. The larger species may dig in the soil or toss aside leaf litter as they search for food.

Nesting   Nest sites chosen are usually in dense low shrubs (or in cactus), only a few feet above the ground. Some tropical species may nest on the ground or in cavities in tree trunks. The bulky, bowl-shaped nests are built of twigs and other coarse plant material, and they are often very well protected by surrounding dense or thorny branches. The eggs (usually 3–5 per clutch) are typically pale blue or blue-green, with or without brown spots; incubation may be by both parents or by the female only. In several of the mimids, incubation begins before the last egg is laid, so the eggs may not all hatch on the same day. Both parents help to feed the young.

Displays   The songs of the males apparently are important both in defending the nesting territory and in attracting a mate. Courtship displays vary among species. The Mockingbird's habit of leaping in the air while singing is apparently a display to attract females, since unmated males do it far more often. Male catbirds and thrashers often posture in front of females. In courtship, either member of a pair may pick up a leaf or stick and present it to the other bird, or the male may feed the female.

GENUS *Dumetella*

GRAY CATBIRD   *Dumetella carolinensis*

Rather plain but with lots of personality, the Gray Catbird often hides in the shrubbery, making an odd variety of musical and harsh sounds—including the catlike mewing responsible for its name. At other times it moves about boldly in the open, jerking its long tail expressively. Most catbirds winter in the southern United States or the tropics, but a few linger far to the north if they have access to a reliable source of berries or a well-stocked bird feeder.

HABITAT   *Undergrowth, brush, thorn scrub, suburban gardens.* At all seasons, favors dense low growth. Most common in leafy thickets along the edges of woods and streams, shrubby swamps, overgrown brushy fields, and hedges in gardens. Avoids unbroken forest and coniferous woods.

FEEDING   **Diet:** *Mostly insects and berries.* Especially in early summer, eats many beetles, ants, caterpillars, grasshoppers, crickets, true bugs, and other insects, as well as spiders and millipedes. Nestlings are fed almost entirely on insects. More than half the annual diet of adults may be vegetable matter, especially in fall and winter, when they eat many kinds of wild berries and some cultivated fruit. Rarely catches small fish. At feeders, will eat a bizarre assortment of items including doughnuts, cheese, boiled potato, and corn flakes. **Behavior:** Does much foraging on ground, flipping leaves aside with bill as it seeks insects. Feeds on berries up in shrubs and trees.

Gray Catbird

NESTING   Early in breeding season, male sings constantly in morning and evening, sometimes at night. Courtship may involve male chasing female, posturing and bowing with wings drooped and tail raised; male may face away from female to show off patch of chestnut under tail. When Brown-headed Cowbirds lay eggs in nests of this species, the cowbird eggs are usually punctured and ejected by the adult catbirds. **Nest:** Placed in dense shrubs, thickets, brier tangles, or low trees, usually 3–10 feet above the ground. Nest (built mostly by female) is a large bulky cup of twigs, weeds, grass, leaves, and sometimes pieces of trash, lined with rootlets and other fine materials. **Eggs:** 3–4, sometimes 2–5, rarely 1–6. Greenish blue, rarely with some red spots. Incubation is by female only, about 12–14 days. **Young:** Both parents feed the nestlings. Young leave the nest about 10–11 days after hatching. Two broods per year.

MIGRATION   Apparently migrates mostly at night. Birds breeding in the northwest seem to migrate east before turning south in fall, since they are rarely seen in the southwest.

CONSERVATION STATUS   In recent years, populations declining in some areas, mainly in southeast.

GENUS *Melanotis*

BLUE MOCKINGBIRD   *Melanotis caerulescens*

Only distantly related to our Northern Mockingbird, this slaty blue Mexican specialty is an elusive skulker of dense thickets. It has strayed north very rarely into southern Arizona, where some individuals have been known to linger for several months.

MOCKINGBIRDS — GENUS *Mimus*

This group includes about 10 species, all mostly pale gray with white markings in the wings or tail. Most kinds are found in semi-open country of South America or the Caribbean. Our representative from this genus is most common in the Deep South, but it is a "Northern" Mockingbird in comparison with the others.

NORTHERN MOCKINGBIRD   *Mimus polyglottos*

This bird's famous song, with its varied repetitions and artful imitations, is heard all day during nesting season (and often all night as well). Very common in towns and cities, especially in southern areas, the Mockingbird often seeks insects on open lawns. When running in the open it may stop every few feet and partly spread its wings, flashing the white wing patches. Mockingbirds are bold in defense of their nests, attacking cats and even humans that venture too close.

HABITAT   *Towns, farms, roadsides, thickets, brushy areas.* Favors areas with dense low shrubs and open ground, either short grass or open soil, thus often common around

suburban hedges and lawns. Also in many kinds of second growth, woodland edges, farmland. In west, often very numerous in desert thickets or streamsides in canyons.

FEEDING   **Diet:** *Mostly insects and berries.* Annual diet is about half insects and other arthropods, half berries and fruits. Feeds heavily on insects in late spring and summer, especially beetles, grasshoppers, caterpillars, ants, wasps, also many others. Also eats spiders, snails, sowbugs, earthworms, and rarely crayfish and small lizards. Fall and winter diet leans heavily to berries and wild fruits, sometimes a few cultivated fruits. **Behavior:** Captures insects mostly while walking and running on ground. Also watches from low perch and flies down to capture items on ground below.

Northern Mockingbird

Perches in shrubs and trees to eat berries.

NESTING   Nesting begins early, by late winter in southern areas. Male sings to defend territory and attract a mate, often leaping a few feet in the air and flapping his wings while singing. Early stage of courtship involves male and female chasing each other rapidly around territory. **Nest:** Placed in a dense shrub or tree, usually 3–10 feet above the ground, sometimes lower or higher (rarely up to 60 feet). Nest has bulky foundation of twigs supporting open cup of weeds, grass, leaves, lined with fine material such as rootlets, moss, animal hair, plant down. Male builds most of foundation, female adds most of lining. **Eggs:** 3–4, sometimes 2–6. Variably greenish to bluish gray, with blotches of brown usually concentrated at larger end. Incubation is by female, 12–13 days. **Young:** Both parents feed the nestlings. Young leave the nest about 12 days after hatching, not able to fly well for about another week. 2–3 broods per year.

MIGRATION   Migration poorly understood; some move southward in fall, at least short distances, but some remain through winter at northern limits of range.

CONSERVATION STATUS   This species was often captured for sale as a pet from the late 1700s to the early 1900s, and probably as a result it became scarce along much of the northern edge of its range. After the cagebird trade was stopped, the Mockingbird again became common in many areas. During recent decades it has expanded its range north, especially in the northeast; its success there may have been partly due to widespread planting of multiflora rose, a source of favorite berries and good nest sites.

BAHAMA MOCKINGBIRD   *Mimus gundlachii*

A localized resident of the Bahamas and a few other islands in the western Caribbean, this hefty mockingbird has strayed to southern Florida more than a dozen times. One male returned for several springs to Key West, where it may have interbred with local Northern Mockingbirds.

GENUS *Oreoscoptes*

SAGE THRASHER   *Oreoscoptes montanus*

This well-named bird is seldom found in summer away from stands of sagebrush. Smaller and shorter billed than most thrashers, it may suggest a washed-out robin.

During the breeding season, its melodious song can be heard incessantly at dawn on the sagebrush flats. The Sage Thrasher is sometimes elusive; if pursued closely it may seem to disappear, only to pop up on a bush top a hundred yards away.

HABITAT *Sagebrush, brushy slopes, mesas; in winter, also deserts.* Breeds almost entirely in sagebrush areas, either in wide-open flats or where sagelands meet open pinyon-juniper woods. Rarely breeds in other brushy habitats. More widespread in migration and winter, occurring in grassland with scattered shrubs, desert, pinyon-juniper woods, and other semi-open areas.

FEEDING **Diet:** *Mostly insects and berries.* Especially in summer, feeds on grasshoppers, beetles, caterpillars, true bugs, wasps, and other insects, plus some spiders. Berries and wild fruits are eaten especially in winter, but the birds may concentrate at any season to feed on gooseberries, wild currants, mistletoe berries, juniper berries, and others, sometimes including cultivated fruits. **Behavior:** Does much of its foraging on the ground, running about rapidly on open ground in scrubby territory. Perches in shrubs and low trees to feed on berries.

Sage Thrasher

NESTING Male sings to defend breeding territory. May also perform flight display, singing while flying in low zigzag over brush, then alighting and holding the wings raised and fluttering for a moment. **Nest:** Site is in sagebrush or other low bush such as greasewood, saltbush, or rabbitbrush, sometimes low in juniper or on ground. Nest (thought to be built by both sexes) is a bulky cup of twigs, lined with fine rootlets, grass, and animal hair. **Eggs:** 3–5, sometimes more or fewer. Deep greenish blue with brown spots concentrated at larger end. Incubation is by both parents, about 13–17 days. Brown-headed Cowbirds sometimes lay eggs in nest, but cowbird eggs are rejected and tossed out by the adult thrashers. **Young:** Both parents feed the nestlings. Young leave nest about 11–14 days after hatching. Adults may raise two broods per year.

MIGRATION Somewhat irregular in its migrations and its wintering range, perhaps concentrating where there are good wild crops of berries. Strays sometimes wander to Atlantic coast, mainly in fall.

CONSERVATION STATUS Has declined in a number of areas with clearing of sagebrush flats. Still common in appropriate habitat.

TYPICAL THRASHERS — GENUS *Toxostoma*

The 10 members of this genus are almost entirely restricted to the United States and Mexico, with only the Brown Thrasher reaching Canada and the West Indies. Several species are common in our southwest. All are some shade of brown or gray-brown, and some are spotted below. The common name of the group comes from their habit of "thrashing" the ground with their bills, digging up soil or tossing leaf litter aside as they search for food.

BROWN THRASHER *Toxostoma rufum*

The big, foxy red Brown Thrasher is a familiar bird over much of the east. Sometimes it forages boldly on open lawns; more often it scoots into dense cover at any disturbance, hiding among the brier tangles and making loud crackling call notes. Although the species spends most of its time close to the ground, the male Brown Thrasher sometimes will deliver its rich, melodious song of doubled phrases from the top of a tall tree.

HABITAT   *Thickets, brush, shrubbery, thorn scrub.* Breeds in areas of dense low growth, especially thickets around edges of deciduous or mixed woods, shrubby edges of swamps, or undergrowth in open pine woods; also in suburban neighborhoods with many shrubs and hedges. Winters in similar areas or in any habitat with dense brush.

FEEDING   **Diet:** *Varied, includes insects, berries, nuts.* More than half of diet is insects, including beetles, caterpillars, true bugs, grasshoppers, cicadas, and many others; also eats spiders, sowbugs, earthworms, snails, crayfish, and sometimes lizards and frogs. Berries and small fruits also very important in diet, especially in fall and winter, and eats many nuts and seeds, particularly acorns. **Behavior:** Does much foraging on the ground, using its bill to flip dead leaves aside or dig in the soil as it rummages for insects. Perches in shrubs and trees to eat berries. Will crack open acorns by pounding them with its bill.

NESTING   Male defends territory by singing loudly from prominent perches. In courtship, male approaches female, singing softly; either bird may pick up leaves or sticks and present them to the other bird. **Nest:** Usually placed 2–7 feet above the ground in a dense shrub, vine tangle, or low tree. Sometimes on the ground under dense cover, or as high as 12 feet up. Nest (built by both sexes) is a bulky structure with foundation of sticks supporting a loose cup of twigs, leaves, weeds, grass, bark fibers, lined with finer materials such as grass or rootlets. **Eggs:** 4, sometimes 3–5, rarely 2–6. Pale blue to bluish white, finely dotted with reddish brown. Incubation is by both parents, about 11–14 days. **Young:** Both parents feed nestlings. Young leave nest about 9–13 days after hatching. Two broods per year, perhaps sometimes three.

MIGRATION   Permanent resident in parts of south; mostly migratory in north, but small numbers may remain far north around feeders or in thickets with many berries. Strays may appear well west of normal range during fall, winter, and spring.

CONSERVATION STATUS   Declining numbers have been noted in some regions; the species remains widespread and common in most areas.

Brown Thrasher

LONG-BILLED THRASHER   *Toxostoma longirostre*

This tropical relative of the Brown Thrasher enters our area only in southern Texas. There it is a common permanent resident of native woodland and thickets, foraging on the ground under dense cover, often singing from a hidden position within the brush. When Brown Thrashers move into southern Texas in winter, the two species of thrashers maintain separate wintering territories.

HABITAT   *Woodland undergrowth, mesquites.* In Texas, found in the brushy undergrowth of native woodlands of hackberry, acacia, ebony, and other trees, especially near water, and in dense thickets of mesquite and other thorny shrubs. In Mexico, lives in various kinds of woodland and semi-open areas.

FEEDING   Diet: *Mostly insects and berries.* Diet not known in detail, but probably similar to that of Brown Thrasher. Known to eat many insects, including beetles, ants, true bugs, moths, grasshoppers, and ant lions; also spiders and centipedes, probably small vertebrates such as frogs and lizards. Also eats many berries and wild fruits and probably some seeds. **Behavior:** Does much foraging on the ground, using its long bill to flip dead leaves aside as it rummages in the leaf litter for insects; also will use its bill to dig in soil within an inch of the surface. Perches in shrubs and trees to eat berries.

NESTING   Pairs may remain together at all seasons, at least in some cases. **Nest:** Placed in dense and often spiny plants such as shrubby mesquite, acacia, prickly-pear, or yucca, usually 4–10 feet above the ground. Site is usually well shaded in undergrowth of woods and in an almost impenetrable position. Nest (probably built by both sexes) is a bulky and loosely constructed open cup of sticks, twigs, leaves, weeds, grass, and other material, lined with softer matter such as rootlets and fine grass. **Eggs:** 3–4, sometimes 2–5. Pale blue to bluish white, finely dotted with reddish brown. Incubation is by both parents, about 13–14 days. **Young:** Both parents feed the nestlings. Young leave the nest about 12–14 days after hatching. Probably two broods per year.

MIGRATION   Mostly a permanent resident. Strays have wandered north into western Texas and even Colorado.

CONSERVATION STATUS   Undoubtedly declined in southern Texas with initial clearing of brushland and river woods for agriculture. Still common in remaining habitat.

Long-billed Thrasher

BENDIRE'S THRASHER   *Toxostoma bendirei*

Bendire's Thrasher

One of the last resident birds in the southwest to be discovered, this thrasher was overlooked until the 1870s, when Charles Bendire noticed that it was different from the common Curve-billed Thrasher. The bird is still easily overlooked as it runs about on the desert floor or flies from bush to bush, but its sweet, melodious song is quite distinctive. With its relatively small bill, it does less digging in the soil than other desert thrashers.

HABITAT   *Desert, farmland; cholla, thorny bushes.* Lives in various kinds of dry, semi-open habitats. Perhaps most common in Sonoran desert with variety of shrubs and cholla cactus and with some understory of grass. Also found where dense hedges or shrubs are next to farmland and in grassland with scattered shrubs and yuccas.

FEEDING   Diet: *Mostly insects, some seeds and berries.* Feeds mainly on insects, especially ants, termites, beetles, ant lions, grasshoppers, and others; also spiders. Also feeds on seeds of grasses and other plants, various berries, and cactus fruits, including

those of giant saguaro. **Behavior:** Forages mostly on the ground. Picks up insects from the surface or uses its bill to scratch or dig slightly in the soil or to turn over rocks or other items. Has a small bill and does not dig as effectively as most thrashers.

NESTING   Male sings in spring and summer to defend nesting territory. **Nest:** Usually placed in dense low shrub, tree, or cactus, commonly in cholla, yucca, mesquite, acacia, desert hackberry, also in other low growth, usually 3–10 feet above the ground. Nest is typically a bit smaller, more compact, and made of finer materials than the nests of most thrashers; usually has outer layer of twigs, inner layer of soft material such as grass, rootlets, feathers, animal hair. **Eggs:** Usually 3, sometimes 4, rarely 5. Whitish to pale gray-green, blotched with brown and buff. Incubation period and role of the parents in incubation are poorly known. **Young:** Both parents feed the nestlings. Young leave nest about 12 days after hatching. Two broods per year, perhaps rarely three.

MIGRATION   Migratory in northern part of range, and even in southern Arizona is partly migratory, being numerous mostly from February to September.

CONSERVATION STATUS   Has declined in a few areas recently because of development, but overall population is holding up well.

CURVE-BILLED THRASHER   *Toxostoma curvirostre*

Of the various thrashers in the southwestern deserts, the Curve-bill is the most familiar and most often seen. It makes itself more conspicuous than the rest, dashing about in the open, calling a loud *whit-wheet!* from the tops of mesquites. This thrasher readily moves into suburbs and cities in the southwest as long as some native vegetation is planted there—especially cholla cactus, its top choice for nest sites.

HABITAT   *Deserts, arid brush.* Lives in Sonoran desert (with its varied vegetation) or in dry brushy country, mainly in lowlands. Avoids extreme deserts with sparse plant life. Often in suburban neighborhoods, especially where cholla cactus grows. In southern Texas, lives in chaparral with prickly-pear cactus. Sometimes on open grassland around stands of cholla.

FEEDING   **Diet:** *Mostly insects and berries.* Feeds on a wide variety of insects and their larvae, including beetles, ants, grasshoppers, wasps, and many others; also spiders, centipedes, snails, and sowbugs.

Curve-billed Thrasher

Also eats many berries and feeds heavily on the fruits and seeds of cactus, including those of prickly-pear and saguaro. **Behavior:** Forages mostly on the ground, using its heavy curved bill to dig in the soil, to flip leaf litter aside, and to turn over small rocks and other items. When digging in hard dirt, braces its tail against the ground and pounds straight down with heavy blows of bill.

NESTING   Pair may remain together all year on permanent territory. Especially in spring, male defends territory by singing. In courtship, male may follow female, giving a soft song. **Nest:** Most commonly placed in fork of cholla cactus, 3–5 feet above the ground. Sometimes in yucca, prickly-pear, or thorny shrub, or on top of mistletoe clump in shrub or low tree. May build on top of old Cactus Wren nest. May sometimes reuse same nest sites. Nest (probably built by both sexes) is bulky, loose cup of thorny twigs, lined with fine grasses, rootlets, feathers, animal hair. **Eggs:** 3, sometimes 2–4. Pale blue-green with tiny brown dots. Incubation is by both parents during the day, apparently only by female at night; incubation period 12–15 days. **Young:** Both parents feed young. If nest site is exposed to sun, female may spend much time shading the nestlings. Young leave nest about 14–18 days after hatching. Two broods per year, sometimes three.

MIGRATION Permanent resident. Rarely wanders out of range, mainly in fall and winter.

CONSERVATION STATUS Surveys suggest slight declines in Texas in recent decades. Farther west, still abundant.

CALIFORNIA THRASHER *Toxostoma redivivum*

Several kinds of dull gray-brown thrashers occur in the west, but this is the only one along the California coast. The bird's normal range is limited to California and a corner of Baja, but within that range it is quite common in the chaparral, even coming into brushy suburbs. It spends most of its time on the ground, walking and running with its tail often held high, stopping to dig in the dirt with its sickle-shaped bill.

California Thrasher

HABITAT *Chaparral, foothills, valley thickets, parks, gardens.* Within its range, found in practically any lowland habitat with dense low brush. Most common in chaparral, also occurs in streamside thickets and in suburban neighborhoods that have enough vegetation. Extends into edges of desert regions, and in chaparral in mountains up to about 6,000 feet.

FEEDING **Diet:** *Mostly insects and berries.* Feeds on a wide variety of insects, including ants, wasps, bees, beetles, caterpillars, and moths. Also eats some spiders and centipedes. Berries and small fruits are important in diet, and eats seeds, acorns, and other plant material. Will come to bird feeders for miscellaneous scraps. **Behavior:** Forages mostly on the ground, using its heavy curved bill to flip leaf litter aside and to dig in the soil.

NESTING Pairs may remain together on territory all year. Male sings to defend nesting territory, usually from top of shrub or tree; song often includes imitations of other birds. **Nest:** Placed in a dense shrub or extensive thickets, less than 10 feet above the ground, usually 2–4 feet up. Nest (built by both sexes) is a bulky open cup of sticks and twigs, lined with fine grass, weeds, rootlets, strips of bark, and other soft items. **Eggs:** 3–4, sometimes 2. Pale blue, evenly spotted with pale brown. Incubation is by both parents, about 14 days. **Young:** Both parents feed nestlings. Young leave the nest after about 12–14 days, are unable to fly well for several more days. Male may care for young from first brood while female begins laying second clutch. Two broods per year, perhaps sometimes three.

MIGRATION Strictly permanent resident, rarely wandering even a short distance from breeding areas.

CONSERVATION STATUS Has disappeared in many coastal areas with increasing urbanization, but still fairly widespread and common.

CRISSAL THRASHER *Toxostoma crissale*

This big dark thrasher of the desert regions manages to stay out of sight most of the time, hiding in thickets. At some seasons its presence is revealed mainly by its rolling call notes, heard especially at dawn and dusk. The observer who seeks it may find the Crissal Thrasher foraging on the ground under dense cover, using its long curved bill to dig in the desert soil. In spring, males move up to higher perches to sing their musical but disjointed song.

HABITAT *Dense brush along desert streams, mesquite thickets.* Habitat varies; in Sonoran desert found only in the densest mesquite thickets along washes, but in Chihuahuan desert it lives in sparse brush in open areas. Also occurs in dense chaparral among manzanita and other scrub in the southwestern mountains.

FEEDING **Diet:** *Mostly insects, some berries.* Feeds on a wide variety of insects, including beetles, grasshoppers, ants, and caterpillars; also spiders, centipedes, and other arthropods. Sometimes eats small lizards. Berries and small fruits make up an important minority of diet. **Behavior:** Forages almost entirely on the ground under dense brush; finds much of its food by digging in the soil or among debris with its heavy, curved bill. Perches in bushes to eat berries.

NESTING Pairs may remain together on territory at all seasons. Males sing in spring to defend nesting territory. When cowbirds lay eggs in the nest of this species, the adult thrashers generally throw the

Crissal Thrasher

cowbird eggs out of the nest immediately. **Nest:** Site is well concealed in dense low growth, often in mesquites but also in other shrubs such as willows, greasewood, saltbush, even exotic saltcedar, usually 2–8 feet above the ground. Nest (built by both parents) is a bulky open cup of thorny twigs, lined with softer materials such as fine grass, weeds, bark fibers, and sometimes feathers. **Eggs:** 2–3, sometimes 4. Blue-green; unmarked, unlike those of other thrashers. Incubation is by both parents, about 14 days. **Young:** Both parents feed nestlings. Young leave nest about 11–13 days after hatching, are unable to fly well for several more days. Two broods per year.

MIGRATION Mostly a permanent resident, but a few may appear in fall and winter away from breeding areas.

LE CONTE'S THRASHER *Toxostoma lecontei*

This wraith of the arid saltbush flats is as pale as desert sand. It seldom flies unless closely pressed, instead running about with great speed on the open ground, its tail cocked up above its back. For many years after its discovery, Le Conte's Thrasher was considered a rare bird, because it lives in desert so barren and forbidding that few people thought to seek birds there.

HABITAT *Desert flats with sparse growth of saltbush.* Lives in more open habitats than other thrashers, on dry flats with only scattered low shrubs. Found especially in areas of sparse saltbush, also on creosote bush flats in some areas; mainly where there are a few slightly larger mesquites or cholla cactus.

FEEDING **Diet:** *Mostly insects.* Diet not known in detail, but feeds mainly on insects, including grasshoppers, ants, and beetles. Also eats spiders, centipedes, and other arthropods, and sometimes small lizards; eats a few berries and seeds. **Behavior:** Forages almost entirely on the ground, walking and running rapidly on bare open soil. Finds much of its food by digging in the soil with its bill.

NESTING May mate for life. Pairs remain together at all seasons on permanent territories. In courtship, male may present female with twig or insect. Male sings to defend

MOCKINGBIRDS AND THRASHERS

Le Conte's Thrasher

territory, beginning in midwinter; nesting may begin in February or even January, but lasts until June in some areas. **Nest:** Usually placed less than 5 feet above the ground. Low, dense cholla cactus favored as nest sites; will also nest in saltbush, mesquite, or other low shrubs. Nest (built by both sexes) is a bulky open cup of thorny twigs, lined with rootlets, leaves, plant fibers, sometimes with softer inner lining of plant down. **Eggs:** 3–4, sometimes 2. Pale greenish blue, lightly dotted with brown. Incubation is by both parents, about 15 days. **Young:** Both parents feed nestlings. Young leave nest about 13–17 days after hatching. Two broods per year, perhaps rarely three.

MIGRATION   Probably permanent resident, although it has been recorded in some parts of range only in breeding season.

CONSERVATION STATUS   Has disappeared from some areas where irrigation has converted desert to farmland. Still common in appropriate habitat.

ACCENTORS (Family Prunellidae)

This Old World family, which includes only about 13 species, has no close counterparts in the Americas. Accentors are rather secretive birds that spend much of their time on the ground, where they move with an odd shuffling walk or hop. They have fairly thin bills and feed mostly on insects, although they may take many seeds and berries in winter. All of the accentors are classified in the genus *Prunella*.

SIBERIAN ACCENTOR   *Prunella montanella*

This species has strayed to Alaska several times, not only to the islands of western Alaska but also to the interior and southeastern parts of the state; as an accidental visitor, it has occurred on the Pacific coast south to Washington.

WAGTAILS AND PIPITS (Family Motacillidae)

Naturalists in most parts of North America can expect to see only one member of this family, but worldwide there are about 60 species. Wagtails and pipits are songbirds adapted to living on the ground, mostly in open country. They walk and run along the ground, often pumping their tails up and down, as they search for insects and seeds.

Since they are often in open terrain where there are few raised song perches, the males of many wagtails and pipits sing in flight, circling or hovering above their nesting territories. All species are strong fliers, and many are long-distance migrants. Several species from Europe and Asia have gone off-course and appeared at various points in North America.

Most of the typical pipits are brown and streaky, colored for camouflage. Brighter colors are shown by the wagtails and by some African members of the family such as the Golden Pipit and the longclaws.

Feeding	Insects make up the great majority of the diet for most species. Other invertebrates may also be taken, such as spiders, earthworms, or snails; species that forage around water may eat small crustaceans or even tiny fish. Some species also eat many seeds and sometimes berries, especially in fall and winter. Most members of the family do all of their foraging while walking or running on the ground, sometimes making short flights to capture fleeing insects. A few of the pipits in the Old World will also forage while walking along horizontal limbs of trees.
Nesting	Typical nest sites are well hidden on the ground, often under an overhanging grass clump or in a crevice among rocks. The nest itself is usually a compact open cup of grass or weed stalks, lined with finer materials. Eggs usually have spots and streaks on a whitish ground color; incubation is typically by the female only among the pipits, by both parents among the wagtails. The young birds are cared for and fed by both parents.
Displays	Males of many species perform a flight song display, flying up and then circling or fluttering down while singing. Some species may remain airborne for many minutes at a time while singing repeatedly. In courtship displays on the ground, males often fluff up their feathers, spread their tails, droop their wings, and strut about near the females; species that have contrasting colors on the throat may point their bills up in the air, showing off these colors.

Wagtails — genus *Motacilla*

Wagtails are small birds that walk and run on the ground in open areas, wagging their long tails up and down. Several kinds are widespread in the Old World, but in our area they occur mostly as visitors to Alaska.

YELLOW WAGTAIL   *Motacilla flava*

This Eurasian species is common over much of western and northern Alaska in summer, nesting around scrub willow thickets on the tundra. If a birder intrudes on their nesting territory, a pair of Yellow Wagtails will often hover overhead, repeatedly calling in shrill voices.

   HABITAT   *Willow scrub on tundra, marshy country.* In Alaska, breeds on tundra, especially in areas with low thickets of dwarf willow or birch. In the Old World, various races of Yellow Wagtail are found in practically any kind of open country.

   FEEDING   **Diet:** *Mostly insects.* Diet in North America not known in detail. In Eurasia, feeds on a wide variety of insects including midges and other flies, beetles, aphids, and ants. Also eats spiders, plus a few small snails, worms, berries, and seeds. **Behavior:** Feeds on ground or along edge of very shallow water. Forages by walking and picking up items, by making quick dashes to grab active insects, or by flying up to catch insects in the air. Sometimes may pick insects from foliage while hovering.

   NESTING   Male may sing in flight to defend territory and attract a mate. In courtship on ground, male may crouch with drooped wings and tail, body feathers fluffed up, while he runs around female; also may hover over her with tail spread wide. **Nest:** Site is on ground, usually well hidden under low matted shrub or overhanging grass or tucked into side of sedge hummock. Nest (probably built by female only) is a cup of grass, leaves, weeds, moss, lichens, lined with softer material such as animal hair or feathers. **Eggs:** In Alaska, 4–5 eggs, sometimes 3–6. Whitish to buff, heavily dotted with brown. Incubation is by both parents (but female may do more), 11–13 days. **Young:** Both parents feed nestlings. Young leave the nest about 10–13 days after hatching, but often unable to fly for another 3–6 days.

MIGRATION   In Alaska, mostly arrives in late May and departs in August. Birds from Alaska probably winter mostly in the Australasian region.

CITRINE WAGTAIL   *Motacilla citreola*

A close relative of the Yellow Wagtail, this species has a more limited range. It nests mostly in western and central Russia and western China and winters mainly in India and Southeast Asia. Although its normal range is very far from our shores, wagtails are known to be capable of straying long distances; a single Citrine Wagtail once reached North America, appearing in Mississippi in midwinter.

GRAY WAGTAIL   *Motacilla cinerea*

The very long tail of this Eurasian bird is noticeable both in flight and on the ground. A rare spring visitor to western Alaskan islands, the Gray Wagtail favors the edges of small streams. It is often elusive and hard to approach.

WHITE WAGTAIL   *Motacilla alba*

One of the most common birds of open country across Europe and Asia, the White Wagtail enters North America only as a scarce and local summer resident of western Alaska. There it seems to favor the vicinity of artificial structures: most of the nests found in Alaska have been in abandoned fishing huts, old gold dredges, empty fuel tanks, or piles of debris on the beach. Birders are likely to spot this wagtail first as it flies past, giving a metallic call, trailing its long tail in undulating flight.

White Wagtail

HABITAT   *Rocky places, towns, rivers.* In Alaska, very localized in summer. Seldom on open tundra, usually around low sea cliffs, coastal villages, or shacks on beaches, sometimes on gravel flats of rivers well inland. In the Old World, found in almost any kind of open or semi-open terrain.

FEEDING   **Diet:** *Insects.* Diet in Alaska not known in detail. In Old World, eats mostly insects, including midges, crane flies, and other flies, beetles, mayflies, dragonfly larvae, caterpillars, and moths. Feeds on a variety of aquatic insect larvae and adults. Also eats some spiders, earthworms, tiny fish, and seeds. **Behavior:** Feeds on ground or along edge of water. Forages by walking and picking up items, by making quick dashes to grab active insects, or by flying up to catch insects in the air. Sometimes walks on floating vegetation or in shallow water.

NESTING   In courtship, male pursues female. On ground, male points bill up to show off throat pattern, runs in zigzags near female, postures with deep bowing, tail lowered and spread wide; may raise one wing over back. **Nest:** Natural sites are in crevices among rocks or cliffs; many in Alaska nest in artificial sites such as abandoned gold dredges, buildings, or empty oil drums, or under debris. Usually nests low. Nest (usually built by both sexes, but female may do more) is open cup of twigs, grass, rootlets, moss, lined with hair and feathers. **Eggs:** 5–7, sometimes 3–8. Whitish to gray, finely spotted with gray or brown. Incubation is by both parents (female does more), about 12–13 days. **Young:** Both parents feed nestlings. Young leave nest about 11–16 days after hatching, are tended by parents for up to another week.

MIGRATION   Those nesting in Alaska spend the winter mostly in Southeast Asia. Outside of Alaska, only an accidental stray in the New World.

CONSERVATION STATUS   Small population in Alaska is probably stable. Widespread and abundant in Eurasia.

BLACK-BACKED WAGTAIL   *Motacilla lugens*

A very close relative of the White Wagtail, breeding mainly along the coast of northeastern Asia and occurring as a rare visitor in Alaska. South of Alaska along our Pacific coast, it occurs surprisingly often as a casual stray—at least as frequently as the White Wagtail.

PIPITS — GENUS *Anthus*

Pipits are rather plain birds that walk on the ground in open country. Worldwide there are more than 30 species, nesting on six continents and even reaching islands on the edge of the Antarctic region. Only one pipit is widespread in North America, another is a specialty of the prairie heartland, and four more reach us from Asia.

TREE PIPIT   *Anthus trivialis*

Common across much of Europe and Asia, this species often perches in trees, although (like other pipits) it does most of its feeding on the ground. Single Tree Pipits have strayed to Cape Prince of Wales and St. Lawrence Island in western Alaska.

OLIVE-BACKED PIPIT   *Anthus hodgsoni*

Although it forages mostly on the ground like other pipits, this Asian species also regularly perches in bushes and trees. It is a rare migrant in western Alaska, mostly in the outer Aleutians. A lone stray, very far off course, was once found in western Nevada.

PECHORA PIPIT   *Anthus gustavi*

Nesting across northern Siberia and wintering mostly in the Philippines and Indonesia, the Pechora Pipit is a long-distance migrant that has strayed to Alaska at least a dozen times. It is even more elusive and harder to see than most pipits, hiding in dense grass and other low growth, flushing only at close range.

RED-THROATED PIPIT   *Anthus cervinus*

Widespread across northern Europe and Asia, this pipit enters North America as a nesting bird only in a very limited area of western Alaska. There it breeds mostly at the western end of the Seward Peninsula and on offshore islands such as St. Lawrence and Little Diomede. Surprisingly, a few Red-throated Pipits often show up along the California coast in fall. These lost migrants usually associate with flocks of American Pipits in open fields.

HABITAT *Tundra in summer; during migration, fields.* In Alaska, breeds on tundra, mostly in fairly dry rocky areas next to hummocky sedge meadows. Migrants elsewhere in North America have been mostly in short grass or plowed fields, occasionally at edge of water.

Red-throated Pipit

FEEDING **Diet:** *Mostly insects.* Diet in North America is not well known. In Eurasia, summer diet is mostly insects, including many midges, crane flies, mosquitoes, beetles, caterpillars, small bees, and moths. Also eats spiders, centipedes, small snails, and seeds of grasses and other plants. **Behavior:** Forages by walking on the ground, picking up items from ground or from low growth. Often probes with its bill among low vegetation. Large insects may be pounded on the ground before they are eaten.

NESTING To defend nesting territory, male performs flight-song: flies up, glides a short distance, then sails or parachutes down while singing. In courtship, male faces female, quivers wings and tail, and raises bill to show off red throat. **Nest:** Site is on ground, usually against side of hummock or partly sheltered by rock or low shrub. Male apparently begins nest by scraping small hollow in moss; female builds nest, with male bringing much of material. Nest is cup of grass, leaves, moss, lined with finer grass and sometimes with animal hair or feathers. **Eggs:** 5–6, sometimes 3–7. Pale gray to buff, finely spotted with brown and gray. Incubation is by female only, about 11–13 days. Male feeds female during incubation. **Young:** Both parents feed nestlings. Young leave nest about 11–15 days after hatching.

MIGRATION Most birds breeding in Alaska probably migrate south in Asia. Small but variable numbers (mostly immatures) go down Pacific coast in fall; in California, seen mostly in October.

AMERICAN PIPIT *Anthus rubescens*

Nesting in the far north and on mountaintops, American Pipits can be found throughout the continent during migration or winter. At those seasons they are usually in flocks, walking on shores or plowed fields, wagging their tails as they go. Often they are detected first as they fly over high, giving sharp *pi-pit* calls.

HABITAT *Tundra, alpine slopes; in migration and winter, plains, bare fields, shores.* Breeds on tundra, both in far north and in high mountains above treeline, in areas with very low growth such as sedges, grass, and dwarf willows. During migration and in winter found on flat open ground such as plowed fields, shortgrass prairie, mudflats, shores, river sandbars.

FEEDING **Diet:** *Mostly insects, also some seeds.* Insects make up great majority of summer diet; included are many flies, true bugs, beetles, caterpillars, and moths. Also eats some spiders, millipedes, ticks. Migrants along coast may eat tiny crustaceans and marine worms. Inland in fall and winter, seeds of grasses and weeds may make up close to half of diet. **Behavior:** Forages by walking on the ground, taking insects from the ground or from low plants. Sometimes forages while walking in very shallow water. Except in the breeding season, usually forages in flocks.

NESTING Male performs song-flight display to defend nesting territory and attract a mate. In display, male begins singing on ground, flies up (often to 100 feet or more), then glides or parachutes down again with wings fully opened, singing

American Pipit

all the way. **Nest:** Site is on ground in sheltered spot, usually protected under overhanging grass, small rock ledge, or piece of sod. Nest (built by female only) is a cup of grass, sedges, and weeds, lined with finer grass and sometimes with animal hair or feathers. **Eggs:** 4–6, sometimes 3–7. Whitish to pale buff, heavily spotted with brown and gray. Incubation is by female only, 13–16 days. Male feeds female during incubation period. **Young:** Both parents feed nestlings. Female broods young much of the time during first few days; male may bring food for her and for young. Young usually leave nest at about 14 days, are fed by parents for about another 2 weeks.

MIGRATION   Migrates in flocks, apparently traveling mostly by day.

CONSERVATION STATUS   Some analyses of Christmas Bird Counts have suggested declining numbers; however, species is still widespread and common.

SPRAGUE'S PIPIT *Anthus spragueii*

Sprague's Pipit

Audubon called this bird the "Missouri skylark" because he found it singing in the sky over the prairies along the upper Missouri River. Sprague's Pipit delivers its breathy flight-song while hovering high in the air, often for minutes at a time, over the northern Great Plains in summer. In winter, it becomes an elusive skulker in the short grass of dry prairies. Unlike the American Pipit, Sprague's never occurs in flocks. Even where it is common in winter, the birds flush singly from the grass, to circle high in the air before diving steeply to land again.

HABITAT   *Plains, shortgrass prairies.* Breeds in relatively dry grassland, especially native prairie, avoiding brushy areas and cultivated fields. Winters in similar shortgrass habitats including pastures and prairies and grassy patches within fields of crops such as alfalfa.

FEEDING   **Diet:** *Mostly insects, some seeds.* Diet not known in detail. Apparently eats mainly insects, especially in summer, including grasshoppers, crickets, various beetles, and moths. Also eats many small seeds of grasses and weeds, perhaps more in fall and winter. Young birds are fed almost entirely on insects. **Behavior:** Forages by walking on the ground, usually among fairly dense short grass, searching for insects and seeds. Forages alone, not in flocks.

NESTING   Male sings to defend nesting territory, spiraling up to 300 feet or even higher, then hovering and circling for several minutes while singing repeatedly. In some cases, a single song-flight may last half an hour or even longer. **Nest:** Site is on ground in grassy field, usually in a slight depression or tucked into the side of a clump of grass. Nest (probably built by female) is a solidly woven cup of dry grass stems, sometimes lined with finer grass. Often has grass arched over the top, with entrance at the side. **Eggs:** 4–5, rarely 3–6. Whitish, heavily spotted with maroon or purplish brown. Incubation is probably by female; incubation period not well known.

Adult does not fly to nest but lands several feet away and walks there. Incubating bird may not flush from nest until approached within a few feet. **Young:** Fed by female, possibly by male, but details not well known. May leave nest as early as 10–11 days after hatching, before able to fly well. Adults may raise two broods per year.

MIGRATION — Migrates relatively late in fall and early in spring.

CONSERVATION STATUS — Numbers have declined in much of range as breeding habitat has been converted to agricultural fields.

WAXWINGS (Family Bombycillidae)

Soft colors and soft voices are typical of the waxwings, gentle birds that feed on berries and small insects. There are only three species of waxwings in the world, and two of them are common in North America; the third is the Japanese Waxwing, found in eastern Asia, similar to our Bohemian Waxwing but more colorful, with a red band at the tip of its tail. All three species have similar habits. Members of this family are very sociable, gathering in large flocks when they are not nesting and often even nesting in small colonies. The name "waxwing" refers to waxy red tips on certain wing feathers of adults.

BOHEMIAN WAXWING *Bombycilla garrulus*

In summer in Alaska and western Canada, scattered Bohemian Waxwings may be seen perching on spruce tops and flying out to catch insects in midair. In winter these same birds become sociable nomads, with large flocks wandering the northwest in search of berries. Sometimes they stray as far east as New England, but in most areas their numbers are quite variable from year to year (the name "Bohemian" reflects their unconventional and seemingly carefree lifestyle). However, in some cities in the prairie provinces of Canada, Bohemians can be found by the thousands every winter, no doubt lured by plantings of mountain-ash and other fruiting trees.

Bohemian Waxwing

HABITAT — *In summer, boreal forests, muskeg; in winter, widespread, including towns.* Breeds in far northern forest in open areas, around edges of burns or bogs or in places with scattered taller trees above brushy understory. Winters in wooded semi-open country where food is available; often concentrates in towns where plantings of fruiting trees provide abundant berries.

FEEDING — **Diet:** *Mainly insects and berries.* Feeds mostly on insects in summer, especially flying insects. Eats more berries and fruits as they become available, and these make up most of winter diet; important are berries of mountain-ash and junipers, also many others. Also eats seeds of birch and other trees, and will drink oozing sap. **Behavior:** Takes insects by watching from high perch, then flying out to catch them in midair. Also forages in trees. Takes berries while perched or hovering. Except when nesting, almost always forages in flocks.

NESTING — Courtship displays may include both birds perching close together with body feathers puffed out; male passes berry, flower, or other item to female. **Nest:** Placed on

horizontal branch of tree, often spruce, usually 6–20 feet above the ground, sometimes much higher. Nest (built by both sexes) is an open cup of twigs, grass, and moss, lined with soft materials such as fine grass and feathers. **Eggs:** 4–6, sometimes fewer. Pale bluish gray, heavily dotted with black, especially toward larger end. Incubation is probably by female only, about 14–15 days. **Young:** Both parents feed nestlings. Young leave the nest about 14–18 days after hatching, continue to associate with parents for some time thereafter, perhaps remaining with them through first fall and winter migration.

MIGRATION   Movements highly variable. In some winters, big flights extend as far east and south as New England, while in other years they are almost absent there. Similarly irregular south of Canada in the west.

CONSERVATION STATUS   Breeding population is impossible to census, but numbers reaching some southerly areas in winter seem to have increased in recent years.

CEDAR WAXWING   *Bombycilla cedrorum*

With thin, lisping cries, flocks of Cedar Waxwings descend on berry-laden trees and hedges, to flutter among the branches as they feast. These birds are sociable at all seasons, and it is rare to see just one waxwing. Occasionally a line of waxwings perched on a branch will pass a berry back and forth from bill to bill, until one of them swallows it. This species has a more southerly range than the Bohemian Waxwing and is a familiar visitor to most parts of this continent south of the Arctic.

HABITAT   *Open woodlands, fruiting trees, orchards; in winter, widespread, including towns.* Breeding habitat is influenced by availability of fruiting trees and shrubs, often most common in "edge" situations, as along forest edges, streamsides, overgrown fields, edges of swamps, suburban yards. In winter, may be in any wooded or semi-open area where berries are abundant.

Cedar Waxwing

FEEDING   **Diet:** *Mostly berries and insects.* Majority of annual diet is berries and small fruits; feeds on very wide variety of berries, with some important sources including juniper, dogwood, and wild cherries. Also eats some flowers and will drink oozing sap. Eats many insects in summer, including beetles, caterpillars, ants. Young nestlings are fed mostly insects at first, then more berries after a few days. **Behavior:** Except when nesting, almost always forages in flocks. May hover briefly while plucking berries or taking insects from foliage. Often flies out to catch insects in midair.

NESTING   In many areas, nesting is late, not beginning until midsummer. Only a small territory is defended, and birds may nest near others in small colonies. In courtship, two birds may perch close together, posturing, touching bills, and passing food items back and forth. **Nest:** Placed in tree, on horizontal limb or in fork, usually 6–20 feet above the ground but can be lower or much higher (up to 50 feet). Nest (built by both sexes) is a rather loosely built open cup of grass, weeds, twigs, plant fibers, lined with finer materials such as moss, rootlets, fine grass, hair. **Eggs:** 3–5, rarely 2–6. Pale gray to bluish gray, finely spotted with brown and black.

Incubation is probably by female only, averaging about 12–13 days. **Young:** Both parents feed nestlings. Young leave the nest about 14–18 days after hatching. Two broods per year.

MIGRATION Nomadic, moving about irregularly; both breeding and wintering areas may change from year to year, depending on food supplies. Some may linger south of breeding range into late spring or early summer.

CONSERVATION STATUS Local numbers vary widely, but overall population apparently is holding up well or even increasing.

SILKY-FLYCATCHERS (Family Ptilogonatidae)

Not related to our tyrant flycatchers, these birds are probably closer to the waxwings. The four species in this family occur only in a limited area between the southwestern United States and western Panama. All of them feed heavily on berries at most seasons, although they also eat many insects.

GENUS *Ptilogonys*

GRAY SILKY-FLYCATCHER *Ptilogonys cinereus*

This relative of our Phainopepla is fairly common in forested mountains and foothills in Mexico. Somewhat nomadic, it moves around in flocks, feeding on berries of mistletoe and other plants. Stray individuals have wandered north into Texas and perhaps other parts of the southwest.

GENUS *Phainopepla*

PHAINOPEPLA *Phainopepla nitens*

Phainopepla

In the desert southwest, Phainopeplas and mistletoe rely on each other. Phainopeplas feed heavily on berries of this parasitic plant; after the berries pass through the bird's digestive tract, the seeds often stick to branches of mesquite or other trees, where they can sprout new mistletoe clumps. Flocks of these slim and elegant birds may gather to feed on seasonally abundant crops such as elderberries. At other times, Phainopeplas are solitary, each bird defending a few small trees with several large clumps of mistletoe and attempting to drive away any other fruit-eating birds that come close.

HABITAT *Desert scrub, mesquites, oak foothills, mistletoe clumps.* Occurs in many lowland and foothills habitats, moving around with availability of berries. Often in Sonoran desert areas and mesquite groves at various times of year; at some seasons moves into chaparral, streamside trees, and oak woodlands.

FEEDING **Diet:** *Mostly berries and insects.* Mistletoe berries are mainstays of diet when available. Also feeds heavily on berries of elder, buckthorn, and sometimes juniper; in settled

areas, eats many berries of pepper trees. Also eats many insects, especially in warmer weather, including beetles, flies, true bugs, and caterpillars. **Behavior:** Feeds on berries mostly while perched; also hovers briefly to pluck berries or insects. Catches insects in midair by flying out from a perch and pursuing them in quick fluttery flight.

NESTING   Male displays over nesting territory by flying in high circles and zigzags. In courtship, male may chase female in flight; while perched, male may feed female. **Nest:** Often placed in center of clump of mistletoe, where it is very difficult to see; sometimes in fork of branch. Nest height varies with habitat, typically low (4–12 feet above ground) in desert mesquites, higher (up to 50 feet) in streamside oaks or sycamores. Nest, built primarily by male, is a rather small shallow cup of twigs, weeds, leaves, plant fibers, bound together with spider webs and lined with animal hair or plant down. **Eggs:** 2–3, rarely 4. Grayish, heavily dotted with lavender and black. Incubation is by both parents, 14–16 days. Male noted to do most of incubation during daylight hours. **Young:** Fed by both parents, receiving mostly crushed insects at first, then also berries. Young leave the nest about 19–20 days after hatching.

MIGRATION   Movements are complex and poorly understood. May nest in spring in the desert and then depart for other areas, possibly to nest again elsewhere.

CONSERVATION STATUS   Numbers vary from year to year, but overall population seems stable.

SHRIKES (Family Laniidae)

Classified as songbirds but living like little birds of prey, the typical shrikes betray their predatory habits by the shape of their hooked bills. This family is widespread in Eurasia and Africa, but only two species reach the Americas, and they are absent south of Mexico.

Scientists disagree on the size of this family; the number of species may be placed at about 30 or more than 100, depending on whether or not one includes here some typically African birds known as bush-shrikes and helmet-shrikes. Members of those groups are often strongly patterned or very colorful, and some of them have remarkable duet songs, with the male and female each contributing half the notes to a rapid-fire melody. Although these birds have thick bills like shrikes, they may not be closely related at all; a fair total for the true shrikes would be about 30 species.

Typical shrikes are often called "butcher birds," because they store uneaten prey, leaving it impaled on thorns or on barbs of fence wires. A shrike's larder in a thorny bush may have several dried-up grasshoppers or other creatures.

Most kinds of true shrikes seem to have habits similar to those of our Loggerhead and Northern shrikes, and most of them belong to the same genus, *Lanius*. Several species in various parts of the world have been declining in numbers recently, making this a family of special concern for conservationists.

GENUS *Lanius*

BROWN SHRIKE   *Lanius cristatus*

Common in Asia, this species is similar in habits to our shrikes, but it may tend to be more elusive, spending less time perched prominently in the open. Brown Shrikes have strayed to Alaska a few times; they have also reached California at least twice, and one spent a whole winter there.

NORTHERN SHRIKE   *Lanius excubitor*

This tough bird feeds on rodents and smaller birds for much of the year. It spends the summer in the far north, appearing in southern Canada and the lower 48 states only in winter. Solitary and wary, the shrike is likely to be seen perched at the top of a lone tree in an open field, watching for prey.

HABITAT   *Semi-open country with lookout posts; trees, scrub.* Breeds in far north in partly open or scattered spruce woods and in willow and alder scrub along streams or edges of

tundra. Winters in similar semi-open areas, sometimes in open grassland with a few high perches, but seems to prefer some brushy areas nearby.

FEEDING   **Diet:** *Includes small birds, rodents, large insects.* Varied diet includes many small songbirds, especially in winter and early spring; also many voles and other small rodents, and many large insects when available. Especially in Eurasia, also known to eat lizards, frogs, snakes. **Behavior:** Forages by watching from an exposed perch, then darting out in swift, powerful flight when prey is spotted. Uses its heavy hooked bill to kill its prey, although small birds attacked in flight may be forced to the ground first with the shrike's feet. Dead prey is sometimes impaled on a thorn and then eaten later.

Northern Shrike

NESTING   Male sings to defend nesting territory and perhaps to attract a mate, giving a surprisingly complex song that includes imitations of other birds. **Nest:** Placed in a low tree or large shrub, often in spruce or willow, usually 6-15 feet above the ground. Nest (probably built by both sexes) is a loosely made, bulky open cup of twigs, grass, bark strips, moss, lined with feathers and animal hair. **Eggs:** Clutch size varies, often 4–7 eggs, up to 9 in Alaska. Eggs pale gray or greenish white, spotted with brown, olive, and gray. Incubation is probably mostly or entirely by female, about 15–17 days. **Young:** Both parents feed nestlings. Young leave the nest about 19–20 days after hatching, are tended by parents for several more weeks.

MIGRATION   Moves south rather late in fall, returning north early in spring. Numbers on the wintering grounds vary from year to year, with many more appearing in the occasional "invasion winters."

CONSERVATION STATUS   No clear evidence of decreasing numbers in North America, but the species should be watched, since various kinds of shrikes around the world are showing declines. An odd historical note: In the 1870s, when the House Sparrow from Europe had just been introduced here, a warden was hired to shoot Northern Shrikes on the Boston Common in winter to protect the sparrows! Although the warden killed as many as 50 shrikes one winter, this episode probably had little effect on the total population of the species.

LOGGERHEAD SHRIKE   *Lanius ludovicianus*

In open terrain, this predatory songbird watches from a wire or other high perch, then pounces on its prey: often a large insect, sometimes a small bird or a rodent. The Loggerhead is gradually disappearing from many areas, for reasons that are poorly understood.

HABITAT *Semi-open country with lookout posts; wires, trees, scrub.* Breeds in any kind of semi-open terrain, from large clearings in wooded regions to open grassland or desert with a few scattered trees or large shrubs. In winter, may be in treeless country if fences or wires provide hunting perches.

FEEDING **Diet:** *Mostly large insects, also rodents and small birds.* Diet in summer is mainly insects, especially grasshoppers and crickets, also beetles, wasps, and others. Eats mice and other rodents at all seasons, especially in winter, and eats small birds. Also sometimes included in diet are spiders, snails, frogs, lizards, snakes, crayfish, small fish, and other items. **Behavior:** Forages mostly by watching from an exposed perch, then swooping down to take prey on or near ground or from low vegetation. Kills prey using its hooked bill. Often stores uneaten prey by impaling it on thorn or barbed wire, returning to eat it later.

NESTING In many regions, nesting begins quite early in spring. In courtship, male performs short flight displays; male feeds female. **Nest:** Placed in a dense (and often thorny) tree or shrub, usually 5–30

Loggerhead Shrike

feet above the ground, occasionally higher, in a spot well hidden by foliage. Nest (built by both sexes) is a solidly constructed but bulky cup of twigs, grass, weeds, strips of bark, lined with softer materials such as rootlets, animal hair, feathers, plant down. **Eggs:** 5–6, sometimes 4–8. Grayish white to pale buff, with spots of brown and gray often concentrated at large end. Incubation is by female, about 16–17 days. Male feeds female during incubation (sometimes bringing her food he has stored on thorns earlier). **Young:** Both parents feed nestlings. Young leave nest at about 17–21 days, are tended by parents for another 3–4 weeks.

MIGRATION Migrates rather early in spring, but in some southern areas, local birds may begin nesting while winter residents from north are still present.

CONSERVATION STATUS During recent decades, numbers have declined in many areas; now essentially gone from the northeast. Reasons for decline poorly understood, may be related to pesticides and changes in habitat.

STARLINGS AND MYNAS (Family Sturnidae)

We often think of starlings only in terms of the chunky black birds that waddle about on our lawns. However, the family includes more than 100 species, many of them brilliantly colored. All are native to the Old World, mainly tropical regions of Africa and Australasia. Starlings and mynas typically are social birds, traveling in flocks at most seasons. Some kinds search for food mainly on the ground in open country, while others live mostly in the treetops in tropical forest. Although none of them have really musical voices, several kinds are good mimics and may learn to imitate human words when kept as pets.

In North America we have only one widespread starling, introduced over a century ago and now common from coast to coast. Several species of mynas have escaped from captivity and nested in the wild in our area, but only one seems to have established itself here (and it may now be disappearing).

EUROPEAN STARLING   *Sturnus vulgaris*

Often regarded as a pest, the Starling wins our grudging admiration for its adaptability, toughness, and seeming intelligence. Brought to North America in 1890, it has spread to occupy most of the continent and is now abundant in many areas. Sociable at most seasons, Starlings may gather in immense flocks in fall and winter. When the flocks break up for the breeding season, males reveal a skill for mimicry, interrupting their wheezing and sputtering songs with perfect imitations of other birds.

HABITAT   *Cities, parks, farms, open groves, fields.* Most numerous in farm country and in suburbs and cities, but inhabits almost any kind of disturbed habitat. Usually scarce or absent in extensive wild areas of forest, scrub, or desert, but will breed around buildings or settlements in the midst of such habitats.

European Starling

FEEDING   **Diet:** *Mostly insects, berries, and seeds.* Diet is quite varied. Eats mostly insects when available, especially beetles, grasshoppers, flies, and caterpillars, also spiders, snails, earthworms, and other invertebrates. Especially in fall and winter, eats a wide variety of berries, fruits, and seeds. Sometimes visits flowers for nectar. Will come to bird feeders for a variety of items. **Behavior:** Forages mostly on the ground in open areas, often probing in soil with bill. Sometimes feeds on fruit up in trees, and sometimes catches flying insects in the air. Usually forages in flocks.

NESTING   Male establishes territory and chooses nest site, singing to attract a mate. When a female arrives, male perches next to nest site and sings, often waving his wings. Male sometimes has more than one mate. **Nest:** Site is in any kind of cavity; usually in natural hollow or woodpecker hole in tree, in birdhouse, or (in southwest) in hole in giant cactus. Sometimes in holes or crevices in buildings or other odd spots. Nest construction begun by male, often completed by female (who may throw out some of male's nest material). Nest is a loose mass of twigs, weeds, grass, leaves, trash, feathers, with slight depression for eggs. **Eggs:** 4–6, rarely 7. Greenish white to bluish white, unmarked. Incubation is by both parents (female does more), about 12 days. Starlings sometimes lay eggs in each other's nests. **Young:** Both parents feed nestlings. Young leave nest about 21 days after hatching. Two broods per year.

MIGRATION   Southern birds may be permanent residents, while many (but not all) northern birds move south in fall. Migrates mostly by day.

CONSERVATION STATUS   Undoubtedly has had a negative impact on some native hole-nesting birds, such as bluebirds and Red-headed Woodpeckers, competing with them for nesting sites.

GENUS *Acridotheres*

CRESTED MYNA   *Acridotheres cristatellus*

Native to southern Asia, the Crested Myna was introduced at Vancouver, British Columbia, in the 1890s. It prospered for many years, with the population building up into the thousands, but it never spread far beyond the Vancouver area. Numbers have been declining gradually for more than half a century; by the mid-1990s, fewer than 100 remained, and the species seemed likely to disappear from our area.

VIREOS (Family Vireonidae)

Found only in the New World, vireos are mostly rather plain birds, often remaining out of sight among the foliage of treetops or dense thickets. The family includes about 50 species. One is called "Solitary Vireo," a name that could apply to practically any of them, because they are all usually seen singly or in pairs, not in flocks.

Vireos are persistent singers. The males repeat their monotonous songs over and over throughout the breeding season, even during the heat of the day and late into the summer, when many other songbirds have fallen silent. The male will even sing from the nest while he is incubating.

In our area, all species belong to the genus *Vireo*. In the tropics there are also several smaller vireos known as greenlets, and a few larger forms called shrike-vireos and peppershrikes.

Feeding   Vireos do almost all of their foraging in trees and bushes, although a few kinds will also descend to the ground. They are usually quite deliberate, moving methodically and rather slowly along branches as they search for food among the foliage. Insects make up most of their diet at most seasons. The birds may hover momentarily to take insects from leaves or twigs, or sometimes make short flights out to capture them in midair. Many vireos also eat substantial amounts of berries, especially in fall or winter.

Nesting   Nest sites chosen by vireos are generally among foliage in trees or shrubs. The typical vireo nest is a compact, basketlike cup, its rim woven onto a horizontal forked twig, the bottom of the nest suspended in the middle of the fork. In most vireos, both parents take part in building the nest and incubating the eggs, but apparently only the female carries out these duties in the Red-eyed Vireo and its close relatives. Both parents bring food for the young.

Displays   Many vireos have distinctive displays used in courtship. Often the male postures in front of the female, with his tail spread and feathers fluffed up, while he calls or sings; sometimes the male sways back and forth or bobs up and down, and either bird may flutter its wings. Other courtship activities may involve examining potential nesting sites.

TYPICAL VIREOS — GENUS *Vireo*

WHITE-EYED VIREO   *Vireo griseus*

A busy bird of the thickets, most common in the southeast. Although the White-eyed Vireo usually stays in dense cover, it is not always hard to see; it will come up to examine and scold a birder who stands near the bushes and makes squeaking sounds. Even when it remains out of sight, its snappy song is distinctive. In Bermuda, where the bird is common, it is widely known as "chick-of-the-village," a good rendition of the song.

HABITAT   *Wood edges, brush, brambles, undergrowth.* Breeds in various kinds of dense low growth, including brier tangles on low swampy ground, shrubby thickets of maple, wild plum, willow, and other saplings in overgrown pastures, and scrub in open woods or near forest edges. Winters in a wide array of similar habitats.

White-eyed Vireo

CONSERVATION STATUS

FEEDING   **Diet:** *Insects and berries.* In the breeding season, takes almost entirely insects, and nearly one-third of diet then may be caterpillars, moths, and butterflies. Diet also includes true bugs, scale insects, many kinds of beetles, ants, wasps, bees, grasshoppers; also spiders, snails, and occasionally small lizards. During migration and in winter, also eats berries and small fruits. **Behavior:** Forages by moving actively among twigs and branches in dense low cover, searching for insects among the foliage. Often hovers momentarily to take insects from leaves.

NESTING   Male sings incessantly from early spring to late summer to defend nesting territory. In courtship, male displays to female by fluffing plumage, spreading tail, and uttering a whining call. **Nest:** Placed low (within 25 feet of ground, usually much lower) in shrub or sapling. Nest is supported by the rim woven onto a horizontal forked twig. Both parents help build nest, a deep, hanging cup made of twigs, roots, shreds of bark, grass stems, leaves, plant down, lichen, moss, sometimes fragments of wasp nests. Nest is bound with spider webs, lined with fine grass and fibers. **Eggs:** 4, sometimes 3–5. White with specks of brown or black. Incubation is by both parents, 13–15 days. Nests are commonly parasitized by cowbirds. **Young:** Both parents feed the nestlings. Young leave the nest about 9–11 days after hatching. One brood per year in the north, two in the south.

MIGRATION   Present all year in many southern areas. Farther north, appears relatively early in spring and lingers fairly late in fall compared with most vireos. A very rare stray in the west.
Northern edge of range varies over time: for example, disappeared from and then reinvaded Massachusetts; spread into Michigan in 1960s. Surveys indicate slight declines over much of range since 1960s.

THICK-BILLED VIREO   *Vireo crassirostris*

A Caribbean relative of the White-eyed Vireo; slightly larger, with a thicker bill. Common in the Bahamas, it has strayed several times to southern Florida. On one occasion, up to three were found together, suggesting that they might have nested locally.

BELL'S VIREO   *Vireo bellii*

Glimpsed in low brushy thickets of the midwest or southwest, this bird looks totally nondescript. When it is heard, however, it is easy to recognize by its jumbled clinking song, as if it had a mouthful of marbles. The species has become less common in recent years in many parts of its range, partly because it is a frequent victim of cowbird parasitism; many pairs of Bell's Vireos succeed in raising only cowbirds, not their own young.

HABITAT   *Willows, streamsides.* Breeds in low dense growth, especially in second-growth scrub or brushy fields in midwest, streamside thickets in southwest, but also locally in chaparral, woodland edges, or scrub oaks. Winters in the tropics in dense low scrub, mostly near water.

FEEDING   **Diet:** *Mostly insects.* In breeding season, feeds almost entirely on insects, especially large ones, including caterpillars, stink bugs, wasps, bees, and weevils, also many

others. Eats some spiders and a very few berries. Winter diet unknown. **Behavior:** Usually forages in low brush, within 12 feet of ground, but occasionally will feed much higher. Searches for insects among foliage, sometimes hovering while picking items from leaves or twigs; occasionally flies out to catch insects in midair.

NESTING   Male defends nesting territory with incessant singing. In courtship, male may chase female; members of pair often posture and display to each other during early stages of nest building. **Nest:** Site is in low shrub or sapling, usually 2–5 feet above the ground and placed in a fork of a horizontal twig. Nest (built by both sexes) is a small hanging cup, its rim firmly woven into

Bell's Vireo

fork; made of grass, weeds, plant fibers, leaves, and strips of bark, bound with spider webs. Inside may be padded with feathers, plant down, moss, then lined with fine grass. Spider egg cases often added to outside. **Eggs:** 3–5, usually 4. White, usually with dots of brown or black concentrated at larger end. Incubation is by both parents (but females do more), about 14 days. **Young:** Both parents feed the nestlings. Young leave the nest about 11–12 days after hatching, are fed by parents for at least another 3 weeks.

MIGRATION   Migrates mostly at night. Arrives in southwest in March, but does not reach northernmost nesting areas until May.

CONSERVATION STATUS   Apparently holding steady in parts of southwest. However, declining in the midwest and especially in California, where it is now endangered. Habitat loss and cowbird parasitism are major threats.

BLACK-CAPPED VIREO   *Vireo atricapillus*

Flitting about actively in the oak scrub, often hanging upside down momentarily, the little Black-cap is our most distinctive vireo. It is also the rarest, nesting only locally in Texas and Oklahoma. Its eggs take an unfortunately long time to hatch; cowbird eggs laid in the same nest usually hatch first, so that the vireos raise only young cowbirds. If cowbird numbers are not controlled, the vireo may face extinction.

HABITAT   *Oak scrub, brushy hills, rocky canyons.* Breeds on hot dry hillsides with dense thickets of brush, especially scrub oaks, often with many openings or gaps rather than solid cover. Winters in Mexico in dense thickets and woodland edges, especially in foothills and lowlands.

FEEDING   **Diet:** *Mostly insects, some berries.* Feeds mainly on insects in summer; diet not known in detail, but eats many caterpillars, beetles, small grasshoppers and crickets, and others, as well as spiders. Also eats some berries and small fruits. Winter diet poorly known, but may include more berries. **Behavior:** Forages more actively than most vireos, moving among branches and twigs in dense cover, sometimes hanging upside down like a chickadee to take items from underside of foliage.

NESTING   Male defends territory by singing frequently through much of breeding season. In courtship, male sings while following female; may also perform short song-flight. **Nest:** Placed in low scrubby oak or other dense shrub, usually 2–6 feet above ground, rarely higher. Both

Black-capped Vireo

parents help build nest, a small hanging cup suspended in the horizontal fork of a twig. Nest is made of grass, strips of bark, weeds, leaves, bound together with spider webs; inside is lined with fine grass. **Eggs:** 3–4, rarely 2-5. White, unmarked (most other vireos lay spotted eggs). Incubation, by both parents, averages about 15 days, surprisingly long for small size of bird. **Young:** Both parents feed nestlings. Young leave the nest about 10–12 days after hatching, and may be cared for by parents for more than another month. Sometimes male is left to care for first brood while female begins second nesting attempt.

MIGRATION   Generally arrives in Texas in April, departs in September. Migrates toward the southwest in fall, wintering along west coast of Mexico.

CONSERVATION STATUS   *Endangered.* Has disappeared from many former haunts and is declining in many current breeding areas. Heavy cowbird parasitism and loss of habitat are major threats. In some areas, projects are under way to control cowbird numbers and to create more nesting habitat through controlled burning.

GRAY VIREO   *Vireo vicinior*

Few birds are as plain as the Gray Vireo, a drab summer resident of juniper woods and open brush in the Great Basin region. What it lacks in color, however, it makes up for with personality, hopping around actively in the scrub, singing, and flopping its tail about. Sometimes the bird seems unafraid, coming quite close to birders who stand still in its habitat.

HABITAT   *Brushy mountain slopes, mesas, open chaparral, scrub oak, junipers.* Breeds in dry thorn scrub, chaparral, pinyon-juniper and oak-juniper scrub, or sagebrush and mesquites of arid foothills and mesas, at 3,000–6,500 feet in elevation. In winter, in northwest Mexico, found near coast in dry thorn scrub of elephant trees and giant cacti.

FEEDING   **Diet:** *Insects and fruits.* During the breeding season, feeds mostly on insects, including beetles, caterpillars, small moths, bugs, treehoppers, tree crickets, dobsonflies, cicadas, grasshoppers, and many others. In winter, eats many berries, especially those of elephant trees, in addition to insects. **Behavior:** Usually forages within 5 feet of the ground, moving about actively in brush on dry slopes. Also does some foraging on the ground. In winter, individuals defend feeding territories, driving away others of their own kind.

Gray Vireo

NESTING   Male defends nesting territory by singing through much of breeding season. **Nest:** Placed in shrub, frequently oak or juniper, 1–12 feet from ground, but most commonly 2–8 feet up. Nest is supported by the rim woven onto a horizontal forked twig. Nest (built by both sexes) is a deep, rounded cup made of weeds, shreds of bark, grass stems, leaves, and plant fibers, bound with spider webs and lined with fine grass. **Eggs:** 4, sometimes 3–5. Pinkish white with brown specks scattered near large end. Incubation is by both parents, 13–14 days. Cowbirds frequently lay eggs in nests of this species. Gray Vireos will sometimes deal with such parasitism by constructing second floor of nest over cowbird eggs. **Young:** Both parents feed nestlings. Young leave the nest 13–14 days after hatching. Two broods per year.

A short-distance migrant, wintering in northwestern Mexico.
CONSERVATION STATUS Population status not well known, but probably stable.

SOLITARY VIREO   *Vireo solitarius*

This vireo is common in summer in mixed forest, where conifers and deciduous trees grow together. When feeding, it works rather deliberately along branches, searching for insects. Its nest, a bulky cup suspended in the fork of a twig, is often easy to find. There are three distinct forms of Solitary Vireos, with different colors and voices; they may be three different species. The Eastern or "Blue-headed" form is widespread east of the Rockies, the "Plumbeous" form is common in the Rocky Mountains and Great Basin region, and the "Cassin's" form nests along the Pacific coast.

Solitary Vireo

HABITAT   *Mixed conifer-deciduous woods.* Breeds in rather open woods, usually containing a mixture of conifers and deciduous trees. Details of habitat differ by region: those in the northeast often in moist coniferous woods, those in the Rockies often in pinyon-juniper areas, those on Pacific coast often in oak woodland. Migrants occur in any kind of woodland.

FEEDING   **Diet:** *Mostly insects.* In summer feeds almost entirely on insects, including caterpillars, stink bugs, beetles, wasps, bees, ants, moths, tree crickets, and many others; also spiders. Also eats some berries and small fruits, especially in winter, when they may make up more than one-fourth of diet. **Behavior:** Forages rather deliberately in upper part of trees, searching for insects along branches and twigs as well as among leaves. Sometimes flies out to catch insects in midair or searches for items on bark of major limbs.

NESTING   Male sings frequently throughout the day to defend nesting territory. In courtship display, male may fluff up plumage and bob his body up and down while singing. **Nest:** Placed in horizontal fork of branch in tree, often quite low (3–12 feet above ground) but can be up to 35 feet or higher. Nest (built by both sexes) is a rather bulky open cup suspended by its rim. Nest is made of grass, strips of bark, weeds, plant fibers, rootlets, lined with plant down and hair. Outside of nest may be decorated with moss, pine needles, pieces of paper. **Eggs:** 3–5, usually 4. Whitish, lightly spotted with brown and black. Incubation is by both parents, probably about 12–14 days. In some areas, nests are often parasitized by cowbirds. **Young:** Both parents feed the nestlings. Young leave the nest about 2 weeks after hatching.

MIGRATION In general, the Solitary migrates earlier in spring and later in fall than other vireos. The two western forms, "Cassin's" and "Plumbeous," both winter in small numbers in the southwest, and the eastern form winters commonly in the southeast.

CONSERVATION STATUS In parts of the east, has expanded its breeding range southward during recent decades, with increasing numbers noted also.

YELLOW-THROATED VIREO   *Vireo flavifrons*

In leafy eastern forests, especially among tall oaks, the slow, husky phrases of the Yellow-throated Vireo can be heard in spring and summer. More colorful than most vireos, it is no easier to see, usually remaining out of sight in the foliage. However, the male sings throughout the breeding season, as late as August and September.

HABITAT *Deciduous woodlands, shade trees.* Breeds in tall trees in open deciduous woods. Prefers trees such as oaks and maples along streams, lakes, and roadsides. Also will summer in tall trees or orchards in towns. Avoids areas with dense undergrowth. Generally absent in mixed or coniferous forest, where it is probably replaced by the Solitary Vireo. Winters in tropical lowlands and foothills, in habitats ranging from rain forest to dry scrub.

FEEDING **Diet:** *Mostly insects, some berries.* Feeds mainly on insects. In summer, over one-third of diet may be caterpillars, moths, and butterflies; also eats true bugs, scale insects, aphids, leafhoppers, beetles, sawflies, tree crickets, dragonflies, cicadas, and others. Will also eat various berries, especially in fall. **Behavior:** Forages by searching for insects rather methodically along the twigs and in foliage high in trees. In winter, defends feeding territory and will drive away others of its own kind, but will associate with mixed foraging flocks of other birds.

Yellow-throated Vireo

NESTING Male defends nesting territory by singing incessantly. In courtship, male leads female to potential nest sites. **Nest:** Placed in tree (usually deciduous), generally 20–40 feet above the ground but can be 3–60 feet up. Both sexes help build open thick-walled cup nest, supported by the rim woven onto a horizontal forked twig. Nest made of weeds, shreds of bark, grass, leaves, and plant fibers. Outside of nest bound with spider webs and camouflaged with lichens and mosses; lined with fine grass and pine needles. **Eggs:** 4, sometimes 3–5. Pinkish or creamy white with heavy spots of brown or lavender near large end. Incubation is by both parents, 14–15 days. Frequently parasitized by cowbirds. **Young:** Both parents feed nestlings. Young leave the nest 14–15 days after hatching. The parents divide the fledglings, each adult caring for part of the brood.

MIGRATION Migrates mostly at night. A rather early spring migrant in the south, often appearing in late March.

CONSERVATION STATUS Over the last century, apparently has declined in the northeast, increased in parts of the upper midwest. Overall numbers probably stable at present.

HUTTON'S VIREO *Vireo huttoni*

In woods of the Pacific coast and the southwest, this little vireo hops about actively in the oaks. The bird bears a surprising resemblance to the Ruby-crowned Kinglet (which is often more common in the same woods in winter); it even twitches its wings in kinglet style when it is excited. Hutton's has the most monotonous song of all the vireos, a single note repeated over and over.

HABITAT *Woods and adjacent brush; prefers oaks.* Breeds in oak and pine-oak forests, preferring evergreen oaks, or in tall chaparral. Also lives in mountain canyons in sycamores, maples, and willows along streams. In Pacific states, may be found in the shrubby understory of humid Douglas-fir and redwood forests. Winters in breeding habitat, also sometimes in thickets along lowland streams.

FEEDING **Diet:** *Mostly insects, some berries.* Diet not known in detail, but feeds mainly on insects (including some that seem large for small size of bird) such as caterpillars,

beetles, and crickets, as well as spiders. Also eats some berries and small fruits, and some plant galls. **Behavior:** Forages in trees and shrubs by hopping from twig to twig, pausing to peer about as it searches for insects. Often hovers momentarily to pick an item from the foliage.

NESTING   Male sings almost constantly during breeding season to defend nesting territory. In courtship display, male approaches female, fluffs out his plumage, spreads his tail, and gives a whining call. **Nest:** Often in oak, sometimes in coniferous tree, usually 6–25 feet above the ground. Round cup-shaped nest is supported by the rim woven onto a forked twig. Nest (built by both sexes) is made of bark fibers, lichens, moss, grass, bound together with spider webs,

Hutton's Vireo

lined with fine grass. Outside of nest often covered with whitish plant down and spider egg cases. **Eggs:** 4, sometimes 3–5, rarely fewer. White with brown specks near larger end. Incubation is by both parents, 14–16 days. Cowbirds often lay eggs in nests of this species. **Young:** Both parents feed nestlings. Young leave the nest at about 14–17 days of age. Parents may care for and feed young for up to 3 weeks after they fledge. One brood per year, perhaps sometimes two.

MIGRATION   Mostly a permanent resident, but a few show up in fall and winter along lowland streams where the species is not present in summer.

WARBLING VIREO   *Vireo gilvus*

Rather plain, but with a cheery warbled song, the Warbling Vireo is a common summer bird in leafy groves and open woods from coast to coast. Because it avoids solid tracts of mature, unbroken forest, it is probably more common and widespread

today than it was when the Pilgrims landed. Some scientists believe that eastern and western Warbling Vireos may represent two different species; if that is true, then the two are very difficult to tell apart in the wild.

HABITAT   *Deciduous and mixed woods, aspen groves, poplars, shade trees.* Breeds in open deciduous or mixed woodland; also in orchards, shade trees of towns. Avoids unbroken mature forest. In the east, often in isolated groves near water. In the west, breeds in broad-leaved trees of mountains, canyons, and prairie groves. Winters in the tropics in open woods.

FEEDING   **Diet:** *Mostly insects, some berries.* In breeding season feeds mainly on insects, including many caterpillars, plus aphids, beetles, grasshoppers, ants, bugs, scale insects, flies, dragonflies; also eats

Warbling Vireo

some spiders and snails. Takes berries and small fruits from bunchberry, dogwood, pokeweed, sumac, elderberry, poison-oak, and many other plants, especially in late summer and fall. **Behavior:** Forages mostly in deciduous trees, sometimes in shrubs, hopping along twigs and searching for insects among the leaves. Also picks insects off the undersides of leaves while hovering briefly.

NESTING   Male defends territory by singing. In courtship, male struts and hops around female with his wings spread and tail fanned, usually not far from potential nest site. **Nest:** In the east, usually placed high in tree, up to 90 feet. In the west, often placed in shrub or tree within 30 feet of ground. Generally in deciduous tree or shrub. Nest (built by both sexes) is a compact, deep cup, suspended by its rim from a forked twig. Nest made of bark strips, grass, leaves, and plant fibers. **Eggs:** 4, sometimes 3–5. White with brown or black specks. Incubation is by both parents, 12–14 days. Male frequently sings from nest while incubating. Commonly parasitized by cowbirds. **Young:** Nestlings are fed and brooded by both parents, leave the nest 12–16 days after hatching.

MIGRATION   Migrates mostly at night. Most eastern breeders apparently travel via Texas and Mexico, rather than flying across Gulf of Mexico.

CONSERVATION STATUS   Since it favors open woods and edges, probably increased in some areas initially with clearing and breaking up of forest. Now common and widespread.

PHILADELPHIA VIREO   *Vireo philadelphicus*

This bird of the treetops is rather uncommon and is often overlooked or passed off as another vireo. It looks somewhat like a Warbling Vireo, and its song of short phrases sounds much like that of a Red-eyed Vireo. In some places where it overlaps with the Red-eye, the two species will even defend territories against each other. Despite its name, this vireo is only an uncommon migrant around Philadelphia and does not nest in that region.

Philadelphia Vireo

HABITAT   *Second growth; poplars, willows, alders.* Breeds in deciduous and mixed woodlands, especially near their edges, or in the young growth of overgrown pastures. Also nests in willows and alders along streams, lakes, and ponds. In winter in the tropics, often in fairly dry forest in lowlands and foothills.

FEEDING   **Diet:** *Mostly insects, some berries.* Feeds mostly on insects, including caterpillars, moths, beetles, wasps, bees, ants, ichneumons, true bugs, and many others; also some spiders. Eats many berries in late summer and fall, including those of bayberry and dogwood. **Behavior:** Forages mostly in deciduous trees and shrubs, moving about actively as it searches for insects. Often hovers to take items from foliage or hangs upside down at the tips of twigs to take insects from underside. Sometimes flies out to catch insects in midair.

NESTING   Male sings to defend nesting territory. In courtship display, male faces female and sways from side to side, fluffing plumage and spreading tail; both members of pair vibrate wings rapidly. **Nest:** Site is 10–90 feet above the ground in deciduous tree such as aspen, willow, alder, or maple. Nest is a compact, basketlike cup, its rim woven onto a horizontal forked twig. Nest (built by both sexes) made of grass, strips of birch bark, lichen, weeds, spider webs, and cocoons, lined with pine needles, grass, and feathers. **Eggs:** 4, sometimes 3–5. White with brown or black spots near large end. Incubation is by both parents, about 14 days. **Young:** Nestlings are fed by both parents. The young leave the nest about 12–14 days after hatching.

MIGRATION   Migrates mostly at night. In spring, most fly north across the Gulf of Mexico and then spread out as they continue northward. Along the Atlantic coast, more likely to be seen in fall than in spring.

CONSERVATION STATUS   Could be vulnerable to loss of habitat, especially on wintering grounds. Current populations seem stable.

RED-EYED VIREO   *Vireo olivaceus*

One of the most numerous summer birds in eastern woods. It is not the most often seen, because it tends to stay out of sight in the leafy treetops, searching methodically among the foliage for insects. However, its song—a series of short, monotonous phrases, as if it were endlessly asking and answering the same question—can be heard constantly during the nesting season, even on hot summer afternoons.

HABITAT   *Woodlands, shade trees, groves.* Breeds in deciduous and mixed forest, occasionally in conifers. Also well-wooded suburbs, orchards, parks. Prefers open woods with undergrowth of saplings, clearings or edges of burns, areas along streams in solid forest, or prairie groves. Winters in lowland tropical forest in South America.

FEEDING   **Diet:** *Mostly insects; also berries.* In summer feeds mainly on insects, including caterpillars, moths, beetles, wasps, bees, ants, bugs, flies, walkingsticks, cicadas, treehoppers, scale insects; also some snails and spiders. Also eats many berries, especially in late summer, including those of Virginia creeper,

Red-eyed Vireo

sumac, elderberry, blackberry, and dogwood. In winter in the tropics, may feed heavily on berries and small fruit. **Behavior:** Forages in trees by picking insects from foliage and from undersides of leaves and flowers, often while hovering momentarily.

NESTING   Male sings persistently throughout the day during the breeding season. In courtship, male displays to female with feathers sleeked down, swaying body and head from side to side; both birds then vibrate wings simultaneously. **Nest:** Placed usually 5–30 feet above the ground, sometimes 2–60 feet up, in deciduous shrub or sapling. Nest (built by female) is a compact, dainty cup, its rim woven onto a horizontal forked twig. Made of strips of bark, grass stems, weeds, rootlets, spider webs, and cocoons. **Eggs:** 4, sometimes 3–5. White with brown or black spots near large end. Incubation is by female only, 11–14 days. Frequently parasitized by cowbirds; rarely deters cowbirds by burying their eggs under a second floor of nest. **Young:** Nestlings are fed by both parents. Young leave the nest 10–12 days after hatching.

MIGRATION   Migrates mostly at night. Peak migration periods in most areas are May and September. Those breeding in northwest apparently move east in fall before turning south.

CONSERVATION STATUS   Undoubtedly declined historically with clearing of eastern forest, but current population seems stable. Could be affected by cutting of forest on wintering grounds in South America.

YELLOW-GREEN VIREO   *Vireo flavoviridis*

This bird enters our area mainly as a rare summer visitor to southern Texas. It is a close relative of the Red-eyed Vireo, and at one time the two were considered to belong to the same species. Yellow-green Vireos nest mostly in tropical areas, from Mexico to Panama, where the climate would seem to be suitable for songbirds all year; yet they are strongly migratory, traveling south to the Amazon Basin for the winter.

HABITAT   *Resaca woodlands, shade trees.* In Texas, a rare nesting bird, usually in native woods near oxbow lakes (resacas) or in shade trees in towns. In Mexico and Central America, breeds in many kinds of open woods, mature forest, second growth, edges of clearings. Winters in lowland tropical forest in South America.

FEEDING   **Diet:** *Mostly insects and spiders, some berries.* Feeds on a wide variety of insects, including tree crickets and various smooth caterpillars. Also eats many spiders. Diet contains berries and small fruits, including those of mistletoe, and some seeds, including those of the tropical shrub *Clusia*. **Behavior:**

Yellow-green Vireo

Forages by searching for insects among the foliage, often hovering briefly to pick insects from the undersides of leaves.

NESTING   Details of breeding behavior have not been well studied. Males sing persistently in spring and summer to defend the nesting territory. **Nest:** Placed 5–40 feet above the ground in branch of tree or shrub. Nest (built by female alone) is a neatly built open cup, its rim woven onto a horizontal forked twig. Nest made of grass blades, plant fibers, cobwebs, strips of papery bark, the outside often heavily decorated with spider webs; lined with fine plant fibers. **Eggs:** Usually 3, sometimes 2. White, with specks of brown. Incubation is by female alone, 13–14 days. **Young:** Both parents feed the nestlings. Young leave the nest 12–14 days after hatching but can fly only poorly at this stage.

MIGRATION   Strictly a summer resident in Mexico and Central America, arriving late in spring. A few from western Mexico apparently go the wrong direction in fall, as there are several fall records along the California coast.

CONSERVATION STATUS   Apparently always has been rare in Texas. In Mexico and Central America, widespread and common, but could be vulnerable to loss of habitat.

BLACK-WHISKERED VIREO   *Vireo altiloquus*

Found almost throughout the West Indies in summer, this is the Caribbean replacement for our common Red-eyed Vireo. In our area, Black-whiskered Vireos are summer residents mainly in southern Florida. There they can be heard singing constantly in the coastal mangrove tangles on hot days in May. Natives of the Caribbean know this bird well by voice, often giving it nicknames that suggest the short emphatic phrases of the song, such as "John-Philip" or "Whip-Tom-Kelly."

HABITAT   *Mangroves; low woods.* In Florida, breeds mainly in coastal mangrove swamps, but also in subtropical hardwoods on dry land, sometimes several miles inland. Migrants wandering beyond southern Florida may be in any kind of forest, but usually close to the coast. In winter in South America, found in open woods and forest edge.

FEEDING   **Diet:** *Mostly insects and other arthropods, some berries.* At times, spiders can be up to 40 percent of diet. Also feeds on many insects, including caterpillars, earwigs, beetles, wasps, bees, true bugs, flies, and mosquitoes. Also eats some berries and possibly seeds during the breeding season. In winter, in the tropics, up

Black-whiskered Vireo

to 50 percent of diet can be berries and small fruit. **Behavior:** Forages by searching rather deliberately among foliage for insects, usually in the upper levels of mangroves or other trees.

NESTING   Males arrive in Florida in April and defend breeding territories by singing continuously throughout the day. **Nest:** Placed 3–20 feet above the ground or water, in a mangrove or a deciduous tree. Nest (built by female) is a compact, basketlike cup, suspended by the rim, which is woven onto a horizontal forked twig. Made of seaweed, grass, weeds, palmetto fibers, spider webs, cocoons, lichen; lined with grass, pine needles, and hair. **Eggs:** Usually 3, sometimes 2. White, with spots of brown, purple, or black. Incubation is by female only; length of incubation period not well known. **Young:** Female feeds the young and probably male does also, but details (including age at which the young leave the nest) are not well known.

MIGRATION   Strictly a summer resident in Florida and nearby islands (may be a permanent resident farther east in the Caribbean). Stray birds appear regularly farther northwest along Gulf coast in spring.

CONSERVATION STATUS   Declined seriously on west coast of Florida in the 1980s, after severe winters killed many mangroves there and after Brown-headed Cowbirds became more common in that area.

YUCATAN VIREO   *Vireo magister*

This is a tropical relative of the Red-eyed Vireo, found locally around the western edge of the Caribbean, especially along the coast of the Yucatan Peninsula. In our area it is known definitely only from one that spent a month on the upper Texas coast one spring, but there have been possible sightings in Florida as well.

BUNTINGS AND THEIR RELATIVES (Family Emberizidae)

This family, as it is now defined, includes about one-sixth of all the bird species known for North America. It is a highly varied group, including birds as different as cardinals and orioles, little wood warblers and big grackles, plain sparrows and brilliant tanagers. These birds were formerly divided among several different families. Although the new classification is probably correct, generalizations about this megafamily are almost useless—hardly any statement will apply to the majority of these diverse species. In this book, the birds are divided and discussed by subfamilies.

WOOD WARBLERS (subfamily Parulinae)

Brightly colored and active, constantly flitting about in the trees, warblers are often called "the butterflies of the bird world." A group found only in the New World, the warbler subfamily includes about 110 species, with over 50 of these occurring regularly in North America. They are so small that most people may fail to notice them at all, but for naturalists in the know they are among the most captivating of birds.

All of our warblers are migratory, with many summering in northern forest and most going to the tropics in winter. During their northward migration in spring, there are places in eastern North America where it is possible to see 20 or even 30 species of warblers in a day. When they return south in fall, many have molted into plainer garb, and experienced birders enjoy the challenge of identifying "confusing fall warblers." Fall is also the season when eastern warblers are most likely to stray west, providing excitement for westerners who seek rare birds. These factors all contribute to the popularity of warblers with active birdwatchers.

Despite the name, hardly any of these birds could be said to warble, and many of them have very thin, dry, or unmusical voices. In general, warblers that sing from the treetops have very high-pitched songs, and those that sing from close to the ground have lower-pitched songs. Males of many warbler species have two distinct song types: one that is used mainly in defense of the nesting territory (to warn other males away) and one that is used mainly for attracting or communicating with a mate.

Many tropical warblers differ from our North American species in important ways. Most warblers in our area are strongly migratory, forage high in trees, and show a big difference between bright-colored males and duller females. A number of the tropical warblers, especially in genera like *Basileuterus*, are permanent residents, stay close to the ground, and have males and females colored alike.

Some warblers may live as long as 10 or 11 years in the wild, but most probably have shorter maximum life spans.

Feeding   All of the warblers feed mainly on insects. A few kinds also eat many berries, and some feed on nectar at flowers, especially in winter in the tropics. However, for the most part, all feed on the same kinds of very small insects, mostly in bushes and trees.

As a general rule, competition makes it hard for two species to exist in the same area if they are seeking exactly the same kinds of food. However, there are places where five or more species of warblers coexist in the same habitats, all eating the same general kinds of insects. They seem to avoid direct competition by foraging in slightly different ways. Some warblers feed high in the trees, others stay low; some forage at the tips of twigs, others stay close to the trunk; some often fly out to catch insects in midair, others forage by walking on the ground.

Nesting   Nest sites for warblers are quite variable. Two species in our area (Prothonotary and Lucy's warblers) nest in holes in trees, and sites chosen by the others range from the ground to the treetops. Most nests are in the shape of compact open cups, and the female usually does most or all of the nest building. The eggs are usually whitish with brown spots, and the female generally does most or all of the incubation. Both parents typically help to feed the young.

Displays   Males of many warblers have notable courtship displays. While moving about near a potential mate, the male may spread his wings and tail, fluff out his body feathers, or raise his head feathers; his postures often seem designed to show off brightly colored areas of his plumage. Some male warblers perform short flights, gliding or fluttering, as part of their courtship display, and some will feed the female.

If a predator threatens their nest, the parent warblers may put on a distraction display. Each adult may spread its tail, flutter its wings, and move away slowly along the ground or along branches. The bird may appear injured, and it may succeed in luring the predator away from the nest.

This genus includes some of the more plainly colored warblers; several of them also have rather simple trilled songs. Unlike many warblers, they often lack white tail spots and strong wing patterns, and they show relatively little change in pattern with the seasons. Most species place their nests on or very close to the ground, although they will forage higher in the bushes and trees. In feeding, many of these warblers probe in buds, flowers, or clusters of dead leaves.

BACHMAN'S WARBLER   *Vermivora bachmanii*

Although it survived at least until the 1960s, this mysterious little bird may now be extinct. Bachman's Warbler was an uncommon summer resident of southeastern swamps, wintering in Cuba. Its exact requirements for nesting habitat are not well understood, but it may have relied on large stands of giant cane (or "canebrakes") growing on higher ground at the edges of swamps. Such habitat is now rare, and its loss could have led to the extinction of the species.

Bachman's Warbler apparently fed mostly on insects, including many caterpillars, and it often probed among clusters of dead leaves. Its nest, placed 1–4 feet above the ground in dense low growth, was a flat open cup of weed stalks and leaves, lined with finer materials. The white eggs (3–5 per clutch) were usually unmarked, sometimes finely dotted near the large end. Incubation may have been by the female only, but both parents helped feed the young. This species was an early migrant in both spring and fall, moving north mostly in March, returning south mostly in August.

BLUE-WINGED WARBLER   *Vermivora pinus*

The simple buzzy song of the Blue-winged Warbler is often heard in brushy overgrown fields and thickets in the east during the summer. Although the bird is not especially shy, it can be a challenge to observe as it forages actively in the dense brush. In recent decades this species has been expanding its range northward, encroaching on the territory of its close relative, the Golden-winged Warbler. The two species often interbreed.

Blue-winged Warbler

HABITAT   *Brushy hillsides, bogs, overgrown pastures, stream and woodland edges.* Breeds in dry uplands in low shrubbery, brier patches, weed-grown fencerows, and bushy thickets; often in neglected fields or at the border of woods. Occasionally in deep swamp woods.

FEEDING   **Diet:** *Insects and spiders.* Details of diet not well known; probably feeds mostly on small insects, including beetles, ants, caterpillars, and grasshoppers, also spiders. **Behavior:** Forages by moving about in shrubs and trees, often fairly low. Preferred method of foraging is by probing with bill into curled leaves. Also searches rather deliberately on outer tips of branches, perhaps probing into buds and flowers.

NESTING   Hybridizes with Golden-winged Warbler. Hybrids, known as "Brewster's Warblers," are fertile, and they backcross with the parent species and with each other;

second-generation hybrids include a rare type known as "Lawrence's Warbler." Males sing two types of songs, one in territorial interactions and one in courting a mate. **Nest:** Site is well concealed in grass or blackberry vines, sometimes under a bush or sapling, close to or on the ground. Attached to upright stems of grass or weeds, especially goldenrod. The bulky nest is a narrow, deep, inverted cone, usually built by the female alone. Constructed of dead leaves, grass, and beech or grapevine bark, lined with plant fibers or animal hair. **Eggs:** 5, sometimes 4–7. White, with fine brown spots on larger end. Female incubates, 10–11 days. **Young:** Both parents feed nestlings. Young leave nest 8–11 days after hatching.

MIGRATION   Migrates mostly at night. Tends to arrive a little earlier in spring than the Golden-winged Warbler.

CONSERVATION STATUS   Despite being parasitized often by cowbirds, seems to be holding up well in numbers. May be gradually outcompeting and replacing the Golden-winged Warbler.

GOLDEN-WINGED WARBLER   *Vermivora chrysoptera*

Golden-winged Warbler

A strikingly patterned warbler of leafy second growth and swamp edges. Once common in the northeast, it has been declining recently in southern parts of its breeding range. As it disappears, its close relative the Blue-winged Warbler has been advancing north. The Blue-wing may be driving the Golden-wing out of the best habitats, but the situation is not well understood. The two species interbreed, creating distinctive hybrid types known as "Brewster's" and "Lawrence's" warblers.

HABITAT   *Open woodlands, brushy clearings, undergrowth.* Breeds in brushy areas with patches of weeds, shrubs, and scattered trees (such as alder or pine). This habitat type is found in places where a cleared field is growing up to woods again, as well as in marshes and tamarack bogs. In winter in the tropics, lives in forest edges and open woodland.

FEEDING   **Diet:** *Mostly insects.* Diet not known in detail, but feeds on many caterpillars and adult moths, especially Tortricid moths, also other insects and spiders. **Behavior:** Forages mostly in the upper level of trees and shrubs in summer. Feeds by probing and picking among foliage, sometimes hanging head downward. Probes in curled leaves and pries them open in search of insects. May forage with Black-capped Chickadees on breeding territories and in migration. On wintering ground, mainly feeds fairly low in trees in mixed flocks with other species.

NESTING   Hybridizes with Blue-winged Warbler. Male arrives on territory in May, a few days before the females. Male defends territory by singing; in aggressive encounters, he postures with raised crown feathers and spread tail, and he may chase and fight with other males. Males have two song types, one used to advertise territory and one mostly for attracting a mate. Courtship includes male chasing female, raising his crown feathers, slow wingbeats as male flies away, and gliding flight as male flies toward female. **Nest:** Built by female on the ground at base of shrub or in a tussock of grass or sedge, usually hidden by foliage. Open cup nest constructed of leaves, grapevine bark, and long strips of grass, lined with fine plant material. **Eggs:** 5, sometimes 4–7. Pale cream or pink with streaks and blotches of brown and lilac. Incubation by female, 10–11 days. Up to 30 percent of nests have cowbird eggs. Hatching of warbler eggs is low when cowbirds present, but cowbird nestlings do not necessarily fare better than warbler nestlings. **Young:** Leave nest after 8–9 days, are fed by parents for up to another month. Parents may divide fledglings into two groups, each parent attending only part of brood. One brood per year.

MIGRATION   Migrants are seen most commonly in late April and May and during September. Probably migrates mostly at night.

CONSERVATION STATUS   Increased and expanded range in late 1800s, probably as clearing of forest created more of the second-growth habitat favored by this species. Now declining seriously in southern part of breeding range. Competition and interbreeding with Blue-winged Warbler probably part of cause, also parasitism by cowbirds.

TENNESSEE WARBLER   *Vermivora peregrina*

This bird is found in Tennessee only briefly, during spring and fall migration; but there is no point in giving it a more descriptive name, because the bird itself is non-descript. The male makes up for his plain appearance with a strident staccato song, surprisingly loud for the size of the bird. Nesting in northern forests, the Tennessee Warbler goes through population cycles: it often becomes very numerous during population explosions of the spruce budworm, a favored food.

HABITAT   *Deciduous and mixed forests; in migration, groves, brush.* Breeds in bogs, swamps, and forests. Prefers openings in second-growth balsam-tamarack bogs, aspen and pine woods, or edges of dense spruce forest. Nests near slight depressions of boggy ground. During spring migration, mostly high in trees. During fall migration, often lower in saplings, brush, weedy fields.

FEEDING   **Diet:** *Mostly insects, some berries and nectar.* In summer feeds mainly on insects, including caterpillars, scale insects, aphids, beetles, flies, ants, and leafhoppers; also spiders. Takes nectar from catkins and some juice from grapes. In winter in the tropics, feeds on nectar, berries, and the protein-rich structures that cecropia trees produce at base of leaves. **Behavior:** Forages in the outer foliage of trees, sometimes hanging head downward. Takes insects in dense patches of weeds. In summer, male may feed mostly in treetops, female remaining nearer the ground. Forages in flocks of up to 200 on wintering grounds, often in coffee plantations.

Tennessee Warbler

NESTING   Male has loud repetitious song on breeding territory. In ideal habitat, nests are closely spaced in loose colonies. During courtship, male performs song-flight up to 60 feet above the ground. **Nest:** Concealed in a depression on ground under bushes or overhanging grass. Site is usually on mossy hummock in a wet area, but will nest on fairly dry ground on steep hillsides. Nest (built by female) is open cup made of thin grass stems; lined with fine dry grass, porcupine quills, or moose hair. **Eggs:** 5–6, sometimes 4–7. May lay more eggs during outbreaks of spruce budworm. Eggs white, with some marks of brown or purple. Rarely parasitized by cowbirds. Incubation by female only, 11–12 days. **Young:** Development and care of the young and age when they leave the nest are not well known. Probably one brood per year.

MIGRATION   In spring, many migrate north across the western part of the Gulf of Mexico. Strays show up regularly in the west, especially along the Pacific coast in fall, where a few may spend the winter.

Local breeding populations rise and fall, apparently in response to outbreaks of certain forest insects, such as spruce budworm. Overall numbers of this warbler seem healthy.

ORANGE-CROWNED WARBLER *Vermivora celata*

One of the plainest of warblers, the orange feathers on its head almost never visible, this species is also among the most hardy. In winter, when most warblers are deep in the tropics, Orange-crowns are common in the southern states. They are usually

Orange-crowned Warbler

seen singly, sometimes loosely associated with flocks of other birds. At all seasons they tend to stay fairly low, in bushes or small trees, flicking their tails frequently as they search among the foliage for insects.

HABITAT *Brushy clearings, aspens, undergrowth.* Breeds in shrubby vegetation, usually deciduous undergrowth in various habitats, including spruce forest, fir-aspen forest, streamside thickets, or chaparral with partly shaded ground. During migration and winter, uses brushy tangles in similar habitat, including gardens and parks.

FEEDING **Diet:** *Mostly insects, some berries.* In summer eats mostly insects, feeding nestlings almost exclusively on insect larvae. In winter, will feed on oozing sap from wells drilled in tree bark by sapsuckers or other woodpeckers. On wintering grounds, feeds on insects, nectar, and berries. Will take suet and peanut butter from feeders. **Behavior:** Forages by flitting from perch to perch, taking insects from foliage and flowers, often fairly low. Will hover to take prey from underside of leaves or sally out from perch for flying insects. Pierces bases of flowers with its bill to take nectar.

NESTING Males arrive on breeding grounds before females and establish territory by singing. Males typically return to territories defended the previous year. **Nest:** Nest site is protected from above by overhanging vegetation, usually on the ground in small depressions or on steep banks. Occasionally low in shrubby bushes or trees. Female builds small, open cup nest of leaves, fine twigs, bark, coarse grass and moss; lined with dry grass or animal hair. Male does not help with nest building but accompanies the female closely. **Eggs:** 4–5, sometimes 3–6. White or creamy, with reddish brown speckles mostly at larger end. Only females incubate, 11–13 days. **Young:** Fed by both parents but brooded only by female. Leave nest at age of 10–13 days, when they still fly poorly. Both parents feed young for at least a few days after they leave nest. One brood per year.

MIGRATION Compared with most warblers, migrates relatively early in spring. Fall migration is relatively late in the east (where uncommon), spread over a long period in the west.

CONSERVATION STATUS Numbers seem stable. Unlike some warblers, because of its wintering range and habitat, unlikely to be affected by cutting of tropical forest habitats.

NASHVILLE WARBLER *Vermivora ruficapilla*

Pioneer birdman Alexander Wilson encountered this bird first near Nashville, Tennessee, and it has been called Nashville Warbler ever since—even though Wilson's birds were just passing through in migration, and the species does not nest anywhere near Tennessee. This small warbler is fairly common in both the east and the west, often seen foraging in thickets and young trees, flicking its short tail frequently as it seeks insects among the foliage.

HABITAT **Cool, open mixed woods with undergrowth; forest edges, bogs.** Breeds in deciduous, coniferous, and streamside woodlands, also bogs and thickets. Favors cedar and spruce bogs in northern part of range, abandoned fields and mountain pastures with saplings and young trees in eastern United States. In the west, breeds in thickets of manzanita and other shrubs near belts of pine and fir.

FEEDING **Diet:** *Insects.* Adults eat beetles, caterpillars, grasshoppers, leafhoppers, aphids, and other insects, including the eggs and larvae of various types. Nestlings are fed caterpillars, small beetles, flies, and other insects. **Behavior:** Forages mainly in the lower parts of trees in open woodlands and in low thickets at forest edges. Takes insects from tips of twigs, undersides of leaves, catkins and flowers in trees.

NESTING Breeding behavior is not well known. On breeding territory, males sing from perches and also sometimes during slow, hovering display flight. **Nest:** Well-hidden, on the ground in a depression made in club mosses, grass, and ferns, usually under scrubby

Nashville Warbler

bushes or saplings. Open cup nest is made of coarse grass, ferns, and strips of bark, rimmed with moss; lined with fine grass, animal hair, or pine needles. Female builds the nest. **Eggs:** Usually 4–5, sometimes 3–6. White, with reddish brown spots concentrated at larger end. Incubation is mostly by female (male may help at times), 11–12 days. Female is fed on nest by male during incubation. **Young:** Nestlings are fed by both parents, but mostly by the female. Young leave the nest about 11 days after hatching.

MIGRATION Birds from both eastern and western breeding populations winter mainly in Mexico. Unlike many warblers, does not migrate north across Gulf of Mexico in spring; instead, travels around Gulf, then spreads northeastward to easternmost breeding areas.

CONSERVATION STATUS Overall populations seem to be stable. Apparently, nests are only seldom parasitized by cowbirds.

VIRGINIA'S WARBLER *Vermivora virginiae*

A rather plain warbler that spends the summer in brush and chaparral on dry mountainsides in the west. The dense low nature of its habitat often makes Virginia's Warbler hard to observe, but its presence is revealed by its simple trilled song and by its hard call note, *tsick*. Although it is common over much of the west, its nesting behavior remains poorly known, partly because its nest is extremely difficult to find.

HABITAT **Oak canyons, brushy slopes, pinyons.** Breeds on dry mountainsides in scrub oak, chaparral, pinyon-juniper woods, or other low brushy habitats. In some areas, prefers mountain-mahogany and Gambel oak. In migration, frequently in woods along streams. In winter in Mexico, at middle elevations in dry scrub.

FEEDING **Diet:** *Presumably mostly insects.* Diet not known in detail; presumed to eat a wide variety of small insects, like other warblers. **Behavior:** During the breeding season, forages mostly by taking insects from among foliage and twigs. Also observed feeding on the ground and catching flying insects in midair. May do much

WARBLERS

Virginia's Warbler

probing of buds and flowers. In winter in Mexico, feeds low, mostly within 15 feet of the ground.

NESTING Breeding behavior not well known. Arriving on breeding grounds in April and early May, the male sings from perches on exposed dead limbs. Pairs begin nesting by early June. Males defend large territories. **Nest:** Usually very difficult to find. Placed under grass tufts in hollow of decaying leaves on ground covered by dense brush. Frequently on steep hillside or talus slope. Nest (probably built by female) is open cup of coarse grass, bark strips, roots, and moss, lined with animal hair and moss. **Eggs:** 4, sometimes 3–5. White to creamy with fine reddish brown spots. Incubation probably by female. Eggs and young frequently fall prey to jays or snakes. Apparently, nests are only rarely parasitized by cowbirds. **Young:** Fed by both parents. Age at leaving nest not well known. Possibly two broods per year.

MIGRATION Probably migrates mostly at night, like other warblers. Southward migration begins quite early, the birds mostly disappearing from the breeding grounds in August.

COLIMA WARBLER *Vermivora crissalis*

In our area, this Mexican species occurs only in Big Bend National Park in western Texas. There it is fairly common in summer at upper elevations in the Chisos Mountains, but seeing it requires a day-long hike or a lengthy horseback ride. The Colima is larger than most warblers and tends to be sluggish, foraging deliberately in the dense undergrowth or in the lower levels of the oaks.

HABITAT *Oak-pine canyons.* Breeds above 6,000 feet in montane forests of pine, juniper, oak, and madrone; or in habitat of oak, maple, and Arizona cypress. Key plants in habitat used by nesting birds in Texas include Mexican pinyon, Grave's oak, gray oak, Texas madrone, beargrass, mountain-mahogany, silktassel, mountain sage, Chisos prickly-pear, and pinyon-ricegrass. Prefers canyons and slopes. In winter in Mexico, found in humid pine-oak habitat with brushy understory.

FEEDING **Diet:** *Mostly insects.* Diet not known in detail; undoubtedly feeds mostly on insects. Wasp galls from oaks, spiders, crane flies, and other flies are among favorite foods early in the breeding season. Nestlings are fed many small green moth larvae. **Behavior:** Moves rather deliberately while foraging, more like a vireo than like most active warblers. Typically, warblers in this genus do much probing of buds and flowers. In winter in Mexico, probably defends feeding territories, usually observed foraging alone or in pairs rather than in flocks.

Colima Warbler

NESTING Males defend nesting territories by singing and calling; sometimes physically attack territorial intruders. **Nest:** Placed on ground among rocks on bank of dry wash or at edge of talus slope. Nest (built by both sexes) is well shaded and hidden in dead leaves beneath grass tufts, rocks, or tree roots. Open cup-shaped nest of loosely woven, coarse grass and cedar bark strips, dead leaves, roots, and mosses; often lined with animal hair. Pinyon-ricegrass is a favorite nest material. **Eggs:** Usually 4. Creamy with wreath of brown spots at larger end. Incubated by both parents, about 12 days. **Young:** Both parents feed nestlings, but males do less than females, spending more time in defending territory. Young leave the nest 11 days after hatching, are independent of parents a few days later.

MIGRATION Only a short-distance migrant, wintering in southwestern Mexico. In Texas, arrives in April and departs mostly in August and early September.

CONSERVATION STATUS Numbers in Texas vary from year to year, probably always fewer than 200 pairs. More numerous in northern Mexico, but would be vulnerable to loss of habitat.

LUCY'S WARBLER *Vermivora luciae*

Small, pale, and plain, this bird is unimpressive in appearance, but it is notable as the only warbler that nests in the hot deserts of the southwest. Lucy's Warblers return to the desert early in spring, and pairs can be found foraging in brush along the washes even before the mesquites have leafed out. Unlike most warblers, they raise their young in cavities, placing their nests inside old woodpecker holes or under loose slabs of bark.

HABITAT *Mesquite along desert streams and washes; willows, cottonwoods.* Breeds mostly in cottonwood-mesquite woods near desert streams or in open groves of mesquite along dry washes in the Sonoran desert. Also found in sycamore and live oak groves near streams in the lower parts of canyons close to arid lowlands.

FEEDING **Diet:** *Mostly or entirely insects.* Diet not known in detail; undoubtedly feeds mostly on insects. **Behavior:** Most common method of foraging is to hop rapidly about in mesquites and other desert trees and bushes, taking insects from the foliage and twigs. Typically, warblers in this genus do much probing of buds and flowers. Sometimes observed flying out to catch insects in midair.

NESTING Male displays to the female during courtship by fluffing plumage, raising crown feathers, and spreading wings and tail. **Nest:** Placed in natural hollows in mesquites, old woodpecker holes, under loose bark (especially bark peeled from trunk by fire), sometimes in deserted Verdin nest or hole in eroded stream bank. Typically nests 5–40 feet above ground. Nest (built by both sexes) is loosely and raggedly made of coarse grass and weeds, bark strips, mesquite leaf stems, surrounding a compact cup of fine grasses. Lined with animal hair or feathers. **Eggs:** 4–5, sometimes 3–7. White or creamy, with red-brown spots near large end. Incubation is by female, possibly also by male. Incubation period unknown. **Young:** Both parents feed nestlings. Age at which young leave the nest is not well known. Probably two broods per year.

Lucy's Warbler

MIGRATION Migrates very early in both spring and fall, with most arriving in the southwest in March, and the species becoming hard to find there after mid-August.

CONSERVATION STATUS Undoubtedly has declined with loss of streamside groves and clearing of mesquite woods in southwest. Still very common in appropriate habitat.

These are very small warblers, with dry, buzzy songs. All are blue-gray above and yellow on the chest, with a contrasting patch of color on the back. Northern and Tropical parulas are very similar, while the Crescent-chested Warbler and the Flame-throated Warbler of Central America are sometimes classified in the genus *Vermivora*.

NORTHERN PARULA *Parula americana*

This small warbler is often hard to see as it forages in dense foliage of the treetops. However, it is easy to hear; the male seems to repeat his buzzy trickle-up song constantly from early spring through midsummer at least. Northern Parulas hide their nests inside hanging Spanish moss in the south or in the similar *Usnea* lichens in the north, where they are impossible to spot except by the actions of the parent birds.

HABITAT *Breeds mainly in humid woods where either* Usnea *or Spanish moss hangs from the trees (but also in some woods where neither is found).* Nests mainly in humid coniferous and deciduous forests, especially those with abundant tree lichens, in swamps or along edges of ponds, lakes, or slow-moving streams. In migration and winter, frequents almost any kind of trees.

FEEDING **Diet:** *Mostly insects.* Feeds on small beetles, flies, moths, caterpillars, egg clusters, true bugs, ants, bees, wasps, and other insects, also spiders. Also eats some small berries. May feed nestlings many soft green larvae. **Behavior:** Forages rather sedately. Searches among leaves and hovers to take insects from foliage, sometimes hanging upside down on twigs like a chickadee or on trunk like a nuthatch. Occasionally darts out after flying insects or forages on ground.

NESTING Pairs often return to same nesting site year after year. Males sing during migration and throughout nesting season, even when feeding young.

Northern Parula

Nest: Placed usually in a hollow excavated in hanging tree lichens (*Usnea*) or Spanish moss, 4–50 feet above the ground. When no lichens or Spanish moss available, also constructed of dangling clumps of twigs or pine needles, or placed in rubbish left by floods in branches hanging over stream. Nest is small hanging pouch of lichen and twigs, unlined or lined sparsely with soft shreds of moss, grass, pine needles, and hair. Built solely by female, but male accompanies her on trips to the nest. **Eggs:** 4–5, occasionally 3–7. Whitish, variably marked with brown. Incubated by both parents, but mostly by female, 12–14 days. **Young:** Both parents feed young, but male may do more. Age at which young leave the nest is not well known.

MIGRATION Southern breeders return very early, often by early March, and may be actively nesting while other parulas are passing through on their way farther north. Strays may appear in west at any time of spring or fall.

TROPICAL PARULA *Parula pitiayumi*

Very similar to our Northern Parula, this bird is widespread in the tropics from northern Mexico to central Argentina. In our area, it is mainly a summer resident of southern Texas, especially in low live oak groves south of Kingsville. Most of these birds seem to disappear in winter, but a few can be found at that season associating with roving flocks of titmice and other birds in woods along the Rio Grande.

HABITAT *Oaks, riverside woods.* In southern Texas, breeds mainly in groves of low live oaks with much Spanish moss (for nest sites), surrounded by mesquites. Also sometimes in dense native woods near Rio Grande where much Spanish moss hangs in trees. In the tropics, nests in many kinds of woodlands, from dry lowland thorn forest to humid forest in the mountains.

FEEDING **Diet:** *Largely insects.* Diet not known in detail; undoubtedly feeds mostly on insects. Known to feed on wasps, ants, flies, and others. **Behavior:** Forages actively from mid-level to the treetops, frequently along streams. Searches among leaves and hovers momentarily to take insects from foliage; sometimes flies out to catch flying insects in midair.

NESTING Details are not well known. In the tropics, may remain paired on territory through-out the year. In Texas, most apparently depart in winter. After returning in spring, males sing persistently to defend territory. **Nest:** Placed 8–40 feet above ground in hanging Spanish moss; sometimes in hollow in orchids or dangling cactus. In Spanish moss, little material may be added. In other sites, nest is cup-shaped and constructed of moss, palmetto bark, grass, roots, and animal hair; lined with plant down and feathers. Nest probably built by female. **Eggs:** Usually 3–4 in south Texas, 2 in the tropics. Creamy white with chestnut speckles around larger end. The incubation period and the roles of the parents are not well known. **Young:** Probably both parents feed the nestlings. Age at which the young leave the nest is not well known.

MIGRATION Returns to nesting areas in south-central Texas early, often in March. A few stay through winter along lower Rio Grande. Strays have reached Louisiana and Arizona.

CONSERVATION STATUS Has disappeared from areas along Rio Grande where it formerly nested. Presence north of there, in Kingsville region, is a recent discovery. Widespread and common in tropics.

CRESCENT-CHESTED WARBLER   *Parula superciliosa*

Common in mountain pine forests in Mexico, sometimes moving to lower elevations in winter, this small warbler has strayed into our area several times. Most sightings are for southeastern Arizona, where one bird returned for two consecutive winters along Sonoita Creek. There is also one possible sighting for southern Texas.

TYPICAL WARBLERS — GENUS *Dendroica*

Included in this genus are many of the most colorful warblers; they provide much of the joy of spring warbler-watching in the east. Some of these species (such as Blackburnian and Blackpoll warblers) are very long-distance migrants, wintering entirely in South America, while others (including Yellow-rumped and Pine warblers) remain through winter in our southern states. Almost all of the *Dendroica* warblers have white spots in the tail feathers, and males are almost always more brightly colored than females.

YELLOW WARBLER   *Dendroica petechia*

The bright, sweet song of the Yellow Warbler is a familiar sound in streamside willows and woodland edges. This is one of our most widely distributed warblers, nesting from the Arctic Circle to Mexico, with closely related forms along tropical coastlines. Their open, cuplike nests are easy to find, and cowbirds often lay eggs in them. Yellow Warblers in some areas thwart these parasites by building a new floor over the cowbird eggs and laying a new clutch of their own. In one case, persistent cowbirds returned five times to lay more eggs in one nest, and an even more persistent warbler built six layers of nest floors to cover up the cowbird eggs.

HABITAT   *Bushes, swamp edges, streams, gardens.* Breeds in a variety of habitats in east, including woods and thickets along edges of streams, lakes, swamps, and marshes, favoring willows, alders, and other moisture-loving plants. Also in drier second-growth woods, orchards, roadside thickets. In west, restricted to streamside thickets. In winter in the tropics, favors semi-open country, woodland edges, towns.

FEEDING   **Diet:** *Mostly insects.* Up to two-thirds of diet may be caterpillars of various kinds. Also feeds on mayflies, moths, mosquitoes, beetles, damselflies, treehoppers, and other insects, plus spiders; also eats a few berries. **Behavior:** Forages from low levels up to treetops. Takes insects from twigs and foliage, hovers briefly to take items from underside of leaves, and flies out after flying insects. Males tend to forage higher and in more open foliage than females. Forages alone in winter in the tropics, defending a winter feeding territory.

Yellow Warbler

NESTING   Males defend nesting territories by singing, sometimes performing fluttering flight displays. Male courts female by actively pursuing her for 1–4 days. **Nest:** Placed in upright fork of branches in shrubs, small trees, and briers from 2–60 feet above ground. Nest (built by female) is compact open cup of weed stalks, shredded bark, grass, lined with plant down or fur. Males accompany females on trips to the nest and will occasionally help build. Females will steal nest material from other nests. **Eggs:** 4–5, sometimes 3–6. Greenish white, with variety of specks or spots of brown, olive, and gray. Incubated solely by female, 11–12 days. Male feeds female on nest. Very frequently parasitized by cowbirds. May defend against parasitism by rebuilding new nest on top of cowbird eggs or by deserting nest. **Young:** Fed by both parents (female does more). Young leave the nest 9–12 days after hatching.

MIGRATION   Migrates mostly at night. Fall migration is very early, with many moving south during August.

CONSERVATION STATUS   Because it favors second growth and edges, less vulnerable to loss of habitat than some warblers. Current populations probably stable.

CHESTNUT-SIDED WARBLER   *Dendroica pensylvanica*

In leafy second-growth woods, clearings, and thickets, this warbler is often common, hopping about in the saplings with its tail cocked up at a jaunty angle. It is apparently much more numerous today than it was historically: John James Audubon, roaming eastern North America in the early 1800s, saw this bird only once. The cutting of forests evidently has created more brushy habitat for Chestnut-sided Warblers, even as it has made other birds less common.

HABITAT   *Slashings, bushy pastures.* A habitat specialist, expanding its range since the 19th century as forests were cut in the eastern United States. Breeds in second-growth

deciduous woods, overgrown fields, and edge habitat. Prefers brushy thickets, briers, and brambles. Winters in tropics in forest edge and second growth.

FEEDING **Diet:** *Mostly insects.* During nesting season, known to eat caterpillars, flies, small moths, small grasshoppers, beetles, spiders; also a few berries. May eat slightly more berries in winter in the tropics, but insects still make up over 90 percent of diet then. **Behavior:** Forages by hopping actively among branches of shrubs and small trees, searching for insects among leaves and twigs, hovering momentarily to take items from foliage. Typically takes insects from undersides of leaves. Also darts out to catch flying insects in midair.

NESTING Male sings to defend nesting territory. During courtship, male displays to the female by fluffing his plumage, raising his yellow crown feathers, spreading and vibrating his wings and tail. **Nest:** Placed in low dense shrubs or tangles such as blackberry or rhododendron, or in deciduous saplings such as alder or maple. Loosely constructed open cup nest (built by female) is made of cedar or grapevine bark strips, fibrous weeds, grasses, roots, and fine plant down, lined with fine grass and animal hair. Nest may be attached to twigs with spider webs. **Eggs:** Usually 4, sometimes 3–5. Whitish with brown markings. Incubated 11–12 days by female. Cowbirds frequently lay eggs in nests of this species. **Young:** Both parents feed the nestlings. Young leave the nest about 10–12 days after hatching.

Chestnut-sided Warbler

MIGRATION Migrates mostly at night. Peak migration in most areas is during May and September. Strays appear regularly in west, especially in fall.

CONSERVATION STATUS Apparently far more common today than in early 19th century, with much greater area of second-growth brush in east. Numbers may have declined somewhat in recent decades.

MAGNOLIA WARBLER *Dendroica magnolia*

Although it is small and very active, the Magnolia Warbler is less difficult to observe than some warblers because it often stays low in shrubbery and short trees. It favors second-growth habitats both summer (in the north woods) and winter (in the tropics), so it has not been hurt by habitat destruction as much as some migrants. Named by chance, since pioneer ornithologist Alexander Wilson happened to spot his first one in a southern magnolia tree during migration.

HABITAT *Low conifers; in migration, other trees.* Breeds most commonly in areas of short young spruce; also in young hemlocks and pines and in dense understory of taller coniferous forest. During migration may be in any kind of deciduous shrubs or low trees. In winter in tropics, often in second growth and scrub as well as edges of taller forest.

FEEDING **Diet:** *Mostly insects.* In breeding season, eats a variety of insects, including beetles, moth caterpillars, leafhoppers, and aphids; also spiders. May eat many spruce budworms when that insect is at epidemic numbers. Occasionally eats berries during inclement weather when insects may be scarce. Diet in migration and winter poorly known. **Behavior:** Forages by hopping along branches, gleaning insects from conifer needles, leaves, and twigs. Takes most insects from underside of vegetation. Sometimes hovers or makes short flights after insects. In summer, males may tend to feed higher than females.

NESTING Male arrives on breeding grounds before female and establishes territory. Has two song types: one to defend territory against intruding males, another apparently to attract and communicate with mate. **Nest:** Site is well hidden in dense low conifer (especially spruce or hemlock), often near trunk on horizontal branch. Usually less than 10 feet above ground, sometimes up to 30 feet. Nest is flimsy cup of grasses, weeds, twigs, with lining of fine black rootlets. Both sexes help build nest, but female does most of work. **Eggs:** Usually 4, sometimes 3 or 5. White, variably marked with brown, lavender, olive, and gray. Incubation is by female only, 11–13 days. **Young:** Fed by both parents. May leave nest at age of 8 days, usually 9–10 days. Young can fly at this stage but may be fed by parents for up to 25 more days. One brood per year, perhaps rarely two.

MIGRATION Migrates at night. Most fly across Gulf of Mexico in spring and fall. Winters in Mexico, Central America, and West Indies, but most common in winter in Yucatan Peninsula. Strays reach west coast in spring and especially in fall.

Magnolia Warbler

CONSERVATION STATUS Numbers apparently stable or even increasing in some areas. Adapts to second-growth woods and cut-over areas better than some other warblers.

CAPE MAY WARBLER   *Dendroica tigrina*

Many of our migratory warblers seem to lead double lives, and the Cape May is a good example. It summers in northern spruce woods but winters in the Caribbean, where it is often seen in palm trees. In summer it eats insects, but during migration and in winter it varies its diet with nectar from flowers and juice that it obtains by piercing fruit. Birders easily recognize the tiger-striped males in spring, but drab fall birds can be perplexing.

HABITAT *Spruce forest; other trees in migration.* Breeds in spruce forest, either in pure stands or mixed with firs or other trees, generally in more open woods or near the forest edge. During migration often favors conifers, but also forages in deciduous trees and thickets. In Florida and the West Indies in winter, often feeds in the crowns of palm trees.

FEEDING **Diet:** *Mostly insects, some fruit, nectar.* Diet includes spruce budworms, parasitic wasps and flies, ants, bees, small moths, beetles, leafhoppers, also spiders. In migration, may pierce grapes and drink the juice. Also feeds on sap from holes drilled by sapsuckers. The Cape May has a tubular tongue, unique among warblers; in winter, it feeds heavily on flower

Cape May Warbler

nectar and fruit juices. **Behavior:** On the breeding grounds, feeds mainly at the tips of spruce branches. Will hang head downward at the tips of branches to pick insects from the undersides of needles. Often flies out several feet to catch flying insects in midair. In winter, may defend flowering plants from hummingbirds and other nectar feeders. **NESTING** Male defends nesting territory against other Cape Mays and other warbler species. During courtship, male displays by flying above female with wings held stiffly out.

GENUS *Dendroica*

Nest: Placed very close to the top of a 35–60-foot spruce or fir, in thick foliage against trunk. Nest is cup-shaped and made of moss, vines, weeds; lined thickly with feathers and fur. Probably built by female. Nest is very hard to find because female flies into the tree low and then sneaks up the trunk to enter the nest; when leaving it, she moves down the trunk instead of flying directly away. **Eggs:** 6–7, sometimes 4–9. May lay more eggs during outbreaks of spruce budworm. Eggs whitish with red-brown spots. Probably incubated by female, unknown number of days. **Young:** Probably fed by both parents. Age at which young leave the nest is not well known.

MIGRATION   Migrates mostly at night. Moves north from Caribbean mostly through Florida in spring. Many move south along Atlantic coast in early fall. A few linger to late fall or even winter, especially outside normal range.

CONSERVATION STATUS   Numbers rise and fall, increasing during population explosions of spruce budworm and other insects in northern forests. Apparently has become more common overall in recent decades.

BLACK-THROATED BLUE WARBLER   *Dendroica caerulescens*

The lazy, buzzy song of the Black-throated Blue Warbler comes from the undergrowth of leafy eastern woods. Although the bird usually keeps to the shady understory, it is not especially shy; a birder who walks quietly on trails inside the forest may observe it closely. It moves about rather actively in its search for insects, but often will forage in the same immediate area for minutes at a time, rather than moving quickly through the forest like some warblers.

HABITAT   *Interior of hardwood and mixed deciduous-coniferous forests.* Breeds in large areas of relatively undisturbed forests of maple, birch, beech, eastern hemlock, spruce, and fir; mainly in forest containing a dense undergrowth of shrubs (especially rhododendron bogs) and vine tangles. During migration, tends to be in shrubby or forested places. In winter, inhabits dense tropical woods as well as fence rows and gardens.

FEEDING   **Diet:** *Mostly insects.* In summer, feeds mostly on insects, especially caterpillars, moths, and crane flies, also spiders. In winter, continues to eat many insects but also takes seeds, berries, small fruits, and flower nectar. Will visit hummingbird feeders for sugar-water. **Behavior:** More methodical in its foraging than many warblers, working over an area thoroughly in the forest understory or lower levels of trees. Forages by gleaning insects among foliage or by hovering briefly to take items from underside of leaves. Males tend to forage higher than females in summer. Frequently seen stealing insects from spider webs. Will join mixed flocks with other birds on migration and in winter. Establishes winter feeding territories, chasing away others of its own kind.

Black-throated Blue Warbler

NESTING   Some males have more than one mate. Pairs are faithful between seasons; 80 percent of returning birds nest with previous year's mate. **Nest:** Site is in thick shrubs (such as laurel, alder, rhododendron, viburnum) or saplings, in a fork within 6 feet of ground, sometimes with leaning dead branch as extra support. Female builds nest, male helps by supplying materials; nest is open cup of bark strips, cobwebs, plant fibers, lined with pine needles, moss, and hair. **Eggs:** 4, sometimes 2–5. Creamy white, with blotches of reddish brown and gray concentrated at larger end. Incubated by female only, 12–13 days. Cowbirds rarely parasitize nests, possibly because this species tends to nest deep in forest interior. **Young:** Fed by both parents. Young leave nest after 8–10 days but fly poorly at this stage. Male often becomes sole provider for fledglings, while female begins second or third nest. Female usually becomes main provider for last brood of season. Two or occasionally three broods per summer.

MIGRATION — Migrates mostly at night. Travels to and from Caribbean mostly via Florida; rare farther west on Gulf coast. Fall migration often lasts through October, and strays in west may appear even later.

CONSERVATION STATUS — Requires tracts of unbroken forest for nesting, so undoubtedly has declined in some areas. Could be vulnerable to continued loss of habitat in both summer and winter ranges.

YELLOW-RUMPED WARBLER   *Dendroica coronata*

Flashing its trademark yellow rump patch as it flies away, calling *check* for confirmation, this is one of our best-known warblers. While most of its relatives migrate to the tropics in fall, the Yellow-rump, able to live on berries, commonly remains as far north as New England and Seattle; it is the main winter warbler in North America. Included in this species are two different-looking forms, the eastern "Myrtle" Warbler and western "Audubon's" Warbler.

HABITAT — *Conifer forests. In winter, varied; open woods, brush, thickets, gardens, even beaches.* In the north, breeds in coniferous and mixed forests, preferring more open stands and edges in pine, fir, spruce, aspen; also spruce-tamarack bogs. In west, breeds up to 12,000 feet in mountain conifer forests. In winter,

Yellow-rumped Warbler

common in many lowland habitats, especially coastal bayberry thickets in east and streamside woods in west.

FEEDING — **Diet:** *Insects and berries.* Feeds on caterpillars, wasps, grasshoppers, gnats, aphids, beetles, and many other insects; also spiders. Feeds in winter on berries of bayberry, juniper, wax myrtle, poison-ivy, and others. Can winter farther north than most warblers because it can digest the wax in berry coatings. **Behavior:** Versatile in its feeding. Searches among twigs and leaves and will hover while taking insects from foliage. Often flies out to catch flying insects. Will forage on ground and will cling to tree trunks and branches. Males tend to forage higher than females during the breeding season. In winter, usually forages in flocks.

NESTING — During courtship, male accompanies female everywhere, fluffs his side feathers, raises his wings and his colorful crown feathers, calls and flutters. **Nest:** Placed 4–50 feet above ground, usually on horizontal branch away from trunk of conifer or sometimes deciduous tree; sometimes in fork where branch meets trunk. Nest (built by female) is open cup made of bark fibers, weeds, twigs, roots; lined with hair and feathers in such a way as to curve over and partly cover the eggs. **Eggs:** 4–5, sometimes only 3. Creamy white with brown and gray marks. Incubated usually by female, 12–13 days. Occasionally the male will cover the eggs. **Young:** Both parents feed nestlings. Young leave nest after 10–12 days, can fly short distances 2–3 days later. First brood probably fed mostly by male after fledging. Normally two broods per year.

MIGRATION Migrates earlier in spring and later in fall than other warblers. The "Myrtle" form, mostly eastern, also winters commonly in streamside trees near coast in Pacific states. "Audubon's" is a very rare stray in the east.

BLACK-THROATED GRAY WARBLER *Dendroica nigrescens*

This strikingly patterned warbler is typical of semi-arid country in the west. It is often common in summer in the foothills, in open woods of juniper, pinyon pine, or oak, where its buzzy song carries well across the dry slopes. Of all the western warblers, this is the one that shows up most often in the east, but it is still rare enough there to provide excitement for eastern birders.

HABITAT *Dry oak slopes, pinyons, junipers, open mixed woods.* Breeds in dry coniferous and mixed woods, especially of oak, juniper, and pinyon pine. Also frequents manzanita thickets and chaparral. Prefers open areas, as in second growth, forest edges, or dry hillsides or canyons. In winter in Mexico, found in lowland dry forest, dense thorn scrub, and pine-oak woods.

FEEDING **Diet:** *Mostly insects.* Diet is not known in detail. Known to feed especially on oakworms and other green caterpillars. **Behavior:** The most common method of foraging during the breeding season is by searching for insects among leaves of low growing foliage; also hovers briefly to pick insects from various

Black-throated Gray Warbler

surfaces. Also flies out after flying insects. In migration and winter, often forages in mixed flocks with other species.

NESTING Details of nesting behavior not well known. Males arrive on breeding grounds in March or April in southern part of the range, in late May in the north. **Nest:** Site varies; may be 4–10 feet from trunk on horizontal branch in larger tree such as fir or oak, or closer to the main trunk in a smaller tree or shrub. Usually placed 7–35 feet above the ground, but can be 1–50 feet up. Nest is a neat, open cup, built probably by both sexes, made of weeds, dry grass, and plant fiber; lined with feathers, fur, hair, and moss. **Eggs:** Usually 4, sometimes 3–5. Creamy white, with brown marks often concentrated at larger end. Incubated by female for unknown number of days. **Young:** Both parents feed the nestlings. Age at which young leave the nest is not well known. Normally only one brood per year.

MIGRATION In the southwest, arrives early in spring and lingers late in fall, with some remaining through the winter. A rare stray east to the Atlantic coast, mostly in fall.

TOWNSEND'S WARBLER *Dendroica townsendi*

The coniferous forest of the Pacific Northwest is the summer home of Townsend's Warbler. There the sharply marked males sing from high in the spruces and hemlocks; their buzzy songs are quite variable, and some are similar to those of the Black-throated Green Warbler, an eastern relative. Most Townsend's go to Mexico or Central America for the winter, but small numbers remain along the coast north to Oregon, Washington, and even Vancouver Island.

HABITAT   *Tall conifers, cool fir forests; in winter, also oaks, madrones, laurels.* Breeds in tall, dense coniferous forest of the Pacific Northwest, both in the humid coastal belt and in the mountains. In winter in the tropics, found mostly in mountain forests of pine, oak, and alder. Along California coast, winters in oak woods and in conifers. Migrants occur in mountain conifer forests and in streamside trees in lowlands.

FEEDING   **Diet:** *Mostly insects.* While nesting, eats mainly insects, including caterpillars, true bugs, beetles, and leafhoppers; also a few spiders, seeds, and plant galls. On tropical wintering grounds, also feeds on some berries and nectar. **Behavior:** Forages mostly in higher parts of trees. Searches actively among twigs for insects, often hovering briefly to take items from foliage. Sometimes flies out to catch insects in the air. Except in nesting season, often feeds in mixed flocks with other warblers and other small birds.

Townsend's Warbler

NESTING   Males arrive on breeding grounds in late May, and establish territories by singing. The first eggs are laid by late June. **Nest:** Placed directly on top of branch, usually toward the end of horizontal conifer branch, 7–60 feet above the ground. Nest (probably built by both sexes) is a large shallow cup of grass stems, mosses, cedar bark, and fir twigs; lined with moss, feathers, and hair. **Eggs:** At least 3, commonly 4–5. White with brown marks. Details of incubation not well known; may be incubated by both sexes, estimated at about 12 days. **Young:** Nestlings are fed by female and possibly by male. Young leave the nest about 8–10 days after hatching.

MIGRATION   Migration is spread over a long period in both spring and fall. In the southwest, migrants occur at all elevations but are most common in the mountains.

HERMIT WARBLER   *Dendroica occidentalis*

This warbler nests in forests of fir, hemlock, and other conifers in the mountains and along the coast from California north to Washington. It also winters locally on the California coast, almost always in conifers. No more a "hermit" than other warblers,

Hermit Warbler

it often joins mixed flocks of birds in the mountain pine forests during migration. This species is closely related to Townsend's Warbler, and the two often interbreed where their ranges meet in Washington and Oregon.

HABITAT   *Conifer forests; in migration, conifers and deciduous woods.* Breeds mostly in moist, dense forests near sea level, especially in forests of Douglas-fir, hemlock, and western redcedar. Also nests in cooler, wetter forests of fir and other trees at higher elevations. In winter found in pine-oak forests of mountains in Mexico, also in oaks and conifers along California coast.

FEEDING   **Diet:** *Mostly insects.* Has been observed feeding on caterpillars, tiny beetles, and flying insects; also small spiders. **Behavior:** Forages mainly in the canopy of tall trees, sometimes up to 200 feet above the ground. Males often forage higher than females. Takes insects from twigs while perching and while hovering, and flies out to catch insects in midair. Moves from trunk of tree out to branch tips, then begins again at trunk. Will hang from twigs like a chickadee. In migration and winter, often forages in flocks with other birds.

NESTING Males arrive on the breeding grounds in early May, and establish territories by singing. The first eggs are laid by the first part of June. **Nest:** Typical site is on horizontal branch, well out from trunk and 20–40 feet above the ground. Nest is a compact, deep, open cup of fibrous weed stalks, pine needles, twigs, lichen, moss, cobwebs, and lined with soft material such as soft bark, feathers, and animal hair. Female alone builds nest. **Eggs:** 4–5, sometimes 3. Creamy, with fine brown flecks in wreath at larger end. Incubation is probably by both parents, probably about 12 days. This species apparently is almost never parasitized by cowbirds. **Young:** Fed by female and possibly by male as well. Young leave the nest 8–10 days after hatching.

MIGRATION   Migrates most commonly north along the Pacific coast in spring and south through the mountains in fall. Southward migration begins early, with many on the move in August or even late July.

CONSERVATION STATUS   Could be vulnerable to loss of habitat with cutting of northwestern forests. Still common within its range.

BLACK-THROATED GREEN WARBLER *Dendroica virens*

In the east, some of the easiest warbler voices to recognize are the patterned songs of the Black-throated Green. As if to confirm the identification, the brilliantly colored male often perches out in the open to sing, perhaps on a high twig of a spruce. He actually has two song types, used in different situations: he sings *zoo zee zoo zoo zee* to proclaim and defend his nesting territory, and *zee zee zee zoo zee* in courtship or when communicating with his mate.

Black-throated Green Warbler

HABITAT   *Mainly conifers.* Breeds mostly in coniferous and mixed forests, very locally in deciduous forest. Often nests around spruce, also in white pine, hemlock, redcedar, and jack pine. An isolated race on the southern Atlantic coast breeds in cypress swamps. During migration, occurs widely in woodland and edges. Usually winters in foothills and mountains among oaks and pines.

FEEDING   **Diet:** *Insects, especially caterpillars.* Feeds mainly on nonhairy caterpillars during summer, as well as beetles, true bugs, gnats, aphids, and others, also spiders. Takes poison-ivy berries and other berries in migration. In winter, may eat protein corpuscles of tropical cecropia trees. **Behavior:** Searches for insects among branches, twigs, and bases of leaves, moving rapidly between foraging sites. Frequently hovers to take insects from underside of leaves. Occasionally catches insects in midair. Males tend to forage higher than females while breeding. In late summer, often forages in mixed flocks with chickadees.

NESTING Males establish territories by singing, also by chasing and fighting with intruding males. **Nest:** Sites are next to trunk where two or more small branches fork out of conifer, usually low (often only a few feet above ground). The race nesting in southern swamps places its nest well out from trunk, and often higher (to 50 feet

or more above ground). Nest (built by both sexes) is open cup of twigs, grass, weeds, bark, spider webs, lined with plant fibers, hair, moss, and feathers. **Eggs:** 4, sometimes 3–5. Gray to creamy white with spots or scrawls of reddish brown. Only female incubates, 12 days. In some areas, up to one-third of nests are parasitized by cowbirds. **Young:** Nestlings are fed only by female at first, later by male. Young leave nest 11 days after hatching. Parents split up the fledglings, each adult tending half the brood for up to a month.

MIGRATION   Migrates mostly at night. Fall passage may last fairly late, extending well into October, even in the north.

CONSERVATION STATUS   Has declined as a nesting bird in parts of the northeast during recent decades. Elsewhere, still widespread and common.

GOLDEN-CHEEKED WARBLER   *Dendroica chrysoparia*

This beautiful bird is a central Texas specialty, nesting nowhere else in the world. It returns early in spring; by the end of March, males can be found singing from the tops of junipers on arid slopes in the hill country. Its total range and population are small, and recently it has faced a double threat: its habitat is disappearing as the area becomes more developed, and where it does still breed, cowbirds often lay their eggs in its nest.

HABITAT   *Junipers, oaks; also streamside trees.* Habitat specialist during the nesting season. Breeds on hillsides and slopes in mature woods of Ashe juniper, especially brakes of junipers 10–20 feet tall interspersed with deciduous trees such as oak, walnut, pecan, and hackberry. In winter in the tropics, found in mountain pine-oak forests.

FEEDING   **Diet:** *Almost entirely insects.* Feeds on caterpillars, green lacewings, small cicadas, beetles, ants, katydids, walkingsticks, deer flies, crane flies, moths, aphids, true bugs, and others; also spiders.

Golden-cheeked Warbler

Behavior: During the breeding season, forages in the upper two-thirds of junipers and deciduous trees, apparently never on the ground. Most common method of feeding is gleaning insects in juniper foliage, hopping among the branches. Also makes short flights out to catch flying insects. Beats caterpillars on branch and removes moth wings before eating or feeding to young.

NESTING   Males return to breeding grounds about middle of March. Females follow about 5 days later. Both sexes faithful to site, returning to previous year's breeding territory. In courtship, male fluffs feathers and calls; occasionally displays by facing female and spreading wings. **Nest:** Female chooses site, usually in fork of juniper branches, sometimes in small oak, walnut, or pecan tree. Deep, compact, open cup nest, constructed by the female, always made of bark strips from Ashe juniper. Also can include spider web, lichens, mosses, leaves, and grass. Nest lined with rootlets, feathers, and hair. **Eggs:** 3–4, sometimes 5. White to creamy, with flecks of brown concentrated at large end. Incubation by female only, 12 days. **Young:** Both parents feed nestlings. Young leave nest about 9 days after hatching. Parents split up the fledglings, each adult caring for part of brood for 4–7 weeks. One brood per year.

MIGRATION   An early migrant in both spring and fall, arriving in Texas in March, departing mostly in August. Apparently migrates north and south through mountains of eastern Mexico. Single strays have reached California and Florida.

CONSERVATION STATUS Very localized in range, now threatened by loss of habitat and by heavy parasitism of nests by cowbirds.

BLACKBURNIAN WARBLER *Dendroica fusca*

A fiery gem of the treetops. In the northern forest in summer, the male Blackburnian Warbler may perch on the topmost twig of a spruce, showing off the flaming orange of his throat as he sings his thin, wiry song. The female also stays high in the conifers, and the nest is usually built far above the ground. Long-distance migrants, most Blackburnians spend the winter in South America, where they are often common in mountain forest in the Andes.

HABITAT *Woodlands; conifers in summer.* Breeds in boreal coniferous and mixed forests, especially spruce and hemlock. In southern part of breeding range in Appalachians, can inhabit completely deciduous forests. When migrating, occurs in all kinds of trees and brush. During winter in the tropics, usually in humid mountain forest.

FEEDING **Diet:** *Mostly insects, especially caterpillars.* In summer, feeds on many caterpillars, particularly those of spruce budworm; also eats beetles, ants, flies, and many other insects, also spiders. Especially during winter, will take some berries as well. **Behavior:** Feeds mostly in treetops, searching along small branches and twigs. Also hovers to take insects from undersides and tips of foliage. Will search dead leaf clumps; occasionally flies out to catch flying insects. In spruce forests, males tend to forage higher than females. In winter in the Andes, forages in mixed flocks with various tropical birds.

Blackburnian Warbler

NESTING Details of nesting behavior not well known, partly because nests are high and hard to observe. Male defends nesting territory by singing, sometimes by attacking intruding males. In courtship, male sings, performs displays with gliding flight and fluttering wings and tail. **Nest:** Almost always placed in dense vegetation near tips of branches of conifers, and usually high, sometimes up to 80 feet above ground. Nest (probably built by female) is cup-shaped and made of twigs, bark, and fibers; lined with lichens, moss, grass, hair, and conifer needles. **Eggs:** 4, sometimes 3–5. White to greenish white, with blotches of reddish brown concentrated near the larger end. Only females incubate, probably 12–13 days. Male feeds female during incubation. **Young:** Both parents feed nestlings. When the young leave the nest, the parents separate, each caring for part of the brood.

MIGRATION From wintering areas (mostly in Andes of South America), many apparently move north through Central America, then fly north across Gulf of Mexico. Fall migration may be spread out over a broader front.

CONSERVATION STATUS May be especially vulnerable to loss of wintering habitat, with cutting of forest at midlevels in mountains in the tropics.

YELLOW-THROATED WARBLER *Dendroica dominica*

A clear-voiced singer in the treetops in southern woodlands. Yellow-throated Warblers return very early in spring to the pine woods and cypress swamps, where they may be seen foraging rather deliberately along branches high in the trees. In the Midwest, they are typically found in riverside groves of sycamores. During the winter in Florida and other tropical areas, they are commonly seen creeping about in the crowns of palms, probing among the fronds with their long bills.

HABITAT *Open woodlands, groves, especially live oaks, pines, sycamores.* Breeds in a variety of southern forest types. On southern Atlantic coastal plain, occurs in old live oaks covered with Spanish moss. In south, lives in pine forest and cypress swamps. In Mississippi Valley, also breeds along streams in bottomland woods, especially of sycamores. During winter, often forages in palm groves.

FEEDING **Diet:** *Mostly insects.* Feeds on many insects including beetles, moths, caterpillars, grasshoppers, crickets, flies, mosquitoes, ants, scale insects, aphids, and others; also spiders. **Behavior:** Favorite method of foraging includes much creeping along on branches and leaning trunks. Probes into crevices in bark with its long bill. Also flies out to catch flying insects in midair. In winter in the tropics, frequently seen searching for insects by hanging upside down among leaves of palms.

Yellow-throated Warbler

NESTING Arrives on breeding grounds early in spring, and males defend nesting territory by singing. **Nest:** Placed in Spanish moss at end of branch. Where Spanish moss does not occur, nest is placed on high branch of pine, sycamore, or cypress, usually 30–60 feet up, sometimes 4–120 feet above ground. Nest is an open cup made of grass, moss, bark strips, weeds, and caterpillar webs, lined with plant down and feathers. Built by both sexes, but mostly by female. **Eggs:** Usually 4, sometimes 5. Dull grayish white, with spots of purple, red, and brown. Incubation period is probably 12–13 days. Female incubates, and possibly male does also. **Young:** Probably both parents feed nestlings, but details (including age at which the young leave the nest) are not well known. Usually two broods per year.

MIGRATION Migrates mostly at night. A very early migrant in spring, reaching many parts of the breeding range in March. Also moves south early, departing many areas in August.

CONSERVATION STATUS Has undoubtedly disappeared from some areas with loss of breeding habitat, but current populations probably stable.

GRACE'S WARBLER *Dendroica graciae*

A young man named Elliott Coues, who later became a leading ornithologist, discovered this bird in Arizona in 1864; perhaps homesick, he asked that it be named after his sister. Grace's Warbler is still common in the southwest as a summer resident in mountain forests. It spends most of its time high in pine trees, where the male sings his thin rising chatter and the female builds a neat, cup-shaped nest among a cluster of pine needles.

HABITAT *Pine-oak forests of mountains.* During the breeding season, found mainly in the tops of pines, sometimes also in spruce, fir, and oak thickets in higher mountains of the southwest. In winter in Mexico, inhabits pine-oak woods in the mountains.

FEEDING **Diet:** *Presumably mostly insects.* Details of diet are not well known; undoubtedly eats mostly insects, like other warblers. **Behavior:** During the

Grace's Warbler

breeding season, often forages by flying out from the treetops to catch insects in midair. Also searches among branches and twigs and hovers briefly while picking insects from foliage, spending most of its time in the tops of the taller pine trees.

NESTING   Details of breeding behavior are not well known. In the southwest, arrives on breeding grounds mostly in early April. Males defend nesting territories by singing. **Nest:** Placed on a horizontal branch or in the top crown of tree, usually pine, sometimes fir, 20–60 feet above the ground. Nest (built by female) is a tightly constructed open cup made of plant fibers, oak catkins, plant down, and webs of spiders and caterpillars; lined with animal hair and feathers. Nest is often well hidden in a cluster of pine needles. **Eggs:** 3–4. Creamy white, spotted with browns around larger end. Details and timing of incubation are not well known. **Young:** Nestlings are fed by female, probably by male as well. Age at which young leave the nest is not well known. Normally two broods per year.

MIGRATION   In the southwest, arrives mostly in April and departs mostly by early September. Very rare autumn stray west to California coast, but it has wintered there several times.

CONSERVATION STATUS   Numbers in our area probably stable. Could be vulnerable to loss of habitat in mountains of Mexico and Central America.

PINE WARBLER   *Dendroica pinus*

This well-named bird is not often seen away from pine trees, especially during the breeding season. More sluggish than most of their relatives, Pine Warblers forage in

Pine Warbler

a rather leisurely way at all levels in the pine woods, from the ground to the treetops. This species is only a short-distance migrant, and almost the entire population spends the winter within the southern United States. Unlike most warblers, it regularly comes to bird feeders for suet or other soft foods.

HABITAT   *Chiefly open pine woods, pine barrens.* Usually breeds in open pine woods, especially southern longleaf pine forest, sandy barrens of pitch pine with scrub oak undergrowth, jack-pine barrens, and similar habitats. Also sometimes in cedar or cypress. In winter, occurs in a wider variety of habitats including heavily wooded bottomlands, orchards, thickets, woodland edges.

FEEDING   **Diet:** *Insects, seeds, berries.* Largely feeds on insects and spiders; diet includes grasshoppers, caterpillars, moths, beetles, ants, bugs, others. When few insects available, often eats seeds of pine, grass, and weeds, also some berries. Will visit bird feeders for suet and other items. **Behavior:** Does much climbing on tree trunks and will walk on ground to forage for dormant insects or seeds. Feeds deliberately, gleaning insects from foliage, sometimes hanging from needle clusters like a titmouse. Probes in pine cones for insects. In winter in the south, may forage in flocks with Eastern Bluebirds.

NESTING   Males begin singing on breeding territories in early February in the southern part of their range, in late March or early April in the north. **Nest:** Sites located toward the ends of limbs of pines or occasionally other trees, usually 30–50 feet above the ground, can be 8–135 feet up. Concealed from below by foliage. Nest (built by female) is deep, open cup of weed stalks, grass stems, strips of bark, pine needles, twigs, spider web; lined with feathers. **Eggs:** 3–5, usually 4. Off-white, with brown specks toward the large end. Incubation is by both parents, probably about 10 days. **Young:** Both parents bring food for nestlings. Young leave the nest at 10 days of age. Pairs may raise 2–3 broods annually.

MIGRATION   Tends to migrate early in spring and late in fall, and many southern birds may be nonmigratory. Those living on islands in the Caribbean apparently are also permanent residents.

CONSERVATION STATUS   Surveys suggest that numbers are stable or perhaps even increasing slightly.

KIRTLAND'S WARBLER *Dendroica kirtlandii*

Kirtland's Warbler

One of our rarest songbirds, Kirtland's is a relatively large warbler that forages slowly, close to the ground, wagging its tail up and down. It nests only in stands of young jack pines in central Michigan, a habitat that grows up only briefly after fires, and its nests have been heavily parasitized in recent decades by Brown-headed Cowbirds. Controlled burning to create more habitat and control of cowbird numbers have helped the warbler somewhat, but its total population in most recent years has remained below 1,000.

HABITAT   *Young jack pine; winters in dense understory of pines.* Breeds only in large stands of young jack pines from 5–25 feet tall. Jack pine grows on sandy soils and regenerates only after fires. In migration, seen in thickets and deciduous trees. Rarely seen in winter; winters only in dense undergrowth of pine forests of the Bahamas.

FEEDING   **Diet:** *Mostly small insects, some berries.* In summer, eats many insects, including sawfly adults and larvae, grasshopper nymphs, moths, and flies. Adults also feed on pine sap and blueberries. May feed soft berries to young. In winter in the Bahamas, feeds on insects and small fruits. **Behavior:** Forages for insects near the ground and in lower parts of pines and oaks. Will hop on ground to probe for insects. Gleans insects from pine needles and other vegetation, and occasionally takes items while hovering. Solitary in its foraging in winter.

NESTING   Males arrive on breeding grounds in mid-May, a few days before the females, and establish large territories. Tend to be loosely colonial (lone pairs are rare), and males tend to return to the same colony in which they previously nested. Males sometimes have more than one mate. **Nest:** Placed on ground in sandy soil close to pine. Nest (built by female) is open cup of grass, sedge, pine needles, oak leaves, lined with rootlets, hair, moss, and fibers. **Eggs:** 4, sometimes 3–6. Buff or pinkish white with brown spots at larger end. Incubation is by female only, 13–15 days; males feed females on nest during incubation. Up to 70 percent of nests are parasitized by Brown-headed Cowbirds in areas where cowbirds are not controlled by humans. **Young:** Fed by both parents. Young leave nest at age of 9 days, do not fly well at first. Parents continue to feed young up to 6 weeks. Usually one brood, rarely two.

Arrives on nesting grounds mostly in mid-May, and gradually departs during August and September, migrating to the Bahamas. Very seldom seen in migration, probably because of the needle-in-a-haystack challenge of finding such a rare bird.

CONSERVATION STATUS *Endangered.* Always known as a scarce bird with a limited range, Kirtland's Warbler apparently began to decline seriously in the 1960s; census numbers dropped from 502 singing males in 1961 to only 201 in 1971. Through most of the 1970s and 1980s, the annual counts hovered around 200 males, twice dropping as low as 167. Since 1990 the numbers have gradually increased, surpassing 700 singing males in 1995. Although these are still dangerously low numbers for a songbird, the trend is encouraging. Conservationists are helping the bird by providing more habitat (controlled burning creates the stands of young jack pines needed by the warbler) and by controlling the numbers of parasitic cowbirds in the nesting areas.

PRAIRIE WARBLER *Dendroica discolor*

Not a bird of open prairies, this warbler nests mainly in young second-growth scrub and densely overgrown fields in eastern North America. Such habitats are often temporary, and colonies may shift around from year to year. In Florida, more permanent populations are found in coastal mangroves. In all of these sun-drenched habitats, the thin buzzy song of the male seems suited to the glare of hot summer days. Prairie Warblers usually stay low, moving about actively in the brush and flicking their tails.

HABITAT *Brushy slashings, bushy pastures, low pines.* Breeds in dry old clearings, edges of forest, and sandy pine barrens with undergrowth of scrub oaks, especially on ends of slopes and ridges. Likes thick second growth of hickory, dogwood, hazel, or laurel with blackberry vines. In Florida, breeds in mangrove swamps. In winter, found in flat, grassy lands with scattered trees and bushes in the south.

FEEDING **Diet:** *Mostly insects.* Feeds on many insects including caterpillars, moths, tree crickets, lacewings, true bugs, beetles, ants, flies; also spiders and millipedes. Also eats a few berries and occasionally sap from holes drilled in trees by sapsuckers. Nestlings are fed mostly caterpillars. **Behavior:** Forages mainly by taking insects while perched or hopping on branches or

Prairie Warbler

twigs. Also catches flying insects in midair and takes insects from undersides of leaves (and spiders from their webs) while hovering. Will also feed occasionally by hanging upside down from tips of branches or by flying down to pick up insects from ground.

NESTING Some males have more than one mate. Often breeds in loose colonies. Males return year after year to the same breeding territory, but females often do not. Males utter a loud, harsh rattle during fights with other males. During courtship, male performs slow butterfly-like display flights; also chases female. **Nest:** Site selected by female. Usually rather low in tree, can be 1–45 feet above the ground. In coastal Florida, usually in mangroves. Nest (built by female) an open cup, made of densely felted plant materials such as plant down, and lined with animal hair. **Eggs:** 4, sometimes 3–5. Off-white, with brown spots concentrated at larger end. Incubated by female for usually 12 (11–14) days. Commonly parasitized by cowbirds. **Young:** Fed by both parents; leave the nest at 8–11 days. Fledglings may be divided by parents, each adult caring for part of brood for 40–50 days until young are independent. Often two broods per season.

MIGRATION   Some Florida birds may be permanent residents. In much of range, southward migration begins by late summer, but a few birds may linger quite late in fall.

CONSERVATION STATUS   Surveys show declining numbers in recent decades. Over much of range, requires brushy areas growing up after clearing or fires, and disappears as forests mature. Also hurt by cowbird parasitism.

PALM WARBLER *Dendroica palmarum*

Palm Warbler

A bird of thickets and open areas, usually seen low or on the ground. Birds from the easternmost part of the range ("Yellow Palm Warblers") are rather colorful, but most others are quite drab; however, they can be recognized by the constant bobbing of their tails. Many Palm Warblers spend the winter in the southeastern United States, especially in Florida, where they may be seen near palm groves but not up in the palms themselves.

HABITAT   *Wooded borders of muskeg (summer). In migration, low trees, bushes, ground.* Breeds in sphagnum bogs with scattered cedar, tamarack, and spruce trees. The western race also breeds in dry pine barrens of boreal forests with ground cover of blueberry, bearberry, and sweet fern. In migration, frequents old hedgerows, edges of streams and ponds, overgrown fields, and open pastures.

FEEDING   **Diet:** *Insects and berries.* Feeds mostly on small beetles, mosquitoes, flies, caterpillars, aphids, grasshoppers, ants, bees, and spiders. Eats also a considerable amount of vegetable matter, including raspberries, bayberries, and seeds. **Behavior:** In winter, does much foraging by walking and hopping on the ground. During the breeding season, gleans insects from foliage while perching or while hovering momentarily in black spruce, tamarack, and cedars. Also flies out to catch flying insects in midair. In fall, may join flocks with other warblers, chickadees, juncos, and sparrows.

NESTING   Some males have more than one mate. An early nester; birds arrive on breeding grounds in early April and begin nests by early May. **Nest:** Placed on or near the ground in a stunted spruce tree, close to the trunk. Open cup nest is frequently concealed under a clump of grass and on top of a hummock of sphagnum moss. Constructed by the female of fine, dry grass stems and bark shreds; lined with feathers. **Eggs:** Usually 4–5. Creamy white with brown marks. Incubated possibly by both parents, 12 days. Rarely a host to cowbird eggs; defends against parasitism by covering cowbird eggs with a new floor at the bottom of the nest. **Young:** Fed by both parents. Young leave the nest at about 12 days and are able to fly short distances within 1–2 days after fledging. Probably two broods per year.

MIGRATION   Compared with most warblers, migrates early in spring and late in fall. The duller-plumaged "Western" Palm Warbler is more numerous along the Atlantic coast in fall than in spring. Very small numbers winter regularly on the Pacific coast.

CONSERVATION STATUS   Numbers apparently stable. Faces no major threats to habitat on either breeding or wintering grounds; often winters in open or disturbed areas.

BAY-BREASTED WARBLER   *Dendroica castanea*

This is a characteristic warbler of spruce forest in eastern Canada in summer. Its numbers vary from year to year and are likely to increase quickly during population explosions of the spruce budworm or other forest pests. This species forages rather slowly compared with most warblers, moving deliberately among the branches. The male Bay-breasted Warbler is unmistakable in spring but goes through a striking transformation in fall, becoming a greenish "confusing fall warbler."

HABITAT   *Woodlands, conifers in summer.* Usually breeds in northern coniferous forest, in thick stands of spruce and fir. Where spruce is not found, will nest in deciduous or mixed second-growth woods of birches, maples, firs, and pines. In winter in the tropics, occurs in forest edge, second growth, and open woodland.

FEEDING   **Diet:** *Mostly insects, berries.* In breeding season, eats a variety of insects, including beetles, flies, moths, caterpillars, leafhoppers, and grasshoppers; also Virginia creeper berries and mulberries. May eat many spruce budworms when that insect is at epidemic numbers. In winter in the tropics, also eats many berries. **Behavior:** Appears more sluggish in foraging than do other *Dendroica* warblers feeding in the same spruce forests. Forages in and out along branches, mostly at midlevels in trees. Rarely catches flying insects in midair. In winter in the tropics, joins mixed foraging flocks in the forest canopy.

NESTING   Males may not arrive on breeding grounds until early June. **Nest:** Site is on a horizontal branch of a dense spruce, hemlock, birch, or other tree, 4–40 feet above the ground. Nest is a large, open cup, either loosely built or compact, made of grasses, lichens, roots, mosses, and protruding conifer twigs;

Bay-breasted Warbler

lined with bark strips and hair. **Eggs:** 4–5, sometimes 3–7. Off-white, with brown or black marks at larger end. Incubated by female, 12–13 days. Female is fed on the nest by the male during incubation. Tends to lay more eggs in years of spruce budworm outbreaks, when food is abundant. Rarely parasitized by cowbirds. **Young:** Both parents feed the nestlings. Young leave the nest 10–12 days after hatching.

MIGRATION   In spring, most apparently move north through Central America and then fly north across the Gulf of Mexico, continuing to Canada and the northeast. In fall, evidently moves south on a broader front. Some may linger quite late in fall.

CONSERVATION STATUS   Numbers may rise and fall, increasing after big outbreaks of spruce budworm or other insects. Could be vulnerable to loss of habitat on wintering grounds.

BLACKPOLL WARBLER   *Dendroica striata*

The Blackpoll is among the most numerous warblers in far northern forests in summer, and perhaps the most impressive migrant of all our small birds. Every fall, most Blackpoll Warblers make an over-water migration from our northeastern coast to northern South America; some may pause in Bermuda or the Antilles, but others apparently fly nonstop for more than 72 hours. In spring they are more leisurely, traveling via the West Indies and Florida, pausing to sing in our shade trees on their way north.

HABITAT *Conifers; broadleaf trees in migration.* Breeds in low northern spruce forest and in alder thickets north of the Arctic Circle and north of tree-line. In migration, moves through forests, parks, and gardens. In winter in the tropics, found in wooded areas, often in canopy of trees.

FEEDING **Diet:** *Mostly insects and berries.* During the breeding season eats aphids, scale insects, caterpillars, beetles, gnats, mosquitoes, cankerworms, sawflies, wasps, ants, termites, and other insects. Also eats spiders and their eggs, pokeberries, and a few seeds. In migration, noted feeding on spiders, aphids, and scale insects found on citrus and native plants in Florida. **Behavior:** Forages in a deliberate manner, creeping along on branches in the tops of taller trees, gleaning insects from bark, leaves, and twigs. Also flies out to catch flying insects. In migration, may forage frequently with other warblers.

Blackpoll Warbler

NESTING A few males have more than one mate per nesting season. Females return to nest site of previous year and mate with male holding that territory, whether or not he is already mated. Courtship and nest building are deliberate and protracted, and begin later in the season than in most warblers. **Nest:** Placed next to trunk, on horizontal branch, usually 2–12 feet above ground, rarely more than 30 feet up. Site is in the understory of young spruce or fir saplings, sometimes in alder thickets. Bulky open cup (built by female) is made of twigs, bark, sprays of spruce, grass stems, weeds, moss, and lichens; lined with feathers, hair, rootlets. **Eggs:** 4–5, sometimes 3. Off-white, with brown and lavender spots. Incubation probably about 12 days, by female. Male feeds female on nest during incubation. **Young:** Fed by both parents. Leave nest 11–12 days after hatching. One brood per year, sometimes two.

MIGRATION Spring migration moves north mostly through Florida, spreading west from there. In fall, many fly nonstop from eastern Canada or northeastern United States to northern South America. Every fall, many (to 100 or more) lost strays appear along Pacific coast.

CONSERVATION STATUS Abundant, but may be decreasing in southern parts of breeding distribution. Vulnerable to loss of habitat, especially on winter range.

CERULEAN WARBLER *Dendroica cerulea*

The sky blue upperparts of the male Cerulean Warbler are difficult to observe in summer: at that season, the birds stay high in the tops of leafy trees in the eastern United States and extreme southern Canada. The bird itself has become harder to observe in recent decades, as its numbers have decreased in parts of its range. Cowbirds, which lay their eggs in the warblers' nests, may be finding their unwitting "hosts" more easily as forest patches become smaller.

HABITAT *Deciduous forests, especially in river valleys.* Breeds in mature hardwoods either in uplands or along streams. Prefers elm, soft maple, oak, birch, hickory, beech, basswood, linden, sycamore, or black ash. Nests only in tall forest with clear understory. In winter in tropics, found mostly in forest and woodland borders in foothills and lower slopes.

FEEDING **Diet:** *Insects.* Diet not well known; undoubtedly feeds mostly or entirely on insects, like most warblers. Has been observed feeding on caterpillars. **Behavior:** Forages mostly high in trees, moving rapidly from limb to limb, searching

Cerulean Warbler

among foliage and twigs for insects. Also flies out to catch insects in midair. In winter in the tropics, scattered individuals forage with mixed flocks, ranging from low to high in the trees.

NESTING Males arrive on breeding grounds near the middle of May. Nesting behavior has been little studied because of the difficulty of observing the nests. **Nest:** Placed on horizontal branch of hardwood, far from trunk and usually high, 15–90 feet up. Favors oak, maple, basswood, elm, hickory, sycamore, beech, or tulip trees. Nest is a small, shallow open cup (probably built by female), made of bark strips, grasses, weeds, spider silk, and lichen; lined with moss and hair. **Eggs:** 3–5, usually 4. Gray or creamy off-white, with spots of brown. Incubation by female only, probably 12–13 days. Apparently does not often host cowbird eggs where it can nest in unbroken mature forest, but may be parasitized more frequently in forest fragments. **Young:** Both parents feed the nestlings. Age at which the young leave the nest is not well known.

MIGRATION Moves south relatively early in fall. Spring migrants coming north from South America may make a regular stopover in Belize before continuing north across the Gulf of Mexico to southeastern United States. A very rare stray anywhere in west.

CONSERVATION STATUS Surveys show steadily declining numbers in recent years. Nesting efforts may fail because of increasing cowbird parasitism in smaller patches of forest. May also be losing winter habitat in tropics.

GENUS *Mniotilta*

BLACK-AND-WHITE WARBLER *Mniotilta varia*

This bird is often a favorite warbler of beginning birders because it is easy to see and easy to recognize. It was once known as the "Black-and-white Creeper," a name

Black-and-white Warbler

that describes its behavior quite well. Like a nuthatch or creeper (and unlike other warblers), it climbs about on the trunks and major limbs of trees, seeking insects in the bark crevices. It often feeds low, and nests even lower, usually on the ground.

HABITAT *Woods; trunks, limbs of trees.* Breeds in mature or second-growth forests, deciduous and mixed. Often in woods on dry, rocky hillsides and ravines. Also nests in dry portions of wooded swamps. In migration, seen most often on trunks and low branches of trees within woodlands and thickets. In winter in the tropics, found in trees from sea level to high in the mountains.

FEEDING **Diet:** *Insects.* Feeds on a wide variety of caterpillars (including those of gypsy moths), beetles (including bark beetles, click beetles, and wood borers), ants, flies, bugs, leafhoppers, aphids, and other insects; also spiders and daddy longlegs. **Behavior:** Adapted to creeping along limbs and on tree trunks to feed.

Switches body from side to side at each hop while foraging. In early spring, takes dormant insects from tree trunks and branches. Sometimes flies out to catch insects in midair.

NESTING   Males arrive on breeding grounds in late April, before the females. During courtship, male chases female, with much singing and fluttering. **Nest:** Placed on ground (or less than 2 feet up), under dead leaves or limbs, against a shrub, rock, log, or tree. Often constructed in cavity at top of stump or in a depression in the ground. Open cup (built by female) made of leaves, coarse grass stems, bark strips, pine needles, rootlets; lined with fine grass or hair. **Eggs:** 5, sometimes 4, rarely 6. Creamy white, flecked with brown at large end. Incubated by female only, 10–12 days. Commonly parasitized by cowbirds. **Young:** Fed by both parents. Leave the nest 8–12 days after hatching, before they are able to fly well.

MIGRATION   Spring migration begins rather early; migration is spread over a lengthy period in both spring and fall. Strays may appear in the west at any season. Migrates mostly at night.

CONSERVATION STATUS   Has disappeared from some former nesting areas, especially in south and midwest. Still widespread and common.

GENUS *Setophaga*

AMERICAN REDSTART   *Setophaga ruticilla*

Warblers in general are often called "the butterflies of the bird world," but the Redstart may live up to that nickname more than any other species. This beautiful warbler flits about very actively in the trees, usually holding its wings and tail partly spread as if to show off their patches of color. At times it feeds more like a flycatcher than a typical warbler, hovering among the foliage and often flying out to grab insects in midair.

HABITAT   *Second-growth woods, river groves.* Breeds in open deciduous and mixed woodland, preferring edges of forests or second growth. Attracted also to roadside trees, shrubby and tree-lined stream banks, and ponds. Will nest in second-growth maples, birch, and aspen following fire in coniferous forests. In the northwest, prefers willow and alder thickets. In winter in the tropics, found in lowland woods.

FEEDING   **Diet:** *Mostly insects.* Feeds on a wide variety of insects including beetles, caterpillars, moths, leafhoppers, aphids, midges, crane flies; also spiders and daddy longlegs. Also eats some seeds and berries. **Behavior:** Forages very actively, often flying out to catch insects in midair or hovering to take them from foliage. Flycatches much more than most warblers, drooping its wings, fanning its tail, and leaping high in the air. Males feed higher and make more midair sallies than do females early in the nesting season. Does not cling to tips of branches while hanging upside down as many warblers do. Holds large caterpillars and moths in bill and bangs them on perch before eating.

NESTING   Males sometimes mate with more than one female and raise 2–3 broods simultaneously. Males perform a frequent boundary display flight toward rivals, flying out with stiff wingbeats and gliding in a semicircle back to perch. Male

American Redstart

displays to female during courtship by fluffing plumage, raising crown feathers, spreading wings and tail, and bowing. **Nest:** Site picked by female, usually in fork of tree, 4–70 feet up; rarely on the ground. Open cup nest (built by female) of plant fibers, grass, rootlets, decorated with lichen, birch bark, and feathers; lined with feathers. Sometimes uses old nests of other birds. **Eggs:** 4, sometimes 2–5. Off-white, with brown or gray marks. Incubation by female only, 11–12 days. Often parasitized by cowbirds. **Young:** Fed by both parents. Leave the nest at about 9 days old. The parents divide the brood, each parent attending half the fledglings. Normally one brood per season.

MIGRATION   Migrates mostly at night. Fall migration begins early, with many southbound in August. Small numbers of strays appear throughout the west, and a few may winter in southern California.

CONSERVATION STATUS   Still widespread and very common, but surveys suggest numbers may be declining slightly.

GENUS *Protonotaria*

PROTHONOTARY WARBLER   *Protonotaria citrea*

In southeastern swamps in summer, this bright golden warbler sings from high in the trees. It is unique among eastern warblers in its habit of nesting in holes in trees

rather than in the open; it will sometimes nest in birdhouses placed close to water. The name "Prothonotary" refers to a group of official scribes in the Catholic Church who wore bright yellow hoods, as this bird appears to do.

HABITAT   *Wooded swamps.* Breeds in flooded riverbottom hardwoods including black willow, ash, buttonbush, sweetgum, red maple, hackberry, river birch, and elm; or wetlands with bay trees surrounded by cypress swamp. Also nests near borders of lakes, rivers, and ponds, normally only in areas with slow-moving or standing water. Winters in the tropics in lowland woods and mangrove swamps.

FEEDING   **Diet:** *Insects and snails.* Feeds on adult insects and larvae (especially aquatic insects) including ants, caterpillars, mayflies, and beetles; also

Prothonotary Warbler

snails and other small mollusks, spiders, and some seeds. **Behavior:** Feeds by gleaning insects among foliage, normally low in thickets and usually above water. Sometimes hops about on floating driftwood and mossy logs, peeping into crevices. May occasionally forage by winding its way up the trunks of trees like a nuthatch.

NESTING   Males arrive on nesting grounds in early April, about a week before females. Males establish territories by singing, vigorous displays, chases, and fighting. Males place small amounts of moss into the nest cavity, building dummy nests, but only female builds real nest. Male displays intensively to the female during courtship by fluffing plumage and spreading wings and tail. **Nest:** Site usually 5–10 feet up (sometimes 3–30 feet), above standing water in hole in tree or stump. Cavities are often old Downy Woodpecker nests. Sometimes excavates its own hole in very rotten stumps, and will use birdhouses. Female fills nest cavity nearly to the entrance hole with moss, dry leaves, twigs and bark, then lines it with rootlets and bark strips. **Eggs:** 4–6, sometimes 3–8. Creamy or pink, with spots of brown. Incubation is by female, 12–14 days. **Young:** Fed by both parents. Leave nest 10–11 days after hatching. Supposedly can swim at fledging. Two broods per year.

MIGRATION   Migrates relatively early in both spring and fall, with peaks in many areas during April and August. A very rare stray in the west, mostly in fall.

CONSERVATION STATUS   Undoubtedly declined in past with clearing of southern swamp forests. Still fairly common in remaining habitat. Has been helped in some areas by birdhouses put up by conservationists.

GENUS *Helmitheros*

WORM-EATING WARBLER   *Helmitheros vermivorus*

A dry trilled song in the undergrowth of deciduous woods in summer announces that the Worm-eating Warbler is at home. Less colorful than most of its relatives, it

is also more sluggish, foraging deliberately in the woodland understory or on the ground, probing among dead leaves with its rather long bill. Despite the name, it does not feed on earthworms; it does eat caterpillars, but no more than many other warblers.

HABITAT   *Leafy wooded slopes.* During breeding season, frequents dense deciduous woodlands. Prefers cool, shaded banks, sheer gullies, and steep, forested slopes covered with medium-sized trees and an undergrowth of saplings and shrubs. In winter in the tropics, forages alone in dense thickets or in the forest undergrowth, usually near the ground.

FEEDING   **Diet:** *Mostly insects.* Eats smooth caterpillars, but rarely or never takes the earthworms that the name would seem to imply. Also feeds on small

Worm-eating Warbler

grasshoppers, bugs, ants, bees, walkingsticks, beetles, sawfly larvae, and spiders. Feeds nestlings on moths and grubs. **Behavior:** Forages mostly in trees and shrubs. Probes in curled, dead leaves for insects and searches on bark of trunks and limbs. Forages also on the ground, walking while seeking insects on the leaf litter.

NESTING   Males defend territories by singing from perches at midlevels or on the ground. Besides the usual insectlike trill, male also sings a musical, varied song during flight as part of courtship. **Nest:** Placed on ground, normally on hillside against a deciduous shrub or sapling, well concealed by dead leaves. Nest (constructed by female) is an open cup of dead leaf skeletons; lined with fungus filaments, hair moss, maple seed stems, animal hair. **Eggs:** 4–5, sometimes 3–6. White, with brown spots and blotches. Incubated by female alone, 13 days. In most areas, rarely parasitized by cowbirds, possibly because it breeds mainly in dense woods far from edges. In some areas, parasitism by cowbirds appears to be more common. **Young:** Fed by both parents. Leave the nest at 10 days of age. Probably one brood per year.

MIGRATION   Migrates mostly at night. Fall migration begins early, many moving south in August. Very rare stray in west, mostly in fall.

CONSERVATION STATUS   Has disappeared from some areas with clearing of forest. Current numbers probably stable. Will become more vulnerable to parasitism by cowbirds where forest is broken up into smaller patches.

SWAINSON'S WARBLER   *Limnothlypis swainsonii*

A shy denizen of southern canebrakes, Swainson's Warbler is more often heard than seen. It spends most of its time on or near the ground in dense cover, walking about in search of insects. Quite plain in appearance, and with a relatively heavy bill, it does not suggest a warbler when it is glimpsed foraging in the undergrowth; however, it may be recognized by its rich musical song, audible from some distance away.

HABITAT *Swamps and river floodplain forests.* Breeds both in swamps and bottomlands of the southern coastal plains and in moist Appalachian forests. In swamps, prefers large tract with dense understory and sparse ground cover. Found especially in canebrakes and dwarf palmetto. In Appalachians, prefers rhododendron-laurel-hemlock associations or yellow poplar, oak, and maple with moderate undergrowth. Winters in woodland undergrowth in tropics.

FEEDING **Diet:** *Mostly adult and larval insects.* Feeds on caterpillars, beetles, ants, crickets, grasshoppers, katydids, stink bugs, flies, other insects; also spiders and millipedes.

Apparently takes no berries or nectar. **Behavior:** Forages at a rapid walk in openings in understory, usually on ground or in leaf litter. Probes under leaves by flipping them over, also probes into ground with long heavy bill and occasionally takes items from tree trunks or makes short flights to catch flying insects. Forages alone in winter or with mate in summer.

NESTING Males normally hold very large territories, but in very good habitat will nest in loose colonies. Sings to hold breeding territory and to attract female. Uses visual threat displays to repel rival males. **Nest:** Site is usually at edge of dense growth of cane, vines, or rhododendron. Placed near or over water, or up to 4 feet above ground. Open cup nests are inconspicuous and difficult to locate, even though they are the largest above-ground nests of all North American

Swainson's Warbler

warblers. Constructed of leaves, sticks, vines, lined with soft material such as pine needles, Spanish moss, hair, grass, and ferns. Female builds nest alone. **Eggs:** 3, sometimes 2–5. Normally unmarked white, sometimes faintly spotted. Incubated by female, 13–15 days. Male feeds female, but only when she is off the nest. **Young:** Both parents feed nestlings for 10–12 days. Young then leave nest and follow parents to be fed for another 2–3 weeks. One brood per year.

MIGRATION Apparently migrates mostly at night. Arrives on breeding grounds later in spring than most other southern warblers. Those wintering in Middle America migrate north directly across Gulf of Mexico.

CONSERVATION STATUS Undoubtedly has declined in many areas with clearing of southern forests. Where habitat remains, still fairly common.

GROUND-WALKING WARBLERS — GENUS *Seiurus*

These warblers are patterned more like thrushes, olive or brown above and streaked or spotted underneath. The three species in this genus all walk on the ground inside the forest or at the edge of streams. They have loud, arresting songs and call notes, often betraying their presence when the birds remain out of sight.

OVENBIRD   *Seiurus aurocapillus*

In shady woods, this odd warbler walks deliberately on the forest floor, holding its short tail cocked up higher than its back. Although it is not especially shy, its choice

Ovenbird

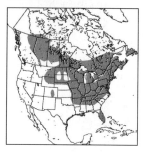

of habitat often makes it hard to observe; its ringing chant of *teacher, teacher* is heard far more often than the bird is seen. The name "Ovenbird" is a reference to the bird's nest, a domed structure with the entrance on the side, like an old-fashioned oven.

HABITAT   *Near ground in leafy woods; in migration, thickets.* Needs large tracts of mature deciduous or mixed forest for successful breeding. Will nest in a wide variety of forest types, as long as they have a closed canopy, large trees, and little ground cover. In winter (mostly in tropics), lives in forests and thickets, from dry lowlands to wet forests in the foothills.

FEEDING   **Diet:** *Mostly insects.* In summer, feeds on a wide variety of insects including adult beetles and their larvae, ants, caterpillars, flies, and true bugs; also worms, spiders, snails. Winter diet not well known, but reportedly includes seeds and other vegetable matter. **Behavior:** Takes insects from leaf litter while walking on ground and rotting logs. (Young Ovenbirds pass through a stage of hopping while they forage.) Sometimes probes among leaf litter, hovers to take insects from foliage, or catches them in midair. Individuals probably defend feeding territories in winter.

NESTING   Male sings to attract female to nesting territory, sings only sporadically during actual courtship. Male threatens rival males by tilting tail up, drooping wings, and kneading with feet. **Nest:** Placed on the ground where ground cover is sparse, especially near trails or roads. Female chooses site, builds domed nest from dead leaves, grass, bark, twigs; lines it with animal hair. **Eggs:** Normally 4–5. White with gray and brown spots. Incubation by female only, fed sometimes by male. Cowbirds parasitize many nests, but Ovenbird nestlings often survive even when sharing the nest with young cowbirds. **Young:** Both parents feed nestlings. Young leave the nest after 7–10 days, can only hop and flutter at this stage; fed by adults for another 10–20 days. One brood per year, but has been known to produce up to three broods in response to a spruce budworm outbreak.

MIGRATION   Migrates mostly at night. Ovenbirds nesting east of the Appalachians may go to the Caribbean for the winter, while those from west of the Appalachians are likely to migrate to Mexico or Central America.

CONSERVATION STATUS   Despite heavy parasitism by cowbirds in some areas, overall numbers seem to be holding up well.

NORTHERN WATERTHRUSH   *Seiurus noveboracensis*

The Northern Waterthrush is likely to be found around bogs and streams inside the forest. Often somewhat shy and hard to approach, it draws attention with its odd "teetering" behavior—bobbing the rear half of its body up and down constantly as it walks—and with its loud metallic call note. It has a wide distribution in both summer (Alaska to New Jersey) and winter (Florida to South America).

HABITAT *Swampy or wet woods, streamsides, lake shores; in migration, also thickets.* Breeds mostly in coniferous forests with standing or sluggish water; found in shrubby bogs and edges of northern lakes, less often along swift streams. In migration, may appear in any habitat; more frequent in thickets along edges of water. In winter in tropics, often in coastal mangrove swamps.

FEEDING **Diet:** *Aquatic and terrestrial insects, crustaceans.* Feeds mainly on insects, including water beetles, water bugs, flea beetles, damselflies, weevils, mosquitoes, ants, fly pupae, caterpillars, moths; also some slugs, snails, crustaceans, and occasionally small fish. Takes mostly insects in winter, also some small crustaceans and other invertebrates. **Behavior:** Walks on ground and wades in shallow water. Often forages on half-submerged logs. Uncovers prey by tossing aside dead and soggy leaves. Defends winter feeding territories against other waterthrushes.

Northern Waterthrush

NESTING Males sing throughout the breeding season, not ceasing after pair formation; song apparently serves to defend territory. Sometimes sings in flight. **Nest:** Site is usually in a small hollow in a moss-covered stump, under a jutting bank, or up to 2 feet above ground in roots of upturned tree, typically very near water. Nest is in shape of open cup, often well hidden among ferns. Constructed by female of leaf skeletons, sphagnum moss, pine needles, twigs, inner bark, and lined with soft material such as red moss filaments. **Eggs:** 4–5, sometimes 3–6. Whitish, with brown and purple-gray spots and blotches. Incubation is by female, 12–13 days. In southern part of range, often parasitized by cowbirds. **Young:** Fed by both parents. Young leave the nest approximately 10 days after hatching, can fly well by about a week later.

MIGRATION Migrates mostly at night. Does not migrate north as early in spring as Louisiana Waterthrush. As a migrant, common in the east, scarce in most parts of the west.

CONSERVATION STATUS Could be vulnerable to loss of habitat, especially on wintering grounds, but surveys suggest that numbers are currently stable.

LOUISIANA WATERTHRUSH *Seiurus motacilla*

A thrushlike warbler that walks on the ground at the water's edge, bobbing the rear part of its body up and down. It is very similar to the Northern Waterthrush but has a more restricted range in both summer and winter. The two species overlap in summer in parts of the northeast but tend to divide up by habitat there, the Louisiana living along flowing streams, the Northern favoring still waters and stagnant bogs.

HABITAT *Brooks, ravines, wooded swamps.* In southern areas, nests in bottomlands, borders of lagoons and swamps, or near sluggish or fast-moving streams. In northern part of range (where it overlaps the range of Northern Waterthrush), favors fast-moving, gravel-bottomed streams flowing through hilly, deciduous forest. In winter in the tropics, near streams in lowland woods, occasionally in coastal mangroves.

FEEDING **Diet:** *Aquatic and terrestrial insects, crustaceans.* Eats many insects including beetles, bugs, adult and larval mayflies, dragonflies, crane fly larvae, ants, caterpillars, scale

insects; also small crustaceans, snails, a few small fish and seeds. Tends to take larger items than Northern Waterthrush. **Behavior:** Walks on ground while foraging, usually along edge or in water, over stones and moss. Turns over dead or wet leaves to find prey. Also flies out over streams to catch flying insects. Defends winter feeding territories against other waterthrushes.

NESTING   Males defend long narrow territories along streams. Each male defends by chasing intruding males, and by singing; sometimes sings in flight, as well as from perches and the ground. Male sings persistently only until eggs are laid, then sings infrequently. **Nest:** Site is concealed in roots of upturned tree, near water, under overhanging banks of streams, or in hollow of rocky ravine. Nest is an open cup, probably built by female, made of leaves, moss, twigs, bark; lined with fine rootlets, ferns, grass stems, and hair. **Eggs:** 3–6, normally 5. Creamy white, with brown and purple-gray spots. Incubation by female only, 12–14 days. Frequently parasitized by cowbirds. **Young:** Both parents feed nestlings. Young leave the nest about 10 days after hatching. One brood per year.

Louisiana Waterthrush

MIGRATION   Migrates mostly at night. Moves north very early in spring, arriving on nesting grounds in March and April; in fall, many have left nesting areas before the end of August.

CONSERVATION STATUS   Undoubtedly has declined with loss of habitat in its range. Surveys suggest that current populations are stable.

THICKET WARBLERS — GENUS *Oporornis*

Although they are brightly colored like many other members of the family, these birds stay low in dense cover, where they are often very hard to see. They have distinctive songs with a richer tone quality than those of most warblers.

KENTUCKY WARBLER   *Oporornis formosus*

During spring and summer, the fast, rolling song of the Kentucky Warbler comes from the undergrowth of eastern forests. This bird spends most of its time on the ground in moist, leafy woodlands, walking on the leaf litter under thickets as it searches for insects. Despite its bright colors, it can be surprisingly hard to see in the shadows of the deep forest interior.

HABITAT   *Woodland undergrowth.* In summer, prefers deep shaded woods with dense, humid thickets, bottomlands near creeks and rivers, ravines in upland deciduous woods, and edges of swamps. In winter in the tropics, requires dense lowland forests and second growth, mostly in lowlands but also in foothills.

FEEDING   **Diet:** *Mostly insects.* Feeds on various insects including moths, bugs, ants, grasshoppers, beetles, caterpillars, aphids, grubs; also spiders, plus a few berries. **Behavior:** Forages mainly by walking on ground, seeking insects among the leaf litter, flipping over dead leaves, sometimes leaping up in the air to take insects from the underside of foliage. In winter in the tropics, sometimes accompanies swarms of army ants, picking up insects that flee the ants. Individuals defend small winter feeding territories.

NESTING   During defense of breeding territories, males are persistent singers, singing as often as every 12 seconds. **Nest:** Placed on ground or within a few inches of it, at foot of shrub, in grass tussocks, bedstraw, or goldenrod, or sometimes in the lowest fork of a small tree. Nest (built by both sexes) is a bulky open cup of leaves, with a core of weeds, grass stems; lined with rootlets and hair. **Eggs:** 4–5, sometimes 3–6. Creamy white, with brown spots. Incubation by female only, 12–13 days. Cowbirds often lay eggs in nests of this species. **Young:** Nestlings are fed by the female and rarely by the male. Young leave the nest 8–10 days after hatching. Both sexes then feed the fledglings for up to 17 days.

Kentucky Warbler

MIGRATION   Migrates mostly at night. Many fly across the Gulf of Mexico in spring and fall. Often departs from breeding grounds in August.

CONSERVATION STATUS   Has declined with clearing of forest in some areas. Becomes more vulnerable to cowbird parasitism as forest is broken up into smaller patches. Also faces loss of habitat on wintering grounds.

CONNECTICUT WARBLER   *Oporornis agilis*

For many birders, the Connecticut Warbler remains a little-known and mysterious bird. A sluggish and secretive warbler, it spends most of its time hidden low in woods and dense thickets, walking on the ground with slow and deliberate steps. It tends to migrate late in spring and early in fall, missing the peak of birding activity. Its northern nesting grounds (well to the north and west of Connecticut) are mostly in dense and impenetrable bogs.

HABITAT   *Poplar bluffs, muskeg, mixed woods near water; in migration, undergrowth.* In breeding season, in United States and eastern Canada, prefers bogs with black spruce or tamarack. In western Canada, nests on dry ridges and in open poplar or aspen stands. In migration, found in undergrowth of lowland woods or in dense thickets in meadows.

FEEDING   **Diet:** *Mostly insects.* Details of diet not well studied. Undoubtedly feeds mostly on insects, like other warblers. Reported to feed its young on green caterpillars, also seen eating spiders, snails; may sometimes eat seeds and raspberries. **Behavior:** Forages mainly by walking on the ground, seeking insects among the leaf litter, sometimes flipping over dead leaves. Also walks along branches, picking prey from crevices in bark. In migration, may forage in small flocks with others of its kind.

NESTING   Males sing from trees to defend nesting territory. **Nest:** Hidden in sphagnum moss hummock. In poplar woods, placed next to clump of dry grass or weeds. Nest is an open cup constructed of leaves, grass, and bark strips, or sometimes a simple hollow in moss lined with finer stems of grass. **Eggs:** Usually 4–5. Creamy white, with black, brown, or lilac spots. Incubation period and roles of the parents are not well known. Apparently only rarely parasitized by cowbirds. **Young:** Both parents apparently care for young; age at which they leave the nest is not well known.

MIGRATION   Migrants enter and leave our area mostly via Florida, moving north-northwest in spring toward Great Lakes, south in fall mostly along Atlantic coast. Migrates relatively late in spring and early in fall.

CONSERVATION STATUS   Status not well known, but no obvious declines in numbers. Would be vulnerable to loss of habitat, especially on wintering grounds.

MOURNING WARBLER   *Oporornis philadelphia*

Often elusive and hard to see well, the Mourning Warbler sings a repetitious chant from thickets and raspberry tangles in the north woods. This bird lives near the ground at all seasons, foraging in low brush and in the forest understory even during migration; it tends to be solitary, not readily joining flocks of other warblers. It got its name because the extensive black throat patch of the male suggested to pioneer naturalists that the bird was dressed in mourning.

HABITAT   *Clearings, thickets, slashings, undergrowth.* Breeds in brushy northern habitats, including dense shrubbery in old deciduous woods clearings, brushy cut-over lands, lowland raspberry and blackberry thickets, or bog and marsh edges; often in temporary habitats, growing up after fires or clearcuts. In winter in the tropics, lives in low, dense thickets and overgrown fields in lowlands and foothills.

Mourning Warbler

FEEDING   **Diet:** *Probably mostly insects.* Details of the diet are poorly known, but has been seen foraging for caterpillars, beetles, and other insects; also eats spiders. In winter in the tropics, sometimes feeds on the protein bodies from the leaf bases of young cecropia trees. **Behavior:** During breeding season, forages primarily in shrubs within a few feet of the ground; hops while feeding on ground. Sometimes makes short flights to catch flying insects. Generally feeds alone rather than joining flocks.

NESTING   Details of the breeding behavior are not well known. Male sings to defend nesting territory; during territorial boundary encounters with rival males, he may bob violently, flip wings outward, and fan his tail. **Nest:** Usually placed on ground next to shrub, at base of weeds, in raspberry or blackberry briers, or among fern, goldenrod, or grass tussocks. Also sometimes in bush within a couple of feet of the ground. Nest (probably built by both sexes) is an open, bulky cup made of leaves, with a core of weeds and coarse grasses, lined with fine grass and hair. **Eggs:** 3–4, sometimes 5. Creamy white with brown spots or blotches. Incubated by female only, about 12 days. Male feeds female on nest during incubation. **Young:** Both parents feed nestlings. Young leave the nest after 7–9 days. Care of fledglings may continue for another 4 weeks or more.

MIGRATION   In spring, apparently moves north overland through Mexico and Texas, rather than crossing the Gulf of Mexico like many other migrants; evidently retraces same route in fall. Migrates relatively late in spring and early in fall.

CONSERVATION STATUS   Current numbers probably stable. Because it inhabits shrubby second growth in both summer and winter, less vulnerable than some warblers to loss of habitat.

MACGILLIVRAY'S WARBLER   *Oporornis tolmiei*

A skulker in dense western brush, sometimes hard to see but readily located by its hurried song and its hard *chip* call note. A close relative of the Mourning Warbler of the east, replacing it from the Rockies westward. Unlike the Mourning Warbler, this species is often seen in substantial numbers during migration—especially in early fall, when practically every thicket in the southwest seems to have one (but only one) MacGillivray's Warbler.

HABITAT *Low dense undergrowth; shady thickets.* Breeds in thickets of willow and alder, near stream bottoms or at edge of coniferous or mixed forest. Favors new growth in logged or burned areas (especially with dead and fallen trees), brushy thickets near low moist ground, and thicketed mountain canyons. In winter in the tropics, occurs in forest undergrowth in foothills and mountains.

FEEDING **Diet:** *Mostly insects.* Details of diet are not well known; undoubtedly feeds mostly on insects. Known to eat click beetles, dung beetles, alfalfa weevils, flea beetles, caterpillars, and other insects. Young birds in Colorado will take sap from borings in willows drilled by sapsuckers. **Behavior:** Forages mostly close to ground in dense thickets, seeking insects on branches and among foliage. Hops when searching for insects on the ground. On wintering grounds, individuals defend feeding territories and usually forage alone.

NESTING Male sings frequently through breeding season to defend nesting territory. **Nest:** Site is well hidden in dense shrubs, often placed in upright fork of fir sapling, scrub oak, alders, salal, chokecherry, or Spiraea. Usually 2–3 feet above ground, sometimes lower or as high as 5 feet. Frequently in shady damp places or amid tall weeds and ferns. Nest is loosely constructed open cup made of weed stems, bark shreds, and dry grass; lined with fine grasses, rootlets, and hair. Both sexes probably help build nest. **Eggs:** Usually 4, sometimes 3–5, rarely 6. Creamy white with brown spots, speckles, or blotches. Incubation is by female alone, about 11–13 days. Apparently cowbirds do not commonly parasitize this warbler's nests. **Young:** Both parents feed the nestlings. Young leave the nest about 8–9 days after hatching.

MIGRATION Probably migrates mostly at night. Migration is spread over a lengthy period in both spring and fall.

CONSERVATION STATUS Still common in its range, although some surveys have suggested a slight decline in numbers.

MacGillivray's Warbler

YELLOWTHROATS — GENUS *Geothlypis*

COMMON YELLOWTHROAT *Geothlypis trichas*

Abundant and well-known, the Common Yellowthroat has succeeded by being a nonconformist. As the only one of our warblers that will nest in open marshes, it is found in practically every reed-bed and patch of cattails from coast to coast. Although it sometimes hides in the marsh, its low rough call note will reveal its presence. The male often perches atop a tall stalk to rap out his distinctive song, *wichity-wichity-wichity.*

HABITAT *Swamps, marshes, wet thickets, edges.* Breeds most abundantly in marshes and other very wet habitats with dense low growth. Also nests in briers, moist brushy places, tangles of rank weeds and shrubbery along streams, and overgrown fields, but is generally scarce in drier places. In migration and winter, still most common in marshes, but also occurs in any kind of brushy or wooded area.

FEEDING **Diet:** *Mostly insects.* Feeds mainly on insects, including small grasshoppers, dragonflies, damselflies, mayflies, beetles, grubs, cankerworms and other caterpillars, moths, flies, ants, aphids, leafhoppers; also eats spiders and a

few seeds. **Behavior:** Forages in marsh and among other dense low growth, searching for insects on surface of plants, sometimes hovering briefly to take insects from foliage. Occasionally makes short flights to catch insects in midair, and sometimes forages on ground.

NESTING Male displays to female during courtship by flicking wings and tail, following her closely, and performing a flight display: flying up to 25–100 feet in the air and returning to another low perch, calling and singing. **Nest:** Prefers to nest low (less than 3 feet up) on tussocks of briers, weeds, grasses, or shrubs, and among cattails, bulrushes, sedges in marshes. Bulky open cup built by female, sometimes with a partial roof of material loosely attached to the rim. Made of weeds, grass stems, sedges, dead leaves, bark, and ferns; lined with fine grass, bark fibers, and hair. **Eggs:** Usually 3–5, sometimes 6. Creamy white with brown and black spots. Incubation is by female only, 12 days. The male feeds the female on the nest during incubation. Very commonly parasitized by cowbirds. **Young:** Fed by both parents. Leave the nest after 8–10 days. Normally two broods per year. Young are dependent on parents for a considerable period, longer than most other warblers.

Common Yellowthroat

MIGRATION Migrates mostly at night. In many areas, migration is spread over a long period in both spring and fall.

CONSERVATION STATUS Has undoubtedly declined in many regions with draining of marshes, and perhaps also in some areas where good habitat still exists. However, still widespread and very common.

GRAY-CROWNED YELLOWTHROAT *Geothlypis poliocephala*

In far southern Texas, this warbler was once a regular resident; today it is only a very rare straggler there. Although its behavior is somewhat like that of the Common Yellowthroat, it is less of a marsh bird, often living in rank weedy or brushy fields.

WILSON'S WARBLER GROUP — GENUS *Wilsonia*

The three species in this genus are all bright yellow below and tend to stay low in deciduous thickets and undergrowth. They do not have oval white tail spots like those of the *Dendroica* warblers, although Hooded Warbler has the outer tail feathers largely white. All three species nest on or very close to the ground.

HOODED WARBLER *Wilsonia citrina*

In the forest undergrowth, this skulking warbler seems to call attention to itself by frequently fanning its tail quickly open and shut, flashing the white outer tail feathers. Hooded Warblers are common in moist leafy woodlands of the southeast. They usually stay low in the shadowy understory, foraging actively in the bushes and nesting close to the ground, although males will move up into the trees to sing.

HABITAT *Forest undergrowth.* Breeds in forest interiors of mixed hardwoods in the north and cypress-gum swamps in the south. During migration, found in deciduous and mixed eastern forests. In winter, males compete for territories in humid lowland forest, and females occupy mainly disturbed scrub or secondary forest.

FEEDING **Diet:** *Insects and other arthropods.* Feeds on a wide variety of insects, including caterpillars, moths, grasshoppers, beetles, flies, and many others; also eats many small spiders. **Behavior:** Hops on ground, low branches, or tree trunks while feeding, often gleaning insects from leaf surfaces in low shrubs. Will also make short flights to catch flying insects in the understory. Males may forage higher than females when feeding young. Both sexes maintain well-defined feeding territories during winter, giving conspicuous *chip* call notes and attacking intruders of their own species.

NESTING Males usually return to occupy the same nesting territory as in previous years, but females usually move to a different territory. **Nest:** Female chooses site in patches of deciduous shrubs within forest or along edge. Site usually 1–4 feet above ground. Nest is open cup of dead leaves, bark, fine grasses, spider webs, hair, and plant down. Usually the female does most or all of the building. **Eggs:** Usually 4. Creamy white, with brown spots at larger end. Incubation is normally by female only, 12 days. Brown-headed

Hooded Warbler

Cowbirds lay eggs in many nests (up to 75 percent in some areas). **Young:** Fed by both parents. Young leave the nest 8–9 days after hatching and can fly 2–3 days later. Fledglings are divided by parents, each adult caring for half the brood for up to 5 weeks. Often two broods per year.

MIGRATION Migrates mostly at night. Many fly north and south across the Gulf of Mexico during migration. A rare stray in the southwest, where many of the records are for spring or summer.

CONSERVATION STATUS Considered vulnerable because it is often parasitized by cowbirds, especially where forest is broken up into small patches, and because it favors undergrowth of tropical forest for wintering.

WILSON'S WARBLER   *Wilsonia pusilla*

A small and spritely warbler that moves actively in bushes and trees, often flipping its longish tail about as it hops from branch to branch. Typically stays low in semi-open areas, avoiding the interior of dense forest. Although it nests from coast to coast across Canada, Wilson's Warbler is far more common farther west. In the east it is seen in small numbers, but in the Rockies and westward it is often the most abundant migrant in late spring.

HABITAT *Thickets along wooded streams, moist tangles, low shrubs, willows, alders.* Breeds as far north as timberline, in thickets, second growth, bogs, or in alder and willow groves near streams and ponds. In migration and winter, occurs from hot lowland thickets up to cool mountain woods; always in scrubby overgrown clearings and thin woods, not in the interior of dense forest.

FEEDING **Diet:** *Mostly insects.* Presumably feeds mostly on insects, like other warblers. Frequent items in diet include bees, wasps, beetles, caterpillars, and aphids. Also eats some spiders and sometimes berries. In winter in the tropics, sometimes feeds on protein corpuscles found at the bases of leaves of cecropia trees. **Behavior:** Feeds usually within 10 feet of ground, searching actively among foliage

Wilson's Warbler

of bushes. Hops on ground to probe among fallen leaves and flutters up to take items from the undersides of leaves. Frequently flies out to catch flying insects in midair.

NESTING   Populations that nest along Pacific coast tend to lay fewer eggs and raise fewer offspring per nesting attempt, and males mate with only one female. Populations that nest in high mountains of west tend to lay more eggs per clutch and fledge more young, and some males have more than one mate. **Nest:** Usually on ground, sunken in moss or sedges, often at base of shrub. Along Pacific coast, nests often placed up to 3 feet above ground, in shrubs or vines. Nest is bulky open cup, built by female, made of dead leaves, grass, and moss; lined with fine grass and hair. **Eggs:** 4–6, sometimes 2–7. Creamy white with variable marks of brown. Incubation is by female only, 10–13 days. Cowbirds regularly lay eggs in nests of this species. **Young:** Fed by both parents; brooded by female only. Young leave the nest about 8–13 days after hatching. Normally one brood per year.

MIGRATION   Birds wintering in Mexico apparently migrate around west side of Gulf of Mexico, not across it. In the west, those nesting along the Pacific coast arrive earlier in spring than those nesting in the mountains of the interior.

CONSERVATION STATUS   Numbers probably stable. Adaptable in its choice of wintering habitats, probably not threatened by cutting of forests in the tropics.

CANADA WARBLER   *Wilsonia canadensis*

Known by its necklace of short stripes, the Canada Warbler is a summer resident of moist, shady woods in the east. It usually stays in the understory, feeding in the bushes or on the ground. Sometimes hard to see in this dense cover, it is not especially shy, and a patient observer can usually get good

Canada Warbler

looks. Although it does breed in Canada, it also nests in the higher Appalachians as far south as Georgia.

HABITAT   *Forest undergrowth, shady thickets.* Breeds in mature mixed hardwoods of extensive forests and streamside thickets. Prefers to nest in moist habitat: in luxuriant undergrowth, near swamps, on stream banks, in rhododendron thickets, in deep, rocky ravines, and in moist deciduous second growth. Winters in a variety of habitats in South America, from forest undergrowth to scrub.

FEEDING   **Diet:** *Largely insects.* Feeds on many kinds of insects, including beetles, mosquitoes, flies, moths, and smooth caterpillars such as cankerworms; also spiders. **Behavior:** Very active in foraging, does more flycatching than most warblers. Typically flushes insects from foliage while foraging on twigs and leaves, then frequently darts out to catch escaping insects on the wing. Also searches on the ground among fallen leaves. In winter in the tropics, forages in mixed flocks with other birds, usually 3–30 feet above ground in denser foliage.

Males arrive on breeding grounds during the first two weeks of May. Sometimes pairs may arrive together, as migrants have been seen traveling in pairs in Central America. **Nest:** Placed on or within 6 inches of the ground, on sphagnum hummocks, in hollows in streambanks, on moss-covered logs, or in cavities among the upturned roots of fallen trees. Nest (built by female) is bulky open cup, loosely constructed of dead leaves or leaf skeletons, bark strips, grasses, weeds, ferns; lined with fern roots, horsehair, and plant fibers. **Eggs:** 4, sometimes 3–5. Creamy white with brown spots. Incubation is probably by female, possibly with help from male; length of incubation period not well known. **Young:** Both parents care for nestlings. Age at which young leave the nest not well known.

MIGRATION   Migrates late in spring and early in fall; peak passage in many areas is during May and August. In spring, most apparently move north through Central America and Mexico, then around west side of Gulf of Mexico, rather than flying across it.

CONSERVATION STATUS   Favoring shady forest undergrowth in summer and probably in winter, this warbler could be vulnerable to loss of habitat with clearing of forest.

GENUS *Cardellina*

RED-FACED WARBLER   *Cardellina rubrifrons*

In New Mexico and Arizona, the brisk song of the Red-faced Warbler is heard in summer in leafy groves surrounded by conifer forest, high in the mountains. This bird and the Painted Redstart, both Mexican border specialties, are our only warblers that wear bright red. In both, unlike many warblers, the females are nearly or quite as brightly colored as the males. Despite their conspicuous colors, both make the seemingly risky move of placing their nests on the ground.

HABITAT   *Open pine-oak forests in high mountains.* In our area, breeds mostly in forests of Douglas-fir, Engelmann spruce, ponderosa pine, and southwestern white pine, at elevations of 6,400–9,000 feet, mainly where small groves of deciduous trees such as oak, maple, or aspen grow among the conifers. In winter in the tropics, found in forests of pine, oak, alder, and other trees, at upper elevations in mountains.

Red-faced Warbler

FEEDING   *Diet: Probably mostly insects.* Diet not known in detail, but undoubtedly feeds mostly on insects. Caterpillars may be important in diet; nestlings are fed many small green caterpillars. Also eats small flies, leafhoppers, and other insects. **Behavior:** Prefers to forage in trees with dense foliage. Searches actively on outer parts of branches and twigs, and hovers to take insects from foliage. At times, does much of its foraging by flying out to take insects in midair. In summer, males tend to feed higher than females, pausing to sing as they forage. When not nesting, typically forages in mixed flocks with other birds.

NESTING   In most areas, males defend nesting territories by singing. In a few places, males are reported not to defend territories very strongly, regularly crossing near each other's nest sites and even congregating in loose singing groups to attract females. **Nest:** On the ground, well hidden at base of shrub, rock, grass tuft, tree trunk, or under log. Usually placed in leaf litter on slope

or steep bank. Open cup is built by female on mass of dry leaves and conifer needles; constructed of grasses, weeds, and bark, lined with plant fibers and hair. **Eggs:** Usually 3–4. Pinkish white, flecked with brown. Incubated by female only, 13–15 days, sometimes 12–17. **Young:** Fed by both parents. Leave the nest 11–13 days after hatching. Parents may divide the fledglings, each adult attending half the brood for up to 4–5 weeks. All fledglings leave nesting territories by early August in Arizona, even though the adults are still on territory. Probably one brood per year.

MIGRATION   In our area, migrants arrive in April, and most depart before mid-September. Migrants are very rarely seen in the lowlands.

CONSERVATION STATUS   Has expanded its nesting range northward slightly in Arizona during recent decades. Could be vulnerable to loss of mountain forest habitat in Mexico.

TROPICAL REDSTARTS — GENUS *Myioborus*

PAINTED REDSTART   *Myioborus pictus*

Painted Redstart

The incredible Painted Redstart, a specialty of the southwestern mountains, is perhaps the most beautiful of the warblers. It almost seems to be consciously showing off as it flits through the oaks, turning this way and that, posturing with its wings and tail partly spread. Unlike most of our northern warblers, females of this species are just as showy as males. Painted Redstarts build their nests on the ground, on steep hillsides in pine-oak woods.

HABITAT   *Oak canyons, pine-oak forests in mountains.* Breeds in mixed oak and pine forests and in streamside woods of steep canyons above 5,000 feet. Prefers to nest under oaks, sycamores, ashes, maples, junipers, and pines. In winter in the tropics, found most often in dry open woodlands of oak and pine.

FEEDING   **Diet:** *Mostly insects.* Diet not known in detail, but undoubtedly eats mostly insects, including caterpillars, flies, and small beetles. Also comes to hummingbird feeders to drink sugar-water. **Behavior:** Forages actively at all levels, from ground to treetops. With wings and tail partly spread, hops quickly among branches, searching for insects. Often hovers while taking items from foliage, or darts out to catch insects in flight. May move up and down vertical trunks, clinging to bark. Sometimes joins mixed flocks with other birds, but often forages in pairs or alone.

NESTING   Males arrive on nesting territories 2–10 days before the females. During courtship, male chases female, and sometimes the pair sing duets together. Some males have more than one mate. **Nest:** Site selected by both members of pair. Placed on ground in a shady spot on steep slope, often on walls of narrow canyons, on low cliffs, beneath overhanging banks, or under a small boulder. Usually near a small stream. Nest is hidden in a shallow depression or crevice. Shallow, open cup is constructed by female out of grass, pine needles, leaves, bark; thinly lined with fine grass and hair. **Eggs:** Normally 3–4. Creamy white, with fine spots of brown. Incubation is by female only, 13–14 days. **Young:** Fed by both parents. Young leave the nest about 9–13 days after hatching. Often two broods per year.

Probably permanent resident over most of range, but most of those in the southwest depart in fall, returning early in spring. A few remain through the winter. Rarely strays far afield, having wandered as far as British Columbia and Massachusetts.

SLATE-THROATED REDSTART *Myioborus miniatus*

Related to our Painted Redstart but not quite as showy, this warbler is very widespread in the American tropics. Throughout its extensive range it is a bird of forests in the foothills and mountains. The Slate-throated Redstart has wandered north from Mexico into the American southwest only a few times, mostly in spring.

GENUS *Euthlypis*

FAN-TAILED WARBLER *Euthlypis lachrymosa*

In Mexico and Central America, this large warbler is a shy denizen of the understory in dense woods. As it skulks near the ground, it often flips its long tail about or fans it wide open, displaying the white spots at the tip. Lone Fan-tailed Warblers have strayed into Arizona a few times, appearing in late spring in canyons just north of the border.

GENUS *Basileuterus*

GOLDEN-CROWNED WARBLER *Basileuterus culicivorus*

In the tropics, this warbler inhabits a variety of wooded areas, from fairly dry lowland woods to humid cloud forest in the mountains. Within our area it is known only as a rare stray into southern Texas, mostly in winter. The golden color on its crown is often inconspicuous, but the bird may draw attention by its insectlike ticking call notes.

RUFOUS-CAPPED WARBLER *Basileuterus rufifrons*

This tropical warbler often behaves somewhat like a wren, flitting about within dense thickets, cocking its tail up higher than its back. It is an irregular and very rare visitor to our area, but strays to Texas and Arizona have sometimes remained for many weeks, and the species has attempted to nest in Arizona at least once.

GENUS *Icteria*

YELLOW-BREASTED CHAT *Icteria virens*

A bizarre series of hoots, whistles, and clucks coming from the brier tangles announces the presence of the Yellow-breasted Chat. The bird is often hard to see, but sometimes it launches into the air to sing its odd song as it flies, with floppy wingbeats and dangling legs, above the thickets. This is our largest warbler, and surely the strangest as well, seeming to suggest a cross between a warbler and a Mockingbird.

HABITAT *Brushy tangles, briers, stream thickets.* Breeds in very dense scrub (such as willow thickets) and briery tangles, often along streams and at the edges of swamps or ponds. Sometimes in dry overgrown pastures and in upland thickets along margins of woods. In winter in the tropics, found in open scrub and woodland edges in the lowlands.

FEEDING **Diet:** *Insects and berries.* Feeds on a wide variety of insects, including moths, beetles, bugs, ants, bees, wasps, mayflies, grasshoppers, katydids, caterpillars, and praying mantises; also spiders. Up to half of diet (or more in fall) may be berries and wild fruit, including blackberries, elderberries, wild grapes, and others. Wintering birds in the northeast often come to bird feeders, where they will take many items such as suet or peanut butter. **Behavior:** Forages by searching among foliage in dense low tangles or by perching to eat berries. Unlike any other warbler, will hold its food with one foot while it feeds. Forages alone during migration and winter, rather than joining feeding flocks.

NESTING During courtship, male displays to female by pointing bill up and swaying from side to side. In flight song display, male flies up singing, hovers, drops slowly with wings flapping over its back and legs dangling loosely, then returns to perch. Occasionally nests in loose colonies. **Nest:** Placed 1–8 feet above the ground, well concealed in dense shrub or tangled vines. Large open cup nest is constructed by female. Outer base of dead leaves, straw, and weeds provides support for a tightly woven inner nest of vine bark, lined with fine weed stems and grass. **Eggs:** 3–4, up to 6. Eggs large, creamy white, with brown spots at large end. Incubation by female only, 11 days. Commonly parasitized by Brown-headed Cowbirds. **Young:** Fed by both parents. Leave the nest about 8 days after hatching. Normally two broods per year.

Yellow-breasted Chat

MIGRATION Most leave our area in fall to winter in the tropics. Every fall, however, many show up along the northeastern coast, and some of these stay through the winter, even as far north as New England.

CONSERVATION STATUS May have increased historically in the east as clearing of forest created more brushy habitat. Current population probably stable, although it has declined in parts of southwest and elsewhere.

GENUS *Peucedramus*

OLIVE WARBLER *Peucedramus taeniatus*

In forests of pine, fir, and oak in southwestern mountains, the Olive Warbler is common in summer and sometimes remains through winter. As it searches for insects high in the trees, it might seem like a typical warbler, aside from its soft whistled call note and the copper-colored head of the adult male. However, studies suggest that it is not related to our warblers at all, that it may be closer to certain Old World birds or to the finches.

HABITAT *Pine and fir forests of high mountains.* Breeds in mountain pine forests, generally at elevations of 6,000 feet and above. Prefers ponderosa pine but also occurs in other pines, firs, Douglas-firs, and adjacent oaks. In winter, at least some individuals move down into oak woodlands in lower foothills.

FEEDING **Diet:** *Probably mostly insects.* Details of diet are not well known. Has been observed feeding on insects, and these undoubtedly make up majority of

food. **Behavior:** Usually forages in the upper one-third of pines and other trees. Creeps over branches and twigs of pines, taking insects from the twigs and from the bases of needle clusters. When not breeding, often seen foraging in mixed flocks including other warblers and also titmice, nuthatches, and other birds.

NESTING   Details of breeding behavior not well studied, partly because of the placement of its nest in the upper reaches of trees. **Nest:** Placed from 30–70 feet up, usually in pine and usually 15–20 feet out from the trunk on a branch. Nest (built by female) is an open cup of moss, lichen, pine bud scales, pine needles; lined with the soft white plant fibers from the underside of silver oak leaves, and rootlets. **Eggs:** Usu-

Olive Warbler

ally 3–4. Bluish white with olive and brown marks at large end. Female incubates (male might also?), but length of incubation period and roles of the parents are poorly known. **Young:** Probably both parents feed the nestlings, but details (including age at which young leave the nest) are not well known.

MIGRATION   Thought to be mostly a summer resident in our area, but at least some remain through winter. Becomes common in mountain forests by March and can still be found in numbers into October.

CONSERVATION STATUS   Within its limited range in our area, numbers probably stable. Could be vulnerable to loss of habitat with cutting of forest farther south.

BANANAQUIT (subfamily Coerebinae)

As defined at the moment, this subfamily contains only one species. The Bananaquit is an active little bird, shaped like a warbler with a slightly curved bill. It often feeds on nectar at flowers, and it was formerly placed in the same group with several tropical American birds known as honeycreepers. Many scientists now believe that the Bananaquit is more closely related to the tanagers.

GENUS *Coereba*

BANANAQUIT   *Coereba flaveola*

Fond of nectar, this little bird often creeps about in flowering trees, probing the blossoms. It is widespread in the American tropics and especially numerous in the West Indies, including the Bahamas. Strays from the Bahamas have turned up a number of times in southern Florida, mainly in winter.

TANAGERS (subfamily Thraupinae)

A dazzling galaxy of bright-colored little birds, the tanagers are among the true delights of the American tropics. Scientists disagree as to how many birds really belong to this group, but the typical tanagers number at least 200 species. In South America they occur in every color imaginable, including brilliant blues, greens, and purples. The few that reach our area are mostly red or yellow; they bring a touch of the tropics to our local woodlots.

Most members of this subfamily are rather sociable. Usually a tanager species will be found in pairs or family groups, not in large flocks of its own kind; however, these small groups of one species are often part of a large mixed flock containing many kinds of birds. In tropical forests, especially on the lower slopes of mountains, flocks may include more than a dozen kinds of tanagers.

Feeding Insects and berries are the main foods of tanagers in general, but the relative importance of these two menu items depends on the species. Many tropical species, including some of the most colorful ones, feed mainly on berries and small fruits. The tanagers in our area eat mostly insects, although they also take many berries at times.

Most tanagers do most foraging in trees and shrubs. They tend to move slowly and methodically, whether they are seeking berries or small insects; but some (including our species) are more active, often hovering to take insects from foliage or flying out to catch insects in midair. Some tropical tanagers accompany swarms of army ants, feeding on insects flushed by the ants, and some other kinds forage on the ground.

Nesting The nests of many tropical tanagers remain undiscovered. Those that are known are mostly open cup-shaped nests among the branches of trees or shrubs. The small tanagers known as euphonias may build domed nests, with the entrance on the side, and a few tropical tanagers nest on the ground or in cavities in trees. Females do most of the work of nest-building. Our species usually lay four eggs, but many in the tropics typically lay only two or three. Incubation is generally by the female alone, but both parents usually help feed the young.

Displays Courtship displays of most tanagers are not well known. However, in several cases they involve postures that seem designed to show off the brightest parts of the male's plumage. Early stages of courtship in some species may involve the male chasing the female in flight through the trees.

GENUS *Spindalis*

STRIPE-HEADED TANAGER   *Spindalis zena*

Apparently specialized for life on islands, the Stripe-headed Tanager is widespread in the Caribbean, but it seldom visits the mainland. In our area it is a rare visitor to southern Florida. Most records have been of single birds in winter, but reports of small groups present in spring suggest the possibility that the bird might nest in Florida someday.

RED TANAGERS — GENUS *Piranga*

The nine tanagers in this genus all show at least some red or red-orange in adult male plumage. The four species that nest regularly in North America are the northernmost tanagers and are among the most colorful birds in our area (even if they are outnumbered and outshone by the rainbow-colored tanagers in the tropics). Most of the *Piranga* species are treetop birds, feeding mainly on insects. While tanagers in general are often poor singers, the ones in this genus have rich whistled songs.

HEPATIC TANAGER   *Piranga flava*

In mountain forests of the southwest, this tanager is fairly common in summer among the pines and oaks. Members of a pair are often found foraging together, moving about rather slowly in the tall pines as they search deliberately for insects in the foliage. The name "Hepatic" is a reference to the color of the male, a more liver-red or duller shade than that of our other red tanagers.

HABITAT *Open mountain forests, oaks, pines.* In our area, breeds at middle elevations in mountains and canyons, in forest of oaks and tall pines; also in some regions in low pinyon pine woods with a scattering of taller trees. In the tropics, lives mostly in the mountains, also locally in lowland pine savanna.

FEEDING **Diet:** *Mainly insects, also berries.* Apparently feeds largely on insects, including caterpillars and beetles, probably many others. Also eats berries and small fruits, especially in late summer, including wild grapes. **Behavior:** Forages rather slowly and deliberately, hopping along branches and pausing to peer about at the foliage. Mostly feeds high in trees,

Hepatic Tanager

but sometimes forages in low shrubs and rarely on the ground. Sometimes flies out to catch insects in midair.

NESTING Male sings to defend nesting ter-ritory. **Nest:** Site is in tall tree, often pine, oak, or syca-more, usually 15–50 feet above ground. Usually placed at a fork of a horizontal branch well out from the trunk. Nest is a shallow open cup made of grass and weed stems, lined with fine grass. Apparently built mostly by the female, although male may accompany her and may help carry nest material. **Eggs:** 3–5, typically 4. Bluish green, with brown spots often concentrated at the larger end. Incubation behavior and length of incubation period not well known. **Young:** Probably both parents feed the nestlings. Age at which the young leave the nest is not well known.

MIGRATION Probably only a short-distance migrant, retreating into Mexico in fall; a few may stay through winter in southern Arizona. Strays sometimes reach California coast, and have wintered there.

CONSERVATION STATUS Has probably declined in some areas of southwest in recent decades. Nests may be parasitized fairly often by cowbirds.

SUMMER TANAGER   *Piranga rubra*

Summer Tanager

A languid song in southern woods, sounding like a lazy robin, is the voice of the Summer Tanager. Seeing the bird may require some patience, because it usually moves rather slowly in the treetops, often remaining hidden among the leaves. At times, however, it flies out conspicuously to catch insects in midair. This bird apparently has no fear of stinging insects, often raiding wasp nests and occasionally becoming a minor nuisance around beehives.

HABITAT *Woods, groves (especially oaks).* In the southeast, breeds in dry open woods, especially those of oak, hickory, or pine. In the southwest, breeds in cottonwood-willow forests along streams. Winters in the tropics, mainly in lowlands but also up to middle elevations in mountains, both in solid forest and in edges and clearings with scattered trees.

FEEDING **Diet:** *Mostly insects, some berries.* Diet in summer is mainly insects; often noted feeding on bees and wasps, and also eats many beetles, cicadas, caterpillars, and grasshoppers, plus bugs, flies, and others; also eats some spiders. Feeds on berries and small fruits at times. **Behavior:** Forages mainly in the tops of trees. Moves rather deliberately, pausing to peer around. Often makes short flights to capture insects in midair, or hovers momentarily while picking them from branches or foliage. Will break into wasp nests to eat the larvae inside.

NESTING Male sings in spring to defend nesting territory. In early stages of courtship, male frequently chases female. **Nest:** Site is in a tree, often an oak, pine, or cottonwood. Placed on a horizontal branch, usually well out from trunk and 10–35 feet above the ground. Nest is a loosely made shallow cup of grass, weed stems, bark strips, leaves, spider webs, Spanish moss (where available), lined with fine grass. Apparently built only by female, although male accompanies her during nest building. **Eggs:** 3–5, typically 4. Pale green or blue-green, with brown and gray spots sometimes concentrated at larger end. Incubation is apparently by female only, 11–12 days. **Young:** Both parents feed the nestlings. Age at which young leave the nest is not well known.

MIGRATION The wintering range is surprisingly extensive, from central Mexico to Bolivia and Brazil. Migrates north and south on a broad front, with some crossing Gulf of Mexico and others traveling overland.

CONSERVATION STATUS Numbers have declined sharply along the lower Colorado River and in a few other localities. Still common and widespread in other areas.

SCARLET TANAGER *Piranga olivacea*

Scarlet Tanager

Tanagers are mostly tropical birds, and male Scarlet Tanagers seem almost too bright and exotic for northeastern woodlands. These birds are fairly common in oak forests in summer, but they often remain out of sight as they forage in the leafy upper branches. Sometimes in spring, when the Scarlet Tanagers have just arrived from their winter home in South America, a late freeze will force them out in the open as they search for insects on roadsides or in gardens.

HABITAT *Forests and shade trees (especially oaks).* Breeds mostly in deciduous forest, mainly where oaks are common but also in maple, beech, and other trees; sometimes in mixed pine-oak woods, and occasionally in coniferous woods dominated by pine or hemlock. Winters in tropical rain forest in lowlands just east of the Andes.

FEEDING **Diet:** *Mostly insects, some berries.* In summer, feeds mainly on insects, including caterpillars, moths, beetles, wasps, bees, aphids, and many others; also some spiders, snails, worms, millipedes. Also eats wild fruits and berries, including those of mulberry, elder, sumac, and others. Winter diet poorly known. **Behavior:** Forages mostly in tall trees (especially oaks), seeking insects rather deliberately among the foliage. May hover momentarily while taking an item, and sometimes flies out to catch insects in midair. Also forages in low shrubs or on the ground, especially in cold weather.

NESTING In courtship, male hops about on branches below perched female, with wings drooped and tail partly spread, showing off contrast between red back and black wings and tail. **Nest:** Site is in tree (usually deciduous), typically 20–30 feet above ground, sometimes lower or much higher. Placed on horizontal branch, usually well out from the trunk. Nest (built by female) is a shallow open cup of twigs, weeds, grass, lined with fine grass and rootlets. **Eggs:** 2–5, usually 4. Pale blue-green, with spots of brown or reddish brown often concentrated at larger end. Incubation is by female only, about 12–14 days. **Young:** Both parents feed the nestlings, although the male may do less of the feeding in some cases. Young leave the nest about 9–15 days after hatching, are tended by parents (or by female only) for about 2 more weeks.

MIGRATION   Most spring migrants enter our area by coming north across Gulf of Mexico. Apparently migrates mostly at night.

CONSERVATION STATUS   Vulnerable to loss of habitat on both summer and winter ranges. Seems to require large blocks of forest for breeding. Does poorly in smaller forest fragments, often being parasitized by cowbirds.

WESTERN TANAGER   *Piranga ludoviciana*

Western Tanager

A western counterpart to the Scarlet Tanager, this species occurs in summer farther north than any other tanager—far up into northwestern Canada. Western Tanagers nest in coniferous forests of the north and the high mountains, but during migration they may show up in any habitat, including grassland and desert; the bright males often draw attention by pausing in suburban yards in late spring.

HABITAT   *Open conifer or mixed forests; widespread in migration.* Breeds mostly in the high mountains or in the north, in forest of spruce, fir, pine, aspen, rarely in lower elevation woods mostly of oak. In migration may occur in any habitat, even desert. Winters in the tropics mostly in pine-oak woods or forest edge. In California, may winter in eucalyptus groves.

FEEDING   **Diet:** *Mostly insects, some fruit and berries.* Feeds mainly on insects, including wasps, bees, ants, beetles, grasshoppers, termites, cicadas. Also feeds on many berries, such as mulberries and elderberries, and takes some cultivated fruit. **Behavior:** Forages mostly in tops of trees. Usually feeds deliberately, peering about slowly for insects in foliage. Also flies out to catch insects in midair. Regularly visits flowers, probably to feed both on nectar and on insects found there.

NESTING   Male sings during late spring and summer to defend nesting territory. Early stages of courtship may involve male chasing female among the trees. **Nest:** Site is usually in coniferous tree such as fir or pine, sometimes in aspen, oak, or other deciduous tree. Usually placed at a fork in a horizontal branch well out from the trunk and 15–65 feet above the ground, rarely lower. Nest (probably built mostly by female) is a shallow open cup made of twigs, grass, rootlets, lined with animal hair and fine rootlets. **Eggs:** 3–5. Pale blue or bluish green, with brown blotches sometimes concentrated at larger end. Incubation is by female, about 13 days. **Young:** Both parents bring food for the nestlings. Young probably leave the nest about 2 weeks after hatching.

MIGRATION   Protracted migration lasts late in spring and begins early in fall, with some birds seen away from breeding areas as late as mid-June and as early as mid-July.

FLAME-COLORED TANAGER   *Piranga bidentata*

Native to mountain forests of Mexico and Central America, this tanager was never found in our area until 1985, when a male spent the breeding season in Arizona's Chiricahua Mountains, paired with a female Western Tanager. Since then the species has appeared several more times in Arizona and has nested there more than once.

This group of about 40 species is found exclusively in the New World, many of them in the tropics. All have thickened bills, a good shape for cracking hard seeds, and in some the bill is very large. Many of these birds are quite colorful, and males are often more brightly colored than females, at least among those species found in the temperate zone.

One species classified here lives in open fields and grasslands (that one is the Dickcissel, a rather odd bird that may not truly belong to this subfamily). All the rest live in heavy cover, such as brushy places, thickets, and woodlands. Many of the grosbeaks and buntings have rich whistled or warbled songs, and most have sharp call notes.

Some species in this group have been known to live as long as 12 to 15 years in the wild.

Feeding   Members of this subfamily usually hunt for food by hopping about among branches or on the ground. Sometimes they will hover for a moment while picking an item from foliage, and a few kinds will sometimes fly out to catch an insect in midair. The species found in our area feed on large amounts of both seeds and insects. In many cases, insects make up most of the diet in summer (and are fed to the young), while seeds become the most important foods in winter. Several of our species also eat berries. Some tropical members of this group, including some of the strongly patterned grosbeaks known as Saltators, are more seriously vegetarian in their diet; they eat many small fruits and berries, as well as seeds, buds, and flowers.

Nesting   The typical nest built by members of this group is in the shape of an open cup, made of twigs, weeds, and grass, lined with finer and softer material. Females do most of the nest building, and usually the nests are well hidden in dense parts of shrubs or trees, although a few kinds will nest on the ground. The eggs are usually white to pale blue or green, with or without brown spots. Incubation is usually by the female only, sometimes by both parents; in most cases, however, the male will help to feed the young.

Displays   Courtship displays of males usually involve singing. The songs are often accompanied by elaborate posturing and fluttering, and males of some kinds will sing in short flights as part of their display. In a few species, the male will feed the female during courtship.

GENUS *Rhodothraupis*

CRIMSON-COLLARED GROSBEAK   *Rhodothraupis celaeno*

Native to only a limited area of northeastern Mexico, this strikingly patterned grosbeak has wandered into southern Texas several times. It tends to stay low in dense cover, where it is often difficult to observe. The first Texas record was of a singing male in midsummer, but subsequent reports have been in winter.

CARDINALS — GENUS *Cardinalis*

This is a group of three medium-sized songbirds, two in our area and one in South America, each having a thick bill, crested head, and at least some bright red in the plumage of the male. All are nonmigratory, and all live in areas with dense brush or other low cover. They have clear, whistled songs, usually given from a conspicuous perch.

NORTHERN CARDINAL *Cardinalis cardinalis*

One of our most popular birds, the Cardinal is the official state bird of no fewer than seven eastern states. Abundant in the southeast, it has been extending its range northward for decades, and it now brightens winter days with its color and its whistled song as far north as southeastern Canada. Feeders stocked with sunflower seeds may have aided its northward spread. West of the Great Plains, the Cardinal is mostly absent, but it is locally common in the desert southwest.

HABITAT *Woodland edges, thickets, suburban gardens, towns, desert washes.* Found in a wide variety of brushy or semi-open habitats in the east, from forest clearings and swamps to city parks, almost wherever there are some dense bushes for nesting. In the southwest, more local; occurs in tall brush, streamside thickets, groves of mesquites in desert.

FEEDING **Diet:** *Mostly seeds, insects, berries.* Diet is quite varied. Feeds on many insects, including beetles, true bugs, grasshoppers, caterpillars, ants, flies,

Northern Cardinal

and many others, also spiders, centipedes, and snails. Most of diet is vegetable matter, including seeds of weeds and grasses, waste grain, leaf buds, flowers, and many berries and wild fruits. Young are fed mostly insects. **Behavior:** Forages mostly while hopping on ground or in low bushes, sometimes higher in trees. Readily comes to bird feeders, where it favors sunflower seeds.

NESTING Male sings to defend nesting territory, actively attacking intruding males (and attacking his own reflection in windows and mirrors). In courtship, male and female raise heads high, sway back and forth while singing softly; male often feeds female early in breeding season. Female sings mainly in spring before start of nesting. **Nest:** Usually well hidden in dense shrubs, vines, or low trees, placed 3–10 feet above ground, sometimes higher. Nest (built by female) is open cup made of twigs, weeds, grass, bark strips, leaves, rootlets, lined with fine grass or hair. **Eggs:** 3–4, sometimes 2–5. Whitish to pale bluish or greenish white, marked with brown, purple, and gray. Incubation is almost always by female alone, 12–13 days. **Young:** Both parents feed nestlings. Young leave nest about 9–11 days after hatching. Male may feed fledglings while female begins next nesting attempt. 2–3 broods per year, rarely 4.

MIGRATION Permanent resident throughout its range.

CONSERVATION STATUS Widespread and abundant, having expanded its range over the last century or more. Current numbers probably stable.

PYRRHULOXIA *Cardinalis sinuatus*

This "desert cardinal" is common in dry country of the southwest. It is similar to the Northern Cardinal in song and behavior, and the two overlap in many desert areas. However, the Pyrrhuloxia can tolerate drier and more open habitats; it is less sedentary and more social than southwestern Cardinals, with flocks often wandering away from nesting areas in winter. The odd name "Pyrrhuloxia," formerly part of this bird's scientific name, combines the Latin term for the Bullfinch with a Greek reference to the bird's bill shape.

HABITAT *Mesquites, thorn scrub, deserts.* Present at all seasons in dense brush in very dry country, including mesquite groves, desert washes, lower stretches of arid canyons,

dry plains with mesquite and acacia scrub, streamside brush in desert regions. In winter, also wanders into open woods, forest edges, hedgerows in farm country.

FEEDING **Diet:** *Mostly insects, seeds, berries.* Diet is varied. Feeds on many insects, including beetles, caterpillars, grasshoppers, and many others, also other arthropods. Eats many seeds, including those of weeds and grasses, and also frequently eats mesquite seeds. Feeds on berries and wild fruits, including cactus fruits. Will come to feeders for sunflower seeds. **Behavior:** Forages mostly while hopping on ground; also does some foraging up in shrubs and low trees. Except when nesting, often forages in small flocks.

Pyrrhuloxia

NESTING Male sings in spring to defend territory; at beginning of breeding season, both male and female may actively chase intruders of their own species. In courtship, male often feeds female. **Nest:** Placed 4–15 feet above the ground, usually in a thorny shrub or low tree, sometimes within a clump of mistletoe. Nest (built mostly or entirely by female) is an open cup made of thorny twigs, weeds, grass, strips of bark, lined with rootlets, plant fibers, fine grass. **Eggs:** 3–4, sometimes 2–5. Pale grayish white to greenish white, spotted with brown and gray. Incubation is by female only, about 14 days. Male often feeds female on nest during incubation period. **Young:** Both parents bring food for the nestlings. Young leave the nest about 10 days after hatching.

MIGRATION Not truly migratory, but strays often show up outside breeding range in fall and winter, and flocks regularly winter in areas not occupied during nesting season.

GROSBEAKS — GENUS *Pheucticus*

Well named for their large bills (or "gross beaks"), these are colorful woodland birds, often hidden among the foliage of leafy trees. The genus includes two species nesting in our area, and about four types of yellow grosbeaks in the American tropics. Unlike most related birds, the male takes part in incubating the eggs, at least in our two regular species. He may even sing while he is sitting on the nest. Sometimes a naturalist will find a grosbeak's nest after hearing the male sing softly and continuously from one spot.

YELLOW GROSBEAK *Pheucticus chrysopeplus*

A tropical relative of our Rose-breasted and Black-headed grosbeaks. The Yellow Grosbeak is quite similar to those birds in shape, behavior, song, and call notes, but its bill is even more massive. Reaching far northwestern Mexico in summer, it has wandered into Arizona at that season on several occasions.

ROSE-BREASTED GROSBEAK *Pheucticus ludovicianus*

In leafy woodlands of the east, the Rose-breasted Grosbeak often stays out of sight among the treetops. Its song, however—rich whistled phrases, like an improved version of the American Robin's voice—is heard frequently in spring and summer. Where the range of this species overlaps with that of the Black-headed Grosbeak on the Great Plains, the two sometimes interbreed.

HABITAT   *Deciduous woods, orchards, groves.* Breeds mostly in open deciduous woods, sometimes in mixed woods, favoring edges or openings with combination of shrubs and tall trees rather than unbroken forest. In migration, may occur in any wooded or semi-open area. Winters in the tropics, mostly at forest edge or in second-growth woods in lowlands and foothills.

FEEDING   **Diet:** *Mostly insects, seeds, and berries.* About half of annual diet may be insects, including beetles, caterpillars, grasshoppers, true bugs, and others, also spiders and snails. Eats many seeds, including those of trees such as elms, and sometimes eats buds and flowers. May feed heavily on berries and small fruits in late summer and fall. Young are fed mostly insects. **Behavior:** Forages mostly in shrubs and trees, searching for food among foliage. Sometimes hovers to take insects from foliage or bark, or flies out to catch insects in midair.

Rose-breasted Grosbeak

NESTING   Male sings to defend nesting territory, and may fight actively with intruding males. In courtship, male may partly spread wings and tail, draw head back, and approach female while singing. **Nest:** Placed in deciduous tree or large shrub (occasionally in conifer), usually 5–20 feet above ground, sometimes much higher. Nest (built mostly by female) is an open cup, rather loosely made of twigs, weeds, leaves, lined with finer twigs, rootlets, and sometimes animal hair. May be so flimsy that eggs are visible through the nest from below. **Eggs:** 3–5, typically 4. Pale greenish blue, spotted with reddish brown. Incubation is by both parents, 13–14 days. **Young:** Both parents feed the nestlings. Young leave nest about 9–12 days after hatching. Male may care for fledglings while female begins a new nest. One or two broods per year.

MIGRATION   Tends to migrate relatively late in spring and early in fall. Migrates at night. Strays appear widely in west during spring and fall.

CONSERVATION STATUS   Could be vulnerable to loss of habitat, but current numbers apparently stable.

BLACK-HEADED GROSBEAK   *Pheucticus melanocephalus*

In foothills and riverside woods of the west, this species is often very common as a nesting bird. In midsummer, the oak woodlands often resound with the insistent whining whistle of young Black-headed Grosbeaks begging for food. This is one of the few birds able to eat Monarch butterflies, despite the noxious chemicals those insects contain from eating milkweeds in the larval stage; in Mexico in winter, grosbeaks eat large numbers of Monarchs.

HABITAT   *Deciduous and mixed woods.* Breeds mainly in oak woodland, streamside groves of cottonwood and willow, pine-oak woods in mountains, pinyon-juniper woodland; seldom in purely coniferous forest. In migration, occurs in any kind of open woods, streamside trees, suburbs, mesquite groves, desert washes. Winters in open woods and brush of the tropics, from lowlands to mountains.

FEEDING   **Diet:** *Mostly insects, seeds, and berries.* In summer, feeds on many insects, including beetles, caterpillars, wasps, bees, flies, and many others, also spiders and snails. Feeds on seeds of various weeds, and eats berries of many plants (including mistletoe and poison-oak) as well as some cultivated fruit. Young are fed mostly insects at first. **Behavior:** Forages mostly in shrubs and trees, searching for food among foliage. Also may forage on ground and in low growth. Sometimes hovers to take insects from foliage or catches them in midair.

NESTING   Male sings to defend nesting territory. In courtship, male performs song-flights above female, flying with wings and tail fully spread while singing almost continuously. **Nest:** Placed in tree or large shrub (usually deciduous), 3–25 feet above the ground, usually about 10–12 feet up. Nest (built mostly or entirely by female) is an open cup, loosely constructed and bulky, made of twigs, weeds, rootlets, pine needles, lined with fine plant fibers, rootlets, and animal hair. **Eggs:** 3–4, sometimes 2–5. Pale greenish blue, spotted with reddish brown. Incubation is by both parents, 12–14 days; only female incubates at night. **Young:** Both parents feed the nestlings. Young climb out of nest after about 11–12 days but are unable to fly for about 2 more weeks; they remain in nearby trees wait-

Black-headed Grosbeak

ing to be fed. Probably one brood per year.

MIGRATION   Tends to migrate late in spring and early in fall. Some birds begin to appear away from nesting areas as early as mid-July. Strays rarely reach Atlantic coast, generally in late fall or winter.

GENUS *Cyanocompsa*

BLUE BUNTING   *Cyanocompsa parellina*

In dense thickets and woodland edges of Mexico and northern Central America, this dark bunting is fairly common. In our area it is a rare and irregular visitor to far southern Texas, mostly occurring in winter. It has very rarely strayed farther up the Texas coast, once reaching Louisiana.

GENUS *Guiraca*

BLUE GROSBEAK   *Guiraca caerulea*

The husky warbling song of the Blue Grosbeak is a common sound in summer around thickets and hedgerows in the southern states. Often the bird hides in those thickets; sometimes it perches up in the open, looking like an overgrown Indigo Bunting, flicking and spreading its tail in a nervous action. During migration and in the tropics in winter, Blue Grosbeaks may gather in flocks to feed in open weedy fields.

HABITAT   *Brush, roadsides, streamside thickets.* Breeds in dense low growth in semi-open country, including woodland edges, brushy fields, young second-growth woods, hedgerows. In the southwest, most common near water, in streamside thickets and mesquite groves. Outside the breeding season, often in open weedy fields. Native forms in Central America inhabit dry tropical forest and edges of other woods.

FEEDING   **Diet:** *Mostly insects and seeds.* Eats many insects, especially in summer, including grasshoppers, beetles, caterpillars, cicadas, and praying mantises, also spiders and snails. Also eats many seeds (may be majority of diet at some seasons), including those of weeds and grass, also waste grain. **Behavior:** Forages mostly on the ground, also in low vegetation. Picks up items from ground and from plants; will hover while taking insects from foliage, and will make short flights to catch insects in midair. Except when nesting, often forages in flocks.

NESTING Male sings to defend nesting territory. Nesting activity may last late in summer in some areas. **Nest:** Placed low in shrubs, trees, or vines, usually 3–10 feet above the ground, rarely up to 25 feet high. Nest (built by female) is compact open cup of twigs, weeds, rootlets, leaves, strips of bark; often adds odd materials such as snakeskin or pieces of paper, string, or rags. Nest lined with fine grass, rootlets, animal hair. **Eggs:** 3–5, usually 4. Pale blue to bluish white, usually unmarked, rarely with brown spots. Incubation is by female only, 11–12 days. Male may feed female during incubation. Cowbirds often lay eggs in nests of this species. **Young:** Nestlings are fed mostly by the female. Young leave the nest about 9–10 days after hatching. Male may feed young more after they fledge, especially if female is starting second nest.

MIGRATION Eastern birds probably migrate across Gulf of Mexico, while those farther west travel south overland. Strays appear north of breeding range in both spring and fall.

Blue Grosbeak

CONSERVATION STATUS Has been expanding breeding range toward the north in recent decades. Surveys suggest that overall population is stable or even increasing slightly.

AMERICAN BUNTINGS — GENUS *Passerina*

In this group (which also includes a couple of Mexican species), adult males are very brightly colored, while females and young birds are very plain. These buntings live in areas with dense low brush, where they often remain out of sight, but males will perch up in the open to sing their bright musical songs. In most species, the eggs and young are cared for mostly or entirely by the female. Generally foraging low or on the ground, these buntings may feed mainly on seeds in winter, but insects are a major part of their summer diet.

LAZULI BUNTING   *Passerina amoena*

Around thickets and streamside trees of the west, this sky blue bunting is common in summer. Males are conspicuous in summer, singing in the open, but the plainer brown females are far more elusive as they tend their nests in the thick bushes. During migration, flocks are more easily observed as they forage in brushy fields. Where Lazuli and Indigo buntings overlap in breeding range, on the Great Plains and parts of the southwest, they often interbreed.

HABITAT *Open brush, streamside shrubs.* Breeds in brushy areas with open grassy ground nearby, such as patches of scrub oak, chaparral, streamside thickets, sometimes in areas of sagebrush or pinyon-juniper woods. In migration and winter, occurs in weedy fields, open woods, brushy places.

FEEDING **Diet:** *Mostly seeds and insects.* More than half of summer diet may be insects, including grasshoppers, caterpillars, beetles, true bugs, wild bees, ants, and others. Also eats many seeds, mainly those of grasses, also weed seeds and

waste grain; seeds may make up most of winter diet. Young are fed mostly insects. **Behavior:** Forages mainly on the ground, also up in low growth. May bend grass stalks down to the ground to eat the seeds from them. Sometimes takes insects from foliage while hovering.

Lazuli Bunting

NESTING   Male sings to defend nesting territory. Where Lazuli and Indigo buntings overlap in range, they will defend territories against each other. **Nest:** Placed in shrubs, vines, or low trees, usually 2–4 feet above the ground, firmly attached to vertical stems or to forked branch. Nest (built by female) is an open cup of grass, weeds, leaves, lined with fine grass and sometimes animal hair. **Eggs:** 3–5, usually 4. Pale bluish white, unmarked. Incubation is by female only, about 12 days. **Young:** At some nests, nestlings are fed entirely by the female, although at others the male helps to feed them. Young leave the nest about 10–12 days after hatching. Male may feed the young more after they fledge, while female begins second nesting attempt.

Two broods per year, perhaps sometimes three.

MIGRATION   Fall migration begins early, with many birds on the move by late July. Migrants stray east of breeding range on Great Plains, especially in spring.

INDIGO BUNTING   *Passerina cyanea*

In parts of the east, the Indigo Bunting may be the most abundant songbird, with the deep blue males singing along every roadside. The plain brown females are seen far less often, and they have good reason to be inconspicuous: they do almost all the work of caring for the eggs and young, hidden away in dense thickets. This species favors brushy edges rather than unbroken forest and is probably far more common today than when the Pilgrims landed.

Indigo Bunting

HABITAT   *Brushy pastures, bushy wood edges.* For nesting favors roadsides, old fields growing up to bushes, edges of woodlands, and other edge habitats such as along rights-of-way for power lines or railroads. Also in clearings within deciduous woods, edges of swamps. In the west, usually near streams. During winter in the tropics, most common around brushy edges of farm fields.

FEEDING   **Diet:** *Mostly seeds and insects.* In breeding season feeds mostly on insects and spiders, also some seeds, berries. Young in the nest are fed mostly insects at first. In winter, eats many seeds, also some insects. **Behavior:** Forages at all levels from ground up into shrubs and trees. Takes insects from leaves, seeds from ground or stems, berries from shrubs.

Forages alone in summer, in flocks in winter.

NESTING   Male establishes territory in spring, defends it with song. Male may have more than one mate at a time living on his territory. **Nest:** Site is usually 1–3 feet above ground, rarely up to 30 feet or more, in dense shrub or low tree. Late in season, may nest in large weed such as goldenrod. Nest (built by female) is an open cup of grass, leaves,

weeds, bark strips, lined with finer materials. **Eggs:** 3–4, rarely 1–2. White to bluish white, rarely with brown or purple spots. Incubation is by female only, 12–13 days, sometimes 11–14 days. **Young:** Fed only by female in most cases. At some nests, male helps feed young when they are nearly old enough to fly. Young usually leave nest 9–12 days after hatching. Male sometimes takes over feeding of fledged young while female begins second nesting attempt. Two broods per year.

MIGRATION   Many migrate across Gulf of Mexico in both spring and fall. Migrates at night and can navigate by the stars. Important studies of bird navigation and migration have involved this species.

CONSERVATION STATUS   Does well in brushy rural areas but not in urbanized areas or regions of intense agriculture. Since about 1940s, has extended breeding range to include much of southwest.

VARIED BUNTING   *Passerina versicolor*

Brushy country near the Mexican border provides a summer home for this elegant bunting. The dense and thorny nature of its habitat may make it seem hard to approach, but the bird is not especially shy and sometimes may be watched at very close range. In Arizona, where its nesting is timed to the summer rains, male Varied Buntings may be in full song on mornings in August.

Varied Bunting

HABITAT   *Streamside thickets, brush.* In United States found mostly in areas of dense thorny brush, often with an upper story of scattered trees. Prime habitat is usually in canyons and along streams, but in some areas may be in flat desert away from water if brush is dense.

FEEDING   **Diet:** *Probably seeds and insects.* Diet poorly known. In breeding season probably feeds mostly on insects, also some seeds, berries. Food brought to young at nest is mostly insects. Winter diet probably includes more seeds. **Behavior:** Forages at various levels from ground up into shrubs and trees. Probably takes insects from leaves, seeds from ground or stems, berries from shrubs. Forages alone in summer but may gather in small flocks in winter.

NESTING   Nests mostly in late summer in Arizona (after summer rains begin), in early summer in Texas. Male defends territory with song and with fluttering flight display directed at intruding males. **Nest:** Site is in dense shrub, low tree, or vine, usually 2–5 feet above ground, sometimes up to 12 feet. Nest (built by both parents) is compact open cup, mostly of dry grass and weeds, lined with finer materials. **Eggs:** 4, sometimes 3, rarely 5. White to bluish white, unmarked. Incubation is by female only, about 12–13 days. **Young:** Fed by both parents; leave nest after about 12 days. For a few days after fledging, parents may divide brood, each caring for half; then male may take over care of all young while female starts another nesting attempt. Often two broods per year, perhaps sometimes three.

MIGRATION   Most leave the United States in winter, probably moving only a short distance south into Mexico. Recently discovered wintering in small numbers in Big Bend region of Texas.

CONSERVATION STATUS   Still locally common in southwestern United States, although some habitat has been lost. Probably declining in parts of its Mexican range, as overgrazing (especially by goats) degrades its habitat.

PAINTED BUNTING *Passerina ciris*

Sometimes called the "Nonpareil," meaning "unrivaled," a fair way to describe the unbelievable colors of the male Painted Bunting. This species is locally common in the southeast, around brushy areas and woodland edges. It is often secretive, staying

low in dense cover. However, males sing their bright warbling songs from higher in the trees, partly hidden among foliage or sometimes out in the sun on an exposed perch. Some lucky Floridians have Painted Buntings coming to their bird feeders in winter.

HABITAT *Woodland edges, roadsides, brush, towns, gardens.* Favors semi-open areas with dense low growth at all seasons. Breeds around thickets, hedgerows, woodland clearings and edges, and undergrowth of open woods. Winters in similar habitats in Florida, plus areas of scrub and second growth in the tropics.

FEEDING **Diet:** *Mostly seeds and insects.* Reported to feed mainly on seeds, primarily those of grasses and weeds; sometimes eats berries and fruits. Also eats many insects, including beetles, caterpillars, grasshoppers, flies, and others. Probably eats more in-

Painted Bunting

sects in early summer, and feeds them to its young. **Behavior:** Forages mostly on the ground. Also does some foraging up in shrubs and low trees. During migration, may forage in mixed flocks with Indigo Buntings.

NESTING To defend territory, male sings from a raised perch, often partly hidden among foliage near treetop. Males will also engage in serious physical fights, probably in disputes over territorial boundaries. One male may have more than one mate. **Nest:** Placed in dense bushes, vines, or low in trees, usually 3–9 feet above the ground, sometimes higher. Nest (built by female) is open cup woven of grass, weeds, leaves, lined with fine grass, rootlets, and animal hair. **Eggs:** 3–4, sometimes 5. Whitish to bluish white or pale gray, with reddish brown spots often concentrated at larger end. Incubation is by female only, 11–12 days. **Young:** Nestlings are fed by the female. Young leave the nest about 12–14 days after hatching, and male may take over feeding them if female begins second nesting attempt. Two broods per year, sometimes three, perhaps rarely four.

MIGRATION Those nesting on southern Atlantic coast probably winter in Florida and northwestern Caribbean; those nesting farther west probably winter in Mexico and Central America.

CONSERVATION STATUS Surveys show declining numbers in recent decades. Nests are frequently parasitized by cowbirds. Often captured and kept as a cagebird on wintering grounds in tropics.

GENUS *Spiza*

DICKCISSEL *Spiza americana*

In the Midwest in summer, male Dickcissels sometimes seem to sing their name from every wire, fencepost, or weed stalk in prairie or farm country. Very erratic in summer occurrence; they may nest in large numbers in an area one year and be totally absent there the next, presumably as a response to rainfall and its effect on habitat. Away from their midcontinent stronghold, migrant Dickcissels are often detected by their electric-buzzer call note as they fly overhead. Most winter in the

Dickcissel

MIGRATION

CONSERVATION STATUS

tropics, but a few spend the winter at bird feeders in the northeast, where they usually flock with House Sparrows.

HABITAT   *Alfalfa and other fields; meadows, prairies.* Originally nested in native prairies and meadows. Today, many nest in fields of alfalfa, clover, timothy, or other crops. In migration, may be found in any kind of grassy or weedy fields.

FEEDING   **Diet:** *Mostly insects and seeds.* Insects make up majority of diet in early summer; included are many grasshoppers, also crickets, caterpillars, beetles, and many others. At other seasons, may feed mainly on seeds, including those of weeds and grasses, also cultivated grain. **Behavior:** Forages mostly on the ground and in low vegetation. Except when nesting, usually forages in flocks.

NESTING   In many areas, numbers of nesting Dickcissels are wildly variable from year to year. Males arrive on breeding grounds about a week before females and sing to defend nesting territory. One male may have more than one mate. **Nest:** Site is usually on or near the ground, typically well concealed in dense growth of grass, weeds, alfalfa, clover, or other plants. Sometimes placed in shrub or low tree, up to 6 feet above ground, exceptionally higher. Nest (built by female) is a bulky open cup made of weeds, grass, leaves, lined with fine grass, rootlets, sometimes animal hair. **Eggs:** 4, sometimes 3–5, rarely 2–6. Pale blue, unmarked. Incubation is by female only, about 12–13 days. **Young:** Nestlings are fed by female only. Young leave the nest about 7–10 days after hatching, are unable to fly for several more days.

Migrates in flocks, sometimes in flocks of many hundreds. Strays reach both coasts in autumn. Rarely found in our area in winter except in northeast, where a few may spend the season at bird feeders.

Formerly nested commonly along Atlantic seaboard, but disappeared during late 19th century; has reappeared as a breeding bird in the east since the 1920s, but only in small numbers. Overall populations recently have been declining again.

AMERICAN SPARROWS AND OLD WORLD BUNTINGS (subfamily Emberizinae)

Most of the birds included here live on the ground or close to it, and many of them are colored in some shade of brown. Short thick bills, good for crushing hard seeds, are typical of the birds in this subfamily. This is a large and varied group. Experts disagree on just which birds to include in this subfamily, but the number of species is over 150, perhaps well over 250.

Birders in North America know this mainly as the group that includes our native sparrows, more than 30 species of them, several of which can be hard to see and hard to identify. Beginners may find these birds frustrating, but experienced naturalists appreciate the sparrows for their intricate patterns and for the attractive songs of many.

Although most members of this group nest as isolated pairs, vigorously driving away intruders of their own species from the nesting territory, many of them gather in flocks at other seasons. Some of the most secretive species remain solitary all year, and these birds are usually quiet and easily overlooked outside the nesting season.

Feeding	We often think of these as seed-eating birds, but most of them eat many insects in summer, and the food brought to nestlings is almost entirely insects and other invertebrates in most cases. At least in winter, however, most kinds feed heavily on seeds, especially those of grasses and weeds. The thick bill shapes of sparrows seem to be adapted mainly for cracking seeds; apparently any bill shape will work for eating insects when they are available, so the evolution of these birds' bills seems to be driven by their feeding habits in winter.

Our species feed mostly on the ground or in low growth such as grass, weeds, or bushes. This seems to be true for most members of this subfamily around the world. A few of them will occasionally make short flights to capture flying insects, perhaps those they have flushed from the grass.

Many of the sparrows and their relatives, like various other seed-eating birds, are known to swallow bits of coarse sand. This grit probably helps with the grinding action of the gizzard when the bird is digesting tough seeds.

Nesting	Nest-building for most birds in this group is carried out mostly or entirely by the female. The typical nest type is an open cup made of grass, weeds, or twigs, usually placed in dense low bushes or on the ground. Some species make a domed top over the nest or choose a site under an overhanging grass clump that will provide such a canopy. The eggs may be unmarked or spotted; in most cases, incubation is by the female only, although the male may feed her during the incubation period in some species. Usually both parents help to feed the young.

Displays	In most members of this subfamily, males defend their nesting territories mainly by voice, singing very frequently during the breeding season. Males of some species living in very open country will perform flight-song displays, flying up and then fluttering or gliding back down while singing; this is typical of the longspurs, Lark Bunting, and Cassin's Sparrow, among others. Some sparrows and towhees live in pairs on their territories at all seasons, and when the members of a pair meet after being separated by some disturbance, they may perform a squealing or chattering "duet."

GENUS *Arremonops*

OLIVE SPARROW *Arremonops rufivirgatus*

Olive Sparrow

In brushy country of far southern Texas, this plain little sparrow moves about quietly in the undergrowth. With its secretive behavior and soft ticking call notes, it often goes unnoticed at most seasons; in spring, however, its song of accelerating musical chips may be conspicuous. Despite the name, this bird is probably related more closely to the towhees than to our other sparrows; it often forages like a towhee, using its feet to scratch for food in the leaf litter.

HABITAT *Woodland undergrowth, weedy thickets.* In southern Texas, lives in the understory of dense low woods and in areas of low native brush. Farther south in the tropics, inhabits drier woods and semi-open scrub, avoiding humid tropical forest.

FEEDING **Diet:** *Probably insects and seeds.* Diet is thought to be mainly insects (including caterpillars) and the seeds of wild plants. **Behavior:** Does at least the majority of its feeding on the ground, under dense thickets or near their edges. Often forages rather like a towhee, scratching with its feet among the leaf litter. Members of a pair may forage together.

NESTING   Little is known of the nesting habits. Birds may remain in pairs or small groups during the winter, separating into isolated pairs in spring. Males sing in spring to defend nesting territories. **Nest:** Site is in dense thickets, usually placed in shrub or cactus, typically 2–3 feet above ground but sometimes up to 5 feet high. Nest is large for size of bird, a bulky cup with a domed top above it, so that entrance is on the side; made of dry weed stems, grass, twigs, leaves, strips of bark, lined with fine grass and sometimes with hair. **Eggs:** 3–5, typically 4. Glossy white, unmarked. Incubation period and roles of the parents in incubating are not well known. **Young:** Probably both parents feed the nestlings. Pairs probably raise two broods per year.

MIGRATION   Apparently a permanent resident throughout its range.

CONSERVATION STATUS   Undoubtedly has decreased in southern Texas as land has been cleared for farming; still common in remaining habitat.

Towhees — genus *Pipilo*

This is a distinctive group of large sparrows that live mostly on the ground, with six species in our area and two more in Mexico. Typical of the towhees is their habit of scratching with their feet in the dirt or in leaf litter as they hunt for food. In this characteristic action, the bird makes a little jump forward and then scratches back with both feet at once. All of the towhees have distinctive songs and call notes, heard more often than the birds are seen.

GREEN-TAILED TOWHEE   *Pipilo chlorurus*

A catlike mewing call in the bushes may reveal the presence of the Green-tailed Towhee. Fairly common in western mountains in summer, this bird spends most of

Green-tailed Towhee

its time in dense low thickets, where it forages on the ground. Like other towhees, it scratches in the leaf litter with both feet as it searches for food. It sometimes wanders east in fall, and strays may show up at bird feeders in winter as far east as the Atlantic coast.

HABITAT   *Brushy mountain slopes, low chaparral, open pines, sage, manzanita, riverine woods.* Breeds in a variety of semi-open habitats, mostly in mountains; typically where there is dense low cover of sagebrush, manzanita, or other bushes, and a few taller trees such as scattered pines. In migration and winter, mostly in dense low brush, often near streams.

FEEDING   **Diet:** *Mainly insects and seeds.* Diet is not known in detail, but includes various insects such as beetles, crickets, and caterpillars. Also eats many seeds of weeds and grasses, and sometimes feeds on berries and small fruits. **Behavior:** Forages mostly on the ground under thickets, often scratching in the leaf litter like other towhees. Also sometimes forages up in low bushes. Will come to bird feeders, but typically forages on the ground below the feeding tray.

NESTING   Nesting behavior is not well studied. Male defends nesting territory by singing, often from a prominent raised perch. **Nest:** Site is on the ground or in low shrubs such as sagebrush, usually lower than 3 feet above ground. Nest is a large, deep cup,

loosely made of twigs, grass, weeds, strips of bark, lined with fine grass, rootlets, animal hair. **Eggs:** 3–4, sometimes 2–5. White, with heavy dotting of brown and gray often concentrated at larger end. Details of incubation are not well known. If adult is disturbed at nest, the bird may slip away quietly through the brush or may drop to the ground and scurry away like a rodent. **Young:** Probably both parents feed the nestlings. Age at which the young leave the nest is not well known. Possibly two broods per year.

MIGRATION   Migrates relatively early in fall and late in spring. Wanderers east of the normal range occur mostly in fall, although some may stay through the winter.

EASTERN TOWHEE   *Pipilo erythrophthalmus*

Eastern Towhee

Sometimes secretive but often common, this bird may be noticed first by the sound of industrious scratching in the leaf litter under dense thickets. In the nesting season, males become bolder, singing from high perches. In some areas this bird is commonly known as "Chewink," after the sound of its call note. In parts of the southeast and Florida, the towhees have white eyes.

HABITAT   *Open woods, undergrowth, brushy edges.* Habitat varies with region, but always in brushy areas. In the northeast, typically in understory of open woods.

FEEDING   **Diet:** *Mostly insects, seeds, berries.* Diet varies with season and region. Eats many insects, especially in summer, including beetles, caterpillars, moths, true bugs, ants, and many others, also spiders, snails, and millipedes. Rarely may eat small salamanders, lizards, or snakes. Also eats many seeds, plus acorns, berries, and small fruits. **Behavior:** Forages mostly on the ground, frequently scratching in the leaf litter. Also sometimes forages up in shrubs and low trees.

NESTING   Male defends nesting territory by singing, often from a high perch. In courtship, male may give a soft "whispered" version of song, chase female, or rapidly spread tail to show off white spots. **Nest:** Site is on the ground under a shrub or in low bushes, usually less than 5 feet above the ground. Nest (built by female) is an open cup of grass, twigs, weeds, rootlets, strips of bark, lined with finer materials, sometimes including animal hair. **Eggs:** 3–4, sometimes 5, rarely 2–6. Creamy white to very pale gray, with spots of brown often concentrated at larger end. Incubation is mostly or entirely by female, about 12–13 days. **Young:** Both parents feed the nestlings. Young leave the nest about 10–12 days after hatching, may remain with parents for some time thereafter. Often two broods per year, sometimes three in southern part of range.

MIGRATION   Many southern birds are permanent residents; most in the north are migratory.
CONSERVATION STATUS   Population in northeast has declined seriously in recent decades. Elsewhere, numbers are probably stable.

SPOTTED TOWHEE   *Pipilo maculatus*

A widespread towhee of the west, sometimes abundant in chaparral and on brushy mountain slopes. For many years it was considered to belong to the same species as

the unspotted Eastern Towhees found east of the Great Plains, under the combined name of "Rufous-sided Towhee," but recent research suggests that the two are distinct. The Spotted Towhee differs in the heavy white spotting on its upperparts, and its songs and call notes are more variable and much harsher in tone. Male Spotted Towhees look very similar throughout their range, but females are quite variable in the color of their upperparts, from brown to gray or black.

In the varied terrain of the west, this towhee often lives in chaparral, mountain manzanita thickets, scrub oaks, or pinyon-juniper woods with dense understory. Its behavior is mostly similar to that of the Eastern Towhee. Nest sites in most regions are typically on the ground, but birds may nest up in bushes more often in some areas.

Spotted Towhee

Spotted Towhees from the far northwest spread eastward in winter onto the Great Plains, and they rarely stray east all the way to the Atlantic coast.

In the southwest, some individuals may move to lower elevations in winter, while others may be permanent residents.

At the southern end of its range, in southwestern Mexico, this species often interbreeds with a related bird, the Collared Towhee. Their interactions have been the subject of some important field studies in the past.

CALIFORNIA TOWHEE   *Pipilo crissalis*

Along the Pacific seaboard from southern Oregon to Baja, this plain brown bird is a common denizen of brushy places, from wild chaparral hillsides to the borders of gardens and city parks. California Towhees sometimes hide in the shrubbery, where

they may be noticed mainly by their sharp call notes and the squealing duets of mated pairs. At other times they come out on open ground, to scratch in the leaf litter with both feet as they search for food.

HABITAT   *Brushy areas, chaparral, coastal scrub, gardens.* Found in a wide variety of dense low habitats, including streamside thickets, chaparral, pinyon-juniper woods, coastal sage scrub, semi-desert scrub, edges and openings in oak woodland, and well-vegetated gardens and city parks.

FEEDING   **Diet:** *Mostly seeds and insects.* Majority of diet, especially in winter, consists of seeds of weeds and grasses, also some waste grain. Also eats insects (including caterpillars and beetles), especially in summer, and eats some berries and small fruits. Young are fed mostly or entirely on insects.

California Towhee

Behavior: Forages mostly on the ground, sometimes scratching among the leaf litter. Often comes to bird feeders, but may do much of its foraging on the ground under the feeding tray.

AMERICAN SPARROWS AND THEIR RELATIVES

NESTING   May mate for life, and pairs may remain together on breeding territory all year. Male is very aggressive in defending this territory, actively attacking intruding males or even his own reflection. **Nest:** Site is usually in a dense shrub or low tree, typically 4–12 feet above the ground, but may be very low (sometimes on the ground) or up to 30 feet or higher. Nest is a bulky open cup, rather loosely made of twigs, grass, weeds, strips of bark, lined with finer grass, rootlets, animal hair. **Eggs:** 3–4, rarely 2–5. Pale bluish white, marked with brown and black. Incubation is by the female, about 11 days. **Young:** Both parents feed the nestlings. Young may leave the nest after as little as 8 days, before they are able to fly well; remain with parents for several more weeks. A pair may raise two or three broods per year.

MIGRATION   Permanent resident, rarely moving even short distances away from nesting areas.

CONSERVATION STATUS   Probably has declined locally, with increasing development and urbanization along California coast, but still very common in much of its range.

CANYON TOWHEE   *Pipilo fuscus*

Canyon Towhee

In dry foothills and canyons in the interior of the southwest, Canyon Towhees are common in the low brush. They spend most of their time on or near the ground, often scratching in the soil with both feet as they search for food. This bird and the California Towhee were once regarded as the same species under the name "Brown Towhee," but their voices are very different.

HABITAT   *Brushy areas, chaparral, desert foothills, canyons, pinyon-juniper woods.* Habitat varies in different parts of range, but always in brushy areas, avoiding forest and open desert. Found in open pinyon-juniper woodland, chaparral on dry hillsides, grasslands with cholla and mesquite, thickets of scrub oak, similar habitats.

FEEDING   **Diet:** *Mostly seeds and insects.* Diet includes mostly seeds in winter, more insects in summer. Young are fed almost entirely on insects. May eat some berries and small fruits at times. **Behavior:** Forages mostly or entirely on the ground. Often scratches in the dirt, but not as much as some towhees. Frequently seen feeding under things, such as logs, bushes, or parked cars.

NESTING   May mate for life, and pairs often stay together all year on permanent territories. Does not seem very aggressive in defense of nesting territory, sometimes tolerating intrusion by other towhees. **Nest:** Site is usually in small tree, dense shrub, or cactus, 3–12 feet above the ground, often placed at the base of a branch against the trunk. Nest is a bulky open cup, solidly built of twigs, weeds, grass, lined with leaves, fine grass, strips of bark, and animal hair. **Eggs:** 3–4, sometimes 2–5, rarely 6. Off-white, spotted and scrawled with reddish brown. Incubation is by female only, probably about 11 days. **Young:** Both parents feed the nestlings. Young may leave the nest before they are able to fly, and climb about in bushes while waiting to be fed. A pair may raise two or sometimes three broods per year.

MIGRATION   Permanent resident and very sedentary, rarely moving even a short distance away from nesting areas.

ABERT'S TOWHEE   *Pipilo aberti*

Along streams in the desert southwest, a sharp pinging note in the thickets announces the presence of Abert's Towhee. If an observer tries to approach, a pair of these towhees may stay just ahead and out of sight, calling in an odd squealing duet when pressed too closely. When undisturbed, they feed on the ground under dense bushes, scratching among the leaf litter. Many southwestern "specialty birds" have extensive ranges in the tropics, but this towhee barely gets across the border into northwestern Mexico.

HABITAT   *Desert streams, brush, mesquite.* Typically found in dense brush near water in arid lowlands, as in streamside thickets, edges of ponds or irrigation ditches, understory of cottonwood-willow groves, even riverside marshes. In some areas (such as around Phoenix), comes into yards in well-watered suburbs. Overlaps in habitat with Canyon Towhee in some places, but Abert's stays closer to water in dense cover, avoiding dry open hillsides.

Abert's Towhee

FEEDING   **Diet:** *Mostly insects and seeds.* Insects make up majority of diet, especially in summer; major items include beetles, ants, caterpillars, grasshoppers, and cicadas. Also eats many seeds, including those of saltbush, weeds, and grasses. **Behavior:** Forages mostly on the ground, often scratching with both feet. Also forages on bark at base of trees, and in low bushes. Members of a pair often forage together.

NESTING   Members of pair remain together all year on permanent territories; courtship and pair formation may occur at any season, but nesting is mainly March through July. Both members of pair evidently defend nesting territory. **Nest:** Site is in dense shrub or tree such as mesquite, willow, baccharis, or elderberry, often well hidden within clump of mistletoe; usually 5–8 feet above the ground but can be higher. Nest (built by female) is a bulky open cup, loosely made of weeds, bark strips, grass, leaves, vines, lined with dry grass and sometimes hair. **Eggs:** 1–4, usually 3. Pale blue or whitish with markings of dark brown and black. Incubation is apparently by female only, about 14 days. **Young:** Both parents feed the nestlings. Young leave nest about 12–13 days after hatching, before they are full-grown, and are unable to fly for another week; tended by parents for a month or more. Often two broods per year.

MIGRATION   Permanent resident, rarely wandering even short distances away from favored habitat.

CONSERVATION STATUS   Still very common in parts of its limited range. Could be vulnerable to loss of streamside habitat.

SEEDEATERS — GENUS *Sporophila*

WHITE-COLLARED SEEDEATER   *Sporophila torqueola*

This tiny finch is abundant in Mexico and Central America, but it has a checkered history in our area. In extreme southern Texas, the seedeater was common as recently as the 1940s, but by the mid-1970s it had all but vanished north of the border. In recent years it has reappeared in small numbers in the Falcon Dam area. Flocks of White-collared Seedeaters feed low in rank weedy places, calling to each other in soft voices. They may roost in tall marsh growth along the Rio Grande. The surprisingly clear whistled song of the male is not often heard in our area.

HABITAT *Weedy places, tall grass, brush.* In Texas, found mainly in weedy overgrown fields or brushy open woods, typically close to water; may roost in tall marsh growth. Farther south in tropics, found in a wide variety of open habitats, from marshes and open grassy fields to brushy edges of woods.

FEEDING **Diet:** *Seeds and insects.* Diet probably includes many small seeds, especially those of grasses. Also probably feeds on a variety of small insects. **Behavior:** Forages in low growth or sometimes on the ground, clambering about among grasses and weeds and plucking seeds from grass stalks. Occasionally will feed higher in dense bushes or low trees. Except in nesting season, almost always forages in flocks.

NESTING Often nests in small colonies, with several pairs fairly close together. Male sings to defend nesting territory. **Nest:** In Texas, nests have been found in shrubs or in large weeds such as giant ragweed, usually 3–5 feet above the ground. Nest (probably built by female) is a small and compact open cup of grass, small twigs, rootlets, plant fibers, and plant down, sometimes with the addition of spider webs or animal hair. **Eggs:** Probably 2–4. Pale blue to pale gray, with spots of brown often concentrated at the larger end. Incubation is probably by female only, about 13 days. **Young:** Both parents feed the nestlings. Young leave the nest about 9–11 days after hatching.

MIGRATION Apparently a permanent resident throughout its range. When the species was more common in Texas, the birds apparently would move around somewhat in flocks during the winter.

CONSERVATION STATUS Reasons for sharp decline in Texas are poorly understood. Still widespread and common in Mexico and Central America, and has probably increased in some areas with clearing of forest.

GRASSQUITS — GENUS *Tiaris*

YELLOW-FACED GRASSQUIT *Tiaris olivacea*

Grassquits are tiny seed-eating birds of the tropics. This species is common and widespread, from northern Mexico and the West Indies to northern South America, living in semi-open country and woodland edges. Single birds have strayed north into Texas and southern Florida.

BLACK-FACED GRASSQUIT *Tiaris bicolor*

Widespread in the Caribbean region is this dark, stubby little finch. Black-faced Grassquits live in brushy fields, clearings, and the edges of woods, often gathering in small flocks. Common in the Bahamas, they have strayed to Florida on several occasions.

LONG-TAILED SKULKERS — GENUS *Aimophila*

Most of the American sparrows live in northern or temperate regions, but this genus is typical of warmer climates. Ten of the 13 species are found in Mexico; five extend north into our area, and there are two in South America. All have rather long tails, and all are elusive, hiding in dense low cover or tall grass. They often live in pairs or in family groups, but never in flocks.

BACHMAN'S SPARROW   *Aimophila aestivalis*

Bachman's Sparrow

Plain in appearance but with a beautiful whistled song, Bachman's Sparrow is an uncommon and elusive resident of the southeast. Its classic habitat is mature pine forest, where it lives in the open grassy understory, flying up to low pine branches only to sing. As such forests have become scarce, it has also nested in brushy open fields. When not singing, this sparrow is extremely secretive, hiding in the undergrowth, and it is easily overlooked.

HABITAT   *Open pine or oak woods, palmetto scrub, bushy pastures.* Favors relatively open grassy areas. Historically was most common in understory of mature pine forest, where frequent fires limited the amount of brush; as mature forest has become scarce, more Bachman's Sparrows are found in clearcuts, power line rights-of-way, old pastures, and other open areas.

FEEDING   **Diet:** *Mostly seeds and insects.* Diet is not known in detail. In summer, majority of diet apparently is insects, especially beetles, caterpillars, grasshoppers, also other insects and spiders. Also eats many seeds, particularly those of grasses; seeds may be especially important in diet in winter. **Behavior:** Forages almost entirely on the ground, moving rather slowly in a limited area. Picks up items from ground or jumps up to take items from low vegetation.

NESTING   In southern areas, members of a pair may remain together at all seasons. Beginning in early spring, male sings to defend nesting territory. **Nest:** Site is almost always on the ground, typically placed at the base of a shrub, clump of grass, or palmetto. Occasionally placed a few inches above the ground, within the base of a weed or grass clump. Nest (built by female) is an open cup made of grass, weeds, rootlets, lined with fine grass and animal hair. Often has a domed top of woven grasses at least partially covering nest. **Eggs:** 3–4, sometimes 2–5. White, unmarked. Incubation is by female only, about 12–14 days. **Young:** Both parents bring food to the nestlings. Young leave the nest about 9–10 days after hatching. One or two broods per year, perhaps rarely three.

MIGRATION   Southern birds probably permanent residents, northern ones probably migratory; status is hard to assess in many areas because nonbreeding birds are so difficult to detect.

CONSERVATION STATUS   Around beginning of 20th century, range of species expanded well to the north, as the bird moved into brushy areas and second growth created by cutting of forests. The range has since contracted sharply again. Bird is now uncommon and possibly declining in the south. Loss of habitat is a major current problem.

BOTTERI'S SPARROW   *Aimophila botterii*

Two kinds of plain, long-tailed sparrows live side by side in southwestern grasslands. While Cassin's is fairly widespread, Botteri's Sparrow is found only in a few areas of southern Texas and Arizona. Although it will perch up on a shrub or an ocotillo stalk to sing its series of accelerating *chip* notes, Botteri's Sparrow is quite secretive at other times, hiding in dense grass.

HABITAT   *Desert grassland, coastal prairie.* In our area, found mostly in drier grassland areas with relatively tall grass and scattered taller shrubs; mainly desert grassland in

Botteri's Sparrow

Arizona, coastal prairie in Texas. Avoids true desert and heavily grazed areas. Farther south in Mexico and Central America, also found on dry scrub areas, overgrazed pastures, and open savanna.

FEEDING   **Diet:** *Mostly insects and seeds.* Diet is not known in detail. In summer feeds mainly on insects, especially grasshoppers, crickets, caterpillars, and beetles, plus many others. Also eats many seeds, probably more so in winter. **Behavior:** Forages almost entirely while hopping or running on the ground, picking up items from the ground or from plants. Usually forages alone, sometimes in pairs or family groups.

NESTING   Nesting activity is mostly in early summer in Texas, mostly in late summer (after onset of summer rainy season) in Arizona. Male sings from a raised perch to defend nesting territory. Details of nesting behavior are not well known. **Nest:** Nest is usually on the ground, often in a slight depression in soil and hidden under grass and weeds; sometimes slightly elevated in base of grass clump and occasionally a few inches up in the base of a bush. Nest is a shallow open cup made of grass. **Eggs:** 2–5, probably usually 4. White to pale bluish white, unmarked. Details of incubation are not well known. **Young:** Probably both parents help feed the nestlings.

MIGRATION   Timing of migration not well known, since birds are very secretive when not singing.

CONSERVATION STATUS   Probably has declined in both Arizona and Texas with loss of habitat, but still common in some localities.

CASSIN'S SPARROW   *Aimophila cassinii*

In dry grassland country of the southwest in summer, this plain brown sparrow is often seen flying up from a bush top and then parachuting down in a "skylarking" display, giving a song of sweet trills and notes. Cassin's Sparrows are sometimes very common, but they are irregular, big numbers often appearing in an area after good rains have turned the prairies green. With their nomadic tendencies, they sometimes turn up far outside their normal range, with scattered records from coast to coast.

HABITAT   *Desert grassland, brushy fields.* Breeds in a variety of situations having good ground cover of grass and low shrubs; ranges from open grassland with only scattered shrubs to brushy areas with grassy understory. In migration and winter, also found in pure grassland, brushy areas, deserts.

FEEDING   **Diet:** *Mainly insects and seeds.* Summer diet is partly to mostly insects, especially grasshoppers, caterpillars, moths, and beetles, also many others. Young are fed almost entirely on insects. Also eats

Cassin's Sparrow

seeds, especially in fall and winter, mainly those of weeds and grasses. **Behavior:** Forages mostly or entirely on the ground, hopping about in relatively open areas, taking items from the ground or from plant stems.

NESTING   Somewhat irregular in its nesting, especially in western and northern parts of range; may appear in numbers and breed only in years of good rainfall. Male advertises

territory with flight-song display, flying up to about 20 feet and then gliding and fluttering down while singing. In courtship, male may chase female or display with wings and tail partly spread and fluttering. **Nest:** Site is either on the ground, well hidden among weeds or at the base of a bush, or up to a foot above ground in a low shrub. Nest is an open cup made of dry grass, weed stems, bark, plant fibers, lined with fine grass. **Eggs:** 3–5, usually 4. White, unmarked. Incubation lasts about 9–11 days. **Young:** Both parents feed the nestlings. Young leave the nest after about 8–10 days.

MIGRATION   In many areas, seasonal occurrence is very irregular; may be present in large numbers one summer, absent the next. Winter numbers in southwest are also quite variable. Strays sometimes wander far, having reached eastern Canada.

CONSERVATION STATUS   Great variation in annual numbers makes it difficult to monitor overall population. Apparently still widespread and common.

RUFOUS-WINGED SPARROW   *Aimophila carpalis*

One of the last birds new to science to be found in North America, the Rufous-winged Sparrow was discovered in 1872 at Tucson. It was common there into the 1880s, but then disappeared for half a century. Since the 1930s it has gradually increased again in southern Arizona, but it is still uncommon and local, found in desert areas with good grass cover. Nesting mainly after the summer rains begin, it may be heard singing in the desert in late summer.

HABITAT   *Tall desert grass, thorn brush.* Quite local in our area, favoring areas with good growth of grass and numerous shrubs, especially mesquite and desert hackberry. Avoids areas that have been heavily grazed, but may occur in suburban areas where houses are scattered and good vegetation remains.

FEEDING   **Diet:** *Mostly insects and seeds.* Summer diet is mostly insects, especially caterpillars and grasshoppers, also many other insects and some spiders. Eats more seeds at other seasons, especially those of grasses and weeds, and winter diet may be almost entirely seeds. **Behavior:** Forages mostly while hopping

Rufous-winged Sparrow

about on the ground. Also forages up in low bushes, especially in summer. Picks up items from ground or from stems of plants, and occasionally makes short flights to catch insects in midair. Usually forages in pairs or family groups, sometimes loosely associated with Black-throated Sparrows or Brewer's Sparrows.

NESTING   Members of a pair may remain together on territory at all seasons. Nesting in Arizona is usually in late summer, after beginning of rainy season; in wet years, may also nest in spring. Male defends nesting territory by singing from a raised perch. **Nest:** Site is usually in low shrub or cactus, from a few inches to 7 feet above ground; often placed in desert hackberry or mesquite, sometimes in cholla or prickly-pear cactus. Nest (probably built by female only) is a deep open cup of dry weeds, grass, and small twigs, lined with fine grass and often with animal hair. **Eggs:** Usually 4, sometimes 2–3. A century ago, may have typically laid clutches of 4–5 in Arizona. Eggs pale bluish white, unmarked. Incubation is apparently by female only, length of incubation period not well known. **Young:** Both parents feed the nestlings. Young leave the nest about 8–9 days after hatching. One brood per year, or two in years with good rains.

RUFOUS-CROWNED SPARROW   *Aimophila ruficeps*

In dry southwestern hills and canyons, where sparse brush covers the rocky slopes, pairs of Rufous-crowned Sparrows lurk in the thickets. Usually they are easy to overlook; but if they are alarmed, or if members of a pair become separated, they reveal

their presence with a harsh nasal call, *dear-dear-dear*. Although they live in dense cover, they are not especially shy if undisturbed, and a birder who sits quietly in their habitat may be able to observe them closely.

HABITAT   *Grassy or rocky slopes with sparse low bushes; open pine-oak woods.* Habitat varies in different parts of range, but always in brushy areas. In southwest, usually in rocky areas of foothills and lower canyons, in understory of pine-oak woods, or in chaparral or coastal scrub. On southern Great Plains, found in rocky outcrops with cover of dense grass and scattered bushes.

FEEDING   **Diet:** *Mostly insects and seeds.* Diet varies with season and locality, but tends to eat more insects in summer, more seeds in winter. Major items in diet may include caterpillars, beetle larvae and adults,

Rufous-crowned Sparrow

grasshoppers, ants, and other insects and spiders. Also eats many seeds of grasses and weeds at all seasons, but especially in winter. **Behavior:** Forages mostly while walking or hopping on the ground, but also will feed up in weeds and low bushes. Tends to move slowly, foraging in a limited area. Usually forages in pairs or family groups.

NESTING   Members of a pair may remain together all year on permanent home range. In spring and summer, male sings to defend nesting territory. **Nest:** Site is usually on the ground, typically well hidden at base of bush or grass clump, placed in a slight depression so that rim of nest is near ground level. Occasionally in low shrub, up to 1–3 feet above ground, especially in eastern part of range. Nest is an open cup made of small twigs, grass, weeds, plant fibers, often with some animal hair in lining. **Eggs:** 3–4, sometimes 2–5. Pale bluish white, unmarked. Incubation is probably by female, but details not well known. **Young:** Both parents feed the nestlings. Young probably leave the nest after about 8–9 days, before they are able to fly; young may remain with parents for up to several months.

MIGRATION   Generally a permanent resident. Thought to retreat from some northern areas of range in winter, but may be simply overlooked at that season.

SMALL, SLIM SPARROWS — GENUS *Spizella*

Unlike some sparrows, the ones in this genus are often rather tame and easy to observe. All are rather small and slender, with rounded heads and small bills; their tails are medium length to rather long. These sparrows all live in semi-open or brushy country. When they are not nesting, they usually gather in small flocks. All seven kinds of *Spizella* are known from our area, but one of them has not been seen here for over a century.

AMERICAN TREE SPARROW   *Spizella arborea*

This sparrow nests and winters farther north than any of its close relatives. Despite the name, it is not particularly associated with trees, and many of its nesting areas are on the tundra north of treeline. In winter in the northern states, flocks of Tree Sparrows are common in open country. They often come to bird feeders with Dark-eyed Juncos and other birds. Males may begin singing their musical songs in late winter, before they start their northward migration.

American Tree Sparrow

HABITAT   *Arctic scrub, willow thickets; in winter, brushy roadsides, weedy edges, marshes.* In summer most common near treeline, where northern forest gives way to tundra. May be in openings in stunted spruce forest, or on open tundra if a few taller shrubs are present. In winter in open fields, woodland edges, marshes, suburban areas.

FEEDING   **Diet:** *Seeds and insects.* Diet in winter is almost entirely seeds, from grasses, weeds, and other plants; also a few insects and berries. In summer eats mostly insects and other small invertebrates, plus a few seeds. Young are fed mostly insects. **Behavior:** Forages on ground or in low bushes, sometimes in trees up to 30 feet or more above ground. Except when nesting, usually forages in small flocks.

NESTING   Pairs form shortly after birds arrive on breeding grounds. Male actively defends territory, chasing away other members of same species. **Nest:** Site is on or near ground, in grass clumps beneath shrubs. Sometimes on hummock in open tundra; rarely up to 4 feet above ground in willow or spruce. Nest is an open cup of twigs, grasses, moss, lined with fine grass and feathers (usually ptarmigan feathers). Female builds nest in about 7 days. **Eggs:** 4–6, usually 5. Pale bluish or greenish, with brownish spots often concentrated at larger end. Incubation is by female, 11–13 days; male visits nest often but does not incubate. **Young:** Both parents feed nestlings. Young leave nest at age 8–10 days, when flight feathers not yet fully grown. Parents may lure them away from nest by offering food. Young are able to fly at about 14–15 days after hatching; parents continue to feed them for about 2 more weeks. One brood per season, but may try to renest if first attempt fails.

MIGRATION   All wintering areas are well to the south of breeding areas. Migrates relatively late in fall and early in spring. Apparently migrates mainly at night. On average, females winter somewhat farther south than males.

CONSERVATION STATUS   Abundant and widespread. Most nesting areas are remote from human disturbance. Wintering numbers in some areas are thought to have declined, but no evidence of decrease in total population.

CHIPPING SPARROW   *Spizella passerina*

The little Chipping Sparrow is common over much of the continent. Originally a bird of open pine woods and edges, it has adapted well to altered landscapes. It now nests in gardens and parks in many areas, its tame behavior making it well-known and popular. Evidently it was even more common in towns in the 19th century; but

Chipping Sparrow

then the House Sparrow, introduced from Europe, took over its place as our number one city "sparrow."

HABITAT *Open woods, conifers, orchards, farms, towns.* Original breeding habitat probably was mainly open pine woods, coniferous forest edges, savanna with scattered conifers. Still breeds in such areas but now also very common in suburbs, city parks, orchards, pastures, other altered habitats. Winters in open woods, thickets, farmland, brush.

FEEDING **Diet:** *Mostly insects and seeds.* Diet varies with season. In summer, feeds mostly on insects, including grasshoppers, caterpillars, beetles, leafhoppers, and true bugs, plus some spiders. Also eats many seeds, especially in fall and winter, including those of grasses, weeds, some waste grain. **Behavior:** Forages mostly on the ground, also up in shrubs and low trees. Occasionally makes short flights to catch insects in midair. Except when nesting, usually forages in flocks.

NESTING A few males have more than one mate. **Nest:** Site varies. Usually in a conifer, but can be in a deciduous tree or sometimes on the ground; usually lower than 15 feet above ground, but can be up to 60 feet or even higher. Nest (built by female) is a compact open cup made of grass, weeds, rootlets, lined with fine grass and animal hair. At one time, when Americans were more rural, the Chipping Sparrow was well known for using horsehair in its nest lining. **Eggs:** 3–4, rarely 2–5. Pale blue-green, with markings of brown, purple, and black mostly at larger end. Incubation is by female, about 11–14 days; male may feed female during incubation. **Young:** Both parents feed the nestlings. Young leave the nest about 8–12 days after hatching. Two broods per year.

MIGRATION Often migrates in flocks. Migration is spread over a long period in both spring and fall.

CONSERVATION STATUS Common and widespread, numbers probably stable. Nests often parasitized by Brown-headed Cowbird.

CLAY-COLORED SPARROW *Spizella pallida*

Clay-colored Sparrow

This rather plain and pale little sparrow is a typical summer bird of the northern prairies, where the males perch in the tops of low thickets to sing their flat, monotonous buzzes. It is sometimes a very common migrant in a narrow corridor through the Great Plains; to the east and west of there it is a rare stray, but small numbers reach both the Atlantic and Pacific coasts every year, mainly in fall. Clay-colored Sparrows seen out of range are usually with flocks of Chipping or Brewer's sparrows, close relatives with similar habits.

HABITAT *Scrub, brushy prairies, jack pines.* Breeds in shrubby areas including stands of bushes on open prairies, edges of woodlands, young second growth, understory in jack pine woods. May overlap with similar sparrows, but generally in more open areas than Chipping Sparrow, heavier brush than Brewer's Sparrow. In migration and winter, found in brushy fields, thickets, dry scrub, desert grassland.

FEEDING   **Diet:** *Mostly seeds and insects.* Diet not known in detail, but feeds mostly on seeds at most times of year, especially those of weeds and grasses; also some leaf buds, catkins, berries. Also eats many insects, especially in summer, including caterpillars, grasshoppers, true bugs, ants, and damselflies, as well as spiders. Young are fed mostly insects. **Behavior:** Forages mostly while hopping on the ground, occasionally up in shrubs. Except when nesting, usually forages in flocks, sometimes mixed with other sparrows.

NESTING   Males sing in spring to establish and defend nesting territories. During the breeding season, adults often forage away from nesting area, unlike most songbirds, which do all their foraging within the breeding territory. **Nest:** Site is usually very low, either on ground or in low shrubs, up to 5 feet high. In some areas, nests built early in season are placed on ground, later ones higher. Local populations often specialize in nest sites; in one Manitoba study, almost all nests were built in snowberry bushes; other common sites include rosebushes and clumps of grass. Nest (built by female) is open cup of grass, weeds, twigs, rootlets, lined with fine grass, more rootlets, animal hair. **Eggs:** 3–5, usually 4. Pale blue-green, with dark brown spots usually concentrated at larger end. Incubation is mostly by female, about 10–14 days. **Young:** Both parents feed the nestlings. Young leave the nest about 7–9 days after hatching, jumping to ground and then scrambling into cover; unable to fly for about another week. One brood per year, sometimes two.

MIGRATION   Often migrates in flocks. Migration is mostly through Great Plains; in fall, some strays reach both Atlantic and Pacific coasts.

CONSERVATION STATUS   Surveys indicate a slight decline in numbers during recent decades; reasons not apparent. Nests often parasitized by Brown-headed Cowbirds.

BREWER'S SPARROW   *Spizella breweri*

Brewer's Sparrow

This drab little sparrow is one of the most characteristic summer birds of the sagebrush flats of the Great Basin. The plainness of its plumage is compensated for by the remarkable variety in its song. The song is most fully developed in summer, but winter flocks may perch up in the tops of desert shrubs with several birds singing at once, creating a jumbled chorus.

HABITAT   *Sagebrush, brushy plains; also near treeline in Rockies; in winter, also weedy fields.* In summer typically in open flats covered with sagebrush; sometimes in stands of saltbush, on open prairie, or in pinyon-juniper woodland. Northern race (sometimes considered a separate species, called "Timberline Sparrow") summers at and above treeline in Canadian Rockies, in stunted thickets of willow, birch, and fir. In winter, found in open country, especially desert dominated by creosote bush.

FEEDING   **Diet:** *Mostly seeds and insects.* Diet in summer is mostly insects, including beetles and beetle larvae, plant lice, caterpillars. By late summer more seeds are eaten, and winter diet is mostly seeds. Can survive for an extended period on dry seeds, with no water. **Behavior:** Forages on the ground and in low shrubs. Except during nesting season, usually forages in flocks, often with other kinds of sparrows.

NESTING   Male sings in spring to defend nesting territory. **Nest:** Site is almost always well concealed in low shrub, no more than 4 feet above ground, rarely on ground. Nest is a small, compact, open cup of grasses, weeds, twigs, rootlets, lined with finer plant

material and with animal hair. **Eggs:** 3–4, sometimes 5. Pale blue-green, with variable brown spots often concentrated toward larger end. Incubation lasts 11–13 days, roles of sexes in incubation not well known. The incubating bird may sit motionless on nest until very closely approached. If disturbed, adult may fly away or may drop to the ground and sneak away through the grass. **Young:** Both parents probably feed the nestlings. Young birds leave nest about 8–9 days after hatching, before fully capable of flight. Adults may raise more than one brood per season.

MIGRATION   Migrates south relatively early in fall, and migrates north in mid- to late spring; some are present on wintering grounds for more than 9 months of year.

FIELD SPARROW *Spizella pusilla*

The plaintive whistled song of the Field Sparrow often can be heard in brushy pastures, even on hot summer days when most birds are silent. Despite the name, this is not one of the sparrows inhabiting open fields of grass; it prefers brushy places, overgrown meadows with many bushes. It looks distinctively small and long-tailed, and its plain face gives it an innocent expression to match the sweetness of its song. In winter, Field Sparrows gather in small flocks.

HABITAT   *Bushy pastures, brush, scrub.* Found at all seasons in brushy overgrown fields, second growth, woodland edges, hedgerows in open country. Sometimes around brushy edges of marshes. Does not usually live in wide-open grassy fields unless they contain scattered shrubs.

FEEDING   **Diet:** *Seeds and insects.* Diet is more than 90 percent seeds in winter, mainly small seeds of grasses. Also eats many grass seeds in summer, but insects make up more than 50 percent of summer diet. Nestlings are fed spiders and insects, especially caterpillars, with many grasshoppers fed to larger young.

Field Sparrow

Behavior: Forages on ground or in low vegetation. When feeding on grass seeds, will fly up to perch on grass stems, bending them to ground.

NESTING   Male defends nesting territory by singing persistently. Adults with young may put on "broken-wing" act at approach of danger. **Nest:** Site on or near the ground in clumps of grass or dense low bushes or saplings. Early nests generally on or near ground, later nests often higher. Nest is open cup woven of grasses, lined with finer plant material and hair. Female builds nest, although male may bring nest material. **Eggs:** 3–5, rarely 2–6. Whitish to pale bluish white, with brownish spots often concentrated at larger end. Incubation is by female only, 10–12 days, rarely up to 17 days in cold spring. Nests parasitized by Brown-headed Cowbirds are often deserted. **Young:** Both parents feed young. Female may begin a second nesting attempt, leaving male to finish rearing first brood. If disturbed, young may leave nest as early as 5 days after hatching, more typically 7–8 days. Remain in low vegetation near nest for several days; able to fly at age 13–14 days. Parents continue to feed them for about another 2 weeks. If nesting is interrupted by predators or other disturbance, pairs quickly attempt to renest; one persistent female in Illinois made 10 nesting attempts in one season. If nesting successful, two broods per season, sometimes three.

Partial migrant. Northernmost breeders move south in fall; southern breeders may move only short distance or may be permanent residents. In spring in northern areas, males arrive 2–3 weeks before females.

CONSERVATION STATUS Population probably increased with clearing of forest following European settlement of North America. Today widespread and abundant, although surveys show overall decline in recent decades.

WORTHEN'S SPARROW *Spizella wortheni*

The high, dry grasslands of north-central Mexico are home to this enigmatic little sparrow. Worthen's Sparrow was actually first discovered in the United States—near Silver City, New Mexico, in 1884—but it has not been found north of the border since then.

BLACK-CHINNED SPARROW *Spizella atrogularis*

A small, long-tailed bird of arid southwestern hills, the Black-chinned Sparrow is quite localized and sometimes overlooked. It often nests on steep hillsides covered with dense low scrub, areas that tend to be ignored by birders. In winter it may occur in small flocks, foraging inconspicuously on the ground in brushy areas, sometimes associating with Chipping or Brewer's sparrows. The black chin advertised in the name is present only on males in breeding plumage.

Black-chinned Sparrow

HABITAT *Brushy mountain slopes, open chaparral, sagebrush.* Found mostly in arid scrub on hillsides, from low foothills up to almost 7,000 feet in mountains, in chaparral and open thickets of manzanita, scrub oak, sagebrush, chamise, and other low shrubs. In winter also found locally in desert areas, mesquite thickets.

FEEDING **Diet:** *Probably seeds and insects.* Diet not well known; probably eats mostly seeds in winter, many insects in summer, like related sparrows. Probably feeds its young mostly on insects. **Behavior:** Does most of its foraging on the ground, often moving about slowly and spending much time feeding in a limited area. Also forages up in low shrubs. Except when nesting, often forages in small, loose flocks, sometimes associated with other sparrows.

NESTING Often nests in small loose colonies. Male sings in spring to defend nesting territory. **Nest:** Site is close to ground (from a few inches up to 4 feet high) in a low shrub, often a sagebrush. Nest is a shallow open cup made of dry grass, weed stems, yucca fibers, lined with fine grass, plant fibers, sometimes feathers or animal hair. **Eggs:** 2–4, sometimes 5. Very pale blue, often unmarked, sometimes dotted with dark brown. Incubation probably about 13 days, and may be mostly by female. **Young:** Both parents bring food to the young. Age at which young leave the nest is not well known.

MIGRATION Fall migration begins early, with many leaving their breeding grounds during August. May be a permanent resident in some areas near the Mexican border.

CONSERVATION STATUS Fairly common in its habitat, numbers probably stable.

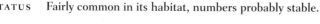

VESPER SPARROW   *Pooecetes gramineus*

A rather chunky sparrow of the open fields, known at all seasons by its streaked appearance and its white outer tail feathers. In summer, its clear musical song may be heard at any time of day; but the naturalist John Burroughs, feeling that it sang most impressively in the evening, gave it the name Vesper Sparrow. Not as shy as many grassland sparrows, it can be observed rather easily. It is often found dust-bathing in bare soil of fields or dirt roads.

Vesper Sparrow

HABITAT   *Meadows, fields, prairies, roadsides.* At all seasons, favors open grassy or weedy fields, often in rather dry situations with much open soil. May be in weedy roadsides, gravel pits, high mountain grasslands, stubble fields, grassy areas just above sandy beaches. Often breeds where there are a few taller plants for use as song perches.

FEEDING   **Diet:** *Mostly insects and seeds.* Feeds on many insects, especially in summer, including beetles, grasshoppers, caterpillars, moths, and true bugs, also spiders and other invertebrates. Also eats many seeds, especially in winter, mainly those of weeds and grasses. **Behavior:** Forages mostly or entirely on the ground, often on bare soil between grass or weed clumps. Except in nesting season, often forages in small, loose flocks.

NESTING   Male defends nesting territory by singing from a prominent raised perch. Courtship may involve male running about on ground near female with his wings and tail spread, sometimes fluttering into the air. **Nest:** Site is on the ground, often in a slight depression and placed at the base of a grass clump, weed, or shrub. Nest is a bulky open cup of grass and weeds, lined with fine grass, rootlets, animal hair. **Eggs:** 3–4, sometimes 2–6. Whitish to pale greenish white, blotched with brown and gray. Incubation is mostly by female, about 11–13 days. When disturbed at the nest, the female may flutter away as if injured, perhaps to lure intruders away. **Young:** Both parents feed the nestlings. Young leave the nest 1–2 weeks after hatching, usually around 9–10 days. One or two broods per year, sometimes three.

MIGRATION   Migrates relatively early in spring and late in fall, with peak migration in many areas during April and October.

CONSERVATION STATUS   Has declined seriously in numbers in some parts of the east, probably owing to loss of habitat. In the west, still widespread and common.

LARK SPARROW   *Chondestes grammacus*

Many sparrows are challenging to identify, but this one is a striking exception, with its bold face pattern and broad, white-edged tail. Lark Sparrows favor areas with bare open ground and scattered bushes, habitats that are more common in the west and midwest than in the east; they often forage conspicuously out in the open. When going from place to place, they tend to fly higher than most sparrows, giving a sharp call note as they pass overhead.

HABITAT   *Open country with bushes, trees; pastures, farms, roadsides.* For nesting, generally favors areas with some open bare ground and some taller plants; included are overgrazed pastures, sandy barrens, hedgerows near fallow fields, brushy dry grasslands, sometimes open pinyon-juniper woods. In migration and winter, found in similar areas, also open weedy fields.

FEEDING   **Diet:** *Mostly seeds and insects.* Feeds heavily on seeds, especially in winter, including those of grasses and weeds as well as waste grain. Also eats many insects, especially in summer, including grasshoppers, beetles, caterpillars, and many others. Young are fed mostly insects, also some grass seeds. **Behavior:** Does almost all its foraging while walking about on the ground in open areas. Typically forages in small, loose flocks.

NESTING   In courtship, male may strut about on the ground near the female, his bill pointed up and tail spread wide to show off the white corners. **Nest:** Both sexes may take part in choosing nest site, with male placing twigs at potential site, but female does actual building. Site varies; often on ground near base of tall weed, but may be up in shrubs or low trees, up to 7 feet above the ground, sometimes higher. Sometimes may nest in crevices in rocky cliffs. Nest is an open cup of grass, weeds, twigs, lined with fine grass, rootlets, animal hair. **Eggs:** 4–5, sometimes 3–6. Creamy to grayish white, spotted with brown and black. Incubation is by female, 11–12 days. **Young:** Both parents feed the nestlings. Young leave the nest about 9–10 days after hatching.

MIGRATION   Migrates relatively late in spring and early in fall. Small numbers appear on the Atlantic seaboard in fall, mostly along the immediate coast.

CONSERVATION STATUS   In recent decades, has declined or disappeared in some former nesting areas east of the Mississippi River. Still fairly common and widespread in west.

Lark Sparrow

DESERT SPARROWS — GENUS *Amphispiza*

These three smartly patterned birds live in dry country, from open sagebrush flats to rocky canyons. Their songs and call notes have a metallic or tinkling quality. Black-throated and Sage sparrows are often rather approachable, but the Five-striped Sparrow is usually quite elusive when it is not singing.

BLACK-THROATED SPARROW   *Amphispiza bilineata*

A sharply marked little bird of the arid zones. Black-throated Sparrows are very common in parts of the southwest, even in some relatively barren flats of creosote bush where few other birds occur; loose winter flocks feed on the ground in open areas, making little tinkling call notes. In spring, males perch atop low bushes to sing their metallic notes and trills.

HABITAT   *Arid brush, creosote-bush deserts.* Lives in a variety of dry open habitats, from Sonoran desert with its mix of shrubs and cactus to very barren flats of creosote bush or saltbush. Also locally in grassland with scattered cactus, sagebrush flats, open pinyon-juniper woods.

FEEDING **Diet:** *Mostly seeds and insects.* In general, probably eats more seeds in winter, more insects in summer. Also feeds on fresh green shoots, other green vegetation, and ripe berries and fruits when available. Can survive without water at some times of year, drawing liquid from insects and green plants it eats. Young are fed mostly insects. **Behavior:** Forages mostly while running about on the ground; also does some foraging up in shrubs and desert trees. Occasionally makes short flights to catch insects in midair.

NESTING Male sings in breeding season to defend nesting territory. Timing of nesting activity may vary from year to year, depending on timing of rains. **Nest:** Site is in a low shrub or branching cactus, typically well hidden and usually within 2 feet of ground;

Black-throated Sparrow

sometimes placed on ground at base of shrub. Nest is a rather bulky, sturdy open cup of grass, weeds, plant fibers, and small twigs, lined with fine grass, plant down, and often with animal hair. **Eggs:** 3–4, sometimes 2. Whitish to very pale blue. Details of incubation not well known. **Young:** Probably both parents feed the nestlings. Age at which young leave the nest not well known. May raise two broods per year.

MIGRATION Permanent resident in much of southwest, migratory farther north. Northern limit of breeding range may vary from year to year, with occasional northward "invasions." Strays sometimes wander far east, even to Atlantic coast.

CONSERVATION STATUS Has declined in some areas with increasing development in desert areas; unlike some desert birds, does not adapt well to suburbs. In proper habitat, still widespread and common.

SAGE SPARROW *Amphispiza belli*

In shrubby open flats of the west, such as the broad sagebrush plains of the Great Basin, the Sage Sparrow is a common bird. It is often seen running about on the ground with its longish tail cocked up above the level of its back; when perched up on a shrub, it twitches its tail in a down-up motion like a Phoebe. Recent research suggests that the Sage Sparrow, as currently defined, may actually represent more than one species.

HABITAT *Dry brushy foothills, chaparral, sage; in winter, also deserts.* Breeds in brushy open country. In northern and eastern part of range, mainly in stands of big sagebrush; farther southwest, mainly in saltbush, chamise, and other low shrubs of arid flats. Winters in dry chaparral, open flats with scattered brush, deserts.

FEEDING **Diet:** *Mostly seeds and insects.* Feeds on many insects, especially in summer, including grasshoppers, beetles, true bugs, leafhoppers, and ants, also spiders. Also eats many seeds of weeds, grasses, and shrubs. Young are fed mostly insects. **Behavior:** Forages

Sage Sparrow

mostly on the ground, picking up items from the soil or from plant stems, sometimes scratching with its feet. Also does some feeding up in low bushes. When not nesting, often forages in small flocks.

NESTING   Male returns to same nesting territory each year, defends it by singing from a raised perch. **Nest:** Site is usually in low shrub (usually in sagebrush or saltbush, depending on habitat), less than 4 feet above ground. Sometimes placed on the ground under a shrub. Nest is a bulky open cup of twigs, sticks, lined with fine dry grass, weeds, sometimes animal hair. **Eggs:** 3–4, sometimes 2–5. Bluish white to pale blue, variably spotted or blotched with brown, gray, and black. Incubation lasts about 13–16 days. **Young:** Probably both parents feed the nestlings. Young leave the nest about 9–11 days after hatching. A pair may raise two broods per year.

MIGRATION   Birds from Great Basin mostly move south into deserts in winter; those found west of the Sierra in California are mostly permanent residents. Still common and widespread in Great Basin; populations west of the Sierra in California may be vulnerable to loss of habitat. Endemic race on San Clemente Island, California, is endangered.

FIVE-STRIPED SPARROW   *Amphispiza quinquestriata*

This elegant Mexican sparrow was never found in our area until the late 1950s. It is now known to be a rare and local nesting bird in several canyons in southern Arizona, but no one knows if it was simply overlooked in the past or if it is actually a recent arrival north of the border. The Five-striped Sparrow favors steep brushy hillsides, where the male often sings his metallic song while perched on the spindly stems of ocotillo.

HABITAT   *Dry canyon slopes, rocky hillsides.* In Arizona found on steep hillsides, generally above streams, with dense growth of low shrubs such as mesquite, acacia, and hackberry, and taller stands of ocotillo. Known Arizona sites are at elevations of 3,400–4,000 feet. In Mexico, also found in dry tropical woods on rocky ground, usually on hillsides.

Five-striped Sparrow

FEEDING   **Diet:** *Mostly insects and seeds.* Feeds mainly on insects in summer, particularly caterpillars, moths, and grasshoppers, also ants and others. Also eats seeds and some small berries. Young are fed mostly caterpillars and grasshoppers. **Behavior:** Forages mostly on the ground and in low vegetation, moving rather slowly and deliberately, picking up small items with bill. Sometimes takes insects from spider webs; rarely makes short flights to catch insects in midair.

NESTING   In Arizona, nests mostly in mid- to late summer, after onset of summer rainy season, but pairs may occupy territories by late spring. Male sings persistently to defend nesting territory. **Nest:** Site is in dense clump of grass, in low shrub such as hackberry, hopbush, or condalia, or at base of ocotillo, from a few inches to 5 feet above ground. Nest (built by female) is a deep open cup of grass, lined with finer grass and often with animal hair. **Eggs:** 3–4. White, unmarked. Incubation is by female only, about 12–13 days. **Young:** Both parents feed young, although female may do more at first. On hot days, female may spend time standing on edge of nest to shade young. Young leave nest about 9–10 days after hatching, but able to make only short flights at this stage. Young are fed by parents for at least 2 weeks after fledging, may associate with them up to 7 weeks. Usually one or two broods per year, sometimes three.

MIGRATION	Migratory status is poorly known. Has been found in winter in Arizona only a few times, suggesting that most probably leave in fall, but species is extremely secretive and hard to detect in winter.
CONSERVATION STATUS	Very uncommon and local in our area, but habitat faces no immediate threats, and numbers are probably stable.

GENUS *Calamospiza*

LARK BUNTING *Calamospiza melanocorys*

On the western plains in early summer, the male Lark Bunting is impossible to overlook, as it flutters up from the grass to deliver its varied flight-song. In winter, when males and females alike are patterned in streaky brown, the species is more subtle. Winter flocks of Lark Buntings occur in dry open fields, where they suggest chunky,

big-billed sparrows. When they fly, however, in compact flocks sweeping low over the ground, some of them will flash patches of white or buff in the wings.

HABITAT   *Plains, prairies.* Breeds mostly on native shortgrass prairie; also on sagebrush plains with understory of grass and weeds. During migration and winter, found in many kinds of open country, including prairies, farm fields, desert grassland, weedy vacant lots.

FEEDING   **Diet:** *Mostly insects and seeds.* Summer diet is predominantly insects, especially grasshoppers, also beetles, true bugs, bees, and ants. Also eats many seeds, especially in winter, mainly those of weeds and grasses, also some waste grain. **Behavior:** Forages mostly while running and walking on the ground, picking up items from soil or plant stems.

Lark Bunting

After flushing insects from ground, will pursue them in short flights. During migration and winter, almost always feeds in flocks, sometimes loosely associated with other seed-eating birds.

NESTING   Arrives on breeding grounds in flocks, then flocks break up and males set up territories. In courtship, male performs a flight-song display, flying up to 20–30 feet above ground and floating or fluttering back to ground on outstretched wings, singing. One male may have more than one mate. **Nest:** Site is on ground in grassy area, usually sheltered or protected by overhanging grass or weeds. Often sunken in small depression in soil so that rim of nest is level with ground or only slightly above it. Nest is an open cup made of grass, weeds, rootlets, lined with fine grass, plant down, animal hair. **Eggs:** 4–5, sometimes 3–7. Pale blue to greenish blue, usually unmarked, sometimes dotted with reddish brown. Incubation is mostly by female (male may help at times), 11–12 days. **Young:** Both parents feed the nestlings. Young probably leave the nest about 9 days after hatching. One brood per year, sometimes two.

MIGRATION	Fall migration begins very early, with some appearing south of the breeding range by late July; some linger in wintering areas into May. Migrates in flocks.
CONSERVATION STATUS	Was extremely common at one time; has lost ground with conversion of prairies to farmland. Still common, but surveys suggest declines in recent decades. Numbers vary widely from year to year in many areas, making it difficult to monitor populations.

SAVANNAH SPARROW   *Passerculus sandwichensis*

A small, streaky bird of open fields, the Savannah Sparrow often confuses birders because it is so variable. Some of its well-marked local forms, such as the pale "Ipswich" Sparrow of Atlantic beaches and the blackish "Belding's" Sparrow of western salt marshes, were once regarded as separate species. Unlike many grassland sparrows, Savannahs are not particularly shy; they often perch up on weeds or fence wires, and their small winter flocks usually can be observed with ease.

Savannah Sparrow

HABITAT   *Open fields, meadows, salt marshes, prairies, dunes, shores.* Over most of range, found in open meadows, pastures, edges of marshes, alfalfa fields; also tundra in summer, shores and weedy vacant lots in winter. Northeastern "Ipswich" Savannah Sparrow lives on grassy coastal dunes; southwestern "Belding's" and "Large-billed" races inhabit salt marshes.

FEEDING   **Diet:** *Mostly insects and seeds.* Feeds on many insects, especially in summer, including beetles, grasshoppers, caterpillars, flies, and others, plus spiders. Coastal populations will also consume tiny crustaceans and mollusks. Also eats many seeds, mainly of grasses and weeds, and some berries. Young are fed mostly insects. **Behavior:** Does most foraging while walking or running on the ground; also sometimes forages in shrubs or low trees. Sometimes makes short flights to catch insects in midair, and occasionally scratches in soil or leaf litter to find food. Except when nesting, often forages in small, loose flocks.

NESTING   Male sings to defend nesting territory and to attract a mate. In interactions with rivals or with mate, male performs a flight display, with tail raised and feet dangling as he flutters slowly over the grass. In some regions, males may have more than one mate. **Nest:** Site is on ground, usually well hidden among grass or weeds. Usually placed under matted dead plants or under overhanging grass, so that nest can only be approached by a "tunnel" from one side. Nest (built by female) is open cup made of grass, lined with finer grass. **Eggs:** 2–6, typically 4; tends to lay more eggs in the north. Eggs whitish to pale tan or greenish, with brown markings usually concentrated at larger end. Female incubates, about 10–13 days. **Young:** Both parents bring food to the nestlings. Young leave the nest about 8–11 days after hatching (average timing varies among different populations). One or two broods per year.

MIGRATION   Migrates mostly at night. Migration is generally early in spring and late in fall, although it may spread over a considerable period in both seasons.

CONSERVATION STATUS   Some coastal marsh races have small populations and may be vulnerable to loss of habitat. Species as a whole is abundant and widespread.

SHORT-TAILED SPARROWS — GENUS *Ammodramus*

These are elusive little birds that hide in dense grass or marshes, where they are usually very hard to see except when they climb to the top of a stalk to sing. They have rather short tails, often with spiky points on the tail feathers, and most kinds are heavily striped on the back, providing good camouflage. Solitary when not nesting, these birds are never found in flocks. The songs of most species are poor efforts, flat hissing or buzzing sounds.

BAIRD'S SPARROW *Ammodramus bairdii*

A grassland sparrow, breeding on the northern Great Plains, wintering locally in the southwest. Audubon discovered this bird in 1843 and named it for the young Spencer Baird (who later became a leading ornithologist). The bird then dropped out of sight and was not seen again for almost 30 years. This kind of disappearing act seems appropriate for Baird's Sparrow, which runs through the grass like a mouse, almost never perching up in the open, and is very difficult to flush. On the nesting grounds, however, males will give a surprisingly musical song, much more attractive than those of related sparrows.

HABITAT   *Mostly native prairies.* Breeds mainly in northern prairies with fairly tall grass and scattered tall weeds or low bushes; also sometimes nests in fields of wheat or other crops. In migration and winter, found mostly on shortgrass prairie and in weedy fields.

FEEDING   **Diet:** *Mostly insects and seeds.* Diet varies with season. In summer feeds mainly on insects, including grasshoppers, caterpillars, moths, beetles, and leafhoppers, as well as spiders and seeds. Young birds are fed mostly grasshoppers and caterpillars. Diet at other seasons is mostly seeds of weeds and grasses. **Behavior:** Forages on the ground, moving about rather slowly among grass clumps. Almost always forages alone.

Baird's Sparrow

NESTING   May nest in small, loose colonies. To defend nesting territory, male sings from the top of a tall grass stem, weed, or low bush. Courtship display of male may involve walking on ground, fluttering one wing at a time over his back, repeatedly bowing. **Nest:** Site is on the ground in a grassy area, well hidden and hard to find. Usually in a slight depression so the rim of the nest is level with the ground, sometimes tucked under a dense overhanging grass clump or built within the base of such a clump. Nest (probably built by the female) is a shallow open cup made of dry grass, sometimes with some weeds added; may be lined with fine grass, animal hair, moss. **Eggs:** 4–5, sometimes 3–6. Grayish white, heavily spotted with reddish brown. Incubation is by the female only, about 11–12 days. **Young:** Both parents feed young (but the female may do more at first). Young leave the nest after about 8–10 days, before they are able to fly, and are fed by their parents for at least another 1–2 weeks. One brood per year.

MIGRATION   Seldom detected during migration. Arrives on wintering areas during October and November, departs in April. Extremely rare stray east or west of normal migration route through prairies.

CONSERVATION STATUS   Originally was a very common bird within its range, now uncommon and local. Loss of habitat on summer range (to farming) and winter range (to overgrazing) probably played a part in decline.

GRASSHOPPER SPARROW *Ammodramus savannarum*

A flat-headed, short-tailed little sparrow of the fields, the Grasshopper Sparrow may go unnoticed even when it is singing, because its song is much like the buzz of a grasshopper. The birder who learns this sound may spot the bird perched on a weed stalk or the lowest wire of a fence. When not singing, the bird stays out of sight; if disturbed it flies away low for a few yards before diving head first back into the grass.

HABITAT   *Grassland, hayfields, prairies.* Breeds in rather dry fields and prairies, especially those with fairly tall grass and weeds and a few scattered shrubs. Also nests in overgrown pastures and hayfields, and sometimes in fields of other crops. In Florida, nests in prairie with scattered palmettos. During migration and winter, found in many types of open fields.

FEEDING   **Diet:** *Mostly insects and seeds.* In summer feeds mostly on insects, including many grasshoppers, also beetles, caterpillars, ants, true bugs, and many others. Also eats spiders, snails, centipedes, and earthworms. Seeds are also important in diet, probably more so in winter, including those of weeds and grasses as well as waste grain. **Behavior:** Forages while hopping or running on the ground, picking up items from the soil or from plant stems. Almost always forages alone.

Grasshopper Sparrow

NESTING   May nest in small colonies; numbers in a given area often change markedly from year to year. Male sings from a low perch to defend territory; sometimes sings at night. In courtship, sometimes sings in flight. **Nest:** Site is on the ground, very well hidden at base of weed, shrub, or clump of grass. Often placed in slight depression, so that rim of nest is even with level of ground. Nest (probably built by female) is an open cup of dry grass, lined with fine grass, rootlets, sometimes animal hair. Usually has partly domed back and sides of grass woven into overhanging vegetation, leaving opening at front. **Eggs:** 4–5, sometimes 3–6. Creamy white, spotted with reddish brown and gray. Incubation is by female only, about 11–12 days. **Young:** Both parents feed the nestlings. Young leave the nest about 9 days after hatching, before they are able to fly well.

MIGRATION   Apparently migrates mostly at night. Peak of migration in many areas during late April and October.

CONSERVATION STATUS   Still common in some areas but has declined seriously in others. Florida race is endangered, with very limited range, population probably under 200.

HENSLOW'S SPARROW *Ammodramus henslowii*

In weedy eastern fields in summer, this little sparrow climbs to the top of a weed stalk, throws its head back, and delivers one of the least impressive of all bird songs, a short *tsilick*. When not singing, it hides in dense grass and is extremely hard to observe. If flushed, it flies away low for a short distance before dropping into the weeds. Despite its lack of vocal prowess, Henslow's Sparrow shows beautiful markings if seen well. Local populations vary from year to year; overall, the species is becoming quite scarce over most of its range.

HABITAT   *Weedy fields.* Requirements not well understood; often absent from seemingly suitable habitat. Breeds in fields and meadows, often in low-lying or damp areas, with tall grass, standing dead weeds, and scattered shrubs. Sometimes in old pastures, occasionally in hayfields. Winters in various kinds of rank weedy fields.

AMERICAN SPARROWS AND THEIR RELATIVES

Henslow's Sparrow

FEEDING **Diet:** *Mostly insects and seeds.* Summer diet is mainly insects, including crickets, grasshoppers, beetles, stink bugs, caterpillars, small wasps, and many others, also some spiders and snails. Many seeds are also eaten, probably making up the majority of the winter diet; included are seeds of weeds, grasses, and sedges. **Behavior:** Apparently does all its foraging on the ground. Almost always forages alone, not associating in flocks with its own kind or other sparrows.

NESTING May breed in small, loose colonies that change location from year to year; territories within these colonies are often separated by unoccupied ground, so there is little conflict among the birds. Males perch on exposed weeds to deliver their short, inconspicuous song. Courtship may involve male leading female to potential nest sites, carrying bits of grass in his bill. **Nest:** Site is on or near the ground, very well hidden. Usually placed in the base of a clump of grass, sometimes in a slight depression in the ground, occasionally more than a foot up among vertical stems. Ground nests often have grass partly arched over them, adding to concealment. Nest (built mostly by female) is an open cup of grass and weeds, lined with finer grass and sometimes with animal hair. **Eggs:** 3–5. Whitish to pale greenish white, with reddish brown and gray spots concentrated toward the larger end. Incubation is by female only, about 11 days. **Young:** Both parents feed the nestlings. Young leave the nest about 9–10 days after hatching.

MIGRATION Apparently migrates at night. Difficult to detect during migration, but most probably move during late April and September.

CONSERVATION STATUS Has declined seriously in much of its former range, should be considered threatened. Loss of proper habitat is likely cause; habitat requirements are still not thoroughly understood.

LE CONTE'S SPARROW   *Ammodramus leconteii*

Le Conte's Sparrow

Small and inconspicuous, but beautifully patterned, Le Conte's Sparrow is a bird of damp meadows and shallow marshes. It breeds across the northern prairies and winters in the southeast. Often very secretive, it hides in dense low growth, flying away weakly when disturbed or simply scurrying away through the grass. In summer on the prairies its quiet song, a soft gasping buzz, may be heard to best advantage very late in the evening on still nights.

HABITAT *Tall grass, weedy hayfields, marshes.* Breeds in wet meadows or the edges of marshes, in areas with damp soil or very shallow water and dense growth of grass, sedges, or rushes. Winters mostly in damp weedy fields, shallow freshwater marshes, coastal prairies.

FEEDING **Diet:** *Mostly insects and seeds.* Diet not well known, but apparently eats mostly insects in summer, mostly seeds in winter. Eats caterpillars, leafhoppers, stink bugs, and many other insects, as well as spiders. Also eats seeds of grasses and weeds. Young

are fed almost exclusively on insects. **Behavior:** Does its foraging on or near the ground, often feeding on the ground under dense cover, sometimes moving about in low vegetation seeking insects. Almost always forages alone.

NESTING   Nesting behavior is not well known, partly because the nests are very difficult to find. Male defends nesting territory by singing from a perch within tall grass; may sing by day or night. **Nest:** Site is usually a few inches above ground, sometimes on the ground, well hidden in areas with large amounts of dead grass, rushes, or sedges remaining from preceding seasons. The nest (probably built by the female), attached to standing stems, is an open cup of grass and rushes, lined with fine grass and sometimes with animal hair. **Eggs:** 3–5, usually 4. Grayish white, spotted with brown and gray. Incubation is by female only, probably about 12–13 days. **Young:** Nestlings are fed by the female and possibly by the male. Age at which young leave the nest is not well known.

MIGRATION   Migrates relatively late in fall and early in spring, with peak passage in many areas during October, March, and April. Rarely strays to Atlantic or Pacific coast, mostly in fall.

CONSERVATION STATUS   May have declined in some parts of range as damp fields have been converted to farmland; however, still very common in available habitat.

SALTMARSH SHARP-TAILED SPARROW   *Ammodramus caudacutus*

A bird of the coast, named for the spiky tips on its tail feathers (a trait it shares with several related kinds of sparrows). Sharp-tails have an unusual mating system for a songbird, with males simply roving about looking for females rather than defending a nesting territory. Recent research has shown that the Sharp-tails nesting from southern Maine to Virginia make up a separate species from those nesting farther north on the coast and inland on the northern prairies.

HABITAT   *Coastal marshes.* Found mostly in salt marshes with sedges, rushes, cordgrass, saltgrass, and other typical plants; sometimes in fresh marshes or fields adjacent to coast.

FEEDING   **Diet:** *Mostly insects and other invertebrates, some seeds.* Animal matter makes up much of winter diet and almost all of summer diet. Feeds on insects (including grasshoppers, beetles, caterpillars, ants, wasps, others), spiders, amphipods, small crabs and snails, marine worms, other invertebrates. Also eats seeds of grasses and other marsh plants, especially in fall and winter. **Behavior:** Forages while walking on the ground or climbing in marsh plants. Picks items from surface of plants, ground, or water, and sometimes probes in mud.

NESTING   Unusual breeding system. Males do not defend territories but move around large area of marsh, singing to attract females. Both sexes are promiscuous, and no pairs are formed; males take no part in caring for the eggs or young. **Nest:** Site is in marsh, usually where standing plants are mixed with much dead grass remaining from preceding seasons. Nests usually placed just above normal high tide mark; many nests are destroyed by extreme tides. Nest (built by female) is a bulky open cup of grass, sometimes partially domed over, with lining of finer grass. **Eggs:** 3–5, sometimes 2–6. Greenish white to pale blue-green, heavily dotted with reddish brown. Incubation is by female only, 11–12 days. **Young:** Nestlings are fed by female alone. Young leave nest about 8–11 days after hatching, may remain with female for another 2–3 weeks. Often two broods per year.

MIGRATION   Migrates at night, traveling along coastline. Apparently moves only short distances, with most wintering along southern Atlantic coast, and many present through the winter in much of the breeding range.

CONSERVATION STATUS   Undoubtedly has declined in many regions with loss of coastal marsh habitat.

AMERICAN SPARROWS AND THEIR RELATIVES

NELSON'S SHARP-TAILED SPARROW *Ammodramus nelsoni*

Recent research has found that the Sharp-tailed Sparrows really represent two species. The "Nelson's" form has an unusual distribution, breeding both far inland and on the coast. In the interior, it summers on the northern Great Plains, in freshwater marsh with growth of cordgrass, phragmites, and other grasses. It also nests in coastal marshes along the southern edges of Hudson Bay and James Bay, and on the Atlantic coast from Quebec south to Maine.

Nelson's Sharp-tail is more migratory than the Saltmarsh Sharp-tail. It leaves its nesting range completely in fall to spend the winter along the Gulf of Mexico and on the southern Atlantic coast, where it often may be found in the same places as its Saltmarsh relative. Small numbers also reach the California coast, and a few are present in coastal marshes there every winter.

Nelson's Sharp-tailed Sparrow

This bird is similar to the Saltmarsh Sharp-tail in its habits, including the odd breeding behavior. However, male Nelson's Sharp-tails sing more often, and sometimes sing in flight. Nesting activity may begin later in the spring, with the first eggs not being laid until early June (or even mid-June for the birds around James Bay). Females in Maine and the Maritime provinces often place their nests in the highest and driest sections of the salt marsh. In the interior, however, they often nest in wetter areas than the Le Conte's Sparrows sharing the same marshes. Male Nelson's may sometimes help to feed the young in the nest.

SEASIDE SPARROW *Ammodramus maritimus*

No other songbird in North America is so closely tied to salt marsh as the Seaside Sparrow. Except for a few populations in Florida, it is almost never found away from tidal marshes along the immediate coast. With a patchy and disjunct habitat, this

Seaside Sparrow

species has evolved a number of well-marked local races. One of these, the "Cape Sable" Seaside Sparrow, was not discovered until 1918; another, the "Dusky" Seaside Sparrow, recently became extinct despite major efforts by conservationists.

HABITAT *Salt marshes.* Lives in tidal marshes along coast, favoring areas with dense tall growth above level of highest tides and with openings and edges for foraging. Habitats often feature spartina, rushes, and saltgrass. In Florida, extinct "Dusky" Seaside Sparrow nested in fresh or brackish marsh in some areas, and "Cape Sable" form still does so in parts of extreme southern Florida.

FEEDING **Diet:** *Mostly insects, other invertebrates, and seeds.* Diet varies with season and location,

but major items include grasshoppers, beetles, caterpillars, spiders, small crabs, snails, amphipods, and marine worms. Also eats many seeds, especially in fall and winter, including those of cordgrass and saltbush. **Behavior:** Forages on the ground at edge of water and in low growth such as cordgrass and salicornia. May probe in mud or pick items from surface of vegetation.

NESTING   During courtship, male follows female, frequently raising his wings and singing. In nonmigratory southern populations, members of pair may remain together on nesting territory all year. **Nest:** Site is in low marsh vegetation, a few inches above level of highest tides. Nest (built by female alone) is an open cup of grass, lined with finer grasses. Usually has at least a partial cover or canopy built by bird or provided by surrounding plants. **Eggs:** 3–4, sometimes 2–5. Bluish white to very pale gray, with blotches of brown often concentrated at larger end. Incubation is by female only, about 12–13 days. **Young:** Both parents feed the nestlings. Young leave the nest about 9–11 days after hatching but are unable to fly well for at least another week. Parents may feed young for 2–3 weeks after they fledge. One or two broods per year.

MIGRATION   Many birds probably nonmigratory, although some depart in fall from northernmost part of breeding range and a few spend the winter south of known breeding areas in Florida and Texas.

CONSERVATION STATUS   "Dusky" Seaside Sparrow became extinct in 1987; "Cape Sable" form is localized and vulnerable, as are some other populations. Species as a whole has declined because of destruction of coastal marshes.

GENUS *Passerella*

FOX SPARROW   *Passerella iliaca*

Fox Sparrow

This big chunky sparrow nests in the far north and in western mountains, and many birders know it only as a migrant or winter visitor. It is usually found on the ground under dense thickets, scratching busily in the leaf litter with both feet. On its breeding grounds, it gives a beautifully clear whistled song. The bird's name refers to the bright foxy red color of the most eastern and northern populations, but many Fox Sparrows in the west are predominantly gray or sooty brown.

HABITAT   *Wooded areas, undergrowth, brush.* Breeds in brushy areas including woodland edges and clearings, streamside thickets, scrubby second growth, stunted coastal forest. Winters in similar habitats, also in brushy fields, chaparral, well-vegetated suburbs and parks.

FEEDING   **Diet:** *Mostly seeds and insects.* During breeding season, con-sumes many insects, including beetles, flies, true bugs, and others, also spiders and millipedes. Majority of diet at other seasons consists of seeds, mainly of weeds (such as smartweed) and grasses. Also eats some berries; in coastal areas, may feed on tiny crustaceans and other marine life on beaches. Young are fed mostly insects. **Behavior:** Forages on ground, characteristically scratching in the soil or snow, making a little forward jump and then scratching back with both feet at once.

NESTING   Male sings in spring to defend nesting territory; may be ag-gressive toward intruders of other species as well as his own. **Nest:** Site is often on ground under dense cover of low shrubs. Sometimes nests up in shrubs or low trees, rarely more than

8 feet above ground. Nest (probably built by female) is open cup of grass, weeds, moss, lined with fine dry grass. Nests built above ground are usually larger and more bulky, with more twigs used in outer walls. **Eggs:** 2–5. Tends to lay fewer eggs in southern part of breeding range. Eggs pale green to greenish white, heavily blotched with reddish brown. Incubation is by female only, about 12–14 days. **Young:** Both parents feed the nestlings. Young leave the nest about 9–11 days after hatching.

MIGRATION   Typically migrates early in spring and late in fall, with peak passage in many areas during late March and early November. Migrates at night.

CONSERVATION STATUS   Some counts of migrants suggest that the species has decreased in recent decades, at least in the east.

SONG SPARROW GROUP — GENUS *Melospiza*

The three sparrows in this genus all live in dense low cover of thickets or marshes, where they are sometimes rather secretive. All have sharp, conspicuous call notes and distinctive songs. They are solitary when not nesting, never forming flocks of their own kind, although they may associate loosely with mixed flocks of other sparrows.

SONG SPARROW   *Melospiza melodia*

Very widespread in North America, this melodious sparrow is among the most familiar birds in some areas, such as the northeast and midwest. At times it is rather

skulking in behavior, hiding in the thickets, seen only when it flies from bush to bush with a typical pumping motion of its tail. Usually, however, sheer numbers make it conspicuous. Song Sparrows vary in appearance over their wide range, from large dark birds on the Aleutians to small pale ones in the desert southwest.

HABITAT   *Thickets, brush, marshes, roadsides, gardens.* Habitat varies over its wide range. In most areas, found in brushy fields, streamsides, shrubby marsh edges, woodland edges, hedgerows, well-vegetated gardens. Some coastal populations live in salt marshes. Nests in dense streamside brush in southwestern desert regions, and in any kind of dense low cover on Aleutian Islands, Alaska.

FEEDING   **Diet:** *Mostly insects and seeds.* Eats many insects, especially in summer, including beetles,

Song Sparrow

grasshoppers, caterpillars, ants, and wasps, also spiders. Feeds heavily on seeds, especially in winter, mainly those of grasses and weeds. Birds in coastal marshes and on islands also feed on small crustaceans and mollusks, perhaps rarely on small fish. **Behavior:** Forages mostly on the ground, sometimes scratching in the soil to turn up items. Also sometimes forages in very shallow water (fractions of an inch deep) and up in shrubs and trees. Will come to bird feeders placed close to good cover.

NESTING   Males often defend only small nesting territories, so high densities of Song Sparrows may be present in good habitat. In courtship, male may chase female; may perform fluttering flight among the bushes with neck outstretched and head held high. **Nest:** Site varies, usually on ground under clump of grass or shrub or less than 4 feet above ground, sometimes up to 10 feet or higher. Raised sites may be in shrubs, low trees, or marsh vegetation, often above water. Rarely nests in cavities in trees. Nest (built mostly or entirely by female) is an open cup of weeds, grass, leaves, strips of bark, lined with fine grass, rootlets, animal hair. **Eggs:** Typically 4, often 3–5, rarely 2–6. Pale greenish white, heavily spotted with reddish brown. Incubation is apparently by female only, about 12–14 days. **Young:** Both parents feed the nestlings. Young normally leave the nest about 10–12 days after hatching, remain with their parents about another 3 weeks.

MIGRATION   Present all year in many parts of range, but birds from northern interior move south to southern United States or extreme northern Mexico in winter.

CONSERVATION STATUS   Some local populations are vulnerable to loss of habitat, especially those in coastal marshes, but species as a whole is still widespread and abundant.

LINCOLN'S SPARROW   *Melospiza lincolnii*

Generally a skulker in dense low cover, this sparrow often goes unnoticed during migration and winter—especially in the east, where it is quite uncommon. In the

west, birders soon learn to find it by its hard *chep* call note in the bushes. Even where they are common, Lincoln's Sparrows tend to be solitary, not joining flocks. The musical song of the males is heard in summer in willow thickets of the north and the mountain west.

HABITAT   *Willow and alder thickets, muskeg, brushy bogs. In winter, thickets, weeds, bushes.* Breeds in northern and mountainous areas in dense low vegetation near water, such as streamside willow groves, bushy edges of bogs, brushy clearings in wet coniferous forest. Winters in dense thickets, overgrown fields.

FEEDING   **Diet:** *Mostly insects and seeds.* Feeds on many insects, especially in summer, including caterpillars, beetles, moths, ants, and flies, also spiders and millipedes. Seeds probably make up majority of diet, especially in winter; included are seeds of weeds and

Lincoln's Sparrow

grasses. Young are probably fed entirely on insects. **Behavior:** Forages mostly while hopping on the ground, typically under or close to dense thickets.

NESTING   Male defends nesting territory by singing. In some areas, may compete with Song Sparrows for territories, but Song Sparrows usually dominate. **Nest:** Site is on the ground, very well hidden under clump of grass or under dense shrubbery, often sunken in a depression in sphagnum moss or other ground cover. Nest (built by female only) is a shallow open cup of grasses or sedges, lined with fine grass and sometimes with animal hair. **Eggs:** 3–5, sometimes 6. Pale green to greenish white, heavily spotted with reddish brown. Incubation is by female only, about 10–14 days. Female may remain on nest until approached very closely, then scurry away over the ground like a rodent. **Young:** Both parents feed the nestlings. Young leave the nest about 9–12 days after hatching, may be tended by the parents for another 2–3 weeks or more.

MIGRATION   Season of migration is spread over a long period in both spring and fall, with some birds migrating both early and late, especially in the west.

SWAMP SPARROW   *Melospiza georgiana*

The reddish cap might suggest a Chipping Sparrow, but this bird of the marshes is bigger and bulkier, a solitary skulker in dense cover. Swamp Sparrows are common in summer in cattail marshes and brushy swamps across the northeast, midwest, and much of Canada. In winter they live not only in marshes but also in thickets and weedy fields away from water. Although they often stay out of sight, they may

AMERICAN SPARROWS AND THEIR RELATIVES

be detected by their sharp call notes, and they will come up to investigate a birder who makes loud "squeaking" sounds next to the marsh.

HABITAT *Fresh marshes with tussocks, bushes, or cattails; sedgy swamps.* Breeds mostly in freshwater marshes with good growth of sedges, grass, or cattails, often with thickets of alder or willow; sometimes in swampy thickets around ponds and rivers. Also breeds locally in salt marshes on middle Atlantic coast. During migration and winter found mainly in marshes, but also in streamside thickets, rank weedy fields.

FEEDING *Diet: Mostly insects and seeds.* Feeds heavily on insects, perhaps more so than related sparrows, especially in summer. Diet includes many beetles, caterpillars, grasshoppers, crickets, ants, and many

Swamp Sparrow

others, as well as other arthropods. Also eats many seeds, especially in fall and winter, including those of grasses, weeds, and sedges. **Behavior:** Forages mostly on the ground, especially on wet mud near the water's edge, and sometimes feeds while wading in very shallow water. Also does some foraging up in marsh vegetation.

NESTING To defend nesting territory, male sings from a raised perch, such as the top of a cattail or a shrub in the marsh. May sing by day or night. **Nest:** Placed in marsh vegetation such as cattails, sedge tussocks, or bushes, often directly above the water, up to 5 feet high; perhaps sometimes on the ground. Nest (probably built by female only) often has bulky foundation of coarse grass and other marsh plants, with inner cup of fine grass. Dead cattail blades or other leaves often arch over the nest, so that the birds must enter from the side. **Eggs:** 4–5, sometimes 3–6. Pale green to greenish white, heavily marked with reddish brown. Incubation is by female only, probably about 12–13 days. Male may feed female on the nest during incubation. **Young:** Both parents bring food to the nestlings. Young leave the nest about 10–13 days after hatching. Often two broods per year.

MIGRATION Most of those breeding in western Canada probably move eastward in fall to winter in the southeast; however, small numbers occur widely in the west in winter.

CONSERVATION STATUS Undoubtedly has declined with loss of marsh habitat, but still widespread and common. Localized salt marsh race on Atlantic coast could be vulnerable to habitat loss.

"CROWNED" SPARROWS — GENUS *Zonotrichia*

Five species of large, strongly patterned sparrows make up this genus. Four live in our area, and the fifth is common from southern Mexico to the southern tip of South America. Crowned sparrows usually live in brushy or semi-open places and gather in flocks when they are not nesting; unlike some sparrows, they are not particularly shy or elusive. All have sharp, ringing call notes and whistled songs.

WHITE-THROATED SPARROW *Zonotrichia albicollis*

A common winter bird of eastern woodlots, shuffling about on the ground in loose flocks, often coming to bird feeders placed close enough to the shelter of thickets. It is also widespread in the west in winter, but in much smaller numbers. In summer, White-throated Sparrows sing their clear whistles in northern forests. Adults may have head stripes of either white or tan, and scientists have found some odd differences in behavior between these two color morphs.

Thickets, brush, undergrowth of conifer and mixed woodlands. Breeds in zone of coniferous and mixed forest, mainly in openings having dense thickets of deciduous shrubs, such as around ponds, clearings, edges, roadsides, second growth. Winters in areas with dense low cover, including forest undergrowth and edges, well-vegetated suburbs and parks.

FEEDING **Diet:** *Mostly seeds and insects.* Feeds heavily on insects during breeding season, including damselflies, ants, wasps, true bugs, beetles, flies, and caterpillars, plus spiders, millipedes, and snails. Winter diet is mostly seeds of weeds and grasses. Also eats many berries, especially in fall. Young are fed mostly insects. **Behavior:** Forages mostly on ground under or close to dense thickets. Often scratches briefly in leaf litter with both feet. Also forages up in shrubs and low trees, mainly in summer.

NESTING The two color morphs (with tan-striped and white-striped heads) may be either male or female; adults almost always mate with the opposite color morph. Male sings to defend nesting territory.

White-throated Sparrow

Nest: Site usually on ground, well hidden by low shrubs (such as blueberry), grass, or ferns. Sometimes nests above ground in shrubs, brushpiles, or low trees, rarely up to 10 feet high. Nest (built by female) is open cup made of grass, twigs, weeds, pine needles, lined with fine grass, rootlets, animal hair. **Eggs:** 4–5, sometimes 3–6, rarely 2–7. Pale blue or greenish blue, marked with reddish brown and lavender. Incubation is by female only, about 11–14 days. **Young:** Both parents feed nestlings. Young usually leave nest 8–9 days after hatching, are tended by parents for at least 2 more weeks. One or two broods per year.

A few differences between color morphs: white-striped males are usually more aggressive and do more singing than tan-striped males. White-striped females also sing, but tan-striped females usually do not. Pairs involving a tan-striped male and white-striped female usually form more quickly than those of the opposite combination. Tan-striped adults tend to feed their young more often than white-striped adults.

MIGRATION Migrates mostly at night. Tends to migrate relatively late in fall, gradually moving south toward wintering areas.

CONSERVATION STATUS Widespread and common. Surveys suggest slight declines in total numbers during recent decades.

GOLDEN-CROWNED SPARROW *Zonotrichia atricapilla*

This big sparrow is a specialty of the far west. Golden-crowned Sparrows nest in Alaska and western Canada; in summer, open scrubby areas near treeline there may resound with their sad, minor-key whistles. In fall, the birds move south along the Pacific slope. They are common in winter from Vancouver to San Diego, with flocks foraging on the ground under dense thickets, often mixed with equal numbers of White-crowned Sparrows.

HABITAT *Boreal scrub, spruce; in winter, forest edges, thickets, chaparral, gardens.* Breeds in shrubby habitats of north and of high mountains, including willow thickets at edge of dry tundra, stunted spruce near treeline. Winters in many kinds of brushy habitats, from wild chaparral to parks and gardens. Winter habitat like that of White-crowned Sparrow, but tends to be in denser brush.

Golden-crowned Sparrow

FEEDING   **Diet:** *Mostly seeds and insects.* Diet in winter is mostly seeds of weeds and grasses, also some other plant material such as buds, flowers, new shoots, and berries. Also eats some insects and spiders, probably more so in summer. Young are probably fed mostly insects. **Behavior:** Forages mostly on the ground, under or near dense thickets. Sometimes feeds up in shrubs or low trees. Except when nesting, usually forages in flocks.

NESTING   Details of nesting behavior are not well known. Male sings from a prominent perch in summer to defend nesting territory. **Nest:** Site is usually on the ground, very well hidden under thickets of dwarf willow or other shrubs; typically placed in slight depression so that rim of nest is nearly level with ground. Rarely placed a couple of feet up in a dense shrub. Nest is a bulky cup of grass, weeds, ferns, leaves, lined with fine grass and sometimes with animal hair. **Eggs:** 3–5. Creamy white to pale greenish, heavily spotted with reddish brown. Incubation is probably by female and probably lasts 11–12 days. Male may bring food to the female while she is incubating. **Young:** Both parents feed the nestlings. Young probably leave nest at about 9 days.

MIGRATION   Apparently migrates at night. Tends to migrate late in fall and early in spring, with biggest numbers on wintering grounds from late October to early April.

WHITE-CROWNED SPARROW   *Zonotrichia leucophrys*

In most parts of the west, the smartly patterned White-crown is very common at one season or another: summering in the mountains and the north, wintering in the southwestern lowlands, present all year along the coast. Winter birds usually live in flocks, rummaging on the ground near brushy thickets, perching in the tops of bushes when a birder approaches too closely. In the east, the White-crowned

White-crowned Sparrow

Sparrow is generally an uncommon migrant or wintering bird. Different populations of White-crowns often have local "dialects" in their songs, and these have been intensively studied by scientists in some regions.

HABITAT   *Boreal scrub, forest edges, thickets, chaparral, gardens, parks; in winter, also farms and desert washes.* Breeding habitat varies, but always in brushy places such as dwarf willow thickets at edge of tundra, bushy clearings in northern forest, scrub just below timberline in mountains, chaparral and well-wooded suburbs along Pacific coast. In winter, also found in hedgerows, overgrown fields, desert washes.

FEEDING   **Diet:** *Mostly seeds, other vegetable matter, and insects.* Apparently feeds mostly on seeds in winter, mainly those of weeds and grasses. Feeds on other vegetable matter at various seasons, including buds, flowers, moss capsules, willow catkins, berries, and small fruits. Also eats many insects and spiders, especially in summer. Young are fed mostly insects. **Behavior:** Forages mainly while hopping and running on ground. Sometimes feeds up in low shrubs, and occasionally

will make short flights to catch insects in midair. Except during nesting season, usually forages in flocks.

NESTING   In southernmost coastal populations, pairs may remain together all year on permanent territories. Elsewhere, males arrive on nesting grounds before females, defend territories by singing. **Nest:** In north, site is usually on ground at base of shrub or grass clump, often placed in shallow depression in ground; along west coast, nest often placed a few feet up in shrubs. Nest (built by female) is open cup made of grass, twigs, weeds, rootlets, strips of bark, lined with fine grass, feathers, animal hair. **Eggs:** 4–5, sometimes 3, rarely 2–6. Creamy white to pale greenish, heavily spotted with reddish brown. Incubation is by female only, 11–14 days, usually 12. **Young:** Both parents feed nestlings, although female may do more at first. Young leave the nest about 7–12 days after hatching, with those in far north tending to leave earlier than those farther south. Male may care for fledglings while female begins second nesting attempt. One brood per year in far north, 2–3 (even 4) farther south.

MIGRATION   Some populations on Pacific coast are permanent residents; those from northern and mountain regions are strongly migratory. Mostly migrates at night. On average, females winter farther south than males.

HARRIS'S SPARROW *Zonotrichia querula*

Harris's Sparrow

This big, elegant sparrow is a bird of the heartland, nesting in north-central Canada, wintering mainly on the southern Great Plains. Because of its remote habitat and shy behavior in summer, its nest was not discovered until 1931, long after those of most North American birds. Harris's Sparrow is more easily observed in winter on the southern plains. Flocks feed on the ground near brushy places, flying up when disturbed to perch in the tops of thickets, giving sharp call notes.

HABITAT   *Stunted boreal forest; in winter, brush, open woods.* Breeds in the zone where northern forest gives way to tundra, in areas with mixture of stunted spruce or larch trees, shrubby thickets, and open tundra. During migration and winter, found in thickets, woodland edges, brushy fields, hedgerows, shelterbelts.

FEEDING   **Diet:** *Mostly seeds, insects, berries.* Diet varies with season, may include more seeds in winter, berries in late spring after arrival on breeding grounds, insects during summer nesting season. Items important at some seasons include seeds of weeds and grasses, fruits of crowberry and bearberry, and various beetles, flies, caterpillars, true bugs, and other insects, as well as spiders. Also eats some flowers and conifer needles. **Behavior:** Forages mostly while hopping on ground, sometimes scratching in leaf litter with feet. Also does some foraging up in bushes.

NESTING   Male defends nesting territory by singing and by actively chasing intruding males. Pairs form quickly after arrival on breeding grounds, soon after territories established. **Nest:** Site is on ground, usually on small hummock, well hidden under dwarf birch, alder, spruce, or other shrub or low tree. Typically in shallow depression scraped out of moss or other ground cover, sometimes placed under overhang of rock or soil. Nest (probably built by female) is a cup of moss, lichens, twigs, lined with fine grass and sometimes animal hair. **Eggs:** 3–5, usually 4. Pale green, marked with brown. Incubation is by female only, 12–15 days. **Young:** Both parents feed the nestlings. Young leave nest about 8–10 days after hatching, unable to fly until a few days later. One brood per year.

MIGRATION Travels slowly between summer and winter ranges, leaving nesting grounds by early September, arriving on wintering areas mostly in November. Migrates mainly at night.

CONSERVATION STATUS Common within its range, numbers apparently stable. Breeding range is mostly remote from effects of human activity.

JUNCOS — GENUS *Junco*

Attractive gray sparrows of open woodlands, juncos usually have white outer tail feathers, conspicuous when they fly up from the ground. The various kinds are found from northern Canada and Alaska to Panama, but they are mainly birds of cooler climates; toward the south, they live mainly in high mountains. In many parts of North America, juncos occur only as winter visitors, with little flocks coming to backyard bird feeders.

DARK-EYED JUNCO *Junco hyemalis*

In winter over much of the continent, flocks of these juncos can be found around woodland edges and suburban yards, feeding on the ground, making ticking calls as

Dark-eyed Junco

they fly up into the bushes. East of the plains the birds are all gray and white, but in the west they come in various color patterns, with reddish brown on the back or sides or both; some of these were once regarded as different species. The forms have separate ranges in summer, but in winter several types may occur in the same flock in parts of the west.

HABITAT *Conifer and mixed woods. In winter, open woods, undergrowth, roadsides, brush.* Over its wide range, breeding habitat is consistently coniferous or mixed woodland, usually in rather open situations such as edges or clearings. Winters in many kinds of semi-open habitats including woodland edges, thickets, brushy places, suburban areas.

FEEDING **Diet:** *Mostly seeds and insects.* Close to half of summer diet of adults consists of insects, including caterpillars, beetles, grasshoppers, and true bugs, also spiders. Feeds heavily on seeds of weeds and grasses, especially in winter. Also eats some berries. Young are fed mostly insects. **Behavior:** Forages mostly while hopping and running on the ground. Sometimes scratches with its feet in leaf litter or snow. Will come to bird feeders, but tends to forage on the ground under the feeding tray.

NESTING Male sings from high perch to defend nesting territory. In courtship, both members of pair may hop about on ground with wings drooped and tail spread wide to show off white outer tail feathers; male may give soft song. **Nest:** Site is almost always on ground, well hidden under overhanging grass, log, rock, or exposed roots, or in shallow hole in dirt bank. Sometimes up in shrub, tree, or ledge of building, rarely more than 10 feet above ground. Nest (built mostly by female) is an open cup of grass, weeds, leaves, lined with fine grass and sometimes with hair or feathers. **Eggs:** 3–5, rarely 6. Whitish to bluish white or pale gray, with markings of brown and gray often concentrated at larger end. Incubation is by female, about 11–13 days. **Young:** Both parents feed the nestlings.

Young leave the nest 9–13 days after hatching. One or two broods per year, sometimes three.

MIGRATION   Most populations are migratory, but some in southwestern mountains and on southern Pacific coast may be permanent residents. Males tend to winter slightly farther north than females.

YELLOW-EYED JUNCO *Junco phaeonotus*

Mountain forests near the Mexican border are home to this distinctive junco. Unlike its dark-eyed relatives to the north, it moves over the ground with an odd shuffling walk; it also has a much more musical and varied song. Its bright yellow or yellow-orange eye gives it an almost fierce look, all out of proportion to the small size of the bird.

HABITAT   *Conifer forests, pine-oak woods.* A bird of mountain forests throughout its range. In our area, breeds at middle and upper elevations of mountains near Mexican border, mostly in forests of pine and Douglas-fir but also down into pine-oak woods. Slight downhill movement in winter may bring a few into areas of scrub oak and pinyon-juniper woods.

FEEDING   **Diet:** *Mostly seeds and insects.* Diet not known in detail; apparently feeds on insects more in summer than in winter. May eat mostly seeds, including those of weeds and grasses. Also known to eat some flowers, buds, and berries. **Behavior:** Does most of its foraging on the ground. Will scratch in the soil or leaf litter to find food, making a little forward jump and then scratching back with both feet at once. Also does some foraging up in shrubs and sometimes in trees. Will hunt for food around picnic areas and campgrounds in the mountains.

Yellow-eyed Junco

NESTING   Male sings to defend nesting territory, often from a perch high in a tree. Males also may be very aggressive in territorial defense, actively fighting with intruders of their own kind. In courtship, male may strut about near female with his tail spread wide, while giving a soft song. **Nest:** Site is usually on the ground, sometimes in a shrub or low tree but rarely more than a few feet high. Nests on ground are often placed in a slight depression and hidden under something such as a log, rock, base of a shrub, or overhanging clump of grass. Nest (built by female, sometimes with help from male) is shallow cup of grass, lined with fine grass and sometimes animal hair. **Eggs:** 3–4, sometimes 5. Pale gray or bluish white, spotted with reddish brown. Incubation is by female only, about 15 days. **Young:** Both parents feed the nestlings. Young leave the nest about 10 days after hatching, cannot fly well for about another week. Two or three broods per year.

MIGRATION   Mostly sedentary, but flocks may move to slightly lower elevations in the mountains in winter. A very rare visitor to lowland valleys.

LONGSPURS — GENUS *Calcarius*

Named for the very long nail on the hind toe, longspurs are chunky relatives of the sparrows that walk and run on the ground in open country. In summer the males have bright patterns, and they often sing in short flights over their nesting territories.

In winter, wearing plainer garb, longspurs gather in large flocks. All have white in the outer tail feathers, conspicuous when the birds fly up from the ground. One of the four species in this genus is widely found across Eurasia (where it is called Lapland Bunting), but the other three are North American specialties.

McCOWN'S LONGSPUR   *Calcarius mccownii*

An uncommon bird of the high plains, nesting on shortgrass prairies and wintering in dry fields of the southwest. McCown's Longspurs are most conspicuous in summer, when the males perform flight-song displays, singing as they parachute down with their white tail feathers spread wide. In winter they are often in forbiddingly

barren areas such as plowed fields or dry lake beds, where there are few other birds except flocks of hardy Horned Larks. Like other longspurs, however, they are attracted to water, and swirling flocks often descend on the margins of ponds.

HABITAT   *Plains, prairies.* Breeds in rather dry open prairie with short grass, sometimes with patches of open ground or low cactus. Winters on similar shortgrass plains, also on bare soil such as dry lake beds, plowed fields. At all seasons, favors shorter grass and more open ground than that chosen by Chestnut-collared Longspurs occurring in same region.

FEEDING   **Diet:** *Mostly seeds and insects.* Seeds make up more than half of summer diet of adults, and most of winter diet; included are seeds of grasses, weeds, sedges, shrubs. Also eats many insects, especially in

McCown's Longspur

summer, including grasshoppers, caterpillars, ants, and moths. Young fed mostly insects. **Behavior:** Forages while running and walking on ground, picking up items from soil or from plant stems. After flushing insects (such as grasshoppers) from ground, will chase actively, sometimes pursuing them in short flights. Except during nesting season, usually forages in flocks.

NESTING   Male defends nesting territory by performing flight-song display, flying up to about 30 feet and then sailing or gliding down with wings outstretched and tail fanned while singing. Will also fight aggressively with intruding males. In courtship, male may circle female on ground, raising one wing high to show off white wing lining while singing. **Nest:** Site is on open ground, usually placed very close to a large grass clump or weed, small shrub, dried cow manure, or other object. Nest is built by female in slight depression in ground, an open cup made mostly of grass, sometimes with weeds, rootlets, and lichens added, lined with fine grass, plant fibers, animal hair. **Eggs:** 2–4, sometimes 5, perhaps rarely 6. White to pale olive, marked with brown and lavender. Incubation is by female only, about 12 days. **Young:** Both parents feed nestlings. Young leave the nest about 10 days after hatching; can run well at this stage but fly only poorly until a few days later. May remain with parents for at least another 3 weeks.

MIGRATION   Migrates in flocks. Northward migration begins by early spring; southward migration spread over much of fall. Rarely strays west to Pacific coast, accidental east of Great Plains.

CONSERVATION STATUS   Species is far less numerous today than at beginning of 20th century, probably because of loss of short-grass prairie habitat. In recent decades, population probably stable or possibly increasing.

LAPLAND LONGSPUR   *Calcarius lapponicus*

Found throughout the Arctic zones of Europe, Asia, and North America in summer, this is one of the most abundant breeding birds of the far north. Birders who visit the tundra in summer will find Lapland Longspurs very common almost everywhere, the bright males singing their short warbling songs from hummocks or rocks or while flying. In winter the birds come south in flocks to forage in windswept fields. Although they range widely across the continent, the vast majority winter on the Great Plains, where flocks in the thousands seem to reflect the abundance of the species on its northern nesting grounds.

Lapland Longspur

HABITAT   *In summer, tundra; in winter, fields, prairies.* Breeds in various kinds of treeless Arctic habitats, from open wet tundra and sedge meadows to drier upland tundra. Winters in open country including shortgrass prairie, overgrazed pastures, stubble fields, plowed fields, lake shores, and similar areas.

FEEDING   **Diet:** *Mostly seeds and insects.* Seeds make up about half of diet of adults in summer, and great majority of diet in winter; included are seeds of grasses, weeds, and sedges, also waste grain in winter. Also eats many insects in summer, including crane flies, other flies, beetles, caterpillars, and true bugs, as well as spiders. Young fed mostly insects. **Behavior:** Forages by walking on ground, searching methodically for food. Except when nesting, usually forages in flocks; sometimes feeds in association with Horned Larks in winter.

NESTING   Males arrive before females on the nesting grounds and establish territories with flight-song displays: flying up from ground to 30 feet or higher, then gliding down while singing. In courtship on ground, male may sing while running about with wings drooped, bill pointed up. In the short Arctic summer, with little time available, courtship and pairing are accomplished quickly, and females may begin nest-building within days after they arrive. **Nest:** Site is on ground, tucked into shallow depression in moss or other tundra vegetation. Nest (built by female) is cup of grass, sometimes with moss added, lined with fine grass and often with feathers. **Eggs:** 4–6, sometimes 3–7. Greenish white to pale gray-green, marked with brown and black. Incubation is by female only, about 12–13 days. Male sometimes feeds female during incubation. **Young:** Both parents feed nestlings. Young leave the nest about 8–10 days after hatching. Adults may split up the fledglings, each parent caring for part of brood. One brood per year.

MIGRATION   Migrates in flocks. Tends to migrate late in fall and early in spring; in most areas south of Canada, peak passage is in November and March.

CONSERVATION STATUS   Abundant and widespread. Most of breeding range is remote from the effects of human activity.

SMITH'S LONGSPUR   *Calcarius pictus*

Rather uncommon and mysterious birds, Smith's Longspurs nest in the Arctic, in a narrow zone where the last stunted trees give way to open tundra. They spend the winter on the southern Great Plains. On the wintering grounds, the birds live in flocks in open fields of short grass, where they are difficult to see well; if a birder

Smith's Longspur

gets too close, the longspurs take wing with dry rattling calls, to circle over the prairie before alighting again some distance away.

HABITAT *Prairies, fields, airports; in summer, tundra.* Breeds along treeline in the north, where stunted forest gives way to tundra, mainly in areas of grassy or sedgy tundra with scattered low shrubs and short conifers. Winters on shortgrass plains, heavily grazed pastures, airport fields.

FEEDING **Diet:** *Mostly seeds and insects.* Diet is mainly seeds for much of year, especially in winter, including seeds of weeds and grasses, also waste grain. Also eats insects, and these become major part of diet during breeding season; included are caterpillars, beetles, grasshoppers, flies, moths, damselflies, and others, as well as spiders and snails. **Behavior:** Does all its foraging while walking or running on the ground. Except when nesting, usually forages in flocks.

NESTING Unusual breeding system. Breeds in small colonies, where males sing to attract females but do not defend territories. Both males and females are promiscuous; the young in a single nest are often of mixed parentage and may be fed by more than one male. **Nest:** Site is on ground on dry hummock of tundra, among grass clumps or near base of low shrub. Often sunken in shallow depression, but not as well hidden as nests of some longspurs. Nest (built by female) is open cup of grass and sedges, lined with lichens, animal hair, and particularly feathers (ptarmigan feathers are especially favored). **Eggs:** 4, sometimes 3–5, rarely 1–6. Pale tan to pale green, marked with lavender and dark brown. Incubation is by female only, 11–13 days. **Young:** Fed by female and by one or more males. Young leave the nest about 7–9 days after hatching, unable to fly well for about another week. One brood per year.

MIGRATION Tends to migrate late in fall and early in spring; present on wintering areas mostly from November to March. Migrates in flocks.

CONSERVATION STATUS Numbers probably stable. Most of breeding range is remote from human disturbance.

CHESTNUT-COLLARED LONGSPUR *Calcarius ornatus*

Male Chestnut-collared Longspurs can be found in summer singing their flight-songs over the northern prairies. In winter, flocks invade the grasslands of the southwest. They can be hard to see well on the ground, flushing when a birder approaches and swirling away over the fields with soft musical call notes; they are more easily observed when they come to drink at ponds.

HABITAT *Plains, prairies.* Breeds in the general region of shortgrass prairie, but in areas of slightly longer grass and scattered taller weeds. Winters in shortgrass prairies and fields. Overlaps broadly in range with McCown's Longspur, but tends to occur in areas with taller and denser grass.

FEEDING **Diet:** *Mostly seeds and insects.* Seeds may make up close to half of summer diet of adults and great majority of winter diet; included are seeds of weeds and grasses. Also feeds on many insects in summer, including grasshoppers, crickets, and beetles, as well as spiders. Young are fed mostly insects. **Behavior:** Forages while running and walking on ground, picking up items from soil or plants. After flushing insects from ground, sometimes will chase them, even in short flights.

NESTING   To defend nesting territory, male performs flight-song display, fluttering up about 20 feet, flying in undulating circles while singing, then fluttering down again.

Also often sings from a raised perch. **Nest:** Site is on ground, often at base of grass clump or weed or next to dried cow manure or other object. Placed in shallow depression, either a natural hollow or one scraped out by bird, so that rim of nest is about level with ground. Female builds nest, a shallow cup of grass lined with finer grass and sometimes with rootlets, feathers, or animal hair. **Eggs:** 4–5, sometimes 3, rarely 6. Whitish, marked with brown, black, purple. Incubation is by female only, about 10–13 days. **Young:** Both parents feed the nestlings. Young leave the nest about 10 days after hatching; can fly well by a few days later. Two broods per year.

MIGRATION   Migrates in flocks. Occurs in small numbers west to the Pacific coast and as an accidental stray east to the Atlantic coast.

CONSERVATION STATUS   Has disappeared from some former nesting areas, but still fairly widespread and common.

Chestnut-collared Longspur

OLD WORLD BUNTINGS — GENUS *Emberiza*

This is a very important group in Europe, Asia, and Africa, with more than 35 species. In many, the males are brightly colored. Seven species from Asia have strayed into Alaska, but only one of these, the Rustic Bunting, comes close to being a regular migrant there.

PINE BUNTING   *Emberiza leucocephalos*

This bunting nests in forests across northern Siberia and generally migrates south quite late in fall. It has been found twice in fall on Attu Island, Alaska; it might occur regularly there in small numbers at that season, but observers are seldom on hand in fall to find it.

LITTLE BUNTING   *Emberiza pusilla*

Widespread across northern Scandinavia and Siberia in summer, the Little Bunting winters mostly in southern Asia. Off-course migrants have appeared in the outer Aleutian Islands, Alaska, a few times, and one very lost bird made it all the way to San Diego, California.

RUSTIC BUNTING   *Emberiza rustica*

Several related species of buntings from Asia have strayed into Alaska. The most frequent of these, the Rustic Bunting, is a rare but almost regular migrant on the western Aleutians, mostly in spring, and shows up occasionally elsewhere in western Alaska. Fall and winter strays have also appeared at several points along the Pacific coast south to California.

AMERICAN SPARROWS AND THEIR RELATIVES

YELLOW-BREASTED BUNTING *Emberiza aureola*

During the summer, this colorful bunting is widespread across northern Siberia and northeastern Europe, nesting in bogs, wet meadows, and thickets. It spends the winter mostly in Southeast Asia. In our area, it is a very rare spring visitor to islands of western Alaska.

GRAY BUNTING *Emberiza variabilis*

This rather large bunting has a limited range in eastern Asia, in coastal regions and on islands, from the Kamchatka Peninsula south to southern Japan. In its normal range, it inhabits the undergrowth of open woods. In our area, it is a rare spring vagrant to the western Aleutian Islands.

PALLAS'S BUNTING *Emberiza pallasi*

An inhabitant of marshes, thickets, and weedy fields in Asia, Pallas's Bunting is a very rare vagrant to western and northern Alaska. Adult males are easily identified, but females or young birds would be very difficult to separate from Reed Bunting, another rare Alaska stray.

REED BUNTING *Emberiza schoeniclus*

Across Europe and Asia, this chunky bird is a common resident of marshes and other rank low growth. Although it may be skulking and hard to approach, it will perch on top of the reeds if undisturbed. The species has strayed to the western Aleutian Islands, Alaska, several times during spring migration.

WHITE BUNTINGS — GENUS *Plectrophenax*

These are hardy songbirds, adapted for survival in the harshest regions of the high Arctic. One of the two species is found around the world in the far north, and the other nests only on a few islands off western Alaska.

SNOW BUNTING *Plectrophenax nivalis*

They sometimes have been called "Snowflakes," and flocks of Snow Buntings may seem like snowflakes as they swirl through the air and then settle on winter fields. South of the Arctic, these are strictly winter birds, arriving in late fall and generally departing at the first signs of spring. In summer they retire to barren northern tundra, with some breeding on the northernmost islands of Canada and the mountains of Greenland. In some high Arctic communities, Snow Buntings nest in birdhouses put out for them.

HABITAT *Prairies, fields, dunes, shores. In summer, tundra.* Breeds on northern tundra, mainly in areas with rocky outcrops, boulder fields, cliffs, or rocky beaches, generally avoiding unbroken wet tundra. Winters in various kinds of open country, including shortgrass prairie, farmland, beaches, lake shores.

FEEDING **Diet:** *Mostly seeds and insects.* Seeds of grasses, weeds, and sedges make up a major part of diet at most seasons, especially in winter; may also consume buds and leaves in spring. Also eats many insects in summer, including crane flies, other flies, beetles, caterpillars, and true bugs, plus some spiders. Young are fed mostly on insects. In coastal areas, may eat tiny crustaceans and other marine life. **Behavior:** Forages while walking and running on the ground. Except when nesting, usually forages in flocks.

Snow Bunting

NESTING   Males arrive on breeding grounds 3–6 weeks before females to stake out territories containing suitable nest sites. In territorial and courtship display, male flies up 20–30 feet, then glides down while singing. In courtship on ground, male spreads wings and tail, turns his back to female to show off contrasting pattern, and makes short runs away from her. **Nest:** Site is in some protected cavity, as in a deep fissure among rocks; sometimes under man-made debris or in hole in ground. Nest (built by female) is a bulky cup of grass and moss lined with fine grass, rootlets, plant down, and especially with feathers or hair. **Eggs:** 4–7, sometimes 2–9. Whitish to pale blue-green, marked with brown and black. Incubation is by female, 10–16 days. In some parts of range, male feeds female on nest throughout incubation period, allowing her to spend more time on eggs—important in cold northern climate. **Young:** Both parents feed nestlings. Young leave the nest about 10–17 days after hatching. One brood per year.

MIGRATION   Migrates mostly late in fall and early in spring. Strays south of main winter range may be most likely to appear in November.

CONSERVATION STATUS   Common and widespread, numbers probably stable. Most of breeding range is remote from effects of human activity.

McKAY'S BUNTING   *Plectrophenax hyperboreus*

McKay's Bunting

Few birders ever get to see this whitest of North American songbirds on its main nesting grounds, remote St. Matthew and Hall islands in the Bering Sea. During many summers, however, a few McKay's Buntings appear on St. Lawrence Island or the Pribilofs, sites more easily visited. On those islands the bird may interbreed with the local Snow Buntings, as the two species apparently are very closely related.

HABITAT   *Tundra, barrens, shores.* Probably breeds in most available habitats in its very limited range, including open tundra with numerous rocky outcrops, stony beaches, and rocky scree slopes with little vegetation. Winters mostly on coastal beaches and low tundra near the shore.

FEEDING   **Diet:** *Probably mostly insects and seeds.* Diet is not known in detail, but undoubtedly feeds on many insects (and some spiders) in summer, mainly or entirely on seeds in winter. Along shorelines, may also eat tiny crustaceans or other marine life. **Behavior:** Forages while walking and running on the ground, picking up items from the ground or from plants. Except when nesting, usually forages in flocks.

NESTING	Nesting behavior not well known, but probably similar to that of Snow Bunting. In display on breeding grounds, may sing while flying in a wide circle. **Nest:** Site is usually in some protected cavity, such as a deep crevice in cliff, among or underneath rocks, or inside hollow pieces of driftwood; these secure sites may be chosen for protection from Arctic foxes. Nest is a shallow cup of grass, lined with finer grasses. **Eggs:** Probably about 5. Pale green, dotted with pale brown. Incubation poorly known; probably similar to Snow Bunting, but it is possible that male may help incubate. **Young:** Probably fed by both parents, and probably leave nest about 10–17 days after hatching, as in the Snow Bunting.
MIGRATION	Winter status on the islands where it breeds is poorly known; most may migrate to west coast of Alaska in fall. Only a casual to accidental stray farther south.
CONSERVATION STATUS	Total population is no more than a few thousand. Could be seriously threatened if rats or other predators were introduced to its nesting islands.

BLACKBIRDS AND ORIOLES (subfamily Icterinae)

With colors ranging from glossy black to flaming orange, this group includes some of our most striking birds. The blackbird subfamily, found only in the Americas, contains nearly 100 species. Most of those in our area live in rather open habitats such as fields or marshes, or in the edge of woodlands, but some in the tropics are denizens of deep forests.

Many of the blackbirds and orioles are quite sociable, living in flocks when they are not nesting, and several kinds even nest in colonies. Most kinds have impressive voices, although these may be anything from rich and melodious to harsh and grating.

Members of this group may have rather long life spans for songbirds, with some kinds known to have lived more than 15 years in the wild.

Feeding The typical blackbirds in our area feed mainly on insects and seeds, often with insects predominating in summer and seeds making up more of the diet at other seasons. The orioles eat very few seeds, but they do eat berries, sometimes in large numbers; they also visit flowers to feed on nectar. Some of the larger species, such as the big grackles, are omnivores that will eat practically anything.

Most foraging by blackbirds and orioles is rather slow and methodical, the birds walking on the ground or hopping about deliberately among tree branches.

Nesting The blackbird group demonstrates a wide variety of approaches to nesting. Some species are solitary breeders, while others nest in dense colonies, with large numbers of nests packed into an acre of marsh or into one big tree. Some nest on the ground, others in the treetops. And some of the cowbirds never raise their own young; they are brood parasites, leaving their eggs in the nests of other birds.

Among those blackbirds that do care for their own young, many build open cup-shaped nests. Others make elaborate, carefully woven hanging bags constructed of long plant fibers; such hanging nests are typical of the orioles and the tropical oropendolas and caciques. Generally the female incubates the eggs, but both parents usually take part in feeding the young.

Displays The males of some blackbird species have spectacular displays that they use to defend their territories or to attract a mate. These visual displays are usually accompanied by songs. There are many different variations, including the posturing and wing-flapping of the large grackles, the puffing up and hovering of the Bronzed Cowbird, and the flight-song of the Bobolink. Perhaps most bizarre is the performance of certain oropendolas: these very large blackbirds of the tropics will perch on a branch and then fall so far forward that they are practically hanging upside down, wings out and crests raised, while they make loud gurgling and popping noises.

GENUS *Dolichonyx*

BOBOLINK   *Dolichonyx oryzivorus*

Fluttering over meadows and hayfields in summer, the male Bobolink delivers a bubbling, tinkling song that, loosely interpreted, gives the species its name. The male is unmistakable in spring finery, but before fall migration he molts into a striped brown appearance like that of the female. Bobolinks in this plumage were once known as "ricebirds" in the south, where they occasionally used to cause serious damage in the rice fields.

HABITAT   *Hayfields, meadows. In migration, marshes.* Original prime breeding areas were damp meadows and natural prairies with dense growth of grass and weeds and a few low bushes. Such habitats are still favored but hard to find, and today most Bobolinks in eastern United States nest in hayfields. Migrants stop over in fields and marshes, often feeding in rice fields.

FEEDING   **Diet:** *Mostly insects and seeds.* Majority of summer diet is insects, including beetles, grasshoppers, caterpillars, wasps, ants, and many others, also spiders and millipedes. Also eats many seeds of weeds, grasses, and grains. May feed more heavily on grain during migration, and in former times caused much damage in southern rice fields. In winter in the tropics, may also eat some berries. **Behavior:** Forages for insects and seeds both on the ground and while perched up in grass and weed stalks. Except when nesting, usually forages in flocks.

Bobolink

NESTING   Males arrive on nesting grounds before females and display by flying over fields, with shallow fluttering wingbeats, while singing. In courtship on the ground, male spreads tail, droops wings, points bill down so that yellow nape is prominent. **Nest:** Placed on the ground (or rarely just above it), well hidden among dense grass and weeds. Typical ground nest is a slight depression holding a shallow open cup of grass and weed stems, lined with finer grasses. **Eggs:** 5–6, sometimes 3–7. Grayish to pale reddish brown, heavily blotched with brown and lavender. Incubation is by female only, about 11–13 days. **Young:** Both parents feed the nestlings. Young leave the nest about 8–14 days after hatching, generally before they are able to fly. One brood per year.

MIGRATION   Migrates in flocks. A long-distance migrant, wintering in southern South America, traveling mostly via Florida and the West Indies, with few occurring in Mexico or Central America.

CONSERVATION STATUS   Declining significantly in recent decades; loss of nesting habitat is a likely cause.

MARSH BLACKBIRDS — GENUS *Agelaius*

Most of the 10 species in this genus spend most of their time in marshes, although they also may forage in open fields away from water. Males are black, and most of them have contrasting patches of red or yellow; most females are duller and browner, with streaks. Generally they are sociable birds, foraging in flocks and often nesting in colonies.

RED-WINGED BLACKBIRD *Agelaius phoeniceus*

Among our most familiar birds, Red-wings seem to sing their nasal songs in every marsh and wet field from coast to coast. They are notably bold, and several will often attack a larger bird such as a hawk or crow that flies over their nesting area. The red shoulder patches of the male, hidden under body feathers much of the time, are brilliantly displayed when he is singing. Outside the nesting season, Red-wings sometimes roost in huge concentrations.

HABITAT   *Breeds in marshes, brushy swamps, hayfields; forages also in cultivated land and along edges of water.* Breeds most commonly in freshwater marsh, but also in wooded or brushy swamps, rank weedy fields, hayfields, upper edges of salt marsh. Often forages in other open habitats, such as fields and mudflats; outside the breeding season, flocks gather in farm fields, pastures, feedlots.

FEEDING   **Diet:** *Mostly insects and seeds.*

Red-winged Blackbird

Feeds on many insects, especially in summer, including beetles, caterpillars, and grasshoppers; also spiders, millipedes, snails. Majority of adult's annual diet (roughly three-fourths) is seeds, including those of grasses, weeds, and waste grain. Also eats some berries and small fruits. **Behavior:** Forages mostly while walking on ground; also sometimes up in shrubs and trees. Outside the breeding season, usually forages in flocks, often associated with other blackbirds and starlings.

NESTING   To defend his territory and attract a mate, male perches on high stalk with feathers fluffed out and tail partly spread, lifts leading edge of wing so that red shoulder patches are prominent, and sings. Also sings in slow, fluttering flight. One male often has more than one mate. Adults are very aggressive in nesting territory, attacking larger birds that approach and loudly protesting human intruders. **Nest:** Placed in marsh growth such as cattails or bulrushes, in bushes or saplings close to water, or in dense grass in fields. Nest (built by female) is bulky open cup lashed to standing vegetation, made of grass, reeds, leaves, rootlets, lined with fine grass. **Eggs:** 3–4, rarely 2–6. Pale blue-green, with markings of black, brown, purple concentrated at larger end. Incubation is by female only, 10–13 days. **Young:** Both parents feed nestlings (but female does more). Young leave nest about 11–14 days after hatching.

MIGRATION   Present throughout the year in many areas. In the north, migrants appear quite early in spring, with males arriving before females. Migrates in flocks.

TRICOLORED BLACKBIRD *Agelaius tricolor*

While the Red-winged Blackbird is abundant over most of the continent, the very similar Tricolored Blackbird has a very small range in the Pacific states. It differs in its highly social nesting: in a dense cattail marsh, nests may be packed in close together, only a foot or two apart. Some colonies may have over 100,000 nests, although such large concentrations seem to be growing scarcer in recent years, as the birds shift to smaller (but, we hope, more numerous) colonies.

HABITAT   *Cattail or tule marshes; forages in fields, farms.* Breeds in large freshwater marshes, in dense stands of cattails or bulrushes. At all seasons (including when breeding), does most of its foraging in open habitats such as farm fields, pastures, cattle pens, large lawns.

FEEDING   **Diet:** *Mostly insects and seeds.* Feeds on many insects, especially in summer, including caterpillars, beetles, grasshoppers, and others; also spiders. Especially in fall and winter, eats many seeds of grasses and weeds, and waste grain. **Behavior:** Forages mostly while walking on ground; also sometimes up in shrubs and trees. Usually forages in flocks, particularly outside the breeding season; often associated with Red-winged Blackbirds, other blackbirds, and starlings.

Tricolored Blackbird

NESTING   Nests in colonies more densely packed than those of Red-winged Blackbirds, with nests often only a couple of feet apart. In displaying to attract a mate, male perches on high stalk with feathers fluffed out and tail partly spread, lifts leading edge of wing so that red shoulder patches are prominent, lowers head, and sings. **Nest:** Placed in marsh in cattails or bulrushes, or in willows at water's edge, sometimes in tall growth in drier fields. Nest (built by female) is bulky open cup lashed to standing vegetation, made of grass, reeds, leaves, rootlets, lined with fine grass. **Eggs:** 4, sometimes 3–5, rarely 2–6. Pale blue-green, with markings of black, brown, and purple concentrated at larger end. Incubation is by female, about 11 days. **Young:** Both parents feed nestlings (but female does more). Young leave the nest about 11–14 days after hatching.

MIGRATION   Not very migratory, withdrawing only from northernmost nesting areas in winter, but moves around considerably with the seasons within its limited range. Colony sites also may shift from year to year.

CONSERVATION STATUS   Has declined in numbers in recent decades, probably because of loss of habitat.

TAWNY-SHOULDERED BLACKBIRD   *Agelaius humeralis*

A Caribbean relative of our Red-winged Blackbird, found only in Cuba and a very limited area of Haiti. It lives in semi-open country and woodland edges, and often occurs in flocks. Strays have reached the Florida Keys at least twice.

MEADOWLARKS — GENUS *Sturnella*

Not larks at all but close relatives of the blackbirds and orioles, these chunky birds stalk about on the ground in open fields. If alarmed, they fly away low over the grass with bursts of quick wingbeats and stiff glides. Besides the species in our area, another three to five kinds of meadowlarks live in South America, but those birds are red on the chest instead of yellow.

EASTERN MEADOWLARK   *Sturnella magna*

A familiar bird, known by the black "V" on its chest when it sings from a fencepost or by the flash of white tail feathers when it flushes from the grass. The clear whistled song of the Eastern Meadowlark can be heard in spring not only in the east but also in desert grasslands of the southwest. Some scientists believe that the southwestern form is actually a different species. Other races of the Eastern Meadowlark are widespread in Central America and northern South America.

HABITAT *Open fields and pastures, meadows, prairies.* Breeds in natural grasslands, meadows, weedy pastures, also in hayfields and sometimes in fields of other crops. Winters in many kinds of natural and cultivated fields. In the midwest, tends to prefer taller and lusher grass than Western Meadowlark, but in the southwest it lives in very arid desert grasslands.

FEEDING **Diet:** *Mostly insects and seeds.* Majority of diet consists of insects, especially in summer, when it eats many grasshoppers, crickets, beetles and their larvae, caterpillars, ants, true bugs, and others; also spiders. Seeds and waste grain make up over one-fourth of annual diet and are eaten especially in fall and winter. **Behavior:** Forages by walking on the ground, taking insects and seeds from the ground and from low plants. May probe in the soil with its

Eastern Meadowlark

bill. In winter, may forage in flocks.

NESTING Male defends nesting territory by singing. In courtship, male faces female, puffs out chest feathers and points bill straight up to show off black "V," spreads tail wide, and flicks wings; he may even jump in the air in this posture. Male may have more than one mate. **Nest:** Placed on the ground, in areas with dense grass and other low cover, in a small depression in soil. Nest (built by female) is a domed structure with the entrance on the side, made of grass stems interwoven with surrounding growth. Usually has narrow trails or "runways" leading to nest through the grass. **Eggs:** 3–5, sometimes up to 7. White, heavily spotted with brown and purple. Incubation is by female, about 13–15 days. **Young:** Both parents feed nestlings (but female does more). Young leave nest after 11–12 days, when still unable to fly, and are tended by parents for at least 2 more weeks. Two broods per year.

MIGRATION Present all year in most of range, although only small numbers usually remain through winter in north. Migrants arrive rather early in spring and linger late in fall.

CONSERVATION STATUS The species probably increased in numbers during the 1700s and 1800s as forests were cleared and turned into farmland. However, populations generally have been declining in the east in recent decades. The decrease in amount and quality of habitat is the most likely cause.

WESTERN MEADOWLARK   *Sturnella neglecta*

Remarkably similar to the Eastern Meadowlark in colors and pattern, this bird is recognized by its very different song and call notes. The two species of meadowlarks evidently can easily recognize their own kind the same way; even where their ranges overlap in the midwest and southwest, they almost never interbreed. However, the two species do seem to see each other as potential rivals, and they actively defend territories against each other.

HABITAT *Grasslands, cultivated fields and pastures, meadows, prairies.* Breeds mostly in natural grasslands, abandoned weedy fields, rangeland, also sometimes on cultivated land. In the midwest, seems to prefer shorter grass and drier fields than the sites chosen by Eastern Meadowlark. In winter, often in stubble fields and other farmland.

Diet: *Mostly insects and seeds.* Majority of diet consists of insects, especially in summer, when it eats many beetles, grasshoppers, crickets, caterpillars, ants, true bugs, and others; also spiders, snails, sowbugs. Seeds and waste grain make up about one-third of annual diet and are eaten especially in fall and winter. **Behavior:** Forages by walking on the ground, taking insects and seeds from the ground and from low plants. Often probes in the soil with its bill. In winter, usually forages in flocks.

Western Meadowlark

NESTING   Male sings to defend nesting territory. One male may have more than one mate. In courtship, male faces female, puffs out chest feathers and points bill straight up to show off black "V," spreads tail wide, and flicks wings. **Nest:** Placed on the ground, in areas with dense cover of grass, in a small hollow or depression in ground. Nest (built by female) is a domed structure with the entrance on the side, made of grass stems interwoven with the surrounding growth. Usually has narrow trails or "runways" leading to nest through the grass. **Eggs:** 3–7, usually about 5. White, heavily spotted with brown and purple, especially at larger end. Incubation is by female, about 13–15 days. **Young:** Both parents feed nestlings (but female does more). Young leave the nest after about 12 days, before they are able to fly, and are tended by parents for at least another 2 weeks. Two broods per year.

MIGRATION   Migrates relatively late in fall and early in spring. Summer range and numbers may vary in drier parts of west, with numbers of breeding birds dependent on amount of spring rainfall.

CONSERVATION STATUS   Has declined in some areas recently, but surveys suggest that overall populations are more or less stable.

GENUS *Xanthocephalus*

YELLOW-HEADED BLACKBIRD   *Xanthocephalus xanthocephalus*

Yellow-headed Blackbird

The male Yellow-headed Blackbird is impressive to see, but not to hear: it may have the worst song of any North American bird, a hoarse, harsh scraping. Yellowheads nest in noisy colonies in big cattail marshes of the west and midwest; when not nesting, they gather in flocks in open fields, often with other blackbirds. At some favored places in the southwest in winter, they may be seen in flocks of thousands.

HABITAT   *Fresh marshes. Forages in fields, open country.* Breeds in freshwater sloughs, marshy lake borders, tall cattails growing in water up to 3–4 feet deep. Forages around marshes and also commonly in open pastures, plowed fields, cattle pens, feedlots.

FEEDING   **Diet:** *Mostly insects and seeds.* Feeds heavily on insects in summer, especially beetles, caterpillars, and grasshoppers, also ants, wasps, and others, plus a few spiders and snails. Young are fed mostly insects. Probably two-thirds of diet consists of seeds, including grass and weed seeds plus waste grain. **Behavior:** Forages mostly by walking on the ground in open fields or near the water's edge; also forages low in marsh vegetation. Sometimes catches insects in flight. May follow farm machinery in fields to feed on insects and grubs turned up by the plow. Except in nesting season, usually forages in flocks, often associated with other blackbirds.

NESTING   Typically nests in colonies in marshes, each male selecting territory within colony and defending it against rivals by singing. One male may have as many as five mates. **Nest:** Placed in marsh, firmly lashed to standing vegetation (cattails, bulrushes, reeds) growing in water, usually no more than 3 feet above water's surface. Nest (built by female) is a bulky, deep cup woven of aquatic plants, lined with dry grass or with fine, dry marsh plants. **Eggs:** 4, sometimes 3–5, rarely 1–2. Pale gray to pale green, blotched and dotted with brown or gray. Incubation is by female only, 11–13 days. **Young:** Both parents feed nestlings. Young leave nest after about 9–12 days, but remain among dense marsh plants until they are ready to fly, about 3 weeks after hatching. One brood per year, possibly two.

MIGRATION   Migrates in flocks. Males may tend to winter farther north than females, on average. Strays reach Atlantic coast, especially in fall.

CONSERVATION STATUS   Undoubtedly has declined in some areas with draining of marshes; however, still widespread and very common.

MEDIUM-SIZED BLACKBIRDS — GENUS *Euphagus*

These two species are very similar in appearance, but not in their choice of habitats. Brewer's Blackbird is common in the arid west, while the Rusty Blackbird summers in bogs of the far north and spends the winter mainly around swamps in the southeastern states. Both have harsh, grating songs.

RUSTY BLACKBIRD   *Euphagus carolinus*

Birders might say that this blackbird is rusty because it spends so much time in the water. In migration and winter it is usually in swampy places, wading in very shallow water at the edges of wooded streams. In summer it retires to northern spruce bogs; no other blackbird has such a northerly breeding distribution. The name "Rusty" applies to the colors of fall birds, but it could also describe the rusty-hinge sound of the creaking song.

Rusty Blackbird

HABITAT   *River groves, wooded swamps; muskeg in summer.* Breeds in the muskeg region, in wet northern coniferous forest with many lakes and bogs. During migration and winter, favors areas with trees near water, as in wooded swamps and riverside forest; will also forage in open fields and cattle feedlots with other blackbirds.

FEEDING   **Diet:** *Mostly insects and seeds.* Majority of annual diet is insects, including many aquatic insects such as caddisflies, mayflies, dragonflies, and water beetles, plus land insects such as grasshoppers and others. Also eats snails, crustaceans, small fish, small salamanders. Eats many seeds and waste grain, especially in winter, also a few berries. **Behavior:** Forages mostly by walking on wet ground or wading in shallow water. May be solitary or in flocks. May join flocks of other blackbirds and feed with them in dry fields.

NESTING   Sometimes nests in small, loose colonies, but more typically in isolated pairs. Male gives harsh, grating song in spring to defend nesting territory or attract a mate. **Nest:** Site is in dense cover, usually in conifer or in shrubs above the water; placed very low, typically only a few feet above water or ground but can be up to 20 feet high in coniferous tree. Nest (built by female) is a bulky open cup of twigs and grass, often with foundation of *Usnea* lichens, the inner bowl shaped of mudlike decaying plant material from the forest floor; lined with fine grass. **Eggs:** 4–5, sometimes 3–6. Pale blue-green, spotted with brown and gray. Incubation is by female only, probably about 14 days. **Young:** Both parents feed nestlings. Young leave the nest about 11–14 days after hatching.

MIGRATION   Migrates relatively late in fall and early in spring. Strays appear in the west and southwest most often in late fall.

CONSERVATION STATUS   Most of breeding range is remote from effects of human activities; has adapted to changing habitats on winter range. Numbers probably stable or perhaps declining slowly.

BREWER'S BLACKBIRD   *Euphagus cyanocephalus*

This is the common blackbird of open country in the west, often seen walking on the ground with short forward jerks of its head. It adapts well to habitats altered by humans, and in places it may walk about on suburban sidewalks or scavenge for crumbs around beachfront restaurants. In winter, Brewer's Blackbirds gather in large flocks, often with other blackbirds, and may be seen foraging in farmland all across the western and southern states.

HABITAT   *Fields, prairies, farms, parks.* Occurs in many kinds of open and semi-open country, including shrubby areas near water, streamside woods, aspen groves in mountain meadows, shores, farmland, irrigated or plowed fields. Often around human habitations, foraging on suburban lawns and in city parking lots.

Brewer's Blackbird

FEEDING   **Diet:** *Mostly insects and seeds, some berries.* Feeds on a wide variety of insects, including grasshoppers, crickets, beetles, aphids, caterpillars, termites; also some spiders, snails, tiny crustaceans. Eats many seeds of grasses and weeds, plus much waste grain. Also eats berries, especially in summer. **Behavior:** Walks on the ground as it searches for food. Sometimes wades in very shallow water. Sometimes catches insects in flight. May follow farm machinery in fields to feed on insects turned up by the plow. Except in nesting season, usually forages in flocks.

NESTING   Often nests in loose colonies of up to 20–30 pairs. In courtship display (or sometimes in aggressive display), male points bill straight up or forward, fluffs out body feathers, and partly spreads wings and tail. **Nest:** Site is quite variable; usually in tree 20–40 feet above ground, but may be on ground among tall grass, in bushes, or in crevice in cliff. Nest (built by female) is a rather bulky open cup made of twigs, grass, weeds, and pine needles, lined with fine grass, rootlets, animal hair. Often has mud or dried manure added to base. **Eggs:** 4–6, sometimes 3–7. Pale gray to greenish gray, spotted with brown. Incubation is by female, 12–14 days. **Young:** Both parents feed nestlings. Young leave the nest about 13–14 days after hatching. One brood per year, sometimes two.

Present all year in parts of west. Spreads eastward in fall, with winter range including much of southeast. Migrates north relatively early in spring.

CONSERVATION STATUS Widespread and abundant. Expanded its range eastward in Great Lakes region during 20th century. In some areas, may be affected by competition with Common Grackle, increasing in west.

GRACKLES — GENUS *Quiscalus*

In the six species of grackles, males are glossy black and females are duller, often brownish. All have oddly creased or keeled tails, with the central feathers lower than the outer ones, looking like a shallow "V" in cross section. Grackles live in open or semi-open country, usually near water, and the males have harsh and discordant voices.

GREAT-TAILED GRACKLE   *Quiscalus mexicanus*

Wherever it occurs, this big blackbird is impossible to overlook—especially the male, with his great oversized tail and incredible variety of call notes. In the southwest, flocks of Great-tailed Grackles feed in open country during the day but often come

into towns at night, forming noisy roosting aggregations in the trees in city parks. During recent decades, this species has greatly expanded its range within our area, and it is still spreading north in some areas.

HABITAT   *Groves, thickets, farms, towns, city parks.* Found in many kinds of open and semi-open country, mostly in the lowlands, including farmland, marshes, irrigated fields, suburban lawns, brushy areas. Avoids true desert situations but may be common around streams or ponds in dry country.

FEEDING   **Diet:** *Omnivorous.* Diet is extremely varied; includes many insects, also spiders, millipedes, snails, crayfish, tadpoles, small fish, lizards, eggs and nestlings of other birds, and sometimes adult birds. Also eats a wide variety of seeds, waste grain, berries, fruits, and nuts. **Behavior:** Forages mostly on the ground

Great-tailed Grackle

or by wading in very shallow water. Also forages in trees and shrubs, especially searching for nests to rob. Generally feeds in flocks.

NESTING   Nests in colonies, from a few pairs to hundreds at times. In courtship and territorial display, male perches in the open, fluffs out feathers, partly spreads wings and tail, rapidly flutters wings while making harsh calls. Also postures with bill pointed straight up, mainly as a threat display to other birds. Both males and females may have more than one mate. **Nest:** Site varies; usually in dense vegetation near water, including dense shrubs or low trees, but also in marsh or in tall trees. Often 2–20 feet above ground or water, but can be as high as 50 feet. Nest (built by female) is a bulky open cup made of twigs, grass, weeds, cattails, rushes, whatever materials are readily available; lined with fine grass. Mud or manure often added to base of nest. Females may steal nest material from each other. **Eggs:** 3–4, sometimes 5. Pale greenish blue, irregularly marked with brown, gray, and black. Incubation is by female only, about 13–14 days. **Young:** Fed by female only. Young leave the nest about 3 weeks after hatching.

Mostly migratory in northern parts of its range; however, it has recently become a permanent resident in some areas where it formerly occurred only in summer. Still expanding its range and increasing in numbers. Competition with this species may have played a part in the extinction of the Slender-billed Grackle in central Mexico many years ago.

BOAT-TAILED GRACKLE *Quiscalus major*

Until the 1970s, this big blackbird was considered to be the same species as the Great-tailed Grackle, but the two forms overlap on the coasts of Texas and Louisiana without interbreeding. The Boat-tail is a more aquatic creature, nesting in marshes, scavenging on beaches. Except in Florida, it is seldom found far away from tidewater. Boat-tailed Grackles nest in noisy colonies, the males displaying conspicuously with much wing-fluttering and harsh repeated calls.

HABITAT   *Marshes, beaches, areas near coast; also inland in Florida.* Almost always near water and very close to coast, in marshes, flooded fields, mudflats. Sometimes forages in drier fields in coastal regions. Occurs well inland in Florida, but generally near marshes and lakes.

FEEDING   **Diet:** *Omnivorous.* Much of diet is taken from water, including many aquatic insects, snails, crayfish, crabs, mussels, shrimp, tadpoles, frogs, and small fish. Also eats land insects (including grass-hoppers and caterpillars), eggs and young of other birds. Seeds and grain important in diet at some sea-

Boat-tailed Grackle

sons. **Behavior:** Forages mostly near water by walking on shore or in shallow water, catching items with rapid thrusts of its bill. Sometimes steals food from larger birds. Will enter heron colonies to feed on unguarded eggs.

NESTING   Nests in colonies. In courtship and territorial display, male perches in the open, fluffs out feathers, spreads tail, and rapidly flutters wings above back while making a variety of harsh and rattling calls. Also postures with bill pointed straight up, especially when threatening another bird. Several males may display together. Both males and females often promiscuous. **Nest:** Site is usually near water: in cattails, sawgrass, or bulrushes, in bushes or saplings at edge of marsh, or in taller trees. Generally less than 12 feet above ground or water, but can be much higher. Nest (built by female) is large, bulky cup of twigs, grass, weeds, bul-rushes, Spanish moss, or other available materials, often with mud added to base; lined with fine grass. **Eggs:** Usually 2–4, sometimes 1–5. Pale greenish blue, irregularly marked with brown, gray, and black. Incubation is by female only, about 13–15 days. **Young:** Fed by female only. Young leave the nest about 12–15 days after hatching.

MIGRATION
CONSERVATION STATUS Generally a permanent resident, but a few northern breeders may move south in fall. Very common within its range; has extended its breeding range northward on At-lantic coast in recent decades.

COMMON GRACKLE *Quiscalus quiscula*

Throughout the east and midwest, this big blackbird is a very familiar species on suburban lawns, striding about deliberately as it searches for insects. Common Grackles often nest in small colonies, and several males may perch in adjacent treetops to sing their creaking, grating songs. Big flocks are often seen flying over-head in the evening, heading for major communal roosts, especially from late summer through winter.

HABITAT *Farmland, towns, groves, streamsides.* Common in many kinds of open or semi-open country. Often forages in farm fields, pastures, suburban lawns, feedlots, marshes. Nests and roosts in places with dense trees (especially conifers) close to open areas, as in groves, woodland edges, parks.

FEEDING **Diet:** *Omnivorous.* Feeds on insects, including beetle grubs, grasshoppers, caterpillars, many others; also spiders, millipedes, earthworms, and such diverse items as crayfish, minnows, frogs, lizards, eggs and young of other birds, and small rodents. Vegetable matter also important in diet, may be majority in winter; includes berries, seeds, waste grain, acorns. **Behavior:** Forages mostly by walking on ground or wading in very shallow water; also up in trees and shrubs. When not nesting, usually forages in flocks. Sometimes steals food from Robins or other birds. Has been seen killing an adult House Sparrow.

Common Grackle

Will come to feeders for various items. May soak dry bread crumbs in water before eating them.

NESTING   Typically nests in small colonies of 10–30 pairs, sometimes to 100 or more. In courtship, male fluffs out body feathers, partly spreads wings and tail, and gives short scraping song; also postures with bill pointing straight up. **Nest:** Site is often well hidden among branches of dense tree or shrubs near water, less than 20 feet above ground; sometimes much higher, or very low in marsh growth. Unusual sites include hole in tree or hollow stump, in lower part of active Osprey nest, or inside old building. Nest (built by female) is bulky open cup of weeds, grass, twigs, usually with some mud added; inside lined with fine grass. **Eggs:** 4–5, sometimes 2–6. Pale blue, blotched with brown. Incubation is by female only, 12–14 days. **Young:** Both parents feed nestlings, bringing them mostly insects. Young leave the nest about 16–20 days after hatching. One brood per year, sometimes two.

MIGRATION   Migrates in flocks. Present all year in much of range. In the north, migration is quite early in spring and fairly late in fall.

CONSERVATION STATUS   Widespread and very common, and has been expanding its range to the west in recent decades.

Cowbirds — genus *Molothrus*

The main claim to fame of the cowbirds is a negative one: they are brood parasites, laying their eggs in the nests of other birds and leaving their unwitting "hosts" to incubate the eggs and raise the young. In places where cowbirds have become very common (especially where clearing of forest has fostered their spread), they may seriously hurt the populations of some other songbirds.

Not all of the five species in this genus are parasitic. In South America, the Bay-winged Cowbird raises its own young, although it may take over nests built by other birds to do so. The Screaming Cowbird is a specialized parasite, laying its eggs in the nests of Bay-winged Cowbirds! At the other extreme is our Brown-headed Cowbird, known to have parasitized over 220 species of birds.

Cowbirds travel in flocks at most seasons. The group name comes from the habit of some species of associating with cattle, horses, or other livestock in pastures, catching the insects that are flushed from the grass by the grazing animals.

SHINY COWBIRD *Molothrus bonariensis*

Originally native to South America, this little blackbird spread gradually through the West Indies in recent decades, island-hopping north through the Lesser Antilles and then west toward Cuba. It arrived in Florida in 1985 and has become locally common there, with some seen elsewhere in the southeast. Like other cowbirds, this species is a parasite, so its arrival in our area was not welcomed by conservationists.

HABITAT
Semi-open country. In North America, found mostly near the coast, often foraging on extensive lawns. In the tropics, found in any kind of open or semi-open terrain, mostly in the lowlands.

FEEDING
Diet: *Mostly seeds and insects.* Diet in North America has not been studied. In the tropics, feeds on insects and other arthropods, and many seeds. **Behavior:** Forages mostly by walking on the ground in open areas. Often forages in small flocks, and

Shiny Cowbird

may associate with other kinds of cowbirds or other blackbirds. In the tropics, will feed in association with horses or cattle in pastures.

NESTING A brood parasite, never raising its own young. Early in breeding season, males sing to attract females. A male singing to a female on the ground may take off and fly in a wide circle around her with fluttering wingbeats. **Nest:** Builds no nest of its own; lays its eggs in nests of other birds. **Eggs:** Quite variable in color: may be unmarked white or have gray dots, large red spots, dark lines, brown blotches, or rarely can be all dark red. Number of eggs laid by a female in one season is unknown, but may be many. Female sometimes punctures eggs already in a nest before she lays her own. In South America, parasitizes nests of many species. May specialize in other areas: in Puerto Rico, mostly parasitizes Yellow-shouldered Blackbird. **Young:** Cowbird nestling is fed by "host" parents and develops rapidly, probably leaving nest after about 10–12 days.

MIGRATION
Pattern of migration within North America still poorly known. In some recent years, numbers have been seen moving through southern Florida in spring, suggesting flocks arriving from Caribbean. Strays have dispersed as far as Texas, Oklahoma, and Maine.

CONSERVATION STATUS
Impact of this parasite on North American birds remains to be seen. In Puerto Rico, has driven Yellow-shouldered Blackbird to endangered status.

BRONZED COWBIRD *Molothrus aeneus*

Larger than the Brown-headed Cowbird and mostly restricted to the southwest, this species is another brood parasite. It may be more specialized in its choice of "hosts" and is thought to have seriously affected populations of some species, such as Hooded Orioles in southern Texas. The Bronzed Cowbird has expanded its range in our area during the last century; in Arizona, where it is now common, it was unrecorded before 1909.

| HABITAT | *Farmland, brush, semi-open country, feedlots.* Outside the breeding season, generally in very open habitats in the lowlands, foraging in open fields and around cattle feedlots and roosting in brushy woods. In breeding season, wanders widely through many kinds of habitats including forest edge, desert, open woods in mountains. |

FEEDING **Diet:** *Seeds and insects.* Much of annual diet is seeds, including those of grasses and weeds, and waste grain. Occasionally eats berries. Also eats insects, including caterpillars, beetles, flies, and others, plus snails and spiders. While females are laying eggs, snails may be important as a source of calcium. **Behavior:** Forages mostly by walking on the ground in the open. May associate with cattle or horses in pastures, catching insects flushed from the grass by the grazing animals. Reportedly may sometimes take ticks or insects from backs of cattle.

Bronzed Cowbird

NESTING A brood parasite, never raising its own young. In courtship display on ground, male puffs out his feathers so that he appears almost round, spreads and lowers his tail, and points his bill down as he sings; in more intense version, he vibrates his wings and rises slowly a few feet in air, then slowly descends again. Both sexes are promiscuous, not forming pairs. **Nest:** Builds no nest; eggs are laid in nests of other birds. **Eggs:** Pale blue-green, unmarked. Number of eggs laid per female is unknown, but may be nearly one egg per day for up to several weeks. When laying eggs, female cowbird may pierce eggs already in nest. Frequent "hosts" for Bronzed Cowbirds include orioles, thrashers, towhees, many others, including smaller birds like warblers and gnatcatchers. **Young:** Nestling is fed by the "host" parents and develops rapidly, leaves nest 10–12 days after hatching.

MIGRATION Only a short-distance migrant, but becomes very uncommon and local in southwest in winter. Some stray eastward in winter along Gulf coast, reaching Florida almost regularly.

CONSERVATION STATUS Has greatly expanded its range and numbers north of Mexico during 20th century; undoubtedly having a negative impact on its "host" species in some areas.

BROWN-HEADED COWBIRD *Molothrus ater*

Centuries ago this bird probably followed bison herds on the Great Plains, feeding on insects flushed from the grass by the grazers. Today it follows cattle, and occurs abundantly from coast to coast. Its spread has been bad news for other songbirds: Cowbirds lay their eggs in nests of other birds. Heavy parasitism by cowbirds has pushed some species to "endangered" status and has probably hurt populations of some others.

HABITAT *Farms, fields, prairies, wood edges, river groves.* Favors open or semi-open country at all seasons. In winter often concentrates in farmland, pastures, or feedlots, where foraging is easy. More widespread in breeding season, in grassland, brushy country, forest edges, even desert, but tends to avoid dense unbroken forest.

FEEDING **Diet:** *Mostly seeds and insects.* Seeds (including those of grasses, weeds, and waste grain) make up about half of diet in summer and more than 90 percent in winter. Rest of diet is mostly insects, especially grasshoppers, beetles, and caterpillars, plus many others, also spiders and millipedes. **Behavior:** Forages mostly by walking on the ground. Often associates with cattle or horses in pastures, catching

Brown-headed Cowbird

the insects flushed from the grass by the grazing animals. Originally, was closely associated with bison herds on the Great Plains.

NESTING   A brood parasite, its eggs and young being cared for by other bird species. In breeding season, male displays by fluffing up body feathers, partly spreading wings and tail, and bowing deeply while singing. Groups of males sometimes perch together, singing and displaying. **Nest:** No nest built; eggs laid in nests of other birds. **Eggs:** Whitish with brown and gray spots concentrated at larger end. Female may lay nearly one egg per day for several weeks, up to 40 in a season, exceptionally 70 or more. Female often removes an egg from "host" nest before laying one of her own. Known to have laid eggs in nests of over 220 species of birds, and over 140 of those are known to have raised young cowbirds. **Young:** Fed by "host" parents. Develop rapidly and usually leave nest after 10–11 days.

MIGRATION   Present all year in many southern areas. Very widespread in nesting season, localized at other times. May begin to depart from nesting areas by August or even July.

CONSERVATION STATUS   Undoubtedly far more abundant and widespread today than it was originally, and having a negative impact on other species. Surveys suggest slight declines in total numbers in recent decades.

AMERICAN ORIOLES — GENUS *Icterus*

Colorful birds of the treetops, most orioles are patterned with black and yellow or orange. There are more than 25 species, the majority in the American tropics. Many of them have rich whistled songs, and most will supplement their main diet of insects with nectar from flowers. The Old World has yellow and black birds called orioles as well, but they are unrelated birds belonging to a different family.

BLACK-VENTED ORIOLE   *Icterus wagleri*

In Mexico and Central America, this large oriole lives mostly in dry forest or semi-open woods of the foothills and lower mountain slopes. It has wandered north into Texas and Arizona on only a few occasions, but some of these strays have remained for months.

ORCHARD ORIOLE   *Icterus spurius*

This small oriole is most common in the midwest and south. It favors open areas with scattered groves of trees, so human activities may have helped it in some areas, opening up the eastern woodlands and planting groves of trees on the prairies. Orchard Orioles often gather in flocks during migration. The black-throated, yellowish young male, sitting alone in a treetop and singing his jumbled song, is often confusing to beginning birders.

HABITAT   *Wood edges, orchards, shade trees.* Breeds in semi-open habitats with deciduous trees and open space, including riverside trees, orchards, suburbs, forest edges and clearings, prairie groves. Usually avoids unbroken forest. Winters in brushy areas and woodland edges in lowlands of the tropics.

Diet: *Mostly insects, some berries and nectar.* Diet in summer is mostly insects, especially caterpillars, beetles, and grasshoppers, plus many others, also spiders. Eats some berries, perhaps more in fall and winter. Often feeds on nectar and may eat parts of flowers. **Behavior:** Forages mostly by searching for insects among the foliage of trees and bushes. Regularly visits flowers, probing in the blossoms with its bill. In winter in the tropics, often forages in flocks.

Orchard Oriole

NESTING Male sings in spring to attract a mate. Often not strongly territorial; in some cases, more than one pair may nest in the same tree. Also sometimes nests in the same tree with Eastern Kingbirds. **Nest:** Site is in tree (usually deciduous) or tall shrub, rarely in tall dense marsh growth. Often 10–20 feet above ground, can be much lower or higher (3–70 feet up); typically placed in fork of horizontal branch, sometimes in clump of Spanish moss or other site. Nest (built by female, possibly with help from male) is a hanging pouch or basket, not as deep as some oriole nests, woven of grass and plant fibers, lined with fine grass and plant down. **Eggs:** 4–5, sometimes 3–7. Pale bluish white, blotched with brown, gray, purple. Incubation is probably mostly or entirely by the female, about 12–15 days; reportedly, the male may feed the female during incubation. **Young:** Both parents feed the nestlings. Young leave the nest about 11–14 days after hatching, may remain with one or both parents for several weeks. One brood per year.

MIGRATION Migrates in flocks; many move north across the Gulf of Mexico in spring. Fall migration begins very early, with some southbound by late July.

CONSERVATION STATUS In recent decades, has decreased in many parts of range, but has increased in some regions, such as northern Great Plains.

HOODED ORIOLE *Icterus cucullatus*

Hooded Oriole

In the hot lowlands of the southwest, this slim oriole is often common in the trees along streams and in suburbs. It is especially likely to be seen around palms, frequently attaching its hanging nest to the underside of a palm frond. In yards and gardens it often visits hummingbird feeders to drink sugar-water. The jumbled, musical song of the male sometimes includes imitations of other birds.

HABITAT *Open woods, shade trees, palms.* Breeds in groves of trees (such as cottonwood, walnut, sycamore) along streams and in canyons, and in open woods in lowlands. Often common in suburbs and city parks. Especially favors palm trees, and will nest in isolated groups of palms even in cities.

FEEDING **Diet:** *Includes insects, berries, nectar.* Feeds on a variety of insects. May especially favor caterpillars, also eats beetles, wasps, ants, and many others. Feeds on many wild berries and sometimes on cultivated fruit. Takes nectar from flowers and will come to feeders to drink sugar-water. **Behavior:** Forages rather slowly and deliberately in trees and large shrubs, gleaning insects from

among foliage or feeding on berries. Regularly probes in flowers for nectar and probably takes insects there as well. A common visitor to hummingbird feeders.

NESTING   In courtship, male moves around female, posturing with deep bows and then pointing bill straight up while singing softly. Female may respond with similar posturing. **Nest:** Often placed in palm or large yucca, sewn to underside of large overhanging leaf; usually 10–50 feet above ground but can be lower. Sometimes placed under banana leaf, in clump of mistletoe or Spanish moss, or suspended from branch of deciduous tree. Nest is a woven hanging pouch of grass and plant fibers, lined with plant down, hair, feathers. Female builds nest, but male may help bring material. **Eggs:** 4, sometimes 3–5. Whitish, irregularly blotched with brown, lavender, and gray. Incubation is by female, about 12–14 days. Bronzed Cowbirds very frequently lay eggs in nests of this species. **Young:** Fed by both parents. Leave nest about 14 days after hatching. Two broods per year, sometimes three.

MIGRATION   Most in our area are migratory, but a few remain through winter, especially where sugar-water feeders are provided. An early migrant in both spring and fall, with many arriving in March and departing in August.

CONSERVATION STATUS   Declined sharply in southern Texas in recent decades, perhaps because of cowbird parasitism. May be making a slight comeback in that area. Still fairly common farther west.

STREAK-BACKED ORIOLE   *Icterus pustulatus*

Dry tropical forests from northwestern Mexico to Costa Rica are the usual haunts of this colorful oriole. The bird is a rare stray into the southwest, mostly southern Arizona and southern California. Most records in the past were for fall and winter, but recently a couple of pairs have stayed through the summer and have even nested in Arizona.

SPOT-BREASTED ORIOLE   *Icterus pectoralis*

Native to southwestern Mexico and Central America and sometimes kept as a cagebird, this large oriole apparently escaped from captivity in the Miami area in the late 1940s. The suburbs of southern Florida, with their gardens of exotic plants, provided a suitable habitat for some tropical birds, so the Spot-breasted Oriole thrived there. Its numbers have been hurt occasionally by exceptionally cold winters, but it is currently doing well in some areas between Miami and West Palm Beach.

HABITAT   *Tall trees, suburbs.* In our area, found only in suburbs of southern Florida, in neighborhoods with many exotic trees and shrubs bearing berries and flowers at all seasons. In native range in the tropics, found mostly in dry woods, thorn scrub, trees along rivers, trees in towns.

FEEDING   **Diet:** *Includes berries, nectar, insects.* Diet has not been studied in detail, but includes many berries and small fruits, also some cultivated fruit. Takes nectar from flowers, and may eat parts of the flowers as well. Also eats many insects. **Behavior:** Forages mostly by moving rather slowly and deliberately among branches and foliage of trees. Often visits flowers; may use its bill to break off long blossoms to get at nectar at the base.

NESTING   In spring, male sings rich, whistled song to defend nesting territory; female may sing at times also. **Nest:** Placed in tree, near end of slender branch and often well above ground (in the tropics, may also nest in yuccas or other low plants). Nest (apparently built by female) is long hanging pouch woven of grass, palm fibers, and other plant fibers, its rim firmly attached to branch and the rest hanging free. **Eggs:** Probably about 2–5. Whitish to pale blue, marked with brown and black. Incubation is probably by female, but incubation behavior and timing are not well known. **Young:** Both parents bring food to the nestlings. Age at which the young leave the nest is not well known. Young may stay with parents for some time after fledging.

MIGRATION Apparently a permanent resident throughout its tropical range; introduced population in Florida is also resident.

CONSERVATION STATUS Seems not to have competed seriously with any native birds in our area. Numbers in Florida declined sharply after cold winters in late 1970s and early 1980s but have partly recovered.

ALTAMIRA ORIOLE *Icterus gularis*

Altamira Oriole

This big tropical oriole is common in northeastern Mexico but was not found in our area until 1939. It has since become common year-round in native woods of far southern Texas. It may go unseen at times as it forages in dense trees, but it draws attention with its harsh fussing call notes. Even before the bird is heard or seen, an observer may notice its oversized nest, a pouch up to 2 feet long hanging from the end of a branch.

HABITAT *Open tropical woodland and edges.* In our area, resident mostly in native woodland near Rio Grande in southern Texas. Farther south in Mexico and Central America, widespread in lowlands and lower foothills in open dry woods, forest edges, streamside groves, scattered trees in open country; usually avoids unbroken humid forest.

FEEDING **Diet:** *Mostly insects and berries.* Diet is not known in detail; feeds on many insects, especially grasshoppers, crickets, and caterpillars, also ants and many others, plus spiders. Also feeds on ber-ries and small fruits, including those of hackberries and figs. **Behavior:** Forages rather slowly and deliberately in trees, mostly high but also in low undergrowth, searching for insects. Will come to feeders for sugar-water and sometimes for other items.

NESTING In Texas, breeds mostly from late April to late July. **Nest:** Placed quite conspicuously out at the end of a horizontal branch of a tree, averages about 30 feet up, can be 10–80 feet above the ground. In the tropics, nest may be suspended from telephone wires. Nest is a very long hanging bag or pouch with entrance at the top, up to 2 feet long; woven of Spanish moss, grass, palm fibers, weeds, strips of bark, lined with plant down, hair, or feathers. Probably built by female; the process may take 3 weeks or more. **Eggs:** 4–6, or fewer in southern part of range. Pale bluish white, blotched with black and lavender. Incubation behavior poorly known, probably lasts about 2 weeks. **Young:** Both parents feed nestlings. Age at which young leave the nest is not well known.

MIGRATION Permanent resident throughout its range.

CONSERVATION STATUS Has become more common in Texas in last half-century. Farther south, remains widespread and common. Perhaps less affected by cowbird parasitism than some orioles.

AUDUBON'S ORIOLE *Icterus graduacauda*

In native woodlands and brushy country of far southern Texas, this large oriole is an uncommon resident. Members of a pair may stay together all year and often forage together in the woods, but they can be hard to see; slow-moving, quiet, and rather

secretive, they often stay low in dense cover. Audubon's Orioles may be noticed first by their hesitant slow whistles from deep in the thickets.

HABITAT *Woodlands, thickets.* In our area, found in southern Texas in native woods near Rio Grande, also locally farther north in mesquite brushland and groves of live oak. In Mexico, often in foothills, in humid oak forest or in pine-oak woodland.

FEEDING **Diet:** *Mostly insects and berries.* Diet is not known in detail but includes a variety of insects; also eats various berries, including those of hackberry. Sometimes takes nectar. **Behavior:** Forages rather quietly and deliberately in trees and shrubs, often staying within dense cover as it searches among the foliage for insects. Sometimes forages on the ground. Will visit flowers for nectar.

NESTING Nesting behavior is not well known. Pairs may remain together on territory throughout the year. In Texas, most nesting activity is from late April through June. Nests are often parasitized by Bronzed Cowbirds. **Nest:** Site is in outer branches of a low tree, often a mesquite, 5–15 feet above the ground and firmly attached to upright twigs. Sometimes placed in a clump of Spanish moss. Nest is a hanging pouch or basket, not as deep as some oriole nests, with the rim firmly woven to the supporting twigs and the entrance somewhat constricted. Nest is made of long grass stems, woven while they are still green, lined with finer grass. **Eggs:** 3–5. Pale grayish to bluish white, with brown and purple markings usually concentrated at larger end. Details of incubation are not well known. **Young:** Probably both parents feed the young, but details are poorly known.

MIGRATION Apparently a permanent resident throughout its range.

CONSERVATION STATUS Numbers in southern Texas apparently have declined during recent decades. Parasitism of nests by cowbirds may have played a part in this decrease.

Audubon's Oriole

BALTIMORE ORIOLE *Icterus galbula*

Baltimore Oriole

One of the most brilliantly colored songbirds in the east, flaming orange and black, sharing the heraldic colors of the coat of arms of 17th-century Lord Baltimore. Widespread east of the Great Plains, Baltimore Orioles are often very common in open woods and groves in summer. Their bag-shaped hanging nests, artfully woven of plant fibers, are familiar sights in the shade trees in towns. This bird was formerly considered to belong to the same species as the western Bullock's Oriole, under the combined name of "Northern Oriole."

HABITAT *Open woods, riverside groves, elms, shade trees.* Breeds in deciduous or mixed woodland, generally in open woods or edges rather than interior of dense forest. May be common in trees in towns. Often favors elms. Winters mostly in the tropics around forest edge and semi-open country.

FEEDING **Diet:** *Insects, berries, nectar.* In summer, feeds mostly on insects, especially caterpillars, including hairy types avoided by many birds; also eats beetles, grasshoppers,

wasps, bugs, and others, plus spiders and snails. Eats many berries and sometimes cultivated fruit. Feeds on nectar and will take sugar-water. **Behavior:** Forages by searching for insects among foliage of trees and shrubs. Sometimes flies out to catch insects in midair. Visits flowers for nectar, and will come to sugar-water feeders; also will come to pieces of fruit put out at feeders.

NESTING   Male sings to defend nesting territory. In courtship, male faces female and stretches upright, then bows deeply with tail spread and wings partly open. **Nest:** Site is in tall deciduous tree, placed near end of slender drooping branch, usually 20–30 feet above the ground but can be 6–60 feet up or higher. Nest (built by female, sometimes with help from male) is a hanging pouch with its rim firmly attached to a branch; tightly woven of plant fibers, strips of bark, grapevines, grass, yarn, string, Spanish moss, lined with fine grass, plant down, hair. **Eggs:** 4–5, sometimes 3–6. Bluish white to pale gray, with brown and black markings concentrated at larger end. Incubation is by female, about 12–14 days. **Young:** Both parents feed the nestlings. Young leave nest about 12–14 days after hatching.

MIGRATION   Migrates in flocks. Fall migration begins early, with many birds departing in July and August. Small numbers may winter in southeast.

BULLOCK'S ORIOLE   *Icterus bullockii*

Common and widespread in the west, this oriole is found in summer in forest edges, isolated groves, and streamside woods, especially in cottonwood trees. For several years it was considered to belong to the same species as the eastern Baltimore Oriole because the two often interbreed where their ranges come in contact on the western Great Plains. The habits of the two are apparently similar, although the nest of the Bullock's Oriole tends to be less deep than that of the Baltimore Oriole. A few Bullock's Orioles stray eastward every year, sometimes even reaching New England. They may be regular in very small numbers during the winter in Florida and perhaps elsewhere in the southeast.

SCOTT'S ORIOLE   *Icterus parisorum*

Scott's Oriole

The rich, melodious whistles of the Scott's Oriole carry well across the slopes of the western foothills and valleys where it spends the summer. This bird occupies a variety of southwestern habitats, from dense oak woods of the lower canyons to open grassland with scattered yuccas, often placing its nest in a yucca and using the long fibers of this plant in nest construction. Scott's Orioles tend to be uncommon, and unlike some orioles, they are seldom seen in flocks.

HABITAT   *Dry woods and scrub in desert mountains, yuccas, Joshua-trees, pinyons.* Breeds in semi-arid zones of southwest in oak zones of lower canyons, open woods of juniper and pinyon pine, stands of Joshua-trees, grassland with many yuccas, palm oases. Avoids true desert.

FEEDING   **Diet:** *Mostly insects, some berries and nectar.* Feeds on a wide variety of insects, including grasshoppers, beetles, caterpillars, and many others. Also eats berries and fruit, including cactus fruit; may feed on cultivated fruit at times. Also feeds on nectar and

will take sugar-water from feeders. **Behavior:** Forages rather slowly and quietly in tree-tops, clambering along branches as it searches for insects. Regularly visits flowers, probing the blossoms deeply for nectar.

NESTING   Males arrive on breeding grounds a few days before females and sing frequently to establish nesting territory. **Nest:** Often placed in yucca, or in Joshua-tree (a tall, branched type of yucca). Also may be in palm or tree such as sycamore, oak, or pine. Usually 4–20 feet above ground. Nest in tree may be hidden in clump of mis-tletoe. Nest (probably built by female) is a hanging basket suspended by its edges, not as deep as the nests of some orioles; woven of grasses, yucca fibers, other plant fibers, lined with fine grass, hair, and plant down. **Eggs:** 2–4, usually 3. Pale bluish white, with dots and lines of brown, gray, and black concentrated at larger end. Incubation is by female, 12–14 days. **Young:** Both parents feed nestlings. Young leave the nest about 2 weeks after hatching. One or two broods per year.

MIGRATION   Migrates rather early in both spring and fall, arriving on nesting grounds in March or April, mostly departing in July and August. Small numbers winter in southern Arizona and California.

CONSERVATION STATUS   Numbers probably stable in most areas. Has expanded breeding range into western Colorado since 1970s.

FINCHES (Family Fringillidae)

The 130-plus members of this family are widespread on five continents but absent from the Australian region except for introduced colonies. All are medium-sized to very small songbirds, and most of them feed mainly on seeds. Most species are quite sociable, gathering in flocks when they are not nesting.

Included in this family are the birds known in North America as "winter finches." These birds breed in the far north and sometimes move well to the south in winter. Such "invasions" are irregular and unpredictable and are probably caused by a failure of the wild food crops in the boreal zones where the birds live. Apparently they are not driven south by cold, since they will remain far north in the coldest winters as long as they have enough food.

When the "winter finches" do move south, they are favorite visitors at bird feeders outside our windows. Many people have a member of this group inside the window as well: the wild ancestor of the Canary belongs to this family. Canaries sold in pet stores are all raised by breeders, but popularity with pet owners has been bad news for some other finches. For example, the Red Siskin of South America is now probably endangered because so many have been captured for the cagebird trade.

Feeding   Members of this family are the greatest vegetarians among North American songbirds. We have many other birds that eat seeds, such as our native sparrows, but those birds also eat many insects in summer, and most of them feed insects to their young (a great source of protein for growing bodies). By contrast, many of the finches continue to eat mostly seeds, buds, and other vegetable matter even when insects are abundant. Several kinds even feed their young on a mash of regurgitated food that is mostly seeds.

While sparrows and buntings usually search for seeds on the ground, the finches are often more acrobatic and will clamber about in trees and bushes and on weed stalks to pluck the seeds before they fall. Most kinds of finches regularly forage in flocks.

Nesting   Some members of this family are flexible in the timing of their nesting season, raising broods at various times of year if food supplies are good. Nest sites vary; usually they are well hidden in shrubs or trees, but rosy-finches nest in crevices in cliffs. The nest, in the shape of an open cup, is usually built by the female. Generally, incubation is by the female only, but in many species, the male feeds her often during the incubation period. Both parents usually feed the young.

Displays Among many finches, the courtship displays of the males involve singing in flight, often circling flight near the female. While perched, one or both members of a pair may posture or bow, with wings drooped or vibrating. In many species, the male feeds the female in courtship.

GENUS *Fringilla*

COMMON CHAFFINCH *Fringilla coelebs*

In Europe and western Asia, this colorful finch is common and widespread. Quite migratory in the northern part of its range, it may stray across the Atlantic at times. Several individuals have been found in New England and eastern Canada (although some have suggested that these birds might be escaped from captivity).

BRAMBLING *Fringilla montifringilla*

A common finch of Europe and Asia, the Brambling appears regularly in small numbers in Alaska during migration, straying the short distance across the Bering Sea. Some of those that stray across in autumn apparently then continue south on the American side, and there have been winter records for numerous states and provinces east to the Atlantic coast and south to Colorado. Many of these vagrant Bramblings have been found visiting bird feeders.

ROSY-FINCHES — GENUS *Leucosticte*

Rosy-finches are "refrigerator birds," living on cold barren tundra of the Arctic and alpine zones. In the high mountains they often feed around snowfields; there they find frozen insects and seeds revealed by snowmelt or pick up insects that have been carried to the heights by updrafts and then have fallen chilled on the snow. During the breeding season, adults develop throat pouches which allow them to carry more food for the young at one time. Except when nesting, they usually forage in flocks.

The distribution of the rosy-finches on isolated mountaintops and islands has allowed many local forms to evolve. Some scientists believe that the three kinds listed here should all be considered part of one variable species.

GRAY-CROWNED ROSY-FINCH *Leucosticte tephrocotis*

The most widespread of our three species of rosy-finches, the Gray-crown nests from the islands of western Alaska south to the high mountains of California and northern Montana. Different populations are variable in size and in the amount of gray on the heads of the males.

HABITAT *Barren tundra, alpine snowfields, rocky islands (off Alaska); winters in open country.* Breeds in barren rocky tundra of high mountains and Alaskan islands; mountain birds often are associated with snowfields. Winters in similar habitats, also in mountain valleys, open plains, towns.

FEEDING **Diet:** *Mostly seeds and insects.* Feeds mainly on seeds of grasses and weeds, especially in winter, when these may make up virtually entire diet. Also eats some buds and leaves, and eats many insects in summer. Young are fed mostly insects.

Gray-crowned Rosy-Finch

Will eat salt. **Behavior:** Forages mostly on ground or on snow. Sometimes flies up to catch insects in midair.

NESTING   One courtship display may involve male facing female, half-spreading and lowering his wings and then raising and lowering them slowly. **Nest:** Typically placed in a niche among boulders, under a rock, or in a crevice in a cliff, sometimes in a hole in a building. Nest (built by female) is a rather bulky cup of grass, rootlets, lichens, moss, lined with fine grass and sometimes with feathers and animal hair. **Eggs:** 4–5, sometimes 3–6. May tend to lay more eggs in some Alaskan populations. Eggs white, rarely with a few reddish brown dots. Incubation is by female only, probably about 14 days. **Young:** Both parents feed the nestlings. Young probably leave the nest about 14–15 days after hatching, but this may vary among populations. One brood per year in mountains, often two among Alaskan island birds.

MIGRATION   Those on the Aleutian and Pribilof islands in Alaska are permanent residents. Mountain populations farther south may move to lower elevations in winter; sometimes stray eastward, well out onto plains.

CONSERVATION STATUS   Fairly widespread and common, numbers probably stable. Most of its breeding range is remote from impact of human disturbance.

BLACK ROSY-FINCH   *Leucosticte atrata*

Black Rosy-Finch

High mountains of the northern Great Basin region, from northeastern Nevada to southwestern Montana, are the stronghold of this uncommon bird. Black Rosy-Finches spend the summer around the snowfields and barren tundra of the rocky crags, where few birders venture. In winter, however, flocks come down into the high valleys. The striking males, their black plumage contrasting with touches of pale rose, make a beautiful spectacle against the snow.

HABITAT   *Rocky summits, alpine snowfields and tundra; winters in open country at lower levels.* Breeds on barren tundra of mountain peaks, mostly in rocky areas and often near persistent snowfields. Winters in open country of mountains and nearby valleys, often coming into towns.

FEEDING   Diet and feeding behaviors are very similar to those of Gray-crowned Rosy-Finch.

NESTING   Males apparently outnumber females, and during the breeding season a male who has a mate usually attends her closely to keep rival males away. **Nest:** Located in a well-protected site in a crevice or hole in a cliff, usually in an inaccessible place; sometimes in a niche among boulders of a rockslide. Nest (built by female) is a bulky open cup of grass and moss, lined with fine grass, animal hair, and sometimes feathers. **Eggs:** 4–5, sometimes 3. White, unmarked. Incubation is by female only, about 12–14 days. **Young:** Both parents feed the nestlings, although the female may do most of it at first. Young probably leave the nest about 20 days after hatching, are fed by their parents for at least another 2 weeks. One brood per year.

MIGRATION   Most apparently move downhill in late fall, with flocks appearing in high valleys and plateaus in winter, including areas some distance to south of breeding range.

CONSERVATION STATUS   Rather uncommon and local, but numbers probably stable. Remote nesting habitat faces few threats.

BROWN-CAPPED ROSY-FINCH   *Leucosticte australis*

Brown-capped Rosy-Finch

Rosy-finches in general are birds of the Arctic and alpine zones, but this one inhabits the high peaks of the Rockies from Wyoming south to New Mexico. Even where highways take the observer to areas above tree-line, this species can be elusive in summer, seeming to favor the most remote and barren cliffs and isolated snowfields. In winter, when the birds move to lower elevations, they are often much easier to find, even coming to feeders in valley towns.

HABITAT   Very much like that of Black Rosy-Finch.

FEEDING   Diet and feeding behavior are very similar to those of Gray-crowned Rosy-Finch.

NESTING   At high elevations where this bird nests, snow may cover nesting sites until late June in some years. Birds may be already paired when they arrive at breeding areas. **Nest:** Site is in a crevice or hole in a cliff, sometimes a very narrow crevice where the nest is quite inaccessible; sometimes under a rock, in mine shaft, or in abandoned building. Nest (built by female) is a bulky cup of moss, grass, weeds, rootlets, lined with fine grass and sometimes with feathers or animal fur. **Eggs:** 3–5. White, unmarked. Incubation is by female only, about 12–14 days. **Young:** Both parents feed the nestlings. Young leave the nest about 18 days after hatching and may remain with parents through end of summer and into the fall. One brood per year.

MIGRATION   Moves to lower elevations in autumn and winter, tending to move farther downhill in winters of heavier snowfall. Migration is all altitudinal; the bird does not seem to move south of breeding range.

GENUS *Pinicola*

PINE GROSBEAK   *Pinicola enucleator*

A big boreal finch, uncommon but widespread in spruce and fir forests of the north and the high mountains. It is often absurdly tame, allowing very close approach; ironically, this sometimes makes it easy to overlook in dense coniferous forest, since it may sit motionless as a birder walks by. On those occasions when Pine Grosbeaks move south in winter, they may be more conspicuous, often feeding on buds in the bare branches of maples or other trees.

HABITAT   *Conifers; in winter, other trees.* Breeds in open coniferous forest, especially of spruce and fir; despite the name, not usually in pines in summer. In winter often found in deciduous trees (especially fruiting trees such as mountain-ash or crabapple), also in groves of pines and other conifers.

Pine Grosbeak

FEEDING   **Diet:** *Seeds, buds, berries, insects.* Feeds mostly on vegetable matter, especially in winter. Major items include the seeds of conifers and other trees, buds of many kinds of trees (such as maples), berries, wild fruits (including crab apples), sometimes seeds of weeds and grasses. Also eats some insects, mainly in summer. Will come to feeders for sunflower seeds and other items. **Behavior:** Forages mostly up in trees and shrubs. Tends to be very methodical in feeding, moving about slowly in trees while feeding on buds, seeds, and fruits. Except during the nesting season, often forages in small flocks.

NESTING   Male sings a mellow continuous warble to defend nesting territory. In courtship, male feeds female. **Nest:** Placed on horizontal branch or in fork of conifer such as spruce or fir, usually 5–15 feet above ground, sometimes as low as 2 feet in deciduous shrub or up to 25 feet high in tree. Nest is a bulky open cup of twigs, weeds, rootlets, lined with fine grass, more rootlets, lichens, moss. **Eggs:** 2–5, usually 4. Bluish green, spotted with brown, purple, and black. Incubation is by female only, about 13–14 days. Male often feeds female during incubation. **Young:** Both parents feed nestlings; during breeding season, both sexes develop throat pouches that allow them to carry more food at once. Young leave the nest about 2–3 weeks after hatching. One brood per year.

MIGRATION   Permanent resident in many areas; may withdraw from northernmost part of breeding range. Sometimes stages small "invasions" southward in winter, probably when food supplies fail in the far north.

RED FINCHES — GENUS *Carpodacus*

This genus includes three species in North America and about 18 in Europe and Asia, with the greatest variety in the Himalayas. Males are marked with red, at least around the head and chest, and females are generally brown. When not nesting, they usually gather in flocks.

COMMON ROSEFINCH   *Carpodacus erythrinus*

A counterpart to our House Finch, this bird is very common in Asia and parts of eastern Europe, inhabiting semi-open country and brushy places. It is a rare spring visitor to the islands of western Alaska, sometimes appearing in small flocks.

PURPLE FINCH   *Carpodacus purpureus*

The male Purple Finch is not really purple but more of an old-rose color. This species is common in the north and east and along the Pacific seaboard, but it is very rare in much of the Rocky Mountain region. Purple Finches feed up in trees and on the ground in open woods. They readily come to bird feeders; but they have become less numerous as feeder visitors in the northeast, where competition with introduced House Sparrows and then House Finches may have driven them back into the woods.

HABITAT   *Woods, groves, suburbs.* Breeds mostly in coniferous and mixed woods, both in forest interior and along edges. In Pacific states, also breeds in oak woodland and streamside trees. In migration and winter, found in a wide variety of wooded and semi-open areas including forest, suburbs, swamps, and overgrown fields.

Purple Finch

FEEDING **Diet:** *Seeds, buds, berries, insects.* Feeds mainly on seeds in winter, including seeds of trees such as ash and elm, as well as weed and grass seeds. Also eats buds of many trees and many berries and small fruits. Eats some insects such as caterpillars and beetles, mainly in summer. Young may be fed mostly on seeds. **Behavior:** Forages for seeds and insects up in trees and shrubs, also in low weeds and sometimes on the ground. When not nesting, may forage in small flocks. Comes to bird feeders.

NESTING In courtship, male hops near female with his wings drooping, tail raised, chest puffed out, then vibrates wings until he rises a short distance in the air. May hold bits of nest material in bill and give soft song during this performance. **Nest:** Placed on horizontal branch or fork of tree (usually conifer in east, deciduous trees often used in far west), often well out from trunk. Typically about 15–20 feet above ground but may be lower or up to 50 feet high. Nest (probably built mostly by female) is compact open cup of twigs, weeds, rootlets, strips of bark, lined with fine grass, moss, animal hair. **Eggs:** 3–5, sometimes 2–7. Pale greenish blue, marked with black and brown. Incubation is by female, about 13 days. **Young:** Both parents feed the nestlings. Young leave nest about 2 weeks after hatching. One brood per year, sometimes two, perhaps rarely three.

MIGRATION Migrates in flocks, mostly traveling by day. Migration is spread over a considerable period in both spring and fall.

CONSERVATION STATUS Probably decreased in northeast in late 19th century after introduction of House Sparrow. In recent decades has declined further in that area, possibly because of competition with House Finch.

CASSIN'S FINCH *Carpodacus cassinii*

Like a slightly larger, longer-billed version of the Purple Finch, Cassin's Finch is a resident of mountains and conifer forests of the west. It is sometimes found at very high elevations, in the scrubby forest just below treeline, especially in late summer. At other times, little roving flocks wander through the woods, often feeding on buds and seeds high in the trees. The complicated song of the male often includes brief imitations of other birds.

Cassin's Finch

HABITAT *Conifers in high mountains; lower levels in winter.* Breeds mostly in mountain forests of conifers, especially spruce and fir, also in pine and Douglas-fir in some areas and sometimes in pinyon-juniper woods. Often at very high elevations, near treeline in mountains. Winters in mountain forests of conifers, sometimes in open woods of lower valleys.

FEEDING **Diet:** *Mostly seeds, buds, berries.* Feeds mainly on vegetable material. Buds of various trees often staple items in diet, also eats seeds of many trees (especially conifers) and some weed seeds. Feeds on berries and small fruits when available. Also eats some insects, perhaps mainly in summer. **Behavior:** Does

much foraging up in trees, especially when ground is snow-covered; also feeds in weedy growth and on ground. Except when nesting, often forages in small flocks.

NESTING   Numbers breeding in an area often change from one year to the next, possibly in response to food supplies. May nest in small colonies. Male often does not defend much of a nesting territory, instead simply staying close to female and driving away rival males. **Nest:** Usually placed in large conifer, commonly about 30–40 feet above ground, may be as low as 10 feet or as high as 80 feet up; sometimes in aspen or other deciduous tree. Nest (probably built by female) is open cup made of twigs, weeds, rootlets, strips of bark, lined with fine grass, plant fibers, animal hair, sometimes decorated with lichens. **Eggs:** 4–5, sometimes 3–6. Bluish green, with brown and black spots often concentrated at larger end. Incubation is by female only, about 12–14 days. Male often feeds female during incubation. **Young:** Both parents feed nestlings. Young leave nest about 2 weeks after hatching, and parents and young may promptly leave nesting area.

MIGRATION   Somewhat nomadic, with numbers in a given locality often changing from year to year. Irregular in winter occurrence in lowlands, but sometimes wanders well out onto plains.

HOUSE FINCH   *Carpodacus mexicanus*

House Finch

Adaptable, colorful, and cheery-voiced, House Finches are common from coast to coast today, familiar visitors to backyard feeders. Native to the southwest, they are recent arrivals in the east. New York pet shop owners, who had been selling the finches illegally, released their birds in 1940 to escape prosecution; the finches survived, and began to colonize the New York suburbs. Fifty years later they had advanced halfway across the continent, meeting their western kin on the Great Plains.

HABITAT   *Cities, suburbs, farms, canyons.* Original habitat was probably streamside trees and brush in dry country, woodland edges, chaparral, other semi-open areas. Now most commonly associated with humans in cities, towns, and farmland, especially in areas with lawns, weedy areas, trees, buildings. Avoids unbroken forest or grassland.

FEEDING   **Diet:** *Mostly seeds, buds, berries.* Almost all of diet is vegetable matter. Feeds mainly on weed seeds. Other important items include buds and flower parts in spring, berries and small fruits in late summer and fall. Also eats a few insects, mostly small ones such as aphids. Young are fed on regurgitated seeds. **Behavior:** Forages on ground, while perching in weeds, or up in trees and shrubs. Except when nesting, usually forages in flocks. Will come to feeders for seeds, bread crumbs, and other items, and to hummingbird feeders for sugar-water.

NESTING   Pairs may begin to form within flocks in winter, and some paired birds may remain together all year. In breeding season, male performs flight-song display, singing while fluttering up with slow wingbeats and then gliding down. Male feeds female during courtship and incubation. Males may sing at any time of year, and females also sing during spring. **Nest:** Wide variety of sites, especially in conifers, palms, ivy on buildings, cactus, holes in man-made structures, averaging about 12–15 feet above ground. Sometimes uses sites such as cavities, hanging planters, old nests of other birds. Nest (built mostly by female) is open cup of grass, weeds, fine twigs, leaves, rootlets, sometimes with feathers, string, or other debris added. **Eggs:** 4–5, sometimes 2–6. Pale blue, with black and lavender dots mostly at larger end. Incubation is by female, about 13–14 days. **Young:** Both parents feed nestlings. Young leave the nest about 12–15 days after hatching. Up to three broods per year, perhaps sometimes more.

MIGRATION — Mostly permanent resident in west, although some may move to lower elevations for winter. In the east, some are permanent residents but others migrate long distances south in fall. Migrates in flocks, mostly by day.

CONSERVATION STATUS — Now abundant over much of North America. In some parts of east, may be competing with Purple Finches to the detriment of the latter.

CROSSBILLS — GENUS *Loxia*

The crossbills are best known for their odd bill shape, with the tips of the mandibles crossed, adapted for prying open evergreen cones to extract the seeds. The birds usually forage on cones still attached to the tree. Crossed bill tips are inserted between cone scales, then spread to pry them apart, and the tongue lifts the seeds out. Cone crops are unpredictable, so the birds wander widely in restless flocks, searching for food. Crossbills may be abundant in an area one year and absent the next, disappearing when the supply of fresh cones is depleted.

RED CROSSBILL   *Loxia curvirostra*

Red Crossbill

These stubby little nomads are often first detected by their hard *kip-kip* call notes as they fly overhead in evergreen woods. Red Crossbills in North America are quite variable, from small-billed birds that feed on spruce cones to large-billed ones that specialize on pines. Scientists have long puzzled over how to classify these different forms. New research suggests that there may be as many as eight different full species of Red Crossbills on this continent. Slight differences in call notes are apparently enough to keep them from mixing, and several kinds may occur in the same area without interbreeding.

HABITAT — *Conifer forests and groves.* Seldom found away from conifers. Depending on region of continent, may breed mainly in pines, or may be in spruce, hemlock, Douglas-fir, or other evergreens. Different races may favor different forest types. Wandering flocks may appear in plantings of conifers in parks or suburbs well away from usual range.

FEEDING — **Diet:** *Mostly seeds of conifers.* Seeds of pines and other conifers are favored foods whenever available. Also eats buds of various trees, seeds of weeds and deciduous trees, some berries, insects. Much attracted to salt. Young are fed regurgitated seeds. **Behavior:** Typically forages by clambering about over cones in evergreens. Forages in flocks. Different forms of Red Crossbill specialize on different kinds of conifers, with large-billed birds often choosing trees with larger cones.

NESTING — Timing and distribution of nesting are quite irregular, the birds often breeding when cone crops are best. In many regions, nesting is typically in winter or spring, but may be at practically any season (except perhaps in mid- to late fall). In courtship, male may perform flight-song display and may feed female. **Nest:** Placed on a horizontal branch in conifer, often well out from trunk, usually 10–40 feet above ground but can be lower or much higher. Nest (built by female) is a bulky open cup, loosely made of twigs, bark strips, grass, rootlets, wood chips, lined with fine grass, moss, lichens, feathers, hair. **Eggs:** 3–4, sometimes 5, rarely 2. Pale greenish white or bluish white, with brown and purple dots mostly concentrated at larger end. Incubation is by female, 12–15 days. Male feeds female during incubation. **Young:** Female spends much time brooding young at first, while male brings food for them and for her; later, both parents feed nestlings. Young leave nest about 18–20 days after hatching.

MIGRATION   No regular migration, but most populations are nomadic, moving about in response to changes in food supplies. Apparently does most traveling by day. Majority of southernmost records (and most lowland records in west) are during winter.

CONSERVATION STATUS   Although Red Crossbills as a group are widespread and common, some of the forms (or evident species) are localized, specialized, and vulnerable to the loss of their particular habitat.

WHITE-WINGED CROSSBILL   *Loxia leucoptera*

Nomads of the spruce woods, White-winged Crossbills wander throughout the boreal zones of the Northern Hemisphere, often in large flocks. Their peculiar crossed

bills are perfectly adapted for prying open spruce cones to get the seeds; flocks will travel long distances, perhaps clear across Canada at times, in search of good spruce cone crops. When they find such crops, they may settle briefly to build nests and raise young, regardless of the season, even in midwinter.

HABITAT   *Spruce forests, tamaracks.* Seldom found away from conifer forests. Breeds mainly in forests having high concentrations of spruce trees, also where tamaracks are common. When not nesting, may also occur in forest of pine, fir, hemlock, juniper, and occasionally in deciduous trees. Isolated race in Hispaniola, West Indies, lives in pine forest.

FEEDING   **Diet:** *Mostly conifer seeds.* Feeds mainly on spruce seeds whenever these are available; also favors seeds of tamarack and hemlock, and will eat

White-winged Crossbill

seeds of many other conifers. Also feeds on buds, weed seeds, berries, insects. Will eat salt. Young are fed mostly regurgitated seeds. **Behavior:** Forages mostly by clambering about in conifers to reach the cones. Usually forages in flocks.

NESTING   May nest whenever and wherever good cone crops are present in spruce forest, which may be at any time of year, including midwinter. Usually nests in loose colonies. In courtship, males may chase females in flight; members of pair may perch close together, touching bills, and male may feed female. **Nest:** Placed on horizontal limb of tree, usually spruce or other conifer, often 10–15 feet above ground, can be lower or much higher (up to 70 feet). Nest (built by female, with male occasionally bringing material) is open cup of twigs, weeds, grass, bark strips, lined with rootlets, lichens, moss, plant fibers, hair. **Eggs:** 2–4, rarely 5. Whitish to pale blue-green, with brown and lavender spots concentrated at larger end. Incubation is by female, probably 12–14 days. Male feeds female during incubation. **Young:**

Female spends much time brooding young at first, while male brings food; later, both parents feed nestlings. Age at which young leave the nest is not well known. Male may care for fledglings while female begins another nesting attempt.

MIGRATION   No regular migration, but flocks may travel long distances at any season in search of good cone crops. Apparently travels mostly by day. Although not yet proven, some birds might nest in Alaska one year and eastern Canada another.

CONSERVATION STATUS   Total population extremely difficult to monitor because of wandering. Numbers may build up when cone crops are good, gradually decline in between.

SMALL FINCHES — GENUS *Carduelis*

This group includes the goldfinches, siskins, redpolls, greenfinches, and others, mostly colorful birds and mostly very small. The 30-plus species in this genus are found mainly in the Northern Hemisphere, but South America also has about a dozen kinds. Most species have mainly vegetarian diets at all seasons.

COMMON REDPOLL   *Carduelis flammea*

Common Redpoll

One of the "winter finches," nesting in the Arctic and sometimes invading southern Canada and the northern states. Redpolls are tiny, restless birds, feeding actively on seeds among trees and weeds, fluttering and climbing about acrobatically, their flocks seemingly always on the move. For such a small bird, they have a remarkable ability to survive cold temperatures; their southward flights are sparked by temporary scarcity of food in the north, not by cold. At bird feeders in winter, redpolls are often remarkably tame.

HABITAT   *Birches, thickets, tundra scrub. In winter, weeds, brush.* Breeds in shrubby habitats of the north, including clearings in birch or spruce forest, thickets of willow, alder, or dwarf birch, bushy areas on tundra. Winters in various kinds of semi-open country, including woodland edges and brushy or weedy fields.

FEEDING   Diet: *Mostly seeds, some insects.* Diet for most of year is mostly seeds and other vegetable matter. Feeds on catkins, seeds, and buds of willows, alders, and birches, small conifer seeds, also seeds of many weeds and grasses. Also eats insects, mainly in summer. **Behavior:** Forages very actively in trees, shrubs, weeds, and on the ground. Except when nesting, usually forages in flocks. Has a pouch within throat where it can store some food for up to several hours; this helps the bird in bitterly cold weather, allowing it to feed rapidly in the open and then digest food over a long period while it rests in a sheltered spot.

NESTING   Males dominate females in winter flocks, but as breeding season approaches, females become dominant and may take the lead in courtship. Does not seem to defend much of a nesting territory; nests of different pairs may be close together. **Nest:** Usually very well hidden in dense low shrubs, within a few feet of the ground, sometimes in grass clumps or under brushpiles. Nest (probably built by female) is an open cup of fine twigs, grass, moss, lined with feathers (especially ptarmigan feathers), plant down, or animal hair. **Eggs:** 4–5, rarely up to 7. Pale green to blue-green, with purplish to reddish brown spots often concentrated at larger end. Incubation is by female only, about 10–11 days. Male feeds female during incubation. **Young:** Fed mostly by female; contribution by male varies. Young leave the nest about 12 days after hatching.

MIGRATION Migrates by day, in flocks. Very irregular in winter range, probably moving only as far south as necessary to find food.

HOARY REDPOLL *Carduelis hornemanni*

A very close relative of the Common Redpoll but adapted to even bleaker conditions, the Hoary Redpoll is only a scarce visitor south of the Arctic. In those winters when

large numbers of redpolls invade southward, a few Hoarys are usually mixed into the flocks. On the breeding grounds, this species extends farther north, onto high Arctic islands of Canada. Where the two redpolls overlap, the Hoary tends to nest on more barren upland tundra, where the patches of shrubs are fewer and smaller.

HABITAT *Thickets, tundra scrub. In winter, also woodland edges, fields.* Breeds in brushy places of far north, especially in low thickets of willow, alder, or dwarf birch on open tundra, sometimes along forest edge. Compared with Common Redpoll, tends to nest in more open or barren habitat. In winter, also found around woodland edges, brushy or weedy fields.

FEEDING Diet and feeding behavior very similar to those of Common Redpoll.

NESTING Does not seem to defend nesting

Hoary Redpoll

territories; several pairs may nest fairly close together, perhaps because good nesting sites tend to be concentrated in small patches surrounded by tundra. In courtship, male feeds female. **Nest:** Placed within a few feet of the ground in dense low shrubs, sometimes on the ground. Nest (built by female) is a small open cup of grass and plant down, sometimes with fine twigs, rootlets, leaves, lined with ptarmigan feathers and sometimes animal hair. **Eggs:** 4–5, sometimes 3–6, rarely 7. Pale green to blue-green, with reddish brown spots concentrated at larger end. Incubation is by female only, about 9–14 days. Male feeds female on nest during incubation. **Young:** Probably both parents feed the nestlings. Young leave the nest about 9–14 days after hatching.

MIGRATION Many apparently remain near Arctic Circle in winter, others moving south, typically only short distances. Apparently migrates by day, in flocks, sometimes mixed with Common Redpolls.

EURASIAN SISKIN *Carduelis spinus*

An Old World relative of our Pine Siskin and goldfinches, this little bird is common across northern Europe and Asia, gathering in active flocks to feed in weedy fields. It has strayed to the western Aleutians at least once; sightings in eastern Canada could refer either to escaped cagebirds or trans-Atlantic wanderers.

PINE SISKIN *Carduelis pinus*

Although it is patterned like a sparrow, its shape, actions, and call notes all reveal that this bird is really a goldfinch in disguise. After nesting in the conifer woods,

Pine Siskins move out into semi-open country, where they roam in twittering flocks. They often descend on fields of thistles or wild sunflowers, where they cling to the dried flower heads, eating seeds. In winter they sometimes invade southward in big numbers, with flocks coming to feeders along with American Goldfinches.

HABITAT   *Conifers, mixed woods, alders, weedy areas.* Breeds mostly in coniferous and mixed woods, often around edges or clearings; sometimes in deciduous woods, isolated conifer groves. In migration and winter occurs in many kinds of semi-open areas, woodland edges, weedy fields.

FEEDING   **Diet:** *Mostly seeds and other vegetable matter, some insects.* Feeds on seeds of alder, birch, spruce, and many other trees, also those of weeds and grasses; eats buds, flower parts, nectar, young shoots. Also feeds on insects, including caterpillars and aphids. May be attracted to salt. **Behavior:** Forages actively in trees, shrubs, and weeds, sometimes hanging upside down to reach seeds. Usually forages in flocks (even during nesting season), often associated with goldfinches in winter.

Pine Siskin

NESTING   Breeding range often changes from year to year. May nest in loose colonies or in isolated pairs. Courtship and formation of pairs may begin in winter flocks; male displays by flying in circle above female, wings and tail spread wide, while singing. Male often feeds female during courtship. **Nest:** Site is well hidden in tree (usually in conifer), on horizontal branch well out from trunk. Typically 10–40 feet above ground, can be lower or higher. Nest (built by female) is a rather large but shallow open cup of twigs, grass, strips of bark, rootlets, lined with moss, animal hair, feathers. **Eggs:** 3–4, sometimes 2–5. Pale greenish blue, with brown and black dots often concentrated at larger end. Incubation is by female, about 13 days. Male feeds female during incubation. **Young:** After eggs hatch, female may spend most of time brooding young at first, while male brings food; later, both feed nestlings. Young leave nest about 14–15 days after hatching.

MIGRATION   Very erratic in winter occurrence, coming south in huge numbers some years, very scarce in others. After big invasion winters, a few may remain to nest south of normal range. Migrates by day in flocks.

CONSERVATION STATUS   Widespread and abundant. Local numbers are quite variable, but overall population is probably stable.

LESSER GOLDFINCH   *Carduelis psaltria*

Very common in parts of the west, this tiny finch is easy to overlook until one learns its chiming and twittering call notes. Small flocks of Lesser Goldfinches are often found feeding in weedy fields or in streamside trees. Two color patterns occur in the United States, and males in some areas may be either green-backed or black-backed. The complicated song of the male usually includes short imitations of the voices of other birds.

HABITAT   *Open brushy country, open woods, wooded streams, gardens.* Generally in semi-open areas where there are thickets and trees close to open weedy fields, from low valleys to high in mountains. In dry country, usually found close to water. In the tropics, found in semi-open terrain, woodland edges.

FEEDING **Diet:** *Mostly seeds, some insects.* Majority of diet at all seasons consists of seeds. Especially favors those of the daisy (composite) family, such as thistle and wild sunflower, also seeds of various weeds. Also feeds on flowers and buds of trees (such as cottonwoods) and on some berries. Eats some insects, especially in summer, mainly small ones such as aphids. Will feed on salt. **Behavior:** Forages actively and acrobatically in trees, shrubs, and weeds. Except when nesting, usually forages in flocks.

NESTING In warmer parts of southwest, breeding season may extend over much of year from early spring to midautumn. In courtship, male feeds female; performs display flight with wings and tail spread wide, fluttering rapidly while singing. **Nest:** Usually placed in vertical fork of twigs in shrub or tree, 5–30 feet above the ground, sometimes higher in tree or very low in bushes or dense weeds. Nest (built mostly or entirely by female) is a compact open cup woven of grass, plant fibers, strips of bark, lined with plant down. **Eggs:** 4–5, sometimes 3–6. Pale blue to pale blue-green, usually unmarked. Incubation is by female only, about 12 days. Male may feed female during incubation. **Young:** Both parents feed the nestlings. Age at which young leave nest is not well known. Two broods per year, perhaps sometimes three.

MIGRATION Permanent resident in much of range, summer resident only in some inland parts of the west, north of the desert regions. Very rare stray east of normal range.

CONSERVATION STATUS Widespread (including much of tropics) and fairly common, numbers probably stable.

Lesser Goldfinch

LAWRENCE'S GOLDFINCH *Carduelis lawrencei*

This little finch of the far west is uncommon and somewhat mysterious. It nests very locally in the foothills of California and Baja, often near streams in fairly dry country. Its winter range varies: in some years, flocks spread well eastward across the southwestern deserts, but the reasons for these "invasions" are not well understood. The twittering song of the male Lawrence's Goldfinch often includes brief imitations of the voices of other birds.

HABITAT *Oak-pine woods, chaparral.* Breeds locally in a variety of habitats including streamside trees, oak woodland, open pine woods, pinyon-juniper woods, chaparral. Often found close to water in fairly dry country. In migration and winter, occurs in weedy fields, farmland, brushy areas, streamsides.

Lawrence's Goldfinch

FEEDING **Diet:** *Mostly seeds, some insects.* Feeds mostly on the seeds of native weeds and other plants, such as fiddleneck, peppergrass, and chamise. Also eats plant galls, buds, and some insects. Will come to feed on salt. **Behavior:** Forages mostly in weeds, shrubs, and trees, often feeding quietly in a limited area, clambering about and occasionally hanging upside down to reach seeds. Sometimes feeds on the ground. Usually forages in flocks, sometimes even during nesting season.

NESTING Does not seem to defend territory strongly; sometimes nests in loose colonies. In courtship, male follows female, perches near her and sings. **Nest:** Site is usually

about 15–20 feet above ground in a tree such as oak, cypress, sycamore, or pine, sometimes lower in shrubs or up to 40 feet above ground. Nest is a small open cup of grass, flower heads, plant down, feathers, animal hair. Female builds nest; male often accompanies her and may carry some material, but rarely provides any real help. **Eggs:** 4–5, sometimes 3–6. Whitish to pale bluish white, usually unmarked, sometimes with reddish spots. Incubation is by female only, probably about 12–13 days. Male feeds female during incubation. **Young:** Both parents feed the nestlings. Young leave the nest about 11–13 days after hatching.

MIGRATION   Movements are poorly understood. Disappears from many breeding areas in winter. In some winters, large numbers spread eastward across Arizona; in other years, whereabouts of most birds unknown, perhaps in Baja.

CONSERVATION STATUS   Uncommon and local, could be vulnerable to loss of habitat.

AMERICAN GOLDFINCH   *Carduelis tristis*

A typical summer sight is a male American Goldfinch flashing golden in the sun over a meadow, calling *perchickory* as it bounds up and down in flight. In winter, when males and females alike are colored in subtler brown, flocks of goldfinches congregate in weedy fields and at feeders, making musical and plaintive calls. In most regions this is a late nester, beginning to nest in midsummer, perhaps to assure a peak supply of late-summer seeds for feeding its young.

American Goldfinch

HABITAT   *Patches of thistles and weeds, roadsides, open woods, edges.* Found at all seasons in semi-open areas having open weedy ground and some trees and bushes for shelter, especially areas of second growth, streamsides, roadsides, woodland edges, orchards, suburban areas. In winter also in some very open fields farther from trees.

FEEDING   **Diet:** *Mostly seeds, some insects.* Diet is primarily seeds, especially those of the daisy (composite) family, also those of weeds and grasses and small seeds of trees such as elm, birch, and alder. Also eats buds, bark of young twigs, maple sap. Feeds on insects to a limited extent in summer. Young are fed regurgitated matter mostly made up of seeds. **Behavior:** Forages actively in weeds, shrubs, and trees, often climbing about acrobatically on plants such as thistles to reach the seeds. Except during breeding season, usually forages in flocks. Commonly comes to feeders for small seeds.

NESTING   Nesting begins late in season in many areas, with most nesting activity during July and August. In courtship, male performs fluttering flight display while singing. **Nest:** Usually in deciduous shrubs or trees, sometimes in conifers or in dense weeds, usually less than 30 feet above ground and placed in horizontal or upright fork. Nest (built by female) is a solid, compact cup of plant fibers, spider webs, plant down (especially from thistles); nest is so well-made that it may even hold water. **Eggs:** 4–6, sometimes 2–7. Pale bluish white, occasionally with light brown spots. Incubation is by female only, about 12–14 days. Male feeds female during incubation. **Young:** Both parents feed nestlings. At first, male brings food and female gives it to young; then both parents feed; role of female gradually declines, so that male may provide most food in later stages. Young leave nest about 11–17 days after hatching.

Irregular in migration, with more remaining in north in winters with good food supply. Peak migration is usually midautumn and early spring, but some linger south of nesting range to late spring or early summer. Migrates mostly by day.

CONSERVATION STATUS Widespread and very common, although possibly has declined recently in some areas.

ORIENTAL GREENFINCH *Carduelis sinica*

This dull olive finch, rather plain except for its yellow wing patches, is common in eastern Asia. It is a rare visitor to the western Aleutian Islands during migration. One that once spent the winter in northern California could have been either a wild stray or an escaped cagebird.

GENUS *Pyrrhula*

EURASIAN BULLFINCH *Pyrrhula pyrrhula*

A colorful and distinctive finch, common across much of Europe and northern Asia. The Bullfinch has appeared more than a dozen times in Alaska, but there is no obvious pattern to its occurrences there, with records for widely scattered places and dates. It may be most regular in spring on St. Lawrence Island, where it has even appeared in small flocks.

GENUS *Coccothraustes*

EVENING GROSBEAK *Coccothraustes vespertinus*

This chunky, big-billed finch wanders widely in winter, descending on bird feeders in colorful, noisy flocks, to thrill feeder-watchers and to consume prodigious amounts of sunflower seeds. Originally a western bird, almost unknown east of the Great Lakes before the 1890s, it now breeds commonly east to New England and the Maritime Provinces. Its eastward spread may have been helped by the planting of box elders (a favorite food tree) across northern prairies, and by the abundance of bird feeders in the northeast.

Evening Grosbeak

HABITAT *Conifer forests; in winter, box elders and other maples, also fruiting shrubs.* Breeds in coniferous and mixed forests; often associated with spruce and fir in northern forest, with pines in western mountains. In migration and winter, may be equally common in deciduous groves in woodlands and semi-open country.

FEEDING **Diet:** *Mostly seeds, some berries and insects.* Seeds make up majority of diet, especially seeds of box elder, ash, maple, locust, and other trees. Also feeds on buds of deciduous trees, berries, small fruits, weed seeds. Will feed on oozing maple sap. Eats some insects in summer. At bird feeders, very fond of sunflower seeds. Will eat fine gravel for minerals and salts. Huge bill allows it to crack large seeds with ease. **Behavior:** Forages mostly in trees and shrubs, sometimes on ground. Except when nesting, usually forages in flocks.

In courtship, male "dances" with head and tail raised, wings drooped and vibrating as he swivels back and forth. Male frequently feeds female. In another courtship display, both members of a pair may bow alternately. **Nest:** Usual site is on horizontal branch (often well out from trunk) or in vertical fork of tree. Height varies, usually 20–60 feet above ground, can be 10–100 feet up. Nest (built by female) is a rather loosely made cup of twigs, lined with fine grass, moss, rootlets, pine needles. **Eggs:** 3–4, sometimes 2–5. Pale blue to blue-green, blotched with brown, gray, purple. Incubation is by female only, about 11–14 days. Male may feed female during incubation. **Young:** Both parents feed the nestlings. Young leave the nest about 2 weeks after hatching. One or two broods per year.

MIGRATION   Winter range in east very irregular, large numbers moving far south in some winters, little apparent movement in others. In west, occasionally invades lowlands from nesting areas in mountains.

CONSERVATION STATUS   Has extended its breeding range eastward since late 19th century. Current numbers probably stable.

HAWFINCH   *Coccothraustes coccothraustes*

In woodlands of Europe and Asia, this big-billed finch is fairly common but easily overlooked, often hiding in the treetops. In our area it is a rare visitor, mainly in spring, to the islands of western Alaska, where it is often elusive and hard to approach.

OLD WORLD SPARROWS (Family Passeridae)

This family only includes about 35 species, but some of them are among the most abundant and familiar birds in the world. This is mainly true of the typical sparrows (of the genus *Passer*), such as our well-known House Sparrow. Several of these species have adopted a winning strategy: they are very good at living alongside humans. It seems not to matter whether the surrounding landscape is open fields or forests, desert or swamp or city; as long as there are houses and buildings and human activity, the sparrows can make a living there.

Native to the Old World, this family has its greatest variety in Africa, where it includes a number of species (such as several kinds of petronias) that live only in wild habitats. Also included in this family are the snowfinches, which live in barren high mountain regions of Europe and Asia. But it is the genus *Passer* that gives the family its claim to fame and its place in this North American book.

GENUS *Passer*

HOUSE SPARROW   *Passer domesticus*

One of the most widespread and abundant songbirds in the world today, the House Sparrow has a simple success formula: it associates with humans. Native to Eurasia and northern Africa, it has succeeded in urban and farming areas all over the world—including North America, where it was first released in New York in 1851. Tough, adaptable, aggressive, it survives on city sidewalks where few birds can make a living; in rural areas, it may evict native birds from their nests.

HABITAT   *Cities, towns, farms.* Surroundings vary, but in North America essentially always found around man-made structures, never in unaltered natural habitats. Lives in city centers, suburbs, farms; also around isolated houses or businesses surrounded

House Sparrow

by terrain unsuited to House Sparrows, such as desert or forest.

FEEDING   **Diet:** *Mostly seeds.* In most situations, great majority of diet is weed and grass seeds or waste grain. Also eats some insects, especially in summer. In urban surroundings, also scavenges crumbs of food left by humans. **Behavior:** Forages mostly while hopping on ground. May perch on weed stalks to reach seeds. Adaptable in seeking food, may take smashed insects from the fronts of parked cars or search tree bark for insects. Comes to bird feeders for a wide variety of items.

NESTING   In courtship, male displays by hopping near female with his tail raised, wings drooped, chest puffed out, bowing and chirping. Often breeds in small colonies. Pairs defend only a small territory in the immediate vicinity of nest, chasing away all intruders. **Nest:** Usually in an enclosed niche such as cavity in tree, hole in building, rain gutter, birdhouse, nests of other birds. Where such sites are scarce, will nest in open in tree branches. Nest (built by both parents) is made of material such as grass, weeds, twigs, trash, often lined with feathers. In enclosed space, material forms foundation; in open sites, nest is a globular mass with entrance on side. **Eggs:** Usually 3–6, sometimes 2–7, rarely 1–8. Whitish to greenish white, with brown and gray dots concentrated toward larger end. Incubation is by both parents, 10–14 days. **Young:** Both parents feed the nestlings. Young leave nest about 2 weeks after hatching. Two or three broods per year.

MIGRATION   Permanent resident over most of its range, including throughout North America.

CONSERVATION STATUS   Probably has affected some native birds by competing for nest sites and food. Eastern population peaked around 1900, has been gradually declining in recent years.

EURASIAN TREE SPARROW   *Passer montanus*

Eurasian Tree Sparrow

Brought from Germany, about 20 of these birds were released in St. Louis in 1870. The population took hold there, and they might have spread except that the House Sparrow, seemingly more aggressive and adaptable, reached the St. Louis area at about the same time. Eurasian Tree Sparrows are still found in parts of Missouri and Illinois, and have reached southeastern Iowa, but they are fairly local in farmland and suburbs. The tougher House Sparrow may keep them out of other areas.

HABITAT   *Farmland, towns.* In North America, fairly local in open country with scattered bushes and trees, also in some suburban and city areas. In Europe and Asia, found in many kinds of semi-open habitats, woodland edges, towns, farms.

FEEDING   **Diet:** *Mostly seeds and insects.* Diet in North America not known in detail, but undoubtedly includes the seeds of various weeds and grasses, also waste grain in fields. Also eats many insects, perhaps especially in summer. **Behavior:**

Forages mostly while hopping on the ground. May also feed up in shrubs or trees at times. Often forages in small flocks.

NESTING   Some adults may remain in pairs at all seasons, or pairs may form well before nesting season starts. **Nest:** Placed inside a cavity, such as a natural hollow in tree, old woodpecker hole, birdhouse, or hole in building or under eaves. Unlike House Sparrow, seldom or never builds nest in open branches. Nest (probably built by both parents) is a bulky mass of grass, weeds, straw, trash, sometimes lined with feathers. **Eggs:** 4–6, rarely up to 8. White to grayish white, marked with brown. Incubation is by both parents, about 13–14 days. **Young:** Both parents feed the nestlings. Young leave the nest about 12–14 days after hatching, may be fed by parents for another week. One pair of adults may raise two or three broods per year.

MIGRATION   Some northern populations in Eurasia are migratory, but those in North America are permanent residents.

CONSERVATION STATUS   Small population in North America more or less stable, probably has little impact on native birds. In Eurasia, widespread and abundant.

REFERENCES

INDEX

REFERENCES

If this book had been written for scientists, it would have a very different sort of text. For example, the section on the nest of Hammond's Flycatcher might include the following:

> Substrate for nest often *Pseudotsuga menziesii* or *Pinus ponderosa* (Sedgwick 1994), or other conifer such as *Abies* or *Larix,* or deciduous *Populus, Acer,* or *Betula* (Bowles and Decker 1927, Bent 1942, Davis 1954, Jewett et al. 1953, KK pers. obs.). Nest height averages about 8–12 m (Johnson 1963, Harrison 1979) but may vary geographically, from mean of 7.5 m (range 3.2–12.2 m) in w. Montana (Sedgwick 1975, 1994) to mean of 18.8 m (range 12–31 m) in n.w. California (Sakai 1987).

That paragraph differs from the text of this book mainly in its use of literature citations—the references to Johnson 1963, Sedgwick 1994, and so on. For proper scientific text, these citations would always be included. A list of Literature Cited at the end would tell us that (Johnson 1963) refers to "Biosystematics of sibling species of flycatchers in the *Empidonax hammondii-oberholseri-wrightii* complex," written by Ned K. Johnson, released in 1963 as part of Volume 66 of the University of California Publications in Zoology. The citation is not just to give credit where it's due, but to allow other scientists to follow up the source of each published statement.

This book, however, was written not for scientists but for a general audience, for people who are just curious about the birds they see. No doubt some professionals will take me to task for leaving out citations to the scientific literature—but I saw no reason to make an already hefty book at least 80 pages longer by adding information that few people would use.

Still, I hope that some readers will be inspired to dig deeper into the subject and to learn more about the lives of birds. This list of recommended reading will point to some excellent sources.

MAJOR SOURCES OF INFORMATION

In researching this book I consulted well over 2,000 separate titles (books, papers in scientific journals, and technical reports). The list below will mention only a fraction of these, mainly ones that are easily accessible and worthwhile for general readers.

BIRDS OF NORTH AMERICA SERIES

My first and best source for many species was the account in the *Birds of North America* series (BNA), published by the American Ornithologists' Union and the Academy of Natural Sciences of Philadelphia. This remarkable series (also described in the introduction to this book) will, when completed, present the most thorough and up-to-date information on all of our birds, with up to 32 pages per species. At the time I was completing this book, almost 200 of the BNA accounts had been published, making my task of researching those species immeasurably easier. Anyone who develops a serious interest in birds should consider subscribing to the entire BNA series; it is expensive, but it is worth every cent.

MAJOR ORNITHOLOGICAL JOURNALS

In researching the book, I went back through about the last 30 years' worth of the major ornithological journals, extracting information from hundreds of different papers. The "big four" bird journals in North America are: *The Auk*, published by the American Ornithologists' Union; *The Condor*, published by the Cooper Ornithological Society; *The Wilson Bulletin*, published by the Wilson Ornithological Society; and *The Journal of Field Ornithology*, published by the Association of Field Ornithologists. Scientists who wish to keep up with the latest on birds read all four of these journals. For amateur birders, these publications make for rather tough reading, especially recent years of *The Auk* and *The Condor*.

MAJOR REFERENCE WORKS

I often consulted these major compilations of facts. They are well worth reading for anyone seeking further information on birds.

The Handbook of North American Birds. Edited by Ralph S. Palmer. Volume 1 (1962), Volumes 2 & 3 (1975), Volumes 4 & 5 (1988). Yale University Press. These five volumes give extensive details on all birds from loons through falcons.

Handbook of the Birds of Europe, the Middle East, and North Africa: The Birds of the Western Palearctic. Edited by Stanley Cramp and others. Nine volumes, published from 1978 to 1994. Oxford University Press. A superb reference covering all birds of that region, many of which are also found in North America.

Handbook of the Birds of the World. Edited by Josep del Hoyo, Andrew Elliot, and Jordi Sargatal. Volume 1 (1992): *Ostrich to ducks.* Volume 2 (1994): *New World vultures to Guineafowl.* Lynx Edicions. This ambitious series, projected at 12 volumes, will eventually give details on every bird species in the world.

The Birder's Handbook. Paul R. Ehrlich, David S. Dobkin, and Darryl Wheye. 1988, Simon & Schuster/Fireside. This book includes only sparse and telegraphic species accounts, but it has wonderful essays on many aspects of bird biology and ecology.

The Audubon Society Encyclopedia of North American Birds. John K. Terres. 1980, Knopf. Somewhat out of date, but still a treasure trove of obscure and offbeat facts.

Life Histories of North American Birds. Edited by Arthur Cleveland Bent. 26 volumes, published from 1919 to 1968. See the discussion of the Bent series in this book's introduction.

GENERAL BIRD BIOLOGY

Ornithology. Frank B. Gill. 2nd edition, 1994. Authoritative and highly readable, the best textbook on the science of bird study.

BREEDING BEHAVIOR, GENERAL

A Field Guide to Birds' Nests (1975) and *A Field Guide to Western Birds' Nests* (1979). Hal H. Harrison. Houghton Mifflin. Photographs of nests and eggs of many species.

Nest Building and Bird Behavior. Nicholas E. Collias and Elsie C. Collias. 1984, Princeton University Press.

Parent Birds and Their Young. Alexander F. Skutch. 1976, University of Texas Press. Slightly outdated, but still a good world overview.

Cooperative Breeding in Birds. Peter B. Stacey and Walter D. Koenig, editors. 1990, Cambridge University Press.

OTHER ASPECTS OF BIRD BEHAVIOR

How Birds Migrate. Paul Kerlinger. 1995, Stackpole Books.

A Guide to Bird Behavior. Volume 1, by Donald W. Stokes, 1979. Volume 2, 1983, and Volume 3, 1989, by Donald W. Stokes and Lillian Q. Stokes. Little, Brown & Co. Each volume covers 25 common species. Good for interpreting displays and other conspicuous kinds of behavior.

Birds Asleep. Alexander F. Skutch. 1989, University of Texas Press.

SPECIES AND GROUP LIFE HISTORIES

Many books treat only one group or birds, or even just one species. A few of the better ones are listed below. Excluded from this list are books that focus mainly on identifying the birds, although a few of these also give details on habitats, behavior, or life history. This is not a complete list by any means, but it includes books that I found particularly helpful.

The Herons of the World. James Hancock and Hugh Elliott. 1978, Harper & Row.

The Ancient Murrelet: A Natural History in the Queen Charlotte Islands. Anthony J. Gaston. 1992, T. & A.D. Poyser.

Pigeons and Doves of the World, third edition. Derek Goodwin. 1983, British Museum of Natural History.

The Life of the Hummingbird. Alexander F. Skutch. 1973, Crown Publishers.

Trogons of the Arizona Borderlands. Richard Cachor Taylor. 1994, Treasure Chest Publications.

Woodpeckers of the World. Lester L. Short. 1982, Delaware Museum of Natural History.

The Black-capped Chickadee. Behavioral Ecology and Natural History. Susan M. Smith. 1991, Comstock/Cornell University Press. An outstanding book, presenting detailed scientific information in a highly readable style.

American Warblers: An Ecological and Behavioral Perspective. Douglas H. Morse. 1989, Harvard University Press.

The Tanagers. Natural History, Distribution, and Identification. by Morton L. Isler and Phyllis R. Isler. 1987, Smithsonian Institution Press.

The Cardinal. June Osborne. 1992, University of Texas Press. A good introductory text on this popular bird.

THE FINAL SOURCE: PERSONAL OBSERVATION

Much remains unknown, or incompletely known, about our birds. In researching this book, I often found that published information on such things as feeding, habitat, and nest locations was lacking or seemed incomplete. In these cases I have often drawn on my own field observations, since I have watched practically all of these birds in life. There is a special satisfaction to writing down something that you know from personal observation, not just from books.

I urge you to apply your own powers of observation to the birds around you. Much remains to be learned. Many things in this book, or in any book, may turn out to be incomplete or just plain wrong. What you learn about birds by watching them will enrich your life, and it may enrich the sum total of human knowledge about our birdlife.

IMPORTANT NOTICE

Scientists often revise their ideas of how birds should be classified. Although the birds themselves have not changed in the short time since this book was written, some of them already have different classifications. For example, the tanagers (p. 558) are now considered to make up a family, not a subfamily; the Sage Grouse (p. 153) is now considered to be two species, not just one. For a complete list and discussion of all such recent changes in bird classification, see Kenn Kaufman's Web site at www.kknature.com.

PHOTO CREDITS

Red-throated Loon: Ervio Sian; Pacific Loon: D. Roby and K. Brink/VIREO; Common Loon: S. J. Lang/VIREO; Yellow-billed Loon: D. Hill/VIREO; Least Grebe: A. & E. Morris/VIREO; Pied-billed Grebe: A. & E. Morris/VIREO; Horned Grebe: E. S. Greene/VIREO; Red-necked Grebe: Don Enger/Cornell; Eared Grebe: Allan Cruickshank/Cornell; Western Grebe: G. Nuechterlein/VIREO; Black-footed Albatross: Eric Pozzo; Laysan Albatross: Doug Wechsler/VIREO; Northern Fulmar: Eric Pozzo; Black-capped Petrel: Mike Danzenbaker; Cory's Shearwater: R. L. Pitman/VIREO; Pink-footed Shearwater: G. Lasley/VIREO; Greater Shearwater: S. LaFrance/VIREO; Buller's Shearwater: R. L. Pitman/VIREO; Sooty Shearwater: Greg W. Lasley; Manx Shearwater: Mike Danzenbaker; Black-vented Shearwater: Rod Norden; Audubon's Shearwater: Greg W. Lasley; Wilson's Storm-Petrel: Roger Tory Peterson; Fork-tailed Storm-Petrel: Ervio Sian; Leach's Storm-Petrel: Adrian Dorst; Ashy Storm-Petrel: Mike Danzenbaker; Black Storm-Petrel: R. L. Pitman/VIREO; Least Storm-Petrel: J. Hoffman/VIREO; White-tailed Tropicbird: F. K. Schleicher/VIREO; Masked Booby: Lloyd McCarthy/Cornell; Brown Booby: Sam Fried/VIREO; Northern Gannet: D. Roby and K. Brink/VIREO; American White Pelican: S. J. Lang/VIREO; Brown Pelican: R. L. Pitman/VIREO; Great Cormorant: A. & E. Morris/VIREO; Double-crested Cormorant: Christopher Crowley/Cornell; Neotropic Cormorant: Roger Tory Peterson; Brandt's Cormorant: H. Clarke/VIREO; Pelagic Cormorant: R. L. Pitman/VIREO; Red-faced Cormorant: A. L. Sowls/VIREO; Anhinga: A. Cruickshank/VIREO; Magnificent Frigatebird: Doug Wechsler/VIREO; American Bittern: Rick and Nora Bowers; Least Bittern: S. J. Lang/VIREO; Great Blue Heron: Lee Kuhn/Cornell; Great Egret: A. & S. Carey/VIREO; Snowy Egret: Tony Leukering; Little Blue Heron: A. & E. Morris/VIREO; Tricolored Heron: Rick and Nora Bowers; Reddish Egret: Roger Tory Peterson; Cattle Egret: Steven Holt/VIREO; Green Heron: A. & E. Morris/VIREO; Black-crowned Night-Heron: A. & E. Morris/VIREO; Yellow-crowned Night-Heron: M. Ludwig/VIREO; White Ibis: Brian Wheeler; Glossy Ibis: W. A. Paff/Cornell; White-faced Ibis: C. H. Greenewalt/VIREO; Roseate Spoonbill: Roger Tory Peterson; Wood Stork: A. Morris/VIREO; Fulvous Whistling-Duck: A. & E. Morris/VIREO; Black-bellied Whistling-Duck: Mitch Smith/VIREO; Tundra Swan: A. & E. Morris/VIREO; Trumpeter Swan: Mike Hopiak/Cornell; Mute Swan: Ervio Sian; Greater White-fronted Goose: Rick and Nora Bowers; Snow Goose: Ervio Sian; Ross's Goose: Rob Curtis/VIREO; Emperor Goose: Mike Hopiak/Cornell; Brant: Mark Wilson/Wildshot; Canada Goose: Roger Tory Peterson; Wood Duck: J. H. Dick/VIREO; Green-winged Teal: Mike Hopiak/Cornell; American Black Duck: Johann Schumacher/VIREO; Mottled Duck: A. & E. Morris/VIREO; Mallard: Roger Tory Peterson; Northern Pintail: A. & E. Morris/VIREO; Blue-winged Teal: A. Cruickshank/VIREO; Cinnamon Teal: A. & E. Morris/VIREO; Northern Shoveler: J. Robert Woodward/Cornell; Gadwall: Johann Schumacher/VIREO; Eurasian Wigeon: Roger Tory Peterson; American Wigeon: Mark Nyhof; Canvasback: Steven Holt/VIREO; Redhead: Rob Curtis/VIREO; Ring-necked Duck: Rick and Nora Bowers; Greater Scaup: Mark Wilson/Wildshot; Lesser Scaup: J. Heidecker/VIREO; Common Eider: T. J. Ulrich/VIREO; King Eider: Roger Tory Peterson; Spectacled Eider: D. Roby/VIREO; Steller's Eider: J. P. Myers/VIREO; Harlequin Duck: A. & E. Morris/VIREO; Oldsquaw: D. Roby and K. Brink/VIREO; Black Scoter: T. H. Davis/VIREO; Surf Scoter: Ervio Sian; White-winged Scoter: S. LaFrance/VIREO; Common Goldeneye: Mark Nyhof; Barrow's Goldeneye: Jim Flynn; Bufflehead: B. Gadsby/VIREO; Hooded Merganser: Mark Wilson/Wildshot; Common Merganser: Mike Hopiak/Cornell; Red-breasted Merganser: Lawrence Wales/Cornell; Ruddy Duck: Rob Curtis/VIREO; Masked Duck: P. W. Sykes/VIREO; Black Vulture: Roger Tory Peterson; Turkey Vulture: William S. Clark ; California Condor: S. LaFrance/VIREO; Osprey: Brian Wheeler; Hook-billed Kite: John C. Arvin; Swallow-tailed Kite: Brian Wheeler; White-tailed Kite: R. & N. Bowers/VIREO; Snail Kite: Brian Wheeler; Mississippi Kite: Brian Wheeler; Bald Eagle: Brian Wheeler; Northern Harrier: B. K. Wheeler/VIREO; Sharp-shinned Hawk: Johann Schumacher/VIREO; Cooper's Hawk: Brian Wheeler; Northern Goshawk: Ervio Sian; Common Black-Hawk: Brian Wheeler; Harris's Hawk: John Cancalosi/VIREO; Gray Hawk: William S. Clark; Red-shouldered Hawk: A. & S. Carey/VIREO; Broad-winged Hawk: Brian Wheeler; Short-tailed Hawk: Brian Wheeler; Swainson's Hawk: Brian Wheeler; White-tailed Hawk: Jim Flynn; Zone-tailed Hawk: B. K. Wheeler/VIREO; Red-tailed Hawk: William S. Clark; Ferruginous Hawk: Scott Kamber/Cornell; Rough-legged Hawk: Brian Wheeler; Golden Eagle: Daniel J. Cox; Crested Caracara: Brian Wheeler; American Kestrel: Roger Tory Peterson; Merlin: Mark Wilson/Wildshot; Peregrine Falcon: F. K. Schleicher/VIREO; Gyrfalcon: Daniel J. Cox; Prairie Falcon: Brian Wheeler; Plain Chachalaca: Brian Wheeler; Gray Partridge: Bob deLange/VIREO; Chukar: Anthony Mercieca/Root Resources; Ring-necked Pheasant: Daniel J. Cox; Spruce Grouse: Rick and Nora Bowers; Blue Grouse: T. J. Ulrich/VIREO; Willow Ptarmigan: Mark Wilson/Wildshot; Rock Ptarmigan: Rick and Nora Bowers; White-tailed Ptarmigan: G. Dremeaux/VIREO; Ruffed Grouse: W. Greene/VIREO; Sage Grouse: Art Biale/Cornell; Greater Prairie-Chicken: Roger Tory Peterson; Lesser Prairie-Chicken: Barbara Magnuson/Photo/Nats; Sharp-tailed Grouse: John Cancalosi/VIREO; Wild Turkey: A. Walther/VIREO; Montezuma Quail: W. S. Clark/VIREO; Northern Bobwhite: Tony Leukering; Scaled Quail: Rick and Nora Bowers; Gambel's Quail: Brian Wheeler; California Quail: Brian Wheeler; Mountain Quail: Daniel Lee Brown; Yellow Rail: Todd Fink/Daybreak; Black Rail: Peter

LaTourrette; Clapper Rail: Rick and Nora Bowers; King Rail: Lawrence Wales/Cornell; Virginia Rail: Mike Hopiak/Cornell; Sora: Lawrence Wales/Cornell; Purple Gallinule: C. Singletary/Cornell; Common Moorhen: A. & E. Morris/VIREO; American Coot: William S. Clark; Limpkin: A. & E. Morris/VIREO; Sandhill Crane: Brian Wheeler; Whooping Crane: Jim Flynn; Black-bellied Plover: W. A. Paff/Cornell; American Golden-Plover: J. R. Woodward/VIREO; Snowy Plover: T. J. Ulrich/VIREO; Wilson's Plover: A. Morris/VIREO; Semipalmated Plover: Mary Tremaine/Cornell; Piping Plover: A. Morris/VIREO; Killdeer: A. & E. Morris/VIREO; Mountain Plover: John Cancalosi/VIREO; American Oystercatcher: J. H. Dick/Cornell; Black Oystercatcher: A. & E. Morris/VIREO; Black-necked Stilt: F. K. Schleicher/VIREO; American Avocet: A. & E. Morris/VIREO; Northern Jacana: R. & N. Bowers/VIREO; Greater Yellowlegs: T. H. Davis/VIREO; Lesser Yellowlegs: A. & E. Morris/VIREO; Solitary Sandpiper: Arnoud B. van den Berg/Cornell; Willet: Roger Tory Peterson; Wandering Tattler: S. LaFrance/VIREO; Spotted Sandpiper: Rob Curtis/VIREO; Upland Sandpiper: Brian Wheeler; Whimbrel: A. & E. Morris/VIREO; Bristle-thighed Curlew: H. C. Kyllingstad/VIREO; Long-billed Curlew: Rick and Nora Bowers; Hudsonian Godwit: D. & M. Zimmerman/VIREO; Bar-tailed Godwit: B. Chudleigh/VIREO; Marbled Godwit: Eric Pozzo; Ruddy Turnstone: Doug Wechsler/VIREO; Black Turnstone: R. & N. Bowers/VIREO; Surfbird: D. Roby/VIREO; Red Knot: Greg W. Lasley; Sanderling: Brian Wheeler; Semipalmated Sandpiper: A. & E. Morris/VIREO; Western Sandpiper: Tony Leukering; Red-necked Stint: Roger Tory Peterson; Least Sandpiper: L. Page Brown/Cornell; White-rumped Sandpiper: A. Morris/VIREO; Baird's Sandpiper: Rob Curtis/VIREO; Pectoral Sandpiper: T. H. Davis/VIREO; Purple Sandpiper: Mitch Smith/VIREO; Rock Sandpiper: Rick and Nora Bowers; Dunlin: Doug Wechsler/VIREO; Curlew Sandpiper: M. Gage/VIREO; Stilt Sandpiper: D. Paulson/VIREO; Buff-breasted Sandpiper: Tony Leukering; Ruff: Sam Fried/Photo/Nats; Long-billed Dowitcher: A. Morris/VIREO; Common Snipe: Roger Tory Peterson; American Woodcock: Mike Hopiak/Cornell; Wilson's Phalarope: Rob Curtis/VIREO; Red-necked Phalarope: R. Villani/VIREO; Red Phalarope: Rick and Nora Bowers; Pomarine Jaeger: R. Crossley/VIREO; Parasitic Jaeger: R. Ricklefs/VIREO; Long-tailed Jaeger: D. Roby and K. Brink/VIREO; South Polar Skua: D. Roby and K. Brink/VIREO; Laughing Gull: A. Cruickshank/VIREO; Franklin's Gull: H. Cruickshank/VIREO; Little Gull: Jim Flynn; Black-headed Gull: Dale and Marian Zimmerman; Bonaparte's Gull: Rick and Nora Bowers; Heermann's Gull: Rick and Nora Bowers; Mew Gull: Rick and Nora Bowers; Ring-billed Gull: Tony Leukering; California Gull: Brian Wheeler; Herring Gull: O. S. Pettingill/Cornell; Thayer's Gull: Ervio Sian; Iceland Gull: William S. Clark; Yellow-footed Gull: Rick and Nora Bowers; Western Gull: William S. Clark; Glaucous-winged Gull: H. Cruickshank/VIREO; Glaucous Gull: O. S. Pettingill, Jr./VIREO; Great Black-backed Gull: Rick and Nora Bowers; Black-legged Kittiwake: H. Cruickshank/VIREO; Red-legged Kittiwake: L. P. Schisler/VIREO; Ross's Gull: L. Page Brown/Cornell; Sabine's Gull: L. Page Brown/Cornell; Ivory Gull: Bruce Mactavish; Gull-billed Tern: Greg W. Lasley; Caspian Tern: A. Morris/VIREO; Royal Tern: Rob Curtis/VIREO; Elegant Tern: A. & E. Morris/VIREO; Sandwich Tern: Rob Curtis/VIREO; Roseate Tern: A. Morris/VIREO; Common Tern: Uve Hublitz/Cornell; Arctic Tern: Rick and Nora Bowers; Forster's Tern: A. & E. Morris/VIREO; Least Tern: Uve Hublitz/Cornell; Aleutian Tern: R. Behrstock/VIREO; Sooty Tern: M. J. Rauzon/VIREO; Black Tern: Mark Nyhof; Brown Noddy: P. G. Connors/VIREO; Black Skimmer: T. Vezo/VIREO; Dovekie: D. Roby and K. Brink/VIREO; Common Murre: R. Villani/VIREO; Thick-billed Murre: Roger Tory Peterson; Razorbill: M. Hebard/VIREO; Black Guillemot: T. J. Ulrich/VIREO; Pigeon Guillemot: M. J. Rauzon/VIREO; Marbled Murrelet: R. L. Pitman/VIREO; Kittlitz's Murrelet: T. Zurowski/VIREO; Xantus's Murrelet: Mike Danzenbaker; Ancient Murrelet: Ervio Sian; Cassin's Auklet: R. L. Pitman/VIREO; Parakeet Auklet: Brian Wheeler; Least Auklet: J. P. Myers/VIREO; Whiskered Auklet: S. V. Byrd/VIREO; Crested Auklet: K. Brink/VIREO; Rhinoceros Auklet: Steven Holt; Tufted Puffin: Rick and Nora Bowers; Atlantic Puffin: A. & E. Morris/VIREO; Horned Puffin: Lloyd McCarthy/Cornell; Rock Dove: Doug Wechsler/VIREO; White-crowned Pigeon: Jim Flynn; Band-tailed Pigeon: D. & M. Zimmerman/VIREO; Eurasian Collared-Dove: B. Schorre/VIREO; Spotted Dove: Rick and Nora Bowers; White-winged Dove: R. K. Bowers/VIREO; Mourning Dove: Roger Tory Peterson; Inca Dove: Roger Tory Peterson; Common Ground-Dove: Steve Bentsen; White-tipped Dove: Steve Bentsen; Black-billed Cuckoo: Mike Hopiak/Cornell; Yellow-billed Cuckoo: Jim Flynn; Mangrove Cuckoo: B. Small/VIREO; Greater Roadrunner: Rick and Nora Bowers; Smooth-billed Ani: Brian Wheeler; Groove-billed Ani: Brian Wheeler; Barn Owl: Jim Flynn; Flammulated Owl: Greg W. Lasley; Eastern Screech-Owl: J. R. Woodward/VIREO; Whiskered Screech-Owl: R. K. Bowers/VIREO; Great Horned Owl: Ervio Sian; Snowy Owl: Mark Wilson/Wildshot; Northern Hawk Owl: Mark Wilson/Wildshot; Northern Pygmy-Owl: Greg W. Lasley; Ferruginous Pygmy-Owl: Rick and Nora Bowers; Elf Owl: Greg W. Lasley; Burrowing Owl: Rob Curtis/VIREO; Spotted Owl: Ervio Sian; Barred Owl: Rick and Nora Bowers; Great Gray Owl: Brian Wheeler; Long-eared Owl: Tony Leukering; Boreal Owl: W. Greene/VIREO; Northern Saw-whet Owl: Brian Wheeler; Lesser Nighthawk: Sam Fried/VIREO; Common Nighthawk: O. S. Pettingill/Cornell; Pauraque: Rick and Nora Bowers; Common Poorwill: R. & N. Bowers/VIREO; Chuck-will's-widow: M.

INDEX